The World of
THE MIDDLE AGES

A REORIENTATION OF MEDIEVAL HISTORY

By

JOHN L. LaMONTE

*Henry C. Lea Professor
of Medieval History
University of Pennsylvania*

APPLETON–CENTURY–CROFTS, Inc.

New York

419

Dedicated to

KATHERINE R. LAMONTE

Ço estoit une sage pucele
E gentilz femme e preuz e bele
Non pas fause ne losengere;

.   .   .   .   .   .

Et . . . l'aveit mult amee.

AMBROISE

CREDO BY WAY OF PROLOGUE

✤

THERE are admittedly two viewpoints in approaching the study of Medieval history. The first studies the past in order to understand the present and stresses in early cultures only those elements which directly contribute to our own modern civilization. The other considers that the past is *per se* worth studying, that there have been civilizations in other ages as significant as our own, and that from a study of their success or failure we can derive not only useful and interesting information but a basis for comparison with the society in which we live. This book attempts to find a middle path between these views, and, while stressing those things which have contributed directly to our modern culture, such as the development of English parliamentary institutions and the universities, places the emphasis in the study of the Middle Ages on institutions, states, and peoples which were the most important in their own time. This has necessitated a reorientation of perspective from the traditional treatment found in most textbooks of medieval history. Instead of Western Europe, Germany, and the papacy, which are usually stressed, the Byzantine Empire and the Moslem caliphates have been made the central theme in the present treatment of the Early Middle Ages. For until the latter part of the eleventh century the East held a clear supremacy over the West. Byzantium was far advanced over the semibarbarous countries of the West, and even the glories of a Charlemagne were meager as compared wtih the splendors of a Leo the Isaurian or a Basil Bulgaroctenos. "The main European nations were already in the process of formation," writes Professor George Vernadsky, "but the center of gravity, both politically and culturally, was located neither in western nor in central Europe but in Byzantium." [1]

With the twelfth century, Western Europe came into much greater importance, and the West took the offensive against the East in the movement of the Crusades. While the East declined, the younger and more vigorous West developed rapidly, establishing institutions and a culture which in time excelled those of the East. Accordingly in the period of the High and Later Middle Ages, the emphasis in this volume has been laid upon the West.

Thus it is, that while the later portions of this volume conform more

[1] G. Vernadsky, *Kievan Russia* (Yale Univ., 1948, pp. 4–5). Unfortunately Vernadsky's book was published only after this volume was in page proofs and could not be used as extensively as I would have wished.

strictly to the accepted pattern of textbooks on medieval history, the earlier sections present radical differences. Instead of the heavy emphasis on the German tribes who invaded the western portions of the Roman Empire, this book stresses developments in the East and gives more adequate attention to the invasions of the Avars, Slavs, Bulgars, and other non-Germanic peoples in the eastern provinces. This point of view leads inevitably to an acceptance of the Pirenne theory which finds the end of the Roman Empire, not in the German *Völkerwanderung,* but in the expansion of the Moslems. Pirenne's theories have recently been attacked with brilliance and erudition, but it is my opinion that, while many of Pirenne's proofs have been destroyed, the essential correctness of his thesis remains unimpaired.

While many American historians now agree with their European colleagues in accepting the greater significance of Byzantium and the East, there may be some to whom the emphasis given them in this book will seem excessive. To such teachers, the author suggests that the sections on the East can be omitted, or assigned as supplementary reading, without impairing the continuity of the Western development. Similarly, if teachers wish to adapt the book to shorter courses, they may omit such sections as those on historiography, Russia, Spain, the Mongols and even the constitutions of the Italian states. In my opinion these constitute one of the most attractive features of the book, but *de gustibus non disputandem est,* and every teacher can select those sections which best fit into his own course-pattern. This book represents my own course as it has developed through a quarter century of teaching.

Interpretation has also been left largely to the teacher. While I have not striven for that impossible, and to me rather terrifying, ideal of "pure historical objectivity," I have tried to keep my own opinions and judgments out of the book as far as possible. I have tried to let the facts speak for themselves, and have deliberately included a multitude of facts. It has been my experience that the student best grasps generalizations if he has been allowed to make them for himself on the basis of a considerable number of factual illustrations. If he does not remember what counties Philip Augustus conquered, he will at least realize that the French monarch was busy adding lands to the royal domain, and if he does not remember (as Heaven forbid he should) how many of the Roman and Byzantine emperors met their end by assassination, he will recognize the fact that the imperial couch was not inevitably a bed of roses.

It has further been my intention to include in this volume a reasonable number of names which are likely to be mentioned in lectures rather hurriedly and on which the teacher, restricted by the exigencies of the clock and calender, has had no time to linger. By consulting the index of this work, the student should be able to find some modicum of information about these names to supplement his often incomplete class notes.

As this book treats the World *of* the Middle Ages and not the World *in* the Middle Ages, such areas as China, India and the Far East have been omitted. From all practical points of view the Far East was no part of the medieval world, at least until the discovery of Cathay in the thirteenth century. In the selection of subject matter I have tried to include those things which were important to medieval men, and to accord them somewhat the importance they might have been given by their contemporaries. This explains what may be considered an overemphasis on the deeds of the mighty to the exclusion of the humbler accomplishments of lesser folk: for in the medieval world it was the aristocracy, not the proletariat, who dominated society. The peasants were all too often lumped with the livestock in the economy of the time; the Middle Ages were distinctly *not* the "era of the common man." If critics may feel that the peasant has received too scant treatment in this volume, it must be admitted that he is accorded here much greater relative space than he received in the annals and chronicles of his own time.

* * * * *

In acknowledging assistance rendered in the preparation of this book, the author is acutely aware that it contains ideas and phrases which he has picked up somewhere and which, through a process of intellectual and literary osmosis, have become part of his own thinking. It would be wholly impossible to pick out the exact source for many statements. While the utmost care has been taken to give credit for all quotations, an exacting reader may well find herein phrases unconsciously derived from some author whose work the present writer has read and admired in years past. There are, I know, several rather good phrases whose origins have long given me cause for curious speculation, and I would be most grateful to any reader who could enlighten me as to their source. For example, whence came the phrase: "Italy has the Papacy, Germany the Empire, but France has the University of Paris"?

It would be difficult to estimate the number of good friends who have assisted me in the course of the preparation of this book for it includes not only those who have offered positive suggestions but those who have patiently suffered through long discussions on my part, and have allowed me to clarify my own ideas through the process of reiteration. The interest shown by two of my older colleagues has been particularly gratifying. Dr. Arthur C. Howland, Emeritus Professor of Medieval History and Curator of the Henry C. Lea Library of the University of Pennsylvania, and Dr. Edgar Holmes McNeal, Emeritus Professor of Medieval History at Ohio State University, who first aroused my interest in the Middle Ages and showed me what true historical scholarship should be, have both been most generous of their time and rich experience in advising and encouraging me throughout the writing of this manuscript. Professor August C. Krey of the University of Minnesota has given the work a most meticulous scrutiny, an editorial criticism, and many suggestions which have proven invaluable. Two of my former students, Mary Elizabeth Nickerson and Betty Waldrop Rhoads, have read the entire manuscript, and have made valuable criticisms and prevented many errors. Miss Marie Paredo willingly and patiently typed and retyped the manuscript. Portions of the book have been read and criticised by Professors Kenneth M. Setton of the University of Manitoba; David M. Robb and Arthur P. Watts of the University of Pennsylvania; Jeremiah F. O'Sullivan of Fordham University; Peter W. Topping of the University of California at Santa Barbara; Joseph McCloskey of LaSalle University; and Joseph Donavan, S. J. of Seattle University. While I have not always followed their suggestions, their interest and advice has been greatly appreciated. My son Robert spent many hours in preparing the maps which were made especially for this volume. Professor David M. Robb also most generously supplied the illustrations for which no other specific credit is given. Miss Ruth Keener, of the editorial department of Appleton-Century-Crofts, has been most patient and co-operative in seeing the book through to final publication. To all of these I wish to express my most sincere thanks and gratitude. Finally, in this as in everything else which I have ever done, I am deeply indebted to my wife, Katherine R. LaMonte, to whom the book is dedicated as a partial expression of my appreciation of her constant encouragement and advice over a long period of composition and of her tireless assistance, willingly given, in reading proofs and preparing the index.

JOHN L. LaMonte

Philadelphia

CONTENTS

✜

Book IV: THE APOGEE OF THE MIDDLE AGES: THE THIRTEENTH CENTURY

Book V: THE CULTURAL REVIVAL OF THE WEST, 1100–1300

Book VI: THE DECLINE OF THE MEDIEVAL WORLD, 1300–1500

CONTENTS

MAPS AND GENEALOGICAL TABLES

✣

MAPS

GENEALOGICAL TABLES

ILLUSTRATIONS

✤

Book I

The Decline of Roman Unity

330-630

In the first era of medieval history the unity of the Roman Empire still continued, the world centering as in Antiquity around the Mediterranean Sea. As Old Rome had dominated the first three centuries of the Christian era, so New Rome—Constantinople—dominated the next three centuries. Christianity had been accepted as the official religion of the Roman Empire and had become the most vital issue to many who sought in the promise of salvation a compensation for the ills of this world.

The barbarian peoples who had long inhabited the fringes of the empire had entered its borders, as individuals and as tribes, until they had taken over the control of the western provinces, but the East still remained Roman and was the one dominant political, economic, and social power in the world. The whole center of gravity of the empire had shifted to the East, and it was there alone that the ancient culture was preserved and the old manner of life maintained. The magnificent opulence of the East stands out the more by contrast with the decline of the West. Seldom has any city so dominated the world as Constantinople did in this period, when it was the center of politics, trade, luxury, amusement, and culture. With the assertion of the political control over the western Mediterranean by Justinian, and with the final defeat of Rome's ancient rival Persia by Heraclius, the supremacy of Constantinople was complete. From the Sacred Palace on the Bosphorus, the emperor ruled over the Roman world, whose industry and trade contributed to the wealth and splendor of the capital.

HAGIA SOPHIA: CONSTANTINOPLE

CHAPTER 1

THE EMPIRE IN THE FOURTH CENTURY

✠

MARE NOSTRUM

MEDIEVAL history has its beginnings in the Roman Empire, but it has too generally been distorted by being considered exclusively the history of the western provinces of that empire. The medieval world, like the Roman, was not centered in western Europe, but in the Mediterranean basin. To divorce Nearer Asia and North Africa from Europe in either ancient or medieval times is to grossly distort the perspective and to lay a wholly wrong emphasis on a single geographical sector.

The Romans in the pride of their empire called the Mediterranean *Mare Nostrum,* and justly, for Roman arms had made of it a Roman lake surrounded on all sides by Roman territory. The sea, not the lands around it, was the center and heart of the empire; its routes were the arteries through which the trade of the empire flowed; its ports were the chief cities of the Roman world; the very existence of the Roman body politic depended upon the successful control and maintenance of the commerce and communications across the Mediterranean.

Rome had first become important when, as a naval power, she defeated her great rival, Carthage, in the second century B.C. If the mighty Julius had gained his great renown through the conquest of Gaul, his predecessor, Pompey, had become the chief citizen of Rome by conquering the pirates who infested the sea. The victory of Augustus over Antony was won in the sea battle of Actium, and throughout the history of the empire the Roman navy was maintained to keep the peace of the central sea. As long as it controlled the sea, the Roman Empire retained dominance over all the old Roman world; as Henri Pirenne has demonstrated, it was only when the new Moslem power challenged its control of the sea in the seventh century that the Roman Empire ceased to be the sole dominant authority both in the East and in the West.[1] Previous to that, Rome had lost many provinces in the West, but her authority had still been recognized by the German kings as a superior authority under whom they ruled at least in theory. For the Roman Empire was more than a political phenomenon: it was one of the eternal verities. Proof of this was to be found in the prophecies of Daniel if anyone was so skeptical as to question it. The shadow of the empire continued to exist in the West until the upstart Napoleon ended it in

[1] H. Pirenne. *Mohammed and Charlemagne.*

3

1806; in the East, the Roman Empire continued as a sovereign state until the Ottoman Turks destroyed it with the capture of Constantinople in 1453. And until the middle of the eleventh century the Roman Empire, with its capital at Constantinople, had remained the chief state of Europe in fact as well as in theory. Medieval history is the history of the period in which the empire continued to be the chief state of Christendom, influencing the life not only of a great part of the Mediterranean world, but of lands in Europe which the Roman of the first century knew only as the unexplored haunts of the barbarians.

In approaching medieval history one must come to it from the point of view of the Roman Empire: it is essentially the history of the lands and peoples who were part of that empire. No attempt is made in this book to consider the history of China, India:—the civilizations which flourished in the East, but which played no role in the Roman world. During the course of centuries the frontier was rolled back, new lands and peoples were brought into the light of knowledge; but it was always as Roman civilization reached these peoples and lands, or as they thrust themselves into the ken of the Roman world, that they become significant in the history of the Middle Ages.

To think of medieval history as covering the period from the fall of the Roman Empire to the beginnings of modern times is a contradiction in terms. For modern times begin with the fall of Constantinople,—with the fall of the Roman Empire, that is to say. It would be better to define medieval as the period of transmutation of Roman civilization and of its decline. The chronological limits of this book are the foundation and the fall of Constantinople (330–1453), and medieval history is that period of man's development in which the Eastern Roman Empire (later called the Byzantine Empire) yet preserved at least the theory of the ancient state and the city of the Caesars on the Bosphorus always stood out as the highest center of a civilization which, however decadent, had once been great.

Not always, throughout this period, did Byzantium dominate the scene; indeed the imperial city suffered badly at the hands of its neighbors (and even worse at the hands of its own children) on many occasions, and when it finally fell it was but a shade of its former greatness. But the passing of the Byzantine Empire is a landmark in history and can justifiably be considered to mark the closing of an era, just as its foundation may be considered to mark the beginning.

Shortly after the fall of Constantinople, the beginning of the Age of Discovery tremendously enlarged the limits of the known world. Already in the thirteenth century Cathay had been visited and described; the discovery of the Americas opened the way for the creation of the great Atlantic empires of modern times. In the Middle Ages the world was still centered, as it had been in Antiquity, around Mare Nostrum.

THE FOUNDING OF CONSTANTINOPLE

Ancient legend, as preserved by the Greek geographer Strabo, tells how the citizens of Megara sought the advice of the Pythian Apollo in connection with the site of a new colony they wished to found. They were told to build their city opposite to the "City of the Blind," whereby was meant on the shore opposite Chalcedon, which had been recently founded on the southern side of the Bosphorus. The intervention of Apollo is not necessary to explain the selection of the site, however, and the naturally favorable position of the northern shore of the Bosphorus is enough to show why the colony of Byzantium was located there in the seventh century B.C. Throughout Antiquity, Byzantium held an important commercial and strategic position, controlling as it did the outlet to the Black Sea, until it was nearly destroyed by Septimus Severus in the civil wars of the second century. But it was only with the selection of its site as the location of his new eastern capital by the emperor Constantine that Byzantium, or Constantinople as it was thereafter called, assumed a position among the chief cities of the world.

That the capital of the empire should be located in the East had long been an idea in the minds of the Caesars. Suetonius credits the great Julius himself with the desire to remove the capital to Troy or to Alexandria; Diocletian made his favorite residence, and practically his capital, in Bithynia at Nicomedia. Constantine's first choice, we are told, was Troy, that the Romans might rebuild and glorify the city of their legendary founders; but celestial intervention again operated in favor of the site on the Bosphorus, and a heavenly vision directed Constantine to Byzantium even as Apollo had formerly directed the Megarians. At any rate the site was selected in 324, building begun the following year, and the city was officially dedicated as the new capital of the empire, the New Rome, on May 11, 330.

The new capital was, moreover, from the outset a Christian city, and in the removal of the capital to the East and the establishment of Christianity as an officially recognized religion of the empire, we have the two events which mark the opening of the fourth century as the border between ancient and medieval times.

CONSTITUTIONAL DECLINE

The Roman Empire, which Constantine adorned with a new capital, had fallen upon sorry times. The glorious state of the early principate had declined considerably, forces from within and from without had robbed it of much of its power and prosperity, and the reforms of Diocletian had been insufficient to re-establish the former condition of internal strength.

The decline of the Roman Empire is an historical fact recognized by all, although it was not evident to those who lived through it and the writings of the time would indicate that few suspected that all was not well within the body politic, but the causes for the decline will probably always afford a fertile field for historical speculation. If we cannot precisely state the causes, however, it is a simple task to indicate some of the more pronounced symptoms of the decay. Politically, economically, socially, and spiritually the empire had declined, and it is wasted breath to try to ascertain which of the many manifestations of decline were primal and which secondary causes. Each cause was the result of other causes, each condition resulted in other conditions, the whole is a perplexing network of cause and effect, and the total result is the decay of ancient civilization.

In the second century of the empire (which is also of course the second century of the Christian era), the Roman Empire flourished. If her government lacked certain desirable elements of stability, it had not yet seriously affected the life of its citizens and the prosperity of the country as a whole cannot be questioned. Industry and commerce, the twin bases for economic welfare, were both carried on extensively under the aegis of the *Pax Romana,* which kept the trade routes open and safe; the wars on the frontiers scarcely disturbed the inhabitants of the interior provinces; taxation was heavy but there was plenty of good money with which to pay all demands; the gods were in their heavens (philosopher-kings were on the throne) and all was well with the world. Of course there was infinite misery and suffering among the lower classes, but there is always suffering among the lower classes and the prosperous Roman citizen was well served by his slaves with delicacies, which were brought to him from the four corners of the known world.

But by the end of the fourth century all this had changed. The Roman citizen was no longer prosperous; there were few who were not poor; the barbarians were no longer held beyond the frontiers, but had penetrated, peacefully enough on the whole but nevertheless noticeably, into the very heart of the empire; trade was disrupted and industry was failing; the gods had been badly shaken up in their heavens and all was very decidedly not well in this world. Instead of purchasing slaves, the Roman had a very fair chance of being sold as a slave, an altogether less appealing prospect. What had happened to cause this change?

In the first place, we must note a serious defect in the constitution of the empire: there was no regular established rule of succession to the throne. Augustus had made himself emperor without giving up any of the old republican forms of government and had merely gathered unto himself all of the offices whereby the state was ruled. His successors still clung to some of these fictions: the years were still numbered by the consuls; the emperor, until the reforms of Diocletian, still employed some of the old titles (Caligula had even been so insistent upon having a colleague in the consulship that he had elevated his favorite horse to that position of honor). At first the succession passed along regularly enough in the Julio-Claudian house, (palace intrigue and an occasional assassination are necessary attributes of any autocracy), but the defect in the matter of succession had only become apparent after the murder of Nero when three emperors followed each other in rapid succession within a single year (68–69 A.D.). The year of turmoil ended when Vespasian was elevated to the throne by his legions, but the precedent had been established—the emperor had been appointed by the army.

Thereafter the most common means of achieving the imperial title was through the army and by force. A popular general would be acclaimed by his legions and they would at once set about placing him on the throne. There were of course other ways of selecting an emperor; the senate could elect him; an emperor could adopt a successor and secure his position during his own lifetime, but the normal way was by selection by the army. The exclusive Praetorian Guard for a time attempted to control all elections, but the provincial armies were not to be ignored, and they were not hesitant about forcing their favorite generals on the state. From the time in 68 that the senate meekly confirmed the election of Galba, who had been proclaimed by his legions, the precedent was set; conspiracy and rebellion were frequent during the second century—after the murder of Commodus in 193 they became chronic. Between 193 and 284 there were twenty-eight emperors who actually ruled, not to mention a host of aspirants who secured temporary support; most of them rose from the ranks of the army; few of them died natural deaths. Most of them, moreover, secured their thrones by means of defeating rivals and through the destructive processes of civil war. It is not the mortality figures among the Caesars that interests us here; it is the almost constant civil war which destroyed the prosperity of the empire, which wiped out the Pax Romana, devastated the fields and destroyed the factories and rendered trade and travel too precarious to be carried on regularly. It was not the civil wars of the third century which brought the extinction of the empire in the West; but they do underly the economic, social, and cultural decay which characterized the last years of the empire. This period of civil war was brought to a temporary end by Diocletian (284–305), a soldier from the ranks who secured the throne through assassination and conquest, but who sincerely tried to give the empire a just and efficient reform administration. It was Diocletian who first divided the empire into East and West, making his own headquarters in the East at Nicomedia and taking Maximianus as a colleague to rule the West. It was his plan that the two Augusti should adopt Caesars who should succeed them when they should retire. Diocletian's idealistic scheme

foundered on the selfishness of his colleague and of their chosen successors and he was forced to return from his self-imposed retirement to
straighten out the political melée. From 305 to 324 the empire was torn
by the struggles of the Augusti and Caesars, and it was only in the latter
year that Flavius Valerius Constantinus was able to overthrow his last
rival Licinius and secure undisputed control of the government. In the
same year he arranged for the transfer of the seat of government from
Rome to the new city which he planned on the Bosphorus.

Diocletian and Constantine were both keenly aware of the problems
which confronted the empire; both tried through legislation to remedy
such defects as they could. But emperors before them had likewise struggled
to reform conditions and institutions: the evils lay too deep for governmental enactments to seriously modify the situation or to check the processes of decay. Reform of administration or of taxation could not restore the
prosperity which had been destroyed during the civil wars; good government could not revive the lost military virtues of the Roman people or
stimulate in them an interest in their state. Further, many of the reforms
only aggravated conditions and made things much worse than before; the
increase in governmental offices and expenditures, which accompanied the
reorganization of the empire, by no means decreased the amount of taxation, and made life even harder to bear than it had been previously.

REORGANIZATION BY DIOCLETIAN

The Roman Empire, as reorganized by Diocletian, consisted of four
great *prefectures* (Italy, Gaul, Illyricum, and the East under prefects) which
were subdivided into *dioceses* (under vicars), in turn subdivided into *provinces* (under governors). These provinces were much smaller than the old
Roman provinces had been, the general rule being to divide each old province into two; this process was continued by later emperors until by the
fifth century there were a total of 120 provinces. But the local unit remained, as it had always been, the municipality or *civitas,* with its local
elective officials and its local municipal *curia.* In the municipalities had
lain the strength of the Roman Empire; the city state was the common
type of government before the rise of Rome, and Rome herself had won her
initial greatness as a city state. The attempt to govern a huge territorial
empire through the machinery which was designed for the city state was
one of the major problems of the late republic and early empire. Rome
answered it by organizing municipalities throughout the entire extent of
her domains. While the city state never took hold in Egypt and Africa as
it did elsewhere, throughout Europe and the west it became the normal
form of local administration, and the tribes of the Gauls were fitted into
the Roman civitates. Each municipality was a miniature Rome, with its

local curia or senate, its local magistrates, courts and administration patterned closely after the model of Rome herself. The local aristocracy were
the *curiales,* the members of the curia, and magistrates whose prosperity
assured the prosperity of the empire.

THE ROMAN EMPIRE

In the 4th Century

PREFECTURES
Gaul
Italy
Illyricum
The East

The municipalities were retained by Diocletian with little change; but
the whole empire was centralized in administration, the military and civil
powers were sharply separated, and all the administrative officials of the
provinces and the larger districts were made appointive by the emperor.
The imperial court took on the character of the oriental monarchies, a
great bureaucracy developing to handle the business of government, and
an elaborate series of hierarchical grades and distinctions appearing as the
ceremonial of the court became increasingly formal and ritualistic.

As has been already noted, Diocletian felt that the responsibility of governing so vast a state was more than one man should attempt to bear, and
so sought a colleague, dividing the empire into Eastern and Western parts
of two prefectures each. For himself Diocletian kept the East with his
capital at Nicomedia; to his colleague Maximianus was given the West
with his capital at Milan. Thus came into being the division of the empire
which was to last until 800, when Charlemagne and the pope took the
crucial step of proclaiming a separate Western empire independent of the
East.

We have already noticed that the system of Diocletian did not work
out exactly as expected; the two Caesars who were supposed to succeed
peacefully to the two senior Augusti quarrelled and there was a renewal

of civil war, until Constantine again reunited the empire under his sole control. Under the immediate successors of Constantine (337–363) the empire remained united with the capital in the East, but in 364 at the death of the emperor Jovian, a new division was made, Valentinian I taking the West and Valens the East. When Valentinian died in 375 he was succeeded in the West by his two sons Gratian and Valentinian II, while Valens in the East was succeeded in 379 by Theodosius. At the death of his Western colleagues, Theodosius again reunited the empire and ruled alone 394 to 395, but at his death the empire was once again divided between his sons: Arcadius who ruled the East and Honorius who held the West. From 395 to 476, the two parts of the empire followed separate courses under their own lines of rulers and it was not until the deposition of the last Western emperor, Romulus Augustulus, in 476 that the unity of the empire was again accomplished, at least in theory, by the recognition in the West of the sovereignty of the Eastern emperor Zeno. As we shall see, this was hardly more than a fiction however, as the West had passed into the hands of German military leaders who actually ruled in the name of the distant emperor.

BARBARIAN PENETRATION

The penetration of the empire by these barbarians is one of the most striking features of the history of the later empire. The failure of Rome to absorb them properly is one of the most significant features of her decline. The Roman Empire was from the first a heterogeneous mass of conflicting races and nationalities: Italian, Greek, Phoenician, Berber, Gaul, Syrian, Egyptian had been subjected and had been largely assimilated into the Roman melting pot. But in every case Rome had taken over something from the conquered and her own civilization had become an amalgam of all the various elements which went into it. From Greece, she had derived most of her culture—art, literature, philosophy, so that we refer to Roman culture as Graeco-Roman. From the Eastern races, Rome had received the salvationist religions which played so important a role in the religious history of her decline. Every people who come into contact with a higher civilization invariably draw from the higher culture; Rome drew from the older civilizations of the East and gave to the younger peoples of the West. Aside from her genius in engineering, law and government, Rome herself made few original contributions to civilization, but she handed on to less well-endowed peoples the high civilization which she herself had absorbed from her eastern conquests. Of all the peoples conquered by Rome in her earlier history, only the Jews, inspired by an exclusive religion and a feeling of racial and national isolationism, successfully resisted Romanization and absorption into the general culture which was Rome's. Later we shall see another Semitic people, the Arabs, likewise inspired by religious fervor, not only resisting absorption by the Graeco-Roman civilization, but overthrowing it and spreading over former Romanized territories their own peculiar Arabic civilization.

But the cosmopolitan Roman civilization which had been able to absorb so many different peoples had reached a saturation point before the Germans entered its sphere of influence. The Germans were quite ready to be absorbed (and were to a large extent) but their assimilation was never complete.

Though they held the highest positions in the army and in the government service, though they latinized their names, though they adopted Roman dress and manners, the Germans always remained a bit outside the pale; they could rule the state through puppet emperors, but they could not themselves aspire to the purple. Professor Lot sees in this one of the causes for the overthrow of the Roman government in the West and points out that the Germans would have preferred to rule as Roman emperors had that possibility been open to them, as it was to the Isaurians in the Eastern empire.[2] Barred from the purple, they ruled as kings under the theoretical suzerainty of the Eastern emperors, but actually as independent despots. The substitution of the Germanic kingdoms for the imperial rule in the West was only the final stage in a development which had been going on for years, wherein individual Germans had risen to positions of supreme importance in the Roman administration and army.

The careers of some of these such as Stilicho, Ricimer, Aspar, and Odoacer will be discussed later in connection with the Germanic invasions. It is enough here to indicate the phenomenon of which they are examples and to point out that it is one of the most evident symptoms of Roman decay.

That barbarians could gain control of the army and the administration was due largely to the fact that the Roman citizens no longer felt inspired by any amount of patriotism and had no desire to serve personally in the armies which defended their empire. The rustic military spirit which had given Rome the mastery of the civilized world had died out in the breasts of its children and Romans were glad to have their military burdens assumed by hired mercenaries recruited from the provinces or from the barbarians who bordered the frontiers. This was in part the result of a general softening, which resulted from the economic position of the Romans. Also it was due to the loss of any feeling of their unity as Romans in opposition to outsiders. In the early empire, Roman citizenship was a cherished thing, accorded only to those actually born in Italy or those who had earned it by service to the state. St. Paul proudly insisted *"Cives*

[2] Lot, Pfister, and Ganshof, *Les Destinées de l'Empire en Occident, 395–888*, p. 23.

Romanus sum" and secured the benefits which accrued to Roman citizenship.

The first attempt to extend the citizenship had been made by Julius Caesar, but this policy had been reversed by Augustus, and citizenship was guarded and kept restrictive in the early empire. Then the bars began to be let down, and more and more provincials were admitted to citizenship until at last, in 212, Caracalla granted citizenship to all the inhabitants of the empire. This at once reduced the value of the status; when the poorest Egyptian fellah or Gallic peasant was a citizen, what was there in citizenship to attract the Roman aristocrat? What everyone had was valued by none. The privileged Roman aristocrat had better things to do than serve in the army, let the poor provincial do that. Further, since the reign of Gallienus the army had actually been closed to men of senatorial rank. This had been done in an attempt to keep ambitious and powerful aristocrats from gaining control of legions and aspiring to the purple. Constantine carried the matter a step further when he forbade members of the municipal curiae (the *decuriones*) to enlist in the army. The result was just the opposite from that desired, however. The army did not become less troublesome or withdraw at all from politics; instead the one result was that its leaders came to be men drawn from the ranks, for the most part barbarians or semi-illiterate peasants, producing a general barbarization of the high commands. In civilian life, the aristocrats continued to dominate politically; only instead of the rulers of the empire being drawn from its citizen body, the state was dominated by a small group of great wealthy lords who ruled over large bodies of servile dependents.

Not only was the army barbarized but its efficiency was reduced. The defence of the long frontier had necessitated so large a force that a sort of militia had been organized along the frontiers. The legionnaires were permitted to marry and live out of barracks; they tilled the fields or engaged in trade on the side in addition to their military duties; consequently they became inferior soldiers. Diocletian did something to reform this situation by dividing the army into two branches; the frontier garrison militia, called *limitanei,* which continued much as it had been before; and a new mobile force, stationed at strategic points within the empire and ready to strike out in any direction, called *comitatensi.* This mobile army was largely a cavalry force which was in itself an innovation, as the Roman armies were traditionally chiefly infantry. While any exact figures of the number of men enrolled in the army are lacking, it has been estimated that in the late empire there were approximately 25,000 to 40,000 cavalry and 200,000 infantry, to which should be added about another 200,000 auxiliary troops, chiefly barbarian *foederati,* who served under their own leaders as dependent allies. The forces of the empire often outnumbered those of the German tribes which overthrew them, for the largest of German tribal armies was only some 40,000 men (the army led by Alaric), but there were two factors which operated in favor of the Germans. First, the wide distribution of the Roman armies and the long frontier over which they were scattered, which gave them fewer effectives to throw against any given point, and secondly, the large number of Germans in the armies of the empire which reduced the effectiveness of the legions. These barbarian mercenaries had no especial loyalty to the Roman state, their allegiance was to their leader, and to a Burgundian mercenary it mattered little whether he served under an independent Gothic king or a Vandal general in the service of Rome. Many of these men were not even employed by the state, but were hired by the generals privately. These private troops, called *bucellarii*, were utterly devoted to their leader, to whom they were bound by the most solemn oaths, but they had no further loyalty and would follow their general in any treason or change of sides. It was not uncommon for them to join the forces of an enemy leader if their own master was killed and they were left unemployed. The use of these bucellarii increased through the fourth and fifth centuries, until by the time of Justinian, we find them outnumbering the regular imperial soldiers in the army of Belisarius which conquered Italy.

THE EAST IN THE FOURTH CENTURY

By far the most important developments of the fourth century were the economic and the religious, but some notice of the political events of the century is necessary. The great problem of the emperors was the defense of the frontiers both against the German barbarians from the north and against the Persian Sassanids on the east.

Three emperors of the fourth century were men of great distinction. Constantine the Great (306–337) is of course famous for founding Constantinople and for establishing Christianity as an official religion of the state. His sons, Constans, Constantine and Constantius, engaged in fratricidal war after his death and the next ruler of any significance was Constantine's nephew Julian, who ruled the empire 361 to 363. Julian is famous for his attempt to turn back the course of history and restore the old pagan religions. He was a scholar and philosopher as well as a first-class soldier, but he opposed himself to forces far beyond his strength and his short and brilliant reign was entirely futile. The empire was again divided between Valentinian and his brother Valens in 364, and it was this Valens who lost his life in the first great victory won by Germans over Roman troops on Roman soil at Adrianople in 378. Valentinian's son, Gratian, chose as his colleague in the East, Theodosius, who was to be known as the Great and who again united the empire in 394 only in time to die, leaving it to his two sons.

Theodosius did much to solve the German problems temporarily by further recognizing the services of the Germans as auxiliaries and by giving their leaders high ranks and titles in the Roman service. His championship of orthodoxy and his reforms earned him the title of the Great—perhaps by contrast with his immediate predecessors.

The defense of the eastern frontier was an important problem throughout, as here Rome was faced by the strong power of the Sassanid Persian Empire. Founded in 226 on the ruins of the Parthian Empire, the new state of the Persian Sassanids was vigorous and ambitious. Rome first encountered the strength of the Sassanids in 229 when Ardashir, the founder of the dynasty, demanded that Rome withdraw from all her Asiatic provinces. Alexander Severus was defeated in battle and the Persians occupied Roman Armenia. Wars between the two powers continued throughout the third century, Mesopotamia passing from one to the other in a series of campaigns. The most important event of this struggle was the capture of the Roman emperor Valerian in 260. In the general confusion, there arose the buffer Arab state of Palmyra, which successfully withheld and even invaded Persia, reaching its height under the romantic Queen Zenobia, only to be completely destroyed by the Romans. In 296–297 Rome and Persia again came to immediate conflict; Galerius was routed at Carrhae, but more than made up for his defeat by annihilating the Persian army the following year and forcing on Persia a most unfavorable treaty, which ceded to Rome all the disputed border lands and moved the frontier from the Euphrates east to the Tigris.

In the reign of Shapur II of Persia (309–379), there were three major wars with Rome. Constantius was defeated in the first; in the second, Julian made a brilliant campaign into Persia and very nearly succeeded in capturing the capital of Ctesiphon but died on the campaign, and his successor Jovian made a most humiliating peace (363). The third war was desultory and inconclusive, but the peace concluded in 384 lasted, with minor exceptions, until the sixth century.

In this interval Persia was busy with the Epthalites, or White Huns, a nomadic people of the Asiatic steppes, who appeared on her northern frontier in 425. For ninety years the Persians and the Huns kept up a war which swayed back and forth across the Oxus, until Kobad finally destroyed the Hun power in 513.

ECONOMIC DECLINE

However important the military situation may have been as a factor in the decline of Rome, it is not in the politics or armies but in the spirit of its people that the strength of any state lies. And the economic, social and moral conditions of the empire are just as important in studying the symptoms of Roman decline as the political and military.

As has been noted above, the general prosperity of the empire was destroyed by the incessant civil wars of the third century. In a vain attempt to maintain the appearance of prosperity by keeping prices up, the emperors of the third century had inaugurated a ruinous policy of inflation and currency debasement. By the end of the century, the Roman coinage was practically meaningless as only supposedly gold and silver coins were issued instead of pure bullion. Diocletian, and after him Constantine, grappled with this problem and the latter succeeded in re-establishing a gold standard, based on the new *solidus* which became the standard coin for several centuries thereafter.

Meanwhile, however, the use of money as a medium of exchange had suffered badly. Barter and exchange began to replace the use of money in simpler business transactions. The government itself began to collect some of its extraordinary requisitions in produce. It was an old custom to demand a special tax for the support of the army, and these special taxes came to be collected not in money but in produce. This tax collected in kind was called the *annona*. Diocletian made this extraordinary tax a regular institution, and passed laws which reformed completely the tax system of the empire. The whole wealth of the empire, including labor, was assessed in a system of units called *iuga* or *capita*. The caput was the value of one man's labor and was used for the assessment of slaves, tenant farmers, servants, factory employees, etc. The iugum was the unit for assessing land or other property. It was not based on acreage but on the productivity of the soil.

The number of iuga in the municipality was reported to the provincial capital and on into the imperial treasury. When a tax was desired, the total amount asked for would be divided by the total number of iuga and capita in the empire and the amount to be paid from each iuga determined. Then each man paid according to the number of iuga and capita which he possessed. This system, although it might not meet the approval of modern tax experts, had much to commend it, as it was a great improvement over the older Roman system of farming taxes. But it had one terrible defect which caused it to become an unbearable grievance. The success of the system depended entirely upon the accurate knowledge of the number of iuga which any individual possessed; this required frequent appraisals and re-evaluations of the land. Such an appraisal was made at the time of the census which enumerated the population and also its property. At the beginning, the census was taken every five years, but the time between one taking of the census and the next was allowed to become longer so that later they were taken only every fifteen years. The decree ordering a census was called an *indictio* and so regular did it become to issue them only at fifteen-year intervals that the term indiction still means a fifteen-year period, and was for centuries employed as a chronological division.

Many changes may come to a property in the course of fifteen years under the best of circumstances. When there is civil war and the country-side is ravaged by armies passing across it, the depreciation of values is rapid. Yet until the next census, the farmer was forced to pay the taxes on the full valuation of his property made at the previous census. This became not only unbearable but impossible. When we realize that the same conditions applied to industry and city property, we can understand some of the misery which the taxes caused. Men found themselves unable to pay their taxes and were willing to abandon their property completely rather than be held for the taxes, which often amounted to more than the property was worth. The taxes levied were not heavier than they had been at earlier times in the history of Rome, but the ability of the people to pay them was greatly diminished. For it was found necessary to use capital to meet the taxes which could no longer be paid out of income. Heavy taxation can be borne when the national income is high, but it was altogether impossible to maintain a tax system which required the liquidation of capital to meet the tax assessments.

Before the inability of the people to pay the taxes, the old system of tax collection broke down. To assure the regular receipt of the taxes new laws were passed which laid the responsibility for the collection of local taxes on the local curiales—members of the local senate, the upper middle class landholders. They were compelled to pay the government the entire amount of the tax assessed against the district; it was up to them to collect it as best they could from the people, and what they could not collect had to be paid out of their own pockets. This obviously made the position of curiales undesirable and men sought to evade entrance into that class. To prevent the avoidance of this obligation, membership in the curia was made compulsory by a law of 325 which forced all citizens possessed of a stated amount of property to become enrolled in the local curiae. They were forbidden to seek escape by entrance into the army, which had been closed to them as a class. In 320 they were forbidden to enter the clergy. They were tied to their property and to their responsibilities. For them there was no legitimate escape; only one good way existed whereby they might avoid the unbearable obligations of their caste. They could give all their lands and properties to some Roman senator who was tax exempt locally and who would rent them back their lands for a stipulated sum. But in doing this they gave up their title to the lands and deprived their children of their inheritance. This transaction was called a *precarium* and the man who gave up his lands and got them back for rent was termed a *precarist,* terms derived from the verb *precor,* meaning to pray or request.

We shall return to a discussion of this important institution in later sections of this work.

The curial was not the only class of society which was bound to its obligations. There developed throughout the late empire a definite caste system; men in all stations and occupations of life were forced by law to remain in those exact occupations or stations and their status became hereditary. This applied not only to the curiales but to the army, to agricultural workers, artisans, sailors, porters, and every class and occupational group. Birth determined a man's rank and occupation and there was no escaping his lot. (It is interesting to note that the children of soldiers could escape from the army only by becoming members of the curiae, showing the position of that unfortunate class.[3]) The pauperization and virtual destruction of the curiales was the destruction of the middle class. The system was no less hard on the lower classes, who were reduced to a servile state.

Early in the empire, the land had come chiefly into the hands of a small class of great landowners, mostly of the senatorial class. These privileged aristocrats worked their great estates, called *latifundia,* by means of slave gangs or by renting out portions of their estates to free tenant farmers called *coloni.* The greatest of all these landlords was the emperor himself, whose private domains were scattered all through the empire. Several elements combined to reduce the status of the free coloni and to bring them closer to the slaves, who were their fellow workers. In the first place the supply of slaves was cut off when Rome ceased to expand and conquer new territories and peoples; as the supply was decreased the cost went up and soon it became economically unsound to try to run the farms by means of costly slave labor. Slaves continued as domestic servants, and as tutors and personal attendants, but the agricultural slave became a luxury and was gradually given up. Landlords found that it was cheaper and better economy to rent the land to tenant farmers and even to free the slaves and put them out on the land as dependent tenants. The freedman was of course socially and economically inferior to the free tenant farmer, but hard times tended to draw them together into a single class. A bad harvest would cause the free farmer to run behind in his rent, which was usually paid in produce. He would borrow from the lord for seed and would be unable to repay the loan. As his debt increased, he would be forced to pay it through extra labor for the lord. This same process also reduced many independent free farmers to the servile level; they would mortgage their lands to the lord and would be unable to pay off the mortgage. The lord foreclosed and the farmer found himself left with no means of existence; he would accordingly pray the lord to let him have his farm back in turn for rent and services, in other words he became a precarist. We have already seen how the curiales would use the precarium to escape from their caste.

[3] D. M. Parker, *History of Roman World, 138–337, A.D.* p. 289.

All of these groups, curial, precarist, free farmer, tenant farmer, and freed-man tended to become confused as they all paid for their lands in produce and in services. In the late empire they were all termed coloni, in the Middle Ages they became *serfs*.

After the time of Constantine, the coloni were bound to the soil. When life had become unbearable for the colonus, he would try to leave. But that could not be permitted as he was taxed along with the land and live-stock as part of the property of the estate. When the colonus ran away he was returned to his master and his land; the master could transfer him from one piece of property to another, but the colonus was fixed on the estate and could not leave it. Like all the rest of society, he was caught in his caste and was tied to the land he worked.

The system of paying for things in service rather than in money was not restricted to the dependents of the great estates. It was used by the state and the services which men rendered were called *liturgies* or *corvées*. These services were compulsory services demanded by the state of the civilian population; they included work on the public roads, messenger service, hauling government supplies, and a thousand kinds of labor which the government was able to force the people to do. If it reduced the actual burden of taxation, it increased the obligations of the individual; but it was found possible to collect labor services from a man who was incapable of being distrained further for taxes. The records of a man's status, his taxes, his liturgies, were all kept by the local government, and, if he were unfree, by his lord as well. Is it any wonder that the Roman populace welcomed the barbarian armies which destroyed the records and gave them a chance to break away from the galling restrictions under which they lived? In many cases the Germans did not, of course, destroy the records, but the poor Roman could always hope that they might. If they kept them as the basis for their own administration he was not worse off, and he *might* profit by the disorders.

Only one real hope was held out to the oppressed Roman—a happy life in another and better world hereafter. The spread of the salvationist cults will be the subject of our next chapter, but it must be noted here that "otherworldliness" was one of the most important manifestations of the decline of Roman secular society. Men cared but little for the things of this life and sought consolation in the prospects of the hereafter. The spread of Christianity and the other oriental salvationist cults did much to undermine the interest in this world by focusing their attention on the world beyond.

Before closing this summary of the decline of the Roman world in the fourth century, let us look for a moment at the brighter side. With all its weakness, Roman civilization yet managed to survive the impact of the barbarians; its political institutions continued in the East, and in the

West they were carried on in the administrations of the German kingdoms. The society which seemed about to collapse from its own inward weakness managed to last on with increasing decadence, but nevertheless without any fundamental change, for another two or three centuries. As Professor Lot says: "Summing it all up, on the eve of its dismemberment, the Mediterranean world, unified under the domination of Rome, did not cut a bad figure in view of the other civilizations of the world: Persia, India or China. In spite of its faults and its vices, it did not seem to deserve the condemnation which is heaped upon it." [4]

[4] Lot, Pfister, and Ganshof, *Destinées*, pp. 6–7. Reprinted by permission of the publishers, Presses Universitaires de France.

CHAPTER 2

THE GROWTH OF THE CHRISTIAN CHURCH

✦

THE SALVATIONIST RELIGIONS

IN 325, the same year that construction was begun on the new capital of the empire, Constantine held the first oecumenical council of the Christian church at Nicea, in Asia Minor across the strait from his new city. Twelve years previously, by the Edict of Milan, in 313, he had declared Christianity one of the recognized religions of the empire. This is the second great event which marks the opening of the fourth century as the obvious starting point for the history of the medieval world.

By the time Christianity was recognized as an official religion, it had had three centuries of existence in which it had developed its organization and its doctrines. At first regarded as merely a sect of Judaism, it had spread to the Gentiles with the preaching of St. Paul, whose activities created Christian communities in the chief cities of the empire. Making its initial appeal to the downtrodden and oppressed, Christianity had spread throughout the Mediterranean world and had slowly forged ahead, taking its place among the other salvationist religions which the East gave to the West. Finally it outdistanced even its most formidable rivals, and by the beginning of the fourth century the Christian church had become so strong that Constantine found political strength in allying to himself the many adherents of the new faith.

In his *Five Stages of Greek Religion,* Professor Gilbert Murray devotes a chapter to what he terms "The Failure of Nerve"; in this chapter he discusses the rise of the salvationist cults, which developed as men lost confidence in the things of this world and turned to a hope for a better world beyond. Ancient paganism was essentially designed for a prosperous world where religion was a matter of civic life; the gods were attended by civic colleges of priests and showered their favors on the communities that worshipped them. There was nothing individual about it; the ancient gods and the city states were necessarily joined in a common concept and shared a common destiny. The destruction of the city state brought down in its ruins the pagan deities who had aforetime protected it. But as long as the world was good, men gave little thought to religion and the old official paganism sufficed for the general needs. Then after the conquests of

Philip and Alexander, the Greeks had found that the old order had crumbled; their happy (if turbulent) world was gone, and a harder existence lay before them. The man who had previously been satisfied with the things of this world and gave little thought to the future, suddenly found himself longing for something better than he could achieve here. Two avenues of thought lay before him: one was the way of philosophy— and it was in the Hellenistic age that both the Stoic and Epicurean philosophies developed—the other was the salvationist religious concept, which had been popular for so many centuries in the East, where men had always been oppressed by tyrants and conquerors.

Both of these lines of religious speculation developed in the Hellenistic world. The appeal of the philosophies was to the intellectuals; Epicureanism offered men the highest concept of self-development possible within the limits of a physical universe. It scorned the need of a hereafter and taught that the fullest accomplishment of man's existence could be made in this world, that the individual could perfect himself through service and uprightness in society and that beyond this earth there was nothing to fear or to hope for. Stoicism too taught a philosophy of service to one's fellowmen, though its eschatology did make dangerous compromises with popular beliefs and was distinctly on a lower plane than the high rationalism of the Epicureans. Yet Stoicism produced the finest of the Roman emperors in the person of Marcus Aurelius, and the high quality of its ethics are evident in the writings of Seneca and Marcus Aurelius.

But any of these philosophies had a cold intellectual appeal and did not involve the emotions; they were excellent for those who could understand them, but could never hope to reach the hearts of the great masses who aspired for something more than this world could give them. To these people the salvationist religions of the East, with their promise of salvation in another world, offered consolation and hope. Introduced into Rome in the days of the republic, the salvationist cults did not spread appreciably until the troubled times of the empire. Then, as hardships increased and men became more and more dissatisfied with the conditions of life, the salvationist religions came into their own.

There were several of these salvationist religions which Rome took over from the East. From Egypt came the trinity of Isis, Osirus, and Horus, as well as a host of lesser deities, and the worship of the Queen Goddess Isis gained many converts throughout the Roman world. The finest exposition of the inspiring effects of the mysteries of Isis is to be found in the last chapters of Apuleius' *Golden Ass*, where the redemption of the soul through the initiation into the cult of Isis is described with fervor. From Asia Minor came the cult of Cybele or Magna Mater, the great earth goddess, giver of life. From Persia came the religion of Mithra, god of the undying sun, the militant, conquering god, who led his votaries to victories here and hereafter. The religion of Isis has been called the religion of the merchants; Mithra was the god of the army. All of these cults had several things in common; all promised to their believers an individual salvation in an afterlife; all were esoteric and could only be entered through participation in certain mysterious rites; all were served by a priestly class, dedicated to the service of the deity and set apart from the common herd. And none of them were necessarily exclusive.

Like them in its promise of salvation, its esoteric character and its priest-hood, but wholly unlike them in its monotheistic exclusiveness was Juda-ism. Unlike them too in that it was the religion of a single people and not fundamentally evangelical, Judaism preached its doctrine of salvation for the chosen people whom God had selected as his own. Conversion was per-mitted and new members were initiated into the faith, but Judaism never made the great efforts to obtain converts which any of the other salvationist cults did.

Christianity made its first converts from among the Jews. It resembled Judaism more than any of the other religions and was as rigidly mono-theistic as the religion of Israel; but it was an evangelical sect from the time of Paul on, and it soon came into conflict with the other religions as Judaism, which sought no converts, had not. An interesting commentary on the early rise of the Christian church is the book of Celsus (preserved to us in Origen's *Contra Celsum,* a work refuting it) which gives the reac-tions of a cultured Roman pagan to the spread of the new faith. With its appeal essentially to the outcast and downtrodden, with its emphasis on the redemption of the sinner and the salvation of the lost sheep, the teach-ings of Christianity seem to Celsus a faith which could have but little attraction to any but the lowest elements of society. That it was among the poor and lowly that the church got its first start is beyond quesion. But the teachings of Jesus and of St. Paul (who incorporated no small amount of Platonism into the Christian doctrine) won converts in all classes of society and it was not long before Roman matrons of the highest social classes were to be found among the ranks of the converts.

At first the Roman government paid little attention to the new faith. Then two things became apparent as the movement spread; the Christians under no circumstances would worship any other God and refused even the conventional emperor worship of the Divine Augustus which was required of all Romans; moreover, the meetings of the Christians were secret and they refused to divulge to those not initiated into the sect the proceedings of their gatherings. It was because of these two factors that Christianity was persecuted. Throughout the ages any exclusive, secret, easily isolatable group has invariably been suspect as subversive, and has suffered accordingly.

"The Blood of the Martyrs"

Emperor worship had come to Rome from the Orient through Greece and the Greek apotheosis of their rulers. Alexander the Great was the first to be proclaimed a god in his own lifetime, but the apotheosis of the ruler was common in the empires of the Ptolemies in Egypt and the Seleucids of Syria. Deification had been avoided as much as possible by the early Julio-Claudian emperors of Rome, although they accepted altars and statues to the *genius* of their house. But the worship of the emperor (or his genius) became an official cult in Rome, and worship at the altar of the reigning Augustus was a necessary act of allegiance required of every citizen. It was far more an act of civic obedience and political allegiance than of religious faith, but the monotheistic fervor of the Jew or the Christian could brook no compromise with the idolatry implied therein, and both sects stalwartly refused to comply with the law in this respect. As this refusal to adore the emperor was then about the equivalent of refusal to salute the flag or to swear allegiance to the Constitution today, the Roman government and people became very suspicious of the loyalty of the groups concerned. When, moreover, they consistently refused to open the doors of their meetings to any outsiders or to reveal even to government officials what went on in their conventicles, the Jews and Christians were marked down as subversive groups to be carefully watched. It was because of this foundation of general suspicion that Nero and the Roman populace could be led so readily to believe that the burning of Rome was the work of the Christians.

The early martyrs went to their deaths because they were suspected of politically subversive activities. The government had, at first, no complaint against their faith, only the fear that it masked antisocial and antigovernmental conspiracies. Later on, in the persecutions of the era of Diocletian, the basis of the charges shifted and membership in the sect which had been officially proscribed was *per se* sufficient to invoke martyrdom; but that was after the emperors had convinced themselves that allegiance to the Christian church and allegiance to the empire were mutually incompatible and that a confirmed Christian could not be a good Roman. The early persecutions were entirely political. Diocletian, one of the best emperors, who re-established strong government in the empire, was most active in persecuting the Christians.

Persecution, as everyone knows, merely strengthened the church. It gave the new sect publicity which called the attention of all classes to its existence. The steadfast courage of the martyrs, and their apparent joy in the horrible sufferings which liberated them from the shackles of this earthly life and opened for them the gates of the Heavenly Jerusalem, impressed even the most bitter opponents. That men were willing to die so readily for an ideal seemed to demonstrate the inherent quality of that ideal; men who came to the arena to see the show, when some Christians were to be thrown to the wild beasts, left with a feeling of wonder which often led them to the faith. Indeed, by the fourth century, Christianity had spread so widely in all classes of society that it probably commanded the allegiance of a larger number of people than any other religion within the empire. At least, there can be little doubt but that this was the opinion of Constantine, and, without going into the matter of his own miraculous conversion, it is safe to affirm that Constantine secured the support of a large percentage of the people by accepting the Christian faith as an official religion of the empire and allowing men to openly profess the religion to which they had so long secretly adhered. Instead of pursuing the policy of his predecessors, who felt that as the Christians gave their only real loyalty and allegiance to their church they could not give loyalty to the empire and must therefore be destroyed as antisocial characters, Constantine wisely saw that by joining the state and the church as closely as possible, he could turn to the advantage of the state that undying loyalty which the Christians gave to their church. By ending the antagonism between church and state and substituting therefor a community of interests between the two, Constantine was able to strengthen his political control and materially bolster up the unity of his empire.

ORGANIZATION OF THE EARLY CHURCH

The statement that Constantine acquired strength by winning over the Christians may seem inconsistent with the remark in the previous chapter that the otherworldliness of the salvationist religions was a sign of the decline, and requires some explanation. Early Christianity was an aloof and self-conscious sect. Persecuted by the state and scoffed at by outsiders, the Christians withdrew into themselves and turned their thoughts to the accomplishment of their individual salvation. This individualism was a characteristic of all the salvationist cults, which stressed the salvation of the individual soul. The world in general was corrupt and headed for perdition but the true believer could avoid the general damnation and secure for himself that salvation which his soul craved. This preoccupation with the life after death, this otherworldliness, tended to make Christians as well as other salvationists indifferent to political, economic, or social problems of this world, and caused them to subordinate all temporal matters to the prime business of saving their own souls. Thus they became at best indifferent citizens. Moreover, the early Christians were pacifists and refused to fight, even when conscripted into the army. They were the meek who waited for their inheritance, not in this world, but the next, and they stolidly refused to bear arms in the defense of any temporal power.

As the faith spread, however, it came to include many who were less rigidly ascetic and more practical-minded. Christians began to assume their normal obligations towards the state and society and to strive for the improvement of conditions here as well as salvation hereafter. By the beginning of the fourth century, there were whole legions in the army made up almost exclusively of Christians, and members of the faith were to be found in all departments of the administration as well as in the humbler walks of life.

They still clung closely together and tried to present a united front to the outside world. Instead of appealing to the law when they had disputes among themselves, Christians would submit their differences to their bishop who would settle the cases without recourse to the secular courts. Thus the bishops developed an extensive judicial power. Constantine recognized this and continued the bishop's courts, recognizing their competency and permitting them to function together with the secular courts. As long as men were taking their cases to the bishops, it was much better to give the bishops legal power to adjudicate them.

By the time the church was recognized, it had developed a complete organization. Originally each community of Christians had organized independently under their pastor or bishop, and the only connection they had with the other Christian communities was through the missionary activities of the preachers who visted the various communities. There are two lines of development in organization: the growth of organization within the individual community, and that of the affiliation of the communities into a single universal church. Within the community developed the assistants to the bishop—the priests, deacons, lectors, and the other minor officials who assisted him in the duties of his office. At first the bishop was the head of the Christian group within the city and ministered to his flock almost unaided, save for some assistance by the deacons in preparing the feasts. As the communities grew, so extensive did the demands on the bishop become that it was necessary for him to have many assistants; the priests were those who assisted the bishop in the observation of the service of the altar and in the absence of the bishop said Mass and performed the sacraments of baptism, marriage, and the eucharist. They were his assistants in things spiritual. The deacons aided him in the administration of the church and in the social work of the community; they helped prepare the church and the altar for services, but they also assisted in the bishop's court, in keeping the records of the community and kindred temporal matters.

Originally every city that had a Christian community had its own bishop. Christianity was essentially an urban religion and the survival of the word *pagan* which is the same stem as *peasant* shows how a country-fellow and a believer in the old gods were considered as one and the same. As the faith spread into the rural districts, the bishops had to extend their spheres of activity so far that they divided their communities, which were called dioceses, into smaller units and delegated priests to take care of smaller outlying churches called parishes. The limits of the episcopal diocese generally coincided with the Roman secular district of the civitas or municipality, which we have seen above was the standard local unit in the imperial administration. Above the civitates in the civil administration were the provinces; the church took over this organization exactly, and the various churches were brought together under an administrative head in the province. This head was the metropolitan (the bishop of the capital city of the province) or the archbishop. In the East, it was an invariable custom that the bishop of the secular provincial metropolis should be the head of the province. The Eastern church still uses the title of metropolitan, but in the Western church the identity was not always preserved, if, for example, a large Christian community existed in one of the other towns of the province but not in the capital city. The ecclesiastical metropolitans thus occasionally were not located in the secular metropolis—and the title of archbishop became the standard one in the Western church.

Above the archbishops or metropolitans were the patriarchs. When the church was first officially recognized there were only three patriarchates: Rome, Antioch, and Alexandria, the three largest Christian communities, whose churches had all been founded by apostles in the earliest days of the faith. Jerusalem and Constantinople subsequently became patriarchates, but could not boast apostolic foundation and were at first not so important as the elder three. If it seems strange that Jerusalem should not be an apostolic foundation, it must be remembered that the city of Jerusalem had been destroyed and her people scattered by the emperor Titus in 70 A.D.; the apostolic church there was destroyed and the patriarchate which later arose was founded only after the city had been rebuilt. The patriarch had certain administrative powers over the bishops and archbishops in his patriarchate. Before the recognition of Christianity, it was impossible for the organization of the church to function very smoothly, as they could not hold great councils, and even provincial and diocesian councils were dangerous. After the official recognition of the church, however, the archbishops exercised a real control over their suffragan bishops and the patriarchs had considerable administrative power over the archbishops whose sees lay within their patriarchates. While Rome, Antioch, and Alexandria were all considered equal, actually Rome had the greatest power from the beginning, for the sphere of influence of the Roman patriarch included all of the Western empire, bishops from Gaul, Spain and north Africa as well as those of Italy being subject to the patriarch of Rome, while the Eastern patriarchs had of necessity more restricted areas.

DOCTRINAL DISPUTES

Not only was the organization of the church dependent upon its ability to come out in the open, its doctrine also had suffered from the inability to straighten out different theories through open discussion. As long as the church had to work underground (literally, for in Rome they met in the catacombs in the earliest days) differences in interpretation and doctrinal detail were bound to develop. In the pre-Constantinian period several heresies developed—notably those of the Ebionites, who denied any divinity to Christ; the Sabellians, who taught that Christ and the Holy Spirit were but revelations of God and had no separate existence; the Montanists, who preached the approaching end of the world and the second coming of Christ; and the Gnostics, who fused Christianity with Persian mysteries of Zoroastrianism, the Greek philosophy of Platonism and crude superstition, to arrive at a belief in two gods and an elaborate system of charms and incantations. The Gnostics parted so far from orthodox Christianity that they may be considered a separate religion, but the others were all variations of theological belief which developed within the Christian fold. Most important of all was the schism which had developed at Alexandria between a deacon, Athanasius, and a priest, Arius, over the nature of the Trinity. The dispute, known as the Arian Heresy, or the Trinitarian Controversy, threw the church into a turmoil and very nearly wrecked the unity of the faith. According to Arius, within the Trinity, the Son was inferior to the Father, was not of the same divine substance and was not coexistent in eternity with the Father, but had been created by Him; his doctrines approximated Unitarianism today. Anthanasius, supported by the patriarch Alexander, championed the Trinity with the doctrine that Christ was coeternal, consubstantial, begotten and not created, and in every respect one with God. Both sides gained adherents and the question became a bitter one. It is extremely difficult for us to comprehend today the excitement and personal vindictiveness with which men fought out theological questions in the fourth and fifth centuries. Theology was the preoccupation of everyone and theological orthodoxy was sufficient to redeem a life of the worst vice and cruelty, whereas the noblest soul was considered damned if infected with the virus of heresy. It has been said that theology and the circuses were the two interests of the populace of Constantinople, and history demonstrates that men were willing to fight to the death for some fine point of theology far more readily than they were to lift a hand to prevent the most inhuman tyranny and oppression.

To Constantine, who had expected harmony, unity and strength through the recognition of Christianity, it came as a grievous blow to find the church so divided against itself over this matter of the Trinity. In order to settle the question and restore unity and peace to the church, the emperor summoned all the bishops to assemble for a general council at Nicaea in 325. This First Oecumenical Council, which was attended by over three hundred bishops, set about defining the dogma of the faith and clearing up moot points. It decided the question of the Trinity in favor of the Athanasian creed and declared Arius and his followers to be heretics. It then drew up the famous Nicene Creed which, with emendations and changes, has been the basis for Christian doctrine ever since.

The Council of Nicaea was only the first of many councils needed to define the exact doctrine of the church. The Arians, although defeated in the decrees of Nicaea, were not yet destroyed, and the ban of exile which had been imposed on Arius and his partisans by the Council was soon revoked. Both parties continued their agitation, the Arians gaining important support. For half a century after Nicaea, the theological world was torn between the two factions, with the Arians securing the victory in local councils and enforcing their doctrines through the power of friendly emperors. For a short time under the emperor Julian there was a temporary revival of paganism, but the new faith proved too strong for Julian's attempted classical revival.

The last emperor to support the Arians was Valens, who died on the field of Adrianople in 378, and at the Second Oecumenical Council, held at Constantinople in 381, the Arians were finally routed. The position of the Holy Spirit had become the subject of a dispute known as the Pneuma-tomachic Heresy, which starting from the Arian view of the Trinity, had declared that the Holy Spirit was not an integral part of the Trinity at all but was in substance akin to the angels, a doctrine most repulsive to good Trinitarians. The Council of Constantinople in condemning this heresy repeated the condemnation of the Arians. It was this same Council of Constantinople which recognized the importance of the city where it was holding its sessions by elevating the new capital to the rank of a patriarchate, inferior only to the see of Rome.

But if the Arians were crushed within the empire, their influence was to continue, for it was during the period of their supremacy that the greatest gains had been made in the conversion of the German tribes through the missionary activities of Ulfilas, who translated the Gospels into the Gothic vernacular. As a result the Christianity of the Germans, when they first crossed into the empire, was of the Arian persuasion.

The end of the Trinitarian Controversy did not bring peace for long within the ranks of the clergy. It was Nestorius, the patriarch of Constan-tinople (428–431), who started the next great dispute, the so-called Christo-logical Controversy, which agitated the church through the fifth and sixth centuries. The basis of the argument was laid in the writings of Theodore of Mopsuesta, who maintained that as Christ's God-head was the incar-nation of the Word in man, there must have been two distinct persons in

Christ, the divine and the human. The human man, born of Mary, was made divine by the indwelling of the Logos which was sent from God; Mary was the mother of the man Christ, but not of the God Christ; it was wrong to refer to her, as was commonly done as *Theotokos* (Mother of God) since she was in actuality merely *Christotokos* (Mother of Christ). This doctrine, which gained enthusiastic support at the great school at Antioch was officially advanced by Nestorius in a sermon at Constantinople. At once Celestine, the bishop of Rome, and Cyril of Alexandria leaped to the defense of the Theotokos. A council was summoned to meet at Ephesus in 431 (Third Oecumenical Council) to settle the dispute. The selection of Ephesus was a first victory for the anti-Nestorian party for Ephesus was the ancient city of Diana, and since its conversion to Christianity had become the center of the worship of Mary. Without waiting for the arrival of John of Antioch, Nestorius' chief supporter, who was bringing a large delegation of clergy and who had been delayed, the Council voted the condemnation of Nestorius and his doctrines. When John of Antioch arrived too late, he seceded and held his own council which approved Nestorianism and condemned Cyril. The emperor Theodosius II, to whom the issue may well have seemed confusing, obligingly confirmed the acts of both councils; but later when the situation had been more fully explained, ratified the decisions of the Council of Ephesus and condemned those of the Nestorians. Nestorius was himself driven from his see and from the empire; he retired to Persia where his followers founded a church which spread into India and China, at one time numbering millions of adherents. It still exists in small numbers in the Middle East and India.

The triumph of Cyril over Nestorius led his followers into a heresy no less dangerous than that of the Nestorians. Having established that Christ was not two persons but one, it was argued that the divine and the human natures must be indivisibly fused into a single nature. This doctrine was called Monophysitism from its insistence on the single nature of Christ, and was supported by the churches of Alexandria and Jerusalem. Flavian of Constantinople ruled that this dogma was heresy, and Leo I of Rome wrote his famous *Tome* to support the anti-Monophysite position. A council was summoned to meet at Ephesus (449) which, under the presidency of Dioscorus of Alexandria, himself a Monophysite, proclaimed the Monophysite belief the true doctrine of the church. At once there rose a storm of protest. Rome, which had supported Alexandria against the pretentions of Constantinople, now saw herself ignored by the Egyptians, who seemed to be aspiring to universal leadership. Dioscorus had not permitted the Roman delegates to Ephesus to present their case; Leo replied by refusing to recognize the Council of Ephesus and breaking completely with Dioscorus. Meanwhile the emperor Theodosius II, who had been favorable to the Egyptians, died and was succeeded by Marcian and Pulcheria who inclined towards Constantinople and Rome.

A new council was summoned to meet at Chalcedon in 451. The Council of Chalcedon (Fourth Oecumenical Council) was the largest ever held up to that time and was attended by 630 prelates. It repudiated the decisions of the "Robber Council" of Ephesus which was declared to be no true council at all, denied the doctrines of the Monophysites and deposed Dioscorus from his see. The creed which the Council adopted was based essentially on the *Tome* of Leo and provided that the orthodox must believe that Christ was one person, with two natures, without confusion or conversion, the properties of each nature being complete, but united into a single person.

Monophysitism had gained too strong a foothold to be easily routed however, and although the sect was declared heretical and orthodox bishops were appointed to fill the sees of the Monophysites, the heretic clergy continued to carry on their work and the people continued to support them. It was altogether impossible to rout out the heresy; for thirty years the Monophysites held out against the condemnation of the orthodox and the temporal power. In desperation the emperor Zeno in 482 issued the *Henoticon,* an attempt at compromise, which was accepted by the orthodox patriarch of Constantinople and the Monophysite of Alexandria. But Rome rejected any compromise; Felix II excommunicated both the patriarchs who had subscribed to the offensive document. The persistency of the Roman see was finally rewarded in 519 when the emperor Justin I ordered that all the clergy subscribe to a profession of faith drawn up by Hormisdas, which condemned Nestorians and Monophysites equally, and asserted that, as St. Peter spoke through the Rome bishop, the orthodoxy of Rome was by divine ordination and was at all times unimpeachable. To this humiliating document the proud prelates of the East were forced to subscribe. Rome alone of the great patriarchates had never fallen into heresy, Rome alone was infallibly orthodox; through Rome and through Rome alone came the voice of God; the supremacy of the Roman see was well in process of establishment.

PRIMACY OF ROME

Rome itself always based its primacy on the firm rock of the Petrine theory. Christ had built his church on St. Peter, Peter had located his church at Rome, the bishops of Rome were the successors of Peter and on them naturally developed the headship of the church. Beyond this scriptural basis there were, however, other reasons why Rome should have assumed a primacy. Not only Peter but Paul had governed the church at Rome—it had a double apostolic foundation. Rome was the ancient capital of the state and as such should be the first of the churches. This claim needed to be urged with extreme care, however, for Constantinople pointed out that the capital had been moved, and that she therefore was by right the first church of the empire. In fact, it was at Constantinople more than at Rome that this cause was advanced as a reason for Rome's claim to primacy, Rome always minimizing its importance. There were, moreover, certain practical considerations which facilitated the establishment of the Roman primacy. Rome had, as we have seen, by far the largest body of dependent churches of any of the great patriarchal sees; for a time its control over the Western churches was contested, either by other patriarchs, or more commonly by the bishops themselves who resented subjection to Rome, but an imperial decree of 445 definitely placed all the churches of the West under the authority of Rome and rendered it supreme throughout the Western empire. This primacy of Rome was further affirmed by the "Perpetual Edict" of Valentinian III and by a decree of Phocas in 607 which stated that, "the See of Blessed Peter the Apostle should be head of all the churches."

Its geographical position also helped Rome. Not only was it not involved in the intense rivalries of the Eastern patriarchs, but it was far removed from the seat of imperial control at Constantinople. The patriarch at Constantinople never could quite shake off the imperial control and always remained too much of an imperial chaplain, dominated by the court. The Roman bishop, however, as we shall see, became the chief political representative of the empire in Italy, and added political and governmental duties to his spiritual powers. The misfortunes of the Western empire were the opportunity for the Roman see, and bishops of the fifth and sixth centuries were men able to meet the emergency and to profit from the confusion to increase their own power. Indeed, one of the chief causes for the ascendency of Rome lay in the strong characters and vigorous personalities of its bishops, men like Innocent, Damasus, Leo, Pelagius, and Gregory the Great. When John the Faster of Constantinople took the title of Oecumenical Patriarch, Gregory replied with an equal superlative by assuming the humble *"Servus servorum Dei"*; but the "servant" was the strongest power in the Western world at the time. At a later date the extensive missionary activities which were carried on under the guidance of Rome and the acquisition of great landed wealth in the Patrimony of St. Peter added to the strength and influence of Rome, but, by the end of the sixth century the Roman see, or, as it is proper to term it by then, the papacy, had achieved an acknowledged primacy throughout the West.

In discussing the primacy of Rome it must always be borne in mind that even today its supremacy is not recognized by the patriarch of Constantinople. The Moslem conquests which destroyed the sees of Antioch, Jerusalem, and Alexandria narrowed the field down to the two prelates at

Rome and Constantinople, and though we are accustomed to speak of the primacy of Rome, as if to imply that it made good its claims to universal dominion, the Greek church does not recognize these claims and still insists on the parity of the patriarchs. Nor is this supremacy admitted by the schismatic Eastern churches which continued throughout the Moslem domination.

ASCETICISM AND RISE OF MONASTICISM

While the church was straightening out its dogma, and the pope was establishing his control over the entire church of the West, a movement had begun within Christianity which was to have an immeasurable effect on the history and organization of the church. In the early days, before Christianity had been recognized, membership in the church had set the believers apart from the rest of the world and martyrdom had sanctified them as men who strove not for the things of this world but for everlasting glory. The official recognition of Christianity and the rapid spread of the church brought into the fold, however, many individuals who were less inspired than the early martyrs and who lowered considerably the high moral and spiritual tone of the Christian community. As soon as Christianity became socially correct, people joined the church for worldly reasons, and the moral level of the Christians became hardly different from their compatriots of the world outside.

This brought despair to the souls of rigid ascetics, who felt that the world was going to perdition and that the church no longer offered sufficient guarantees against the pollutions of the world, the flesh, and the devil. Despairing of the world and all that it contained, these timorous souls withdrew into themselves and the desert, that in solitude they might prepare themselves, through mortification of the flesh, for the blessed raptures of their heavenly homes.

Asceticism was not original with the Christian hermits; it had long flourished in the East, one of the most conspicuous exemplars being that Hindu prince, who withdrew from the world to become the Buddha. Asceticism was practiced by the devotees of each of the oriental salvationist cults, which came to Rome from the East, and even the philosophies produced "holy men" who scorned the world and retreated in isolation to the contemplation of the eternal verities.

Isolation, self-flagellation, and other forms of mortification of the flesh, excessive fasting, uncleanliness and hours spent in intensive prayer were characteristics of the early hermits. They resembled more than anything else the Hindu fakirs of today who lie on beds of nails and scourge themselves in the excesses of their religious zeal. The company of their fellows, decent and palatable food, comfortable clothing, and the pleasures of a bath were spurned by them as concessions to the corrupt flesh. They strove to outdo each other in their austerities and happy was the hermit who could set a new record. This may have been considered good sport, but on the whole Kingsley is correct when he characterizes their attitude as, "a superstition which ended by enervating instead of ennobling humanity." [1]

The earliest and perhaps most famous of all these anchorites was that St. Anthony (ob. 356) who withdrew to the desert of the Egyptian Thebaid and there wrestled with the devil and innumerable demons, who, concealing their wicked characters under the disguise of loose and lovely ladies were unceasing in their efforts to entrap his soul. More picturesque perhaps was St. Simeon Stylites (ob. 459), who perched for several decades on the top of a high pillar in the neighborhood of Antioch. He was accustomed to fast for forty days at a time, and when he could no longer stand would tie himself to a pillar so that he would not be forced through weakness to lie down or even sit. On the rare occasions when he permitted himself any food at all it was only water with a few beans or millet or other common vegetable. He never washed and his body was covered with vermin; there can be little doubt that at his death he ascended to heaven amid a great odor of sanctity; indeed it is specifically attested by one of his admirers who has left us a biography of the saint. Both in life and death he is reported to have performed miracles, but as Kingsley says, "these good hermits, by continual fasts and vigils, must have put themselves into a state of mental disease in which their evidence was worth nothing." [2]

At first the hermits were completely isolated, each man occupying his own patch of waste land, wholly cut off from the world; but as the fame of a holy hermit spread, admiring followers congregated around him so that he found that he was no longer a lonely solitary. Probably it was not because the waste spaces of the Thebaid became too crowded for each hermit to live alone (although the picture of the hermits in the Campo Santa at Pisa gives the impression of distinctly crowded conditions), but rather that the hordes of adoring imitators might be better regulated that the first cenoebitic establishments were created. At any rate, establishments soon developed where the hermits lived together communally, although they were liable to go through life without speaking to the men whose board they shared.

These communal establishments, called *lavra*, but which later came to be called monasteries, first developed in the East, under the influence of St. Basil, who wrote the first monastic (as opposed to eremitic) rule at the end of the fourth century. The anchorites of the Thebaid never took well to any community life, and although rules were written for their conduct

1 C. Kingsley: *The Hermits: Their Lives and Works.* (London, 1885) p. 170.
2 *Ibid.*, p. 205.

by St. Anthony and St. Pachomius (ob. 346) their disciples always remained solitaries, though the rule of Pachomius was followed by several thousand ascetics of both sexes. St. Basil (ob. 379), however, postulated a community life for his disciples, wherein they shared a common labor and common worship, a common roof and a common table. Extreme asceticism was eschewed, being replaced by hard manual labor and frequent prayers. The Basilian rule set the duties of the monk for each hour of the day and night and made no provision for individual ascetic excesses. It became extremely popular throughout the East, and is still the rule followed by the great majority of Eastern monasteries.

In the West, monasticism was introduced by Athanasius and spread by St. Martin of Tours (ob. 397) and St. Honoratus of Arles (c. 410). These early establishments followed the rule of St. Pachomius, but the Egyptian system was not found suited to Gaul, and Caesarius of Arles (fl. c. 500) wrote the first Western monastic rule. This early form of monasticism had been carried to Ireland by St. Patrick (c. 389-ob. 461), who had been a monk at Honoratus' establishment at Lérins, and in the Emerald Isle monasticism developed with unusual results. The Irish accepted the monastic ideal, but adapted it to their own clan organization, so that whole families entered monasteries without especially altering their mode of life. On the other hand, other Irish monks became the most violent ascetics, practicing the most rigid austerities. The Irish monasteries were responsible for a tremendous missionary effort which converted much of Gaul and Germany, and also for developing the finest of the "national hands" of majuscule writing and the loveliest illuminated manuscripts.

Although the Irish form of monasticism spread through the activities of missionaries such as St. Columba (521–597) and St. Columban (c. 545–615), who founded the monasteries of Bobbio and Luxeuil, the great monastic rule which became almost universal throughout the West was that of St. Benedict of Nursia (c. 480–543).

St. Benedict was a noble Roman from Nursia, who, after receiving the secular education of his time, turned from the world in disgust and became a solitary at Subiaco near Rome. There his austerities attracted disciples until he became the head of a considerable community which in time aroused the enmity of rival monastic houses. Benedict withdrew to the heights of Monte Cassino on the road towards Naples, and there in 529 established what was to become the most famous of all Western monasteries and the mother of thousands of similar establishments. For his monks St. Benedict drew up his celebrated Rule, a practical set of regulations for the life of a community devoted to the worship of God. Like St. Basil he rejected flagellation and excesses of mortification. Prayer, meditation, and work occupied the time of the monks, whose lives were regulated by the daily routine of the canonical hours. The monks could possess no individual property and had no will apart from that of their abbot. Poverty, chastity, and obedience were the essential things which the monk must swear to observe; the individual lost his identity and became a part of the monastic whole. His life was severe but not fantastic, and food, drink, and sleep were his portion as well as work and prayer. The one thing to be avoided above all else was idleness; self indulgence was forbidden, and the monk was to eat no more than he needed to keep fit for his tasks, but he should not eat less than was necessary, and though meat was in general forbidden, it was permitted to the sick or infirm. Drink was limited to a pint of wine a day, with more if the monk was engaged in hard labor, and while drunkenness is especially condemned, Benedict especially repudiated total prohibition. Clothing was to be simple and of coarse cloth, but warm and sufficient for comfort. In short the Benedictine Rule, while strict and austere, was in no wise fanatical or excessive; it was designed for men who aspired to humble themselves in the service of God and denied the vainglories of the extreme ascetics as much as the vanities of the worldly rich.

The monks who lived under the rule were termed regular clergy (*sub regula*) in distinction to the secular clergy who lived in the world (*in saecula*). Monks were originally laymen and did not receive ordination; as men set apart and devoted to religion they were considered clerics, but they were in no respect able to minister to others and themselves required the ministrations of priests in their religious life. To the monasteries were attached chaplains and other priests, who might or might not be monks themselves. It was only later that it became common for the monks to take holy orders, and even today not all monks are ordained clergy.

CHAPTER 3

THE EMPIRE IN THE FIFTH CENTURY
✠

PRACTICALLY, the empire, after the death of Theodosius (395), was divided into Eastern and Western halves, but it was only *de facto* never *de jure,* and no one would have admitted that the sacred unity of the empire had been rent. Nor was the actual division of the empire a fact before the seventh century. While it is traditional to speak of the "Fall of the Western Empire" in 476 and to discuss the various states which emerged within the former western provinces of the empire as Germanic kingdoms, they never actually or theoretically cut themselves off from the parent state, they were never more than autonomous provinces, always recognizing and always aping the metropolis. And the disturbances which afflicted the West never diminished in any way the continuity of life and institutions in the East. When the Arabs came in the seventh century, destroying much that existed of the Roman institutions and replacing them with a truly oriental culture—when they broke the unity of the Mediterranean world— the empire really was divided and began to disintegrate. But the German invasions did not produce this effect; they were never more than local disturbances, provincial affairs, which affected the more remote provinces without materially altering the life of the capital.

The Germans presented a problem both to the Eastern and Western parts of the empire. But whereas their incursions resulted in the setting up of autonomous principalities in the West, in the East the superior diplomacy and the persuasive qualities of the imperial treasury reduced them to raids and incursions which had little lasting effects.

Never has any state been so dominated by its capital as was the Roman Empire. Situated at the crossroads between east and west, north and south, Constantinople soon became the commercial and industrial center of the Roman world. Its position was geographically far more favorable than Rome's, and men were not slow to take advantage of the splendid facilities offered by the new metropolis. In it were centered not only the merchants who dominated the carrying trade, but the artisans and manufacturers, who produced articles of luxury for domestic consumption and for export. Textiles, jewelry, mosaics, and glass were made in the general vicinity of Constantinople; the furs of the north were treated there and fashioned into cloaks and garments for the wealthy nobles. Spices from the Orient, fine wines, and table delicacies of all kinds added to the pleasure of life there. Constantinople enjoyed, moreover, not only an economic superiority but a social supremacy. The seat of the court, it set the styles for the entire Roman world; and the barbarians copied the manners, dress, and customs of the aristocracy of the capital. Throughout its history, until after the ravages of the Fourth Crusade, Constantinople was the wonder city of the world to the rough barbarians who saw her magnificence. Brilliant, luxurious, sophisticated, Constantinople was the city of splendor and gay life, as well as the financial, industrial, and commercial hub of the empire. In Constantinople were the most magnificent buildings, in its circuses were held the most spectacular games and chariot races. Constantinople was the New York and Hollywood of the Mediterranean world from the fourth to the thirteenth century.

Situated serenely on the Bosphorus, the New Rome dominated the empire and focused on herself all the energies and interests of her wide territories. Byzantinization has come to mean excessive centralization and bureaucracy. Paris has often been considered the heart of France, but Paris never absorbed the country as Constantinople did. The government, the church, civil and military life all centered in the capital city and in the Sacred Palace of the Basileus. The concept of Byzantium as a state ridden with palace intrigue, a government overloaded with bureaucratic red tape, is not incorrect in so far as it reflects the concentration of power and authority in the capital. When the great Roumanian scholar Nicholas Iorga and his students sought to prove that Roumania was *par excellence* the heir of Byzantium, most faithfully reflecting the traditions of the ancient empire, it was facetiously remarked that in her intrigue and palace coteries, Bucharest did more closely resemble Byzantium than any other modern state.

In two respects this absorption of the empire by the capital is especially apparent: in the influence on politics exercised by the city populace, and in the lavishness with which the emperors devoted the best energies of the empire to the beautification of the city.

The *populus Romanus* had always enjoyed a large role in imperial politics. With the transfer of the capital to the Bosphorus, this role increased rather than diminished. Centering in the circus, the factions became political machines which forced their will on emperors and ministers alike. The Niké riots under Justinian were only the culmination of a long growth of political mob rule which made the emperors the creatures of the populace.

In the same way the beautification of the city was always a matter of prime importance to its rulers. While the reign of Justinian was the apogée of this building, the emperors who preceded him had not been neglectful of their city, and churches and palaces had been erected by several of them.

Of the emperors of the fifth century few are worthy of special notice. Theodosius II (408–450) is notable for the walls which he built around the city and for the code of laws which was promulgated in his name. Both were to be superseded within a few generations by the later works of Anastasius and Justinian. Zeno (474–491) is memorable as an astute diplomat who cleverly played the various barbarian leaders off against each other. This established the policy which was followed so successfully by the Eastern emperors in their relations with the barbarians as long as their money held out. It was he who received from Odoacer the scepter and buskins of the West thus reuniting in fact as in theory the two segments of the empire. The remaining emperors of this period, both in East and West, belong fittingly in that frieze of shadowy figures which marches across the pages of Gibbon.

The chief problems of the empire in the fifth century were the preservation of the frontiers, the absorption of the barbarians, and the ever present matter of religious schism and heresy. The course of the Persian War and the religious disputes have already been discussed. The barbarian problem as it presented itself in the East and the West is the subject of this chapter. In the main the barbarians were Germans, but other non-Germanic people, such as the Huns and the Isaurians also played important roles in the drama of the century.

THE BARBARIANS BEFORE THE VÖLKERWANDERUNG

Actually very little is known about the Germans before they entered the lands of the Roman Empire. A few paragraphs in Caesar's *Commentaries* and the *Germania* of Tacitus are our only sources for them in their earlier periods and both of these are subject to question, as Caesar had little contact with the Germans and Tacitus was writing a moral book to shame the Romans by stressing the virtues of the noble savages as compared to their own decadent ways.

We do know that they had a tribal organization, had passed the purely nomadic stages and had become cultivators of the soil, and that they were divided into social classes, with the nobility enjoying special privileges. Below the freemen was a class of slaves. Their religion was nature worship with an elaborate mythology; at some time they developed what may be called a national literature with legendary heroes; and as we can see from their laws after they entered the empire, they were legally minded and had courts and law codes, the latter based essentially on the custom of the tribe.

By the time they came into the empire, we can distinguish several important federations of tribes, which seem to have approximated national status. To the east, north of the Black Sea were the Ostrogoths; just west of them and north of the Danube were the Visigoths. Along the lower Rhine were the Franks, divided into the two peoples of the Salian (on the

sea coast) and the Ripuarian (on the river bank). South of the Franks
were the Allemani, Burgundians, Suevi, and others. In inner Germany
wandered the Vandals, Heruls, Gepids, Lombards, and Saxons, while the
Jutes and Angles occupied the Danish peninsula. To the east beyond the
German lands in what is now Russia were the non-Germanic peoples of
the Huns, which included the Bulgars, Avars, Alans, and Slavs.

Among the institutions of the Germans the most interesting are those
of the *comitatus* and their system of trials with compurgation and ordeal.
The comitatus was a system of associating young or poorer warriors as dependents of a chosen war chief. The chieftain commanded them in battle
and raid, shared with them the booty captured, swore never to desert
them, and always to lead them well. The members of the comitatus swore
to follow their leader faithfully and never to desert him; they always attempted to equal his valor and prowess; they were faithful unto death
and beyond. This institution, which is the first appearance in Germany
of the principle of blind allegiance to a leader and which is the first known
institution of the Germans, was destined to have an influence on the development of feudal institutions at a later date.

In the matter of courts and trials, the Germans (at least after they settled
in the lands of the empire) had tribal *moots* or *things* in which the male
members of the tribe met to settle any necessary policies (usually whom to
fight that season) and to administer justice. The use of the oath was an essential feature of their justice, as the whole proceeding hinged on the oath of
the defendant. When a case was brought against a man, if the case was not
too serious and if the defendant had a good reputation, he was allowed to
clear himself by his own oath supported by those of compurgators—friends
or relatives who swore not to the truth of the oath, but to the honesty of the
oathtaker. Each man had a value depending on his place in society and
the weight of his oath varied with his position, that of a *twelfhundman*
being worth as much as that of six *twahundmen*. Likewise damages inflicted on an individual could be paid for according to a set scale of prices,
the cost being greater with the importance of the injured party. In cases
where the offense or the amount of the matter in question was too great
for compurgation, resort was had to the Judgment of God through means
of the ordeal. This could be of several kinds but the principle was the
same in all cases: God would protect the innocent and reveal the guilty.
The ordeal by fire would consist of a man walking through open flames or
carrying a red hot iron a stated number of paces; that of hot water was
plunging the hand or arm into a pail of boiling water. In all of these ordeals
the judgment of his fellows played an important role as they could determine the weight of the iron, the size of the fire, the number of minutes
which the arm must be held in the water. After the ordeal had been
performed the arm was bandaged up and the bandages removed several

days later. If the wounds had begun to heal he was declared innocent—if not, he was guilty. The worst of the ordeals was that of cold water, in which a man was bound and thrown into a pond or stream. In this case if he floated he was guilty and if he sank innocent, as water will cast out impure substances. If however the accused was compelled to remain under water any great length of time to prove his innocence the acquittal must have been but an empty victory and small consolation to his widow and children. Priests were not subject to these ordeals, but were required instead to swallow a piece of cheese, the size of which was determined by the court. Sufficient practice in the art of cheese-swallowing may well have rendered a life of crime somewhat easier for the clergy than for the laity, but then they were assumed to be men of higher moral caliber than their erring flocks. Later among the Franks, though not among the Anglo-Saxons, the ordeal by combat developed and became most popular. This was simply a duel fought by plaintiff and defendent under the supervision of the court. It remained a popular method of settling disputes long after the other ordeals had been outlawed by the pope, and in its extra-legal form the duel is still used as a means of settling points of honor in some Continental countries.

THE PENETRATION OF THE BARBARIANS

The barbarians entered the empire in two ways; by peaceful penetration of individuals or small groups or by national mass migrations. The latter were a phenomena of the fifth century, but the former method had been employed for centuries.

Under Theodosius, the Goths and other Germans were taken into the Roman system and entrusted with important positions. The "peaceful penetration" of the Germans within the empire, while less dramatic than the migrations of whole peoples, was no less conducive to the Germanization of the Empire than the larger mass movements which affected individual provinces. The fact that the Germans had, in general, been converted to the Arian form of Christianity, largely through the efforts of the great missionary Ulfilas, complicated the situation as it increased the natural antagonism between the Arian Germans and the orthodox Romans. In the fifth century Germans held many of the most powerful positions in the empire and the leading names among the imperial ministers, especially the generals, were nearly all Germans. Under Arcadius (395–408) whose wife was a Frank, the Gothic general Gainas virtually ruled the Eastern half of the empire for years, opposed by the eunuch Eutropius and by an "old Roman" faction who found their most eloquent spokesman in Synesius of Cyrene. Synesius submitted to Arcadius a most explicit memorandum warning him of the dangers of the Germanic penetration, a document which Bury refers to as the "anti-German manifesto of the Roman party." [1]

Gainas' career is typical of how completely the Germans ran matters. Taking the occasion of a revolt of some Goths settled in Phrygia, he gathered an army; then instead of putting down the revolt he joined the rebels and returned to the capital where he forced the execution of his rival Eutropius. Gainas at once demanded concessions for his Arian friends and so extreme did he become that in a popular outburst in the capital many Germans were massacred: Arcadius dispatched against him an army commanded by another Goth, Fravitta, a pagan, who managed to defeat Gainas. Gainas fled to Thrace where he was captured and executed by the Huns. Thus the ruin of a Gothic general was accomplished only through the agency of another Goth and the Huns. It must be remembered in all accounts of the wars of the *völkerwanderung* (migration of the peoples) that the so-called Roman armies, which opposed the German invaders, were made up principally of Germans and were commanded generally by German officers.

Even more important than Gainas in the East, were the succession of Germans who ruled the Western part of the empire. Under Valentinian II, the Frank Arbogast in 392 had murdered the emperor and set up a puppet emperor Eugenius; his defeat by Theodosius reunited the empire. Under Honorius, the Vandal Stilicho ruled from 395 to 408, during which time he defeated the Visigoths and several other barbarian armies, and married his daughter to the emperor (thus emulating the Frank Bauto who had married his daughter to Arcadius in 395). In 408, Honorius, tired of this tutelage and weary of his in-laws, caused Stilicho to be murdered. Even greater than Stilicho was Ricimer, the Suevian who dominated the Western empire 456 to 472, setting up no less than four emperors and himself ruling on occasion in the interims. The Herule (or Hun), Odoacer, who finally suppressed the Western line of emperors and returned the symbols of state to Zeno in Constantinople was only the last of a long line of barbarian generals who ruled the empire through appointees and puppets. Like the emperors they succeeded, few of them died in their beds.

When Odoacer in 476 deposed the young Romulus Augustulus and officially reunited the Western to the Eastern part of the empire, he brought about what historians for generations have considered the end of the Roman Empire. Of course it was no such thing and actually 476 is not a date worth remembering at all, for the reunion of the halves of the empire was not an unusual thing; since Diocletian the two halves had been joining and separating spasmodically so it was nothing new, and as the empire went on undisturbed in the East until Charlemagne became the agent of reviving the Western branch in 800, there was nothing particularly lasting

[1] J. B. Bury, *History of the Later Roman Empire* (1889) I, 83.

about the work of Odoacer. However by 476 the dominion of the empire had been considerably cut down by the incursions of the Germanic peoples, several of whom had settled in force in various provinces and had set up semi-autonomous states.

THE GERMANIC INVASIONS

The German invasions, commonly called the völkerwanderung, were a general displacement of the German tribes, which was precipitated by the incursions of new peoples from the east. It first affected the Roman Empire when the Visigoths, who were settled north of the Danube, feeling the pressure from other barbarian peoples to the north and east, petitioned the emperor to be allowed to cross over into the lands of the empire. This permission was granted them in 376 by the emperor Valens, who granted them lands in Lower Moesia. By the terms of the agreement, the Goths were disarmed, and they soon found themselves easy prey for unscrupulous officials who exploited them unmercifully. After putting up with just so much exploitation the Visigoths revolted. Under Fritigern, a native leader, they invaded Thrace and Macedonia where they defeated and killed the emperor Valens at the battle of Adrianople in 378. This battle was long considered one of the decisive battles of the world.

After winning this initial victory, the Goths were unable to take any real advantage of it. They ravaged Thrace for several years, but were finally pacified by Theodosius, who became the patron of a Gothic prince, Alaric, holding out to him promise of honors in the service of the empire. When, at the death of the emperor, Alaric found himself cheated out of what he had assumed was to be his reward, he too began to ravage Thrace, and advanced to the very walls of Constantinople. He was bought off by Arcadius with the title of *magister militum* (commander of the army) for Illyria, and took his hordes into that province. There he was met and defeated by the armies of Stilicho. Leaving Illyria, he turned west and arrived in Italy where in 410 he sacked the city of Rome itself. This sack of Rome is another event, which has made a tremendous impression on historians through the centuries but which actually was only one of many sieges and sacks which that venerable city was to undergo. Having sacked Rome, Alaric marched south to meet his death. After the dramatic burial of their king in the waters of the Busento River which was turned out of its course so that no man might know where the king lay buried, the Visigoths elected Alaric's brother, Ataulf, as king and returned north whence they moved west into southern Gaul. After establishing themselves along the Riviera, they pressed on in 415 into Spain where they established their final kingdom. Thus the first of the Germanic states was established in Spain and southern Gaul. Ataulf was an ardent Romanophile and copied things Roman in every respect. He was moreover strongly influenced by his patrician wife, Galla Placidia, the sister of the Roman emperors, Arcadius and Honorius.

This Visigothic state, which lasted until it was destroyed by the Arabs in the eighth century, became practically independent, but its king recognized the vague suzerainty of the emperor and copied in his institutions and titles those of the imperial court. Its laws became famous, as it had separate codes for the Germans and for their Ibero-Roman subject peoples; the latter code, the famous *Breviary of Alaric* being one of the most celebrated codes of medieval Europe. Although the Visigoths were themselves Arians at first, the country was very largely then as now under the influence of the clergy and Visigothic Spain has been characterized by Professor Merriman as distinctly "priest ridden."

While the Visigoths were establishing themselves in southern Gaul and Spain, indeed before this while they were wandering about in the Balkans and Italy, other Germanic tribes crossed the borders of the empire and found for themselves homes on imperial soil.

The Vandals were one of the first to move. About the beginning of the fifth century the Vandals, together with the Burgundians, Alans, and Suevi, crossed the Rhine into Gaul. Sweeping across Gaul the Vandals kept on till they had crossed the Pyrenees into Spain. There they set up an ephemeral state which was soon destroyed in 419 by the Visigoths. The Vandals fled on across the Straits to Africa, where they were invited to settle by the Roman general Boniface who dreamed of establishing an independent state with their aid. But Gaiseric (or Genseric) the Vandal king proved an untrustworthy ally and an ambitious monarch; he defeated Boniface and kept Africa for himself. During the Vandal siege of Hippo in 430–431, the learned bishop of that city, Augustine, entered the Heavenly City of which he had so eloquently written. Carthage fell in 439, and the Vandal kingdom was supreme in Africa. Emulating the earlier Carthaginians, the Vandals took to the sea and infested the waters of the Mediterranean. So potent did their sea power become that in 455 they raided Italy, sacking Rome itself,[2] thereby giving their name to acts of useless destruction. The Vandal kingdom hardly outlived its founder however, and after the death of Gaiseric a disputed succession opened the opportunity for the reconquest of Africa by the legions of Justinian (533–534). The Vandals were always a small minority ruling over a much larger subject population; apart from their reputation for double-dealing and brutality, they have left little impress upon history.

[2] Certain Eastern chroniclers report the story, not mentioned in any Western sources, that Gaiseric was invited to Rome by the Empress Eudoxia who called him in to overthrow her husband, Maximus, a usurper who had forced her to marry him. But the invitation episode appears too frequently to be entirely creditable. Bury, *Later Roman Empire* (1923 ed.) I, 324, accepts it as possible but not certainly true.

The Burgundians, who had crossed the Rhine about the same time as the Vandals, did not go so far afield. They settled down just across the river and to the south, in a region that has ever since been known as Burgundy. Like the other German tribes they held their lands by (forced) authority from the emperor and patterned their institutions after the Roman. The chief claim to fame which the Burgundian kingdom may have is that it became the scene for the heroic deeds of Siegfried and the heroes of the later Nibelungenlied. The Suevi followed the Vandals into Spain; after the conquest by the Visigoths they were quietly absorbed into that people.

The cause for all this migration of the Germans was the westward sweep of the Huns. They had moved west from Asia in the fourth century displacing the Goths and starting the whole movement of the peoples. The Huns were a Mongolian people of what was once called the Turanian race, akin to the Turks, Mongols, Bulgars, and Esquimaux; they were short, with sparse hair and oriental features, and seemed veritable centaurs as they rode their swift ponies, so completely did man and beast blend into an efficient war machine. Without any particular civilization of their own, they were extremely receptive to other cultures. The court of Attila, their king, unflatteringly termed by his Western enemies "The Scourge of God," although it was a city of tents and was wholly itinerant, none the less harbored distinguished Romans and members of all the other races and peoples the Huns had conquered. When delegations were exchanged between Rome and the Huns, the Hunnic envoys were Romans, the Roman, Germans.

About 450 Attila decided to move west; the Huns had already overrun South Russia and the Balkans as far as the Danube, forcing the empire to pay them an annual subsidy. In this case there can be no doubt that the Huns were summoned into the empire by Honoria, the sister of Valentinian III, who sent Attila a ring and money asking his aid against her brother. Attila took the ring to be a marriage proposal, accepted, and demanded half the Western Empire as his bride's portion. He was also urged to invade the west by Gaiseric, who wished to use him against the Visigoths. Consequently when Valentinian refused his demands Attila advanced against the empire with his army made up of all the eastern barbarian tribes whom he had conquered including Burgundians, Ostrogoths, and Alans. He met unexpectedly serious opposition at a battlefield near Châlons (451) in a Roman force under the general Aetius assisted by the Visigoths and other Western barbarians.

Aetius and his allies were successful; the battle of Châlons has come down as one of the truly significant encounters in world history, for by it the advance of Attila towards the west was stopped. However important the battle may have been in perspective, it helped but little at the moment and although it stopped Attila's westward march it merely diverted him to the south where he attacked Italy and laid siege to Rome. That his whole desire in the western campaign was plunder rather than conquest is proven by the readiness with which he accepted the terms offered by the Roman bishop Leo, who offered and paid tribute on condition that the city be spared, although disease among his troops and the expected arrival of imperial reinforcements also influenced him. Attila accepted the offer and returned north; Rome was spared from the ravages of the Huns in 452— to be the fatter for the Vandals in 455.

The year after his meeting with the pope at Rome, in 453, Attila died, murdered on one of his many wedding nights by a jealous wife. His empire vanished with him. The various heterogeneous elements of the Hunnic state broke up into their component parts after a great battle between the various nations at Nedao in Pannonia, and the empire disintegrated entirely. It left the various Germans, however, somewhat reshuffled.

Among the most important of these were the Ostrogoths. They had been north of the Black Sea when the Huns came west, and had been incorporated in the Hunnic state. With the end of the Hun Empire, the Ostrogoths reappeared as an entity under their own kings; Theodoric the Amal and Theodoric, son of Strabo, were rivals for the kingship, and the wily emperor Zeno used their rivalry for his own ends, thus keeping the Goths under control. The death of Theodoric, the son of Strabo, left Theodoric the Amal supreme, and Zeno at once recognized him as his magister militum, gave him the rank of patrician and suggested that he could find much greener pastures in Italy than he could in the Balkans.

This was astute diplomacy. For Italy was ruled by Odoacer, who, however much he protested his allegiance to Zeno and however faithfully he put the emperor's name on edicts and coins, nevertheless gave him no real obedience. Zeno was confronted with the prospect of losing the Balkans to Theodoric and that would have been painful to him. It was a master stroke of diplomacy when he armed Theodoric with imperial titles and sent him off to recapture Italy from Odoacer who was ruling it as the subregulus of the Empire. The comedy was about played out—two German armies were fighting for imperial soil, but both claimed to represent the emperor, and the emperor had nothing to gain or lose whichever won or lost. As it resulted, Theodoric chased Odoacer around the Italian peninsula for some time, caught him in Ravenna where he besieged him for three years and finally forced his surrender in 493. Then inviting Odoacer to dinner, Theodoric calmly murdered him and seized all power in Italy (still in the name of Zeno in whose name Odoacer had ruled!).

Although his acquisition of the kingdom of Italy was not done without some questionable practices (even for those days), Theodoric became one of the eminent rulers of Italian history and his reign from 493 to 526 is considered one of the glorious periods in the history of that country.

Modeling his government on that of his Roman predecessors, Theodoric built solidly and founded a state in which the balance between German and Roman was well-controlled; the church was given its due rights, but was not pampered by the Arian monarch; the king's justice was enforced and became proverbial. Theodoric had himself been brought up as a hostage in Constantinople and was personally a cultured Roman gentleman, and he brought this culture to his more barbarous subjects. He easily became the leading figure in the western portion of the empire and was the arbitrator in disputes between other German monarchs, several of whom he attached to himself by marriage alliances. His capital at Ravenna became one of the leading cities of the West, and his tomb still stands there as a monument to his greatness.

The state he founded fell before Justinian, but the tenacious resistance it showed, demonstrated the soundness of the principles on which Theodoric built, as the population was largely loyal to the Gothic cause, even though they were alien in race and religion.

Two other Germanic states were established in the old boundaries of the empire; states which were destined to be more permanent than any of those discussed so far; the Frankish and the Anglo-Saxon.

The Franks were a Germanic people settled along the shores of the North Sea (the Salian Franks) and along the banks of the Rhine (the Ripuarian). In their migrations they differed from all of the other Germanic peoples in the important fact that they never abandoned their original homeland, but merely expanded from it. All the others picked up and moved somewhere, leaving their original homes entirely; the Franks kept what they had and merely added to it. Their expansion differed also in one other most important respect; the Goths, Burgundians etc. had all been Arians and were thus considered heretics by the Roman population over which they ruled. The Franks first started their expansion when they were still pagans, but their first king Clovis, after his great victory over the Allemani, accepted Christianity at the hands of the orthodox St. Martin of Tours. This orthodoxy of the Franks made them acceptable to the Gallo-Roman clergy and people and greatly facilitated their conquests from their Arian neighbors. Under Clovis (481–511) the Franks destroyed and absorbed the states of the Ripuarian Franks, the Allemani, and the Roman principality of Syagrius (a Roman general who had set himself up as an independent ruler in the district around Paris). The duplicity and guile of this founder of the French monarchy are narrated naively and graphically in the *History* of Gregory of Tours, who saw in Clovis the instrument of God's will. The conquest of Aquitaine from the Visigoths which was begun under Clovis was continued under his sons; the stream of conquest being sadly and periodically interrupted by civil wars among the descendants of the old conqueror. The family affairs of this dipsomaniac house, whose marital troubles were only equaled by their murderous tendencies, make exciting, if not elevating, reading as revealed by the worthy bishop, and the Frankish monarchy under the Merovingians, as the descendants of Clovis were called, is truly one of those states which can be aptly termed "despotism tempered with assassination."

Four states emerged in the Frankish kingdom: Austrasia in the northeast, Neustria in the northwest, Aquitaine in the southwest, and Burgundy in the southeast; they were continually being united, separated and reunited as the brothers murdered each other and seized each other's property. In each generation there was this process of unification by means of murdering one's relatives, only to end in the division of the kingdom among the sons of the final victor and the beginning of the business all over again. Clovis and his successors, like the Gothic kings, prided themselves on their Roman titles and considered themselves regents for the emperor in Constantinople. Their administration was a poor replica of the Roman and the elaborate Roman titles rested but badly on the shoulders of the half-civilized Frankish lords. This kingdom escaped the reconquest by Justinian and continued to develop until it eventually emerged as the French monarchy.

The other state which developed without re-absorption into the empire was Britain. In 407 the Romans had withdrawn from the island when a local general was proclaimed emperor by his troops and started out to assert his claims in Italy. He failed, but the legions never returned to Britain, where the evidences of Roman rule soon disappeared. In no other place where the Romans had been did they leave so little behind them; only a few roads and buildings and the Christianization of the people remained as evidences that the Roman rule had once existed there. The country relapsed into the semi-barbarism of its Celtic inhabitants and was soon thereafter overrun by particularly uncivilized and savage tribes from northern Germany and the Danish peninsula. The landings of the Jutes, Angles and Saxons are traditionally dated at 449, and while there is no historical evidence to properly attest the existence of the mythical leaders Hengist and Horsa, there is reason to believe that the German occupation does date from about the middle of the fifth century.

In spite of the lamentations of the British monk Gildas who affirms that the native population of Britain was exterminated by the hordes of Germans who swept over the land, historical evidence indicates that the Germans were always a very small minority group. So slight were the remains of Roman civilization, however, that the entire country was quickly Germanized and we find in Britain the most completely German states founded within the empire. Nor were the Anglo-Saxon princes greatly influenced by the idea of the empire; their institutions were hardly tinged by Roman examples and they did not assume Roman titles. Romanism came to them, not through their subjects, but through the conversion to Christianity, which was accomplished by the famous mission of St. Augustine of Canterbury in 597; and when it came, it was not the Romanism of the empire but that of the church. It is interesting to note that no attempts seem to have been made by the Christian Britons to convert their conquerors; presumably they felt that if the Germans had everything on this earth, it was the least they could do to keep closed to them the doors to Paradise, and thus prevent them ruling in heaven as they did on earth. It may have been some spiritual consolation to the Celts to picture their oppressors suffering in Hell, while they basked in the joys of Paradise.

Apart from the German kingdoms of Britain, the states set up by the Teutonic conquerors were not designedly independent entities. As we have seen, the kings considered themselves regents for the emperor; they used Roman titles for their courtiers and ministers; they carried on in a half-hearted and misunderstood manner the main principles of Roman administration and even taxation. While the laws for the conquerors were the old German tribal laws, the subject people were governed by an adaptation of the Roman law, or Roman principles entered into the German laws themselves. The unity of the empire, however demolished it may have been in practice, was never lost in theory in most of the provinces of the empire. Lip service, if nothing else, was given the emperors and behind the German king always stood the half-mythical figure of the Roman basileus.

BARBARIANS IN THE EASTERN EMPIRE

The Eastern part of the empire was more fortunate than the Western in its relations with the Germans. This was due to several factors, among which should be noted the superior diplomacy of the Eastern ministers, the greater wealth of the Eastern cities and provinces, which enabled the emperors to bribe the Germans, and the presence of non-Germanic barbarians, who were used as a counterirritant against the Germans.

We have already noticed the career of Gainas the Goth, who lorded it in Constantinople for a while under Arcadius and who was overthrown only by employing other Gothic and Hunnic troops. The anti-German massacre, which took place in the capital in 400 at the time of the overthrow of Gainas, greatly reduced the number of Germans in Constantinople and temporarily brought an end to their influence. In the reign of Theodosius II (408–450) during the domination of Pulcheria, the emperor's sister, a new general arose in the person of the Alan, Aspar. So powerful did Aspar become that on the death of Theodosius he secured the marriage of Pulcheria to his friend Marcian and the coronation of the latter as Roman emperor (450–457). On the death of Marcian, Aspar again controlled the election and secured the elevation of a Dacian soldier, Leo I (457–474).

Leo, however, was not minded to remain the puppet of the powerful general and he called in the wild Isaurians of the Anatolian highlands as a counter-balance to the German influence. A new guard regiment, the Excubitores, was organized from the Isaurians and its commander, one Tarasicodissa, was married to Leo's daughter Adriane. Fortunately for future students of history, Tarasicodissa changed his name to the Greek name of Zeno.

Aspar meanwhile had engaged in a disastrous naval war against the Vandals in Africa, the reverses in which caused him much loss of prestige at home. In 471 Leo called out his Isaurians to put an end to the Alan's rule, and in the fighting which followed Aspar was killed and the German threat to Constantinople ended forever.

When Leo I died leaving the throne to his grandson Leo II, who was six years old, the new emperor invited his father to assume the purple as co-emperor and Tarasicodissa ascended the throne as the emperor Zeno (474–491). The accession of Zeno to the purple was an important event in that it showed a different line of development in the East from the West. In the latter, barbarian generals who dared not aspire to the throne because of their race dominated the puppet emperors of purer Roman stock. In the East, barbarians (although not Germans) ascended the throne. The institution of the major domo or regent did not have to develop.

We have already noticed Zeno as the emperor under whom the empire was reunited after more than eighty years of division in 476. His career is worthy of closer attention as it illustrates the way in which court intrigue, conflicting interests, and playing one group off against another, preserved the Eastern empire.

Zeno was personally disagreeable and unpleasant and soon became extremely unpopular. He was forced to rely more than ever on the loyalty of his Isaurian guard and their commander Illus. But Illus sold him out to a court party headed by Verina, the widow of Leo I and Zeno's mother-in-law, who temporarily succeeded in driving Zeno out of the capital and putting her brother Basiliscus on the throne. Zeno was reinstated after a year by Illus who returned to his former allegiance, but Verina continued to oppose him, setting up still another pretender. The Germans and the city populace supported this revolt and it was put down by Illus and his Isaurians. Shortly thereafter Zeno broke with Illus due to the machinations of Verina, and Illus revolted. To gain support against the Isaurians, Zeno called in Germans. Theodoric the Ostrogoth was the means of Zeno's regaining his throne; then as we have seen, the wily emperor sent Theodoric off to Italy to recover that province from Odoacer.

Zeno was succeeded on the throne by Anastasius (491–518), a civil official, whom Adriane married as her second husband. A riot in the Hippodrome gave Anastasius the opportunity to attack the Isaurians and to drive them from the city. In the twenty-seven years of his rather uneventful reign Anastasius gave the empire one of the best governments in its long history, being especially notable not only for ending the barbarian menace, but for his abolition of hated taxes and general reform in administration. He also had built the long walls, which defended Constantinople on the land side 40 miles inland.

The destruction, however, of the German and Isaurian threats to Constantinople by no means ended the barbarian menace to the city. In 493 first appeared a new barbarian people, the Bulgars, formerly part of the Hun Empire, who were destined to play an important role in the history of the Eastern empire and the Balkan peninsula. Further the whole reign of Anastasius was marked by desultory war with the hereditary enemy of the empire, the Sassanids of Persia.

CHAPTER 4

THE EMPIRE OF JUSTINIAN

✣

JUSTINIAN AND THEODORA, 518–565

THE sixth century is commonly called, from the rulers who dominated most of it, the Age of Justinian and Theodora. It marks in many ways the apogee of the Eastern Roman Empire and the history of the century is the history of the imperial revival.

Anastasius was succeeded by a rude soldier from Macedonia, Justin, who was count of the Excubitores. Justin was given large sums of money to purchase, by bribery, support for the grand chamberlain, but secretly used his bribes to his own advantage so that he was himself proclaimed emperor. As he was a simple, if crafty, soldier and recognized his limitations, he entrusted the real government from the beginning to his more highly educated nephew Justinian, so that the reign of Justin (518–527) was in reality merely the preliminary to Justinian's personal rule.

Justinian is one of those rulers who, without any great personal merits, has succeeded in dominating his times. He fancied himself a theologian and was actually something of a pedant. His character, as we know it, was vain, ambitious but somewhat vacillating and extremely bigoted; but he surrounded himself with a remarkable group of ministers and generals, and he followed an imperial policy, which brought great glory to his empire, so that he is called "great." That he nearly ruined the economic resources of the country and that his ambitions were far in excess of his abilities did not seem so disastrous until the course of time had shown the fruits of his errors. He brought the empire glory—and men have always been willing to pay heavily for national glory and prestige, however transient and unsubstantial.

The most interesting of the persons associated with Justinian was undoubtedly his consort, the famous (or infamous) empress Theodora. We are told that she was a woman of great beauty, and while the mosaic portrait of her at San Vitale in Ravenna shows only the dignified conventional empress, the literary accounts of her reveal a seductive and alluring, if cruel and domineering woman.

Our chief source for the career of Theodora is the *Secret History* of Procopius, and Procopius was admittedly angry with the empress and anxious to besmirch her. However, there is every reason to believe that a part at least of what he tells is the truth, and only a small part would be

51

needed to make Theodora one of the most amazing figures of history. According to Procopius, she began life as the daughter of the bear-keeper in the circus. When she was still a child, she began the practice of that most ancient of all occupations open to women, which was a concomitant part of every actress' life in those days. Theodora soon developed a remarkable reputation. She went to Egypt with a petty government official, worked her way home through Syria, and returned to the capital where she met the young Justinian. *Amor vincit omnia:* they met, fell in love and subsequently married, Justinian causing his uncle to elevate the former courtesan to the highest grade of the Roman aristocracy. With marriage, Theodora changed her mode of life entirely; she became a model of propriety, active in all kinds of good works and especially interested in religion. She did not forget her former colleagues and built on the Bosphorus a home for wayward women (in which it was reported that women were kept by force much against their will). Throughout her life Theodora exercised a tremendous influence on Justinian and may be considered responsible for much of the activity of the reign.

Others of the coterie around Justinian who made the reign illustrious were the two great generals, Belisarius and Narses, Tribonian, the great jurist, and the unpopular and hated, but extremely efficient John of Cappadocia, whose tax extortions enabled the government to engage in its expensive wars and its orgy of building.

The reign of Justinian and Theodora can best be studied under several topics: 1. the Niké riot and the breaking of the circus factions; 2. the wars with Persia; 3. legislative activity; 4. building; and 5. religious policy.

THE NIKÉ RIOT OF 532

As we have seen, the urban populace exercised a considerable influence over politics in Constantinople, as it had done in old Rome. The center of their activities in Constantinople was the Hippodrome where the public games were held, especially the popular chariot races. There were originally four teams, designated by the colors worn by the drivers, who competed in the races; and the populace was divided into four factions, each of which supported one of the teams. Gradually two of the teams dropped into insignificance, leaving the two great factions of the Blues and the Greens. These factions developed into far more than sporting clubs, however, and became political parties, with what approximates our ward organizations. They backed rival candidates for the imperial throne and indulged, often riotously, in every political issue of the time.

The great Niké Riot began with a smaller fracas between the two parties, in which several rioters were arrested and sentenced to be hanged. By some mistake, which was interpreted by the people as a miracle, the ropes broke and some of the condemned men escaped the death by hanging, to which they had been sentenced. They at once became popular heroes and all attempts to arrest them again were met with violence. Both factions combined to resist all efforts to recapture the rioters and a general uprising developed. The crowds shouted "Niké" (Victory) and demanded the deposition of the unpopular Tribonian and the even less-liked John of Cappadocia. The troops sent out to quell the riot either joined the rioters or were driven back by them. Fires were set at various parts of the city and several of the chief buildings, the Senate House, the Chalké, and Hagia Sophia were among the buildings destroyed.

The senatorial party, which resented the control of the military faction under Justinian, supported the rioters and proclaimed Hypatius, the nephew of Anastasius, as emperor. Justinian was besieged in the imperial palace while his enemies occupied the streets. All seemed lost and the emperor made plans to flee the city. It was then that Theodora intervened. Her speech, as reported by Procopius, is one of the most pungent declarations in history:

If there were left me no safety but in flight, I would not fly. Those who have worn the crown should never survive its loss. Never will I see the day when I am not hailed Empress. If you wish to fly, Caesar, well and good, you have money, the ships are ready, the sea is clear; but I shall stay. For I love the old proverb that says "The purple is the best winding-sheet." [1]

Thus shamed by the courage and the uncompromising ambition of a woman, the emperor and his councillors took heart. Belisarius again led his men out against the mob, and at last the troops proved successful. The rioting lasted almost a week and in the course of it some 30,000 people are said to have been killed; but when it was over the pretender was dead, the emperor had saved his throne, and the political power of the city factions had been destroyed as a threatening force forever. The factions reappeared several times to disturb the government, but they never acquired again the strength they had before the Niké Riot.

THE RECONQUEST OF THE WEST

Justinian oriented his policy to the West. He considered himself a Roman emperor in the tradition of Augustus, and he set for himself the goal of reuniting the ancient empire, and especially of regaining control over the old capital of Rome.

When Justinian ascended the imperial throne, the western provinces were all in the hands of German princes: the Ostrogoths held Italy; the

[1] Translation from C. Diehl, *Byzantine Portraits*, p. 63. Reprinted by permission of the publisher, Alfred A. Knopf, Inc.

Vandals, Africa; the Visigoths, Spain; the Franks, Gaul; and the Anglo-Saxons, Britain. In regard to the two latter Justinian accomplished nothing, but Italy and Africa he brought back under the empire, and he made the power of the emperor felt in Spain.

His first task was in the Vandal state in North Africa. There the descendants of Gaiseric had indulged in a civil war which gave the Romans a good occasion for intervention. One Gelimer had usurped the throne at the expense of Rome's ally, Hilderic, in 531; when revolts broke out in Tripolitana and Sardinia, Gelimer sent his armies to reduce Sardinia, thus leaving Tripolitana, nearer home, festering. The reconquest of Africa was as much the result of Gelimer's mistakes as of Belisarius' strategy. The empire made an alliance with the Ostrogoths of Italy, which gave them a needed base in Sicily. Then in 533 Belisarius was sent with a force of some 15,000 men to Africa. He landed 162 miles south of Carthage and began a march towards the capital. At *Ad Decimum* (10-mile post) south of Tunis, he encountered the Vandal forces and routed them. It is to be noted that this battle was entirely a cavalry engagement, the Roman infantry arriving on the scene only after the battle had been won. A second victory at Tricamaron (December 533) completely destroyed the resistance of Gelimer and placed all Africa in Roman hands. Gelimer was sent a prisoner to Constantinople, but instead of restoring the old Vandal dynasty, the province was brought back under the empire. Maladministration of local matters, and especially rapaciousness in tax-collecting, produced local revolts which took some years to put down, but ultimately Africa was completely reduced and restored to its former status as a Roman province. New forts were built at strategic points and Roman officials took over the administration of the province. The Vandal kingdom disappeared forever.

Justinian next turned to Italy. Here again a civil war offered him the needed excuse for intervention. Amalasuntha, the daughter of Theodoric the Great, was regent for her son, Athalaric. She married, as a second husband, her cousin, Theodahad, who promptly murdered his wife and seized the throne for himself. Justinian took up the cause of Amalasuntha. Two armies were despatched against the Ostrogoths: one against Illyria and the second against Sicily and south Italy. In 536, Belisarius victoriously captured Naples after a long siege. The Goths, mistrusting the abilities of their king, deposed Theodahad and elected Witigis as their ruler. The empire countered by an alliance with the Franks, who were persuaded to invade from the north while the Romans marched up from the south. While Witigis turned north to meet the Franks, Belisarius captured Rome. But Witigis returned and besieged Belisarius in Rome; for a year and nine days the city held out; the aqueducts were cut and the water supply shut off; many of the ancient buildings were destroyed. Rome suffered more in the wars between the Goths and the imperial forces than she did at the

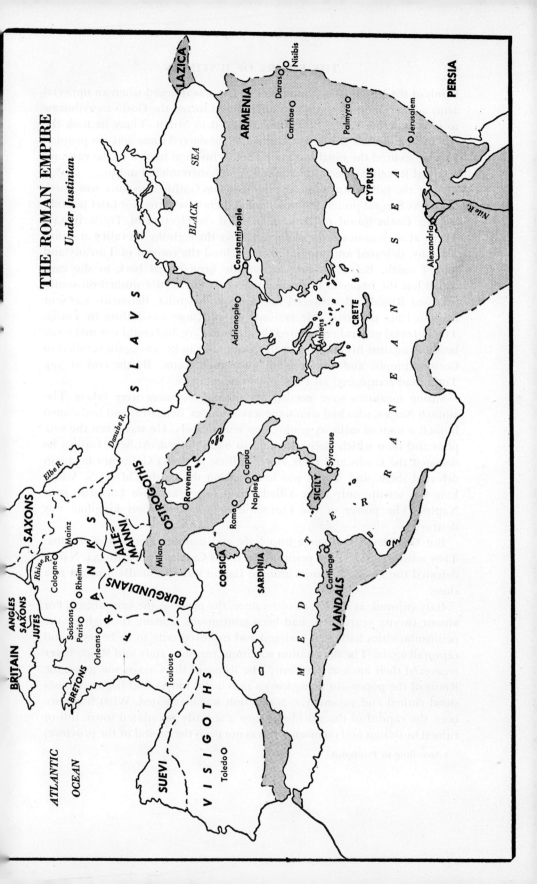

THE ROMAN EMPIRE
Under Justinian

PERSIA

LAZICA

Nisibis

ARMENIA

Daras

Carrhae

Palmyra

Jerusalem

BLACK SEA

CYPRUS

Nile R.

Alexandria

Constantinople

Adrianople

CRETE

Athens

M E D I T E R R A N E A N   S E A

S L A V S

Danube R.

Elbe R.

Rhine R.

Mainz

Cologne

Rheims

OSTROGOTHS

Ravenna

Capua

Rome

Naples

Milano

ALLE-
MANNI

F R A N K S

BURGUNDIANS

CORSICA

SARDINIA

SICILY

Syracuse

Carthage

VANDALS

SAXONS

BRITAIN

ANGLES
SAXONS

JUTES

BRETONS

Soissons

Paris

Orleans

Toulouse

VISIGOTHS

Toledo

SUEVI

ATLANTIC

OCEAN

hands of the Visigoths or Vandals. The city was relieved when an imperial army advanced up the east coast of Italy and forced the Goths to withdraw to meet it. From Rome Belisarius advanced to Milan. There he took the city in 539, but not before the Goths had massacred some 300,000 people.[2] Having secured the northern plain, Belisarius then turned to the east and attacked Ravenna, the Gothic capital, which surrendered in 540.

After the fall of Ravenna, the only serious Gothic resistance was north of the Po. Several pretenders proclaimed themselves kings for brief periods, but the Goths found no real leader until the election of Totila in 541. Totila at once assumed the offensive, drove through the Po valley and into Tuscany, defeated an imperial army, secured the control of Tuscany and moved south. Belisarius had meanwhile been called back to the east, which left the imperial forces in inferior hands. Totila pushed on south, bypassed Rome and advanced to Naples and Apulia. Belisarius was sent back to Italy posthaste. He arrived just as Rome was falling to Totila. The imperial general recaptured the Eternal City, but could not make any headway against his enemies in the south. In 549 he was again recalled to Constantinople, and Totila again recaptured Rome. By the end of 549, Totila had recaptured all Italy and invaded Sicily.

Strong measures were needed and strong measures were taken. The eunuch Narses, who had seen some service under Belisarius and had shown himself a man of military genius, was sent to Italy. He was given the supplies and men which Belisarius had so badly lacked. At Sena Gallica he defeated the Goths and their Herule allies; at Busta Gallorum he again defeated them, and Totila was left dead on the battlefield (552). A new king was set up, only to be killed and defeated at Mons Lactarius near Naples. The power of the Ostrogoths was ended; their kingdom was destroyed.

But the Franks had come into Italy and had no intention of leaving. They advanced down the peninsula as far as Capua. There, in 554, Narses defeated the Frankish armies and the Italian war was finally brought to a close.

Italy enjoyed, as she has so often since, the peace of the vanquished. For almost twenty years there had been continuous fighting throughout the peninsula; cities had been besieged and captured only to be besieged and captured again. The devastation was immeasurable. Italy and Rome never recovered their ancient grandeur. The Rome of the Caesars was gone; the Rome of the popes—in many ways a provincial town—had begun. Houses stood ruined and vacant; the population was decimated. What had once been the capital of the world was now a scantily populated town, full of ruined buildings and memories. It was not even the capital of the province;

---

[2] According to Procopius.

Ravenna, which had been the capital under the Goths, was retained as the administrative center, and there later, under the emperor Maurice, the Byzantine government was officially established.

With Africa and Italy restored to the empire, Justinian next turned to Spain. There again civil war among Visigothic contenders offered cause for intervention and the imperial forces invaded the country to support Anathagild against Agila. The conquest was only partial, however, the Romans occupying only the southwestern territories around Cordova and Cadiz. This was to be the most ephemeral of Justinian's reconquests.

THE EASTERN FRONTIERS AND THE PERSIAN WARS

Part of the cost of the reconquest of the West was paid on the Eastern frontier. After the long peace of the fifth century, war broke out again between Persia and Rome in 503 when the Persian Kobad invaded Roman Armenia and northern Mesopotamia. The immediate cause of the war was the refusal of Rome to continue payments towards the defense of the pass of Derbend, which both powers maintained as a check on the inroads of the northern barbarians. The underlying causes were much more significant and complex. Both Rome and Persia had attempted to set up buffer states in Armenia and Lazica and there was a constant struggle for influence in these regions. Further, Rome resented the Persian persecution of orthodox Christians and the favoritism shown heretical sects. The most important cause was, however, the economic rivalry which centered in the silk trade.

Silk was brought to the Roman Empire from China by a series of stages. The Chinese themselves brought it to Ceylon or Turkestan. There the Persians picked it up and brought it to the Roman frontier at Nisibis in Mesopotamia or Artaxata in Armenia. Thus all the silk which reached Rome passed through Persian hands, and the Romans paid a premium to the middlemen. The silk industry was an imperial monopoly in the Roman Empire, all the silk being worked in the imperial factories in Tyre and Beirut. Rome had long desired to break the Persian monopoly on the silk trade, and the development of alternate routes was one of Justinian's pet projects. This traffic was largely responsible for the Persian wars and also for Justinian's attempts to set up competitive routes by sea through Abyssinia or by land through the territories of the Turks to the north of Persia. In their struggle with the Persians, the Romans made consistent use of the Epthalites and other Hunnic peoples whom they secured as allies against the Persians. In general, Rome sought to handle the Persian question through diplomacy and by subsidizing barbarians rather than by direct appeal to arms.

It was the Epthalites who forced Kobad to conclude the war with Rome which he began in 503, but during the next decade he crushed the power of this people and in 524 again attacked the empire. Persia protested the building near Nisibis of the Roman border fortress of Daras and attacked the new colony. At first the war favored the Persians and the Romans suffered several defeats, the Persians reaching Antioch on a raid, but in 528 Belisarius won a great victory at Daras. In 533 the new Persian emperor, the famous Chosroes Nushirwan (531–579), made a "perpetual peace" with the empire whereby Rome was allowed to retain the fortress of Daras but paid 11,000 pounds of gold a year towards the upkeep of the border forts in the Caucasus.

Chosroes Nushirwan was the greatest of the Sassanid rulers; he strengthened the internal government of the empire, favored trade and industry, and generally brought Persia to its height. Naturally such a monarch aspired to foreign conquests, and the "perpetual peace" was soon shattered by conflict over the control of border territories. Dissident Armenians and ambassadors from Witigis, the Ostrogothic king, persuaded the Persian monarch to attack the empire and force Justinian to fight on two fronts at once. Witigis was destined to be disappointed as Justinian did not reduce his efforts in the West, considering the Eastern always the second front. Much of the fighting was done by rival Arab states, the Ghazanids supported by Rome and the Lakhmids of Hera supported by Persia. Every year from 540 to 545 Chosroes invaded Syria; Antioch, Daras, and Edessa were all besieged on occasion, Antioch being burned to the ground; but Belisarius, who had been recalled from Italy, made a brilliant campaign in Armenia which resulted in a treaty in 545 whereby Rome secured peace by paying 2,000 pounds of gold to Persia. This peace was of short duration, however, and as soon as Rome was able to do so, she denounced the treaty. The immediate cause offered was that the king of Lazica, a state in the Caucasus dependent on Rome, transferred his allegiance to Persia, whereupon Rome invaded his country. The Lazic War lasted from 549 to 557 when the Persians were finally driven out of the province. The final peace was only concluded in 562 by a treaty whereby Rome received Lazica and paid Persia 30,000 gold pieces a year. An interesting provision of this treaty was the restriction of trade to certain specified cities where Roman and Persian merchants could meet and exchange wares.

Thus Justinian sacrificed considerable power and prestige in the East in order to be free for his wars in the West. Each treaty increased the amount to be paid by Rome, and it was only by tribute and by diplomacy that the Eastern frontier was made at all secure. Fortunately for Rome, Persia was bordered on the north by vigorous and warlike peoples, and the Turks and the Khazars, as well as the Abyssinians on the south, assisted the empire in keeping Persia engaged.

LEGISLATION AND GOVERNMENT

The true fame of Justinian rests not on his conquests but on the great legislative work which was accomplished under his auspices. The *Corpus Juris Civilis,* or, as it is more commonly known, the Justinian Code, was the summation of Roman law and has remained the chief source of the law of most nations to our own day.

Roman law in the days of the republic and early empire was made up of a number of types of regulations. There were the ancient laws of the assemblies, the decrees of the senate, the edicts of emperors: there was also a large body of law which had developed from the opinions of eminent jurists and which served as precedents in the absence of explicit law. By the time of Diocletian, this vast body of legislation had become very confusing, as it included laws from many periods and from many variant types of government and political development. Some simplification of this mass of material was obviously necessary, and, as stated, in the reign of Diocletian two compilations of the laws were made. These were wholly unofficial however and the first official code was proposed by Theodosius II in 429. The great compilation, which Theodosius proposed was never made, but a smaller collection of imperial laws was prepared and issued in 438—the Theodosian Code which was promulgated throughout all parts of the empire.

Justinian revived the project of Theodosius, and through the efforts of a commission headed by Tribonian, his Code was promulgated in 529. It was based on the earlier codes and was done rather hurriedly, but it accomplished its purpose of stating what laws were to be considered in force and eliminating all laws which were not found in it. In a revised form, published in 534, the Code contains 12 books with 4652 separate laws.

The Code was, however, only the first part of Justinian's corpus; even more important was the Digest or Pandects, issued in 533. The Digest did for jurisprudence what the Code did for the laws. The commission went through some 2000 books containing the opinions of the greatest jurists of Rome and winnowed them out into a work of 50 books in some 150,000 lines, which discussed the principles and problems of jurisprudence. Obsolete matters were discarded and only the most important subjects were retained. Extracts were made from the writings of Gaius, Papinian, Ulpian, Paulus, Modestinus, and others of the great legal minds of earlier periods (most of them from the Antonine age), and they were so arranged that decisions on legal matters could be supported by the opinions of the greatest authorities. Later in the West, the emperors were to find in the Digest theoretical support for their assertions of supremacy over the popes, and many of the quotations from the Digest (*"quod principi placuit leges habet vigorem." "Rex legibus solutus est"*) were to appear and reappear in the political writings of pamphleteers for centuries thereafter.

In the same year as the appearance of the Digest, Tribonian and his colleagues issued the Institutes. This was a manual of law, based on an earlier work by Gaius, to be used as a text book for the study of the law. This students' manual was a convenient guide to the larger works and was the first introduction to the study of the laws. These three works were promulgated with imperial authority and became the official law of the empire. At the end of his reign a fourth part of the Corpus was issued— the Novellae—which included all the supplementary legislation of Justinian. While the Code, Digest and Institutes were issued in Latin, the Novellae were published in Greek. Although Latin was Justinian's own tongue, the lawyers who made up the commission were mostly Greeks and Constantinople was a Greek city, so that the new laws which were promulgated to supplement the Code were issued in that language.

The Justinian law marks a great improvement over the old Roman law; the old concept of the paterfamilias was done away with, laws of succession and inheritance were made more liberal, emancipation of slaves was made easier and the rights of slaves against cruel masters were protected. The influence of the church appeared in more stringent divorce laws, with penalties for the parties to divorces. But the law still differentiated between men on the basis of their position in society, and criminal law continued to be different for the powerful and the obscure.

Subsequent emperors issued new laws, but it was not until Leo the Isaurian issued the *Ecloga* in 739 that a new code was promulgated in the East. In the West, the Justinian legislation was officially promulgated in Italy and the other provinces reunited to the empire, but it seems to have had little general effect. Gaul and Spain were almost entirely uninfluenced by it (although much of their law was based on the earlier Theodosian code), and it was not until the "revival of Roman law" in the schools of the twelfth century that the Justinian Corpus was accepted as the basic body of laws in Western Europe.

In the field of government Justinian tried to be a reformer, but here his work was less lasting or significant. The government of the Roman Empire after the removal of the capital to Constantinople became a ponderous bureaucracy. We have already seen how Diocletian divided the empire into the four great prefectures with the Augusti and Caesars at their heads. Over each prefecture was a praetorian prefect who was the chief civil authority, having charge of finances, the corn supply, transport, and exercising jurisdiction over all the lower officials and appelate jurisdiction over the provincial courts. Under the prefect was the vicar in charge of the diocese [3] and the governor over the province. While the vicar

[3] It is from these that the ecclesiastical titles were derived.

was under the prefect, appeal from his court was directly to the emperor, and he acted as a check on the prefect. The civil administration was kept separate and distinct from the military, and only in his control over corn and transport did the prefect have any connection with the army. *Magistri militi* commanded the troops in the prefectures and dioceses. When Diocletian separated the civil and military powers it was considered a great reform; generations later, when the two powers were reunited in the person of a single official in the new system of *themes,* it was thought to be a great improvement insuring greater efficiency and security. The provincial administration was simple as compared to the central bureaucracy; it was there that officialdom burgeoned forth in all its formality, cloth-of-gold and red tape.

At the head of all was the emperor, *Dominus et Deus* he had been called at the time of Diocletian; at later times he was to be called Autocrator, Basileus, God-Given Emperor, Sacred Majesty, Glory of the Purple, and always there was about him that divinity which "doth hedge a king." He was sent by God to rule the people; his person, his palace, his treasury were sacred. Before him men knelt in suppliance, they backed out of his presence, they kissed the hem of his garment or the toe of his boot, they prostrated themselves before him and no man spoke in the august presence without special permission. The emperor was the sole source of law; his word was law; he alone could dispense with the law. There is a nice paradox in the fact that the emperor was always considered as subject to the law, but was always able to dispense with it. It may even seem paradoxical to some that while the sacred majesty was so awesome so many emperors were murdered. But that is the way of despotisms and of the East. The Moslem caliphate shows just the same meteoric rises and falls as does the Byzantine Empire; from the gutter to the throne to the grave was not an uncommon *cursus honorum* anywhere in the East.

Around the sacred person of the emperor stood his council, called *consistorium* because they stood around him. This small and powerful group included the chief officials of the empire, the secretaries, chamberlains, treasurers, generals, admirals, and commanders of the special guard regiments, of which there were six.

Each of these regiments had its own magnificent uniform, with bright cloaks and plumed helmets, and each sought to outdo the other in splendor. With the elaborate court costume prescribed by custom, the thick cloth-of-gold, the sweeping robes, the jewel-encrusted belts and caps, and the general profusion of ornament everywhere, the rooms and corridors of the Sacred Palace must have been a most colorful sight. Certainly the splendor of the Roman court gravely impressed the emissaries of any barbarian rulers who came there, and the ostentatious display of wealth and luxury was a studied aspect of Byzantine diplomacy.

In such a formal court society, social grades were many and rigid. Above all, aloof and alone was the sacred person of the *Basileus*. Theodora was the first empress to secure for the Divine Augusta, the Beauty of the Purple, the reverence and adoration accorded the Augustus, her spouse. Caesars had originally been, in Diocletian's system, younger colleagues and successors-elect of the Augusti. The title remained to indicate the heir apparent or presumptive, and later was extended to other members of the imperial house. Imperial relatives who had no pretentions to the throne were known as *Nobilissimi*. Justinian introduced the new grade of *Curopalates,* just below that of Nobilissimus. The old senators were the *Clarissimi,* the highest order of the aristocracy; below them were the *Perfectissimi* (the former equestrians), the *Spectabilis,* the *Gloriosi,* and the *Illustres*. The old grade of *Patrician,* which had been popular in the fourth and fifth centuries dropped out; it had been used for rulers of barbarian tribes and was still continued somewhat in the West, where it was conferred in the eighth century on Charles Martel. These various grades of the nobility carefully guarded their privileges and precedence, and everything at the court went strictly according to protocol. Diplomatic procedure of today would have seemed pure confusion and anarchy to a Roman courtier of the sixth century.

As all of these officials and courtiers derived their living from the public treasury, the cost of the court was a considerable item. The empire was always trying to find new ways to raise money for its continual overhead, not to mention extraordinary expenses due to wars and diplomatic bribes. Lactantius in the fourth century said that more people lived off the taxes than paid them so many were there who enjoyed the imperial bounty or were exempt from taxation. This necessitated an elaborate system of taxation. And everything was taxed. We have seen Diocletian's tax system on agriculture. There were also taxes on commerce and manufactures; taxes on senators as a class; surtaxes for the troops; or special taxes for any special occasion. Much of this was probably not collected owing to special exemptions however. And vast sums came into the treasury from the royal monopolies (such as silk) and from all sorts of indirect taxes. In addition to the taxes there were services which took care of many of the expenses of the government; the postal service, supply of horses for the army, maintenance of roads and bridges, maintenance of public buildings were all supported by special services or liturgies.

Fortunately the empire was, in spite of all its tribulations, wealthy. Unlike the Western provinces where agriculture was almost the only occupation practised, the Eastern provinces were also important commercially and industrially. Agriculture was, of course, the chief occupation, and Egypt was still the granary of the empire; but there was also considerable industry. There were the great state monopolies: mines, quarries, arms factories, silk factories. There was an extensive business in pottery, glazed stones for mosaics, which were in demand in all ecclesiastical as well as secular buildings, crucifixes, fine cloths. Commerce was active and ships of Constantinople dominated the Mediterranean. The trade with the West and with the Black Sea ports was active (i.e. conducted in Roman ships), although the trade with Persia and the East was largely passive (i.e. goods carried in Persian ships). In the reign of Justinian, the empire could boast of many large and prosperous ports: Alexandria, Damietta, Rosetta, Tinnis, and Pelusium in Egypt; Antioch, Sidon, Tyre, Jaffa, Beirut, Ephesus, Smyrna, Sinope, Trebizond in Asia; Constantinople, Corinth, Cherson, Thessalonica in Europe. The greatest, of course, were Constantinople and Alexandria, the two chief centers of trade throughout all the centuries of the later Roman Empire.

Much wealth was derived from the mines, an imperial monopoly, and the mineral wealth of the empire did much to enable her to finance her diplomacy and wars. When Justinian introduced the culture of the silk worm (smuggled from China by a couple of monks), another lucrative source of profit was established.

Perhaps the economic position of Constantinople can best be seen in the quotation from P. Boissonade's *Life and Work in Medieval Europe:*

Nowhere was agricultural production as far advanced and as well balanced as in the East . . . The Eastern Empire held the first place in the cultivation of dye plants and medical herbs, a monopoly in the cultivation of sugar cane, cotton, mulberries and the rearing of silk worms. It was from agricultural produce that it drew the greater part of that wealth for which it was admired and envied by all men in the Middle Ages. . . . Industrial and commercial activity also contributed to bring about the economic supremacy of Byzantium, as well as to enrich the state. Indeed, urban economy, completely shattered in the countries of the West, remained intact and even developed in the Eastern Empire. . . . In the early Middle Ages the Byzantine Empire enjoyed a monopoly of the international commerce of Christendom, which continued to be centered in the Mediterranean. Byzantium lay at the meeting place of all the great trade routes, both maritime and territorial, of Western Asia and Europe, and possessed, moreover, a regular system of land and sea transport and highly perfected methods of exchange, which the West lacked.[4]

JUSTINIAN'S BUILDINGS

Justinian is also remembered as the great builder who beautified the capital and many of the provincial cities. Constantine and other emperors had lavished treasure in buildings in the city, but Justinian surpassed them all. The destruction wrought by the Niké Riot gave him a good opportu-

[4] Translated by Eileen Power, 1927, pp. 35, 46, 50. Reprinted by permission of the publisher, Alfred A. Knopf, Inc.

nity to indulge his passion for building and he gratified himself without stint.

The greatest monument to Justinian's zeal, and the greatest Byzantine church in the world, is the great basilica of Hagia Sophia in Constantinople. The daring of the architects, who swung the great dome across a square opening by the creation of pendentives, was magnificently rewarded. Resting on its four piers the great dome reaches 180 feet into the air— low, judged by modern standards, but terrifyingly high when one considers the materials with which it was constructed and the daring inventiveness of its architects.

For centuries the mosaics of Hagia Sophia, reputed to be the finest in the world, had been covered by the whitewash of the Turks. Now they are again revealed to view, thanks to the secularism of the Turkish Republic and labors of the Byzantine Institute, and justify all that was rumored about them.

More familiar are the mosaics of Justinian's churches in Ravenna. There is found at San Vitale a domed church, while San Apollinare Nuovo is the old traditional basilica. Both are resplendent with mosaics, San Vitale having the famous composition which shows us Justinian on one side and Theodora on the other surrounded by their courtiers. Other churches built and adorned by Justinian's largesse were St. Demetrius at Salonica, St. Irene, Sts. Sergius and Bacchus and the Holy Apostles, at Constantinople.

But Justinian did not restrict himself to ecclesiastical building. He rebuilt the Senate House, the Chalké (the splendid monumental entrance to the Sacred Palace) and other porticoes and baths. And in rebuilding he improved and beautified so that Constantinople was a fitting monument to its glorious ruler. Further, throughout the empire he built baths, aquaducts, theatres, churches, walls, roads, and especially fortresses.

THE RELIGIOUS PROBLEM

We have already seen how the church in the East was split by the various schisms of the Christological controversy and how the Monophysite sect continued to claim adherents in Syria and Egypt. This dissention in the church was most painful to Justinian, who considered the church an integral part of the state and who felt himself divinely appointed to preserve the true religion. The term Caesaro-papism has been used to describe Justinian's position in regard to the church: as head of the state he was obliged to interfere in matters of church policy and to enforce orthodoxy. He was a mighty persecutor of Jews, pagans and heretics, and it was due to his influence that the pagans were forbidden ever to teach in any of the schools of the empire and that the University of Athens was closed down in 529.

In general Justinian's religious policy, like his political, was oriented to the West. He was most anxious to keep on good terms with the pope, and, although not personally unwilling to make some concessions to the Monophysites, he followed the papal dictates and kept Eastern orthodoxy in line with Rome. The Monophysites had a powerful champion in the empress Theodora, who favored their cult, and who interceded on their behalf with the emperor. So strong was Theodora's influence that Justinian's own religious policy became extremely vacillating, at one time favoring Rome and again making concessions to the Monophysites. In 536 a synod at Constantinople anathematized the schismatics and affirmed the papal doctrine; then in 553 another council at Constantinople criticized the dogma of Chalcedon and brought the emperor into conflict with Pope Vigilius. Although he fancied himself quite a theologian, Justinian actually seemed very vague about matters of dogma and his policy was inconsistent. The result of the council of 553 was only to promote further schism and to antagonize all factions. Once again an imperial policy of compromise had failed. It was during this reign that Jacobus Baradaeus revitalized and extended the Monophysite faith in Syria, so that today Syrian Monophysites are called Jacobites.

THE BARBARIAN PEOPLES

The sixth century is an unimportant one in the history of the German states of Western Europe. The imperial reconquest, which wiped out the Vandal and Ostrogothic kingdoms, and touched the fringe of the Visigothic state in Spain only involved the Franks indirectly (in their invasions of Italy) and had no effect whatever on Anglo-Saxon England.

The Franks spent their time in conquering their neighbors and in destroying themselves in fratricidal war. As stated before, the kingdom was divided into four states: Austrasia, Neustria, Burgundy and Aquitaine with their capitals at Rheims, Paris, Soissons, and Orleans. The Merovingians were chronic dipsomaniacs and their conquest of Aquitaine and Burgundy have been attributed in part to their desire to possess these excellent and wine-producing provinces. The four sons of Clovis enthusiastically exterminated each other until only Clothar was left. The reign of Clothar (511–561) nearly parallels that of Justinian; it was his nephew Theodebert who invaded Italy as the ally and then as the enemy of the imperial armies. At Clothar's death, the kingdom was once again divided among his sons, and again the civil war started. This second civil war is high-lighted by the amazing personality of Chilperic and by the ambitious and determined queen Brunehild, who carried on the war for her sons and grandsons until she was finally defeated and killed in 613. The execution of the seventy-year-old queen by tieing her to wild horses, who pulled her limbs apart, gives some idea of the utter brutality of Merovingian manners.

It is hardly to be expected that we would find much institutional or cultural development in Gaul at this time. The one thing of significance to note is the rise of important local families, who combined governmental positions with local lordships and became the dominant aristocratic class. As celibacy of the clergy was an idea which had hardly reached Gaul at this time, these lords also often held bishoprics or other important church offices.

Anglo-Saxon England in the sixth century developed the seven states of the Heptarchy: Kent, Essex, Wessex, Sussex, East Anglia, Mercia, and Northumbria. These kingdoms completed the conquest of the Celtic Britons and also struggled for power among themselves, finally passing under the vague and general leadership of Kent in the reign of Ethelbert (560–616). It was under Ethelbert that St. Augustine brought Roman Christianity to the Anglo-Saxons in 597, establishing the first English bishopric at Canterbury. This conversion, which occurred at the very end of the century, is the only important single event in English history in this period.

More important than the civil wars of the Franks or the petty conquests of the Saxons were the invasions of eastern Europe by new tribes of barbarians. In 454 the German subjects of the Hun Empire had revolted and destroyed their masters at the battle of Nedao. The Hun Empire then split up into many tribal states, of which we have already traced the rise and fall of the Ostrogoths. The Gepids, Heruls, and Lombards all settled to the north of the Danube, whence some of them entered the empire as federates. Justinian played an astute diplomatic game with these peoples, keeping them inflamed against each other and preventing their uniting against the empire. In general he favored the Lombards against the Gepids and Heruls.

The Germans were, however, only a few of the peoples of the Hun Empire. The Slavs or Sclavenes were also settled along the Danube, whence they made raids across the border into imperial territory. In 540 they allied with the Bulgars and invaded Greece, ravaged Thrace and Thessaly and even got as far as the long walls of Constantinople itself. From then on war between the empire and the Slavs continued spasmodically, imperial armies entering the Slav country, and Slavs invading deep into the empire. Two Hunnic or Turkish peoples, the Kotrigurs and the Utrigurs, also played important roles in the Balkans at this time. The empire was successful in general in playing them off against each other, but in 558 the Kotrigur king, Zabergan, invaded the empire, ravaging both Greece and

Thrace, and reaching the walls of the capital itself. Only by the genius of Belisarius was the city saved from pillage at the hands of these barbarians, and the panic caused by their presence was long remembered.

In 558 there came to Constantinople for the first time ambassadors from a ruler of a savage people to the north of the Caspian, the Avars. From their home between the Caspian and the Black Seas they raided into Europe, defeating the Kotrigurs, Utrigurs, Slavs, and reaching the frontier of the Frankish kingdom on the Elbe. Justinian treated with them and they refrained from invading the lands of the empire for the time being. The weight of the Avars was to be felt by Justinian's less fortunate successors.

The only other peoples with whom the empire entered into relations of any importance were the Abyssinians and the Himyarites of Arabia. There had been almost a traditional friendship between New Rome and Abyssinia, the two Christian states making common cause against the Jewish state of the Himyarites. It was the aim of Justinian to unite the two states with Rome in a common struggle against Persia and several embassies were sent to the southern kings. While treaties were arranged with both powers, little was accomplished. The Persians got the better of the Abyssinians in their struggle for the silk trade of Ceylon; and the men of Yemen refused to engage in a campaign against distant Persia.

THE SUCCESSORS OF JUSTINIAN, 565–628

The history of the empire from the death of Justinian to the accession of Heraclius in 610 is largely an aftermath to the reign of the great Justinian, and shows the defects in his work.

At the death of Justinian in 565, Justin II, the nephew of the late emperor who was married to Sophia, the niece of Theodora, was elevated to the throne by the acclamation of both senate and army. Justin was a stern and sombre man, greatly impressed with the dignity of his imperial position and unwilling to make any sort of compromise. He was disdainful of the populace and relied exclusively on the support of the aristocratic party. In his pride he abandoned the policy of his predecessors of paying for peace, with the result that his reign was marked by numerous barbarian incursions as well as by a renewal of the war with Persia.

The Persian war began in 572 when Justin refused to pay the tribute due under the old treaty, but it was also a struggle for influence in Armenia and among the Arabs of Mesopotamia. The Persians invaded the empire, ravaged Syria to the walls of Antioch, and captured the fort at Daras. The news of the loss of Daras is reputed to have been the cause of Justin's going insane. Sophia took over the regency and associated with herself Tiberius, the count of the Excubitores, whom she had Justin adopt as his son and successor. For four years Tiberius ruled with the title of Caesar while

Justin lived on alternately sane and insane; then in 578 he ascended the throne with the title of Augustus.

Tiberius II (578–582) was the opposite of Justin. He was lavish and open-handed, he distributed large bonuses to the army, gave the populace bread and circuses and sought in every way to purchase popularity. He brought an end to the Persian war and bribed the Slavs to moderate their attacks on the lands of the empire. In so doing he exhausted the treasury and virtually bankrupted the state. When he died, after four years of reign, he left the throne to his son-in-law, a general Maurice, who had distinguished himself in the Persian war under Justin II and who had married Tiberius' daughter. Maurice was confronted by serious problems: the Slavs had overrun the Danubian border and settled in Thrace and Greece; the Lombards had moved into Italy and had conquered most of the northern part of the peninsula (giving their name Lombardy to the Po valley); the Avars, who had been brought to the border of the empire by the westward migration of the Lombards, seriously threatened the frontier; and the state was without money. Maurice met these problems as best he could; he cut expenses to the bone—unwisely, as it developed, for he economized by cutting the pay of the army, always a dangerous practice. His chief defect was that he appointed officials of dubious ability and then stuck to them, so that he was ill served as well as unpopular.

The Persian problem was resolved for him by a fortuitous event. The son of Chosroes I, Hormisdas, was driven from his throne in 590 by a military rebellion which set up a usurper, Vahram. Chosroes II, the son of Hormisdas, fled to Constantinople and appealed for aid to the emperor. Maurice willingly gave him men and money to re-establish himself on his ancestral throne, with the result that a close alliance was formed between the two emperors.

To the north, however, the troubles were intensified. The Avars invaded across the Danube and in 591 reached the very gates of Constantinople. Maurice sent his armies against them and they carried the war into the Avar country across the river. In the winter of 601–602, the troops were ordered to remain in the enemy country instead of returning home to winter quarters. This, plus the disaffection already produced by the reduction in pay, was too much for the troops. Under the lead of an illiterate and uncouth centurion, Phocas, they revolted and marched on the capital. The Green faction in the city joined the troops in revolt; Maurice fled but was captured, and, together with his five sons, was killed by Phocas, who immediately proclaimed himself emperor.

Phocas (602–610) is one of the few rulers in history about whom no good has ever been said. He was a brutal soldier who had risen to power through treachery and murder and had no qualifications for rule. His one virtue was a certain bravado. While his accession to the throne was recognized

in Constantinople, the provinces never accepted him, and at once conspiracies were set afoot to remove him. The most important of these
conspiracies was that of Heraclius, the governor of Africa. An elaborate
campaign was planned whereby Heraclius' son Heraclius was to attack
Constantinople by sea, while Nicetas, a cousin, was to lead an army through
Egypt and Syria against the capital. The younger Heraclius reached the city
first and, with almost no opposition, entered the capital. The fickle populace deserted Phocas, who was dragged into the presence of his conqueror
before he was executed. Heraclius then had himself proclaimed emperor.

The usurpation of Phocas had given rise to a renewal of the Persian
wars. Chosroes had a perfect excuse for his attack in that he was avenging
his ally, Maurice. In order to meet the Persian advance, Phocas bought
peace from the Avars by paying a large tribute, but it availed but little as
the Persians continued their advance, coming through Asia Minor as far
as Chalcedon. Unfortunately for the ideology of this campaign, Phocas
was overthrown and Maurice avenged by Heraclius, but the practical
Persian refused to give up anything he had taken and the war continued
on into the reign of Heraclius. The reign of Heraclius is the end of an
age of transition in the history of the empire. He is generally conceded
to be the first Byzantine, as opposed to Roman, emperor. It was during his
reign that Greek completely replaced Latin as the language of court and
army in the empire; his interests, although he came himself from Africa,
were entirely focused on the East. He completed victoriously the centuries-
long struggle with the Persians, which had marked the entire history of the
late Roman Empire, and it was in his reign that the new, peculiarly
medieval, menace of the Arabs first appeared.

When Heraclius came to the throne in 610, the Persians were threatening the very capital. They had gotten as far as Chalcedon in 608 and the
Asiatic provinces of the empire were all threatened. In 613, they overran
all Syria; a great victory at Antioch laid open the whole province and they
quickly overran Damascus, pushing up into Cilicia where they reduced
Tarsus. In the following year (614), they mortally affronted all Christendom
by capturing Jerusalem and carrying off the Holy Cross. In the same year
they overran Egypt. Five years later they besieged Constantinople itself.

In the face of all these Persian victories, Heraclius seemed to do nothing.
He made only a show of resistance, and it seemed that the might of Rome
had definitely fallen before their ancient enemy. But Heraclius was preparing for a crushing blow. He was slowly building up a superior army and
an effective navy. Finally, in 622, he felt himself in a position to strike.
Heraclius' six Persian compaigns in the years 622 to 628 are among the
most famous masterpieces of strategy in history. Instead of attacking the
strong Persian army which faced Constantinople, he cut south, went by sea
to Alexandretta and thence marched inland, cutting off the Persian army of

Anatolia from its bases. After tieing up the Anatolian army so that he felt it could not seriously threaten his rear, he boldly struck east into Armenia and the Caucasus.

The Persians obviously did all they could to oppose him. They formed an alliance with the Avars, and in 626 the two allies besieged the city of Constantinople. But a Byzantine fleet controlled the Straits and the Marmora, and the allies could never get together well. Instead of returning from Armenia to rescue his capital, Heraclius boldly struck south and invaded Persia proper. He pushed into Assyria, won a great victory at Ninevah, and captured the Persian capital of Ctesiphon in 628. This threw the Persians into hopeless confusion; Chosroes II fled; his son, Siroes, revolted and overthrew his father; Shah Barz the general in Anatolia also revolted. Heraclius was able almost to dictate his own terms to the new monarch. Siroes agreed to restore the Holy Cross, and all provinces captured from the empire. Heraclius carried the Cross back to Constantinople in triumph. In Persia, Siroes died and was succeeded on the throne by Shah Barz, who followed a thoroughly Romanophile policy. The ancient struggle between Rome and Persia was ended forever.

But in the course of this war both Rome and Persia had exhausted themselves. If in 628 Rome seemed utterly victorious, an ancient foe prostrate at her feet and her influence supreme, the picture was but ephemeral. For five years later, in 633, both states were to feel the sharp impact of a hitherto unheard nation—the Arabs. J. B. Bury has remarked: "These five years [between 628 and 633] might be considered the ultimate between the Old and the Middle Ages; the appearance of the Saracen launches us into the medieval high seas, and few vestiges of antiquity remain." [5]

As the rise of Muhammad and the Saracens brings us into the medieval world, the Byzantine-Saracen struggle, as well as other aspects of the reign of Heraclius, will be reserved for treatment in a later chapter. But with the defeat of the Persians, a characteristic feature of the late Roman period passed away.

THE LOMBARD CONQUEST OF ITALY: GREGORY THE GREAT

A most significant event of the last part of the sixth century was the conquest of Italy by the Lombards. This German people had freed themselves successively from the overlordship of the Huns, Heruls, and Gepids and as allies of the empire had assisted in the wars of Justinian. The arrival of the Avars in the trans-Danubian region stirred up the Lombards, who allied with them to destroy the Gepids, after which, abandoning their own former lands to the Avars, they moved west into Italy.

The Lombards were always a small nation and in all their conquests they

5 J. B. Bury, *History of the Later Roman Empire* (1889 ed.) II, 246.

were assisted by other peoples. They derived their name, according to legend, from the fact that they had so few warriors that the women braided their hair below their chins to give the impression of beards so that they might be mistaken for fighting men. From the length of these beards the nation took its name of Longobards or Lombards.

It was under their king, Alboin, that they migrated west into Italy. They found the country devastated by the Ostrogothic-imperial wars and seem to have met with but little resistance as they overran the northern part of the peninsula. The Lombard conquest of Italy was extremely spotty; they conquered the interior without gaining control of the sea coast. Rome, Ancona, Ravenna, Naples, and the extreme south were still left in imperial hands; while any of the land below Naples was only partially occupied. In fact, the Lombard conquest was not the conquest by a people, so much as by a number of independent chiefs. The king of the Lombards ruled at Pavia in the north, but the dukes of Spoleto and Benevento, further south, recognized only the vaguest suzerainty of the king. At one time in the sixth century there were some thirty-six Lombard dukes, all aspiring to supremacy. In the seventh century, the power of the kings increased considerably, but the great duchies of the south were never brought effectively under their control.

The Lombards were in many ways the most adaptive of any of the German peoples. They took immediately to the Roman titles, government, and institutions. Arians at first, they quickly accepted Roman Christianity. As they were constantly at war with the empire, and with the popes, they have left a very bad name and are probably most maligned. They dreamed unsuccessfully of uniting all Italy, thereby arousing the antagonism of the popes who prefered to rule Rome themselves. Had they been successful, the whole history of Italy would undoubtedly have been quite different and might have been less disastrous. Papal, imperial, and Frankish historians unite in condemning the Lombards as savage, cruel, and uncivilized, but apart from the calumnies of their enemies, there is nothing in the history of the Lombards to indicate that they could not have founded as good a state as any of the other German peoples. They allowed the cities of northern Italy to develop and produced a civilization superior to most of their neighbors.

Imperial Italy had, meanwhile, been reorganized, Maurice establishing at Ravenna a governor, known as the Exarch, who held authority, usually vague, over the other imperial dukes in Italy. The imperial fleet continued to control the waters around Italy, and as long as the empire had the sea power the Lombards could never complete their conquest of the peninsula. Only in the last years of their existence in the eighth century did the Lombard kings succeed in conquering the Exarchate.

One of the most significant developments in Italy in this time was the rise of Venice. The islands in the lagoons were first settled by fugitives fleeing before the advance of the Huns in the fifth century, but it remained only a few scattered fishing villages on several islands until the Lombard invasion caused a further influx of colonists. The chief settlements developed on the islands of Rialto, Grado, Torcello, Malamocco, Murano and Chioggia, the settlements continuing through the seventh century. The fishermen of the lagoons had given some aid to Belisarius in his campaigns, but it was only after 568 that there was any organization of the town with elective officials to govern the confederated island villages. Venice was always theoretically subject to the empire but actually little imperial control was exercised over it. While it admitted the suzerainty of the empire, Venice was always virtually independent; safe behind her lagoons and her walls of wood, the maritime republic early developed an independence of spirit which was to mark its history to the end of its days.

It was also during the Lombard invasion that Rome became definitely the Rome of the popes. Rome of the Caesars passed out of existence during the struggle between the imperialists and the Ostrogoths, when her wealth and prosperity were destroyed by a series of sieges. During the new Lombard invasions the Eternal City passed definitely under the control of her bishops and became the medieval city of the popes. The greatest figure in this change was Gregory the Great (590–604). Born of an aristocratic Roman family, Gregory had achieved some position and honor in the secular administration of the city before he renounced the world to enter a monastery. But Gregory was not suited for the contemplative life; he left the monastery to become a deacon at Rome, and was sent on a mission to the emperor Maurice in Constantinople to secure aid against the Lombards. In this he failed, as Maurice was not interested in expensive campaigns in Italy, and Gregory developed a dislike of all things Greek during this time that was to color his whole career. Returning to Rome, he was elevated to the papacy in 590, and at once the defense of the city became his chief goal. Ignoring his imperial overlord, Gregory negotiated peace with the Lombards, and proceeded to reorganize the government of Rome independently of the Exarch at Ravenna. It is from his pontificate that the Patrimony of St. Peter may be said to date.

Gregory was most emphatic in his assertion of the claims of papal supremacy based on the Petrine theory, claiming overlordship over the churches of Italy, Gaul, Africa, and the West. Missionaries sent out from Rome penetrated into all parts of western Europe, the famous mission of St. Augustine converting King Ethelbert of Kent and establishing Roman Christianity in England. Gregory worked through the Benedictine monks; it was a partnership which brought mutual advantages. The pope favored Benedictines, and they carried the idea of submission to Rome wherever they went. We have already noted that he affirmed his position of supremacy as against the patriarch of Constantinople, and when John the Faster assumed the title of Oecumenical Patriarch, Gregory replied by adopting the famous "Servant of the Servants of God." Gregory is one of the greatest of the popes; he is rightly one of the Fathers of the Church. In the intellectual field, his influence, as we shall see in the next chapter, was unfortunate, as he set himself against pagan learning; and although he lived many years in Constantinople, he remained wholly ignorant of Greek. But in the matter of defending the position of the pope in regard to ecclesiastical and secular rivals, and in his organization of the church and its property, Gregory deserves to stand among the highest group of the elect. His little volume on *Pastoral Care,* while not one of the great literary works of the ages, is probably the finest exposition of the duties of a bishop that has ever been penned. Pious, sincere, with a singleness of purpose, Gregory represents the best of the militant churchmen of his time. And he affixed on Rome the seal of St. Peter so that until most recent times it remained a city apart from secular control—the home of the Catholic papacy.

CHAPTER 5

INTELLECTUAL ACHIEVEMENTS

✣

THE CLASSICS AND THE CHURCHMEN

FROM the vantage point of modern times, it is evident that the empire in the fourth to sixth centuries was in a state of sad decline and disrepair, but the same evidences were not so apparent to the men who were living in that age. Looking back we can now see that the empire was divided, never really to be whole again, that the new barbarian elements were assuming an importance and gaining an ascendency that was to bring about the utter disintegration of the empire, that the old world was dying. But to those who participated in these fateful events none of this was evident. They felt, of course, that the world had fallen on hard times, but that is an emotion felt by every generation of mankind and each successive era brings forth nostalgic lamentations for "the good old days." In many ways the Romans of this time felt that they were considerably advanced over their ancestors, and the protagonists of that artificial and sterile literature which flourished in Gaul in the days of Ausonius considered themselves much superior to the poets of an older age. They could not know, as we do, that the Golden Age had slipped into the Silver, and that the Silver was becoming badly tarnished.

To attempt to discuss the cultural and intellectual achievements of a period of three centuries in a single chapter would be an impossible task were it not that the culture of the fourth to sixth centuries was a particularly uninspired one, with but few really great figures looming up above the general level of dull mediocrity.

Intellectual life in the late Roman Empire was directed into one of two channels: theological speculation or classical appropriation. The greatest number, and the dullest, were the theologians, but the protagonists of classical culture also cut a sorry figure.

It was a period of extremely prolix theological works and of extremely concise epitomes of secular knowledge. With a tendency, which is unfortunately too prevalent today, the Romans endeavored to compress all knowledge into a few handbooks or manuals. And like many of our textbooks today, they endeavored to sugar-coat their facts to suit the appetite of a not too particularly interested audience. Flowery phraseology, recondite expressions, allegory and allusion characterize the writings of the secular authors of this period, and the most esteemed authors were those who could express their thoughts in the most ornate and confusing language.

The humanists of the Italian Renaissance claimed that they rediscovered the classical authors and were the first to appreciate them after centuries of neglect. This was entirely false, as classical authors were read and studied throughout the Middle Ages both in the East and West. C. H. Haskins has shown that the true renaissance occurred not in the fifteenth but in the twelfth century, and E. K. Rand, in his *Founders of the Middle Ages* has pointed out the humanistic qualities of some of the Latin Fathers. While it is true that certain elements in the church denounced the classical pagan authors and considered them pernicious and demoralizing, while it is true that Gregory the Great did "deem it exceedingly inept to fetter the words of the Heavenly Oracle to the rules of Donatus," while it is true that St. Jerome dreamed that he stood condemned before the bar of Heaven not as a Christian but a Ciceronian, nevertheless, as Rand points out, the fathers denounced the pagan authors in classic style, which owed much to the study of those very authors whom they decried. Both in East and West the classical authors formed the basis of education in the schools of the empire, and the Church Fathers, who denounced them, were themselves thoroughly imbued with classical learning.

It was St. Jerome who developed the doctrine of the "Spoils of the Egyptians," which was to justify the study of the classics in the consciences of so many medieval humanists. Even as the Children of Israel brought out from Egypt with them the spoils of the Egyptians, so should Christians take from pagan authors those things which were of value, eschewing meanwhile the dross of error. And if it be argued that medieval humanists studied the classics more for their application to Christian thought than for any pure sensual pleasure in the writing themselves, we must remember that in all periods words have been the tools of men to express their thoughts rather than the end in themselves. Sorry indeed those fortunately few periods when the phrase was the thing and when ideas were consistently subordinated to correct phraseology and elegant expression.

The great trouble was, and this is even more evident in the East than in the West, that secular studies did not progress. They remained entirely static where they did not retrograde. There were plenty of scholars, scientists, philosophers, poets and literary men of all types, but they were quite content generally to repeat the ideas of the ancients without adding anything to them. The late Roman and Byzantine scholars transmitted the learning of Antiquity to posterity but they only transmitted; therein lies the great contrast between them and the Arabs who were both transmitters and transmuters, who added their own thoughts, ideas, and experiments to the learning which they received from the ancients.

The Patristic Writers

Only in the field of theology were truly great works produced in the fourth to sixth centuries. Christian theology was a new and living subject; it was a field in which men could think originally and produce profound works. Not that all of the writings of this period were profound by any means, but the intellectual level was high. Later, as theology became set, theological writing became the dullest and most depressing of all subjects, but the early centuries of the Christian era were the great age of theology. Philosophy had stagnated since the great days of Greece, but theology was in its Golden Age both in the Greek and Latin worlds.

It is difficult for us today to understand the role which theology played in the minds of medieval men. Religion today is, in most countries, no longer a sufficiently vital issue to be seriously controversial. Economics has taken the place in our thinking that religion occupied throughout the Middle Ages, and we worry about Fascism, Communism, Syndicalism, and Anarchism as the sixth century man worried about Gnosticism, Arianism, Nestorianism, or Monophysitism. A well-known quotation from Gregory of Nyssa, describing Constantinople in the fourth century, illustrates this point:

> The city is full of mechanics and slaves, who are all of them profound theologians, and preach in the shops and in the streets. If you desire a man to change a piece of silver, he informs you wherein the Son differs from the Father; if you ask the price of a loaf, you are told by way of reply that the Son is inferior to the Father; if you inquire whether the bath is ready, the answer is that the Son was made out of nothing.[1]

In the fourth century, the Eastern Empire produced a remarkable group of theologians. The so-called Cappadocians: St. Basil the Great, Gregory Nazianzus, and Gregory of Nyssa are among the most venerated fathers of the Greek Church today. These men represented the application to Christian thought of the training still to be received in the old schools of Athens and Alexandria. They wrote doctrinal essays, sermons, letters, poems. They were ardent defenders of the orthodox faith against the Arians and used the subtleties of classical education to defend the position of Christian orthodoxy. Perhaps most famous of the Greek theologians was the great orator and preacher John Chrysostum, who occupied the see of Constantinople from 398 to 403. A product of the schools of Antioch, John was the greatest preacher of his times, and so insulted the Augusta Eudoxia by his tirades against luxurious and lascivious dress and manners that he ended his days in exile. His literary works—sermons, letters, and

---

[1] Quoted from J. W. Thompson: *Economic and Social History of the Middle Ages*, p. 80.

orations—show a firm basis of classical knowledge and a mastery of the Greek tongue.

The Christological controversy, of course, produced a large crop of theologians. Nestorius, Cyril of Alexandria, Theodore of Mopsuesta, Ibas of Edessa all wrote tracts and sermons on this all-important subject. In the reign of Justinian, Leontius of Byzantium brilliantly defended the orthodox position in a series of works refuting the heresies of both Nestorians and Monophysites.

These are but the most brilliant lights in the galaxy of theologians produced in the Eastern Empire in the fourth to sixth centuries; the list could be extended into the hundreds and a glance at Migne's *Patrologia Graeca* evidences the extent of Greek patristic writings; but even the greatest are but names to most of us today and their works are among that vast library of great literature about which we know, but about which we know nothing at first hand.

More familiar to us, though no more important in the realm of theology than the great Greek Fathers, were the Latin Fathers, especially the great triumvirate of Saints—Ambrose, Jerome, and Augustine. These three giants of Latin thought were all roughly contemporaries: Ambrose (340–397) and Jerome (340–420) being exact contemporaries, while Augustine (354–430) was somewhat younger. Of the three, Augustine was undoubtedly the greatest theologian, but the work of Jerome in defining the Vulgate and in establishing monasticism, and that of Ambrose in developing church organization and setting the basis for allegorical interpretation is hardly less significant.

Ambrose is chosen by E. K. Rand as representing the mystic. While most of his life was spent in practical business matters and in ordering his see of Milan, to which he was elevated direct from a secular career, Ambrose deserves the appellation mystic for the popularization of allegory. In his *De Officiis Ministrorum* Ambrose assimilated to Christian ethics the best ethical precepts of the ancients. In his commentaries on various books of the Bible, he set up the standard allegorical interpretation, which was to be so popular throughout the Middle Ages. It is sometimes difficult to decide whether Ambrose or Dr. Freud could read more into a simple statement, but Ambrose certainly did not lag far behind the great Viennese psychiatrist. To him every statement had four meanings; the literal, the moral (its application to human character), the allegorical (prophecy), and the anagogical (escatological). Ambrose's moral interpretation was later called tropological, and these four meanings were read into Scripture by pious scholars for centuries to come. "A sure path to mysticism is through allegory" says Rand; and certainly we cannot deny Ambrose the title of mystic.

St. Jerome is to Rand the humanist, and with this characterization no one can quibble. Jerome is best known for his great work in compiling the Vulgate; he sorted out all the sacred writings of Judaism and Christianity and established the canons of the Old and New Testaments which he translated into Latin, and the Apocrypha. His *De Viris illustribus* is a *Who's Who* of early Christian writers; his letters did much to popularize monasticism and the ascetic life. In all of his writings, Jerome showed the classical scholar; even at the time when he had most violently repented of his Ciceronianism and eschewed pagan authors, numerous quotations from the classics creep into his own writing. He developed the idea of "the spoils of the Egyptians" to justify in his own soul the love of literature, and though his themes were ascetic and religious, his phrases were classical and urbane. But Jerome had another idea; that of giving Christian readers good literary Christian literature. He wrote three saint's lives; popular stories of the edifying careers of holy men, which could be read by all with profit and pleasure. He was, as Rand points out, "without doubt the greatest scholar among the Latin fathers" and deserves the characterization with which Rand closes his brilliant chapter on him, *"Tu et Christianus es et Ciceronianus."*

Theologically the greatest contribution was made by St. Augustine, bishop of Hippo (not to be confused with the later and less important St. Augustine of Canterbury). Augustine is best known for two works, his *Confessions,* an autobiography in which he relates how the pagan rhetor found salvation and the gratification of his soul in the teachings of Christ, and the *City of God,* his greatest philosophical work. For centuries men have disputed over the meaning of the two cities which Augustine described: the City of Man and the City of God, but the accepted view now is that he referred to this earth and to heaven, though clerics long maintained he meant the secular and ecclesiastical states. The *City of God* traces the course of Roman history to show the ills and tribulations which came to Rome through her adherence to false gods; then he goes on to discuss the plan of God for mankind; the creation of the world, the fall of Satan, the redemption of man through Christ, and the establishment of the sacraments, whereby man can be saved and brought to God's eternal city. This work has probably had a greater influence on religious thought in the West than any other single book; not only was Augustine studied and revered by medieval theologians, but his teachings strongly influenced both modern Catholic and Protestant thought.

Augustine was a prolific writer and these works are but a small part of his total output. He lived in an age when heresies were undermining the Faith, and he stoutly raised his pen to refute the errors of the heretics; against Pelagius, the Donatists, the Arians, the Manichaeans and others he joyfully fought God's battle. Some of his doctrines have proven almost embarrassing to the church since; for example, in his arguments against the free-will theories of the Pelagians, he asserted a doctrine of predestination, which was later taken over by Calvin as the basis of his teachings. The church meanwhile had receded somewhat from the extreme position of Augustine, so that Calvin's extension of Augustine's teachings was distinctly heretical. According to Augustine, God willed all men to be saved and men were predestined to salvation; this the church accepts and believes. But Calvin (following Gottschalk, a ninth-century monk) interpreted predestination to mean not a general predestination to salvation, but a specific predestination of the individual to salvation or to damnation. This same argument had been raised by Gottschalk and had been denounced by Hrabanus Maurus as early as 848. Hincmar of Rheims and Remegius of Lyons took up the quarrel, and the question split French councils throughout the ninth century until it was settled by compromise at the Council of Tusey (860), by a formula which accepted only universal redemption. Calvin's unbending rigidity accepted no such compromise and the doctrine which he claimed to have found in Augustine was one of the chief points of conflict between the Calvinists and the Catholics in the sixteenth century. This discussion may well seem to have little bearing on Augustine himself, but it illustrates the tremendous influence which Augustine had on future generations and on all Christian theology.

A fourth great ecclesiastical writer, sometimes ranked as one of the great Latin Fathers, was Gregory the Great, whose activities as pope we have already noticed. Gregory was the reverse of Jerome in that he opposed any classical influence, and resolutely shut his mind against any pernicious pagan doctrines. Yet the religion which he advocated was, while pure of any pagan philosophical ideology, full to overflowing with the darkest type of pagan superstition. It is largely due to Gregory that much of the crass superstition of medieval Christianity developed. His was a world peopled with demons and devils of all sorts. The infernal hierarchy was fully as developed as the heavenly, and man must be always on the alert to outwit the wiles of the devils. In his *Pastoral Care,* as stated above, Gregory wrote a magnificent exposition of the duties and obligations of the episcopal office; his sermons and commentaries reveal a fervid, sincere, passionate belief; but the hosts of angels, devils, and demons which fill his writings almost obscure the clarity of the faith behind them.[2]

---

[2] In this short space we cannot attempt to do more than scratch the surface of the Latin Fathers any more than we could the Greek. Lactantius, Prudentius, Arnobius, Hilary of Poitiers, Paulinus and a host of others must be passed over without comment, and the student is referred to E. K. Rand's *Founders of the Middle Ages* or to P. de Labriolle's *History and Literature of Latin Christianity* for further discussion of them.

PHILOSOPHY

In the realm of philosophy, as apart from theology, the period of the late empire produced but few important names. Pagan thought was generally proscribed and the pagan philosophers had to keep more or less obscure if they wished to live to philosophize another day. The most famous of the philosophers of the East is best known for precisely the fact that martyrdom crowned her teachings. Hypatia, the learned woman professor of philosophy at Alexandria, whose beauty and erudition made her the center of interest in the Alexandrian academic world, was assaulted in the street and brutally murdered in 415, by a gang of monks who relied on the protection of Cyril of Alexandria. Earlier, Libanius of Antioch, the teacher of Chrysostom, St. Basil, and Gregory Naziansus, had acquired the reputation as the first teacher and philosopher of the fourth century. In the fifth century, Proclus of Constantinople taught at Athens, which remained the last stronghold of pagan philosophy until its university was closed by Justinian.

The greatest single work in philosophy was not done, however, by any pagan philosopher but by a Western Christian, who in prison and awaiting death, turned to philosophy for spiritual consolation. *The Consolation of Philosophy* of Anicius Manlius Boethius is still considered one of the world's classics and one of the finest examples of prison literature extant. We will have more to say about Boethius below, but must here indicate this important philosophical work which had such an influence on such people as King Alfred (who had it translated into Anglo-Saxon), Chaucer, and Dante, as well as on thousands more. Though himself a Christian, Boethius turned entirely to philosophy in his last hours, and was so uninfluenced by any Christian doctrine in the *Consolation* that many scholars have insisted that Boethius could not have been a Christian at all. This work, written around 524, has properly been called the last important work of classical philosophy.

We must be careful, however, both in this and in later periods of medieval history, to avoid the idea that men were interested only in theology and philosophy. One of the most popular misconceptions of the Middle Ages comes from this idea that men were all spiritually minded and that secular matters were neglected in favor of otherworldly pursuits. While this was true of a certain section of society, it did not apply to all men then or at any time. Gregory's picture of the theologians of Constantinople is exaggerated for effect and must not be taken too literally. The Middle Ages were in fact the Age of Faith; but even then there were many dissenters.

The Transmitters of Classical Learning

The years of the decline of the empire were years of confusion, especially in the West. Barbarian inroads upset the ordered way of life and forced many families to flee their homes and seek refuge elsewhere. They had less time to read, less leisure in which to peruse the long works of the ancient authors; further, they developed less inclination to do so. They preferred summaries, manuals, compendiums of science or history. Moreover, in moving about it was impossible to carry along several cartloads of books; people took along the short manuals which gave them the most reading in the least space: "Bedside Pliny," "The Pocket Ovid," "Tales from Livy," "The Horatian Omnibus" might well have been fifth century bestsellers, second only to Outlines of History, Compendiums of Science and Handbooks of Philosophy.

This same tendency affected the schools; textbooks were preferred to the original sources. The most popular book in the early Middle Ages was probably the amazing *Marriage of Mercury and Philology* of Martianus Capella, who wrote in Africa in the early years of the fifth century. This little book was a compendium of all essential knowledge and fixed the Seven Liberal Arts of our educational system. The book is a rather silly allegory of the marriage of Mercury to Philology, which occurred on the Milky Way with all the gods in attendance. At the wedding, Mercury presents his bride with seven handmaidens and as each is introduced, she steps up and recites her attributes. These seven recitations are seven textbooks on the seven arts: Grammar, Rhetoric, and Dialectic (the *Trivium*) represent the literary arts; Arithmetic, Geometry, Astronomy, and Music (the *Quadrivium*) represent the mathematical sciences. And therein was contained all that people need to know. These arts, as has been pointed out, were really vocational subjects for the clergy, since all were more or less important to the education of a priest. He must know grammar and rhetoric to prepare sermons, and it were as well if he had some idea of logic for the same purpose. He must know arithmetic to keep the books of the parish, geometry to settle boundary disputes over property (for geometry included surveying), astronomy so that he could fix the movable dates in the ecclesiastical calendar, and music that he might chant the hymns of the service. Architecture and medicine, which had been included among the arts in the ancient schools were dropped from the new Christian educational system as unnecessary to the needs of the priest.

Although today Martianus' book seems the most ridiculous sort of performance, it enjoyed a tremendous vogue. People liked the sugar-coating; they enjoyed being slipped into their texts via the allegorical wedding. It made the plunge into learning less noticeable to slide down the greased skids of the allegory. And the book retained its popularity for centuries.

There were other authors who, however, approached learning in a more sedate fashion. Basic texts in grammar (which included the study of literature) were the manuals of Donatus (fourth century) and Priscan (fifth century). These books laid down rules of grammar and illustrated them with copious quotations from the classical authors. Virgil, Horace, Ovid, Cicero, Juvenal, Sallust, Lucretius—all the popular classical authors were combed to provide illustrations, and the quotations from their works in these grammars made their names, if not their writings, familiar to generations of students in the medieval schools.

First place among the transmitters of classical learning in the West must go however to that Boethius whom we have previously encountered as a philosopher *in extremis*. Boethius was a Roman patrician who held the office of consul under Theodoric the Ostrogoth, and whose political ventures resulted in his imprisonment, execution, and literary immortality. But his great work, in his own mind, was his attempt to reconcile Plato and Aristotle. He set himself the goal of translating all the works of both of these philosophers and synchronizing their teachings. Of course he never accomplished this gargantuan task, but he did translate the *Timaeus* of Plato and several of the Aristotelian logical works (subsequently known as the *Old Organon*). In translating Aristotle he found that commentaries were needed; from this he was further sidetracked by the necessity of preparing usable manuals on the Liberal Arts so that the commentaries would be understandable. In the course of these discursions Boethius translated standard Greek handbooks on most of the seven Arts, which showed no originality but enjoyed a considerable vogue, though they were less popular than Martianus.

Boethius is called by Rand the "first of the scholastics" because he introduced into the thought of the Middle Ages that attempt to synchronize Aristotle and the Bible. This he did in four theological tracts which he wrote towards the end of his life, one of which bears the significant title "How Substances can be good in virtue of their being, although they are not Substantial Goods." The arguments of Abelard or of Anselm are already ringing in our ears; the road from Rome leads to the Rue du Fouarre and the Place St. Michel.

Cassiodorus, Boethius' contemporary, and like him a public official under Theodoric, ranks with Boethius as one of the great transmitters. Cassiodorus' great work lies not so much in his own writings, although they show a good classical education, but in the influence he had in causing the Benedictine monks to engage in the copying of classical texts. Copying had always been one of the labors favored by Benedict, but at first it had been only copying sacred writings. Cassiodorus, who became a monk when he was sixty, in 540, was able to get the copying of classical authors accepted as equally meritorious work. Without this many of our texts of ancient authors would undoubtedly have been lost, as we have them almost entirely preserved in monastic codices.

The third and last of the great trilogy of transmitters (note how prevalent is the sacred number three in all our classifications of these early churchmen) was a much later and much less well-informed person. Isidore, bishop of Seville (died 636), is the last scholar to partake at all fully of the ancient learning, and he imbibed but little. His *Etymologies* was a compendium of all secular knowledge of his time and was considered as the authoritative reference work, enjoying a position not unlike that of the *Encyclopedia Britannica* today. Isidore wrote of the cosmos, the heavens, the earth, man, angels, and devils, animals, medicine, games and sports, economic and political geography; in fact, everything that he could think of went into his work. It is based on words, hence the title *Etymologies,* and the derivation of words is given. While some of Isidore's derivations have some sense, most of them sound wholly ridiculous today. His geography is a strange mixture of fact and fable, much of it being derived from Solinus, a third century writer who took it from Pliny. The trouble was that Solinus took from Pliny the most amazing phenomena, while disregarding familiar things, and Isidore culled only the most bizarre things from Solinus, so that the result was a most startling world inhabited by most unusual animals and people. We can read Isidore today with considerable amusement (in the excellent translation by Brehaut), but it gives us pause to consider when we realize that he was the great scholar whose erudition surpassed that of his contemporaries. Nothing shows more clearly the depths to which culture had fallen in the West.

This decline in education is one of the most outstanding characteristics of the last centuries of the empire. In the fourth century, secular schools flourished all over the empire, and Constantine issued an edict to secure adequate pay for the teachers. In the fifth century while the old learning went on in the East, it declined sadly in the West and the same decline continued throughout the next century. While the schools of the Eastern Empire continued to flourish, those of the West disappeared. In the West, learning retreated into the monasteries where it played but a secondary role to piety. But throughout the East and in parts of Italy secular schools continued to teach the youth Greek grammar and the Greek authors. Athens continued its pagan university until the reign of Justinian; Alexandria accepted Christian ethics and continued her university as a Christian school, specializing in logic, a subject on which pagan and Christian authorities could agree. But even the higher education of the Eastern Empire was somewhat sterile and stagnant; the old forms were preserved but there was little life left in them, and no new blood.

POETRY

Poetry was especially cultivated, the art of poetical composition being considered one of the essentials of a proper education. Martianus Capella's remarkable textbook was written partly in prose and partly in verse, a form which remained very popular throughout the Middle Ages. In the Greek provinces of the empire, there is no name in poetry in this period comparable with that of Romanus the Melode, a Syrian, who came to Constantinople in the reign of Anastasius, and whose hymns have such elegance that he has been termed the "Pindar of rhythmical poetry" and "The greatest poet of the Byzantine period." [3]

Latin poetry enjoyed almost a renaissance although it was a rather formal and lifeless affair in many ways. In the fourth century, Claudian and Ausonius wrote almost perfectly classical verse which was technically very superior. Claudian was the poet-chronicler of Honorius and of Stilicho and wrote many poems celebrating the deeds of his patrons. His poems are not only thoroughly classical in form but also in spirit, and, although he was a professed Christian, there is no influence of the new religion in any of his verse. Ausonius, prefect of Gaul, wrote verse which carried on the classical love of nature and which reflects the society of Gaul at the time. His poems are technically correct, but although greatly admired by contemporaries, seem somewhat stilted and artificial. Much more spirit is found in the religious poems of his student, Paulinus of Nola, and in the works of the Spaniard, Prudentius, both of whom wrote hymns and other sacred verse. Some of the finest hymns of this time, moreover, were written by St. Ambrose.

The secular tradition was carried on in Gaul by Apollonaris Sidonius, who was bishop of Clermont-Ferrand in the fifth century, but whose poems show little religious influence, giving instead a pleasing picture of the cultivated urbane life of the Gallo-Roman aristocracy of the time. He also strove for mechanical perfection, which he achieved at the expense of any real emotion. Ennodius, a Gaul, bishop of Pavia (ob. 521), was another poet whose works show the stilted, artificial correctness of a classical style with little vitality. Venantius Fortunatus, who has a somewhat higher place among poets, was an Italian who came to Gaul and became secretary to Queen Radegonda, whose life he "immortalized" in a poem; he also wrote versified lives of several saints, the most important being a life of St. Martin of Tours. With Fortunatus, who lived at the end of the sixth century, the decline in classical knowledge had strongly set in, and we find in his works little of the classical influence that marked his predecessors. Other Latin poets of this period are Avitus, Commodian, Juvenecus, Sedulius, Dracontius et al.

[3] A. A. Vasiliev, *History of the Byzantine Empire*, I, 153.

HISTORICAL LITERATURE

In the field of historical writing, we note the same characteristics of transition from the antique secular to the medieval ecclesiastical emphasis. Whereas some historians continue the classical traditions of historiography, others color all their history with a religious bias. Edifying history which traces the triumph of the godly over the ungodly becomes a popular theme, and biography generally becomes no longer the deeds of military or political heroes but the pious lives of the saints.

Hagiography, the writing of the lives of the saints, became one of the most popular forms of literature. Athanasius, the great opponent of Arius, wrote the Life of St. Anthony; St. Jerome wrote the lives of three saints; Sulpicius Severus wrote a life of St. Martin of Tours, as did Fortunatus; Paladius of Helenopolis wrote a general history of monasticism. The pious and edifying deeds of the saints were considered the very best kind of reading, and saints' lives multiplied throughout the entire Middle Ages. Some of these lives are first-rate historical documents, and many episodes in history are only known to us through being incorporated in a saint's life, but on the whole they are quite inferior as history. Every proper saint had to have his miracles, and as the miracles increase the historical value goes down. Many of the lives were but pious fabrications in which a string of miracles were attributed to a saint in order to give him greater standing and sanctity. Later on the miracles became almost standardized, so that each saint performed the same miracles as the others; no biographer could allow his saint to be less holy than his rivals.

These saints' lives were probably the most popular reading of the time. They took the place not only of popular biography today but also of much fiction, as the fictional romance had made little headway in Antiquity, and the miraculous exploits of the saints lent romance to the lives of their readers.

Apart from these pseudo-historical popular saints' lives, the historical writings of the late empire break down into two major groups: world chronicles and histories of special events or periods. A very popular type of history was the universal world chronicle which began with the Creation and carried events to the present. Generally the history would be divided into two parts—sacred history of the Jews derived from the Scriptures, and profane history of the Gentiles derived from pagan sources. The two channels of history would be carried down separately until they joined in the Age of Augustus and the life of Christ. Thereafter there would be but one stream of history, but the ecclesiastical history would predominate in it. The victory of Christianity over paganism was the theme of many of these histories, and all historical happenings were interpreted to prove this point.

Another characteristic of medieval historiography which it will be well to mention here is the tendency of authors to plagarize and epitomize. When a man sat down to write a history he would have to have some previous sources for earlier periods; therefore he simply copied out what to him seemed the best accounts available until he got to that part of his work which he intended to do at first hand. As time went on there was an increasing tendency to abridge these earlier accounts and to stress more the later periods. But much of the best history written was done as a continuation of some celebrated earlier work, as we shall see.

In general the Greek historians were far superior to the Latin. This was probably due to the fact that through the sixth century history in the East was written largely by laymen, especially lawyers, and they adopted a more objective and unprejudiced view than their ecclesiastical colleagues of the West. Also, as we have insisted upon elsewhere, the general state of learning was far superior in the East and the ancient models were more familiar.

The first great historian in the East in this period was Eusebius of Caesarea who wrote in the early fourth century. He was the author of a *Life of Constantine,* a *Chronicle,* and an *Ecclesiastical History,* as well as of some saints' lives and lesser works. The *Life of Constantine* does not redound to his credit as a historian, as it is thoroughly unreliable, but the *Chronicle* and the *Ecclesiastical History* were both of the utmost importance.

Eusebius' *Chronicle* (called *Chronographia*) was one of the world chronicles described above. It began with Abraham and came down to 324 A.D. It included chronological tables of all the peoples, Assyrians, Greeks, Romans, Hebrews, showing the correlation of their dates and the chief events in the history of each. After the birth of Christ, sacred history and Roman history converged. This work became immensely popular. It was translated into Latin by St. Jerome, who continued it from 324 to 378. This Latin translation was continued by Prosper of Aquitaine (to 455) and by other authors including Cassiodorus, Isidore of Seville, and Bede. Eusebius' *Chronicle* is lost in the original and is only known to us through the Latin adaptations and through Armenian and Syriac translations, but his *Ecclesiastical History* is available in its original. This first history of the Christian church covers the period from the birth of Christ to the triumph of Constantine and Christianity in ten books. It is much more detailed than the *Chronicle* and does not attempt to cover secular history, devoting itself to the rise and growth of the church and the martyrdoms and persecutions of the early Christians. The *Ecclesiastical History* was continued in Greek by Socrates in 439; and by Evagrios (431–593) while similar ecclesiastical histories were written by Sozomen to 439,

Theodoret to 428, and Philostorgius (an Arian) to 425. Eusebius was also translated into Latin by Rufinus.

The next important historian in the East after Eusebius was Ammianus Marcellinus, who wrote in Latin a history which was meant to continue the history of Tacitus. Of his work only the last eighteen books, covering the years 353–373, has been preserved. Thus, what we have of Ammianus covers the reign of Julian, a fortunate chance, as Ammianus was himself a pagan and sympathetic with the Apostate. He belonged rather to the past than to the future and was the last important pagan historian. The only other pagan of any significance was Zosimus, who wrote in the early sixth century a history of Rome to the fall of the city before Alaric. Zosimus blamed the abandonment of the old gods for the troubles which had afflicted the empire and considered Constantine the villain of the piece.

The greatest name in the historiography of the fifth century is that of Orosius. Orosius was a Spanish Christian, a pupil of St. Augustine, who at Augustine's suggestion composed a history to show that it was not the failure to adhere to the old religion that caused the travail of the empire, as empires were accustomed to fall. His *Seven Books of History against the Pagans* is a dull apologetic which narrates the sins of the pagans and the workings of Divine Justice, which sent the barbarians to destroy them. It nevertheless had considerable influence on succeeding generations.[4]

The reign of Justinian brought a veritable deluge of historical writing in the East. Foremost amongst the historians of the sixth century is Procopius of Caesarea who wrote three important histories: the *Wars,* the *Buildings,* and the *Secret History.* In the *Wars,* Procopius tells with great detail of Justinian's reconquest of the West; in the *Buildings* he extolls his beautification of Constantinople; but in the *Secret History* (which was not discovered for many centuries after his death) he narrates the scandals of the life of Theodora and the corruption of the court. Procopius was an ardent admirer of Thucydides and followed him both in narrative style and in vocabulary. It is largely due to his splendid descriptions that we are so familiar with the personalities of Justinian's entourage, especially with Belisarius who was the hero of Procopius' piece. Procopius was a Christian, but not a very devout one, and his prejudice against monks and the evils of monasticism appears throughout his writings. The history of Procopius was continued to the death of Maurice in 602 by three writers of lesser note: Agathias (552–558), Menander Protector (558–582) and Theophylactus Simocatta (582–602). The chronicle of John Malalas, which

---

4 The only other fifth-century historian of note is Priscus of Thrace who wrote a history of the period 434–474, valuable for his account of the Huns. Much of our information for the events of this century is derived from the historical poems of Claudian mentioned above.

covered the history of the world from ancient Egypt to the death of Justinian, is significant in that it was composed in the vulgar spoken Greek
of the time and was intended for popular consumption. While the historical accuracy of Malalas is poor, the very inclusion of fables in his work
added to its popularity and it had a great influence especially on Slavic
chroniclers.

Latin historiography on the whole did not produce the great world
chronicles which the Greek did. We have already seen that Eusebius'
Chronicle was translated and continued in the West; also Orosius wrote
his history of the fate of empires. There were several minor universal histories, such as those of Cassiodorus, and Fulgentius and Victor bishop of
Carthage, both sixth century, but nothing of any importance.

The really significant historical writing in the West was the histories
of the various nations which established themselves in the former provinces of the empire. While the Visigoths of Spain were treated only in
relatively unimportant histories, the best of which was that by Isidore
of Seville, the Ostrogoths were the subject of a tremendous history by
Cassiodorus in twelve books. Unfortunately Cassiodorus' *Gothic History*
is now lost and we know it only in the abridgement made in the middle
of the sixth century by Jordanes. Jordanes did more than condense
Cassiodorus however; he wrote a history of the German migrations based
on the legends and traditions of the people. He wrote in rather bad Latin
and the history is full of superstition and fable, but it is the first history
written from the German point of view.

Although the Anglo-Saxons were to have no great historian until Bede
(673–735), the story of their conquest was told by a Celtic monk, Gildas,
who witnessed the events of the conquest and fled before the invading
Germans. Gildas' narrative is a dirge and a lament rather than a history,
but it does give some contemporary evidence for the conquest.

By far the greatest of the Germanic national histories, before we come
to Bede, is the *History of the Franks* by Gregory, bishop of Tours (538–
594). Gregory was of a wealthy and influential Gallo-Roman family of
Auvergne and inherited what was left of the culture of the society of
Ausonius and Sidonius. The quality of his Latin shows to what depth
education in the West had fallen, as it is ungrammatical and full of bar-
barisms; further, he is superstitious and credulous, recording miracles and
omens along with more sober facts. But Gregory wrote in a vivid style
and he shows considerable critical ability in regard to secular events. The
society he described was one of peculiar violence and brutality; Gregory
does not attempt to gloss over the crimes of his characters. But he did
justify them with a certain casuistry which seems a bit shocking to modern
ideas. For example, after describing one of Clovis' more exceptionally
treacherous crimes, in which he caused two of his relatives to be mur-

dered and then seized their kingdom, Gregory concludes: "He received Sigibert's kingdom with his treasures, and placed his people too under his rule. For God was laying his enemies low every day under his hand, and was increasing his kingdom, because he walked with an upright heart before Him, and did what was pleasing in His eyes." [5]

Elsewhere Gregory attributes Clovis' attack on the Aquitanian Visigoths to his reluctance that such fair lands should be held by heretics. However, in Merovingian society it did not do to be too squeamish, and little matters like murder, arson, and theft were inconsequential in view of the unfaltering orthodoxy of Clovis' theological convictions. In another age Gregory of Tours might not have rated so highly as scholar or historian, but in Merovingian Gaul he was great. And between the ancient historians and Bede there is none other of his caliber.

GEOGRAPHICAL LORE

In one other field of writing interesting work was done in this period. That was in geography, in which two important works were produced, both in the reign of Justinian. Hierocles, a grammarian, wrote a Travelers' Guide (*Vade-mecum*), which described the political geography of the empire, discussing its 64 provinces with descriptions of some 912 cities. This early Baedeker, though dry and factual, was employed by subsequent geographers for many centuries.

More interesting is the *Christian Topography* of Cosmos Indicopleustes (c. 550). Cosmos was a merchant who made a number of trading voyages to the Further East. Retiring from business to become a monk in Alexandria, he wrote his *Topography* to refute the pagan heretical idea that the world was round and to prove that it was shaped like an oblong box. The universe, according to Cosmos, was designed like the Tabernacle of Moses with the earth resembling the sanctuary. Cosmos was not too successful in selling this idea, as the more popular concept of the world was that of Isidore—a saucer inverted. But it is not for his cosmography that Cosmos deserves to be remembered; it is for the accurate and circumstantial descriptions of places he had seen on his voyages that his book is important. He had visited the shores of the Red Sea and the Indian Ocean, and he describes the ports and cities of the East. Especially important is his account of Ceylon, which was the great mart where Chinese and Western merchants met and traded. His is the most important description of the Far East by any Christian writer until the thirteenth century.

Thus in summary we can see that the period of the fourth to sixth centuries was an active intellectual era. While much of the work done was distinctly second-rate or worse, in some fields, especially theology, it was of first

[5] E. Brehaut, *Gregory of Tours* (Columbia Univ. Press: "Records"), p. 48.

importance; and while classical education was declining in the West, it was preserved in the East. There were few secular writers of any marked genius; there was a lamentable tendency to emphasize style and forms of expression rather than content of ideas; old forms were decaying and new forms were not yet developed. Yet it must be remembered that writers of this time did not know that they were in a decline; much that offends us now they thought to be the height of elegance and taste; if some authors recognized and lamented the rusticity of their style, others prided themselves on the niceties of theirs. And in comparison to the age that followed it was certainly a Silver Age.

✛✛

Book II

The Ascendancy of the East
630-1050

In this period the unity of the Roman Empire was destroyed by the rise of the Arab caliphate, which overran Africa and gained control over the western Mediterranean. The Western provinces of the empire were isolated from the capital, which became so completely Greek, that we now speak of the Byzantine (or Greek) rather than the Roman Empire. Byzantium still retained its position of superiority to any other state in Europe, but its position was not so unique, since the Moslem Empire in the East and the new Frankish Empire of Charlemagne in the West both challenged its absolute supremacy. However Byzantium was still far ahead of the West in material and intellectual culture, in military power and wealth, and Byzantine trade was the most important of any Christian state. The Moslem cities, Damascus, Baghdad, and Cordova, were also centers of a flourishing economic and cultural development, and Western Europe played but a sorry role in comparison with the East.

The Arab power rose and declined within the limits of this era. Byzantium suffered some reverses, but reached its apogee of power and glory under the Macedonian emperors in the tenth century. At the very end of the period, however, Byzantium was badly hurt by the Turkish invasion, which destroyed its military power at Manzikert. However it can clearly be said to have held its position as the first power of the European world throughout this entire period.

In the West meanwhile the Frankish Empire had been formed and had broken up into several states. Feudalism was developing and the Western nations were laying the basis for the resurgence of vitality, which they were to experience in the following era. The old dependence on Constantinople had been broken by the erection of the Carolingian and later the German Roman empires. The papacy had asserted its independence from Constantinople, but had fallen under the control of the Germans. Intellectual life was beginning to revive, but was still infinitely inferior to the East.

MOSQUE OF OMAR: JERUSALEM

Chapter 6

THE MOSLEM CALIPHATES[1]

✛

The Arabs before Muhammad

IF the Persian wars of Heraclius were in the ancient tradition, the Moslem wars were characteristically medieval. The rise of the Moslem Empire and the struggle between Cross and Crescent was one of the most typical aspects of the medieval period which may be said to lie between the Arab offensive of the seventh century and the Turkish conquests of the fifteenth.

When Heraclius and Chosroes were battling for supremacy in the early years of the seventh century neither had ever heard of Muhammad or of his religion of Islam. But it was the Moslem Arabs who were to benefit from the long and exhausting Byzantino-Persian War and who reaped the fruits of the victory over both states.

The Arabs, before Muhammad, had for centuries been a small, loosely organized people, some of which were under the Byzantine and some under the Persian influence. Arab tribes had assisted both the great empires in their struggle as minor dependent allies. That they would completely overthrow the Persian and tear away some of the best provinces of the Byzantine Empire would have been considered ridiculous to anyone. But in the early years of the seventh century the Arabs were provided with a new impetus, in the form of a new religion, which gave them a unity to carry the banner of the Prophet in a series of campaigns whereby they stretched their control in all directions until they possessed all the lands from the Atlantic to the Indus and from the Loire and the Oxus to the Sahara.

When we speak of the Arabs we are too inclined to think of them as the tent-dwelling sons of the desert who roamed about in the center of the Arabian peninsula with their herds of camels, engaged in perpetual raids and skirmishes under the leadership of their tribal sheiks. These are the Bedouin, and they are an important element of the Arab people, but they are only one part, and the real development of the Arabs was done by the urban dwellers who inhabited the cities of Hedjaz, southern Palestine, and Mesopotamia. There had been Arab kingdoms in southern and in

[1] In transliterating Arabic names the form used by P. K. Hitti in his *History of the Arabs* has been used except for place names and such words as Hegira, which are more familiar in the usual English spelling.

northern Arabia since before the Christian era, those of the Himyarites in the south (115 B.C.–525 A.D.) and the Nabateans in the north (c. 300 B.C.– 105 A.D.) having achieved considerable importance. Palmyra in the third century had been a formidable state which stretched from Ankara to Alexandria until it was overthrown by the emperor Aurelian. In the sixth century, the two chief Arab kingdoms were the Ghazanids and the Lakh-mids, both in the north, both Christian, and allies, respectively, of Jus-tinian and Persia. There was a constant movement of the Arab peoples from south to north in the peninsula, with the result that enclaves of southern Arabs were often found to the north of the northern Arabs; thus Mecca was inhabited by northern Arabs while Medina to the north was a south-Arab city. Medina had a large Jewish population and the name of the city was derived from the Jews, not as tradition asserts from Muham-mad.

In the city of Mecca the governing tribe was that of the Quraysh. This powerful tribe was divided into two main branches, the wealthy and aristo-cratic Banu-Harb or Umayyads and the poorer, more plebeian Hashimites. Mecca was the center of a local religion which looked to the Kabah, a black meteorite, as a god, the shrine being a center of pilgrimage for tribes of the neighboring districts. Much of the prosperity of the city was based on the pilgrim traffic and any attack on it was bound to be vigorously opposed by the rulers of the city.

LIFE AND TEACHINGS OF MUHAMMAD

In Mecca Muhammad was born about 571 in the Hashimite branch of the Banu-Quraysh. Left an orphan at an early age, he was brought up by his grandfather, Abd al Muttalib, and his uncle, Abu Talib. His life was humble and he found a suitable career as the agent of a wealthy widow, Kadijah. He would serve as the custodian of her goods in the caravans, guarding them and selling them for her; this work took Muhammad along the caravan routes to the north and brought him in contact with Christians and Jews in the Palestinian and Syrian cities to which he went to trade. Damascus he did not visit, as he found the city so beautiful that he re-fused to enter it, feeling that man could only enter paradise once and if he should do so then he would forfeit his right to do so later.

Muhammad seems to have pleased his employer in more than a strictly business way, for in 596 Khadijah married him, thus making him a man of substance and removing the necessity of his working for his living. This gave him the opportunity to take those trips into the desert in which he communed with God and conversed with the Archangel Gabriel.

Muhammad's first revelations came to him while he was alone in the desert; he had visions of Gabriel and felt that God spoke to him. Many authors have disputed as to the sincerity of Muhammad's visions, a foolish waste of time, as Muhammad undoubtedly shared that same sincere conviction that all great religious prophets felt. It is not for us to decide whether the visions he saw were real or imagined, any more than it is for us to decide as to the authenticity of Constantine's vision or as to the stigmata of St. Francis. Muhammad was a sincere reformer who felt that God had chosen him as the unworthy instrument of his Divine Grace to impart His will to men. As God had previously revealed himself to Abraham, Moses, and Christ, so now He revealed Himself to Muhammad. Each prophet brought to men some portion of God's will and intent towards them, each revelation was greater than those preceding. While Muhammad stoutly denied to Christ any divinity, he insisted on Christ's inspiration as a prophet, next only to Muhammad himself as the expounder of God's will to man.

THE TRIBE OF THE QURAYSH

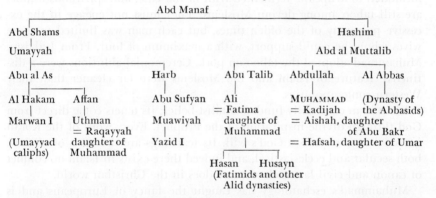

The central theme of the religion which Muhammad brought back from his communions with God was rigid monotheism. "There is no God but God, and Muhammad is His Prophet." The Christians err in attributing to Christ any divinity; their Trinity is sacrilegious, for God is but One. This belief in the Oneness of God may be termed the essential cornerstone of Islam (Subjection to God's Will), the name which Muhammad gave to his new faith.

The complete revelation of Islam covered all the years of Muhammad's life, and the precepts are written down in the sacred script of the Moslems, the Koran. This book was not compiled until after the death of the Prophet; it was first put together under Abu Bakr and then revised under Uthman. In its present format the *suras* (chapters) are arranged according to length, the longest coming first and on to the shortest, last. There are 114 suras and an introductory prayer. All the suras are considered to be the word of God as revealed to Muhammad and are therefore sacrosanct.

The Koran is the supreme expression of God's will; its words are sacred and every letter of it is blessed. To memorize the Koran is a pious work which has been accomplished by an amazing number of devout Moslems.

The articles of faith are few and simple. Muhammad laid upon his followers five injunctions: they must believe in the Oneness of God; they must pray five times a day, kneeling and facing Mecca; they must give alms to the poor and needy; they must fast during the sacred month of Ramadan; and they must (if in any way possible) make at least once during their lives a pilgrimage to Mecca. A further admonition, to engage in the Holy War or *Jihad* against the enemies of the faith was not, as commonly believed, one of Muhammad's prescribed duties of the true Moslem; but like Christianity, Islam early developed the idea of the Holy War and the fanaticism of the new converts made it an important part of their lives.

In addition to these articles of faith, Muhammad laid upon his followers several other rules, governing their lives and conduct. They were forbidden to drink the fermented fruit of the vine, and spirituous liquors are still taboo among devout Moslems. They must not engage in the excessive polygamy of the olden times, but each man was limited to those wives whom he could support, with a maximum of four. From Judaism, Muhammad adopted the taboo on pork. Ceremonial ablutions were a distinctive feature of Islam and the Moslems were far cleaner than their Western contemporaries.

Islam is an essentially fundamentalist belief; its tenets come direct from God through divine inspiration of the Prophet. Every word of the Koran is sacred as it expresses God's will. Its teachings are the basis of all law, both secular and ecclesiastical, and indeed there exists in Islam no conflict of canon and civil law such as there does in the Christian world.

Muhammad's eschatology has caught the fancy of Europeans and is given a disproportionate emphasis in Christian discussions of Islam. To Muhammad, a desert Arab, paradise was a cool, verdant, well-watered spot, where the sun never shone too hot and where man never suffered from thirst. Damascus, lying in its oasis, seemed to Muhammad as a young man the very realization on earth of what paradise must be. In paradise the souls of the blessed enjoyed those things which had been denied them here on earth; lying at their ease in the cool shade they were waited on by the beautiful *houris,* the ever young and lovely maidens whose duty it was to attend to the wants of the blessed. There they could drink to satiety of a wondrous wine which exhilarated, but never intoxicated. There was always soft music, sweet singing, luxury, and rest. To Western minds this has seemed a sensuous place, comparing unfavorably to the more austere beauties of the Christian heaven where marble palaces line streets paved with gold, and where angels continually play on celestial harps incessantly uniting their voices in a great hymn to the glory of God. But to the desert Arab this cool oasis, where men could be at ease after the strenuous exertions of their ordinary life, seemed a realization of all that they longed for and never found on earth.

Paradise was also peopled with hosts of angels, who are quite as common in Islamic as in Christian theology. In fact the same angels appear in both, Gabriel having an honored post in both religions as the spokesman of God. Nor would St. Gregory have felt a stranger amidst the hordes of demons and genii with which Muhammad populated the heavens and the regions under the earth. But Islamic superstition developed much as did Christian, and we must not blame Muhammad for all the tales of genii sealed up in bottles by King Solomon, which we are familiar with in the *Arabian Nights,* any more than we should credit St. Paul with the stories of devils being eaten on a leaf of lettuce, which we find in Western monkish lore.

Muhammad began his career as a prophet of the Word of God in Mecca, and it is a tribute to his persuasiveness and genius that his first convert was his wife. Thereafter he gathered around himself a small group of intimate converts, those "Companions of the Prophet" who were to have such great influence in the years after his death. Among these were Abu Bakr (whose daughter Aishah Muhammad married), Muhammad's own nephew Ali (who married Muhammad's daughter Fatimah), the wealthy patrician Umar ibn al Khattab (whose daughter Hafsah Muhammad married), Abu Ubaydah, Abd ar Rahman, Az-Zubair, Talhah, and the Umayyad Uthman ibn Affan.

As the little sect became more vociferous and the teachings of the Prophet threatened to disturb the *status quo* in Mecca, the Umayyads under the leadership of Abu Sufyan began to persecute the little group. Muhammad made some compromises: he made Mecca a Holy City, incorporated the Kabah into his religion as a holy symbol of God's greatness, but was unable to win over the old conservative party of the city. Under the persecution, Uthman ibn Affan led a party of Moslems (as the followers of the new faith called themselves) to exile in Abyssinia in 615, but Muhammad himself chose to remain at Mecca. It was not for long however. Merchants from the neighboring, and rival, city of Medina to the north of Mecca heard of the Prophet and offered him a refuge in their city. They even offered to accept his religion as the religion of their city and to accept him as their honored leader. This naturally was opposed by the Banu-Harb and the conservatives in Mecca, and they plotted to do away with Muhammad. On the night of September 24, 622, two years after the migration had first been planned, Muhammad and a few chosen companions fled Mecca and went north to Medina. When Abu Sufyan came to take the Prophet, he found only Ali there in his place. Muhammad went to the city of refuge and there established a theocratic state, dedicated to the glory of God and the strict observance of His will. It was during his sojourn at Medina that Muhammad received the inspiration for those suras of the Koran which deal with administration and public and private law and which became the basis for the law of the Moslem world.

For ten years Muhammad ruled at Medina. During most of that time there was intermittent warfare between the Medinites and the Meccans. The first great victory for the arms of the Prophet was in 624, when at the battle of the Badr a thousand Meccans under Abu Sufyan were defeated by three hundred Medinites under Muhammad and a rich caravan was carried home as plunder. Four years later, in 628, Muhammad raided Mecca with 1400 men and forced a treaty from the Meccans. It was about this time that two of the greatest generals of the Moslems accepted Islam, Khalid ibn al Walid and Amr ibn al-As.

After the defeat of the Meccans, Muhammad's political influence spread rapidly throughout the peninsula and most of the tribes accepted the new faith and the governance of the Prophet. The crowning glory of Muhammad's life came in his last year, in the famous "farewell pilgrimage" to Mecca which the Prophet led in person. He died shortly thereafter on June 8, 632.

THE ORTHODOX CALIPHATE, 632–661

The death of the Prophet brought a falling away among the more recent converts. Although the theologians maintained that he did not die an ordinary death but ascended into paradise on his favorite horse, the death of the leader caused a diminution in the prestige of the cult, and a number of pseudo-prophets set themselves up in various parts of the peninsula. During Muhammad's lifetime the Moslems had brought under control nearly all the peninsula and even raided into Byzantine lands across the border, but this expansion was interrupted by the necessity of reducing to obedience the tribes who broke away, and the reign of Abu Bakr, who succeeded Muhammad as the first caliph (khalif), was largely devoted to the so-called Riddah wars in which the desert tribes were brought back into submission to the true faith. Foremost in the accomplishing of this was Khalid ibn al Walid, whose military genius was only matched by his brutality and barbarism, and who offended deeply the more sensitive Umar by his brutal excesses, so that Umar never had any great confidence in or affection for this redoubtable warrior.

Muhammad's theocratic state had no provision for any successor to the Prophet when he should die. Consequently at his death there was a division among his followers, the Medinites endeavoring to assert themselves against the Companions. However the Companions prevailed in the council and Abu Bakr was elected as caliph (successor), and invested with the leadership in the state. It was Abu Bakr to whom the Prophet had entrusted the leading of the prayers during his sickness and this gave him a lead over all other candidates. The support of Umar, Abu Ubeydah, and others of the Companions secured the election, although Ali refused to recognize him for some time.

Before discussing the expansion of the Moslems during the period of the Orthodox caliphs, it will be well to trace the succession to the caliphate during these formative years. Abu Bakr reigned only two years (632–634). On his deathbed he designated Umar as his successor and the succession was approved while Abu Bakr still lived. Umar ruled for ten years (634–644), the most important in the expansion of Islam. Before his death Umar appointed an electoral college to ensure a peaceful succession. The election was hotly disputed between Ali, the nephew and son-in-law of the Prophet, and Uthman ibn Affan, one of the early Companions, but a member of the Umayyad branch of the Quraysh. For three days the college was deadlocked. Then Abd ar Rahman, who was presiding, went to the great mosque of Medina where he solemnly interrogated both candidates. As Uthman's answers pleased him the better, he conferred the title on him, Ali accepting the decision with extremely bad grace. Here for the first time we find the struggle between the two factions which were to rend Islam: the family of the Prophet on the one hand and the old ruling aristocratic house of the Umayyads on the other. In spite of the earlier opposition of Abu Sufyan, when the Umayyads had accepted Islam they had stepped into a position as leaders in the movement and now a member of their house had ascended the throne of the caliphate. Uthman was not a strong man nor an especially good ruler; he relied too much on personal friends and made some very bad appointments to provincial governorships which caused widespread discontent against him. After twelve years of rule (644–656) he was confronted by a serious rebellion in which troops from Kufah, Basrah, and Egypt were all involved. Each of the rebel parties had a favorite candidate for the caliphate, Ali being supported by the Kufans. At first, Ali, Az-Zubair, and Talhah, the three candidates, all maintained a most correct attitude and supported Uthman, but, when Marwan (an Umayyad) accused Ali of fomenting the entire rebellion, the three leaders abandoned the caliph and joined the rebels. They marched on Medina and captured the city. While Ali, Talhah and Az-Zubair stood aloof the rebels cruelly murdered the old Uthman. Then they proclaimed Ali as caliph, and Talhah and Az-Zubair gave him homage, though they later claimed it was only with reluctance. Thus Ali came to the throne stained with the blood of the murdered Uthman, if not on his own hands on those of his supporters.

Ali's tenure of the caliphate was a short and disturbed one. The Umayyads, led by Muawiyah ibn Abu Sufyan, the nephew of Uthman, who was

governor of Syria, refused to accept his election and broke out into revolt.
The bloody robe of Uthman was hung in the mosque at Damascus and
Muawiyah called for vengeance on the murderers. Meanwhile Aishah,
Muhammad's widow, raised a revolt at Mecca. She was joined by Talhah
and Az-Zubair, and with a considerable army they marched from Mecca
to Basrah. Ali had moved his headquarters to Kufah where he had his
greatest support. In December, 656, the Kufans under Ali met the Meccans
and Basrans under Aishah at the Battle of the Camel.

The Battle of the Camel was the first war among the Moslems. It resulted
in the defeat of Aishah and her allies, Aishah escaping on her camel and
retiring to Medina where she lived for several years, maintaining a shrine
for Muhammad.

Feeling stronger as the result of this battle, Ali removed all the governors
appointed by Uthman, including Muawiyah (although he had been appointed by Umar). He did nothing to punish the regicides, but in fact
relied on them more than ever, and definitely moved the capital of the
Moslem Empire from Medina to Kufah. Muawiyah refused to accept the
new regime and raised an army which attacked Ali. On July 26, 657 the two
armies met at Siffin on the Euphrates. Amr ibn al-As, who commanded the
army of Muawiyah, affixed leaves of the Koran to the lance-heads of his
men so that Ali's troops would not dare strike them for fear of committing
sacrilege. For four days the battle was fought more or less desultorily,
with no result. Then both sides agreed to arbitrate. Amr represented
Muawiyah while Abu Musa was the spokesman for Ali. At the suggestion
of the wily Amr both agreed to abdicate on behalf of their principals.
Abu Musa accordingly abdicated on behalf of Ali; then Amr pointed out
that Muawiyah had nothing to abdicate as he had never been caliph.
For the next few years things were at deadlock, but the very agreement
to arbitrate had caused dissention in the ranks of the Alids. A fanatical
party, known as the Kharadjites, felt that arbitration of the sacred office
of the caliph was sacrilegious and that both leaders had betrayed the
faith. While some of their members vainly attempted to murder Muawiyah
and Amr, others successfully assassinated Ali on January 24, 661. Muawiyah
immediately proclaimed himself caliph at Jerusalem, while Hasan, the
son of Ali, was proclaimed at Kufah. Hasan, however, lacked the ambitions of his father and allowed himself to be bought off. In return for
a generous pension, he abdicated his pretensions and retired to Medina
where he spent his time marrying, accumulating over a hundred wives.
Not until the revival of the Alid claims by Husayn, the younger brother
of Hasan, in 680 was there really an Alid party or a definite schism within
Islam.

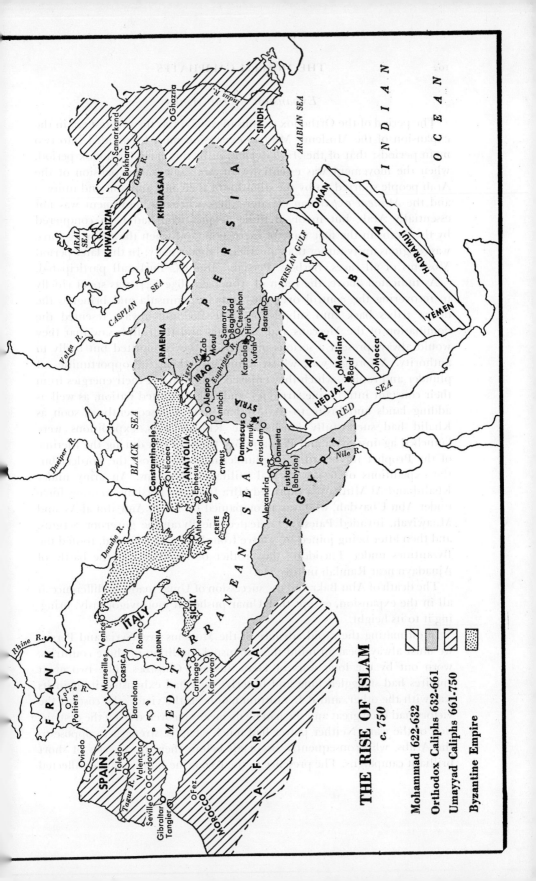

THE RISE OF ISLAM
c. 750

Mohammad 622-632
Orthodox Caliphs 632-661
Umayyad Caliphs 661-750
Byzantine Empire

INDIAN OCEAN

ARABIAN SEA

SINDH

Indus R.

Ghazna

KHURASAN

Samarkand
Bukhara
Oxus R.

KHWARIZM

ARAL SEA

OMAN

ARABIA

HADRAMAUT

YEMEN

Aral Sea

CASPIAN SEA

Volga R.

ARMENIA

PERSIA

Medina
Mecca
Badr

HEDJAZ

RED SEA

Baghdad
Samarra
Ctesiphon
Mosul
Zab
Tigris R.
Euphrates R.
Karbala
Kufah
Basrah
Hira

IRAQ

Aleppo
Antioch

SYRIA

Damascus
Yarmuk
Jerusalem

BLACK SEA

Dnieper R.

Constantinople
Nicaea
Ephesus

ANATOLIA

CYPRUS

Athens

CRETE

Danube R.

PERSIAN GULF

EGYPT

Nile R.

Alexandria
Damietta
Fustat
(Babylon)

MEDITERRANEAN SEA

Rome
Venice
SARDINIA
CORSICA

ITALY

SICILY

AFRICA

Carthage
Kairowan

Marseilles
Barcelona
Valencia
Cordova
Seville
Gibraltar
Tangier
Toledo
Oviedo
Poitiers
Loire R.
Rhine R.

FRANKS

SPAIN

Tagus R.

MOROCCO
Fez

Expansion of the Arabs

The period of the Orthodox caliphs (632–661) was the greatest era in the expansion of the Moslems. Moslem expansion must be divided into two main periods: that of the *Arab expansion* in this early Orthodox period, when the movement was essentially an Arab one—an expansion of the Arab people spurred on by the stimulus of their new religion and unity—and the *Moslem expansion* of later times, when the movement was not essentially Arab, but involved those peoples who had been conquered by the Arabs in the first wave of expansion, and when the unifying force was religious unity rather than any racial homogeneity. In this later period Moslems of all races, Berbers, Persians, Iraquis, Turks all participated.

As indicated above, the reign of Abu Bakr (632–634) was spent chiefly in recovering the control over the Arabian peninsula and bringing the desert tribes back into submission. The Bedouin always resented the domination of the Meccans and Medinites and the caliph saw that they would always present a serious problem, as they submitted but badly to authority. A foreign war, which would give them the opportunities of plunder and rapine, which they enjoyed, would divert their energies from their constant internecine struggles, and forge a united nation, as well as adding lands and lustre to the Moslem state. Consequently as soon as Khalid had successfully finished the Riddah wars, expeditions were launched against Syria and Persia in 633 to 634. Even during the lifetime of the Prophet there had been plundering raids across the border; but the expeditions of 634 were real military campaigns. An army under Khalid and Al Muthanna captured Hira from the Persians, another force under Abu Ubaydah, who was accompanied by Yazid, Amr ibn al-As, and Muawiyah, invaded Palestine, defeated the Byzantine governor Sergius, and then after being joined by a force from Iraq under Khalid, routed the Byzantines under Theodore, the brother of Heraclius, at the battle of Ajnadayn near Ramlah in July 634.

The death of Abu Bakr and the succession of Umar made no difference at all in the expansion, except that Umar pushed it more vigorously, bringing it to its height.

In estimating the rapid advance of the Moslems over Syria and Persia, we must always bear in mind the exhausted condition of those countries, worn out by the long wars of Heraclius and Chosroes. The two great empires had struggled long and bitterly; each had exhausted itself in its war with the other, and if Byzantium had been the victor, the costs of the victory had been great and she had by no means recovered from the destruction of the wars. Neither power had much effective strength to oppose to the Arabs, who consequently swept all before them in a series of short brilliant campaigns. The presence in the Byzantine Empire of a disaffected minority who welcomed the Arabs was another important factor, demonstrated especially in the conquest of Egypt. The Monophysites loathed and hated the Orthodox Christians; they were persecuted by them, and welcomed the Moslems as deliverers. To the Monophysites, who were in the majority in Egypt, Palestine, and Syria, the Oneness of God proclaimed by Muhammad seemed nearer the truth than the two natures maintained by the Chalcedonians.

The conquest of Syria and that of Persia took place simultaneously, but Syria fell more rapidly than Persia. The army which Khalid and Al Muthanna had led into Iraq divided after the capture of Hira, Al Muthanna moving east while Khalid turned west, marched across the desert and joined the force moving north from Arabia. Eastern Syria was conquered before coastal, and Damascus was taken in 635. On August 20, 636, Khalid broke the Byzantine power in Syria by defeating the chief Byzantine army at the decisive battle of the Yarmuk (a small river near the Lake of Tiberias). The emperor Heraclius, who was at Antioch on his way to command in the defense of the province, abandoned all hopes and retreated to Constantinople.

Khalid was not left to complete the conquest however. As we have seen, Umar distrusted and disliked him because of his savage brutalities, so he was recalled and Abu Ubaydah, who had commanded the southern army was left as governor of Syria with the task of finishing the conquest. It proved an easy task: along the coast, Acre, Tyre, Sidon, Beirut, even great Antioch herself fell in rapid succession, while inland Homs and Aleppo were captured before the end of 636. Jerusalem was not taken until 638 after a long siege by Amr ibn al-As, and the caliph Umar himself came up to receive the surrender of this city, the third Holy City of Islam. The last town in Syria to hold out was Caesarea in Palestine, which did not fall until 640 when Muawiyah finally took it.

Meanwhile Al Muthanna had been badly defeated by the Persians near Hira in November of 634 and had been succeeded by S'ad ibn abi-Waqqas as commander in Iraq. In June 637 he defeated the Persian governor Rustem at the battle of Qadisiyah, following up his victory by the capture of the old capital of Ctesiphon. New bases for operations were established at Basrah and Kufah, which were long to remain the chief Arab cities in Iraq. The battle of Nihawand and the capture of Mosul in 641 completed the defeat of the Persians; all of Iraq was secured and the Arabs pushed east along the south coast through all Persia and Baluchistan to the frontier of India which they reached about 643. The reduction of central Persia, the conquest of Khurasan and the invasion of Armenia all followed during the reign of Uthman in the years 649 to 652. The murder of Yzdegerd III by one of his own men put an end to the old Persian dynasty and to any semblance of Persian resistance. While the conquest of Persia

had been more difficult than that of Syria, it nevertheless succumbed reasonably rapidly to the Arab advance.

Egypt was conquered by Amr ibn al-As in the years 639 to 642. Ignoring
orders of Umar not to undertake the invasion, Amr crossed into Egypt
in December 639 and quickly reduced Pelusium and Bilbeis. The siege
of Babylon [2] took seven months in 641, and Amr built a new town at
Fustat, where his camp had stood, to serve as the new capital of Arab
Egypt. Alexandria still held out under the command of the patriarch
Cyrus, but in November 641, Cyrus accepted a treaty which he thought
would secure him in his own position under the caliph. Amr, however,
drove him from his city and occupied it in September, 642. The conquest
of Alexandria was made more difficult, as it was a Byzantine naval base and
able to get support from Constantinople. In 645, the Byzantines sent a
fleet which temporarily recaptured the city, but Amr defeated them and
secured Alexandria to the caliphate. Under Uthman, Abdullah, who
succeeded Amr as governor of Egypt, pushed west and subjected the
Berber tribes of Tripoli and Tunis.

After securing the coast, the Moslems first took to the sea, where they
were later to have such predominant control. In 649, Muawiyah with a
newly built fleet captured the island of Cyprus, the first insular possession
acquired by the Arabs; and in 652 and 655, Moslem fleets defeated the
Byzantines, gaining a supremacy in the eastern Mediterranean.

In all their conquests the Moslems gave most liberal terms to the conquered. This was an important factor in explaining the rapid spread of
their conquests. The old idea that Moslems invaded a country with a
sword in one hand and the Koran in the other, offering the conquered
people their choice between conversion and death, is utterly false. Muhammad had recognized the "peoples of the Book" (Christians and Jews) as
acceptable, if misguided, religions. They could retain their own religion
and customs, but were forced to pay tribute which was not demanded from
Moslems. Only to those who did not worship the True God in any of his
forms—the fire worshippers of Persia for example—was conversion obligatory. This is one reason why Persia was harder to conquer than Syria or
Egypt. In the conquest of Egypt, the native Coptic Christians (Monophysites) offered no resistance whatever to the Arabs; in fact so many
embraced Islam that there was some concern that there would be enough
taxable subjects left to make the expedition a financial success. Jews and
heretics found the rule of the caliph much lighter and their freedom much
greater than under the Christian emperor; also a common Semitism drew
Copt, Jew, and Arab together in opposition to the European Byzantines.

---

[2] Babylon in Egypt was an old city on the Nile at approximately the site of modern
Cairo. Medieval chroniclers frequently referred to Cairo as Babylon.

THE UMAYYAD CALIPHATE, 661–750 [3]

When Muawiyah secured the caliphate in 661, he established his dynasty on the throne for ninety years, making the previously elective caliphate hereditary. Ali had moved the capital of Islam from Medina to Kufah, Muawiyah moved it to Damascus, and the Umayyads always relied on the Syrians as their chief source of support. The Umayyad period is often described as one in which the Moslems were Hellenized and in which they absorbed the culture of Greece, Rome, and Byzantium, slowly adapting it to their own needs.

As long as Muawiyah lived there was no revival of the Alid claims. Hasan had retired to Medina, his brother Husayn had never abandoned his claims, but did not see fit to press them while the old conqueror lived to defend himself. After the death of Muawiyah in 680, and when his son Yazid I had ascended the caliphal throne, Husayn proclaimed himself caliph at Kufah and raised the standard of the Alids in revolt.

The revolt of Husayn marks the beginning of the great schism which still rends Islam. Husayn was himself defeated and slain at the Battle of Karbala in October 680, but his followers refused to accept the decision of the battle and continued to maintain the claims of the descendants of the Prophet. Thus were founded the two great sects of Islam; the *Sunna* who accept the Umayyad caliphate, the traditional *hadith* or sayings of Muhammad, and the Orthodox faith; and the *Shia* who deny the Umayyad caliphate and insist that the true caliphs ended with Husayn the martyr, that the descendants of Husayn are the true Immans of Islam, and that the Traditions are not to be accepted as the sayings of Muhammad. The Shia have broken down into a number of heretical sects. Sunna Islam has often been compared to Roman Catholicism with its accepted body of faith and doctrine, the Apostolic succession etc., while Shia is like the Protestant sects, agreeing in their opposition to Catholicism, but disagreeing on almost every possible point of doctrine. This schism within Islam is of the first importance and was largely instrumental in overthrowing the Umayyad caliphate in 750. While most Moslems today are Sunna, there are still numerous Shia sects, scattered from Africa to farthest Asia, especially strong in Persia and the Sudan.

The Alid revolt was not the only challenge to Yazid's inheritance of the caliphate. In 683, Abdullah ibn Az-Zubair proclaimed himself in the Hedjaz. The importance of the revolt is that Yazid sent an army to Mecca, which burned the Holy City and damaged the Kabah. The revolt was not ended however until Abdullah was killed in 692.

Among the thirteen Umayyad caliphs who followed Muawiyah there

[3] See list of Umayyad Caliphs, Appendix p. 763.

are few outstanding personalities, Marwan I (683–685) and Sulayman (715–717) being perhaps the most important. It was a period when the Moslem state was developing its organization and Moslem society was settling into definite classes. The empire was divided into five viceroyalties: Iraq, Arabia, Egypt, Jazirah, and Africa, while Transoxiana and the Punjab had independent governors. The viceroy appointed all local governors and officials in his district, controlled the judiciary and local government. Finance was under a special sect of officials and the chief revenues were income from state lands, state monopolies and the tax on all non-Moslems. Originally Moslems and their property had been tax exempt but land soon came under taxation, the Moslems being however exempt from a poll tax which non-Moslems paid. One of the most important developments of the Umayyads was the chancery which registered all documents, with elaborate archives at Damascus. The army and navy were both based on Byzantine models and were armed like the Greeks.

Meanwhile the races of the Moslem empire were falling into several recognized groups: 1. Arab Moslems; 2. Non-Arab Moslems; 3. *Dhimmis,* the tolerated non-Moslem peoples (Christians, Jews, etc.); 4. Slaves (captives taken chiefly in war). Moslems could not legally be slaves, though this was never observed, and the slaves were able to rise to positions of great importance, especially the eunuchs who held high offices in the palace.

Intellectually the Umayyad period is only the precursor of the more brilliant development of the Abbasid. During these years the Arabic language spread and became the universal language of government and theology; its rules of grammar developed and became fixed, and there grew up a considerable literature in poetry, oratory, and epistolography, although the Umayyad period is notably lacking in the historical writing which was to develop so prominently later. In science, the Arabs were learning the lore of the Greeks; their own contributions came at a later date after they had completely mastered the older sciences. Perhaps the greatest cultural feature of the Umayyad period is the progress made in architecture. Syrian, Persian, Indian, and Spanish schools of architecture were all drawn upon by the Arab architects, resulting in the erection of the magnificent mosques of Jerusalem and Damascus and in many secular buildings.

Conquest of Spain

Politically the Umayyads continued the expansionist movement which they inherited from the Orthodox caliphs, and began the long struggle with the Byzantines for the control of Constantinople itself. To the east they pushed into Transoxiania, capturing Balkh, Bukhara, Samarkand, and Khwarizm (706–712); they drove into India taking Sindh, Hyderabad, and the southern Punjab (710–713). Towards the west, they pushed along the north coast of Africa; Carthage was taken in 698, Algeria and Morocco were overrun and the Berbers conquered. In 711 Tarik, a Berber freedman of Musa ibn Nusayr, the commanding general, crossed the straits and landed in Spain at the rock, which has borne his name since (Gib al Tarik). What started as a mere foraging raid developed into the conquest of a peninsula.

The conquest of Spain was unplanned and unexpected. Tarik went over on a raid and found no opposition to speak of. He defeated Roderick the Visigothic king in a quick battle, and, by-passing the strongly fortified towns, occupied those which offered less resistance. Three columns advanced towards the north, taking Granada, Cordova, Malaga, and finally Toledo. The unexpected success of Tarik aroused the jealousies of Musa, who came over with a larger force to reap the fruits of victory. Seville, Medina Sidonia, and other places by-passed by Tarik were reduced; Tarik was disgraced for having exceeded his orders so flagrantly, and Musa pushed on to the conquest of Saragossa. But Musa met the same fate as Tarik. The caliph Walid became jealous of the glories being won by his general. Musa was called home to Damascus in 715, his march back across North Africa with his slaves and booty being a long triumph, but his arrival at Damascus bringing quick and complete disgrace.

Meanwhile the conquest was carried on under new leaders. The hatred of the old native Celt-Iberians for their Visigothic lords, and the feuds among the Goths themselves greatly facilitated the conquest, while a large and disaffected Jewish population proved an invaluable assistance. The Spanish Christians accepted the Moslem conqueror except in one small corner in the mountains of northwest Galicia, where they maintained the independence of the tiny principality of the Asturias. In 720, the Pyrenees were crossed and Narbonne and Septimania were taken. The first reverse encountered was in the failure to capture Toulouse in 721. Aquitaine was overrun, Bordeaux fell, and in 732 Abd ar Rahman pushed as far north as Poitiers, where he was met between Poitiers and Tours in October, 732, by Charles Martel, the Frank, and forced to turn back. This battle of Tours or Poitiers has long ranked as one of the great battles of history but in fact it had little real significance beyond marking the point of the farthest advance of the Arabs in the north. Abd ar Rahman was only on a raid; there is nothing to indicate that he was attempting a serious conquest of that country. The Moslems had established themselves in Spain and in southern Gaul and the battle of Poitiers did not disturb them where they had established themselves. In no wise did the defeat they suffered diminish the empire they were building or cause them to lose any territory where they had permanently settled.

Wars with Byzantium

Far more important in checking the advance of Islam were the defeats suffered outside the walls of Constantinople. Legend says that the caliphs planned a great encircling movement whereby Europe would be attacked from both east and west, with the armies pouring through Byzantium and Spain to meet in central Europe. If this is true (which it probably is not) the defeat at Poitiers came later and was of much less importance than that at Constantinople.

The development of the Moslem naval power, which challenged that of the Byzantines and succeeded in winning from them the control of the eastern Mediterranean, as well as the conquests in Syria and Armenia, brought Islam directly into conflict with Byzantium. Though there were repeated incursions into Anatolia, the frontier was well guarded and border war around the Taurus passes shifted the frontier back and forth without much result for the entire period. But the Arabs drove straight for the heart of Byzantium in a series of daring naval attacks. The first Arab siege of Constantinople occurred in 669. Yazid, the son of Muawiyah, commanded the Moslem forces. While a land army captured Chalcedon, Yazid subjected Constantinople to a siege for several months. The Arabs were finally beaten off by Constantine IV, but only to return in 674 when they established a naval base at Cyzicus and besieged Constantinople every summer, until, in 677, they withdrew their fleet (which was destroyed on the way back to Syria). Peace was finally secured in 680, the year of Muawiyah's death. It was during this siege of 674 to 677 that the famous Greek fire was first employed by the Byzantines to beat off the Moslem ships.[4]

The greatest effort made by the Umayyads against Constantinople came under Sulayman in a great siege which lasted from August 716 to September 717. A large force, both by land and by sea, was sent against Constantinople under the command of Maslamah, the brother of the caliph. The defense of the city by Leo the Isaurian, who came to the Byzantine throne during the siege, is one of the great heroic stories of history. At first it seemed that the Arabs must be successful; the defense was disorganized, the odds were overwhelming against the Byzantines. But the new emperor infused a new life into his people; they offered a stubborn and heroic resistance and, after securing the defection of the Coptic sailors on the ships from Egypt, were able to beat off the Arab fleet. The siege was brought to an end by the death of Sulayman and the accession of Umar II, who sought peace and a treaty. Not until the advent of the Turks in the eleventh century was Byzantium to be so seriously threatened by the Mos-

---

[4] Greek fire was a compound of naphtha and sulphur which would burn on water. It was thrown in buckets or casks from catapults or squirted from tubes (early flame-throwers) and would ignite on the water, burning the ships.

lems again. The Byzantine use of Mardaites, native Christians who were enticed to revolt against the Arabs, materially assisted the Greeks in these campaigns. The war between the empire and the caliphate continued throughout the Umayyad period, but it was generally a matter of raids and border fighting, with treaties wherein one power would agree to pay tribute to the other for a time. The caliphs had much to occupy their attention in other regions, in Africa, Spain, and the East, and made no further serious attempt against Byzantium. But if any one man should be credited with saving Europe from a Moslem conquest, it is not Charles Martel, but Leo the Isaurian.

Revolt of the Abbasids

The Umayyad caliphate fell before a combination of forces which developed in the East. Shia sectaries, Persian malcontents, a general resentment on the part of non-Arab Moslems against the dominance of the Arab-Syrian element, combined to support the claims of a descendent of the Prophet. The revolt began in Khurasan in 747, when Abu Muslim unfurled the black banner of the Prophet (as opposed to the Umayyad green) and occupied the cities of Merv (747) and Kufah (749). The rebels proclaimed at Kufah the true caliph, Abu al-Abbas al-Saffah, the great-great-grandson of Abbas, the uncle of Muhammad. Although the Abbasids were themselves Sunnite, the old Alid sympathizers rallied to the Abbasid banner against the hated Umayyads; Kufah saw itself again the center of the empire; the eastern provinces would have their revenge on the west.

The revolution was accomplished in one major battle; at the Zab in January 750, Abu al-Abbas defeated the Umayyad caliph, Marwan, and broke the power of the Umayyads. The capture of Damascus and the execution of Marwan followed. Then Abu al Abbas justified his sobriquet of al-Saffah (the Bloodshedder) by systematically exterminating every member of the hated house of the Umayyads. Only one escaped, Abd ar Rahman, who fled west across Africa, until, after many dramatic escapes, he came to Spain where he was recognized by the troops and governors loyal to the old regime. He was to set up the independent emirate of Cordova; his descendants became caliphs of the West.

The rise of Islam and the expansion of the Arabs really marks an end to the old conditions of the ancient world. As Professor Pirenne has pointed out, not the German invasions, but the Moslem ended the Roman Empire. They broke the unity of the Mediterranean world; they introduced a new oriental type of culture which was widely different from the classical; they set up an empire which included half of the old Roman, but which was based on principles totally different from Rome. With the Arab shattering of the unity of the Mediterranean world, the various parts of the old em-

pire began to go their various ways. Byzantium became more Greek as it
was limited to the Greek lands of Anatolia, the Balkans, and the Aegean.
The German kingdoms were cut off from the trade of Byzantium and fell
back on themselves, becoming more Germanic. The old ties which had
held the ancient world together—the ties of commerce and culture flowing
along the waterways of the Mediterranean—were broken by the Arab invasions. An alien body had been inserted into the scene. The old problems
of the days of Constantine and Justinian have given way to new conditions,
to the struggle between Cross and Crescent (which was to culminate in
the Crusades), to the local particularism which was to be feudalism, to the
blending of oriental and occidental civilizations which was to become the
Renaissance.

The Abbasid Caliphate, 750–1055 [5]

When Abu-al-Abbas al-Saffah overthrew the Umayyad caliphate and
established that of the Abbasids in 750 it was more than a mere dynastic
revolution; it was a complete change in the character of the Moslem
Empire. Under the Umayyads the world of Islam had been ruled by the
Arabs, led by the members of the Quraysh house and with the Arabs enjoying political and social superiority over all other non-Arab Moslems.
The Abbasid revolution overthrew this regime and substituted one in
which all Moslems, irrespective of race, were equal under the rule of the
Commander of the Faithful. The center of the Moslem world shifted from
the Hellenized Syrian provinces to the more oriental Iranian and Iraqi;
the family of the Prophet—of the line of al-Abbas—ruled supreme, with a
bureaucracy made up of ministers from all parts of the empire; the old
democracy of the Orthodox caliphs and the aristocratic rule of the Umayyads were both discarded in favor of a new theocratic despotism. All men
were alike in their subjection to the caliph; all men had equal opportunity
to rise in his service. As a sign of the changed regime, the capital was
moved from Damascus to Kufah and then in 762 to Baghdad, a new city
built on the Tigris as the home of the new caliphate.

Baghdad and the Abbasids will always be connected; the "Golden prime
of the Abbasids" coincided with the great development of the "City of the
Arabian Nights." Baghdad reflected the glory and wealth of its rulers; its
luxury was unequaled in the Western world; its stately and ornate palaces,
its schools and observatories, its teeming markets and bustling quays, where
the silks and spices of China and the Indies were offered for sale together
with the furs of Russia and the products of western Europe, made it a fitting
capital for a state which stretched (at least theoretically) from the Atlantic

[5] See list of Abbasid Caliphs, Appendix p. 763.

to the Indus. It is difficult for modern Western readers to comprehend the difference between the high material civilization of a Baghdad or a Constantinople and the primitive squalor of a Paris or London of the ninth and tenth centuries.

The great period of the Abbasids lasted only about a century, from the accession of Al Mansur in 754 to the death of Al Mutawakkil in 861. This includes the splendid reigns of Harun al Rashid (786–809) and Al Mamun (813–833) in which the Abbasid power reached its height. There were in all thirty-seven caliphs of the dynasty, of whom thirty-five were descended from Al Mansur, the brother and successor of Abu-al Abbas, but none after the first few are worthy of special notice. They became impotent figureheads dominated by powerful viziers and palace guards, who remained immured in their harems, only to appear for religious festivals or state occasions.

The first great family of grand viziers was that of the Barmakids. Under Al Mansur, Khalid al Barmaki, a Persian son of a Buddhist priest, became minister of finance in Tabaristan and established the fortunes of his house. His son Yahya became the tutor and chief minister of Harun al Rashid. During the early years of Harun's reign, Yahya and his sons Jafar and Al Fadl ruled the empire, dispensing justice and patronage throughout. As their power and influence increased so did their splendor and magnificence, until Jafar made the fatal blunder of building a palace in Baghdad, which was more luxurious and resplendent than that of the caliph himself. Jafar had been Harun's closest friend, the companion of his nocturnal adventures and his sports; he had been given the caliph's sister to wife; then in 803 Harun suddenly asserted himself against his erstwhile crony. Jafar was arrested and executed, Yahya and Al Fadl fell immediately thereafter; their offices were given to others, their goods confiscated to the caliphal fisc. The history of this family is illustrative of how men could rise from nothing to the heights of glory and power only to be plunged into disgrace and destruction at the whim of the caliph—a phenomenon which recurred consistently throughout the history of the Eastern absolutisms. The name of the Barmakids has passed into the English language (via the *Arabian Nights*) as synonymous with illusory and unreal.

During this great period of Abbasid power there were several wars with Byzantium. In 782 while his father was still caliph, Harun led a great expedition into Anatolia which reached the Bosphorus and was only bought off by heavy payments of tribute. Under Irene there was desultory fighting, but in general the Greeks paid tribute throughout her reign. Then Nicephorus stopped the tribute and Harun led another invasion which ravaged Anatolia and succeeded in getting the amount of tribute increased. The last Abbasid attack on the empire occurred in 838 when the

Moslems penetrated deep into Anatolia and captured Amorion. The next wars between the two powers were to find the Byzantines taking the offensive against weakened Moslem dynasties.

Meanwhile, as will be seen, Harun entered into an alliance with Charlemagne and the Franks, embassies passing back and forth between the two. It is worthy of note that these embassies which made so great an impression on the Western chroniclers are not mentioned by the more sophisticated Arabs; the Franks were forging ahead when they could deal with the caliph; to the Arabs the relations with the Franks were probably no more important than those with the Khazars or Bulgars—all barbarian peoples with whom the caliph consented to treat.

It is not in the realm of political history that the Abbasid caliphate is significant however. After Al Mamun there was no truly great ruler; the history is one of palace intrigue, plot, rebellion, and assassination. In the reign of Al Mutasim (833–842) the caliphs first established a special palace guard of Turkish mercenaries from Transoxiana, some 4000 men in all. This guard soon developed a predominant influence over the caliph and the guardsmen adopted a very superior and arrogant attitude towards the other soldiers and towards the civilian population of Baghdad. The troops from Khurasan and the citizens of Baghdad united to drive out the Turks. The guardsmen fled—but they took the caliph with them, retreating to Samarra, a new city, where from 836 to 892 the caliphate had its seat. The caliphs became the puppets of the guards; when in 861 the guards murdered Al Mutawakkil the complete decline of the caliphate set in. Thereafter the empire was run by guards, slaves, harem favorites, and eunuchs, all endlessly scheming against each other and wholly disregarding the interests of the state. In 862, Al Mustain fled from Samarra to Baghdad to escape the control of his own guards, but they forced him to return and it was not until 892 that the capital was restored to Baghdad. In 869 a great slave rebellion broke out among the slaves who worked in the imperial mines, a rebellion which lasted fourteen years and cost the lives of half a million people. This condition of anarchy continued until 945 when Ahmed ibn Buwayh, a Shiite Persian who had revolted and seized Isfahan, Khuzistan, Kirman, and Shiraz—captured Baghdad, drove out the Turkish guard and made himself master of the capital and state.

For a century (945–1055) the Buwayhids ruled the caliphate from their capital at Shiraz. Under the title of amir-al-umara (commander of commanders) the Buwayhids set up and deposed caliphs at will. Controlling the caliphate, they established therein all the Shia festivals, thus forcing the orthodox Abbasid caliph to condone the schismatic beliefs. While they kept great palaces and offices at Baghdad, the real capital of the state was transferred further east to their own city of Shiraz, the Persian influence becoming more than ever dominant. They were finally overthrown by a new Sunna people, the Saljuq Turks, who in 1037 began a career of conquest in the northeastern provinces (Merv, Nishapur, Balkh, Tabaristan, Khwarizm, Hamadhan, Isfahan) and then in 1055 captured Baghdad and the caliph.

The caliph hailed the Saljuqs as deliverers; Tughril Beg, their leader, was invested with the administration of the government with the new title of *sultan* (one with authority) and declared regent over all the lands ruled by the caliph. The Abbasid remained a figurehead, but it must be admitted that he received generally more courteous treatment from his new master than he had from his old. A new era in Moslem history had begun, and the early Saljuqs were to rival the glories of the early Abbasids.

Rise of the Independent Moslem States

Meanwhile the empire had slowly been falling apart. The first province to secede was Spain where the Umayyad Abd ar Rahman had established himself in 755–756. Arriving as a fugitive, after a long and perilous flight from Damascus, Abd ar Rahman was accepted as lord by the Syrian troops stationed in Spain. He defeated the Abbasid governor Yusuf, captured Cordova and began to make himself lord of all Spain. Local resistance was quickly put down, Toledo finally submitting in 764. It was in support of some of the local rulers who opposed Abd ar Rahman, that Charlemagne invaded Spain in 778 to meet defeat at Saragossa and disaster at Roncevalles. The Franks did, however, as we have seen, establish a march in Spain in the lands around Barcelona. Abd ar Rahman meanwhile had made himself emir of all Spain, passing the title and the power on to his descendants.[6] In 929 Abd ar Rahman III (the eighth emir) proclaimed himself caliph, completely repudiating any ties with Baghdad. Thereafter from 929 to 1031 the Umayyad caliphate at Cordova maintained an independent existence as a rival caliphate to that of Baghdad.

Cordova reached its height under this Abd ar Rahman III. Reconquering those cities which had broken away, he made himself supreme over all of Moslem Spain. His capital rivaled Baghdad in splendor and luxury; here magnificent palaces and mosques attested the superiority of the Moslem civilization; here too the commerce of the world supported the luxury of a brilliant court and culture. But the Cordovan caliphate went the way of the Abbasid; the caliph organized a special guard (called the slavic guard from the number of European slaves in it) which gradually took over the control of the government, leaving the caliph only a puppet. Usurpers set themselves up in Tangier and in Spain itself; the caliph was powerless to suppress them, and finally the last Umayyad caliph, Hisham III, was quietly deposed by his own viziers in 1031. Thereafter Moorish Spain broke down into a number of independent states, the so-called

[6] See list of Umayyads Caliphs of Cordova, Appendix p. 763.

Taifas, at Seville, Granada, Toledo, Cordova, Badajoz, Valencia, Cadiz, Jaen, Elvira, and Saragossa. The Christian states in the north (Navarre, Leon, and Castile) emerged and began the long process of the *Reconquista.* How this was halted by the Almoravides (1090–1147) and by the Almohades (1145–1269) will be discussed in a later chapter. Suffice it here to note that Spain was never really subject to the Abbasids, but had its own state and caliphate during most of the Abbasid period.

While Spain was lost completely, other provinces set up autonomous governments which rendered at most the merest lip service to the caliph at Baghdad. Morocco became independent under the Idrisid dynasty (788–974); Tunis and Algiers became the seat of the Aghlabids, who ruled from Kairowan from 800 to 909, extending their power into the islands of the Mediterranean through the conquest of Sicily and Sardinia. A series of independent dynasties established themselves in Egypt: the Tulunids (870–905) and Ikhshidids (935–969) both ruling there before the final loss of the province to the Fatimids. Arabia fell under the control of the Qarmatians, a communistic Shia sect, while in Syria, the Shia dynasty of the Hamdanids held Aleppo, Homs, and Mosul from 923 to 1003. Farther east in Transoxiana, Khurasan, and northern Persia the dynasties of the Tahirids (820–872), Saffarids (867–903), Samanids (874–999) and Ghaznavids (962–1186), divided the control of the country, warring with each other and with outside powers and extending their dominion into India as far as Lahore. Under these dynasties, Bukhara, Samarkand, Kabul, Herat, and Ghaznah became cities of first importance, both economically and culturally. Both Rhazes and Avicenna were for a time connected with the Samanids, while Mahmud of Ghaznah (999–1030) made his kingdom for a time the political and cultural center of the Middle East.

The Fatimid Caliphate of Egypt, 909–1171 [7]

The most important of all the dynasties which challenged the power of the Abbasids was the Fatimids of Kairowan and Egypt.

Said ibn Husayn, who claimed to be descended from Fatimah and to be the Mahdi of the Shia Ismalians, gained the support of Ismalian sectaries in North Africa and first set himself up in 909 in Tunis, which he wrested from the Aghlabids. Taking the title of Ubaydullah al Madhi, Said established his capital in Kairowan from which he expanded west into Morocco which he took from the Idrisids, and east into Egypt where he overthrew the Ikshidids. Alexandria was taken in 914, but it was not until 969 that the Fatimids completely defeated the Ikshidid power and captured Fustat. There they built a new city, Cairo, which they made their capital in 973 and which soon rose to be the rival of Baghdad. Under the com-

---

[7] See list of the Fatimid Caliphs, Appendix p. 764.

mand of a former Christian slave from Sicily, Jawhar al Rumi, their victorious armies and fleets overran Africa and raided Sicily, Corsica, Malta,
and the coasts of Italy and southern France. With the fanaticism of religious
zealots they pushed into Arabia, defeated the Qarmatians, captured Mecca,
Medina, and the Hedjaz, and then turned against the Hamdanids in Syria,
overthrowing them and even temporarily occupying Damascus. Under the
caliph Al Aziz (975–996), the Fatimids ruled over an empire which stretched
from Morocco to Mosul and which greatly exceeded that of the Abbasids
both in extent and in wealth.

The Fatimids set themselves up as the only true caliphs and denied the
authority of the Abbasids. They were Shia, and not only Shia but of the
sect of the Ismalians. This peculiar and eccentric sect believed that after
the Prophet there would appear a series of *imams* ending in a Madhi who
would remain hidden until the Day of Judgement. The religion was one
which allowed of considerable latitude in belief and observance, and
variations which produced new sects within the Ismalian body were constantly appearing. One of the most bizarre of these sects of the Ismalians
was that founded by Fatimid caliph Al Hakim (996–1021). There can be
little doubt that Al Hakim was insane, but the medieval mind approximated insanity to godliness and Al Hakim ended by founding a new sect
in which he was God. One of the most amazing characters of history, Al
Hakim is famous for his intense religious persecution and for his distruc-
tion of the Church of the Holy Sepulchre in Jerusalem. He closed all
churches, destroying not a few; Christians and Jews were forced to wear
distinctive dress; Moslems were prohibited from making the pilgrimage
to Mecca; edicts were issued wherein Al Hakim ordered that all dogs be
exterminated, that all chessboards be burned, that women be forbidden
to appear in the streets or at windows (and to enforce this he forbade
women to possess shoes so that they could not venture out of their apartments). At one time he decreed that all shops and places of public con-
course should be strictly closed all day and all business must be transacted
at night. Finally he burned down his own capital city of Cairo. Perhaps the
most remarkable thing about Al Hakim was that he ruled twenty-five years
before he was assassinated. But the murder of the God did not end the exist-
ance of his sect and the Druze people of Syria today are descended from
the adherents of his cult.

Perhaps the most interesting of the sects of the Ismalians was that of
the Assassins, founded in the late eleventh century by Hasan ibn al Sabbah
in Persia, with headquarters at Alamut (The Eagle's Castle) in northern
Persia, and a branch in the Lebanon. What made them notorious (and
feared) was their doctrine of the leveling off of mankind by the simple
process of murdering anyone who became too eminent in any field. Inflamed with hashish, whence they derived the name Assassins, these sec-

taries would recklessly murder anyone designated by their superiors. Their leader, the Shaykh al Jabal, or as the Christians called him "the Old Man of the Mountain," was one of the most feared figures in the Moslem world, and the power of the sect was only destroyed in the thirteenth century by the armies of the Mongols, who had no respect for human life and who refused to be terrorized by the daggers of the Assassins.

Another sect of the Ismalians, the Nusayris, founded about 870, with the belief that Ali was the incarnation of God, took over many Christian practices, while the Qarmatians, who possessed Arabia in the tenth century, were Ismalians, remarkable chiefly for their communism of wives and property.

The decline of the Fatimids was quite similar to that of the Abbasids, being largely due to the civil disturbances caused by rival guard regiments. The Fatimid caliphs had three guards, a Turkish, a Berber, and a Negro. These regiments struggled for power and periodically liquidated each other amid scenes of carnage. The caliphs, like their Abbasid counterparts became more and more figureheads under the domination of palace ministers and guardsmen. Internal corruption bred external weakness; the outlying provinces were wrested from the feeble hands of the Fatimids. Local dynasties set themselves up throughout Africa; the Normans captured Sicily in the eleventh century while the Turks deprived them of most of their Syrian and Palestinian lands. By the end of the eleventh century, the Fatimids were reduced to a feeble control over Egypt, western Arabia, and southern Palestine. The loss of Palestine to the Crusaders and the eventual overthrow of the Fatimid caliphate by Saladin in 1171 will be discussed in a later chapter.

The Fatimids were never the great patrons of learning that the Abbasids were. There was some scientific work at their court, especially in medicine and optics, but the realm in which the Fatimids excelled was in architecture and building. The mosques of al-Ashar (972) and al-Aqmar (1125) in Cairo are still among the greatest monuments of Moslem architectural achievement. The walls and gates of Cairo were built by the Fatimids to stand for centuries. But Egypt was to reach her zenith culturally and artistically under the later dynasties of the Ayyubids and Mameluks rather than under the Fatimids. While their civilization was high as compared to that of the West, it was not one of the great centers of Arabic culture and cannot be compared to Baghdad.

CHAPTER 7

BYZANTIUM IN THE ERA OF ICONOCLASM

❖

AFTER the beginning of the seventh century it is customary to refer to the empire as Byzantine (or Greek) rather than Roman since in language and population it was largely Greek. While the Western provinces remained to trouble the dreams and ambitions of the Eastern emperors, the country under their control was primarily Greek, and the Greek and Latin worlds began to draw apart as they had not done before. This was due largely to the incursions of the Arabs, who, as we have seen, destroyed the Mediterranean unity and forced the Eastern empire to fall back on its eastern European and Asiatic possessions. The Eastern emperors continued to style themselves emperors of the Romans, but they did so in the Greek language; Latin remained the language of the old Justinian law, but it was soon to be superseded by the later Greek codes (it had already given way to Greek in Justinian's Novellae), and pleading in the courts, as well as commands in the army or bickerings in the market place, were expressed in Greek. Until the very end of the empire in 1453 the rulers called themselves Roman emperors, and the Turks called them Romans, but they were in fact Greeks ruling over a Greek state. Thus the term Byzantine, derived from the old Greek city on whose site Constantinople was built, is properly applied to the empire after this date.

HERACLIUS AND MONOTHELITISM, 610–641

The reign of Heraclius has always been considered in relation to the Persian and Arab wars. Under his able leadership, Byzantium emerged at last triumphant over her old enemy, Persia, just to lose all she had gained to the new power of the Moslems. But it is not only in his relations with the Persians and Arabs that Heraclius merits our attention. The dynasty he founded ruled the empire until 711 and gave it, in the earlier reigns, a new upsurge of power and importance. Byzantine history follows a marked pattern: a new dynasty will bring a fresh vigor into the state and there will be a period of greatness, then the energy of the dynasty and of the people seems to fade, and the ruling house will die out in a series of incompetents or worse, which produces a short period of anarchy until a new dynasty asserts itself and brings another resurgence. In this chapter we shall trace the rise and decline of the Heraclian, Isaurian, and Amorian dynasties, ending with the establishment of the Macedonian.

The main features of the period as a whole are the wars against the Arabs, some of which have already been noted, the relations with the barbarians to the north, the loss of the Italian possessions, relations with the Western powers of the Franks and papacy, and the ever-present religious controversy. In the Isaurian period, the religious developments—the Iconoclastic Controversy—assume the most important place in the history of the empire. The period is highlighted by such dramatic characters as Heraclius, Justinian II, Leo III, Irene, Caesar Bardas, Plato and Theodore of the Studion, and the Patriarch Photius.

The Persian and Arab wars emphasized the religious disunity of the empire. Monophysitism was the prevalent belief throughout the Asiatic provinces, and the Monophysites, as we have seen, proved very effective allies for enemy invaders. To combat this schism, Heraclius sought a formula which would reconcile the divergent factions, and facilitate the recovery of the lost provinces. At first the emperor and Sergius, the patriarch of Constantinople, sought to effect this unity by a formula which explained that while Christ had two *natures* as the Chalcedonians maintained, He had but one *energy*. This was acceptable to the Monophysites, but not to the Chalcedonians, and Sophronius, a monk of Palestine, raised a storm of protest. In the hope of winning him over, Sophronius was elevated to the see of Jerusalem, but this merely gave him greater prestige when he denounced the compromise. Failing in this attempt, Sergius and Heraclius worked out a new formula. In the *Ecthesis,* issued in 638, it was forbidden to mention *energies,* but was asserted that Christ was possessed of two natures and of a single *will* (Monothelitism). All four of the Eastern patriarchs were willing to accept this formula, but Pope John IV of Rome rejected it emphatically. While the schism seemed healed somewhat as regarded the Monophysite East, the Roman West was now antagonized. The pope followed up his denunciation of the *Ecthesis* by excommunicating the patriarch of Constantinople. Constans II (641–668), who had succeeded to the throne by this time, tried to end the matter by another imperial decree. He issued the *Type* in 648, in which he forbade any mention of *wills.* But Pope Martin refused to accept this, as he maintained it left open the whole matter and indicated that either view might be correct. He denounced the *Type,* was summoned to Constantinople, arrested for treason and banished to Cherson, where he died in 655.

Thus the imperial attempts to solve the Monophysite problem only resulted in causing Monothelitism and a serious breach with Rome. And, as most of the Monophysite provinces had already been irrevocably lost to the Moslems, nothing had been gained by the effort. Italy was still one of the most important possessions of the empire and the alienation of the pope merely weakened the imperial control there.

However, the reign of Heraclius did bring some benefits to the empire. In the field of administration there was a notable tightening up and reform. The army improved and Heraclius left his state, if reduced in territory, at least improved in efficiency.

Successors of Heraclius, 641–685

At the death of Heraclius there was a struggle for the succession which lasted until the senate, with a sudden revival of authority, proclaimed Constans II, the grandson of Heraclius, emperor at the age of eleven. The twenty-six years (641–668) of Constans II's reign were marked by the religious troubles mentioned above and by continued losses to the Arabs, who occupied Rhodes and invaded the Aegean, and also by the mass migration of Slavs into Thrace and Greece. In 662, so desperate did the situation seem that Constans revived a scheme of his grandfather's to transfer the capital back to the West. Landing in southern Italy, he recaptured part of it from the Lombards (but failed to take Benevento), marched north long enough to visit Naples and Rome, and then retired to Syracuse where he set up his seat of government. The move was ephemeral, however; Constans was murdred in his bath in 668 (some say smothered in soap), and the empire reverted to his son Constantine IV, who had remained at Constantinople.

Constantine IV (668–685), surnamed Pogonatos (The Bearded), was the emperor in whose reign occurred the first two Arab sieges of Constantinople in 669 and 674 to 680. Also in his reign was held the Sixth Oecumenical Council of the church at Constantinople (680–681), which condemned Monothelitism, thus bringing an official reconciliation with Rome. It is also at this time that the Bulgars, who had first appeared about 619 and had allied with Heraclius against the Avars, were driven west by the Khazars and moved into the Balkans, settling around the mouth of the Danube in Bessarabia and the Dobrudja.

There had been considerable movement among the barbarian peoples beyond the Danube. The old Avar Empire had broken up and what remained of it was centered in what was to become Bohemia. The Avars last appeared as a threat to Constantinople when they besieged the city in 619 and when they allied with the Persians in 626. Thereafter they moved on west and north to pass into the orbit of the Frankish rather than the Byzantine Empire. The Bulgars, however, had cut loose from the Avars and settled, under their king Kubrat, in the lands along the lower Don and upper Caucasus. There they bore the brunt of the attack

of a new nomadic people from Asia, the Khazars. Driven out of the
Don area by the Khazars, the Bulgars, under Asperuch, the grandson of
Kubrat, migrated into Bessarabia and the Dobrudja. Under Terbel, the
successor of Asperuch, they developed a powerful state on both sides of the
Danube, with an important city at Pliska on the border of the Dobrudja
and eastern Bulgaria. In the eighth century, their empire stretched out to
include most of the Balkans along the south bank of the Danube (the state
of modern Bulgaria and parts of Jugoslavia) and they were the most
formidable neighbors of Byzantium on her northern frontier.

Behind the Bulgars, in the Ukraine, Crimea and the Caucasus, the
Khazar Empire was a consistent ally of Byzantium. The Khazars were in
many ways the most enlightened of any of these Asiatic nomads and developed a high degree of civilization. Their state is unique in history as
being the only one which, on relinquishing paganism, accepted the Jewish faith. Not all the subjects of the Khazars were Jews, but the ruling
class became Jewish, and the religious tolerance of the Khazars was conspicuous in an age of bigotry.

Meanwhile the Slavs had been pushed about by their more vigorous
neighbors. The kingdoms which they established in Serbia and Croatia
were both conquered by the Bulgars in the eighth century and the Slavs
migrated in large numbers into the lands of the empire, largely populat-
ing Macedonia, Greece, and especially the Peloponnesus (known throughout the Middle Ages as Morea). This Slav migration was going on in the
seventh century and continued throughout the eighth.

It must be borne in mind that these migrations of the Slavs, Bulgars,
and other Asiatic peoples were just as important as were the earlier migrations of the Germans. Because the Germans settled in countries nearer
to our own, we are inclined to make much of them and to ignore the
equally significant migrations of the eastern barbarians. From the point
of view of the empire, the loss of Gaul, Spain, or Britain to German invaders was of far less moment than the settlements of the Slavs and Bulgars
in the Balkans, or of the Arabs in the Levant.

Justinian II, 685–711

Constantine IV was succeeded by his son Justinian II (685–695, 705–711)
one of the worst of the many bad emperors who tyrannized over Byzantium.
Despotic and capricious, Justinian attacked the privileges of the clergy
and the nobles, enforcing an unpopular government by means of a highly
organized secret police. Nor did he bring his people glory, for he provoked wars with both Arabs and Bulgars in neither of which was he successful. Finally the opposition broke out into revolt, and in 695, after
ten years of Justinian's evil rule, Leontius, the general of the troops of

the Anatolic theme, rebelled, marched on Constantinople, overthrew Justinian and proclaimed himself emperor. Justinian had his nose and tongue slit and was banished to the colony of Cherson in the Crimea.

Leontius was, however, not destined for a brilliant reign. He engaged in a war with the Arabs in which he sent an army and fleet against the Moslems in Africa. In 698 the troops mutinied, proclaimed their admiral emperor, and returned to Constantinople to put Tiberius III on the throne. Leontius in turn had his tongue slit and was immured in a monastery. Tiberius (698–705) engaged in the usual wars with the Arabs, but the chief interest in his reign was in the machinations and restoration of Justinian II.

When Justinian had been banished to Cherson, he had not taken his disgrace meekly. At once he began conspiring to regain the throne and sought help from the Chersonese. They however reported his schemes to the emperor, who ordered that Justinian be arrested and returned to the capital. Not waiting for arrest, Justinian fled to Khazaria where he took refuge with the khan of the Khazars, and so won his friendship that he married his daughter. Tiberius at once sent agents to win over the khan, who agreed to dispose of his son-in-law, but Justinian's wife warned her husband, who again fled, this time to Bulgaria. There he allied himself with King Terbel, who agreed to supply an army to restore him to the throne of Constantinople.

The Bulgar forces, aided by partisans of Justinian's within the empire, proved more than Tiberius could withstand. Justinian was restored to the throne, both Leontius and Tiberius were beheaded (Justinian had little faith in mutilation) and Justinian began a reign of terror in which he hunted down all his enemies with a passion that suggested insanity. Especially was he enraged at the city of Cherson, which he felt had betrayed him, and he vowed to destroy it utterly. An army was sent to the Crimea with instructions to wipe out all traces of the city of Cherson; when the general in charge seemed to show some lenience, another general was sent to replace him. The army, however, could not stomach the senseless brutalities of the emperor. Revolting, they proclaimed their general, Philip Bardanes, emperor, and, with the assistance of the Chersonese and the Khazars defeated a fleet sent out against them by Justinian and moved on Constantinople. The rebels were welcomed; Justinian and his son Tiberius were both murdered, and the house of Heraclius perished in an orgy of vengeance against its last unworthy member.

ANARCHY AFTER THE FALL OF THE HERACLIAN DYNASTY

Philip (711–713) was not the man to restore the empire. He was luxurious, a spendthrift, and above all an Armenian heretic. He did one important thing in removing many Armenians from Armenia to Cilicia where they settled and founded the Armenian states of Little or Cicilian Armenia. But his reign was disturbed by an invasion by Terbel of Bulgaria, who ostensibly came down to avenge his former ally Justinian, and by renewed Arab incursions into Anatolia which lost considerable land to the empire. Finally a revolt of the Opsikian guard resulted in the overthrow and blinding of Philip and the proclamation of Anastasius (713–715) a former secretary of state, who was elevated to the throne by the election of the senate. Anastasius was always the emperor of the civilian bureaucracy and never had the support of the army, so that his tenure of the throne was most precarious. At this moment Caliph Sulayman decided on his great attempt to take Constantinople. A fleet was hurriedly prepared and sent to meet the Moslems off Rhodes. Instead of attacking the Moslems, the fleet mutinied, picked up a tax collector whom they happened to encounter and who was cursed with the imperial-sounding name of Theodosius, forced him against his will to accept the purple and returned to Constantinople, where they deposed Anastasius and proclaimed Theodosius III.

The Arabs meanwhile invaded Anatolia. Leo the Isaurian, general of the Anatolic army, revolted against Theodosius, was recognized by the Moslems as emperor, and having secured a temporary truce, marched on the capital. Patriarch, senators, army, and the chief officials of the government all joined in hailing Leo and proclaiming him emperor. The empire, in her hour of stress, had at last found a saviour.

LEO THE ISAURIAN, 717–741

Leo III, the Isaurian (717–741) was in many ways the greatest emperor to rule Byzantium; the dynasty he founded lasted only until 802, but the results of his reign were of far more lasting importance. We have already seen how he organized the defense of the city against the Arabs and saved Constantinople from the greatest attack made on her by the caliphate. His defense of the city and the lifting of the siege made him a national hero. It did not, however, end the war with the Arabs. After a few years of comparative peace, the war broke out again in Anatolia. From 726 to 739 there was constant campaigning, ending in Leo's brilliant victory at Acroinon (near Dorylaeum), which drove the Arabs back and permanently ended any attempts of the Umayyads to expand at the expense of the empire. Few rulers can boast so splendid a military achievement as Leo: saving his city when it was on the verge of being conquered and carrying his arms victoriously into the field to utterly defeat his enemy and render the Moslems impotent for years to come.

But while Leo was a great military leader, his abilities did not stop there.

In the field of legislation and administration, he ranks second only to Justinian I for his promulgation in 726 of the *Ecloga*, a revision of the Justinian Corpus in Greek, a Maritime Code, Military Code, and Agricultural Code. The Latin law of the old Corpus was no longer intelligible to the Byzantines; a Greek code was badly needed. Also, increased Christian influence had greatly modified some of the laws of Justinian's time and it was necessary to recodify the laws to incorporate these changes. The Ecloga is a Christian Greek code: divorce is made almost impossible, concubinage is banned, sex crimes are punished with utmost severity, mutilation was substituted for capital punishment, and ecclesiastical influences are evident throughout. The Agricultural Code is of interest as showing the existence of free peasants and free village communities, with no evidence of unfree peasantry. Slaves, of course, still persisted, but there was no unfree villeinage. This has been explained as the result of the new Slavic settlements and the universal military service levied on all males.

The Maritime Code (edited under the name of the Rhodian Sea Law) is one of the most elaborate of the medieval maritime codes, with detailed provisions for flotsam, jetsam, and responsibility for jettisoning cargo. At the same time the army and the provincial administration was extensively overhauled and reformed to promote greater efficiency.

It is under Leo that it is customary to discuss the development of the system of *themes*. The history of imperial provincial administration is one of alternation between strong and weak provincial government. Whichever is abandoned and the other instituted constitutes a great reform. In the days of Diocletian, when the provincial governors had been too strong, a great reform was instituted by separating the civil and military functions and making the civilian governor and the military general of the province distinct individuals, who could be used as checks on each other. However, this proved ineffective in defending the provinces, when a union of powers was often desirable. The result was the development of a new system, that of the themes, military districts under generals, who also ruled as civil governors. We have already noticed the power of some of these generals of the Anatolic, Opsikian, and other themes. The creation of the themes was a slow process; at first they developed on the frontiers, then the system was extended to include the interior regions. One of the most interesting of the themes was the naval command, which was rated as a theme. This organization continued until the end of the empire, and the names of the Armenian, Bucellarian, Opsikian, Thracian, Cibyrrhaeot, Optimatian, and other themes constantly recur throughout Byzantine history. While much of the work of organizing the themes had taken place before the accession of Leo and there was a continuous development after his time, his reforms extended and regularized this system.

SILESIA

BOHEMIANS

POLES

MORAVIANS

MAGYARS

PETCHENEC

Venice

Ravenna

DALMATIA

ADRIATIC SEA

SERBS

Danube R.

Nish

Plis

DYRRHACHIUM

Rome

Ragusa

Preslav

Tirnovo

BULGARIA

Gaeta

Benevento

NAPLES

Salerno

Bari

Durazzo

Ochrida

Adrianopl

LONGOBARDIA

Brindisi

Avlona

MACEDONIA

STRYMON

THESSALONICA

Salonica

CALABRIA

NICOPOLIS

CEPHALLENIA

OPSIKIAN

HELLAS

SICILY

AEGEAN

Smyr

Syracuse

Athens

PELOPONNESUS

MEDITERRANEAN

CRETE

Boundaries before 960

Conquests of the Macedonians

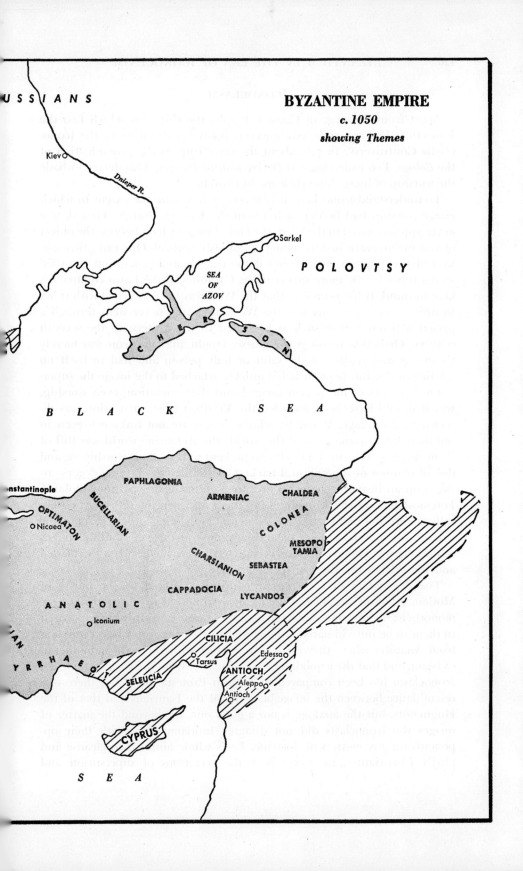

BYZANTINE EMPIRE
c. 1050
showing Themes

RUSSIANS

Kiev

Dnieper R.

Sarkel

SEA
OF
AZOV

POLOVTSY

CHERSON

B L A C K   S E A

PAPHLAGONIA

Constantinople

OPTIMATON

Nicaea

BUCELLARIAN

ARMENIAC

CHALDEA

COLONEA

MESOPO
TAMIA

CHARSIANION

SEBASTEA

CAPPADOCIA

LYCANDOS

A N A T O L I C

Iconium

CILICIA

Edessa

YRRHAEOT

Tarsus

ANTIOCH

Aleppo

SELEUCIA

Antioch

CYPRUS

S E A

ICONOCLASM

Apart from the siege of Constantinople, the thing for which Leo the Isaurian is best remembered, however, is his inauguration of the Iconoclastic Controversy. In 726, about the same time as the promulgation of the *Ecloga,* Leo issued his first *Decree against Images.* This decree forbade the worship of images and their use in churches.

To understand iconoclasm it is necessary to realize the extent to which image worship had become a fetish in the Eastern church. To a degree never approximated in the West, the Holy Image or Icon became the object of veneration and worship among the piously faithful. One can gain some idea of this popular superstition if the exaggerated veneration accorded sacred relics by the more superstitious Catholics in the Latin countries is kept in mind. It has been said that the West was too concerned with relics to turn to images; at any rate the Western church never went through a period of iconodolatry such as prevailed in the Eastern in the seventh century. Orthodox theology, of course, taught that the icon was merely the image and replica of the saint or holy person and had in itself no mystic powers. But popular belief quickly attached to the image the supernatural powers of the person imaged and the veneration, even worship, which should have been accorded the Virgin, Christ, or a saint, was directed to the image. Wonder-working images are not unknown even in our own day in some parts of the world: the Byzantine world was full of them. Statues performed miracles, wept, bent to bless their worshipers, and did all manner of supernatural tricks. Christianity was rapidly degenerating from an inspired monotheism into a welter of superstitious idolatry. Foremost among the iconodules, as the worshipers of the images were called, were the monks and the women. The leading protagonists of the iconoclastic movement were the military, the court officials and the higher secular clergy. The struggle has been described as one between the mailed and the skirted members of society.

The degeneracy of Christian worship was pointed by the purity of Moslem monotheism. The Moslems always referred to Christians as non-monotheist Trinitarians and ridiculed the image worship which appeared to them to be pure idolatry. It is significant that the iconoclasts came first from Anatolia where they came into contact with the rigid monotheism of Islam, and that the iconodules were primarily from the Greek provinces. Iconoclasm has been compared to modern Protestantism, and there is a resemblance between the image-breaking of the Isaurians and that of the Huguenots, but the analogy is not a good one, for beyond the matter of images the iconoclasts did not disagree fundamentally with their opponents on any matters of doctrine. Leo's whole aim was to cleanse and purify Christianity, to sweep away the accretions of superstition and paganism, and to reinstate Christian worship on the high ethical plane of the Fathers.

The iconoclast movement was not in its inception an anti-clerical one. Some of the higher clergy of Constantinople helped draw up the decree against images; the more educated secular clergy generally supported the movement. It was the illiterate, superstitious, bigoted monks, who infested Constantinople like a swarm of parasites, who were the arch defenders of the images. That iconoclasm became an anti-clerical movement was due to the illogical, intransigeant bigotry of the monks who brought down on their own heads the rigors of persecution. There seems no need to accept the view of Uspensky that the movement was from its inception an attempt to break the power of the monasteries; the monks drove Leo to that.

Under Leo there was no real persecution of inconodules. The decree against images was issued and soldiers removed from their places the most conspicuous images throughout the city. When a huge image of Christ was taken down from the Chalké (the entrance to the imperial palace) hysterical women, spurred on by monks, stirred up a riot in which the officer commanding the soldiers was killed. Naturally the rioters were punished; but the civil crime was forgotten by their partisans and they became the first martyrs in the cause of the images. A church council was held on the matter in 729; Patriarch Germanus objected to the decree and resigned his office, to be succeeded by Anastasius, an ardent iconoclast. The new patriarch issued a new decree forbidding the employment of the images in Christian worship, which Pope Gregory II in Rome promptly denounced.

To understand the position of the pope in this matter, one must remember that image worship was not prevalent in the West as in the East, so that there is some excuse for the pope aligning himself with the forces of superstition and reaction in this case. The church had recognized the use of images in churches from the earliest times, and to the pope the decree seemed an unjustified attack by the secular power on an established custom of the church. At any rate, whether through ignorance of the true conditions or through a natural conservatism which made him champion the cause of the monks, the pope threw his weight in on the side of the images, thereby precipitating a schism which was to have most important political as well as religious results.

The charge has been made that Leo closed the schools of Constantinople. This is not true. He did close some monastic schools where iconodolatry was taught, but there was no general suppression of education by the iconoclasts. Rather, they favored it; for theirs was the side of reason and logic against superstition.

Under Constantine V (741–775), who succeeded his father on the throne, the iconoclast struggle became much more bitter and real persecution did develop. Constantine was more of a unitarian in theology and had less patience than Leo with the obtuseness of his opponents. A church council in 753 to 754 drew up a strictly iconoclast policy, which the monks uniformly rejected. In the decade 761 to 771 several monks were executed for their refusal to accept the official pronouncements in regard to images and a real persecution of iconodules was inaugurated. In Asia, the general Michael Lakanodracon carried the persecution to extremes, closing monasteries and (like the agents of the Committee of Public Safety in the French Revolution) forcing the monks and nuns to marry. Thousands of monks are said to have fled to southern Italy to escape persecution at this time.

The Iconoclast Controversy produced a definite breach between Constantinople and the West. There were revolts in Greece; and Ravenna, which had been having trouble for some years over the matter of taxation, declared itself independent of the empire, opening its gates to the Lombard king Luitprand. Imperial troops were able to recover the Exarchate but it was lost again shortly thereafter. Although the emperors never attempted to enforce iconoclasm in Italy, the pope broke off all relations with the heretic. Gregory III was the last pope to seek confirmation of his election from Constantinople and in 781 the popes ceased mentioning the name of the emperor in the dating of their documents. Cut off from the empire, the popes turned to the Franks, and the Franco-papal alliance with all its consequences may be attributed largely to the struggle over images. South Italy and Sicily were transferred by the emperor from the Roman to the Constantinopolitan allegiance administratively, but the churches and monks of Magna Graecia adhered to Roman doctrine and repudiated that of the East.

THE ISAURIAN EMPERORS, 741–802

Iconoclasm was not, however, the only concern of Constantine V; the reign opened with a revolt of the Opsikian army under Artavasdos, the brother-in-law of the emperor, which was not quelled until 742. Wars with the Arabs, carried on in a more or less desultory fashion on both sides, characterized the whole reign, the Byzantines taking the offensive in a series of campaigns in Syria and temporarily re-occupying Cyprus. More important were seven campaigns against the Bulgars in which the imperial arms were in general successful. An invasion of Bulgaria in 762 resulted in the overthrow of King Teletz and plunged Bulgaria into civil war, in which the Byzantines interfered to their own advantage. The alliance with the Khazars was maintained, Constantine marrying a Khazar princess. Meanwhile the Slavs were continuing their migrations into Greece, and, when a great plague in 744 to 747 decimated the population of the empire and caused many Greeks to move to Constantinople, the Slavs moved into Greece filling in the lands vacated by the Greek emigrees.

Constantine was succeeded by his son Leo IV "the Khazar" (775–780), who continued his father's iconoclast policies and who won a great victory over the Arabs in 778. He is perhaps most important for his marriage to the Athenian Irene.

Byzantine empresses were chosen by a method which seems extremely modern in its general features and which we associate more with Atlantic City than Byzantium. In every province a beauty contest was held; the provincial winners would compete in a larger contest at the capital and after the field had been limited to a few of the most pulchritudinous and likely candidates, the emperor himself would interview the girls and select the one he preferred to share his throne and bed. Intelligence was a factor as well as beauty, family influence was not without its place in the eliminations, but most of the empresses selected in this manner (which was of course not always resorted to) came of middle-class stock. Irene was the daughter of a teacher at Athens; her beauty and wit appealed to Leo and she became the "basilissa of the Romans." Unfortunately Irene was a woman of pronounced religious feelings and an ardent iconodule; she was also inordinately ambitious and possessed with a consuming lust for power. She was always the empress, never the woman, and if she is a saint because of her religious policy, she is a scandal because of her unmaternal character.

When Leo died in 780 the throne went to his ten-year-old son, Constantine VI, with Irene as regent. The boy's uncles, Leo's brothers, conspired to seize the power but were firmly suppressed by Irene, who put them all into monasteries. Throughout Constantine's minority, Irene ruled thereafter alone with the advice of a favorite minister, Stauracius. She did not at once attempt to restore the images but began by relaxing the penalties on iconodolatry. Then in 786 she summoned a church council to repeal the iconoclast decrees. The army was, however, still strongly iconoclast and the troops broke up the council, driving the clergy out of the hall.

Irene was not to be foiled so easily. She engaged in a war with the Moslems, sent the army on campaign in Asia and reconvened the council at Nicaea (Seventh Oecumenical Council). There, undisturbed by the army, the iconodule clergy solemnly restored the images to the churches and drew up an impressive body of arguments in favor of their use. This ended the first period of iconoclasm, which had lasted sixty years from 726 to 786.

In 790, Constantine VI reached his twentieth year and began to have dreams of ruling by himself. Unwilling to give up any of her power, Irene imprisoned him in his rooms in the palace and ordered the army to take an oath of allegiance to her personally. The troops of the Armeniac theme refused and revolted, proclaimed Constantine sole emperor and were joined by other armies. Constantine, released from his captivity, deposed Stauracius and in turn imprisoned Irene in her palace apartments. Within the year, however, she had regained her old ascendency over her son and was again in control of the government. Again the Armeniacs revolted, led by the Caesar Nicephorus, one of Constantine's uncles. This time Constantine himself suppressed the revolt; Nicephorus was blinded, and it became evident that Constantine was not to be relied on against his mother.

The affection was entirely one-sided. Irene viewed her son as an obstacle to her full exercise of power. She deliberately set about a campaign to discredit him with clergy, army, and people. In 795, Constantine divorced his wife to marry one of his mother's maids-in-waiting, Theodote. It would seem that Irene secretly encouraged the affair and deliberately exposed her son to the girl in an attempt to make him divorce his wife. The clergy at once protested the divorce. Abbot Plato, the most influential monk in Constantinople, was most emphatic in his denunciations of the emperor and his harlot and was accordingly imprisoned by Constantine. The clergy rose in wrath—and Irene stepped forward as the champion of the monks. Then Irene turned to the army. The war with the Moslems was still going on in Asia and the imperial troops were winning rather consistently. Irene tampered with the loyalty of officers and men, she deliberately bribed the troops to lose the campaign less Constantine gain some prestige from victories. Finally in 797 she hired ruffians to attack the emperor and blind him. The only redeeming thing in this whole picture of depravity is that Theodote proved herself completely faithful to Constantine and stayed by him loyally through some five years of blind captivity in the palace until he died.

Irene recalled Stauracius and they ruled the empire unhindered until the death of the minister in 800. It was at this time that the pope transferred the crown of the empire to Charles, king of the Franks, and set up the Western as opposed to the Eastern Roman Empire. It is an evidence of Charles' heroic valor that he contemplated and even negotiated a union of the two empires by offering to marry Irene. That other great figure of this dramatic age, Harun al Rashid, had meanwhile successfully invaded Anatolia, and Irene bought peace with the Moslems by paying a heavy tribute under the treaty of 798.

By 802 the rule of Irene had grown too oppressive. A coterie of generals rebelled, seized the palace and quietly deposed Irene who was banished to Lesbos. The grand logothete, Nicephorus, was proclaimed emperor, and the house of Leo the Isaurian came to an end.

Irene is one of the most intriguing characters in history. She ranks with Theodora in the sixth century and Theophano and Zoe in the tenth and eleventh as one of the great empresses of Byzantium. The Greek church considers her a saint for her work in restoring the images, but she is more generally remembered as the unnatural mother and ambitious sovereign who destroyed her own son that she might rule alone.

The Amorian Emperors, 802–843

Nicephorus I (802–811) was a mildly iconoclastic state official, who was anxious to bring the church under the control of the secular authority. He encountered the violent opposition of Theodore of the Studion, abbot of the most important monastery in Constantinople, and one of the eminent literary figures of the period, who denounced him bitterly in his letters and sermons. Foreign affairs prevented Nicephorus from accomplishing anything in the religious field, and the reopening of the iconoclast controversy had to await the accession of Leo V. Nicephorus' reign was a series of calamities: the Arabs took Crete and Sicily, the Franks occupied Italy, and the Bulgars expanded in the Balkans in imperial territory. The Bulgars found a strong leader in Tsar Krum (a. 808–814) who pushed west in the Balkans, took Sofia, and occupied the country that is still known as Bulgaria. Nicephorus invaded Bulgaria in 809–810, defeating Krum and capturing his capital city of Pliska. Then in 811 he determined to put an end to the Bulgar state and again invaded and sacked Pliska. Krum offered terms which were refused; as Nicephorus was victoriously returning home he was ambushed by the Bulgars, his army annihilated and Nicephorus himself was killed on the field of battle. With grim humor Krum had his skull encased in gold, making of it a macabre drinking cup out of which the Byzantine envoys subsequently had to drink to the friendship of the two nations. Stauracius, Nicephorus' son, though severely wounded in the battle, escaped to Constantinople, where he was recognized for a few weeks. He is reported to have had some idea of turning Byzantium into a republic but died before he could do anything, overthrown by his brother-in-law, Michael I Rangabé.

Michael I (811–813) was an iconodule, strongly influenced by Theodore of the Studion, and immediately restored all the images to the churches, a move which lost him the support of the army. He is most important for his recognition of the division of the empire and acceptance of the Frankish Empire in the West. His chief problem was Krum and the Bulgars, who had invaded deep into Thrace and approached Adrianople. Michael went out to meet them, was defeated near Adrianople (not without some question of treachery on the part of Leo, the general of the Anatolics) and the Bulgars moved in to besiege Constantinople. Michael abdicated and Leo the Armenian, the general of the Anatolics, was proclaimed emperor by the army.

Leo V, the Armenian (813–820), began his reign by defeating the Bulgars, driving them back from Constantinople and defeating them in battle at Mesembria (813). Krum died the next year and his son Omurtag made a peace for thirty years, so that the Bulgar menace was averted for the time being. Leo was a soldier and an iconoclast; he at once revived all the old iconoclast legislation and began anew the struggle over images. This time however the controversy had a broader aspect. It was the struggle of the state to destroy the power of the church and particularly the monks. Theodore of the Studion denounced Leo and was exiled for his pains. Monasteries were broken up all over the empire, the monks dispersed and their properties confiscated by the state. The monks demanded complete independence from any secular control and appealed to Rome. Leo continued to persecute them and make them feel the force of the secular arm. The second phase of the inconoclast struggle which Leo began in 815 lasted until 843, when once again the work of an Anatolian soldier was undone by an empress selected in a beauty contest.

In his elevation to the throne and in his governance, Leo had been supported by his good friend, Michael the Amorian. Elevated to the post of count and commander of the Excubitores (the elite palace guards), Michael developed ideas of grandeur and plotted against his friend. Leo learned of his treason, arrested Michael, and precipitated a rebellion. Leo was murdered while singing in church and Michael, rescued from his prison, was proclaimed emperor.

Michael II, the Amorian (820–829), aimed at a policy of conciliation in religious matters. He was personally indifferent to religion and sought to make peace between the warring religious factions, recalling all exiles of either party. But compromise was not in the nature of Theodore of the Studion. As soon as he was back from exile, Theodore began virulently to attack the iconoclasts and the emperor who tolerated them. His intransigeance drove Michael into the camp of the iconoclasts, so that he renewed all the decrees against images and their worshipers, although he was always lenient in enforcing them. Theodore retired into his monastery where he died in 826, thus removing the most eloquent leader of the iconodule party.

A new leader of quite a different stamp had developed however: Thomas the Sclavonian, a general and former companion of Leo V and Michael II, had revolted in Asia and declared himself the champion of the iconodules. The revolt had begun under Leo, but assumed importance only under Michael. It was more than a military or religious revolt and took on the aspects of a social war, for Thomas supported the lower classes against the aristocracy and aimed at the destruction of the large estates for the benefit of the peasants. Allied with the caliph Al Mamun, who recognized him as emperor, Thomas gained control of most of Anatolia and in 821 to 822 attacked the capital which he besieged by land and sea for a full year. It was a Bulgar army, under Omurtag, come to the aid of his ally, which rescued the city from the rebels. The revolt of Thomas has caused considerable attention among historians as being the first serious social war in Byzantine history. It shows how religion, economic and social grievances, and personal ambition can be fused into a single cause. Its failure may be the cause of the reappearance in Anatolia of the large estates and the crushing of the small farmers, a phenomenon which was most important in the tenth century.

Michael II was succeeded by his son, Theophilius (829–842), who gave the empire one of its most prosperous and glorious reigns. An ardent iconoclast, Theophilius enforced the laws against the images with rigor, subjecting the monks to a severe persecution. Like most happy and prosperous periods the reign is not marked by any political events of importance. There was war with the Abbasids (838) and alliances were concluded against them with both the Khazars and the Umayyads of Cordova. A new people appeared on the northern frontier—the nomadic Patzinaks or Petchenegs, probably the lowest in civilization of any of the nomads who came out of Asia, but they did not become a serious menace during this period.

Theophilius was able to devote himself to the internal improvement of his empire; he organized new themes, recast the administrative system, reformed finances and built new fortresses along the frontiers to hold back the barbarians. Inside his capital city he built magnificent palaces with every luxury which oriental splendor could afford, especially equipped with many mechanical devices, which caused amazement to less sophisticated visitors. Golden birds sang on the branches of bejewelled trees, mechanical lions roared as the visitors approached; it was all rather gaudy and ostentatious and exceedingly impressive to ambassadors and dignitaries from barbarian countries.

Like Leo IV, Theophilius selected his wife through a beauty competition, preferring, we are told, the more modest graces of the Paphlagonian Theodora to the ready and caustic wit of the aristocratic poetess Kasia. Theodora was a pious girl from a family of provincial officials and cherished her rustic love of images. During the lifetime of her husband she secreted holy images in her wardrobe and brought up her son to love and adore the pretty dolls. When Theophilius died in 842, the child Michael was only three years old, and he ascended the throne under the regency of Theodora and her brother the Caesar Bardas.

Theodora (she is "The Blessed" in the Greek Church) at once set about restoring the use of images when her husband was dead. But she struck a shrewd bargain with the clergy, as she would not permit them to anathametize all those who had persecuted the iconodules, and only permitted the restoration of the images on assurance that the soul of Theophilius would not suffer from her act. In 843 a church council officially restored the images and the iconoclast controversy, which had torn the empire intermittently since 726, was ended. The Paulicians, a heretical sect of Armenia, who were rabid in their hatred of images, were persecuted and driven into exile, whereupon they spread into Bulgaria and the Slavic lands where they were to reappear as the Bogomiles and to extend their influence into the West as the predecessors of the Cathari.

CAESAR BARDAS AND MICHAEL III, 843–867

From 842 to 856, Theodora and her brother ruled the empire in comparative harmony. But Bardas was too ambitious to want to share the rule permanently and conspired against his sister, overthrowing her and assuming sole control in the name of Michael III. At the same time he encouraged Michael in all manner of vices and depravity, so that he would have no political aspirations. Michael III, the Drunkard, was thoroughly corrupted by the education given him by his uncle; his chief amusements were heavy drinking, wenching, horse racing, and athletic competitions. He loved to sleep in the stable surrounded by his horses; his favorite companions were grooms and wrestlers, and his amusements sometimes involved sacrilege which profoundly shocked the clergy. Among the intimates whom Michael acquired was one Basil, a groom from Macedonia, who could break the spirits of unruly horses and the necks of opposing wrestlers. Basil seemed a stupid irresponsible lout and Bardas favored the friendship. Michael heaped honors on Basil, even arranging for Basil to marry Eudocia Ingerina, his own mistress. Bardas was content as it kept Michael's mind off politics and gave him a free hand to rule the empire.

Caesar Bardas continued the same wise rule which Theophilius had given the empire. But he added more, for he was a great patron of letters and the arts. Under his patronage schools developed, literature flourished, and under Photius, an encyclopedic scholar who gathered around himself a group of scholars and litterati, the court of Bardas became a great cultural center.

It should be noted here that we are entirely without any iconoclast historians. After the restoration of the images, the works of all the iconoclasts were collected and destroyed so that the only historical accounts we have of the iconoclast emperors come from the pens of their opponents. That they should stand out as they do when only revealed to us by their enemies attests eloquently their real virtues and accomplishments. The chief historical work for this whole period is the chronicle of Theophanes which will be discussed in Chapter 13.

The reign of Bardas is also noteworthy for the Russian attack on Constantinople in 860, when the barbarians were bought off by a favorable treaty, and for the Photian schism with Rome. In 858, Bardas arrested the patriarch Ignatius (a son of Michael I who had taken Holy Orders) for treason, deposed him, and appointed Photius patriarch. Pope Nicholas I excommunicated Photius as an usurper, Photius excommunicated Nicholas as a meddler, and a Greek council in 867 broke off relations with Rome. Photius disagreed with the pope on several points of doctrine as well as on the question of the relation of the two sees to each other. Among the points at issue were differences concerning the use of the seven-fold amen, leavened or unleavened bread in the Eucharist, bearded or clean-shaven clergy, and the thorny question of the Procession of the Holy Spirit. The Fathers had never settled the question as to whether the Holy Spirit proceeded from the Father *and* the Son or from the Father *through* the Son. A Spanish council had decided that it was from the Father *and* the Son; this idea had been accepted by the Gallican church and by Rome and was considered the orthodox belief throughout the West. The Eastern church had never accepted this interpretation, which they termed a heretical innovation, and the *Filioque* arose to be the doctrinal point on which the two churches split apart. Far more important really was the matter of the patriarch's refusal to accept the supremacy of the pope, but the Filioque enabled them to put the argument on a higher spiritual plane. Although the schism was officially healed rather promptly, the seeds of disunion were planted in this Photian schism and only waited a favorable opportunity to sprout up again in the eleventh century.

Ignatius was not without strong support even in Constantinople and the elevation of Photius caused Bardas to lose considerable influence and power at home. It was not this, however, which precipitated his downfall, but the ambitions of the erstwhile groom Basil, who was a far more crafty and astute individual than anyone considered him. With aspirations for the imperial buskins for himself, Basil persuaded the besotted Michael to join him in a plot to murder Bardas. They were successful; Bardas was killed in 866 and Basil was elevated to the title of Caesar. But he found his own position now too uncertain; while Basil governed, Michael developed new favorites so that Basil felt himself about to be replaced. Without waiting for Michael to overthrow him, Basil in 867 quietly murdered Michael and proclaimed himself sole emperor. The Macedonian dynasty ascended the throne through a series of debaucheries and murders, but in the ex-groom and drinking companion of Michael the empire found again a man whose dynasty raised it to a period of unsurpassed splendor.

CHAPTER 8

THE BYZANTINE APOGEE:
KIEVAN RUSSIA

✦

BYZANTIUM UNDER THE MACEDONIANS

THE EARLY MACEDONIANS, 867–963

IN spite of his lurid and unsavory past and the unscrupulous means employed to acquire the imperial purple, Basil the Macedonian (867–886) proved to be in every respect a strong, intelligent and able emperor. In the matter of internal administration, he carried out extensive reforms, adopting a policy of favoring the small landholders against the growing power of the owners of great estates. He also instituted a new code of law, a revision of the codes of Justinian and Leo the Isaurian, which was published after his death under the name of the *Basilics*. He seems to have attempted to parallel the career of Justinian in all possible respects, as legislator, administrator, and conqueror. Under his direction, Byzantine armies conquered south Italy with the port of Bari, and his wars in the Mediterranean indicate a revival of Justinian's dream. It was in his reign that Sicily was finally lost to the Moslems, but his conquests on the Italian peninsula and in Asia Minor more than compensated for this loss and left his reign one of military splendor. He also emulated Justinian in beautifying the capital with new churches and palaces.

One of the first acts of Basil as emperor was the recall of the former patriarch Ignatius and the deposition of Photius. This should have ended the schism with Rome, as Rome had protested the elevation of Photius, but a new source of conflict broke out immediately over the matter of the ecclesiastical organization of the Bulgarian kingdom. Bulgaria had been converted to Christianity largely through the efforts of missionaries from Constantinople, and had accepted obedience to the patriarch. But when Rome protested, the Bulgarian tsar Boris broke his allegiance to Constantinople and placed himself under the papacy. Thus the schism between the two churches was continued over this matter of jurisdiction. Further, when Ignatius died in 877, Photius was reinstated as patriarch, which did nothing to mend matters with Rome. During the last years of Basil's rule, Photius conspired against the emperor, persuading his son

Leo to turn against his father and causing an open breach between the emperor and his heir.

At Basil's death in 886, he was succeeded by his two sons, Leo and Alexander. Alexander, however, actually exercised no power whatever, although an attempt on the part of Leo to liquidate him in 900 failed and he remained titular co-emperor. Leo VI (886–912), known as Leo the Wise, was a scholarly man, interested in the science of government and in legal and administrative works. He completed the Basilics which his father had inaugurated; issued also the famous *Book of the Prefect,* which regulated the guilds and the industries of the empire, and himself wrote a volume on *Tactics.* In 886 he deposed Photius from the patriarchate for the second time and thus officially healed the schism with Rome. The causes for the breach remained, however, and reappeared again when a strong pope and independent patriarch came into conflict in 1054.

The reign of Leo was one of military disaster. In a war with the Bulgarians, which began in 889, the Byzantines were seriously defeated in 897. The Moslems resumed their advance in Asia Minor and struck out from Sicily. In 904, Moslem pirates from Crete sacked and pillaged the city of Salonica.

Leo is best remembered, however, for his marital rather than for his martial difficulties. The Greek Church recognized only reluctantly a second marriage for widowers, and under no circumstances would tolerate a third. But the emperor, who desired an heir, married three times in spite of the patriarchal opposition. When his third wife died still leaving him childless, Leo remained single for six years, the patriarch and clergy absolutely refusing to permit a fourth marriage. Then in 906, in spite of the church, Leo married Zoe Carbonupsina who produced the longed-for heir, Constantine Porphyrogenitus (born in the imperial porphyry chamber). To accomplish this Leo was obliged to banish the patriarch Nicholas; and it should be noted that the clergy were still arguing the merits of his case (whether dynastic necessity justified the relaxation of the church law) for many years after the death of the emperor who had so offended.

Leo died in 912 when his son was only seven years old, leaving the child to the care of Alexander, who had been resentfully sulking in the background for many years. Alexander at once banished Zoe Carbonupsina, recalled the patriarch Nicholas, dismissed all the advisors and ministers of Leo and set about securing the throne for himself alone. It is generally believed that he was actively plotting to murder Constantine when his years of dissipation got the better of him and he died in 913. Immediately a struggle for the throne began between the patriarch, empress dowager and several powerful nobles. In the course of this struggle Romanus Lecapenus, who had come up from the humblest origins to the position of admiral of the fleet, secured a great influence over the boy-emperor. Romanus married Constantine to his daughter Helena, and had himself proclaimed first *Basileopater,* then Caesar, and finally in 919 Emperor. Within the next four years Romanus had his wife crowned empress and three of his sons proclaimed emperors: for his youngest son he subsequently secured the patriarchate. Romanus Lecapenus had much in common with Basil I. They were both illiterate, unscrupulous adventurers of low birth and considerable ability. Romanus spent most of his reign in a long-drawn-out war with the Bulgarians, during which Tsar Simeon twice (913 and 924) besieged Constantinople itself. At Simeon's death however, Romanus arranged a treaty with the new tsar Peter, to whom he married his daughter. Against the Hamdanids, the leading Moslem power of Syria, Romanus conducted several successful campaigns around Daras and Nisibis; and in 941 he defended his capital against an attack by the rising power of the Russians, who under their prince Igor raided the city of the Bosphorus.

Romanus ruled unchallenged until 944. In that year his own sons, ambitious for a greater share in the government, revolted and forced their father into a monastery. But their revolt was without profit for them, as the partisans of Constantine asserted themselves, overthrew and banished all the Lecapanids and established Constantine (now a man of 39) on the throne whence he had been so long excluded.

Constantine Porphyrogenitus, who had been titular emperor since 912 only began his personal rule in 944. He was a scholarly man, more interested in writing than in government, and better suited to the recluse existence he enjoyed in his earlier years than to the cares of state which he bore until 959. Constantine's literary accomplishments will be discussed in Chapter 13; they were of a higher quality than his government.

In foreign affairs he suffered some defeats by the Moslems on the sea, offset by some gains in the vicinity of Aleppo. The most significant event in foreign affairs was the visit in 957 of the tsarina Olga of Kiev, who came to Constantinople and there received baptism into the Christian faith. Although Russia relapsed into paganism after her death, the conversion of Olga was the first step in the establishment of Byzantine religious and cultural dominance of Russia.

The death of Constantine VII was caused in all probability by poison administered to him by his son, Romanus II, at the instigation of his wife Theophano. This Theophano was a notorious courtesan, the daughter of a tavern keeper, who had won the affection of the young Romanus, a dissipated and generally worthless youth, so that he married her and associated her on the throne. With her father-in-law removed and her debauched husband on the throne, Theophano took into her own hands the reins of power, ruling with the advice of the eunuch Joseph Bringas, an old functionary of Constantine's.

In spite of the utter worthlesssness of the emperor, the reign of Romanus II (959–963) was a brilliant one, due entirely to the genius of two nobles, the brothers Leo and Nicephorus Phocas, who defeated the pirates of Crete, secured the maritime supremacy of the eastern Mediterranean once more in Byzantine hands, and made signal advances against the Hamdanids in Asia, capturing Cilicia and Aleppo. With his conquest of Crete, Nicephorus Phocas became the leading man in the Byzantine Empire. Of an aristocratic Anatolian family, he had shown himself the first soldier of his day; but he was spirtually a monk and had lavished his wealth in building a monastery on Mount Athos, to which he intended eventually to retire.

Just as Nicephorus reached his great triumph after the capture of Crete, Romanus II died. Whether it was the result of the excesses of dissipation in which he had always indulged, or whether, as was claimed by many, due to poison administered by his wife, Romanus departed this world in 963 leaving Theophano a widow at the age of twenty with two small sons, Basil and Constantine. What could be more natural than that the widowed empress should seek a supporter and helpmate in the gallant soldier? Bringas attempted to assume the custody for the two young princes at the death of their father, but Theophano and the patriarch engaged in an unholy alliance to confer the government on the hero Nicephorus. As a result, Nicephorus was declared protector and regent for the young princes; soon thereafter he was proclaimed emperor by his troops; then six months after the death of Romanus, Nicephorus married Theophano. The marriage, however, antagonized the patriarch; Nicephorus' monastic friends despaired of him; the Church showed her displeasure at this offensive union. Nicephorus, "the fool of love," retaliated by an imperial law which drove all monks from the cities of the empire and confiscated their goods. It should be noted that the money thus obtained from the spóliation of the monks helped finance some of Nicephorus' campaigns, but even so Nicephorus has the questionable distinction of being the first Byzantine emperor to debase the coinage.

THE MILITARY EMPERORS, 963–1025

The reign of Nicephorus Phocas (963–969) is one of the most glorious in the military annals of the empire. Northern Syria with the great city of Antioch was captured from the Hamdanids; Mesopotamia was invaded; Byzantine fleets raided Sicily and captured Cyprus. In 967 war with Bulgaria was resumed: Nicephorus allied with the Russian Sviatoslav who

took Preslav, the Bulgarian capital, and the eastern Bulgarian empire was
badly shattered. With the West there were some negotiations with Otto
I, which, while unsuccessful diplomatically, are most important historically as Liutprand of Cremona, Otto's ambassador to Constantinople,
has left us a detailed account of his legation which throws an intimate light
on the court of Nicephorus and gives interesting information as to the
Greek attitude towards the Western barbarians.

Nicephorus is also remembered as a precursor of the crusades. He attempted to secure from the clergy the honor of martyrdom for all those
soldiers who gave their lives in combat against the Moslems, and to have
erected in their honor a new basilica. He was unsuccessful and the clergy
withstood his demands, but this previsioning of the crusade is not without
its interest.

In the campaigns of Nicephorus a leading role had been played by a
younger cousin of the emperor, John Tzmisces. The two cousins were
alike in military ability but unalike in personality and appearance. While
Nicephorus was hairy, unkempt, heavy and mystical, John was handsome,
urbane and sophisticated. The new general was thrown into intimate contact with the empress; Nicephorus spent much of his time away at the wars.
Further, his conscience troubled him and he took to wearing a hair shirt.
It must be admitted that Nicephorus showed greater prowess in battle
than in the boudoir, and he undoubtedly insulted the empress by his
habit of sleeping on a panther-skin on the floor. Before long Theophano
began to find solace for her loneliness during her husband's absences in
the company of Tzmisces. Nicephorus deprived Tzmisces of his military
rank and banished him to the provinces, but Theophano had other plans
and, thinking to replace Nicephorus with John in every capacity, plotted
the murder of her husband. The empress arranged for John and his men
to be admitted into the palace; they found Nicephorus asleep on his
panther-skin and fell upon him, stabbing and hacking his face and body
(December 11, 969). Tzmisces had himself immediately proclaimed emperor.

Theophano saw herself now the wife of a new and handsome emperor.
But she had been duped; when the patriarch refused to recognize Tzmisces
as emperor until he had "driven from the Sacred Palace the adultress . . .
who had been the chief mover in the crime" he cheerfully repudiated
Theophano, who was banished to a nunnery (she was then 27 years old).
John married Theodora, the daughter of Constantine VII. To further
propitiate the clergy, Tzmisces rescinded all the anticlerical legislation
of Nicephorus and made great gifts to churches and monasteries.

The reign of John Tzmisces (969–976) was no less brilliant on the military side than that of his predecessor. He completed the conquest of eastern
Bulgaria, capturing Preslav in 971 and completely destroying the old Bul-

garian empire so that the Bulgarians retreated to Ochrida in the west, where they set up a new capital. In the following year, he attacked the Russians, drove Sviatoslav out of Bulgaria, and stirred up the Petchenegs to attack Kiev. In the south, he invaded Armenia and Syria, raided Damascus, and even pushed temporarily into Palestine. Relations with the West were cemented by the marriage of Theophano, a daughter of Romanus II and sister of the princes Basil and Constantine, to Otto II. In the height of his glory, just after his return from his victorious campaign in Syria, John died, probably from the typhus, on January 10, 976.

The death of Tzmisces left the control of the empire in dispute between the court officials and the military. While the young princes Basil II and Constantine proclaimed themselves emperors and recalled their mother from her nunnery, the generals prepared to strike for the throne. The decade from 976 to 989 is marked by almost continuous revolts, led by Bardas Phocas and Bardas Scleros, who fought against each other and then in alliance against Basil. The emperor allied with Vladimir of Kiev to defeat them, an alliance which was to have the most profound results as Vladimir accepted, with the hand of Basil's sister Anne and the province of Cherson, baptism to Christianity which he enforced on the Russians.

The reign of Basil II (976–1025) marks the apogee of Byzantine history. Although technically Constantine VIII ruled concurrently with his older brother, actually he played no greater role in government than had Alexander in the reign of Leo VI. In fact, Constantine and Alexander had much in common, both being primarily interested in personal debaucheries and pleasures, and being apparently quite willing to allow their brothers to assume the burdens of government. Basil II more closely resembled his stepfather Nicephorus Phocas whose virtues he seems to have emulated. He was above all a soldier, happiest in the camp and in battle; rough and indifferent to the amenities of culture, he was equally indifferent to women and, perhaps scared off by the precedent of his parents, never married.

Basil is best known for, and indeed received his nickname "Bulgaroctenos" from, his campaigns against the western Bulgarian state. From 986 to 1018 he engaged in a series of campaigns in Bulgaria and Serbia, which resulted in the total destruction of the Bulgarian kingdom. With the capture of Ochrida in 1016, the Bulgarian power was ended and the whole Balkan peninsula fell under the rule of Byzantium. Meanwhile he extended his power in Asia, where he further consolidated the Byzantine rule in northern Syria, secured Homs and defeated the Fatimids, who were encroaching on Syria from the south. Peace was finally made with the Fatimids in 1001 with the Byzantines strongly entrenched in the north. Further accretions of territory in Asia came to Basil through the bequests of the kings of Iberia and Armenia, both of whom willed their kingdoms to the emperor, while an expedition into Khazaria made the power of Basil felt north of the Black Sea.

Basil also played an important part in Italian politics. He allied with Crescentius of Rome against Otto III and in 998 the two emperors set up rival popes. In 992, Byzantium made a treaty of alliance with the new power of Venice and benefited therefrom shortly thereafter when a Venetian fleet saved Bari from Moslem attack (1002). Byzantine rule in southern Italy was difficult to maintain, however, and there were constant revolts by Lombard princes and others. It was during this confusion of Byzantine, Moslem, and Lombard parties that the first Normans made their appearance in Italy in 1017.

Although foreign affairs and military campaigns form the most spectacular parts of Basil's rule, his internal policies were not without interest. He consistently renewed the legislation against the great landed estates and attempted to safeguard the interests of the small proprietors. In 989 occurred a great earthquake which did much damage throughout the empire, and which gave Basil the opportunity to indulge in rebuilding many of the great edifices of his predecessors, among which the reconstruction of Hagia Sophia was probably the most important. At Basil's death in 1025 he left an empire strong and respected, a dynasty well established, and Byzantine dominion rose to its greatest extent since the days of Justinian.

THE DECLINE OF THE MACEDONIANS, 1025–57

How secure the Macedonian dynasty was on the Byzantine throne was amply proven in the thirty years that followed the death of Basil II, when the throne was occupied by Constantine VIII (1025–28) and his daughters, Zoe (1028–50) and Theodora (1028–56). That the Byzantine people remained loyal to such rulers proves conclusively how firmly the able members of the family had seated the house on the throne.

Constantine had theoretically been ruling throughout the long reign of his older brother, but he had little ambition and no desire to play any active role. As a result, at the age of 65, this degenerate and extravagant old man came to a throne for which he was altogether unfitted. His reign was brief and stormy, being marked by wars with the Petchenegs and Moslems, and by a major revolt of Nicephorus Comnenus in Anatolia. After three miserable years, Constantine died, leaving the throne to Zoe, the eldest of his three daughters.

Zoe (1028–50) presents rather a pathetic figure, an elderly lady seeking romance and glamor, fighting vainly to preserve her youth and collecting about her throne young men who flattered her vanity and coldly exploited her weaknesses. She was fifty when she ascended the throne, seventy-two when she died, but until her death she tried to appear young, spending hours at her toilette and turning a part of the palace into a factory for perfumes. Four men shared the throne with her: Romanus Argyrus (1028–34), Michael IV (1034–41), Michael V (1041–42), and Constantine IX Monomachus (1042–54).

The chief events of this period in foreign affairs were the campaigns of the general George Maniakes in southern Italy and Sicily, and a war against the Bulgarians, who besieged Salonica in 1040. Otherwise the chief interest of Zoe's reign lies in the demonstration of loyalty to the dynasty made by the Byzantine people. In spite of the worthlessness of Zoe and the inertia of her husbands, the old empress managed to retain the loyalty of her subjects. In 1042, Michael V, the nephew of Michael IV and Zoe's adopted son, attempted to seize the throne for himself. A popular rising overthrew him and recalled Zoe and Theodora to the throne. Zoe's third husband, Constantine IX Monomachus, whom she married when she was sixty-four, was an urbane, refined, genial gentleman with great literary and artistic accomplishments and little ambition. He is well spoken of by a number of historians who enjoyed his patronage, but cannot be considered an effective emperor.

Zoe at last ended her life at the age of seventy-two in 1050. Constantine followed her to the grave five years later; for another year Theodora ruled alone, until she too died at the age of seventy-five in 1056. When the old empress was on her deathbed she nominated as her successor Michael VI Stratiocus (1056–57) an old patrician and close friend of the eunuch Leo Paraspondylus, who had been the chief minister of the aged Theodora. Michael was never accepted by the senate or the army; senators and generals alike rejected his rule and broke into revolt; riots broke out in the capital. The patriarch, Michael Cerularius, declared for the general Isaac Comnenus whom he proclaimed emperor. Isaac defeated an army which Michael sent against him, marched on Constantinople, deposed Michael and banished him to a monastery. The last vestiges of the Macedonian dynasty passed away and the rising sun of the Comneni appeared in the ascendent. The years 1042 to 1057 were more important in the external history of the empire than they were in the capital. While the old ladies and the elderly roué were amusing themselves in their own ways in the Sacred Palace, the Normans began the conquest of south Italy, the Turks invaded Anatolia, and the Petchenegs overran Thrace and Macedonia. In 1043, the imperial armies carried out a successful campaign against the Russians, but this was more than offset by the losses in Italy and Asia.

In southern Italy, George Maniakes had reconquered considerable territory for the empire from the Moslems and the Lombards. But Maniakes revolted against the government of Constantine IX and invaded Greece assisted by a band of Norman adventurers. The rebellion was suppressed, but the Greek power in Italy was destroyed, and the Normans, under Robert Guiscard, captured one after another of the Byzantine towns there. While the end of this conquest came only with the capture of Bari in 1071, Greek rule after the departure of Maniakes was always precarious.

In Anatolia also the empire was losing ground. In 1044, the Saljuq Turks invaded Armenia, at the time a satellite state of the empire. Constantine proclaimed the annexation of Armenia in order to defend it, but was unable to hold the land and was forced to retreat before the Turks in a series of campaigns which lasted throughout his reign. Here too the climax was reached only in 1071 when the Turks defeated Romanus Diogenes at Manzikert, but the foundations of their conquest were laid in the earlier period.

It was also during the reign of Constantine and Zoe that Michael Cerularius, the patriarch, brought on the schism of the Greek and Roman churches. Constantine himself supported the Roman side in this schism, but the patriarch was strong enough so that he forced the emperor to submit. The Latin churches in Constantinople were closed as heretical in 1053, and on July 20, 1054, Cerularius anathematized the pope at Rome, rejecting at one time both the Filioque in the Creed and the papal claims to universal supremacy.

The last years of the Macedonian dynasty produced, however, as we have said, a notable intellectual movement. Constantine gathered around his court the best minds of the age, founding anew the University of Constantinople. True, the university was compelled to close its doors after five years due to the persistent quarrels of the faculty, but nonetheless their presence shed the light of learning over the capital. Michal Psellos, John Xiphilinos, Michael Attaliates were all objects of the imperial patronage and have all left histories of the period which show at one time the intellectual glory and the moral decay of the empire in the eleventh century.

BARBARIAN PEOPLES OF EASTERN EUROPE

Passing mention has been made on several occasions of the barbarian neighbors of the Byzantines:—the Bulgars, Slavs, Avars and others. As the movements of these peoples are just as important for Eastern Europe as those of the Germanic tribes are for the West, some further notice must be taken of them here.

The earlier history of the Slavic peoples is shrouded in the mists of uncertainty and legend. They were generally disorganized tribes inhabiting the great plains of east-central Europe, with little civilization and no political unity. Stronger peoples came, saw, and conquered them, and they became parts of the greater empires of the Huns, the Avars, and other more aggressive nations. It is really only after the breakup of the Avar Empire that most of the Slavic nations emerge as distinct units at all.

THE BULGARIANS

We have already noticed the rise and fall of the first Bulgarian Empire in our discussion of the Byzantine Empire. The Bulgars, a Turkish people, first appeared after the breakup of the Hun Empire, when they were settled in Bessarabia. Under the names of Kotrigurs and Utrigurs they crossed the Danube and fought the Byzantines in the seventh century. Under Kubrat and Asparuch they founded a state with its capital at Pliska in the Dobrudja, whence they expanded south into the Balkans. We have noted how they interfered in Byzantine politics when they allied with the deposed Justinian II and replaced him on his throne.

It was in the eighth century that the Turkish Bulgars assimilated with their Slavic subjects to become the Bulgarians, who are now essentially a Slavic people.

The height of the first Bulgarian Empire was reached in the ninth and tenth centuries in the reigns of Krum (808–814), Boris I (852–889), and Simeon (893–927). Krum gained great glory by his victorious wars with the Avars and the Byzantines, during the course of which he killed the emperor Nicephorus I. Under Boris, the Bulgarians accepted Christianity and moved their capital to Preslav farther south in what is today Bulgaria. Simeon was the first Bulgarian ruler to assume the title of Tsar, and under him Bulgaria became a highly civilized state, reflecting faithfully the culture of the Byzantines, and establishing at Preslav and Ochrida centers of trade and culture. Simeon attempted repeatedly to conquer Constantinople and dreamed of making himself in fact as well as in title "Emperor of the Romans and the Bulgars," but although he conquered Nish and Belgrade, overran Macedonia, Albania and Thrace, and defeated the Byzantines severely at Anchialus in 917, he was himself defeated by the Magyars and by the Petchenegs, whom the Greeks stirred up against him, and he was never able to fulfill his dream.

Under Peter (927–969), the son of Simeon, the Bulgarians completed the conquest of Serbia, but it was during his reign that Sviatoslav of Kiev invaded Bulgaria, and under his son Boris II (969–972) the Russians and Byzantines overran and destroyed completely the empire in the east, reducing it to a small state around Ochrida, which was in turn conquered by Basil II in the opening years of the eleventh century. For the next century and a half Bulgaria was a province of the Byzantine Empire.

At its height under Simeon, the Bulgarian Empire had included all of the Balkans except a few towns on the coast of Epirus, Morea, and eastern

Thrace. It possessed its own metropolitan and its own autocephalous church. The culture of the Bulgarians was a replica of the Byzantine, and Preslav was considered one of the most beautiful cities of Europe. For a time the Byzantine Empire paid tribute to the Bulgarians, and we know from the testimony of Luitprand of Cremona that the Bulgarian ambassador took precedence in the court of Constantinople over that of the German emperor.

THE KHAZARS, PETCHENEGS, AND POLOVTSY

It is undoubtedly insulting to the respectably civilized Khazars to associate them in the same section with the utterly barbarous and savage Petchenegs and Polovtsy, but all three of these peoples founded ephemeral states in the region north of the Black Sea, and all passed out of existence as political entities without leaving any marked traces.

The Khazars are first encountered settled in the lands across the Caucasus when they allied with Julian against the Persians, but they seem by then to have been inhabiting that region for some time. They supported the empire against the Persians, giving valuable aid to Heraclius in his Persian wars, and later assisting the empire in its wars against the Arabs. They were defeated by the Arabs and made tributary to the caliphs, but they were for long a powerful state checking the Arab advance to the north. From the Caucasus, the Khazars spread across the plains north of the Black Sea establishing great trading cities at Itil on the Volga and Sarkel on the Don. They were a remarkably civilized people, addicted to trade which they pursued in the Caspian and Black seas, as well as taking part in the China trade, and playing a leading role in the commerce between Constantinople and the north.

We have already noted that the khan of the Khazars accepted the Jewish religion for himself and his nobles, and that religious toleration was practised throughout their empire. They reached their height in the seventh to tenth centuries when they controlled much of southern Russia, and when they played an important part in Byzantine history. When the Petchenegs invaded the west they formed a buffer against them, diverting them from the Black Sea, but their power declined and they fell before the Russians in the reign of Sviatoslav at the end of the tenth century.

Far removed from the urbane Khazars were the wild Petchenegs or Patzinaks. This Turkish people came into eastern Europe from the district of the Urals in the ninth century, and were first employed by the Byzantines as a check upon the Russians of Kiev. Pushed west by the Khazars, they settled in the plains north of the Danube, whence they invaded Thrace in 1027 and 1051. The Petchenegs were finally destroyed as a power by the Byzantine emperors Alexius and John Comnenus. Of them nothing good

can be said. They were complete savages, dirty and unkempt, nomadic warriors without any vestiges of culture. They brought devastation wherever
they went and seem never to have settled down or to have assimilated any
of the civilization of the peoples with whom they came into warlike contact.

The Polovtsy or Cumans were a little better than the Petchenegs whom
they closely followed. They first appear in the lands north of the Black
Sea in the eleventh century when they threatened Kiev in 1061. In the
years 1060 to 1210 they made no less than fifty recorded raids on the Russian
cities, burning, robbing, raping and carrying off slaves and plunder. They
engaged in a lively traffic in slaves whom they sold in the Crimean ports.
The raids of the Polovtsy are among the chief causes for the decline of
Kievan Russia, but they did not confine themselves to Russia, raiding
across the Danube as well. They were repeatedly driven out of Thrace,
and were severely defeated by Igor, prince of Sieversk, in 1185, but they
continued their wild nomadic life in southern Russia and the Ukraine
until they were destroyed by the Mongols in the thirteenth century. Meanwhile they had rendered valuable assistance to the Byzantines in helping
to destroy the Petchenegs, their kinsmen and deadly enemies. With the
break up of the Polovtsy confederacy, most of the people were absorbed
into the Mongols, while a few tribes fled west to be assimilated by the
Hungarians. Beyond a record of devastation, and a few songs and dances,
the Polovtsy have left nothing to record their existence.

THE RISE OF RUSSIA UNDER THE VARANGIANS TO 1113

Of all the northern neighbors of the Byzantine empire, the only ones
destined to any considerable future greatness were the Russians. Here
as in Bulgaria the Slavs remained relatively backward until stimulated
by the conquest of a stronger more aggressive people,—in this case the
Scandinavian Varangians.

We shall later have occasion to notice the expansion of the Norsemen
among whom were the Swedes who came to the eastern end of the Baltic
and thence through Novgorod and Pskov down the river Dnieper to Kiev
and on to the Black Sea. Legend attributes the first conquest by these
vikings to three brothers: Rurik, Sinius and Truvor, who conquered the
old Slav towns and established a thriving commercial state. The first
authenticated fact we know about the Russ was their raid on Constantinople in 860, which was repulsed by Caesar Bardas. In 911 a second Russian attack was made on Constantinople, this time by Oleg (c. 880–912),
the Varangian prince, who united Novgorod and Kiev into a single principality. By this time we know that they had established an important
trade along the Dnieper and the Don with prosperous towns at Novgorod,
Smolensk, Kiev, Chernigov and Tmutorokan. In 945, the Byzantines signed

a commercial treaty with the Russ whereby the trade between the two peoples was strictly regulated. The prince of Kiev was to inform the emperor of the names of all the merchants who made up the company trading with Constantinople. When the merchants arrived at the city, they were quartered at government expense in one of the suburbs, and only fifty Russ were permitted to enter the city at a time. It was particularly specified that they must remain unarmed and that they were to be accompanied by a Byzantine official while within the walls. Although the Varangians established a state in Russia, they were in their earlier years more traders and pirates than politicians, and their whole policy seems to have been devoted towards the development of commerce. Many of them turned mercenary soldiers, and they formed the nucleus of the emperors' famous Varangian guard, which later included Saxons, Normans, and adventurers from all over Europe.

Oleg ruled over Novgorod and Kiev, and left his throne to his son Igor (912–945). Igor twice raided Constantinople and made the commercial treaty noted above. When he died he left his throne to his infant son Sviatoslav while the actual rule was taken over by his widow Olga. Olga continued the policy of establishing trade relations with Constantinople, and even went to the capital on a mission in 957 where she was baptized a Christian, with Constantine Porphyrogenitus standing as her godfather. Her conversion had little effect on Russia however, as Sviatoslav, who came to the throne in 964, was a pagan and refused to accept the new faith of his mother.

Sviatoslav (964–972) was the first prince of Kiev to attempt conquest outside of Russia proper. He invaded Bulgaria, took Preslav in 968 and seriously thought of moving his capital from Kiev to the more centrally located Bulgar city. His famous explanation that Preslav was on all the trade routes and was a better site for an active trading center shows how the Russians were still motivated by the desire to secure commercial advantages. Sviatoslav was forced to withdraw from Bulgaria by John Tzmisces, and on his way home was killed in a battle with the Petchenegs, whom the Byzantines had employed to attack him.

The succession was disputed between his sons Yaropolk I and Vladimir (978–1015) with the final victory going to the younger brother. St. Vladimir was the ruler under whom the Russians were officially converted to Christianity, legend reporting that Vladimir refused Islam because no one could live happily in Russia if prohibited to drink intoxicating liquor. With the conversion of the Russians, the church was organized throughout their dominions and Byzantine culture was carried to them by the missionaries. From then on Russia became a cultural outpost of Byzantium, and Kiev soon after became a second Constantinople, with churches in the Byzantine style and a life patterned entirely after the Byzantine. It is worthy of note that Vladimir's conversion was definitely part of a policy of drawing closer to Byzantium. He had just captured the Byzantine city of Cherson in the Crimea; by a treaty he accepted Christianity, the hand of the princess Anne,—and retained Cherson.

At the death of Vladimir the throne was disputed by his sons Sviatopolk of Kiev, Mstislav of Tmutorokan and Yaroslav of Novgorod. After several years of war, Yaroslav secured the whole country and moved to Kiev.

Yaroslav "the Wise" (1019–54) brought Kievan Russia to its height both internally and in foreign affairs. In many ways his reign resembles that of Justinian in Constantinople: he built a cathedral which he called Santa Sophia and many other buildings to beautify Kiev; he issued a code of laws (strongly influenced by the Byzantine); he expanded to the west, conquering Galicia from the Poles; he defeated the Petchenegs, and attempted a campaign against the Byzantines, in which he was unsuccessful. Most significant were the marriage alliances which he negotiated: his own wife was a Swedish princess; his son Vsevelod married a Byzantine princess, and three of his other sons married German ladies of noble birth; his daughter Elizabeth married Harold Hardrada, king of Norway; another daughter Anastasia married Andrew of Hungary; a third, Anne, was given to Henry I of France; and Casimir of Poland was brought into the family by marrying Mary, Yaroslav's sister. These alliances are of interest as showing the importance of the prince of Kiev at his time.

Modern students are too inclined to remember how Russia came up out of Eastern darkness into the light of Western reason in the sixteenth century when the princes of Moscow had thrown off the Mongol yoke and set up a new state, and are liable to overlook altogether the high civilization of Russia in her Kievan period before the Mongols came. It must be borne in mind that Russia had in the eleventh century a culture and civilization far superior to that of England, France, or Western Europe generally; that Russia partook of the glories of the Byzantine East; and that Kiev was the greatest capital of Christendom after Constantinople. The Mongol conquest ended all this and reduced Russia to the position of a backward country from which it had to drag itself up. When it did, it was in Moscow not in Kiev that the new state appeared, but it would seem safe to say that never since has Russia achieved the relatively high status of culture apropos of the other nations that Kiev enjoyed in the age of Yaroslav.

For all his greatness and wisdom, Yaroslav initiated an institution that was destined to lead to the weakening and downfall of his house and his country. Determined that his family must always stick together and never indulge in fratricidal strife, he established the succession to the throne on the famous *rota* system whereby each son received a province, which he held until the death of his elder brother when he moved up a notch. Thus

GRAND PRINCES OF KIEVAN RUSSIA TO 1212 *

1. Rurik, 879 *

2. Oleg, 912

3. Igor, 945 = Olga, 964

4. Sviatoslav, 973

5. Yaropolk, 980   6. Vladimir, 1015

Yziaslav of Polotsk   7. Sviatopolk, 1019   8. Yaroslav, 1054

Anne = Henry of France   Anastasia = Andrew of Hungary   Elizabeth = Harold Hardrada of Norway

Mstislav

Vladimir   9. Yziaslav, 1078   Sviatoslav   Vyacheslav   Igor   10. Vsevelod 1093

Rostislav   11. Sviatopolk 1113   Oleg   David   Yaroslav of Riazan   12. Vladimir Monomakh 1125

Rurik of Galicia   15. Vsevelod 16. Igor 1146 1147   20. Yziaslav 1161   13. Mstislav, 1132   14. Iaropolk, 1139   19. Yuri Dolgoruki of Suzdal 1167

17. Yziaslav, 1154   18. Rostislav, 1167   22. Andrei Bogolubski 1174   23. Michael 1176   24. Vsevelod of the Big Nest 1212

21. Mstislav, 1170   Mstislav the Brave

Roman of Galicia   Mstislav the Daring

* Dates are those of death. Table based on Stokvis, *Manuel d'histoire, de généalogie et de chronologie* (1889).

Yaroslav ordered that his sons should divide the country as follows: Yziaslav, the eldest, received Kiev, Sviatoslav got Chernigov, Vsevelod was given Pereiaslav, Vyacheslav got Smolensk, and Igor received Volhynia. Only Kiev was really sovereign, but all the brothers were supposed to rule together harmoniously. Each of these princes was to rule his territory in this order while the eldest lived. When Yziaslav died Sviatoslav should move up to Kiev, leaving Chernigov to Vsevelod, who in turn left Pereiaslav to Vyacheslav, each brother moving up one place. While the names of the princes are quite unimportant, the principle involved is an interesting one, and bears a certain resemblance to Diocletian's system of Augusti and Caesars.

Yaroslav's intention in this amazing scheme of succession was to bind his sons together into a single family policy. But the system had exactly the opposite result from that desired by its founder. Instead of each brother working harmoniously with the others, each only waited for his elder brothers to die so that he could acquire the better province. Also men refused to give up what they held but tried to pass their lands on to their own sons. The whole scheme hardly worked out even in the first generation. Yziaslav was driven out of Kiev by a rising of his subjects aided by his brothers Sviatoslav and Vsevelod. Sviatoslav died and Yziaslav returned to Kiev, and as Sviatoslav had broken the line of succession the claims of his sons to Chernigov were recognized by neither Yziaslav nor Vsevelod, who himself took Kiev at the death of Yziaslav. A general civil war followed in which the dispossessed princes joined forces with each other against their relatives who had refused to surrender their proper heritages. The whole matter was straightened out at a conference at Liubeck in 1097 whereby it was decided that each prince should keep the province originally assigned to his father by Yaroslav. But even this did not end the perniciousness of the thing, for when Sviatopolk of Kiev died in 1113, Vladimir Monomakh of Perieslavl was chosen grand prince over the better claims of his cousin Sviatoslav of Chernigov. The civil wars which resulted from this mad scheme to promote family unity eventually wrecked Kievan Russia, which was suffering from the attacks of the Polovtsy in addition to the civil wars.

The net result was the creation of a series of principalities in Kiev, Chernigov, Volhynia, Galicia, Novgorod, Rostov-Suzdal, Polotsk, and Riazan. How these states were overthrown by the Mongols and how a new principality emerged in Moscow, a dependency of Suzdal, will be discussed in a later chapter.

CHAPTER 9

WESTERN EUROPE AND
THE CAROLINGIANS

✦

THE GERMAN KINGDOMS

NOTHING in Western Europe in the seventh to the ninth centuries can compare in significance to the rise and expansion of Islam, nor was there anywhere in the West any civilization in any way comparable with the Byzantine; but the very fact of the Arab expansion threw the West back on its own resources and caused it to produce a culture of its own, less dependent on Constantinople, more Germanic and local, more native to its own soil. That the coins of the Merovingians were gold while those of the Carolingians were silver attests the decline in international trade and the self-sufficiency of the Frankish Empire. The Middle Ages of Western Europe began when the Arabs cut the Mediterranean and severed the connections with the East. Medieval society, as it is generally thought of, emerged from the Germanic states of the West, which began to develop in this period, and the empire of the Franks and Charlemagne, although emphemeral, was destined to have a tremendous influence on later history.

Of the barbarian nations of the West, by far the most important in the period under consideration was the Frankish. Visigothic Spain dragged out an uneventful existence, punctuated by local wars and feuds until it was overrun and destroyed by the Moslems in the first decades of the eighth century. Anglo-Saxon England continued to be divided into the seven states of the Heptarchy, with the supremacy passing from Northumbria to Mercia and finally to Wessex. Roman Christianity, introduced by Augustine in 597, was spread throughout the kingdoms, coming into conflict with the Celtic church which had been established during the Roman occupation. Differences as to the date of Easter, tonsure of priests, and use of the Halleluiah, and the missionary zeal of both churches brought the two churches into direct conflict. The ultimate victory of the Roman church was assured after the Council of Whitby in 664, when King Oswy of Northumbria elected to follow the Roman road to salvation and secure a friend in St. Peter at Heaven's gate. Soon after this Theodore of Tarsus came to Britain (669–690) to organize the church, establishing the Roman system of dioceses and parishes and giving a great impetus to a national unity, which was seriously impaired when a second archbishopric was established at York in 735. The one thing worth noting about Saxon England before the Danish invasions of the ninth century is the development of laws and local government, but this can better be studied at a later period, when they were more fully developed. One can only regret that a historian of Bede's genius did not have a more worthy subject for his narrative.

Nor was the history of Lombard Italy of great importance until it entered the orbit of the Franks. The kingdom was given a semblance of unity by Agilulf (590–615), but the great dukes of the south remained independent, and the church secured such immunities that the bishops became virtually autonomous rulers over their cities. The war with the Exarchate was chronic but uneventful. Luitprand (712–744) succeeded in temporarily conquering the Exarchate and was able to bring the dukes of Spoleto and Benevento into submission, but his successes so alarmed the pope that Rome turned to the Franks and the Lombard kingdom was destroyed by the Carolingians. Paul the Deacon's *History of the Langobards* is as dismal a chronicle of petty wars as that of Bede or Gregory of Tours.

THE FRANKS UNDER THE LAST MEROVINGIANS

If the history of the Franks is no more edifying, it is at least more significant. We last observed the Franks emerging from a civil war and executing Queen Brunhild in 613. The fall of Brunhild is notable for the fact that it was a coalition of Austrasian nobles headed by Bishop Arnulf of Metz and Pepin of Landen who called in Clothar of Neustria and encompassed the destruction of the aged queen. The real power in all of the Frankish states was passing out of the hands of the kings into that of the landed nobility, and the mayors of the palace, who managed the king's household and estates, were usurping royal prerogatives and reducing the kingship to nothing. This process was temporarily stopped by Dagobert (629–639), who secured the control over all of the Frankish kingdoms and who gave them a short period of strong royal administration. But it was only an Indian summer and was ended soon, Dagobert's successors dropping into a position of second place to their great noble councillors and rapidly degenerating into *rois fainéants*. The real power in the kingdom rested in the great mayors of the palace in Austrasia and Neustria and in the great landed nobility. From 639 to 687 the mayors gradually increased their powers, sometimes the Neustrian, sometimes the Austrasian, being the more powerful. Then in 687 Pepin of Heristal, the grandson of Pepin of Landen and Arnulf of Metz, mayor of Austrasia, completely defeated his rival of Neustria at the battle of Testry and secured unchallenged domination over the whole Frankish realm.

When Pepin died in 714 he left no legitimate sons and his grandchildren were too young to assume the burdens of state; the position of mayor fell to his illegitimate son Charles Martel (714–741). Charles' accession was not accepted without opposition and he was virtually forced to reconquer most of Neustria, Aquitaine, and the eastern border districts. In the process of re-establishing his power over Aquitaine, Charles came into conflict with the Moors who had pushed across the Pyrenees from Spain; the battle of Poitiers (732) put a term to their raids and they withdrew to the southern part of the province where they were firmly ensconced. The real reconquest of Aquitaine and the pushing back of the Moors to the Narbonnaise was the work of Charles' son Pepin.

The Moorish war determined Charles political affiliations and his attitude towards the church. To secure help against the Moors, he allied with the Lombards, so that when the pope approached him with an offer of alliance against them, Charles refused to accept the position of defender of the papacy against the Lombards, leaving that role to be assumed by his son at a later date. Also, in order to secure lands with which to pay his warriors, Charles confiscated great amounts of church lands in Gaul, thus bringing down on himself the condemnation of the clergy. This confiscation of lands to pay soldiers has been seen as one of the important steps in the growth of feudalism. The old Frankish armies were essentially infantry, and the equipment of the Frankish soldier was that of a heavy armed infantryman. As the Moors were primarily cavalry, Charles found it necessary to raise mounted troops to oppose them, and mounting the troops meant that they would have to be paid more. Charles got the land wherewith to compensate his men for the added expense of supplying horses from the church. His great-grandson Louis the Pious was to do heavy penance for this almost a century later.

During the last four years of Charles' tenure of office there was no king and Charles ruled alone without benefit of any puppet monarch. At his death, like any Merovingian king, he partioned his lands between his sons, giving Pepin "the Short," Austrasia, and Carloman, Neustria. Rivalry between the brothers threatened the peace of the state, but Carloman in 747 abdicated his honors and sought the refuge of a monastery, leaving the field free to his brother.

Pepin completely reversed the policy of his father in regard to the church. He made an arrangement whereby the title of the lands was returned to the church, though the military service obtained from them was rendered to the state, which partially appeased the clergy for the confiscations of the previous regime. He encouraged and closely co-operated with St. Boniface in a general overhauling and reform of the Gallic church and in missionary endeavors to the East. While Charles Martel had encouraged missionaries, Pepin made them instruments of his policy as

Charles had not. Most important of all, he accepted the papal alliance and became the protector of the papacy against the Lombards.

In 751, Aistulf, king of Lombardy, conquered the Exarchate of Ravenna. Fearful for Rome, Pope Zacharias appealed to Pepin for assistance and protection against the Lombard menace. Pepin was willing to give the aid, but at a price. When he had come to power, Pepin had appeased the nobles by re-establishing the Merovingian monarchy, appointing a puppet king Childebert III. It irked Pepin that he had the substance of power without the title; he saw in the necessity of the popes an opportunity to regularize his position and requested, as the price of his alliance, recognition as king of the Franks. It was all done very diplomatically; Pepin wrote the pope asking whether it was not proper that he who exercised the power should have the title; the pope approved. Pepin with papal approbation deposed Childebert and proclaimed himself king (751). In 754, Pope Stephen came to Gaul where he solemnly crowned Pepin king of the Franks and appointed him Patrician of Rome (a title which should have been conferred only by the emperor). The shadow and substance were united and the house of the Carolingians was seated on the throne of the Franks with the blessing and support of the Roman church.

It remained for Pepin to live up to his part of the bargain. The same year he descended into Italy, defeated the Lombards and granted the Exarchate of Ravenna to Rome. But the Lombards failed to make the stipulated surrender and Pepin had to come back two years later (756), defeat the Lombards again, and see that Ravenna and the disputed lands were turned over to papal officials. It was a this time that he made the famous *Donation of Pepin,* which created that strip of territory across Italy, including Rome, Ravenna, Ancona and most of the lands that were later known as the Papal States.

Having secured his royal title, fulfilled his obligations to his papal ally, halted the expansion of the Lombards, and made the Franks a power in Italy, Pepin turned to Aquitaine where he drove the Moors back, suppressed local rebellions and established his authority to the Pyrenees.

CHARLEMAGNE, 768–814

When Pepin died in 768 he divided his kingdom, according to custom, between his two sons Charles and Carloman, whose wives were sisters, the daughters of the Lombard king. Charles and Carloman never did get along; Carloman refused to support Charles in his campaigns and often war between the brothers seemed imminent. Then Carloman died in 771 leaving minor heirs. Charles swept aside the claims of his nephews and added Carloman's domains to his own. Carloman's wife fled with her children to the court of her father Desiderius at Pavia; as Charles' own wife had already gone back to her father the diplomatic, as well as the domestic, relations between Charles and Desiderius became rather strained. But it was the papacy, more than his daughters or grandchildren, that finally brought Desiderius into war with Charles. Desiderius had dabbled in Roman and papal politics, which had become hopelessly confused with rival factions setting up opposing popes. Adrian I appealed to Charles, and his appeal, coupled with Desiderius championing the cause of Carloman's sons, brought Charles down into Italy in 773. While Desiderius held out in Pavia which Charles besieged, the Franks overran all Lombardy as far as Benevento; at Easter 774, Charles in Rome renewed (and probably increased) the Donation of his father, and the pope conferred on him the title of Patrician of Rome. Returning to Pavia, Charles was able to force the surrender of the city; Desiderius was tonsured and sent to a monastery thus effectively withdrawing him from political circulation; Charles assumed the Iron Crown of the Lombards and the Lombard kingdom became a possession of the Frank. It was not incorporated into the Frankish monarchy, but ruled as a separate possession.

Charles, who is known variously as Charlemagne or Karl der Grosse, so outshadowed his predecessors that he gave his name to the dynasty of the Pepins. We know him well from the intimate biography of him written by Einhard who lived at his court. He represents the finest accomplishment of the barbarian monarch—the conquering warrior, the legislator, patron of the clergy and of scholars, a shrewd diplomat and just judge, pious but practical, servant and master of the church at the same time; he very nearly deserved much of the reputation which history and legend have combined to give him.

Most of his life was given over to incessant wars. From 772 to 804 he was more or less constantly at war with the Saxons of northern Germany, destroying their independence and reducing them to submission to the Frankish crown and the Christian church. In thirty years there were eighteen campaigns in which the Franks would invade and conquer the Saxons, convert them to Christianity and set up churches, which began at once to collect tithes; the Franks then withdrew, the Saxons burned the churches, killed the priests and relapsed into paganism—and the whole business started again the next year or so. As the wars continued, the Franks became more zealous in enforcing their laws and customs on the Saxons and the Saxons more obstinate in refusing to be assimilated. A national leader rose up among the Saxons in the person of Widikind (778), but Charles eventually put him down and crushed all opposition so that by the end of the reign Saxony had been incorporated into the Frankish empire. Bavaria under its duke, Tassilo, was also subjugated (787–788); six campaigns were conducted against the Avars in Bohemia (788–805) which succeeded in destroying the power of that once ferocious people; and Spain was invaded. The Spanish expedition in 778 was one of Charles' few un-successful campaigns. Although invited into Spain by a faction of Moorish malcontents, and assured of the assistance of some Moorish and many Christian Spaniards, Charles found that his allies were powerless or un-reliable, and his expedition bogged down before Saragossa. The campaign was abandoned when news of a Saxon revolt called Charles back to the east, and on the way home the Frankish rearguard was ambushed and destroyed at Roncevalles, in the most famous battle in Carolingian history, for it is the scene of the *Chanson de Roland*. Neither the participants or the events of the campaign are very recognizable in the poem, but the story of the heroism of Roland at Roncevalles inspired future generations of French knights as no more prosaic account of any of the great king's vic-tories could have done. Charles never went back to Spain, but the Frankish control was established over the northeastern corner of the peninsula by local rulers who created what became in 812 the Spanish March or County of Barcelona.

In one other opponent did Charles find his match; he was never able to reduce Venice. In 805 and again in 809, Frankish armies attempted to capture the city of the lagoons, but the Venetians received help from Constantinople and maintained their independence of the Frankish goliath.

Charles was also disturbed in the later years of his reign by raids by the savage Norsemen and by incursions by the Moslems from Africa. On the borders of his empire Charles established a series of marches (or marks), military districts established for the specific purpose of guarding the frontier against outside invasion. The marches thus established included the Spanish, the East, and Friulian (between the Danube and the Adriatic), the Altmark (lands across the Elbe), the Marches of Thuringia, Bohemia and Moravia, and the Danish Mark. The possessions of Charles thus ex-tended from the Atlantic to beyond the Elbe and upper Danube, and from Denmark to Barcelona and Benevento.

The Imperial Coronation

On Christmas day 800 (it was really 799 as Christmas was the first day of the year 800 according to the reckoning of time then) Charles added the final touch to his aggrandisement by receiving the imperial crown of the Roman Empire from Pope Leo III. For some time he had had imperial ideas and had entered into negotiations for marrying his daughter to Constantine VI and later even contemplated marrying Irene himself. But the crown was presented him by the pope as a result of his championing the papal cause and reinstating Leo in Rome whence he had been driven by a city faction. Einhard in telling of the coronation says: "He received the title of Emperor and Augustus, to which he was so averse that he remarked that had he known the intention of the Pope, he would not have entered the Church on that day, great festival though it was." [1]

This statement has been variously received by historians, some feeling that this attitude was mere hypocrisy on the part of Charles. There is now a tendency, however, to accept Einhard's statement as a true expression of Charles' sentiments. That he sought the imperial crown cannot be questioned, but that he wanted it from the hands of the pope is quite another matter. Charles was negotiating to secure the crown by agreement with the Byzantine empress; the pope's precipitate action upset his diplomacy, further it placed him in the position of having received his crown from the papacy, an idea that could not have appealed to him. However the deed was done; the crowd in St. Peters acclaimed the Divine Emperor Elect of God, and the seat of the Roman Empire was transferred from the Bosphorus back to the Tiber. No woman could be emperor, so the imperial throne was vacant. The pope took it upon himself to fill it. What a Pandora's box of troubles was opened when the pope thus set up his right to create emperors!

Charles immediately set about trying to get recognition of his title from the emperor in the East. The difficulties of travel, the rapid turnover in Byzantine rulers and the inevitable delays attendant on any diplomatic exchanges prevented the accomplishment of this recognition until 812 when Michael I finally, officially, accepted the existence of the Western emperor. It is worthy of note that Charles aligned himself with the emperors against the clergy in passing iconoclastic decrees for the Frankish church.

Meanwhile Charles had extended his influence diplomatically to the far corners of the world; Einhard tells us that the kings of the Asturias and of Scotland called themselves the lieges and servants of the emperor, and that he formed an alliance with Harun al Rashid, who granted him the protectorship over the Holy Places of Jerusalem.[2] More tangible and most impressive was the elephant which Harun sent to Charles as a token of friendship. While Einhard does not mention the fact, it is generally accepted that the alliance with Harun was aimed at their mutual enemies, the Umayyads of Cordova and perhaps the emperors of Constantinople.

The Government of the Carolingian State

Like Leo the Isaurian, Charles was legislator as well as conqueror. He reorganized the system of local government, curtailing the powers of the counts and dukes, and sending out his royal emissaries, the *missi dominici*,

---

[1] Einhard, *Life of Charlemagne*, trans. W. Glaister; reprinted in Scott, Hyma, Noyes, *Readings in Medieval History*, p. 165.

[2] Although this rests on the authority of Einhard, there is considerable reason to doubt that such a grant was really made by Harun.

to keep a close check on the activities of his local governors. By means of his *capitularies* he legislated on all sorts of matters from the most minute details of the administration of an estate to matters of national and provincial administration. Political, economic, ecclesiastical, social and educational matters were all treated in the capitularies wherein Charles tried to lay down rules for the operation of his domains. But the legislation and administration of Charles presents a marked difference from that of Leo. While the Byzantine emperor was recodifying a great body of highly developed law for a well-developed bureaucratic state, Charles was never more than a barbarian tribal ruler, ruling through his personal attendants and treating his empire like his own personal estates. The concept of empire, as opposed to the private possessions of the emperor, hardly developed at all in the Carolingian system. The land was the king's, to be divided among his heirs as any private estate would be; it was managed and controlled by the personal servants and followers of the monarch, counts—originally members of the king's *comitatus*—governing the provinces which came to be called counties.

The development of the grand officers had been a Merovingian institution. These personal servants of the king grew to hold high offices of state. The seneschal, who was originally the steward of the estate, became the king's viceroy with command in the army and authority to represent the king in courts or administration. The constable, originally the chief groom of the king's household, became, through his control of the horses, the chief commander of the army (who rode the horses). His assistant groom, the marshal, became a high military figure, while the butler became the grand commander of the fleet. The pantler and the cook never developed more than their domestic duties, but the chancellor, originally the priest who could write and was therefore secretary to the king, became the head of the royal secretariat (called chancery or chancellory). The development of these grand officers, which began with the Merovingians, continued into the Capetian period, but the Carolingian was one of the periods of its development.

Charles never developed a regular army or navy. The army was still the general levy where all freemen assembled under arms to participate in a campaign. The growth of the use of cavalry changed this in that not every free proprietor could afford to provide himself with a horse, and *benefices* were given those who came mounted. Charles Martel, as we have seen, obtained the lands to create these benefices from the church; Charles continued the system, but paid in lands newly conquered or parceled out of the royal domain. The alienation of crown lands to provide military effectiveness is one of the tendencies which must be followed throughout the Carolingian period, and one which resulted in the rapid decline of the monarchy to the benefit of the landed nobility. Charles further stimulated the growth of a military aristocracy by his capitularies which provided that for distant campaigns small farmers should band together to send one man on horse instead of several on foot—a process which tended to raise the one who went on horseback above the level of his fellows who remained unmounted and gradually made him the lord over the others who worked on his lands while he was away at the wars.

The "Carolingian Renaissance"

One of the most important aspects of the reign of Charles is the so-called "Carolingian Renaissance," that great revival of learning which occurred under the patronage of the monarch and which centered in the famous palace school at Aix-la-Chapelle under the leadership of Alcuin. The Frankish lands had fallen far behind Italy or Britain in matters of education and general culture. Charles determined to bring Gaul up to and, if possible, beyond her neighbors. To accomplish this he imported the leading scholars from all the neighboring countries: Alcuin of York, exemplar of the culture of the Northumbrian monasteries, which had maintained a higher level of culture than any other portion of northern Europe; Theodolphus, a Spaniard, who was the finest poet of the age; Peter of Pisa the grammarian, Paul the Deacon the historian (who found the rigors of the north too much to bear and retired to Monte Cassino), and Paulinus of Aquilea, all products of the Italo-Lombard civilization. These scholars and others like them were gathered together at Aix by Charles in the school at the palace, where they educated the noble youth of the Franks. They also served as royal agents, Theodolphus was made bishop of Orleans and was one of Charles most trusted *missi*. The results of their labors are to be seen in the next generation of Franks: Einhard, the biographer of Charles, Smaragdus, and Hrabanus Maurus, scholars and teachers themselves, who carried on the educational revival to their own pupils. In the generation of Charles' grandsons and great-grandsons, Gaul had become the center of cultural activities; John Scotus Eriugena, Lupus of Ferrières, Agobard of Lyons, Sedulius Scotus, and Hincmar of Rheims were the intellectual leaders of the West. It is interesting to note that while Charles sent to England for Alcuin to educate Gaul, at the end of the century Alfred of Wessex sent to Gaul for scholars to re-educate England.

The Carolingian educational revival did not stop at the palace school and the education of a select few. Charles issued capitularies ordering that in every cathedral there should be a teacher of grammar and in every archepiscopal cathedral a professor of theology for the education of the youth of the districts. That these schools did not develop appreciably for some centuries was not the fault of the Carolingian legislator, who never quite learned to write his own name, but who had the greatest respect for education and learning.

The Successors of Charles the Great, 814–887

Like any German tribal king, Charles had, during his lifetime, divided his lands among his sons. Charles the eldest was given Neustria, Pepin, Italy, and Louis, Aquitaine, with the title of kings. But both Charles and Pepin predeceased their father, so that in 814, when the old king died, the whole realm went to Louis I, rightly called the Pious, while Bernard, the son of Pepin, ruled Italy as a subking under his uncle.

Louis I (814–840) began his reign by expelling from court the numerous illegitimate relations resulting from his father's and sisters' amours. Fanatically religious, Louis surrounded himself with monks, and his first reforms were the imposition of a stricter discipline on the rather lax Gallican clergy. He permitted Pope Stephen IV to be crowned pope without obtaining his imperial approval before the event, and then further demonstrated his dependence on the church by having himself recrowned in 816 by the pope, although he had once been crowned previously. Paschal I succeeded Stephen in 817, also without benefit of imperial approbation, but without any objection on the part of Louis.

The main event of interest in the over-long reign of Louis I was his repeated attempts to insure the succession. By his first wife, Louis had three sons, Lothaire, Pepin, and Louis, among whom he made a division of his inheritance as early as 817. But the matter was complicated by a second marriage and the birth of a son, Charles, to Louis' young wife, Judith, and the king then sought to carve out a kingdom for this youngest child. As the new division inevitably cut down the lands previously awarded the elder sons, they revolted and the next few years were marked by a confusion of civil wars, in which Louis was deposed, restored and deposed again. The sons were, however, unable to get along among themselves and a rebellion of Louis and Pepin against Lothaire resulted in the re-establishment of Louis I on the throne in 834. The death of Pepin relieved the situation somewhat, as Louis was then able to substitute Charles for Pepin in the division of his lands, but young Louis and the sons of Pepin revolted against this scheme and war broke out again. During the campaign which followed Louis I died (840), an old and broken man, whose whole life had been made miserable by his attempts to provide for his ungrateful sons. General anarchy followed the death of Louis; everyone advanced his own claims, alliances formed and reformed. Lothaire, who wanted to rule everything, tried to divide his brothers and nephews against each other and was successful up to a point, but Louis and Charles joined together against Lothaire and defeated him at a great battle at Fontenoy (841). But Lothaire was far from subdued, and Charles and Louis met at Strasbourg to strengthen their alliance against their brother. There they took the famous Strasbourg Oaths (842).

The Strasbourg Oaths and Treaty of Verdun

These famous oaths show how the empire had divided into Latin and German parts. In order that the oaths should be understood by the followers of each other, Louis swore in the Roman tongue employed by the Aquitanian and western followers of Charles; while to be understood by Louis' Saxon, Bavarian, and other eastern soldiers, Charles swore in the German tongue they used. These oaths have a tremendous philological

CAROLINGIAN DYNASTY

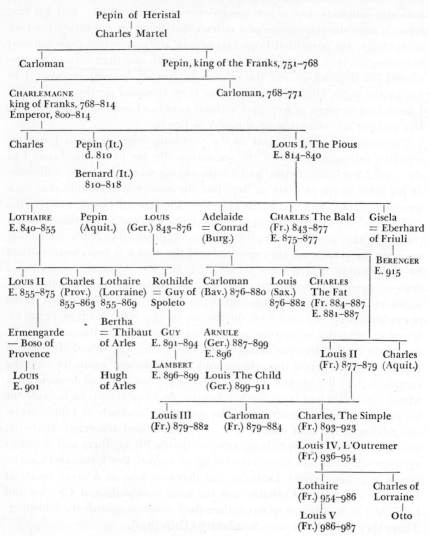

Pepin of Heristal

Charles Martel

Carloman   Pepin, king of the Franks, 751–768

CHARLEMAGNE   Carloman, 768–771
king of Franks, 768–814
Emperor, 800–814

Charles   Pepin (It.)   LOUIS I, The Pious
             d. 810   E. 814–840

             Bernard (It.)
             810–818

LOTHAIRE   Pepin   LOUIS   Adelaide   CHARLES The Bald   Gisela
E. 840–855 (Aquit.)   (Ger.) 843–876 = Conrad (Fr.) 843–877   = Eberhard
                                  (Burg.)   E. 875–877   of Friuli

                                                                BERENGER
                                                                E. 915

LOUIS II   Charles Lothaire Rothilde Carloman   Louis   CHARLES
E. 855–875 (Prov.) (Lorraine) = Guy of (Bav.) 876–880 (Sax.) The Fat
           855–863 855–869 Spoleto   876–882 (Fr. 884–887
                                                        E. 881–887

                   Bertha
Ermengarde   = Thibaut GUY   ARNULE
— Boso of   of Arles   E. 891–894 (Ger.) 887–899
Provence   E. 896   Louis II   Charles
                             LAMBERT   (Fr.) 877–879 (Aquit.)
LOUIS   E. 896–899 Louis The Child
E. 901   Hugh   (Ger.) 899–911
                  of Arles

                   Louis III   Carloman   Charles, The Simple
                   (Fr.) 879–882 (Fr.) 879–884 (Fr.) 893–923

                                             Louis IV, L'Outremer
                                             (Fr.) 936–954

                                   Lothaire   Charles of
                                   (Fr.) 954–986   Lorraine

                                   Louis V   Otto
                                   (Fr.) 986–987

importance as they show the development of language at this point; whether the Roman form was the last appearance of Vulgar Latin or the first appearance of Old French is entirely immaterial and can be left to philologists to wrangle over. That it was something neither classical Latin nor yet French will be apparent:

Louis swore:

Pro deo amur et pro christian poblo et nostro commun salvament, d'ist di in avant, in quant deus savir et podir me dunat, si salvaraeio cist meon fradre Karlo et in aiudha et in cadhuna cosa, si cum om per dreit son fradra salvar dist, in o quid il mi altresi fazet, et ab Ludher nul plaid numquam prindrai, qui meon vol cist meon fradre Karle in damno sit.[3]

To this Charles in the German of the time swore:

In godes minna ind in thes christanes folches ind unser bedhero gehaltnissi, fon thesemo dage frammordes, so fram so mir got geuuizci indi mahd furgibit, so haldih thesan minan bruodher, soso man mit rehtu sinan bruodher seal, in thiu thaz er mig so sama duo, indi mit Ludheren in nohheiniu thing ne gegango, the minan uuilon imo ce scadhen uuerdhen.

Whereupon Charles' followers swore:

Si Lodhuuigs sagrament, que son fradre Karlo iurat, conservat, et Karlus meos sendra de suo part non los tanit, si io returnar non l'int pois; ne io ne neuls, cui eo returnar int pois, in nulla aiudha contra Lodhuuuig nun li iv er.[4]

And Louis' men swore:

Oba Karl then eid, then er sinemo bruodher Ludhuuuige gesuor, geleistit, indi Ludhuuuig min herro then er imo gesuor forbrihchit, ob ih inan es iruuenden ne mag; noh ih noh thero nohein, then ih es iruuenden mag, uuidhar Karle imo ce follusti ne uuirdhit.

As it happened both kings did keep the oath; they invaded Lothaire's lands and drove him from one place to another, but were distracted by rebellions and invasions in their own lands so that they were willing to accept the mediation of the bishops and agreed to a peace. The Treaty of Verdun (843), which resulted, laid out the general lines of the national development of western Europe and began some of the thorniest problems, which have troubled European statesmen even until our own day.

The Treaty of Verdun divided the empire into an eastern, western and

[3] By God's love and by this Christian people and our common salvation, from this day forth as far as God gives me to know and to have power, I will so aid this my brother Charles (Louis) in each and every thing as a man ought to aid his brother, in so far as he shall do the same for me; and I will never have any dealings with Lothaire that may by my wish injure this my brother Charles (Louis).

[4] If Louis (Charles) keeps the oath which he swore to his brother Charles (Louis) and Charles (Louis) my lord, on his part does not keep it, if I cannot prevent it, then neither I nor anyone whom I can prevent shall ever defend him against Louis (Charles).

(Text and translation from Thatcher & McNeal Source Book, 1907, pp. 61–62. Reprinted by permission of the publishers, Charles Scribner's Sons).

central part. No account was taken of national feelings for there were no national feelings to consider. The whole thing was feudal, being based on domain lands, abbeys, old counties, and benefices. Charles was given the west including old Neustria and Aquitaine; Louis had Saxony, Bavaria, and the lands east of the Rhine (except Frisia in the north); Lothaire had the middle kingdom, Italy, Burgundy, the land along the Rhine, Meuse, Rhone, and Scheldt, including the two capitals of Rome and Aix-la-Chapelle. Louis' lands later became Germany, Charles' evolved gradually into France and Lothaire's became Italy, Provence, Burgundy, and Lotharingia or Lorraine. But these were all developments of the future; while Charles' subjects generally spoke the Roman speech and Louis', the German, Lothaire's were hopelessly mixed. The middle kingdom which Lothaire ruled has never been successfully divided, and the idea of reviving it was the cardinal point in the dreams of Charles the Bold of Burgundy in the fifteenth century.

THE BREAKDOWN OF THE CAROLINGIAN EMPIRE

Too much emphasis must not, however, be placed on the Treaty of Verdun. Its provisions were, in fact, quite ephemeral. Lothaire died in 855 and his kingdom was divided between his three sons: Louis II received Italy, Lothaire got the northern lands to the Alps, and Charles took Provence. When Lothaire died his uncles Charles and Louis divided his lands at the Treaty of Meersen in 870, splitting Lotharingia down the middle and creating the vexing problem of Alsace-Lorraine which with the growth of nationalism in modern times has been such a bone of contention between France and Germany.

The treaties of Verdun and Meersen only emphasized the breakdown which was affecting the empire throughout. Although there was theoretically an emperor ruling over the entire state, and though kings fought desperately for this empty title, the unity of the empire did not survive Louis I and the various parts thereof went their own ways with their own separate histories, sometimes converging, but often quite independent.

The imperial title was one of the first casualties. From Lothaire I, it passed on his death in 855 to his eldest son Louis II (855–875). At Louis' death, the crown was offered by various factions to each of his uncles, Louis the German and Charles the Bald; Charles got there first and was crowned emperor (875–877). Carloman, the son of Louis the German, opposed his pretensions, and was able to secure the crown of Italy at Charles' death in 877; but he was himself never crowned emperor and died soon thereafter. For a time there was no emperor at all, then Charles the Fat of Germany, the younger brother of Carloman, was crowned emperor in 881. He completed the unification of the realms by securing his election as king of the west Franks in 884, but was deposed from all his titles and offices by the nobles in 887. With him the Carolingian empire as any sort of a unit came to an end.

During this period of confusion two new states developed in the old middle kingdom. Boso of Provence, who had married the daughter of Louis II, established himself with a virtually independent state in Southern Burgundy around the mouth of the Rhone, and another state was carved out of northern Burgundy (Besançon, Geneva, Lausanne, western Switzerland, and Franche Comté) by a certain Rudolph who styled himself king of Burgundy.

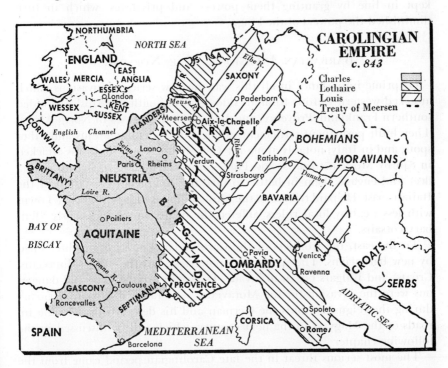

Meanwhile, in the western kingdom, the Carolingians were dragging out a miserable existence. Charles the Bald was succeeded by his son Louis II (877–879), who in turn left the kingdom to his sons Louis III (879–882) and Carloman (879–884). When Carloman died the nobles passed over Charles the Simple, a younger brother of Louis and Carloman, and elected Charles the Fat of Germany (884–887).

This dismal chronicle of successions is fortunately the least important aspect of the history of any of the Carolingian states at this time. It is necessary to show the division of the empire, but apart from the main fact it is of little significance.

Of far greater importance was the growth of the great noble houses, the complete breakdown of the central state into a complex of feudal states, and the new wave of barbarian invasion which threatened the empire from without.

The rise of the great duchies and feudal principalities will be discussed in later chapters on France and Germany. Suffice it to note here how the feudal principle was undermining the imperial or tribal. Larger territorial units were breaking down everywhere into smaller; royal powers and duties were everywhere being usurped by private individuals; the crown was helpless without the support of the barons and the barons could only be kept in line by granting them powers and privileges, which in turn diminished the powers of the king.

Barbarian Invasions: The Norsemen

Of prime importance in all this was the new series of invasions which attacked western Europe from all sides. To the south the Moslems raided southern Frankland, Provence, and Italy from their bases in North Africa. They built permanent settlements along the Riviera at Frejus and other spots, and in Italy, notably along the Garigliano. Rome itself was attacked in 846 by Moslem corsairs, and Pope John VIII (872–882) had to raise a fleet and engage them in battle to save the complete devastation of the Italian coast. He paid tribute to the Moslems to save his capital city. Towns with less wealthy local rulers suffered the incursions of these early "Barbary corsairs."

To the east, the frontiers of the Carolingian Empire were threatened by new barbarians. The Avars were powerless, but the Slavs (Moravians, Croats) and Bulgars began to invade. Especially troublesome and dangerous were the invasions of the Moravians, who ravaged eastern Germany during the reigns of Louis the German and his descendants, and the inroads of the Magyars in the next century, which will be discussed in the following chapter.

The most serious threat in the late Carolingian period came from the Norsemen. These inhabitants of the Scandinavian peninsula erupted over Europe under a number of names; in England they were known as the Danes, in France as the Norsemen, in the eastern Baltic regions as the Varangs. The causes of their sudden eruption have been given variously as overpopulation and as the fleeing of the local tribal chieftains before the centralizing efforts of the newly founded monarchies. At any rate the first Norsemen to take to the sea in their long ships were known as Vikings, a term which designated these refugees.

The Norse invasions covered a period of over two centuries, but the later movements were expeditions directed by kings of Denmark or Norway and were not the same type of movement as the early invasions of the late eighth and ninth centuries. At first they appeared as mere traders, indulging in a bit of piracy or plunder if the occasion arose, but often as not purely peaceful in their purpose. Thus they traded with the Frisians in the early eighth century. Then they gave up trade for the more profitable pursuit of piracy; every spring they would come down in their long ships, land on the coasts or sail up the rivers and raid a town or abbey. Having plundered, they would depart for home with their loot and there would be peace for another season. One of the first places to be attacked was England. There they landed at Lindisfarne and burned the monastery (794); next they overran all Northumbria; by 798 they had entered the mouth of the Thames and by 837 were pillaging all the way around the coast of Cornwall. The winter of 851 marked an epoch in these raids, for then for the first time the Danes wintered on the isle of Thanet. Once landed they elected to stay; they overran Northumbria, Mercia, East Anglia, and forced the Saxon kingdoms into an unprecedented union against them. Alfred the Great in 879 made a treaty with their chief Gunthram, whereby Gunthram accepted Christianity and was recognized as lord of the Danelaw, the whole of northeastern England and southern Scotland.

As a matter of fact these Norse were not so different from either the Saxons or the Franks. They were the same race and stock, only a bit less civilized, more brutal, not yet affected by the restraining influences of Christianity or Roman culture. One of the remarkable things about the Norsemen was the rapidity with which they assimilated the customs and characteristics of the lands they conquered: how quickly the Norsemen became the Normans. In England, even by the time of the Norman Conquest, it would have been hard to distinguish the Danelaw from Saxon England; a few differences in names, a few variations in local custom, but essentially the same culture and the same folk.

On the continent, the Norsemen turned their attention first to the Low Countries and to the mouths of the Seine and the Loire. As long as the imperial defenses held up at all, the Norse raids on the empire were not of tremendous gravity, but when the civil wars began during the latter years of Louis I's reign, the Norse seized the opportunity to increase their raids. In 840 they burned Rouen, and in the following years they made repeated raids up the Seine, in 845 reaching Paris. They pushed on, sailed up the Loire to Tours and Orleans, up the Somme to Amiens, up the Garonne to Toulouse. Annually the Norsemen raided the fields of western Frankland; towns and monasteries were burned, all valuables were carried off, massacre and rape attended the raids and the people seemed powerless against this new scourge. Tribute proved ineffective; the monks of St. Denis began in 845 to pay the marauders to spare them, the Norsemen took the money and then pillaged. All they could do was pray: "From the fury of the Norsemen, good Lord, deliver us."

The Carolingian monarchs were apparently powerless to prevent these ravages. They had so dissipated their power in civil war and imperial quarreling that they had none left for local defense. Occasionally they bestirred themselves; Paris was the key city in the defense of northern Frankland against the Norse, and Charles the Bald endeavored to build up there strong defenses. He also created in the lands between the Seine and the Loire a new march under the powerful noble, Robert the Strong, count of Anjou, Blois, and Touraine (861). For a time under the able rule of Robert, the Seine-Loire region enjoyed comparative peace, while the Norse devoted all their energies to England. Then in 879 there was a grand invasion on a truly great scale; encamped near Ghent, the Norsemen raided the Low Countries; they came up the Rhine to Aix and Cologne. In 881 Louis of Saxony (the son of Louis the German) defeated them at Saucourt, but Charles the Fat let all advantage slip out of his hands. In 882 he ceded to the Norse the province of Frisia (setting a precedent for the treaty of Charles the Simple in 911). Meanwhile the long ships had carried their crews to the south where they twice took Bordeaux, and sailed up the Tagus, Duoro, and Guadalquivir rivers in Spain. Passing through the straits of Gibraltar, they came around to the Rhone and pillaged Nîmes and Avignon. What the Moslem left the Norseman carried away.

A turning point in the Norse invasions of Frankland and of the Franks themselves was the great siege of Paris of 885–886. Count Eudes, the son of Robert the Strong, defended his city with heroic zeal. For almost a year the city held out while Charles the Fat tarried in Italy. When the king-emperor did arrive it was to purchase peace by tribute. Nothing could have been a greater contrast than the conduct of Eudes and Charles on this occasion; the Franks were not men to forget such an incident. When the German nobles became disaffected, those of the west supported the movement to unseat Charles, and with his fall in 888 Eudes was elevated to the throne of the western Franks.

England and the Frankish empire were not the only places to feel the brunt of the Norse invasions. Ireland, which had been unaffected by the German invasions and had preserved a relatively high culture in her monasteries, was attacked by the sea-rovers in 795, their inroads assuming serious proportions around 830 and thereafter. They settled, as in England and the continent, at the mouths of rivers, Danish settlements being established at Dublin, Cork, Limerick, and Wexford. The Danes organized a kingdom at Dublin, which lasted until overthrown by the Irish in 1014.

Beyond Ireland to the west, the Norse settled Iceland (874) whence they expanded on to establish colonies in Greenland (986) and, under Leif

Ericson, even reached the coast of North America which they called Vinland (c. 1000). Greenland was never more than a small fishing colony, but Iceland developed into an important state with its own institutions and, after conversion to Christianity, its own bishop.

While the Norse and Danes were expanding to the west, a group of Swedes pushed east along the coasts of the Baltic and down the rivers along its southern shore, to found the Russian states discussed in Chapter 8 above.

And as we shall see in a later chapter, the Norse, become Normans, continued the work of expansion carrying with them the culture of the Franks modified by the contributions of their own peculiar genius.

CHAPTER 10

GERMANY AND THE PAPACY

✤

WHILE the Byzantine Empire was reaching its apogee under the Macedonian dynasty, Western Europe was rearranging itself after the breakup of the Carolingian Empire. While there always remained an imperial idea in the west, the substance of power passed into the hands of the local dukes and counts, and the new monarchs who developed were feudal rather than tribal rulers. From this maze of local authorities a new empire arose, the Holy Roman Empire of the German people, which carried on the traditions of the Roman and Carolingian empires, but in a purely teutonic and feudal manner. The papacy meanwhile declined to be the pawn of local Italian magnates, until it was revived to become the chaplains of the German emperors. In southern Italy the Normans founded a new monarchy.

CAROLINGIAN AND SAXON KINGS, 877–936

In the East Frankish kingdom decentralization under the last Carolingians resulted in the growth of five great states, called "stem duchies." These duchies, which were once thought to have been tribal states, were in reality only feudal principalities established by the counts of the Carolingians, the tendency in Germany exactly paralleling that in France, though the feudalization was not so complete. The Liudolfs in Saxony and the Luitpolds in Bavaria set themselves up as practically independent rulers, assuming the title of dukes, a similar process following in Swabia under the descendants of Burchard, in Franconia under the Conradins, and in Lorraine.

At the deposition of Charles the Fat in 887, the throne of Germany passed to an illegitimate Carolingian, Arnulf (887–889), who spent his reign in fighting off the Magyars who invaded Germany from the east and in endeavoring to make his authority felt in Italy, which had broken down into the most frightful anarchy. There Berenger of Friuli and Guy of Spoleto, both of whom claimed Carolingian descent, were fighting for the empty title of emperor and the control of Italy, while the actual power was passing into the hands of the local nobles. Though Arnulf made expeditions to Italy and secured some authority over the Italian nobles, his control was ephemeral and shadowy, all authority ending with the withdrawal of the German forces. While his rule in Germany was unchallenged,

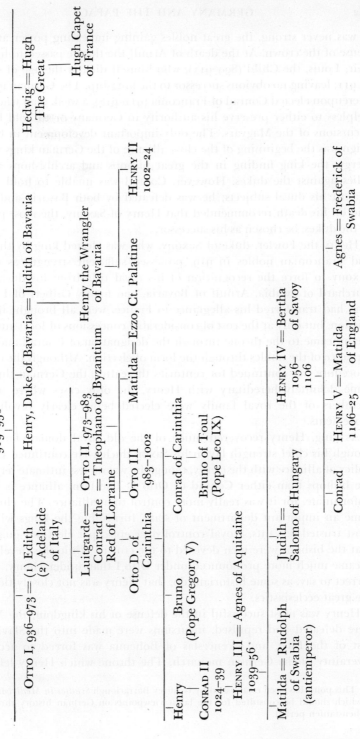

SAXON AND SALIAN EMPERORS OF THE HOLY ROMAN EMPIRE

Henry I, the Fowler = Matilda
919–936

Otto I, 936–973 = (1) Edith
          = (2) Adelaide of Italy

Hedwig = Hugh The Great

Hugh Capet of France

Henry, Duke of Bavaria = Judith of Bavaria

Luitgarde = Otto II, 973–983 = Theophano of Byzantium
Conrad the Red of Lorraine

Henry the Wrangler of Bavaria

Matilda = Ezzo, Ct. Palatine

Henry II 1002–24

Otto D. of Carinthia

Otto III 983–1002

Conrad of Carinthia

Bruno of Toul (Pope Leo IX)

Henry

Bruno (Pope Gregory V)

Conrad II 1024–39

Henry III = Agnes of Aquitaine
1039–56

Henry IV = Bertha of Savoy
1056–1106

Agnes = Frederick of Swabia

Matilda = Rudolph of Swabia (antiemperor)

Judith = Salomo of Hungary

Conrad

Henry V = Matilda of England
1106–25

it was never strong, the great nobles gaining increasing power at the expense of the crown. At the death of Arnulf the throne passed to his minor heir, Louis, the Child (899–911), who himself died at the age of eighteen in 911, leaving no obvious successor to the kingship. The German magnates thereupon elected Conrad of Franconia (911–918), a weak man who proved helpless to either preserve his authority in Germany or to hold back the incursions of the Magyars. The only important development in Conrad's reign was the beginning of the close alliance of the German kings with the clergy, the king finding in the great bishops and archbishops valuable allies against the dukes. However, Conrad was unable to hold his own against his ducal subjects; he was defeated by both Bavaria and Swabia and on his death recommended that Henry of Saxony, the most powerful of the dukes, be chosen as his successor.

Henry the Fowler, duke of Saxony, who was elected king by the Saxon and Franconian nobles in 919, possessed sufficient strength as duke of Saxony to force the recognition of his royal title from his ducal rivals. Burchard of Swabia, Arnulf of Bavaria, and finally Gilbert of Lorraine, who had transferred his allegiance to France, were all brought into submission, but only at the cost of considerable concessions of local autonomy. Henry came to the throne through the designation of Conrad and the acceptance of the nobles through the form of election. Although the electoral procedure was continued for centuries thereafter, the German throne became definitely hereditary with Henry, the only cases where men not members of the royal family were elected being clearly revolutionary movements.[1]

As king, Henry recovered much of the old royal domain in Swabia, though his chief strength lay in his Saxon duchy. He continued Conrad's policy of alliance with the clergy, though he was on less intimate terms with the bishops than either Conrad or Otto I. The term alliance is perhaps unfortunate, for it was really more control than alliance. The church became an important department of state, furnishing the kings with their most trusted servants. Royal control over episcopal elections guaranteed that the bishops were men devoted to the crown. While this development became much more pronounced under Otto I than under Henry, it is not correct to say, as some historians do, that Henry was not closely tied up to the great ecclesiastics.

Henry was most successful in the defense of his kingdom; the Magyars were defeated and repulsed, incursions were made into the Slavic lands east of the Elbe, and Wenceslas of Bohemia was forced to accept the suzerainty of the German monarch. The throne which Henry left to his

---

[1] This point has been established by Geoffrey Barraclough *Studies in Medieval History*, I, which should be consulted for the latest viewpoints on German history through the Hohenstaufen period.

son Otto I (936–973) was a much stronger one than that which he had
mounted seventeen years before. His succession was guaranteed by his
father's securing the assent of the nobles before his own death, the only
serious opposition coming from his younger brother, Henry, who claimed
the throne as porphyrogenitus.[2]

THE REIGN OF OTTO I: IMPERIAL REVIVAL OF 962

Unlike his father who was interested principally in Germany and even
in Saxony, Otto I dreamed of the imperial throne. "His objective was
Empire, and his model was Charlemagne." [3] But if he dreamed of empire,
Otto kept a firm hand on the realities of German politics; it is under him
that the administrative machinery of government was established with the
establishment of the royal chanceries and other royal officials. Throughout
his reign he was forced to withstand revolts at home and pressure of foreign
enemies from without. To meet the problem of the insurgent dukes, Otto
developed a system of dynastic alliances whereby he succeeded in securing
all of the great duchies to relatives or in-laws. At the same time he increased the domain lands of the crown and made the counts directly subordinate to himself, rather than through the dukes.

Otto's plan in regard to the duchies proved singularly unsuccessful.
Although the dukes were all related to the king, this did not ensure their
loyalty, and Otto had to fight his relatives in many campaigns. His brother
Henry, who had revolted spasmodically until 941, was made duke of
Bavaria and remained loyal to the king thereafter, but Otto's son Liudolf,
whom he had made duke of Swabia, and his son-in-law, Conrad of Lorraine, revolted in 953, and had to be deprived of their fiefs. Abandoning
his policy of appanages, Otto appointed new dukes chosen from the nobility
of the regions concerned.

In regard to his neighbors, Otto's policies were most successful. He
reconstituted the old Danish mark, built a new mark in the northeast,
which he entrusted to Herman Billung; put down a rebellion in Bohemia,
and forced it back under the German suzerainty; and played the part of
mediator between the rival claimants to the throne of France, both of
whom were married to his sisters. His greatest fame in this connection was,
however, in his crushing of the Magyars.

In 937 the Magyars had invaded Germany in force, pushing straight
through Germany to sack Rheims and Sens in France; in the following year
they raided Saxony. Although Otto was able to defeat them in Saxony, he
was unable to defend all Germany from these fierce invaders, and often

---

[2] As we have seen above, this means born in the porphyry chamber, and is the term
used to designate the child of a crowned monarch as opposed to children born before his
accession to the throne.

[3] Z. N. Brooke, *History of Europe, 911–1198*, p. 26.

in his reign, eastern Germany, especially Bavaria, was subject to Magyar raids. Finally in 955 they made a great incursion which took them to Augsburg. Assembling troops from Saxony, Franconia, Swabia, Bavaria, and Bohemia, Otto met the Magyars at the battle of the Lech, where the Magyar host was destroyed and their power was broken forever. The invasion of 955 was the last great raid the Magyars made on the West; after this defeat, they retired to the Danubian plains where they settled down to build the kingdom of Hungary and to take their place among the civilized nations of Europe. Under King St. Stephen, the Magyars were converted to Christianity at the end of the century, becoming a vassal state of the papacy, and moving generally in the orbit of German-Roman policy.

Otto I not only saved Germany from the Magyars and gave it a strong internal administration, he also revived the Roman Empire. In 951 he made his first Italian expedition to rescue Queen Adelaide, the beautiful sister of Conrad of Burgundy and widow of King Lothaire, who had been dispossessed of her kingdom of Italy by Berenger II of Ivrea who was establishing himself as king in Italy. Otto's aims in this expedition were multiple: he sought to marry Adelaide, secure control of Italy, and be crowned emperor at Rome. In the first he was successful; Adelaide escaped from the prison where Berenger had placed her, joined Otto and married him (thus allying him to the old Carolingian house). But when Otto sought the imperial crown at the hands of Pope Agapetus, the pope, who was the tool of Alberic, the senator of Rome, refused. Rebellion in Germany called Otto home and he left Italy with his mission only partly accomplished.

Ten years later he returned and fulfilled his ambition. Pope John XII appealed to him for help against Berenger; Otto marched south, entered Rome and on February 2, 962 was crowned emperor. For the rest of his reign Otto was kept busy with the affairs of Italy. Not only did he have to beat down Berenger, but he was compelled to force his authority over the unruly Roman nobles. In 963, he made the Romans swear that they would never elect a pope without the approval of the emperor, thus gaining control over the papacy.

But the control over central Italy and the assumption of the imperial title brought Otto into conflict with the Byzantine emperor. Adalbert, the son of Berenger, appealed to Nicephorus Phocas for help. To counter this Otto sought control over Byzantine south Italy and moved down to Capua and Benevento. At first he sought the friendship of the basileus, but a mission headed by Archbishop Luitprand of Cremona failed. Luitprand's account of his "Mission to Constantinople" is one of the most interesting documents of the tenth century, valuable not only for his description of Constantinople under Nicephorus, but for the light it throws on the comparative civilizations of the East and West. On the failure of negotiations,

Otto invaded Apulia to be defeated in an attempt to capture Bari, but the assassination of Nicephorus and the accession of John Tzmisces in Byzantium opened the way for negotiation again and a treaty was arranged whereby Otto kept the suzerainty over Capua and Benevento, but gave up all attempts against Apulia. At the same time a marriage alliance was concluded between his son Otto II and Theophano, the daughter of Romanus II (972). Shortly thereafter Otto I died (May 7, 973) passing his thrones on to Otto II, his son by Adelaide.

THE PAPACY IN THE TENTH CENTURY

Before proceeding further with the history of the empire it will be necessary to turn briefly to the story of the papacy, which Otto I brought under the control of the emperors. Since the days of Nicholas I (858–867) the papacy had been steadily declining, and the popes had become the tools of the local Roman nobility. Towards the beginning of the tenth century a powerful noble, Theophylact, aided by his beautiful and unscrupulous wife, Theodora, secured control of Rome. Their daughter Marozia became the central figure of a corrupt society which completely dominated both the city and the papacy. Marozia herself married as her third husband Hugh of Provence, then king of Italy. One of her sons became pope as John XI (931–936), while another, Alberic, assumed the title of "prince and senator of the Romans" and ruled Rome, appointing four popes in the years 932 to 954.

Meanwhile the struggle for the somewhat empty title of King of Italy was being fought out by a number of pretenders, who traced their claims to Carolingian decent. Berenger of Friuli and his grandson Berenger of Ivrea represented one line; Hugh of Provence and his son Lothaire another; Rudolph of Burgundy a third. Berenger I was able to hold the royal title until his death in 924; then Hugh of Provence secured it for himself and for his son. To gain the support of Burgundy in his plans, Hugh ceded Provence to Rudolph, who gave his daughter Adelaide in marriage to Hugh's son Lothaire. But in 947 Berenger of Ivrea, the grandson of Berenger I, overthrew Hugh and seized the crown. Lothaire opposed him but died two years later, and Berenger captured and imprisoned Lothaire's widow, Adelaide. It was in answer to the appeal of Adelaide that Otto I came down in 951.

As we have seen, Otto was not able to receive the imperial crown in 951 because of the opposition of Alberic, who forbade his pope, Agapetus, to crown the German monarch. It was only after the death of Alberic that his son John XII, who had broken with Berenger over the control of Rome, called Otto back and accorded him the crown. After the imperial intervention, the papacy passed from the hands of the local nobles into that of

the emperors, who appointed candidates to the Holy See for several generations until the rise of the counts of Tusculum once again made the papacy
the pawn of local Italian politics in the eleventh century.

Perhaps the most remarkable thing about the history of the papacy in
the tenth century is that in spite of the degradation of the popes and the
utterly unworthy characters of many of them, the papal office increased in
prestige abroad. The scandals were kept at Rome and the prestige of the
papacy as the head of the church was enhanced by the missionary activities
in the north and east and by the Cluniac reform movement which began
in this period. Though the persons declined, the office increased and the
institution of the papacy showed no ill effects from the period of degradation.

Otto II and Otto III, 973–1002

Otto II (973–983) ascended the throne at the age of only eighteen; with
an Italian mother and a Byzantine wife, he was even more interested in
Italy than his father had been, but he had to spend much of his reign
struggling in Germany against the ambitions of his cousin Henry the
Wrangler of Bavaria. It was in the course of his struggle with Bavaria that
Otto II created the East Mark (Austria) under Luitpold of Babenberg.
He was also compelled to fight the Bohemians and Poles, both of whom
he forced back into submission, to drive back an invasion by Harold
Bluetooth of Denmark, and to fight Lothaire of France for the possession
of Lorraine. By 980, however, Otto had defeated all his enemies in the
north and was able to turn his undivided attention to Italy. Marching
south through Pavia and Rome, Otto came to southern Italy where he
found himself involved in struggles with both the Byzantines and Moslems.
Severely defeated in battle by the Moslems, Otto was compelled to retreat
to the north, where he died while planning a second expedition south
(December, 983). He is the only emperor of the Holy Roman Empire who
was buried in St. Peter's cathedral at Rome.

The news of the death of Otto II and the accession of his three-year-old
son was the signal for general revolt in the north. The Slavs east of the Elbe
rose in a concerted rebellion, which destroyed most of the German colonies
that had been planted in their country: not until the colonizing activity of
the Welfs in the twelfth century was the district between the Elbe and the
Oder brought again under German control. At the same time Sweyn Fork-
beard of Denmark, who had deposed his Christian father Harold and
re-established the old paganism, overran the Danish mark and made it
independent of Germany. Henry the Wrangler demanded the regency for
Otto III and captured the king, but Adelaide and Theophano, supported
by the archbishop of Maintz and the nobles of Saxony, Franconia, Swabia

and Lorraine, were able to overpower him and get control of the king and government. Theophano edged out Adelaide after a year, and for the remainder of her life, until 991, the Byzantine princess ruled Germany and Italy with remarkably efficient skill. Meanwhile she indoctrinated her son with a Byzantine concept of empire, so that he considered himself not only a second Charlemagne, but also a second Constantine.

The control of Rome and the papacy had again fallen into the hands of a Roman family, the Crescentii, whose position was much like that of Theophylact or Alberic in the preceding century. Although Theophano had been recognized as empress, Crescentius continued to rule Rome as Patrician. A quarrel between Crescentius and his appointee, Pope John XV, gave Otto III an excuse to intervene in Roman affairs in 996. He came to Rome to find John dead; the Romans asked him to appoint the next pope and his choice fell on his twenty-four-year-old cousin, Bruno, the first German to ascend the papal throne. Bruno, who took the name of Gregory V (996–999) obligingly crowned Otto emperor, and Otto returned to Aix-la-Chapelle where he attempted a revival of the court of Charle-magne. It was at this time that Otto became intimate with Gerbert, the great teacher of Rheims, who became the imperial favorite, and who as Pope Sylvester II (999–1003) was to co-operate with Otto in the most per-fect accord, showing the reality of the old Gelasian theory of emperor and pope as two co-ordinate leaders of a single society.

Gerbert undoubtedly influenced Otto in his idea of the *"Renovatio Imperii Romanorum"* which Otto used as his motto on his seals. The new Constantine was seconded in his work by the new Sylvester, as Constantine I was believed to have been aided by Sylvester I. Rome, to which Otto removed in 999, was to be the center of the Christian empire, whose head was the emperor "servant of the apostles," with the pope his chief lieu-tenant. In pursuance of his ideal, Otto made a great pilgrimage in 1000 to Poland which he hoped to bind more closely to both church and em-pire. He even sent an embassy to Russia in the hope of winning it over to Roman allegiance. In 1001 he made a new Donation of Constantine, grant-ing the papacy by imperial favor the eight counties of the Pentapolis. In Rome he constructed a new palace on the Aventine, at the same time showering favors on the people and nobles of the city, especially on the counts of Tusculum, descendants of Alberic and rivals of the disgraced Crescentii.

But the Roman people are traditionally known for their fickle tempers; under the leadership of this same count of Tusculum, the Romans revolted against the emperor because he refused to destroy utterly the rival town of Tivoli. The populace rose in the streets; Otto was besieged in the Castle Sant'Angelo, whence he withdrew to Ravenna. While he was preparing his forces to recapture Rome he died of a fever at the age of twenty-one.

The death of the emperor brought the end of this imperial dream. Otto, mystic and visionary, had in reality only weakened the imperial position by his far-flung schemes. He had lost power in Germany and had gained nothing in Italy. On the death of Gerbert in 1003, the Crescentii and the counts of Tusculum again began their struggle for the control of Rome and the papacy, which latter declined again from the high place it held under Gerbert to become once more the puppet of the Roman nobility. Otto's seven years were splendid and magnificent, but both Germany and Italy reaped the whirlwind at the end.

THE IMPERIAL SUCCESSION, 1002-39

As Otto III left no direct heirs, the throne passed at his death to his cousin, Henry II (1002-24), duke of Bavaria, the son of Henry the Wrangler and great-grandson of Henry I. Henry II is the only German emperor to achieve the honor of canonization, which he received not only for his great personal piety, but for his zeal for church reform. Henry had the usual trouble with the dukes and was also forced to struggle with some of the greater churchmen, who were not sympathetic with the reform movement within the church. Although successful in maintaining his suzerainty over Bohemia and Hungary, he was defeated by Boleslav of Poland (992-1025), who defeated the Germans in a series of campaigns and proclaimed himself independent king of Poland.

Italy had broken away from the empire at the death of Otto; Ardoin of Ivrea proclaimed himself king of Italy, defeating an army sent against him by Henry in 1002, while in Rome the counts of Tusculum and the Crescentii struggled for control. Henry made three expeditions into the peninsula: in 1004 he defeated Ardoin and burned Pavia but was called back to Germany by troubles in Bohemia; in 1013 to 1014 he came to Rome where he was crowned emperor and ordered the affairs of central Italy; and in 1021 to 1022 he was brought back by the pope (Benedict VIII, 1012-24) to help papal designs against the Byzantines in Apulia. During this expedition a synod was held which promulgated ecclesiastical reform measures, especially in the matter of clerical celibacy.

When Henry II died in 1024 without heirs, the nobles chose as his successor the nearest relative descended from the old royal house in the person of Conrad of Franconia, a great-great-grandson of Otto I through the female line, thus inaugurating the Salian line of emperors.

Conrad II (1024-39) was fortunate in his relations with the great dukes, the only serious ducal rebellion being that of his step-son Ernest of Swabia. Eventually both Swabia and Bavaria passed into the royal hands and were given by Conrad to his son Henry. Conrad was also able to secure the inheritance of the kingdom of Burgundy, which he inherited from Ru-

dolph III in 1033, and to which he made good his claims against the aspirations of Eudes of Champagne, who was backed by the king of France.
In the east, Conrad reasserted the German control over Poland after the
death of Boleslav, but was defeated in a campaign in Hungary. The
northern frontier was assured by a close alliance with King Canute of
Denmark to whom he ceded Schleswig, the alliance being reinforced by
the marriage of Prince Henry to Canute's daughter, Gunnhild.

In Italy Conrad made several campaigns. In 1027 he went to Rome
to receive the imperial crown; in 1036 he went back to restore order in the
north where civil war had broken out among the nobles. Conrad systematically favored the lesser nobles against the greater, at the same time
appointing Germans to key positions in the administration. He tied Italy
and Germany together by a series of marriage alliances which united the
German and Italian houses: one of these, the marriage of Azzo d'Este
marquis of Tuscany to Kunigunde the heiress of the Welf lands in Swabia,
was to result in the formation of the fortune of the Welf house. The introduction of Germans into the government of Italy antagonized the bishops,
who had previously been the chief agents of the empire in the peninsula,
archbishop Aribert of Milan especially leading his city into open revolt
against the emperor.

In all his administration, Conrad relied on a new class of officials, the
ministeriales, servile tenants of the crown domains whom he employed
as royal agents. These unfree ministeriales, who were wholly dependent
on the royal favor, proved effective agents and became an important element in the German administration.

Conrad died in June 1039 as the result of a fever contracted during an
expedition to south Italy the previous year. He was succeeded by his son
Henry III (1039–56), under whom the medieval German empire is generally conceded to have reached its height. Henry III had already been
crowned king during his father's lifetime, so had no difficulty on his own
accession to the throne. Personally very devout, he threw himself into the
cause of ecclesiastical reform, winning back the support of the clergy which
had been weakened somewhat under Conrad. Germany and Italy were
both relatively peaceful during his reign, and he succeeded in putting
down revolts and securing the full submission and vassalage of the rulers
of Bohemia, Poland and Hungary.

HENRY III AND THE REFORM OF THE PAPACY, 1039–49

The greatest accomplishment of Henry III was, however, his intervention in papal affairs and his re-establishment of the imperial control
over the church.

In 1012 Alberic, count of Tusculum, had seized control of Rome and had established his dominance over the papacy. His brother Benedict VIII (1012–24) was an able warrior, who defeated the Saracens in Italy and encouraged the republics of Pisa and Genoa to unite in the conquest of Sardinia from the Moslems. Benedict was indifferent to church reform but was willing to give it lip-service to gain the support of Henry II. At his death he was followed by another brother, John XIX (1024–32), who was content to let abuses run rife and who ruled chiefly for the benefit of his house. At the end of his uneventful pontificate he was succeeded by Alberic's ten-year-old son who became pope with the name of Benedict IX (1032–45).

Benedict IX brought the papacy to a new depth of degradation; young and naturally vicious by temperament, he scandalized even the disreputable Roman society by the licentiousness of his amours and the corruption of his rule. After twelve years of this regime, the Romans rose, and, under the leadership of the rival house of Crescentii, drove Benedict out of the city. A nominee of the Crescentii was then elected pope as Sylvester III. Sylvester never gained complete control and was soon thereafter driven out in turn by Benedict, who returned to the papal throne. He seems to have wearied of it, however, as the following May he suddenly sold the papacy to an arch-priest, John Gratian, who ascended the throne as Gregory VI. Benedict is said to have done this so that he could marry, but he soon repented of his actions and returned to drive out Gregory.

The open sale of the papacy was an act of flagrant simony such as the church had never witnessed before. There was considerable question as to whether a pope could dispose of the holy office, and certainly to sell it openly broke every canon of the law. But Gratian was backed by the reforming party in the church; two of his most ardent supporters were the deacon Hildebrand and the monk Peter Damiani, and he bought the papacy to reform it. However, whatever his motives, the means taken were illegal and scandalous in the extreme, and decent men repudiated the whole transaction. The stench of Rome reached into Germany where it offended the nostrils of the pious emperor. Henry III came down into Italy intent on cleaning the Augean stables of the church. At Sutri he held a synod in 1046; Sylvester was deposed; Gregory voluntarily deposed himself, regretting his great sin; Benedict was formally tried and declared deposed, and a German, Suidiger, bishop of Bamberg, was elected pope under the eyes of the emperor. Under the name of Clement II, Suidiger began the series of reforming German popes.

Clement only enjoyed the papal office for a few months. Benedict IX tried to come back, and is credited with having poisoned Clement. But his attempt to regain the papacy failed, and Henry III filled the papal chair by appointing the bishop of Brixen as Damasus II (1048). There was not even a consultation of the Roman clergy in this most irregular appointment. Damasus lived only twenty-three days as pope; Henry again appointed a pope in the person of his cousin, Bruno of Toul, who took the papal name of Leo IX (1049–54). Bruno was, however, an ardent reformer. He refused to accept the papacy as the appointee of the emperor and demanded election by the clergy and people of Rome. Coming to Rome as a humble pilgrim, he refused any papal honors until he had been properly and officially elected by the clergy and acclaimed by the people. Then he began the reform of the church which is connected with the name of his friend Hildebrand. How this reform brought the papacy into conflict with Henry IV, who succeeded his father in 1056, will be the subject of Chapter 14 below.

MORAVIA, BOHEMIA, AND POLAND

While we are accustomed to think of the Slavs as essentially Eastern and dependent on Byzantium for their civilization, certain groups of the more western Slavs fell distinctly under the influence of Germany rather than Greece. These people are today referred to as the "Western Slavs" and their history, after their initial foundations, comes under the general history of the West rather than that of the East.

The first Slavic state of any consequence to develop was Moravia, which became an extensive kingdom in the ninth century. As far back as the seventh century, one Samo had united the Czechs and eastern Wends and had thrown off the overlordship of the Avars, but his state had collapsed at his death. The Moravians, however, again reasserted their independence in the early ninth century and under Sviatopolk (870–894) established a state which occupied the lands along the Danube, Theiss, and Saale rivers and included the Czechs, Moravians, Slovenes, Silesians, Serbs and western Galicians. This "empire" was in general oriented towards Byzantium, and it was from Byzantium that there came the great missionaries Cyril and Methodius, "the Apostles of the Slavs," who converted these peoples to Christianity. In order that the Slavs might read the Scriptures in their own language, St. Cyril invented the Cyrillic alphabet, which he adapted from the Greek, and established the language now known as "Old Church Slavic."

But although the Moravians began with close relations with Byzantium and received their conversion from Constantinople, they were also friendly with their German neighbors to the west, and after the death of Methodius (ob. 885) the organization of the church was carried on by German clergy, with the result that Moravia fell into the Roman obedience rather than the Byzantine. Also Sviatopolk was the vassal of Charles the Fat, for some of his lands, and his political orientation, as well as the ecclesiastical, turned to the west.

In 906, the Moravian kingdom was overthrown and destroyed by the Magyars. When it revived it was a much smaller affair, consisting of only Bohemia, to which Moravia was added later.

The new Bohemian state was founded by St. Wenceslas (ob. 929), who founded the Premyslid dynasty which was to last until 1306. Wenceslas was from the beginning dependent on the Germans and became the vassal of King Henry the Fowler for his duchy. Although the dukes of Bohemia attempted on occasion to free themselves from the German overlordship, they were never successful, and after 1041 ceased to try, contenting themselves with the position of honored and influential vassals. In 1156, they were granted the title of king as a reward for their faithful support of Frederick Barbarossa.

About the same time that the Bohemian duchy was reviving after the Magyar conquest, the Poles first united into a state under Mieszko I (c. 960–992). They accepted Christianity in 966 from Bohemian missionaries, and like the Bohemians became the vassals of the German emperors. But they aspired to greater things, and under Boleslav the Brave (992–1025) attempted to unite all the western Slavs in a single kingdom. Boleslav conquered Pomerania, Silesia, Moravia, Slovakia, Ruthenia, Bohemia, and Lusatia, but was forced by the emperor Henry II to relinquish Bohemia and to hold Lusatia as a fief from the emperor. In 1025, Boleslav was successful in obtaining the title of King of Poland, but his empire fell to pieces at his death. Moravia and Silesia fell to Bohemia, Pomerania to Denmark, Slovakia to Hungary, Ruthenia to Russia, and Poland itself was divided between two rulers.

Part of these losses were recaptured by Casimir I (1038–58), who secured the help of Henry III in regaining Silesia at the cost of surrendering his royal title and contenting himself with that of Grand Duke. His work was carried on by his son Boleslav the Bold (1058–79) who supported the pope against the German emperor, regained his royal title, reconquered Slovakia, and even invaded Russia. But he was deposed by the nobles who feared his strong rule, and Poland went into a decline, the king once more surrendering his royal title and relapsing to a grand duke.

As there is little to interest us in the history of Poland in the next two hundred years we will disregard chronology long enough to notice the developments there through the next couple of centuries. Under Boleslav III (1102–38) the power of the king was again reasserted, the Germans were defeated and Pomerania was recaptured. But the Polish hold on Pomerania was insecure and it was wrested from them within a few decades by the Germans under Albert the Bear and Henry the Lion. Following the death of Boleslav III, Poland slipped into the condition of anarchy which we are inclined to think of as the natural state of that unhappy country. Menaced from without and helpless within his state, the Polish duke declined in importance until he was merely another noble. In 1228 the Poles received a severe blow when the Teutonic Knights established themselves in Prussia and the final blow was given when the Mongols overran the country. Not until the fourteenth century was Poland to become an important state again.

THE MAGYARS OR HUNGARIANS

The Hungarians, or as they term themselves, the Magyars, first appear along the Don and Dnieper rivers in the empire of the Khazars. From this home they were driven west by the attacks of the Petchenegs, a people even more savage than themselves. Throughout the later ninth and early tenth centuries the Magyars pushed west, raiding Germany and even reaching eastern France. Legend says that they first came into Germany at the invitation of Arnulf, who wished to use them to combat the Moravians, but this story is so familiar in connection with the migrations of so many peoples as to attract no credence. What is sure is that about 896 they left Wallachia and established themselves in the plains of Hungary (to which they gave their name) under their first king, Arpad (ob. 907). In 906 they overran and destroyed Moravia, and thereafter until 933 they raided Germany at will. In 933 they were badly defeated by Henry the Fowler at the battle of the Unstrut, and Otto I completed their defeat at the River Lech near Augsburg in 955.

After their defeat at the Lech, the Magyars seem to have given up their raids in the west and settled down in their own region of Hungary. There Duke Geza (972–997) began to organize them into a nation, suppressing the more troublesome leaders, establishing a royal authority, and encouraging the activities of missionaries.

Under Geza's son St. Stephen (997–1038) the Magyars became not only Christian, but an organized monarchy. Stephen accepted the faith himself, brought in numbers of Benedictine monks, suppressed pagan revolts (which were at the same time rebellions against his royal authority) and, with the help of the clergy, forced a peaceful civilization on his people. In 1001, Pope Sylvester II sent him the royal crown in recognition of his work. Although the German emperors tried to reduce him to vassalage, Stephen was able to resist them successfully. At Stephen's death the Hungarian throne passed to Peter Orseolo, the son of the Doge of Venice, and the sister of Stephen, who brought in Venetian and German favorites and was driven out in 1041. Henry III replaced Peter on the throne in return for which Peter did homage to the German, but he was again overthrown in 1046 in the course of a pagan uprising against the Christian church and state. The rebellion was put down by Andrew I (1047–61) who reestablished the royal power and beat back the Germans, regaining Hun-

garian independence. At the end of the eleventh century Ladislas I
(1077–95) increased the fortunes of his kingdom by annexing Bosnia and
Croatia and paving the way for the subsequent conquest of Dalmatia
(1097–1102). He also strengthened the ties between Hungary and the
papacy, and was eventually canonized.

CHAPTER 11

FRANCE AND ENGLAND TO
THE NORMAN CONQUEST

✤

FRANCE

CAROLINGIAN AND ROBERTIAN KINGS, 877–987

W HEN in 887 Charles the Fat was deposed from the Carolingian thrones
by an infuriated nobility, and while Arnulf secured for himself
the throne of Germany, the western Franks sought for a man who could
rule over them. The legitimate Carolingian, Charles the Simple, the
younger brother of Louis III and Carloman, was in Aquitaine and removed
from the center of things. Although his succession was recognized in the
south, Guy of Spoleto tried to place himself at the head of the Carolingian
party in the west. However, a new man, Eudes, count of Paris, son of
Robert the Strong (whence the name Robertian for the early generations of
the Capetian house) seized the throne and in 888 secured recognition
from Arnulf by doing homage to him for the kingdom. Eudes had already
won for himself an enviable reputation by his heroic defense of Paris
from the Norse invasion of 885, and was considered the strongest noble
of the west.

Eudes was, however, unable to withstand renewed Norse invasions. For
five years (888–893) he struggled to maintain himself on the throne and to
repel the invaders, but the Carolingian tradition was too strong. Charles
the Simple was supported by the Archbishop of Rheims, the counts of
Flanders, Vermandois, and the barons of Champagne and the east, who
proclaimed Charles king. As a result of the war which followed, Eudes
agreed to a treaty which granted Charles half the kingdom and the succession to the throne. In 898 Eudes died and Charles became sole king,
but Robert, Eudes' brother, was given the counties of Paris, Anjou, Touraine, and Blois, which left him the most powerful man in the kingdom.

Charles the Simple (898–923) is best known for his treaty with Rollo the
leader of the Norsemen in 911, whereby the invaders were granted the
district at the mouth of the Seine. Rollo received Christian baptism,
changed his name to Robert, and began at once to extend his possessions
until by 933 he had conquered what we know as Normandy. The Norse-

men showed an amazing receptiveness for the civilization of any country in which they settled, and within a few generations they had become French in speech and in custom, though always retaining a special character, an adventurousness and legal-mindedness, which marked them off from other peoples.

For the rest, the reign of Charles the Simple is marked chiefly by a struggle for Lorraine, which the west Frankish monarch annexed on the death of Louis the Child in Germany (911). Lorraine was strongly Carolingian and consistently supported the claims of the Carolingians against any other house. Twice Charles defeated attempts of Conrad II of Germany to recapture the duchy, but it was ultimately lost to Henry the Fowler.

The preoccupation of Charles with Lorraine produced disaffection among his barons. Under the leadership of Robert of Paris they revolted and in 922 proclaimed Robert king. In a battle at Soissons, Robert was killed but his son Hugh the Great won the victory, and Raoul, duke of Burgundy, Hugh's brother-in-law, was elected king. Charles the Simple was imprisoned while his wife fled to the court of her father, Edward of England, with her son Louis, known thereafter as Louis l'Outremer. Louis remained in England until the death of Raoul in 936, when he was summoned back to the throne by Hugh the Great who expected to completely dominate the young king. But Louis showed himself unamenable to the designs of Hugh, who appealed to Otto I of Germany and revolted. The king was captured and released only after he surrendered Laon to Hugh, but this action cost Hugh the support of Germany, and Louis was able to conquer back his kingdom with the aid of the Germans and English. Louis l'Outremer reigned from 936 to 954, largely by the grace of Otto I and always troubled by revolts of the great feudatories and by incursions of the Magyars, who made a particularly severe raid in 951. On his death in 954 his son Lothaire was crowned, but he gained his throne only by great concessions to Hugh the Great. On Hugh's death in 956 his possessions were divided between his sons, Hugh Capet receiving the Ile de France and his brother, Eudes, taking Burgundy.

Lothaire (954–986) ruled largely with the support of Germany, Otto I and Otto II supporting him against Hugh Capet who stood in opposition. A dominant position was acquired, meanwhile, by Adalberon, archbishop of Rheims, who with the assistance of his *scholasticus* Gerbert, tried to hold the balance of power between contending parties in both France and Germany. They favored Otto III against Henry of Bavaria in Germany and Hugh against Lothaire in France, but Lothaire was able to hold his own and Adalberon was ordered to appear before the king's court to answer charges of treason. Lothaire died, his son Louis V succeeded him for a few months, but died in turn before Adalberon could be tried, and the claims to the throne passed to an uncle of the late king, Charles duke of Lorraine. In 987 an assembly of the nobles rejected the claims of Charles and elected Hugh Capet as king of France.

The election of Hugh has been seen as variously the triumph of feudalism over the old German tribal kingship, which it was, and as the triumph of the French over the German elements in the western Frankish kingdom, which it was not, as the Robertians were a Saxon family who had been introduced into the west after Charlemagne's conquest of Saxony. The new dynasty which ascended the throne in 987 was to create the kingdom of France, and was to last as long as the French monarchy, its last representative being driven out in 1848, but Capetian pretenders still exist in Europe today. When Louis XVI was executed by the revolutionists in 1793 it was as "Citizen Capet" that he was condemned and beheaded.

THE STATES OF FEUDAL FRANCE

Throughout most of the Middle Ages the history of France is the history of the great fiefs, which made up the kingdom by recognizing the often titular suzerainty of the king in Paris. The story of the medieval French monarch is the story of the slow conquest of these counties by the king and their absorption into the domain of the kings of France, a process which was completed only at the very end of our period in the fifteenth century. It is therefore necessary to turn briefly to survey the map of feudal France and the great counties which composed the kingdom. The *Île de France* was the royal domain of the Capetian house. It consisted of Paris, Orleans, and the middle Seine basin, its extent varying considerably with the alienations and acquisitions of the individual rulers. From its name, the duchy of Francia, the kingdom was known as France, and its rulers had at least theoretical suzerainty over all the other counts and dukes of the west. At the time of Hugh Capet the royal domain included not only the Paris basin but Rheims, Châlons, Sens, Laon, and several other important bishoprics.

Within this domain the king was relatively weak. To gain support the early Capetians granted away their domain lands until they had weakened themselves below the level of many of their great vassals. Within the domain itself there developed a class of robber barons, the Coucys, Le Puisets, Monthléris, Roucys, and others, who successfully defied the attempts of the king to bring them into subjection and who were only reduced after more than a century of struggle.

The great *county of Flanders* lay across the border of France and Germany with fiefs dependent on both countries. The Scheldt marked roughly the border between the lands held from the emperor and those held from the king of France, and the count of Flanders used this position to play off both of his suzerains against each other to his own advantage. No great fiefs were allowed to develop in Flanders, but the towns soon achieved a degree of autonomy which was unique in northern Europe; Bruges, Ghent, Ypres, Lille, St. Omer, and Arras all becoming important towns at a relatively early period.

Due to her trade and industry, Flanders was one of the wealthiest regions in western Europe and her counts were less troubled with financial difficulties than most of their contemporaries. The county had first been created by Charles the Bald for one Baldwin Ironarm in 862, and his descendants ruled Flanders for ten generations until the house died out and was succeeded by a dynasty from Alsace in the twelfth century.

The *duchy of Normandy* occupied the land at the mouth of the Seine. Founded in 911, this strong state, under the descendants of Rollo, became the most highly centralized and strongest feudal state in the west. The Duke of Normandy had a stricter control over his vassals than any of his contemporaries, the church was under his domination, and the natural agricultural wealth of the district afforded him means above those of some of his neighbors. Normandy was always somewhat oriented towards the Scandinavian homeland and kept up relations with Denmark, England, and the northern countries. The Norman dukes steadily increased their power, reaching an apogee in the reigns of Robert the Devil and William the Bastard in the early eleventh century.

The *county of Brittany* occupied the American peninsula, southwest of Normandy, which included the cities of Rennes, Dol, and Nantes. Conon of Rennes became count in 987, founding a dynasty which lasted for the next century, but as their power was always challenged by rival counts of Nantes, they were never able to gain any very effective control over the county. The Bretons were only partly French, as the county was settled by Celts, who had fled there before the Anglo-Saxon invasion of England, and they have always retained many ancient local customs, even to the present day. Brittany was really united for the first time in the twelfth century under the Plantagenet dukes of Normandy, who claimed suzerainty over the county. Its population was largely sailors and fishermen, both religious and conservative.

The *county of Anjou* lay along the Loire River, centering in the city of Angers. The first count of Anjou was Foulque the Red who died in 941–942 and the dynasty he founded continued on into the Plantagenet house of Normandy and England. These early Angevins, all named either Foulque or Geoffrey, were mighty warriors who beat down their rivals of Samur, Thouars, and Maine, and fought their neighbors of Normandy, Brittany, Poitou, and Blois. Typical of them all was Geoffrey Martel (1040–60) whose biography, written by his nephew and successor, is one of the finest bits of feudal history to be found anywhere.

My uncle Geoffrey became a knight in his father's lifetime and began his knighthood by wars against his neighbors, one against the Poitevins, whose count he captured at Mont Couer, and another against the people of Maine, whose count, named Herbert Bacon, he likewise took. He also carried on war against his own father, in the course of which he committed many evil deeds of which he afterward bitterly repented. After his father died on his return from Jerusalem, Geoffrey possessed his lands and the city of Angers, and fought Count Thibaud of Blois, son of Count Odo, and by gift of King Henry received the city of Tours, which led to another war with Count Thibaud, in the course of which, at a battle between Tours and Amboise, Thibaud was captured with a thousand of his knights. And so, besides the part of Touraine inherited from his father, he acquired Tours and the castles round about—Chinon, l'Ile-Bouchard, Chateaurenault, and Saint-Aignan. After this he had a war with William, count of the Normans, who later acquired the kingdom of England and was a magnificent king, and with the people of France and of Bourges, and with William count of Poitou and Aimeri viscount of Thouars and Hoel count of Nantes and the Breton counts of Rennes and with Hugh count of Maine, who had thrown off his fealty. Because of all these wars and the prowess he showed therein he was rightly called the Hammer, as one who hammered down his enemies.

In the last year of his life he made me his nephew a knight at the age of seventeen in the city of Angers, at the feast of Pentecost, in the year of the Incarnation 1060, and granted me Saintonge and the city of Saintes because of a quarrel he had with Peter of Didonne. In this same year King Henry died on the nativity of St. John, and my uncle Geoffrey on the third day after Martinmas came to a good end. For in the night which preceded his death, laying aside all care of knighthood and secular things, he became a monk in the monastery of St. Nicholas, which his father and he had built with much devotion and endowed with their goods.[1]

The *county of Blois* had been the original fief of the Robertian counts of Paris, and was for a time included in their domains. Towards the middle of the tenth century it was given in fief to Thibaut, the brother-in-law of Robert, who founded a dynasty, which in the early eleventh century extended its power to include the *county of Champagne* as well. This house (in which the common names were Thibaut, Eudes and Stephen) became one of the most powerful in northern Europe, supplying kings to England (Stephen), Jerusalem, and Navarre, and queens to France and Cyprus. As it surrounded the Ile de France on the east and south it was closely tied up with the fortunes of the royal domain. Champagne became famous and wealthy through the great fairs held there, and it was not until these developed in the twelfth century that Champagne really came into the first rank of French states. The count of Champagne held his lands from a variety of suzerains, of which the king of France was only one.

The great *duchy of Aquitaine* occupied all of southwestern France south of the Loire and included the great counties of Poitou, Limousin, Perigord, La Marche, and Gascony as well as many smaller seigneuries. Aquitaine

---

[1] Translated by C. H. Haskins, *The Normans in European History*, pp. 62–63. Reprinted by permission of the publishers, Houghton Mifflin Co.

was one of the old Frankish kingdoms and became a duchy in the ninth century under the counts of Poitou, most of whom were named William. It was too large ever to acquire any centralized government and the dukes were never able to make their power felt effectively throughout their wide domains. Gascony, inhabited by the Basques, especially showed a tendency to independence and feudal anarchy, the nobles of Gascony achieving a reputation for contentiousness which has been immortalized in D'Artagnan and Cyrano de Bergerac. The English to whom the whole duchy passed with the marriage of Eleanor of Aquitaine to Henry II in the twelfth century, always called the whole region Guyenne and long cherished it, especially for the fine Bordeaux wines. Aquitaine was the great center of the Provençal literature and courtly chivalry in the High Middle Ages.

The *county of Toulouse* was a constant rival of Aquitaine. Centering in the city of Toulouse, it later spread out to include much of the region known as Languedoc along the coast of the Mediterranean. It was the strongest feudal state in the south, but never became really strong as its counts were constantly confronted by coalitions of rebellious vassals and independent bishops. Toulouse recognized only the most shadowy dependence on the king of France and hardly entered into the orbit of France at all until it was reduced by the Albigensian crusade of the thirteenth century. Its counts played illustrious roles both in the wars in Spain and in the crusades to Syria.

The *duchy of Septimania* or Gothia, which included the lands around the cities of Narbonne and Nîmes with territories along the coast, was a loosely held state whose fortunes were closely bound up with its neighbors of Toulouse and Barcelona, under both of whom it was held at various times. The *duchy of Barcelona,* the old Carolingian Spanish March, maintained close relations with France, its bishops depending on the archbishop of Narbonne. At first cut off from the other Christian states of Spain by intervening Moslem states, Barcelona ultimately was joined to Aragon, and the Catalans contributed much to the development of Aragonese power in Spain and in the Mediterranean. Across the Rhone from Languedoc and including the city of Marseilles, lay the *county of Provence,* which in the Middle Ages was not included in France but was a part of the Holy Roman Empire. As the residue of the old Carolingian kingdom of Arles, it was incorporated into the empire in the early eleventh century. It should be remembered that Provençal culture developed not in Provence, but in Aquitaine.

To the north of Provence along the Saone, lay the great *duchy of Burgundy* with its capital at Dijon. Across the Saone lay the *county* centering around Besançon which was in the empire. The dynasty of the dukes of Burgundy stemmed from the Carolingian and later from the Robertian house. In 965 Henry, the third son of Hugh the Great of Paris, received the fief from his brother Hugh Capet. The land was brought back into domain, only to be alienated again, and the dynasty of the Burgundian dukes were descendants of King Robert of France from 1015 on. Burgundy was one of the weakest of all feudal states. Its powerful bishops and abbots (Cluny, Cîteaux, Molesme) ignored the duke and paid allegiance only to the pope; its nobles were independent and rebellious, and the duke was always limited by his personal ability to make his influence felt over his vassals.

The *duchy of Lorraine* in the northeast was generally in the empire, though sometimes in France. It was finally divided into Upper and Lower Lorraine, of which Lower Lorraine broke down into a number of independent bishoprics, while Upper remained a duchy of the empire. At the very end of the Middle Ages it was incorporated into France, and it was from Lorraine that Joan of Arc came to bring nationalist sentiments to the French during the Hundred Years War.

In addition to the great counties were a number of lesser seigneuries and ecclesiastical fiefs. Among the latter were: Rheims, Laon, Langres, Châlons, Beauvais, Lyon, and Le Puy, the incumbents of which ranked among the great feudal nobles of France. Among the lesser secular fiefs were: Vermandois and Ponthieu in the north; Nevers, Bourbon, Auvergne, in central France; and Rouerge, Albi, Velay, Quercy, Agenais, Foix, and Bearn in Aquitaine and the south. Many of these achieved special prominence at one time or another but they never rivaled the greater states mentioned above.

THE EARLY CAPETIANS, 987–1108

When Hugh Capet ascended the throne of France on July 3, 987, he gave up his position as a strong baron to become a weak king. His election was the triumph of feudalism over hereditary monarchy, and his chief concern was in the securing of his dynasty on the throne. Until the end of the twelfth century the kings of France regularly crowned their sons during their own lifetime to insure a peaceful succession. Although Hugh alienated lands in an effort to secure support, and managed to keep himself on the throne against the opposition of Charles of Lorraine and Arnoul, a Carolingian who became archbishop of Rheims in 989, he was never strong and had no more control over the more distant counties than his weak Carolingian predecessors had enjoyed. His influence was much less than that formerly exercised by his grandfather, and it was merely as an equal that he engaged in the feudal wars of the counts of Blois, Anjou, and Normandy. At first he had secured the alliance of the count of Blois by ceding him Dreux, but later in the reign Blois conspired with Otto III and the Carolingians, and Hugh allied with Anjou and Normandy to attack it. Most of his reign was spent in fighting the Carolingians; Charles

CAPETIAN KINGS OF FRANCE, 888–1314

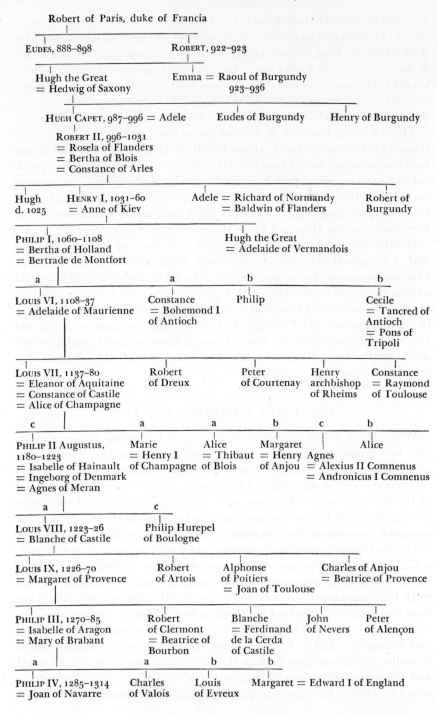

Robert of Paris, duke of Francia

EUDES, 888–898   ROBERT, 922–923

Hugh the Great   Emma = Raoul of Burgundy
= Hedwig of Saxony   923–936

HUGH CAPET, 987–996 = Adele   Eudes of Burgundy   Henry of Burgundy

ROBERT II, 996–1031
= Rosela of Flanders
= Bertha of Blois
= Constance of Arles

Hugh   HENRY I, 1031–60   Adele = Richard of Normandy   Robert of
d. 1025   = Anne of Kiev   = Baldwin of Flanders   Burgundy

PHILIP I, 1060–1108   Hugh the Great
= Bertha of Holland   = Adelaide of Vermandois
= Bertrade de Montfort

a   **a**   **b**   **b**

LOUIS VI, 1108–37   Constance   Philip   Cecile
= Adelaide of Maurienne   = Bohemond I   = Tancred of
                   of Antioch   Antioch
                                        = Pons of
                                        Tripoli

LOUIS VII, 1137–80   Robert   Peter   Henry   Constance
= Eleanor of Aquitaine   of Dreux   of Courtenay   archbishop   = Raymond
= Constance of Castile   of Rheims   of Toulouse
= Alice of Champagne

c   **a**   **a**   **b**   **c**   **b**

PHILIP II Augustus,   Marie   Alice   Margaret   Alice
1180–1223   = Henry I   = Thibaut   = Henry   Agnes
= Isabelle of Hainault   of Champagne   of Blois   of Anjou   = Alexius II Comnenus
= Ingeborg of Denmark   = Andronicus I Comnenus
= Agnes of Meran

a   **c**

LOUIS VIII, 1223–26   Philip Hurepel
= Blanche of Castile   of Boulogne

LOUIS IX, 1226–70   Robert   Alphonse   Charles of Anjou
= Margaret of Provence   of Artois   of Poitiers   = Beatrice of Provence
                                = Joan of Toulouse

PHILIP III, 1270–85   Robert   Blanche   John   Peter
= Isabelle of Aragon   of Clermont   = Ferdinand   of Nevers   of Alençon
= Mary of Brabant   = Beatrice of   de la Cerda
                    Bourbon   of Castile
a   **a**   **b**   **b**

PHILIP IV, 1285–1314   Charles   Louis   Margaret = Edward I of England
= Joan of Navarre   of Valois   of Evreux

of Lorraine was captured and imprisoned, Arnoul of Rheims was deposed
by a council over which Hugh presided, and Gerbert, his old friend, was
installed in his place. This interference in Rheims brought down on Hugh
the enmity of both Otto of Germany and the pope. Hugh countered with
an attempted alliance with Basil II of Constantinople, but this was unsuccessful. He died in 996 leaving the throne to his son Robert II the
Pious, but the throne he left was rather a feudal suzerainty over equals
than any royal sovereignty over subjects.

Robert II (996–1031) was a student of Gerbert's and was better educated
than most laymen of his time. He was noted for his piety and was at the
same time a warrior of no mean ability, but his reign is unimportant and he
was never able to exert any great influence over his vassals. Much of the
troubles of the reign came from his marital difficulties. Before his accession
he had been married to Rosela of Flanders who was considerably his
senior. Falling in love with Bertha of Blois, Robert divorced Rosela and
married Bertha, an act which necessitated breaking his alliance with Anjou
and joining Blois. The pope objected to this marriage, and to win him over
Robert allowed the return of Arnoul to the archbishopric of Rheims. Gerbert fled to Germany where Otto III subsequently made him archbishop of
Ravenna and finally pope. But Pope Gregory V refused to be placated and
still opposed the marriage to Bertha, so Robert finally divorced her and
married Constance of Arles. This marriage of convenience did not long
suit Robert, however, and he soon repudiated Constance and called back
Bertha. The pope again objected and as Constance was strongly supported
by Anjou, Robert was forced to submit. Bertha was once again repudiated
and Constance returned to become the mother of Robert's three sons. Her
support of Robert, the third son, against his father resulted in a civil war
at the end of the reign.

Meanwhile, from 1002 to 1015, Robert was busy trying to conquer Bur-
gundy. He was finally able to gain possession of ducal Burgundy, but
King Rudolph ceded the county to the empire so that it was lost to
France. In his relations with the great counts he was opposed by Anjou and
Blois, but supported by Normandy. The acquisition of Champagne by
Blois weakened the king as it surrounded his domain by a hostile power.
He allied with Flanders, giving his daughter in marriage to the count, and
in 1026 he unsuccessfully backed William of Aquitaine for the throne of
Italy. His relations with the empire were generally hostile throughout
the reign. On the other hand, he was most successful in establishing his
control over the clergy. He interfered in episcopal elections and secured
the election of his candidates in several instances, installing his illegitimate
brother in the see of Bourges in 1013.

He associated his eldest son Hugh on the throne in 1017 but Hugh died
soon thereafter and he crowned his second son Henry in 1026, whereupon

Constance and Robert the third son, joined in a revolt against the king in 1030. King Robert died the following year and Henry came to the throne. His brother Robert continued his rebellion supported by Constance and Blois. Normandy, Anjou, and Flanders supported the king, but he was unable to suppress the revolt, and it was only after the death of Constance in 1034 that Robert gave up his claims to the throne in return for the cession of the duchy of Burgundy.

The reign of Henry I (1031–60) shows how completely the king was only one of the great counts. His authority south of the Loire was nil, and in the north he was forced to ally with one great feudatory to counteract another. In 1034 to 1039 Henry allied with Anjou, Normandy, and Conrad II of Germany against Eudes II of Blois and Robert of Burgundy; to gain the support of Normandy in this war, Henry ceded the Vexin to Robert the Devil and at the end of the war Anjou got Touraine and France received Sens. When Robert of Normandy went on a pilgrimage to Jerusalem he appointed the king as regent for his young and illegitimate son William: the Norman barons promptly revolted and Henry aided William in the battle of Val des Dunes (1047), in which he broke the resistance of the Norman nobles and reduced the duchy to obedience. But the alliance between William and Henry was of but short duration, and in 1054 Henry was supporting a coalition of Anjou, Burgundy, Champagne, Aquitaine, and Auvergne against William. It is eloquent testimony of the strength of William and the weakness of Henry, that William managed to defeat this coalition in 1055 and to administer a second defeat on the king three years later. Meanwhile Henry had supported a revolt of Geoffrey of Lorraine against the empire in 1044, but had been unable to prevent the deposition of his protégé by the emperor Henry III. His relations with the papacy were strained, partly because he tried to maintain a royal control over the French bishops, and partly because the popes were imperial appointees. When Leo IX summoned the clergy of France to a council at Rheims in 1049, Henry called them all out for military service and prevented their attendance.

In 1051 Henry married Anne of Kiev, daughter of Yaroslav the Wise, quite a fine marriage for the French monarch. Their son Philip was associated with his father on the throne in 1059 at the age of seven, and Henry died the following year, leaving Philip under the regency of Anne and Baldwin of Flanders.

The reign of Philip I (1060–1108) differed but little from that of his father and grandfather. He did manage to annex a few parcels of land; Vermandois was acquired and given to his brother Hugh; the Vexin and Valois were annexed when Count Simon entered a monastery; Corbie was won in a war with Robert the Frisian of Flanders, and Chateau Landon and the Gatinais were ceded by Foulque of Anjou as the price of the king's neutrality when Foulque usurped the thrones of Anjou and Touraine. Philip supported Robert Curthose in 1079 against his father William of Normandy and received Gisors; and in 1101 he purchased Bourges from its viscount who was going on a crusade. In 1087 he fought against the combined forces of Normandy, England, and Aquitaine. But all this was merely the action of any feudal noble, and the king was still weaker in his own domain than were his vassals in theirs.

Like Robert, Philip had trouble with the church over his marital life. He had married Bertha of Holland by whom he had a son Louis, whom he associated with himself on the throne in 1098. But in 1092 he repudiated Bertha to marry Bertrade de Montfort, the wife of Foulque of Anjou. Foulque protested, but accepted the situation. Not so Pope Urban II, who excommunicated Philip and Bertrade at the Councils of Clermont in 1095, Tours in 1096, and Poitiers in 1101. In 1104 they finally submitted and Bertrade was deposed as queen, although they continued to live together. Meanwhile prince Louis had actually taken over the control of government in 1100 and really ruled from that time until his father's death in 1108. In the last year of the reign the king gained possession of the castle of Month-léri by arranging the marriage of its heiress to a royal bastard Philip. It was the first step in the consolidation of the strength of the king over the barons of his own domain, which was to be the chief work of Louis VI.

The Government of the Capetians

The early Capetians sacrificed real power in their own domain for shadowy attempts to control their great vassals. Not until Louis VI did they begin the policy of strengthening themselves at home before they attempted to extend their influence. While they were the heirs of the old Carolingian monarchy, and their coronation by the clergy kept up this aspect of their rule, actually they were only feudal lords exercising a not too real suzerainty over their vassals. One thing they did accomplish: they made the throne definitely hereditary in the eldest son of the reigning house.

Their administration was exceedingly simple. They continued the use of the old household officers, and as the great offices tended to become hereditary in the families of the great feudatories, they employed meaner men to perform their duties. Their chancery developed but slightly: Hugh Capet issued but a dozen charters as compared to 200 issued by Otto the Great, and while Robert issued more than his father the number was still insignificant throughout the early Capetian period. The king's curia, composed of all his vassals, was theoretically the chief advisory, administrative, and judicial body of the kingdom, but a smaller curia, composed of the intimates of the king, handled most of the business. There were a few royal proclamations but no legislation. The king was in theory the fountain of justice and the royal will was supreme, the king superseding the curia as a judge from whom there was no appeal. But practical factors entered into the picture to minimize this power of the king and render him no greater than the other great counts.

In local government, as the counts ruled almost absolutely over their fiefs, the only part that remained to the king was the royal domain. Even here the barons and chatelains took the law and administration into their own hands with little regard for the royal prerogatives. *Prevots* were established by Henry I as royal agents to administer justice, collect revenues and lead the army, but they were paid in land so that the office soon became feudalized, and the prevots became as hard to control as the local nobility. The first really serious attempt to gain a real control over local officials came with the introduction of the *baillies* under Philip II.

The king of necessity "lived on his own." His chief revenues were the produce of the domain farms, the feudal aids and reliefs collected from his vassals, and the revenues of churches and monasteries for which the king had the protection as *avoué* or *vidame*. This was one of the sources of the Capetian power, as the kings were the secular representatives of several important abbeys, such as St. Denis, and of a number of bishoprics.

Thus at the end of the eleventh century France was a feudalized state, divided into a number of counties and fiefs under the nominal suzerainty of a weak monarchy which had developed no institutions other than those of every feudal state. It was the work of the kings in the twelfth and thirteenth centuries to make the king the strongest power in France and to develop a truly royal administration.

ENGLAND

Saxons and Danes, 802–1016

In our history so far England has played no very significant role, and in truth, until the Danish invasions of the eighth and ninth centuries, English history presents little of interest. The Angles, Saxons and Jutes had established seven kingdoms: Kent, East Anglia, Mercia, Northumbria, Essex, Wessex, and Sussex, and for several centuries English history is a wearisome story of the struggle for supremacy between the rulers of these petty kingdoms. With the coming of the Danes, England was united for the first time under the house of Wessex, and Alfred the Great (871–899) is justly the first English king to merit our serious attention.

It is precisely in the time of the first Danish invasion at the opening of the ninth century that King Egbert of Wessex (802–839), seized the foremost position in the Heptarchy, conquering all the other Anglo-Saxon states and defeating the Danes and Welsh. His rule, as overlord of the local kings, was accepted throughout England as far as the Firth of Forth, with the exception of Celtic Strathclyde. It was in the reign of Egbert's son Ethelwulf (839–856) that the Danes first wintered in England in 855. Ethelwulf allied with Charles the Bald against the Norsemen and even sought help in a pilgrimage to Rome, but was unable to withstand successfully the attacks of the invaders, who continued to raid England and who began to make permanent settlements there. These Danish invasions continued unabated through the reigns of the three elder sons of Ethelwulf—Ethelbald, Ethelbert, and Ethelred—who followed each other in succession on the throne in the years 856 to 871. In 866 the Danes captured York and overran Northumbria, which they made into a Danish kingdom; this was followed by the reduction of Mercia and East Anglia (868–870), and it was not until they were met by an army from Wessex under the command of Alfred, the youngest of the sons of Ethelwulf, in 871 that their drive was stopped.

Alfred (871–899) came to the Wessex throne after the death of his brother Ethelred in the battle of Merton. He carried on a desultory war against Gunthrum, the leader of the Danes, in which the Danes were generally successful by land, but the Saxons at sea. Finally in 878, after he had won a signal victory at Ethandun, Alfred made peace with Gunthrum at Wedmore. By this treaty Gunthrum accepted Christianity and was recognized as ruler over all the territory north of the Thames and east of the old Roman Watling Street, a road which bisected Mercia. This territory included Essex, East Anglia, Northumbria, and eastern Mercia, and was thereafter known as the Danelaw. Alfred retained Kent, Wessex, Sussex, and the western part of Mercia.

To hold the lands which he still ruled, Alfred built a series of forts and towns throughout his kingdom, perhaps to offset the towns which the Danes had built. He also reorganized his army and founded a navy with which he patrolled the coasts, warding off further Danish landings. But Alfred is known as the Great more for his administrative reforms and contributions to culture than for his military accomplishments. He codified the laws and set up a system of courts through Saxon England; he rebuilt the monasteries which had been ravaged by the Danes and filled them with clergy. And in order that the clergy should be literate he sent to the continent for scholars, who could bring back to England the learning which a century before Alcuin and his fellows had transplanted to Gaul. Alfred is also famous for his translations into Anglo-Saxon of such works as Boethius' *Consolation of Philosophy,* and the histories of Orosius and Bede, and for the founding of the *Anglo-Saxon Chronicle,* which, continued until 1154, was the first great historical work in any Western vernacular tongue.

The consolidation of England under Alfred was continued under his son Edward (899–924) who, ably assisted by his sister Ethelfleda, lady of the Mercians, began the reconquest of the Danelaw. He re-established the Saxon rule over Essex, Mercia, and East Anglia, and forced the submission of the Welsh, Northumbrians, Danes, and Scots. This work was completed by his son Ethelstane (924–939), who absorbed Wales and Northumbria into the kingdom of Wessex and reorganized the administration of the kingdom, establishing his own ealdormen as royal representatives in the various provinces. When the Scots and Welsh revolted he defeated them utterly at Brunanburh (937) and brought Wales, Strathclyde, and Scotland into vassalage. Under Ethelstane, England became one of the leading powers of the West; his sisters married: Otto I, Charles the Simple, Hugh the Great, and Louis of Arles. Ethelstane was succeeded by his brothers Edmund (939–946) and Edred (946–955). At the death of Edred, the throne passed to the two sons of Edmund, Edwig (955–959) and Edgar (959–975).

During this period considerable progress was made in fusing Saxons and Danes into a single people; Danish revolts were suppressed when they arose, Strathclyde was ceded to Malcolm of Scotland, and a better frontier was established on the north. So successful was this assimilation that Edgar's reign of sixteen years is unmarked by any wars and he is known as Edgar the Pacific. Much of the credit for this policy must be given to Dunstan, bishop of London and later archbishop of Canterbury, who was the chief advisor of Edred and Edgar. Church and state were reorganized, new bishoprics and monasteries established, ecclesiastical reforms introduced, a stronger royal administration effected and the local courts strengthened. Commerce was fostered, laws were recodified, and England seemed about to enter into a period of great prosperity under a strong monarchy.

This hope was, however, to prove illusory, and the years following the death of Edgar in 975 were filled not only with renewed Danish invasions, but with civil war and the breakdown of the royal power. Edgar had been twice married and left sons by both wives. At his death his eldest son Edward (975–978) was crowned by Dunstan, but the surviving queen sought the throne for her son Ethelred, and Edward earned his name of "the martyr" when he was murdered by the queen's agents to clear the way for the ten-year-old Ethelred.

With the accession of Ethelred "the Unready" (978–1016), the power in the kingdom passed from the hands of the king to that of the great nobles, ealdormen and thegns. Dunstan was driven from court and the first place was taken by a group of the nobles who imposed their will on the youthful king in a manner not unworthy of their feudal counterparts across the Channel.

Then in 980 the Danes again began to invade England. This invasion differed from the earlier ones in that it was a planned affair led by the kings of Denmark and Sweden. As we have seen, the early Norse invasions were conducted by tribal chieftains, who were trying to escape the controls placed on them by the growing power of the kings; now the kings themselves sought to expand, and having been turned back from Germany, descended on England. Beginning in 980, the Danes once more attacked the shores of England; in 991, Ethelred resorted to a general tax, called the Danegeld, with which he bought them off, but this policy of appeasement only whetted their appetites and in the years that followed both Olaf of Norway and Sweyn of Denmark led fresh expeditions to collect further tribute. Ethelred sought an ally against these invasions in Duke Richard of Normandy, whose sister Emma he married (1002); in the same year he perpetrated a massacre of the Danes in England which brought fierce reprisals from Sweyn. From 1003 to 1013 Sweyn waged continuous war on England; he attacked in the north, in the Midlands, on the coasts of Kent. Ethelred's forces were defeated, his lands overrun and occupied. Finally, in 1013 the unhappy king fled to Normandy, leaving his country to the invader. The English Witan, the king's council, recognized Sweyn as king. But Sweyn did not live to be crowned king of England, for he died in 1014, and it was his son Canute who ascended the English throne. The inhabitants of the old Danelaw gladly recognized Canute, but the English members of the Witan refused allegiance and recalled Ethelred from Normandy. Once again England was torn by war between Saxon and Dane; Ethelred died in 1016 and the Witan proclaimed his son Edmund Ironside (1016). Edmund brought to the war a vigor wholly lacking in his father, with the result that the English won several engagements and were able to force from Canute a treaty re-establishing two kingdoms. Edmund held the south and Canute the north, with the understanding that when either died the other should succeed to the whole kingdom. Hardly had this treaty been arranged than Edmund was treacherously murdered by one of his own men and Canute entered into possession of the realm.

DANISH AND LAST SAXON KINGS, 1017–66

Canute (1017–35) was ultimately king of England, Denmark and Norway, and overlord of Sweden. It is a tribute to his greatness that he is the hero of numerous English legends and that his rule is recognized as one of the best in the annals of England. Under his wise administration England was made a part of a northern empire, oriented towards the Baltic, and drawn into its active economic life. Commercial treaties with Germany facilitated English as well as Scandinavian trade with Europe; Normandy became Canute's ally; and he married Emma, the widow of Ethelred. In his administration Canute sought to favor equally his Danish and English subjects. England was divided into four great earldoms: East Anglia and Northumbria being given to Danes and Mercia and Wessex to Englishmen. Godwin, the Englishman whom Canute made earl of Wessex, was given the hand of his niece in marriage and was made the king's chief lieutenant in all matters pertaining to England. English laws were respected and enforced; the nobles were held in check and the lesser folk and clergy were placed under the protection of the crown. Religion was encouraged, monks and clergy patronized, and the king made a personal pilgrimage to Rome in 1027. It is from his reign that the collection of the special church tax of Peter's Pence in England is to be dated.

That a foreign conqueror should be able to become one of the best and most respected of England's kings, and that his reign should be one of the most peaceful in her history proves only that there was among the English little national consciousness at this time and that the differences between Englishman and Dane were in fact but slight. The assimilation of the two peoples, which had begun under the English Edgar the Pacific, was continued by the Danish Canute.

The peaceful reign of Canute was followed by a period of troubles while his sons disputed the throne. By his first wife Elgifu, Canute was the father of Sweyn and Harold, while by Emma he had Harthacanute. It was Canute's intention that Harthacanute should succeed him in Denmark and England while Sweyn received Norway. But, as is so often the case, the great man had produced only degenerate offspring. While Harthacanute was accepted in Denmark, the Norwegians refused Sweyn and called back Magnus, the son of their former king Olaf, while the English elected Harold to rule over them. Harold at once murdered Alfred, the elder son of Ethelred and Emma, and the queen fled to the continent with her younger son Edward, while she tried to stir up Harthacanute to press his claims to England.

Harold "Harefoot" (1035–40), although he had nothing to recommend him as a king, managed to hold the throne until his death in 1040, when Harthacanute peacefully annexed the English to the Danish crown. He proved himself no better than Harold, and the two years he ruled England were marked by tyranny, murders, and the complete subordination of England to Denmark. Fortunately he died in 1042 and the Witan, led by Godwin, recalled Edward, the son of Ethelred and Emma.

Edward, "the Confessor," (1042–66) had been brought up in Normandy and was more Norman than English in his manners and ideas. With his accession to the throne, the Norman Conquest is sometimes said to have begun, for he brought with him from the continent Norman clergy, Norman officials, and Norman administration. Robert of Jumieges, a Norman, was made archbishop of Canterbury; Norman favorites surrounded the king; but the strongest man in England was neither the king nor any of his protégés, but Godwin, earl of Wessex, who married his daughter Edith to the new monarch, and secured earldoms for his sons Sweyn and Harold.

The ascendancy of Godwin angered the other nobles both Norman and Saxon, and even irritated beyond endurance the peaceful and gentle Edward. In 1051, the king took the occasion of a minor quarrel to expel Godwin and his five sons from England and to draw closer to Normandy. It was at this time that he promised the succession to William, duke of Normandy, who came to visit him and who presented claims as his nearest blood relative. However, Godwin was too strong and too popular to remain long in exile. He returned the following year, the Normans fled; Robert of Jumieges was deposed as archbishop and replaced by Stigand. a nominee of Godwin's. Unfortunately for Godwin the deposition of Robert and the election of Stigand were done without consulting the pope, who refused to recognize the *fait accompli* and became the confirmed enemy of the house of Godwin. The earl, however, completely controlled the king and the kingdom; his enemies were banished, his sons given earldoms. When he died in 1053 his son Harold stepped into his place, and until the death of Edward in January, 1066, Harold virtually ruled England.

The death of Edward the Confessor threw the question of the succession into the open. The best claimant was probably Edgar the Atheling, the grandson of Edmund Ironside, but he was only a small child. William of Normandy pressed his claims:—relationship to Edward through Emma, Edward's promise, and a pledge wrested from Harold, when the latter had been shipwrecked in Normandy in 1064, to accept him as the next king. The Witan, however, disregarded all these claims and placed the crown on the head of Earl Harold.

There can be little question as to the legal right of the Witan to elect Harold, for the English throne had always been elective, though the king was expected to be chosen from the members of the reigning house. In consideration of the complete unsuitability of Edgar Atheling, the Witan was entirely within its rights in disregarding any claims made by William (who was not related to the old house of Alfred, but only to Edward the Confessor through his mother) and elect that man who seemed to them best fitted to rule. But however legal his title, Harold had to defend it by arms, for William fully intended to make good his claims, however shadowy.

Further, the situation was complicated by a feud which had broken out between Harold and his brother Tostig. Tostig had been made earl of Northumbria, but had been driven out of his earldom because of his cruelty and bad government. Harold had accepted his brother's overthrow and had married the sister of Morcar, who had received Northumbria at Tostig's deposition. Morcar was the brother of Edwin, earl of Mercia, so that the marriage with Edith brought Harold into alliance with both these powerful earldoms. But Tostig had no intention of standing by and seeing his brother profit while he lost out; he allied himself with Harold Hardrada, the king of Norway, to recapture his earldom. Thus Harold was threatened with invasion from both Norway and Normandy. Tostig and Harold Hardrada were the first to invade. Landing in the north, they defeated Edwin and Morcar near York, but Harold came up from the south and met them at Stamford Bridge in September, defeating them and killing them both in the battle.

While Harold was winning the north, William of Normandy, with his banners blessed by the papacy, landed on the south coast at Pevensey on September 28. Slowly William moved inland while Harold rushed down from the north. Edwin and Morcar were to follow him, but were delayed in getting under way. On October 14, 1066, Harold met the Norman invaders at a field between Hastings and Senlac. By a feinted retreat, one of the oldest stratagems in the history of warfare, the Normans dislodged the English from their prepared positions and routed them. Harold was killed in the battle; William had made good his claims; the road to London and the crown lay open. The Norman Conquest of England had been accomplished. After having been oriented towards Denmark and the north, England was now to be turned for five hundred years towards France.

ANGLO-SAXON INSTITUTIONS

The institutions of the Anglo-Saxons are of interest especially in that they show the old German institutions almost wholly unmodified by Roman influences. The day has fortunately passed when historians sought to find in the laws and institutions of the Saxons the origins of all the modern institutions of England and America; but while we no longer consider them of prime importance in the development of later institutions, it must be admitted that they did contribute some elements to the later institutional development.

The kingship was, as we have seen, elective by the Witan, but the choice of the councillors was limited by the understanding that the king should normally be chosen from among the members of the ruling house. The rule of primogeniture never developed in old German laws, being a purely feudal contribution. To the selection by the Witan was added the ecclesiastical benediction of the coronation. This gave the king a semi-religious character: in return for his promise to protect the church and the weak, the king was anointed with holy oil which gave him an almost sacerdotal quality. The legend of the "king's touch" as a panacea for all ills is a development from this sacred character of the monarch.

The king was the commander-in-chief of the army and the supreme governor of the realm. He appointed the sheriffs (shire-reeves) who governed the local districts (shires). The Saxon monarchs never developed the character of supreme lawgivers that their Frankish counterparts achieved, and England before the Conquest did not know any system of judges sent out from the royal court to carry the king's justice into the shires. On the other hand, the king did have special prerogatives: he had a special peace or *grith;* wherever the king himself was, or certain designated places, were considered under the king's peace and any violence committed there was subject to a special fine. When the king was dead his peace lapsed, and it was from this that the custom arose of proclaiming "The king is dead, long live the king." The king's highways were protected by this special peace and were much safer than the ordinary roads. The fines for the violation of the king's peace or his highway were heavy and were paid directly to the crown.

The king's advisory council was termed the Witan or Witanagemot. It was composed of the chief nobles and bishops of the realm, and amounted in the tenth century to a body of fifty to one hundred men. The Witan elected the king and had a theoretical right to depose him, but the whole matter of both election and deposition was really one of the nobles giving their personal allegiance to a particular man, or withdrawing it. Depositions were invariably accompanied by violence and it is a mistake to see too much of a constitutional practice in the turbulent politics of the Saxons. The Witan was the chief advisory body of the king, but he was not compelled to follow the advice given, and the king always controlled the agenda of the meetings. It was the supreme court of the kingdom, the body which approved laws and treaties, and was often consulted in the appointment of bishops and officials.

Special taxes, such as the Danegeld, were voted in the Witan, but otherwise the king "lived on his own," that is to say, he derived his revenues from his own private estates and from the fines which came to him in his courts. The crown also derived considerable revenue from tolls and tariff charges at the ports, from a special inheritance tax levied on all earls and thegns, and from the mint right.

The army was composed of the *landwehr* or *fyrd,* the army of free farmers who owed military service to the crown, the royal house-carls, professional soldiers retained by the king; and the troops supplied by the thegns with their followers. A special *shipwehr* provided for the navy, as the landwehr did for the army. The thegns were the military vassals of the king, similar to the feudal vassals of the continent or the old Germanic comitatus. While most of the thegns were the men of the king, thegns of the great earls were not unknown, but the Saxons never developed the elaborate system of dependent tenures, which marked the feudal relationship of the continent, nor were their relationships governed by any reciprocal contract as in feudalism.

More important than the organs of the central government were the local institutions. The kingdom was divided into shires, hundreds, and vills, each of which had its own court. The vill-court was an extremely simple affair, which met on market days and in the phrase of the great historian of English law, F. W. Maitland "had more to do with pigs than with politics."

While much of England had a fully developed manorial system, a considerable part operated under the village community; all land was divided into folkland which was held directly from the king under the old customary law, and bookland which was held under charter by a lord. The bookland had been carved out of the folkland, and its spread shows the weakening of the older clan organization in favor of the newer lordships. This same tendency is shown in the development of *bohr* or securities. Originally a man had to be vouched for by the members of his clan who stood security for him; as time progressed, it became more and more common for him to be vouched for by a lord. Finally all men who did not have lords to go security for them were organized into "tithing groups," which were organized to provide security for each other. This organization acted not only as a means of guaranteeing adequate financial responsibility for the members, but also acted as a preventive police force, since the members of the group were always anxious to restrain any of their fellows from engaging in any misdeeds which would cost them heavily if discovered.

The hundred was a much more important unit than the vill. It was probably the territory inhabited by a hundred families and supplying a hundred men to the fyrd, though there were many different theories as to its origin. The hundred is first encountered as a local unit in the tenth century, there being no mention of it in Bede. Its court was a judicial body as well as a court of record, and met one day every four weeks under the presidency of the hundred reeve. The peculiar importance of the hundred court is that it was attended by the reeve, priest, and four men from each vill in the hundred, thus being the first representative institution in history. The court could act for all the inhabitants of the hundred and the constituents were bound by any action taken.

The shire court met twice a year, and, like the hundred court, was a representative body, being composed again of the reeve, priest, and four men from each vill. It must be pointed out that the vill was the unit of representation in both the hundred and shire courts, and that the shire court did not represent the hundreds. It was presided over by the ealdorman (later earl), the bishop, and the sheriff. The ealdorman was originally the elected ruler of the shire, but the office early became a hereditary one; he was the chief military leader of the shire and commanded the local fyrd. In the eleventh century, the title of ealdorman was changed to that of earl (a fusion of the older office with the Danish jarl), and the earls normally ruled over several shires. The sheriff, or shire reeve, was the king's representative in the shire; when the earl took over several shires, the sheriff became the chief judge and military leader in the shire. The shire court was a court of first instance and also an appelate court from the hundred courts, although a case must prove miscarriage of justice three times before it could be appealed from the hundred to the shire court. From the shire court there was no appeal to any higher tribunal, though cases could by-pass it and go directly to the king's court.

The procedure in these courts was the familiar ordeal, or compurgation. The members of the court could, of course, exercise their discretion in awarding the verdict, and an option was sometimes given the defendent by the court giving the "two-tongued" verdict of submitting to an ordeal or paying a fine.

One striking feature of the Saxon system was the control over the church exercised by the secular government. Church and state were practically one throughout the Saxon period, the clergy playing important roles in the secular courts and being wholly amenable to them. Secular courts enforced the collection of tithes and the imposition of ecclesiastical penalties, and the church enjoyed a special peace like that of the king. On the other hand, the bishops were entirely under the royal control and were regularly appointed by the crown, whose most trusted advisors and ministers they often became. Relations with Rome were sketchy and the papacy exercised but little control in England, although the pope reserved the right to grant to archbishops the *pallium,* the distinctive mark of their status, and England was one of the few countries which paid Peter's Pence (a special tax of a penny a hearth paid directly to Rome and collected only in England, Scandinavia and Poland). We have already noted how Stigand was appointed archbishop of Canterbury without the pope being consulted; in the earlier days this might well have passed unnoticed, but the Hildebrandine papacy and William of Normandy made the most of it, William making the reform of the English ecclesiastical system one of the cardinal points in his program and gaining thereby the support of the papacy. The separation of church and state and the introduction of continental feudalism into England by the Normans will be discussed in a later chapter.

Chapter 12

THE FEUDAL REGIME

✠

Definitions and Characteristics of Feudalism

THERE has already been occasion to speak of feudal states and feudal conditions; what precisely is meant by feudal? While there was much fighting in feudal society the distinction between feudalism and feuding must always be preserved and one must not fall into the error of the student, probably from Kentucky, who defined a feudal tenement as a crowded apartment house where all the families were continually fighting!

An exact definition of what feudalism was is practically impossible to evolve, for whatever criteria are selected there seem to be more exceptions than there are cases to prove the rule. Any definition is either simple and wrong, or involved, approximately correct and unintelligible.

Certain elements can be isolated; feudalism was political, economic, and social. It included the relationship of lord to vassal and of vassal to lord; it included the system of government employed in the medieval monarchies; it included the system of land tenure whereby land was held in return for definite stipulated services rendered and whereby services were paid for by grants of land to be held for life or in perpetuity. It included the means whereby the military establishment, the judicial machinery, the bases of taxation, and the monarch's advisory council were obtained. It was extremely complex and fundamentally simple. It was the natural and inevitable development in countries where the central government had broken down and where public functions, obligations, and privileges had been usurped by private individuals operating under bilateral private agreements. Feudalism has been almost universal, being found in various forms in Byzantium, the Moslem world, and Japan as well as throughout Western Europe. But it was never really complete even in Europe and there were always non-feudal elements confusing the picture even in the most completely feudalized countries. Feudalism is commonly broken down into two "systems": the feudal and the manorial. In the feudal system are included the essentially political relationships between people of the governing class, while the manorial includes the relationships between the lord and his servile or semi-servile dependents. The manorial system is the economic organization which underlay the feudal. From his manors the feudal lord derived the means of life, which enabled him to devote his own time and energies to warfare, government,

206

and sometimes brigandage. In the feudal society are found nobles, knights, and territorial lords of all degree; in the manorial, baillies, serfs, villeins, and the semi-free laboring classes. Medieval society was sharply divided into the three classes of those who prayed, those who fought, and those who worked. The fighters were in the feudal system, the workers in the manorial, though both overlapped a bit into the other.

The same man and the same piece of land entered into both systems. As a *vassal* of a lord for the landed fief which he held, the man was in the feudal system; as the lord of the manor he was in the manorial. And the same piece of land could be a manor and a fief, though generally a fief was composed of several manors.

Another thing that makes feudalism so hard to talk about intelligently is the confusion of time and place. As the system in one form or another lasted from the ninth to the fourteenth centuries, as it changed materially during that time, and as it was found all over the world with local variations everywhere, what can be said about one place at one time may be wholly wrong about another place at another time. For years English historians have tried to find a single "typical English manor;" everyone knows what such a manor should be like—but to date no one has ever found a manor that was in every respect typical, there are always local variations and discrepancies. The same can and must be said for feudalism. The only safe thing is to take a single feudal country in a single period and try to give from it as clear a picture as possible of what the general situation was.

Feudalism, as stated above, was the inevitable development when, as happened throughout western Europe, the agencies of central government broke down; when public powers were incapable of fulfilling their functions and private arrangements were made to fill in for the failure of public authorities. A modern analogy is to be found in Chicago of the 1920's, the "Age of Capone," when law enforcement practically broke down and gangs of racketeers carried on a brisk war. In this each gang leader gathered his mob who fought and died for him, as well as hijacking, "muscling-in" and other picturesque activities. When a man entered a mob, he and his family were protected by that mob; the gang leader "took care of his boys," if they were killed, the boss gave them spectacular funerals (to which it was customary for the rival mob which had just "rubbed him out" to send the largest wreath); he moreover pensioned their wives and guaranteed jobs to their sons. If a gangster was arrested, as occasionally happened in more flagrant crimes, the boss always had a "mouthpiece" to "spring him." Professor James Westfall Thompson, who taught at Chicago at the time, used to say that if one could only imagine the armored car as a mailed horse, and the tommy-gun as a lance, the conditions in Chicago were such as to make feudalism very easy to understand.

It is quite probable that had Al Capone lived in the tenth instead of the twentieth century, he would have ended up as a count if not a duke. When a particular mob-war was ended a regular treaty was arranged and a man of one party married the daughter of a leader of the opposite faction, the young couple being given a specified area in which they could run the show unhindered by either gang. It sounded like any medieval baronial marriage contract.

THE ORIGINS OF FEUDALISM

The origins of feudalism are to be found in the Roman Empire. While it was once popular to believe that feudalism was derived from the tribal practices of the early Germans (and some historians still adhere to this theory, at least in part) it is now generally recognized that both feudal and manorial origins stem from the conditions of the late empire. The Germans made some modifications to the Roman institutions, but their influence was on the whole slight.

In discussing the early development of feudal institutions it will be convenient to describe three relationships which combined to make the feudal: 1. the growth of tenurial dependence; 2. the growth of personal dependence; and 3. the development of immunities and the usurpation of public functions by private individuals. Development along these three lines gave birth to the system of relationships which we term feudalism.

Taking up first the matter of *tenurial dependence*—the relation of man to man by reason of his landed interests, the feudal and manorial practices find their origins in the late Roman mortgage tenure and in the *precarium*. With the increasing load of taxation which fell on the farmers of the empire, with the taxation which had to be paid out of capital and not income, the farmers found that a bad season would often throw them into practical bankruptcy. To get enough to continue operations, they resorted to mortgages even as now. The obvious person from whom to borrow, and the man who would lend the most on the security of the land, was the great landed proprietor of the neighborhood. He advanced seed and supplies against the mortgage of the land. When the farmer was unable to pay back, as was only too often the case, he foreclosed. The once independent small farmer thus found himself a tenant on the lord's estate. This procedure was also used as a means of tax-evasion (another modern institution with roots in antiquity); as we have seen earlier, the taxes bore hardest on the free farmers and the curiales of the local municipalities. They found that their taxes were greater than their income. To avoid this they would give their land to the neighboring great landowner, who might be a senator and tax exempt, or who at any rate bargained for his taxes with the imperial fisc and got off much lighter than the individual small farmer could. The arrangement was that the lord (as he will be called eventually) took title to the land and allowed the farmer to occupy it for life. It was a purely private transaction—the farmer ceded the land, he then requested the right to use it which the lord granted, the terms being usually much lighter than the taxes the farmer would have to pay. But this contract, called *precarium*, was not enforceable in the courts, so there was nothing to constrain the lord to abide by it if he chose to violate it. Later it became recognized as a legal contract, but at first it was merely a personal agreement and the only legal part was the outright cession of title to the lord.

This one-way gift by the original owner to the lord was often made more attractive to the precarist (he who received the land back at his prayer) by an augmentation of land granted by the lord. For example, if a farmer gave his lord his own land, the lord would grant him the use for life of double the amount of land,—the farmer's own property and an equal amount of his (the lord's) land. Thus the farmer got a larger acreage for life by ceding his title to the smaller amount, which he formerly held in perpetuity. As the institution of the precarium developed, it also became customary for lords, who had extensive tracts of land which they desired to get under cultivation, to grant land to landless farmers on the same terms that they had granted the land to precarists. Subsequently the plural form of the word slipped over into the singular and the three types of precarium were known as the: *precaria oblata, precaria remunerata* and *precaria data.* What the whole thing amounted to was that in the late empire, there was a great decline of free peasant holdings and an absorption of them into the great estates (*latifundia*), with the erstwhile free farmers staying on as tenant sharecroppers. This class was increased by the *coloni.* As the supply of slave labor became scarce and costly with the decline of Rome's conquests, proprietors found it much cheaper to work their lands with sharecroppers than with slaves. These peasants were settled on the estates by the lords and received the name of coloni. Practically the coloni and the precarists merged into a single class before long; eventually they both became villeins or serfs.

The legal status of these peasants was fixed by imperial legislation which bound the worker to his job. This legislation affected both urban and rural workers and resulted in the condition of the peasant bound to his land; he could not be removed while he fulfilled the terms of his tenure, and he could not voluntarily abandon his land and his work at any time. This legislation had been necessitated by men abandoning their farms rather than pay the taxes on them any longer. Under the taxation system worked out by Diocletian, where labor units were taxed along with livestock and land, it was necessary to assure the laborers remaining on the land, and appropriate legislation provided for this. Thus in the late empire developed the conditions which led directly to the manor with its serfs and semi-free villeins.

There were, moreover, in the empire large stretches of unreclaimed land which it was the desire of the government to bring under cultivation. To secure this a system was devised whereby the land was granted in large estates to an individual who would guarantee to work it and bring it under tillage. He received the land tax free for a stipulated number of years, so that he would not be paying taxes on land which was still unproductive and would have a chance to recoup some of his expenses before he did begin to pay. This system was termed *emphyteusis* and greatly facilitated the growth of the large estates. The holder of the estate then got the land worked by coloni or precarists—and the manor was created. There is every evidence to show that the manorial system, at least in its economic aspect, was quite prevalent in the late empire.

When the Germans entered the empire and took over the administration of it, they appropriated this system of land tenure. The ancient rule of *hospitium* was invoked,—that the district should support the soldiers who "protected" it. There were large confiscations of land for the benefit of the German soldiery, but it should be observed that these confiscations hardly affected the small farmers at all, as they were made almost entirely at the expense of the large estates, either the imperial estates or those of the large landowners. The peasants went along with the land and merely changed masters.

So far we have been concerned with tenurial dependence; let us now examine the other side of the coin, *personal* dependence. This too had its origin in Rome, though here the German modifications are more noticeable.

In the Roman republic there had existed the institution of *patronage*. A wealthy and powerful patrician would take under his protection lesser men who became his clients. He would represent them in court, would generally look after their interests and act as a patron to them. In return they would form a retinue for him when he went out on state occasions and would serve him in many small ways. The greatest lords took whole nations under their patronage, the Scipios being patrons of all Greeks who came to Rome. This system of patronage continued and increased in the empire. Further, if a lord freed any of his slaves they automatically became free clients of his. As a lord's influence and prestige increased, men desired to place themselves under his protection. When the lord received them into his patronage they were known as *suscepti*. In the more or less anarchic days of the empire, it was the customary thing for a lord to organize these clients into a guard, who accompanied him when he went abroad, who served as a claque when he spoke in public, who hung around his house, lived off his bounty, and served him. Arming slaves was always a dangerous practice and the lords felt much safer if they had a guard of faithful suscepti.

With the infiltration of Germans into the empire, they were seized upon as ideal clients. They were warlike fellows who made excellent guards; they certainly needed patrons if they were to get along in the complexities of Roman life. By the fourth century most important lords had their bands of German guards who lived in their houses and watched over them.

The introduction of Germans into this relationship brought in a new modification. As we have seen, in their tribal communities the Germans had been familiar with a lord and follower system known as the *comitatus*. The lord supplied his followers with arms and food, he shared with them the booty gained in raids or battles; when not engaged in warfare they all drank together, indulging in drunken brawls and tremendous boasting sessions. There was a far greater comradery among these Germans than there ever was between the Roman patron and his clients, and any member of the comitatus might aspire to founding his own company. It was the normal thing for a young German of high birth to enter the comitatus of one of his father's friends and thus serve his military apprenticeship.

Now when the Germans entered the empire and became suscepti of the Roman lords, they brought with them the institution of the comitatus; they swore mighty oaths to the lord, and required that he swear an oath to them. They assumed more of a social equality with him and became his companions as well as his guards.

As the imperial power declined in the anarchy of the third century, it became the practice for the great nobles to organize larger and larger private guards. By the fifth century, regular private armies were common. A general found that his position was considerably strengthened if he had, in addition to the regular Roman troops under his command, a corps of private armed retainers, who served not the state but him personally. These private troops were called *bucellarians* from the fact that they ate a special ration (bucellae) superior to the food issued the ordinary troops. Belisarius, the great general of Justinian, had been the commander of Justinian's bucellarians before Justinian became emperor. In his own army he had as great a number of bucellarians as he did imperial troops. The fifth and sixth centuries were the great period for the employment of these private armies.

The loyalty of these troops to their lord was a matter of great pride. The illustrous Roman general Aetius, the victor of Châlons, had a corps of bucellarians; when he was murdered by Valentinian III, his bucellarians were taken over by the emperor; but they were loyal to their former lord, to whom they had sworn fidelity, and two of them quickly avenged his death by murdering the emperor.

In the Germanic states which developed in the West, the bucellarian system provided a large part of the military force of the state. The Germans were familiar with the old comitatus, they adapted the bucellarian system; in ordering their kingdoms the personal contract played a large part in securing the agents and agencies of government. It was in Visigothic Gaul and Spain that a new departure was made when the bucellarians were for the first time paid not in arms and booty, but in land.

The payment of the armed retainer by granting him a piece of land is characteristically feudal; although the term did not develop quite so early the soldier can well be termed, as he was later called, the vassal.

Due perhaps to the immense popularity of the opera *The Bohemian Girl* with its unfortunate song about dwelling in marble halls "with vassals and serfs at my side," there is a popular misconception as to the status of a vassal. To couple him with a serf is the rankest heresy and comes only from a base misunderstanding of his true position. The vassal was always a free warrior in the same general social class as his lord, while the serf was a poor lowly creature separated from the lord by an impassable social and economic chasm. The vassal was himself usually a lord with serfs under his dominion.

The real development of vassalage comes when the tenurial and the personal dependencies fused—when it became common to pay the personal dependent by granting him a piece of land, when it became customary to bind the tenurial dependent by requiring from him an oath of fidelity. This process worked, of course, both ways; if the lord had land to give out he would give it to a man who was already his personal dependent; a man holding land from a lord would bind himself closer to his lord by assuming a personal dependency, by *commending* himself to the lord and being received by him into his company.

Thus far we have been talking about paying a man for services by granting him land. This has undoubtedly been somewhat misleading. While in some cases the warrior might conceivably have worked the land himself, it was really *rights over the land* that were granted him. The land came all equipped with peasants who did the work; the warrior was given enough land so that he could live off the returns without having to work himself and could devote his time to fighting—or carousing in his lord's hall.

These rights are what distinguish real feudalism from the semi-feudal arrangements from which it sprung, and will be discussed later on in discussing the manorial system.

Before the grants of land in payment of services could be really feudal, it was necessary to have the *immunity*. This developed in the Merovingian period and started as a privilege given the church. As the royal power declined, it spread to secular holdings. The immunity did not, as has been often claimed, create private justice; what it did was to declare a certain territory immune from interference by the agents of the ruler. This created a judicial vacuum, which was then filled by the private courts. The Merovingian kings granted to the church and monasteries complete immunity from any outside interference; the king's agents did not enter the domains to collect taxes, to administer justice, to recruit troops. The immune land was a small state within a state and its administration and government were left to the owner of the immunity. Gradually these same immunities were extended to secular lords, and other lords usurped immunities, so that by the end of the Carolingian period there were few lands which were not under the control of their own lord. In Capetian France the rule prevailed that there should be *"Nulle terre sans Seigneur."*

The earlier form of the fief was the *benefice*. This later became an ecclesiastical tenure essentially, but originally it was the tenure from which the fief developed. A benefice was granted by a monarch in return for some stipulated service; it might be prayers for his soul or those of his ancestors by the clergy, it might be military service by warriors. The benefice was for life only, and limited the holder to the use of the land and the consumption of its products (*usufruct*). The eminent domain always rested with the lord, and this was true of fully developed feudalism. When in the Carolingian period the benefices became hereditary, they are commonly called fiefs, and this heritability is the distinguishing mark between benefices and fiefs. In general, benefice is the earlier term, fief the later, but both were used interchangeably as late as the twelfth century.

As we have stated above, feudalism developed when the central government broke down. In the Merovingian times local government was entrusted by the king to counts (*comites*, members of the *comitatus*), companions of the king who were sent out to rule the local districts in the king's name. This practice continued under the Carolingians. In some border districts it was found better to allow the country to be ruled by a member of the old local kingly house, who had made submission and become the vassal of the king; in these cases the local ruler was called duke (*dux*). At first these agents ruled in the king's behalf, but as the royal power grew weaker they inclined to rule more for themselves and less for the monarch. Charlemagne checked this tendency with his *missi dominici*, itinerant agents who went around checking up on the counts and bringing them to obedience. But as the Carolingians declined the counts grew stronger and soon assumed to themselves the royal powers which had earlier been delegated to them. Thus the count would hold court, collect taxes and raise an army, but it was for himself not his king that he did these things; he kept the taxes and the army served him in his private wars. Lands were granted out for military service—but the service was

due to the count who granted the lands, not to the king who held the ultimate legal title to the land. As the kings were too weak to do anything
about this, they compromised and recognized the counts as holding the
land in return for services to the crown—usually military service with a
given number of retainers and whatever taxes the crown could force them
to disgorge. When we find the local lord holding his land in return for
stipulated services, administering his own justice, collecting his own
revenues from the lands and paying the king only occasional sums, leading his own army of men sworn to follow him, then we have arrived at
feudalism.

TYPES OF TENURES

In the first place, let us examine the various types of feudal tenures of
which there were three main varieties: frankalmoin, military, and sergeanty.

Frankalmoin was a strictly ecclesiastical tenure. By it land was given
to the church with no strings attached. The church did nothing in return
for the land, and the benefit to the donor was spiritual in that he had done
a good deed in giving to the church. Frankalmoin is, however, generally
confused with the ecclesiastical benefice whereby land was ·given to the
church in return for spiritual service, such as prayers. Men would give a
tract of land to endow a perpetual mass for their souls and the church
held the land as long as the mass was celebrated. Although there is a very
definite distinction between the ecclesiastical benefice and frankalmoin,
there is a popular tendency among many of our writers on the subject
to confuse the two. Both frankalmoin and tenure by ecclesiastical services
are sharply opposed to lands held by the church for secular service, which
lands were commonly referred to as being held by barony or by lay fee.

The most common type of feudal tenure is the ordinary *military tenure*.
By it a man was given a fief for the service of a given number of knights.
The number of knights depended on the value of the fief, the bargaining
power of the vassal, the circumstances of the crown at the moment and
many other variables. But the personal service of the knight to whom
the fief was given was always required. The amount of time that he had to
serve was, in France in the twelfth century, limited to forty days at his
own expense, all service in excess thereof being at the expense of the
lord.

Military service was divided into two categories: *ost and chevauchée*
and *castle guard*. Ost and chevauché was service in the field and the vassal
owed forty days of this, castle guard was service as a guard at the lord's
castle and the vassal owed a specified amount of this in addition to the
time in the field. The distinction between ost and chevauchée is uncer-

tain, the present tendency being to believe that ost refers to service in the king's army in company with the lord, while chevauchée means service in the lord's army in his private campaigns, though some scholars think the difference lay in the length of the expedition, ost being a long campaign, chevauchée a short raid. In England, theoretically, the vassal owed service only when the king summoned the host, but that was purely theoretical and vassals served their lords just as they did in France in their private quarrels.

In most countries there was a territorial limitation on military service in that the vassal was not forced to accompany the lord against his will outside the limits of the realm. Nor were vassals compelled to serve in person before they were fifteen or after they had passed sixty years of age. Women were, of course, exempt from personal service, but had to supply a knight to serve for them.

Sergeanty has been defined as that tenure which was not any other tenure; it was tenure by service not ecclesiastical nor knightly. Military sergeanty was tenure by serving as a sergeant, that is, a lightly armed horseman or a footman. Sergeanty by supply was tenure in return for supplying a certain number of horses, spears, arrowheads or a given amount of provender. Then there were such sergeanties of service as cook, butler, stable groom, et al. There is the celebrated English sergeanty of holding the king's head when he crossed the Channel, for which its holder received a manor in Kent. Sergeanty could be made a very nominal type of tenure. A fief could be held in return for a rose, or a pair of gauntlets, a goblet of wine or any other token payment. When we remember that cash was relatively unused and that service of any kind was paid for by granting land, sergeanty is the only answer, although it may seem strange to us today to think of enfeoffing your cook with a plot of land in return for her services. Still, it had its advantages, as it probably guaranteed a certain modicum of permanency among domestic servants, which is sadly lacking today. Clerks in the lord's household were sergeants, one of the most famous sergeants of all time being Geoffrey Chaucer whose name appears on the royal rolls as holding a sergeanty. But by Chaucer's time the fief he held was a money fief—a payment of a certain sum annually from the royal treasury in lieu of the land.

This worked both ways and eventually ended feudalism. The vassals paid cash instead of rendering their services; the rulers granted fiefs in cash instead of in land. It may seem more natural to us, but it took time to work out the idea—time and a greater amount of cash than was extant in the halcyon days of feudalism. For feudalism was essentially a non-monetary system.

In addition to the above tenures there were other tenures which were not strictly feudal, and which were in fact non-feudal. Such are the *allods* and *socages*. The allods were the old free tenures, where the holder held his land directly from the king without any intermediary lords. These were more common in the south of Europe than in the north, but even in highly feudalized Normandy we find occasional allods. But these tenures in fee-simple became increasingly rarer as time went on, becoming almost extinct in the north by the thirteenth century.

Closely allied to the allod was the English socage tenure; in this tenure the holder of the land paid a rent, sometimes in money, sometimes in agricultural produce and service. The rental might be merely a token payment or it might be a considerable sum, and occasionally the socage tenant is hard to distinguish from either the sergeant or the servile tenant. Both socage and allod were remnants from an older period and not properly feudal themselves.

The Feudal Contract

The basis of all feudal relations lay in the feudal contract. This was formed by a ceremony whereby the vassal swore *fealty* and performed *homage* to his lord, in return receiving the *seisin* of the fief.

The vassal knelt before his lord, placed his hands between those of the lord and swore to be faithful to him in all things and to serve him loyally. He promised to become his man (*homo*) and in return for benefits received to serve him with a stipulated service. The lord then received him as a vassal and invested him with the seisin (i.e. possession) of the fief. According to the *Establissements de St. Louis,* a code of thirteenth century French law, this cermony should be conducted as follows: [1]

with hands joined [the vassal should] speak as follows: "Sir, I become your man and promise to you fealty for the future as my lord towards all men who may live or die, rendering to you such service as the fief requires, making to you your relief as you are the lord" . . . The lord should immediately reply to him "And I receive you and take you as my man, and give you this kiss as a sign of faith saving my right and that of others according to the usage of the various districts."

At first all homage was the same, the vassal pledging unrestricted service and allegiance to his lord. As the feudal relationship became complicated with a vassal holding lands from more than one lord, homage was divided into liege and simple homage. *Liege homage* was the homage taken to the first lord from whom the vassal held his fief and was unlimited. To other later lords, he took *simple homage,* which reserved the homage done the liege lord. In Normandy, England and the other Norman states, liege homage was always reserved for the duke or king, and a vassal pledged

[1] Univ. of Penna. "Translations and Reprints," First Series, IV, 3; *Documents Illustrative of Feudalism,* p. 21. A very fine selection of illustrative documents to illustrate homage and fealty is also found in Thatcher and McNeal, *Source Book* (Scribners, 1907), pp. 363–65.

liege homage to both the king and his first suzerain, that to the king taking precedence over all others. Ordinarily, however, liege homage could only be taken to one's chief lord, or him from whom one held his first enfeoffment.

The performance and reception of homage carried with it very real obligations. The suzerain who received the man into his homage was bound to give him protection in his person and in his tenement, to render him justice in his court, to defend him against outside attack and always to treat the vassal and members of his family honorably.

The vassal, on the other hand, undertook considerably greater obligations to his lord. In the first place, he must serve him according to the obligation of the fief by military service, sergeanty, or whatever the service was. This must be personal service unless the vassal was too young or too old to perform it, in which case a substitute could be sent. If the fief was a military one held for the service of ten knights, the vassal was held to serve in person accompanied by nine other knights. This personal service always accompanied liege homage, and was assumed in simple homage unless the vassal was personally serving his liege lord at the time, in which case a substitute was sent. Secondly, the vassal was obliged to perform court service; he must attend his lord's court when summoned and give counsel and advice to the lord in any matter which he might request. This is most important as it was from this feudal court service that the great curias of the kings developed, to become the governing bodies of the feudal monarchies.

Beside military and court service, the vassal owed many other services and payments. When the lord was traveling he had the right to visit his vassal and stay with him a stipulated number of days at the vassal's expense. This right, called *purveyance* or *gite,* was most unpopular and was one of the first to be commuted into a regular money payment. In addition, the vassal owed a cash payment when he inherited the fief, called *relief.* In theory the fief was not hereditary and reverted to the lord at the death of the holder. The heir then had to pay the relief to lift (re-lever) the fief and assume occupancy. Then there were the *feudal aids,* which the vassal paid to the lord when the latter was put to some extraordinary expense. These were at first three: when the lord's eldest son was knighted, when his eldest daughter was married for the first time, and when the lord was captured and had to be ransomed. To these later was added the aid for the crusade; when the lord went on a crusade and the vassal did not go too, the latter was held to contribute to the expenses of his lord. These payments were due from all military fiefs, but were not collected from sergeanties or lesser holdings.

In addition to the feudal aids were the feudal incidents, events in the life of the vassal on which the lord enjoyed special privileges. Thus, if a vassal died leaving a minor heir, the lord assumed the guardianship of the child by his right of *wardship*. He would administer the fief during the minority of the heir, but was held to turn it over at his majority without payment of relief. If a woman inherited a fief, the suzerain could assume the right of *marriage* by which he could stipulate whom the heiress should marry or collect a fee for permission to marry freely. This was a most important right, as the lord must be guaranteed that a vassal heiress should not marry a man who was the enemy of her lord. It was often abused and became a means of extortion in the hands of unscrupulous lords, as they would stipulate that an heiress marry a thoroughly unacceptable person or pay a large fine to avoid it. In many feudal countries if the vassal became a leper, or went insane, the lord occupied the fief until the heir came of age, though in more centralized states this was frequently a royal prerogative.

If the family of the vassal died out the land *escheated* to the lord, who was then free to grant it to someone else. Similarly, if the vassal was guilty of treason or failure to perform his feudal obligations the land could be declared *forfeit* and the lord could enter into possession, although this could only be done by the action of the lord's court and the judgment of the vassal's peers.

Subinfeudation: the Feudal Hierarchy

We have seen that a vassal might owe several knights in service to his lord. Where did he get these knights? The answer lies in the process of *sub-infeudation* whereby a vassal granted out to his own vassals portions of the land which he held in fief from his own suzerain. Everyone in the feudal organization was at the same time vassal and suzerain, except the king at the top, who "held only from God," and the lowliest knight at the bottom who had no one holding from him. All the others, called mesne lords, were at the same time vassals of their own suzerains and suzerains of their own vassals.

In theory the picture is a simple one; the king grants lands to the great counts who in turn grant them the lesser barons who grant them to knights. Unfortunately, this was not the way it worked out. Barons and knights held directly from the king, counts held from other counts, barons from other barons, knights from other knights. Barons could even hold from knights and counts from barons. There was absolutely no system about feudalism: it developed utterly casually and without any *a priori* theory. Only after the reality was well established, in fact only after feudal institutions had become out-worn and were beginning to decline, do we find any clear theory of feudalism developing; before that time it grew as the practical solution to an immediate problem. In the later Middle

Ages there was a pseudo-feudalism which conformed to a theory, but the real vigorous feudalism of the tenth and eleventh centuries developed without benefit of theory or plan.

When a man had land and needed service, he would subinfeudate to acquire the service required; if he could acquire more land by becoming the vassal of another lord he would gladly do so. In all of his fiefs, a noble would retain a portion for himself as his *domain,* where he personally owned the manors and enjoyed the produce. The greater the domain, the more wealthy the lord, for domain land was under his direct control and all the revenues from it went into his treasury, while the fruits of land granted in fief went to the feudatory and the lord received only the stipulated service.

In the composition of any large seigneury, the lands would be divided into domain lands kept by the lord and fiefs granted to vassals. These vassals might be great lords holding many fiefs or simple knights with a single manor. The same vassal might hold many separate holdings in various parts of the lord's seigneury; and the same baron might hold fiefs of any number of lords. The count of Champagne, for example, possessed a seigneury, which was made up of fiefs held from the emperor, the king of France, the duke of Burgundy, the archbishops of Rheims and Sens, the abbot of St. Denis, the bishops of Chalons, Langres, Auxerre, and Autun. From his seigneury he had, in addition to his domains, lands enfeoffed to the extent of 2,036 knights. The largest fief was that of Chatillon and Fismes which owed 160 knights, and in which lands were held by the counts of Rethel, Grandpré, Roucy, Chiny, and the lords of Rozoy, Montmort, Oisy, Chatillon and others.[2] To some of these the count of Champagne was liege lord while some held their lands from him by simple homage. From all of them, however, he would exact military service with its attendant court service and feudal aids and incidents.

Thus it will be seen that a feudal lordship was made up of a great number of rights over different parcels of land. The lord tried to fill in his lands and acquire as compact a fief as possible, but this was often impossible and the average baron held lands in many counties and parts of the country, often separated by large estates belonging to others.

Any right over the land could be granted as a fief: the same land might be held by different lords for different services, and land granted in knight service could be subinfeudated in frankalmoin, sergeanty, or socage. Land held by sergeanty or frankalmoin could equally be subinfeudated in knight service. There was a general tendency in the twelfth century for the great vassals to enfeoff many more knights than they owed their suzerains. Thus the bishop of Bayeaux, who had 119 knights owing to him, owed but

[2] The documents for the county of Champagne are translated in Thatcher-McNeal, *Source Book,* pp. 368–82.

10 knights to the king of France and 40 to the duke of Normandy; the bishop of Countances owed but 5 knights to the duke, but had 18 owing to him.[3]

In his *Studies in the History of the English Feudal Barony*, Sidney Painter has shown that in an analysis of eight great English baronies of the twelfth century, five had about 70 per cent of their lands subinfeudated to mesne lords, who produced from 80 to 100 per cent of the knights due from the entire barony. The rest of the knights were hired with revenues from the domain. With the introduction of *scutage*, a money payment in lieu of knight service, there was a general tendency to retain more land in domain and to subinfeudate less.[4]

The process of subinfeudation caused innumerable complexities. In France the rule prevailed that "the vassal of my vassal is not my vassal" (*vassalus vassali mei non est meus vassalus*) and the superior lord had no control whatever over the arriére-vassals (i.e. those who held from his vassals). In the Norman lands, owing to the reservation of liege homage noted above, the king or duke could directly control the arriére vassals, but this was a Norman innovation and not generally known elsewhere. Matters became complicated when a man held from two lords who became engaged in war with each other. Theoretically, he served in person in the army of his liege lord, sending the required number of knights to the army of his secondary lord. Actually, he probably threw all his resources onto the side of one or the other and trusted to victory to straighten out his situation later. Or he might be able to arrange for a neutrality; but in theory he served each with the quota of knights owed.

Private warfare was one of the prerogatives of the feudal baron, and save in the Norman countries, his vassals were legally bound to follow him in his private quarrels. This right permeated all ranks of feudal so-ciety, every man held his own castle against every other save his feudal lord, and war was the common condition of life. Indeed these feudal gentry had little value save in war, and perforce kept in practice in the one art and occupation which they knew.

As will have been noted, the organization of feudalism was entirely vertical. While there was a definite arrangement of relationship between a man and his superiors and inferiors, there was no relationship between men of the same status not bound by ties of either lordship or vassalage. Between the vassals of the count of Champagne and those of the count of Anjou there was no possible tie or any ordered relationship provided. If a lord wished to attach to himself a man of conspicuous valor and worth,

---

[3] Pollock and Maitland, *English Law*, I, 264.

[4] S. Painter, *Studies in the History of the English Feudal Barony*, p. 28 ff. The Mande-villes, who enjoyed a very low quota of service due, were able to raise 175 per cent of their obligations on only half of their lands; but this was most unusual. Other barons had to enfeoff almost all their lands to procure the necessary quotas of knights.

he could do so by making him his vassal for a fief given, but there was no other way, unless a marriage alliance could be contracted between two houses.

This very lack of horizontal relationships made for a general attitude of democracy among the members of the feudal noble classes. Whether a man was a duke or a mere knight, if he was noble, he enjoyed the freedom of society and could mingle unabashedly with any other noble. Throughout most of the feudal era he was cut off by an almost impassable gulf from all non-nobles, but within the caste distinctions of rank mattered comparatively little. The poor knight-bachelor might well marry the daughter of the count and become himself a great lord. Even the king was only one among social equals in this select society; he was always first among equals (*primus inter pares*), and the oath taken by the Aragonese nobles to their king shows how completely the monarch was merely a feudal lord: "We who are as good as you, swear to you who are no better than we, to accept you as our king and sovereign lord, provided you observe our liberties and laws; but if not, not." [5]

About such a monarch there was little divinity: he was the lord bound by the feudal contract to vassals who were his equals. This equality among the nobility is one of the most striking features of feudal society and resulted in a rough limitation of the monarch which preceded the more elaborate constitutional limitation of later days.

FEUDAL COURTS AND JUSTICE

Judgment by his peers was one of the most valued rights of the vassal. Every action was taken in the lord's court which was made up of his vassals, and all vassals of a common lord were *peers*. This term which now means merely social equals, originally meant a common vassal of a mutual overlord: thus all the vassals of the count of Champagne were peers, as were those of the count of Anjou, but the vassals of Champagne were not the peers of the Angevins. Counts, viscounts, chatelains, knights were all peers as long as they held their fiefs from a common lord, but only those holding from a mutual lord were peers, irrespective of their social status.

Every feudal lord who had vassals had a court to which the vassals brought their litigation. The lord merely presided over the court and the decisions were made by the other vassals. This guaranteed that the lord could not illegally oppress his vassal, for the other vassals would stand together to preserve their legal rights against the suzerain. And as every lord was himself the vassal of some higher lord, it was to his interest to preserve the rights of vassals.

[5] R. B. Merriman; *Spanish Empire* (Macmillan, 1918) I, 458–59.

If the vassal had a suit against his lord he must first bring it into the lord's court for judgment by his fellow-vassals. If, however, justice could not be obtained in the lord's court, the vassal could appeal to the court of his lord's suzerain. Thus a vassal of Champagne, who failed to receive justice in the court of the count, could appeal to the court of the king of France as suzerain of Champagne. Usually this involved difficulties, as the lord would probably attack the vassal while he was appealing, so that the king, should he decide in favor of the vassal, would have to defeat the count and force him to reinstate the vassal in his tenement. In some countries, Normandy, England, crusader Jerusalem et al., the vassals had a legal right to revolt against their lord if he refused to abide by the decisions of the court.

The law enforced in these courts was the custom of the fief. Until the later days of feudalism we find no elaborate codes of law and even when they do appear they are largely codes of custom written down. The law existed: it was the duty of the court to find it and declare it. Legislation was utterly unknown in medieval society; all law was court-made law, and the consensus of the opinions of the wiser members of the court established what was the custom and what was respected as the law of the land. "The memory of the oldest inhabitant runneth not to the contrary" was a formula whereby law was declared throughout the feudal world. After the reintroduction of the Roman Law into western Europe, there was a sharp division between the lands of the custom law and those of the written law, but in the high feudal age of the tenth and eleventh centuries there was no law save custom in northern Europe.

Every locality had its own custom and the principle of the territoriality of the law was inherent in feudalism. The Île de France, Flanders, Normandy, Anjou, Champagne, Poitou, Burgundy, all had their own laws based on the traditional customs of the country, and often differing widely in detail. Such matters as female inheritance, the right of representation whereby a man inherited through a deceased parent, and the rights of collateral heirs were all subjects in which local variation was common. Every fief that had high justice could have its own law, and the gallows which hanged a man for an offense in one fief might be unused for the same crime a hundred miles away. Medieval law as localized as medieval currency, and justice and the mint right were equally attributes of the seigneury.

The king's court was only the feudal court writ large. It was made up of the tenants-in-chief of the crown who served in fulfillment of their feudal court duty. The greatness of the accomplishment of Henry II of England in establishing the common law, common to all the realm, can only be properly understood by bearing in mind the complexities of feudal justice before his innovations.

Procedure in the court was by ordeal and combat. Trial by battle was the normal means of deciding a case in the feudal court, a system which tended to give right to the strong at the expense of their weaker brethren. But the terms of the combat were fixed by the members of the court who could and did exercise their judgment in regulating the rules of the battle to give the advantage to one side or the other. The same applied to the use of the ordeal which could be made difficult or easy at the discretion of the court.

Appeal from a feudal court could be made to that of the overlord, but a decision once given was immutable, unless the appellant could prove failure of justice. Beyond the royal high court there was no appeal in any case. Appeals were discouraged by a rule in some countries that an appeal could be made only by individually challenging all of the members of the court to the judicial duel and defeating them all between sunrise and sunset, a privilege rarely if ever invoked.

Only members of the feudal nobility were amenable in the feudal court; lesser folk were tried in their own courts—the manor courts, market, and burgess courts, which were presided over by the lord's bailiff. Churchmen and ecclesiastical property fell under the jurisdiction of the canon law courts, though for a lay holding a churchman was amenable in the feudal court.

FEUDALIZATION OF THE CHURCH

The church did not escape the influence of feudalism but became in almost every way feudalized. The wealth of the church lay in its lands and endowments, which fell naturally into the feudal relationships. As has been noted, much land was held by the church in frankalmoin or in return for ecclesiastical services, but the clergy also held land as secular barons. One of the great problems which the church was always having to contend with was the question as to whether the bishop (for example) was a dignitary of the church or a feudal magnate. Prelates held high office in the state, which naturally emphasized their feudal position at the expense of their ecclesiastical. This was the basis for the Investiture Controversy which was to play so important a part in the history of the late eleventh century.

When a lord built a church or chapel on his own lands, he naturally expected to appoint the priest who should serve it. Thus developed the so-called "owned churches" over which the bishops exercised an unsatisfactory control and which they were always trying to bring under more complete subjection. Even monasteries and nunneries were somewhat feudalized, as they were often founded and endowed by secular nobles who preserved rights of appointment over them. The endowment of a church or monastery was a common way of a noble's seeking to compensate for a life of questionable morality: the noble would endow a monastery with lands on condition that he be allowed immediate entry into the house without passing through the novitiate. The life of Geoffrey of Anjou quoted above in Chapter 11 shows how convenient this could be.

Many of the clergy who held their office by virtue of the appointment by the feudal lord were hardly worthy of their divine offices. The lord of a manor would appoint the son of a favored serf as the local priest irrespective of his qualifications, with the result that the local clergy were often illiterate. The younger son of a great noble would be awarded a bishopric over which his father had certain claims. This resulted in the rise of a class of princely warrior prelates, more noted of their prowess in arms than for the sanctity of their lives. Especially was this true in Germany where, under the Ottos, the higher clergy were favored at the expense of the secular nobles. The fighting bishops of Germany were legendary throughout western Europe.

But the church was the one institution which sought to soften the harshness and brutality of the feudal society. The most effective means devised were the Peace and the Truce of God. The Peace of God was a prohibition against fighting women, children, or clergy, and endeavored to save these classes from the brutalities of constant warfare. The Truce was an attempt to impose a period of cessation of hostilities every weekend; there should be no fighting from sundown Friday until sunrise Monday. These devices were not too successful but they did something to mitigate the incessant warfare of the feudal nobles and to render it more humane. If the church was itself somewhat brutalized, it was the church alone which ameliorated conditions and forced men to keep faith. Without the sanction of the church, the whole feudal organization would have fallen apart, for it was based on a reciprocal oath and only through the church was the validity of an oath preserved.

CHAPTER 13

ECONOMIC AND CULTURAL DEVELOPMENTS

✣

ECONOMIC ASPECTS

IN discussing the economic life of the early Middle Ages a sharp distinction must be made between the highly developed economy of the Byzantine and Moslem world and the crude agricultural conditions of Western Europe. Even more than in politics or intellectual accomplishments, the superiority of the East is revealed in her economic life. In agriculture, industry and commerce the Eastern world was incomparably advanced over the West until the eleventh century, when Western Europe began to gain the ascendency which it was to preserve to the present. If the Middle East today seems a backward and undeveloped area, it must be remembered that it was a center of economic activity and great material luxury at a time when Western Europe was a crude agricultural community. A brief description of these two civilizations between the seventh and eleventh centuries will point the contrast.

THE BYZANTINE EMPIRE

Although the greatest development of the Byzantine Empire was in the period before the Arab conquests, until the eleventh century Byzantium remained the dominant power in Mediterranean economic life. Located at the crossroads of the trade routes from East to West and commanding the road from Asia to western Europe, Constantinople was the chief emporium of the Christian world. Her merchant marine covered the Mediterranean and her bazaars were filled with the produce of every country of the known world.

Agriculture was, of course, still the chief means of livelihood to the majority of her inhabitants, and Byzantium shared with the Moslem countries a superiority of agricultural development far in advance of the ruder methods employed in the West. Horticulture, viniculture, and scientific agricultural techniques were practised throughout the empire, as through the lands of the caliphate; while producing the ordinary cereals found in Europe, the lands of the empire also brought forth citrus fruits, mulberries for the production of silk, flax, and herbs used in medicine. The

225

wealth of the great Byzantine families was largely based on great landed estates, worked by servile dependents, in the manner of the old Roman *latifundia*. But it was in her commerce and industry that Byzantium presented the greatest contrast to Western Europe.

Constantinople was the natural meeting place of East and West. To her port came merchants from the Arab lands, from Italy and the West, from Russia and the Slavic north. The silk and jewels of China, India and Ceylon reached her either along the "old silk route" through Turkestan or through the Arab-controlled routes of the Persian Gulf, Red Sea, Tigris, and Nile valleys. From the Caspian and Black Sea trade came the spices, jewels, rugs and tapestries of central Asia. From Russia came the amber, furs, and honey of the north. Western Europe sent timber, wine and furs. Ivory from Africa, pearls from Ceylon, steel from Damascus, Moroccan and Spanish leather, and slaves from all parts of the world were to be found in her markets.

The main street of Constantinople was the Mesé, along which were located the shops of the artisans. In the Palace Square were the perfumers, so located that the sweetness of their wares would be wafted into the sacred precincts; along the street were the jewelers, leather workers, bakers, grocers, and butchers, silk merchants and money changers. Byzantine industry was rigidly regulated, and the *Book of the Prefect,* which shows the regulations in effect in the late ninth century, includes rules for the governance of the bankers and money-changers, manufacturers and merchants of silk, linen, and cotton cloths, silver and copper smiths, soap makers, butchers, confectioners, spice merchants, salt dealers, and other lesser trades.

Among the products of Byzantine industry were many items of the luxury trade: gold embroidery, cloisonné work, mosaic icons, inlaid enamels, jewelry, cloths of gold, silver and purple, carved ivories, all were produced to cater to the exquisite taste of the Byzantine nobility. The sumptiousness of their dress is evidenced by portraits of the time: the luxury of their manners is revealed in their own literature and in the descriptions left by foreign visitors. The magnificence of their churches, the mosaics, inlaid furniture, tapestries, ivory and sandalwood boxes, jeweled chalices and dishes, icons and crucifixes which have been preserved all attest the degree of refinement and artistic achievement reached by the Byzantines.

Perhaps the best proof of the supremacy of Byzantium was the fact that her hyperper, called the *besant,* was the standard coin used throughout the world, and was copied in both Moslem and Christian mints wherever a firm currency was needed for international trade.

The economic policy followed by the emperors was not an especially intelligent one, and Byzantine commerce and industry flourished almost in spite of governmental restrictions and monopolies. Her great carrying trade declined, and long before Constantinople ceased to be the chief commercial center of Christendom, the products came to be carried in the ships of the Moslems, Russians, and Italians. Venice built her greatness on her Eastern trade which she acquired at the expense of Byzantium, of which she was at first only a western outpost.

THE MOSLEM CALIPHATES

By the ninth and tenth centuries the economic supremacy of Byzantium was seriously challenged by the Moslem caliphates. Baghdad, Basrah, Cairo, Alexandria, Damascus, and Cordova all became centers of active economic life, which disputed with Constantinople and with each other the dominance of industry and trade. Baghdad as the city of the *Arabian Nights* is familiar to all, with its magnificent palaces, teeming bazaars, mysterious side-streets, and sumptious apartments in which Al Rashid and his companions engaged in their fabulous adventures. The luxury of the wealthy and the squalor of the poor reflect the varied life of this city where kings and beggars, viziers and porters mingled in a world filled with genii and monstrous beasts. Of course, the *Arabian Nights* do not accurately portray the life of Baghdad any more than the old French *romans d'adventure* revealed the life of Arthurian Camelot; they were written in Egypt under the Mameluks and much more closely reflect fifteenth-century Cairo than ninth-century Baghdad, but they do show the ideas of luxury and of material and intellectual accomplishment, which the Moslem considered the height of civilization. Every Arab boy could dream of finding a marvelous lamp as did Aladdin, or of falling into a robbers' cache of treasure as did Ali Baba, and the marvelous adventures of Sinbad are actually based on travel accounts of Abbasid merchants, who visited Ceylon, Zanzibar, and the farthest reaches of Africa and the Spice Islands.

The Arabs took over the control of the Eastern trade routes from the Persians and extended their own carrying trade to the Far East, Africa and the southern coast of the Mediterranean. Arab coins have been found in Russia and Scandinavia; we have records of Arab merchants in China, India, and the East Indies; the works of the Arab geographers show how well-informed they were on the far reaches of Asia and Africa and how intimately they knew the customs and manners of the peoples of distant lands.

The Arabs themselves looked upon trade as an honorable profession, reserving their disdain for agricultural labor, which they left to the native peasantry; and the ports of the eastern Mediterranean and Middle East generally experienced an increase of economic activity with the Moslem conquest. "Apes and ivory," slaves, spices, precious stones, textiles, and all the products of the East, which we have already noticed, passing through Constantinople likewise appeared on the quais and in the markets of the Moslem cities. Moslem trade did not equal that of Byzantium in the Mediterranean, or extend much into the Black Sea area, but in the Indian Ocean, Persian Gulf, Red Sea, and the Caspian Sea the Moslems enjoyed the great bulk of all commerce.

Moslem industry produced many of the articles of commerce. From Iraq, Persia, Transoxiana, and Khurasan came rugs, carpets and tapestries—the prayer rugs of Bukhara achieving world renown. Among Moslem textiles were damask from Damascus, taffeta from Persia, striped "tabby" cloth from the Attab quarter of Baghdad, brocades, silk, woolen and cotton cloth from Iraq, Persia, Syria, Armenia and Khurasan, and furs and felt from Samarkand and Bukhara. Syria was famous for its dyes, glass, sweetmeats, and Damascus steel; Egypt, Iraq, Khurasan, and Sogdiana were great agricultural areas, producing sugar cane, oranges, lemons, rice, wheat, dates, cotton, flax, sesame, cucumbers, grapes, apples, peaches, figs, spices, and other fruits and cereals; mines in Khurasan, Transoxiana, Persia, and Syria yielded up gold, silver, rubies, lapis lazuli, turquoise, iron, sulphur, and asbestos. Paper was made at Samarkand as early as the eighth century, and the industry spread to Iraq and Egypt in the ninth. From there it passed to Morocco and Spain in the twelfth century and thence to western Europe.

The cultivation of flowers reached a high point among the Moslems, and the gardens which surrounded their cities yielded roses, lilies, and other flowers used in the preparation of perfumes. Most of these products of the Arab countries are commonplaces in our life today, but in the Middle Ages many of them were objects of the greatest rarity and were practically unknown in Western Europe. It must be borne in mind that the English, French, and Germans of the tenth century were either unacquainted with many of these oriental products which we take for granted, or, if they knew them at all, possessed but one or two examples which they prized as great treasures. To the Byzantine or Moslem they were probably as familiar as they are to us today.

Although the consumption of alcoholic beverages is strictly prohibited by the Koran, viniculture was practiced throughout the Moslem world, and wines were made and consumed by the less pious Moslems as well as by the non-Moslem population. The breeding of livestock was a major industry; the primitive Arab reckoned his wealth in camels, and Arabian horses enjoyed a deserved renown the world over. Sheep, goats and cattle were found everywhere, though pigs were less popular throughout the Islamic world than in Europe.

In both the Byzantine and Moslem empires we find, then, in the early Middle Ages a highly developed industrial and commercial civilization centering around urban communities, where men led comfortable lives

with many refinements which we consider essentially modern. Every town
had its public baths, and personal cleanliness was a religious duty for all
Moslems. Among the upper classes their diet was varied and rich, their
mode of living comfortable and often luxurious. In all they preserved
the creature comforts of the Romans and Hellenistic Greeks and more
closely approached our own manner of living than did the Europeans
of their time.

WESTERN EUROPE

By comparison with the East, the commerce and industry of Western
Europe hardly existed at all. In the Mediterranean there was some trade,
and an active commerce was maintained by the Scandinavians in the
Baltic, but inland trade dwindled down to a mere trickle. Only Venice,
which was more Byzantine than Western, could really be considered an
important mercantile city.

With the establishment of the German kingdoms the trade of the Roman
world in the West was disrupted, and while for a time merchants continued
to trade along the old Roman roads, by the end of the Merovingian period
they had largely disappeared. There was never a complete cessation of
commerce, and there were always a few merchants who risked their lives
and merchandise on the ruined roads, but they were mostly Levantine
peddlers who carried their stock of goods in packs on horse or mule back.
Indeed, the condition of the roads practically prevented transport by
wagon.

The classic description of travel in the ninth century is the account of
his journey from Rheims to Chartres by Richer the canon of Rheims. After
narrating his difficulties with rain and flood, and his wandering six leagues
out of his way when he got lost in a forest, Richer describes his crossing
of the bridge at Meaux:

When I reached the bridge it was scarcely light enough to see. Carefully examining the structure I was once more overwhelmed with new misfortunes. For it had
so many holes and such great gaps in it that the citizens of the town could scarcely
cross it even by daylight in the course of their necessary business. But my quick-
witted guide, who was pretty well experienced in traveling, searched about on
every side for a skiff. Finding none, he came back to the dangerous task of trying
to cross over the bridge. With the aid of heaven he managed to get the horses over
safely. Where there were holes he would sometimes lay his shield down for the
horses to step on, sometimes place boards across that were lying around, and now
bending over, now standing up, first running ahead, then coming back, he finally
got safely across with me and the horses. Night had fallen and covered the earth in
darkness when at length I entered the cloister of St. Pharo, where the brothers were
just preparing the love-drink.[1]

[1] Translation by A. C. Howland in D. C. Munro, *Syllabus of Medieval History* (Philadelphia, 1900), p. 77.

Richer made this trip to read a classical manuscript, but such conditions of travel impeded the merchants as well as scholars. The arrival of the peddler with his pack at the manor house or castle was a great event and the ladies had great pleasure in examining his stock of cloth, jewels and other luxury items.

The only international trade was in luxury goods. The cost of transportation was so exorbitant that only small items of great value could be profitably carried. During the Carolingian period even these peddlers became few, and so cut off was the Frankish empire from outside trade that Charlemagne could substitute a silver coinage for the older gold, thus establishing a standard valid only within the limits of his own state. The decrease in commerce in this period was directly due to the Moslem conquest of the Mediterranean littoral and the decline in Christian trade there.

Towns died out as did trade. The old Roman settlements declined into mere villages inhabited by agricultural workers. Thus the urban industry of western Europe declined drastically, except for a few places in Italy, and Europe retreated to a self-sufficient local domestic economy. Most of the things needed were produced on the manor itself, and there was neither the making of nor demand for manufactured goods. Some cities there were and some manufacture for export, but outside of the ports and Italy there was little urban economy in western Europe between the seventh and the eleventh centuries.

The Manor: Agriculture in Western Europe

The ordinary economic unit in western European society was the manor. We have already seen something of its development from the estates of the Roman empire and have noted that it was the economic basis on which the political and social edifice of feudalism was built. A fief was composed of several manors and it was from them that the lord derived the produce, which enabled him to live a life of war and economic inactivity. There were always some money-fiefs, but these were few and they occur much more frequently in the later than in the earlier Middle Ages. Generally speaking the economy of the feudal world was a barter economy rather than one based on cash until in the age of the crusades the needs of the nobility for ready cash and the revival of international trade brought about a renewal of town life. This will be discussed in a later chapter; in the earlier period we need concern ourselves only with the agricultural organization.

As stated above, no one has been able to find a "typical manor" but we know what manors were like generally, though there were always local variations. The manor consisted of the lord's manor house, the village where the peasants lived, usually along one street, a church, smithy, bakery, and mill. The lands of the manor were divided into the lord's domain and the lands allotted to the peasants. These were laid out into three great fields, so that a rotation of crops could be practiced, and one field could be left fallow. Within the fields the land was divided into strips, each peasant having a strip or two and several strips being reserved for the lord's domain. In some manors each peasant worked his own strips and then did his required share of the work on the lord's strips. In others they co-operatively plowed and harvested the whole field, dividing up the produce in proportion to their share of the land. There was always a common pasture, and the peasants had the right to take wood from the woodland and fish from the pools belonging to the lord.

The peasant was protected in his tenement and only obliged to perform the customary services and pay the customary rents. A percentage of all he harvested went to the lord, a tithe went to the priest, the steward of the manor might demand an additional share. These payments were, of course, made in produce. In addition, the peasant was held to give special gifts on certain holidays such as a chicken at Easter or Lady's Day. Besides the work in the field which they did for the lord, they were required to do certain boon-work, such as collecting wood for the lord's fireplace, hauling his produce, repairing the roads or bridges of the manor, going on errands at the lord's demand. Their wives worked in the kitchens of the manor house and assisted the lady and her staff on certain days each week.[2]

When the peasant worked for the lord on boon-work he received from the lord his meals for the day, and the quantity, quality, and nature of the food was strictly regulated according to custom. At one time, meat, soup, cheese, bread and ale were required, at another fish and water were ordered instead of meat and ale, and the exact amounts of each were specified for each occasion. One of the reasons for the decline of serfdom in the later Middle Ages was the fact that these meals often cost the lord more than it would to hire the work done, but that was a much later de-velopment.

The lord also enjoyed certain monopolies, known as *banalités*. The peasants were bound to have their grain ground in the lord's mill, their grapes pressed in his winepress (though they could make their own beer at home); the lord could hunt through the fields without considering any damage he might do the holdings of the peasants. The peasants were sub-ject to the jurisdiction of the lord's manor-court, and depending on their status, whether free or serf, required to make payments to the lord.

The poll tax was in many communities the sign of serfdom. It was the head tax collected from all non-free peasants and served as a mark of servi-tude. It is probably due to this that among Anglo-Saxons everywhere the

---

[2] An excellent picture of the life of a ninth century peasant is found in Eileen Power's *Medieval People* (London, 1924) in her study of the Carolingian serf, Bodo.

poll tax has always been an especially hated form of taxation. Other servile taxes were the *formariage,* or *merchet,* which the serf paid for permission to marry his daughter outside the manor, and the *heriot* which the lord collected as an inheritance tax on the death of the serf and which was usually the best chattel which he possessed.

The serf was "tallagable at will" by the lord—that is to say the lord could arbitrarily impose any charges he wished on the serf, but actually manor custom regulated the services or payments which the serf must make. If the serf was practically bound to the land he was also secure in his tenancy. He could not be dispossessed as long as he performed the required services and made the prescribed payments. His position was inferior to that of the free peasant more in the legal and social than in the economic sphere. Free villein and serf alike paid farm rents and hearth taxes, both used the lord's banalities and performed the *corvées* (labor services). The free man could come and go as he willed, while the serf was obliged to stay on his land; the freeman was not burdened with the marriage tax or the heriot, and in the court of the manor the free man had an undoubted advantage as he was a free legal person, which the serf was not. But they did the same work under the same circumstances, lived in the same kind of huts in the same village and were economically not very different from each other. The cotter, who was free, was below the serf, for the cotter had no land and could only work as the serf's assistant. He might aspire to become a serf and move into the village, but as a cotter he lived in the field with his equals, the livestock. Peasants and livestock had much in common in the Middle Ages; they often shared their quarters, and were both listed as appurtenances of the farm which was stocked with men and beasts. It is difficult not to paint either too dismal or too roseate a picture of the medieval peasant. Contemporary literature describes him as a black and grimy creature, clothed in rags and giving off a stench which offended the nostrils of the gentlefolk. He was stupid and uncouth, but possessed of a sharp animal craftiness, unfeeling and boorish, the natural object of the derision and contempt of the upper classes. Some modern authors have depicted the life of the peasant in his village as a round of dancing and sporting on the green, while others portray it as an endless round of daily drudgery in the most laborious manual work. While there was undoubtedly some of each, the darker side of the picture would seem the more accurate, especially for the earlier period. Too often we are asked to accept evidence from the fourteenth century, when peasant conditions had improved tremendously, as descriptive of the life of the medieval peasant. By that time he had gained considerable freedom of action and had greatly improved his status; in the tenth century his lot must have been thoroughly uncomfortable.

Freedom could be acquired by the serf by purchase, if he could get the purchase price, or by flight. While the lords organized to prevent the escape of serfs, there was a constant flight of serfs to towns after town life had revived. The fact that the earliest townsmen were merchants from the servile class attests that even in the earlier period serfs did break away and seek their fortunes elsewhere. On the other hand, free men dropped into the servile class by marrying serfs or by acquiring servile lands. Occasionally a lord would emancipate some of his serfs as an act of grace, but such instances are comparatively rare until serfdom became economically unprofitable in the later centuries. Serfs on ecclesiastical lands, while treated better on the whole than those on secular manors, had less chance of attaining their freedom from the corporation of the church.

The horizon of the medieval peasant was a narrow one. While some sought and found the world outside, the majority began and ended their days within the limits of their own manor, their food and their clothing were produced there, and beyond food and clothing they had few possessions. The steward of the estate was the authority that they knew and recognized; count, king, and emperor were but vague rulers far beyond their personal ken. God was in heaven as the king was on his throne, but to the peasant it was the local saint and the local steward who represented religion and government; he obeyed the steward and prayed to the saint and did not bother his head with higher powers.

INTELLECTUAL ASPECTS

The greatest cultural developments of the period between the seventh and the twelfth centuries were those of the Arabs. Moslem science forged far ahead of anything in the contemporary Christian world; Arabic astronomy, mathematics, medicine and geography developed to a high level while Christendom developed nothing new and hardly held on to the knowledge of Antiquity. But in Christian Europe, although there was nothing comparable to the accomplishments of the Arabs, the Byzantines continued to preserve a high level of culture, and Western Europe began to lift itself out of the depth of illiteracy which characterized the period immediately following the barbarian invasions.

THE BYZANTINE EMPIRE

The cultural history of the Byzantine empire breaks into three periods in this era. First, during the iconoclastic period, there was little literary or scientific work, what writing there was being devoted largely to the problems presented by the religio-political controversy. Then towards the end of the Amorian dynasty, under the patronage of Caesar Bardas (ob. 866) there was a literary revival, which extended through the reign of

Constantine Porphyrogenitus (ob. 959), and finally there was a second renaissance under Constantine Monomachus (1042–54), which carried on to the end of the century.

Among the theological writers of the iconoclast period John of Damascus (ob. 750) and Theodore of the Studion (759–826) occupy first place. Although he lived in Damascus under the caliphs, John was one of the most active partisans of the images, writing several dogmatic works, hymns, and theological tracts. He is also credited with the authorship of the story of *Barlaam and Josephat,* a version of the Buddha legend which gained great popularity in Europe. The attribution of this work to John has been seriously challenged, but the most recent scholars of the question seem to incline towards accepting his authorship. Theodore also wrote hymns, sermons and theological books. Of more general interest is his sermon on the death of his mother Theoctista, from which Diehl derived the materials for his charming study of a "Middle Class Woman of the Eighth Century" in his *Byzantine Portraits.* Among other defenders of the images was the patriarch Nicephorus (806–815), who wrote not only many religious treatises, but a history of the years 602 to 769 in which he presents the recent events with a distinctly iconodule coloring. This history is especially valuable for a long discussion of the Bulgarians, who played so large a role in Byzantine politics at the time. Nicephorus also wrote a shorter and less valuable universal history from Adam to his own time.

The iconodule point of view on the history of the time was also presented in two world chronicles written in the ninth century. Theophanes the Confessor wrote a chronicle of the world from 284 to 813, continuing a work begun by George Syncellus which reached only 284. This chronicle is one of our main sources for this period of Byzantine history and it is from this hostile and prejudiced account that we must glean much of our knowledge of the iconoclast emperors. Theophanes' chronicle enjoyed great popularity and was continued by an anonymous writer to 961 as well as by the chronicle of John Skylitzes for the period 811 to 1079. The other iconodule chronicle mentioned above was that of George the Monk, whose work covered the period from the Creation to 842. This chronicle is especially valuable for the religious history of the time, as George was a monk and an ardent iconodule and devoted much attention to the monastic and religious developments. This chronicle was also continued, the various recensions coming down to 948, 1071, 1081, and even 1143.

It is unfortunate that the fury of the iconodules destroyed completely all the writings, historical as well as theological, of the iconoclasts. What all was destroyed we cannot tell, but the net result is that Byzantine literature in the period is rather meagre and uninspiring. We do know the work of one great iconoclast, Leo the Mathematician, who taught in Con-

stantinople under Theophilius and under Caesar Bardas, and whose fame
was such that the caliph al Mamun offered a treaty of perpetual peace and
2000 pounds of gold if he would come to Damascus, but Theophilius kept
him in Constantinople. Leo was for a time bishop of Salonica, but his iconoclastic beliefs caused him to be deprived of his see and he returned to Constantinople to teach. While his reputation has remained, we know nothing
of his actual writings. The same is true of the patriarch John the Grammarian (834–843) whose reputation for learning was so great that he was
accused of occult arts, but whose works were destroyed by his enemies.

At the close of the iconoclast era, under Caesar Bardas, was the revival
of learning which is associated with the person of Photius (ob. 891). We
have already seen Photius as a patriarch of Constantinople who precipitated a schism with Rome, but even more important than his political
career was his position in the world of scholarship. Caesar Bardas founded
at the palace a school for the teaching of the liberal arts, with free tuition
to students, but with a highly paid faculty maintained by the state. Of this
school Photius was the recognized leader, and around him were gathered
the greatest minds of the age, among them Leo the Mathematician. Photius
was possessed of a magnificent library and to make his treasures more ac-
cessible to his friends and students he prepared his *Myriobiblon,* a great
synthetic work in which he abridged the great works of both ancient and
modern authors, many of whom are known to us only through this book.
Learned in theology, philosophy, sciences, law, medicine, history and literature, Photius was a prolific writer as well as a great teacher. He has been
called the most learned man since Aristotle and the variety and extent of
his erudition would seem to justify this appellation, though there seems to
have been in his work none of the freshness or originality of the earlier
philosopher. Like the civilization of which he was so illustrous a representative, Photius was learned and brilliant, with an encyclopedic knowledge but without any great depth or originality of thought—stagnant at
a very high level.

But the education imparted by Photius and his colleagues was a sound
one; both the emperor Leo the Wise and the missionary Cyril, the apostle
to the Slavs, were students at his school, and Cyril was for a time a teacher
there.

The emperor Constantine Porphyrogenitus (913–959) carried on in the
tradition of Bardas and Photius. He gathered around himself a group of
scholars, among whom were Simeon the logothete who wrote a history of
the world from the Creation to 948, and Joseph Genesios who prepared, at
the suggestion of the emperor, a history of the empire in the years 813 to
886. But Constantine was himself the great scholar in his own court. He
willingly gave over the business of state to others and devoted himself to
scholarly pursuits, achieving thereby a reputation as a scholar, which off-

set somewhat his deficiencies as an emperor. His own written works include a *Life of Basil I, On the Themes, On the Administration of the Empire* and the famous *Book of Ceremonies.* These treatises, written by the scholar-emperor, are invaluable sources for the administration and customs of tenth century Byzantium, revealing a combination of practical administrative sense, a love of rigid protocol, and a great antiquarian knowledge on the part of their author.

In the latter part of the century appeared the *Lexicon* of Suidas, an encyclopedic compilation of grammatical, philological, literary, and historical information, which enjoyed considerable popularity as a reference book among later scholars. In the same period were written the poems, epigrams, and hymns of John Kyriotes Geometres, one of the most brilliant of Byzantine poets. This was also the time of the historian Leo the Deacon who wrote an account of the military campaigns of the years 959 to 975, when the empire was waging victorious wars against both Bulgar and Moslem.

At the very end of this period, under the patronage of the emperor Constantine IX Monomachus (1042–54) was another renaissance of learning, again associated with the development of new schools at Constantinople. The two chief figures of this movement are John Xiphilinos, who was head of the school of law and author of several legal works, and Michael Psellos. Xiphilinos became patriarch of Constantinople (1064–75) and played an important role in the religious and political as well as in the intellectual life of his age.

The colleague of Xiphilinos in the schools of Constantinople, Michael Psellos, the head of the school of philosophy, also rose to great heights in the world of politics, becoming prime minister of the empire (1071–78). Learned in all the arts and sciences, Psellos has left books on philosophy, philology, law, theology, natural science, and history as well as volumes of letters and some poetry. Psellos cannot be called a modest man. Of himself he wrote: "It was certified that my tongue has been adorned with flowers even in simple utterances; and without any effort natural sweetness falls in drops from it." [3] Psellos' history covers the years 976 to 1077, continuing where Leo the Deacon stopped. In the latter part, the work is a partisan account marred by the personal prejudices of the author, but as the first-hand testimony of one who played an important role in the events he describes Psellos' history has a unique value for the history of the period. It is, moreover, written in an elegent style and stands as an example of the finest literary style of eleventh century Byzantium.

The history of the later Macedonians and of the following time of troubles is also told by Michael Attaliates, who wrote an account of the years 1034 to 1079, much of which is based on the author's personal experiences

[3] Quoted in A. A. Vasiliev, *History of the Byzantine Empire,* I, 445.

and recollections. Attaliates was also the author of several treatises on the law.

One of the most important literary developments of the Macedonian period in Byzantium was the growth of the epic legend of Digenes Akrites. This Greek equivalent of the *Chanson de Roland* told the story of a legendary hero of the Moslem wars, and became the greatest popular epic of the Byzantine empire. The place of the *Akritis* in the history of European literature has only recently been fully appreciated through the studies of the Belgian Byzantinist, Henri Grégoire.

THE MOSLEM CALIPHATES

The culture of the Moslem lands was immeasurably higher than that of the Western Christian in the eighth to tenth centuries. It was even superior to the Byzantine in that it was more virile and vigorous. Byzantium maintained a high level of culture but it was largely stagnant; Byzantine scholars were too absorbed in theological speculation and argument; they threshed over old straw until little was left, and their writings, while elegant, are stultified and moribund. The Arabic culture, on the other hand, was young, vigorous and alert. In the Ummayad period the Arabs had begun to absorb something of the classical heritage through Syria and Byzantium. In the Abbasid era they added to this the Persian and Indian cultures until they had produced a civilization of their own, which incorporated elements of the older East and West and outshone the earlier cultures in many respects. The Arabs have well been termed the "transmitters and transmuters" of the earlier cultures.

There are several causes of this apogee of Moslem culture at this time. In the first place, the Moslem civilization was uniform throughout the Moslem world; it was based on a single language, the Arabic of the Koran, which was the language of scholars and savants through all Islamic countries. The grammar and rules of the language had been set during the Umayyad period; by the Abbasid times it was capable of allowing free intercourse of ideas from Spain to India. Secondly, there was a uniformity of interests: men lived under the same law, that of the Koran, they worshiped in the same kind of mosques, they engaged in the same pursuits. There were no great barriers separating the Moor of Spain from the Turk of Afghanistan, as there were between the Byzantine and the Englishman of that epoch. Thirdly, there was in Islam a religious toleration which allowed the Moslems to exploit to the best advantage the brains and abilities of non-Moslem populations. Many of the greatest Arabic scholars were not Moslems; Jews, Christians of all creeds, Nestorian, Jacobite, Coptic, Orthodox, all contributed to Moslem culture and all were patronized by Moslem princes. Lastly, the simplicity of the Moslem faith allowed greater opportunity for secular study than did contemporary Christianity. The greater part of Christian thought and speculation was devoted to intricate theological problems: the nature of the Trinity, the nature and persons of Christ, free will and predestination, these were the topics on which the best Christian minds labored. Moslem theology was much simpler; the Word of God was revealed in the Koran by the prophet Muhammad, there was little to argue about. Muhammad was a man not a God, and there was no disagreement on his nature. There were of course many theological arguments, and as we have seen a great multitude of sects, especially among the Shia; there were arguments as to the Traditions (out of 600,000 traditional sayings of Muhammad only some 7275 were generally accepted as genuine and this gave rise to some argument), but on the whole the Moslem scholars were much more free to turn their thoughts to secular problems than were the Christian. Islam developed her scholastic philosophy as did Christianity. Like the Christians, the Arabic scholastics labored to reconcile the revealed truth of their holy book with the scientific statements derived from Aristotle. Even as Thomas Aquinas sought to reconcile Aristotle and the Bible, so did Al Farabi, Ibn Sina (Avicenna), and Ibn Rushd (Averroes) seek to reconcile him with the Koran. But on the whole the Arabic scholars were much less concerned with science and revelation and more with science *per se*. This is at once evident when one notes the works of Aristotle which we derived from the Arabs: the *Politics, Laws,* and *Poetics* were ignored, it was the scientific works which interested the Moslem scholars and which they translated and used as the bases for their own works.

The modern world has been torn by the conflict between science and religion. The Moslem world of the eighth to tenth centuries accepted their revealed religion on faith, and turned their intellectual interests to science. In mathematics, astronomy, medicine, chemistry, and geography the Arabs became the leaders in the scientific world, leaving an impress which is still strongly felt in most of these subjects.

In mathematics, the Arabs took over the Greek geometry and added algebra. They brought from India the Hindu numerals (called Arabic by the Western world), first adapting the numerals and finally in the ninth century adding the use of the zero. When one stops to consider the difficulty of mathematical calculation with Roman numerals [divide MDCLXVIII by CXVII without transposing] the debt owed the Arabs in this matter is at once evident. The "Sindhian Tables," Hindu mathematical tables, were first brought to Baghdad about 753. Using the works of the Greek Ptolemy and the Sindhian Tables, Muhammad Al-Khwarizmi wrote his *Book of the Restoration and Opposition of Numbers,*—commonly called "The Book"—*Al Gebra* whence we name the science algebra,—in the first quarter of the ninth century. However much modern schoolboys may regret the invention of algebra, we must admit that it was a great development in mathematics and very useful to those who can comprehend it properly.

In astronomy, the Arabs started with the classical text of Ptolemy and added thereto. To the theoretical study they added experimental science; astronomical observatories were built in Baghdad, Damascus, Shiraz, Samarkand, Nishapur and other Moslem cities. Al Kindi (fl.c. 880) was one of the greatest Arabic astronomers; Al Fargani built the Nilometer in 861; Al Battani and Umar al-Khayyam in the eleventh century invented new calendars. Among Moslems the fame of Umar al-Khayyam rests more on his mathematical and astronomical research than on the quatrains with which he passed his leisure moments. The application of astronomy to the individual was astrology and this pseudo-science flourished along with the more genuine article. Albumasar (d. 886), Thabit ibn Qurrah (836–901) and Costa ben Lucca (fl. c. 860) all wrote on astrology, interpreting the heavens in their relation to man's destiny but with a solid foundation of astronomy as their basis.

Chemistry, as studied by the Arabs, was largely alchemy (al chemie) based on the old Aristotelian concept of the four prime substances of earth, air, fire and water, and on the lore of the ancient Egyptian Hermetic cults. The first Arabic alchemy was translation from the Egyptian Hellenistic material, but they soon added ideas of their own. The doctrine developed that sulphur and mercury were the two prime bases for all metals, and that by experimentation it should be possible to transmute any baser metal into gold. The essence of mercury would accomplish this feat, and the essence of gold would give eternal life. Scholars were divided as to the truth of these alchemical doctrines, Al-Razi defending them while Al Kindi vigorously attacked them. In the course of their experimentation, while they never found the essences of mercury or gold, these alchemists laid the basis for the science of chemistry, and the failure of the alchemist was the success of the chemist. Many of our common chemical terms show the Arabic influence: such as alcohol, alkali, alembic [but not alum or albumen] and spirits of camphor.

Arabic accomplishments in medicine were perhaps the most significant. While Western Europeans were attempting to cure sickness with incantations, holy water, and exorcism, Arabic scholars were studying disease in the laboratory and the hospital. Hunayn (809–873) is the first great name among Arabic doctors; al Tabari (fl. c. 850), Al Razi (Rhazes) (865–925) and Ibn Sina (980–1037) carried on the great tradition. It was Al Razi who, while head of the great hospital at Baghdad, is supposed to have first written a clinical account of the symptoms and progress of smallpox; in all he was the author of some 140 works. Ibn Sina (Avicenna) was less prolific than Al Razi (he is only credited with 99 books), but he was the most universal scholar of the Islamic world, excelling in medicine, mathematics, philosophy, and every branch of learning. He came from Bukhara and died at Hamadhan, but is considered among the luminaries of the Abbasid caliphate.

Geography was also studied by the Arabs. Here a practical consideration entered into the picture as the Arabs were traders with all parts of the world and their geographical knowledge was both a result of and an aid to their commerce. But they were thoroughly familiar with the location, products, peoples and needs of the Mediterranean and Asiatic worlds at a time when Western Europeans knew only their own locality and imagined all sorts of strange creatures and countries beyond the seas or mountains. That Arabic lore could also populate the world with all manner of strange creatures is evident to anyone who has read *Sinbad the Sailor,* a legendary composition based on actual travelers' accounts. The greatest names among Arabic geographers were Yaqut (1179–1229) of Baghdad, who wrote a great geographical dictionary, and Idrisi, who flourished in the twelfth century at the court of Roger of Sicily, but they were the heirs of a long tradition of geographical study, which was well developed in the days of the Abbasids.

In all this discussion of Moslem culture we have gone beyond the chronological limits of the Abbasid period, and will close with a brief notice of a great Arabic intellectual center which developed in the eleventh and twelfth centuries in the West. In Moorish Spain the height of Moslem culture came late. It was this group which especially influenced the thought of Western Europe in the Twelfth-Century Renaissance. In Spain, as in the East, there were hospitals, observatories, and schools far superior to those of Christian Europe. Agriculture was especially studied and scientific horticulture and astronomy were developed among the Moors. The greatest names in the Western Moslem intellectual history are those of Al Zahrawi (d. 1013) who wrote on surgery and who practiced dissection in his hospital; Ibn Bajjah (Avenpace d. 1138) the great physician of Seville, whose experimental clinical studies rank him next after Rhazes in the field of Arabic medicine; Ibn Rushd (Averroes, 1126–98) the great commentator on Aristotle ("he who wrote the great commentary" according to Dante), philosopher, grammarian, astronomer, medical writer, whose influence on Christian thought was so great and who played a greater role in Christian than in Moslem scholasticism; and the great Jewish physician and philosopher Musa ben Maymum (Maimonides, 1132–1204), who deserted Spain to become the physician to Saladin in Egypt.

Moslem art and architecture also developed its own forms, taking from the Graeco-Syrian, Armenian, Iranian and Indian to produce a new synthesis. Suffice it here to note that the prohibition in the Koran on reproducing pictorially the human figure caused an extremely ingenious development of floral and geometric designs, and an extensive use of animal and flower figures. Several schools of architecture developed (Syrian, African, Egyptian, Indian, Persian) but all followed the basically same form of the mosque with its minarets, domes and carved stone or mosaic decoration. Calligraphy became a fine art and some of the finest examples of Moslem art are the illuminated copies of the Koran. Also, most familiar to Westerners, the Arabs developed wonderful patterns in weaving of rugs, which spread on the floors or hung on the walls added color and life to the otherwise dead white of their buildings. Rugs from Bukhara, Shiraz, Hamadhan and other Moslem provinces are still considered the finest in the world, commanding in some cases fabulous prices.

Arabic literature has affected that of the West less than most of the Moslem cultural contributions. Poetry was always popular, and extemporaneous poetizing was considered one of the accomplishments of the educated gentleman. Few of the poets of Islam are known to Western readers, Hafiz and Umar al-Khayyam being the exceptions, but Arabic literature provides many poets who are honored by their own people. History was also highly developed, Arabic authors being scrupulously careful to indicate the source of their information for any historical fact. The Arabs inherited the historical traditions of the Persians; it was not until the Abbasid period that Arabic historiography developed, and even then though the works were in Arabic the authors were generally Persians. The end of the ninth century witnessed a great flowering in Arabic historiography, the chief writers being al-Waqidi, al Tabari, Yaqubi, and al-Baladhuri, who wrote of the expansion of the Arabs and the founding of the Moslem state. After these great historians there was a steady stream of Arabic historical writing, mostly world histories, annals, local histories, and biographies, which reached its culmination in the work of Ibn Khaldun in the fourteenth century.

As can be seen from the above in almost every aspect of civilization and culture the Moslem world was far advanced over anything in contemporary Christendom. The only possible comparison is Byzantium, and while it maintained an equally splendid material culture and a comparatively active intellectual life, it lacked the vigor of the Moslem. The modern Arab has for centuries been oppressed and kept down by Turkish masters, but it must never be forgotten that in the eighth to tenth centuries the Arabic world was far ahead of the Christian in all respects save only the political. A resurgent Arab people, Westernized and industrialized, may yet again recall the glories of their past and become once more a cultural and political factor of prime importance in the destinies of the world.

WESTERN EUROPE

Bede

While the Arabs were developing a virile and aggressive new culture and the Byzantines were maintaining a magnificent, if static, one, Western

Europe was losing what it had inherited from Rome save in a few isolated cases. There was still some considerable culture in the Irish monasteries, secular education still persisted in some of the Italian towns (though in a rather shabby state), but for the most part the "Dark Ages" had settled down over the West. In all of this darkness, but one really great figure stands out, that of the Northumbrian monk of Jarrow; the Venerable Bede (673–735).

In Bede we find the fusion of the Celtic learning with that of the Romans as transmitted by Isidore of Seville, and with the patristic lore of the Latin church. Bede knew Latin, Greek, and some Hebrew; his works include many commentaries on various books of the Bible, lives of saints, a *De Natura Rerum* (based on Isidore), a book on poetry, sets of Easter tables and other chronological works, and above all the *Ecclesiastical History of the English People*. This history, which begins with Caesar's conquest of Britain and comes down to the year 731, relates the great story of the conversion of the heathen Saxons to Christianity and of the triumph of the Roman over the Celtic church. It is based, as the author tells us, on written records and on conversations with men who took part in the events and recalled the happenings. Bede's history, which is our only source for most of the matters chronicled there, has rightly deserved the high esteem in which it has been held ever since its first appearance. Professor Wilbur Abbott, in a charming essay on Bede sums up in a style which Bede could have envied:

So he lives today, the man of a book. He is among the Fathers; but not among the saints, for he wrought no miracles—except the crowning miracle of his history. He converted none—save those who read it. He held no office—save that of the first great English, if not the first great modern, historian. He was not canonized— save by the men of his own craft. And, seeking to immortalize the achievements of others, he somehow managed to immortalize himself.[4]

The Carolingians

After Bede there is no scholar of first importance in England until we come to Alcuin of York, who is associated not with England but with the court of Charlemagne at Aix. And it is in the "Carolingian renaissance" that the intellectual life of western Europe really begins to revive. We have already noticed this "renaissance" in our discussion of the Carolingians and seen how Charles gathered around himself as illustrious a group of scholars as could be found in western Europe in his day. That they were not what we would call highly educated men at all is beside the point—they were the intellectual giants of their own age and brought a deserved lustre to the court of the great king. Of all their writings prob-

[4] Reprinted by permission of the publishers, Harvard University Press, from W. C. Abbott, *Conflicts with Oblivion*, 1924, p. 278.

ably only the *History of the Longobards* by Paul the Deacon [5] and the *Life of Charlemagne* by Einhard have many readers today; Alcuin's dialogues and Theodolphus' poems have small attraction for modern readers, and the theological and philosophical speculations of Eriugena and Hincmar can now excite but a limited audience; but these men laid the foundations of the educational development, which was to prove receptive to the Arabic science and the rediscovered Aristotle in the twelfth century.

A comparison of the works of Paul the Deacon and Einhard shows in itself what the Carolingian renaissance accomplished. While Paul's history is a simple chronicle of the Lombards' actions, the work of Einhard shows a strong classical influence, being copied from Suetonius. This classical influence is even more marked in the writings of Lupus of Ferrières, a genuine humanist in the ninth century, who was enamored of classical literature for itself. Further, the education of the Carolingian school bred in its students an independence of thought and a critical capacity which set them apart from the herd. Agobard of Lyons and Claudius of Turin were both outspoken critics of the superstitions of their times, Claudius boldly attacking the prevalent worship of images and relics. John Scotus Eriugena, undoubtedly the most original thinker among them all, even went so far as to assert the dangerous doctrine that reason was superior to authority!

The Carolingian revival had an important effect on the writing of history. In addition to the histories of Paul the Deacon and Einhard already mentioned, the palace school produced Nithard, an illegitimate grandson of the emperor, who wrote the history of the reign of Louis the Pious and the wars among his sons. It is in his history that the text of the Strasbourg Oaths, quoted above, is to be found.

Charlemagne was personally interested in the writing of history and tried to guarantee that the history of his country should always be known and recorded. To this end he ordered that each monastery should keep annals of local and national events, each years' happenings recorded at the time. While many of these remained merely local annals or died out altogether, several became works of prime importance. The *Annals of Lorsch* (741–829) are the most famous for the earlier period, and have been thought by some modern scholars to have official status. At any rate they form the basis for the earlier entries in most of the other major annals, such as those of St. Bertin (741–882, and continued by St. Vaast to 900), Fulda (680–901), Xanten (831–873), and the *Chronicon* of Regino of Prum (843–906). In the west the annals of Fontanelle, near Rouen, are especially important for the information they afford on the Norse raids of 834 to 850.

---

[5] Translated by W. D. Foulke in Univ. of Penna. "Translations and Reprints," second series (1907). Einhard is translated by W. Glaister (London, 1877) and reprinted almost entire in Scott, Hyma, Noyes, *Readings*, pp. 149–66.

In addition to the monastic annals, the ninth and tenth century produced a number of saints' lives, another matter in which Charlemagne had interested himself. While these are essentially works of edification, they often contain mention of events of considerable historical importance.

The Carolingian period also produced several important works in the field of political theory. Hincmar of Rheims, Jonas of Orleans, Sedulius Scotus, Smaragdus, and Hrabanus Maurus all wrote treatises in which statements of political theory are to be found. In general these writers of the ninth century agreed that the king was an office ordained by God and that all men owed him obedience, but they are also in agreement in insisting that the king must rule justly and mercifully. The king is under the law and can be judged for his own offenses by the clergy according to Hincmar, who goes further to assert that the king held his position by election by the bishops and other men of realm. It was through the coronation by the bishops that the king received his special character, and only with the counsel of the bishops should he presume to act. This statement of the dependence of the king on the clergy is important as being one of the earliest affirmations of ecclesiastical superiority, foreshadowing the arguments of the eleventh and twelfth centuries.

Tenth and Eleventh Centuries

The tenth and early eleventh centuries are a bleak period in the cultural history of western Europe, what learning there was being largely connected with monastic or cathedral schools. There was a considerable amount of monastic writing, historical and dogmatic, but the only figure of first rate importance is that of Gerbert, the scholasticus of Rheims who later became Pope Sylvester II. The chief intellectual development of the period was the growth of the cathedral schools, which gradually replaced the monasteries as educational centers. While this was not complete until the twelfth century the movement began in the tenth.

Gerbert of Aurillac (c. 946–1003), a Frenchman from Auvergne, was not only one of the learned men of his time, but a great teacher, an astute politician, and one of the few great popes of this rather dismal age. We have already seen his political activities in connection with the ascension of Hugh Capet and his alliance with Otto III to produce that harmonious co-operation of empire and papacy which was the Gelasian dream. No less significant was his role as a scholar and especially as a teacher; under him the school at Rheims became the intellectual center whence learning spread throughout France and Germany.

Educated at the monastery of Aurillac and at Barcelona, Gerbert became proficient in grammar, philosophy and especially mathematics. Whether he studied Arabic mathematics there or not has never been satisfactorily decided,[6] but that he possessed a peculiar mathematical knowledge and genius is amply evident. From 972 until 989 (with the exception of one year) he taught the Trivium and the Quadrivium at Rheims, excelling especially in his teaching of mathematics and astronomy for which he not only wrote textbooks, but prepared various mechanical aids to teaching for which he became famous. He made a sphere surrounded by planets, a hydraulic organ, a mechanical clock, and other mechanical wonders. At the same time he instilled into his students a real love for classical authors for themselves, in his teaching and writing showing himself to be devoted to Cicero. Gerbert was never an original scholar and his learning was not phenomenal, but he was a great teacher and his influence was conspicuous in laying the foundations for the educational revival of the twelfth century.

Among Gerbert's pupils were King Robert of France, Richer the historian who gives us the details of Gerbert's teachings, Adalberon of Laon, John of Auxerre, and above all Fulbert of Chartres. Fulbert carried to Chartres the enthusiasm for learning which he had acquired at Rheims and built up at Chartres what was to be in many ways the most famous of all cathedral schools. The cathedral schools of Chartres, Laon, Auxerre, Rouen, Sens, Cambrai, Cologne, and Utrecht all owe their foundations to pupils of Gerbert. Chartres became famous as the great center of humanism: Laon was the home of mathematics.

Apart from Gerbert and his pupils the chief interest in this period centers in the historians and annalists. In England the *Anglo-Saxon Chronicle* was founded, as we have seen, by Alfred, the first great historical work in any vernacular. In Germany the monastic annals, such as those of St. Gall, Reichenau, Altaich and Hersfeld, were supplemented by the annals of the episcopal sees of Hildesheim, Salzburg, and Cologne. Especially important among these episcopal annals are those of Notger of Liége and Alpert of Metz. Alpert also wrote a history of the district around Utrecht in the years 1002 to 1018. Among the more general and less strictly local histories of this period should be noted Widikind's *History of the Saxons,* the *Chronicon* of Theitmar of Merseberg and the *Life of Conrad II* by Wipo. There were also a number of lives of bishops and abbots which supply considerable historical information for Germany of the Saxon and early Salian period.

The most important Italian historian in this era was Luitprand bishop of Cremona who wrote the *Antipodosis,* a history of Italy and the Western empire from 887 to 950, a *History of Otto I,* and the celebrated *Relatio* of

---

[6] The last word on this problem is Oscar Darlington's "Gerbert, the Teacher," in the *American Historical Review,* LII, 3 (April 1947) 456–76. Darlington opines "Gerbert might easily have visited Cordova" but defers any definite conclusions until the Spanish records can be studied more exhaustively.

his embassy to Constantinople in 968. Luitprand was a well-educated man who knew Latin and Greek well and who wrote in a breezy narrative style, which makes him delightful reading at any time.[7] His descriptions of people he met are written with the most scathing satire and throughout his works his rather earthy humor intrudes with little anecdotes and character sketches worthy of his successors in a more enlightened and secular age.

Apart from Luitprand, Italian historiography offers little but the *Liber Pontificalis* which was begun in this period, and Leo of Ostia's history of Monte Cassino (to 1075) written at the request of Abbot Desiderius. Leo's work was continued by the equally important chronicle of Peter the Deacon who brought the history of the abbey and the papacy down to 1139. Archbishop Arnulph of Milan's *History of His Own Times* (925–1077) anticipated the great flowering of Italian city chronicles, which were to be so important for the twelfth century and after.

The story of the last Carolingians in France was told by Flodoard of Rheims who wrote annals of the years 922 to 966 and a *History of the Church of Rheims* in the same period. Flodoard is valuable for the inclusion of many documents, but his annals are rather factual and dull. Much more readable and interesting is the history of Richer, a canon of Rheims and a pupil of Gerbert, which gives us great detail about not only Gerbert, but about the rise of Hugh Capet and the period to 999, in a vivid narrative style which reveals a genuine familiarity with classical historical writing. His description of his journey to Chartres, quoted in part above, is characteristic of the detail and descriptive power of his work.

Monastic historians are represented by Adhelmar de Chabannes of St. Martial of Limoges and Raoul Glaber, a Cluniac. Adhelmar was the author of a *Chronicle* of the history of France from Clovis to 1028, an *Annals of Limoges* (687–1030), a *Chronicle of Aquitaine* (830–1028), and lesser historical works. His *Chronicle* is especially valuable in the latter portions for the history of southern France. Raoul Glaber's work is an amazing compilation of tales and anecdotes with little value for political history but of great significance for the intellectual and cultural history of the time. Raoul, himself mystical and superstitious, allowed much of his personality to appear in his writings with the result that his chronicle is valuable not for the facts contained, but for the picture it affords of the mind of the eleventh-century monk.

French historiography, like French history at the time, was largely local and there are few really important histories of this era. The *Deeds*

---

[7] His works are translated by F. A. Wright in The Broadway Medieval Library (London, 1930). The description of Constantinople, and the good bishop's righteous indignation at the scant treatment he received there are especially fine.

of the Counts of Anjou, from which we have quoted the life of Geoffrey, is one of the most valuable local histories to appear in this period.[8]

In the field of religious literature there was considerable writing, little of which holds much interest for modern readers. Othloh (ob. c. 1075) and Peter Damiani (c. 1007–72) have left letters and writings which reveal the struggles of the pious and mystical soul in this world of sin and corruption. Hroswitha, a nun of Gandersheim, wrote religious poems and dramas in which she combined great piety with classical style and form in a manner not followed by later religious dramatists. There were several dogmatic disputes which produced a considerable literature, notably the controversy over predestination between Gottschalk and Hincmar of Rheims, and that over the Eucharist and the relative necessity of faith and reason which was argued out between Berenger of Tours and Lanfranc of Bec. While important in the history of doctrine, these controversies had but little importance beyond the limited world of the ecclesiastics who participated in them.

The greatest literary work of the period was in a field far removed from church dogma. In the vernacular languages, in Anglo-Saxon, German, Norse, and Old French there developed an epic literature that far outshadows any of the learned Latin writings of the era.

The expansion of the Scandinavians gave rise to a literature in the Norse sagas, which told the story of the intrepid Norsemen taking to their long ships and seeking adventure and profit over the cold seas. While many of these sagas, in their present forms, date only from the twelfth century, they stem from the earlier period and should be considered as the products of the past. The same should be said for the German epics which were later cast into the cycle of the *Nibelungenlied,* although only the *Hildebrandslied* actually dates in its present form from the early eleventh century. The greatest of the early Teutonic epics is, however, the Anglo-Saxon *Beowulf.* This fantastic story, full of marvelous deeds of valor against foes natural and supernatural, is the outstanding literary composition of the Anglo-Saxon period and the first great monument in the history of English literature. In it, as in the Norse sagas, one sees the wild untamed spirits of these Teutonic adventurers.

Far superior to the Germanic epics however was the epic of medieval France, which grew up during the eleventh century along the pilgrim road to Santiago de Compostella. While the Saxons were telling of Beowulf's battles with dragons and of Siegfried's struggles with magic wiles, there grew up in France the less fanciful, more realistic, more truly heroic *Chanson de Roland.* This magnificent story of warfare against the infidels, of knightly loyalty and base treason, and of gallant death defending one's honor—this epic of the fighting man in which there are no

[8] See pp. 188–89 above.

major feminine characters and no feminine influence, is the first great
literary work in the Old French vernacular and the core around which
later developed the whole cycle of Carolingian romances. Henry Adams,
in his *Mont Saint Michel and Chartres*, brilliantly shows how it reflects
the ideals of the eleventh century military caste and is the literary expression of the same emotion which built the Abbey of Mont Saint
Michel. In an age that can be termed intellectually sterile, the *Chanson*
stands out as the supreme literary achievement of the Frankish people.
Its heroic stanzas reflect the vigor of the new race, its ideas their ideals.
Let us stop to read, in the translation of Henry Adams, of the death of
Roland. The "iron age" of feudalism has no more fitting epitaph.

> Then Roland feels that death is taking him;
> Down from the head upon the heart it falls.
> Beneath a pine he hastens running:
> On the green grass he throws himself down;
> Beneath him puts his sword and oliphant,
> Turns his face towards the pagan army.
> For this he does it, that he wished greatly
> That Charles should say, and all his men
> The gentle Count has died a conqueror.[9]

[9] Henry Adams, *Mont Saint Michel and Chartres*, p. 28. Reprinted by permission
of the publishers, Houghton Mifflin Co.

✥✥

BOOK III

The Ascendancy of the West

1050-1200

In this period the ascendancy which had formerly been held by the East passed to the West. Both the Byzantine and Moslem worlds declined in the twelfth century. Although both the Byzantines under the Comneni and the Moslems under the Saljuq Turks underwent a temporary revival, these empires were rather in the nature of Indian summers, and it is clear that the real center of power and importance had shifted back to the West. Constantinople and Baghdad were still the greatest cities of the world, but the life was largely gone out of their empires. The Franks (a term which had expanded to include all the nations of the old Frankish Empire: Italians, French, Germans, and, indeed, any Latin-speaking people) and the Roman Church were in the ascendancy. This shift is shown most dramatically by the crusades, when Latin Christendom took the offensive against the East, establishing Latin colonies in the Levant.

In this new Western world the two chief powers were the German Roman Empire and the papacy, and this period is marked by the first phases of the struggle for supremacy between these two. At the same time the feudal monarchies of France and England were developing, their natural growth being impeded by the struggle for the control of western France. In Spain, the Christian states also took the offensive against the Moors, and the wars of the Reconquista were launched. A new political and cultural center developed in Sicily in the court of the Normans, who seized control of much of the western Mediterranean from the Arabs and the Byzantines.

This is the period in which the great political power of the papacy is developed and brought to its climax in the pontificate of Innocent III. The center of world dominion had shifted back from the Bosphorus to the Tiber, and the pope more than any other one man could claim to rule the medieval world.

MONREALE CATHEDRAL: SICILY

CHAPTER 14

THE WESTERN EMPIRE AND
THE PAPACY

✛

THE HILDEBRANDINE REFORM, 1049–73

WHEN Bruno of Toul ascended the papal throne in 1049 with the title of Leo IX, a new period in the history of the church and of Europe began. The worst excesses of the decadent Roman papacy of the tenth and early eleventh centuries had been checked, and a new sincere reforming group of prelates came into power under the aegis of the emperors. The reform program, which had begun in the monasteries at Cluny, and had been carried over to the secular clergy in Lorraine, reached the center of the church and began to operate in respect to the papacy and to the church entire. This reform was not the work of one man, a number of popes and cardinals contributed largely to it, but one man so consistently pursued the reform program and so influenced the course of events that the whole movement is known as the Hildebrandine Reform, and the age is termed that of Hildebrand.

But, although the figure of Hildebrand dominates the scene, his work would have been impossible without the efforts of others of that great group who took over the church in the latter half of the eleventh century. Leo IX, Peter Damiani, Humbert of Silva Candida, Frederick of Lorraine (Stephen IX), Anselm of Lucca (Alexander II), Desiderius of Monte Cassino (Victor III) were all ardent reformers and all contributed largely to the movement. And the problems which faced them taxed to the utmost the abilities of all of them.

In general, the objectives of the reform party may be said to have been roughly four: 1. to put an end to simony, that flagrant sale of church offices which had become such a scandal in the church; 2. to enforce clerical celibacy and put an end to Nicolaitism, as the marriage of the clergy was called; 3. to emancipate the church from any form of secular control; and 4. to assure the primacy of the papacy and its unquestioned headship over the church universal. In all of these policies the reformers met determined opposition; the struggle which they carried on to gain these objectives is the main theme in the history of the church for the next two and a half centuries.

Simony was an evil which had long troubled the church. Sylvester II

(999–1003) had especially worked against it, but it was too inherent in the position of the church in a feudal world. Simony and the secular control of ecclesiastical positions are all part of the same picture and all stem from the dual position of the clergy under feudalism. As we have seen, when a noble built a church on his own estates he naturally retained the right to appoint the priest who should serve that church; likewise when a bishop was one of the chief ministers and one of the greatest landholders in a kingdom, the king naturally felt that he had a right to control the appointment of the incumbent. And if the secular lord had a right to appoint a cleric, why should he not derive some financial profit from it, as he did from his other rights over land and property? Therefore the sale of church offices flourished to the benefit of the lords and to the detriment of the church. Nor were the men who indulged in this practice necessarily opposed to ecclesiastical reform; the reforming emperors freely appointed bishops, who were sometimes their agents in enforcing reform; William the Conqueror, the friend of the reforming popes, was a chronic seller of the church offices; popes and higher clergy practiced simony, the depth of degradation in this matter being reached when Benedict IX sold the papacy to the highest bidder in 1045. And the reform party among the clergy stooped to simony when they purchased the papacy for Gregory VI. Leo IX himself received the appointment to the papal throne from Henry III, but, true reformer that he was, refused to accept the tiara at secular hands and insisted on being regularly elected by the clergy and people of Rome before he would allow himself to be crowned.

Most reformers recognized that the feudal position of the clergy necessarily placed them under a certain amount of secular control. They sought primarily to put an end to the outright sale of offices, but Peter Damiani included under simony the rewarding clerics who had proven themselves valuable to a ruler by granting them high position in the church. This extreme of asceticism was fortunately not followed by most reformers, and both the church and secular princes long continued to reward their ministers with lucrative prebends and benefices.

The method employed by the church to stamp out simony was the same as that applied to Nicolaitism and other evils. Church councils were held in which decrees against the evil were promulgated and then an attempt was made to enforce these decrees through the use of excommunication. In general the attack on simony was most effective and that portion of the Hilderbrandine reform was one of the first and most easily accomplished.

Ecclesiastical celibacy proved a harder matter to handle. The clergy in the early days of the church had regularly married; the Council of Nicaea had rejected the rule of celibacy, and it was only with the rapid spread of monasticism that ecclesiastical celibacy became a cardinal point in the program of reforming clerics. These men, mostly monks themselves, held up the higher standard of personal life presumed by the celibate state as that desired of all clergy, but the average run of the clergy who were themselves married had no interest in this and strenuously opposed the movement. It is extremely doubtful if celibacy, merely as a nobler mode of life, would ever have gained many adherents among even the secular clergy, had not economic and other consideration entered into the picture.

The church must at all times be kept a career open to talents; it must never be allowed to degenerate into a priestly caste; there must never develop in Christianity a class of Pharisees. Yet this was precisely what was tending to grow in the medieval church. Married clergy naturally looked out for the interests of their families and heirs; church lands were alienated to provide fiefs for the sons of bishops; high offices were passed down from father to son. That the father may have been able but the son unworthy was seldom considered. It was this economic aspect of the problem which stirred the reform clergy to action. Under the inspiration of Hildebrand, a number of decrees were issued against the married clergy. By these all priests were declared bachelors, their wives were stated to be no wives at all but concubines, and their children bastards. This naturally aroused a storm of protest among the properly married clergy. In Milan there were open revolts and one party among the secular clergy repudiated the authority of Rome. The Milanese considered themselves far more moral, being married, than their Roman bretheren who were celebate but not chaste.

It is unfortunate that Hildebrand was so uncompromising in this matter. Had he adopted the policy later employed by the church with the Uniate Greeks and Maronites, which permitted the married clergy to retain their offices, but refused to allow the future ordination of any married man, much of the grief which attended the enforcement of ecclesiastical celibacy in the Middle Ages would have been avoided.

Omitting for the moment the third part of the reform program to pass to the fourth, the assurance of the unquestioned primacy of Rome was secured by the reforming popes only at the expense of a complete schism with Constantinople and the creation of two separate communions in Christianity. As we have seen, the patriarchs of Constantinople were always loathe to admit any supremacy of Rome and schisms between Rome and Constantinople had occurred repeatedly during the early Middle Ages. The Photian schism of the ninth century had been healed, but the causes had never been remedied, so that all that was needed was a strong and ambitious patriarch and an ambitious and intransigeant pope to break the two churches apart. This happened in 1054 when the patriarch Michael Cerularius and the papal delegation to Constantinople, headed by Humbert, mutually anathematized each other and broke the communion of the two churches. The theological basis for the schism was the Greek rejection of the Filioque, the doctrine approved by Rome and rejected by Constantinople that the Holy Spirit proceeded from the Father and the Son. There was also much argument about the use of unleavened bread in the Eucharist, the use of Halleluiahs, the marriage of clergy, and other points on which the two churches differed; but the one real cause was the Roman demand for, and the Byzantine rejection of, the universal headship of the church by Rome. Although many attempts have been made through the centuries to heal the schism, the two communions are still separate today. The Greek church seized upon the term Orthodox for itself, so Rome replied with the adjective Catholic or universal. The supremacy of Rome over the church was established; but it was only over a part of the church universal; the seamless garment of Christ was badly rent, and the unity of Christendom was destroyed for centuries if not for all time. In this respect the program of the reformers distinctly failed, and those who glibly speak of the "unity of Christendom in the High Middle Ages" must be reminded that the unity was merely the unity of the part and that in actuality this aspect of the Hildebrandine movement caused only failure and disaster.

The loss of the East was probably a factor in making the popes more than ever determined to control the West. And the first step in accomplishing this must of necessity be the emancipation of the church from any secular control. The "owned churches" of the feudal regime must be eliminated, but even more important, the secular control over the election of bishops and popes must be ended. As noted above, Leo IX prepared for this by refusing to accept the papal crown from Henry III and demanding election by the clergy and people of Rome. Thus his skirts were clear and he was able to take a firm stand against any secular interference in church affairs.

The relation of church and state was one which had troubled both theoretical and actual politics for many years. The popes claimed a certain right in the selection of emperors, based on the acceptance of the Donation of Constantine, and on the precedent of the coronation of Charlemagne. The emperors on the other hand claimed a right to interfere in papal elections, basing this claim on the precedent of the appointment of such popes as Sylvester II by Otto III, Benedict VIII by Henry II, and Clement II, Damasus II and Leo IX by Henry III. Both found apologists for their claims; both found scriptural arguments to support their contentions. The most commonly cited papal arguments were those which involved the sun (church) and moon (state), the latter deriving its light entirely from the former, and the argument from the Two Swords. When Christ said to St. Peter "Art thou armed?", Peter said "Yea, here are two swords," to which Christ replied "Put them away." This obviously, as any good papalist could tell, proved that to Peter were accorded the spiritual and the temporal swords, and that the pope, as Peter's successor, wielded the spiritual directly and the temporal through delegation. Thus any power that the empire had it had as the delegate of the church. The fact that Samuel deposed Saul gave Biblical precedent to any claims the church might have to dispose of emperors. But in the earlier stages of the struggle the claim of the papacy was essentially based on the position of the emperor as a man, and all men were subject to the discipline of the church when they transgressed the will of God.

The imperialists had, of course, their arguments too. Their best Biblical authority was in the statement of Christ that one should "Render unto Caesar those things which are Caesar's and unto God those things which are God's"; but they also argued that the execution of Christ by Tiberius proved that Christ Himself recognized the authority of the emperor; further, Christ sat on the throne of David the king, not Aaron the high priest; it was as a king that Christ was to rule mankind, in itself proof of the divine recognition of the kingly office.

This argument among the theorists developed throughout the twelfth and thirteenth centuries, reaching its height at the pontificate of Boniface VIII, but the beginnings were laid in the days of the reform party of the late eleventh century.[1] As a practical measure to prevent imperial interference in papal elections, the pope in 1059 issued an electoral decree. In the earliest days of the church, the pope, like all other bishops, had been elected by the clergy of his diocese and by the members of his flock. The consent of the emperor had customarily been sought before the election was held, although often the emperor was merely notified after the event. As we have seen, during the Iconoclast schism the popes ceased to be in communion with the Eastern emperors and so ceased to seek their confirmation of elections; but in the creation of the revived empire of the West, both Carolingian and Holy Roman, the popes acquired new temporal sovereigns, whose consent to their election was assumed necessary, at least by the sovereigns. As we have just noticed in the period between 800 and 1049, both the emperors and the popes established precedents whereby they later claimed the right to control the election of the other, and which side dominated was largely a matter of the relative strength of the two heads of society. The old Gelasian theory of the equality of emperor and pope, although temporarily put into practice by Otto III and Sylvester II, had rather generally disappeared before the asserted claims of one or the other to complete supremacy. The purpose of the electoral decree of 1059 was to clarify the process of papal election by returning it

---

[1] The history of the development of theory during the struggle of empire and papacy is one of the most fascinating studies in medieval history and the student is strongly recommended to investigate it in the excellent studies of C. H. McIlwain and A. J. Carlyle.

to the body originally responsible for it—the clergy and people of Rome. The method employed was by establishing a College of Cardinals, Roman clergy especially and exclusively designated as the electors of the pope. The term cardinal merely means the most important (as in our cardinal and ordinal numerals) and there had long existed in the major churches a division between the cardinal and ordinal clergy. What this decree did was to set up a college composed of cardinal bishops, cardinal priests and cardinal deacons attached to the churches of Rome, who were to elect the pope. Only after they had elected a pope was the emperor to be notified and his approval requested. In the first College there were 7 cardinal bishops, 28 cardinal priests, and 18 cardinal deacons. The bishops selected a candidate, the priests and deacons voted, and the pope-elect was then acclaimed by the other clergy and the people of Rome.

The great drawback to this system was one inherent in all medieval electoral colleges; the theory of the weighted vote. The medieval man did not have our modern democratic idea of all votes being equal; "one vote one value" was unknown until modern times, and it was taken for granted (after the manner of the Roman Senate) that the votes of men of greater dignity and experience should bear more weight than did those of lesser electors. Thus a cardinal bishop could outvote several cardinal priests or deacons. This system was not unique in the papacy but was standard in all medieval assemblies, both ecclesiastical and lay. It resulted in several disputed elections, where one candidate would have the majority of votes, but the other those of the greatest value. The *pars valentior,* that part having the greatest importance or value, was uniformly accepted as properly dominating any medieval election, and this theory prevailed into modern times. England still gives certain universities parliamentary representation so that the graduate enjoys an extra vote through his university, an obvious relic from this medieval practice.

Although the issues between empire and papacy were drawn with the accession to power of the reform party in the papal curia, the actual conflict did not break out until the accession of Hildebrand himself as Pope Gregory VII in 1073. Before that time under Popes Leo IX, Stephen IX, Alexander II, and others there was comparative harmony between the papacy and the emperor. Henry III, until his death in 1056, was most friendly to the popes, and Henry IV ascended the throne a minor and found himself far too busy with troubles at home to quarrel with the church. Politically, the chief struggle which the popes engaged in was war with the Normans of South Italy, and after the disastrous defeat of Leo IX by Robert Guiscard in 1053, a truce was arranged with them whereby the pope recognized the position of the Normans and conferred upon Guiscard the title of duke, accepting his homage for his holdings in 1059.

The Pontificate of Gregory VII, 1073-85

When Pope Alexander II died in 1073, the choice of his successor seemed obvious. For twenty-four years the archdeacon Hildebrand had played an important role in the councils of the papacy and had been the guiding genius of the reform party. There was no other candidate even approximating his stature and his election was assured. So assured was it that, even before the election was announced, the people of Rome gathered outside the hall of the conclave and shouted his name, cheering his election. This episode, which had no real significance, later enabled the emperor to challenge his election on the ground that it had been obtained through pressure of the populace.

Hildebrand was not an extremist in his claims of temporal power. He never advanced any theory of universal political domination by the church, but he did steadfastly maintain the right of the pope, as the spokesman of St. Peter who could judge all men and and be judged by none, to excommunicate wicked princes (who were but mortal men), and to relieve their subjects from any obedience which they owed their wicked rulers. He did claim political suzerainty over Spain, Hungary, Denmark, Poland, and Apulia, but these were vassal states of the papacy—at least in the opinion of the church—and the relationship was feudal and not any evidence of claim to universal dominion.

In memory of his former friend Gregory VI, Hildebrand assumed the pontifical name of Gregory VII. It was a clear statement that he intended to pursue the policy of the reform party and to insist on the emancipation of the church. At first there seemed to be no particular opposition. Henry IV was involved in a war with rebels in Saxony and unquestioningly approved the election of Gregory. Then in 1075 Gregory launched his First Decree against Lay Investiture.

The Investiture Controversy became so important that, during its progress, the major issue was obscured by the detail. When a bishop was elected he was supposed to receive a double investiture: the investiture with his spiritual authority by his ecclesiastical superior, and the investiture with his temporal authority by his secular suzerain. But the secular lords, especially the emperors, had developed the habit of investing with both the temporal and the spiritual authority. This the pope justly protested. It was over this question of lay investiture of spiritualities that the issue between pope and emperor was to be fought out in its earliest stages.

The trouble started over Milan. There virtual civil war had been raging for some years as a result largely of the attempts of the papacy to enforce ecclesiastical celibacy. The reformed party, known as the Patarini, fought the established clergy of the city and the whole district was thrown into turmoil. In 1071 when the archbishop died, each party elected its own archbishop; the pope supported one, the emperor the other. But Henry had backed down during the Saxon war to secure the support of Rome and had abandoned his candidate entirely. When in 1075 the Saxons had been properly subdued, Henry felt himself strong enough to assert his authority in Milan and appointed a new bishop. He followed this by appointing two bishops in the Romagna. Gregory replied with a threat of excommunication unless Henry ceased his meddling in church affairs. Henry summoned a council of the German bishops at Worms in January 1076.

From this council Henry sent a letter to Gregory which began: "Henry, king not through usurpation but through the holy ordination of God, to Hildebrand at present not pope but false monk . . ." and which went on to denounce him as the persecutor of the Lord's annointed, ending with the injunction: "Thou, therefore, damned by this curse and by the judgment of all our bishops and by our own, descend and relinquish the apostolic chair which thou hast usurped. Let another ascend the throne of St. Peter, who shall not practice violence under the cloak of religion, but shall teach the sound doctrine of St. Peter. I, Henry, king by the grace of God, to say unto thee, altogether with all our bishops: Descend, descend, to be damned throughout the ages." [2]

Gregory's answer to this epistle was immediate and effective. He deposed all the bishops who had signed the letter, deprived Henry of both his German and Italian thrones and excommunicated him. Further he absolved all Henry's subjects from their allegiance to the emperor, and invited them to elect a new emperor whom the pope could approve. The dukes of Swabia, Carinthia, and Bavaria promptly revolted; the unruly Saxons renewed their rebellion; the nobles of the empire held a diet at Tribur and demanded that Henry surrender and secure absolution within the year or they would deprive him of his kingdom. Then they invited Gregory to come to a diet to be held at Augsburg in February 1077 where the case of Henry would be tried, and, if necessary, a successor would be elected.

Henry recognized when he was beaten. Only by abject humiliation could he hope to maintain his royal position. With a few followers, Henry slunk over the Alps to meet Gregory, who had begun his journey towards Germany. The pope had gotten as far as the castle of Canossa in Tuscany, where he was protected by the powerful Countess Matilda. There Henry sought him, asking forgiveness. For three days the pope kept Henry waiting outside the castle, dressed in penitential garb, humbly beseeching absolution. Then he finally received him, removed the ban of excommunication and administered to him the Holy Sacrament. Henry promised in

[2] Translation from E. F. Henderson, *Select Historical Documents* reprinted in Scott, Hyma, Noyes, *Readings*, pp. 241-42.

return to return to Germany to be tried by the barons and to accept without objection or resistance whatever decision the council and the pope should make.

The real significance of this humiliation at Canossa has been the subject of much learned discussion. One school of historians affirm that it was an out-and-out victory for the church since Henry gave in abjectly to all of Gregory's demands. The other group (mostly Germans) claim that Henry won a distinct victory, that he knew that the pope could not refuse absolution to a penitent, and that by a mere act of humiliation he actually regained his kingdom and prevented the pope from joining his enemies at Augsburg. Certainly Henry did regain his kingdom and was the immediate gainer by the act; but in the realm of theory the papacy had won a signal victory; Henry had back his kingdom by the grace of the pope, the right of the pope to judge emperors was admitted.

Unfortunately for the peace of Germany, the nobles did not seem to recognize what had happened at Canossa. Like so many crucial events, its importance was hardly recognized at all by its contemporaries. The revolting nobles refused to lay down their arms and held a diet at Florscheim, where they elected Rudolph of Swabia emperor. Henry retaliated by confiscating Swabia, which he gave to his son-in-law, Frederick of Hohenstaufen. For three years civil war continued in Germany. Then the pope finally gave his decision. In 1080 he again excommunicated and deposed Henry and recognized Rudolph as emperor. In his decision he asserted the right of the papacy to depose monarchs and to judge kings.

But if the German bishops and barons had favored the pope in 1076, they now rallied around Henry. They resented the arrogance of the papal claims. It was one thing to excommunicate and depose a sinning emperor and summon the barons to try him and elect a successor if they wished. It was quite another thing to depose one emperor and appoint another, asserting at the same time the right to do so. Henry had done nothing to Gregory since Canossa; in 1080 it was Gregory who deliberately interfered in German affairs. With the general support of his clergy and nobles, Henry summoned a diet which deposed Gregory and elected Archbishop Guibert of Ravenna, who assumed the papal name of Clement III.

For the next eight years fortune favored Henry. Rudolph of Swabia was killed in battle in 1080; Herman von Salm was elected to succeed him, but gained almost no recognition. Henry carried the war into the enemy's country by invading Italy and capturing Rome (1083). Gregory arranged an alliance with Robert Guiscard the Norman ruler of southern Italy [3] to counter it. Henry built up a coalition with Alexius Comnenus and Jordan of Capua. The Germans took Rome and installed their anti-pope.

[3] The story of the Norman conquest of south Italy and Sicily is to be found in the following chapter.

Gregory called for help, but Guiscard was busy in a war with Comnenus. Not until 1084 was Guiscard ready to march on Rome. When they did finally take the city the Normans knew they could not hope to hold it long so they submitted it to sack and burning. The Norman destruction of Rome was the most serious which the eternal city experienced in a millennium of warfare and pillage. When the Normans withdrew, taking Gregory VII back with them to Salerno, Rome was a mass of smouldering ruins. Nevertheless Guibert came back and again occupied the Castle San' Angelo. Gregory, worn out with the troubles of the last years, died at Salerno in May 25, 1085. He is reported to have said: "I have loved righteousness and hated iniquity: therefore I die in exile."

THE END OF THE INVESTITURE CONTROVERSY, 1085–1122

For a year after the death of the great pope there was no attempt to fill his place. Finally Desiderius of Monte Cassino, the good friend of the Normans, was elected under the name of Victor III, but he only ruled from May to September 1087. At his death he was succeeded by the French Cluniac Eudes, cardinal bishop of Ostia, who took the name of Urban II (1088–1099).

With the advent of Urban, a vigorous papal policy reversed the position of the two contestants. The pope arranged an alliance with Duke Welf of Bavaria and the Countess Matilda of Tuscany (who married Welf the younger), which stirred up a revolt in both Germany and Italy. Conrad, the son of Henry IV, was persuaded to revolt against his father; a league was organized among the Lombard towns to oppose the emperor; Urban reconquered Rome (though he was not to get possession of the Castle). It was during this struggle with Henry that Pope Urban held his councils at Piacenza and at Clermont in 1095, which resulted in the proclamation of the crusade, and the crusade must be considered as a part of the papal show of force in his campaign to reduce the emperor.

Henry was, however, a tough old warrior and hard to beat. He battered down the rebellion of the German nobles; he won over Welf of Bavaria; he secured the succession to his younger son, Henry. At Urban's death in 1099, the old emperor was still defying the papacy. But he had not long to go. Pope Paschal II continued the policy of Urban in stirring up revolt in Germany. In 1104 he incited young prince Henry to revolt against his father, supported by the margrave of Austria, the duke of Bohemia and other nobles. Henry, supported by the German towns, defeated the rebels on several occasions, but was captured by his son and forced to abdicate in December 1105. He retreated into the Rhineland to carry on the war against his son and his papal allies, but there he died in August 1106, an old defeated man, deserted by all but the faithful cities, which had rewarded his favors to them with unflinching loyalty. The pope was unforgiving in death as in life and refused to allow his body to be buried in consecrated ground.

Henry V (1106–25) came to the throne as the ally of the church. But he was a selfish, unscrupulous, ungrateful deceiver with no honor in his soul, and he quickly turned against his former allies, asserting to the full his father's claims to control ecclesiastical appointments and affairs. The papacy soon discovered that it had merely replaced an old wornout opponent by a young vigorous one.

The struggle between empire and papacy continued unabated throughout his reign, but it came down from the rather high plane on which Henry IV and Gregory VII had fought and concentrated entirely on the detail of lay investiture. From 1106 until 1122 this question was the predominant issue between emperor and pope.

Paschal II, though a milder man than Gregory, was no less inclined to affirm the prerogatives of the papacy. He reissued the decree against lay investiture. Henry V, who like his father was always concerned in Italy, marched on Rome. At this crisis, Paschal offered a solution to the question which was, to say the least, unexpected; he proposed that the church give up all its temporal possessions and that the clergy thus be removed from any secular control. Henry promptly accepted this astounding proposal and agreed for his part to abandon completely lay investiture. But the clergy were of no mind to follow the pope in such a step. They looked forward with no enthusiasm to being reduced to apostolic poverty and forced to live on the alms of the faithful. There was a near riot in St. Peter's and Henry had to carry off the pope in protective custody. The upshot of the whole affair was that Paschal had to give up his decree against lay investiture and to crown Henry emperor. For the next couple of years Henry was busy in Germany, but trouble broke out again in 1115 on the death of the Countess Matilda of Tuscany. This ancient ally of Gregory VII's had placed herself in vassalage to the papacy in the days of the great Gregory. But when she died she bequeathed her lands to Henry V. The pope refused to recognize the legacy, but Henry came down into Italy to collect his heritage. Paschal fled to the south, while Henry occupied Rome and had himself crowned anew. Then in 1118 Paschal died and Gelasius II ascended the papal throne. Henry set up an anti-pope whom he took to Rome, while Gelasius excommunicated emperor and anti-pope from his refuge at Cluny. His brief reign ended the next year and he was succeeded by Calixtus II (1119–24). He promptly renewed the excommunications of Henry and his pope and backed it up by capturing Rome and installing himself there. The German bishops on the whole favored the pope; the barons favored the emperor, but were sick of the unending struggle. Frederick of Swabia and Henry the Black of Bavaria (the heads of the great houses of Hohenstaufen and Welf) brought pressure to bear on the emperor to make his peace with Rome. Under their urging Henry summoned a diet to arrange the peace. The result of this negotiation was the famous Concordat of Worms (1122) which ended the investiture controversy. By its terms Henry gave up investiture with ring and staff and swore to permit free ecclesiastical elections. The compromise was made, however, that while in Italy and Burgundy the bishops were to be elected and consecrated before being invested with their temporalities; in Germany the elections were to take place in the presence of the emperor or his agent and the investiture with the temporalities preceded the consecration with the spiritual powers. This agreement was solemnly confirmed by a diet of the German people and by a Lateran Council of the church (1123).

Thus ended in compromise the long drawn out struggle over investiture. The compromise was not original; it was the same as that reached between Anselm of Canterbury and Henry I of England. It settled nothing, as the emperor continued to interfere in ecclesiastical matters in Germany, though he did to some extent withdraw from Italy. But only the detail had been settled; the real struggle was to appear in a starker and more open form in the succeeding reigns.

GERMANY, 1056–1152: THE WELFS AND HOHENSTAUFENS

Although the struggle with the papacy is the chief interest in the reigns of both Henry IV and Henry V, the developments in the internal history of Germany were also of considerable importance. There is a realignment of power and a constitution of a new group of ducal families.

Most important were the Hohenstaufens of Swabia. When Henry IV confiscated the duchy of Swabia from Rudolph the anti-emperor, he bestowed it on his son-in-law, Frederick of Hohenstaufen. Frederick in turn served him loyally throughout his lifetime, and his sons were the chief allies of Henry V. A family connection with Austria was made when Agnes, the widow of Frederick, married as her second husband, Leopold, the duke of Austria, by whom she was the mother of the famous Henry Jasomirgott.

Next in importance was the house of Welf which ruled over Bavaria. This family was never so close to the emperor, and we have already seen Welf allying with Gregory VII and marrying his son to the Countess Matilda of Tuscany. Nothing came of this however, and Tuscany was lost to the family, being given as we have seen to Henry V. Meanwhile Henry the Black (1101–26), the successor of Welf, continued to build up his strength in Bavaria and managed to acquire some of Saxony at the extinction of the old house of the Billungs, though the bulk of Saxony with the ducal title went to Lothaire of Supplinburg. An alliance between the Welf and Hohenstaufen families was concluded with the marriage of Judith, the daughter of Henry the Black, to Frederick of Swabia, the eldest son of Frederick and Agnes. (Consult genealogical table, p. 265.)

During both the reigns of Henry IV and Henry V, the Hohenstaufens were the one great house on whom the emperors could rely. While Henry IV was popular in the Rhineland and had his chief strength there, Henry V was as unpopular as his father had been beloved, and the great archbishops of the west, led by Adalbert of Maintz, continuously stirred up rebellion against him.

Henry V himself married Matilda the daughter of Henry I of England and Normandy but they had no issue, so that when Henry died in 1125, the succession to the throne was disputed. Henry had nominated as his successor his nephew, Frederick of Swabia. But the anti-Salian clerical party, under the leadership of Adalbert, refused to permit the continuance of the dynasty and secured the election of Lothaire of Supplinburg, duke of Saxony. Henry the Black was won over to the Saxon party by arranging the marriage of his son, Henry the Proud, to Gertrude, the only daughter of Lothaire.

At once civil war broke out. Frederick of Swabia did not oppose the election of Lothaire, but he did put in a claim for all the lands held by Henry V as his personal inheritance from his uncle. Lothaire claimed them as crown lands rather than as personal property and the two parties engaged in conflict, Frederick and his brother, Conrad, rebelling in 1125.

Lothaire (1125–37) relied strongly on the papal clerical party. He gave up all claims to investiture and did not even attempt to enforce the imperial rights granted under the Concordant of Worms. With the strong support of the bishops and the house of Welf, he was able to crush the Hohenstaufen revolt both in Germany and in Tuscany, where Conrad had gone to gather in his inheritance of that duchy. The only support which Conrad received in Italy came from the city of Milan which was strongly anti-papal.

It is from this period of civil war that the great party names of Guelph and Ghibelline are thought to date. Guelph is of course merely a softening of Welf, while Ghibelline is the Italian pronounciation of the Hohenstaufen castle (and battle cry) of Wiblin. Supporters of the two families assumed the party names and the struggle continued in Italy for centuries, until the original meaning of the names had been long forgotten. In general it can be stated however that the Guelphs were usually pro-papal and the Ghibellines anti-papal and pro-imperial.

In 1130, occurred a papal schism which gave Lothaire an opportunity to increase his prestige and authority. At the death of Honorius II there was a split in the College of Cardinals, with the resultant election of two popes. The cardinal bishops, supported by the great Roman house of the Frangipani, elected Innocent II; the majority of the cardinal priests and deacons, supported by the house of Pierleoni, elected Anacletus II. As the one had the votes of the more important members of the College, but the other had the majority, each had a legitimate claim and considered himself properly elected. Lothaire, Louis VII of France, and Henry I of England all recognized Innocent; Roger II of Sicily recognized Anacletus, and received from him a royal title. The election was finally settled through the influence of St. Bernard of Clairvaux, who dominated the ecclesiastical and much of the political scene from his monastic cell, and who declared for Innocent II.

Anacletus, however, held Rome, and though Innocent had the support of most of the world, his rival was ensconced in the Eternal City. Lothaire, defender of the papacy, made an expedition to Italy in 1132–33 to place Innocent on the papal throne and to secure his own imperial coronation. He had to fight his way through Lombardy, which was hostile, and he

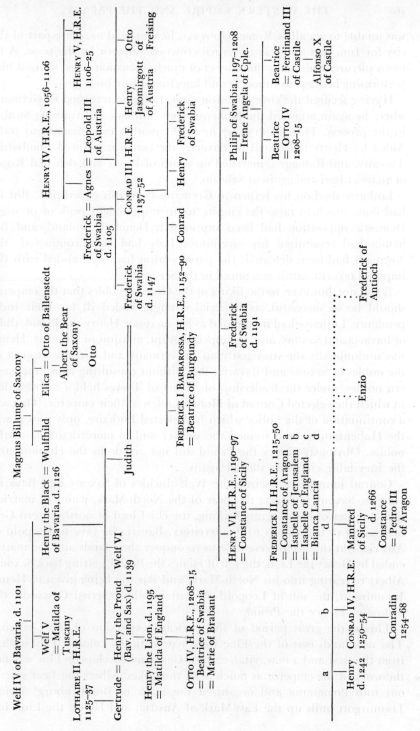

THE WELFS AND HOHENSTAUFENS

was unable to get all of Rome. However, he managed to secure part of the city for Innocent and was in return crowned emperor by the pope. A famous picture, which was the subject of much discussion later, showed him performing homage to Innocent and kneeling before him.

Having secured the coveted coronation, Lothaire returned to Germany where he again attacked the Hohenstaufen brothers, overrunning Swabia in the process. Then in 1136–37 he made another expedition into Italy. Aided by Henry the Proud of Bavaria, the emperor reduced Lombardy, Tuscany, and Romagna, marched on south of Rome and defeated Roger of Sicily at Bari and again at Salerno.

Lothaire died on his return to Germany from this expedition. But he had done much to raise the empire to an unprecedent peak of prestige. Domestic opposition had been suppressed; Denmark, Poland, and Bohemia had recognized his suzerainty; Italy had been conquered; the Normans had been defeated; the papal schism had been ended with the imperial favorite firmly ensconced in the See of Peter.

It was not, however, to the liking of the German nobles that the emperor should be so successful, as imperial strength boded ill for their independence. Lothaire had nominated as his successor Henry the Proud, duke of Bavaria and Saxony, and, by imperial grant, marquis of Tuscany. Henry was undoubtedly the strongest man in Germany and had the support of the nobles of Saxony and Bavaria. But without consulting these, the western nobles, under the leadership of Albert of Treves held a hurried diet in which they elected Conrad of Hohenstaufen as their emperor. This was a continuation of the policy which had elected Lothaire, only now it was the Hohenstaufen who seemed the weaker and so more desirable to the nobles. Obviously Henry the Proud did not accede to the election, and the inevitable civil war started again.

Conrad immediately seized the Welf duchies of Saxony and Bavaria. He gave Saxony to Albert the Bear of the North-Mark, who had married the daughter of old Magnus Billung, the chief lord of north-eastern Germany, and so had claims to this territory. Bavaria he gave to Leopold of Austria. But the Welfs were able to reconquer their lands and the matter ended by Henry the Lion, the son of Henry the Proud, getting back Saxony, Albert retreating into his North-Mark, and Bavaria being given to Henry Jasomirgott, the son of Leopold of Austria, who married Gertrude, the widow of Henry the Proud.

This is the great period of the eastward expansion of the Germans. The new lands east of the Elbe were systematically colonized by settlers from the west and a new, vital, eastern Germany developed. This was not the work of the emperor as much as of the dukes. Albert the Bear spread out into Pomerania and organized the mark of Brandenburg; Henry Jasomirgott built up the East-Mark of Austria, and Henry the Lion fostered colonization in the lands east of Saxony. In 1147 there was a crusade of the German princes against the Slavs east of the Elbe, which further increased the power of the great nobles.

Conrad III (1138–52) was not a strong ruler. While his great vassals were building themselves states in the east, he piously went off on the Second Crusade against the Moslems of Syria, returning in defeat and disgrace after a wholly unsuccessful expedition. He recognized that the Welfs and other houses had grown too strong for him, and passed over his own sons in the matter of the succession, selecting as his successor his nephew Frederick, the son of his elder brother Frederick of Swabia. When he died in 1152, the nobles were willing to accept the nomination of Frederick because the royal power had been reduced to such an extent that anarchy rather than imperial despotism was their chief concern. It was with little opposition, therefore, that Frederick Barbarossa ascended the throne.

FREDERICK I BARBAROSSA, 1152–90

Frederick Barbarossa has often been thought to have brought the medieval German empire to its height of power and prestige. Once considered the greatest of all German emperors, his reputation was subsequently attacked by historians, who felt that his Italian schemes operated to the prejudice of Germany. The most recent scholarship has, however, vindicated his position and shown that while he attempted to impose his rule over Italy he nevertheless kept a firm hand on Germany, and consistently built up the position of the emperor at home.

Frederick was undoubtedly influenced by the ideas of the Roman Law which was being revived at the school of Bologna: he felt sincerely that the emperor was God's agent on earth and that his was a holy office, ordained by God, and that he was responsible only to God for his actions. His ideal was an autocratic empire with all power concentrated in the hands of the emperor, but he was enough of a realist to see that he could best maintain his control by an alliance with the great dukes, and that only by the concerted action of the emperor and the dukes could the independence of the petty local dynasts be checked.

The great threat to the imperial power in Germany lay in the allodial counts who were making themselves virtually independent and breaking down all centralized government. Against them Frederick built up not only the domain lands of the emperor, but the strength of the great dukes. He aimed at building up a group of strong states, of which the royal domain should be the strongest, which would be bound together by feudal ties under the emperor. With this in view, he supported the early activities of his cousin, Henry the Lion of Saxony, and built up the Wittelsbach and Zahringen principalities. It was with imperial support that Henry engaged in his eastward expansion. When Frederick turned against Henry the latter fell before the attack of his own vassal counts; and it should be noted that the breach between Frederick and Henry was caused, not by any difference in policy over Italy, but because Henry demanded and Frederick refused to surrender, the city of Goslar. It was only after Frederick refused to give him this city that Henry refused to campaign in Italy, and only after this that Frederick turned against his cousin and destroyed the Welf duchies.

At first Frederick supported the Welfs. Henry the Lion was restored in Saxony and Bavaria, Welf VI was granted the marquisate of Tuscany. Later, after they had quarreled over Goslar and Henry deserted him in Italy, Frederick turned against Henry and in 1180 deprived him of his lands, leaving him only Brunswick. But Bavaria was given to the Wittelsbachs, whom Frederick systematically built up, and the emperor continued to support the formation of a strong state in the Zahringen lands of Switzerland and the Burgundian Alps.

Likewise Frederick favored the growth of towns in Germany. He did not approve of the independence of the communes, but he did favor the growth of towns as centers of royal administration. The rural districts were made dependent on royal towns, which became the centers of the emperor's strength.

As long as there were strong emperors in Germany this policy was successful. It was only after the fall of the Hohenstaufens, when the strong imperial control was removed, that the dukes and towns asserted a virtual independence and took over the control of the state.[4]

But Frederick aimed at more than control of Germany: he aspired to actual rule in Italy, to a real revival of the empire. In his Italian ambitions, he was less successful. He made six expeditions into Italy, and although at times he was able to assert considerable authority there, the net result was the increased independence of the Italian communes and the increased power of the papacy.

The spirit of municipal independence was rife in Italy. The Lombard towns had in general won their independence of their feudal lords and set up communes. This movement had begun in north Italy, but had spread even to Rome itself where a commune had been established by a popular revolt against Pope Lucius II (1144-45) and the nobles. The pope had been killed in the fighting; his successor Eugenius III (1145-53) had been

---

[4] The modern point of view followed in this discussion is developed by Geoffrey Barraclough, *Medieval Germany* (1938). J. W. Thompson's *Feudal Germany* (1928) gives the older view which condemned Frederick for his imperial aspirations and accused him of neglecting Germany and opposing the development of towns. Thompson said (*The Middle Ages*, I, 498) "His policy was based on castles and agricultural conditions . . . Cities were hotbeds of insurrection and independence and did not fit into his scheme of government," a point of view which Barraclough shows to be wholly mistaken.

forced to recognize the commune, but even so had been unable to enter the city and had taken refuge in France. The leadership of the Roman commune had passed into the hands of Arnold of Brescia, a well known heretic, who advocated the secularization of all church property and similar subversive ideas. Of Arnold, St. Bernard wrote: "A man of amiable and seductive conversation but his teaching is poisoned; he has the head of a dove and the tail of a scorpion, a monstrous creature whom the city of Brescia has vomited out, whom Rome has rejected, whom France has repulsed, whom Germany hates and whom Italy is no longer willing to receive." [5] This arch-enemy of the papacy took over the control of the Roman commune after it had been organized and kept the successor of St. Peter in exile from his proper city.

At the death of Eugenius III, Nicholas Breakspear, the only Englishman ever to become pope, ascended the papal throne with the name of Adrian IV (1154–59). He placed an interdict on Rome and opened up negotiations with Frederick for joint action against the commune and the arch-heretic, Arnold. Arnold was as obnoxious to the emperor as he was to the pope, for he stood for the independence of the towns against the rights of the emperor, and Frederick gladly made common cause with Adrian in this matter. In 1154–56 he accordingly set out on his first Italian expedition, for the purpose of extirpating Arnold from Rome and securing for himself the imperial coronation. These ends were gained; Arnold was captured and executed and Frederick was crowned in Rome. On the way down into Italy, however, Frederick had encountered the first sample of that Lombard opposition which was to be the bane of his life. He held high diet at Roncaglia on his way south, and there came to him there representatives of Lodi and Como demanding vengeance on Milan for her aggressions against them. Frederick did not have time to besiege mighty Milan, but he did lay siege to her ally Tortona, a comparatively small and ill-defended place. That it took two months to besiege Tortona showed how much longer the capture of any really strong city would take. The art of defense was much more highly developed throughout the Middle Ages than was that of offense, and even a weak town could stand off a considerable army for months. Frederick finally took Tortona, razed it, and then, anxious to be on his way, went on down to Sutri where he first met Adrian in person.

At this meeting at Sutri occurred another incident which was significant of future events. By traditional protocol the emperor, when he met the pope, would descend from his horse and hold the stirrup of the pope while the latter alighted. This Frederick refused to do: the pope (who had to dismount unaided) reproached him, but Frederick refused to act as the pope's squire. Ultimately, after much argument, Frederick relented and consented

---

[5] Munro and Sellery, *Medieval Civilization* (Century Co. 1907) p. 427.

to hold the pope's bridle and stirrup, but the incident is of real importance as it shows Frederick's determination not to seem to do homage to the pope in any way. After this point was amicably settled, the two proceeded to Rome where Adrian crowned Frederick emperor. On the very night of his coronation, however, rioting broke out in the city so that the emperor had to withdraw outside the town. Disgusted he turned back north, refusing to engage in a campaign against William of Sicily into which the pope was trying to inveigle him. That the Sicilian king followed up this failure of the emperor to attack him by taking the offensive and forcing the pope to recognize him as king of Apulia and all south Italy, was a blow to both papal and imperial prestige.

But though Adrian and Frederick had ostensibly co-operated amicably, there was a considerable element of distrust between them. They might agree about the destruction of Arnold, but his death was an insufficient bond to hold them together long. The first incident to show actual conflict between them occurred when Frederick was holding diet at Besançon in 1157 to proclaim the unification of Burgundy with Germany, and is accordingly known as the "Besançon episode." To Frederick, holding court at Besançon, came two legates from the pope, one of whom was the celebrated Master Roland Bandinelli, a famous canon lawyer, bearing a letter from Adrian protesting against the violent seizure of the bishop of Lund as he was returning from Rome, a crime which had gone unpunished by Frederick. In the course of the letter Adrian wrote:

> You should remember, most glorious son, how graciously your mother, the holy Roman Church, received you last year, how kindly she treated you, and how gladly she conferred upon you the imperial crown, the highest mark of dignity and honor; how she has always fostered you on her kindly bosom, and has always striven to do only what would be pleasing and advantageous to you. We do not regret having granted the desires of your heart; nay, we would be glad to confer even greater benefits *(beneficia)* upon you if that were possible . . .

The trouble arose over the translation of the word *beneficia,* which could mean benefits or could mean benefices, i.e. feudal tenures. Coupled with the statement that the papacy had conferred upon Frederick the imperial crown, this interpretation was entirely logical, and Frederick's good friend, Otto of Wittelsbach, drew his sword to attack the legate, Roland, who had dared to make such an assertion. Frederick interfered to save the life of the legate; there is a supreme irony that he thus rescued the man who, as Pope Alexander III, was to become his most implacable enemy. But Frederick was not inclined to take this statement without protest. Indignantly he wrote back to Adrian, relating the events at Besançon and ending:

> We hold this kingdom and empire through the election of the princes from God alone, who by the passion of his Son placed this world under the rule of two swords;

moreover the apostle Peter says "Fear God, honor the king." Therefore whoever says that we hold the imperial crown as a benefice from the pope resists the divine institution, contradicts the teaching of Peter, and is a liar.

Adrian was in no position to antagonize the emperor. His answer was a complete withdrawal of any claim to feudal suzerainty.

We are informed that you were enraged because we used the word *beneficium,* at which surely the mind of so great a person as yourself should not have been disturbed. For although with some that word has come to have a meaning different from its original sense, yet it ought to be taken in the sense in which we have used it and which it had from the beginning. For *beneficium* comes from *bonum* and *factum,* and we used it to mean not a *feudum* but a good deed, in which sense it is used throughout the holy scriptures. . . . We meant by the words "we conferred" no more than "we placed" as we have said above.[6]

This may seem trivial; but who can say what might have been the future papal claims had Frederick not thus forced the pope to explain and to deny any intent to claim suzerainty? Frederick was right in being suspicious of this statement; as it was his successors faced definite papal claims to suzerainty; had he let this pass, what a precedent the popes could have cited in his acknowledgement of their pretentions!

In 1158 to 1162, Frederick made his second expedition into Italy. Again he held diet at Roncaglia to which the representatives of the Italian cities and the greatest doctors of the law schools came. A committee of these lawyers approved the award to the emperor of all the regalia. There he asserted his supremacy over the Italian towns and the Italian nation. The imperial aims and principles were set forth at length: the emperor alone was to enforce the peace of Italy; private war was prohibited; imperial *podestas* were appointed to rule each of the towns in the name of the emperor; and all rights not specifically granted the towns by charter were to be henceforth invalid.

To understand the significance of this diet, we must turn momentarily to a discussion of the situation in Italy, and especially Lombardy in the twelfth century. Throughout Italy the towns had grown in size, strength, and political independence. They had cast off their obligations to their old feudal lords and had defeated the country nobles, establishing self-governing communes. In many cases the bishops played a leading role in this emancipation of the towns and were recognized as the rulers of the communities; in others the bishops had been the chief objects of the communal hatred and were considered the enemies of the communes. On the whole, the bishops were quite loyal towards the emperor, as they were often the imperial governors, but in every town there had developed two parties, the one proimperial, the other anti; they took the party names

---

[6] All quotations are from the translation in Thatcher and McNeal, *Source Book,* pp. 185–88. Reprinted by permission of the publishers, Charles Scribner's Sons.

of Ghibelline and Guelph. The situation was further complicated by the intense rivalry among the towns; if one important town was Guelph, its nearest neighbors (and hence rivals) would probably be Ghibelline. Thus Milan was strongly Guelph at the accession of Barbarossa, and Pavia and Cremona, her rivals were Ghibelline. Beyond these, Brescia, Piacenza, Bergamo, Tortona, and others were pro-Milanese, while Lodi and Como were anti.

We have already seen how in 1154, Como and Lodi had appealed to the emperor against Milan, and Frederick had punished Milan by destroying her ally, Tortona. Then in 1158 Frederick determined to punish Milan herself. He besieged the city for a month and forced it to surrender, but the terms he demanded of the proud city were relatively light: Como and Lodi were to be compensated for damages done them, Milan was to give up all the regalia it had usurped and to accept imperial confirmation of her consuls and communal officers, but her territory was to be guaranteed and she was to retain her fortifications and her autonomy. To this Milan agreed; at Roncaglia the Milanese archbishop was most servile in his submission to Frederick. But at the diet at Roncaglia, Frederick broke his guarantee of Milanese territorial integrity and took away from the city the territory of Monza, which was made an official coronation site for the Italian kingdom. The commune protested against both this attack on her territory and on accepting podestas appointed by the emperor. Supported by her allied towns, Milan prepared to resist decrees of the diet. Frederick replied by attacking Crema, one of Milan's smaller allies. For six months he besieged the little city in 1159-60; then he pressed on to besiege Milan itself. The siege of Milan took two years (1160-62); when it was finally taken the noble city was ordered razed and its inhabitants dispersed. To ensure the completeness of its destruction, the razing of Milan was entrusted to the citizens of Pavia, Cremona, Lodi, Como, and Novara, all of whom had suffered at Milanese hands in the past. Brescia and Piacenza were also reduced, and Frederick was supreme in Lombardy.

While Frederick was busy with Milan in 1159, Adrian IV had died and the election had resulted, as in 1130, in a schism. Roland Bandinelli of Parma was elected by one faction with the name of Alexander III, while their opponents, probably inspired by Frederick, elected Octavian under the name of Victor IV. Frederick ordered a council to convene and summoned both candidates to appear and accept the judgment of his council. Victor appeared, but Alexander refused to recognize the competence of the imperial council and stayed away. Victor was proclaimed true pope by the council, which consisted only of imperial clergy, but Alexander fled to France where he was recognized. Both popes promptly excommunicated each other and all the other's partisans.

Trouble in Germany took Frederick back north in 1162, but he returned to Italy in 1163 for an administrative tour. He found things in a very unsatisfactory state indeed, but he had insufficient forces to accomplish much, and this expedition did little but increase anti-imperial sentiment among the Italians.

When in 1164 Victor IV died, Frederick appointed, with hardly any form of election, Paschal III. But Paschal had no support outside of Germany and even there opinion was divided. In the years 1164 to 1180 Frederick appointed three anti-popes to oppose Alexander III (1159–81), but all were imperial puppets without any power.

In 1165 Alexander occupied Rome; Frederick came down on his fourth Italian expedition to drive him out (1166–68). He succeeded in capturing Rome and driving Alexander into the south where he sought refuge with the Normans. Frederick planned to move on against the Normans, but malaria infected his army, causing so many losses that he was compelled to leave the "pestilential humors" of Rome and retreat to the north.

No sooner was Frederick out of Italy than Alexander began to build up alliances against him. Thirty-six of the Lombard cities had organized themselves into the Lombard League to defend their liberties. To this League Alexander allied the papacy, King William of Sicily, and the Byzantine emperor, Manuel Comnenus. As a sign of its independence and resistance to Frederick, the League built the new town of Alessandria (named after Alexander), which was populated with the former citizens of Milan and which stood as a symbol of the Lombard resistance against the empire.

Frederick accepted the challenge and led a fifth expedition into Italy (1174–77). But this time he had fewer troops than his enemies were able to put in the field against him, primarily because Henry the Lion had refused to accompany the army with any of his forces. Frederick began a siege of Alessandria, but was forced to abandon the operation after six months and send back to Germany for reinforcements. Henry the Lion still refused to come unless Frederick would purchase his support by ceding him the city and district of Goslar. Frederick refused to do this and so remained short of troops. On May 28, 1176 he met the army of the League in open battle at Legnano near Como. The German knights were outnumbered and outfought by the soldiers of the communes; the imperial army was routed. The Italians still talk of the great day of Legnano, when they completely whipped the hated Germans. Italian military glory has been sufficiently limited that this victory still looms large in their annals. At Legnano, Frederick's hopes of Italian empire crashed. The following year he was forced to make a humiliating peace with Alexander at Venice, whereby he recognized Alexander as the legitimate pope, and meekly held his stirrup. A six-year truce was made with the Lombard towns, which was later made permanent at the Peace of Constance (1183), whereby the independence of the Italian towns was guaranteed. They were to have their own governments, their own laws, administration, armies, and the collection of their own taxes.

Thus at the end of a quarter century of fighting in Italy, Frederick had to admit total defeat. The papacy had preserved its independence of the empire and the Lombard towns had gained theirs. But Frederick had stopped extreme papal claims at Besançon, and while no emperor thereafter ever ventured to set up an anti-pope, the papacy had still admitted that it had no claim to feudal suzerainty over the empire. Little had been decided; the issue was still in doubt and another century of struggle lay ahead.

Alexander III celebrated his triumph by summoning the Third Lateran Council of 1179. Here it was ordained that in papal elections a two-thirds vote should prevail. Legislation for the suppression of heresy and the establishment of schools was passed and decrees banning tournaments were issued. Frederick tried to console himself by holding a great diet at Maintz in 1184, but it was a thing of tinsel. The great show of pomp and ceremony could not conceal the fact that there was little real power behind it all; it was attended by small dukes and petty nobles, but Italy was lost and the emperor's power in Germany had suffered as a result of his defeat in Italy.

Frederick made one last expedition into Italy. William II of Sicily had become embroiled with the Byzantine Empire and sought help. Pope Lucius III (1181–85), who was anxious to renew friendly relations with the empire, approved of an alliance between Germany and Sicily. In 1184, this alliance was cemented by the betrothal of Frederick's son and heir, Henry, to Constance, the aunt of King William. In 1186, Frederick made his last visit to Italy to see his son married and crowned. Then in 1189, turning the administration of the empire over to Henry, the old emperor started off to Jerusalem on the Third Crusade. After marching across Europe into Asia Minor, Frederick was drowned in a small river in Anatolia in June 1190, some say while attempting to ford it, others while taking a bath.

Although unsuccessful in his schemes for Italy, Frederick nevertheless had been a strong king in Germany and had made himself feared and respected throughout the Western world. Saladin dreaded his coming more than that of any of the other crusaders and his death brought great comfort to the Moslems. The old emperor soon became a legendary figure of heroic proportions, and the legend of the great emperor, sitting in a cave waiting for Germany's hour of peril to come back and lead his people, which was originally attributed to Frederick II, was later transferred to Barbarossa. A great feudal monarch, he epitomizes the ideals of the medieval German Empire.

Chapter 15

NORMAN ITALY AND SICILY: SPAIN

✤

THE NORMANS IN THE SOUTH

Robert Guiscard and the Conquest

In the tenth century, southern Italy was the battle ground between the warring factions of the Byzantines, Moslems, and Lombard dukes. The Aghlabids of North Africa had conquered Sicily in the ninth century and had begun to raid the Italian mainland. Naples and Bari were captured, Amalfi and the southern cities were laid waste, and in 846 the Moslems plundered Ostia at the mouth of the Tiber. In 915 Pope John X defeated the Moslems at the battle of the Garigliano, and Benedict VIII similarly inflicted a defeat on them in Italy, while the Genoese and Pisans took the offensive driving the Moslems out of Sardinia.

Meanwhile, the Byzantines had attempted to reassert their control over Apulia and Calabria. In 876 they had captured Bari and Tarento and established the theme of Longobardia. By the opening of the eleventh century, the Byzantines held the east and south, the Moslems were in possession of Sicily and the rest of the south was divided among the Lombard principalities and republics of Capua, Benevento, Salerno, Naples, Amalfi and Gaeta.

Into this melee were intruded the Normans in 1016. A band of Norman pilgrims, returning from a pilgrimage to Jerusalem, landed in southern Italy where they joined some Lombard rebels who were trying to secure their independence from the Byzantines. This first band was followed by small groups of Norman knights who took service as mercenaries under the various Lombard dukes. In 1029, the Lombard duke of Naples granted the leader of one of these Norman bands the county of Aversa, which then became the center of the Norman adventurers. These mercenaries served anyone who would pay them most, forming part of the army which the Byzantine general George Maniakes led against the Moslems and also fighting against the Greeks in the service of Lombard princes.

About 1036 there appeared the brothers William of the Iron Arm, Drogo, and Humphrey, sons of Tancred of Hauteville, who soon became recognized as leaders of the Norman freebooters. They allied with Guimar of Salerno against Maniakes, then assisted Maniakes when he revolted against the Byzantine emperor. When William of the Iron Arm died in

THE HAUTEVILLES OF APULIA, SICILY, AND ANTIOCH

Tancred of Hauteville

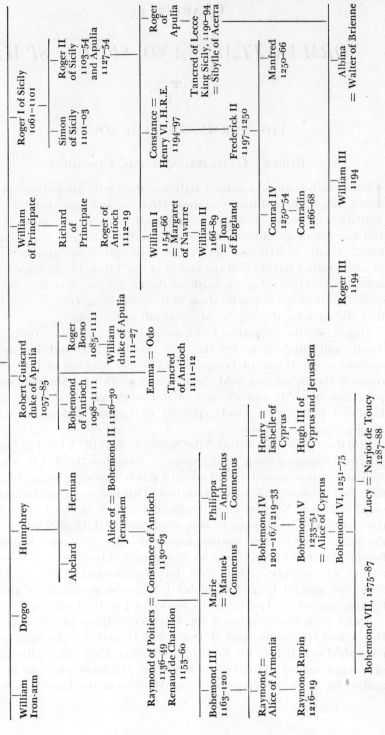

1046 he had created a Norman state in Apulia and had become, with Rainulf II of Aversa, the chief leader of the Normans of the south. At William's death, Drogo took over his brother's possessions in Apulia and was recognized as count of Apulia by Henry III. Meanwhile, other Hauteville brothers were arriving, notably a younger half-brother, Robert Guiscard. Drogo was murdered in 1051 and Humphrey succeeded, Robert Guiscard being left in control of a small territory he had conquered in Calabria. The Normans were still, in spite of the recognition, hardly more than robber barons and mercenaries, who throve on the civil wars between the Lombards and Greeks, but their position as territorial lords was rapidly developing. In 1053 Pope Leo IX, angered at their incursions into papal territory, led an army against them only to be defeated and captured at Civitate. Humphrey then conferred upon another brother, William, the county of the Principate, taking the lands for this investiture from Salerno.

In 1057 Humphrey died and Robert succeeded as count of Apulia. Moving to Melfi, Robert entrusted the conquest of Calabria to his younger brother Roger who had recently come south, while he pushed on his conquests in the east. Robert's rule was opposed by the other Norman barons, who felt that the conquest had been undertaken by them all equally and resented Robert's assumption of superiority. Although troubled by revolts of his nephews and his barons throughout his life, Robert managed to put them all down and to establish a firm rule in his territories.

Robert's official position was recognized when, in 1059, through the intermediacy of Abbot Desiderius of Monte Cassino, an alliance was concluded between the Norman chiefs and Pope Nicholas II whereby the pope invested Robert with the duchies of Apulia, Calabria, and Sicily, and Richard of Aversa was granted the principality of Capua which he had taken from the Lombards.

Having secured papal recognition of his titles, Robert, aided by Roger, began the intensive attack on the Byzantine towns. Reggio, Tarento, and Brindisi were taken in 1060 and the conquest of Sicily was begun in the same year. The conquest of Sicily differed from that of Apulia in that it was entirely the work of the two brothers, and principally of Roger. In 1061 Messina fell, but the brothers were repulsed before Palermo in 1064. While Roger continued to campaign in Sicily, Robert returned to the mainland where he captured Bari in 1071, taking advantage of the difficulties the Byzantines were having in Asia with the Turks to attack them while they were preoccupied elsewhere. The capture of Bari ended any Greek dominion in Italy: Robert returned to help Roger in Sicily and Palermo fell in 1072.

But Robert had grown great too fast to please his papal suzerain; playing off one group of Norman leaders against another, the popes helped stir up rebellion which broke out in 1072 when Richard of Capua and Guiscard's nephew Abelard, the son of Humphrey, defied the duke. Robert crushed Abelard, won over Richard and captured Salerno from Gisulf, a Lombard ally of the pope. Then he invaded the papal states, which brought down on his head not only a sentence of excommunication (1078) but a renewal of the revolt. Then war with Henry IV of the empire, which broke out in 1080, forced Gregory VII to make peace with Robert and even seek his alliance, recognizing the conquests which the Normans had made in the papal lands.

Robert, meanwhile, had boldly struck out against Byzantium. Taking advantage of the civil wars which distracted that unfortunate empire, Robert invaded Greece, capturing Corfu, Avlona, and Durazzo and pushing inland towards the capital. The diplomacy and military skill of Alexius Comnenus, who allied with Venice to cut the communications of the Norman armies, saved Byzantium, and Robert was forced to return to Italy to put down another revolt of the barons. While back in Italy, Robert "rescued" Gregory VII from Rome, which he sacked in 1084. He died the following year while preparing for another invasion of Greece.

The state which Robert Guiscard passed on to his son was one of the strongest in Europe. Built out of nothing, the Norman principality, in one generation, had developed to be a strong military power, encompassing all southern Italy and closely allied with a sister Norman state in Sicily. Out of the anarchy of the tenth century had emerged a powerful centralized state which was to play a leading role in the history of Europe in the period following.

The Kingdom of Sicily

When Robert Guiscard died in 1085 he left his son, Roger Borsa, as duke of Apulia and his brother, Roger, as count of Sicily. For forty-two years the two states maintained a separate existence before they were united in 1127 into the single kingdom of Sicily. The history of Apulia in this period is not important; it consists largely of the familiar baronial outbreaks and the slow but steady assertion of the ducal authority over the tempestuous lords. In 1098, Richard of Capua accepted the suzerainty of Roger Borsa over his domains, thus uniting all the Norman lands on the mainland into a single state, but otherwise the reigns of Roger Borsa (1085–1111) and his son, William (1111–27), are relatively unimportant. The most significant developments in connection with this side of the house were the conquests in the East made by Roger's half-brother, Bohemond of Tarento, in connection with the First Crusade and the establishment of a Norman state in Antioch in Syria.

Meanwhile Count Roger (1061–1101) had continued the reduction of the island of Sicily, a task which he completed in 1091. His next step was to secure from the pope the title of Apostolic Legate in his own domains, a position which gave him control over the Sicilian bishoprics by virtue of his ecclesiastical, if not his feudal, office. His rule was a stern and efficient one and at his death in 1101, he left a secure throne to his son, Simon (1101-03). On Simon's premature death in 1103, the county passed to his younger brother, Roger, under the regency of his mother, Adelaide (1103-12).

In 1127, Roger, taking advantage of the death of William of Apulia and the absence in the East of the proper heir Bohemond II, seized the control over the continental possessions of his house, uniting Apulia to Sicily. Then in 1130 he secured from Anacletus II, whom he supported for the papacy, the investiture with the royal title making Sicily into a kingdom, held from the papacy.

Roger II, King of Sicily, 1130-54

Roger had already ruled for twenty-seven years as count when he assumed the royal title, and for the last seventeen years it had been a personal rule. He was one of the ablest rulers in a century of great kings, and under him Sicily became one of the most powerful states of Europe.

The first event of his reign as king was a war with the papacy. As he had supported Anacletus and been crowned by him, Innocent II refused to recognize the title and attacked the usurper. Roger defeated the pope at the battle of the Garigliano in 1130 and forced the legitimate pope to approve the title conferred by his rival. Then occurred a period of intricate three-cornered diplomatic intrigue between the German emperors, the Byzantine emperors, and the Sicilian king, all of whom sought to dominate Italy. Resentful of royal control and abetted by Innocent II, the Norman barons revolted in 1131-34 but were put down by Roger. Then in 1136 when Lothaire made his Italian expedition there was another general revolt, the barons giving assistance to the German emperor, so that he was able to occupy temporarily Bari and Salerno. Although Roger had inherited from Robert Guiscard a generally anti-Byzantine policy, he modified it to meet the menace of the German attack and we find him negotiating with both John and Manuel Comnenus against the German emperors. When Conrad and Manuel allied in spite of Roger, the Sicilian king made a naval attack on Greece in which he destroyed the cities of Corinth and Thebes (1147); and to offset the German-Byzantine alliance, Roger allied with the Welfs against Conrad and stirred up Louis VII of France against the Greeks.

Although he played an active role in the wars and diplomacy of Italy, Roger was always more concerned with the development of Sicilian sea power. His main policy, which he pursued with unflagging zeal, was to secure control of the mouth of the Adriatic and of the passage between Tunis and Sicily so that his fleets could command completely all shipping in the western Mediterranean. In pursuance of this policy, Roger began sending expeditions to North Africa as early as 1118 but attempts to establish Norman colonies in Africa, which were repeatedly made in the years 1118–27 generally failed. In 1134 Roger interfered in North African affairs as the ally of the sultan of Madiyah over whom he secured an hegemony. Then in 1146 he captured Tripoli to the east, a conquest which he followed up two years later by the capture of Gabes, Sus, and Madiyah. The Normans increased their control in North Africa until they held the whole coast from Tripoli to Tunis and advanced into the interior as far as Kairowan. As he had at the same time secured the control of the mouth of the Adriatic, this gave Roger his desired predominance in the western Mediterranean and made Sicily easily the greatest Western naval power of the time. It also brought him the active enmity of Venice, Genoa, Pisa, and the other Italian commercial republics.

Institutions of Norman Sicily

The state which Roger II built up was in many ways the strongest in Europe. Its king was the strongest of any of the Western monarchs, and the Norman "baptized sultan" rested his power on a highly centralized bureaucracy in which he fused elements from the Norman, papal, Byzantine, and Arabic. Logothetes, catapans, and emirs served together with constables and justiciars in the court of the Sicilian king; his chancery issued documents in Latin, Greek, and Arabic, employing a French miniscule script, but copying the style of the Latin charters from the Lombard and the Greek from the Byzantine. While the Sicilian institutions most closely resembled the English and were for years thought to be derived from them, Professor Haskins has shown that the Sicilian in all probability antedated the English and that English influences were not extensive.[1]

While the old feudal law was respected by the king, and while the Moslems were governed by their own laws, Roger was strongly under the influence of the revived Roman law [2] and a series of royal decrees modified the old established customs of the realm. The judicial system was staffed by professional lawyers and judges like the Byzantine courts; royal justices were established in specified districts, but in addition, Roger added the strictly Norman institution of the itinerant justices, who went on circuits throughout the kingdom hearing pleas. The king's justiciars had jurisdiction over all pleas of homicide, robbery, rape, and such major offenses and after c. 1168 the old *curia regis* ceased to have many judicial functions, these all being handled by the royal justices and courts. The unusual position of the king as papal legate in the realm gave Roger a

[1] See especially Haskins: "England and Sicily in the Twelfth Century," *English Historical Review*, XXVI (1911), 433–47, 641–65.

[2] For the revival of Roman law in Western Europe, see below pp. 575–77.

unique control over the ecclesiastical courts, and Sicilian clergy did not enjoy the right of appeal to Rome as the king handled all appeals in his own legatine court.

The exchequer which was founded under Roger II, showed the influence of the Moslem *Diwans*. Two bureaus, the *Duana de Secretis* and the *Duana baronum* had competence over the royal and feudal revenues respectively. Nothing shows better the cosmopolitan character of the Sicilian institutions than the financial administration where a *Secreton*, (a title taken from the Greek) had charge of a group of Moslem clerks and officials, who handled finance in the Moslem manner, but added to the oriental financial office the Norman judicial powers and functions of the exchequer. A Thomas Brown, whom we first encounter in the exchequer in Sicily, also held a similar position in England and there is reason to believe that there was a strong reciprocal influence between the Sicilian and English exchequers.

The military establishment was essentially feudal, but the king always preserved the Norman reservation of allegiance to the crown, and the king could always summon out directly the arrière vassals. Knights fees in the five and ten knights units were found in Sicily as in England and Normandy; the forty-day limitation on service and the established feudal aids were also similar to the Anglo-Norman practice. But the king held a tight check on his vassals and Roger compiled a *Catalogus Baronum*, which listed all services due, some time earlier than Henry II's famous Inquest of Service of 1166. In this the Sicilian monarch got around the diminution of service to the crown by arbitrarily doubling all services due the king. Castleguard and coastguard were owed in addition to the regular service, the king controlling all castles and the building of them. The fleet, which played so large a part in Roger's military arrangements, was made up of ships and mariners supplied by certain feudatories and by the maritime cities, though the crews were largely Moslems and Moslem mercenaries were also continuously employed in both the navy and the army.

The towns of southern Italy and Sicily enjoyed a great revival under the Norman kings. The fleets of Amalfi, Salerno, Naples, and the Sicilian cities carried their wares throughout the Mediterranean and brought wealth and prosperity to the towns. There were no communes in the Norman kingdom, but the towns flourished under the benevolent patronage of the king. Industry was fostered; mining of iron, salt and sulphur was one of the chief industries of the kingdom; pottery and glass making flourished. Palermo became the commercial crossroads of the western Mediterranean, and ships from all nations entered her roadstead. The wealth of Palermo became fabulous, its income alone being greater than that of the entire kingdom of England.

Intellectual and Cultural Life

The wealth of Palermo brought about a great era of building, which beautified the capital and made it the loveliest city of the West. The church of the Martorana is a pure Byzantine edifice, that of San Giovanni degli Eremiti is pure Saracenic; but the greatest church in Sicily is the great basilica of Monreale just outside Palermo, with its Romanesque floor plan and construction, beautified by magnificent Byzantine mosaics. The mosaics at Cefalu are said to be even finer than those of Monreale, though not so well preserved, and the Capella Palatina in Palermo is a gem of medieval art, which combines the best of the Norman and Arabic elements and which ranks with the Sainte Chapelle in Paris.

In every way Palermo reflected the combination of Greek, Arabic, and Latin civilizations, which marked its architecture and art. In material luxury, it partook of the character of an oriental city; in the ceremonial and elaborate costuming of its courtiers it reflected Byzantium; in the military prowess of its nobles and in their distinctive legal genius it was the child of Normandy, while thriving commerce and wealthy bourgeoisie placed it well in the ranks of the Italian towns. Under the Norman kings, Sicily enjoyed almost complete religious toleration; the official clergy were Latin, the monks were mostly Greek, but Moslem cadis touched shoulders with Basilians and Benedictines in the streets, and the call of the muzzein competed with the tolling of the monastic bells.

The culture of his court also showed Roger's cosmopolitanism. Roger II was one of the great patrons of learning in the Twelfth Century Renaissance. His special interest was in geography; he had a great silver map made on the wall of his palace, and the most honored scholar at his court was the geographer, Idrisi. It was at Palermo that Aristippus translated Plato and Aristotle from the Greek (as well as engaging in political conspiracy as we shall see below), and it was there that Eugene the Emir wrote his treatises on mathematics and astronomy. Men came from all over the world to the court of Palermo, and Sicily ranked second only to Spain as the great center for translations of the Arabic and transmission of the oriental culture. Adelard of Bath studied there as well as in Spain. This scientific activity reached its height under Roger's talented grandson Frederick II in the thirteenth century, but it had achieved a remarkably high plane under Roger himself.

The Two Williams and Tancred, 1154–94

When Roger II died in 1154 he was succeeded by his son William I (1154–66) called the Bad. His reign is marked chiefly by a long struggle with the Byzantines, loss of the African colonies, and troubles with Frederick Barbarossa due to the Sicilian support rendered Alexander III. In

1155, Manuel Comnenus directed a Byzantine invasion of Apulia and stirred up a rebellion among the Sicilian nobles which resulted in the fall of Bari, Brindisi, Tarento, and other towns to the Byzantines. The following year however, William was able to put down the rebellion in Sicily and to bring his forces into Italy where they defeated the Greeks at Brindisi, reconquering all that had previously been lost. William followed up this victory by besieging Pope Adrian, who had assisted Manuel, and forcing him, at the Treaty of Benevento, to accede to the Norman position in the south and to accept the Sicilian king as the protector of the papacy. He further took the war into the Greek Empire by sending his fleet to ravage Greece, while he opposed in Apulia the attack made by a Greek army from Ancona. In the following year (1158) a peace was concluded between the rivals and an alliance was drawn up between the pope, the Byzantines, and the Sicilians to oppose the ambitions of Frederick.

The height of Sicilian power in Italy was effected in 1159 when the Sicilians were able to secure the election to the papal throne of their friend Roland of Parma as Alexander III. The alliance already established was extended to include the Lombard League. Frederick replied with an alliance with Pisa and a grand scheme for a naval attack on Sicily, which however never came off.

Sicilian gains on the mainland were offset in the years 1156 to 1160 by the total loss of the North African colonies, which were systematically destroyed, with great massacres of the inhabitants, by the rising power of the Moslem Almohades, who conquered all the north coast of Africa as well as Spain. Towards the end of the reign, in 1161, William had to face a general revolt on the part of the Sicilian baronage, who were roused to rebellion by the exactions of Maio of Bari, the king's chief minister. The rebels led by Henry Aristippus, the scholar and translator, succeeded in killing Maio and imprisoning William for a time, while Aristippus was made governor of the realm. But William got loose and wreaked his vengeance on the conspirators, replacing Aristippus with a new chief minister, the notorious Matthew of Ajello. In 1166, just after he had sent an army to restore Alexander III to Rome, William the Bad died, and was succeeded by his son William II (1166–89) called the Good, although as Haskins has remarked he was no better than his father.

William the Good, the son of William I, ascended the throne under the regency of his mother, Margaret of Navarre. A baronial rebellion marked the inauguration of the new reign, and a Council of Ten was set up to govern the kingdom, in which the chief power soon passed to the Englishman, Walter, archbishop of Palermo. Under his guidance, Sicily maintained its support of Alexander III and the Lombard League against Frederick I until the battle of Legnano and the Peace of Venice (1177) brought an end to the conflict. Thereafter the Sicilian government made peace with the German Empire, even allying with it in the marriage of Henry, the son of Barbarossa, to Constance, the aunt of King William in 1186. At the time few suspected that Constance would ever inherit the throne, as William and his wife, Joan of England, the daughter of Henry II, were both young and there seemed no reason to think that they would not have heirs, but William had the barons swear to accept Constance as queen in case of his death without issue.

The last years of the reign were marked by a war which began in 1185 against the Byzantines. In 1185 Tancred of Lecce, an illegitimate grandson of Roger II, led a naval expedition against the Byzantines which captured both Durazzo and Salonica and invaded the empire, advancing towards Constantinople. This invasion was the cause of the fall of Andronicus Comnenus, and when Isaac Angelus revolted, William sent a fleet to his assistance under the command of the famous admiral Margarit.

Even farther east, William interfered in the politics of the eastern Mediterranean and carried on a naval war against Egypt. He had earlier allied with King Amaury of Jerusalem to invade Egypt, but the death of Amaury in 1174 had put an end to that project. William however continued his naval attacks on the Egyptians, and had taken the cross for the Third Crusade when he died in 1189.

At the time of her marriage to Henry VI, Constance had received the allegiances of the Sicilian barons to her as queen should her nephew die without issue. When William died in 1189 she should have succeeded to the throne without opposition and one party, headed by Archbishop Walter, favored this; but another party of the nobles led by Matthew of Ajello refused to accept her German husband as their king, and elected instead Tancred of Lecce, the illegitimate grandson of the great Roger, who had already distinguished himself in the campaign against Salonica. The opposition to Constance was not at all objection to her, but entirely to her husband.

Constance and Henry were in Germany; Tancred was proclaimed king and crowned; the papacy, which dreaded the union of the German and Sicilian crowns, approved the election. When Richard of England arrived at Messina on his way to the East in the Third Crusade, he found Tancred king, albeit on a somewhat shaky throne. Richard was much concerned over the repayment of the dower of his sister Joan (the widow of William II) and as Tancred seemed reluctant to pay the money, the Anglo-Norman army attacked and stormed the city of Messina. After this preliminary encounter, however, the two kings came to an agreement whereby Tancred paid the equivalent of the dower and Richard recognized him as king.

Meanwhile Henry VI, who had become emperor of Germany on the death of his father in 1190, was planning how to regain his southern kingdom. In 1191 he allied with Pisa and Genoa to attack Sicily. Naples fell after a siege and most of the other cities along the coast soon passed into the hands of the Germans. But the southern climate and the outbreak of an epidemic were too much for the northern warriors and Henry retreated to the north, leaving Constance behind him in Salerno. There she fell into the hands of Tancred, who was, however, too chivalrous to imprison a lady, and he released her at the request of the pope. Thereby Tancred's heirs lost the throne, for Constance and Henry continued to press their claims. Tancred was able to maintain himself on the throne until his death in 1194, but his son William III (1194) who succeeded under the regency of his mother Sibylle of Acerra, was soon dispossessed by Henry VI. In a rapid campaign in 1194 Henry reduced the Italian mainland and then crossed into Sicily. On Christmas 1194, he was solemnly crowned king of Sicily at Palermo. William was reduced to the county of Lecce, which his father had held before his election as king; Markward of Anweiler was appointed as the royal governor of the southern kingdom, and Henry returned to the north.

The Norman kingdom of Sicily had finished its first phase; in the next century it was to rise to even greater glories under Frederick II, but it was by then part of the empire and inextricably involved in it. Its great independent period, when as an Italian power it had gained the supremacy of the Mediterranean, was ended.

SPAIN TO THE END OF THE TWELFTH CENTURY

While the Normans were driving the Moslems out of Sicily, the Spanish peninsula was also being recovered from the Moors and a new group of Christian states was emerging south of the Pyrenees.

The history of these Christian states in Spain is complicated by the fact that several centers developed which became independent kingdoms, all of whom sought to beat back the Moors, but who were, as often as not, also engaged in wars with each other. Not until the end of the fifteenth century was most of the peninsula united into a single kingdom, and Portugal is still a separate state. The states whose individual histories we shall have to discuss were Leon, Castile, Navarre, Aragon, Barcelona, and Portugal.

MOORISH SPAIN

As we have seen, the Moslems conquered Spain in the eighth century, pushing their conquests even across the Pyrenees into southern France. They were pushed back by the Carolingians and the Spanish March was established around Barcelona; but only in the extreme northeast at

Barcelona and the extreme northwest around Oviedo and Santiago de Compostella were the Christians in control. The rest of the peninsula was held by Moorish emirs, who were united for a time under the Ummayad caliphate at Cordova (929–1031). When the caliphate fell, independent emirates were again established at Toledo, Valencia, Saragossa, Seville, Cordova, Murcia, Badajoz, Granada and Malaga. Among these *Taifas* states, as they were called, there was constant fighting, each trying to gain the ascendency over its neighbors. In the middle of the eleventh century, Seville gained a supremacy over the other southern emirates, under the rule of Abu'l Qasim and his son Mu'tadid.

As we have seen Moorish Spain developed a high cultural and economic civilization, very similar to that of Baghdad or Egypt. Agriculture was practised on advanced scientific lines, and horticulture, viniculture, and stock raising were highly cultivated. Olives, citrus fruits, and wines were among the chief agricultural products, while Spanish or Cordovan leather early gained an international reputation. Toledo became the rival of Damascus for the production of fine steel and armor, and the trade between the Spanish Moslems and their co-religionists in Africa and the Levant was a flourishing business. We have already noted Spain as the home of considerable intellectual activity, with such great names as Averroes and Maimonides in the twelfth century and Ibn Khaldun in the fourteenth.

Spain was also par excellence the center from which Arabic learning reached the West. The greatest center for translation from the Arabic to Latin was at Toledo, where men from all over Europe came to learn and translate the Arabic sciences.

CHRISTIAN STATES IN SPAIN

When the Moors overthrew the Visigothic kingdom in the early eighth century, some of the native Christians retreated into the mountains in the extreme northwest of the peninsula, in the district known as the Asturias where, under the leadership of the legendary Pelayo, they kept up a resistance to the invaders. With the slackening of the first drive of the Moors, these Christians were able to gain back some slight territory, until by the end of the eighth century they had established a small state around Oviedo. This little state was called first the Asturias and then later the Kingdom of Leon. The whole thing was very gradual; from their original holdings they spread south and east into Galicia, Burgos, and into a new territory which they wrested from the Moors in the southeast. In this new land, which was occupied in the early tenth century, they built castles to defend the districts, until the territory was known as the land of castles or Castile. Under Fernando Gonzales (930–970), this territory

THE SPANISH MONARCHIES TO THE THIRTEENTH CENTURY

Sancho III of Navarre, 970–1035

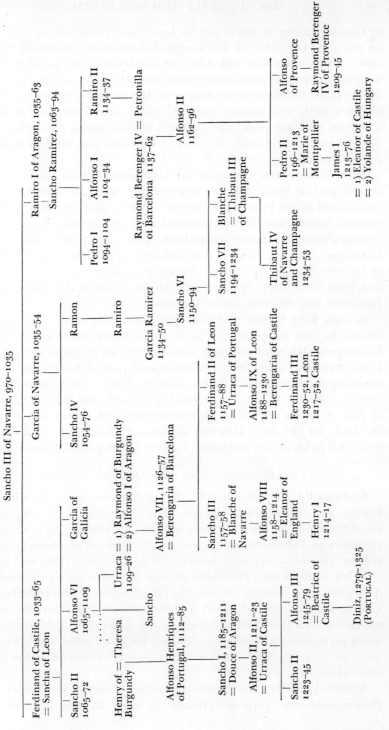

of Castile became as important as Leon, and threw off its dependence
on the older kingdom. In this struggle for autonomy, it should be noted
that the Castilians were aided by the Cordovans. This tendency to ally
with the infidel reappears throughout Spanish history, as throughout that
of the states founded in the East after the crusades. While the men of
an alien faith were natural enemies, and it was always easy to stir up
a war on religious principles, political considerations generally entered
into the picture and made alliances of Christian and Moslem matters of
common occurrence.

While Castile was becoming an autonomous county in the north-
central part of Spain, Navarre was growing up in the Pyrenees. In the
eastern end of the Pyrenees the county of Barcelona, the old Carolingian
Spanish March, was closely connected with France; but in the western
Pyrenees, as the Moors were driven back, there grew up in the ninth century
an independent state which in the tenth century took the name of Kingdom
of Navarre. Both of these states were quite separate from the rest of Spain
and from each other. Navarre was inhabited chiefly by Basques, while
Barcelona was the home of the Catalans.

In 1029, King Sancho of Navarre managed, as a result of marriage alliances, to gain possession of Castile, to which he added a part of Leon
by conquest. His son Ferdinand, who married the daughter of the king of
Leon, received Castile from his father and part of Leon with his wife,
assuming the title King of Castile in 1033. The rest of Sancho's domains
went to his other sons, Garcia receiving Navarre, and Ramiro the county
of Jaca, to which was later added Ribagorce. This county was to become
the basis for the later kingdom of Aragon. Meanwhile Ferdinand defeated his father-in-law and added Leon to his kingdom of Castile in 1037.

The Reconquista in the Eleventh Century

Ferdinand I (1033–65) having thus gotten control of Castile, Leon,
Galicia and Asturias, next turned against the Moors. In 1064 he captured Coimbra and made the emir of Badajoz tributary; then he attacked
the emirs of Toledo, Saragossa, and Seville from all of whom he exacted
tribute. He was unsuccessful, however, in an attempted drive on Valencia.

At his death in 1065, Ferdinand divided his realm among his three sons.
This policy of constantly dividing the kingdoms among the children of the
king produced endless difficulty and constant civil war, but the Spanish
monarchs, like the Merovingians, blindly adhered to the practice. For
seven years after the death of Ferdinand, his sons fought with each other,
until in 1072 Alfonso VI succeeded in getting possession of his father's
inheritance.

Alfonso VI (1072–1109) is one of the great kings in the history of the
Reconquista—the "perpetual crusade" in Spain. In 1085, aided by volun-

teers from Burgundy and France, by the king of Aragon and the emirs of Seville and Valencia, he attacked and conquered Toledo. The conquest of Toledo was the high point in the Christian reconquest for many years to come, for it brought a vigorous Moslem reaction. The Taifas emirs were alarmed at the advance of the Castilians; in desperation they sought help from Ibn Tashfin, the head of the Almoravides, who had recently established an empire in north Africa. On the invitation of some of the Moorish princes, Ibn Tashfin crossed over into Spain in 1086. The Taifas emirs rallied to his banner, and war was begun against the Christians. In October 1086, the allied Moslems met the Castilians at Zalaca: it was a crushing defeat for Alfonso, hardly a hundred of his knights escaping from the field. But the Moslems were unable to follow up their victory as Ibn Tashfin returned almost at once to Africa. When he came back to Spain somewhat later, he was not interested in wars with Castile, but began systematically to conquer his former allies, whose weakness he had observed earlier, until he had accomplished the conquest of all of Moorish Spain (with the exception of Saragossa) and added it to his African empire.

It was during the reign of Alfonso that there flourished Roderigo Diaz y Vivar, the famous Cid Campeador, who became the national hero of Spain and whose legend became the first great epic of Spanish literature. Actually the Cid was an adventurer who fought with equal enthusiasm against Christian and Moslem enemies, only seeking his own profit. He became ruler of Valencia in 1094 and waged continuous wars against both his Moorish and Christian neighbors. However, the freebooter was transmuted by later legend into the great Christian hero, and still remains the great heroic figure of medieval Spain.

When Ibn Tashfin died in 1106, his empire passed to his son Ali, who renewed the wars against the Christians. In 1108 he attacked Castile and defeated Alfonso at the battle of Ucles, where Sancho, Alfonso's only son, was killed. Thus when Alfonso died the next year, the throne passed, for lack of male heirs, to his daughter Urraca. As Urraca's husband, Raymond of Burgundy, was dead and a king was obviously needed, the Castilian nobles promptly married her off to Alfonso of Aragon.

Aragon had been made into a kingdom by Sancho Ramirez (1076–94), the grandson of Sancho the Great of Navarre, who annexed Navarre at the murder of its king in 1076. Sancho increased his holdings at the expense of Saragossa, and his son Pedro I in 1095 further strengthened his monarchy by placing his kingdom under the protection of Pope Urban II. Thus it was, that when Urban preached the First Crusade at Clermont that same year, he specifically excepted the Spaniards, who were ordered to remain at home and carry on their own Holy War against the Moors.

The Reconquista in the Twelfth Century

The union of Castile and Aragon under Alfonso and Urraca was not, however, destined to be long-lasting. Urraca made no secret of her dislike for her husband, and Alfonso attempted to console himself for the lack of his wife's affections by getting personal control over her kingdom. In this he was opposed not only by his wife, but by the Castilian nobles and clergy, so that a civil war broke out. Alfonso was ultimately driven out of Castile, which remained in the hands of Urraca until her death in 1126, when it passed peacefully to her son by Raymond of Burgundy, Alfonso VII.

It was during the civil war in Castile that Portugal first became an important state. The county of Portugal, on the west coast north of the Duero river, had been given by Alfonso VI to Henry of Burgundy, the brother of Raymond, who had married a younger sister of Urraca. During the civil war Henry played off both sides against each other to his own advantage until he had secured a considerable holding in the west. His son, Alfonso Henriques, further increased his possessions by conquests south of the Duero, and in 1139 assumed the title of King of Portugal (though this was not officially recognized by the pope until 1179).

The growth of Aragon on the east coast and Portugal on the west, cut Castile off from expansion in either of those directions and virtually necessitated that its expansion must be through the center of the peninsula. The history of the twelfth and thirteenth centuries is the story of the expansion of the three Christian kingdoms at the expense of the Moslems. But while Portugal drove straight south along the west coast, and Castile pushed south through the heart of the peninsula, conquering by far the greatest amount of land, Aragon turned to the sea, winning her empire in the islands of the Mediterranean. However, these lines of development were not as clear in 1100, as they were to be a century later.

When Alfonso of Aragon was driven out of Castile he returned to his ancestral kingdom and began to expand south against the Moors. In 1118 he conquered Saragossa, which he made his new capital. This was a conquest comparable to the Castilian capture of Toledo, but his further advances were stopped by a defeat which he suffered at the hands of the Almoravides in 1134 at Fraga.

When Alfonso died in 1134 without heirs he bequeathed his kingdom to the crusader military religious orders of the Knights Hospitallers and Templars, but the Aragonese and Navarrese nobles had no intention of accepting any such bequest and at once chose other kings. Navarre broke off from Aragon under Garcia V, descendant of the old line of kings of Navarre, while the Aragonese proclaimed Ramiro II, a younger brother of Alfonso, whom they brought out of a monastery to put on the throne.

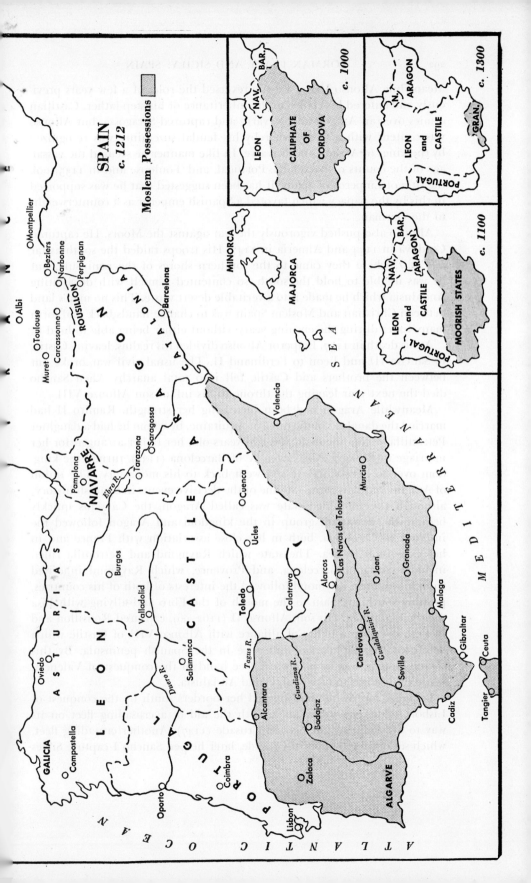

SPAIN
c. 1212

Moslem Possessions

c. 1000

LEON

NAV.
BAR.

CALIPHATE
OF
CORDOVA

c. 1100

PORTUGAL

LEON
and
CASTILE

NAV.
ARAGON
BAR.

MOORISH STATES

c. 1300

PORTUGAL

LEON
and
CASTILE

N.
ARAGON
BAR.

GRAN.

Montpellier
Beziers
Narbonne
Perpignan
Albi
Toulouse
Muret
Carcassonne
ROUSILLON

Barcelona

CATALONIA

MINORCA

MAJORCA

MEDITERRANEAN SEA

Pamplona
NAVARRE
Ebro R.
Tarazona
Saragossa
Tarragona

Valencia

Murcia

Cuenca
Ucles

Las Navas de Tolosa
Alarcos
Colatrava
Guadalquivir R.
Jaen
Granada
Cordova
Seville
Malaga
Gibraltar
Ceuta
Tangier

Burgos
CASTILE
Valladolid
Toledo
Tagus R.
Alcantara
Guadiana R.
Badajoz
Zalaca
ALGARVE
Cadiz

OVIEDO
ASTURIAS
GALICIA
Compostella
LEON
Salamanca
Duero R.
PORTUGAL
Coimbra
Oporto
Lisbon

ATLANTIC OCEAN

Meanwhile Alfonso VII of Castile reversed the roles of a few years previously and entered his claims to the inheritance of his step-father. Castilian armies overran Aragon and Navarre and captured Saragossa, but Alfonso was content with a treaty whereby his feudal suzerainty was recognized by the kings of Aragon and Navarre. In like manner he secured the vassalage of the counts of Barcelona, Portugal, and Toulouse and in 1135 took the title of Emperor of Spain. It has been suggested that he was supported in this by the papacy which favored a Spanish emperor as a counterweight to the German.

Alfonso also pushed vigorously the war against the Moors. He captured Cordova in 1144 and Almeria in 1147. His troops raided the south as far as Cadiz, where they came to the southern shores of the peninsula, but he was unable to hold the south, so contented himself with devastating Andalusia which he made into a veritable desert waste. This no man's land between Christian and Moslem Spain was to change hands back and forth many times during the ensuing years without either being able to hold it.

At his death in 1157, Emperor Alfonso divided his realms, leaving Castile to Sancho III and Leon to Ferdinand II. The usual civil war broke out between the brothers and Castile fell into total anarchy when Sancho died the next year leaving the throne to his infant son Alfonzo VIII.

Meanwhile Aragon had been increasing her strength. Ramiro II had married the daughter of the duke of Aquitaine, by whom he had a daughter Petronilla. When the child was two years old, her father arranged for her marriage to Raymond Berenger IV of Barcelona (1137), turned the kingdom over to his son-in-law and went back to his monastery. The union of Aragon and Barcelona was one of the decisive events in Spanish history; although the combined state was called Aragon, the Catalans quickly became the dominant group in the kingdom and Aragon followed the interests of Catalonia, both in her close association with France and in her expansion by sea. The state which Raymond and Petronilla ruled included Aragon, Barcelona, and Provence, which Raymond inherited from his mother. Raymond followed the interests of both of his countries, pushing south in Spain to the mouth of the Ebro and allying with Pisa to attack Majorca. His son, Alfonso II (1162–96), captured Rousillon and in 1179 drew up a treaty of alliance with Alfonso VIII of Castile which delimited their spheres of influence in the Spanish peninsula. By this treaty, Aragon was to be given a free hand in the conquest of Valencia, while Castile was to take Murcia and Andalusia.

Portugal meanwhile had pushed her borders south by the conquest of Lisbon, which was undertaken with the aid of a crusading fleet on its way to Syria during the Second Crusade (1147). Another crusading fleet, which set out for the Third Crusade, later helped Sancho I capture Silves and the Algarve in 1189, though these lands were lost again and were only captured permanently in 1249.

The latter part of the twelfth century witnessed the growth of several military religious orders in Spain, patterned after the great crusader orders of the Temple and Hospital in Syria. Chief among these were the orders of Calatrava (founded 1164), Alcantara (1183), and Santiago de Compostella (1171), of which the first two followed the Cistercian rule and the third the Augustinian. In Portugal, the order of Avis started as a branch of Calatrava, later becoming independent. These orders, like their prototypes in the East, rendered invaluable service in the wars of the reconquest and provided a skilled force on which the Christian kings could always count for their campaigns against the Moors.

Meanwhile the Moors had undergone a second revitalizing. In Africa had arisen the new power of the Almohades, which destroyed the old Almoravid empire, extending their power all along the African coast and pushing over into Spain in 1146. Although the Moorish emirs turned to the Christians for help against these new conquerors, the Almohades overran Moslem Spain with little difficulty. The Christian states took up arms: a crusade was preached throughout Europe against the Almohades and crusaders came from France and the north to join the forces of the Castilians. At Cuenca in 1177, Alfonso VIII won a victory over the Almohades and drove south to Cordova, but the Almohades counterattacked and in 1196 won the decisive battle of Alarcos, which enabled them to push the frontier back north of Toledo. While Castile was reeling from the blow of this attack, Leon and Navarre took the the occasion to attack in the rear. Aragon however supported her Castilian ally; Navarre was defeated and forced to surrender some territory to Castile, while Leon was bought off with a marriage alliance of the princess Berengaria of Castile to Alfonso IX of Leon. Although the marriage was nullified almost immediately by the pope, their son Ferdinand III united the crowns of Castile and Leon after the death of his uncle Henry I of Castile in 1217.

Meanwhile Innocent III preached another crusade for Spain. The kings of Aragon, Navarre and Portugal rallied to Alfonzo VIII, bands of crusaders came from across the Pyrenees, and the newly organized military orders came out in force. Only Alfonzo of Leon refused to co-operate in this great concerted effort to rid Spain of the infidel. The armies met at Toledo and advanced to meet the Almohades. At Las Navas de Tolosa, on July 16, 1212 the Christians won the greatest single victory in the long history of the reconquest. Thousands of the enemy were left dead on the field, their army was routed and the Almohade power broken forever.

The Christians were however unable to stick together long enough to really finish up the job. Disputes broke out at once between the allies.

Pedro II of Aragon became involved in the Albigensian war in southern France in which he lost his life at the battle of Muret (1213). Alfonzo VIII died the following year (1214) leaving the throne of Castile to a minor heir Henry, who lived only three years and died in 1217 before attaining his majority. The throne of Castile then passed to Ferdinand III of Leon (1217–52). James I (1213–76) had meanwhile ascended the throne of Aragon. With these two monarchs began a new phase of the reconquest which will be discussed in a later chapter.

CHAPTER 16

CAPETIAN AND NORMAN MONARCHIES

✛

THE twelfth century witnessed the growth of the two great national monarchies of the West, France and England. When the century opened the two states were far apart institutionally, as the Norman Conquest of England gave that kingdom a strong and absolute monarch, who contrasted greatly with the feeble Capetian in France. While the French monarch was hardly more than *primus inter pares* (first among equals) apropos of his great vassals, the English king was the supreme ruler of his domains and none of his barons could presume to question his will.

During the course of the century, the English kings developed a powerful royal administration which further reduced the power of the nobles; under the Plantagenets they possessed a considerable empire in France—more than the kings of France possessed in their own kingdom—and until the end of the century the English far outshone the French kings in breadth of lands and strength of government.

FRANCE UNDER LOUIS VI AND LOUIS VII, 1108–80

When Louis VI came to the throne in 1108, he had already had several years practice in ruling, as he had actually controlled the government for the last eight years of his father's reign. With him the Capetians developed a new policy: instead of trying to maintain his rather vague rights over the great vassals, as the earlier Capetians had done, Louis contented himself with ensuring his own unquestioned supremacy in his own royal domain. While he interfered in the wars of the great counts, it was as one of them, and his real concern was the establishment of his power at home. Most of the reign of Louis VI was spent in fighting the local barons, Hugh Le Puiset, Guy de Rochefort, Thomas de Marle of Couci and others who had lorded it in their castles in the Île de France until they were finally brought into subjection and their power destroyed. When a rebellious baron was defeated, Louis would often give a considerable part of his lands to his ally, the church.

Throughout most of the reign Louis VI was dominated by Etienne de Garlande who held the high offices of chancellor and seneschal and, with his three brothers, effectively controlled royal policy. But the Garlandes were attacked by St. Bernard, the great abbot of Clairvaux, and Louis became suspicious of them, with the result that they were deposed from their offices and honors. For three years (1127–30) the king had to fight with his former seneschal before he was able to break him. The office of seneschal was thereafter allowed to remain vacant for several years and to no one was given such extensive authority.

The greatest of Louis' advisors, and one whose influence lasted well into the reign of Louis VII, was Suger, abbot of St. Denis (1081–1151). Suger had been brought up in the royal abbey, and before his elevation to the abbacy had already proven himself useful to the king in many ways. After he became abbot in 1122, he divided his time between his duties as a churchman and those as a royal minister. He was the intimate advisor of both Louis VI and his son, being made regent of the kingdom when Louis VII went on the Second Crusade in 1147–49. Suger built the great abbey church at St. Denis, reformed the monastery, enforced discipline among the monks, and in his spare time wrote an account of his governance of the abbey and biographies of Louis VI and Louis VII. He is the first of the great ecclesiastical ministers of France and was a worthy predecessor of Mazarin and Richelieu centuries later.

Louis VI relied heavily on the clergy. He was closely allied with Pope Calixtus II, whose niece he married, and was in general a supporter of the Cluniac reform movement except where it conflicted with his own policies. He gave extensive lands to the church, and received in return money and support against the nobles. He yielded completely in the matter of lay investiture, which was so disturbing the church at the time, but reserved for himself the right to approve all election of bishops and to hear appeals from ecclesiastical courts. Likewise he was the great patron of the towns, granting many charters of limited bourgeois liberties, but he put down communes when they developed within his own domains, granting communal charters only in the lands of his enemies.

Louis' relations with the great counts were influenced by the chronic war with Henry of Normany (Henry I of England) with whom he fought throughout the reign. There were two major wars (1109–12; 1116–20) in which Louis supported the pretentions of William Clito, Henry's nephew, to the throne of Normandy. For a time he secured the suzerainty over Brittany and Maine, but these were soon lost and the war was on the whole unsuccessful. Anjou, which had supported him in the early stages of this war was won over to Normandy, when Henry I gave his daughter Matilda in marriage to Geoffrey of Anjou and bound the latter to his cause. In Flanders, Louis had a strong ally in the person of Count Baldwin, but his successor Charles veered to Normandy. On the murder of Charles in 1127, Louis installed William Clito in Flanders, but Clito was defeated and killed by Thierry of Alsace, with whom Louis was forced to make his peace (1128). Louis was successful in a couple of expeditions he made into Auvergne and the Bourbonnais to protect the clergy, and he repulsed an abortive attempt of the Emperor Henry V to invade eastern France, but on the whole the king only held his own against his great vassals.

In the last year of his life Louis accomplished his greatest diplomatic triumph when, with the support of the clergy, he arranged the marriage of his son Louis to Eleanor, the daughter and heiress of William X of Aquitaine, a marriage which gave the crown the alliance and later the control of the wide lands of Aquitaine in the south.

Louis VI is considered the real founder of the strength of the Capetian house. Fat to the point of unwieldiness (he could hardly mount a horse in his later years), Louis was a brave warrior and a wise ruler. He recognized the limitations of his strength and did not try to accomplish more than he could achieve. His son Louis VII, who came to the throne at the death of his father in 1137, inherited a strong principality in the Île de France which was entirely the work of Louis VI.

Louis VII (1137–80) was a totally different character from his father. He has been described as "a monk in king's clothing" and, although historians have recently rehabilitated his reign somewhat, his weak administration stands in marked contrast to the strong reigns of his father and his son. It is interesting to note how the Capetian house regularly skipped generations in producing able men: every other reign is a strong one, but there is always the unimportant reign between the significant ones.

In his early years Louis VII was vigorous and active, almost rash and impetuous. He began his career by unsuccessfully attempting to conquer Toulouse in 1141; he followed this up by an equally unsuccessful struggle with Thibaut of Champagne, during the course of which he became estranged from the pope. The only real success of his early years was the annexation of the Vexin, a small territory on the border between France and Normandy, which he got from Normandy during the struggle between Matilda and Stephen for the thrones of Normandy and England.

In 1147 to 1149 Louis and Eleanor went on the Second Crusade. This dismal fiasco brought the king no military glory and only resulted in his estrangement from his wife, whom he divorced in 1152, after death had removed the restraining influence of Suger. The divorce of Eleanor of Aquitaine marks a turning point in the history of twelfth-century France. When Eleanor was married to Louis, Aquitaine and France were united and the king was the greatest territorial lord in the kingdom. When Louis divorced her he lost control of the south, and when she promptly married Henry of Anjou the control of Aquitaine was carried over to Louis' great rival who already held Normandy, Anjou, and Maine, and claimed the throne of England.

The growth of the Angevin state was the most important single factor in the history of the time. Henry Plantagenet was the son of Geoffrey of Anjou and Matilda of Normandy, from both of whom he inherited; in

1152 he married Eleanor and became lord of Aquitaine; in 1154 he finally secured the inheritance of his grandfather Henry I of England from his rival Stephen and ascended the English throne. His "empire" ran from the Pyrenees to the border of Scotland (which he made a vassal), far outstripping in extent of territory, as in efficiency of administration, the domains of his royal rival.

The long struggle between Louis VII and Henry II will be discussed in the following chapter. But before leaving Louis VII it must be noted that, although his reign was rendered inglorious by his failures against the Plantagenets, it was not without its good points. The royal power increased at home, the lesser barons were held in firm control, the alliance with the clergy and the towns which his father had built up was continued and royal justice was made generally enforced throughout the limited domains of the king. Champagne was brought into close alliance with France by a double marriage, whereby Louis married Alice, the sister of count Henry, while Henry married Marie, daughter of Louis and Eleanor. By his marriage to Alice, Louis became the father of his longed-for son whom he named Philip. In the reign of this Philip, the roles of France and England were to be reversed and France was to gain all that she had lost during the great days of the Plantagenets.

ENGLAND UNDER WILLIAM THE CONQUEROR, 1066–87

When William the Bastard, duke of Normandy, defeated Harold Godwinson of Wessex and won the throne of England at Hastings in 1066, the real work of the conquest had only begun. The great work of William and of his sons was the amalgamation of the Normans and Saxons into the English people.

William's reign was marked by a series of revolts; from 1066 to 1070 he was kept busy putting down Saxon revolts, then for the rest of the reign he was confronted with a series of rebellions by his discontented Norman vassals, which were more dangerous to the king than had been those of the Saxons. The rebellion of Hereward the Wake in 1070 may be the most famous in romance, but that of Odo of Kent in 1082 was a far more serious affair from the point of view of the king.

William's great task was the fusion of Norman and Saxon institutions to produce the strongest possible monarchy. To accomplish this end he wisely selected those elements from each of the two systems, Norman and Saxon, which best fitted into the scheme of a centralized state. Norman feudalism was introduced into England in all its rigor, with the king keeping a close check on his vassals. William was all too aware of his own strength as duke of Normandy in relation to the king of France to want a similar situation in his own kingdom, so he resolutely kept the power in his own hands, allowing his vassals but little of that freedom which accompanied French feudalism. Every man was the liegeman of the king, and, in theory at least, all private war was outlawed and all military sub-tenants were held to serve only in the army of the king. In addition to the feudal array thus provided, William retained the old Saxon fyrd, the "citizen militia" of the Saxon kings. Thus he had a Norman feudal army to use against the Saxons and a Saxon force to use against his Norman vassals.

In the same way William retained a double system of courts. He kept the old Saxon courts of the shire and the hundred, but superimposed on them the feudal courts. Hundred courts were often granted out as fiefs, becoming what were termed "courts leet" or "liberties," but alongside of the feudal courts-baron there functioned the old free courts of the shire and hundred, presided over by the king's sheriff. The sheriff as an office underwent a change: it became more the equivalent of the Norman viscount, the agent of the king in the shire, and as time went on there was a tendency for sheriffs to hold authority over a number of shires. The law which the courts enforced was carefully preserved; in the Saxon courts the "laws of King Edward my predecessor" were scrupulously en-forced and no attempt was made to force strange Norman customs on the Saxon people. The ancient law was respected throughout, and Normans were on the whole more rigorously dealt with than were Saxons.

But if William preserved elements of the Saxon system which seemed useful to him, he brought with him the centralization of government which he had known in Normandy and which had been conspicuously lacking in England. The old Witan was replaced by the new *curia regis,* the court composed of the king's tenants-in-chief. No longer did an earl or bishop have a place in the Witan by virtue of his rank; if he sat in the new curia it was by virtue of a fief, which he held from the crown, and tenure was the only basis for inclusion in the king's council. This curia was nothing more or less than the feudal court of the suzerain to which his vassals owed court service and which they attended as one of the obligations of their tenure.

It was formerly maintained that William, in distributing the fiefs to his vassals, carefully granted them their lands in small parcels distributed throughout the realm so that no one man would have too large a holding in any one place. The two exceptions to this rule were Odo of Kent, William's half-brother, and Roger Fitz-Osborn of Norfolk, and the fact that these two men subsequently led baronial revolts was used to prove the wisdom of the conqueror's policy. Unfortunately for this fine theory, the facts have now been interpreted to prove that this distribution of fiefs among the various shires was not at all owing to William's pre-conceived theory, but due entirely to the fact that the barons insisted on being given a share in each county as it was conquered. Since the conquest and occupation of the country was a slow affair, William had to allot fiefs in each district as he occupied it, with the result that the great barons received lands in various counties and not in single blocks.[1] That this arrangement worked to the eventual advantage of the crown was entirely fortuitous, but there can be no doubt as to the conscious strengthening of the royal position involved in William's making his council exclusively his tenants, and in his enforcing attendance at the council on these tenants. It has been often pointed out that one of the ways in which a feudal monarch best secured the loyalty of his vassals was by forcing them to continuous attendance at his courts, where he could keep his finger on them at all times.

William was always a feudal monarch; it is problematical that he ever really understood any relationship other than the feudal. This is indicated by the great oath which he caused all the landholding men of England to take to him at Salisbury Plain in 1086, when every landed man had to come and swear allegiance and fealty to the king as his liege lord. It is the opinion of the present author that this was an attempt on the part of the king to express in feudal terminology the subjection which everyone owed him as king, but which he knew no means of expressing other than by the feudal oath.

Professor George B. Adams has claimed that William established complete tenurial feudalism in England, but modified some of its political characteristics.[2] It is my belief that he did not consciously modify the political aspects any more than necessary, and that he endeavored throughout to express in feudal terms the royal position which he inherited from his Saxon predecessors.

In the matter of finances, William retained the old Saxon Danegeld as a general tax, but on the whole his financial arrangements were those of any feudal noble. In the main he "lived on his own," on the proceeds from his domain lands, the fines from his courts and the other ordinary sources of feudal revenue. One of the most important of these was the heavy relief which he collected from the Saxon landholders. At the time of the conquest, the lands of those Saxon lords who had openly opposed him were confiscated and distributed among his Norman followers, but many Saxons, who had not been openly opposed to him, were allowed to retain their holdings on payment of a heavy relief. However, William felt that he was not securing from his lands the amount which could be legitimately derived from them, and to remedy this he caused to be held in 1086 a

[1] For a full discussion of this point see S. Painter, *Studies in the History of the Medieval English Barony*, where the whole matter is discussed in detail, with illustrations.
[2] G. B. Adams, *Origin of the English Constitution*.

great inquest. This famous Domesday Inquest, which resulted in the Domesday Book, was an attempt to determine what had been the value of each manor and farm in the days of King Edward and what revenues the king had derived from it then in comparison to the value at the moment. This inquest is important for two things: from Domesday Book we are able to learn more about the social and economic conditions of eleventh-century England than we can know of any other Western country (though the Book is utterly valueless for information as to knight's fees and military tenures), and also this is the first time in English history when we find the use of the royal inquest.

Charlemagne, as will be recalled, had sent out his *missi dominici* throughout his realm to enforce justice, check the counts, and obtain information for the king. In like manner William now sent out inquisitors from his central curia to obtain the information needed. This first use of the royal inquisitors was the precursor of the itinerant justices, which were employed in a limited field by Henry I and to a much larger extent and on regular circuits by Henry II.

William also brought extensive changes into the church in England. His banners had been blessed by the pope and he had come to England as the champion of the reformed papacy against the errant Saxons. Therefore, as was to be expected, he tried to bring England into line with the accepted continental practices. In this, as in all his administrative work, he was ably assisted by Lanfranc, former abbot of Bec, whom he made archbishop of Canterbury. The old Saxon confusion of ecclesiastical and secular jurisdiction was ended; separate church courts were established with competence over cases affecting clergy or clerical property, a measure much desired by Rome. But though William was willing to co-operate with the church to a certain extent, he was not subservient to it, and established rules for the English clergy which were quite contrary to the ideals of the reformed papacy. In the years 1070 to 1075, William issued a series of decrees whereby he required that all bishoprics and abbeys were liable to military service for the lands they held, that no acts of church councils in England were valid unless approved by the king, that no excommunications could be published or legates admitted into England without the royal approval, and that only the king had the power to recognize the pope who was to be accepted in England. He stoutly refused to accept papal overlordship over his new kingdom, and always kept the appointment and investiture of bishops in his own hands. But he enforced clerical celibacy, encouraged monasticism, founded new abbeys and brought many monks into England, and filled the sees of England with Norman and French clergy who were in sympathy to the reformed program. Although he undoubtedly fell far short of what Gregory VII might have wished of him, his attitude was sufficiently conciliatory and the pope was sufficiently preoccupied with his struggle with Germany, to make relations between England and Rome of the best throughout the reign.

By his wife, Matilda of Flanders, William had three sons and a daughter: Robert, William, Henry, and Adele. The eldest son, Robert Curthose, was always a thorn in the flesh of his father; they were opposite in character, Robert being impractical, prodigal and vacillating. He frequently quarreled with his father, actually engaging in open revolts in Normandy. But as he was the eldest son, the Conqueror could not help leaving him the duchy of Normandy. To his second son, William Rufus, who was more like his father, William bequeathed the kingdom of England. The third son Henry Beauclerc was educated for the church, and the daughter was married to Stephen of Blois.

THE NORMAN KINGS, 1087–1154

When the Conqueror died in 1087, the Anglo-Norman kingdom was in consequence divided, Robert taking Normandy and William II England. Both brothers aspired to reunite the inheritance and both invaded each other's domains, supported by parties of disaffected barons. Robert showed real strength in England and the rebellion in his favor in 1088 assumed serious proportions, several of the most important earls participating, but William II was able to beat them down, and in 1091 and again in 1094 William invaded Normandy. Then in 1096 Robert took the cross for the First Crusade. To obtain funds needed for this expedition, he pawned Normandy to William Rufus, granting his brother the control of the duchy for a term of not less than three years in return for a cash advance of 10,000 marks. This being arranged, Robert went off to Jerusalem, and William occupied Normandy. As lord of Normandy he promptly attacked the French Vexin and Maine, but was not able to conquer them.

The reign of William Rufus (1087–1100) is little more than a continuation of his father's, though Rufus lacked the political good judgment of the Conqueror and aroused a more general opposition than had ever developed previously. In his administration of his kingdom, William was assisted by Ranulf Flambard, who tried to further the concentration of power in the king's hands. But what Henry II could accomplish in the middle of the twelfth century was too much for Flambard at the end of the eleventh, and the nobles resented what they felt were his usurpations and tyrannies. William and Flambard systematically pushed to the extreme all the royal and feudal prerogatives of the crown, attacking the rights of the barons in jurisdiction, in matters of wardships and in other of the feudal privileges. Especially were financial demands exorbitant, which above all antagonized the barons. The result was that Willaim had to put down two major baronial revolts, as well as an attempted invasion from Scotland. In all of these he was successful (in fact imposing feudal vassalage on the Scottish king) but the opposition smouldered, and when William was hunting in the Great Forest in August 1100, an arrow mysteriously pierced his back and brought him to the ground dead. It has never been positively proven whether this was accident or murder, and William Tirel

THE NORMAN AND PLANTAGENET KINGS OF ENGLAND, 1066–1377

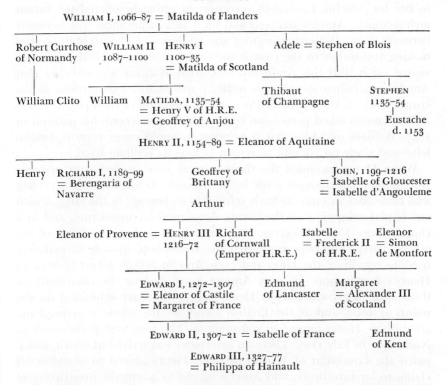

who was accused always pleaded innocence, but there were few who wept over the fallen monarch. His brother Henry, as soon as he heard of the tragedy, rushed to Winchester where he seized the royal crown and treasure and proclaimed himself king. Although there were some who put forward the claims of Robert, most of the clergy and barons were quick to accept Henry, and he was crowned three days after his brother's death. At this time he issued a coronation charter in which he made many promises as to the nature of his rule. This charter, which can only be considered a set of campaign promises, was never adhered to in the least by Henry, but it did become a sort of ideal and was later used by the barons when they were working up their demands on John in 1215. In it Henry promised to protect and respect not only the feudal rights of the barons, but the privileges of the church.

This matter of the privileges of the church was a critical one at the moment. As long as Lanfranc lived there had been complete harmony between the archbishop and the king, but at his death in 1089 William II had left the see of Canterbury vacant until 1093, while he himself enjoyed the revenues from it. Then in 1093 William had been taken acutely sick and had repented his sins. As a visible sign of his repentance he sent to Bec for Anselm, Lanfranc's successor, to whom he offered the vacant archbishopric. Anselm accepted and for a short time there was harmony between them, William accepting the guidance of the archbishop and making restitution to the church for the oppressions he had previously visited on it. But this could not last; soon William was insisting that Anselm was falling short in his military and financial obligations to the crown. Further, they quarreled over the recognition of rival popes. When at last Anselm asked permission to go to Rome to receive his pallium in 1097, William told him that if he went he could never return. Anselm left—and made no attempt to return as long as William lived.

When Henry ascended the throne, he at once invited Anselm back. But Anselm had changed while he was in exile. It was a different prelate who came back in 1100: he flatly refused to do homage to the king, denied any feudal obligations to the crown, denounced lay investiture, and in a church council issued decrees which denied altogether the claims of the secular party. The pope supported the archbishop, though he privately tried to conciliate the king, and even Anselm accepted two bishops of Henry's nomination. In 1103 Anselm again fled to the continent; he threatened to excommunicate Henry unless the latter submitted on the points at issue, and as the English clergy on the whole supported the archbishop, Henry agreed to compromise. The king and prelate met in Normandy in July 1105. There an agreement was arrived at which anticipated the Concordat of Worms of 1122; Henry agreed to abandon all claims to lay investiture, and Anselm agreed to accept the investitures of bishops already installed by the king. The pope approved the compromise and Anselm returned to England where he died in 1109. In fact, Henry had won, for as it worked out the king appointed the bishops, invested them with the temporalities and then the archbishop invested with the spiritualities; but in the narrow matter of lay investiture with spiritualities the church had had its way.

The return of Robert Curthose from the crusade in 1101 precipitated a series of wars between the brothers, as neither was willing to leave the other in peaceful possession of his lands. Robert invaded England in 1101 but was bought off by Henry; then Henry invaded Normandy and defeated Robert at Tinchebrai in 1106. Robert was forced to renounce his duchy and to come to honorable retirement in England, but his claims were taken up by his son William Clito, who, backed by Louis VI, continued to stir up rebellion in Normandy for the next two decades. Against France Henry allied with Germany and Blois, and was able to ward off all attacks, finally securing his southern frontier by an alliance with Anjou in 1128.

Far more important than these feudal wars, which were at best a matter of skirmishes and sieges of castles, was the work of Henry in building up the English administration. More than either of his immediate predecessors, Henry tried to be the Saxon king as well as the Norman overlord. He married Matilda, the daughter of Malcolm of Scotland and last representative of the old house of Wessex, so that his children inherited the blood of both the Norman and Saxon houses. In his administration he favored Saxons, so that his Norman barons often contemptuously referred to the king and queen as Godric and Godgifu, but in the process he went far towards accomplishing the fusion of the two peoples into a single English nation. His chief minister, throughout the reign, was Roger, bishop of Salisbury and chancellor, who, with his talented family, provided Henry with able and loyal officials.

It was in the reign of Henry I that the curia regis began to break down in personnel and function into a number of separate administrative bodies. Originally the curia was like any feudal court, at once the judicial, the law-finding, and the administrative organ of government. Its breakdown into separate bodies, each especially qualified to handle a certain type of business, began with the break-off of the court of the exchequer. The exchequer was the financial chamber to which the sheriffs brought in the returns of their farms; it received its name "exchequer" from the checkered table on which the accounts were rendered. Quite often there were cases involving at one time the financial rights of the crown and matters of law, wherefor there developed a special court to handle these cases. The barons who made up this court were at first any members of the curia who were delegated to that special duty; then as certain men became expert in the kind of business which came before the exchequer, they tended to be used primarily for that duty. Thus the barons *in* the exchequer gradually came to be the barons *of* the exchequer. We are indebted for our information as to the composition and functions of this court to a contemporary work, the *Dialogus de Scaccario* by Richard Fitz-Neal, the great-nephew of Roger of Salisbury.

In addition to the exchequer, the reign of Henry I saw the establishment of the itinerant justices. These members of the curia went out into the county courts to hear the king's pleas and to bring the king's justice into the local districts. The justices brought the king's court to the counties.

At first, presumably, they were used to expedite justice; the agenda before the king's court got too great to be handled and so part of it was delegated to these itinerant justices. But they were also used for administrative purposes; they inquired into the local conditions, checked up on the sheriffs, looked into matters of local taxation and defense and did all manner of odd jobs for the king. Both the judicial and administrative work of these justices was greatly enlarged and increased under Henry II; while under Henry I they had been sent out occasionally on their missions, under his grandson they were established in regular circuits which they covered every few months. While all of the institutions of Henry I were brought to a greater degree of standardization and efficiency by Henry II, it is important to note that the germ of the administration was found under Henry I, and, indeed, to a certain extent, as we have seen, under William the Conqueror.

Henry I had only one son, William, who was drowned in the famous sinking of the *White Ship* in 1120. Henry's only other legitimate child was his daughter Matilda who had been married in 1114 to Henry V of Germany. When Henry V died in 1125 and Matilda returned to England, Henry caused all his barons to take an oath to accept her as his successor. Then he married her to Geoffrey of Anjou, to the great resentment of the barons. It should be noted that the first English baron to swear fealty was Stephen of Boulogne, the largest landholder in England, the son of Adele of Normandy and Stephen of Blois, the nephew of King Henry and the grandson of the Conqueror.

When Henry died in 1135, he expected his daughter, now the wife of Geoffrey Plantagenet of Anjou, to succeed peacefully to his various domains. But Stephen broke his oath and himself claimed the throne of England while his brother, Thibaut of Champagne, was proclaimed duke in Normandy. Stephen was popular in London, where he was at once acclaimed by the people; from there he rushed to Winchester where he received the homages of the clergy and barons.

King Stephen (1135–54) began his reign with an unjustified usurpation, but he was essentially an honest man who tried sincerely to live up to the promises he made in his coronation charters. Like his uncle, he promised to respect the liberties of the church and the rights of the barons, but unlike Henry he made an honest endeavor to keep his promises. And therein lay the essential weakness of his reign, for a king could not retain his position and at the same time give away all his royal rights by catering to the constant demands of the baronage. Stephen's reign is sometimes known as the Period of Anarchy, and it was almost that, for civil war and rebellion marked nearly the entire reign.

When Stephen seized the throne he was supported by a strong party of the clergy, led by his brother Henry, bishop of Winchester, and Roger, bishop of Salisbury, and by a powerful group of the barons led by Hugh Bigod. To bolster up his strength further, Stephen created a large number of new earls, the first with whom the title was merely a title and not an office. Until 1139 it seemed that Stephen, supported by the officials of Henry I and the barons, might be able to enjoy a reasonably peaceful and secure reign.

Matilda and Geoffrey had, of course, not taken the succession without protest. They had invaded Normandy from Anjou in 1135, but the barons there had declared first for Thibaut, until they learned of the coronation of Stephen in England when they transferred their allegiance to him. In England, Robert of Gloucester, an illegitimate son of Henry I's, rebelled in behalf of his sister, and David of Scotland invaded the north as Matilda's ally, but Stephen was able to defeat them both, and his coronation was accepted in 1136 by the pope.

Then in 1139 Stephen made a cardinal mistake—he broke with Roger of Salisbury and his house, with the result that he lost the support of the old administrative officials and also of the clergy. Matilda was not slow to take advantage of this situation. She invaded England, was defeated at Bristol, and captured by Stephen. Then Stephen made his second great error; he released his prisoner and allowed her to join her partisans at Gloucester. Stephen had previously shown himself too lenient in his treatment of rebels; now he proved himself too chivalrous. There was a general reaction against the king; Hugh Bigod and Robert of Chester declared for Matilda and revolted. Stephen marched against the rebels, but was defeated and captured at Lincoln (1141). With the capture of the king, his party collapsed; even his own brother, Henry of Winchester, deserted him, and Matilda was crowned queen of England. Matilda, however, proved no improvement over Stephen; London, which had always supported the king, was first to revolt; a number of clergy and barons soon reversed themselves and again declared for the former king. Robert of Gloucester was captured by Stephen's partisans and exchanged for the king, who promptly created some new earls and gathered support wherever he could. Meanwhile, Geoffrey of Anjou had overrun Normandy and reduced it completely to obedience, being recognized as duke by Louis VII.

Things remained at more or less of a deadlock for the next few years. Neither side would give in and there was desultory war throughout England. Then in 1147 Robert of Gloucester died; Matilda had grown weary of the war and when her son Henry reached the age of sixteen in 1150 she made over to him her title to Normandy and her claims to England. The following year Geoffrey died and Henry received Anjou, to which he added Aquitaine in 1152 by marrying Eleanor, the divorced wife of King Louis. By 1153, Henry felt himself ready to assert his claims to England and invaded the island. Stephen was at Wallingford fighting the earl of Chester when Henry invaded. But while he was still engaged in this campaign, his only son, Eustache, died, leaving him no heir to succeed him. This made a peace easy, as Henry was young and in no great hurry to rule England. A treaty was agreed upon whereby Stephen should retain the throne as long as he lived, but Henry should succeed him. Henry did not have long to wait, for Stephen died within the year, and Henry was peacefully crowned king on December 19, 1154.

The reign of Stephen is an important one in English history. For almost twenty years a weak king ruled, and in that period the barons had things pretty much their own way. The land was filled with adulterine castles (castles built without royal permission); the barons had greatly increased their holdings and decreased their obligations by turning coat at every propitious occasion and wringing concessions from both of the rival claimants. The work of William I and Henry I had been checked; but the country was so sick of war that it welcomed a man who would restore peace and a regular system of government. This Henry II proved more than able to do.

CHAPTER 17

THE ANGLO-NORMAN EMPIRE: HENRY II

✥

HENRY PLANTAGENET, 1154–89

HENRY II stands out as perhaps the greatest English king; his great accomplishments in creating a royal administration and a system of law common to all the realm have won him a high place among English sovereigns; but it must always be borne in mind that, however great an Englishman he may have been, Henry was above all else a French duke. He was duke of Normandy, count of Anjou, Touraine and Maine, duke of Aquitaine, count of Poitou and a host of other French titles as well as king of England, and his French "empire" took up more of his effort and attention than his insular kingdom ever did. Rouen was his favorite capital in life; he died at Chinon and lies buried at Fontevraud near the Loire. French was his native tongue and he never learned to speak English.

Henry Plantagenet was in appearance short, barrel chested, red haired and too fat. He was violent, passionate, inclined to fierce outbursts of anger and to lavish demonstrations of affection. Restless and tireless, he drove himself as he drove others, and if he was a failure as a husband he was overly indulgent as a father, his affection for his ungrateful sons being pathetic in its intensity. But, though he loved his sons excessively, he never learned to trust them and consequently spent the better part of his life plagued by rebellions in which one or another of his sons was the leader.

Against Henry was pitted the weak and vacillating Louis VII. Not until the later years of his reign (1180–89) was Henry confronted by an antagonist who was his match in political ability. Had it not been for the incessant wars between Henry and his sons, France might well have been pushed back into a position of complete subordination to the Angevin empire. But Louis was astute enough to take advantage of the civil disturbances within Henry's family and to press every advantage against his great rival. His son was to turn the incompetence of Henry's son to good account and to destroy utterly the great state of the Plantagenets.

The political history of Henry's reign is largely a chronicle of the wars between the king and his sons, Henry, Richard (Coeur-de-Lion), Geoffrey, and finally John. The reign opened with an attack on Brittany which was brought into feudal vassalage; an attempt to take Toulouse was defeated by the intervention of King Louis (1159). Thereafter for a decade Henry was relatively peaceful in France, his English interests and struggle with Archbishop Thomas Becket occupying most of his attention, but in 1170 Henry laid the foundations for untold grief by allotting each of his sons a portion of his inheritance. Henry, the eldest, was given the title of king of England, and was assigned the territories of Normandy, Maine, and Anjou; Richard was given Aquitaine and all the lands of his mother's inheritance; Geoffrey was granted Brittany; and John, who was too young to participate in this distribution, was given nothing, whence he derived the nickname "Lackland," which he was to bear all his life. But although Henry was most generous in assigning lands and titles to his sons, he gave them neither the control of the lands nor any of the revenues. This was especially galling to young king Henry, who was naturally extravagant and lavish. In his discontent he was encouraged by his mother Eleanor, who had grown to hate her demanding and unfaithful husband, and by his father-in-law Louis of France. However, there was no open revolt until 1173 when Henry II alienated some castles in Anjou, which had been allotted young Henry, to make up a marriage portion for John. This was too much; Henry fled to Paris where he was joined by his brothers Richard and Geoffrey, who had been inspired by their mother to join the coalition against the king. The princes, France, Scotland and a few Anglo-Norman barons supported the revolt, but in the main the nobles as well as the clergy stood behind the king. By 1174, Henry had defeated the Scots and the rebels, driven the French from Normandy and forced his sons to complete submission. By the treaty of Falaise the young princes were restored to their titles and given pensions, but John was given the castles which had started the whole war, and the king of Scotland was forced to do homage for his kingdom. While this rebellion of 1173–74 was the most violent of the rebellions of the young king, from 1173 until his death in 1183, young Henry consistently fought the friends and partisans of his father and stirred up trouble between his brothers and the old king. At the time of his death young Henry and Geoffrey were at war with Richard, who was supported by their father.

The death of young Henry necessitated a redistribution of his inheritance. Henry II accordingly asked Richard to surrender Aquitaine to John; but Richard refused and John and Geoffrey took up arms against him. There can be no question but that John was his father's favorite, and Henry did everything to procure for his youngest a suitable share of his empire. It was John who was proclaimed Lord of Ireland when that island was brought under the royal control in 1177; it was for him that Henry antagonized both Richard and Geoffrey. True, a peace was made between the king and Richard, but Geoffrey was about to revolt against his father when he died in 1186. It was then that Henry showed his great preference for John and completely antagonized Richard. When Henry the young king had died, his widow Margaret of France had returned to her brother,

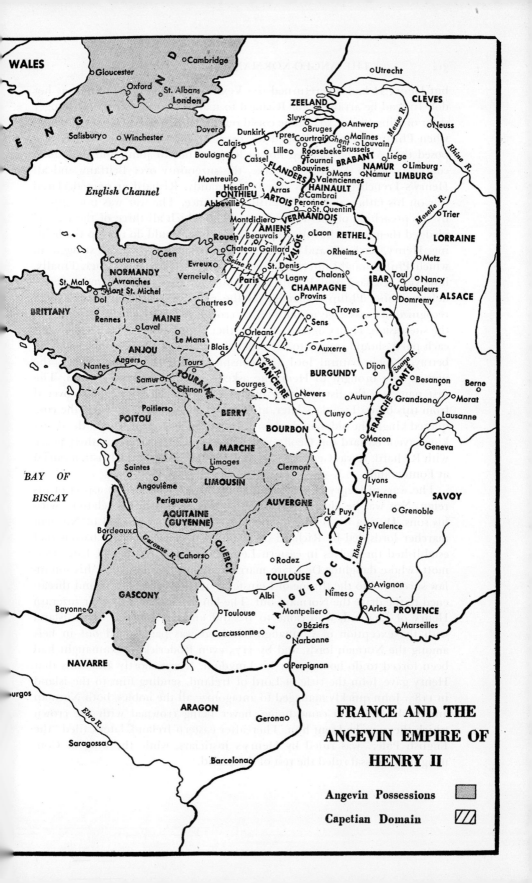

FRANCE AND THE
ANGEVIN EMPIRE OF
HENRY II

Angevin Possessions
Capetian Domain

but Henry II had not returned the Vexin which she had brought as her dot. Instead he arranged for Richard to marry Alice of France, a younger sister of King Philip, so that he could retain the Vexin. At Geoffrey's death, when Philip of France claimed the overlordship of Brittany, Henry proposed that Alice be married not to Richard but to John, and the young couple be given Anjou, Aquitaine, the suzerainty over Brittany and all Henry's French possessions except Normandy. Richard at once declared war on his father and joined Philip in France. The war was interrupted by the preaching of the Third Crusade, to which all three of the leaders pledged themselves. But in spite of all the pope could do to stop the fighting, Henry, Richard, and Philip engaged in a three-cornered struggle in which Philip fought alternately against Richard and his father. Finally, however, Richard and Philip joined forces against Henry and severely defeated him. Philip demanded as the price of peace only that Henry recognize his vassalage to the French crown and the rights of Richard to the succession. Henry agreed. As a further stipulation it was decided that each party should supply to the other the names of those barons who had betrayed their natural lord and conspired with the enemy. When the names were brought to Henry he asked that they be read to him. The first name on the list was that of his son John. Henry never recovered from this blow. Two days later, at Chinon, muttering "Shame on the conquered king," the old man died on July 6, 1189. No one attended the dying king save a bastard son Geoffrey; all the rest were off making their peace with Richard. It was Geoffrey who took the body to give it Christian burial at Fontevraud.

The wars of Henry II are, fortunately, the least important aspect of his reign. Nor was he always as unsuccessful as he was in his relations with his sons. During his reign Ireland was conquered by a band of Norman marcher lords, led by Richard de Clare of Pembroke. These barons had established themselves in eastern Leinster in 1170 as allies of King Dermott, whose daughter De Clare married. When Dermott died, his son-in-law succeeded to the throne of Leinster, but the Irish revolted and threatened to the drive the Normans out. The barons appealed to their suzerain Henry of England, who came to Ireland and overran the whole island with the exception of Connaught. Ireland was partitioned out in fiefs among the Norman lords, and by 1175 even Roderick of Connaught had been forced to do homage for his kingdom. It was shortly after this that Henry gave John the title of Lord of Ireland, sending him to the island in 1185. John quickly managed to antagonize all the nobles, both Norman and Irish, and soon came home, never being crowned with the crown which the pope had sent him. Thereafter eastern Ireland, later called "the English Pale," was ruled by Henry's justiciars, while the king of Connaught as a vassal ruled the rest of the island.

Likewise Henry had made his power felt in Scotland, where he defeated King William and forced him to do homage for his kingdom.

Thomas Becket

But it is for his internal policies in England that Henry best deserves our attention. Henry's policy was so to strengthen the administration that there would be no power in England, whether ecclesiastical or lay, which could dare to oppose the will of the king in any matter. To effect this end he attacked the privileges of the church and the barons as a class, destroying many of their prerogatives and establishing in England a single "common law, common to all the realm."

While Henry was most successful in his limitation of the powers of the barons and in establishing his authority over the secular courts, he failed signally in his policy of forcing the church into obedience. In this struggle he was pitted against one of England's greatest churchmen, Thomas Becket. The career of Becket in its earlier stages somewhat parallels that of Wolsey in the sixteenth century, but Wolsey never achieved sainthood. Becket began his career as a chancery clerk, rose to a high place in the chancery and was appointed chancellor of the kingdom by Henry in the early years of the reign. No one proved himself more devoted to the interest of the king than the new chancellor and Henry grew to rely on him greatly. Consequently, when the archbishopric of Canterbury became vacant in 1162, Henry appointed his protégé to this high position. And then occurred a most unexpected transformation in the character of Becket. While he had been the king's minister he had labored in the interests of the crown, now that he was archbishop he devoted himself to defending the rights and privileges of the church against any royal aggression. The faithful ally had become the most vigorous and militant opponent. Not only did he himself resign the chancellorship, but he ordered that no clerks who held high office in the church could at the same time serve the king. Then he refused to pay a tax which Henry had regularly collected from the church, but which the archbishop claimed was not permissible. In 1163 matters came to a head when Henry arraigned a clerk charged with a crime in the secular court, although he had previously cleared himself by oath in a church court. Becket defended the clerk on the grounds of clerical immunity. Henry then brought the matter into the open by demanding that clerks accused of crimes should be amenable to sentence in the secular courts. Becket and the clergy refused. When Henry next demanded that Becket and the clergy take an oath to observe the ancient customs of the realm, they did so only "saving their order" which meant a refusal. Henry convened his council at Clarendon. There in 1164 he issued the Constitutions of Clarendon, one of whose provisions was the paragraph which provided that a criminous clerk should be arraigned in the secular court, turned over to the ecclesiastical court for trial, and then be brought back to the secular court for sentence. It also demanded that cases affecting land which was disputedly frankalmoin or lay fee and all cases relating to the presentment of clergy be heard in the secular courts. The king's right to supervise the election of bishops was reaffirmed, and in every way the church was restored to the position it had occupied before it had secured its emancipation during the reign of Stephen.

Not long after this Henry was able to cite Becket for contempt of court and to impose on him a fine; then he went further and demanded of Becket an accounting of all the funds he had controlled while chancellor. Against these charges Becket appealed to Rome, which was contrary to the Constitutions. The king offered to drop all the charges if Becket would resign as archbishop, but the prelate refused such a compromise. The secular lords sat in trial on him (he had forbidden any clergy to take part in the trial), found him guilty of violating the Constitutions, and Becket fled to France. For six years the archbishop remained in exile, supported by Louis VII, who was only too glad to succor any enemy of Henry's. The pope and King Louis offered to mediate, but nothing came of their efforts until 1170 when a peace was patched up between Henry and the archbishop. In December 1170, Becket returned to England. But he seems to have deliberately courted martyrdom, for he began at once to excommunicate all those clergy who had opposed him during his exile. Especially was he furious at the archbishop of York who had dared to crown young king Henry in the absence of his colleague of Canterbury. He renewed the excommunication of the advisors of the king which he had previously launched from France. In fact, he seems to have done everything he could think of to deliberately annoy and infuriate Henry.

Henry was in Normandy when he heard that Becket had issued a new set of excommunications against his advisors. "My subjects are sluggards," he is reported to have said, "men of no spirit. They keep no faith with their lord; they allow me to be made a laughing stock of by a low-born clerk." This was enough for four knights of the king's retinue. They hastened to Canterbury where they found Becket in the cathedral. When they demanded that he recall the bans of excommunication he had issued, he refused, and they fell upon him. Standing in front of the altar the archbishop defied his attackers: if he sought martyrdom, he at least knew how to meet it. Finally Hugh of Horsea split open his skull and he fell dead at the foot of the altar.

Becket dead was infinitely more powerful and more dangerous to the king than Becket alive. The martyr was at once popularly canonized; miracles began to take place at his tomb. Henry did a severe and ostentatious penance in the cemetery at Avranches and denied any guilt in the murder of the martyr, but the saint was avenged only when in 1172 Henry abandoned all his claims against the church and granted complete control over clerks to the ecclesiastical courts. "Benefit of Clergy," thus established, was to become one of the plagues of English justice, but the pilgrimage to Becket's tomb at Canterbury was to give the setting for the first great literary masterpiece in the English language.

THE ENGLISH CONSTITUTION

Although Henry II was unfortunate in his attempt to bring the church under the royal control, he was more than successful in the administrative reforms which he instituted as parts of his policy of reducing the barons and increasing the revenues of the crown. By an extension of the royal justice, through the use of writs, new assizes, itinerant justices and the jury trial, Henry brilliantly attacked the system of private feudal jurisdictions and gave to England her common law. "The most important thing in English medieval history on the whole is that England had the common law instead of the Roman law" said Professor McIlwain,[1] and that England had the common law was the result of the work of Henry II.

As all of Henry's administrative reforms were closely interlocked, it is difficult to know where to begin. Each depended on the others, in part deriving from and in part serving as a cause for their development. Henry's aim was two-fold: he wished to break down the power of the barons and he wished to divert to the royal exchequer the revenues from justice which were collected in the feudal courts. Medieval justice was always considered primarily as a source of revenue for the person holding the court: the more cases Henry could get into his courts, the more money found its way into his coffers. And Henry was wise enough to see that the best way to get the cases and the fines into his own hands was to provide better justice at a cheaper price. This was the fundamental principle which governed his judicial reforms.

If the royal courts were to handle more cases they must first be increased in number; accordingly Henry established regular circuits for the itinerant justices so that they made the rounds of the county courts at stated intervals. As we have seen, the use of the justices for both judicial and administrative purposes had been begun by Henry I, but their *iters* or *eyres* were regularized and increased by Henry II. Three justices went to the meeting of the shire court, which became, as long as they were presiding over it, a session of the king's court. By the regular use of the itinerant justices, litigation which would have taken years to handle in the king's own court, could be cleared off quickly and only cases of utmost importance reserved for the attention of the royal court. In addition to establishing

[1] In a lecture in his course on English Constitutional History, at Harvard University.

the circuits, Henry made another judicial reform designed to expedite business by establishing the Court of Common Pleas to handle private civil suits in which the crown had no interest. Previously anyone having business to bring before the king's court would have to follow it around wherever the king happened to be, and, as it often took months or years for a case to be heard, a litigant would spend much time and money journeying around the country in the wake of the king and court. In 1178 Henry established a court of five justices to hear these private cases. This court, which after 1215 sat regularly at Westminster, served as a court of first instance equal to the curia and cases could be remanded to it by the itinerant justices.[2]

Important private cases and the king's pleas (all cases in which the crown was a party, except exchequer cases), were heard by the king's curia; at a somewhat later date the king's pleas came to be heard by a subsection of the curia known as the King's Bench court, and as G. B. Adams has pointed out, the development of the King's Bench was a necessary corollary of the creation of the Common Pleas court in 1178.[3]

To assure that it was possible to get cases into these royal courts, writs were devised which ordered that the case be heard in the king's court. These writs were the very cornerstone of Henry's policy. They had been employed by Henry I and here again the work of Henry II was rather a matter of extension and regularization of an older institution than any new innovation. A man having a case to be heard could only apply to the curia for a writ which would order that the case be begun in the king's court. These writs were issued by the chancellor as the secretary of the curia, and developed into two types—writs *de cursu* for ordinary cases where a standard form of writ could be used, and original writs where a special writ would be evolved to meet the special circumstances of the case. This power to make and issue writs became one of the chief functions of the chancellor and ultimately led to the development of the chancery equity jurisdiction in the fourteenth century. These writs also became a source of law, for by ordering that a case should be heard by a set procedure in a specified court, the chancellor unconsciously helped fix the law which should be applied. That the writs *de cursu* were uniform throughout the realm was one of the chief factors in establishing the common law.

The writs embodied the new assizes as they called for the application of new laws and in fact created them. Thus the Grand Assize, which provided for a jury trial to determine the ownership of land, was called for by the Writ of Right and the action is known by either name. The writ

---

[2] Article 17 of Magna Carta required that the Court of Common Pleas should sit permanently at Westminister, thus showing the popularity of the institution.

[3] G. B. Adams, *Councils and Courts in Anglo-Norman England*, p. 227 ff.

Praecipe was the most unpopular of Henry's writs as it ordered that a case be stopped in a baronial court and transferred to the king's court immediately. In general the new assizes, especially the possessory assizes, were popular. By these laws a jury was impaneled to determine the right or wrong of a case, thus substituting the information of one's fellows for the somewhat unsatisfactory judgment of God as revealed through combat or the ordeal.

As we have seen, in the earlier judicial practice, the members of the court actually used considerable judgment in the awarding of the proof of the ordeal, but even then the matter was unsatisfactory as too much depended on the physical qualifications of the litigants. The new method, provided by the assizes, called for the selection of a jury of the men of the district who would state their knowledge in regard to the case in dispute. The most popular of these assizes were the *possessory assizes* which determined not the right to hold land, but merely the fact of possession. The assize *mort d'ancestor* asked the question whether a man's ancestor possessed the land "on the day that he was living and dead"; if the ancestor was known to have possessed it, the assumption was that the heir had a right to it and he was at once put in seisin of the fief. *Novel desseisin* asked whether the man had himself formerly possessed the land and had been dispossessed from it; if so, he was reinstated. *Darein presentment* dealt with the presentment of clerks to livings, and if it was established that a man had presented the last incumbent, he was allowed to present the next. All of these possessory assizes could be tried by a jury of simple freemen, but for the Grand Assize, which determined the legal right of a man to hold a fief, a jury of knights was required. Another important assize was the assize *Utrum,* which determined whether a piece of land was held in frankalmoin or as a lay fee. Depending on the answer to this assize, litigation concerning the property would be tried in the secular or ecclesiastical courts; it was one of the points of dispute between Henry and Becket whether this assize should itself be heard in lay or church courts.

In connection with the establishment of the jury trial it is interesting to note that the jury and the dreaded Inquisition were offshoots of the same process. Both were a method of obtaining information by asking questions of people who might be presumed to know something about the case. These medieval jurors were quite different from our modern ones; today if a person has any knowledge of or opinions concerning a case he is automatically disbarred from serving on the jury. In the twelfth century, it was quite another matter: only those who had some knowledge of the case in point could be jurors. For they were not so much what we term jurors as witnesses. "Unlike our jurors these were witnesses of fact; unlike the compurgators of earlier English law they swore to tell the truth,

not to assent to a fixed formula; unlike the doomsmen who found judgment they merely gave answer to a specific question." [4]

Trial by jury was at first a monopoly of the royal courts. If a man sought
to have his case tried by this new and more efficient system he had to bring
his case into the king's court as the baronial courts had not the right to
impanel juries; and if he brought his case to the king's court he had not
only to pay the court fines and costs, but he had to pay for the writ which
would order the case heard in the king's court. Thus the system paid the
king well and the increased revenues probably influenced Henry more
than the desire for abstract justice in the establishment of the system.

So far we have been discussing only civil juries; equally important was
the introduction of the jury system into the field of criminal jurisdiction.
In the early days, under the Saxons, crime was not a matter of public
concern. If a man was killed, his relatives could appeal the case as they
would any other civil injury, and if the murderer could be found and
convicted he (and his family or tithing-group) had to pay an enormous
fine, which was divided up among the relatives of the deceased. But there
were many crimes which were never brought to justice through lack of
anyone to prosecute them. Gradually it dawned on the kings that there
was in the fines from crimes a lucrative source of income which they had
never so far tapped. The crown began to interest itself in crime, and one
of the obligations of the itinerant justices was to discover all the crimes
that had been committed in the districts and to bring the cases into court.
To effect this a presentment jury was established; twelve men from each
hundred and four from each vill were sworn in the county court before
the itinerate justices to state what they knew about any crimes which had
been committed in their district. This presentment jury did not declare
any special person to be guilty, they merely stated that a certain individual
was suspected of the crime. In fact their procedure was identical with our
modern Grand Jury. At first the indictment by the jury was followed by a
trial by ordeal, but this began to die out and after 1215 the ordeal was
prohibited by the pope. As a result the jury was then required not only
to bring the indictment but to try the case. As the jurors were held to be
guilty themselves if the person they had accused were found innocent, the
number of acquittals by medieval juries was conspicuously small. The
purpose of the criminal trials was to bring in fines to the crown which
prosecuted the case, and the juries were found extremely co-operative in
returning verdicts of guilty. When one bears this procedure in mind it is
easier to identify the jury and the Inquisition as related institutions, and
it becomes apparent how far the system of jury trial has developed since
its beginnings in the twelfth century.

The use of the jury, writs, and assizes was not the only administrative

[4] W. A. Morris, *Constitutional History of England*, (Macmillan, 1930) p. 285.

reform of Henry II. By the Inquest of Sheriffs (1170) he called on the counties to give evidence as to how the sheriffs had been performing their duties, and, on the basis of the information gathered, rectified abuses and brought these powerful officials into line. The character of the sheriff of Nottingham in the Robin Hood legends shows how the sheriff was often a popular villain, hated as the oppressor of the community. In general Henry reduced the powers of the sheriffs and made them more amenable to the will of the crown. By the Assize of Arms (1181) the old national military force which could be used against the barons was reorganized. In 1166 a great Inquest of Service checked on the military services which were due from the feudal vassals to curb the process that was going on whereby a vassal would subinfeudate many more military tenantry than he owed service to the king, thus building up a private army. This was particularly important as it was under Henry that the use of *scutage* developed. This was the payment of money in lieu of personal military service and was supposed to be the amount of money which would be needed to hire a knight to perform the service owed by the vassal. This commutation of military service was immensely popular with both king and vassals, as the king could hire mercenaries on whom he could rely more completely than he could on the feudal army, and the barons were able to avoid the rigors of a military campaign for no more expense than it would have cost them to attend personally.

The king did not collect scutage from his own vassals; he summoned them to appear and, when they did not, took a fine from them. But he would permit them to collect a scutage from their vassals at a fixed rate. When the vassal had collected his scutages from his arrière vassals he would then pay his fine to the king. Since many vassals had subinfeudated many more subvassals than they owed the king, this enabled them to collect from a large number and to pay for relatively few. The Inquest of 1166 checked up on this and saw that the tenants-in-chief paid the king for all the scutages they collected. Under Henry II scutages were only collected some seven times, under Richard four, but in the seventeen years of John's reign they were collected eleven times, and at markedly advanced rates. This was one of the great grievances of the barons in 1215.

The most famous financial measure of Henry II was the Saladin Tithe of 1188. This was a special tax on movable goods and personal property levied to raise money for the crusade. An inquest was employed to see that the returns were properly reported, and this tax is notable as the first general tax on personal property in English history. The old Danegeld, which Henry continued to collect, was a tax on land, and the Saladin tithe is justly celebrated as inaugurating a new development in the field of taxation.

RICHARD LIONHEART, 1189–99

Richard Coeur-de-Lion or Lionheart, as he is popularly called, is best known for his exploits on the Third Crusade of which he was the Christian hero. As an English king he is not conspicuous. That he has been able to become a national hero is probably due to the fact that he almost never visited England and spent only a few months there during the ten years of his reign. A Poitevan by preference, Richard stayed in the south of France when he was not engaged in military campaigns in the east or in Normandy, and his only visits to England were on the occasion of his coronation when he came to London to receive the crown and raise money for his crusade, and after his release from captivity when he came back to raise money for his ransom.

In England, Richard's reign is merely a continuation of his father's. He retained many of his father's ministers, among them the famous William Marshal, but his chief minister was William Longchamp, bishop of Ely, whom he left as justiciar and regent of England while he was on the crusade. Longchamp proved a most rapacious regent and soon raised up a storm of opposition which centered around Prince John who attempted to seize the crown during his brother's absence. In 1191 the barons of the curia forcibly removed Longchamp and appointed Walter, bishop of Rouen, as justiciar with power, while John was given the title of regent and heir apparent. This overthrow of the unpopular justiciar has been recognized by modern historians as the first constitutional opposition to develop in England and to be the precursor of the baronial revolt of 1215.[5]

In 1194 the governance of England passed into the hands of Hubert Walter who combined the offices of archbishop of Canterbury, papal legate, and justiciar. He showed himself extremely able in devising new means of taxation and in extending the principle of the Saladin Tithe when money had to be raised to ransom the king from his captivity. Also under his administration we find the first appearance of the *coroners,* officials whose duty it was to reserve the pleas of the crown from the jurisdiction of the county courts. The duty of the modern coroner to decide whether a person has died by violence (in which case the state would interest itself in him) or by natural causes is a shabby remnant of the once extensive powers of this royal official, who for a time exercised an important check on the sheriffs.

When Richard returned from his crusade he found that Philip Augustus had attacked his lands in Normandy and the rest of his life was spent chiefly in a desultory war with France. During the course of this war

<hr />

[5] R. F. Treharne, *The Baronial Plan of Reform;* E. A. Joliffe, *Constitutional History of Medieval England.*

Richard built his Chateau Gaillard at Les Andelys on the Norman-French frontier—the finest example of military architecture of the twelfth century and a formidable castle, which transplanted to the West the best principles of Byzantine and Arabic fortification.

Richard was killed in a private war with the viscount of Limoges over a bit of treasure which the viscount had discovered and which Richard claimed. His death, like most of his life, was dramatic, chivalrous and useless. Apart from his exploits in the East, which brought him glory without any material benefits, Richard is chiefly important in that his continued absence gave England a taste of governing herself without a resident king, and like the famous Flight to Varennes of Louis XVI, engendered the idea that a regency might well be in many ways preferable to the royal presence.

On the death of Richard his brother John seized the throne; in his reign the work of his father was largely undone. Throughout the twelfth century the Norman-Angevin-English state had held a dominant position as opposed to France and had developed institutionally far beyond her neighbor kingdom. In the thirteenth century, the roles were to be reversed and a strong French king was to take advantage of his weak English rival.

CHAPTER 18

THE BYZANTINE REVIVAL: SALJUQ SULTANATES

✢

BYZANTIUM UNDER THE COMNENI AND ANGELI

THE TIME OF TROUBLES, 1057–81

THE accession of Isaac Comnenus, after the deposition of Michael VI, represented, as we have seen, the triumph of the military over the court officials. It inaugurated a new "time of troubles" which lasted until the establishment of the new dynasty in the person of Alexius Comnenus in 1081. During this period the imperial title passed back and forth between the military and the bureaucratic factions, the country was devastated by civil war within and by the inroads of aggressive hostile neighbors from without, the treasury was emptied and a general condition of anarchy prevailed, in which the only gains were those made by the great landed aristocracy.

Isaac reigned for only two years (1057–59). He gave the empire a strong rule devoted mainly to suppressing rival factions at home, the most important of which was that of the patriarch Michael Cerularius, who dreamed of setting up the church superior to the state. Isaac had ordered the arrest of the ambitious patriarch when the death of Cerularius brought an end to his career. But the "persecution" of Cerularius caused the development of considerable opposition, which probably played a large part in deciding Isaac to abdicate.

In 1059 Isaac abdicated the throne, which he turned over to Constantine X Ducas (1059–67). Constantine was a financial official of the government and represents the return to power of the bureaucrats, although he, like Comnenus, was a member of one of the great landed families. Constantine's reign was marked by a series of wars against the Petchenegs and the Polovtsy (or Cumans), in the course of which the Polovtsy took Salonica in 1065. Of even greater danger to the empire was the advance of the Saljuq Turks under Alp Arslan, the nephew and successor of Tughril Beg, who overran Armenia and advanced into the heart of Anatolia.

As a civilian, Constantine opposed the military group and reduced drastically the army estimates so that the military forces of the empire were badly reduced at a time when they were most needed. Constantine established for the defense of the capital a new guard recruited from the Norsemen of Russia and the West. This Varangian Guard became one of the great regiments of history and was later filled with English Saxons and western Danes. But the organization of a single new guard regiment was insufficient to offset the general decline of the army which Constantine forwarded in his attempt to reduce military political control.

When Constantine died in 1067 he left the throne to his widow Eudocia as regent for his son Michael, compelling her to swear that she would never remarry. But the military leaders persuaded her to remarry almost at once, and she gave herself to the general Romanus Diogenes, who ascended the throne as Romanus IV (1067–71). With Romanus the nadir of Byzantine fortune was reached. In the West the Normans conquered Bari and completed the conquest of Byzantine Italy. But the greatest blow to Byzantium came when Romanus, in an attempt to drive back the Saljuqs in Asia, was defeated and captured by Alp Arslan at Manzikert in 1071. The battle of Manzikert was utterly disastrous for the empire; its army destroyed, its emperor a prison of the Turks, the empire lay at the mercy of any enemy.

Romanus had always been opposed by the bureaucratic faction at the court. His capture was the signal for them to proclaim Michael VII Ducas, the son of Constantine and Eudocia, who ascended the throne under the tutelage of his uncle John Ducas, though the eunuch Nicephorus actually wielded most of the power. The reign of Michael VII (1071–78) was one of uniform defeat and demoralization; the Bulgars and Serbs rose and overran most of the Balkans, the Turks continued their advance in Anatolia, establishing a state at Iconium, Petchenegs and Polovtsy harassed the northern frontiers, while at home palace intrigue corrupted the government and the leading generals revolted. Typical of the anarchy of this period was the revolt in 1074 of Roussel de Baliol, a Norman mercenary, who had been employed by the empire against the Turks in Asia Minor. He proclaimed himself independent in Anatolia and defied the government. The Caesar John Ducas was sent against him, but Balliol won him over by proclaiming him emperor. To meet this rebellion Michael allied with the Turks, and a combined attack by the Saljuqs and the Byzantine general Alexius Comnenus succeeded in suppressing the revolt. But the emperor could not control his own forces; the generals Nicephorus Bryennius and Nicephorus Botaniates revolted, the latter allying with the Turks. Michael was deposed in 1078 and made bishop of Ephesus, while Botaniates ascended the throne as Nicephorus III (1078–81).

Total anarchy followed. The other generals refused to recognize Nicephorus and the armies of both Anatolia and Thrace revolted. Further, Robert Guiscard invaded Epirus, ostensibly to avenge the insult to his daughter, who had been betrothed to the son of Michael VII and had then been forced into a convent. In this anarchy the strongest figure was that of Alexius Comnenus, a nephew of Isaac, the general of the Thracian armies, who was supported by the three great houses of the Comneni, Duci, and Palaeologi. In 1081, Comnenus marched on Constantinople, took the city and deposed Nicephorus. Once again the empire had found a savior in her hour of greatest peril.

THE RESTORATION UNDER ALEXIUS I, 1081–1118

The throne which Alexius ascended was a tattered and unstable one. On every side enemies pressed hard on the empire, and the new emperor found himself without either troops or money wherewith to defend himself. Fortunately he was a master of diplomacy and adept at playing off one enemy against another to his own advantage.

The most immediate danger was the Norman invasion of Illyria. Guiscard had landed in Illyria and begun to penetrate inland during the reign of Nicephorus, at the accession of Alexius the Normans were in possession of Avlona and were beseiging Durazzo. Alexius attempted to form an alliance with Pope Gregory VII and with Emperor Henry IV against Robert, but was not successful. He did however secure the alliance of Venice, by granting the Venetians extensive commercial privileges throughout the empire, and a Venetian fleet won the first victory of the war by destroying the Norman fleet in the southern Adriatic. Guiscard was still able to defeat Alexius in the field however, and to capture Durazzo. But the diplomacy of Alexius began to show results when a group of Norman barons revolted and, coupled with an appeal from the pope, caused Robert to return to Italy. But even with Robert gone, the Normans continued their advance, for Bohemond, Robert's son, carried on into Thessaly and pushed as far east as Larissa, defeating Alexius enroute. In 1083, Alexius was finally able to defeat Bohemond and drive him back west; at the same time the Venetians recaptured Durazzo for the empire. The death of Guiscard in 1085 brought an end to the whole expedition and the Normans withdrew to Italy.

Before the Norman attack had been repulsed, Alexius had to meet other troubles in the Balkans. A revolt of the Bogomile heretics in Macedonia and Thrace was complicated by an invasion by Petchenegs and Polovtsy. The barbarians overran all Bulgaria, defeating Alexius at Drystra in 1087. The emperor was able to avenge himself in 1091 when he bought over the Polovtsy and by heavy subsidies secured their co-operation in a campaign against the Petchenegs. The battle of Leburnium stopped the Petchenegs and reduced them to impotence for the rest of the reign.

In Asia Minor the Turks had advanced to the Straits and occupied Nicaea and Nicomedia; Alexius fished in the troubled waters of Turkish politics after the death of Sulayman ibn Qutlumish (1085) and was able to recapture Nicomedia and Cyzicus. But the position of the empire both in Asia and Europe was most precarious and it was with considerable reason that Alexius made his appeal to Robert of Flanders and to the pope for mercenaries whom he might use against the Turks. What Alexius wanted was a mercenary army who would serve him in fighting in Anatolia; what he got was the First Crusade which opened up a whole new set of problems for his dynasty. The crusade will be discussed in the next chapter; here we must point out that Alexius profited by the crusade to recapture much of Anatolia from the Turks in the years which followed the passage of the crusaders through Asia. The capture of Antioch by Bohemond of Tarento and the subsequent quarrel over the suzerainty of Antioch led Alexius into another war with the Norman leader. In 1107, Bohemond, who had raised a new army in Europe, invaded the empire at Avlona again. Once again he started on the road to the capital, but once again he was stopped by Alexius. Without risking a pitched battle Alexius wore down the Norman's forces so that Bohemond was forced to accept the treaty of Deabolis whereby he recognized the suzerainty of Alexius (1108).

By the end of his reign Alexius had put an end for the time being to the Norman threat, had broken the power of the Petchenegs, had carried his arms victoriously into Anatolia, and had increased the power and prestige of the empire on all sides. Internally he had put down a dangerous revolt in Thrace and had taken some measures to reduce the power of the great landed families. At his death in 1118, his daughter Anna conspired to put her husband Nicephorus Bryennius (the son of the former pretender) on the throne, but was unsuccessful, and the throne went to Alexius' son and chosen successor John.

JOHN AND MANUEL COMNENUS, 1118–80

The reign of John II Comnenus (1118–43) was in many ways a continuation of the work of his father. In 1122 to 1123 he completed the destruction of the power of the Petchenegs; he intervened successfully in the internal affairs of Hungary, was victorious in a war with the Turks of Iconium, and increased the prestige of the empire in Syria by establishing his suzerainty firmly over Antioch. His one major defeat was in a war with Venice in 1126 which resulted in a new and more favorable commercial treaty between Venice and the empire. John died in Cilicia in 1143 while on a campaign to recover Syria.

Manuel I (1143–80), his son who succeeded him, was in many respects the most interesting of the Comneni princes. He was imbued with Western ideas of chivalry and knightly prowess and endeavored to introduce into

Byzantium the chivalrous concepts of the Franks. Both of his wives, Bertha of Salzbach and Marie of Antioch, were Latins, and although he engaged in many struggles with the Latins, Manuel was throughout a great admirer of Latin institutions and culture. He greatly advanced the interests of the Italian commercial cities, granting most favorable treaties to the Venetians, Genoese, and Pisans for trade in the empire. In his relations with the crusader states, Manuel again enforced his suzerainty over Antioch, and may even have extended it to a shadowy hegemony over Jerusalem. He allied with the kings of Jerusalem in a common struggle with the rising power of the Zanghids of Syria, and Byzantine armies and fleets co-operated with the Latins in campaigns in both Syria and Egypt. During the ill-fated Second Crusade, Manuel was charged by the Latins with treachery towards the Christian armies, but there is little to substantiate the charges, although they persisted in Europe and built up an anti-Greek sentiment, which was to bear fruit in the Fourth Crusade.

Manuel dreamed of re-establishing the power of the empire in the West and engaged in a series of wars against the Normans and Venetians to this effect. A Norman fleet attacked and pillaged Corinth and Thebes in 1147. Manuel retaliated by attacking Italy. He made an alliance with Conrad III and attempted to make one with Frederick Barbarossa against the Normans, but nothing came of these attempts. However, the Greeks were able to capture Ancona and to gain control of the eastern coast as far as Tarento (1155). The Normans recaptured this territory after some delay, but Manuel had meanwhile become enamored of the idea of restoring the imperial control over all Italy. Unable to make terms with Barbarossa, Manuel allied himself with Pope Alexander III and the Lombard towns, an alliance which necessitated the conclusion of temporary peace with William of Sicily, also an ally of the pope. Manuel tried to get the pope to crown him emperor of the West, but was never able to manage this, and the reunion of the churches which he advocated as part of this policy met with stern refusal on the part of the Greek clergy. The ambitions of the emperor in Italy greatly alarmed the Venetians as well as the Sicilians. In 1171 Manuel broke off relations with Venice and arrested all Venetians in the empire, confiscating their goods. Venice replied by pillaging the coastal towns of Greece, assisting the Germans to attack the Greek towns in Italy and making an alliance with Sicily against the empire.

More practical gains were made by Manuel in Hungary. There he interfered in the troubled politics of that kingdom, espousing the cause of Bela for whom he secured the throne at the death of Stephen III, receiving as his reward control over Dalmatia, which had been Bela's appanage.

Manuel's European schemes had caused him to neglect somewhat the relations with the Turks of Asia Minor. He had interfered on occasion and had even won some concessions from Qilij Arslan (which were never carried out). In 1175, the emperor broke relations with the sultan who had formed an alliance with Barbarossa and had refused to live up to his promises. In 1176, Manuel led an expedition against Iconium. The imperial army was caught in the pass at Myriocephalum and cut to pieces. Manuel fled with the shattered remnants of his army. Although Qilij Arslan granted a remarkably lenient peace treaty, this battle ended forever Byzantine attempts to reconquer Asia Minor. As Chalandon says: "The battle of Myriocephalum sealed the fate of the Comnenian dynasty, if not the fate of the Byzantine Empire." [1] The disaster of Manzikert was repeated with even greater intensity, and imperial prestige and authority in Anatolia were ended forever. Barbarossa took the occasion of this defeat of his rival to write a most insulting letter in which he stressed the superiority of the Roman emperors over the kings of the Greeks. William of Tyre tells us that Manuel never got over this defeat and that he never smiled again or enjoyed himself as he had in his earlier years.

Manuel died in September 1180, leaving the throne to his son Alexius II, under the regency of his widow, Marie of Antioch.

THE LAST COMNENI, 1180–85

Marie of Antioch, who ruled in the name of her son Alexius II (1180–84), was herself a Latin and continued the policy of Manuel of favoring Latins in the government of the empire. The court became a hotbed of intrigue and rival factions, among which developed a considerable party of Greeks who resented the Latin dominance and determined to rid themselves of "the foreign woman." There were several abortive attempts to overthrow Marie, but it was not until Andronicus Comnenus entered the scene that the Greeks had a leader who could accomplish the revolution. Andronicus was a man of amazing character and vigor. He was a cousin of Manuel's and had been a thorn in the flesh of that emperor for many years. His scandalous life had become legendary; he had seduced successively his cousin Eudocia, Philippa of Antioch the sister of the empress, and another cousin Theodora queen of Jerusalem. He had been exiled several times and had found refuge at various times with the Russians and Turks, where his conspiracies so alarmed the emperor that he had ordered him back to the capital each time. In 1183 Andronicus felt the time was ripe for him to strike for the throne. He marched on the capital followed by his own retainers, and found the city ready to welcome him as the leader of an anti-Latin party. A great massacre of Latins in Constantinople attended his usurpation of the throne. Marie was condemned to death, and Andronicus associated himself on the throne with young Alexius. But that was only the first step. The next year he mur-

[1] *Cambridge Medieval History*, IV, 378.

dered Alexius and himself married Alexius' widow, Agnes, daughter of Louis VII of France.

The reign of Andronicus (1183–85) is one unbroken reign of terror. As he was opposed by the great aristocratic families, Andronicus systematically liquidated the chief nobles of the empire. His secret police carried the fear of his name into every home in the capital, and although his administration of the provinces was a just one, his excesses in Constantinople soon made him hated by all alike. Losses of territory to both the Turks and the Hungarians increased the precariousness of his position and increased the severity of his rule. Then in 1185 William II of Sicily declared war and attacked Greece. The victorious Normans captured the city of Salonica; the empire was thrown into a state of hopeless confusion. Disaffection broke out in the capital and Andronicus could only arrest more leaders. It was the arrest of Isaac Angelus that precipitated rebellion. Isaac escaped the troops who had been sent to arrest him, and even won them over to his side. Taking refuge in Hagia Sophia, he proclaimed his resistance to Andronicus. The populace rallied to his support; Isaac was taken out of the cathedral and proclaimed emperor; Andronicus was captured and tortured. The excesses of his execution show the extreme of hatred which he had engendered during his two years on the throne. He was hung head down between two pillars in the Hippodrome and the flesh was cut away from his still living body, until he expired under the torture. Thus ended the dynasty of the Comneni. Unfortunately they were succeeded by a house which had no abilities save for fratricidal war. The last glory of the empire passed away in an orgy of civil war and bloodshed.

DECLINE OF BYZANTIUM UNDER THE ANGELI, 1185–1204

Isaac Angelus (1185–95) had little to recommend him as an emperor, and his reign was a series of misfortunes. While the court wasted the resources of the empire in a series of useless extravagances, the great families secured an increasing control over the government. Isaac was at first successful in his conduct of foreign affairs, and his general Alexius Branias was able to recapture the lands in Macedonia which had been taken by the Normans. The victory at Demetricia (1185) ended the Norman attempts on Greece, but the Norman kingdom itself fell shortly thereafter into the possession of Henry VI, who dreamed of a total conquest of the East. Meanwhile the Bulgarians and Vlachs revolted. They were suppressed by Branias, who then proclaimed himself emperor (1186). Branias was defeated, captured and beheaded, but the Bulgarians broke loose again and set up an independent state in the Balkans.

When the armies of the Third Crusade prepared to move to the East, Isaac, who mistrusted Barbarossa, allied himself with Saladin against the German emperor, but when Barbarossa refused to help the Bulgarians against the empire, he reversed his policy and allied with Frederick, marrying his daughter, Irene, to Frederick's son, Philip of Swabia. He further renewed the old alliances with the Italian towns, granting new and increased privileges in the empire to Venice, Genoa, and Pisa and trying to make up to them for their losses in the massacre of 1182. With Venice a close alliance was established in 1193 against the pretensions of Henry VI.

The wasteful extravagance of the court, the indecision of the emperor, the excessive taxation, and the increased arrogance of the great nobility, led to a number of attempted revolts. Finally, the brother of the emperor, Alexius, supported by a considerable group of the nobles, rebelled, captured, and blinded the emperor and proclaimed himself. Alexius III (1195–1203) was, however, no improvement on his brother. He recognized the new Bulgarian state by force of necessity, and allowed the formidable Johannitza to establish himself firmly in Bulgaria. Inside the empire the great nobles got more than ever out of hand, the great families of the Cantacuzeni, Branias, Sguri, and others becoming virtually independent in their own great estates.

Meanwhile Alexius, the son of the deposed Isaac, had fled to the West to seek aid in restoring his father and himself to the imperial throne. He sought and found support at the court of his brother-in-law, Philip of Swabia, and a series of negotiations were begun with the barons who had assembled for the Fourth Crusade. How the crusaders agreed to restore Isaac and Alexius and how the crusade was diverted will be discussed in a later chapter. With the assistance of the crusaders and the Venetians, Isaac and his son were restored and Alexius III driven from the throne. But Isaac and Alexius IV were unable to fulfill their promises to the crusaders and in 1204 they too were driven from the throne, and the Byzantine empire was captured by the Latins, who set up a new Latin Empire. During the attack by the Latins, the Greeks tried to rally around the person of Alexius V Ducas "Murtzuphles," but he was unable to save the city and fled. Theodore Lascaris, the son-in-law of Alexius III, was then proclaimed emperor, but he made no attempt to hold Constantinople and fled to Nicaea.

For the next half century the Byzantine empire existed in a number of fragments. The Latins held Constantinople; Lascaris ruled at Nicaea; a collateral line of the Comneni declared their independence at Trebizond, and a Greek despotate in Epirus was set up by Michael Angelus Comnenus, an illegitimate child of a cadet line of the Angeli house. Although the empire was officially re-established in 1261, the greatness of Byzantium was forever passed, and the empire of Constantinople which dragged out its miserable existence for two centuries had little in common with the great empire of the Isaurians, the Macedonians, and the Comneni.

THE RISE OF THE SALJUQ EMPIRE

The two worst defeats that the Byzantines suffered in the Comneni period were both inflicted on them by the Saljuqs in Asia Minor. We must now look at the establishment of the Saljuq states, which brought a new life into the world of Islam in the late eleventh century.

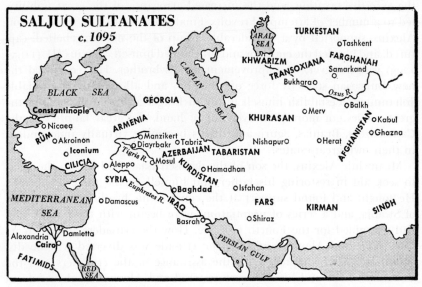

As has already been mentioned, the Saljuqs first became important when Tughril Beg occupied Baghdad in 1055 and made himself the protector of the caliph. Tughril established himself as master of the old Abbasid state, but he did not transfer his seat to Baghdad, preferring to rule from Merv. At his death in 1063, he was succeeded by his nephew Alp Arslan (1063–72) who expanded the limits of his power both to the east in Khwarizm and Turkestan and to the west in Asia Minor. In 1071 he won the great victory of Manzikert over the Byzantines, which gave the Saljuqs a strong foothold in Anatolia. The conquest of Asia Minor was entrusted by Alp Arslan to a distant cousin, Sulayman ibn Qutlumish, who founded the sultanate of Rum at Iconium (1077). Pressing on towards the Straits, Sulayman captured Nicaea which he made his capital, but after the reconquest of Nicaea by Alexius and the Crusaders in 1097, the capital was transferred to Iconium where it remained until the extinction of the dynasty (1300). Meanwhile Alp Arslan returned to Isfahan whence he

ruled over his scattered empire. The real ruler, and the guiding genius of
the early Saljuqs was the gifted vizier, Nizam al Mulk, who served both
under Alp Arslan and Malik Shah, and who was primarily responsible
for the renaissance of culture which marked the height of the Saljuq
empire. Nizam al Mulk is most celebrated for his foundations of universities in Baghdad and in Nishapur called after him *Nizamiyahs*, which became the great centers of Moslem learning, and which were graced by
such scholars as Umar al Khayyam, Al-Ghazzali, and the great poet, Sa'di.
The calendar, which was prepared at his direction by a commission of
which Umar al Khayyam was a member, has been stated to be the most
exact calendar that has ever been formulated. Nizam al Mulk is equally
famous for his great work, a *Treatise on Politics,* the best work on political science produced in the Islamic world at the time.

When Alp Arslan died in 1072 the throne went to his son Malik Shah
(1072–92), under whom the Saljuq state reached its zenith. He ruled from
the Oxus to the Mediterranean, from the Bosphorus and the Caspian to
Mecca and Karman; and throughout his empire so well was order kept
that caravans or even individual merchants could travel in peace without
fear of robbery or spoliation. Throughout most of his reign Nizam al
Mulk continued to be the chief advisor of the sultan, and it is largely due
to his genius that the administration of the empire was so efficient and ran
so smoothly.

During the reign of Malik Shah, the conquest of Syria was undertaken
by the brother of the sultan, Tutush, who established himself in Syria
with his chief centers at Aleppo and Damascus, which he subsequently
left to his two sons, Ridwan and Duqaq. Other parts of the empire were
ruled by officers of the sultan known as *atabegs.* These atabegs or regents
held the provinces in the name of the sultan or one of his sons, and became
a regular institution in Islam. Among the great dynasties of atabegs were
the Burids of Damascus, the Urtukids of Maridin and Diyarbakr, the
Zanghids of Aleppo, and the Khwarizm shahs. While they were theoretically only the regents for the sultan, these atabegs actually ruled absolutely,
founding dynasties which had little connection with the sultanate.

The Saljuq empire was as short lived as it was brilliant. At the death
of Malik Shah in 1092, civil war broke out between his sons. The throne
finally went to Barkiyaruk (1094–1104), who devoted himself almost exclusively to the eastern portions of the empire, neglecting the west. It was
during his reign that the First Crusade took place, and the preoccupation
of the sultan with the east in part explains the indifference with which
he viewed the events of that movement. "To the main body of the Moslem
community the Crusades, viewed from headquarters, were but an insignificant episode" says P. K. Hitti,[2] and to Barkiyaruk at Baghdad they

---

[2] *History of the Arabs,* (3rd ed.), p. 480.

undoubtedly seemed less important than events in the Persian or Trans-oxianian povinces. When Barqiyaruk was confronted with a rebellion of his brother Muhammad in 1098 and was forced to compromise with him by dividing the empire, he retained for himself the eastern portion, giving Muhammad: Armenia, Georgia, Syria, Iraq, and Media. At Barkiyaruk's death in 1104, this Muhammad reunited the empire into his own hands and ruled from 1104 till 1117, when the throne passed to a third brother

THE SALJUQ SULTANS

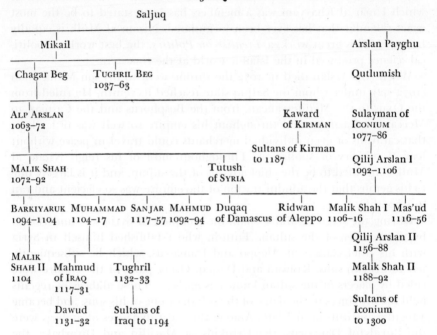

Saljuq

| Mikail | | | | | | | Arslan Payghu |

Chagar Beg — Tughril Beg 1037-63 — Qutlumish

Alp Arslan 1063-72 — Kaward of Kirman — Sulayman of Iconium 1077-86

Sultans of Kirman to 1187

Malik Shah 1072-92 — Tutush of Syria — Qilij Arslan I 1092-1106

Barkiyaruk 1094-1104 — Muhammad 1104-17 — Sanjar 1117-57 — Mahmud 1092-94 — Duqaq of Damascus — Ridwan of Aleppo — Malik Shah I 1106-16 — Mas'ud 1116-56

Malik Shah II 1104 — Mahmud of Iraq 1117-31 — Tughril 1132-33 — Qilij Arslan II 1156-88

Malik Shah II 1188-92

Dawud 1131-32 — Sultans of Iraq to 1194 — Sultans of Iconium to 1300

Sanjar (1117-57) the last of the great Saljuq sultans. Sanjar spent much of his time in wars with the Khata (Cathayans) and Turkomans from across the Oxus and with the rebellious shahs of Khwarizm, in neither of which did he enjoy great success.

With the death of Sanjar the line of great Saljuqs ends. Thereafter the empire was divided into several independent parts. In southern Persia, the Saljuqs of Kirman ruled till 1187; in Syria, the descendants of Tutush continued until the atabeg dynasties of the Burids and Urtukids replaced them in Damascus and Aleppo about 1117; in Iraq and Kurdistan a dynasty descended from Muhammad ibn Malik Shah ruled until 1194; while at Iconium the independent line continued, as we have seen, until 1300. This branch of Iconium is by far the most important for European history, as it was they who were in contact with both the Byzantines and the crusaders. In the east, meanwhile, the chief power passed into the hands of the dynasty of the shahs of Khwarizm, who extended their rule over Persia, Bukhara, Samarkand, and Ghaznah, and built up a strong state which wrested the control of Baghdad and the caliph from the Saljuqs of Iraq in 1194. Ala-al-Din Muhammad, the shah, planned to depose the Abbasid caliph and replace him with an Alid, but the caliph Al Nasir called in as his protector a new power of the east, the formidable Chingiz Khan of the Mongols. Chingiz routed Ala-al-Din, who abandoned his empire and took refuge in an island in the Caspian (1220), while the Mongols ravished his cities and destroyed his people. The conquests of the Mongols will be discussed below in Chapter 31. With their advent the old world of Islam was shattered and reshaped.

CHAPTER 19

THE FIRST CRUSADE

✦

THE twelfth and thirteenth centuries are often called the Age of the Crusades and it was once current practice to attribute almost everything which characterized these centuries to the influence of the crusades. Now however it is realized that the crusades themselves were but a part, though a conspicuous part, of that revival of energy and activity which is termed the Twelfth Century Renaissance, and these expeditions have been reduced from a prime cause to a sort of catalytic agent, which hurried along tendencies which were already well under way. For example the growth of trade and the development of the towns, which were once thought to be a result of the crusades, are now seen to have been developing long before the beginning of the crusades, though they did receive a tremendous acceleration from them. But the crusades do show, as does nothing else, how the center of the medieval world had shifted from the East to the West, for with them it is the active, virile, aggressive West which takes the offensive against the more disorganized and somewhat outworn East in the age-long struggle between East and West. By the twelfth century neither Byzantium nor the caliphate was capable of attempting to conquer western Europe: it was the West which attempted to conquer the East, and which for a time at least succeeded in that attempt.

Urban II and the Launching of the Crusades

The idea of the crusade did not spring full grown from the head of Urban II, though that pontiff was responsible for its launching. The old legend which attributes the idea of the crusade to Peter the Hermit must be dismissed as purely fictitious, since Peter is now known to have been merely one of the clerics who were commissioned to preach the crusade, and his own role in the movement was a distinctly inglorious one. Urban II proclaimed the crusade at the Council of Clermont in November 1095 largely because at that moment the circumstances in both East and West seemed particularly advantageous for such an expedition, which had been in the minds of the popes for some time.

The first expression of the idea of a military campaign to rescue the Holy Land from the Moslems may have been put forth in certain schemes of Pope Sylvester II (Gerbert) about the year 1000, but it was the great Gregory VII who first made serious plans for it. Gregory, however, never found himself in a position where he could indulge in such ambitions, as he was constantly preoccupied with his struggle with the empire. By 1095, Urban II had carried the offensive into enemy country, stirring up rebellion against Henry IV, and the situation at home was less critical. Also Urban was given a special occasion by the request which the emperor Alexius I made of him to send troops to assist him in his wars against the Saljuqs, a request which was presented the pope at the Council of Piacenza in 1095.

There has been much scholarly argument as to what motives prompted Urban to launch the crusade. Several theories have been advanced, all of which probably played some part. That the pope was moved by a sincere desire to aid the sufferings of the oriental Christians and to rescue the Holy Sepulchre is undoubted; that he was influenced by the desire to heal the schism between the Eastern and Western churches, which was then only fifty years old and the termination of which he considered would be a consequence of the aid which he would send Alexius, cannot be questioned; and there is much reason to believe that he also felt that the crusade would materially strengthen the position of the papacy in respect to the German empire, as the possession of such military might as the crusade showed would inevitably enhance the temporal position of the church. It is immaterial whether Urban first determined on the crusade during his journey from Piacenza to Clermont or not. By the time he had arrived at Clermont, he had worked out the scheme for the crusade as a great expedition to be launched under papal guidance for the redemption of the Holy Land. It was this that he preached at Clermont, after the business of the council had been completed. Not merely mercenaries to aid Alexius against the Turks, but a Christian army to capture Jerusalem for Christ was the objective of the pope. He could not raise a huge army to unseat the German emperor, but he could and did raise the largest military force that western Europe had witnessed since the days of the Roman empire to march across the limits of the known world to capture Jerusalem in the name of Christ and the papacy. Such strength could not pass unnoticed by the enemies of the church at home.

Further, the crusade promised to help out in a program at home to which the pope was devoted. Urban at the Council of Clermont had reissued the bans of the Peace and the Truce of God. The Peace of God prohibited any war waged against women, children, or clerics; the Truce prohibited any fighting over weekends. This seriously curtailed the freedom of the turbulent nobles to engage in their cherished pastime of private war; Urban offered them as a substitute unlimited warfare against the enemies of Christ in Palestine and the East. It must be noted that Urban specifically exempted the Spanish from the crusade; he did not want to divert from the "perpetual crusade" in Spain any efforts of those engaged in it. But to those who were not fighting for Christ in Spain, a new field was opened up in the East. Urban appealed to the religious zeal of his listeners and promised absolution to those who should lose their lives in the crusade; he also appealed to their cupidity in pointing out the great wealth of the East, which was to be had for the taking. Salvation, glory, and wealth waited those who went; for the stay-at-homes were only the ordinary cares and obligations of their positions and the restriction of their warlike temperaments.

The response to the appeal had very probably been planned in advance. Bishop Adhemar of Le Puy and Count Raymond of Toulouse, both of whom had discussed the matter earlier with the pope, led the clergy and the nobles in their enthusiastic reply to the pope's appeal. With cries of *"Deus vult,"* they placed crosses on their shoulders in sign of their dedication to the crusade. Hundreds of others present followed their example. Then the pope sent preachers to carry the word of the crusade throughout the lands of Catholic Christendom.

The First Crusade was no spontaneous affair; it was well worked out in the mind of the pope before any action was taken. The leadership of the expedition was entrusted to the bishop of Puy; preachers were warned to enlist only knights and soldiers who could properly bear arms against the infidel. That the preachers, like Peter the Hermit, gave the cross to all and sundry was not the fault of the pope, nor was it in accordance with his plan or desires. Urban planned a well-organized military expedition under experienced leaders, the whole under the guidance of the papal legate, Adhemar. It was to give aid to Alexius, but was also to push on to Jerusalem and wrest from the Moslems the control of the Holy Places. It is going too far to claim that Urban contemplated the erection in Palestine of a theocratic state directly ruled by the church: that was the idea of Daimbert of Pisa and cannot be found in the plan of Urban; but we can argue that Urban hoped for the erection of a Christian kingdom, which would be a vassal of the Church.

PEASANT CRUSADE

Although Urban projected only a military force under competent leadership and fixed the time for departure and the rendezvous at Constantinople, the preachers of the crusade gave the cross to all comers and allowed several ill-equipped and poorly led groups of smaller folk to start off on their own on the holy pilgrimage. This first movement, known as the Crusade of the Peasants, was undertaken by lesser folk, not actually peasants, but poorer knights and sergeants, who took their wives and belongings and started off on the road to the Sepulchre. Several bands can be distinguished, led by Peter the Hermit, Walter the Penniless, Count

Emicho, Gottschalk, and others, but the expeditions were all essentially alike in their character and in their fates.

They generally began their pilgrimage by massacring the Jews at home. Why should they go to Palestine to fight Christ's enemies when those who had killed Him were close to hand? Pogroms took place in most of the towns of western Germany, though some Jews were able to buy protection by contributing largely to the war chests of the local nobles. Then the ill-ordered bands started out across Germany and Hungary and into the Balkans on their way to Jerusalem. As they had no provisions for the journey and little money they were forced to live off the land and that largely by pillage; this naturally caused considerable trouble with the inhabitants of the countries through which they passed. At Belgrade a number of the crusaders were hanged for pillaging; a second band stormed the city to avenge their fellows; markets were established for them, but, when they stole rather than bought, the markets were closed and they were forced to pillage. Large numbers were lost on the long march through the Balkans and only a portion reached Constantinople. There Alexius, who had no possible use for such an unruly mob, quartered them outside the city to wait for the princes and the regular armies (October 1096). But their depredations made them so obnoxious to the inhabitants of the Byzantine capital that the emperor transferred them across the Straits to a camp in Asia Minor where they could wait less destructively. Alexius furnished them with food and supplies and settled them at Civitot, but they were unwilling to remain idle and bands set out to pillage in the Moslem lands nearby. The answer of the Turks was prompt and decisive: the camp at Civetot was attacked, the pilgrims slaughtered and only a few thousand, who had secured themselves in a fort, were rescued by the Byzantines and brought back to safety. Thus ingloriously ended the Crusade of the Peasants; the remnants joined the main body of the crusade when it left Constantinople and marched south the following spring.

THE FIRST CRUSADE: TO NICAEA

The main body of the crusade, the army of the princes, was led by a number of prominent leaders, though there was no crowned head among them. From Provence and southern France came a large host under the leadership of Raymond de St. Gilles, count of Toulouse, an old warrior who had served through many campaigns in Spain and who had been one of Urban's earliest consultants on the matter of the crusade. The men of Flanders marched out under their count Robert; those of Normandy under Duke Robert Curthose, the eldest son of William the Conqueror, who had pawned his duchy to his brother William Rufus of England for money to pay his crusade expenses; the French came under Hugh de Vermandois, the brother of King Philip; while a large contingent of Champagnois was led by Stephen of Blois, the son-in-law of the Conqueror and one of the wealthiest barons of France. As might be expected there were no great German contingents, but a large force of Lorrainers and men from the Low Countries were led by Godfrey de Bouillon, marquis of Antwerp and Duke of Lower Lorraine, and his brother Baldwin.

Three main routes were followed by these various groups. The old overland route, the traditional pilgrim road, across Germany, down the Danube, across Hungary, through Bulgaria to Adrianople and thence to Constantinople was followed by the Lorrainers. The Provençals marched across north Italy, through Venetia and down the eastern shore of the Adriatic to Durazzo whence they turned east and followed the old Roman Via Egnatia to Adrianople and Constantinople. A third route was down the length of Italy, where they stopped to deliver to Urban that portion of Rome which still was held by the anti-pope, into the Norman duchy, where they took ship at Bari or Brindisi to Durazzo or Avlona and thence across the Via Egnatia. This route was the one followed by the Normans, Flemings, Champagnois, and French. When they reached southern Italy they were joined by the warrior who was to become the most important leader of the whole crusade, Bohemond, prince of Tarento, the son of Robert Guiscard, who had been cheated out of his inheritance and who was trying to win some portion of it from his brother, Roger Borsa. Bohemond had led Guiscard's forces in the Greek campaign of 1081 to 1085 and was a soldier of great ability; with his nephew Tancred and other members of his house (Richard of the Principate et al.) he joined the crusaders, prompted by the practical desire to gain conquests in the East, which would compensate for his lack of fortune in Italy. That Bohemond had any religious principles or was in any way motivated by religious zeal is seldom even suggested; he was an adventurer who saw a large army going off to conquer something and felt he might as well be the man to rule the lands they conquered.

Alexius had asked for mercenaries to assist him against the Saljuqs: what he got was the tremendous host of the crusaders who had come, not to serve the empire, but to conquer Jerusalem for Christ. There was considerable trouble for a time before the proper relations between emperor and crusader chiefs could be established. Alexius tried intimidation and bribery, imprisoning some and lavishing gifts on others of the leaders. Finally an agreement was reached whereby the princes swore allegiance to the emperor and promised to restore to him all lands they should recapture, which had been parts of the empire. Only Tancred and Raymond of Toulouse refused to take this oath, but it was Bohemond who first broke it, and the interpretation thereof was to cause trouble between the Byzantines and the crusaders for years to come.

Finally the host was shipped across the Straits to Asia Minor, where from May to June 1097 the combined Byzantine-crusader army besieged the Turkish city of Nicaea. This was finally captured and duly surrendered to Alexius. Then while the emperor campaigned in northern Anatolia and regained much of the territory previously lost to the Turks there, the crusader host pushed on through central Anatolia towards the south.

NICAEA TO JERUSALEM, 1097–99

As Anatolia is a mountainous and rugged country and it was felt that the needs of the whole army could not be met if they all followed a single road, the army split into two sections which followed parallel roads south. On July 1, 1097 one section of the host that was led by Bohemond and Robert of Normandy, was attacked by the forces of Iconium at Dorylaeum. The battle seemed desperate, for the crusaders were greatly outnumbered, but help came from the other section of the army which attacked the Turks and the Western knights defeated the Turkish warriors and won an unexpected victory. This battle, which destroyed the flower of the Turkish army, gave the crusaders free passage thereafter through Anatolia and gave the Turks a paralyzing fear of the strength and ferocity of the Franks. It also greatly facilitated the conquests of Alexius from the defeated Turks.

After the great victory at Dorylaeum, the crusaders marched south until they reached the Taurus passes from Anatolia into Syria. Then, while the main body of the army went on towards Antioch, Tancred and Baldwin separately went into Cilicia to conquer for themselves principalities in the east. Tancred besieged Tarsus and had the siege well advanced when Baldwin joined him. But when the city surrendered it was to Baldwin, and Tancred found himself deprived of any part of the conquest. Fighting broke out between the two Christian armies, but Baldwin suddenly decamped and went on east to Edessa, while Tancred rejoined the main army at Antioch.

Before continuing with the exploits of the crusader host, some mention must be made of the local conditions in Syria at the time of the arrival of the Franks. As we have seen in Chapter 18 above, the Saljuqs had overrun Syria and Anatolia, but had not established any single state; rather a number of rival Saljuq principalities were at constant feud with each other. While the descendants of Sulayman ibn Qutlumish ruled at Iconium (Rum), the governors of Barkiyaruk held Mosul and Antioch, and the sons of Tutush ruled in Damascus and Aleppo. Thoros, an Armenian, held

Edessa as the vassal of Tutush; Jerusalem which had been held by the Urtukids as vassals of Tutush was recaptured by the Fatimids in 1096 and the Urtukids removed themselves to Diyarbakr. There were also several native Arab families who held out in such places as Shaizar. Between few of these various parties was there anything but hostility and they could not be counted on to assist each other even against a wholly foreign foe.

When Baldwin left Tarsus, he moved eastward towards Edessa. There Thoros, the Armenian, welcomed him and adopted him as his son, declaring his independence of his Moslem overlord. Exactly what happened next is a bit confused in the chroniclers, but Thoros was overthrown by a rebellion in which Baldwin may or may not have had a hand and Baldwin emerged from the confusion as lord of Edessa (Easter 1098). Thus was founded the first of the Latin crusader states of Syria.

Meanwhile the main crusader host had settled down to besiege the powerful city of Antioch. The siege began in October 1097 and lasted until June 1098. The crusaders suffered extremely during the hard winter, as they ran out of food and supplies periodically, and the morale of the army sank to a low ebb. Finally Bohemond contacted an officer inside the city and persuaded him to betray the tower of which he was the guardian. Then calling the princes together Bohemond proposed that the city be given to whichever of the leaders should first effect an entrance into its walls. The others, ignorant of Bohemond's negotiations with the traitor within, thought this an equitable arrangement and agreed to the plan. The tower was surrendered as agreed and Bohemond placed his standard on it; the gates were opened, the crusader army was admitted and the city was taken. The citadel held out however and the crusaders were unable to reduce it.

Meanwhile the emir of Antioch had sought help from his Moslem neighbors, and Karbuqa of Mosul armed to relieve the city. He arrived shortly after the capture and promptly besieged the crusaders within the town. Once again the Christian army underwent the rigors of a siege, this time themselves besieged. Many deserted and let themselves down over the walls on ropes, among the deserters being Peter the Hermit, who was ignominiously captured and brought back. At about this same time Stephen of Blois, who was recuperating from an illness in Cilicia, grew discouraged and fled towards Constantinople.

Hugh de Vermandois had meanwhile been sent by the crusaders to ask Alexius to bring aid quickly. The emperor was on his way through Anatolia bringing reinforcements when he was met by Stephen, who assured him that all was lost and the crusader host surely wiped out. Feeling that further advance was useless, Alexius turned back, accompanied by Hugh and Stephen. When after the battle word reached the crusader leaders in Antioch that the emperor had abandoned them they were most bitter in their denunciation of his perfidy.

On June 28 the leaders decided to risk all on the fortunes of battle and came out to meet Karbuqa's host which was made up of contingents from Mosul, Damascus, Aleppo, and the other Moslem cities. The accounts of the battle differ; Bohemond certainly displayed real leadership and tactical genius in arranging and deploying his men, and it is probably not necessary to explain the victory which he won by stating, as the Moslem chroniclers do, that the Damascene and Aleppan soldiers deserted, or as the pious Raymond does, that celestial assistance was given the crusaders by the Holy Lance which had been discovered in Antioch a few days before the battle. As a result of the defeat of Karbuqa, the garrison of the citadel of Antioch surrendered to Count Raymond, who refused to surrender it to Bohemond, but claimed that he was holding it for Alexius to whom it rightly belonged. As Adhemar had died shortly after the siege, there was no one to decide the matter whom both princes would accept as their superior.

Raymond and Bohemond had disagreed earlier. When the Holy Lance was discovered by one of Raymond's men, the Provençals had hailed the miracle and the hard-headed Normans had questioned its veracity. Personal friction between Bohemond and Raymond reached an open breach, and their rivalry threatened to tie up the whole crusade. Finally Raymond was forced to surrender Antioch to Bohemond and the army moved south, leaving the Norman leader behind in his new domain. But Raymond wanted to recoup his lost city and attempted to take other towns on the road south. At Marra and at Archas, Raymond lost much time for the army by besieging the cities, while the host clamored to be led on to Jerusalem. It was at this time that Godfrey de Bouillon first appears as an important leader of the army; for he and Robert of Normandy placed themselves at the head of those who insisted on marching directly to Jerusalem without stopping to capture the towns on the route. In accordance with this policy the crusaders bypassed most of the cities along the coast, accepting safe-conducts and supplies from the emirs and leaving them in Moslem hands until they could be picked up later after Jerusalem itself should have been captured.

Finally in June 1099, the crusader army reached Jerusalem and invested the city. Godfrey, Raymond, Tancred, and the two Roberts of Normandy and Flanders arranged their forces to surround the city, except on the eastern side where there was no hope of storming the walls. In a raid made during the siege, Tancred captured Bethlehem with the Church of the Nativity. Aid was rendered the besiegers by the Christians within the city and also by a group of Genoese who had arrived by sea at Jaffa and had come to join them before Jerusalem. Siege machinery was constructed and the attack was pressed. On July 13 the first crusaders gained an entrance into the city and the rest soon followed. The slaughter which accompanied the capture of Jerusalem was barbarous and revolting.

On the top of Solomon's Temple, to which they (the Moslems) had climbed in fleeing, many were shot to death with arrows and cast down headlong from the roof. Within the Temple about ten thousand were beheaded. If you had been there, your feet would have been stained up to the ankles with the blood of the slain. What more shall I tell? Not one of them was allowed to live. They did not spare the women and children.

wrote Fulcher of Chartres; [1] while an even more revolting picture is given by Raymond of Agiles: [2]

But now that our men had possession of the walls and towers, wonderful sights were to be seen. Some of our men (and this was the more merciful) cut off the heads of their enemies; others shot them with arrows, so that they fell from the towers; others tortured them longer by casting them into the flames. Piles of heads, hands and feet were to be seen in the streets of the city. It was necessary to pick one's way over the bodies of men and horses. But these were small matters compared to what happened in the Temple of Solomon, a place where religious services are ordinarily chanted. . . . In the Temple and porch of Solomon, men rode in blood up to their knees and bridle reins. Indeed it was a just and splendid judgment of God that this place should be filled with the blood of the unbelievers, since it had suffered so long from their blasphemies. The city was filled with corpses and blood.

ESTABLISHMENT OF THE KINGDOM OF JERUSALEM, 1099–1118

As soon as the Holy City had fallen into their hands, and the objective of the crusade had been accomplished, the crusaders set about organizing their conquest. First they proceeded to elect a ruler for the new state, their choice falling on Godfrey de Bouillon. Although William of Tyre says that this was because of the personal piety and qualities of Godfrey, the real reason for his election must be sought in the feuds which divided the crusaders themselves. The Normans would never consent to the election of Raymond of Toulouse, and the Provençals would not accept a Norman. As Robert of Flanders and Robert of Normandy were both anxious to get home as soon as possible, that left but one available candidate, Godfrey, who had acquired no great personal enemies and whose ambitions were feared by neither party. Godfrey accepted the election but refused to be crowned king, contenting himself with the title of Protector

[1] *Fulcher of Chartres*, trans., E. McGinty. Univ. of Penna. "Trans. and Reprints," Third Series, pp. 68–69. Reprinted by permission of the publishers, Univ. of Pennsylvania Press.
[2] A. C. Krey, *The First Crusade* (1921), p. 261. Reprinted by permission of the publishers, Princeton Univ. Press.

(Advocate) of the Holy Sepulchre. This may have been a tacit recognition of the suzerainty of the church over the new kingdom, as the title Advocate was applied to the secular administrators of ecclesiastical estates. Godfrey later did homage to the patriarch Daimbert for his kingdom, thus recognizing the suzerainty of the church.

The secular ruler having been selected, the barons and clergy next elected a patriarch, choosing for this honor Arnulf, the chaplain of Robert of Normandy, a man of superior intellect and education, though worldly and ambitious, and not without enemies. Arnulf's tenure of the patriarchate was short, as he was soon displaced by Daimbert, archbishop of Pisa, who arrived in Syria shortly after the crusade and was elected patriarch through the influence of Bohemond. Daimbert was to go far beyond any plan we can attribute to Urban in his attempt to make of Jerusalem a purely theocratic state with the patriarch at its head.

But although Jerusalem had been captured, the crusade was not yet ended. The Fatimids of Egypt had no intention of accepting the victory of the crusaders without protest. A great Egyptian army came up into Palestine to drive out the invaders. Gathering all possible forces, Godfrey marched to meet them at Ascalon. Here on August 12, 1099, the crusaders gained a signal victory over the Egyptians. After this battle of Ascalon, with which the First Crusade really ended, many of the crusaders returned to Europe: the minority remained to find new homes in the Promised Land.

Hardly had the rough outlines of a state been established when Duke Godfrey died after only one year of rule in 1100. The succession to the kingship fell, by the choice of the leading barons of the principality, to Baldwin, his brother, who had been ruling at Edessa. Bohemond and the new patriarch, Daimbert, opposed this election and conspired to prevent Baldwin's ascending the throne, but Baldwin won through to Jerusalem and forced the reluctant patriarch to crown him king at Bethlehem on Christmas Day 1100. Unlike Godfrey, Balwin assumed a royal crown and title, and with his coronation a certain amount of oriental formality entered the Latin Kingdom.

Baldwin I (1100–18) was the real founder of the kingdom. When the crusaders had marched to Jerusalem, they had, as we have seen, passed by most of the coastal cities on their route, accepting from these supplies and titular submission. The task of filling in these gaps and conquering the coastal towns had been begun by Godfrey and he had invested Caiphas (Haifa), which was captured about the time of his death, but it was Baldwin who in the years 1101 to 1110 captured Arsur, Caesarea, Acre, Sidon, and Beirut, thus pushing the northern frontier of the principality to the Dog River between Beirut and Djebail. The capture of these cities was made possible by aid rendered by Venetian, Pisan, Genoese, and Scandinavian fleets, which blocked the towns from the sea while the Frankish armies attacked them by land. In return for this service the Italians received large shares of the booty and also extensive trading privileges, warehouses, and whole quarters of the towns captured. Baldwin also defeated the Egyptians at Ramlah in 1101 and 1105 (and was himself defeated in 1102) and secured the southern frontier of the kingdom. Towards the interior Baldwin expanded towards the Jordan River and beyond, establishing fiefs with strong castles at Tiberias and across the Jordan at Montréal. He died while on an expedition into Egypt in 1118; at the time of his death the kingdom had reached in general the frontiers which it was to retain for most of its troubled existence. Of the coastal cities only Tyre, between Sidon and Caiphas, and Ascalon, to the extreme south on the border of Egypt, remained in Moslem hands.

Baldwin was the first Latin king of Jerusalem, and from him the other kings numbered themselves. While the rough outlines of a government were probably set up by Godfrey, it was under Baldwin that the constitution of the kingdom really appears.

As the only type of government with which they were at all acquainted was a feudal state, it was a feudal monarchy that the crusaders established in Syria. Already before Jerusalem had been captured, two feudal principalities had been established at Edessa and Antioch; Jerusalem made a third, and a fourth was to be added soon thereafter when Raymond of Toulouse laid the foundations of the county of Tripoli between Jerusalem and Antioch. All were organized, as far as the nobles were concerned, on strictly feudal principles. Godfrey had begun by distributing fiefs among his barons, allotting them in the main titles to lands as yet unconquered, but also parceling out what lands had been taken already. Baldwin continued this practice. These were to be held from the king as prince of the principality of Jerusalem, and the relation of the king to the great counts of Antioch, Edessa, and Tripoli was somewhat indefinite. These counts had organized their states on feudal lines with their own vassals and institutions; they remained separate entities throughout the history of the kingdom. Although the suzerainty of the king of Jerusalem as a superior lord was recognized, the position of the king of the whole kingdom was shadowy and enforceable only by strong men. The power of the king of Jerusalem rested entirely on his position as chief feudal lord in the principality of Jerusalem itself. Unfortunately for clarity in understanding their institutions, the term Kingdom of Jerusalem was applied to both the southern principality and the whole over-all kingdom, which probably was, as Professor Stephenson has claimed "at most an afterthought." [3]

The first thing Godfrey had done was to establish a system of courts.

[3] Carl Stephenson, *Medieval Feudalism*, p. 95.

A High Court, the baronial court of the suzerain, was established for the nobles; bourgeois courts, presided over by viscounts, were established in the chief cities where there were Frankish settlers; and native courts under native judges were set up for the local Syrian population.

Local tradition also credited Godfrey with establishing a code of laws for the kingdom. According to this tradition, Godfrey assembled the leaders of the crusaders and caused them to draw up a code of laws, which would incorporate the general principles of the laws of their various provinces and home lands. This composite code was then declared to be the law for Jerusalem. While there is considerable doubt that Godfrey established a real code, there can be no question but that some fundamental laws were established at this time which were known as the "Letters of the Sepulchre." [4] We know that Baldwin, at any rate, left several laws.

Although the feudal state which the crusaders set up has been properly claimed to be the ideal feudal state, inasmuch as it never contained elements which were anything but feudal, it must not be thought that the crusaders deliberately set out to establish an ideal feudal state. They would not have known what this meant; they simply set up the only kind of political and economic organization which they understood; that it happened to be almost the ideal feudal state was purely fortuitous. They were all feudal barons themselves and the state they established was one which reflected their former position and the type of organization they were familiar with and wanted to perpetuate.

Meanwhile the northern states had been expanding and consolidating themselves also. Bohemond had engaged in war with Aleppo and with the other Moslem emirs of the north, and had been captured in 1100. During his captivity, Tancred served as regent in Antioch, continuing Bohemond's aggressive policies. When Bohemond was released he returned to Europe to raise a new army, but he was diverted into an unsuccessful war against the Byzantine Empire in 1107–08 in which he was badly defeated and had to recognize the suzerainty of the emperor over Antioch. As Bohemond returned to Europe again after this defeat and died there in 1111, this recognition of suzerainty, which was never accepted by Tancred, who was ruling in Antioch during his absence, had little material value.

Tancred, who was regent and then prince of Antioch from 1104 to 1112, carried on wars indiscriminately with the Byzantines and Moslems, allying with one Moslem emir against another. Laodicea (Lattakiya) was captured from the Byzantines; Aleppo was besieged and forced to pay tribute; Antioch under Tancred was easily the dominant state in northern Syria.

4 See La Monte, "Three Questions concerning the Assises de Jerusalem," *Byzantina-Metabyzantina,* I (1946), 201–12.

Raymond of Toulouse had meanwhile begun the conquest of the county of Tripoli. In 1102 he captured Tortosa, and two years later with the help of the Genoese took Gibelet (Djebail). He was engaged in an unsuccessful siege of Tripoli itself when he died in 1105, and the city fell to his successors only in 1109. The creation of the county of Tripoli filled in the gap along the coast between the southern boundary of Antioch and the northern limits of Jerusalem, so that the Latins held an unbroken coastline (except for Tyre) from Lattakiya to Jaffa.

Throughout this whole period of conquest several elements favored the Latins. First of all, they received priceless assistance from the navies of Genoa, Pisa, and Venice. Also Moslem resistance was weak and scattered, there was still no unity among the Moslem states, and the rivalry between Aleppo, Damascus, Mosul, Diayrbakr, and others, coupled with the comparative indifference of the sultan to the affairs of his westernmost provinces, afforded the Latins a splendid opportunity for conquest. Moreover the name of the Franks still brought fear to the hearts of the Moslems, a reputation which Tancred did much to keep up.

The capture of Jerusalem had brought an immediate response in western Europe. When the news of the capture of the Holy City reached the West, several bands of crusaders set out for Palestine. This expedition, the crusade of 1101, was led by Stephen of Blois (who hoped to redeem himself from the obloquy he had earned in his desertion at Antioch), Stephen of Burgundy, the Count of Nevers, Welf of Bavaria, and Duke William of Aquitaine, as well as a large number of Lombard and German ecclesiastics. The expedition reached the East in three divisions, each of which was destroyed before the other arrived. The whole crusade was lost in Asia Minor, and only a few members reached Jerusalem to be slaughtered in the battle of Ramlah in 1102. Stephen of Blois achieved martyrdom and removed the blot from his honor; but the results of the crusade were negligible.[5]

Of much greater importance to the crusader kingdom was the founding in the last year of the reign of King Baldwin I, of the military-religious Order of the Knights Templar. A number of Christian knights, led by Hugh de Payns, organized themselves into a semi-monastic order dedicated to the protection of pilgrims and to perpetual war with the Moslems. They were given as their headquarters a building on the site of the ancient Temple of Solomon, whence they called themselves the Knights of the Temple. The order was given a rule by St. Bernard in 1128 and at once became the recipient of the gifts of the faithful all over Europe. Combining as it did the ideals of religious monasticism with the warlike virtues of feudal chivalry, the Temple was the most popular religious order among

---

[5] The best account of this crusade is in James L. Cate, "A Gay Crusader, William of Aquitaine," *Byzantion*, XVI (1942–43), 503–26.

the military nobility. Membership into the class of knights was restricted to men of noble birth, but lesser folk could join the order as sergeants or lay brethren. The Templars soon acquired much property in both Syria and Europe and became extremely wealthy and powerful. They built strong castles to hold the roads and passes of Syria and gave the kingdom of Jerusalem its strongest and most reliable military force.

In this they were soon equaled by the Knights Hospitaller (the Knights of St. John of Jerusalem). This order was originally founded at the time of the First Crusade as a hospitaller order to care for the sick and injured during the siege of Jerusalem. It had its origin in an old Amalfitan hospice for pilgrims in Jerusalem, which was taken over by the noble hospitallers when the city was captured. The Hospitallers remained a strictly hospital order until after the foundation of the Templars; then under their second Master, Raymond du Puy (1125–58) they turned into a military order like the Templars, whose bitter rivals they soon became. They too built fortresses in Syria, the most famous being the great Crac-des-Chevaliers (see our frontispiece) and received grants of land throughout Syria and Europe. These two orders provided Jerusalem with a strong, effective fighting force, but unfortunately the rivalry between them became so intense that in the later years of the kingdom they caused almost as much damage as they did good. Further they were both pledged to perpetual warfare against the Moslems and never respected well the truces which the secular princes made. The Hospitallers remained always something of a hospital order, their hospice at Jerusalem continuing to care for pilgrims long after the kingdom was lost. In the 1160's they were reported by the traveler, John of Wurzburg, as having as many as two thousand beds in their hospital and administering to the needs of countless outpatients and pilgrims, and as late as the 1480's, Felix Fabri found them capable of housing one thousand pilgrims at the nominal charge of two Venetian marks for an indefinite stay of up to a year.[6]

[6] John of Wurzburg and Felix Fabri are to be found in the Palestine Pilgrims' Text Society publications, Vols. XIV and XX.

CHAPTER 20

THE KINGDOM OF THE CRUSADERS

✛

THE GROWTH OF THE KINGDOM, 1118–44: ZANGHI

IF the rounding out of the frontiers of the kingdom was the work of Baldwin I the firm establishment of the royal power was the task of his successor Baldwin (1118–31). Baldwin du Burg, a cousin of Baldwin I's, had been given Edessa when Baldwin I became king of Jerusalem, and he succeeded him in the royal position by the election of the barons in 1118. Baldwin completed the filling in of the coast by capturing Tyre in 1124 with the aid of the Venetians, and he carried on an almost continuous war with the Egyptians and the Damascenes in which little was accomplished by either side, but he is most notable for his successful intervention in the affairs of the northern counties and for making his power as suzerain respected in Antioch, Edessa, and Tripoli. During the captivity or minority of the rulers of these states, Baldwin served as regent for both Antioch and Tripoli, both of which he tied to himself by marrying one of his daughters to the ruling prince.

The Moslems had finally shaken off the lethargy concerning the crusaders which had affected them in the earlier years, and attempted a definite revanche in the west. New governors were sent out by the sultan at Baghdad to lead the war against the Christians, and serious inroads into the Latin lands were made by Nur-al-Daula Balaq of Aleppo and by Aksunkur Al-Burski of Mosul. The real Moslem offensive began however with the capture of Aleppo by Imad al-Din Zanghi, atabeg of Mosul, in 1128. Zanghi united the two northern states of Mosul and Aleppo and then attacked the Latins. He was not primarily interested in fighting the *jihad* against the Franks, but in consolidating his power in northern Syria, and when the Franks got in his way he attacked them as he would any rival Moslem ruler. In 1144, Zanghi rounded out his possessions by overrunning the county and capturing the city of Edessa. It was not until later that this was seen to have been the crowning glory in the career of the hero of Islam.

Meanwhile Baldwin II had been succeeded on the throne of Jerusalem by his eldest daughter Melissende and her husband Foulque of Anjou (1131–43). Foulque was an old and experienced warrior and had already lived a full life in Anjou when he was selected to become the husband of the princess of Jerusalem. Leaving his son Geoffrey Plantagenet to rule

348

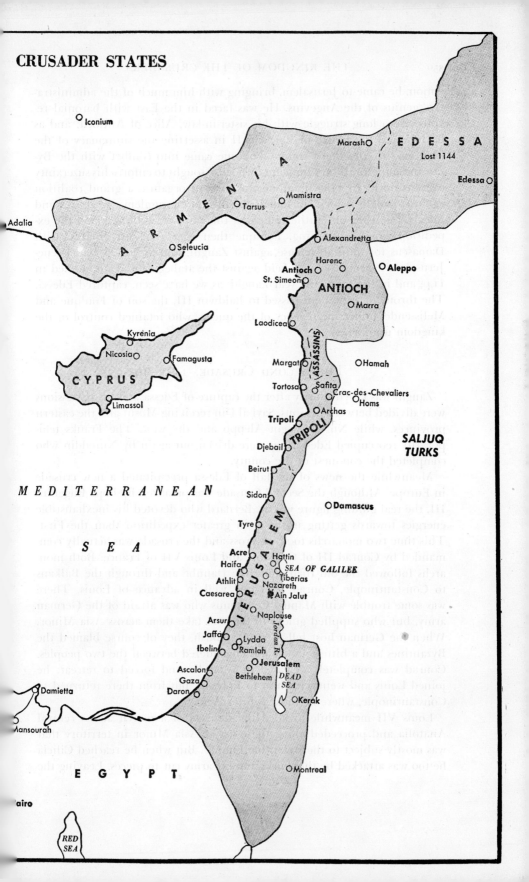

CRUSADER STATES

- Iconium

EDESSA

Marash

Lost 1144

Edessa

A R M E N I A

Mamistra

Tarsus

Adalia

Seleucia

Alexandretta

Harenc

Antioch **Aleppo**

St. Simeon

ANTIOCH

Marra

Laodicea

Kyrenia

Hamah

Nicosia Famagusta

Margat

CYPRUS

Tortosa Safita

Crac-des-Chevaliers

Limassol

Homs

Archas

Tripoli

SALJUQ
TURKS

Djebail

TRIPOLI

Beirut

M E D I T E R R A N E A N

Sidon

Damascus

S E A

Tyre

Acre Hattin

Haifa *SEA OF GALILEE*

Tiberias

Athlit Nazareth

Caesarea **Ain Jalut**

Naplouse

Arsur

Jaffa

Lydda

Ibelin Ramlah

Jerusalem

Ascalon Bethlehem *DEAD*

Gaza *SEA*

Damietta Daron

E G Y P T

Mansourah

Cairo

Montreal

Kerak

RED
SEA

(ASSASSINS)

JERUSALEM

Jordan R.

Anjou, he came to Jerusalem, bringing with him much of the administrative genius of the Angevins. He was faced in the East with baronial revolts and a long struggle with his sister-in-law, Alice of Antioch; and as he followed the policy of Baldwin II in asserting the supremacy of the king over the northern counts, Foulque came into conflict with the Byzantine emperor, John Comnenus, who also sought to enforce his suzerainty over Antioch. In 1138, Foulque was able to organize a grand coalition against Zanghi which included Byzantium, Jerusalem, Antioch, and Edessa, but after one futile campaign the emperor withdrew and the expedition came to nothing. Foulque then concluded an alliance with Damascus for mutual defense against Zanghi, and an allied Damascene-Jerusalemite army took the field against the atabeg. But Foulque died in 1143 and in the following year Zanghi, as we have seen, captured Edessa. The throne of Jerusalem passed to Baldwin III, the son of Foulque and Melissende, under the regency of the queen, who retained control of the kingdom until 1152.

THE SECOND CRUSADE, 1147–49

Zanghi was killed shortly after the capture of Edessa and his possessions were divided between his sons, Sayf al-Din receiving Mosul and the eastern provinces, while Nureddin got Aleppo and the west. The Franks temporarily reoccupied Edessa, but were driven out again by Nureddin who completed the conquest of the county.

Meanwhile the news of the fall of Edessa precipitated a new crusade in Europe. Although the Second Crusade was preached by Pope Eugenius III, the real guiding figure was St. Bernard who devoted his inexhaustible energies towards getting up an even greater expedition than the First. This time two monarchs took the cross and the crusade was actually commanded by Conrad III of Germany and Louis VII of France. Both monarchs followed the old road along the Danube and through the Balkans to Constantinople, Conrad marching well in advance of Louis. There was some trouble with Manuel Comnenus who was afraid of the German army, but who supplied guides to them to take them across Asia Minor. When the German host fell into an ambush, they of course blamed the Byzantines and a bitter enmity was engendered between the two peoples. Conrad was completely defeated in Anatolia and forced to retreat; he joined Louis and went with him to Ephesus, but from there returned to Constantinople, where he took ship for Acre.

Louis VII meanwhile avoided the dangers of a march across central Anatolia and proceeded along the coast of Asia Minor in territory that was mostly subject to the Byzantine Empire. But when he reached Cilicia he too was attacked by the Turks and his army cut to pieces. Leaving the infantry to manage as best they could, the French king and his nobles took ship from Adalia for Antioch. The crusade was doomed before it ever reached Syria.

When Louis reached Antioch he was lavishly received by Raymond of Poitiers, who had become prince of Antioch by marrying the princess Constance. Raymond was of the ancient house of Aquitaine and was himself the uncle of Eleanor of Aquitaine, Louis' queen. His reception of the queen was such that when Louis later divorced her on grounds of consanguinity, it was rumored that the real reason was because of her conduct in Antioch. At any rate the French king steadfastly refused to countenance a campaign for the benefit of Antioch, and insisted on pushing on to Jerusalem.

When the crusaders had reached Acre a great council was held to determine a plan of campaign. Although the rescue of Edessa was the announced objective of the crusade, it was agreed that Nureddin was too powerful to be attacked and a more likely opponent was sought. As the barons of Jerusalem were far more concerned in securing themselves than in succoring their northern neighbors, it was decided that the resources of the crusade should be devoted to the conquest of Damascus. That Damascus was the ally of Jerusalem against Nureddin did not matter; there was no chance of defeating Nureddin and there was a good possibility that Damascus might be taken. So the crusade moved against Damascus, "a city of great menace to us." [1]

The campaign against Damascus was one of the most ill-organized and futile in the history of warfare. After besieging the city from one side and bringing great distress on the inhabitants, the crusaders moved their camp to the other side of the city and began the siege anew from that point. Then, when their supplies began to run out, after holding a council it was determined to abandon the siege altogether. Many causes for this fiasco have been offered by contemporary and by modern writers. Some say that Thierry of Flanders wanted to keep Damascus when it was captured and that the Palestinian Franks had no interest in fighting for him; others say that Anar, the governor of Damascus, bribed some of the leaders to abandon the siege; others affirm that Anar threatened to turn the city over to Nureddin and that the Franks withdrew rather than have this happen. It is also suggested that Raymond of Antioch used his influence to make the siege fail as Louis had refused to help him in any way. Whatever the cause for the abandonment of the siege, the whole scheme was ridiculous, and the enterprise deserved no better success than it achieved. Conrad returned to Europe at once; Louis remained in Palestine for another year but accomplished nothing at all during that time. The only real result of the crusade, as far as Syria was concerned, was that the

[1] *William of Tyre*, trans. by Babcock and Krey, II, 186.

LATIN KINGS OF JERUSALEM AND CYPRUS

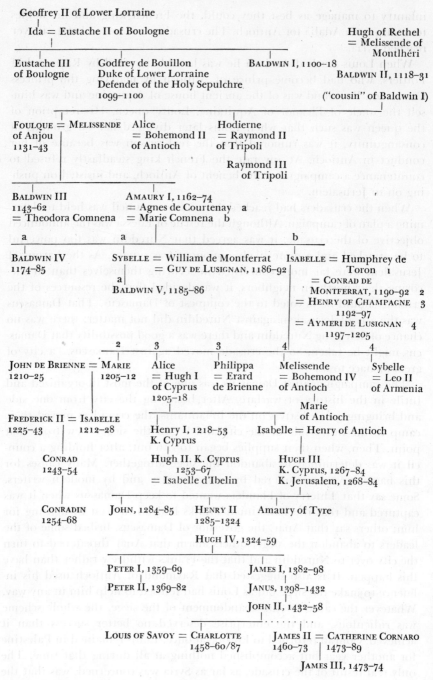

Geoffrey II of Lower Lorraine
  |
  Ida = Eustache II of Boulogne

Hugh of Rethel
= Melissende of
  Montlhéri

Eustache III
of Boulogne

Godfrey de Bouillon
Duke of Lower Lorraine
Defender of the Holy Sepulchre
1099–1100

BALDWIN I, 1100–18

BALDWIN II, 1118–31

("cousin" of Baldwin I)

FOULQUE = MELISSENDE
of Anjou
1131–43

Alice
= Bohemond II
of Antioch

Hodierne
= Raymond II
of Tripoli

Raymond III
of Tripoli

BALDWIN III
1143–62
= Theodora Comnena

AMAURY I, 1162–74
= Agnes de Courtenay   a
= Marie Comnena   b

a   a   b

BALDWIN IV
1174–85

SYBELLE = William de Montferrat
        = GUY DE LUSIGNAN, 1186–92
a
BALDWIN V, 1185–86

ISABELLE = Humphrey de
         Toron   1
      = CONRAD DE
        MONTFERRAT, 1190–92   2
      = HENRY OF CHAMPAGNE   3
        1192–97
      = AYMERI DE LUSIGNAN   4
        1197–1205

       2   3   3   4   4

JOHN DE BRIENNE = MARIE
1210–25   1205–12

Alice
= Hugh I
of Cyprus
1205–18

Philippa
= Erard
de Brienne

Melissende
= Bohemond IV
of Antioch
  |
Marie
of Antioch

Sybelle
= Leo II
of Armenia

FREDERICK II = ISABELLE
1225–43   1212–28

Henry I, 1218–53
K. Cyprus

Isabelle = Henry of Antioch

CONRAD
1243–54

Hugh II. K. Cyprus
1253–67
= Isabelle d'Ibelin

HUGH III
K. Cyprus, 1267–84
K. Jerusalem, 1268–84

CONRADIN
1254–68

JOHN, 1284–85

HENRY II
1285–1324

Amaury of Tyre

HUGH IV, 1324–59

PETER I, 1359–69

JAMES I, 1382–98

PETER II, 1369–82

JANUS, 1398–1432

JOHN II, 1432–58

LOUIS OF SAVOY = CHARLOTTE
         1458–60/87

JAMES II = CATHERINE CORNARO
1460–73 | 1473–89

JAMES III, 1473–74

Moslems ceased to fear the Franks and instead began to feel that they could be easily defeated. It also left bad blood between the Byzantines and the Latins.

The most important result of the crusade was incidental. A fleet of Flemish, English, Scandinavian, and German vessels had sailed for Syria from the harbors of northern Europe. On their way south they stopped in the county of Portugal and assisted its count to capture the city of Lisbon, which was later to become the capital of the Portuguese kingdom.[2]

NUREDDIN AND THE RISE OF SALADIN, 1148–74

The period between the Second and Third Crusades is marked primarily by the steady progress of Nureddin and after him Saladin in unifying Moslem Syria. The Latin states play out their little roles against the greater background of Moslem developments which they are powerless to prevent. Internally the kings grow stronger and under Amaury the Latin kingdom reaches its height of international power, but this greatness is wholly overshadowed by the steadily increasing power of Nureddin.

Baldwin III (1143–62) was one of the best and strongest kings Jerusalem had. His conquest of Ascalon in 1153 brought the kingdom to the farthest limit of its territorial expansion, but it was more than offset by Nureddin's capture of Damascus the year following, as this gave the Latin states a continuous frontier with Nureddin's empire and removed their last possible Syrian ally against the great conqueror. Baldwin was keenly aware of the seriousness of his position and made a close alliance with Byzantium, but got but little help. Before he could accomplish more, Baldwin died at the age of only thirty-three.

Amaury, his brother who succeeded him, brought the kingdom to its height of prestige in both external and internal affairs. He was a great legislator and secured the passage of assizes which strengthened the king in his relations with his barons, as well as compiling a commercial and maritime code for his kingdom. But he is best known for his campaigns in Egypt, in the course of which he succeeded temporarily in making Egypt subject to the Latin rule. This very expansion was, however, to lay the foundations for the destruction of his kingdom.

Fatimid Egypt had fallen on bitter days. The fainéant caliphs were dominated by viziers and by palace guards, until all power rested in the hands of their ministers and they were but puppets on gilded thrones. Ever since the capture of Ascalon, the Egyptians had paid tribute to the Franks of Jerusalem to purchase peace, but the payments were suddenly stopped

[2] The story of this expedition is told in C. W. David, *The Conquest of Lisbon*, Columbia: "Records." A similar expedition on the Third Crusade assisted in the capture of Silves and southern Portugal.

by the vizier in control at the moment. Urged on by the Hospitallers, Amaury invaded Egypt in 1163, only to become embroiled in Egyptian politics. Rival viziers allied respectively with the Franks and with Nureddin, and each invited their allies into the country to establish their own positions. Four times Amaury invaded Egypt in the years 1163 to 1168, and each time Shirkuh, the general of Nureddin, made a counter-invasion. For a time the Franks held Cairo, but were ultimately routed by Shirkuh, who deposed the Egyptian ministers and proclaimed the rule of Nureddin over the southern kingdom.

In his expeditions against Egypt, Shirkuh was accompanied by his nephew, Salah al-Din Yusuf ibn Ayyub, the famous Saladin, and at the death of Shirkuh in 1169 Saladin succeeded to the position of vizier of Egypt. Two years later (1171) Saladin quietly suppressed the Fatimid caliphate and proclaimed the name of the orthodox Sunna caliph of Baghdad in the Friday prayer. Thus easily, at the death of the last Fatimid caliph, was the Shia rule in Egypt ended and Saladin established as uncontested master of the Southern kingdom.

Nureddin naturally viewed with alarm the rapid rise of his lieutenant, but Saladin was most circumspect in his relations with his master; he always addressed him in the most humble manner and pretended to be only his officer and slave. Actually he avoided meeting the old sultan and stalled off any open conflict until the death of Nureddin in 1174, the same year in which Amaury of Jerusalem died.

SALADIN AND THE CONQUEST OF JERUSALEM, 1174–87

When Nureddin died, he left his dominions to his son, Salah, whom Saladin recognized to be "a young man unequal to the cares and responsibilities of sovereignty, and to the task of driving the enemies of God from the land." [3] Saladin therefore set out from Egypt and advanced into Syria where he took possession of Damascus so that he could "take upon himself the education of that prince, the administration of government and the re-establishment of order." To do this he had to fight and defeat Izz al-Din and Sayf al-Din of Mosul, as well as several of Nureddin's former generals. Nor was Salah properly grateful to his protector, for he allied himself with his kinsmen against Saladin. When he died in 1181 he deliberately willed his kingdom to his cousin, Izz al-Din of Mosul, but Saladin was able to defeat the Zanghids and bring Syria into his own possession by 1183. While engaged in the conquest of Moslem Syria, Saladin fought a few campaigns against the Christians, but he awaited the consolidation of his Moslem lands before attacking the Franks in force.

The kingdom of Jerusalem had meanwhile been ruled by a hopeless

---

[3] Beha ed Din: *Life of Saladin* (Palestine Pilgrims' Text Society XIII), 68–69.

leper. Baldwin IV (1174–85), the son of Amaury and his first wife Agnes de Courtenay, had been a leper from his earliest childhood. He was still a minor when he came to the throne so the regency was entrusted to his father's cousin, Count Raymond III of Tripoli, who was not only count of Tripoli and the king's nearest male relative in line of succession, but also by marriage lord of Tiberias, one of the largest fiefs of the southern kingdom.

While Saladin was busy getting control of Moslem Syria, he had little time for the Franks, but there was some fighting in which fortune favored first one side and then the other. The most spectacular event of this period was a mad expedition against Mecca in 1182–83 undertaken by Renaud de Chatillon, lord of Montréal, which accomplished nothing but to insult the Moslems and provoke against himself the undying hatred of the sultan. In 1182 Saladin raided into Frankish Syria and besieged Beirut, and in the next year, while Saladin was busy at Aleppo, the Franks besieged Damascus; but neither campaign had any results.

Then Baldwin's disease became so severe that he became totally blind and could no longer hope to attend to affairs of state. The question of the regency brought into open conflict two parties which had been developing during his reign. The "court party" was composed of the extremists, mostly first generation immigrants from Europe; while the "baronial party" was made up of the old Franco-Syrian aristocracy. The barons especially feared the influence and possible succession of Guy de Lusignan, the husband of Baldwin's sister, Sibylle, whom they felt with considerable justice to be incompetent and irresponsible. To prevent Guy's inheritance of the throne, the barons secured the coronation of Baldwin V, Sibylle's son by a former husband, but young Baldwin died after ruling only a few months (March 1185–September 1186) and Guy and Sibylle seized the throne. An attempt to crown Isabelle, the youngest sister of Baldwin IV and Sibylle, and her husband Humphrey de Toron failed, due to the weakness of Humphrey, and the barons were forced for lack of another candidate to accept the rule of Guy. Count Raymond, however, hedged his position by contracting an alliance with Saladin, and refused to accept the coronation of Guy. The count was only reconciled with the king after the invasion of the kingdom by Saladin had already begun in 1187.

It was Renaud de Chatillon, lord of Montréal, one of Guy's closest friends and supporters who broke the truce by attacking a Moslem caravan which was passing through his territories. It so happened that Saladin's own sister was captured in this raid, and when Renaud refused to surrender to the sultan, Saladin vowed personal vengeance on the lord of Montréal, and summoned his forces for the invasion of the kingdom of Jerusalem.

The barons at once sought to reconcile Raymond with the king, as they recognized their need of his leadership in the emergency. While an embassy was seeking Raymond, the Templars fought an engagement with some of Saladin's troops near Nazareth (May 1, 1187), in which the Knights were almost entirely wiped out. The news of this defeat moved Raymond to end his feud with Guy in the interests of the national safety, and while the count accompanied the king's envoys back to Jerusalem, Saladin moved in to besiege Raymond's castle and city of Tiberias, which was defended by his wife.

Thereafter events moved rapidly towards the climax. Guy summoned the Christian host to assemble at the fountain of Sephoria, a familiar rendezvous for campaigns towards the Jordan. There the leaders took counsel as to their tactics. Raymond urged that they remain quiet and await Saladin's attack; Renaud and the Templars insisted that they advance and attack Saladin, as he was besieging Tiberias. Raymond pointed out that it was his wife and his city that were being besieged, but that he yet could not sanction a march across the desert to meet the enemy. When the council broke up it had been agreed to follow this sage counsel, but during the night the Templars and Renaud persuaded Guy to change the plans and order an immediate advance.

The order was given to move out; in the blazing July sun the Frankish army tramped across the desert towards Tiberias. They soon became parched with thirst; Moslem raiders harassed them as they marched; their morale ebbed. Finally they camped, but as they had no water at their camp their discomfort was not abated. In the morning the Moslems attacked. The battle of Hattin sealed the fate of the kingdom of Jerusalem. Contemporaries report 20,000 men involved in the battle on the Christian side, and while the Moslems had roughly only the same number, they were fresh. Confusion overcame the Franks, whose lines were broken. Men threw down their arms and asked for water. Raymond, Balian d'Ibelin, and some of the knights cut their way through the Moslems and fled from the field. Guy, Renaud, and most of the leaders were captured; thousands of the lesser folk, the archers and infantry, were killed, as were great numbers of horses.

When the battle was ended Guy and Renaud were brought to Saladin's tent. There the sultan fulfilled his vow to wreak personal vengeance on the lord of Montréal, and Renaud was killed while Guy looked on in terror. But apart from Renaud, against whom he had a private grievance, Saladin did not kill his prisoners. All the Templars and Hospitallers were executed, as they were sworn enemies of Islam and would never ransom themselves save by their swords, but the secular lords were sent into captivity to Damascus, Aleppo, and other Moslem cities.

To raise the forces for the battle of Hattin, Guy had denuded the forts and cities of his kingdom of all defenders. Consequently the conquest of the country was easy after the one battle had been won. Hattin took place on July 4; on the 10th, Acre was captured; Djebail and Beirut fell in August, the refugees fleeing or being escorted by Saladin to Tyre. Then in September, Jerusalem itself was besieged. Balian d'Ibelin, who had come back to attempt the defense of the capital, was forced to arm and knight merchants and burgesses to obtain fighting men. The besieged resisted valiantly, but their cause was hopeless and when Saladin offered them liberal terms, the city capitulated on October 2, 1187. The contrast between the capture of Jerusalem in 1099 and that in 1187 is striking. Saladin allowed all those who could pay a ransom to do so; further, a thousand of the poorer folk were released at the request of Saphadin, Saladin's brother, another twelve hundred at that of the patriarch and Balian d'Ibelin, and finally Saladin freed all the aged and infirm himself as an act of grace. At the same time the patriarch was permitted to take away with him the treasure of the cathedral, Saladin scorning to confiscate what the patriarch held dearer than the lives of his co-religionists.

All the refugees sought shelter in Tyre, which soon became hopelessly overcrowded and ran short of provisions. The city was then besieged by Saladin and was on the point of surrender, when a fleet from Constantinople under the command of Conrad de Montferrat sailed into the harbor bringing them food, supplies, and reinforcements. More than that it brought them, in Conrad, a new leader around whom the resistance could center. Saladin abandoned the siege until a more promising time and turned to Ascalon, which surrendered in return for the liberation of King Guy. In doing this Saladin was wise, for he thus released the king whom he would rather have command against him than anyone else, since Guy's incompetency had been well proven. When Guy came before Tyre and demanded admission, Conrad refused to let him come in and forced him to encamp outside the city.

In his rapid conquest of the Latin kingdom, Saladin had systematically bypassed the strongest fortresses. Some of these he now besieged and took; others he merely isolated so that they could neither give nor receive any help. Apart from the northern counties, nothing remained in Christian hands except Tyre and a few scattered forts. The work of the First Crusade seemed wholly undone.

THE THIRD CRUSADE, 1189–92

When the word of the loss of Jerusalem reached Europe there was general lamentation and special masses of mourning were ordered for the Holy City. The pope immediately proclaimed a new crusade, and brought pressure to bear on the secular monarchs to take the cross. Frederick Barbarossa was the first to prepare. Henry II of England, his son Richard, and Philip II of France all took the cross, but it took much papal effort to stop their fighting in France and make them give thought to the crusade. Money was raised all over Europe to defray the expenses of the crusade: the pope levied a special tax on all ecclesiastics; Henry II established his famous Saladin Tithe on all movable goods, a measure which was quickly copied by Philip. But the leaders were slow in getting under way. Henry II died before his preparations were completed, Richard had to take care of the business of his succession to the throne before he could go, and Philip was always a reluctant crusader in no great hurry to depart. Smaller contingents got under way sooner however, and parties led by Jacques d'Avesnes, Henry of Champagne, Thibaut of Blois, the archbishop of Canterbury, the bishop of Beauvais, and others all started for the East before their monarchs were ready.

The locale for most of the action of the Third Crusade was selected by Guy de Lusignan. When Conrad refused to allow him to enter Tyre, Guy organized an army and went to besiege Acre where he was joined by the first contingents of crusaders from the West. But Saladin moved in against him and while the Christians besieged Acre the Moslems besieged the Christian camp. There both Moslems and Christians suffered great hardship and privation. From August 1189 to the spring of 1191 when the French and English kings arrived, the Christians besieged Acre without any noticeable effect, while Saladin lay behind them harassing them constantly. As usual with medieval armies their supply was haphazard and they feasted and starved alternately, depending on the ability of supply ships to get through to them.

Frederick Barbarossa was the first of the rulers to depart from the West. He left Germany in 1189 and followed the old pilgrim road to Constantinople, where he allied himself with Isaac Angelus, although Isaac had already made an alliance with Saladin. From Constantinople Frederick advanced into Asia Minor, to the great concern of Saladin who kept a close watch on him. But the sultan's fears were groundless, for Frederick drowned in the Saleph River (June 10, 1190). With the emperor's death his crusade broke up, and while some of the Germans went on to Acre, a good number returned to their homes.

Richard and Philip had meanwhile gotten under way, the two armies meeting at Vezelay and marching south along the Rhone. Richard took ship from Marseilles and Philip from Genoa, agreeing to meet at Messina. After a leisurely trip south, Richard came to Messina September 23, 1190, to find Philip awaiting him. Trouble broke out between the Sicilians and the English troops, which resulted in a riot to which Richard replied by storming the city and capturing it by force of arms, much to the annoyance of Philip.

After capturing Messina, Richard turned to King Tancred and demanded from him the dower of his sister Joan, the widow of William II. Tancred offered to repay the amount of the dower and to give his daughter in marriage to Richard's nephew, Arthur of Brittany, on which an alliance was concluded between the two kings, whereby Richard officially recognized Tancred as king of Sicily. This was to cost him dear when he later fell into the hands of Tancred's rival Henry VI of Germany. It was while they were wintering at Messina that arrangements were made for Richard's marriage to Berengaria of Navarre, whose dot brought him added supplies and money for the crusade.

Both monarchs left Messina in the spring of 1191, Philip proceeding directly to Acre where he arrived in April. Richard followed somewhat more slowly. While his main fleet was approaching Rhodes, a storm hit them, blowing several of the ships, among them the galley carrying Berengaria, off their track and onto the coast of Cyprus. Isaac Comnenus, the emperor of Cyprus,[4] captured the English ships, taking the queen prisoner. Richard again abandoning Acre for the time being immediately set out to avenge the honor of his crown and rescue his fiancée. He chased the unfortunate Isaac all over the island, rescued Berengaria whom he married at Limassol, captured the daughter of the Cypriot monarch, and forced the surrender of the emperor and the island. Having promised Isaac that he would never put him in irons, Richard kept his word by binding the emperor in special silver chains.

While Richard was in Cyprus, he was joined by Guy de Lusignan who came to seek his support against Conrad. During the siege of Acre Queen Sibylle had died and with her death Guy lost his title to the throne, at least in the opinion of his opponents. The barons seized upon Isabelle, the younger sister of Sibylle, with the intention of proclaiming her queen, but she was married to Humphrey de Toron, who had already failed the barons in 1186 when they tried to make him king. The bishop of Beauvais was willing to arrange a divorce so that Isabelle could marry a more worthy husband, and Isabelle was forced to divorce Humphrey and marry Conrad de Montferrat, whom the majority of the barons wished to be their king. As Conrad was recognized as the legitimate ruler by Philip when he arrived at Acre, Guy sought the aid of Richard, which that monarch was only too glad to give. Then, finally, after turning Cyprus over to the Templars, Richard went on to Acre.

The siege of Acre, after the arrival of the French and British contingents, was pushed on apace. But as the two monarchs were seldom willing to press the attack at the same time the siege dragged on longer than was necessary. Finally however they so weakened the defenses of the city, and

[4] Isaac declared himself an independent emperor at the time of the usurpation of Isaac Angelus.

wore out its garrison whose supplies were cut off by the superior Christian fleets, that the governor offered to surrender. On July 12, 1191 Acre fell; the crusaders made a triumphal entry; prisoners and plunder were divided; and Philip, who had been sick during the siege and who was at any rate sick of the crusade, prepared to return home. Leaving his men under the command of the duke of Burgundy, Philip departed at the end of July, while Richard planned a campaign which would liberate the Holy City of Jerusalem. By the terms of the capitulation there was to be a general exchange of prisoners, but when the Moslems failed to return their prisoners on exactly the day appointed, Richard executed some three thousand Moslems.

For the next year (July 1191–October 1192), Richard campaigned in Palestine. Marching south he defeated the Moslems in the battle of Arsur in September 1191 and engaged in a futile march towards Jerusalem during the winter months. He felt unable to capture the city, however, and so retreated to the coast where he turned south and refortified Ascalon. After some further futile campaigning and another major battle at Jaffa in August 1192, Richard finally agreed to a peace with the Moslems whereby the Christians were allowed to visit Jerusalem as pilgrims, and Jaffa, Caesarea, Arsur, and Caiphas were returned to the Latins. By this treaty the kingdom of Jerusalem was reconstructed only along the coast, with the Moslems holding the entire interior. Neither side considered the treaty more than a truce for three years and both expected that the war would be resumed after each had rested and strengthened himself. Richard then departed from Acre on October 9, 1192. Fearing that he might be waylaid on his way home, Richard chose to sneak back in disguise. He was captured in Austria, sold to the Emperor Henry VI and held for some months until a ransom could be arranged. Philip Augustus and Richard's brother, John, tried to purchase his continued imprisonment but the emperor finally released him after terms had been agreed upon.

The expedition of Richard has been a favorite theme for romantic writers. The personalities of both Richard and Saladin easily lend themselves to fabrication, and their relationships, as perverted and falsified by Sir Walter Scott and others, are the common knowledge of all schoolboys. The last word in corruption of the legend was said by Cecil B. DeMille in a cinema purporting to depict the crusade, but that was only the culmination of an old romantic trend. Actually the two monarchs never met, though Saladin did send Richard medicine and refreshments when the latter lay ill at Acre.

Saladin did not long outlive the crusade. He died in 1193 and his empire was divided between his three sons and his brother, Saphadin. But the division was only temporary as Saphadin was able to reunite the whole empire in his own hands before his death. The unification of the

Moslems, which had been begun by Zanghi and completed by Saladin, continued until it was broken by the contending sons of Saphadin in the second decade of the next century. Before Richard left Palestine he had had to surrender on one point. The barons of Jerusalem were so insistent on the dispossession of Guy de Lusignan and the recognition of Conrad as king that Richard finally gave in and accepted Conrad. Guy was compensated for the loss of his kingdom by being sold Cyprus which the Templars had recently returned to the English king. Conrad never enjoyed the throne as a crowned king, for on the eve of his coronation he was murdered by members of the dread sect of Assassins (April 28, 1192). That the throne should not be vacant, a compromise candidate was chosen in the person of Henry of Champagne, who was nephew of both Richard and Philip. Henry married Isabelle a few days after the murder of Conrad and received the homages of the Syrian barons. He never allowed himself to be crowned as he always expected to return to France, a vain hope, since he lost his life in 1197 when he fell from a tower window in Acre.

The Third Crusade was, from the papal point of view, a failure. While it had succeeded in recapturing Acre, Jaffa, and others of the coastal towns, Jerusalem still remained in the hands of the unbelievers. How the character of the crusades had changed is well illustrated in this movement. Of the leaders, only Frederick entered it with any religious motives, Richard went because it gave him a chance to win military glory, and Philip came along because he felt it was the correct thing to do. The main objective of the crusade was not Jerusalem but Acre, not the city of the holy places but the commercial capital of the Levant. The armies of Richard and Philip were both transported to the East in the galleys of the Mediterranean towns, whose increased importance is shown thereby. More and more the commercial interests of the Venetians, Genoese, Pisans, and Provençals took precedence over the religious aims of the pilgrims. The cities gained great wealth from the traffic in pilgrims and in Eastern wares. In the thirteenth century, the commercial greatly outstripped the religious in the motives of the Europeans, who attempted to preserve the Latin colonies on the Syrian coast, and the tendency had already shown itself by the Third Crusade.

CHAPTER 21

COMMERCE AND THE TOWNS

✣

REVIVAL OF COMMERCE

ONE of the real results of the crusades was the revival of international commerce between western Europe and the Levant. It was once thought that this revival was due entirely to the crusades: now we know that the crusades merely stimulated a commercial revival which was already under way when they began, but their influence was nevertheless great. The reappearance of international commerce on a comparatively large scale was due primarily to the commercial activities of the Venetians and other Italian cities in the Mediterranean, and to the trade of the Scandinavians in the Baltic. European trade never actually died out, but it diminished to a meagre trickle throughout most of the Continent; Venetian trade with Byzantium and the commerce of the Scandinavians in the north however always kept alive some measure of international activity.[1]

As long as the Mediterranean was in Moslem hands, Christian trade languished; Venice always maintained trade relations with Constantinople, however, and with the opening of the Mediterranean on a larger scale, the Republic of St. Mark was in a good position to take the lead in the new commercial activity. Genoa and Pisa, too, entered early into the competition, their combined fleets sweeping the Moslems out of the Tyrrhenian sea and gaining the mastery over the western Mediterranean in the early years of the eleventh century. But it was the First Crusade which opened up the Levant and the eastern Mediterranean and inaugurated the great revival of East-West trade between the ports of Syria and those of Italy. We have already seen how the Italian cities gained concessions in the ports of the crusader states, founding there commercial colonies.

It is important to note that international commerce developed before internal; it was from the stimulus of the international trade that the local traffic within western Europe developed. As the Eastern goods were made available in the Mediterranean ports, new markets developed in the inland

---

[1] H. Pirenne, *Economic and Social History of Medieval Europe,* a translation of Pirenne's chapter in the Glotz, *Histoire du Moyen Age,* VIII, is, in my opinion, the best single work on medieval commerce and the towns and is the basis for most of the ideas and information contained in this chapter. Since the work of Pirenne older histories of medieval trade and towns have been rendered completely obsolete. This little volume sums up the theories of the great master in a short, clear, readable volume of 250 pages.

cities of the West, and new trade routes across country were opened up. Along the trade routes, with the growth of the trade, rose the new towns, which in turn became both commercial and industrial centers, producing their own wares to add to the stream of commerce. The towns developed especially where merchants had to unload their wares for trans-shipment, where they transferred from ship to caravan, where they left ocean-going ships to be loaded into smaller craft, where the main roads crossed rivers, or where two main routes crossed. This accounts for the importance not only of the great ports, but for the Lombard towns and those of Champagne and Flanders.

The quantity of medieval trade was, of course, slight by modern standards, and the difficulties of travel were immense. Ships were small: Venetian ships of the thirteenth century averaged about five hundred tons cargo while those of Genoa were only slightly larger, and English ships of the fourteenth century rarely surpassed two hundred to three hundred tons capacity. For the Mediterranean coastal trade, oared galleys were employed, sailing ships or mixed oared-and-sail ships being used for the Levantine trade. Cabins were first developed in the thirteenth century, and even then they were reserved for royalty or such distinguished passengers, the ordinary merchants and travelers sleeping on deck, each man having his space marked off by chalk lines. Instead of our modern system where a passenger can take along baggage, in the Middle Ages passengers went with the freight, and if a merchant contracted for a certain amount of cargo space he was given passage for a factor to represent him and to watch over the safety of his goods. In case of storm and danger, the master of the ship had the right to lighten ship by throwing overboard any of the cargo, but the factor could stipulate which of his bales should be jettisoned first. In the age of the crusades, so much more important was the East-West than the West-East trade, that a merchant buying cargo space from Acre to Genoa would often be given an equivalent amount on the outward voyage.

Transport of goods by ship was the most satisfactory and easiest method throughout the Middle Ages, but even so it was attended by many hazards. The ships were small and light and often fell victims of storm. And for those which could weather the elements there was always the danger from pirates and privateers. Piracy, throughout the Middle Ages as in Antiquity, was a popular profession among sea-faring men, and the line between the honest merchant and the buccaneer was often a thin one, especially as letters of reprisal were in general use. If a Venetian ship should be plundered by a Genoese corsair, the captain of the ship would apply to the Venetian government for letters of reprisal, which granted him the right to take the equivalent of the goods stolen from any Genoese ship. He would promptly despoil the first Genoese ship he found; the Genoese merchant would then get letters from his government permitting him to avenge himself on the first Venetian he encountered. Thus an unending chain would be started, which very often spread to the merchants of other cities as the holders of the letters were not always too scrupulous in collecting their damages to ascertain for sure that the person attacked was of the enemy city, and a Marseillais or Barcelonian would serve as well as a Genoese or Venetian. The slowness of communications also made for trouble; many a merchant lost his ship and cargo by sailing into what he considered to be a friendly port, only to find that war had been declared while he was at sea.

Elaborate codes of maritime law were developed by the commercial cities, some of which received international acceptance. The Byzantine sea code, known as the Rhodian Sea Law, the Usages of Barcelona, and the Customs of Oleron were all widely recognized codes of maritime law, providing laws for maritime contracts, flotsam and jetsam, and the responsibility of shipper and carrier. In many of the ports special courts, known as Courts of the Chain (from the chain which guarded the harbors), were established to handle maritime disputes.

In the Mediterranean shipping, there were two great *passages* each year when the winds were most favorable. The best time to go from Italy to Syria was in April or June; the return trip was made in August by the galleys, and in September or October by the heavier sailing ships. The cargoes carried were usually pilgrims, timber, and woolen goods from Europe to the East, and spices, cottons, alum, fruits, silk, perfumes, and other luxury goods from the East to Europe.

When the traffic had to be done by land conditions of transport were even more difficult. The roads were terrible: the old Roman roads had fallen into disrepair, and great ruts furrowed the highways. Light carts with two huge wheels, which were common throughout the Middle Ages and are found in some rural areas still today, were designed to straddle the ruts and holes of the medieval road. Many roads were utterly unusable by carts, so that goods had to be carried in packs on horses or donkeys. Bridges were another hazard, as they were generally non-existent until the bridge-building associations of the thirteenth century began to remedy the situation. Monasteries would undertake the building or repair of bridges in their neighborhoods, but the great work was done by the townsmen or by the religious associations of bridge builders, sponsored by the church, which put up most of the more important bridges built in the late twelfth and thirteenth centuries. The possession of a good bridge was a source of income to a town, and a feature which often influenced its growth. Some of the great bridges of the time were those of London, Paris, Rouen, and Avignon.

Even where there were roads and bridges the merchants suffered disadvantages from the very improvements, as tolls were collected everywhere. There were 74 toll stops on the Loire river, 64 on the Rhine, 77 on the Danube, and 35 on the Elbe, even after a number had been abolished. And travel on the roads was even more expensive than on rivers or canals. Travelers were taxed when they entered the gate of a town or the territory of a lord, each merchant had to give something from his wares, and jongleurs and trouvères were compelled to sing a song or put on a trick or two before entering the gate. Robbers and brigands were common, and while some lords endeavored to keep the roads through their domains free of bandits, others joined in the sport themselves and preyed on the merchants who did not buy their protection. We have already seen how Renaud de Chatillon precipitated a war by attacking a caravan which went through his lands at Montréal in Syria. Only in the Moslem lands and in Norman Sicily and South Italy were the roads kept safe by the government.

One of the results of the hazards of travel was that merchants did not move about alone, but always went in caravans, grouped together for protection. Another was the development of joint stock companies.

The joint stock company seems to have been engendered in Italy for the Levantine trade. At first a merchant would entrust his goods or money to the master or supercargo of a ship, who would carry it East, sell it there, reinvest the money in Asiatic wares, and bring it back to Italy, the merchant and the sailor dividing the profits equally. Later merchants hired vessels to take their wares, in which case they made a larger profit. But if a merchant put all his goods in one ship and that was lost he would probably be ruined, so the practice developed whereby several merchants would go together to charter several ships. Thus each had an interest in each ship and if one or two were lost, they could still show a profit on the remainder. When the voyage was over, each merchant would take out his profits and the association was disbanded. From this it was a natural step to the stock company where people could invest smaller sums in a voyage, receiving proportionate shares of the profits. The longest step was when the association ceased to end with the voyage, but remained in existence to conduct expeditions from year to year. The greatest of these companies was the famous Bank of St. George of Genoa which was to be pre-eminent in the following centuries.

MONEY, BANKING, AND INSURANCE

Maritime insurance developed with the great expansion of trade. As part of the process described in the paragraph above, banks arose in Italy, which would insure the investment of the merchant for a voyage, and from this maritime insurance rose the whole structure of modern insurance practice.

Banking also became a recognized profession in this period. It is quite wrong to believe that the Middle Ages were a period of pure barter economy, and Pirenne has proven that there was always a certain amount of exchange of currency. In the early Middle Ages it was not great, and the manorial economy probably got along with very little ready cash, but there was always some need for money and Europe has never been without some circulation of currency. Of course, in the Byzantine and Moslem East a money economy flourished in the days of the lowest ebb of Western business, but even in Europe there was always some. The local currencies which prevailed throughout Europe were naturally a great hindrance to trade, but in 1192 the Venetians issued their silver *groat* which almost immediately found great popularity and was copied by other cities. In 1266 Louis IX of France issued the *gros tournois* and the *gros parisis* at Tours and Paris respectively, which soon became the standard coins of northern Europe. The resumption of a gold currency in the West came with the *augustales* of Frederick II in 1231, but the first gold coin to become popular was the Florentine *florin* of 1252. Gold was found necessary when international trade developed extensively, and we find gold coins minted by St. Louis in France, and by the kings of England, Castile, Bohemia, and the counts of the Low Countries in the fourteenth century.

The use of money brought with it the development of credit. Jews had always loaned money against security, such as modern pawnbrokers do today, and had received therefrom interest of about 43 per cent. But banking on a larger scale was undertaken by the Italian merchants, who would loan their extra money on good security at rates of interest that varied from 10 to 16 per cent. While the Church banned usury, it recognized the right of the lender to receive compensation at a just rate for the inconvenience endured while his money was out at loan. A man would borrow money to be repaid at a given date, and when he did not repay on the date assigned would be charged damages for the time until restitution was made.

One of the difficulties about early banking was that so many of the loans were strictly consumption loans. A lord would borrow money for his ordinary expenses which he found it difficult to repay. Insolvency was not considered a disgrace among even the highest nobility, and the securities put up were often in the form of a lien on future revenues. In this way the Templars became the creditors and at the same time the tax gatherers for the papacy. Kings followed the same procedure and it was the loans made by the Templars to the king of France that caused their downfall, when Philip IV found himself unable to repay and took the easy way out by liquidating his creditor.

Banking was, in fact, the chief business of the Templars for some time. With strong castles both in Europe and the East, the Templars had developed a system whereby the pilgrim to Jerusalem could deposit funds in the Temple at Paris, London, or any other European city, and be given a letter of credit payable at houses of the order on his route and in the East. Thus a Parisian would deposit in Paris, cash some at Marseilles, and finally cash his letter at Acre. He could reverse the process for his return trip. This was most useful as it got around the serious problem of transporting cash, the Templars sending bullion under heavy guard when necessary to bring up the balances at either end. From this it was an easy step to loaning money, and the Templars soon became the creditors of most of the great of Europe.

The same general process took place in the Italian towns. Merchants would go together to loan money to the papacy or to a king or count. The great commercial houses became bankers, and the "Lombards" soon secured the greater part of the banking business of the West. The Bardi, Peruzzi, Frescobaldi, Scotti, were all merchant houses which engaged in banking along with their trade. In the twelfth century we find a great development of commercial credit, the borrowing of money for investment and further profit.

An interesting development was that of the "life rents" whereby the towns financed themselves. Loans against real estate had been common for some time, but a new form of loan was worked out whereby the lender loaned his money to the municipal corporation against a "life rent"— an income to be paid the holder until his death. These early annuities could be purchased for the term of one or two lives, and proved most popular. Thus early did the towns fund their indebtedness. It is noteworthy that these municipal bonds, if we may so term them, paid a very low rate of interest and yet nevertheless were much more in demand than the promissory notes of rulers, who offered higher interest, but whose credit was much less sure.

DEVELOPMENT OF INDUSTRY

As commerce expanded, local industry arose to participate in the flow of trade. The crude manorial economy was unsuited to the needs of towns and trade, and various crafts developed in the towns, some devoted to the production of the necessities for local usage, others to that of manufacturing goods for the export market. In every town we find gilds of bakers, blacksmiths, tailors, butchers, and in the larger towns the gilds of wool and silk merchants, armorers, and vintners who dealt in commodities essentially for export.

The gilds were associations of workers in the same craft, banded together, under the auspices of a patron saint, into a fraternity which regulated prices, conditions of manufacture and sale, and standards of quality. The gild was made up of masters, under whom worked apprentices who were learning the trade, and journeymen. These journeymen were hired laborers and made up the urban proletariat. The gild was at the same time the creation of the workers themselves and of the municipal authorities who used the gilds to regulate industry.

Work was all done in the home. The master would have his *atelier,* where he worked and where he sold his wares. Two or three apprentices lived in his house and assisted him in his labors, while for extra help he could hire journeymen at a fixed wage. How similar were industrial conditions in the Middle Ages and today is evidenced by the strikes of journeymen, with which the industrial history of the thirteenth century is marked. The tools and the raw materials of the craft were the property of the master, who made up his goods and sold them direct to his customers. The middleman did not appear at first, but the merchant who bought in one town to sell in another soon developed, and it was in this way that the Italian merchants grew so wealthy. Only at the end of the Middle Ages did the masters sell their services to Italian merchants, who supplied the raw materials and hired them by the piece to make up the finished goods.

The great staple of Western European manufacture was woolen cloth. In this industry the towns of Flanders—Ghent, Ypres, Bruges—were preeminent. In Flanders was found the precious fuller's earth, which was necessary to the treatment of wool, and in Flanders developed the greatest weaving centers. The raw wool was generally imported from England, which, together with Spain, produced the finest wool of medieval Europe. This had a tremendous effect on the economy of both England and Flanders, as the English became essentially a nation of sheep raisers, while the Flemings bought the wool to make into woolen cloth, which they sold for export all over the world. Woolen cloth was the one Western product to be exported in any great quantity to the East. In Florence, where the weaving industry also developed to a high degree, a special process of treating the rough woolen cloth to make a smoother finer fabric was the monopoly of the famous and wealthy Calimalla Gild.

It is worthy of notice that mining developed very little during the Middle Ages, iron mining being a very small industry and coal mining hardly existing at all except in one or two localities. The scepticism shown Marco Polo when he described how the Chinese burned black stones shows how little Europe had learned the use of coal at the end of the thirteenth century.

THE FAIRS

An important part in medieval commerce was played by the great fairs. While there were local markets in the towns, the fairs were the great international markets where the great bulk of trade was carried on. Most important of the medieval fairs were those of Champagne: Lagny in January,

Bar in Lent, Provins in May, Troyes in June, Provins again in September, and a second fair at Troyes in October. As each fair lasted about six weeks there was not much time between them, and merchants went from one fair to another.

These fairs, as Pirenne has defined them, "were periodical meeting-places for professional merchants. They were centers of exchange, and especially of wholesale exchange, and set out to attract the greatest possible number of people and of goods, independent of all local consideration." [2]

Merchants from every part of Europe attended these fairs. After a formal opening, a period of days would be set aside for the dealing in each product: wool, hides, wine, so that each man would be free to sell his own wares and at the same time to purchase the goods of others. At the end of the fair some time was reserved for the exchange of money and the clearing up of accounts. These "money fairs" were great centers for financial exchange. During the fair operations were generally conducted on credit, and at the end the merchants would exchange their bills of credit. Thus if a Bruges merchant sold to a Genoese, who in turn sold to a man from Cologne, who had sold to a merchant from Bruges, the note would probably pass along until it came to the Bruges merchant, thus avoiding payment in all sorts of specie. But there was also a regular exchange of money, where the values of the various currencies were established and exchange of bills effected.

The fairs of Champagne were, of course, not the only fairs. Equally famous was the great Fair of the Lendit at St. Denis outside of Paris. This fair was opened annually by a solemn procession from the University, when the faculty and students went out to the fair to buy pens, inks, and parchments for their current use. The students seem to have tarried to participate in the wine fair also, though here their purchases were at retail and for immediate consumption. Other great fairs were those of Beaucaire (near Marseilles) and Aix in France, Frankfort in Germany, Ypres and Bruges in Flanders, Stamford and Winchester in England, and Nizhni-Novgorod in Russia.

Business was not the only attraction of the fairs; like our county and state fairs today, they were centers of all sorts of amusements; jugglers, dancing and fighting bears, cockfights, races, and all manner of attractions were offered for the enjoyment of the visitors. While the type of entertainment probably differed considerably, the "midways" of the medieval fairs probably attracted people just as those of our expositions do now, and there is no reason to think that they did not have dancing girls and similar side-shows along with the cockfighting, dancing, and bear-baiting.

But if the great international wholesale business was conducted at the

[2] Pirenne, *Economic and Social History of Medieval Europe*, p. 98, reprinted by permission of the publishers, Harcourt, Brace and Co.

fairs, the bulk of the trade took place in the permanent markets set up in the towns. It was there that the goods generally reached the ultimate consumers and to the towns we must now turn our attention.

THE RISE OF THE TOWNS

The problem of the origins of the medieval towns was one which produced much controversial literature, several theories being advanced by eminent historians to explain why the towns grew up where they did and why they developed the institutions that they had. One theory as to the origin of the towns was that they were the relics of the old Roman towns; another was that they developed around monasteries; a third saw their origin in the manorial villages. However, the researches of the great Belgian scholar, Henri Pirenne, have finally put an end to such speculation and there are only a few die-hards who do not today accept as correct the Pirenne theory of the growth of the towns from commercial settlements. One school for long held that the towns caused the development of the trade instead of being the result, but statistical studies show that the great increase in population of the towns developed only *after* the establishment of permanent markets, and that the town clearly resulted from and did not cause the growth of commerce.

The location of the town was due primarily to its position in relation to routes of trade. Towns developed, as we have stated above, at the crossings of roads and at places where goods were unloaded for transshipment. The merchants at first came to the old feudal *burg* where they brought luxury goods for the lord of the castle; but they had to pay a toll to enter the gate of the burg, so they set up their stands outside the walls. Gradually a permanent market developed; the merchants established a "factory," a permanent depot for their goods with a small settlement of traders permanently settled there. Without the walls, however, they found themselves in dire need of protection, and they early purchased the rights to fortify their settlements. These mercantile settlements, outside the walls, were termed faubourgs (*foris burgensis*), and it is in them that the institutions of the medieval town developed. The merchants banded together to obtain rights from the lord of the burg; they purchased a charter which gave them the right to fortify their faubourg, to have their own elected officials, and to deal collectively with the lord or his agent.

It must always be remembered that these merchants were free men; the inhabitants of the burgs were servile. That the merchants were often the younger sons of serfs, who had run away and thus secured their freedom, is irrelevant; they were originally landless men, but they devoted themselves to trade and acquired wealth or at least a moderate substance. And they were free.

Without liberty, that is to say, without the power to come and go, to do business, to sell goods, a power not enjoyed by serfdom, trade would be impossible. Thus they claimed it, simply for the advantages which it conferred, and nothing was further from the mind of the bourgeoisie than any idea of freedom as a natural right; in their eyes it was merely a useful one.[3]

The essential characteristic of the organization of the mercantile community was its free association. They were not subject to the arbitrary tallage of any lord, but for their own common needs they voted taxes on themselves; for their common defense they subjected themselves to military liability; for their own security, they established their own merchants courts and developed a law to deal with mercantile problems unthought of in the older feudal laws.

The presence of these mercantile settlements outside their walls acted as a great leavening force on the inhabitants of the burgs. They, too, sought this liberty of action, this freedom from tallage and from the jurisdiction of the lord's court. Following the lead of the merchants, they sought charters granting them liberties.

These charters were secured by rebellion and violence, by gift or by purchase. Those which were secured by violence were liable to be ephemeral for the lords rescinded them as soon as they had the power. Such towns as Laon fought for decades before they finally secured their liberties. The most common and most satisfactory way to procure a charter of liberties was by purchase, and the crusades gave a great impetus to this movement as the lords needed ready cash for their pilgrimage and so were willing to sell charters to the townsmen. Some lords, sensing the value of towns in their territories, voluntarily gave charters to their towns, but these were the exception. Civil war was often advantageous to the towns, both contestants giving charters to secure the support of the townsmen. Thus the Flemish towns got great concessions during the war between William Clito and Thierry of Alsace in the early twelfth century, London secured privileges under Stephen and John, and the German cities profited from the struggle between Hohenstaufen and Guelph. The kings of France, Louis VI and Philip II, granted charters of liberties to their towns to secure their aid against the feudal nobility; the Hohenstaufen likewise sought the support of the towns in their struggles with the petty dynasts of their domain lands. A city like Venice developed independently of any control; Venice was always a merchant town and never knew anything but the freedom of the mercantile communities.[4]

[3] Pirenne, *Economic and Social History of Medieval Europe*, p. 51. Reprinted by permission of the publishers, Harcourt, Brace and Co.

[4] For the rise of the medieval towns Carl Stephenson, *Borough and Town: A Study of Urban Origins*, (1933), is a most scholarly and excellent study. See especially his first appendix where he discusses the various theories concerning the communes.

TYPES OF TOWNS: COMMUNES

The charters procured by the towns brought varying degrees of emancipation. Medieval towns were generally divided into three categories: 1. completely unprivileged towns whose inhabitants were the serfs of the lord and who were exploited at will; 2. towns of limited liberties (*villes de bourgeoisie*); and 3. communes. The term *city* throughout the Middle Ages had nothing to do with the size of the town, but indicated that it was the seat of a bishop; the smallest village with a cathedral church was a city, while the largest without was merely a town.

Between the domainial town and either of the chartered towns was a wide gap, but between the towns of limited liberties and the communes there was less actual difference. The town of limited liberties had a charter which protected the inhabitants against any extraordinary exactions on the part of the lord. Their charter guaranteed that they would receive justice in the lord's court held in the town; that they would not be amenable to any jurisdiction outside the town; that they would not be arbitrarily summoned for military duty; that they would not be tallaged at will, but would be allowed to pay their taxes at stated intervals and at stated rates. Such charters were popular with both townsmen and lords, and were the most commonly used throughout northern Europe; the townsmen remained under the control of the lord but their rights as individuals were guaranteed. A number of these charters of limited liberties gained great popularity and were copied throughout extensive regions. Thus the charter of Lorris was the model for charters throughout France, Berry, and Burgundy; that of Peronne was copied in Vermandois, Picardy, and Artois; Rouen influenced Gascony, Poitou, and Guyenne; the famous charter of Beaumont, given by Archbishop William of the White Hands of Rheims, was copied by more than five hundred towns in Champagne, Lorraine, France, and Flanders; Normandy and England followed the charter of Bretueil, granted by William the Conqueror, or that of Newcastle-on-Tyne given by Henry I. The most popular charter in Germany was that of Freiburg-im-Breisgau, of 1120, which was based on the liberties of Cologne, and which in turn was copied by towns throughout western Germany. Paris throughout the Middle Ages was only a ville de bourgeoisie and not a commune.

The communes were corporate self-governing communities. Luchaire has defined them as "corporate feudal persons" and pointed out that as collective seigneuries they fitted themselves into the pattern of feudalism, the signs of their corporate lordship being the bell tower, the *hôtel de ville*, the corporation seal, and often a gallows. This distinction does not, however, always hold up, and Professor Carl Stephenson in his *Borough and*

Town, has proven that these emblems of the seigneury were often found in towns of limited liberties. The communes did, however, have their own municipal officers who governed the town on behalf of the citizen body. In England, Normandy, France, and Germany these were usually a mayor and council; in Flanders and Picardy a committee of *jurées* or *eschevins;* in Genoa two *consuls;* in the Italian cities generally a *podesta.* Luchaire's theory is supported by the fact that in greater towns the mayor was termed the Lord Mayor and ranked with the nobles of the realm while he held office.

The citizens of the commune by no means included all the people living within the town; citizenship was restricted to a small group, usually those who had helped obtain the charter. In many towns the members of the gilds had gone together to secure the charter and only gild members were voting citizens of the commune. To the noncitizens the commune gave less liberty than did the charters of the villes de bourgeoisie as they were left unprotected against the exactions of the commune, but to the citizens it gave self-government.

In the cases of those communes which had won their charters through revolt, the franchise was generally much larger. In these cases there was generally a "sworn commune," i.e. the people got together and swore to win their freedom and charter and to obey only the communal officers. At one time it was thought that the sworn association was the essential characteristic of the commune, but this theory, supported by the English scholar J. H. Round among others, has been discredited by the scholars of the Pirenne school. However, sworn communes were prevalent in many towns, the movement spreading as far as crusader Syria, where sworn communes are found at Antioch, Acre, and Tripoli in the thirteenth century. We have already seen how the Italian towns secured their liberties from their feudal lords and struggled to maintain them against Frederick Barbarossa. In northern Europe charters were won by revolt in the years between 957 and 1127 by Cambrai, Morville, Chateau-Cambreisis, St. Quentin, Beauvais, Arras, Amiens, Soissons, Bruges, Lille, St. Omer, and other towns. The movement spread to southern France somewhat later, communes being established in Montpellier, Beziers, Toulouse, and Nîmes between 1142 and 1207.

Not all the communal revolts were even eventually successful. Chateauneuf revolted twelve times and was always defeated; Orleans was defeated twice and her communes destroyed, Laon won her charter in 1106, lost it in 1112, revolted again and was suppressed by the king, and only finally won her independence in 1128.

The nobles and the churchmen hated the communes which they felt were destroying their legitimate control over their serfs;

Now Commune is a new and bad name of an arrangement for all the poorest classes to pay their usual due of servitude to their lords once only in the year, and to make good any breach of the laws they have committed by the payment fixed by law, and to be entirely free from all other exactions usually imposed on serfs.[4]

This definition, taken from Abbot Guibert de Nogent, shows clearly the attitude of the clergy towards the communes in the early twelfth century.

In the communes of the north, the nobles had no place and were, indeed, the traditional enemies. In the south, on the other hand, the nobles were forced to come into the communes, where, after submitting to the commune, they were allowed special privileges, such as putting towers on their town houses.

Many lords recognized the value of having towns on their domains and deliberately built towns, to which they tried to attract their neighbors' serfs. These towns, called *villes neuves, bastides* or *freiburgen* were regularly laid out and granted charters of limited liberties on their foundation. The number of villeneuves and villefranches in France, of freiburgs in Germany, of newtowns in England and of villenovas and villafrancas in Italy attest the spread of these "made" towns.

An interesting extension of the idea of urban liberties occurred in the "rural communes" of France, where a number of rural villages would go together to secure a charter of urban liberties. This was especially prevalent in Alsace and in the region of the Pyrenees.

TOWN LEAGUES

The greatest concentrations of cities were in northern Italy, Flanders, along the Rhine and on the shores of the Baltic. And in most of these districts we find the development of town leagues, organized for the mutual protection of their liberties. We have already encountered the Lombard League of Milan, Crema, Brescia, Bergamo, and other cities of northern Italy which united to oppose Frederick Barbarossa. Other leagues, less important politically but more so economically, were the leagues of the Flemish towns (Ghent, Bruges, Ypres, Antwerp, Lille, Liége, St. Omer, et al) and the Baltic Hanse (Lübeck, Bremen, Hamburg, etc.). Similar leagues were developed among the Rhine towns and elsewhere. The Flemish League, known as the Hanse of London, because it traded with England, was very powerful in the thirteenth and fourteenth centuries, while the Baltic Hanse reached its height politically and economically in the fifteenth. These leagues provided for favorable reciprocal tariffs among the members cities, and even maintained navies to protect their shipping. The Hanse became the master of the Baltic, controlling the island of Wisby, and planting colonies in London (the Steelyard) and in distant Novgorod.

[4] Guibert de Nogent, *Autobiography*, quoted from Scott, Hyma, Noyes, *Readings*, p. 304.

The money of the Baltic Hanse, the currency of the "Easterlings," gave England her pound sterling, but in the thirteenth century the chief trading center of the north was the city of Bruges. Bruges was unique in that she was not only a great commercial, but also a wealthy industrial town, and much of the trade that passed through her port consisted in the export of her own produce.

In the south, Venice, Genoa, Pisa, Marseilles, and Barcelona were the chief ports of the western Mediterranean, but their trade was challenged by the southern towns of Palermo, Salerno, Amalfi, and Naples. The intense rivalries of the Italian cities prevented their even getting together for more than short periods and kept any of them (with the possible exception of Venice) from developing to the fullest capacities. Lisbon in Portugal, and Bordeaux and Bayonne in Gascony were important Atlantic ports, Bordeaux doing a thriving trade both in wines and in salt.

EFFECT OF THE TOWNS ON INSTITUTIONS AND SOCIETY

The rise of the towns gave Europe a new class, the bourgeoisie, which fitted but badly into the feudal scheme of society. Sprung from the serfs, they were able, through the wealth they controlled, to mingle with the nobles, though they seldom achieved social equality. And the feudal nobility did well to mistrust the bourgeoisie for they represented the forces which were to destroy feudalism and the nobles themselves. Money began to replace land as a criteria of wealth; the landed noble could no longer have everything his own way for the *nouveaux riches* of the towns challenged his position.

It was from these bourgeoisie, who went to the universities and became the professional classes, that the kings of the late thirteenth and fourteenth centuries were to find their ablest ministers. In Italy the thirteenh century saw the triumph of the *populo* over the nobles in such cities as Florence and Bologna. The new mercantile society gradually replaced the old feudal and left the nobles mere anachronisms—but that was a development of the period after the limits of this chapter. Suffice it here to note that while the bourgeoisie were the butt of jokes on the part of the nobles and were generally looked down on socially, they were, by the end of the thirteenth century, making their power felt politically and socially as well as economically, and the future was all theirs.

CHAPTER 22

FEUDAL SOCIETY

✤

CASTLE LIFE

OF the three major classes of society—nobles, bourgeoisie and peasants,
—the nobles in the twelfth century had by far the most comfortable
life, but even their living conditions left much to be desired from our
modern point of view. It is difficult to describe social conditions in the
Middle Ages as they were not static, and between the rude castle life of the
tenth century and the greater comfort and ease of the fourteenth there is a
tremendous difference. We shall endeavor to describe the life of the nobles
in the twelfth century, but some of our remarks will be more applicable
to the thirteenth, as institutions, like chivalry, which began in the twelfth,
only reached their full development in the century following.

The center of the noble's life was his castle; whether he be lord of a vast
county or owner of but a single castellany, the living conditions did not
vary considerably. The castle was his home and his fortress, and in the
early days the fortress predominated. The early castles, known as the motte
and bailey type, followed a general plan. There would be the great tower
of the dungeon or keep, situated when possible on a hill, which served as
the main fortress and as the living quarters for the lord and his family. At
some distance around the dungeon was an outer wall equipped with
towers, fencing off an enclosure in which were the buildings of the castle,
barns, brew-house, smithy, store houses, buttery, kitchens, and often barracks for the castle guards. These buildings were often built along the outer
wall, leaving an open space or courtyard before the dungeon. Around the
outer wall was the moat, a deep ditch filled with water, which served as
further defense. Entrance to the castle was gained over a drawbridge across
the moat, which was usually built between two towers of the outer wall.
Between the towers, at the head of the drawbridge, was the portcullis, an
iron drop-gate or grill, which was lowered to keep out invaders. The
portcullis was often equipped with heavy spikes at the bottom, so that if
it fell on a person it would not only crush but pierce him. At night the
portcullis would be lowered and the bridge drawn up, thus effectively
cutting the castle off from all outside visitors.

In the tenth century the castles were generally built of wood, but stone
came into general use during the eleventh and twelfth centuries. The
towers on the walls, like the dungeon itself, were built with crenellations

on the roofs—parapets behind which defenders could crouch to drop missils on attackers. Platforms were built out over the outer side of the walls and towers, which were pierced with slits, through which hot oil, melted lead, and other discomforting substances were poured on the heads of enemies attempting to scale the walls by ladders. The early castles were square, but as a result of observation during the crusades, round keeps were brought back from the East, and the highest perfection of defensive castle building was the concentric circle type, where the towers came out in semi-circles from the walls, thus eliminating any corners where ladders could be set up with comparative impunity, and giving a wider target for the arrows of the defenders. Chateau-Gaillard, built by Richard I of England at Les Andelys in Normandy, is probably the finest example of twelfth-century military architecture in western Europe.

The inside of the castle was still more of a fortress than a house. The dungeon was always dark, as its windows were narrow slits designed to shoot out of rather than for the transmission of light. A deep windowseat, in which a bowman could crouch, was topped by a narrow slit-window, and while it afforded a potential resting place which was most useful in the absence of many chairs, it served but badly as a means of illumination. Ventilation it did give, especially in winter, for glass was practically unknown before the fourteenth century in domestic building.

The rooms were cold, as the stone walls retained cold and damp. To mitigate against this, tapestries were hung on the walls a few inches out from the wall, making an air-pocket insulation, which did something to reduce the damp. As the tapestries became more elaborate, this also added much to the decoration of the rooms, the embroidered tapestries adding color and interest to the gray walls.

In Spain and southern France, where contact with the Moors suggested the idea, carpets were laid on the floors, but in the north, at least through the twelfth century, floors were commonly covered with reeds which were changed seasonally. The reeds had an advantage over carpets in that, when a meal was finished, the tressel tables could be tipped and the table scraps dumped into the reeds, where they would be ferreted out by the ever-present dogs.

The dungeon consisted of several stories. In the cellar were the wine vaults and prisons, dark holes where the lord's enemies or poor unfortunates who had roused his anger were thrown to rot in dark airless confinement, often shackled to the walls by heavy irons. The ground floor (sometimes elevated and reached by a short flight of steps) contained the great hall of the castle. Here the lord and his retainers ate and drank, held court, and passed most of the cold months. It was furnished with several long tressel tables and benches, and perhaps a few chairs for the lord, lady and especially honored guests. By the thirteenth century the pennons and shields of the lord and the knights of his menage were hung around the walls, along with trophies won in battle, tournament, or the chase. At one end of the hall was the huge fireplace which heated the whole building and where roasts were cooked. The fireplace was generally a tremendous affair, big enough to cook an entire steer or boar on a spit.

A stair, or often merely a ladder, went from the main hall to the lord's sleeping quarters above. This too was a large apartment scantily furnished. A great bed was the chief piece of furniture, and indeed except for some chests and a few benches and stools, the only furniture of the room. The beds were big and high with curtains to afford what little privacy the lord and his lady enjoyed. Other members of the household—the ladies in waiting—slept on straw mattresses on the floor around the room. Honored guests were generally given the bed, sometimes sharing it with the hosts. The men-at-arms slept on straw mats in the great hall below. In the fourteenth century there developed the parlor, a small room where the lord and lady could retire privately to talk, but even then privacy was not one of the concomitants of life, and the puritanical modesty of the Victorian age would have suffered severe strains in the rather free and naturally uninhibited life of the medieval castle. With any sort of plumbing still several centuries in the future, our ancestors can be forgiven if they were less addicted to baths and personal cleanliness than would be considered good form today.

The clothing of the medieval knight or lady was simple. Buttons were only discovered towards the end of the thirteenth century, and the usual male garment was a shirt which came to the knees, and in cold weather did double duty as a nightshirt as well. Trousers, leggings, and shoes completed the ordinary costume. The fancy doublets, long hose, and pointed shoes which we associate with medieval costumes were innovations of the fourteenth century, when dress blossomed forth and went to extremes. In the earlier period, men wore simple garments which protected them from the cold. Over the shirt was worn a tunic, on which in the late twelfth and thirteenth century was embroidered the arms of the noble, and which was held in at the waist by a broad belt. The ladies wore simple dresses somewhat devoid of lines, ornamented by embroideries, and belted. By the fourteenth century they had devised most attractive dresses which followed the contours of the wearer, and were topped by hats with long wimples, but the twelfth century styles were much less elaborate. The main difference between the clothing of the rich and poor lay in the quality of the cloth and in the fur trimming which the nobles affected.

The food they ate would have shocked any modern dietitian. They were blissfully ignorant of vitamins, calories, and all the other accepted standards of modern eating. Green vegetables were eaten in season, but the medieval diet consisted largely of starches and proteins—meat, bread, and wine or ale being the standard foods. What they lacked in variety they made up in quantity, and a medieval banquet with its roasts of beef, mutton, venison, and pork, its fish, eels, lampreys, and shell fish, its chickens, pheasants, capons, quails, and ducks, its wheat cakes, pastries and custards, all washed down with great quantities of beer, ale, and wine at once titillates and shocks our senses of taste and fitness.

The meat was usually more tasty in the autumn than in the spring, for the livestock was slaughtered in the autumn and hung on rafters to smoke. By spring it had generally gotten a bit "gamey," and the extensive use of pepper and spices, once they became available, is readily understood when one remembers that a dose of spice would kill the game flavor and make the food much more palatable. Spices from the East adorned the tables of the wealthy, and enriched the purveyors of these products. Likewise perfumes had a practical as well as ornamental use in those days, and a strong scent of perfume covered up for a lack of baths, making social intercourse considerably more pleasant.

Table manners were somewhat casual, but there were rules and books of etiquette which were followed by the more sophisticated. While wearing hats at table was considered acceptable, it was most unmannerly to pick one's teeth with a knife, to drink or to talk with the mouth full of food, to spit while at table, or to sit back at ease with the feet on the table before the repast had been finished.

Knives and spoons were the only table utensils, forks not having been invented as yet. After using a knife or spoon, the user should, if well mannered, carefully wipe it off and not leave it in his dish or lying on the table unwiped. Food was served in large dishes and several people often used the same dish; slabs of bread were used as plates on which to lay meats, and correct etiquette demanded that a person cut or tear off a piece of meat from the roast and eat it from his own trencher of bread or wood. One utensil on which no expense was spared was the goblet which was of copper, silver, or even gold encrusted with gems in the wealthiest houses. Poor folk drank from wooden goblets, but all alike were large, and goblets which held a full litre were standard. In some monasteries, where the monks were forbidden by rule to drink more than one cup of wine a day, the goblets held as much as two quarts.

When the weather permitted, the nobles spent as little time as possible inside their castles. Medieval life was outdoor life and the parks, gardens, fields and woods played a far greater role in the life of the twelfth century than they do in ours today. Winter was a dull season when men were confined to their castles with virtually nothing to do, and it is small wonder that so much of the medieval lyric poetry is devoted to songs about the coming of spring. In winter recreations were limited to sitting around the fire, drinking, listening to occasional minstrels, and telling tall tales. But in spring one could go hunting, or visiting one's neighbors, or take exercise in the courtyard, or occasionally take part in a tournament or even in a public or private war.

The feudal noble had as his *raison d'être*—war, and his whole life was geared to it. When he was not fighting (and the church had made this much more difficult with its limitations of the Peace and Truce of God) he was practising for war, either by exercise or by tournament. In most courtyards were to be found posts with revolving bars to which were hung dummies. The knights would charge the dummy and try to pierce it. If they missed they would be hit by a sandbag on the other end of the bar which swung around. This sport was very popular with the squires and young men of the castle, who developed their aim thereby.

Hunting was also good sport and much indulged in. Hunting had the double advantage that it not only served as pleasant recreation, but also filled the larders with tasty meat and fowl. In the earlier ages, hunting was largely restricted to men, and boars, wolves, and deer were the chief objects of the hunt, but by the twelfth century the ladies had entered into the sport, and falconing, the hunting of birds with birds, had become the approved sport for mixed company. Fishing lacked excitement and was not a popular sport in the Middle Ages, being left to the peasants and professional fishermen.

But the supreme recreation of the noble was the tournament. It was the best substitute for war which could be devised, and in its earlier forms differed very little from actual warfare. In the eleventh century, tournaments were miniature wars which extended over large areas. A district would be indicated as the field of play, two rival armies, often of several hundred knights each, would prepare, and on a given day the tournament would begin. It differed from actual warfare in that the lives of the contestants were spared; when a knight was unhorsed and captured he must return to the pavilion of his captor and wait there until he could make arrangements for ransoming himself, his horse and his armor. Defeat was costly, but victory brought rich rewards in the shape of ransoms, and many a knight supported himself on the proceeds of tournaments. William Marshal, later earl of Pembroke and regent of England, maintained himself for several years in his youth by going from one tournament to another and taking prisoners. Tournaments were also less destructive to the property of the peasants who lived in the vicinity than were real wars. But even so they were often bloody affairs and men were frequently killed in the greater tournaments, so that the church banned them. The ecclesiastical ban however did nothing to mitigate the popularity of the tournaments and they continued to thrive through the fourteenth century. A great change came over them, however, during the thirteenth century.

Instead of being fought over large areas they were held in small fields; the lists were marked out, stands were erected for noble spectators, and the ladies came to watch their champions carry their colors to victory or defeat. These later tournaments, which are the ones familiar to us in fiction and art, were strictly regulated affairs. There would be a series of individual encounters between knights. Each knight would start at one end of the lists and charge his opponent; if they missed, they would wheel and charge back. This they kept up until one knight unhorsed the other. Then they would dismount and fight with swords until one was beaten to his knees or otherwise defeated. Judges could put a stop to the fighting when they felt that one contestant was defeated, and the fight was not carried on to the death as it would have been in battle. Usually at the end of the tournament, after the individual jousts had been completed, there was the melee, when whole companies of knights charged each other. It was still a dangerous sport, and if fewer were killed, there were yet many broken bones and injured bodies.

By the fourteenth century the practice had developed for each knight to wear the colors of a chosen lady. Then after the tournament the victor would ride up to the stands to where his lady sat and receive from her the crown of victory. In the fifteenth century, tournaments became mere displays of horsemanship with less real fighting.

The development of body armor paralleled the changes in tournaments. In the eleventh and early twelfth centuries the armor consisted of a long shirt of mail, a conical helmet, and a large kite-shaped shield. Then plate mail began to be used on the legs and arms, and the pot-helm came into vogue. The pot-helm, as its name suggests, looked like an inverted pot. It was heavy and ably protected the wearer's head, but had the disadvantage that the eye-slits, which were all the knight had to see through, might be turned to the side or back of the head by a glancing blow. With his helm turned sideways the knight was blind and *hors-de-combat*. This was met by shaping the helmet to the head and putting a visor on the front. When not in actual battle the visor was worn open, giving the knight more air; during battle it was closed, but eye-slits enabled him to see, and the shape of the helm prevented its being knocked sideways easily.

Plate armor also became increasingly used to protect the body: legs, arms, feet, breast, back and thighs—all came to be encased in heavy plate. This did away with the necessity of a large shield and the great kite-shield gave way to the small round targe.

As the plate increased, and the knight became more and more encased in steel armor, his freedom of action decreased proportionately. It was quite possible to move about in a shirt of chain-mail, but in a suit of plate armor the wearer was virtually immobilized. In the tournaments of the fourteenth century it was customary for the knights to ride to the field unarmed, while their armor was carried along behind them on a spare horse led by a squire. Arrived at the lists, the knight would either don his armor, assisted by his squires, and then be hoisted on to the back of his special heavy war-horse (Percherons were preferred in France) by means of a derrick set up for the purpose, or lacking a derrick, the knight would mount the horse and the armor be placed on him piece by piece by his squires. Once unhorsed the knight was helpless and could only lie on the ground waiting rescue or capture. It was in part this factor which gave the victory to the lightly armed English infantry at Crécy and Agincourt, and to the Turkish Janissaries at Nicopolis.

Closely associated with the development of armor is the growth of heraldry. During the crusades, the Western knights had observed that their Moslem antagonists wore emblems on their shields and surcoats which readily identified them to both friend and foe. With the increasing coverage of the features by the heavier helmets and armor, this method of identification spread into general use in Western Europe. At first a man would select a symbol: a cross, lion, panther, lily, or castle, which he would have painted on his shield and embroidered on his surcoat. Then they put the same symbol on a pennant attached to the lance. At first these insignia were purely personal, but they quickly became hereditary, and each noble house was distinguished by some emblem. Playing on the name was common: Louis of France used the lily, the kings of Castile used castles, those of Leon, lions. Crosses in various forms were the most popular heraldic symbols, and are found on thousands of coats of arms, especially the earlier ones. Lions in all sorts of positions—rampant, dormant, halved —eagles with one or two heads, birds, serpents, fishes, and mythical monsters were used equally with circles, bars, and geometric designs. When the science of heraldry really developed, a man would combine the insignia of his various ancestors, halving or quartering them on his shield. By the fourteenth century elaborate coats combining many insignia were made, although sixteen quarterings was about the most that anyone actually placed on his shield or coat. The tomb of Charles the Bold of Burgundy at Bruges is a veritable manual of heraldry, showing as it does, all the coats of arms which the duke held from his various ancestors. Younger sons bore the heraldic arms of their father, but indicated that they were the cadet line by adding some extra figure to the insignia. The term "bar sinister" indicating illegitimacy comes to us from the heraldic practice of crossing the coat with a bar from left to right in the case of illegitimate sons.

CHIVALRY AND THE COURTS OF LOVE

The feudal noble lived for war. His whole education was for war from the time he became a squire until he took his place among the knights of the realm. But in the twelfth century this essentially military character was modified and softened somewhat by the development of the idea of chivalry. Sidney Painter, whose *French Chivalry* lightly but learnedly analyzes the whole matter of chivalry in medieval Europe, finds three forms of chivalry—that of the knights, that of the clergy, and that of the ladies. All had their effects on the society of the twelfth through fifteenth centuries.

The chivalry of the knights was the earliest form. A knight should be always brave and loyal, true to his given word, faithful and obedient to his lord, eager to destroy the enemies of his God or his king, but generous and magnanimous towards a defeated foe. He would never attack in ambush, never strike a fallen enemy while he was down, never betray a trust or desert his post, never surrender while there was any hope of victory. To this concept the clergy added the idea of protecting the poor and weak, of fighting always in the righteous cause, of defending the church and clergy and constantly warring on the enemies of the Faith. The Knights Templar and Hospitaller in many ways expressed the clerical ideal of chivalry: brave knights vowed to God and devoting their lives to fighting the enemies of Christendom. The clergy and the knights disagreed in the matter of tournaments; to the clergy they were sinful and wasteful shows, while to the knights they were a noble sport where a man could best show his prowess and daring. But the real conflict of ideas came in the concept of chivalry advanced by the ladies, which ran directly counter to that of the churchmen in many respects.

To the ladies, the chivalric knight was one who was ever ready to serve his lady in her lightest whim. He would face dishonor and disgrace for her sake, would imperil his soul and defy the angers of the church for love. The fair name of his lady was the chief concern of the knight, and knights-errant wandered about the country challenging all and sundry to fight or admit that their particular lady was the fairest, gentlest, noblest, and most accomplished in all the world. This feminine conception of chivalry was the one which was followed in the famous courts of love, and the one which we find reflected in the *romans d'aventure* of the Arthurian cycle.

The effect of chivalry on knighthood was tremendous, even though it did not make the tough warriors into refined gentlemen. The status of knighthood ceased to be a military and economic one and became social. No longer was the knight a warrior who held enough land to enable him to serve heavily armed and mounted in the army; the knight was now a member of an exclusive social class, and even princes and dukes could not be called knights until they had formally been dubbed and received into the select company. In place of the old system of dubbing by a blow of the fist or the sword, a new and elaborate ceremony developed. The candidate for knighthood fasted and spent the night before his dubbing in prayer. Then he bathed, put on entirely clean garments, confessed his sins, and, thus purified within and without, came to the ceremony of his knighting. The knight who was to dub him touched him lightly on the shoulder with the flat of the sword; the armor of the new knight was put on him by friends and relatives, ending with the girding on of the sword. Then he would demonstrate in the courtyard his ability as a rider and lanceman. It became increasingly the custom to have dubbings to knighthood on a large scale. The sons of lesser knights would have been brought up as pages and squires in the castles of their fathers' lord. When the lord's son was of age for knighting, there would be a general ceremony in which a number of young knights were created. This would be followed by a banquet and tournament, in which the new knights would show their accomplishments. Minstrels would sing the songs of the heroes of old, food would be distributed to all the guests and to the poor, and the celebration might well last for days or even weeks. This was, of course, paid for by the special feudal aid for knighting the lord's son, but the vassals often got their own sons knighted in the process. At the time of his knighting, the new knight took an oath to protect the church, the weak and the defenseless, and to respect all noble ladies everywhere. It is worthy of note that this respect for women applied only to the noble classes and in no wise limited the predatory nature of the knight as regarded women of the lower classes.

The courts of love were centers for the growth of this feminine chivalry. They first developed in the south of France, the court of William IX of Aquitaine being most important. They were introduced into the north by William's granddaughter, Eleanor of Aquitaine, and even more by her daughter, Marie of Champagne, who made Troyes a center of chivalrous courtesy and of vernacular literature. But their true home was in the Midi and it is there that they flourished most profusely. These courts would hold sessions in which they would try the various lovers and judge who loved the most. The whole thing was extremely artificial, conventional, formal—and intimate. Andreas Capellanus wrote a manual for these courts, the *De Amore,* in which he stated the rigid rules regulating courtly love. The whole thing was distinctly ethereal in theory: the lover should ideally hardly know his lady; it was best if he had but glimpsed her once or twice at church. His love must always be hopeless and he must never allow either the lady herself or anyone else to discover the identity of his beloved. Ideally she should be married to someone else, for young girls were strictly watched and were not allowed to associate with men until they were married. The lover must sigh for his lady and compose in her honor songs and poems. He must defend her charms and beauty against all the world, asserting her superiority over all other women. Each lover strove to prove himself the most distraught by love and his beloved the most delectable of womankind. Of course this was the theory; the practice obviously differed widely from it, and the ladies certainly knew their admirers and rewarded them as suited their lovers' devotion and their own consciences. In the Catharist Midi, where marriage was a greater sin than illicit affairs, the ideal undoubtedly suffered badly and the sighs of the lovers did not always go unheeded and unrewarded. It must be remembered that these ladies and knights were married not according to any idea of personal feeling but because a suitable marriage properly arranged by the families would unite two fiefs or cement a political alliance between two houses. Small wonder that they sought romance outside the marriage vows, and that they attempted to sublimate their natural desire for love in the artificial trappings of the chivalrous code of courtesy.

For the life of the medieval lady was not too soul-satisfying. She was busy (as what housekeeper is not) in managing the domestic affairs of the castle, and in supervising her women and the servants around the house. But her recreations were limited: she could embroider and sew; she could listen to the minstrels in the great hall, she could occasionally join her husband in falconing and the hunt. But to her, too, winter was a deadly season and she must have looked forward to the warm months when she could picnic in the forest, or pay a call on some other castle, or even break the monotony of her life by engaging in a pilgrimage. The arrival of an itinerant peddler with his pack of trinkets was a gala day, as he brought not only rare luxuries to tempt her, but the gossip of other castles and news of the world outside. This was also done by the minstrels who wandered from castle to castle, singing their songs, or by the jongleurs and mountebanks, who came around with their tricks and performing animals to amuse the gentry.

By the twelfth century a goodly number of both the knights and ladies had learned to read, and a well brought up woman would spend hours over her breviary or books of religious edification. For more entertaining literature she usually had to await the arrival of the minstrels, and fortunate indeed was that lady who could hold her own court of love and thus pleasantly while away the dull hours. Chess had been imported from the East and was avidly played; playing cards were not invented until the fifteenth century.

As we have noted above, women were still most valuable as means of securing title to desirable real estate, and their use as a convenient form of land conveyance governed their marriages. The medieval lady who inherited a fief could not long remain unwed as she must have a baron to serve for her fief, and for the average noble dame of the early thirteenth century, according to the estimate of A. Luchaire, "to have three or four husbands was a minimum." [1]

Noble girls were married off at the age of twelve or fourteen, and sometimes even younger. From then on they continued to marry, the mortality among men being much higher than among women, until they had a son old enough to take over their fiefs. In some countries feudal law permitted the suzerain to stipulate three suitors for the hand of an heiress of whom she had to select one, and in no country was the heiress permitted to marry without the consent of her suzerain. The case of Queen Isabelle of Jerusalem who was married four times in eighteen years and all before she was thirty, amply illustrates the fate of the feudal heiress, especially when we recall that Isabelle personally opposed, or was indifferent to, all but her first marriage.

Only occasionally do we find any outbursts of revolt on the part of the medieval women. In general they accepted their lots and made the best of conditions. William of Tyre tells the story of one noble Frankish lady of crusader Syria who revolted, but her fate was not such as to encourage the practice. A lady of Banias in the early twelfth century ably defended her castle against the Moslems in the absence of her husband, but was finally forced to surrender. She was taken to Damascus where she was put in the harem of her captor. Some years later her husband was able to secure the return of his castle and his wife, but after returning to her home the lady let it be known that she had apparently enjoyed her sojourn in the luxurious surroundings of her captivity. Such infidelity was of course punished by immuring her in a convent while her husband married another heiress; but one cannot but sympathize with the woman who preferred the comfortable luxury of imprisonment in a harem in Damascus to the liberty and boredom of the Frankish castle.

In southern Europe in the twelfth century the lives of many of the nobles were completely revolutionized by the rise of the towns. While the nobles in the north remained purely rural and never moved into the new communities, in the south, as the towns defeated the nobles in the neighborhood, they forced them to move inside the town where they could keep a closer watch over them. Thus there developed an urban nobility in southern France and Italy, which caused great difficulty to the towns by their constant feuding and quarreling. Their living conditions did not differ greatly in town or in country, save that in the country they had more room and were less crowded in their houses. In the towns the houses were built close together on narrow streets and neither ventilation nor

---

[1] A. Luchaire, *Social France at the Time of Philip Augustus* (Holt), p. 363.

sanitation was what would today be termed adequate. The nobles generally set their houses flush with the street, but built around a courtyard where they could take the air in privacy.

The habit of throwing slops from the upper stories of the houses into the narrow and muddy streets gave rise to both an architectural form and a sort of urban annex to the chivalric code. The houses were built with their upper stories projecting over the lower so that there was a pathway under the upper story on which pedestrians could walk; and the custom developed for the gentleman to walk on the outside to protect the lady from any missiles which might be directed from above. The very highest development of courtesy took place in the sixteenth century in the urban courts of northern Italy, such as Urbino where Baldassare Castiglione wrote his *Book of the Courtier,* but it was by then far removed from the chivalry of France of the feudal age, although descended from it.

Chateau Gaillard, France

MEDIEVAL CASTLES

Kenilworth, England

Ghent, Flanders

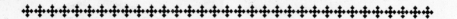

BOOK IV

The Apogee of the Middle Ages: The Thirteenth Century

The thirteenth has been called "the Greatest of Centuries" and certainly it is the height of medieval civilization. In this period the papacy and the German Roman Empire engaged in a death struggle which destroyed the empire and weakened the papacy. Frederick II successfully defied the church, but the empire as an international state died with him. The papacy went on to push its claims to supremacy until it overreached itself and fell during the pontificate of Boniface VIII.

The new power which overthrew Boniface was the national monarchy of France. In France and in England, strong national states were developing, and in the thirteenth century the bases were laid for the constitutional government of England and the royal absolutism of France. This is probably the most permanently significant development of the century.

Europe was still the aggressor in the struggle of East and West, and the century was characterized by continued crusades which generally were unsuccessful, except the Fourth which captured Constantinople and destroyed temporarily the Byzantine Empire. In Egypt a new strong state of the Mameluks, and in farther Asia the great empire of the Mongols arose. The Mongol invasion of western Asia and eastern Europe was the most important single event of the century, but its results were ephemeral save in Russia and the Middle East.

In general throughout this century, except for the Mongols, the states of the West increased in power and importance while those of the East declined. The cities of northern Italy, Flanders, and Germany were growing in wealth and importance while those of the East were devastated by war and destruction. Economically and politically the ascendancy in the medieval world completed its translation to the West.

Great Mosque, Kairawan, Tunis
(*Islamic*)

Monreale Cathedral, Sicily
(*Norman Sicilian*)

MEDIEVAL PORTALS

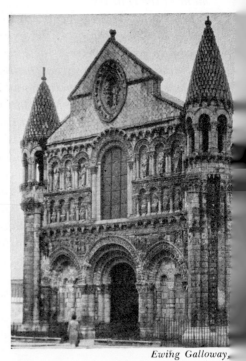

Amiens Cathedral, France
(*Gothic*)

Poitiers Cathedral, France
(*Romanesque*)

CHAPTER 23

THE CHURCH OF INNOCENT III
✣

THE PAPAL MONARCHY

THE papal monarchy had fought a century long struggle with the empire in the period 1049 to 1183 and had emerged triumphant; the church had emancipated itself from the control of the empire and had even begun to assert claims of superiority over the emperors. This development reached its height in the pontificate of Innocent III (1198–1216), who was politically the greatest of all medieval popes.

The church has never canonized Innocent III, for his great contributions were not in the field of dogmatics nor was his life that of a saint. The miracles he performed were political miracles, and these the church does not hold in high esteem. But at no time in history has the See of Peter wielded the political power, at no time was the long arm of the pope felt in so many places and in such diverse things as in the years when Lothario Conti occupied the Fisherman's Seat. The popes of the thirteenth century claimed even more than Innocent, but their claims were largely illusory, and the chart of papal power and prestige runs up from Leo IX to Innocent III and then down from Innocent to a nadir in the collapse of papal authority under Boniface VIII.

Although in his younger days Lothario Conti wrote a book *De contemptu mundi,* mundane affairs occupied almost all of his attention after Innocent came to the papal throne at the age of thirty-seven. Trained in the law, Innocent organized the papal monarchy into the most efficient administration of his time; the papal chancery and the papal financial bureaus were the best in Christian Europe, the papal state spread out, superior to secular states, over all Catholic Christendom. The pope was above all secular rulers and was himself responsible only to God.

The claims to universal dominion advanced by Innocent seem mild and modest as compared with those propounded by the apologists for Boniface VIII a century later, but Innocent's claims were not merely words as were those of Boniface; Innocent made good in fact all that he asserted in theory. Every man was a member of the church, as he was of the state, and the control over him of the church was the more effective of the two. The church *was* the sun whose reflected light illuminated the moon of the state; the spiritual and temporal swords *were* both administered by the successor of Peter, kings *were* but human sinners amenable to the discipline of the Mother Church, the Vicar of Christ *did* judge all and was judged by no one.

The empire over which the pope ruled was coterminous with Latin Christianity, stretching from the isles of the Atlantic to the crusader states of Syria. The organization of the ecclesiastical state was the organization of the church, with its priests, bishops, and archbishops in the provinces and with its curia, as the heart and center of government, in Rome. Its soldiers were the monks who penetrated into every country of Europe; its courts were everywhere, with their elaborate system of appeals from the diocesan to the archdiocesan and primatial courts and eventually to Rome itself. The tremendous variety of the business handled by the papacy is revealed by a glance at the papal correspondence; over 6000 letters have been preserved from the eighteen years of Innocent's reign, addressed to clergy and laity alike and dealing with everything from personal marital matters to issues of national and international policy. Innocent would concern himself equally with the domestic relations of Philip Augustus and Ingeborg, with a disputed election to a bishopric, with the securing of a prebend in a cathedral, with the crusade, or with the suppression of heresy in southern France. Nothing was too large and very little was too small to attract the interest of the pope.

In matters of faith or morals, religious orthodoxy, public decency, and anything which came within the competence of the canon law, the pope was the final judge. In secular matters, while he did not attempt to regulate or judge matters of purely feudal law, the pope was the arbiter, and judgments which he made on rulers as individuals often affected purely secular affairs.

In the administration of his ecclesiastical empire, the pope was assisted by the curia at Rome. This was composed of the cardinals and the officers of the papal household and administration. Since the pope was both bishop and monarch, the papal curia included both ecclesiastical and secular officials. As Sidney M. Brown has stated: "The administration of the Church differed from that of temporal states chiefly in efficiency." [1] There were the ecclesiastical officers, the archpresbyter and the archdeacon, there were the chancellor, treasurer, archivist, almoner, steward of the papal domains, and the vidame, called Patrician of Rome and given as an honorary office to such great lords as Charlemagne, Alberic, or Charles of Anjou. The curia was divided into four major bureaus: the chancery, which handled all correspondence and documentary material of both pope and cardinals and which was unquestionably the most efficient in Europe; the dataria which dealt with indulgences, absolutions, and dispensations; the rota, which heard all judicial appeals and handled legal matters; and the camera, the bureau of finance and taxation.

[1] S. M. Brown, *Medieval Europe*, p. 351.

The sources of papal income were many and extensive. There were first of all the tithes and the *servitia* (with which annates were often confused), the gratuities given by a prelate when he received the investiture of his office; there was the *census* collected from exempt monasteries; the *visitation* collected from clerics visiting Rome; Peter's Pence of a penny a household collected in England, Poland and Scandinavia; and the revenues in *cens* and *tallages* from the papal domain farms and towns. The papacy also collected the *fructus male* from benefices held non-canonically; purveyance for legates and visitors; spoils of deceased prelates who died in Rome; tribute from secular princes who recognized papal suzerainty; and fees from chancery services and for absolutions. Appeals to the papal court also provided considerable income, as did special legacies and outright gifts to the church. The papacy also shared in all oblations to the Roman churches. With the crusades developed special taxes on income (first collected in 1199) and revenues from the issuance of indulgences. Out of these revenues the papacy had to pay for the expenses of the court at Rome, church buildings, alms to the poor, the maintenance of schools and hospitals, and the costs of military expeditions like the crusades to the East or against heretics.

In the administration of the church's business the pope made extensive use of legates, special agents sent out to handle ecclesiastical business. In general these legates checked up on the local clergy and kept them in line. There were three types of legates by the time of Innocent III. The *legatus natus* was a resident legate in a given community, the legatine power being allocated to an important dignitary like the archbishops of Canterbury, Arles, Lyons, Toledo, Treves, Salzburg, and Pisa. In the case of Sicily the legatine power was entrusted to the king, but this was most unusual and greatly reduced the effective control of Rome over the Sicilian clergy. As papal power increased after the middle of the eleventh century these legates came to have less and less real authority and eventually the legatus natus was hardly more than a title. The *legatus missus* developed in the tenth and eleventh centuries as a special agent to settle disputes between local clergy, to represent the pope at coronations or special celebrations, to preside over local provincial church councils, and to act as governors of cities in the Patrimony. By the thirteenth century they were commonly called *nuncios*. The third class of legates, the *legatus a latere* were the most important and were always cardinals. They differed from the nuncios in prestige and power in that they represented the *plenitudo potestatis* of the papacy for the duration of their mission and that there was no appeal from their decisions. The legatus a latere took precedence over all clergy, save only the pope himself, and was used on only the most important missions.

In addition to the ecclesiastical organization of the papal monarchy, the papacy of Innocent III had a definite feudal position. The pope was recognized as the feudal suzerain of the kings of England, Sicily, Spain, Hungary, Serbia, Bulgaria, and the Latin emperor of Constantinople.[2] Much of this was the work of Innocent himself, acquired through the events of his reign, which will be discussed below.

THE CANON LAW

For its ecclesiastical empire the church had its own code of laws called the canon law. The sources of canon law were the Bible, the decrees of the councils, the writings of the Fathers, papal decrees, and the civil law of Rome. Early attempts to codify the canon law were made by Burchard of Worms (ob. 1025) and Ivo of Chartres (c. 1100), but the first standard collection was that of the Bolognese doctor, Gratian, in the years 1139–41. *The Concordance of Discordant Canons*, commonly called the *Decretum*, codified the earlier canons and established the recognized body of the ecclesiastical law.[3]

The competence of the canon law is of two kinds: the *ratio personae*—all cases affecting clerics in any way, based on the old idea of the personality of the law, and the *ratio materiae*, cases dealing with ecclesiastical organization, ecclesiastical property, the sacraments, legitimacy, divorce, testaments, wills, heresy, schism, perjury, usury, sorcery, and blasphemy. Students, crusaders, and employees of churches were considered to be clerical persons for the purposes of the canon law. Also the extension of the competence over sacraments to include wills, oaths, and pledges opened up a fertile field of litigation which often conflicted with the secular courts.

The courts were originally in the hands of the bishops, but the archdeacons got control of them so that they were virtually the archdeacon's courts until, in the twelfth century, the bishop got them back by delegating a special official to hold the court. Cases could be appealed from the bishop to the archbishop and on to the papal curia at Rome. Jurisdiction was one of the largest items in the papal income, and appeals to Rome kept clerics constantly traveling Romeward throughout the later Middle Ages. We shall see elsewhere how the national monarchies opposed these appeals to Rome and tried to legislate against them.

---

2 For the Latin conquest of Constantinople, see below, pp. 494–99.

3 The *Corpus Juris Canonici* includes the *Decretum* and the additions made by subsequent authors. They are: The *Decretals* of Gregory IX (1234); the *Sext* of Boniface VIII (1298); the *Clementines* of Clement V (1313); and the *Extravagantes* of John XXII, continued in a second series to 1484. A *Ius novissimum* includes legislation since the Council of Trent.

The Sacramental System

The whole purpose of the ecclesiastical system was to keep men in the path of the true faith. To accomplish this, the church had developed a fixed theology and a universal practice, based on the system of sacraments, which applied to all Christians. The sacraments guided the believer throughout his life, and the proper reception of them would preserve him in the way of salvation.

The sacraments are as old as the church itself, being found in the teachings and in the life of Christ. Though at first there was some disagreement as to just what the sacraments were—Augustine considering all the ceremonies of the church as sacraments and Isidore of Seville believing only baptism, confirmation, and the eucharist deserving of that appellation—by the twelfth century the number had been recognized as seven, the mystic number having been suggested by Hugh de St. Victor and Roland of Parma (later Alexander III) and definitely established by Peter Lombard in his *Sentences*.

1. Baptism was the reception of the believer into the fold of the church; it washed away all his previous sins and brought him pure into the body of the faithful. At first baptism was administered at the great festivals of Easter and the Saturday before Pentecost. Lent was the period of preparation for the reception of the sacrament and candidates were examined before being baptized. The baptism of infants came into practice early, was the cause of considerable controversy in the fourth century, gained strength in succeeding centuries and was made compulsory by Charlemagne. Until the twelfth century, baptism was administered only by total immersion, but in that century infusion began to be practiced, until by the end of the thirteenth century it became the standard practice.

2. Confirmation was "the reception of the Holy Spirit by the baptized, whereby their faith was strengthened." It could only be performed by the bishop. Confirmation should follow as soon as possible after baptism, and this was easy in the early church when the bishops were the pastors of all congregations. As the church spread and baptism came to be performed by priests in rural areas, it was often impossible for a person to come to the bishop until after some considerable lapse of time. The Council of Cologne in 1280 ordered that children should not receive confirmation under seven years of age, and that has been the practice of the church until modern times.

3. The eucharist incorporates the partaker into Christ and, while not absolutely essential to salvation, was urged as most salutary to all believers. At first the communion was commonly double, the partaker receiving both the bread and the wine. In the third century in the East and in the sixth in the West, it became the custom to dip the bread into the wine and thus

to administer it to the communicant. This practice was, however, banned by the Council of Clermont in 1095 and the custom developed of giving only the bread to the communicant, while the priest alone partook of the wine. By 1250 the wine had practically disappeared as far as the communicants were concerned and by 1400 it had disappeared entirely. This became, in the fifteenth century, one of the complaints of the Hussites, who made double communion one of the major issues in their reform. At first taken every time the Christian attended church, the partaking of the eucharist became less and less frequent, until in 506 it was required that the eucharist be taken at least three times a year, a regulation which prevailed through the twelfth century. The Fourth Lateran Council of 1215, of which more later, decreed that it was sufficient if the believer partook once a year; monks were obliged to partake once weekly.

The Mass was the ceremony of the consecration of the bread and wine. It was the representation and commemoration of the Sacrifice on the Cross and became the very center of Christian worship. The doctrine of transubstantiation, that the bread and wine were miraculously turned into the body and blood of Christ, is found in the earliest teachings of the church, but the theological term transubstantiation was not defined by the pope until the Fourth Lateran Council under Innocent III.

4. Penance was the true repentance of the sinner for his sins, and was the sacrament whereby sinners could regain lost grace. In the earliest days of the church, penance could be performed only once and any sin committed thereafter was irremediable with the result that people delayed baptism until the approach of death. Then the church adopted the doctrine that lapses from virtue should be forgiven those truly repentant, and the system of confession, the imposition of penance, and absolution developed. At first confession was public, the sinner confessing his sins to the bishop in the open congregation, but this often caused embarrassment and a system of private confession was begun, first among the monks of St. Pachomius and then among the laity. The early penances were, however, public affairs: the penitent was excluded from the church and had to remain outside until he gradually worked his way back in. After a portion of the penance had been completed he was admitted to stand on the porch of the church; only after full penance had been performed and he had been given absolution could he join the faithful in the interior. It was the Irish who first developed the system of penitentials with a regular tariff of penances for specific sins. Confession among the Irish could be made to any holy man, who would then assign a penance according to the tariff of the penitential. This system was carried from Ireland to Gaul in the sixth century. By the thirteenth century, private performance of penance had become usual, the general rule being that public scandals must be atoned for by public penance, but that private sins could be satisfied by private

penances. While confession was obligatory as early as St. Patrick (fourth century), the number of times a year that confession should be made remained a moot question for centuries. Frequent confession was favored by the early theologians and Gregory VII lent his support to regular confessions; by the Fourth Lateran Council annual confession to one's parish priest was ordered of all faithful.

5. Ordination to the priesthood consecrated the priest to his duties and empowered him to administer the other sacraments except confirmation. In the early church there was a question whether or not ordination lapsed with heresy, but by the thirteenth century the church agreed on the doctrine of the "indelibility of the priesthood"—that a priest once ordained can never lose his sacred characteristic. Thus a schismatic or heretical priest, himself lost to salvation, can administer valid sacraments to true believers. The religious ceremonies whereby one is admitted to any order or clerical status below that of deacon is not a sacrament. The tonsure, the distinguishing mark of the clergy, was taken over by the clergy in the sixth century from the Egyptian hermits, who had adapted it from the priests of Isis.

6. Marriage was a sacrament constituted by the marriage contract and blessed by the priest. At first not insisted upon by the church, ecclesiastical marriage ceremonies were required by Charlemagne. While civil marriages of non-Catholics are recognized by the church today, the ecclesiastical marriage ceremony is required of Catholics. The indissolubility of marriage was insisted on by the early church, temporarily relaxed in the fifth century, but reaffirmed consistently since the Carolingian era. No grounds for annulment were recognized other than that of consanguinity.

7. Extreme unction is the annointing with consecrated oil, which is administered to the dying. Administered only after the person has been reconciled with the church, the application of the holy oil has a salutary spirtual effect and should be taken by all *in periculo mortis*.

Reception of the sacraments increases Grace and thus helps the Christian to aspire to salvation. But the frailties of human nature are such that the burden of temporal punishment due to sin can be seldom atoned for in this life. Few indeed, save the saints, can hope to attain paradise immediately upon death; for the bulk of humanity, purgatory affords an opportunity to pay this punishment after death. In purgatory, the soul is purged of its sins and made ready for the reception of God's grace in paradise. Absolution granted by the church does not mean that the penitent will not have to serve some further punishment in purgatory for his sins, but he can accept the purgatorial pains since he knows that salvation awaits him finally. Far different is the lot of the unrepentant sinner who must suffer for eternity the agonies of hell without any hope of the relief of salvation; part of the horror of hell is the utter frustration involved.

The duration of a soul's stay in purgatory can be shortened by good works done in his name by his relatives or friends: special Masses can be said for his soul, gifts can be made to the church for his sake, and the love of his relatives can help to shorten the length of his sufferings. The merit from virtuous deeds can be transferred to the sinner, except that few mortals have any superabundance of virtue to transfer. There exists in heaven, however, a Treasury of Merit made up of the superabundant virtue of Christ and the saints. To this treasury the pope has the keys so that he can grant to a worthy soul some portion of that grace. From this Treasury of Merit were issued indulgences, which transferred some of this grace to the individual. "An indulgence" says the *Catholic Encyclopedia,* "is the extra sacramental remission of the temporal punishment due, in God's justice, to sin that has been forgiven, which remission has been granted by the Church in the exercise of the power of the Keys, through the application of the superabundant merits of Christ and the Saints, and for some just and reasonable motive." Indulgences are of two types: plenary —a remission of the entire temporal punishment, and partial—the remission of a certain number of days penance. Thus an indulgence of forty days would be the equivalent of performing a forty-day penance (not as is sometimes believed the remission of forty days suffering in purgatory).

Indulgences had existed as commutation for minor penances throughout the Middle Ages, but greatly increased in the eleventh century, one of the earliest important indulgences being granted by Urban II to William, archbishop of Rouen, whereby William was authorized to remit a fourth of the penances required of them to all who would contribute to the re-building of a certain monastery. Indulgences were then granted to those who visited certain holy shrines or who made pilgrimages. From these early indulgences the papacy derived no financial profit, as the money went to the local shrine or church. Not until the middle of the thirteenth century did the papacy benefit directly from the indulgences. "The commercialization of indulgences began with those issued in connection with the crusades"; [4] it was with the crusades that the great increase of the issuance of indulgences started.

In 1095 at Clermont, Urban II promised the remission of plenary penance to all who went on the crusade; in 1125 a remission of penance was granted those "truly confessed and truly penitent" who fought against the Moors in Spain, or who sent substitutes; in 1145 to 1146 one-seventh of all penance was remitted those who contributed in alms to the Knights Templar; in 1187 partial penance was remitted those who contributed to the cost of the crusade. The amount of penance remitted by indulgence usually depended on the amount of money given or the amount remittable

---

4 W. E. Lunt: *Papal Revenues in the Middle Ages,* I, 115. The examples cited are de-rived from Lunt.

for the act for which the indulgences substituted. If a man took the cross and could not go on a crusade, he could obtain an indulgence which remitted the same amount of penance that he would have received by actually going. As the cost of the indulgence was no more than the cost of the crusade and much less dangerous, the indulgences were employed frequently by those who regretted momentary enthusiasm which had prompted them to take the cross. But though indulgences were issued in increasing numbers throughout the period of the crusades, it should be noted that the papacy derived no gain therefrom until indulgences were issued to those who contributed to the expenses of the crusade which the pope launched against Frederick II.[5]

MEANS OF ENFORCING OBEDIENCE TO THE CHURCH

For those who wandered from the path of obedience and showed no intention of returning, the church had powerful weapons to force them back. Of these the most effective were excommunication (and anathema), the interdict, and the Inquisition.

Excommunication was the cutting off of the sinner from the society of the faithful; it placed him outside the church and banned him the society of his fellowmen. The excommunicate was a pariah and no one dared associate with him in any way; not only was he cursed with the most horrible torments, but all obligations to him were invalidated so that a feudal lord, placed under excommunication, forfeited the homages and allegiance of his vassals, and a merchant found that all debts due him were automatically cancelled.

Excommunication varied in degree and severity, the greater excommunication being known as the anathema.

May he be seized with jaundice and smitten with blindness; and may he bring his present life to a miserable ending by a most wretched death and undergo everlasting damnation with the devil, where bound with red-hot chains, may he groan forever and ever, and may the worm that never dies feed on his flesh, and the fire that cannot be quenched be his food and sustenance eternally.[6]

More immediate than the torments of the future were the civil liabilities which various states imposed in the excommunicated. In France the government seized the property of any one excommunicated for over a year and a day; in England the writ *De excommunicando capiendo* ordered the seizure of an excommunicate after forty days; in Sweden the state executed

---

[5] It was with the issuance of plenary indulgence by Boniface VIII in 1300 to those who attended the Papal Jubilee of that year that the indulgences really became a major item in the papal income.

[6] Univ. of Penna. "Translations and Reprints," First Series, IV, 4, 25 from an act of 988. Other more violent anathemas are found in S. M. Brown, *Medieval Europe*, pp. 354–56.

those who had been under the ban for more than a year. While in Germany, Spain, Italy, and Poland the secular government took no special actions against the excommunicated, in no country were they allowed to plead in court, bear arms, marry, or engage in business of any kind. Those dying under the ban were, of course, refused Christian burial, and their lands were generally confiscated by the state.

There was even a post-mortem excommunication; people who had been able to conceal their sins during their lifetimes could be excommunicated after death, their bodies being disinterred, their goods confiscated. "Their peaceful slumbers might be disturbed by a posthumous excommunication," said Henry C. Lea, "and the Almighty be notified that the zeal of His watchful agents could not rest satisfied with the judgement that He might already have pronounced." [7] It should be remembered, however, that the excommunication was designed not to affect the eternal but the temporal status of the subject; his body suffered—his soul went marching on.

The interdict was a collective excommunication; by it all churches were closed and the administration of the sacraments suspended. This is a development of the principle of the Germanic law (denied by the Roman) that the whole community should be made responsible for the sins of any individual member. Although first used in the fourth century, the interdict was opposed by such authorities as St. Augustine, and its development was slow. In the seventh to eleventh centuries there were instances of local interdicts employed by bishops, but it was not until Innocent III that the interdict was widely applied on a grand scale. During the eighteen years of his pontificate, Innocent placed 57 interdicts, threatened 27 more and may have placed an additional 6, a total of 90, which may not be complete. The interdict could be placed by the pope, a council, or by bishops, archdeacons or canons over the churches within their jurisdiction. The Inquisition after its foundation was also given the power to lay an interdict. In addition to interdicts especially pronounced by an ecclesiastical authority, there were certain offenses which automatically invoked the punishment of the interdict. Such offenses included violence towards the person of a bishop or cardinal or refusal to admit a legate, and grants to churches often carried with them the imposition of either excommunication or the interdict to those who violated the terms of the grant.

The length of the interdict varied, averaging about one or two years, but Mantua lay under the ban for thirty-three years and a chapel in Maidenhead was under interdict from 1274 to 1324, a period of fifty years. They also varied in severity. In general, while churches were closed and the sacraments forbidden, baptism and extreme unction were always permitted, and religious orders were allowed to hold services privately for

[7] H. C. Lea, *Studies in Church History*, p. 264.

themselves so long as no outsiders were admitted. The most severe interdict on record is that which Innocent laid on England in 1208 to 1213, all privileges of the orders being cancelled. We shall note one of the most unusual interdicts when Jerusalem was placed under the ban in 1229.

The ambulatory interdict developed in the twelfth century; this placed the ban on whatever community sheltered the individual who had caused the imposition of the interdict. Legend recounts how the church bells began to toll the minute Robert of France and his wife Bertha left any town, to the amusement of the unrepentant monarch. Perhaps the most famous ambulatory interdict was that which was attached to the person of John Huss, who avoided the consequences of it by preaching in the open fields far removed from any town. At first people whose homes lay under the ban could attend divine offices in neighboring places not affected, but by the end of the thirteenth century the church prohibited this practice.

The third great method employed by the church to enforce obedience was the Inquisition. This was merely a court procedure whereby information was sought from the neighbors and associates of the accused to determine his guilt or innocence. It stems from the same origins as does the English trial by jury, both coming from the old sworn inquest. But whereas the jury trial became one of the bases for the preservation of individual rights, the Inquisition developed a reputation for injustice and arbitrary procedure.

With the spread of heresy (for which see below) the church found it necessary to devise some means of ferreting out heretics. The use of the sworn inquest was applied to the matter, and the bishops were authorized to hold inquests in their dioceses to determine the incidence of heresy and to punish the offenders. But it too often developed that the heretics were people of power and influence, who did not hesitate to intimidate the bishops' court, and who spirited away informers before they could give damaging testimony. The result was the establishment of the papal Inquisition, manned by special inquisitors sent out from Rome. After the founding of the Dominican order, these friars became the usual officers of the Inquisition.

The chief causes of complaint in regard to the inquisition were that a man was considered guilty unless he could prove his innocence and that guilt could be presumed on the bases of anonymous depositions. The use of anonymous depositions came about through the misfortunes which so often attended known informers, with the consequent reluctance of anyone to give evidence. Once accused, the suspected heretic had to clear himself of the charges. As he was not allowed benefit of counsel and as torture was employed to force confession, this was difficult to do. If a man admitted his heresy under torture and then recanted, he was considered to have relapsed into error and the penalties were increased. The impossibility of getting an acquittal under such a procedure gave the Inquisition the bad name that it in large measure deserves.

The ordinary procedure in the court of the Inquisition was as follows; first was the *citation* where the accused was charged; then the *interrogation,* often under torture; if he admitted his error and sought penance and absolution, this was followed by the *reconciliation;* then came the *confirmation* by the accused of the *procès-verbal* of the trial; after which the case was closed by the pronouncing of the *sentence.* When a man abjured his errors, the sentence might be relatively light: a severe penance, a fine, a term of imprisonment in a monastery. Only in the cases of the most hardened sinners or of relapsed heretics who recanted their confessions was the death penalty—the *auto da fé*—employed. For those who think of the Inquisition as an agency which invariably sent its victims to the stake, it must be emphasized how small a portion of the total cases brought before this tribunal ended in that manner. They were the most conspicuous, of course, and attracted the most attention, but the great bulk of the cases heard by the inquisitors were settled by penances, fines, or imprisonment. Nor did the Inquisition concern itself only with such major offenses as heresy: blasphemy was a common charge in the inquisitorial court, and sexual immorality played a large role on its dockets. It must be pointed out that the church never executed anyone. When the death sentence was in order, the Inquisition turned the heretic over to the secular arm for punishment. The worst horrors of the Spanish Inquisition are more Spanish than inquisitorial, the Inquisition in other lands not bringing nearly so many victims to the stake. An illuminating case to show the influence of the secular power over the penalties of the Inquisition is to be found in the celebrated process of the Knights Templar at the opening of the fourteenth century, when all the Templars in France were convicted and most were executed, while in Cyprus, England, Italy, Spain, and Germany, few, if any, were surrendered to the flames, although everywhere their goods were confiscated.[8]

THE FOURTH LATERAN COUNCIL, 1215

The Fourth Lateran Council, held at Rome in November 1215, marked the climax of the pontificate of Innocent III. To it came some 1300 clergy, including 71 primates and archbishops, 412 bishops, and 800 abbots and priors, as well as representatives from most of the secular states of Latin Christendom. Nothing showed better the position of the pope as head of the world state which was the church, and the variety of business attended to equally reflects the wide range of papal influence.

8 For the Inquisition in general see H. C. Lea, *History of the Inquisition in the Middle Ages,* and for the Templars, Vol. III, chap. 5.

Many of the actions of the council were ephemeral: plans were made for a new crusade (the Fifth); the count of Toulouse was excommunicated for heresy; special action was taken in regard to the heretical teachings of Joachim of Flora; but, in the main, the actions of the council have had so lasting an influence on the church that it is quite proper to say that it marked an era in the history of Western Christianity.

The creed of the church was reaffirmed, with the doctrine reasserted that the church was the only road to salvation. The sacraments were defined as the channels through which God's grace was communicated, and special legislation was taken in regard to several of them. Annual confession to the parish priest was required, as was annual reception of the eucharist; transubstantiation was defined and made an article of faith for the church. Nothing that the council did was more important than the declaration of the faith and *credo* of the church.

Reforms were instituted: a minimum age was established for priests at twenty-five and for bishops at thirty; it was ordained that relics must be approved by Rome before their validity could be accepted. Pluralities were forbidden; laws were passed against simony; it was provided that annual synods should be held in every diocese to regulate the local affairs of the church. It was further ordered that the clergy could not be taxed by secular authorities, but that tithes were to be collected by the church from all laymen. Any secular legislation detrimental to the church was declared *ipso facto* null and void, but the secular authorities must co-operate with the church in the suppression of heresy.

Jews were ordered always to wear a distinctive dress and to stay in their ghettos. No new monastic orders could be organized without the special permission of the papacy, but encouragement was given the mendicants. Heresy was clearly defined; the bishops were ordered to ferret it out and extirpate it, and the inquisitorial process was approved. Lastly, but of the utmost importance, it was ordered that every cathedral must support a teacher of grammar and each archepiscopal cathedral a professor of theology.

CHAPTER 24

MONKS, FRIARS, AND HERETICS

✤

THE REFORMS OF MONASTICISM

THE latter half of the eleventh century, which saw the spread of the Hildebrandine reform throughout the church, witnessed a great wave of monastic reform. Throughout the history of monasticism, reform and laxity alternated, a period of worldly decline following one of rigid ascetic enthusiasm. The first great reform of western Benedictine monachism had been that which sprang from the monastery of Cluny in the tenth century, and it was this movement which established the congregations, or definite orders of monks. Between the houses of the Benedictines there was no necessary organizational connection; they all lived under the same rule of St. Benedict, but there was no superior over the abbot of each monastery. Closer ties were often established between houses which had been founded as offshoots of each other (the close relations between Mont St. Michel in Normandy and San Michele in the Norman kingdom of Sicily are famous), but this was purely circumstantial and not due to any legal ties established between them. With the development of the congregation of Cluny, however, a new idea entered monasticism. The mother house at Cluny sent out daughter houses, who were tied to her by definite regulations, the whole congregation being under the headship of the abbot of Cluny. Convocations of the congregation were held at regular intervals to which all the priors of Cluniac houses came, and the abbot of Cluny had the right of visitation and inspection over any of the subordinate monasteries.

But although founded as a reform order, even Cluny became too worldly to suit the temperaments of pious ascetics. The abbots of Cluny were anxious to make their establishment the most magnificent house of God on earth; they built lavishly and beautifully; arts and letters were patronized; poverty and humility seemed to have departed Cluny, yielding place to luxury and worldly power. The abbot of Cluny was one of the great prelates of the church, a confidant of the pope on many occasions, a patron of scholars, the dispenser of alms to thousands of needy and of hospitality to travelers of all ranks and stations. Peter the Venerable, abbot of Cluny (1122–57), perhaps epitomizes the best of the Cluniac order: urbane, scholarly, lover of the Fathers but also of the classics, tolerant rival of St. Bernard but the protector of Peter Abelard, organizer and builder, author and administrator, Peter is one of the most attractive figures in the twelfth century. At the time of his abbacy, Cluny herself housed 460 monks, while 2000 daughter houses recognized the headship of the monastery.

But the cultured urbanity of Cluny failed to satisfy the souls of more ascetic zealots, who felt that they must get farther away from the world than they could do in either the Benedictine or Cluniac houses. The last quarter of the eleventh century witnessed the foundation of a number of new congregations, all more strict and ascetic than the older houses, and all destined to enjoy considerable popularity in the next centuries. Grandmont or Grammont, founded in 1076 by Stephen of Auvergne, was an order of hermits which practiced the most severe austerities and which enjoyed the special patronage of Louis VII; it had sixty houses by the middle of the twelfth century. A similar order of hermits was that of the Carthusians, founded at the Grand Chartreuse near Grenoble in 1084 by St. Bruno of Cologne. The Carthusians occupied separate cells, ate no meat, and were bound by vows of silence. In the thirteenth century the order numbered around one hundred houses. A small order which was founded in 1095 in Anjou and never spread was that of Fontevraud, in which the distinguishing feature was that the houses were always double, a nunnery for women accompanying each monastery, and the headship over the whole establishment was vested in the Mother Superior of the female house.

By far the most important of the new orders founded at this time was the Cistercian, which, founded in 1098 near Dijon by Robert de Molesme, spread rapidly until by 1143 it had 113 houses and by 1300 over 700. The great popularity of this order was due to the personal prestige of St. Bernard of Clairvaux, its most illustrious member. How great was his influence is shown by the fact that the order had nearly died out in 1120, and that it increased during the lifetime of Bernard so that by his death in 1153 it included 288 houses. The Cistercians believed in the most rigid simplicity and are famous for the severity of their churches, which remind one of the Puritan churches of New England. They felt that beautiful decorations in a church took the mind of the worshiper away from the contemplation of the glory of God, so they removed temptation by making their edifices as simple as possible. The Cistercians were also great agriculturalists. They repudiated scholarship as a proper means of work and insisted on manual labor in the fields; as they were always in search of new lands to develop, they became pioneers in the eastward colonization of Germany which took place in the twelfth century.

St. Bernard (1090–1153) was the perfect monastic saint, and was canonized within twenty years after his death. Born of a noble Burgundian family, Bernard entered Cîteaux in 1113, but sought something more challenging than the life of the monastery and so set out with a few companions the next year to found the daughter house of Clairvaux. From the cloister he dominated the ecclesiastical and much of the political life of Europe for a quarter century. It was Bernard who finally secured the acceptance of Innocent II as pope in 1138; it was he who wrote the rule for the Templars in 1128; his influence was largely responsible for the launching of the Second Crusade and it was his persecution that broke Peter Abelard. Bernard was the soldier of Christ, militant, uncompromising, fiery, intolerant. He hated luxury and the comforts of decent living and attacked Peter the Venerable mercilessly; he hated education, which he felt was dangerous to simple faith, and drove Abelard into retirement after securing the burning of his books at Sens. Heretics and schismatics he abhorred and he poured out his best invective on Peter of Bruyes and Arnold of Brescia. Feeling sincerely that only through monastic renunciation of the world could men be saved, he spared no one in his efforts to bring people into the cloistered life. He persuaded his brothers and other relatives to enter religious houses; one of his most famous letters is to the parents of a boy who were trying to prevent their son from becoming a monk, in which he denounces them for their selfishness in trying to destroy the soul of their son. "Oh harsh father! savage mother! parents cruel and impious—parents! rather destroyers, whose grief is the safety of the child, whose consolation is the death of their son," [1] rather harsh words for parents who only desired to have their child return home. But Bernard's fiery intolerance was well suited to the spirit of the times of which he was at once the product and the arbiter.

In addition to the regular monastic orders founded in the late eleventh century, a monastic reform pervaded the chapters of the cathedral canons. These canons were the clergy who administered to the service of the altar and the chapels of the cathedral church, singing in the choir, teaching in the cathedral school, and living on the returns of prebends assigned them from the revenues of the church. They were not all priests but were mostly in minor orders; they formed the advisory council of the bishop, and it was part of the Hildebrandine reform to secure for them the right of serving as the episcopal electors. The first adoption of a rule by a cathedral chapter was that of Metz in the eighth century, but regular canons were few until the twelfth century, when canons regular of the rule of St. Augustine appeared all over Europe. They had a rule, adopted from the preaching and practice of St. Augustine, which ordained community of goods, a common dormitory and board, a white habit and the ordinary monastic obligations of chastity, poverty, and obedience. Like the Benedictines where each house was independent of the others, the Augustinian canons never formed a single congregation, but a number of orders de-

[1] Quoted in H. O. Taylor, *The Medieval Mind* (Macmillan 4th. ed.), I, 413.

veloped within the group, the most important of which was the Praemon-stratensian. This congregation, founded by St. Norbert near Laon in 1119, rapidly spread, especially in Germany, until at its height the order claimed almost a thousand houses. The Praemonstratensians, like the Carthusians, were noted for the abstemiousness of their diet. Other orders of canons regular were the canons of the Holy Sepulchre in Jerusalem, those of St. Geneviève in Paris, those of St. Victor of Paris and the Gilbertines of Sempringham in England.

The military religious orders of the Temple and Hospital were also developments of this period. We have already seen the tremendous popu-larity of these orders; their example was followed by a number of lesser military orders, most important of which were the Knights of St. Mary the Virgin of Jerusalem, called commonly the Teutonic Knights, founded dur-ing the siege of Acre, and the Castilian orders of Calatrava, Alcantara, Santiago, and the Portuguese order of Avis. It is worthy of note that two of the Castilian and the Portuguese orders developed from Cistercian houses, while the order of Santiago followed the Augustinian rule.

THE MENDICANT ORDERS

To many pious people, however, there was something which the regular monastic orders lacked. Monks generally retired from the world searching for the salvation of their own souls; while they provided hospices for travelers and the sick, and while they distributed alms to the needy, the social program was entirely incidental to the main issue of securing per-sonal salvation by withdrawal from the sins and temptations of the world.

There were many who felt much as did Guyot de Provins who found something wrong with all the existent orders,[2] yet who desired some form of regular religious life.

[2] Guyot of Provins (fl. c. 1205) was a trouvère of Champagne who ended his life as a Cluniac monk after trying out several of the other orders. His *Bible* contains short and pithy criticisms of the various congregations: "For nothing in the world would I be a Carthusian; their rule is too harsh. Each monk is obliged to do his own cooking, to eat alone, and to sleep in a solitary cell. When I see them blowing and kindling their fires it seems to me that this is not the duty of honest men. I do not know what the dear Lord thinks of it, but as for me, I do not wish to live isolated even in Paradise. The place where I had no companions would be no paradise for me. It is not good to be alone; solitude is a bad life which often engenders sadness and anger. . . . These men are murderers of the sick. I would not allow a poor man to die before me rather than give him meat." Of Cluny he says: "They give us bad eggs and unshelled beans. What often arouses my wrath is that the wine is too thin; they have put in too much of what the oxen drink. No, I will never get drunk on convent wine. At Cluny it is better to die than to live." The Augustinians come in for better treatment. "Blessed be Saint Augustine. His Canons have good meat and good wine in abundance." For a time he considered the military orders but decided against them. "The Templars are much honored in Syria. The Turks fear them terribly. They defend the chateaus and ramparts, and in battle they never flee. But that is exactly what worries me. If I belonged to that order I know very

Guyot's main criticism of the monks was for their lack of charity:

A congregation is builded in charity and of charity it should be full. A monk can indeed be at great pains to read, to sing, to work, to fast, but if he has not charity in his soul it avails him nothing to my mind. He is like an empty house in which the spiders spin and wind their webs, and then immediately destroy what they have spun. Singing and fasting are not what save the soul, but charity and faith.

It was because they did not withdraw from the world, but entered into every aspect of daily life, and because they practiced charity, humility, and brotherly love that the mendicants became almost at once the most popular and influential of all the religious orders.

Though there are many mendicant orders, the Franciscan and Dominican so greatly overshadow the others that it will be necessary here to study only these two. Founded at about the same time, with totally different aims in view, the two orders soon grew closer and closer, each taking the best of the other, until a century after their foundation they had become utterly alike—and the bitterest of rivals. St. Francis of Assisi (1182–1226) is probably the most Christ-like man that has ever lived. The simplicity of his faith and the absolute sincerity of his convictions, his complete humility, his childlike naïveté, his tender love for all created beings, all go to make up a character of unparalleled charm and appeal. Divinely mad, or at least divinely impractical, Francis approached the world with faith and love, with an empty purse and a firm conviction in the kindness and decency of humanity that could not fail to produce in people the qualities which he so innocently assumed them to have. It is one of the signs of greatness in Innocent III that he recognized the divine inspiration of this seemingly mad beggar, and instead of condemning him as a heretic for the pantheism of his teachings, blessed his group and accepted them as servants of the church. They were to prove one of the strongest allies that the church ever found.

So much has been written concerning St. Francis that it would be useless to repeat here what can be read in so many books.[3] His devotion to Lady Poverty; his refusal to provide for the morrow lest it show lack of confidence in God's will to provide; his dislike of learning which he felt to be a possession of the mind; his pantheism which made him preach to the

---

well that I should flee. I should not tarry for blows for I do not dote on them. They fight too bravely. I do not care to be killed. I would rather pass for a coward and live, than be the most glorious of earth dead. I would sing for hours for them; that would not inconvenience me in the least. I would be very exact in the service, but not at the hour of battle. There I should completely fail." These and the quotation in the text are all taken from A. Luchaire, *Social Life in France at the Time of Philip Augustus* (trans E. B. Krehbiel) pp. 201–03. Reprinted by permission of the publishers, Henry Holt and Co.

[3] Excellent chapters on St. Francis are to be found in Henry Adams, *Mont Saint Michel and Chartres*, Ch. XV, and in H. O. Taylor, *The Medieval Mind*, I, Ch. XVIII.

birds, write a canticle to the sun, and refuse to put out Brother Fire lest he injure it; his naïve preaching of the Gospel to the Egyptian sultan during the Fifth Crusade—these are all familiar aspects of the saint's life. No order founded on the ideal of total poverty that Francis preached could have hoped to survive, and it is as well that his companions and followers modified the strictness of his prohibition of private property to permit the collective ownership of goods, but the life of their founder and his personal holiness, demonstrated to the world in the market place and the camp, did more to bring men back to the faith than all the persuasions of the Inquisition or the theology of the scholastics.

St. Dominic was a man of totally different stamp. Himself well-educated, Dominic felt keenly the need of a thoroughly educated clergy who could preach the gospel so convincingly that they could overcome all hostile arguments. The simple Italian and the cultured Spaniard had little in common beyond a burning desire to serve the church and a realization that the church must be brought to the people in every aspect of their daily lives. Like Francis, Dominic received his first encouragement from Innocent III, and like the Franciscans, the Dominicans established their first houses in crowded cities. The official names of the two orders reveal the difference in their functions; St. Francis termed his order the Little Brothers (Friars Minor) while Dominic called his the Order of Preachers. From the color of their habits they are commonly called the Gray Friars and the Black Friars, a third order, the Carmelites, being known as the White Friars.

Both Gray and Black friars grew with amazing rapidity. Officially approved as an order by Honorius III in 1223, the Franciscans had 1450 houses by 1350; the growth of the Black friars was less spectacular, but by 1300 they counted 562 houses. Both orders had female sister-houses as well as tertiaries, laymen who patronized the order as affiliates and who enjoyed the right to be buried in their churches.

Soon after their foundations each order had borrowed from the other; the Franciscans became scholars and preachers, while the Dominicans adopted the rule of poverty. Both orders had a master in Rome; chapters general where representatives of the houses met with the master; provinces under provincial priors; and the local units, the convents, under conventual priors in the Franciscan, guardians in the Dominican, orders. Both were invaluable to the church as preachers, and the Dominicans proved especially useful as administrators of the Inquisition. Both orders invaded the universities where they contributed the greatest names to the faculties and to the development of scholastic theology.

Lesser mendicant orders were the Carmelites, founded on Mount Carmel in Palestine in 1156 as a monastic order, but transferred to Europe in the thirteenth century as mendicants, and the Austin (Augustinian) friars, a mendicant order created by Innocent IV's unification of the hermits of Tuscany into an order under the Augustinian rule.

Not mendicants but allied to them were the hospitaller orders. While the most famous of these, the Hospitallers of St. John of Jerusalem and the Teutonic Knights, both became essentially military orders, several orders continued as genuine hospitaller organizations devoted to the care of the sick. Among these were: the Order of the Holy Ghost, founded at Montpellier in 1178, which had 900 houses in the fourteenth century, of which 400 were in France; the Order of St. Lazarre for the care of lepers, of which the master had to be himself a leper until 1253; and the Order of the Trinity, founded in 1198, and that of Our Lady of Mercy, founded in 1230, to ransom Christians who were captives of the Moslems.

All of these orders had in common the fact that they were directly under the papacy. While the old Benedictine monasteries had been under the jurisdiction of the local bishops, beginning with Cluny the congregations sought to be exempt from the local supervision and directly under Rome. Each had a general or master, directly responsible to the pope, who ruled the order, usually assisted by a council of representatives of the local chapters. In fact, the thesis has been presented, though not proven, that representative institutions in lay society were modeled after the system of representation worked out in the Dominican order. The independence of the congregations, particularly the mendicants, their special rights to preach, hear confessions, and administer sacraments, irritated extremely the secular clergy who felt that their prerogatives were being usurped by the regulars. But popular sentiment was with the regulars, especially the mendicants, and the secular clergy had eventually to admit defeat in the struggle. Also, the popes recognized too well the immense value to the church of the mendicants, so that they conferred honors and privileges upon them, making many mendicants bishops and cardinals, some of whom in turn rose to become popes themselves.

THE SPREAD OF HERESY

One of the prime objectives of the mendicant orders was the fight against heresy which was spreading rapidly in Europe in the twelfth century. Although the Middle Ages have been characterized as "The Age of Faith," there was certainly sufficient lack of faith to more than prove the rule, and one is tempted to wonder if the faith of the Middle Ages was in fact much more deeply ingrained than ours today. The infinite number of rules and regulations which the church had to ordain to keep men in the path of the true faith shows how inclined they were to wander away, and the spread of heresy evidences the great number of those who squarely set themselves against the faith of the church and sought their own salvation in their own way. They were defeated, but only after great effort on the part of the clergy; and some of their ideas continued to reappear in the later religious reformation of the sixteenth century.

Heresy is, of course, as old as the church itself, for at all times men have differed on their interpretation of the mysteries of religion. The great controversies of the early church which produced the separatist churches of the Arians, Nestorians, Armenians, Copts, and Jacobites have been discussed in an earlier chapter; so has the schism with Byzantium which resulted in the separation of the Greek and Latin churches. In this schism doctrinal differences were distinctly subordinated to organizational, and it was the supremacy of the papacy far more than the *Filioque* of the creed that caused the rupture between Constantinople and Rome. Other earlier heresies had included the Adoptionist, Donatist, Pelagian, Iconoclastic, and the ninth-century controversies over predestination and the eucharist. Some of these disputes were of oecumenical significance, others were hardly more than monkish squabbles.

By the twelfth century there were three main groups of heresies flourishing in western Europe. The Cathari were the most extreme and the most dangerous to the orthodox faith; the Waldensians were less extreme but were immensely popular and threatened to undermine the authority of the church; and the various academic philosophical heresies were sometimes theologically the most dangerous but were so esoteric as to appeal to only the learned and so had the least influence. There were in addition a number of mystics and some practical critics of the church like Arnold of Brescia, who so offended the churchmen as to be termed heretics, although their theology was on the whole sound and their errors lay in their attitude towards the temporal organization and administration of the church.

To take up these groups in reverse order of importance, let us look first at some of the academics. Amaury of Bene taught a pantheism which distressed the orthodox by his assumption that since God was in all men and God cannot sin, it must follow that man cannot sin. Peter Abelard, who will be discussed more fully in our treatment of the intellectual developments of the time, raised a storm of protest, especially from St. Bernard, by his cool and remorseless logic, which postulated the thesis that reason precedes faith and that only that which can be understood was worthy to be believed. Siger of Brabant in the thirteenth century was to carry rationalism even farther by following the great Moslem philosopher, Averroes, in his ideas concerning the eternity of matter and the superiority of intellectual philosophical truth. But these heresies affected only the few; while they greatly agitated the scholarly world they were relatively innocuous to the general run of men.

More immediately dangerous to the church was the simple antisacerdo-talism of an Arnold of Brescia who became the leader of the Roman com-mune in the days of Adrian IV. He taught that the church should go back to apostolic poverty, that as long as the clergy were corrupted by wealth they could not properly administer the sacraments, and he further at-tempted to help along the ecclesiastical reform by confiscating church property. Thus his execution became the common bond uniting empire and papacy, as this was a revolt against the established order of things which no conservative power could tolerate.

The Waldensians were a much more serious challenge to the church than any of the heretical sects other than the Cathari. Founded in Lyons by Peter Waldo, around 1173, the Waldensians started out as a group of reformers who sought to preach the gospel in apostolic poverty. In the be-ginning the fundamental ideas of the Waldensians and the Franciscans were extremely similar, but the Franciscans were fortunate to find in In-nocent III a prelate who appreciated their piety and worth. Peter Waldo was condemned by Alexander III and Lucius III and was driven into heresy. Waldo had requested permission from the archbishop of Lyons to be allowed to preach the gospel; it was refused as he was no priest, but Waldo felt that the admonition in the Bible to go forth and preach unto all the nations was superior to any prohibition given by any bishop, and so went ahead with his preaching. Condemned at the Third Lateran Council and again at Verona, the Waldensians were driven from Lyons, only to spread over Lombardy, Provence, France, the Rhineland, Poland, and Bohemia. In the thirteenth century, the Waldensians split into con-servative and radical parties, of which the conservative was eventually reabsorbed into the church while the radical continued in its heresy, being the object of many crusades, until it finally merged with the Hussites of Bohemia or with the Lutherans and Anabaptists of Germany. As late as the seventeenth century, the Vaudois (Waldensians) of Savoy were the object of a crusade, which was supported, ironically, by Oliver Cromwell.

At first, the Waldensians were hardly heretical at all, but they became more heretical under persecution. They claimed that the Bible should be in the hands of everyone and that any inspired man or woman was capable of preaching the Word of God. They felt that sacraments were invalid when administered by a priest who was himself in mortal sin, and they agreed that the clergy should be reduced to apostolic poverty. They were complete pacifists and like the strict Quakers today refused either to bear arms or to take an oath. The more radical wing developed further the ideas that indulgences or prayers for the dead had no value or efficacy as there was no such thing as purgatory; that neither the pope nor any of the clergy had any special authority as only God need be obeyed; that tithes should go not to the clergy, but to the poor.

They further claimed that the eucharist was not a real transfer of the substance, but only a commemorative ceremony celebrating the Last Supper; that infant baptism was invalid; that all confession must be openly made; all services held outdoors; and all services be in the vernacular. They denied all allegory, and abolished any singing of hymns at their services. Many of the doctrines of the Waldensians seem extremely familiar to Protestants today, and, indeed, the Poor Men of Lyons were the spiritual predecessors of modern Protestantism. But in the thirteenth century they were dissenters and heretics, and so subject to persecution and suppression whenever encountered. These sectarians studied their Scripture and became expert in knowledge of it; in many disputations between Waldensians and Catholic clergy, the heretic evidenced the greater familiarity with holy writ, and it was in part to combat this that St. Dominic organized his society of preaching brothers.

Far different from the pacifist Waldensians were the Cathari. Called Albigensians because their great center in southern France was in the city of Albi near Toulouse, these heretics spread throughout southern France and north Italy, and proved, when in the majority, no less intolerant than did the Catholics. The magnificent fortress which the bishop of Albi built as a cathedral evidences the measures which that worthy had to take to protect himself from the violence of the heretics.

Their religion was in part imported from the East and was made up of many various religious ideas. Combining elements of the Persian Zoroastrian and the Manichean, the religion developed as Paulicianism in Asia Minor. Driven thence, they migrated to Bulgaria where they were known as the Bogomiles; thence the heresy followed the trade routes to northern Italy and southern France, making special headway in the cultured centers of Languedoc.

Catharism (the Pure) started with the assumption that there were two gods, a god of good and a god of evil. The god of evil had originally been an angel, Jehovah, who was something of a mechanic and to whom God assigned the job of constructing the earth. When he had made earth, Jehovah decided to have his creation worship him instead of the true God, and so organized his church on earth. This was the synagogue of the Jews. But God sent His own Son Christ to redeem men and bring them back to the true worship. A few accepted Christ's teachings, but the church of Jehovah foiled Christ's mission and killed Him. The Cross is, therefore, not the symbol of the victory of Christ but of His defeat and death; instead of being worshiped it should be spat upon and hated. Further, the ministers of Jehovah cleverly took up the story of Christ and perverted it, making it appear that only through the Passion could the ministry of Christ be accomplished. Thus these agents of Jehovah, who was by now cast out of Paradise and who lorded it over hell, set themselves up as the representatives of Christ, while in truth they were the ministers of the devil. Thus the pope and all the clergy were actually the servants of hell and the opponents of the true God.

From this assumption the Cathari went on to deny all the sacraments of the church; they rejected purgatory, the resurrection of the flesh, the incarnation of the man Christ; the Virgin Mary was herself only a spirit and not flesh. All flesh was created by the devil and everything that came from the flesh came from the devil. Thus they were forbidden to eat meat, eggs or anything which had an animal origin. All things of the flesh are evil; all sexual intercourse was sinful, and marriage was worse than occasional lapses from virtue for it was a public declaration of an intent to live in sin; women were agents of hell, snares set for the unwary to seduce them from the path of virtue. Some of the Cathari believed in transmigration of souls and felt that the lesser animals were the souls of the unredeemed.

Thus Catharism set up an almost impossible ascetic ideal for its adherents. But the believers were divided into two groups: the *perfecti* and the *credentes*. The credentes were those who believed but who had not taken the one sacrament of their faith—the *consolamentum*. Before taking the consolamentum they could live as they pleased, but after the receipt of this sacrament they must adhere to the most rigid asceticism, shunning all intercourse with women and eating no flesh or animal products. The consolamentum could be received but once and because of this it was usually postponed until the believer was on the point of death. If a man seemed about to die and was given the sacrament, and then started to get well again, his soul could still be saved by the practice of the *endura,* whereby his friends and relatives quietly smothered him and thus saved his soul at the expense of his mortal life. But though they practised this spiritual euthanasia, the Cathari denied all capital punishment, and were, in fact, like the Waldensians, professed pacifists, rejecting war and oaths. This did not, however, stop them from fighting fanatically in the defense of their religion and lives.

Their clergy were drawn from among the perfecti. Learned in their doctrines, these perfecti went about the country teaching their perverse doctrines. They had bishops and deacons as well as lesser clergy known as the *filii major* and the *filii minor.* They believed in an ordination which came from the laying on of hands, with apostolic succession which went back to the few who had truly recognized Christ in His lifetime.

This amazing religion got a tremendous hold in Provence and Languedoc, where it strangely appealed to the urbane and cultured courts of the troubadours. The destruction of the Cathari in southern France carried with it the destruction of the materially advanced culture of the south, and

Provençal civilization did not survive actively the crusade against the Albigensians.

The Albigensian Crusade

In attempting to crush out this pernicious heresy, the church exercised all its weapons. Excommunication and the interdict proved worthless among men who rejected the church altogether. The Inquisition was sent into Languedoc, but the heretics overpowered and overawed the episcopal inquisition, and even killed papal inquisitors. It was to combat these incorrigible heretics that St. Dominic organized his order of preachers, but the real agency which stamped out Catharism in France was the crusade.

As we have seen, the crusade gave the papacy a great military strength. To Innocent III it seemed obvious that this great weapon which had secured so much for the church in its wars with the Moslems should be applied to those even greater enemies of the faith, the heretics nearer home. Accordingly, in 1209 the pope launched the crusade against the Albigensians and the Waldensians. Philip of France refused to accept the leadership in this movement, but he allowed the crusade to be preached in France, and a great army was raised commanded by Simon de Montfort, which invaded the fertile lands of the south. As in the days of Clovis, it seemed a great shame that this fine country should be held by heretics, and the warriors from northern France piously carried orthodoxy, fire, and the sword into Languedoc.

The Cathari put up a fight; this heresy had been accepted by many of the noble knightly class, and even those nobles who were not themselves Cathari resented the invasion of the northerners and lent their support to the heretics. The war became a struggle between Count Raymond of Toulouse and the northern crusaders, in which Raymond was gradually deprived of his lands and fiefs. De Montfort conquered Beziers, Carcassonne, Narbonne and eventually Toulouse itself. The pope backed the crusaders, declaring Raymond's lands confiscated and bestowing them upon the conqerors. Pedro of Aragon, a kinsman of Raymond, and himself overlord of many fiefs in the affected area, interfered on behalf of his vassals, only to be defeated and killed at the disastrous battle of Muret (1213); Montfort assumed the titles of count of Toulouse, duke of Narbonne and viscount of Beziers and Carcasonne. These pretentions were approved at the Fourth Lateran Council, and his homage for them was accepted by Philip Augustus.

In the course of this crusade, the northern French barons lived up to the best traditions of the First Crusaders at Jerusalem. De Montfort is reported to have told his men to kill all, as God would recognize the souls of his own, and the capture of the Provençal cities was effected with the greatest bloodshed and brutality.

Montfort did not retain his titles long; Raymond reasserted himself and de Montfort was killed in 1218 besieging Toulouse which had rebelled. His son Amaury was unable to hold his inheritance against the legitimate house of Toulouse and the papacy called in Louis VIII of France, who invaded the country which he proclaimed to be annexed to the royal domain of France. Louis himself died on this compaign, but the conquest was carried out by his officers, and the union of Languedoc to France was accepted by the Treaty of Meaux of 1229. By this treaty, Raymond VII retained Toulouse until his death, on condition that he assign it as a dot to his daughter who was betrothed to Alphonse of Poitiers, the younger brother of the king. The papacy meanwhile received Avignon for itself. When Alphonse inherited his father-in-law's lands in 1249, the independence of Languedoc was at an end.

The Albigensian crusade is important, however, for more than its effect on southern France or on the heretics, for it set the example which later popes were to follow in diverting crusades from the East to European struggles. Innocent III himself had given it priority over the Eastern crusades. Later popes were to divert men and money intended for the East to wars nearer at hand; political struggles of the papacy were termed crusades and were given the privileges of crusades. Nothing did more than this to undermine the interest in the crusades and to turn men away from them. Political crusades in Europe were waged throughout the thirteenth and fourteenth centuries against heretics or any other enemy of the papacy. The Albigensians, Frederick II, the kings of Aragon, the house of Colonna, and the Hussites, were all the objects of crusades during the next two centuries; crusades against the Turks and Mongols took distinctly second place.

CHAPTER 25

THE CHURCH MILITANT: INNOCENT III AND FREDERICK II

✦

THE end of the twelfth century and the first half of the thirteenth were dominated by two great figures of church and state: from 1198 to 1216 the papacy dominated Europe under Innocent III, then from 1215 to 1250 the Emperor Frederick II (*"Stupor Mundi"*) occupied the center of the stage. The struggle for supremacy was continued, Innocent maintaining a clear supremacy against a divided and disorganized empire, and Frederick reasserting the power of Caesar against the church. In the long run the eternal corporation conquered the man, but as long as Frederick lived the victory of the church was delayed.

INNOCENT III AND THE EMPIRE, 1198–1216

When Frederick I died the imperial throne, as we have seen above, passed to his son Henry VI, who combined with his German titles that of king of Sicily, which he had acquired through his marriage with Constance de Hauteville. Although he planned a great crusade which would conquer the East, and dreamed of an empire which would include Germany, Italy, Greece, and the Levant, Henry VI died in 1197 just after he had made good his pretentions to the Sicilian crown. He left the southern kingdom to his infant son, Frederick, under the regency of Markward of Anweiler, while the leadership of the Hohenstaufen party in Germany passed to Philip of Swabia, the younger brother of Henry VI.

The Ghibelline princes met and dutifully elected Philip king of the Germans in March 1198, but the Guelph nobles, spurred on by English influence, elected Otto of Brunswick, the son of Henry the Lion. While England backed Otto, France supported Philip; both emperors-elect sought the support of the papacy. Meanwhile the north Italian towns established a practical independence of any imperial control, and Lombardy and Tuscany settled down to a gala period of civil strife.

It was in this crisis of European affairs that Innocent III ascended the papal throne on January 8, 1198. As we have seen, Innocent was a firm believer in the temporal lordship of the papacy supreme over all secular rulers. He began his rule by reducing to submission the turbulent nobles of Rome, extending effective papal control over Spoleto and Ancona. At the same time the pope accepted the guardianship of Sicily from Constance, placing the child, Frederick, under the protection of the Holy See. When Philip and Otto in turn sought the approval of the papacy on their elections, Innocent made the most of the situation to affirm the papal control over imperial elections. At first he maintained a policy of neutrality while he studied the claims of the two candidates, but it was but natural that the pope should favor somewhat the claims of the pro-papal Guelph over those of the traditionally hostile Ghibelline. However, he kept up negotiations with both claimants until 1201 when he finally recognized Otto, on the basis of promises made by him to renounce all claims over Italy and to abandon imperial claims to episcopal spoils in Germany.

However, even papal support was not enough to win for Otto the throne of Germany; he quarreled with his chief supporters; Philip steadily gained in power, and by 1207, Otto had been compelled to flee Germany and take refuge in England. Innocent at once resumed negotiations with Philip, endeavoring to salvage what he could from the defeat of his protégé; Philip sought absolution from the excommunication under which he had lain since 1197 and Innocent finally agreed to accept him as emperor, when in June 1208, Philip was murdered as a result of a private quarrel with Otto of Wittelsbach of Bavaria. With the field thus cleared, Otto was able to stage a comeback and secured the votes of the Hohenstaufen nobles on condition that he marry the daughter of Philip.

But Otto, the recognized king of the Germans, proved himself much less pliable than Otto the losing candidate. Although he renewed his promises to respect freedom of ecclesiastical elections in Germany, he embarked on an expedition to Italy in 1209 for the ostensible purpose of receiving the imperial crown at Rome. After his coronation, however, he proceeded to appoint imperial governors throughout Italy, establishing his vicars in Lombardy, Tuscany, Spoleto, and other papal lands, and preparing to conquer Sicily, which he had specifically renounced. In 1210 to 1211, Otto invaded the south and overran the entire mainland; young Frederick prepared to retreat to Africa. To avoid this, Innocent intrigued with the bishops of Germany and secured the election in September 1211 of young Frederick as king of the Germans.

The election of Frederick recalled Otto from Italy, as expected. Frederick promised to abdicate the throne of Sicily in favor of his infant son, Henry, as soon as he should receive the German crown, did homage for Sicily to the pope meanwhile, and with papal support went north through Genoa to Germany where he began to build up a party. The Rhineland accepted Frederick enthusiastically; the Hohenstaufen partisans acclaimed him, and on December 9, 1212 Frederick was crowned king of the Germans in Mainz. French money and influence aided Frederick while English continued to buttress up Otto.

The final victory of Frederick was secured by the battle of Bouvines, July 27, 1214. In this battle the allied forces of Otto IV, John of England, the count of Flanders and others of the lords of the Low Countries were decisively defeated by Philip Augustus of France, who was allied with Frederick. The rout of Otto at Bouvines destroyed his power in Germany and left Frederick free to press his advantage. To purchase the support of the German princes, Frederick made extensive grants of privileges to the nobles which reduced the imperial power in Germany, and to secure the continued support of the papacy, he issued on July 12, 1213, the Golden Bull of Eger, in which he confirmed in a law the promises made to Innocent III. Then with papal and baronial approval, Frederick was again crowned king of the Germans at Aix-la-Chapelle in 1215, at the same time taking the vow of the crusade.

Thus the policy of Innocent III eventually triumphed in Germany. The promises which he had gotten and then lost from Otto were solemnly confirmed by Frederick, the church in Germany was virtually independent of the secular authority and placed squarely under papal control. Neither Innocent nor Frederick could have foreseen the long years of conflict which were to result from the events of 1215.

INNOCENT III, FRANCE AND ENGLAND

If Innocent made the papacy ultimately the arbiter of affairs in the empire he was hardly less powerful in the internal affairs of France and England.

In France, Innocent was to meet his match in the person of Philip Augustus and the papal intervention there was not successful. Philip had married in 1193 Ingeborg, the sister of King Canute of Denmark, but after his marriage had immediately and inexplicably repudiated her. A local council annulled the marriage and Ingeborg was sent to a convent, against her own protests and those of her brother. Celestine III, answering their appeal, had annulled the annulment, but Philip had ignored the papal action, and had instead procured for himself a new wife in the person of Agnes of Meran, daughter of the duke of Meran in eastern Bavaria. The pope replied to this defiance by placing France under the interdict in 1200. At first Philip resisted, but in March 1201 the king yielded; he appeared before the papal legate and solemnly received Ingeborg back to favor, restoring her to her royal position. However, instead of restoring Ingeborg to the palace, Philip imprisoned his queen, depriving her of even the necessities of life. Agnes died, her children were legitimated, but still Philip avoided Ingeborg, until finally, under further pressure from Rome, Philip again yielded in 1213 and this time did restore her to her queenly estate. However, though Innocent ultimately triumphed even over the determination of Philip, the whole business could hardly be called a brilliant victory for the papacy, as Philip evidently gave in only when he was ready to do so. Throughout, Innocent needed Philip more than Philip needed the pope; involved with Germany and England, the pope was forced to tread warily with France which he sorely needed as an ally. In his struggle with Otto, with John Lackland and with the Albigensians, Innocent was dependent on the good will of Philip Augustus, and while he fought with him, he did so with some reserve.

The struggle with John of England was, on the other hand, one of Innocent's greatest triumphs. On July 13, 1205, Hubert Walter, Archbishop of Canterbury, died. The monks of Canterbury Cathedral proceeded secretly and hastily to elect a successor without getting the required permission from the king. Having secretly chosen one of their number, the sub-prior Reginald, the monks despatched him to Rome to secure the papal approval and the pallium, instructing him to avoid any mention of the purpose of his voyage until he should arrive at Rome. But Reginald saw no reason why he should travel humbly as a mere sub-prior when he would be received with honor as the archbishop-elect, and upon reaching France let the news of his election be known.

King John was furious and vowed that never would he accept the election of Reginald. A new election was ordered wherein one of John's protégés, John, bishop of Norwich, was chosen archbishop, and he, too, set out for Rome to secure the papal confirmation. When the two claimants reached Rome, Innocent ordered the whole case to be heard there, and instructed the monks to send a new delegation, who would be empowered to conduct a new election on the spot. The matter was dragged on in the curia for months; finally both candidates were thrown out. The logic of this was irrefutable: Reginald was disqualified as he had been elected illegally, while John was rejected as he had been elected while another candidate was pressing his claims at Rome. With both candidates out of the way, the pope then ordered the monks to elect as archbishop Stephen Langton, an English cardinal, former professor of Paris, canon lawyer, and the man who had broken the chapters of the Bible down into verses. There can be no question but that Langton was the outstanding English ecclesiastic of his day, and the decision of the pope was a manifestly wise one.

However, King John was not minded to accept such dictation from the pope or anyone else. Although Langton was consecrated by Innocent in 1207, John refused to accept the election and confiscated the properties of the see of Canterbury, expelling the monks. Innocent in turn placed an interdict on all England. This interdict, which lasted from 1208 until 1213, was the most severe interdict in history; no ordinary exemptions were valid, the churches of the orders as well as secular churches were closed. While some of the clergy ignored the interdict and stood by the king, the great majority were obedient to the pope. John declared all clergy outside the protection of the law, and himself set the example of the spoliation of the churches. The confiscation of much ecclesiastical property enabled John to live for several years without asking any aids or taxes from his subjects, which helps explain his ability to resist the papal pressure. In 1209, the interdict having failed to bring him to terms, John was formally excommunicated, but this also proved ineffective. The most remarkable thing about this whole business is the resistance which John was able to offer, and the strength which he showed against the church; it speaks well for the royal absolutism of Henry II that it was able to withstand so severe a strain as long as it did.

Finally, in January 1213, Innocent took the last drastic step. He formally absolved all of John's subjects from their oaths of allegiance to the king, and authorized Philip of France to proceed with the conquest of England. Philip enthusiastically collected an army which he entrusted to his son Louis, for whom he claimed the English throne by virtue of Louis' wife, Blanche of Castile, John's niece. John began preparations for the defense of his kingdom—and then suddenly surrendered abjectly. On May 13, 1213 John met Pandulph the papal legate and made complete surrender. He agreed to accept Langton as archbishop, to reinstate all the exiled clergy, to restore all church property alienated and to compensate for all damages done the clergy. Then the king went beyond the papal demands; of his own volition he surrendered the kingdom of England to the papacy, receiving it back as a fief, and paying an annual tribute of seven hundred marks a year for England and three hundred for Ireland.

Nothing could have been more complete than the triumph of Innocent III over England. But at the same time John was the gainer by the form of his submission, for by making himself the vassal of the papacy, he placed himself under the protection of the church, and was able to call on Rome for help against his other enemies. Not only did the French invasion collapse, but John was able to use the papacy to rescind Magna Carta in 1215.

England was, however, as we have seen, only one of the many states which recognized the papal suzerainty. The only two states of Europe to successfully defy the pope were Venice, which took Zara from the papal vassal Hungary, and Norway, where King Sverre (ob. 1202) carried on an antiecclesiastical policy and successfully withstood personal excommunication and the interdict over his kingdom. Elsewhere the power of the papacy was paramount and the Lord Pope Innocent could feel justifiably that he had no equal in European Christendom.

Frederick II, Honorius III, and Gregory IX, 1216–41

When Innocent died in 1216 he was succeeded on the papal throne by Honorius III (1216–27), a mild man who was passionately interested in the crusades against the Moslems. In general, Honorius carried on to the best of his ability the policies of his great predecessor, but his pontificate was chiefly marked by his attempts to get Frederick II to fulfill his vow of the crusade. It was to this end that he arranged the marriage of Frederick to Isabelle or Yolande of Jerusalem. But Honorius, who had been the protector of Frederick in his youth, was constantly put off by the innumerable excuses which the emperor advanced, so that Frederick had not yet left for the East when the good pontiff died in 1227. Gregory IX, who succeeded him, was a man of a different calibre; stern and uncompromising, he admitted no excuses and was not in the least inclined to overlook Frederick's dilatoriness. We will see in the chapter on the later crusades how Frederick was excommunicated for failing to depart on his crusade as scheduled, and how the pope invaded the kingdom of Sicily during the absence of its monarch. In 1230 when Frederick returned from Syria, he defeated the papal armies and at the cost of some concessions, forced the pope to a reconciliation at San Germano.

It was in 1231 that Frederick issued two constitutional documents which regulated the administration of his domains: the Constitutions of Melfi, for the Kingdom of Sicily, and the Constitution in Favor of the Princes, for Germany. In both states Frederick had been building up his strength to the best of his ability; the differences in the two documents show the difference in the success which he achieved in the two countries.

The Constitutions of Melfi was the code of laws for the southern kingdom based on Roman law and establishing the most centralized and bureaucratic secular government organized in medieval Europe.

Under the Constitutions of Melfi, the kingdom was a benevolent despotism with all power emanating from the king-emperor. An elaborate system of courts, itinerant circuit judges, appellate jurisdiction, and a stern enforcement of law brought justice to the state. An equally elaborate financial administration provided the machinery for obtaining the funds which were necessary to maintain it. Ecclesiastical privileges were restricted, although heresy was made a civil crime; the old feudal privileges were abolished; municipal liberties were curtailed and the government of the towns was placed in the hands of royal governors. Representatives of the town were summoned to local assemblies and to general parliaments, but the local government of the towns themselves was wholly controlled by the monarch. Commerce and industry were fostered, a new gold coinage was introduced, local customs barriers were wiped out and trade within and without the kingdom was encouraged. The Sicilian monarchy was

ITALY

In the 13th Century

Como
Bergamo
Legnano Monza Cortenuova Vicenza Treviso
vara Brescia Verona Padua Venice
lli Milan Crema Este Trieste
Pavia Lodi Cremona Chioggia
Piacenza Mantua Po R.
in Roncaglia
andria Tortona Parma Reggio Ferrara
Fornovo Modena
Genoa Canossa Bologna Ravenna
Imola Forli
Lucca Faenza Rimini
Pistoia
Pisa Florence
Arno R. Arezzo Ancona
San Gimignano
Siena Assisi
Montaperti Perugia
Orvieto Spoleto
Viterbo Tiber R.
Rome Tagliacozzo
Anagni
Ostia Monte Cassino
Capua Lucera Foggia
Aversa Benevento Melfi
Naples
Amalfi Salerno
Tarento
Brindisi
Lecce
Otranto

DALMATIA
Zara
Spalato
Ragusa

ADRIATIC SEA

CORSICA

TYRRHENIAN SEA

SARDINIA

APULIA

CALABRIA

Palermo Messina Reggio
Cefalu
SICILY Catania
Girgenti
Syracuse

Tunis

al States

gdom of the Two Sicilies

unquestionably the most modern state of medieval Europe: its very centralization was to prove a liability, both from the high taxation required to finance it, and from the vulnerability implicit in the centralization, whereby the conquest of the capital easily led to the complete subjugation of the country.

The Constitution in Favor of the Princes, on the other hand, reflected a setback of Hohenstaufen policy. Both Frederick I and Frederick II had attempted to increase the royal domain in Germany, erecting a central core of territory directly under the control of the emperor as a territorial prince. So far had Frederick II and his son Henry, who was governing Germany for his father, gone in building up this personal domain, that the German princes were alarmed and forced on the emperor a treaty whereby he granted them the same rights that had previously been accorded the church. Henry had violated the traditional rights of the nobles in his absorption of territories with the inevitable reaction. To insure the continued support of the princes, Frederick was constrained to abate his centralizing policy and to repudiate his son's actions, guaranteeing the nobles their legal rights. This document has been interpreted as a voluntary abdication of imperial authority over Germany: actually, it was merely a return to the accepted feudal practices. "The *constitutio in favorem principum* was not promulgated because Frederick, absorbed in Italy, was forced to leave Germany to the princes, but because he and his son were so intent on building up their Hausmacht in Germany that an opposition was evoked which it was necessary at least to temporize." [1] That the Hohenstaufen power in Germany declined thereafter was through no fault of Frederick, who consistently endeavored to increase his family holdings and to build up in Germany a dynastic principality which could dominate the whole country. And it was really only after the death of Frederick that the decline set in.

The repudiation of his policies, however, antagonized young Henry, who broke into revolt against his father. In 1234 Henry allied himself with the Lombard towns, who had revived the old Lombard League in 1226, and openly defied his father. Frederick marched north in 1235 to be enthusiastically received by the princes. Henry was deposed and sent to Apulia where he died in prison in 1242. Conrad, Frederick's son by Isabelle of Jerusalem, was elected king of the Germans and left in titular control of Germany while Frederick went back to Italy to pacify Lombardy.

In his wars in north Italy, Frederick was ably assisted by Ezzelino da Romano, who was to become his most valuable lieutenant. Originally a partisan of the Lombard League, Ezzelino had swung over to the imperial side in 1232 (driving his rivals, the Estensi of Ferrara, into the Guelph

---

[1] Geoffrey Barraclough, *Medieval Germany* (Blackwell, 1938), I, 122–23.

camp) and had become master of the March of Verona, conquering Vicenza and Padua for the emperor. With the help of Ezzelino, Frederick invaded Lombardy in 1237 and met the forces of the League at Cortenuova (November 27, 1237). The imperial victory which was won that day compensated for the defeat at Legnano sixty-one years before. The League was broken up, most of the towns surrendered, the carroccio of Milan and her podesta were captured on the field, and only the severe terms of unconditional surrender which Frederick demanded of the Milanese prevented them from making submission. As it was, the imperial terms were so stringent that the Milanese and some others continued to resist as best they could, and they were considerably heartened when Brescia was able successfully to withstand a two-month siege in 1238.

Meanwhile, Frederick had further antagonized the papacy by seizing papal territories. He married his illegitimate son, Enzio, to the daughter of the chief lord of Sardinia, which was a papal possession, and set him up as king of Sardinia under the empire. At Easter 1239, Gregory again excommunicated Frederick and armed against him, securing the adherence of both Venice and Genoa to the Lombard League. Frederick besieged Milan unsuccessfully, while the allied forces wrested from him both Ferrara and Ravenna. Cremona, Pavia, Parma, and Pisa as well as Ezzelino supported the emperor who was able to make some gains in Tuscany and the Romagna, but on the whole the war was going against him. Gregory, feeling himself in a strong position, summoned a council to meet at Rome to depose Frederick. The prelates assembled at Genoa where they took ship for Ostia, but Enzio and the Pisan fleet attacked the Genoese ships, capturing the whole body of churchmen who were carried off to prison at Pisa (1241). Shortly thereafter Gregory, who was by then in his nineties, died. He was succeeded by Celestine IV who reigned only a few days (November 1241) after which the cardinals were unable to select a candidate for two years.

FREDERICK II AND INNOCENT IV, 1241–50

The man who was finally selected as Pope Innocent IV was actually the candidate favored by Frederick. Sinibaldo Fieschi, a Genoese, had proven himself the best ally the emperor had in the curia, and it was largely through imperial influence that he was ultimately chosen pope (1243). But as Frederick is said to have remarked "A pope cannot be a Ghibelline," and, once elected pope, Innocent became the most uncompromising enemy of the empire.

The opposition of Gregory IX to Frederick had been bitter and intense, but there had never been a question of personal malice. Gregory fought for his position and principles; with Innocent the struggle became more personal. Innocent was above all else a Genoese and a politician; in him there was but little of the churchman.

The entire armoury and prerogative of the Papacy were turned to secular uses. Provisions, dispensations, appointments, depositions, taxation, excommunication, interdict, crusade were made consistently weapons of diplomacy and war. The spiritual functions of the Papacy and the Church were degraded by bold misuse, and the medieval ecclesiastical system never recovered from the decay induced by his pontificate.[2]

Innocent entered into long and involved negotiations with Frederick, in which the emperor made several major concessions in central Italy to secure himself in Lombardy. Then, in the middle of the negotiations, Innocent suddenly fled from Rome to Genoa, claiming treason on the part of Frederick, and from Genoa went on to Lyons where he summoned a church council to depose Frederick.

At the Council of Lyons (1245) both pope and emperor presented their case to the contemporary world. But the verdict was foreordained and Frederick was anathematized and deposed from all his possessions.

In Germany an antiemperor was set up in the person of Henry Raspe of Thuringia (1246–47) and after his death in William of Holland (1247–56), while the pope began to hawk the throne of Sicily among the princes of Europe. Meanwhile, the mendicant friars were sent throughout Frederick's domains to stir up rebellion and conspiracy against the emperor. A conspiracy of the Sicilian barons in 1246 was discovered and put down; the papal forces were defeated and Frederick, ably supported by Enzio and Ezzelino, actually made considerable gains in northern Italy. The emperor was even contemplating attacking the pope at Lyons itself, when the commune of Parma, which had been one of his most faithful adherents, was captured by the papal partisans. As Parma controlled the route from Italy to the north, Frederick had to abandon his plans until he could reduce the city. Moving up in force he built a fortified camp which he named Victoria outside Parma and sat down for a long siege, but in February 1248, the Parmesians sallied out while the emperor was away hunting and took and destroyed Victoria, capturing his baggage train and treasure. This defeat was followed the next year by the capture of Enzio by the Bolognese, who carried him off to Bologna where he remained in captivity for the rest of his life. Although Parma was eventually recaptured and Ezzelino made marked gains in the northeast, the war was still undecided when Frederick died on December 13, 1250. He bequeathed both the empire and the kingdom to his son Conrad, but appointed his favorite

---

2 C. W. Privité-Orton, *A History of Europe from 1198 to 1378*, p. 74. Reprinted by permission of the publishers, G. P. Putnam's Sons, New York, and Methuen & Co., London.

bastard, Manfred, as regent of the southern kingdom until Conrad should come in person to claim it.

THE CHARACTER OF FREDERICK II

The man who died in 1250, defying the papacy, but professing his adherence to the Christian faith, was one of the most astounding characters in history. The nickname "Stupor Mundi" well characterized the impression he made on his contemporaries, and few figures in history have shown such a versatility of temperament and interest as Frederick.

Frederick has been termed the prototype of the despots of the Italian Renaissance and the ideal *uomo universale*. Certainly few men in history have shown such versatility and such keen intellectual curiosity in everything. He was cruel, unscrupulous, amoral, despotic. But the characteristic that most impressed men, and the sin for which Dante found him suffering in hell, was his complete scepticism. Frederick probably did not say, as the pope claimed, that "The world has been fooled by three great impostors; Moses, Christ, and Mohammed," but the phrase does seem to epitomize his religious sentiments. That he had a harem could be overlooked, but that he included in it Moslem women was an offense to all good Christians. In his struggle with the popes, he was supported by a colony of Moslems which he established at Lucera, on the border of the papal states, whence he derived warriors for his campaigns against Rome. His friendly relations with the Moslem sultans shocked Europe; the popes never forgave him his treaty with Al Kamil, a kindred soul who shared Frederick's broad toleration. When Jerusalem had been surrendered to the Christians, Frederick insisted that the Moslems continue their religious practices even when he was in the city. At his court Moslem and Greek ministers worked together with Latins; Moslems and Jews were tolerated throughout his domains. Heretics he burned, but heretics were rebels against constituted authority and so subversive elements who must be suppressed.

To many churchly writers Frederick was veritably anti-Christ.

He honored serfs and baseborn men. He exalted and defended thieves and murderers and others, which things he alone did more than those others against whom he defended them could do. He was cruel beyond measure so that he had no pity in him. He was treacherous and evil, and no confidence could be placed in him for any oath or promise which he made, and whether it be that he was timid, nevertheless in enforcing the reverence for the Catholic faith he was most active. He without sparing the dignity of the men of the Church, or sex, or age, or youth tortured extensively in manner which was never heard of; widows, children, the aged and infirm, archbishops and bishops, men of religion, were all despoiled by him of their lives and goods. In the matter of lechery he went contrary to nature so

that in his lusts he surpassed Nero: beyond number were his adulteries, his forni-
cations, and with it all he was a sodomist.[3]

But Salimbene, the Franciscan, who should have hated the persecutor of
his order, said of him:

Of faith in God he had none: he was crafty, wily, avaricious, lustful, malicious,
wrathful . . . And yet a gallant man at times, when he would show his kindness
or courtesy; full of solace, jocund, delightful, fertile in devices. He knew to read,
write and sing and make songs and music. He was a comely man and well made,
though of middle stature. I have seen him once and loved him . . . Moreover he
knew how to speak many and varied tongues; and to be brief, if he had been rightly
Catholic and had loved God and His Church, he would have had few Emperors
his equals in the world.[4]

Unquestionably Frederick felt himself above the laws that bound ordinary men, both as emperor and as a man. His political despotism was
matched by his code of sexual morality, but if Frederick was a bad husband,
he was a good father. He was married four times: first to Constance of
Aragon by whom he had Henry; second to Isabelle of Jerusalem by whom
he had Conrad; third to Isabelle of England; and lastly to the one endur-
ing love of his life, his long-time mistress, Bianca Lancia, the mother of
his favorite son, Manfred. By other women he had Enzio, Frederick of
Antioch, and a number of other illegitimate sons and daughters, for all of
whom he provided fiefs and doweries. In addition he maintained at
Palermo a regular harem; yet in his sexual morality Frederick was not
unique in his own or any other time, nor indeed was this one of the major
sins with which he was reproached.

More offensive to contemporary society was his religious indifference,
his scepticism, and his intellectual curiosity. This very curiosity made him
one of the great patrons of science, and much of his interest lies in his devotion to science and in the numerous experiments he caused to be made
to test the truth of old sayings and to find out how things actually happened. Unfortunately, few, if any, of his experiments ever succeeded very
satisfactorily, but his zeal for experimentation went on undiminished.
Among his experiments a few are worthy to be recorded here as samples of
his intense curiosity. It was an accepted belief that the souls of men existed
in heaven before being born on earth: Frederick was anxious to learn what
language was spoken in heaven and so sought to find out by taking a number of children immediately after their birth and confiding them to the
custody of some dumb mutes. Thus, hearing no spoken language they
would ultimately communicate with each other in the language which

[3] The *Gestes de Chiprois*, par. 102, translated by LaMonte in *The Wars of Frederick II
in Syria and Cyprus*, Columbia: "Records," p. 190. Reprinted by permission of the publisher, Columbia University Press.

[4] Scott, Hyma, Noyes: *Readings*, p. 418.

they had spoken in heaven, and Frederick would be able to find out whether it was Hebrew, Arabic, Greek or whatever other tongue that was spoken there. Unfortunately, the children all died of neglect and the experiment never worked out. On another occasion Frederick determined to find out if barnacle geese were really hatched out from barnacles; securing a large batch of barnacles from the bottoms of his ships, he sent for barnacle geese and had them set on nests of barnacles until he was convinced of the falsity of this belief. One of the experiments which he tried repeatedly without success was an attempt to watch the heart beat and the lungs expand and contract. Taking condemned prisoners, he would have an executioner with a sharp sword cut off the ribs of the condemned in the hope that the operation could be conducted swiftly enough to catch the organs at work. This he was never able to do.

Frederick also sent out questionnaires to other courts asking questions of all sorts. Especially did he send these questionnaires to his friend Al Kamil of Egypt, who finally sent him a learned slave to answer them. But Frederick's great love was for birds and animals. From all over the world he collected strange birds and beasts: he even took his zoo with him when on campaign, losing most of it at the disastrous capture of Victoria. He had an elephant, a giraffe, lions, tigers, and all manner of Asiatic and African beasts, sent him by his friends the sultans of Egypt and North Africa.

Concerning birds, Frederick was not only a gifted amateur but a professional expert. He himself wrote a treatise *De Arte Venandi cum Avibus,* which was a complete study of the breeding, care, feeding and training of falcons for hunting. This work has received the highest praise from later specialists in the field and has hardly been surpassed in some respects. Until recently the manuscript of this important work was kept in the Vatican Library; only in our own time did a fire there destroy this last souvenir of the great Hohenstaufen.

The Court of Frederick II at Palermo

Under Frederick the city and court of Palermo became the chief intellectual center of western Europe as well as one of the greatest ports. The income from the port of Palermo under Roger II is said to have been greater than that of the entire kingdom of England, and Frederick increased it even more. But the real glory of the court was not in buildings, but in the men whom the emperor attracted to himself there.

First among all the intimates of Frederick was the scholar poet, Piero della Vigna, "who held both keys to Frederick's heart, and turned the wards opening and shutting with a skill so sweet, that besides me, into his inmost breast scarce any other could admittance find." [5] Piero came up from nothing to be the chancellor of the Kingdom and the private secretary

5 Dante, *Inferno,* XIII, 60–64 (trans. H. F. Carey).

and closest confidante of the emperor. In 1249 he was accused of treasonable conspiracy against Frederick and was arrested and blinded. He committed suicide in prison, and Dante found him in the forest of the suicides, where he protested his innocence. "By the new roots which fix this stem I swear that never faith I broke to my liege lord who merited such honor." [6] Piero's Latin style was considered the most elegant of his time; his letters were collected in books as models of style and he holds a high position as probably the most polished Latin poet of the pre-Petrarchian era.

Other poets connected with Frederick's court were: Henry of Avranches, also a protégé of Henry III of England; Petrus de Ebulo, whom Frederick inherited from his father; and a number of minor poets who made up the Sicilian school of Provençal poets—Guido delle Colonne, Rinaldo d'Aquino, Jacopo da Lentino, and others. More significant even than the poets, however, were the scientists. Foremost among these was Michael Scot, the court astrologer, who translated several Aristotelian scientific works and wrote original treatises in astronomy, alchemy, and zoölogy. Theodore of Antioch, who was sent to Frederick by Al Kamil, was another astrologer and translator from the Arabic, and also served as the emperor's Arabic secretary. It is interesting to note that among his works was the translation of an Arabic treatise on falconry. Eugene the Emir translated Ptolemaic books; Leonard of Pisa wrote mathematical studies; Giordano Ruffo prepared a treatise on the diseases of horses; Jacob Anatoli translated commentaries of Averroes and Ptolemy; and there were a score of lesser scholars who flourished in the patronage of the emperor. As we have seen, not the least among the scientists was Frederick himself, and his son, Manfred, inherited this interest of his father's, continuing his patronage of scholars and authors.

The glories of the court of Palermo were thus closely associated with the princes of the Hauteville and Hohenstaufen houses; after the fall of Manfred, a blight fell over Sicily so that in the flowering of the Italian Renaissance it played no important role.[7]

END OF THE HOUSE OF HOHENSTAUFEN, 1250–68

The empire of Frederick II did not long outlast his life. While the emperor was able to withstand the tremendous forces arrayed against him by the papacy, the great corporation of the church could carry on with

---

[6] Dante, *Inferno*, XIII, 75–77.

[7] For the scientific interests of Frederick and the culture of his court see especially the studies of C. H. Haskins collected in his *Studies in Medieval Science* and *Studies in Medieval Culture* as well as his *Renaissance of the Twelfth Century*. For the literature of the Sicilian court see H. D. Sedgwick, *Italy in the Thirteenth Century* (Houghton-Mifflin, 1912), I, chap. 12. For Henry of Avranches as an international poet see the study by J. C. Russell in *Speculum*, III (1928), 34–63.

an unwavering policy aimed at the destruction of the house of Hohenstaufen, and the sons of Stupor Mundi were unable to withstand the constant blows leveled against them.

In Germany, Conrad found himself opposed by William of Holland,
so that his short reign (1250–54) was a prolonged civil war in which his
opponents steadily gained ground. At his death the electors passed over
his son Conradin, and William was generally accepted for the last two years
of his life. Then in 1256 William also died; the electors divided in their
choice, one party electing Richard of Cornwall, and the other Alfonso
of Castile. Neither ever established any real control in Germany, which
was plunged into practical anarchy, each prince going his own way virtually unlimited by any superior authority. The years 1254 to 1273 are
known as the period of the Great Interregnum, and were only brought to
a close by the election of Rudolph of Hapsburg, who established the "new
Hapsburg policy" of ignoring Italy to build up strength in the Germanies.

Meanwhile, in Italy the Ghibellines had had a period of great success
immediately following the death of the emperor. Manfred in the south,
Ezzelino da Romano in the northeast, Uberto Pallavicini in Lombardy,
and the Marquis Lancia in Tuscany, supported by Ghibelline factions in
the cities, gained an almost complete ascendency throughout the peninsula,
effectively checking the attempts of the papacy to establish Guelph administrations in the various towns. When Conrad IV came to Italy in 1252
he was well received almost everywhere, but his death in 1254 produced
a schism among the ranks of the Ghibellines.

Manfred, who was strongly supported by the nobles of Sicily, had held
the regency from 1250 to 1252 and saw no reason why he should not continue to hold that position. But Conrad had left his throne to his infant
son, Conradin, under the regency of Berthold of Hohenberg, who began
negotiations with the pope to secure the state for his ward. Innocent replied by annexing Sicily to the Papal States, whereupon Manfred defeated
the papal armies and proclaimed himself regent (1254). Innocent IV had
previously attempted to sell the throne of the Sicilies to some foreign
prince without success, Charles of Anjou having been prevented from accepting by the veto of his brother, Louis IX of France. When Innocent
died in December 1254, his successor Alexander IV (1254–61) a member
of the house of Conti, sold the throne of Sicily to Henry III of England
for his younger son, Edmund. With funds obtained from England,
he sent a papal army to invade the kingdom, but it was defeated by Manfred, who then assumed the royal crown of Sicily (1258). Having secured
the south, Manfred resumed his father's policy of attempting to dominate
northern Italy. In alliance with Pallavicini and Ezzelino, he invaded Tuscany and Lombardy, receiving the subjection of Siena in 1259 and assisting
in the great victory at Montaperti, which secured Florence to the Ghibel-

lines in 1260. Recognized as overlord in Tuscany and much of Lombardy, Manfred turned to outside alliances, marrying a daughter of the Greek despot of Epirus and giving his daughter in marriage to the son of the king of Aragon. In 1263, Pope Urban IV (1261–64) who had succeeded Alexander, declared war by excommunicating Manfred and again opened up negotiations with Charles of Anjou. Urban was a Frenchman and was closely bound by ties to the French house; with him began the French domination of the papacy, seven of the fourteen cardinals he appointed being Frenchmen, and Charles of Anjou being made Senator of Rome in 1264. He did not live to complete his arrangements, but his successor Clement IV (1265–68) concluded a treaty with Charles whereby Charles was to receive the kingdom of Sicily, with the stipulation that he would pay 50,000 marks in cash and 8,000 a year tribute thereafter, that Sicily and the empire should never be united, and that the king of Sicily should hold no office of any kind in Rome, Tuscany, or Lombardy.

With a large army of French knights and foot, Charles entered Rome and marched on south towards the end of 1265. Manfred at first avoided him, but finally fell back on Benevento, where the two armies met on February 26, 1266. Manfred, deserted by a considerable number of his Sicilian barons, was killed on the field of battle, supported to the last by the loyal Moslems of Lucera. The defenses of the kingdom seemed to fall completely with the death of the king; only Lucera put up any prolonged resistance, and the rest of the kingdom surrendered promptly to Charles. At once the old officials were dismissed and a new corps of French officers took over the administration of the kingdom.

The fall of Manfred precipitated a revolution throughout Italy. For some time the Ghibelline ascendency had been on the decline: Benevento assured a complete victory for the Guelphs. As far back as 1259 Ezzelino da Romano had been defeated and killed, Verona and Vicenza turning Guelph; in the same year the Guelph, Martino della Torre, had become podesta of Milan, and, although he had maintained friendly relations with Pallavicini until 1263, at that time Milan had broken completely from the Ghibelline alliance and become openly Guelph. After the battle of Benevento, the Guephs rose everywhere; Florence and Arezzo expelled their Ghibelline lords; Pallavicini was driven out of Brescia, Cremona, and Piacenza; Pisa, Lucca, and other Ghibelline towns were forced to submit, and the Guelph hold was as strong in Lombardy and Tuscany in 1267 as had been the Ghibelline seven years earlier.

But the Ghibellines refused to be disposed of so easily. There still existed a Ghibelline pretender, the fifteen-year-old Conradin, or Corradino as he is known in Italian chronicles, the grandson of the great Frederick. Representatives from Pisa, Pavia, and other Italian cities went to Germany to urge Conradin to make good his claims; on his acceptance, the Ghibellines all over Italy began to prepare to aid the invasion. The pope, fearful lest the expedition be too successful, abrogated the terms of the treaty with Charles whereby he was prohibited from holding other offices in Italy and summoned him to become Pacifier of Tuscany and Senator of Rome. However the Romans, ever fickle, would have none of Charles and, swinging violently Ghibelline, called in Don Henry of Castile as their Senator.

In 1268 Conradin invaded Italy. He marched south through the imperialist towns of Verona, Pavia, and Pisa to Rome, receiving enthusiastic receptions throughout. Thence he pushed on into the Kingdom, where a revolt on his behalf had already begun. Charles met him at Tagliacozzo (August 23, 1268); the French knights were fewer but much better marshalled than the German and Spanish forces of the Hohenstaufen; Tagliacozzo completed the work of Benevento, the last hope of a Hohenstaufen restoration was destroyed. The following October young Conradin was beheaded in the public square at Naples, whither Charles had moved the capital from Palermo; with his death ended the legitimate Hohenstaufen dynasty. The papacy had accomplished its purpose of exterminating the house of Frederick.

CHAPTER 26

CHARLES OF ANJOU AND BONIFACE VIII

✛

THE IMPERIAL SCHEMES OF CHARLES OF ANJOU, 1268–85

THE destruction of the Hohenstaufens had removed forever the threat which most disturbed the papacy; no longer need the popes fear a union of the empire and Sicily; but in setting up Charles of Anjou the papacy had created a Frankenstein monster which was to bring the See of Peter to a depth of dependence which it had not experienced for a century past.

For in inheriting the Norman kingdom of Sicily, Charles inherited the Norman dreams of empire in the East. He envisaged himself lord of an empire which would include Sicily and Italy, the Dalmatian coast and the Balkans, Constantinople, Jerusalem, and the states of the Levant. Towards this end Charles labored strenuously until all his plans were destroyed overnight at the Sicilian Vespers of 1282.

Charles was the recognized head of the Guelph party in Italy. Under his aegis the Guelphs had seized control of the Tuscan and Lombard cities, and the papacy had accepted him as its protector. From his capital at Naples, Charles dictated the fortunes of Italy and attempted to dominate the East. To secure a foothold in the Balkans, Charles worked out a series of diplomatic marriages: his daughter Beatrice married Philip, the son of Baldwin of Constantinople; his son Philip married Isabelle de Ville-hardouin, princess of Morea; and Hungary was secured by a double marriage alliance, Charles of Salerno marrying the sister of King Ladislas while Ladislas himself married Isabelle of Anjou.

Then in 1270 his plans were threatened by the crusade which his own brother Louis IX was launching against the Moslems. Whether or not the crusade was diverted to Tunis by Charles, or whether Louis seriously thought he could convert the sultan of Tunis, is uncertain. What is certain was that it was Charles who benefited by it in the long run, for Louis died of a fever in his camp before Tunis and Charles was able to exact double the amount of tribute which the sultan had previously paid to the rulers of Sicily.

Meanwhile a new adversary had developed in the person of Pope Gregory X (1271–76) who was genuinely interested in crusades against the Moslems and who opposed Charles' schemes for Eastern expansion. In 1273 the pope secured the election of Rudolph of Hapsburg to the empire against the candidacy of Charles' nephew, Philip III of France; at the Council of Lyons, Gregory persuaded the representatives of Michael VIII Palaeologus to accept proposals for union of the Greek and Roman churches, thereby eliminating the excuse for an invasion of the Eastern empire. Further, a new electoral decree made the method of papal elections more strict, in an attempt to forestall any interference on the part of the Senator of Rome.

Three popes—Innocent V, Adrian V, and John XXI—followed each other in rapid succession in 1276 to 1277, after which Nicholas III (1277–80) a member of the Roman house of Orsini and a notorious nepotist, ascended the papal throne. During this period, Charles purchased the title of king of Jerusalem from Marie of Antioch, a defeated claimant who had appealed to Rome and whose title had been approved by the pope. It was Nicholas who suggested a division of the empire, whereby Rudolph was to have Germany, Charles to keep the kingdom of Sicily, Charles' grandson, Charles Martel, to receive Provence and the old Arelate, and northern Italy to be made into a principality for the Orsini. The pope was successful to the extent of persuading Charles to renounce all imperial claims over northern Italy, but his death put an end to the whole scheme; his successor Martin IV (1281–85), a former councillor of the king of France, was a most faithful servant of the mighty Angevin, who had secured his election. To further Charles' plans, he appointed him Senator of Rome for life, so that Charles held undisputed sway over the entire Romagna, and broke with Constantinople, so that Charles would have a good excuse for attacking Greece. A great Neapolitan-Venetian fleet was prepared for the invasion of Greece and the conquest of Constantinople when the Sicilian Vespers occurred.

THE SICILIAN VESPERS

The aggrandisement of the Neapolitan king had not taken place without raising serious opposition: Don Pedro of Aragon, who was married to Constance, the daughter of Manfred, allied with Michael Palaeologus of Constantinople to oppose Charles, and prepared a fleet, under the great admiral Roger de Loria, which set out for Tunis with the ostensible purpose of a crusade there, but actually to be within closer striking distance of Sicily. Meanwhile John of Procida, an astute agent of the Aragonese prince, fomented revolt in Sicily, playing upon the anti-French feelings of the native Sicilians. On Easter Monday, 1282, a riot broke out in Palermo which rapidly spread over all Sicily. This rising, known as the Sicilian Vespers, was carefully worked up by the Aragonese, although it seemed to be a spontaneous uprising of the Sicilians due to an insult offered a Sicilian girl by a French soldier. Between three thousand and four thousand French were slaughtered throughout the island, and the leaders of the revolt made haste to offer the crown of Sicily to Don Pedro, whose fleet immediately came up from Tunis. Charles at once besieged Messina, but Pedro landed at Trapani and forced him to withdraw to the mainland. The union of southern Italy which had been effected by Roger II was ended; thereafter Naples remained in Angevin hands while Sicily remained Aragonese until the two realms were united under Alfonso of Aragon in 1443.

The pope, however, came to the aid of his patron. He preached a crusade against Aragon, proclaimed Charles of Valois king of Aragon, and persuaded Philip III of France to lead an invasion whereby Charles was to capture that kingdom. An attempt on the part of the Angevins to attack Sicily by sea was averted by Roger de Loria; Charles, the son and heir of Charles of Anjou, was captured by the Aragonese, and in the midst of the ruin of his schemes, Charles of Anjou died in January 1285.

Charles of Anjou was in character a marked contrast to Frederick II; fully as cruel and more ambitious than Frederick, Charles was motivated by a deep religious zeal which he combined with his personal ambitions. There can be no doubt but that he really felt that he was carrying out the will of God in all that he did; he had the fervor of the zealot, combined with the canny opportunism of the politician. In his youth he had been something of a gay blade, but in his later years he was austere and unbending. Hard and wholly unappealing, Charles ruled by virtue of his real administrative and military genius; he was feared and obeyed but not loved, and the marked favoritism he showed to his French nobles did nothing to endear him to his subjects. "He ruined the Hohenstaufen; he crippled the Papacy. In South Italy he only left a new dynasty, a worse government, and a degenerating people." [1]

In his administration of the kingdom of Sicily, Charles continued the regime of Frederick II, his despotism being the more conspicuous in that it was foreigners who were the agents of his rule. Until destroyed needlessly and maliciously by the Germans in the recent war, the Angevin archives at Naples remained a silent testimony to the efficiency of Charles' government, and a mine of information to those few scholars who had the necessary time to explore them. But excellent archives do not necessarily imply good government, and the rule of Charles brought decline and decay to Sicily generally.

[1] G. W. Previté-Orton in *Cambridge Medieval History* (Cambridge Univ. Press and Macmillan), VI, 200.

THE ANGEVINS OF NAPLES

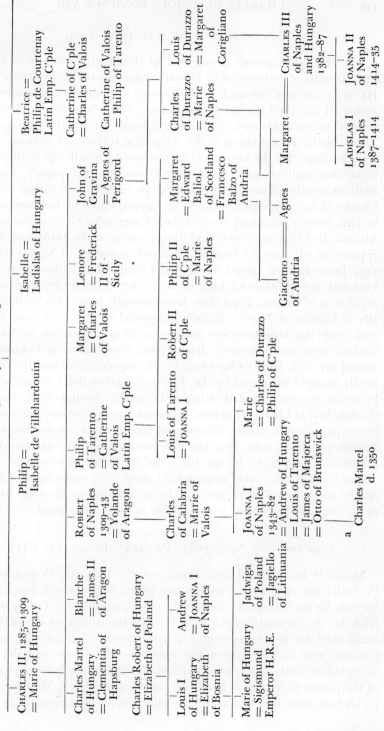

Naples and Sicily, 1285–1309

The chief protagonists of the War of the Sicilian Vespers all died in 1285. Charles of Anjou died in January, Pope Martin IV in March, Philip III of France was defeated before Gerona and died in November, and Pedro III breathed his last in November. The inheritance of Pedro was divided between his two eldest sons, Alfonso III receiving Aragon and James, Sicily. This division of the Aragonese realms was to bring endless complications, for the king of Aragon showed himself repeatedly willing to sacrifice Sicily to gain peace with France and the papacy, while the Sicilians stoutly refused to be sacrificed. In 1288 Alfonso agreed to release Charles of Salerno, now Charles II of Naples, whom he held captive, and in 1291 further promised to make James surrender Sicily to Naples. But Alfonso died that same year and James ascended the throne of Aragon, appointing his younger brother Frederick governor of Sicily. When in 1295 James in turn agreed to surrender Sicily, the Sicilians resisted and Frederick was proclaimed king of Sicily, which thereafter remained independent of Aragon. For a time James actually fought his brother as the ally of Charles of Naples; Sicily was invaded by an allied force in 1299 and, while the Aragonese won the command of the sea, the Sicilians and Catalan mercenaries severely defeated the Neapolitans at Falconaria. A second invasion, led by Charles of Valois, was defeated, and the war was finally brought to an end by the Treaty of Caltabellotta (1302), whereby Frederick was recognized as "King of Trinacria" (insular Sicily) and given the daughter of Charles II as wife. Frederick was to recognize the suzerainty of the papacy, pay annual tribute, and the kingdom was to revert to the Angevins at his death. This last provision was not enforced and when Frederick died in 1337, his son succeeded to the Sicilian throne.

Charles of Naples ruled uneventfully until 1309, when he died leaving Naples to his son, Robert, and his claims to Hungary (through his wife) to his son, Charles Martel, who was able to make them good.

End of the Medieval Papacy: Boniface VIII

Martin IV had been followed in succession by Honorius IV and Nicholas IV, both conscientious but unimportant popes, whose pontificates are notable only for the increased power in the curia gained by the Colonna under Nicholas. At the death of Nicholas in 1292, the college of cardinals were deadlocked for two years while the rival houses of the Orsini and the Colonna who had long been important in both Rome and the Curia struggled for control. Then in 1294 a compromise candidate was suggested in the person of a famous hermit of the Abruzzi, Pietro Morrone, noted for his holy austerities and his otherworldliness. Such an innocent appealed strongly to all parties, and the election was carried through. Morrone was brought down from his hermitage and installed in Rome as Celestine V (1292–94) while the cardinals built up their forces for the next election. Celestine was, as expected, utterly incapable of controlling the administrative machinery of the papacy and the real control fell more and more into the hands of the cardinal Benedetto Gaetani, while Celestine stayed at Naples under the protection of Charles II. The pope further distressed the cardinals by insisting on the reduction of all luxury and ceremony, while he despaired of his own salvation at being thus thrust into the evil world of affairs. Finally, spurred on by angelic voices (actually Gaetani speaking through a tube), the poor pope determined to abdicate, the "great renunciation," which placed him at the gate of hell among those who have never really lived.[2] He was succeeded on the papal throne by Gaetani, much to the chagrin and annoyance of the Colonna.

Benedetto Gaetani, who took the papal name of Boniface VIII (1294–1303), was a nephew of Alexander IV, and had been raised to the cardinalate by Martin IV after a distinguished career as a canon lawyer and papal minister. Learned in the law, able and ambitious, Boniface believed in the absolute supremacy of the papacy, and under him the papal claims to temporal power reached their height, in his own bulls and in the writings of his apologists, Egidius Romanus and James of Viterbo.

To Boniface, as a canon lawyer, the flaw in his title was most apparent. Whether or not a pope could legally abdicate was distinctly questionable, and even though Celestine had issued a special decree stating that abdication was possible, there were many who questioned the legality of the whole business. Therefore, Boniface could not feel safe while Celestine was at large. As a result the poor old hermit, who only wanted to return to his mountain, was arrested by the new pope and imprisoned in a fortress where, after nine months, he died. Ghibelline writers were to fasten on this as the first crime of Boniface.

The new pope's first concern was with the house of Colonna. The two cardinals Colonna, supported by their numerous kinsmen, and jealous of Gaetani's elevation, conspired with Ghibellines in Sicily and issued a statement that Boniface was not a legitimate pope as abdication from the papacy was illegal. Boniface replied by excommunicating them, and, when they refused to submit, preached a crusade against them. A papal army besieged the Colonna's stronghold of Palestrina, which was destroyed completely. According to Dante and the Ghibelline writers, the surrender of the town was gained by promises of liberal terms which the pope then repudiated. Having thus suppressed the Colonna, Boniface turned to Tuscany where he interfered in the civil disturbances of Florence, again preaching a crusade against his opponents. Among the Florentines who

[2] Dante, *Inferno*, III, 55–57.

suffered as a result of papal intervention was Dante, who immortalized his hatred of Boniface in the *Divine Comedy.*

Meanwhile Boniface had become embroiled with the new monarchies which were becoming so strong beyond the Alps. In 1296 he had issued the bull *Clericis laicos* which forbade any taxation of the clergy by secular princes. This was a direct blow at both Philip IV of France and Edward I of England, both of whom reacted vigorously. Edward placed the clergy outside the protection of the law until they requested permission to give him the sums which he could not demand of them; Philip merely confiscated all monies being sent from France to Rome and prohibited any export of money from France. Boniface, who derived a very considerable portion of his revenues from France, was constrained to back down, which he did in the bull *Ineffabilis amor,* in which he explained that the clergy could loan money if it was for the defense of the realm. This was followed by the bull *Romana mater* (February 1297) in which he instructed the clergy to give aids to their respective rulers, and by the bull *Etsi de Statu* in August, which officially revoked *Clericis laicos.* It should be noted that in this controversy the French clergy had generally supported Philip. As Boniface was at the moment engaged with the Colonna and with Sicily, he could not afford to antagonize the kings of France and England at this point. He even went so far as to canonize Louis IX in the hope of placating his grandson.

In 1300 Boniface held at Rome the Papal Jubilee. Thousands of pilgrims came from all over Christendom to gain the indulgence which was granted those attending the Jubilee; the coffers of the Roman churches ran over with the gifts of the faithful; while no great princes of the first rank came, so many of lesser state and such throngs of commoners attended that the pope justifiably received an impression of tremendous papal prestige and authority. After the Jubilee the arrogance of Boniface knew no bounds.

He was consequently in a mood to put the king of France in his proper place. The occasion was offered when Philip seized and imprisoned one Bernard Saiset, bishop of Pamiers and friend of Boniface's, whom he accused of treasonable agitation against the crown in southern France. Bernard demanded trial at Rome, while Philip insisted on trying him in the royal court. The pope sprang to the defense of Saiset; in 1301 he issued the bull *Salvator mundi* which cancelled all privileges, especially the financial ones, previously granted the French king. Then in the *Asculta filii* he warned Philip that the pope was above all kings and summoned the French clergy to a council at Rome, where Philip's offenses against the church would be judged. Philip's ministers, Pierre Flotte and William de Nogaret, issued a corrupt version of this bull in France and openly burned it in Paris. At the same time the king summoned a meeting of the three Estates of France to gain support for the contest with the papacy. The clergy were dumb, but the nobles vociferously expressed their support of the royal policy; a note was sent to the cardinals signed by the nobles and burgesses in which the pope was bitterly denounced.

Although the meeting of the Estates ordered that none of the French clergy should attend the council which Boniface summoned at Rome, before the council met Philip had been defeated by the Flemings at the battle of Courtrai (July 1302) in which Pierre Flotte was killed. Anxious for peace with the pope, Philip permitted the French clergy to attend the council in Rome if they chose, and about a third of the prelates of France, mostly from the southern provinces, were present.

It was at this council in November 1302 that Boniface issued the famous bull *Unam sanctam*.

That there is one Holy Catholic and Apostolic Church we are impelled by our faith to believe and to hold—this we do firmly believe and openly confess—and outside of this there is neither salvation or remission of sins, as the bridegroom proclaims in Canticles, "My dove, my undefiled is but one; she is the only one of her mother; she is the choice one of her that bare her." The Church represents one mystic body and of this body Christ is the head: of Christ, indeed, God is the head. In it is one Lord, and one faith, and one baptism. In the time of the flood, there was one ark of Noah, pre-figuring the one Church, finished in one cubit, having one Noah as steersman and commander. Outside of this, all things upon the face of the earth were, as we read, destroyed. This Church we venerate and this alone, the Lord saying through his prophets, "Deliver my soul, O God, from the sword; my darling from the power of the dog." He prays thus for the soul, that is for Himself, as head, and also for the body which He calls one, namely, the Church on account of the Unity of the bridegroom, of the faith, of the sacraments, and of the charity of the Church. It is that seamless coat of the Lord, which was not rent, but fell by lot. Therefore, in this one and only Church, there is one body and one head, —not two heads as if it were a monster—namely, Christ and Christ's Vicar, Peter and Peter's successor, for the Lord said to Peter himself, "Feed my sheep:" my sheep, he said, using a general term and not designating these or those sheep, so that we must believe that all the sheep were committed to him. If, then, the Greeks, or others, shall say that they were not entrusted to Peter and his successors, they must perforce admit that they are not of Christ's sheep, as the Lord says in John, "there is one fold, and one shepherd."

In this Church and in its power are two swords, to wit, a spiritual and a temporal, and this we are taught by the words of the Gospel, for when the Apostles said, "Behold, here are two swords" (in the Church, namely, since the Apostles were speaking), the Lord did not reply that it was too many, but enough. And surely he who claims that the temporal sword is not in the power of Peter has but ill understood the word of our Lord when he said, "Put up thy sword in its scabbard." Both, therefore, the spiritual and the material swords are in the power of the Church, the latter indeed to be used for the Church, the former by the Church, the one by the priest, the other by the hand of kings and soldiers, but by the will and sufferance of the priest. It is fitting, moreover, that one sword should be under the other, and the temporal authority subject to the spiritual power. For when the Apostle said, "there is no power but of God and the powers that are of God are ordained," they would not be ordained unless one sword were under the other, and one, as inferior, was brought back by the other to the highest place. For, according to the Holy Dionysius, the law of divinity is to lead the lowest through the intermediate, and the inferior through the superior. It behooves us, therefore, the more freely to confess that the spiritual power excels in dignity and nobility any form whatsoever of earthly power, as spiritul interests exceed the temporal importance. All this we see fairly from the giving of tithes, from the benediction and sanctification, from the recognition of this power and the control of the same things. For the truth bearing witness, it is for the spiritual power to establish the earthly power and judge it, if it be not good. Thus, in the case of the Church and the power of the Church, the prophecy of Jeremiah is fulfilled: "See, I have this day set thee over the nations and over the kingdoms"—and so forth. Therefore, if the earthly power shall err, it shall be judged by the spiritual power; if the lesser spiritual power err, it shall be judged by the higher. But if the supreme power err, it can be judged by God alone and not by man, the apostles bearing witness saying, the spiritual man judges all things but he himself is judged by no one. Hence this power, although given to man and exercised by man, is not human, but rather a divine power, given by the divine lips to Peter, and founded on a rock for Him and his successors in Him (Christ) whom he confessed, the Lord saying to Peter himself, "Whatsoever thou shalt bind," etc. Whoever, therefore, shall resist this power, ordained by God, resists the ordination of God, unless there should be two beginnings, as the Manichaean imagines. But this we judge to be false and heretical, since, by the testimony of Moses, not in the beginnings, but in the beginning, God created the heaven and the earth. We, moreover, proclaim, declare and pronounce that it is altogether necessary to salvation for every human being to be subject to the Roman Pontiff.[3]

At the same time the pope sent a legate to France with a series of demands which included recognition of papal rights over investiture, clerical taxation, appellate jurisdiction, et al. Philip demurred but submitted in part; the pope demanded complete submission. De Nogaret then brought charges of simony, heresy, adultery, tyranny, against the pope and proposed to bring him to France for trial; the royal chancery issued a formal accusation of Boniface. Popular sentiment in France strongly supported the king, and the University of Paris gave their official approval. The pope retaliated by suspending the University, and issuing the bull *Super Petri solio* which condemned Philip.

Meanwhile, De Nogaret, who was joined by Sciarra Colonna, had gone to Italy to arrest Boniface. They found him at his native city of Anagni (September 1303). Gaining admission to the city, De Nogaret and Colonna

---

[3] Quoted from the translation by J. H. Robinson in Univ. of Penna. "Translations and Reprints," First Series, III, 6, *Pre-Reformation period*, pp. 20–23. By permission of the publishers, Univ. of Penna. Press.

burst into the cathedral where Boniface awaited them. Colonna would have killed him on the spot, but De Nogaret prevented him, and Boniface was placed under arrest to be taken to France. But before the prisoner could be taken from Anagni, the townspeople rose to rescue him. De Nogaret and Colonna were forced to flee, and Boniface was triumphantly rescued by his loyal people. The Orsini, ever enemies of the Colonna, came to escort him back to Rome, but the experience had been too much for the old man and he died on October 11, 1303.

The "crime of Anagni" was the reversal of Canossa. At Canossa the papacy had freed itself from secular control; thereafter it continued to increase its temporal power until it reached its zenith under Innocent III; then throughout the thirteenth century the papal pretentions had continued to go on until they achieved their maximum theoretical height with Boniface, but actually the real power of the popes had declined during the long struggle with Frederick II and the period of subserviency to Charles of Anjou. The popes had succeeded in destroying the Hohenstaufen empire, but the new national monarchies had in turn destroyed the universal papacy. Both empire and temporal papacy were anachronisms by the beginning of the fourteenth century, and both had in fact, if not in theory, disappeared.

The full significance of the episode of Anagni was not at once apparent. Boniface was succeeded by Benedict XI (1303–04) who absolved Philip, but refused to pardon De Nogaret. He died suddenly, not without some suspicion of foul play; the cardinals haggled over the election of a successor for almost a year before they finally accepted a candidate put forth by Philip. Bertrand de Got, archbishop of Bordeaux, came to the papal throne as the protégé of the French crown. He took the name of Clement V, and, avoiding Rome where the Italian party was in control, settled down in Avignon to await a more favorable opportunity to proceed to the holy city. The Avignon Captivity of the papacy had begun; it was seventy years before the popes returned to Rome. Clement was wholly subservient to Philip, allowing the king to force him into the disgraceful destruction of the Knights Templar.[4] His successors were, on the whole, better men, but they were no less dominated by France.

THE STATES OF NORTHERN ITALY

The latter half of the thirteenth century was a great age in the development of the city states of Lombardy and Tuscany; it is, moreover, one that is especially familiar to us as it is the age of Dante in Florence, and so many Italians of that period are known out of proportion to their importance through the immortalizing verses of the poet.

[4] For the suppression of the Templars, see below pp. 465–66.

We have already seen the Lombard towns in their relations with the two Fredericks and have noted something of the struggles in which they were involved after the death of Frederick II. The period from 1250 to 1300 is one in which tendencies, held in check by the imperial authority in the earlier period, were able to develop freely, the cities profiting by the struggle between the Angevins and the successors of the Hohenstaufen. In general, the period is marked by the rise of the *populo* and the transfer of power from the nobles to the middle class, the constant civil war between Guelph and Ghibelline in every city, and the beginnings of the despotisms which were to characterize the fourteenth century.

It will be remembered that the Italian communes, unlike those of northern Europe, included the nobles of the *contado,* who moved into the cities where they continued their rivalries and feuds to the distress of the burgesses. Nobles in most Italian cities had the right to build towers on their houses, and they used to fight back and forth from tower to tower. The arcaded streets of such towns as Bologna were used not only to keep out the sun, but also the arrows which flew from tower to tower. The one great restriction was that the towers of the nobles' houses must be lower than those of the *palazzo publico* or the palace of the *podesta.*

The podesta was an office which grew out of the constant feuds of the nobles. Realizing that the incessant fighting was dangerous for the prosperity of the town the nobles agreed to the establishment of an outside arbitrator, whose chief duty was to preserve peace. This officer, the podesta, must be a noble but must also be a foreigner with no connections in the city. He was given a palace with a guard and had almost absolute power within the city during his term of office, but he was appointed only for a short period and his acts were carefully scrutinized at the completion of his magistracy. Many important nobles held the office of podesta, going from city to city, and we shall see how such a man as Uberto Pallavicini held the podestate of several cities at the same time.

As the burgesses grew in strength during the course of the century a new officer developed: the *capitano del populo.* He, too, was a noble, but he represented the *populo,* the non-noble burgesses. He was essentially the magistrate of the gilds; within the city he ranked equally with the podesta, but outside he was the commander of all the troops of the commune. Both the podesta and the capitano had their own councils to advise them, but that of the capitano represented the gilds while the nobles were prominent in that of the podesta. Both of these offices afforded a way for an ambitious man to become a tyrant of the city in the fourteenth century.

The struggle between Guelph and Ghibelline, which was rife in every city, added to the general political anarchy. This party spirit affected every aspect of the town life.

There was no standing ground in Italy outside one or the other hostile camps. Society was riven down to its foundations . . . Banners, ensigns, and heraldric colors followed the divisions of the factions. Ghibellines wore the feathers on their caps upon one side, Guelphs upon the other. Ghibellines cut fruit at table crosswise, Guelphs straight down. In Bergamo some Calabrians were murdered by their host, who discovered from their way of slicing garlic that they sided with the hostile party. Ghibellines drank out of smooth, and Gulephs out of chased, goblets. Ghibellines wore white, and Guelphs red, roses. Yawning, passing in the street, throwing dice, gestures in speaking or swearing, were used as pretexts for distinguishing the one half of Italy from the other. So late as the middle of the Fifteenth century, the Ghibellines of Milan tore Christ from the high-altar of the Cathedral of Crema and burned him because he turned his face to the Guelph shoulder.[5]

While we may speak of periods of Guelph or Ghibelline ascendency, we must always remember that the members of the other party were waiting, generally in exile in some neighboring town, for an opportunity to re-establish themselves in their native cities. All victories were local ones, and if a Ghibelline or Guelph lord gained control over a large area it was by getting the power in each of a number of towns. Thus William de Montferrat, who was first Ghibelline and then turned Guelph, was podesta of Turin, Ivrea, and Crema, and capitano del populo in Milan, Pavia, Novara, Vercelli, Como, Asti, Casale, Tortona, Alessandria, Verona, and Mantua when he was captain of the great Ghibelline league, but local revolutions drove him from power in one place after another until he had lost out altogether. Pallavicini was lord of Piacenza and Brescia, copodesta of Cremona and for a time capitano of Milan. Coalitions of Ghibelline or Guelph towns would place themselves under the captaincy of a common ruler, as the Ghibellines did with Manfred and the Guelphs with Charles of Anjou and later Charles of Valois.

In this way it is possible to distinguish periods as either those of Guelph or Ghibelline domination. Under Frederick II and immediately after his death the Ghibellines held the supremacy, after Benevento the Guelphs came in with Charles of Anjou.

Milan and Lombardy

Milan, which was one of the largest and wealthiest cities of Italy, having a population of about 200,000 in the thirteenth century, was one of the most consistently Guelph towns, but reached a height of power as a Ghibelline city. In the twelfth century it had taken the lead in the Lombard League against Frederick I and had repeated the role against Frederick II fifty years later. At this time the archbishop was the chief dignitary

5 J. A. Symonds, *The Age of the Despots*, (1897) p. 57. Reprinted by permission of the publishers, Henry Holt & Co.

of the city, the podesta of the commune, known as the Credenza di San Ambrogio, taking second place.

Defeated at Cortenuovo, Milan submitted to an imperial governor, the Marquis Lancia being podesta in 1250. But after the death of Frederick, the Guelphs came into power under the leadership of Martino della Torre who was elected podesta del populo in 1259. Martino continued to hold this office annually until his death in 1263, sharing his power with Pellavicini whom he made captain (1259–63). At the death of Martino, his brother Filippo, who succeeded him as podesta, broke with Pallavicini and ruled alone for life. He lived only two years and was followed by his nephew Napoleone. But after eight years the Ghibellines got back into power under Otto Visconti, the archbishop, who also held the title of capitano del populo. For a time Milan was part of the coalition under William of Montferrat. The Torrensi called in Charles of Anjou as podesta, but the Guelph rule collapsed after his death and the Visconti returned, Matteo, the nephew of Otto, receiving the title of capitano and later (1294) being appointed Imperial Vicar in Lombardy. In 1302 to 1308 a Guelph reaction brought the della Torre once again into control, but the expedition of Henry VII in 1311 reinstated the Visconti, Matteo taking the title of Lord of Milan and ruling Milan, Tortona, Pavia, Piacenza, Bergamo, and Alessandria until his death in 1322.

It would be useless and boring to attempt to discuss the local history of all, or even many, of the Lombard towns. Milan is the greatest and is typical of the rest. In Pavia, the Langusco and Beccheria families struggled for control; in Piacenza, the Landi and Scotti; in Bergamo, the Soardi and Cleoni; in Brescia, the Brusati and Maggi. In all of these places the rival parties would drive each other out only to be driven out themselves, and the political complexion of each town was influenced not only by its internal situation but by that of its more important neighbors.

At the eastern end of the Lombard plain lay the March of Treviso, which included the cities of Verona and Padua over which Ezzelino da Romano had ruled until his overthrow in 1259. At his death, Verona established a republic with Mastino della Scala as podesta (1259–77). Alberto della Scala, who succeeded him (1277–1301) was made capitano del populo for life with power to amend the constitution as he willed; thereafter the Scaligeri ruled as unchallenged despots, extending their rule over the neighboring Vicenza, Treviso, Padua, Feltre, and Belluno, until under Can Grande (1308–29) they were the most important lords of eastern Italy. Can Grande is better known however for the patronage which he gave to Dante than for his conquests.

The great rival of Ghibelline Verona was Guelph Ferrara. Azzo VII d'Este, a distant relative of the Welf house in Brunswick, was the lifelong opponent of Ezzelino, and his descendants continued to hold the city as a Guelph center. In 1264, Obizzo, the grandson of Azzo, was made hereditary lord of Ferrara, and his son Azzo VIII married a daughter of Charles II of Naples. The dynasty was to become one of the most brilliant of the fifteenth century.

In Ravenna, the house of Polenta and, in Rimini, that of Malatesta had been traditional enemies; it was to bind a peace made between them that Francesca da Polenta married Gianciotto Malatesta, only to find that it was his brother Paolo whom she loved, and to die with Paolo at the hand of her outraged husband. Her love and her death placed her among the immortals: to many today Rimini is important chiefly as the home of Francesca, who consented to "remember days of joy when misery is at hand" and who died for "love that denial takes from none beloved." [6]

At the extreme west, beyond the western end of Lombardy, the republic of Genoa, marquisate of Montferrat and the county of Savoy were both in and outside of Italy. Both Savoy and Montferrat were territorial lordships in the empire, Savoy really becoming important in Italian affairs only in 1280 when the counts acquired the lordship of Turin. William VII of Montferrat played a conspicuous role as a military leader in northern Italy from 1278 to 1290, but the real greatness of his house was in the East, where Conrad and Boniface had distinguished themselves in the crusades.

Like Montferrat, in that its chief glory lay in the East, was Genoa, the great commercial republic of Liguria. The Genoese themselves began their official history with the First Crusade, and the glory of Genoa was in its far-flung maritime empire, with colonies in the Levant and along the Black Sea. This very empire provoked continual struggle with Venice and Pisa, who were also building up colonies in the East: the Fourth Crusade which gave to Venice the control of the commerce of the Eastern Empire was a severe blow to Genoa, but it recouped the losses when, in 1261, Genoa allied with Michael Palaeologus to restore the Greek Empire and oust the Venetians. The wars with Pisa and Venice continued throughout the entire thirteenth century and well into the fourteenth, until first Pisa and then Genoa had completely lost out.

The government of Genoa, like that of Venice, was controlled by the rich merchant nobles, who governed through two consuls. In 1257 a popular revolution brought in a captain or "abbot of the people," but his power was never very extensive and the great houses of Doria, Spinola, Embriaci, and others continued to supply rulers to the republic. The real importance of Genoa lay in the great progress in commerce and banking which took place there, the famous Bank of St. George developing the first joint stock companies as well as maritime insurance.

---

[6] Dante, *Inferno*, V, 118–19, 102 (Carey trans.) *"Amor ch'a null' amato amar perdona."*

Venice

Of greater interest is Genoa's great rival Venice, which also came into its own only with the crusades. The period 1100 to 1380 (the end of the War of Chioggia with Genoa) is the great period in the development of the Venetian empire and constitution. Like Genoa, Venice received important concessions in the crusader states, developing colonies in all the principal ports of the Levant. Its greatest acquisition of territory came with the Fourth Crusade, when the Aegean islands and the ports of the Byzantine Empire were acquired, but already the fleets of Venice had gained control of the Adriatic, and it had played an important role in the struggle between the Normans and the Byzantines.

In the thirteenth century, Venice at first remained on good terms with Frederick II; later it participated in a crusade against Ezzelino, but its chief interest lay not in Italy but in the sea. "Venice pursued wealth with a single-minded devotion, seldom equalled and never surpassed." [7] Not until the accession of Pietro Gradenigo (1289–1311) did Venice engage in any serious wars for territorial expansion on the Italian mainland.

Since 697 Venice had been ruled by a *doge* (duke), and for the first three hundred years the doges were mostly selected from one of the three great houses of the Sanudo, Badoer, and Orseolo. In 1032 the dogeship was declared no longer hereditary and a nebulous council was established, but it was not until 1172, as a result of the disastrous defeat of the republic in a war with Byzantium, that the Great Council was established. This council was the work of the new merchant class who resented the domination of older nobility. The increased trade of the republic had created a new class of merchant nobles who controlled the wealth and who insisted on their share in the government. The creation of the council was followed by the establishment of the six ducal councillors, and the senate (*pregadi*) organized in 1230. The duties of the Great Council, which was composed of 480 members selected from various city wards, were to elect officials and to approve legislation submitted to it. The senate, of 246 members consisting of 123 elected members plus the doge and his councillors was the chief legislative body of the state, passing on measures proposed by the doge or his officials. It had, in addition, some judicial powers. The six ducal councillors were an inner cabinet without whom the doge could do nothing. They were the chief executive of the state, and could act without the doge, though he could not act without them. In addition to the six councillors, there was the Collegio which consisted of the doge, the six councillors, three judges of the appellate court, and the fifteen *savii* (ministers) of the admiralty, war, and exchequer. The most important office in Venice was that of the *Savii grandi,* six lords who acted as a supervisory

---

[7] H. D. Sedgwick, *Italy in the Thirteenth Century,* II, 30.

body over all others, and one of whom acted as prime minister for one day of each week. The doge himself was thus stripped of practically all power, though he remained a magnificent figurehead and represented the dignity and splendor of the republic. He was elected by a complicated combination of lot and examination by a committee of 41 electors chosen from the Great Council.

Venice also had an elaborate system of courts, with three courts of first instance having competence over criminal, civil, and provincial cases respectively. Above them was the appellate court, but before a case could be taken into any court it must be heard and approved for trial by three *avvogadori* (advocates) who prepared the agenda for the courts, and acted as attorneys once the case had been introduced. In cases of appeal in civil pleas, the plaintiff paid a fee to the judge of the court of first instance and another to the avvogadori; then, if the appellate court upheld the decision of the first court, the avvogadori had to refund the fee; if on the other hand, the court reversed the decision, the judge of the first court was the one to refund. In Venice only good justice was to be paid for.

When Gradenigo became doge in 1289 a further reform was instituted in the constitution. The membership of the Great Council had declined in the course of time from its original 480 to a mere 210. The doge secured the passage of a law to reorganize the council and the appointment of a committee to select new members. It was then decided that only those who could show a paternal ancestor in the council at some time since 1176 would be eligible for membership. This decision, made in 1297, is commonly known as the Closing of the Great Council; it was backed up in 1315 by the establishment of a register of all the births in any of the families eligible for the council, a record which became the famous "Golden Book" in 1506. While the members of the council were chosen by lot from the list of eligibles, if a man had been passed over seven times he could demand immediate seating as his due. In spite of the "closure," the Great Council increased its membership by the admission of new families: by 1311 the membership had grown to 1017 and by 1510 had reached 1671 members. Even so, the great old families of the Contarini, Cornaro, Foscari, Morosini, Dandola, Mocenigo, and others kept the ascendency.

The last great constitutional change in Venice came in 1310 as a result of the conspiracy of Bajamonte Tiepolo, a young noble who attempted to overthrow Gradenigo. While the conspiracy was not successful, it was felt that the state had been endangered and a new agency, the Council of Ten, was established with extraordinary powers to try criminal cases and matters affecting the public welfare. At first temporary, it soon became permanent, and its great power coupled with the secrecy of its proceedings made it a terrible, if efficient, weapon. Drawn from the members of the Great Council, with the proviso that not more than one member of any family should ever be included at the same time, the Council of Ten soon became the master of the Great Council and the most important agency of government.

The Venetian constitution preserved perfectly the rule of the oligarchy. Democratic among its members, it was exclusive in the extreme, and represented only the wealthy commercial nobility, whose interests were in the maintenance of Venetian trade and the Venetian empire. Venice showed a continuity of policy and purpose wholly unlike that of any other Italian state, and unlike all the others she was never disturbed by civil strife, having experienced only two major conspiracies in centuries of government. Nothing is more striking than the contrast between the internal calm and consistent foreign policy of Venice and the domestic turbulence and vacillating foreign policy of Florence, her rival republic.

Florence and Tuscany

Like Lombardy, Tuscany was divided among a number of cities which were generally in constant feud with one another. Florence, the largest with a population of some 45,000, was Guelph on the whole, and was supported by the Guelph towns of Lucca and San Giminiano; Pisa, Siena, and Pistoia were usually Ghibelline, and were always on the opposite side politically from Florence. The politics of both the Tuscan and the Lombard towns were governed largely by geography, as an important Guelph town would be surrounded by Ghibellines, and vice versa.

Under Frederick II, Florence had been Ghibelline: the Ghibelline Uberti had seized control and exiled the Guelph Buondelmonti in 1248; but with the reaction after Frederick's death the Guelphs returned to power and organized the Committee of Public Safety of thirty-six commoners, six from each of the city wards. To the earlier podesta with his councils was added the capitano del populo with his. The Ghibellines were exiled and fled to Siena and Pisa, whence they were able to return with the assistance of Manfred and win the decisive battle of Montaperti in 1260. The city barely escaped complete destruction at this time, as its neighbors of Pisa and Siena thought it an excellent opportunity to eliminate it altogether, but Farinata degli Uberti, who wanted to rule the city, saved it for the Ghibelline nobles. For six years the Ghibellines controlled Florence while the Guelphs were in exile; then in 1266 Charles of Anjou restored the Guelphs once more. It was at this time (1267) that the famous Parte Guelpha came into power, with its treasury full of former Ghibelline property. A new constitution was established at the same time. In 1273 the pope forced through a hollow reconciliation ceremony and the exiles were permitted to return. There were by now five major parties in Florence: the Ghibelline nobles (Uberti, Pazzi, Ubaldini) who had little power; the Guelph nobles (Cavalcanti, Cerchi, Donati, Medici);

the seven major gilds (*arte maggiore*) of the Calimalla, wool merchants, money-changers, druggists, furriers, silk merchants, and notaries; the fourteen minor gilds; and lastly the *populo piccolo*.

A new constitution, adopted in 1282, gave more power to the gilds at the expense of the nobles. It provided that a college of six priors, representing six of the major gilds and at the same time the six city wards, should constitute the executive, called the *signoria*. The priors served for only two months each and they must be members of the Guelph party. These new officials completely superceded the older officials, though the others were still retained in subordinate roles. Although the nobles resented the pre-eminence given the gilds by this constitution, Florence was at war with her Ghibelline neighbors and a party of exiles, and little could be done at home. In 1284, Pisa was defeated, Siena soon followed, and in 1289 the battle of Campaldino routed the exiles and their allies from Arezzo, wiping out the Guelph disgrace of Montaperti. With the foreign situation under control, civil strife broke out afresh in Florence. The nobles demanded a greater share in government and the gildsmen became alarmed. Giano della Bella, a wealthy Guelph, in 1293 secured the institution of the Ordinances of Justice, which established a new officer, the *gonfalonier di Giustizia*. The qualifications of this officer showed the power of the gilds: he must be a non-noble and an active member of a gild; he was chosen by the priors for a two-month term, the candidate being selected each term from a different city ward. While in office he commanded a special militia of 1000 men and acted generally as president of the priors. The Ordinances further provided that the priors, who could not hold office more than twice in two years, must be active gildsmen, practicing their trade in one of the twenty-one recognized gilds (in 1295 this was amended to make membership in the gild sufficient). But the most radical provision of the Ordinances was that which placed the nobles under a special law. Every noble was put under bond of 2000 lire; his family were made responsible for his actions; 150 noble families (probably 1000 individuals) were set apart as an unprivileged caste, who could not participate in government or enjoy the privileges of citizenship. If a commoner married a noble he lost his commoner status and was degraded to the nobility. This remarkable constitution, which was the direct antithesis of the Venetian, marked the high point in the triumph of the *populo* over the *grandi,* and it must be admitted that in all its severity it was not of long duration. Giano della Bella fell in 1295 and was exiled for violating his own Ordinances; the nobles got control of the treasury of the Parte Guelpha and, thus fortified, began to recapture some of their former position in the city. Further, the pope, who hated a commune in Rome which had patterned itself after Florence, opposed the constitution and sought to undermine it. This is one of the main reasons for Boniface's intervention in Florentine politics, though he also hoped to secure Florence as a principality for one of his relatives.

Meanwhile the Guelph nobles themselves had split into two sections, to be known subsequently as the Whites and the Blacks. The Whites, led by the Cerchi and Cavalcanti, were willing to accept the Ordinances and to work within them, but the Blacks, led by the Donati, refused. Corso Donati got control of the podesta and so distorted the administration of justice that the signoria exiled both the podesta and the Donati.

It was during this exile of the Donati that Dante held his priorship in 1301 as a member of the White faction. But the exiled Blacks appealed to the pope, who sent Charles of Valois to pacify Florence. In 1301, Charles captured the city and restored the Blacks—the Whites, among them Dante, being forced to flee. While Charles occupied the city, the Blacks carried on a proscription of their opponents; Dante was one of the exiles who was given a death penalty. This Black terror threw the Whites into the arms of the Ghibellines of Arezzo and Pisa where they waited the fall of Boniface VIII to regain their city. Dante went farther afield and found refuge with the Scaliger of Verona, where he wrote his immortal poem, finally ending his life at Ravenna.

In spite of all this political confusion the latter thirteenth century was a great period in Florentine history, for developments in commerce and industry as well as for her literature and art. The Calimalla and the Arte della Lana made Florence the great center of the woolen industry and trade in the south. But the economic greatness of Florence lay in the banking houses which developed in this period. The wool merchants turned their profits into banking and the Bardi and Peruzzi were only the greatest of a number of banking houses among whom the Medici appear as early as 1277. The Florentine bankers financed the papacy in its wars with Frederick II, which may account for the strength of the Guelph party in Florence. These banking houses built commercial empires all over Europe, for they conducted trade as well as banking operations. The *Practica della Mercatura* of Francesco Pegalotti, though written in the fourteenth century, gives a good insight into the interests of these houses. Pegalotti was an agent of the Bardi, serving them in Antwerp, England, Cyprus, and Florence; his book contains information as to rates of exchange of currencies and to the products obtainable or in demand in the various countries.[8] The Bardi and Peruzzi became the official collectors of papal taxes, at the same time making loans to bishops and secular rulers against the security of future income; it was thus that they were ruined when Edward III repudiated his debts in the fourteenth century. But despite the mis-

[8] Edited (without translation) by Allan Evans; Cambridge, Mass.; The Mediaeval Academy, 1936.

fortunes of individual houses, Florence, through its industry and banking, was one of the wealthiest cities of the West.

It was also one of the most beautiful. For the end of the thirteenth century is the age in which Florence began building; the Bargello was begun in 1255, Santa Annunziata in 1250, Santa Maria Novella about 1270, San Marco around 1290. In 1296, the architect Arnolfo di Cambio began the construction of the cathedral of Santa Maria del Fiore (to be continued by Giotto, Andrea Pisano, and Brunelleschi); two years later work was begun on the Palazzo della Signoria (the Palazzo Vecchio). While these buildings reached their perfection only in succeeding generations, the age of Dante saw their inception.

But above all else Florence of the thirteenth century glories in being the home of Dante Aligheri (1265–1321). No attempt can be made here either to discuss the work of this great poet or to estimate his place in history. Unfortunately, any translation of the *Divine Comedy* fails to bring out the true beauty of the Italian verse, but even so every person who even aspires to culture must at some time read this magnificent and monumental work. Dante stands at the end of medieval and the beginning of modern times, and scholars will probably never tire of arguing to which period he really belongs, but his poem is timeless. His concept of paradise is derived from St. Thomas Aquinas, that of hell from Aristotle; most of the figures in his drama are those of contemporary Italy, although classical figures abound. But the spirit of the *Commedia* is of no age and of all ages, the beauty of his verse made the Florentine dialect the Italian language. Whether read in the verse of Carey or the prose of Norton, or even better in the original as edited by Grandgent, the true majesty of his ideas and of his words defies description. Through the writings of this White exile, turned Ghibelline, the Italy of the thirteenth century lives as few other eras of history can ever hope to live; and the honor or infamy of scores of men and women, who would otherwise be unknown, has been immortalized in the work of this poet who shed upon them some portion of his own immortality.

CHAPTER 27

RISE OF THE FRENCH MONARCHY

❖

ESTABLISHMENT OF THE ROYAL POWER

IN our discussion of Italy and the papacy we have had frequent occasions to refer to the French monarchy; we must now go back to the end of the twelfth century and trace the growth of the royal power in France from the accession of Philip II in 1180 to the death of Philip IV in 1314. In general this development can be characterized by saying that Philip II broke down the enemies of his house and established the king as the strongest person in France; his grandson St. Louis made the monarchy popular and represents the feudal monarchy at its finest; *his* grandson Philip IV, whom we have already seen in conflict with Boniface VIII, centralized the government and established a ruthless despotism cloaked in legal formulae. By the end of the century (if we may accept 1314 as marking the turn of the century) the French king was unquestionably the strongest monarch in Europe.

PHILIP AUGUSTUS, 1180–1223

When Philip II ascended the throne of France at the age of fifteen, he inherited a crown which was threatened by the power of his great vassals among whom Henry II was only the most formidable. The real control exercised by the king was limited to the narrow confines of the royal domain, and from Normandy and Anjou in the west, Flanders in the north, and Champagne in the east and south, the young king could look for only trouble. But Philip possessed all the political acumen which his father had lacked and from the very beginning of his reign he played his cards with consummate skill until he had humbled all his rivals and made himself the strongest figure in the realm.

He began by allying himself closely to Henry II, while he fought with his relatives of Champagne and asserted his claims over Artois and Vermandois in the north. This alliance he maintained until he found it expedient to ally with the sons of Henry against the old king, and we have already seen him as the ally of Richard in the war in which Henry II was defeated in 1189. Following the death of Henry II, came the interlude of the Third Crusade, on which Philip went reluctantly and from which he returned as soon as he could do so without losing face. Let

Richard Coeur-de-Lion gain glory in Palestine: Philip was busy occupying lands in France. When Richard was captured on his return from the East, Philip allied with John Lackland to try to bribe the emperor Henry VI to keep the English monarch in captivity, but Richard raised his ransom and returned to begin hostilities with Philip which lasted as long as he lived. In this rather desultory war of skirmishes and sieges Richard came out the winner and Philip had little success or glory as long as Richard held the field against him. But, as we have seen, Richard allowed himself to be drawn off into a petty war with the viscount of Limoges in which he met his death in 1199. With the accession of John in England, Philip had his opportunity and he was not slow to take advantage of it.

It may be remembered that Geoffrey of Brittany, the elder brother of John Lackland, had died during his father's lifetime, leaving a child Arthur to inherit his lands. When Richard died the partisans of this young Arthur of Brittany claimed the throne of England for their principal as the son of the elder brother in preference to John who was younger than Geoffrey. Seeing his chance to profit from a disputed succession, Philip Augustus promptly recognized the claims of Arthur. The barons of Anjou, Maine, and Touraine, led by William des Roches, declared for Arthur, while the English and Normans accepted John, for whom the allegiances of the Aquitainian nobles were also secured by Queen Eleanor.

As Philip accepted the homage of Arthur for all of the Plantagenet dominions, war was inevitable. At first success was with John; William des Roches quarreled with Philip and transferred his allegiance, and that of his partisans, to John which gave the latter not only a firm footing in Anjou and Maine but also the possession of Arthur. Philip meanwhile was distracted from the war by the interdict placed on France by the pope over the question of Queen Ingeborg. Accordingly Philip made a truce whereby he accepted John's homages for all the Plantagenet lands, stipulating only that Arthur should hold Brittany under his uncle. To cement the peace Louis, Philip's son, married John's niece, Blanche of Castile.

But John soon gave Philip a chance to recover his losses. In 1200, John violated one of the cardinal obligations of a feudal suzerain by marrying a girl who was already bethrothed to one of his vassals. While traveling through southern France, John stopped at Angoulême, where he saw the daughter of the count, Isabelle, and also the fertile lands of the county. Although Isabelle was already engaged to Hugh de Lusignan, lord of LaMarche, John carried her off, thus acquiring a bride and preventing the union of Angoulême and LaMarche. Hugh revolted against John and appealed to the court of his lord's lord, demanding justice of Philip as overlord of Poitou. Philip summoned John to appear in his court to answer the charges brought by Hugh. John refused to appear. As a result of John's refusal to present himself at the court of his suzerain when duly summoned, the court of France solemnly declared him forfeit of all the lands which he held as the vassal of the king of France. At the same time Philip recognized Arthur of Brittany as his vassal for all of the Plantagenet lands except Normandy and betrothed him to his own daughter Marie.

The war which broke out in 1202 was to last until the English had been driven out of all their continental possessions save only Guyenne in the south. It opened with a victory for John in which he captured Arthur and Hugh de Lusignan. Arthur was imprisoned at Falaise; William des Roches demanded his immediate release and, when John refused, went over to Philip, accompanied by the Angevin barons of whom he was the recognized leader. Then in 1203 Arthur died; it has never been proven definitely that he was murdered by John, but neither has John's innocence ever been attested, so that there is considerable reason to think that John was responsible for his death. At any rate this further alienated many of the barons, who welcomed Philip as the avenger of Arthur. John's tyranny had already gone far to antagonize his vassals and they offered but little resistance to Philip who quickly overran most of Normandy, Anjou, Maine, Touraine, and Poitou. By the middle of 1204 all of Normandy was in Philip's hands and was incorporated into the royal domain. By 1205 he had conquered the lands as far as the Loire and had even driven as far south as La Rochelle. Only Gascony remained actively loyal to John, and this was not due to any affection for the Plantagenets, but to the fact that the Gascons preferred a king in London to one in Paris who was nearer and could wield a more effective check on them. Also as part of the British domain, the wines of Gascony enjoyed a monopoly of the British trade, whereas were they to become part of France they would have to compete with the Burgundies and wines of other regions. Thus both political and economic reasons motivated the Gascons to adhere to the English cause.

In May 1205, John attempted to raise an army in England to recapture some of his lost possessions, but a baronial opposition led by William Marshal and Hubert Walter forced him to abandon the campaign. In 1206 however he was able to send across an expedition which succeeded in temporarily recapturing most of Poitou and the territories south of the Loire. The loss of Normandy and the continental domains had a profound effect on the English baronage. Most of them held lands on both sides of the Channel and they found themselves forced to decide which they would keep and which sacrifice. Those who chose to stay by John became consequently much more English than they had been before, for they lost their French possessions and were localized in their English holdings.

Others gave up their English lands to become purely French. Many authorities feel that the first appearance of any feeling of English nationalism on the part of the barons can be dated to the loss of the continental lands in the period 1203 to 1208.

In 1207, John became involved in his struggle with Innocent III over the appointment of Stephen Langton which has been discussed above (Chapter 25). In the course of this struggle John formed a coalition with some of the other enemies of France and of the pope for joint action against Philip. A great alliance of England, Otto of Brunswick, Raymond of Toulouse, the count of Flanders, and several of the other lords of the Low Countries was organized in 1212, but John was prevented from taking the field by a war with the Welsh and domestic troubles with some of his own barons. Then in 1213 Innocent authorized Philip to invade England. Philip prepared an expeditionary force under his son Louis for the conquest of England under papal auspices, and it was to avert this that John made his abject surrender to Innocent, giving his kingdom to the pope and receiving it back as a fief. This of course ended any thought of a crusade against England and gave John papal support against any attempted invasion. Philip employed the forces he had collected against Flanders, where they were largely destroyed by a combined Flemish-English army and fleet.

In 1214, John's plans for an attack on Philip were complete. The English were to attack in the south, while Otto was to invade through Flanders, supported by Flemish and English armies. John began the war in Poitou which he overran. Angers was captured and John seemed well on his way to push his conquests north of the Loire when he laid siege to La Roche-sur-Moine, a castle of William des Roches, in June 1214. But Prince Louis marched to the relief of the castle and forced John to withdraw in July. The Poitevain barons revolted, Louis moved south, and Angers and much of the country was reoccupied by the French. Meanwhile in the north Otto had been met by Philip at Bouvines in Flanders on July 27, 1214. The battle of Bouvines was undoubtedly one of the most significant military engagements of medieval times; the utter defeat which Philip inflicted on Otto not only ended that monarch's effective rule in Germany and assured the success of Frederick II, but it gave France a clear supremacy in the West. The value of the communal militia, who appeared for the first time in the army of the king of France, has been exaggerated by many historians, but the importance of the battle itself is not diminished merely because the trainbands did not acquit themselves as heroically as was once believed. As a result of Bouvines and his defeat in the south, John was forced to accept a truce which established peace on the basis of the *status quo,* leaving Philip in possession of most of Poitou. John returned to England to try to raise a new army to avenge his defeat, and thereby stirred up the baronial revolt which resulted in Magna Carta. Philip went on organizing his conquests.

During the course of his wars, Philip increased the royal domain of France fourfold. When he ascended the throne the kings of France ruled over little more than the Île de France, the Orléanais, and a part of Berry. At his death they held Normandy, Anjou, Maine, Touraine, northern Poitou, Artois, Amienois, Valois, Vermandois, Clermont, Beaumont, Ponthieu, and Alençon, besides the suzerainty over Brittany, Auvergne, Toulouse, and Languedoc. Many of these lands had been conquered from the Plantagenets, others had been taken from Flanders, others acquired by purchase or trade. The suzerainty over the south had been gained as a result of the Albigensian crusade.

The history of the Albigensian crusade has already been sketched in Chapter 24. Without directly participating in the movement, Philip profited from it, as the northern barons who conquered the south held their lands as vassals of the king in Paris. It was only after the death of Philip that his son Louis personally invaded the south and brought the country under the direct control of the crown, extending the royal domain from the Channel to the Mediterranean.

In all of this territory Philip established a strong royal government. He had learned much from the administrative experiments of Henry II of England and copied the best of Henry's measures. He ceased to rely on the great officers of the crown, several of which he allowed to lapse entirely while the others became purely titular. A greater reliance was placed on members of the bourgeoisie, among whom the king found some of his ablest officials. Through the use of scutage, Philip was able to build up a royal army, independent of the feudal levies and much more reliable (though the loyalty of these mercenaries was given only to him who paid them most). Like Henry, Philip made extensive use of the inquest as a means of procuring local information, and Henry's Inquest of Service of 1166 was closely paralleled by a similar inquest held in the French royal domain. The use of the justices in local courts, and the establishment of the jury trial were not, however, copied in France.

One of Philip's most significant reforms was the employment of a new class of local governors—the *baillies*. The older *prévots*, although originally non-nobles, had tended to assimilate themselves into the local nobility and to assume the position of local lords rather than royal agents. To curb them and to establish a new group of officials more closely dependent on the crown, Philip selected his new baillies from the lesser nobility, and paid them not in lands but in cash. Each baillie was responsible for a district which included several *prévotries*, and to prevent their developing local roots they were shifted from one district to another after a few years

in any community. They were further required to render accountings to
the king at Paris three times a year. The prévots were continued as the local
agents for the maintenance of roads, bridges, fortifications, and public
works, and continued to hold their offices in farm; but above them the
baillies controlled the collection of all the important revenues, the administration of justice, and the command of the local military levies. In the
south, the office of baillie was not instituted, their duties being performed
by seneschals, who had the same functions, but who differed from the
baillies in that they were of the upper nobility, and their offices were
hereditary.

In addition to the reforms in local government, Philip reorganized the
central *Curia Regis*. It is from his reign that the Twelve Peers of France
are thought to date.[1] These twelve peers formed the highest feudal court
in the realm, but their duties and even their existence as a body was largely
theoretical and the great bulk of the work of the curia was done by trained
lawyers from the bourgeois class. The reign of Philip II is the great period
of the introduction of Roman Law into France, when the old feudal customs of the kingdom were becoming altered by the introduction of principles derived from the revived study of Justinian.

Unlike the English system, there was little breakdown in function or
personnel in the French curia. The whole curia sat as a judicial or administrative body and the Parlement of Paris as a strictly judicial court
does not appear until after the reign of Philip. In the same way the establishment of a separate financial body was delayed in France long after the
appearance of the exchequer in England. These organs of government
will be discussed under Philip IV. In the matter of finances, however, considerable improvement in administration was accomplished by Philip II,
and many new sources of revenue were added to the older feudal and
domainial income. There was an increasing tendency to commute services
into money payments, scutage being only one of many such commutations.
The Saladin Tithe was copied in France shortly after being inaugurated
in England. It is interesting to note that the Knights Templar were the
financial agents of the king and handled most of the collection and dis-
bursement of monies. In similar wise Philip chose as his chief advisor the
famous Guérin, the Hospitaller, whose military genius was in large part
responsible for the great victory at Bouvines.

It was also under Philip that Paris became definitely the royal capital.
After losing his treasure and chancery records when his baggage train was
captured by Richard Lionheart in a skirmish, Philip built in Paris the
great fortress of the Louvre to house the treasure and records of the

---

[1] They were the Archbishop of Rheims; the bishops of Laon, Langres, Chalons, Noyen,
and Beauvais; the dukes of Normandy, Burgundy, and Aquitaine; and the counts of
Champagne, Flanders, and Toulouse.

monarchy. Around the Louvre developed the administrative capital of Paris, which within a generation was to become the very heart of France.

The reign of Louis VIII (1223–26) who followed his father for three years was hardly more than a brief continuation of Philip's regime. Louis invaded the south where he annexed Toulouse and Languedoc, and won Poitou, the Limousin, and Perigord from the Plantagenets, but the most significant development of the reign was the institution of the system of *appanages*. It was the will of Louis VIII that each of his sons should have some portion of his inheritance, but that the essential unity of the king-' dom should not be disrupted. Accordingly, he decreed in his testament that fiefs (appanages) should be created for his younger sons, and, as his eldest son Louis was a man of the utmost honor and filial obedience, his will was carried out. As a result, while Louis received the kingdom, Robert received Artois, Alphonse got Poitiers and Charles was given Anjou. As all of the boys were children when their father died, these grants were only made in later years, but they set the disastrous policy of endowing the younger sons of the royal house with extensive lordships. Louis had hoped that the possession of these fiefs by members of the royal family would prevent the growth of great feudal houses: what resulted was that great feudal houses developed which had claims to the throne should the direct line die out. The trouble which France was to suffer from the appanages was only evident in the fifteenth century during the Hundred Years' War.

St. Louis, 1226–70

Louis IX, or as he is better known, St. Louis, was only twelve years old when he ascended the throne under the regency of his mother Blanche of Castile. Concerning his personality we are better informed than on any other king of medieval France, owing to the biography of him written by his old friend and companion-in-arms John, lord of Joinville. Joinville's book is probably the finest biography written in the Middle Ages, and is certainly one of the great masterpieces of Old French prose; in it the good knight of Champagne tells the story of the crusade of his beloved lord with many anecdotes concerning his reign and life in France, which give us not only an unequaled picture of the king, but an excellent study of Joinville himself. In it we see Louis the man, Louis the warrior, Louis the king—as he appeared to one who served him faithfully and who looked back to the happy days of his reign with nostalgic longing. Funck-Brentano calls his chapter on Louis "The Justiciary in Ermine" [2] and it is a happy phrase, for it suggests both the absolute and uncompromising sense of justice which was so marked a characteristic of Louis, and the gentleness

[2] F. Funck-Brentano, *The Middle Ages* (Putnam, 1923), pp. 289–320; in contrast to Louis VI whom he calls the "Justiciary in Armour."

of the man who wore ermine rather than armor in his governance. St. Louis is the ideal feudal monarch: he is the Platonic philosopher-king, the saint upon the throne, who administered justice to all equally, who was himself humble yet tolerant of the bravado or luxury of others, who was deeply religious but never priest-ridden. Professor Charles Homer Haskins used to say in his lectures at Harvard that St. Louis was a luxury which France could afford after Philip Augustus, but which would have been out of place in an earlier age. For Louis, finding a monarchy strong and feared, made it loved and respected. Without the rule of iron of Philip, the rule of justice and love of Louis would have been impossible, but coming after it, it increased the influence and prestige of the French crown. Since much of Louis' work really only reached fruition under Philip IV the discussion of his administrative reforms will be deferred to the treatment of the administration under Philip.

For the first nine years of the reign, Blanche of Castile was regent, and she kept her son closely under her own control. Louis was destined to be dominated by women, first his mother, then his wife, but at the same time he never lost his own will power and could oppose his womenfolk as well as he could any baron or bishop if the case required. It was primarily that Louis loved both his mother and his wife, and endeavored to do those things which would please them most.

The barons saw in the reign of Blanche a golden opportunity to revolt. They had submitted for years to the stern rule of Philip; now with a child on the throne and a woman as regent (especially a "Spanish woman") they thought the opportunity good for a reassertion of their ancient privileges. A great coalition was organized by Pierre Mauclerc, count of Dreux, who since 1212 had ruled Brittany by virtue of his wife Alice, the sister of Arthur. To him were allied Henry III of England, Philip Hurepel of Boulogne (a son of Philip II by Agnes de Meran), the duke of Burgundy, and others, in a great conspiracy which was "more noisy than methodical and more ambitious than formidable . . . with no concerted plan, no definite programme, completely haphasard." [3]

Pierre's first rebellion in 1226 was ended by the queen buying him off with a royal alliance and the cession of lands in the Avranchin; a second shortly thereafter was ended by the defection of Count Thibaut of Champagne, who fell in love with Blanche and abandoned his former allies. An English invasion which was to co-operate with the rebels was meanwhile defeated by Louis. The south was also pacified during the regency by the Treaty of Paris (1229) whereby Alphonse of Poitiers married the daughter of Raymond of Toulouse, receiving with her the cession of Carcassonne, Nîmes, and Béziers and the inheritance of the rest of the county.

[3] C. Guignebert, *Short History of the French People* (Macmillan, 1930), I, 234–35.

The history of France under Louis IX lacks the drama of the reign of Philip II, but it was nonetheless an important period for the development of the royal power. The suzerainty over Blois, Chartres, Sancerre, and Chateaudun was purchased from Thibaut of Champagne in 1234 when the latter needed cash to buy off the claims of Alice of Cyprus. More significant than acquisitions of territory, however, was the establishment of the king as the source of justice to whom all men could turn for remedy of grievances. Louis extended the system whereby Philip II had made personal agreements with individuals placing them under the royal protection. But his justice and mercy were available to great and small alike: the most famous passage in Joinville is probably the description of Louis meting out justice informally in the wood at Vincennes.

Many a time it happened that in summer time he would go and sit down in the wood at Vincennes, with his back to an oak, and make us take our seats around him. And all those who had complaints to make came to him without hindrance from ushers or other folk. Then he asked them with his own lips: "Is there any one here who has a cause?" Those who had a cause stood up when he would say to them; "Silence all, and you shall be dispatched one after the other." Then he would call Monseigneur de Fontaines or Monseigneur Geoffrey de Villette and would say to one of them: "Dispose of this case for me." When he saw anything to amend in the words of those who spake for others, he would correct it with his own lips. Sometimes in summer I have seen him, in order to administer justice to the people, come into the garden of Paris dressed in a camlet coat, a surcoat of woolen stuff without sleeves, a mantle of black taffety round his neck, his hair well combed and without coif, a hat with white peacock's feathers on his head. Carpets were spread out for us to sit down upon around him, and all the people who had business to dispatch stood about in front of him. Then he would have it dispatched in the same manner as I have already described in the wood of Vincennes.[4]

The most important single event of the reign was the crusade which Louis led to Egypt in 1248, which, with his captivity and his sojourn in Palestine, kept him in the East until 1254. This crusade will be discussed in a later chapter but it should be noted here that Louis' motives, unlike those of so many of the later crusaders, were entirely religious, and that his expedition was in his own mind a pious pilgrimage to redeem the holy places. The failure of this crusade rankled in the breast of the king, and he was never satisfied until he had again taken the cross in the ill-fated crusade which he led to Tunis in 1270, and on which he met his death.

Louis contributed much to making France the recognizedly first power of the West. In his relations with the other great states, he pursued a policy of compromise and adjustment rather than war when possible. In 1258 he signed the treaty of Corbeil with Aragon, whereby he gave up all the French claims to Roussillon and Catalonia (the old Spanish March)

---

[4] Joinville, quoted in Scott, Hyma, Noyes, *Readings*, pp. 464–65.

and James of Aragon in turn relinquished all the Aragonese claims to Languedoc with the exception of the city of Montpellier. Friendly relations were kept up with Navarre, which passed by inheritance to Thibaut of Champagne in 1234. Marriage alliances cemented the good relations with both Aragon and Castile.

The most famous of Louis' concessions to maintain peace was his treaty with England in 1259. Henry III had assisted Pierre Mauclerc in his rebellion in 1229 and had been defeated by Louis. Henry again interfered when Hugh de Lusignan revolted against the king in 1241. After the death of John Lackland, Hugh had married Isabelle of Angoulême, to whom he had previously been engaged, and the imperious queen resented what she thought to be a slight to her dignity at a meeting held by Alphonse of Poitiers. Hugh revolted; Isabelle persuaded her son Henry III to aid his stepfather, and a small English army invaded Poitou. Louis promptly sent an army to meet them, and in the spring of 1242 won the victory of Taillebourg which drove the English back out of the country. But Louis did not take advantage of his position. In 1259, he negotiated with Henry the Treaty of Paris whereby he restored to Henry the districts of Perigord, Quercy, and the Limousin, on condition that Henry relinquish all claims to Normandy and Anjou and perform homage to him for all his lands in France. Louis explained this unnecessary cession of territory to a defeated enemy on the grounds that he would rather have a loyal vassal than enemy, and pointed out that his children and Henry's were cousins, since Louis and Henry had married sisters (daughters of the count of Provence) and he wished that there be perpetual peace between the cousins. In fact this treaty, which Louis hoped would settle for all time the rivalry of France and England in Poitou, was one of the remote causes for the Hundred Years' War which broke out many years later. The position of Louis in Europe, and the confidence which all men had in his impartial justice, is, however, best shown by the fact that he was chosen by the English barons as the man who should arbitrate their grievances with the king at the time of the baronial revolt. The Mise of Amiens, which Louis handed down in 1264, decided against the barons and de Montfort refused to accept it; but the fact that they had agreed to accept Louis' decision shows clearly the position which the king held in the opinions of his contemporaries.

In his relations with the empire and the papacy, Louis showed the same impartial sense of right. Although himself devoted to the church, Louis could not approve of the papal policy towards Frederick II, and refused to allow his brother Charles of Anjou to accept the throne of Sicily when it was first offered him by the pope after the deposition of Frederick at Lyons (1247). He did permit Charles to accept it in 1263 after Frederick's death and assisted Charles in his conquest of southern Italy, but as long as he felt the pope was illegally attacking Frederick, he supported the emperor, whose personal character and actions he could hardly have approved. The conquest of Italy by the French knights under Charles added much to the lustre of the French crown, as their victories gave great prestige to French warriors and to the land whence they sprang.

Thus the reign of the sainted king was a period of steady growth of power and prestige for the French monarchy, and St. Louis is justly reckoned one of the great kings of medieval France. His reign has often been termed an "Indian summer" of feudalism, for Louis, although he had an exalted concept of the royal office and strictly limited the nobles, was above all else a feudal king: the royal absolutism of Philip IV would have been as unthinkable to Louis, as would have been many of the tyrannous acts of his grandson.

At the death of Louis IX in Tunis in 1270 the throne passed to his eldest son Philip III (1270–85). Appanages were created for Philip's younger brothers Robert and Peter in Clermont and Alençon, thus continuing the unfortunate policy begun by Louis VIII. The reign of Philip III marked a setback in the development of the royal power as Philip allowed himself to be dominated by his uncle, Charles of Anjou, and French policy became dependent on Angevin. It was at the instigation of Charles that Philip advanced his own candidacy for the throne of the empire unsuccessfully, and also became involved in the "crusade against Aragon." As we have seen, Aragon supported the Sicilian Vespers which drove the Angevins out of Sicily in 1282; Pope Martin IV preached a crusade against Aragon on behalf of Charles, and Philip led a large army south to support his uncle. He was stopped at Gerona and died while retreating northwards (1285). French prestige in Castile had also suffered in his reign owing to his unsuccessful attempts to secure the throne for his nephews, the Infantes de la Cerda, who were opposing the claims of Sancho IV. In southern France, Philip III did accomplish the final union of Languedoc and Toulouse to the royal domain on the death of Alphonse of Poitiers without direct heirs. However a new appanage had been created when Valois was given to Philip's younger son Charles.

PHILIP IV THE FAIR, 1285–1314

The handsome, friendly, modest man who ascended the throne of France in 1285 was destined to be one of the great builders of the French monarchy. The kingdom at the time of his accession included most of France, having thirty-five bailliages in the domain, only Burgundy, Guyenne, Provence, and Lorraine still remaining outside the royal control. It was not however through any accessions of territory that Philip IV distinguished himself, but through the tremendous development of institutions which took place during his reign. How far the king was personally responsible for any of the institutional developments is a disputed point, but there can be no doubt as to the ability of the ministers with whom he surrounded himself and as to the results accomplished. The day of the old feudal officials was past; the new men from among whom Philip chose his confidantes and ministers were mostly of the bourgeoisie and were generally trained in the law schools. His three chief officials were the lawyers Pierre Flotte and William de Nogaret, and the financier Enguer-raud de Marigni, all of whom exercised a great influence on the king and on his policies.

We have already discussed the struggle of Philip with Boniface VIII which led to the "Crime of Anagni," and the establishment of a French control over the papacy with the election of Clement V (1305–14). It was in alliance with Clement that Philip perpetrated the great crime for which he is rightly condemned, in the suppression of the Knights Templar.

The Templars had served a very useful and valuable purpose as defenders of the kingdom of Jerusalem as long as that state lasted, but after 1291 they had had little objective in life. They had, during the crusades, developed an extensive business in international banking, and this became their chief occupation after the fall of the Holy Land. As bankers they became the creditors of the papacy and of practically all the kings and great lords of Europe, loaning money against future revenues. So deeply was Philip IV in the debt of the Temple that the entire income of the kingdom of France would not suffice to repay their loans. The great wealth of the order naturally made it the object of much jealousy and resentment, and to the true stories of their luxury and pride were coupled utterly unfounded and scurrilous tales of heresy, licentiousness, and strange and secret practices. Further, the refusal of the Templars to be united to the rival order of the Hospital, which had been recommended as far back as the Council of Lyons in 1274, caused people to feel that the Templars were unwilling to devote themselves to proper activities and must be concealing some dark secrets.

In 1305, Philip determined to suppress the order. If they could be declared heretics, all debts owing them would be invalidated, and this seemed by far the easiest way to clear off the huge debt owed them by the French crown. Accordingly Philip began negotiations with Clement on the matter. The pope was reluctant, but Philip forced his hand by threatening to institute a process against the memory of Boniface VIII. As Clement could not willingly allow the memory of the earlier pope to be defiled, he reluctantly consented to institute proceedings against the Temple. In 1307, Philip entrusted the case against the Templars to the tender mercies of de Nogaret, who at once arrested the members of the order in France. They were subjected to the tortures of the Inquisition, and under torture admitted to many crimes and blasphemies which they as promptly recanted when relieved of the torture. When the pope objected, de Nogaret threatened to try him for simony. At last Clement agreed that the king of France could try the Templars as individuals, but that any trial of the order as a whole would have to be done by the papacy. A general council of the church was summoned at Vienne for 1310 to try the order; meanwhile de Nogaret continued his persecution of the individual members.

In the special tribunal at Paris, presided over by the archbishop of Sens, a brother of de Marigni, fifty-four Templars were burned at the stake. A safe-conduct issued by the pope to all Templars who would appear at Vienne to testify was flagrantly violated by the officers of the French crown and a large number of knights, who had hidden themselves, were captured in this manner. At that, 546 Templars came to testify as to the innocence and integrity of their order. From France the Inquisition spread the trial of the Templars over England, Spain, Portugal, and Cyprus, but only where torture was freely applied were any confessions secured. Finally the pope issued the bull *Vox in Excelso* (1311) which dissolved the order as being suspected of heresy though the charges had not been proven; the individual Templars were, however, acquitted. This was far from satisfying Philip or de Nogaret as it did not allow them to confiscate the property of the order, but it was interpreted to mean that any debts due the Templars were cancelled and Philip at once seized all monies found in the various houses of the Temple in France. Theoretically the possessions of the order were forfeited to the pope who bestowed them on the Hospital, but the Hospitallers were forced to purchase them from the king. Jacques de Molay, the last Grand Master, was burned at the stake in Paris in April 1314. Legend recounts that he went to his death stoutly maintaining the innocence of himself and his order, and demanding that Clement, de Nogaret, and Philip appear before the bar of God's judgment seat to answer for their crime within the year. That Clement died within a month, de Nogaret soon after that and Philip within six months, added credence to this story. In the other countries the lands of the Temple were likewise confiscated by the state. In Spain new orders were established and endowed with the properties of the Temple; in England the Temple property was sold to the new corporation of lawyers, who still inhabit the Temple precincts in London.

In the conduct of his foreign affairs Philip IV was moderately successful. The reign was marked by spasmodic war with England over the border of Guyenne, a matter which Louis IX had hoped he had settled forever. There was considerable border warfare along the Gascon frontier and a number of naval engagements between English and Norman sailors in the Channel. A treaty was arranged whereby Edward of England married Margaret, Philip's sister, and Edward of Carnarvon, the son of Edward I, married Philip's daughter Isabelle. From this treaty were to come the dynastic claims which Edward III pressed in the Hundred Years' War,

It was during this period of trouble with England that Philip first negotiated the alliance with Scotland which was to last, with a few interrup-
tions, until the reign of Elizabeth.

Philip was also confronted with a chronic struggle with Flanders.
Count Guy de Dampierre had become most unpopular with the wealthy
upper bourgeoisie of the Flemish towns and had made common cause
with the lower bourgeoisie. The upper bourgeoisie, who were called the
Leilarts, turned to Philip of France, while Guy and the commoners allied
with England. In 1297, Philip invaded Flanders and forced the rule of
the Leilarts on the towns. But the commons began to revolt again, and in
May 1302, at the "Matins of Bruges" the townspeople rose up under Guy
de Namur, the son of the count, and massacred not only the Leilarts but
the occupying French garrison. A fresh army was despatched to Flanders,
only to be destroyed at Courtrai (July 1302) in a disastrous battle in which
Pierre Flotte was killed and in which French control over Flanders was
wholly wiped out. Courtrai was the worst defeat which Philip suffered
from any of his enemies, but he made up for it two years later when he
again invaded Flanders and forced the towns to accept the treaty of Athis
(1305) whereby Lille, Douai, and other Walloon towns were surrendered
to France and an indemnity was collected from the Flemings.

Philip also interfered in the affairs of Germany, at one time even seem-
ing to desire the imperial throne for himself, and later (1308) trying to
secure the imperial title for Charles of Valois. Philip was finally successful
in securing the election of Henry of Luxemburg, a minor prince who
had been brought up at his court, and was rewarded in 1310 by the cession
of Lyons to France.

The real importance of the reign of Philip lies, however, as has been
stated above, in the institutional developments. The last vestiges of feudalism disappeared from the government of France, and a new absolute monarchy, with the supreme royal will carried out by officials and ministers
trained in the law was instituted. Everything that was done was done
legally, with the greatest respect for the letter of the law, but it was Roman
law in which the monarch was all powerful and all the old feudal limitations were disregarded. One of the conspicuous developments of the reign
was the growth of the royal household—the Hotel du Roi—with its army
of petty officials, clerks, huntsmen, chamberlains, and domestic servants.
The Curia Regis was broken down, as it had been in England, into a number of separate bodies each with its own special functions and personnel.
These special functions had been developing throughout the thirteenth
century and came to full growth in the reign of Philip, so that by the
fourteenth century they were functioning as separate units. They were,
however, still parts of the general curia and, when the king personally sat
with any part, it could assume the duties of the whole.

About 1247 to 1250 the first specialization began to appear with the meeting of special judicial commissions of the curia. These commissions at first varied considerably in size and personnel, but from 1254 they began to keep the records of their sessions on rolls, known as *Les Olim*. At first this court met four times a year, but in the fourteenth century it developed the habit of holding only one prolonged session, with special officers to carry on the work between meetings of the court. The whole court was called the *Parlement* and was in turn broken down into four sub-sections: the Chambre des Plaids for ordinary civil pleas, the Chambre des Requêtes for petitions, the Chambre des Enquêtes for inquests on local courts and officials, and the Auditory of the Written (Roman) Law. It came to be permanently resident at Paris and is commonly known as the Parlement of Paris. This was the standard royal court for all judicial matters; it had moreover a semi-legislative function in that no laws or ordinances were valid until registered by the Parlement (much as our own laws are never certain until passed upon by the Supreme Court). It should be observed that the Parlement of Paris was a strictly judicial body and was quite different from the parliaments which developed in England, of which the French equivalent was the Estates General discussed below.

In addition to the Parlement, the French curia also developed a special financial section, called the *Chambre des Comptes*. At first a temporary and occasional commission, this body met three times a year at the Temple in Paris to act on agenda prepared by a sub-committee which met in the Chambre des Deniers in the Louvre. Then in 1295 the occasional committee moved out of the Temple and joined the permanent sub-committee in the Louvre, being later transferred to the palace on the Île de la Cité. The Chambre des Comptes registered all financial ordinances, received the accounts of the baillies and prévots, and controlled expenditures. It reached its final development by an ordinance of Philip V in 1320.

The last section of the curia to develop was the *Conseil*, the advisory council which acted with the king in matters of administration. It was broken into Grand and Privy Councils, the latter called *Conseil étroit* or secret. Like the Chambre des Comptes, the Privy Council received its official organization by a decree of Philip V in 1316, but it had been functioning under Philip IV for some time previously. It was a small group of some twenty-five members who granted pardons, bestowed favors, and took similar special actions. The personnel of this body varied, the members for each monthly session being appointed during the previous month by the king. The Great Council was a larger body composed of the royal advisors and ministers which acted as the official consultative body of the crown. It may be considered to have retained the old rights of the Curia not delegated to any of the other more specialized bodies.

It is in the reign of Philip IV that the Estates General were first summoned as a regular body. Consultation with representatives of the various elements of the realm had taken place throughout the thirteenth century, the king always summoning to a meeting of his curia anyone whom he wished to consult. In 1269 and again in 1284 large assemblies of notables had been summoned to confer with the king, and in 1290 letters were issued to the counts, barons, and communes of France, but beginning with the assembly of 1302 the Estates came to have a more permanent composition.

The occasion for the summoning of the Estates in 1302 was Philip's quarrel with Boniface VIII. The king was embarking on a serious struggle with the papacy and he wished to know that he had the support of all classes of society behind him in his campaign. Consequently clergy, nobles, and representatives of the towns were summoned to meet at Paris to hear and approve what the king set before them. The Estates were consulted separately in the following year, but in 1308 a general meeting was summoned to approve the royal action against the Templars.

It should be noted that these assemblies did not concern themselves with matters of finance which were handled, as previously, in local assemblies. In 1314 however the Estates were summoned together to vote money. The Estates only voted their approval of the tax in principle; the bargaining for the amount and the collection was still done locally by the royal agents.

These assemblies undoubtedly loom much larger now than they did at the time. There was absolutely nothing new in the idea that the king should consult his subjects, and contemporaries saw no innovation in the fact that he summoned them all to come to confer with him at the same time and place. In other years the old system of local assemblies or individual conferences was employed, and men found in the general assemblies only a source of grievance that they had to go to the king rather than have his agents come to them. This is one reason why the French Estates General never developed as did the English parliaments: the cost of attending was excessive and people much preferred to stay home and have the king come to them. France was too big a country to have a single assembly represent the whole; local assemblies, or assemblies of the north and of the south, prospered better than did the national bodies. The French Estates never became the high court which the English Parliament was from the beginning, for the judicial powers of the old curia had been delegated to the Parlement; it did not develop the financial powers as finances were always handled locally; although at first membership in the English Parliament was a duty it ultimately became a privilege, but membership in the Estates General was considered only a duty until that body was revived after more than a century of somnolence in 1789.

In matters of finance Philip instituted few new measures. His expenses were of course extremely heavy as the paid personnel in government service had increased tremendously, but Philip managed to get along with extraordinary expedients. He collected the regular scutages and tallages on towns, taxed the clergy, nobles and commons and employed all the ordinary means of taxation; but these were not enough and he resorted to special confiscations of the property of the Jews in 1306, of the Templars in 1308 to 1311 and of the Lombard bankers in 1311. These spoliations of the Jews and Lombards were severe blows to the prosperity of the country and the fairs of Champagne particularly suffered from the withdrawal of the Italian bankers. Philip also attempted to debase the coinage from the sound standard which had been established by St. Louis. The crisis which resulted from his first debasing of the coinage was so great that he restored it to its full value, only to debase it again somewhat later. This continuous shifting in the value of money was of course the worst possible thing for business; and that French commerce and industry survived at all was not due to any intelligent policy of the crown.

In the field of local government, the only great step taken after the establishment of the baillies by Philip II was the institution of the *enquêteurs* (inquisitors) under St. Louis. These enquêteurs were members of the curia who, like the English itinerant justices, went out into the local districts to hear appeals against the local governors. At first created as special protectors of the people against the tyranny of the baillies and prévots, the enquêteurs quickly degenerated into merely another set of royal officials who were used for all sorts of administrative duties. They did not, however, develop the judicial duties of the itinerate justices.

The use of the sworn inquest was introduced into jurisdiction in France under St. Louis. In 1254 Louis ordered that inquests by royal officials should replace judicial duels in all civil cases, and in 1258 the royal inquests were extended to all criminal trials. But the inquest in France was a far different thing from that in England, for in France it was merely an investigation made, often through the employment of torture, by a royal official and there was never any employment of the jury system. The result was that the inquest facilitated official tyranny in France, while in England it guaranteed the rights of the subject.

Thus it will be seen that during the thirteenth century the French monarchy grew from a small weak feudal suzerainty, which was barely able to hold its own against its great vassals, into a powerful centralized autocracy. This was accomplished gradually by three outstanding kings. At no time was any attack made on the nobles as a class; each conquest was made from some individual noble whose lands were quietly incorporated into the royal domain. At no time did the nobles feel that they need make common cause against a monarch who was destroying their rights and prerogatives until it was too late to do anything about it. The contrast between this development in France and that in England is at once evident.

CHAPTER 28

GROWTH OF THE ENGLISH CONSTITUTION

✤

THE history of England in the thirteenth century presents a striking contrast to that of France in the same period. At the beginning of the century the English kings were practically absolute monarchs with a well organized administration and an empire which included half of France. By the end of the century they had been reduced in territory to England, Wales, and Gascony, and the control of government had passed largely into the hands of the baronial class. Edward I was still a strong ruler, who took every advantage of the royal prerogative, but the elements which were to result in the limited constitutional monarchy were all existent, although as yet but slightly developed.

JOHN LACKLAND AND MAGNA CARTA, 1199–1216

The reign of King John breaks into three main topics of which two have already been discussed. In the early years of the reign John was engaged in his war with Philip Augustus which resulted in the loss of Normandy and all the lands in France north of the Loire; then he became involved in his long struggle with Innocent III as a result of which he surrendered England to the papacy to receive it back as a fief. His third struggle was with his own barons and culminated in the issuance of the Magna Carta.

During the course of his wars in France, John had already had some trouble with the barons who resented being called upon to serve in what they considered—after the loss of Normandy—foreign campaigns. In 1205, as we have seen, the king was forced to abandon his plans for an invasion of Poitou by the refusal of the barons, led by William Marshal and Hubert Walter, to serve overseas. During the great interdict, John developed a system of insuring the loyalties of the barons by demanding hostages from them, and forcing them to sign special charters guaranteeing their fidelity. At the same time he filled England with foreign mercenary troops whom he employed in minor campaigns against any barons who proved recalcitrant. He also collected scutages at increased rates on all occasions, making the scutage not a commutation of service, but another arbitrary and extraordinary tax.

When, therefore, after the disastrous campaign of Bouvines in 1214, the king returned to England and levied a new scutage at the unheard of rate of three marks to the fee, the northern barons refused payment on the grounds that they were not obligated to serve in such a campaign and so were not obliged to pay scutage. John replied by attacking them individually in their castles. Meeting at Bury St. Edmunds, the barons swore to stand together, and demanded a return to the customs guaranteed in the coronation charter of Henry I. In an attempt to divide the opposition, John then issued a new charter guaranteeing the liberties of the church with full freedom of elections, but Archbishop Langton refused to swallow the bait and adhered loyally to the baronial cause. The king then assumed the cross, claimed the privileges of crusaders, and at the same time hired more troops in Flanders and Poitou.

In April 1215, the barons met again at Brackley: five earls and forty barons were present at this meeting which drew up a list of grievances against the king. John sent William Marshal and Stephen Langton to receive the demands of the barons, but when his emissaries reported the nature of the baronial proposals, the king flew into a rage and swore that never would he humiliate himself by granting such unreasonable demands. He proposed instead submitting the entire matter to a papal commission, confident that in his capacity of papal vassal he could count on the support of the pope. The barons refused and on May 5 solemnly affealted themselves and declared war on the king. Choosing Robert Fitz-Walter as their general they occupied London, to which they had been invited by the citizens. John demanded the immediate excommunication of all the baronial leaders, but Langton refused. The barons then proceeded to draw up a charter, known as the Articles of the Barons, which they announced as the goal of their revolt.

John moved down from Oxford to Windsor: the barons moved up from London to Staines. From June 8 to 14th a conference was held at Runnymede between the representatives of the two parties. In this conference a leading part was played by Langton and by William Marshal, the one baron who remained loyal to the king in whom the other barons had any confidence. The result of the conference was the document, known as Magna Carta, which was drawn up article by article between June 15th and 19th, being officially sealed on the 19th. It is now generally conceded that the Charter in its final form was largely the work of Marshal and Langton working from the Articles of the Barons as a point of departure.

Magna Carta is in form a charter granted by the king to his loyal subjects: actually it is a treaty between two opposing forces and represents a compromise between the original demands of the barons and the royal will. While it is generally considered to be the very cornerstone of English liberties, and was subsequently declared to be the first Statute of the Realm, Magna Carta is actually a reactionary feudal document which reaffirms

the old feudal law on many disputed points. It opens with a general promise to respect the privileges of the church including freedom of elections
and benefit of clergy in judicial matters, a chapter which was not in the
Articles and which undoubtedly shows the direct influence of Langton.
Then it goes right to the heart of the matter by defining the proper reliefs
that can be taken and by limiting the power of the king in matters of
wardship, marriage, dower rights, seizure of property for debt and other
purely feudal questions. Article 12 provides that "no scutage or aid shall
be imposed in our kingdom, except with the common assent of our kingdom" save only the legitimate feudal aids. Article 14 explains that this
assent is to be obtained by the convocation of a council of the archbishop,
bishops, abbots, earls, and major barons, who are to be summoned individually, and of all the tenants-in-chief who are to be summoned through
the sheriffs, and it goes on to state that the decision of those present at the
meeting shall be valid for all. Articles 17 and 18 show that the barons
appreciated the value of some of the reforms of Henry II: they provide
that the Common Pleas Court shall sit regularly at Westminster, and that
the judicial eyres shall be held four times a year in each county. Other
articles are aimed at the powers of the sheriffs, delays in justice, amerce-
ments, illegal seizures of the goods of intestates, tally payments for purveyance, commandeering carts and animals, prerogative wardship, forest
laws, and other matters in which the king had been violating custom. The
hated writ *praecipe* is restricted by Article 34. The most celebrated article
in the Charter is article 39 which provides that: "No free man shall be
taken, or imprisoned, or disseised, or outlawed, or exiled, or in any way
destroyed, nor will we go upon him, nor will we send against him, except
by the legal judgment of his peers or by the law of the land." [1] This famous
article was once thought to provide jury trial for all free men in England;
it is now realized that it only refers to nobles in the first place—as the term
liber homo was used only in reference to the privileged classes,—and that
it guarantees only that a man must be given trial either in a feudal or
royal court. Likewise the phrase of Article 36 which was long thought
to provide for *habeas corpus* is now known only to mean that there should
be no charge for the writ which invoked the jury trial in matters concerning
life or limb. Other articles are purely temporary, such as those which
provide for the banishment of the foreign mercenaries. But the general
importance of Magna Carta lies not in any single provision, but in the
principle which underlay the document. By Magna Carta the king was
forced to admit that there existed a body of higher law which he was not

---

[1] All quotations and translations are from the text of Magna Carta given in Stubbs
Select Charters, 9th ed. (Oxford Univ. Press), pp. 292–303. Translations of the Charter
are to be found in Stephenson and Marcham, *Sources of English Constitutional History*
(Harpers) and in Adams, *Select Documents* (Macmillan).

able to ignore—that he was bound by law and was subject to it as were other men. John would gladly have developed a theory of royal absolutism like that which Philip the Fair later enjoyed in France. By forcing him to accept Magna Carta the English barons guaranteed that their kings should always admit that they were not above the law and that their actions were subject to limitations.

The greatest defect in the Charter was in the means of enforcement. In the sixty-first article it was provided that there should be set up a committee of twenty-five barons who represented the community of the realm. If the king violated any provision of the Charter, four of the barons should call upon him to desist and make restitution. If he refused the four should submit the matter to the twenty-five, who could then declare war on the monarch. In other words the only means which the barons could devise to guarantee the Charter was to legalize rebellion and civil war should it be violated.

Magna Carta failed to settle the conflict which produced it. The northern barons, who had left the conference before the Charter was drawn up, refused to lay down their arms; John refused to attend a meeting which was summoned for Oxford. Further, in direct violation of the Charter, John immediately sought from Innocent III a nullification of the Charter on the grounds that it had been wrung from him by violence, and that it diminished his power as king and so reduced the value of the fief which he held from the pope. Innocent's action in annulling the Charter was the worst political mistake made by that normally astute pope, for it turned Englishmen from the papacy, which they now considered an ally of their enemy.

Of course war broke out. It was the usual feudal war of besieging castles and harrying the land. The barons deposed John and invited Prince Louis of France to come to England and rule over them; he landed in May 1216 and soon was in possession of London and the eastern counties. John was forced to retreat to the Welsh border, but he came back and by October the country was about equally divided between the two parties. Then on October 19, the king died from eating too many green peaches and drinking too much hard cider. His partisans, led by William Marshal, at once proclaimed the nine-year-old Henry III.

HENRY III, 1216–72

Minority and Early Years, 1216–44

The death of King John and the coronation of Henry completely changed the situation in England. On November 12, two weeks after Henry had been crowned, William Marshal, as regent, reissued Magna Carta in the name of the young king, thus cutting the ground out from under the baronial party. Already Henry was supported by the papal legate and the majority of the bishops; the reissue of the Charter as the platform of the royalist party won over many of the barons, who preferred a child king to a foreign one.

The war continued, however, through the following year. In May 1217 the royalists won a great victory at Lincoln—called the Fair at Lincoln because of the great quantity of booty captured—and the following August won a naval victory which cut Louis off from his base of supplies in France. On September 11, 1217, Louis consented to the Treaty of Lambeth whereby he surrendered all his claims to the English throne in return for an indemnity of 10,000 marks. A general amnesty was ordered on both sides and Magna Carta was again reissued on November 6. By his prompt action in reissuing the Charter and by his wise negotiations with the barons and Louis, William Marshal had saved the throne of England to the Plantagenet dynasty.

For the next two years, until his death in 1219, William Marshal was the ruler of England. He was aided by the papal legate, and after his death the legate continued to rule for another two years. But in 1221 the legate was recalled and the governance was turned over to two men whose rivalries were to color the next decade. Peter des Roches, bishop of Winchester, was the personal guardian of the young king, while Hubert de Burgh, the justiciar, controlled the administration of the kingdom. These men had both risen to power during the regency of Marshal and the legate, and a bitter rivalry had grown up between them.

In 1223, Pope Honorius III declared Henry III of an age to govern alone, which took him out of the control of des Roches and brought him closer to de Burgh, but Peter hung on desperately until 1227 when Henry declared himself sole ruler and dispensed with any regency. However he continued de Burgh as justiciar—so des Roches went off on the crusade with Frederick II.

The minority of Henry III was an important period in English history. The absence of any real king gave the ministers a feeling that their power lay in their offices, not in the king from whom they held them. The royal ministers, co-operating with the barons of the curia, were able to run the kingdom rather better than it had been run for some years past under the king. "From the exercise of royal authority by ministers without the personal intervention of the monarch arose the ideas of limited monarchy, the responsibility of the official, and the constitutional rights of the baronial council to appoint ministers and control administration." [2]

Henry's first act as king was to reissue once more Magna Carta. This reissue of 1227 is the form in which the Charter was always confirmed later and became the standard text of the document. It is interesting to note that

[2] Tout, *Political History of England, 1216–1377* (Longmans), p. 29.

the last paragraph indicates that the barons in return for the reissue had granted the king a fifteenth of their movable goods—the first time that we have any evidence of the grant of money in return for redress of grievances in England.

As we have already seen, the early years of Henry's reign were marked by a series of invasions of France in an attempt to recapture some of the lands lost by John. The failure of the French war, which ended in 1230, had repercussions in England, for Hubert de Burgh was blamed for its failure with the result that he was overthrown and deprived of his office in 1232. The fall of de Burgh gave the ascendency to Peter des Roches who had returned from the crusade. Des Roches, who lacked the support of much of the council, devised means of controlling the government without consulting council. Under his rule we find the great development of the Wardrobe and the Privy Seal to offset the exchequer and the chancery which had passed entirely under the control of the council.

Originally the Wardrobe had been a spending body under the exchequer. Its functions had been the control of the current expenses of the king's household for which it rendered accounting to the exchequer. Now, under Peter des Rivaux, one of the satellites of des Roches, the Wardrobe developed an independence of action; it received certain revenues and spent them without rendering any accounting to the exchequer. In the same way the Privy Seal developed as a means of sealing charters without consultation of the chancellor, who was the agent of the curia.

But des Roches went too far when he caused de Burgh to be tried for witchcraft. Although de Burgh was imprisoned, a party of the nobles under Richard Marshal, the son of the great William, revolted in 1233. Marshal was killed but the leadership of the insurgents passed into the hands of St. Edmund Rich, archbishop of Canterbury, who threatened to excommunicate the king unless he dismissed des Roches and his minions. Henry, ever fearful of incurring the anger of the church, complied and des Roches was dismissed, while de Burgh was released from prison and restored to his estates.

Meanwhile papal agents had been traveling all over England collecting money for papal purposes. Henry had never said nay as he was always under the thumb of the pope, even agreeing when Otto, the papal legate, demanded a fifth of all clerical revenue in England and provision in England for some three hundred Roman clerics. But if Henry agreed the English clergy did not. Under the leadership of Robert Grosseteste of Lincoln, ably seconded by Edmund Rich, the English clergy resisted the demands of the papal agent. Henry supported the legate however, and Rich fled the country, dying in exile. But even Henry lost his enthusiasm for the papal cause. In 1235, he married his sister Isabelle to the Emperor Frederick II in an attempt to build up an alliance against France. Consequently he was in a most embarrassing position when the papacy started to collect money in England for a crusade against Frederick. While he wanted the friendship of the emperor, he was afraid to oppose the papacy, with the result that he lost the friendship of both parties by his vacillating policies.

Then in 1236 Henry married Eleanor of Provence (the sister of Margaret of France). With the queen there came to England a host of her relatives, known as the Savoyards, among whom William, bishop of Valence, the uncle of the Queen, was particularly important. The Savoyards quickly gained a complete ascendency over the rather irresolute king; the barons were discredited and des Roches and all his group were reinstated. In 1239 both des Roches and William died, but Peter of Savoy came to England in the same year and quickly stepped into the position of the king's chief minister. It was as one of these "foreign favorites" that Simon de Montfort, the son of the conqueror of Toulouse, came to England in the early thirties. He was the grandson of the countess of Leicester and entered a claim for her inheritance, which had escheated to the crown when his father had sided with Philip II in the war with John. In 1238, Simon was given the hand of Henry's sister Eleanor, and in the following year was given the county of Leicester, becoming one of the king's most privileged favorites, and receiving the important post of seneschal of Gascony.

It was just at this time that the second war with France broke out. As we have seen, the battle of Taillebourg resulted in the complete defeat of the English and Lusignan parties, so that the Lusignans all flocked from Poitou to England demanding that their half-brother supply them with fiefs and positions. This second invasion of the king's foreign relatives merely increased the dislike with which the English baronage viewed all these new visitors from across the Channel, and a national party of English barons began to take definite shape.

Relations with the Barons, 1244–72

The first manifestation of the spirit of the baronial opposition occurred in 1244 at a meeting of the council which Henry had summoned to raise funds to pay for the recent French war. Prelates, earls, and barons formed three separate bodies in this meeting, but all agreed in their protest to the king. The leader of the opposition was Grosseteste, but it is notable that such divergent elements as Richard of Cornwall, the king's brother, Boniface of Savoy, Simon de Montfort and Earl Roger Bigod of Norfolk should all agree on a common program. A Committee of Twelve, appointed by the three bodies, drew up a program of reform which they insisted should be put into effect before they would vote any supply. This program called for the appointment of a committee of four councillors, chosen from and responsible to the magnates, who would have complete control over all administration and could only be removed with the consent of the barons. Henry refused the scheme indignantly, and the magnates in return refused the requested supply; but a precedent had been set for a constitutional opposition.

The next few years were marked chiefly by an unsuccessful Welsh war and by the breach between Henry and de Montfort whom he recalled in disgrace from Gascony. In 1254, in Henry's absence in Gascony, Richard of Cornwall convened a meeting of the council to which were summoned two knights from each shire to grant an aid. Then the barons, prelates and representatives of the diocesan clergy were convened for the same purpose. De Montfort became the accepted leader of the opposition at this meeting, and carried the point that the assembly refused to grant the subsidy requested.

Then in 1255 Henry made the move which was to precipitate rebellion. In that year he accepted from the pope the crown of Sicily for his younger son Edmund. The throne had, of course, to be conquered from Manfred, but the pope was willing to raise the army if Henry would pay for it. The barons, however, refused to vote supply for any such scheme. The pope raised an army which was defeated. Then in 1258 the pope revoked the grant of the throne to Edmund, but nevertheless presented to Henry the bill for the unsuccessful campaign which had been waged in his behalf. Meanwhile defeats on the Welsh border had further reduced the prestige of the crown. In April 1258, the king summoned the magnates to meet at London. They came, but were so vociferous concerning their grievances that Henry was only too happy to adjourn the meeting and send the barons away to draft a plan of reform.

The following June the magnates met again, this time at Oxford. To this meeting, known as the Mad Parliament, the barons came under arms, as they expected to proceed on to the Welsh war. At the meeting they demanded the appointment of a committee of twenty-four, representing equally the royal and baronial factions, which should present a program for reform. This program, which was presented by Earl Roger Bigod of Norfolk, was the famous Provisions of Oxford. "It is clear that the voice of the baronial opposition, usually so full of conflicting and inarticulate sounds, became one single coherent cry for reform." [3]

The Provisions of Oxford demanded that a council be established to advise the king in all matters. A Council of Fifteen (seven earls, three barons, five clergy) should be permanently with the king, and without their assent the king would be powerless to act. In addition a separate Committee of Twelve who were to represent the community of the realm, was to meet with the Fifteen three times a year as Parliament. A third Com-

[3] Treharne, *The Baronial Plan for Reform*, p. 66.

mittee of Twenty-four was to control all grants of money. Of these commit-
tees the Twelve were elected entirely by the barons, while the Fifteen were
to be selected by a complicated system to represent both the baronial and
royal factions. It was further provided that in each county a council of
four knights be elected to check on the sheriffs.

The Provisions of Oxford did not establish a permanent government,
and so have been generally underestimated by historians. While they were,
in a way, an amplification of the committee of twenty-five barons established by Magna Carta, there was a great difference between the fundamental concept behind the Charter and the Provisions. In the Charter the
theory was that there was a higher law above the king to which he must
be made to conform. As long as he obeyed this higher law, the king was
free to do as he willed. This concept of a sovereign limited by a fundamental or constitutional law is the basis of the American constitution
today. But in the Provisions the theory had changed. No longer was it
enough that the king be held back when he attempted to break the law.
Now all his actions were to be governed and controlled by a committee of
the nation, which was in fact a committee of the barons, as they considered
themselves to be the nation. In other words, the Provisions placed the
kingship in commission and reduced the king to the "crown" which was
then sovereign. This is the constitutional policy now followed by the
English government. There is no limitation to what the sovereign can do,
but the sovereign is not one man but a group of men, no part of which can
act independently of the others. It is hardly probable that the barons who
met at Oxford realized the constitutional principles they were suggesting.
To read constitutionalism into any of the baronial struggles of the Middle
Ages is probably a mistake, for the barons were simply seeking a means to
control the king and protect their own privileges. But nevertheless, although the theory was undoubtedly far from the minds of the men who
imposed the Provisions on Henry, in this document the barons laid down
the line on which the English constitution was to develop.

The new government called for by the Provisions was established in
1258. It was pledged to the expulsion of all aliens from positions of trust
and importance in England, to establish new officials who would rule in
the interest of the community of the realm (the barons), to reform the royal
household, and to hold inquests to redress grievances throughout the realm.
Hugh Bigod, the brother of the earl of Norfolk, was appointed justiciar
to reform the administration and at once began holding inquests throughout the kingdom. The results of his labors were published the following
year in the Provisions of Westminster, a document of twenty-four articles,
which served as an *ad interim* report of the barons on the conduct of their
program. It dealt with reforms in such subjects as wardships, inheritance,
waste, fines, guarantees, and similar feudal and judicial matters. In gen-

eral the purpose of the Provisions was to protect the mesne tenant in his lands and to reduce the competence of the private courts to the benefit of those of the royal justiciar.

The barons, governing through the Council, in the years 1258 to 1260, removed the foreigners from their posts, negotiated the Treaty of Paris with France, held inquests and brought erring officials to justice, and in general carried out the program to which they had been pledged. But difficulties shortly developed between the leaders of the baronial party. De Montfort seemed too radical for some of the more conservative earls like Gloucester, and a rift began to develop between them. Meanwhile Prince Edward began to form his own reforming royalist party which undercut both of the baronial leaders. By Easter 1260 the rift had grown so wide that de Montfort and Edward armed against the king and Gloucester, and peace was only preserved by the intervention of Richard of Cornwall. Then the pope relieved the king of his oath to accept the Provisions and Henry promptly dismissed all the officials who had been forced upon him. Leicester and Gloucester patched up their quarrel to save the constitution; they summoned an assembly of three knights from each shire to meet at St. Albans—to which the king replied by summoning them to meet at Windsor. The barons were successful in forcing the king once again to approve the Provisions in 1263, and the death of Gloucester and the accession of his son, Gilbert, an ardent admirer of de Montfort's, further increased the power of the earl. Prince Edward had meanwhile been building up his party among the Marcher earls, who were generally bought over by individual concessions.

Both parties armed. The king took refuge in London only to find that the city was strongly for de Montfort; so once again the king swore to accept the Provisions. As a matter of fact neither side was ready for war, so compromise was possible. It was agreed that the whole matter should be submitted to St. Louis of France and that both sides would agree to accept his decision as to whether the king was bound by the Provisions or not. In January 1264, Louis handed down his decision in the Mise of Amiens. As might have been expected from a monarch enjoying practically absolute power in his own domains, Louis declared the Provisions null and void. Henry gladly accepted this decision, but Leicester refused to accede to it, as he had not been personally present to present his case to the king. Both sides took to arms. The two armies met at Lewes on May 14, 1264; Leicester's victory was complete and Henry was taken prisoner by Earl Simon.

From May 1264 until August 1265, de Montfort was the supreme ruler of England. He forced the king to accept the Mise of Lewes, a constitution similar to that established by the Provisions but in which a share in the selection of the committee was given to the knights of the shires. It must not be thought that de Montfort was any great democrat or that he especially sought to advance the rights of the lower classes. The fact was that he was rather generally opposed by the higher nobility and received his strongest support from the knights of the shire and the towns. Consequently it was to his personal interest to give these elements as much share in government as possible. In line with this policy Earl Simon issued writs in the name of the king for a parliament to meet in January 1265. To it were summoned not only selected and friendly earls, barons, and bishops, but also two knights from each shire and two burgesses from each of a carefully chosen list of boroughs. The writs of summons in the case of the burgesses were not sent through the sheriffs, but directly to the borough corporations themselves. Because of this famous parliament, Simon has been credited with being the "father of the House of Commons," an entirely unjustified attribution. In fact the whole parliament hardly deserved the name for it failed to include many of the more prominent earls and barons, and consisted only of the partisans of de Montfort. Nor, even had it been a complete parliament, was there anything spectacularly new in Simon's action. It had long been the custom to summon representatives of the shires and of the towns to meet with the king. All that was new in 1265 was that the representatives of all the groups met in the same place at the same time.

But de Montfort's actions, once he had control of the government, seemed more the deeds of a self-seeking adventurer than those of a great statesman. His partisans began to fear that Simon had won the victory not for the party but for himself. Accordingly a split developed in the baronial party, led by young Gilbert of Gloucester, who found ready allies in Prince Edward and the Marcher earls. To offset the influence of the Marchers, Simon allied himself with Llewelyn, prince of Wales. This alliance with a foreign enemy gave substance to Gloucester's charges that Leicester was himself a foreign tyrant, seeking only his own aggrandisement. It may be questioned how far there was any real nationalism in England at this time, but there was certainly throughout the reign a strong feeling of difference from those not English. The loss of the Norman lands had made the English baronage more insular, and the "foreign favorites" of Henry had accentuated the feeling of England for the English.

The two parties armed, and war broke out afresh. Simon's forces were divided and Edward was able to defeat them separately, first crushing the force under Simon, the younger, at Kenilworth on August 1 and then defeating Earl Simon himself at Evesham on August 3. The earl was killed in this battle, and with his death his party collapsed.

Edward showed himself an astute politician. He had won the battle of Evesham by adopting the same tactics which Simon had used at Lewes; now he took over almost all of Simon's reform program as the royal party platform. It was the same move which William Marshal had made when he reissued the Charter in 1216. But Henry was vengeful and decreed the forfeiture of all those who had supported Simon, so that the rebels continued their resistance until they were beaten down in detail. In October 1267, Edward as the acknowledged leader of the royalist party issued the

Dictum de Kenilworth in which he promised amnesty and reinstatement to those who laid down their arms, and this was reaffirmed by a parliament. The Charter was reissued, the rebels were allowed to recover their estates on payment of a fine of five years income, some specific grievances were remedied:—and the rebellion was ended. A handful of rebels who held out at Ely were conquered and given lenient terms by Edward, and Llewelyn of Wales was pacified by the confirmation of the titles and lands which Simon had granted him. In the same year (1267), Edward showed the sincerity of his purpose by issuing the Statute of Marlborough, which

virtually re-enacted the Provisions of Westminster of 1259, and showed
that the prince was really determined to carry out the policies of the reform
party. Then with the country once more at peace, Edward went to Syria
on a crusade in 1270.

Edward had really been the ruler of England since the battle of Evesham,
his father having slipped into an indolent lethargy. It was while he was in
Sicily on his way home from the crusade, that Edward heard of the death
of his father (November 1272). He returned home leisurely, stopping to
arrange affairs in Gascony, and arrived in England only in August 1274.

EDWARD I, 1272–1307

Wales, Scotland, and Foreign Affairs

Edward Longshanks was a tall, handsome man, brave and impulsive,
violent and dogmatic. Although in his early years he was somewhat shifty,
on the whole he had a remarkable respect for the integrity of the pledged
word, and his respect for the law was profound. However, like his great
rival Philip IV, he was quite willing to violate the spirit while scrupulously observing the letter of the law. Indeed the two monarchs, second
cousins and deadly rivals, were much alike both in appearance, character,
and accomplishment.

Although the real significance of his reign lies in the legal and constitutional development, Edward is perhaps best known for his conquest
of Wales and his wars in Scotland, which for the first time united Great
Britain under the English sceptre.

When Edward ascended the throne, Wales was ruled by Llewelyn, whose
homage for the whole country, except the Marches, had been accepted by
Henry III. This homage Llewelyn refused to renew to Edward, but it was
not until 1277 that Edward was able to invade Wales and drive Llewelyn
back into the north. On his submission he was granted the fief of North
Wales while the south was made into a principality under the direct rule of
England. Then in 1282 the south Welsh revolted and called back Llewelyn.
Edward again invaded and in a prolonged campaign in 1282 to 1284 reduced the entire country. English settlers were moved into new fortresses
which were built throughout the country; Llewelyn was killed in battle;
his brother David was captured, tried, and executed; and the Statute of
Wales of 1284 united Wales to the royal domain, dividing it into shires
and establishing English law and English government. This created a
rather difficult situation in that Wales was completely under English law,
but the Marches, between England and Wales, still enjoyed their special
privileges.

The Welsh were, however, not entirely pacified, and in 1294 they took
the occasion of Edward's becoming embroiled with France to revolt. An-

other campaign, which lasted almost a year, was required to force them once more into submission and during the course of this campaign, especially at the battle of Maes Madog, the English learned the efficiency and power of the Welsh long-bow. The use of the long-bow and a heavier reliance on infantry, which the English learned the hard way in this campaign, served them in good stead in the subsequent wars with France, when it demonstrated its superiority on the fields of Crécy and Agincourt. Meanwhile Wales was pacified, and in 1301 was erected into a special principality to be held by the eldest son of the English monarch. Since the conquest in the thirteenth century, Wales has been an integral part of Great Britain, and there have been those, especially in the recent career of Lloyd George, who felt that Wales governed rather than was governed by England.

If Edward's conquest of Wales united permanently the two peoples, his wars in Scotland produced only ephemeral glory. The kings of Scotland had fought England on several occasions, always unsuccessfully, and had at various times been forced to do homage for their kingdom to the English ruler. Under Henry II, Scotland had performed homage, but Richard had sold it back to the king, although he remained an English vassal for lands which he held south of the border. In 1278, King Alexander III performed homage to Edward, but carefully did not stipulate whether it was homage for Scotland or only for his English lands.

In 1286, Alexander died, leaving only his granddaughter Margaret to succeed him. This "Maid of Norway" (she was the daughter of Eric of Norway and Margaret of Scotland) was proclaimed queen and a regency of Scottish barons was established to rule the country in her name. Meanwhile negotiations were begun for her marriage to Edward of Carnarvon, Edward's eldest son. By the terms of this agreement, it was stipulated that while both the English and Scottish kingdoms should pass to the heirs of Edward and Margaret, the two realms were to be kept separate and Scotland was not to be absorbed into England. Unfortunately this plan for a peaceful union fell through when the Maid died on her way from Norway to England. At once thirteen claimants for the Scottish throne appeared. Of these only three, John Baliol, Robert Bruce, and John Hastings, all of whom were descended from daughters of David of Huntington, the younger brother of William the Lion (1165–1214), had really serious claims. Bruce and Hastings were descended from younger daughters, but were a generation nearer than was Baliol who was descended from the eldest daughter.

At the suggestion of Edward, as overlord of Scotland, it was agreed to submit the matter to him for arbitration. A thorough investigation of the claims of each of the contenders was made by the English court, and in

1292 the throne was awarded to John Baliol, who performed homage to Edward for his kingdom of Scotland.

But if Baliol had the best claims and was acceptable to Edward, he was not the man for the Scots barons. They forced him to accept a Council of Twelve which completely controlled the government, to make an alliance with France in 1295, and to declare war on England. A Scottish invasion of the northern counties was beaten back and an English invasion of Scotland followed. King John surrendered his throne to Edward,— admitting that it was forfeit as a penalty for his violation of his homage— and Edward proceeded to the complete conquest of Scotland in his own name. Within five months he had overrun the entire kingdom and had set up a committee of three barons to rule for him.

The Scots however continued to resist. Under William Wallace and William Douglas they revolted in 1296 to 1297 and seriously defeated an English army at Stirling Bridge. In 1298, Edward, who had made peace with France and his own barons meanwhile, again invaded the northern kingdom. Wallace was overwhelmed at Falkirk in 1298 by heavy English cavalry and Welsh bowmen, but though he was continuously defeated, he repeatedly fought back, so that Edward was engaged in annual campaigns in Scotland from 1298 to 1305. And even the death of Wallace in 1305 did not end the matter, for his place as leader of the resistance was taken by Robert Bruce of Carrick, a grandson of the earlier claimant.

Bruce won his position as leader of the Scots not only by his hereditary claims but by his murder in 1306 of "the Red Comyn," a nephew of John Baliol and one of Edward's regents in Scotland. Fleeing to the highlands after the murder, Bruce gathered around himself a band of determined men (patriots or rebels, depending on the point of view) and defied Edward by having himself crowned king of Scots at Scone on March 27, 1306. With the coronation of a king, the Scottish revolt flamed up with renewed vigor. Edward was on his way north with another army, when he died near Carlisle on July 7, 1307.

After the death of the great king the Scottish war lapsed while Edward II was concerned with domestic matters in England. Finally he marched north in 1314, to be met by Bruce at Bannockburn, near Stirling, on June 23. Here, as in the contemporary Franco-Flemish battle of Courtrai, the pikemen broke the charge of the heavy cavalry, and the English went down in ignominious defeat. Stirling surrendered; the English garrisons were driven out of Scotland; and Bruce was recognized as king of an independent country. Although beyond the chronological limits of this chapter, the battle of Bannockburn was the logical end of Edward I's attempt to conquer the northern kingdom and marks the complete failure of his aspirations to unite the two realms.

Edward I was hardly more successful in his relations with France than he was in those with the Scots. In 1293, Philip IV declared Guyenne forfeit and began the occupation of the country. Edward conducted several campaigns in southern France, none of them brilliantly successful, and there was considerable fighting in the Channel. A truce was arranged in 1298 whereby a double marriage alliance was arranged, both Edward and his son marrying French princesses, but the war still went on in a desultory manner until 1303. By that time Philip, who had been defeated at Courtrai and was deeply involved in his struggle with Boniface VIII, was anxious to make peace with England, and a treaty was negotiated on the basis of Gascony being returned to Edward I, who did homage therefore through his son Edward. The whole business was only a preliminary to the later Hundred Years' War, and the marriage alliance of 1298 only gave the English king a claim to the French throne.

In his relations with the pope, Edward ran afoul of Boniface VIII when the latter prohibited the secular taxation of the clergy by his bull *Clericis laicos.* Edward's answer to this was to declare that the clergy, who paid no taxes, were without the protection of the law. After a certain amount of spoliation the clergy were only too glad to offer the king as a gift what they had refused as a tax, and the matter was ended with the submission of the clergy.

Law and Parliaments

Edward has received the title of "the English Justinian" for the great statutes which were enacted during his reign and which resulted in the reduction of feudal privileges and the end of feudal decentralization. All of his legislation had this as its objective, though much of it was such long-range legislation that the barons could not see how it was destined to bring the power ultimately into the hands of the king to their own detriment. These great statutes were enacted in parliaments which Edward convened with great regularity. "The reign of Edward," says Jolliffe, "was a time of slack water between the dying impulse of feudalism, and that political life of parliament which was as yet in the future. It was possible, therefore, for the crown to emerge in the absence of rivals as legislator by prerogative." [4]

For the first time positive legislation was recognized; the old feudal theory, that all law existed and that man merely interpreted it, was passing away to be replaced by the modern concept of legislation. In this changing period, Edward reaffirmed old laws with new interpretations and at the same time actually laid the principles of new law. By the end of the reign feudalism in England had been destroyed as a living organism and the country had been set well on her way to become a parliamentary monarchy.

[4] J. E. A. Jolliffe, *Constitutional History of Medieval England,* p. 336.

The first attack which Edward made on feudalism was by the statute *Quo Warranto* (Statute of Gloucester) of 1278. This demanded to know by what warrant or right any baron was possessed of his private court. Unless he could show a royal warrant, or prescriptive tenure since the reign of Richard, his right to the court was invalid and he was deprived thereof. This statute thus prevented the further extension of the feudal right of private courts; it destroyed prescriptive right as a future basis for privileges and stopped the growth of new immunities.

After this attack on the barons, Edward next turned to the church. By the Statute of Mortmain (*De viris religiosis*) of 1279 he forbade any grants of land to the church without specific royal permission. The church, as an undying corporation, never paid relief or any of the feudal incidents and so cheated the suzerain out of many of the payments which he received from lay holders. This act did not prohibit the future endowment of churches, but did require that special permission be obtained for it. The statute *Circumspecte agatis* (1285) further limited the church by strictly defining the limits of the ecclesiastical jurisdiction over temporal matters.

In 1285 and in 1290 by the Statutes of Westminster II and III, Edward struck his death blow at feudalism. The first, the famous statute *De donis conditionalibus* created entailed estates, thus stopping the free alienation of estates and requiring that they descend to heirs of the body in legitimate succession. Previously the courts had ruled that as soon as a man had heirs he could convey his property in fee simple to a third party. This statute ended this practice. The gain to the crown was entirely in the future; if the legitimate line died out the estates would escheat to the suzerain; thus ultimately the crown would be sure of acquiring many fiefs with the extermination of the families which held them. The second statute, *Quia emptores,* practically put an end to subinfeudation. It did not prohibit subinfeudation however; it merely ruled that if a man subinfeudated to another, land which he held in fief, the subvassal should become the direct vassal of the overlord. Thus anyone subinfeudating would merely cut himself out and create a relationship directly between his lord and his vassal. As there could be no possible advantage in such a procedure, this amounted in effect to a prohibition of all subinfeudation. This statute undermined the very principle of feudalism and stopped any chance of its further growth. It tended to bring more tenants directly under the crown, and, together with the *De donis,* insured the king's ultimate assimilation of greater holdings. The same Statute of Westminster II which created the *De donis* was also important for the establishment of the *Nisi prius* jurisdiction of the itinerant justices, whereby the Court of Common Pleas was empowered to try a case unless it had previously been heard by the itinerant justices.

The last great statute which we shall need to consider is the *Confirmatio cartorum,* or Confirmation of the Charters of 1297. This arose out of a revolt on the part of both clergy and barons. The clergy were antagonized by Edward's confiscations after *Clericis laicos,* and the barons were refusing to campaign in France. Things almost reached the point of armed revolt, but were settled by the concessions made by the king. The barons drew up a series of demands which Edward met in the *Confirmatio.* Magna Carta and the Charter of the Forest were confirmed and were declared to be part of the common law of England; further it was provided that "for no business from henceforth will we take such manner of aids, mises nor prises from our realm but by the common assent of all the realm and for the common profit thereof, saving the ancient aids and prises due and accustomed." [5] The importance of this document is that by this time the common assent of the realm could only be obtained in parliament, so that this charter grants parliamentary control over all extraordinary financial contributions.[6] The *Confirmatio* also stipulated that *maletote* (a tax on wool) should not be taken without the assent of the realm, save only those customs on wools, skins and leather which had previously been granted for life by parliament.

The customs on wool and leather had by this time become an important part of the king's revenue. To supplement the old revenues from feudal and domainial sources, which were quite inadequate to meet the increased costs of government, to say nothing of the expenses of the wars, Edward had placed a customs duty on wool and leather, the Great and Ancient Customs, in 1275. This had been granted the king for life, but when he found it still inadequate he took a second duty, the Small and New Customs in 1303. This new duty was levied only on Italian merchants who paid a fifty per cent tax for the privilege of trading in England. English merchants refused to pay this duty and the king made no attempt to force them to do so. This new customs was never discussed in Parliament and remained always a strictly prerogative tax. Parliament meanwhile voted subsidies as needed in return for redress of grievances presented.

Edward also profited, as did Philip of France, from confiscations of the goods of the Templars, and of the Jews who were banished from England in 1290.

During the reigns of Henry III and Edward I, considerable progress was made in the development of the royal administration. The King's Bench became a separate section of the curia sometime in the reign of

---

[5] Stubbs, *Select Charters,* pp. 491–93.

[6] The issue of tallages and the *De Tallagio non Concedendo* has not been entered into here. As Adams has pointed out, tallage was not a tax, but a return from investment and so not subject to the restrictions of this act. The barons may have demanded a restriction on tallages; it was not included in the Confirmation as issued.

Henry III, taking unto itself the adjudication of the king's pleas. The powers of the itinerant justices were increased by the new writs of *trial bastion,* which gave them the right to try all disturbers of the peace; *oyer et terminer,* which greatly extended their competence by granting them the right to hear all cases enumerated in their commissions; and *gaol delivery* which commissioned them to clear out the jails by trying all pending criminal cases. While the judicial eyres were becoming more important the general administrative eyres were growing less and less frequent, but the less frequently the justices came around on the general eyre, the more unpopular they became as their exactions each time were more severe. Finally the administrative eyres were abolished by Edward III, the justices having more work than they could handle with their strictly judicial business.

In many ways the most important development of the reign of Edward I was the growth of Parliament. From the point of view of personnel this development was practically completed in the early years of Edward, but his reign saw significant increases in the powers and prerogatives.

"The king holds his curia in his council in his parliament." This phrase from a contemporary law book well describes the early parliaments which were meetings of the curia or council primarily for judicial business as the high court of the realm, but capable also of handling any administrative or financial matters which might be of moment.

The growth of the personnel of Parliament is closely associated with the idea of the *communitas regni,* the community of the realm. As we have seen, in 1215 the barons considered themselves the spokesmen for the entire kingdom. This was still true at the time of the Provisions of Oxford, but during the course of the century the lesser elements, the knights and burgesses, came to have an increasingly important role in representing the community of the realm. The habit of consulting the knights and burgesses did not arise full blown in the mind of de Montfort. As we have shown, it had been customary to call in representatives of the shires and towns to grant aids or to bring the local knowledge of their districts on specified matters to the king since the beginning of the thirteenth century. In 1213 there had been a concentration of juries at St. Albans to determine the damages inflicted on the clergy during the interdict; in the same year John summoned four knights from each shire to deliberate with the barons of the curia meeting at Oxford. In 1254 knights from the shires were summoned to grant an aid, and after they had departed the barons and clergy met for the same purpose. In 1261 the knights were again summoned to confer with the king and then three years later de Montfort had them meet together with the earls, barons, and clergy. The same general development was true of the townsmen. They had, on several occasions, been summoned to consult with the king; de Montfort in 1265 only brought them into the same meeting as the earls, barons, clergy, and knights.

A similar gathering of nobles, clergy, knights, and burgesses was convened by Edward in 1275 to take formal allegiance to him after his coronation. But there was no regularity about the matter. In 1285 the knights and burgesses again met with the barons, but two parliaments were held for different parts of the country. In 1283 the Parliament of Shrewsbury, which met to try and condemn David of Wales, included only the earls, barons, and knights who tried David. The burgesses met separately to pass the Statute of Merchants, and the clergy were not present at all. In 1290 a parliament at Westminster included at first only the barons and clergy who enacted the statute *Quia emptores;* then after the departure of the magnates the knights met to vote an aid. No burgesses attended this session. In 1294 the clergy met in September, the nobles and knights in November. Finally in 1295 was held the famous Model Parliament to which were summoned the earls and barons, knights and burgesses, bishops and abbots, cathedral and parochial clergy. They all met together to hear the royal message, then divided into separate sections to debate, and then came back into a single body to return their answer to the king. This Parliament, though called Model, was in fact inclusive of certain elements which seldom ever appeared in Parliament again, but it does mark the widest extent of parliamentary membership. In the fourteenth century the clergy began to meet separately in Convocation, so that only the higher clergy who were also barons later met with the parliaments.

It will be noted that in these parliaments only those groups came who had business which affected them. Medieval assemblies were all based on the idea of estates or corporations. The upper clergy, the earls and barons, the lower clergy, the knights and the burgesses were all recognized as individual estates having special interests. When there was no business before the parliament which affected any given estate (as at Shrewsbury), that estate was omitted from the summons. "What concerns a part shall be approved by that part but what affects all shall be approved by all" (*Quod omnes tangit ab omnibus approbetur*) was to become one of the cardinal rules for parliamentary practice.

Parliament was above all things a court of justice, and most of its work was judicial. But when the nobles, clergy, and representatives of the shires and towns were all together, it was an excellent time for the king to ask for a vote of supply. The "gracious aids" were given by the representatives to assist the king in his difficulties, and it was soon discovered that the king was far more prone to receive favorably humble petitions from his subjects when he was asking them for gracious aids than at other times. Consequently there developed the custom for the members of the parliaments to present petitions demanding redress of grievances to the king at the meetings of the parliaments. At first there were individual petitions but soon they became collective group petitions. The barons had shown the value of collective bargaining when they granted an aid only after grievances had been redressed in 1236. In 1243 they had refused any aid because the king refused to grant their petitions, and in 1244, 1248, and 1254 they had again refused to vote supply. The refusal of the barons to vote money did not, of course, mean that the king went without. After Parliament had been dissolved, the royal agents would approach the barons individually and extract money from them, but the refusal to approve the grants in Parliament made more trouble for the king and tended to build up a feeling of solidarity among the barons as a class.

This also applied to the knights and burgesses. They were in general more docile than the barons in the matter of voting gracious aids, but they did begin to demand that their grievances be redressed before they would do so. The first "Commons' petition," a collective petition submitted by the burgesses and knights, was presented only in 1309, but individual petitions had been presented for some time before that, and after 1327 Commons' petitions became the standard form of initiating legislation.

The acceptance of the theory that "redress of grievances and supply go hand in hand" was one of the greatest gains made in the early history of Parliament. Throughout the reign of Henry III, although there was nothing definite, the barons had voted supply and the king had redressed grievances—or neither had done their part. Under Edward the essential relationship between the two was more clearly established. The right to participate in granting money was won by the Commons long before that of participating in legislation. For aids were collected from all and therefore all should be consulted in the voting of them, but legislation might concern only a part and so its enactment could be done by that group alone. By the end of the reign of Edward I, Parliament had pretty definitely gotten the right to approve all taxation (this had been won by the *Confirmatio cartarum*), but its right to exclusive control of legislation had to wait considerably longer.

The work of the parliaments was incorporated in statutes. At the end of a session all the legislative work that had been accomplished would be brought together and written into a single document which then became the statute of that parliament. Only later did the term statute come to apply to the individual laws.

In all of these parliaments it must be borne in mind that attendance was a duty and not a privilege. We have seen that this was so in France and it was scarcely less so in England, though it became a privilege there sooner. But in the reign of Edward I, as G. L. Haskins has said:

Attendance at parliament was, like attendance at the borough court or the shire court, clearly in the nature of an obligation. Not only was the knight or burgess not anxious to make a weary and frequently dangerous journey to Westminster to attend to affairs, which for the most part were of little interest to him, but the shires and boroughs themselves were anxious to evade the duty of sending up representatives." [7]

The development of Parliament in the fourteenth and fifteenth centuries will be discussed in a later chapter. To summarize the development this far, by the beginning of the fourteenth century Parliament was complete as far as personnel was concerned and included representatives from the various classes of the community of the realm, it had gained the power to be consulted in matters of taxation and had established the principle that supply followed redress of grievances. After this initial start it could make great progress in the reign of Edward III and in the Lancastrian period.

[7] G. L. Haskins, *Growth of Representative Government in England*, p. 76. Reprinted by permission of the publisher, Univ. of Pennsylvania Press. This is probably the most brilliant recent work on the history of Parliament and should be consulted for the latest points of view on the entire subject.

CHAPTER 29

THE LATER CRUSADES

✠

THE crusades of the thirteenth century, and the history of the Latin states in the East after 1192 have been considered by many historians as merely epilogues to the greater movements of the twelfth century. Certainly they lack the grandeur of purpose and accomplishment of the First Crusade, but in many ways the history of the thirteenth century is more interesting and informative than that of the earlier age.

If the twelfth century produced great religious wars, the thirteenth brought forth important colonial rivalries and struggles. It is as early efforts in colonization that the thirteenth-century crusader states must be studied. While some, such as the crusades of St. Louis, were sincerely religious affairs, in general the thirteenth-century crusades were commercial and colonial wars, in which European states attempted to keep alive valuable commercial colonies in the Levant. Not the papacy but the Italian commercial communes dominate the history of the thirteenth-century Latin states.

That these Christian communities were allowed to exist to the end of the century was due primarily to the civil distractions of the Moslems, which prevented the great powers of Islam from concentrating on destroying them. That and the comparative insignificance of the Latin colonies allowed them a century of precarious existence. When the Moslems were finally united again among themselves the doom of the Latin states descended upon them and they were wiped out.

AFTERMATH OF THE THIRD CRUSADE: HENRY VI

The failure of the Third Crusade to accomplish the liberation of Jerusalem was a great grievance to the papacy. But renewed hope for the accomplishment of this purpose was given the church by the plans of the emperor Henry VI who announced his imminent departure for the crusade as soon as he had completed his conquest of his southern kingdom of Sicily. To Henry the crusade was but a part of a greater scheme of conquest in the East. The son of Barbarossa had even greater imperial dreams than his father, and he planned nothing less than the creation of an empire which should include not only Germany, Italy, and Sicily but the lands of the Byzantine Empire and the states of the Levant. Great preparations were made, the first part of the expedition being sent on to the East in

1197. In line with this program, Henry VI accorded royal titles to the monarchs of Armenia and Cyprus, who became thereby vassals of the empire and allies of the emperor.

The German crusaders arrived in Syria where they engaged in a few futile campaigns while awaiting the arrival of their leader. The fortifications of some of the Latin cities were reconstructed, but the military campaigns were unsuccessful and the whole thing was only a preliminary to the greater effort which would be made when Henry arrived in person. Then the emperor died and the whole affair collapsed.

The Latin states were thus thrown back on their own resources. And it was a new group of Latin states which had emerged from the Third Crusade. The kingdom of Jerusalem was a smaller and weaker state, composed only of a few scattered cities along the coast. To the north, the counties of Antioch and Tripoli had been united when Raymond III willed his county to the son of the prince of Antioch, and the two states were joined into one. The new kingdom of Cyprus under Guy de Lusignan (1192–94) and his brother Aymeri (1194–1205) gave shelter to many of the dispossessed barons of Jerusalem and created a situation similar to that in the West where many barons held lands in both England and Normandy and divided their allegiance between the two. Cilician Armenia had increased in prestige and been made a monarchy, becoming more closely integrated into the community of the Christian states. Saphadin was gradually reuniting in his own hands the inheritance of his brother Saladin, and, fortunately for the Latins, be preserved a policy of friendship to the Christian states which, in their disorganized condition, could hardly have withstood a serious attack by the Moslems.

When Henry of Champagne died in 1197, his widow Isabelle was again remarried, her fourth husband being Aymeri de Lusignan, king of Cyprus. Thus for a short time (1197–1205) Cyprus and Jerusalem were united and the strength of the island kingdom bolstered up its weaker continental neighbor. But at Aymeri's death in 1205 the two kingdoms were separated, Cyprus going to Aymeri's son Hugh, while Jerusalem passed to Maríe la Marquise. The barons of Jerusalem at once sought a husband for their princess, finding a proper candidate in John de Brienne, a noble of Champagne who was recommended to them by Philip Augustus. But when John arrived to assume the crown of Jerusalem in 1210, the forces which the barons had hoped he would bring to the kingdom proved very few indeed.

THE FOURTH CRUSADE

Meanwhile the papacy had passed into the hands of Innocent III, who, as we have seen, was most anxious to promulgate a successful crusade. Determined to compensate for the failure of the Third Crusade and the

German fiasco, Innocent raised money throughout Europe and commissioned preachers to enroll volunteers, the most eminent of the preachers being Foulque de Neuilly. In this expedition the papacy sought to keep a closer control over the armies, and barons rather than kings were enrolled.

The crusade really got under way after a large number of the nobles of northern France, who were at a tournament at Ecri, took the cross together, electing Thibaut of Champagne as their leader. The fact that the crusade began at a tournament was indicative, for throughout it was more of a sporting event than a religious war.

The Fourth Crusade was not to make the same mistakes as the earlier ones. Its transport was carefully worked out in advance and nothing was left to chance. A committee of the barons, one of whom was Geoffrey de Villehardouin, was despatched to Venice to arrange for the carrying of the crusaders to the East, and a treaty was made whereby the crusaders were to pay the Venetians the sum of 85,000 marks of pure silver in return for the transport of 4500 knights, 9000 squires and 20,000 infantry. In addition Venice agreed to supply fifty warships, to be furnished by the Seigneury, and the date of April 1202 was set for the departure from Venice. Before the crusade could get started however Thibaut died and the barons elected a new leader in the person of Boniface de Montferrat, the brother of Conrad.

Although the recapture of Jerusalem was the announced objective of the crusade, there is reason to believe that the plans of the leaders never called for an expedition direct to Syria. The difficulties which Richard had encountered in his campaign in Palestine had shown the crusaders that any attempt to capture the Holy City itself was fraught with innumerable obstacles of terrain and supply. Consequently the strategically sound plan had been advanced that Jerusalem might best be won by attacking a port town of Egypt, such as Damietta or Alexandria, which could be captured by the naval power of the Latins, and then traded back to the sultan for Jerusalem. This plan may have been in the minds of the leaders; it was not communicated to the rank and file.

To insure the success of the expedition it was necessary that all the crusaders follow out the plan of the crusade and meet at Venice. But when the army gathered in the city of the lagoons it was found that many had sailed from Marseilles and other ports, so that its numbers fell far short of the expected total; instead of the 33,500 men who were anticipated only about 12,000 turned up at Venice, so that they were able to pay only a third of the sum agreed upon. As Venice had devoted all her energies for several years to equipping the fleet of transports and the government had been put to great expense to fulfill its part of the bargain, the Venetians naturally insisted on full payment. This the crusaders could not make, though the leaders raised money on everything they possessed. Waiting in Venice for further reinforcements only used up what money the crusaders had and left them worse off than ever, so that they were very glad when the doge Enrico Dandola offered them a way out of their impasse.

The Venetian empire had stretched down the Dalmatian coast including some of the cities there. But the expansion of the Hungarian monarchy had captured some of these places, notably the city of Zara, which Venice was most anxious to regain. The doge accordingly offered the crusaders a proposition whereby they should help Venice recapture Zara in return for which the Venetians would extend them credit until they could easily pay their debts from the profits they would make out of the campaign. This offer the crusader chiefs willingly accepted, though some, among them Simon de Montfort, objected, and a papal prohibition was issued against this attack on a Christian city. It was agreed that the doge himself should lead the expedition, which should go on from Zara to the East, and in an impressive ceremony in St. Marks, Dandola took the cross, followed by many of the Venetian nobles. After stopping by Trieste and forcing its surrender to Venice, the fleet arrived at Zara in November 1202, and laid siege to the city which surrendered after two weeks investment. The pope excommunicated the leaders who had thus diverted the crusade, and many of the crusaders left the host to go on directly to Syria; but the majority waited until after Zara had been captured and then sent messengers to the pope expressing their repentance and desire for absolution. As Innocent could not continue to keep them excommunicated without breaking up the crusade, he was forced to accept their repentance as sincere and to grant them absolution pending the completion of penance assigned. This applied only to the crusaders, and the Venetians, who had not even expressed repentance, continued under the ban of excommunication.

The siege of Zara had kept the army in the West until the dead of winter so that it was impossible to proceed to Syria before the spring crossing. Accordingly they camped at Zara for the rest of the winter. It was while they were waiting there that envoys of Alexius Angelus came to them with a plan which, while it would divert the crusade temporarily, would insure its greater success ultimately. It will be recalled that Isaac Angelus had been deposed from the throne of Byzantium by his brother Alexius III in 1195. His son Alexius now proposed that if the crusaders would go to Constantinople and put his father and himself on the throne, they would give the crusaders 200,000 marks towards their expenses, provide food and supplies for a full year, contribute a Greek army of 10,000 men to fight against the Moslems for a year, support, for as long as Alexius should live, an army of 500 knights for the defense of Jerusalem, and finally bring about the reunion of the Greek and Latin churches by submitting the Greek church to the Roman obedience. There is little doubt that this plan was developed in Germany at the court of Philip of Swabia where Alexius had been staying, and there is reason to believe that Boniface de Montferrat knew about it long before it was submitted to the crusader chiefs. But irrespective of its authorship, the plan must have appealed strongly to the crusaders. It offered them a chance to repay their debt to Venice easily, and guaranteed them assistance, money and supplies for their own campaign.

Modern historians have engaged in spirited academic discussion as to who was responsible for the diversion of the crusade. One school maintains that the whole diversion was the work of Philip of Swabia, who was the brother-in-law of young Alexius and who hoped to profit personally from the expedition to Constantinople. Another school insists with equal certainty that it was the Venetians who engineered the diversion because they did not want the crusade directed against the Egyptians with whom they had made favorable commercial treaties. A third group feels that the whole thing happened, as Villehardouin says, entirely by accident and that one thing led to another circumstantially to produce the diversion. It must be remembered that when the crusaders agreed to go to Constantinople they did not think of that as the goal of their crusade. They were given to believe that the conquest of the city would be an easy and quick affair and that they could then go on, strongly reinforced and enriched, to the capture of Jerusalem.

Having decided to accept the proposition of Alexius, the crusaders left Zara towards the end of April 1203 and sailed to Corfu where they were met by Alexius in person. Simon de Montfort and a considerable number of the crusaders abandoned the expedition and went on direct to Acre, but the majority were persuaded, albeit with great difficulty, to continue on to Constantinople. The force which undertook to conquer Byzantium amounted to no more than about 20,000 men divided about equally between the crusaders and Venetians. On June 23, 1203 they anchored off Constantinople, having met no resistance from the Byzantine fleet even in passing through the Dardanelles.

However Constantinople was not to fall without fighting. The crusaders tried to stir up a rebellion in the city on behalf of their protégé but were unsuccessful and so had to resort to arms. On July 17 the assault began, the crusaders attacking by land, the Venetians by sea. In the first day's fighting they were unable to make any headway and retired discouraged to their ships and camp; but Alexius III proved even more discouraged than they were, for during the night he fled the city. Isaac was brought out from his prison and restored to the throne with his son as coemperor.

Had Alexius been able to live up to his promises at once, the crusade might well have proceeded as planned. But the young emperor found himself unable to fulfill his commitments for the time being. He accordingly persuaded the leaders to wait until the following spring to continue their crusade, meanwhile quartering them comfortably in the suburbs; some of them assisted the emperor in a campaign in Thrace for which they received extra money. Although Alexius and the leaders kept up friendly relations, trouble soon broke out between the Latin soldiers and the Greek populace. There were recurrent street fights, a fire was started by the Latins which burned out a whole quarter of the city, the bad feelings spread from the lesser folk to the leaders and both Alexius and the crusader chiefs developed an attitude of hostility towards each other. The Latins demanded that Alexius pay what he had promised; Alexius procrastinated; the Greeks attempted to burn the Venetian ships in the harbor and the Venetians pillaged several towns along the Straits.

War had practically broken out between the former allies when in January 1204 the Greeks themselves revolted against Isaac and Alexius IV. Under the leadership of Alexius Ducas Murtzuphles, who took the title of Alexius V, a party of Greeks overthrew and assassinated Alexius IV, again deposing Isaac who died almost immediately thereafter. The party of Alexius V was definitely anti-Latin and opposed to any concession to the crusaders.

This revolution decided the Westerners to capture the city for themselves. A treaty was drawn up between crusaders and Venetians providing for the partition of the empire after it should be captured, and for the election of a Latin emperor and patriarch. If the emperor was a crusader, the patriarch should be Venetian and vice versa. After the signing of the partition treaty in March 1204, there was no further thought of a crusade against the Moslems. Each party agreed to keep up its forces for a year to complete the conquest of the Byzantine Empire and all their thoughts were directed towards the permanent occupation and exploitation of the Greek lands.

The second siege of Constantinople was begun April 9, 1204, and lasted only four days. Alexius V fled; Theodore Lascaris was proclaimed by a party of the Greeks but he fled too, so that there was no Greek leader to oppose the Latins. The city was given over to plunder and for several days the Franks and Venetians gorged themselves on the loot of this wealthiest of Christian cities. Not only gold, silver, and other precious stuffs were taken, but great quantities of sacred relics were stolen from the many churches of Constantinople.

The account of the plunder acquired by Abbot Martin of Pairis, a German monastery, includes: a trace of blood of Christ, a piece of the True Cross, "a fair sized piece of St. John, the fore-runner of Our Lord," and many other relics of both saints and holy objects.[1]

---

[1] Univ. of Penna. "Translations and Reprints," First Series, III, 1, pp. 17–19 gives a translation of the account of the looting with a full list of the relics.

When the city had been thoroughly looted and the plunder distributed, the conquerors set about organizing their empire. Baldwin of Flanders was elected emperor and the Venetian, Thomas Morosini, patriarch. Boniface de Montferrat had to content himself with a kingdom to be established at Salonica, while the Venetians took their "fourth and half of a fourth" in Crete, the Aegean islands, and the coastal towns, which were the most valuable trading centers.

Presented with the *fait accompli* of the conquest and the organization of a Latin church in the Byzantine empire, Innocent III forgave the crusaders for the diversion of the expedition and accepted the Latin Empire as a client state of the papacy. Lascaris, meanwhile, fled to Nicaea where he set up a Greek empire. The history of the states founded after the Fourth Crusade will be discussed in the next chapter.

THE FIFTH CRUSADE

Although Innocent accepted the results of the Fourth Crusade, he was nonetheless anxious that Jerusalem should be recaptured, and so set about again preaching a crusade. This time the expedition was to be definitely under papal leadership so that there could be no question of its diversion or failure. While secular princes were enrolled, the most important being the young king of Sicily and Germany Frederick II, papal mercenaries made up a large part of the crusading army of this expedition, and a legate was appointed to take command. But Innocent died before the expedition started. The first of the crusaders to reach the East was Andrew, king of Hungary, who arrived at Acre in 1217. Together with King John de Brienne of Jerusalem and King Hugh of Cyprus the crusaders made an attempt on the fortress of Tabor and an expedition inland towards the Jordan, but their forces were few and nothing came of the campaign. Andrew went home, Hugh died, and John de Brienne was left to carry on alone.

Then in 1218 the great bulk of the crusaders arrived in the East. For this crusade the new strategy was definitely adopted. Instead of attacking Jerusalem and trying to fight in the mountains of Palestine, the crusaders launched their offensive against the wealthy Egyptian city of Damietta, in which their naval superiority would serve them in good stead. Then they hoped to trade the city to the sultan for Jerusalem. King John was accepted as commander of the expedition and the crusade began to besiege Damietta in June 1218.

The siege lasted from June 1218 till November 1219. Attack after attack was launched against the city walls, the ships being maneuvered in the Nile, so that the city was attacked both by land and water. While they kept the Moslems from relieving the town, the crusaders were however unable to capture it. During the siege a new contingent of crusaders arrived from the West, commanded by the Cardinal legate, Pelagius of Albano, who immediately took command of the whole crusade.

It was while the crusaders were besieging Damietta that Saphadin died in 1218 and the throne of Egypt passed to his son, Al Malik al Kamil, while that of Damascus went to another son, Muazzam. Although he was supported by his brothers, al Kamil was anxious to be rid of the crusaders and so offered them what they had hoped:—the return of Jerusalem and all the former territory of the kingdom of Jerusalem, excepting only Montréal and the land across the Jordan, if they would give up besieging his city and depart in peace. The secular leaders were eager to accept these terms as they were all that they could have hoped for from the crusade, but Pelagius intervened and flatly rejected them.

The judgment of the legate seemed to have been justified when Damietta surrendered and the Christians occupied the city. The Moslem population was expelled, and colonists from Europe, especially from the Italian cities, were settled in Damietta, which quickly became a Christian town. Again the sultan renewed his offer, this time promising to release all Christian prisoners who might be found in captivity throughout Egypt; again Pelagius refused. Instead the legate decided to attack Cairo itself and conquer all Egypt. King John had left Damietta and returned to Acre; when word was brought that Pelagius had ordered the army to advance up the Nile the king despaired as he knew that the venture could not succeed. However, lest he be blamed for its failure by absenting himself, John reluctantly joined the army as it marched up the branch of the Nile on its way towards Cairo (July 1221).

One thing which John feared and which the legate ignored was the flooding of the Nile. The Christian army marched south between two branches of the river; where the two branches joined, the Egyptians had taken a stand against the invaders and had built a camp. While the Christians marched south the waters of the Nile began to rise. Soon they were caught, their camp flooded and their escape blocked by the Egyptian forces. Disaster and despair overcame them. Once again al Kamil offered terms but they were quite different terms now:—he would grant the crusaders safety in their retreat to Acre if they surrendered Damietta. After rejecting the earlier offers of the sultan, Pelagius was forced to accept this.

The utter dismal failure of the Fifth Crusade must be laid at the door of Pelagius. Had the advice of John de Brienne been followed, the Fifth would have been rated as the most successful of all the crusades; but the o'erweening ambition of the proud prelate refused to accept the liberal terms offered by the sultan and approved by the secular lords. Overconfident and refusing to accept any advice from those who knew the situation much better than he, Pelagius brought the whole expedition to ruin. His only excuse, and one which he promptly exploited to the full, was that he had been betrayed by Frederick II, who had assumed the cross but had not come on the crusade.

The failure of the Fifth Crusade brings into sharp focus a tendency which had been developing throughout the whole of the twelfth century and which was most marked by the time of the Third Crusade; the utter inability of the new crusaders come fresh out of the West to co-operate with the native Syrian Franks. The native Franks had lived with the Moslems and learned to get along with them; considerable mutual respect was enjoyed by Christians and Moslems in Syria and neither was inclined to underestimate his opponent or neighbor. Truces were common and trade and peaceful relations prevailed between Christian and Moslem in the intervals when there were no new crusades to disturb them. But the Westerners came out to destroy the infidel and could not bear the thought of compromising their religious prejudices to the extent of treating with the Moslems. This difference of view was most marked during the Third Crusade and was increased throughout the crusades of the thirteenth century.[2]

THE CRUSADE OF FREDERICK II

There was some justice in the charge brought by Pelagius against Frederick II, for that monarch had assumed the cross as far back as 1215, but kept finding excuse after excuse for delaying his departure. Pope Honorius had accepted his excuses, always hoping that he would really go at the time he promised, but the emperor was still putting off his departure when the Fifth Crusade ended in disaster. The pope finally hit upon an idea which he thought would surely interest Frederick in the crusade. The throne of Jerusalem would pass from John de Brienne to his daughter Isabelle; Honorius arranged for Frederick to marry her, judging correctly that if Frederick was king of Jerusalem he would be more interested in recapturing the country. Consequently in 1225 Frederick was married to Isabelle and acknowledged by the barons of the kingdom of Jerusalem as their king. John de Brienne, who had wanted to keep the throne as long as he lived, protested in vain. As he had received the crown by marrying the princess, he had no legitimate grievance when it passed to the husband of his daughter. So while John stayed in Europe, Frederick appointed a baillie to represent him in the East and began his plans to acquire possession of the Holy City.

The situation in the East was most favorable. Al Kamil and his brother al Muazzam had become embroiled in a fratricidal war in which both

---

[2] On this point see D. C. Munro, "Christian and Infidel in the Holy Land" in Scott, Hyma and Noyes, *Readings*, pp. 276-86. Also La Monte, "The Significance of the Crusaders' States in Medieval History," *Byzantion*, XV (1940-41), 300-315.

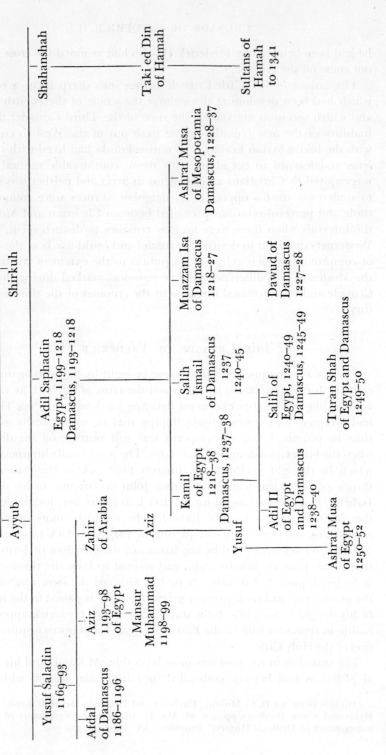

THE AYYUBIDS OF EGYPT AND DAMASCUS

were looking for allies; when Damascus allied with the Khwarizmian Turks, Egypt turned to the "sultan of Sicily" and a treaty was signed between Frederick and al Kamil whereby, in return for help against Damascus, the Egyptian promised the surrender of Jerusalem. This treaty was for obvious reasons not communicated to the pope. In this same year (1227) Honorius III died, to be succeeded by Gregory IX. The new pope was a stern and uncompromising man who lacked his predecessors' faith in Frederick and was little inclined to put up with any procrastination. Frederick took a mighty oath to depart, and began to assemble his forces at Brindisi. Then in September 1227 just as he was about to set out, a plague swept the camp of the crusaders; many of the chief leaders as well as the lesser folk were killed and the emperor himself was taken sick. Nevertheless Frederick started out, but finding himself too ill to proceed, returned to shore, while the fleet went on to Acre where it waited the arrival of the emperor. At once Gregory excommunicated him for failing to keep his oath and depart for the crusade. Frederick's explanations were refused by the pope, who of course did not know that Frederick really wanted to go at this time. Then in face of the papal excommunication, the following June, Frederick again set out. Himself excommunicated, in a fleet which was largely manned by Moslem sailors from Sicily, Frederick II started out on the most amazing of all crusades.

It was not as king of Jerusalem that he set out. For while he was delaying his departure, his wife, Isabelle, had died giving birth to a son in April 1228, so that Frederick was no longer king but merely regent for his infant son, Conrad.

The emperor first landed in Cyprus where he demanded that the regency for the minor king Henry I, who had inherited the throne in 1217 when only eight months old, be surrendered to him as the feudal suzerain of the king. This was done but in the doing, Frederick gained the enmity of the powerful house of Ibelin, the most influential family in Jerusalem and Cyprus. From Cyprus the emperor went on to Acre. There he was met with ecclesiastical opposition, the patriarch denouncing him as an excommunicate and refusing to co-operate with him. What was worse, the sultan, al Kamil, had no longer any need for him and refused to surrender Jerusalem to him. For in the interval al Muazzam had died, al Kamil had invaded Palestine, driven out the son of al Muazzam, and occupied Jerusalem and other Damascene towns. He was far less willing now to give to Frederick, whose assistance he did not need, a city which he now possessed, than he had been willing earlier to pay for assistance needed with a city still to be taken from his brother. But Frederick was determined to have Jerusalem. When the sultan moved from Naplouse to Gaza, Frederick followed him south from Acre to Jaffa. While the emperor's army was too small to be a serious threat to the sultan it did have a considerable nuisance value, as the emperor could cut al Kamil's communications with Egypt if he engaged in a campaign in Syria; and the sultan was afraid to abandon Syria lest his nephew take possession of it. Consequently al Kamil finally agreed to accept Frederick's terms and give over the city of Jerusalem. By the treaty of Jaffa, which was signed in February 1229, the Christians were restored to possession of Jerusalem, Bethlehem, Nazareth, Sidon, Lydda, and a few other towns, and there was to be a complete exchange of prisoners, including some who had been taken during the Fifth Crusade. Moslems were to have freedom of religion in Jerusalem and were to retain the Dome of the Rock and the Temple area; they were to have their own courts in Jerusalem and be ruled by their own officials and laws. Finally the emperor agreed never to make war on the sultan or to allow his people to do so, and he engaged never to give assistance to any crusade aimed against Egypt. The truce was to last for ten years, five months and forty days.

Both the Christian and Moslem worlds were shocked at this treaty. The patriarch of Jerusalem denounced it for allowing Moslems to worship in the Holy City and for the emperor's pledge not to assist further crusades. More legitimate were the Moslem objections that the sultan had ceded too much to Frederick for what he received in return. "If I did not fear to lose my prestige in the eyes of the Franks I should not have sought to impose all this on the sultan," Frederick is quoted as saying to the Moslem ambassador, while al Kamil said: "I have ceded nothing to the Franks but churches and houses in ruins . . . the Moslems remain the masters of the provinces." [3]

Frederick at once moved on to Jerusalem. On March 18 he solemnly crowned himself king of Jerusalem in the Church of the Holy Sepulchre, putting the crown on his own head as no churchman dared crown an excommunicate. Then just at the end of the ceremony, the archbishop of Caesarea, in the name of the patriarch, placed the ban of the interdict over Jerusalem! The Holy City under an interdict was indeed a blow to the crusaders who had expected much benefit from its liberation; sadly they withdrew to Acre where the emperor besieged the patriarch and the Templars in their palaces. While thus pleasantly engaged, Frederick learned that a papal army, commanded by John de Brienne, was invading his territory in Italy. Hurriedly he departed after appointing baillies to represent him in both Syria and Cyprus. The most strictly secular religious war in history had ended, and the most irreligious crusader, operating under a ban of excommunication, had liberated the Holy City only to have it placed under an interdict!

Nothing illustrates better than the crusade of Frederick II the changed

[3] La Monte and Hubert, *Wars of Frederick II in Syria and Cyprus,* Columbia: "Records," p. 35 (Columbia Univ. Press).

attitude of the papacy towards the crusades. When Frederick II liberated Jerusalem, the ostensible goal of all crusades, the papacy denounced him and his works. They would not accept the redemption of the Holy City at the hands of one defiled by political antagonism to the papacy. Not by negotiation but by blood must Jerusalem be rescued—this was the attitude of the papacy as opposed to the tolerance of the native Franks and such rare individuals as Frederick.

It must further be pointed out that it was the papacy of the early thirteenth century, the papacy of Innocent III and Gregory IX, which diverted the energies of the crusades to wars against the heretics at home, and which granted the privileges of the crusade to those who would fight Albigensians or other Western heretics. When the wars against the heretics received preference over the crusades in the opinion of the papacy, the knell of the crusades had sounded. Some popes there were in the thirteenth century and after who sincerely labored to revive the interest of Europe in the crusades and in Jerusalem, but in general the crusade was subordinated to the struggle in the West either against the enemies of the faith or the enemies of the papal monarchy. Any war against a political enemy of the papacy was called a crusade, and when these received the same privileges as the expeditions to Jerusalem, it is small wonder that men lost interest in the *via crucis*. Only so long as the kingdom of Jerusalem brought credit to the papacy did the popes seriously interest themselves in the crusade to the East; when the kingdom was recognized to be a bankrupt and failing concern, the papacy turned to other interests. Whatever had been the motives of Urban II in inaugurating the crusades, before the end of the movement the papacy was supporting them only when politically useful.

Civil Wars in Jerusalem and the Crusade of St. Louis

The period following the crusade of Frederick II was one of civil war in the kingdom of Jerusalem. Frederick had left baillies to govern the kingdom in his name who promptly antagonized the local barons by attacking their cherished privileges. From 1229 to 1243 the Syrian Frankish nobles, led by the house of Ibelin, carried on a war with the baillies of the emperor, the war being fought out in both Syria and Cyprus. Eventually the barons won out in both theatres, the imperialists being driven first out of Cyprus and later out of Tyre. The most interesting feature of this civil war is the way in which it monopolized the attention of the Franks. In reading the account of this war in Philip de Novare there is no mention of the Moslems, save incidentally, and the Syrian Franks seemed totally oblivious to the situation in the Moslem world while they fought among themselves for the preservation of the feudal privileges and liberties which were guaranteed them by their assizes. This was a characteristic of the thirteenth-century Franks of Syria. They fought valiantly to defend their feudal privileges, indifferent to the greater issue developing in the world outside. At the very end of the kingdom, when the Moslems threatened the complete destruction of the crusader states, the Franks were themselves still engaged in petty civil wars. This condition of civil war was further aggravated by the constant quarreling of the military orders and the Italian communes. The Templars and Hospitallers always took opposite sides on any issue, each at times allying with rival Moslem states against each other, while the Venetians, Genoese, and Pisans kept the Syrian ports in constant turmoil with their political and commercial rivalries.

Fortunately the Moslem world was no less divided, the various branches of the Ayyubid house keeping up a constant fratricidal war among themselves. Damascus and Egypt were the two chief contenders and both sought alliances with the Franks. It was during this period of both Moslem and Christian wars that the crusades of Thibaut of Champagne and Richard of Cornwall took place, and it was due to the Ayyubid rivalry that their crusades were able to regain much of the former possessions of the Latins.

When Thibaut arrived in Syria in 1239 his purpose was to strengthen Jerusalem and as the first step towards this end he decided to refortify Ascalon. But his forces were badly defeated at Gaza and he retreated to Acre without accomplishing anything. There he was approached by the Damascenes, who had allied with the Templars, and who offered the return of Safita and several northern positions in return for alliance against Egypt. Thibaut accepted the alliance, and the crusaders and Damascenes marched south to Jaffa. Here the Egyptians and their allies, the Hospitallers, proposed to Thibaut that he ally with them against Damascus, in return for which they would release the prisoners captured at Gaza and make some territorial concessions in the south. Thus by allying with both Moslem factions Thibaut secured considerable increase of territory for the Latin kingdom, and feeling that he had done well, he departed for Europe. Hardly had he left when Richard of Cornwall arrived. Richard was the friend of Frederick II and followed somewhat the Hohenstaufen policy of friendliness with Egypt; he confirmed the treaty with Egypt and fortified Ascalon, finishing up the work begun by Thibaut. Then he too returned home, a successful crusade accomplished. Once again Frederick II's policy of alliance with Egypt had born fruit, but the Franks were not content to adhere to it. The advocates of the Damascene alliance gained the upper hand and the Latins allied with Damascus against Egypt which in turn called in the Khwarizmian Turks. In August 1244 the Khwarizmians captured Jerusalem. This was followed by a second defeat of the Franco-

Damascene allies at Gaza in October; the victorious Egyptians possessed themselves of most of Palestine and went on to take Damascus itself (1245).

The fall of Jerusalem precipitated the crusade of St. Louis. That deeply religious monarch, shocked at the loss of the Holy City, took the cross and brought out a great expedition in 1248. Once again the strategy of attacking Damietta was employed. Huge quantities of supplies were collected in Cyprus, and a great force attacked Egypt. This time the siege of Damietta took only a few weeks and the Franks again started to march up the Nile. Once again the crusaders met the Egyptians at the confluence of the branches of the river, at the town of Mansourah, which the Egyptians had built on the site of their former victory.

The story of the crusade should be read in the stirring prose of Joinville, who made of it one of the great historical classics of all time. The complete defeat of the crusaders, the individual heroism of the Christian knights, the capture of the king, the negotiations for the ranson of the prisoners, are all told most graphically in the narrative of the Champagnoise lord.

While Louis was negotiating a treaty with his captors, a revolution occurred among the Egyptians. Sultan al Salih died (1249) and the throne was seized by his widow the sultana Shajar-al-Durr, the only woman to rule a Moslem state in Africa or the Levant. She ruled alone for eighty days and then associated with herself on the throne Izz-al-Din Aybak, the leader of the former sultan's Mameluk guards. The Mameluks were foreign captives who became slaves of the sultan and formed an elite guard regiment. The accession of Aybak began the Mameluk dynasty which was to rule Egypt until 1517. Succession was, except in rare instances, not from father to son but from master to slave. Made up of men of all races, the Mameluks gave Egypt a strong rule, even though its rulers were Turks, Mongols, Circassians, and anything but Egyptians.

Aybak (1250–57) came to terms with Louis, who after arranging a huge ransom went to Acre where he stayed four years (1250–54) during which time he was accepted as virtual king by the Syrian Franks. While in Palestine, Louis refortified Sidon and other cities and tried to give what assistance he could to the little Latin state. Thus ended the last really important crusade to the East until after the fall of Acre at the end of the century.

The Fall of the Kingdom of Jerusalem, 1254–91

For almost half a century after the failure of the crusade of St. Louis, the kingdom of Jerusalem, or as it has been well named by Grousset, "the republic of Acre," carried on a precarious existence on the coast of Syria. The civil wars which had characterized the earlier period intensified and increased. Especially was this true of the conflicts between the citizens of the Italian communes. In 1256 a war broke out between the Venetians and Genoese in Acre in which some 20,000 men are said to have been killed and in which the whole kingdom was involved.

The Venetians secured the alliance of the commune which had been established at Acre, while the Genoese allied with the lord of Tyre, so that the two chief cities of the kingdom were at war. The Templars, Teutonic Knights, Pisans, and Provençals supported the Venetians and Acre, while the Hospitallers, Catalans, and Anconitans fought for Genoa and Tyre. Naval battles took place in the Acre harbor while street fighting destroyed considerable portions of the city. This war was not really ended until 1277 when peace was finally agreed upon between the lord of Tyre and the Venetians.

Meanwhile civil war had broken out in the north between the prince of Antioch-Tripoli and his chief vassal the lord of Djebail, a quarrel which outlasted the Frankish possession of Antioch. In the kingdom of Jerusalem there was a disputed succession to the throne, when, on the death of Conradin, the last Hohenstaufen, the legitimate line of Jerusalem ended. The throne then passed to a collateral line: Hugh III of Cyprus uniting the thrones of Cyprus and Jerusalem in 1268 against the protest of Marie of Antioch, who, unable to secure support for herself, subsequently sold her claims to Charles of Anjou, king of Sicily. Charles sent his baillies to take over the kingdom in his name and for a time both Cypriot and Angevin attempted to control the remnants of the unfortunate kingdom. Only the Sicilian Vespers (1282) and the collapse of the Angevin dream of oriental empire ended this conflict in which all the rival parties had become involved.

Meanwhile crusades undertaken by the bastards of Aragon (1269), Edward prince of England (1270–72) and the second crusade of St. Louis (1270) accomplished nothing, the crusade of St. Louis being diverted to Tunis where Louis died.

While the Latins were indulging in these civil wars, the fate of Syria and the Levant was being fought out between the Mameluks and the Mongols. The expansion of the Mongols will be treated in a later chapter and it will suffice here to notice only the Mongol invasions of Syria and their effect on the crusader states.

In 1258 the Mongol khan, Hulagu, had captured Baghdad, whence he directed expeditions into Syria. Damascus and Aleppo were captured with horrible slaughter and it seemed that only the sea would check the advance of these wild nomads from central Asia. But Hulagu was called back to the East to take part in a *kuraltai* or election of a great khan, and was forced to withdraw most of his army leaving only reduced forces in Syria under the command of his general, Kitbuqa, a Nestorian Christian. As

Hulagu had favored Christians over Moslems (though he was himself a Buddhist, his wife was Christian) many of the Syrian Christians looked on the Mongols as deliverers. The king of Armenia and the prince of Antioch both accepted his suzerainty and placed themselves under the Mongol protection. The pope and St. Louis both sent ambassadors to the great khan seeking alliance. The nobles of Acre however threw in their lot with the Mameluks of Egypt, whom they dreaded less than the terrible Mongols.

In 1260 the armies of the Mongols and Mameluks met at Ain Jalut. The Armenians, Antiochenes, Georgians, and other Christian troops fought side by side with the Mongols in the army of Kitbuqa, but the Mameluk sultan, Qutuz, and his great general, Baybars al Bunduqdari, defeated them completely and drove them back into the north. The battle of Ain Jalut saved Syria from the Mongols and virtually assured the Mameluk conquest. This was to be accomplished by Baybars who murdered Qutuz and seized the throne as they were returning from Ain Jalut. From 1260 to 1277 the great sultan systematically conquered Syria and reduced it to the Mameluk obedience. While Baybars first attacked Arsur and Jaffa which lay nearest his own border, his special vengeance was reserved for Antioch whose prince had been allied with the Mongols. In 1268 he attacked Antioch and captured it, massacring and enslaving the inhabitants and sending a taunting letter to Bohemond, "no longer prince of Antioch but count of Tripoli." Acre was spared due to the alliances which Baybars made with Hugh of Cyprus and Charles of Anjou whose baillies ruled that city, and to the conciliatory policy of the barons of Acre themselves. When the Mongol Il-Khan of Persia, Abagha (1265–81), offered an alliance to the Christians against the Moslems, the men of Acre remained true to their treaty with Egypt.

It is difficult at this distance to judge the wisdom of policies whose results are now all too apparent. René Grousset has made a great point of lamenting the folly of the Franks who adhered to the Egyptian alliance and rejected the proposals for a "Mongol crusade." But it must be remembered that the Egyptians were generally much more civilized than the Mongols whose terrible devastations had held the whole world paralyzed with fear. It is easy to say that if the Latins had allied with the Persian Mongols in a joint crusade they could have broken the Mameluk power and saved the Christian states, but it is impossible indeed to prove such a contention, and when one considers the reputation of the Mongols it is not hard to see why the Franks preferred to trust themselves to the mercies of the Mameluks. There was little to choose, and their alliance with Baybars at least gave the citizens of Acre a few more years of precarious existence. For the Persian Mongols attempted another invasion of Syria, only to be defeated at Homs in 1281 by Qalawun who became sultan of Egypt in 1279. Qalawun

(1279–90) continued the policies of Baybars, slowly overrunning Syria and consolidating the power of Egypt in opposition to the Mongols. In 1289 Tripoli, which had been embroiled in a civil war of succession for two years after the death of Bohemond VII in 1287, was conquered by the Egyptians. When Qalawun died in 1290 only Acre, Beirut, Tyre, Caiphas, Sidon, Tortosa, and the Templars' castle of Athlit remained in Christian hands.

These might have continued Christian cities for some time had not a group of crusaders from the West broken the truce by raiding into Moslem territory. This gave Qalawun the needed excuse to destroy the last of the Christian colonies in Syria, but the sultan died before he was able to accomplish this purpose and the final conquest of Acre was undertaken by his son, al Ashraf Khalil. The siege of Acre (April 5–May 28, 1291) allowed the Latins to expire in a manner worthy of the best crusading traditions. Forgetting at last their mutual rivalries, Templars, Hospitallers, Venetians, Genoese, Pisans, Cypriots, French, and Syrians all fought valiantly to defend the doomed city. After the town had fallen, the Templars kept up an heroic if futile resistance in their own castle, thus enabling many refugees to escape to Cyprus or Armenia. Only when the last Templar had been killed did the resistance end.

After the fall of Acre, the remaining Latin strongholds gave up without further opposition. By the end of the year al Ashraf had completed the conquest of Tyre, Sidon, Beirut, Caiphas, and Tortosa. The defenders quickly withdrew to Cyprus, which remained for the next two centuries the last outpost of Latin Christianity in the Levant.

THE RESULTS OF THE CRUSADES

To estimate the results of the crusades is no mean task. At one time, as has been mentioned, everything which happened in the thirteenth century was considered to be a result of the crusades. The development of trade, the growth of towns, the decline of feudalism, the emancipation of the lower classes, the formation of national monarchies, and even the intellectual revival were all attributed to the influence of the crusades. Then when a reaction set in the crusades were credited with nothing more than ridding Europe of a number of turbulent warriors. To find the middle ground and to determine what were the results of the movement, as opposed to what developed simultaneously with it, is a matter on which few historians yet agree entirely.

In some respects we now know that the crusades had very little influence. It was not through Syria but through Spain and Sicily that the Arabic science and learning came into Western Europe. The crusaders brought back but little of the intellectual accomplishments of the Moslems. A few literary themes, some verse forms (though these probably came more through Spain than Syria), some translations from the Greek made in Greece after the Fourth Crusade: these are the chief intellectual results. In the science of geography, the crusades did contribute something, as men from the West made a first-hand acquaintance with the East, greatly improving their knowledge of the world. Further it was through the crusades that Europeans came into contact with the Mongols and sent embassies to the court of the great khan. Thus via the crusader states central Asia and even China was discovered by western Europeans. The travels of Marco Polo took off from the commercial colonies, which had been established in the crusaders' states.

In the field of economics however the contribution is much greater. Acquaintance with Eastern products caused the development of a demand for them in the Western markets. Spices, fabrics, jewelry, perfumes—all the exotic wares of the East were greatly in demand in the West and merchants made fabulous fortunes in the Eastern trade. As this trade was largely in the ships of the Italian towns, it was to them that these profits went, and the great days of Venice, Genoa, and Pisa date from the beginning of the crusades. The Mediterranean empires of both Genoa and Venice were closely tied up with the crusader states; the colonies in the Levantine cities were in some instances nearly as important as the mother city, and the power and glory of both Genoa and Venice disappeared with the ending of their commercial empires and the destruction of their control over the Eastern trade.

One very significant development which resulted from the crusades was the return to a money economy and the development of international banking. In the feudal world, where everything was localized, a barter economy with payment in goods was adequate, but with the need of ready cash for the expenses of the crusades, a money economy had to be reestablished. And the currency had to be good currency which could serve in international trade. Thus we find the revival of a gold coinage reappearing in the thirteenth century as a direct result of the crusades. Also the Templars were the fathers of modern banking in that they first developed letters of credit. It was also in the age of the crusades, and probably largely due to them, that there developed new commercial forms in contracts for shipping, joint stock companies and the other commercial and financial developments described above in Chapter 21.

The need for ready cash also had a great effect on the emancipation of the towns as well as upon that of individuals. Needy lords, wanting money for the crusade, would sell to towns in their domains or to individual serfs, charters of liberties, and it was in this way that many of the Western cities gained their independence. It has been argued that the crusades also contributed to leveling off the strata of society, in that peasants went to the East and there became free burgesses, while lesser nobles of the West became great lords in the East. While this can be proven in the case of a few noble houses, the "influence of the frontier" cannot be shown to have greatly affected society, and this thesis rests on extremely shaky grounds.

In the field of military science, the crusades had an undoubted influence. The crusaders found in the East the superior Byzantine and Arabic castles and systems of fortifications and they reproduced them when they returned home. Richard Lionheart's Chateau Gaillard, which he built in Normandy after his crusade, shows clearly the influence of Eastern military architecture.[4] Also in armor the influence of the crusades was felt, for it was from the Arabs that Europeans got the habit of wearing a surcoat over the armor to soften the heat of the sun shining on the metal. Coats of arms and heraldic emblems are also attributed to the crusades, as it was between the Second and Third Crusades that they first appear in the West, while they had been common among the Arabs earlier. The prevalence of the cross on heraldic emblems also indicates the influence of the crusades in this matter.

That the crusades rid Europe of many obstreperous nobles cannot be questioned, but it seems a bit far-fetched to claim that they were in any way responsible for the decline of feudalism or the rise of national monarchies.

In one respect however the crusades did have a tremendous influence; that is in their effect on the medieval papacy. The crusades gave the popes a military power and prestige they had never enjoyed before. In the crusade they found a weapon which could be turned against their enemies at home. True this perversion of the crusade soon blunted the weapon and made people indifferent to the crusade appeal, but while it lasted it was a strong weapon in the papal arsenal. Furthermore it was from the crusades that the system of indulgences got such an impetus. At first when a man had taken the cross he had to go or do a heavy personal penance; then it became customary for him to send a substitute if he could not go in person. From that it was an easy step to giving enough money to support a warrior who could go in his stead. The spiritual benefits accrued to the man who paid the bill rather than to the man who went. The indulgences were but the logical outcome of this development. A man could purchase an indulgence which gave him the same benefits as he would have received had he gone on the crusade.

The privileges of the crusaders raised new points of law which affected

---

[4] The thesis that the reverse was true, so ably stated by T. E. Lawrence in his *Crusaders' Castles* is not accepted by most scholars, who feel that Lawrence's was a brilliant but false presentation of the facts. The accepted belief is found in the works of Paul Deschamps.

both the canon and the secular laws. Special taxes for the crusades greatly increased the scope of both ecclesiastical and secular taxing power. And the criticism of the taxes, coupled with the criticism of the perversion of the crusade idea, led to a general criticism of the church, which did much to build up the anticlericalism of the fourteenth century.

Still the statement made at the beginning of Chapter 19 holds true, that the crusades were hardly the prime cause of anything, but were powerful catalytic agents in speeding up many movements and trends which had already begun to show themselves.

CHAPTER 30

SPAIN AND FRANKISH GREECE

✤

THE SPANISH KINGDOMS

THE history of the Spanish kingdoms up to the early years of the thirteenth century was exclusively the story of the reconquest of the peninsula from the Moors. As far as Castile was concerned this is essentially true of the thirteenth century also, but the history of Aragon and Catalonia in the thirteenth century is more the story of overseas expansion in the Mediterranean. Consequently while it was possible to treat the Spanish states as a unit in an earlier chapter they will now have to be considered as separate entities.

CASTILE, 1214–1314

As we have already seen, the great victory of Las Navas de Tolosa in 1212 broke the power of the Almohades and cleared the way for the re-conquest of the Moorish states. From the wreck of the Almohade Empire in Spain there survived only four important Moslem kingdoms: Murcia, Seville, Jaen (Granada), and Valencia. No one of them was strong enough to withstand a vigorous Christian attack, and they proved themselves unable to unite in the face of a common danger. As a result Valencia was taken by the Aragonese (1233–45) while Seville, Murcia and Jaen fell before Castile, so that by 1270 only Granada, formerly a part of Jaen, remained under Moorish control.

This reconquest was the work of Ferdinand III of Castile (1217–52). Inheriting Castile from his mother, Ferdinand had at first to fight his father Alfonso IX of Leon who attempted to wrest Castile from his son. Ferdinand was able to defeat his father, and in 1230, at the death of Alfonso, united Leon to Castile. The union of 1230 was permanent and the two kingdoms remained together thereafter, so that it was with the combined strength of the two states that Ferdinand turned against the Moors. Also he made a close alliance with James of Aragon, with whom in 1244 he signed a treaty once more delimiting the conquests of the two kingdoms in the peninsula. The Almohade sultan of Morocco also allied with Castile against the Spanish Moors.

Ferdinand began his reconquest by the capture of Badajoz in 1228 and

Cordova in 1236; by 1241 all of Murcia had surrendered to him; the Masrids of Jaen accepted Castilian suzerainty in 1246 ceding Jaen itself to the Christians and retreating to Granada which they held as vassals. Two years later in 1248 Ferdinand captured Seville and in 1250 reached the coast at Cadiz. In 1250 the Algarve was conquered and the southwest cleared of Moors. Meanwhile Aragon had taken Valencia, so that Christian control or Christian suzerainty was effective throughout the peninsula. In 1266 the Murcians revolted, but were quickly put down by James of Aragon who surrendered the country back to Castile which then annexed it outright. Thus by 1270 only Granada remained in Moorish possession. For the next two centuries Granada continued her separate existence, sometimes allied with and often at war with Castile or Morocco.

On the death of Ferdinand in 1252 the Castilian crown passed to his son Alfonso X, "the Learned" (1252–84), who wasted much time and energy in a vain attempt to have himself recognized as emperor of Germany (1254–72). Although a scholar of great ability, and a great legist, Alfonso was a very weak king, and the reign is marked by the increase of the power of the nobles and the Cortes. He is best remembered as the author of the *Siete Partidas,* a great code of law into which was incorporated a considerable amount of political philosophy as well as moral and legal maxims. In addition, Alfonso promulgated the *Fuero Real,* a codification of the old laws of Castile, which remained the official code for over a century. "It has been well said of Alfonso X that he would have had more success in any other role than that of a king. . . . The same extraordinary versatility which marked his activities as a scholar was at once the distinguishing feature and the ruin of his career as a monarch." [1]

Before Alfonso died trouble had broken out over the succession. His eldest son Ferdinand de la Cerda died before his father in 1275 leaving sons, "Infantes," who claimed the throne through representation of their father. Their claims were disputed by Sancho, a younger son of Alfonso, who allied with Granada and had himself proclaimed regent. Alfonso supported the claims of the Infantes de la Cerda and secured the support of France, the pope and the sultan of Morocco, but Sancho was backed by his younger brothers, and by Aragon and Granada, and was able to seize the throne at the death of his father (1284). The first part of the reign of Sancho IV (1284–95) was marked by civil war against the Infantes, in which all parties changed sides as the occasion presented. The Moroccans captured Tarifa, and the threat of a Morroccan conquest caused a temporary alliance of Castile, Aragon, and Granada to drive them out. Sancho followed this up with an attack on Granada in which he was wholly unsuccessful. The war with Granada was still going on at his death

[1] R. B. Merriman, *The Spanish Empire,* I, 99. Reprinted by permission of the publishers, the Macmillan Co.

THE SPANISH MONARCHIES IN THE THIRTEENTH CENTURY

Alfonso VII of Castile and Leon, 1126–57

Sancho III of Castile 1157–58

Ferdinand II of Leon 1157–88

Pedro II of Aragon, 1196–1213 = Marie of Montpellier

Alfonso VIII of Castile, 1158–1214

Alfonso IX of Leon 1188–1230

James I of Aragon, 1213–76

Henry I 1214–17

Blanche = Louis VIII of France

Eleanor = James I of Aragon

Berengaria = Alfonso IX of Leon

Ferdinand III of Castile and Leon 1217–52

Edward I of England = Eleanor

Henry

Alfonso X 1252–84

Violante

Pedro III 1276–85 = Constance of Sicily

Isabelle = Philip III of France

James of Majorca 1276–1311

Ferdinand de la Cerda = Blanche of France

Sancho IV, 1284–95

Alfonso III 1285–91

Frederick I of Sicily 1296–1337

James II 1291–1327

Sancho 1311–24

Ferdinand

James II of Majorca 1324–49 (MAJORCA)

Alfonso de la Cerda

Ferdinand de la Cerda

Ferdinand IV, 1295–1312

Alfonso IV 1327–36 (ARAGON)

Pedro II of Sicily 1337–42 (SICILY)

Alfonso Fadrique (Greece)

Alfonso XI, 1312–50 (CASTILE)

and was continued by his successor Ferdinand IV (1295–1312) who likewise failed to accomplish anything against the Moors.

Of much greater importance than the civil wars and attempted conquests of these Castilian kings was the development of Castilian institutions in this period. Spain had a unique form of feudalism; the nobles were divided into three major classes, the *ricos hombres,* the *hidalgos,* and the *caballeros,* corresponding roughly to the English classification of earls, barons, and knights. All of these classes enjoyed freedom from taxation. The ricos hombres were those great families who were virtually the equals of the king and who were practically free of any royal control; they were free from arrest, could maintain their own armies and could at any time renounce their allegiance to the king. The hidalgos were on the whole royal creations and the title was often sold or awarded to the king's officials. These nobles all cherished their privileges and rights and were as frequently as not in rebellion against the crown.

A unique position was held in Castile by the Cortes, the representative assembly of the clergy, nobles, and townsmen. The early participation of the towns in the Cortes was undoubtedly due to the fact that the kings relied on them for support against the nobles, but their appearance in the Cortes of Leon in 1188 and in those of Castile in 1250 certainly places Spain ahead of England temporally in the development of representative assemblies.

The whole history of Castile favored the growth of privileged towns. As new land was reconquered from the Moors towns were established to hold the territory, and to entice people to settle in these towns, liberal privileges had to be assured. Each town had its own *fuero* or charter of laws guaranteeing the privileges of the townsmen. Thus the Castilian towns like the communes of Italy early became experienced in self-government. "From the middle of the twelfth to the middle of the fourteenth century, when the development attained its climax, the vigor and liberty of the municipal government of Castile was probably unsurpassed anywhere in Western Europe." [2]

One method whereby the towns maintained their privileges and liberties was through the organizations of the *hermandades.* Representatives of different towns would form themselves into a brotherhood to preserve their liberties, organizing regular leagues with constitutions which they had approved by the king. Although there are evidences that these hermandades first began in the twelfth century, they first become important in the latter part of the thirteenth, one of the most famous being an hermandad of the towns of Leon organized in 1282. The early associations were generally temporary and designed only to preserve the towns through some single crisis, but in the fourteenth century they became permanent

[2] R. B. Merriman, *The Spanish Empire,* I, 189.

associations for the preservation of the peace of the kingdom. These larger hermandades became most valuable allies of the kings in their struggle with the nobles, for the same frontier conditions which facilitated the development of self-governing towns tended to make the nobles more independent and unruly, so that the kings needed local allies to check the nobles. The hermandades reached their height of importance in the early fourteenth century and then declined into relative insignificance.

Returning to the Cortes, of which the representatives of the communes were so important a part, by the middle of the thirteenth century the Cortes had gained the right to grant all extraordinary taxation, and by 1307 this right was written into the law. By the end of the thirteenth century they had also the right to petition the crown in matters of legislation. Like the English parliaments, the Cortes greatly increased their powers in the fourteenth century only to lose them in the late fifteenth and sixteenth.

ARAGON, 1213–1327

The kingdom of Aragon could not, by its very composition, pursue a single purpose as Castile devoted herself to the reconquest. While the king took his royal title from the essentially Spanish state of Aragon, the greatest strength of the monarch lay in his principality of Catalonia with its great port of Barcelona. The two states were never completely united as each preserved its own separate Cortes and laws, and the interests of the two did not run at all in the same direction. While Aragon was most interested in expansion within the peninsula, Catalonia turned to the sea and sought an empire in the islands of the Mediterranean.

James I, the Conqueror (1213–76), ably gratified the ambitions of both of his constituent states by his conquests from the Moors. In 1229 to 1235 he led a crusade which captured the Balaeric Isles, long desired by the Catalans, and then in 1233 to 1245 invaded Valencia and incorporated it into his domains to the great satisfaction of the Aragonese. He further strengthened his position in the Mediterranean by an alliance with Manfred of Sicily, which was cemented by the marriage of his son Pedro to Manfred's daughter Constance. At the same time he strengthened his frontier on the north by the treaty of Corbeil with France in 1258, whereby he gave up all his claims to Provence and Languedoc, except Montpellier, in return for Louis' renunciation of all claims over Rousillon, Cerdagne, and Catalonia. While this seemed an abandonment of extensive claims by both monarchs, it fixed a boundary which was maintained with little variation until the seventeenth century.[3]

[3] Montpellier continued to be held as a fief under France until 1349, when Philip VI purchased it from James of Majorca.

Unfortunately James reverted to the old practice of dividing his domains among his sons. While Aragon was left to the eldest, Pedro III, the Balaerics, Roussillon, and Montpellier were made into an appanage kingdom for his younger son, James, who took the title of King of Majorca. This appanage was to cause considerable trouble and fighting before it was eventually reunited to the crown in 1344.

Pedro III, the Great (1276–85), is that king of Aragon whom we have already encountered as profiting from the Sicilian Vespers and conquering Sicily by virtue of the claims of his wife. By the conquest of Sicily, Pedro brought Aragon into the forefront of the Mediterranean powers and greatly enhanced the reputation and position of his state. But internally he was forced to pay for his conquests by concessions, which were exacted from him by the nobles of Aragon who had no interest in this expansion and who resented the heavy costs of it. In the Aragonese Cortes of 1283 the nobles and towns formed a union to oppose the king and were successful in forcing him to grant the General Privilege (*Privilegio general*). By this Privilege it was promised that the ancient *fueros* (custom laws) and privileges of the realm were to be respected; no one was to be convicted without proper trial; ricos hombres could not be distrained for military service outside the limits of the kingdom; and all classes of society were to be included in the royal councils. This Privilege has been called the Aragonese Magna Carta, but it really went far beyond the Charter in the rights guaranteed to the townsmen.

Further concessions were wrested from King Alfonso III (1285–91) by the union in the *Privilegio de la Unión* in 1287 wherein the king granted to the Cortes the right to appoint members of the council, and even recognized the rights of the union to depose him and to elect another king. James II (1291–1327) was able to break the power of the union by dividing the towns from the nobles, but the Privileges remained on the books and the power of the king over the nobles was only assured by the battle of Epila in 1348.

The Cortes of Aragon and those of Catalonia were much like the Castilian, although the nobles were more important in Aragon than in Castile. In both Catalonia and Valencia the capital cities exercized an undue influence in the representation of the communes, but in all the Cortes under the crown of Aragon the nobles held the dominant position. Aragon possessed a unique institution in the *Justicia,* a supreme judge who was especially empowered to try all officials and to decide in cases between the king and his subjects.

The political history of Aragon in the latter thirteenth century is closely bound up with that of Sicily and has already been noticed. Alfonso III tried to support his brother James in Sicily, but was forced by the pope and the French crusade, which supported the Angevins, to withdraw his support in the last year of his life. When James succeeded him on the Aragonese throne, he appointed his younger brother, Frederick, governor of Sicily, but dropped him under pressure from the pope and other powers. Frederick refused to be abandoned, however, and was proclaimed by the Sicilians as an independent king. He was able to defend himself against the attacks of the Angevins and the papacy, even though the latter received naval help from Aragon itself. The Treaty of Caltabellota (1302) left Frederick in possession of Sicily, where his descendants maintained their rule for over a century.

It was during the reign of James II that the Catalan Grand Company, composed of *Almogavares* (the light-armed Catalan infantry) who had been in the service of Frederick of Sicily, carried the fear of the Catalan name to the eastern Mediterranean and the Aegean with their conquest of Frankish Attica. The exploits of this band of adventurers will be noted below in our discussion of Frankish Greece.

THE LESSER STATES OF THE SPANISH PENINSULA

The kingdom of Navarre was practically without any history in the thirteenth century. In 1234 it passed through inheritance to Count Thibaut of Champagne and thus went out of the Spanish and into the French orbit. With the marriage of Joan of Navarre and Champagne to Philip IV of France in 1284, the little kingdom was incorporated into the royal domain of France.

Portugal, which in the time of Innocent III had become a vassal state of the papacy, spent most of the thirteenth century in civil war between the kings and the clergy. The kings were determined to prevent further alienation of land to the church and to make the orders taxable, which of course the clergy fought strenuously. Alfonso II (1211–23) was forced to recognize the superiority of canon law over civil law in the courts of the kingdom, and was defeated by a coalition of clergy and nobles which wrested considerable concessions from him. His son Sancho II (1223–45) continued the struggle with clergy and nobles only to be deposed by Innocent IV and replaced by his brother Alfonso III (1245–79). Alfonso, however, got along with the church no better than his brother and was himself excommunicated and Portugal put under the interdict. But Alfonso was stronger than his predecessors and built up a party in the towns who supported him in the Cortes. It was under his rule that Portugal conquered the Algarve from Castile and fixed the boundary between herself and Castile by the treaty of Badajoz in 1267. Alfonso died in office and his son Dinis (1279–1325) continued the struggle with the church, finally concluding a concordat in 1289 whereby he was able to retain his laws concerning mortmain. The reign of Diniz was one of great progress and development in Portugal, in which the monarchy was strengthened and the foundations were laid for the naval power, which was to bring the country to such heights in the following century.

GREECE AND THE BALKANS

While in the western end of the Mediterranean, Castile and Aragon were winning the Spanish peninsula and laying the foundations for an overseas empire, in the East, in the lands bordering the Aegean and the Black Seas, the Latins were struggling with Greeks and Slavs for supremacy in the former lands of the Byzantine Empire.

A number of states emerged as a result of the Fourth Crusade. The Latins held the empire of Constantinople under Baldwin of Flanders, a kingdom of Salonica under Boniface de Montferrat, the Frankish principalities of Greece and a number of the islands which were primarily under Venetian control. Opposed to them were the two important Greek empires of Nicaea and Epirus and the Bulgaro-Vlach kingdom. Of these the Latin states of Constantinople and Salonica soon fell before the attack of the Greeks of Nicaea, but some of the Latin states in Greece and the islands continued until the very end of the Middle Ages.

CONSTANTINOPLE AND NICAEA

The Latin Empire of Constantinople was of ephemeral importance. Baldwin of Flanders distributed fiefs throughout the Balkans and Anatolia, wholly disregarding the fact that the lands were actually held by the Greeks. At first some headway seemed to be made in conquering these territories, but in 1205 he was defeated and captured by Johannitza, the king of the revived Bulgaro-Vlach kingdom, which had arisen in the western Balkans in the last quarter of the twelfth century.

This "Bulgarian kingdom" had been started when the brothers John and Peter Asen led a revolt of the Vlachs in the region around Ochrida and Tirnovo in 1185, and established what they claimed to be a revival of the old Bulgarian empire of Krum and Simeon. In 1204, Johannitza or Kalojean, their brother who had succeeded them, received a royal crown from Pope Innocent III while the metropolitan of Tirnovo was approved as an archbishop. At first Johannitza had been prepared to welcome the Latins as allies, since they were both enemies of the Greeks, but the Latins haughtily refused his proffered friendship, whereupon the Bulgaro-Vlach monarch became their most powerful enemy.

The capture of Baldwin left the empire of Constantinople to his brother

Henry of Hainault, first as regent and later as emperor in his own name (1206–16). Under Henry, the Latins enjoyed a brief period of success in which they extended their influence both in the Balkans and in Asia Minor, but their victories were ephemeral, and they soon lost their lands in Asia to the Greeks of Nicaea, while those in the Balkans were overrun by the lords of both Nicaea and Epirus. Peter de Courtenay, count of Auxerre, the brother-in-law of Baldwin and Henry, succeeded to the imperial title in 1216 at the death of Henry, but never even reached his capital, being cap-

LATIN EMPERORS OF CONSTANTINOPLE, 1204–1373

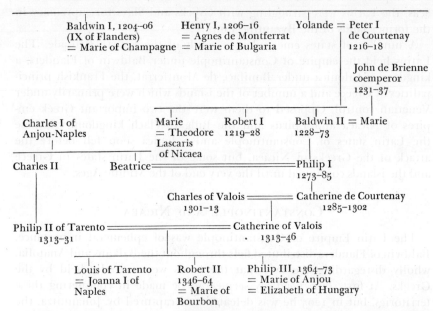

tured by the Epirotes in 1217 and dying in prison the following year. His son Robert was weak and ineffectual, and antagonized his own barons who virtually overthrew him. At his death in 1228, he was succeeded by his younger brother Baldwin II (1228–61) a minor, so the barons sought a ruler in John de Brienne, the former king of Jerusalem, whose daughter was married to Baldwin and who was proclaimed coemperor. John beat off an attack on Constantinople by the combined forces of Nicaea and Vlachia in 1236, but died the next year, and Baldwin dragged out a miserable existence, seeking aid from Europe which never came, and finally losing his city to Michael VIII Palaeologus in 1261.

The kingdom of Salonica was even more short-lived. Founded by Boniface de Montferrat in 1204, it passed at his death to his son Demetrius (1207–22). At first Salonica, which was the most important port of continental Greece, was an important state, the lords of Athens, Bodonitza, and other Frankish rulers in Greece recognizing its suzerainty. But in 1209, Emperor Henry made them all vassals of the empire, and in 1224 Salonica fell before the attack of Theodore, the Greek despot of Epirus.

Epirus had been founded as a Greek despotate by one Michael Angelus-Comnenus-Ducas who had fled there in 1204 and established an independent state. His brother Theodore (1214–30) raised Epirus to a position of first importance in the Balkans, conquering considerable territory from the Bulgarians and annexing Salonica, Durrazzo and most of the western Balkan region. But Theodore's successes stirred up the fear and jealousy of both Vlachia and Nicaea, and in 1230 Theodore was captured by John Asen II of Vlachia who overran Macedonia and Epirus which he annexed to the Vlach kingdom. While Salonica passed to Theodore's brother Manuel (1230–40), Epirus first was incorporated into Bulgaria and then in 1237 reasserted its independence as a revived despotate under Michael II, the son of Michael I.

Meanwhile the Greek Empire of Nicaea had increased its power by the reconquest of much of Anatolia and eastern Thrace. Under John Vatatzes (1222–54), Nicaea became easily the most powerful of any of these states, conquering Salonica in 1246 and asserting its suzerainty over Epirus in 1254. In 1261 the supremacy of Nicaea was assured when Michael VIII Palaeologus (1259–82) conquered Constantinople and restored the empire to its proper capital.

The capture of Constantinople in 1261 affected more than the mere Latin Empire. The Venetians had been the great gainers by the Fourth Crusade and their rivals the Genoese had been driven out of their commercial outposts in the East. Consequently Genoa had allied with Nicaea against Venice and the Latins, and it was largely through Genoese help that Constantinople was retaken. The Venetians of course found themselves deprived of the commerce of the empire which was given to the Genoese, but as they still held many strong positions in the Aegean islands, Greece and Crete, they did not yield passively, and the Venetian-Genoese struggle disturbed the whole region for many years to come.

The Latin Empire had never really had a chance. With the Venetians holding the commercially most important portions of the empire, with Salonica in alien and often hostile hands, with the Greek power concentrated in Nicaea just across the Straits and blocking any chance of expanding into Anatolia, the new little empire of Constantinople was practically doomed from its inception. Under Henry, the only really able ruler it ever had, it had made some progress towards establishing a real power, but Henry died prematurely and his successors were men of an inferior stamp, wholly incapable of wrestling with the problems which faced the infant state. There is less excuse for the fall of Salonica after only eighteen years of existence because the states in Greece founded by vassals of Boniface, which were hardly less exposed than was Salonica itself to outside attack, lasted on for centuries. But caught as she was between Epirus and Nicaea, Salonica did not have the strength or resources to maintain herself and so perished ingloriously.

FRANKISH GREECE AND MOREA

Far different was the fate of the Duchy of Athens, the marquisate of Bodonitza, and the principality of Achaea or Morea (the ancient Peloponnesus) which were all founded in Greece and which were all originally vassals of Salonica. On the very morrow of the first conquest, in 1204 to 1205, Otho de la Roche established himself at Athens and Thebes, Guido Pallavicini founded the marquisate of Bodonitza in the lands around Thermopylae, and William de Champlitte and Geoffrey de Villehardouin, the nephew of the chronicler of the Fourth Crusade, conquered the Peloponnesus. These were not the only states founded by the Latins in Greece, but they were the most important, and were fairly representative of the petty feudal dynasties which were established in Greece and the islands of the Archipelago after the Crusade.

In these states of Frankish Greece, the institutions and culture of thirteenth-century France were planted on Eastern soil as eleventh-century France had been transferred to Syria at an earlier period. In Morea, at the court of the Villehardouin, as good French was spoken as was in Paris or Tours, French literature was read and imitated, French chivalric concepts were practiced, with the usual tournaments and knightly exercises. Of Geoffrey II de Villehardouin (1218–45) the Venetian Marino Sanudo wrote: "At his own court he constantly maintained eighty knights with golden spurs, to whom he gave all that they required besides their pay; so knights came from France, from Burgundy, and, above all, from Champagne, to follow him. Some came to amuse themselves, others to pay their debts, others because of crimes which they had committed at home. . . ." [4]

It was also in Frankish Corinth, where he was bishop, that William of Moerbeke first translated Aristotle's *Politics* from Greek into Latin.

The history of these Greek principalities is similar to that of the empire. Civil wars between the Franks gave opportunity for the Greeks to reestablish themselves in the peninsula, which they did after the celebrated battle of Pelagonia in 1259. There the chivalry of Frankish Greece was defeated by Michael Palaeologus of Nicaea. The despot of Epirus had allied with the Latins in this battle, but his forces proved untrustworthy, and the Franks were left to face the attack of a polyglot army assembled by Michael

---

[4] Marino Sanudo, *Istoria del Regno di Romania*, translated by P. Topping, in *Feudal Institutions* (Univ. of Penna. "Translations and Reprints," Third Series, III), Introduction. Reprinted by permission of the publishers, Univ. of Pennsylvania Press.

from Hungary, Germany, and the Balkan states. So many Frankish knights were captured or killed at Pelagonia that the parliament which met at Nikli to make peace with Michael has been termed "the parliament of dames" as so many noble ladies represented their husbands' fiefs at the meeting. The ladies gladly surrendered to Michael the strong castles of Monemvasia, Maina, and Mistra in Morea, which was Michael's price for the return of their husbands. This gave the Greeks a firm foothold in the peninsula, which they later expanded to include the whole southern part of the Peloponnesus.

Unfortunately for Morea, the direct line of the Villehardouin, who had made the principality a state of the first importance, died out with William I in 1278. The title passed to William's daughter Isabelle, whose marriage to Philip of Anjou, a cadet son of Charles of Anjou, king of Naples, brought Morea into the orbit of the Angevin power which was at this time at its height in the East. Charles of Anjou, after conquering Naples and Sicily, had begun intrigue in the East towards the end of establishing a great empire under Angevin dominance. He had secured the alliance of Hungary, which ultimately passed to his grandson Charles Martel. He purchased the title to the kingdom of Jerusalem from Marie of Antioch in 1277; his daughter Beatrice married Philip de Courtenay, titular emperor of Constantinople (1273–85), and he assumed the title of prince of Morea in 1278 as the guardian of Isabelle de Villehardouin. More practical than this accumulation of titles was his alliance with the Venetians and the Serbs for the conquest of Corfu and a considerable section of the Albanian coast which he took from Epirus. Thus Charles was well on his way to accomplishing his goal in Greece and the Balkans when his whole scheme was destroyed by the Sicilian Vespers in 1282.

The collapse of the Angevin imperial dream nevertheless left Morea as a satellite of Naples. Charles II restored Morea to Isabelle and her second husband, but the Angevins kept a control over the principality and, as the rulers were generally resident in Naples, Angevin baillies actually ruled in Greece, whether they represented the Angevin kings or titularly-independent princes of Morea. The titles of Constantinople and Morea were combined (1333–73) in Catherine de Valois and her sons, Robert and Philip, after which the title to Morea passed to Queen Joanna of Naples. But during this period there were civil wars and pretenders, and even the strong rule of the Angevin baillies could not maintain order. While the Latins quarreled amongst themselves the Greeks of Mistra (ancient Sparta) took the opportunity to expand their frontiers and capture most of the peninsula.

Meanwhile the Frankish duchy of Athens had fallen before the onslaught of the Catalan Grand Company and had been placed under the suzerainty of the house of Aragon. The Company, made up of Catalan Almogavares, light-armed infantry who achieved a great reputation for military efficiency in the wars in the West, had served under Frederick of Sicily in his campaigns against the Angevins. With the peace of Caltabelotta (1302) these mercenaries, having no further business in the West, moved East where they took service under the Byzantine emperor, Andronicus Palaeologus. Under their leader Roger le Flor, they fought the Turks in Anatolia, conquering Ephesus and driving south as far as the Cilician Passes. But it was soon evident that the Catalans, though ostensibly fighting for Andronicus, were actually conquering lands for themselves. They had already quarreled with the Genoese and massacred several thousand Italians in Constantinople, and the emperor, quite reasonably, began to fear them more than any of his earlier enemies. To prevent their gaining complete mastery over Anatolia, the emperor recalled them to Gallipoli. While they were encamped there, Roger, who had demanded and been granted the title of Caesar, was invited to a banquet by Michael Palaeologus, the son of the emperor, and was murdered. But the Catalans elected another leader and began to raid all of Thrace, establishing at Gallipoli a great slave market where they supplied the Moslem slave markets with captives taken in their raids. From Gallipoli they moved over into Thrace and Macedonia, which they ravaged. While they were engaged in this pleasant occupation, Walter de Brienne, duke of Athens, engaged them to conquer Thessaly in his name. They did, but shortly thereafter broke with their employer, who had neglected their wages, and turned against Athens. In the battle of Cephissus (1311) the Catalans wiped out the knights of Athens and gained possession of the duchy. Requesting a prince from King Frederick of Sicily, they then settled down in Boeotia and Attica, where they married the widows of their former foes and established themselves as the rulers of the land. In 1316 Alfonso Fadrique, an illegitimate son of Frederick of Sicily, came out to rule them, and they remained under Sicilian government until 1377–79 when they placed themselves under the rule of the kings of Aragon.

Under the Almogavares, Attica and Boeotia were made as much like Catalonia as possible. Their capital was established, like that of the Burgundian dukes before them, at Thebes: Catalan became the official language, the "Usages of Barcelona" were made the official law code of the duchy of Athens, and Catalan institutions were copied in every aspect of life. As rulers of Greece the Catalans lost their early ferocity and became semi-hellenized; they frequently quarreled among themselves, and so were much weakened. Thus it was with difficulty that they withstood the attack of a new company of adventurers, the Navarrese Company, who attacked Albania and captured Durazzo in 1376. These Navarrese were mercenaries who had been in the service of Charles of Navarre and had been sent to Greece to press the claims of his brother, Louis of Evreux, to the "Kingdom of Albania." Left stranded by the death of Louis, they passed into Morea in

1378. In the spring and early summer of 1379, some of them, under a certain John of Urtubia, captured Thebes, which the Catalans never regained. Athens withstood them, but four years later some of their companions took over Morea.

The Navarrese Company really ended Frankish Greece. The old feudal principal cities were gone. The Florentine Acciaiuoli got possession of the Athenian Acropolis in 1388, while Morea fell to the Greeks, who pushed up from Mistra until they conquered virtually the entire Peloponnesus. By the early fifteenth century a few Italian dynasties and a few Venetian colonies were all that was left of Frankish Greece. Most of these were ultimately reduced by the Ottoman Turks after the middle of the fifteenth century.

However dismal their end, these Frankish states in their prime in the thirteenth century were centers of Western culture and institutions in the East. French feudalism was introduced into both the empire and the Greek principalities. The *Assizes of Romania,* the code of Morea, is a thoroughly Western feudal document. Dukes, counts, marquises, viscounts, and barons were installed in the ancient Greek towns, and the title Duke of Athens which Dante and Shakespeare gave to Theseus is a relic of the Frankish occupation. But like the crusaders in Syria, the Franks of Greece were always a ruling minority over an alien subject majority; they never completely absorbed or were absorbed into the great mass of their subjects. Religion and language especially served to separate them from the Greeks and to prevent the creation of a strong and lasting state.

SERBIA

Our discussion of the principalities of Greece has carried us far beyond the temporal limits of this chapter. Before turning away from the Balkans, we must notice, however cursorily, the erection in the twelfth century of the kingdom of Serbia. The first unification of the Serbs had been begun in the tenth century, but the real founder of Serbia was Stephen Nemanya (1168–96) who united under his control, and that of the Greek church, most of the clans of Serbia and secured their independence of the Byzantine Empire. He was succeeded by his son Stephen Nemanya II (1196–1223) who secured a royal crown from Pope Innocent III in 1217. In 1222 under the influence of his brother St. Saba, Stephen exchanged his Latin crown for a Greek one sent by Nicaea, thus holding the country in the Greek Orthodox obedience ecclesiastically. Stephen was supported by Johannitza of Bulgaria, and for a time relations between the two states were close, Bulgaria exercising an unofficial hegemony over Serbia. Surrounded by the Hungarians, Vlachs, Bulgarians, Greeks, and Angevins, the kings of Serbia sought security and aggrandisement in the quarrels of their neighbors; but foreign intervention, civil war, and dynastic rivalries and murders kept the kingdom weak until the accession of Stephen Dushan (1331–55). Dushan interfered in the civil wars of the Greeks and very nearly secured for himself the possession of the Greek Empire. He conquered Bulgaria, Bosnia, Macedonia, Thrace, defeated the Hungarians and took Belgrade, and was planning to attack Constantinople when he died. His reign marks the apogee of Serbian power and is the last important political development in the Balkans until the Ottoman conquest.

CHAPTER 31

THE MONGOLS, RUSSIA, AND THE BALTIC LANDS

✤

THE MONGOLS

IN many ways the most important single event of the thirteenth century was the establishment of the Mongol Empire. Coming out of eastern Siberia, the Mongols, a confederacy of nomadic tribes of the steppe, conquered in a few decades the largest territorial empire that the world has ever known. Like the Huns, Avars, Bulgars, Magyars, Petchenegs, Cumans, and Turks, the Mongols swept out of the steppes into the civilized lands of western Asia and eastern Europe, bringing destruction and death; but savage as had been the invasions of these earlier peoples the Mongols exceeded them both in the extent of their conquests and in the ferocity of their destruction.

The history of the Mongols knows no geographical boundaries. The settled limits of nations were swiftly and ruthlessly overthrown . . . Wherever their fancy roamed, their hordes followed. Flourishing cities perished in a night, leaving no memorial but ruins and mounds of piled up corpses. The quiet that followed the Mongol invasions was not the calm that settled on a world wearied of strife, eager to foster once again the fruits of civilization: it was the gasp of expiring nations in their death agony, before the eternal silence of the tomb. They made their deserts and they called it peace.[1]

Originally the Mongols were but one of a group of nomadic tribes which roamed the steppes of eastern Asia. Mongols, Tatars (corrupted in Latin to Tartars), Keraits, Naimans, Merkits, Uighurs, Kipchaks, Kankali, and Kara-Khitai were all included in the general name of Mongols or Tartars when they came out of the desert into the sown lands. The welding of these tribes into a great empire which dominated a large portion of the world was the work of a single man, Temujin, better known by his royal title of Chingiz Khan, the greatest conqueror the world has ever known.

The lands of the Mongols were bordered to the east by the empires of China, that of the Kin in the north and the Sung in the south. The Great Wall of China had been built as early as the second century B.C. for the purpose of protecting the northern empire from the raids of the Mongols and

---

[1] *Cambridge Medieval History*, IV, 627–28. Reprinted by permission of the publishers, Cambridge Univ. Press and the Macmillan Co.

529

the other nomad tribes. For a time the nomads were subject to China, but in the twelfth century they broke away and asserted their independence. As long as they were disorganized, however, they fought among themselves and were no great menace to the civilized world. Once united under an aggressive leader they became a destructive force which reduced outside civilized countries to the desert level of their native steppes.

One difference between the Mongols and other conquerors was in their total disregard for human life; to the Mongol a human was worthless, it was a horse which had value. They did not understand or like cities: when they came across a large city they did not know what to do with it, so destroyed it completely. They drove their men to exhaustion, sparing only their animals. It was said that every Mongol warrior had eighteen horses, which he rode one after the other until all were exhausted, but while the horses got rest the riders went on tirelessly. They carried meat under their saddles so that they could eat without dismounting; where other armies made miles in a day the Mongols made leagues. Much of their military success lay in the speed of their attack—they were the inventors of the *blitzkrieg*.

Small, squat, bowlegged men, these savage warriors seemed hardly human to their enemies. In all their battles they counted on numbers, speed, and discipline, and when one battalion had been killed another took its place. With complete disregard of losses they threw their forces into the fight, and their overwhelming numbers, plus their skill in maneuver assured them victory against enemies who may well have been individually braver. The Mongols also developed psychological warfare,—the war of nerves. When they first came to a country they would destroy a city completely, sparing no living soul. Then they would let the word of the massacre spread through the country until their foes were filled with dread. The story is told of one stray Mongol who wandered into a village alone and took it single-handed because the people were so afraid of the very name Mongol that they threw themselves at his feet in abject surrender. How many people were killed during the Mongol invasion we cannot say, but it is estimated that in the conquest of China alone, 18,000,000 were slain.

CHINGIZ KHAN, 1162–1227

Temujin, who led them to victory under the name of Chingiz Khan, was born about 1162, the son of a chieftain of one of the Mongol tribes. His early years were hard for he was dispossessed of his inheritance and wandered as a refugee for a number of years until he was taken into the household of the Wang-khan of the Keraits. With the backing of the Wang-khan, he began to build himself a following, got himself elected chief of all the Mongols, and then started on a career of conquest. He conquered the

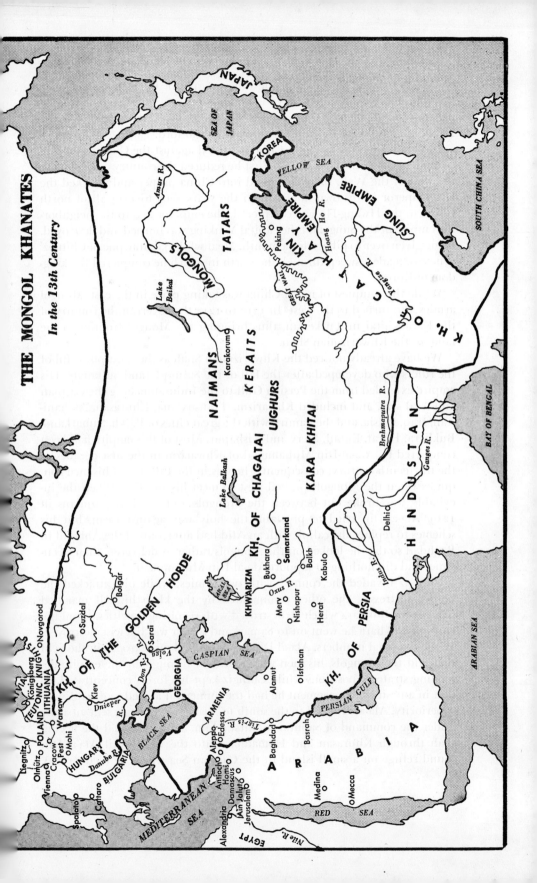

THE MONGOL KHANATES
In the 13th Century

JAPAN

SEA OF JAPAN

KOREA

Amur R.

YELLOW SEA

TATARS

MONGOLS

Lake Baikal

Karakorum

Peking

Hoong Ho R.

KIN EMPIRE

CATHAY

Yangtze R.

SUNG EMPIRE

SOUTH CHINA SEA

NAIMANS

KERAITS

UIGHURS

GREAT WALL

KARA - KHITAI

KH. OF CHAGATAI

Lake Balkash

Samarkand

Bukhara

Oxus R.

Merv

Nishapur

Balkh

Kabulo

Herat

KHWARIZM

Aral Sea

KH. OF PERSIA

Isfahan

Alamut

Brahmaputra R.

HINDUSTAN

Ganges R.

Delhi

Indus R.

BAY OF BENGAL

ARABIAN SEA

Bolgar

Suzdal

Novgorod

THE GOLDEN HORDE

Sarai

Volga R.

Don R.

Kiev

Dnieper R.

CASPIAN SEA

GEORGIA

ARMENIA

BLACK SEA

LATVIA

Königsberg

TEUTONIC KNIGH

LITHUANIA

POLAND

Warsaw

KH. OF

Liegnitz

Olmütz

Cracow

Pest

Vienna

Mohi

HUNGARY

Danube R.

BULGARIA

Spalato

Cattaro

MEDITERRANEAN SEA

Antioch

Aleppo

Edessa

Tigris R.

Homs

Damascus

Ain Jalut

Jerusalem

Alexandria

EGYPT

Nile R.

Baghdad

Basrah

PERSIAN GULF

ARABIA

Medina

Mecca

RED SEA

Tatars, Naimans, Merkits and the other people of the steppe, and overthrew his former suzerain, the Wang-khan of the Keraits. Then in 1206, having reduced all the nomads to subjection, he assumed the title of Chingiz
Khan, a name which indicates great or universal lord.

Having united the nomads, Chingiz turned against the Chinese Empire
of the Kin across the Great Wall. First he reduced the country of the Hia to
the west of the Wall, then he crossed into China proper and attacked the
Kin emperor in his own domains. In the years 1208 to 1214 all of north
China to the Hwang-Ho was conquered; the emperor fled to the neighboring empire of the Sung, and the capital Yenking was burned and destroyed,
being given over to pillage for a month. Meanwhile Sabutai, one of Chingiz'
generals, made a sweep through the north in which he conquered the kingdom of Korea.

While the conquest of north China was taking place in the east, Mongol
armies also turned to the west. In 1212 to 1214 they overran the country of
the Kara-Khitai in Turkestan, thus bringing the Mongol frontier to the
lands of the Khwarizmian Shah.

We have already noticed the Khwarizmian Shah as the most powerful of
the rulers who developed after the fall of the Saljuq Grand Sultanate. His
empire extended from the Persian Gulf to the Indus, touching the Caspian
and Aral seas, and included Khwarizm, Transoxiana, Khurasan, Afghanistan, Iraq, Persia, and the Pamirs, with the great cities of Balkh, Samarkand,
Bukhara, Herat, Kabul, Merv and Nishapur. Most of this empire had been
conquered by Ala-al-Din Muhammad of Khwarizm in the first decades of
the thirteenth century; consequently he was in the full tide of his own conquests when the Mongols pushed west to meet his frontier. When the inevitable war broke out between the Mongols and the Khwarizmians in
1219, Ala-al-Din tried to proclaim the holy war against them, but his
schemes to replace the caliph with an Alid had antagonized the Abbasid in
Baghdad so that he looked on the Mongols rather as deliverers than as enemies and did nothing to support Ala-al-Din Muhammad.

Chingiz invaded the country with two armies; while one attacked the
border fortresses, the other commanded by the khan himself marched
straight for Bukhara which he destroyed with revolting cruelties. From the
ruins of Bukhara he went on to Samarkand which was likewise destroyed.
While in actual numbers, Ala-al-Din probably had more troops in the field
than did the Mongols, his men were scattered throughout the empire defending strategic positions while Chingiz kept his forces concentrated, so
that in any single engagement he had the numerical as well as disciplinary
superiority. Ala-al-Din fled to the south to Nishapur; Chingiz sent an army
under the command of Sabutai to pursue him. Sabutai chased the fleeing
shah through Khurasan and Hamadhan into the west, until Ala-al-Din
found refuge on a small island in the Caspian Sea where he died (1220).

Chingiz proceeded with the reduction and destruction of his empire. Balkh, Merv, and Nishapur were destroyed with a great massacre of the inhabitants. At Nishapur, which had resisted and killed a Mongol general, the entire population was killed, the bodies were decapitated and three great pyramids were built of the heads of men, women, and children. Even the

CHINGIZKHANID KHANS OF THE MONGOLS

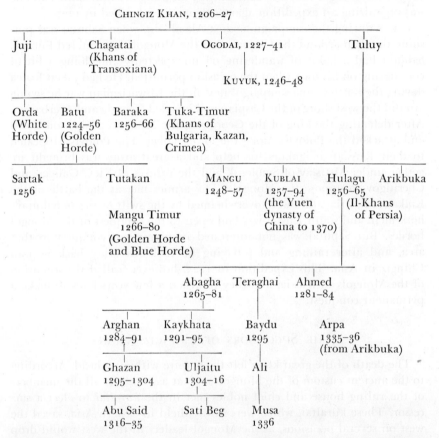

CHINGIZ KHAN, 1206–27

Juji	Chagatai (Khans of Transoxiana)	OGODAI, 1227–41	Tuluy
		KUYUK, 1246–48	

Orda (White Horde)	Batu 1224–56 (Golden Horde)	Baraka 1256–66	Tuka-Timur (Khans of Bulgaria, Kazan, Crimea)				
Sartak 1256	Tutakan			MANGU 1248–57	KUBLAI 1257–94 (the Yuen dynasty of China to 1370)	Hulagu 1256–65 (Il-Khans of Persia)	Arikbuka
	Mangu Timur 1266–80 (Golden Horde and Blue Horde)						

Abagha 1265–81   Teraghai   Ahmed 1281–84

Arghan 1284–91   Kaykhata 1291–95   Baydu 1295   Arpa 1335–36 (from Arikbuka)

Ghazan 1295–1304   Uljaitu 1304–16   Ali

Abu Said 1316–35   Sati Beg   Musa 1336

dogs and cats of the city are said to have been killed, so that no living thing would remain where Nishapur had stood.

But Jalal-al-din, the son of Ala-al-Din Muhammad, continued to resist the conqueror. He gathered his forces in Afghanistan and defied the khan, but Chingiz sought him out. In a battle on the banks of the Indus, Jalal-al-din was defeated and forced to flee to Delhi. Chingiz went on to destroy Herat where 1,600,000 are said to have been massacred. It was the custom of the Mongols when a city was captured to make all the inhabitants come out into an open space outside the walls and there sort them out; artisans, strong-bodied men, and beautiful girls would be taken prisoners, as they could be used by the conquerors; the remainder were slaughtered indiscriminately.

After the fall of Khwarizm, Chingiz returned to the steppes, to his capital at the tent city of Karakorum. But the death of the Kin emperor gave him an excuse to tighten his control over north China which he did in 1223. This brought him into conflict with the Sung of south China, and he was organizing an expedition against them when he died in 1227.

It was during the campaign against Ala-al-Din, when Sabutai was pursuing the shah around the Caspian that the Mongols first entered Europe. Sabutai had a habit of wandering off unexpectedly and doing a bit of conquering on his own when the occasion permitted. He had taken Korea during the north China campaign: now in the Khwarizmian war he swung around the west shore of the Caspian and invaded Georgia and Azerbaijan. After defeating the king of the Georgians, the Mongols pushed on north and attacked the Polovtsy along the lower Volga. The Polovtsy appealed to their Russian neighbors for help and a great army was brought together under Mstislav of Smolensk and the princes of Kiev, Galicia, and Chernigov to oppose the Mongols. The armies met at the battle of the Kalka (1223); the allies were overwhelmed by the swift tactics of Sabutai's horsemen, and south Russia was laid open to the conquest of the Mongol hordes. But Sabutai was not interested in permanent conquest in that area, and after raiding and pillaging he took his army back to join Chingiz in Asia. This expedition of 1223, however, called the attention of the Mongols to Russia, and they returned a few years later to make a permanent conquest.

THE SUCCESSORS OF CHINGIZ KHAN

The death of the great khan left the empire without a head. According to the ancient custom of the Mongols a great assembly of all the members of the ruling house and chief nobles met in the *kuraltai* to elect a successor. These kuraltai, which were always held in eastern Asia, saved the west on several occasions, as the Mongol leaders in the west would drop their conquests to return east to participate in them. It was this which later saved both Europe and Syria from even worse devastation than they suffered.

With the death of Chingiz the empire was divided; while one son held the title of Supreme Khan and was theoretically over the others, the actual control of the vast empire was divided among the descendants of the conqueror, so that several principal states emerged. Chingiz had four sons: Juji, Chagatai, Ogodai, and Tuluy. Of these Juji died before his father, but he left four sons, of whom Batu was the most important. Although by the old Mongol rule of primogeniture, the grand khanate should have gone either to Chagatai or to one of the sons of Juji, by the express will of Chingiz it was awarded to his third son, Ogodai. It was two years after the death of Chingiz before the kuraltai could meet; during this interregnum, the government was carried on by the lieutenants of the old emperor, but in 1229 Ogodai was officially proclaimed. Ogodai granted appanages to his nephews and brothers in the outlying districts. For himself he kept the old ancestral homeland, Karakorum and the steppe; the sons of Juji were allotted the west, Chagatai was given Transoxiana and the country of the Uighur Turks, while Tuluy was kept near the capital as the lieutenant of his brother.

The sons of Chingiz continued the conquests of their father. Immediately after the death of the old khan, the Kin had reasserted themselves in north China and had defeated a Mongol army. This emboldened the Chinese to revolt. Ogodai and Tuluy invaded China; the Kin were again defeated and this time wiped out, and in 1235 the attack was begun on the Sung empire in the south. The Mongols took over the direct administration of north China, and the dynasty they established, known to the Chinese as the Yuan dynasty, lasted in China until 1368.

While one Mongol army was invading the Sung empire and a second was forcing Korea back into subjection, a third, under the command of Sabutai and Batu, the son of Juji, turned to the west. They first attacked the Bulgar state on the Volga which they destroyed in 1237; thence they moved west against the Russian principalities and in 1237 to 1238 overran Riazan, Suzdal, Rostov, and Tver. Two years later Batu captured Chernigov and Pereiaslav, while his lieutenants sacked Kiev. The Russian princes put up but a feeble resistance; they were disunited amongst themselves and utterly incapable of organizing any unified resistance to the rapidly moving Mongol host.

In 1241 after Russia had been reduced to vassalage, the Mongols (they are always referred to as the Tartars in the Western chronicles) pushed on in two columns into Poland and Hungary. The Hungarians were defeated at Mohi near Pesth by the southern army under Sabutai, while the northern army drove through Poland, sacked and burned Cracow, and defeated the combined forces of Poland, the Teutonic Knights, and the duke of Silesia at Liegnitz. Unable to take the well-defended city of Olmutz, this army turned south to join their colleagues in Hungary. After the rout of King Bela of Hungary at Mohi, the Mongols sacked Pesth and ravaged the Hungarian plain. Total destruction was the order of the day and the massacres reached staggering proportions. It seemed to be a rule among the Mongols to destroy more the farther away from home they were, probably on the theory that they could not carry home goods or prisoners from so great a distance. Bela fled to Dalmatia and was pursued by a Mongol army which reached the Adriatic and destroyed the cities of Spalato and Cattaro (1242).

In the midst of his victories, and just after he had crossed the Danube and sacked Gran near Vienna, Batu heard of the death of his uncle Ogodai in Mongolia. Withdrawing to the Volga, where they built the new capital at Sarai, the Mongols abandoned their westernmost conquests, while Batu hurried east to take part in the kuraltai which would elect a new great khan.

Never again did the Mongols reach so far west into Europe as they did in this campaign of 1241 to 1242. From Sarai they ruled Russia through vassal princes, satisfied generally if they received the heavy tribute which they imposed on the conquered people. If there was any sign of revolt they would come out and chastise the rebels, and in 1282 they made a great raid through Galicia and south Russia, but in general they were willing to allow the Russians to govern themselves as long as their overlordship was acknowledged and their tribute received. Several Hordes were established among the Mongols of Russia, the most important being the Golden Horde ruled by Batu and his immediate descendants.

For four years there was an interregnum in the great khanate while the family of Ogodai quarreled over the succession. Then in 1246 his son Kuyuk was proclaimed great khan, but he reigned only two years and was succeeded by his cousin Mangu, the son of Tuluy, who reigned from 1248 to 1257.

It was in the reign of Mangu that the Moslem east was overrun by Hulagu, the younger brother of the great khan. In 1252 Hulagu was sent into Persia by the khan to wipe out the pernicious sect of the Assassins, who were still terrorizing the country with their secret murders. The Mongols were just the men to oppose the Assassins, for they had no respect for life and could not be intimidated by the sectarians. The castle of Alamut was taken and the Assassins as a political force were destroyed. From Alamut, Hulagu turned to Baghdad where the caliph Mustasim had given shelter to enemies of the Mongols. Hulagu demanded the submission of the caliph, which was refused. Accordingly he advanced on Baghdad and in 1258 captured the city with the usual attendant massacre in which 800,000 were thought to have been destroyed. The caliph was killed, Baghdad was razed to the ground and the refugees carried the fear of the Mongol into every country of Islam.

With Baghdad destroyed, Hulagu pushed on to Syria where he sacked Aleppo. Damascus saved itself by immediate surrender, but Antioch was destroyed in spite of its capitulation. The king of Armenia and the prince of Antioch became the vassals of the Mongols, while the inhabitants of the southern Syrian cities threw in their lot with the Mameluks who were clearly the next object of Hulagu's attack. But while he was still at Aleppo, Hulagu was informed of the death of Mangu and had to drop everything to rush back to the kuraltai. He left his army under the command of Kitbuqa who was defeated at Ain Jalut by the Mameluk sultan, Qutuz, in 1260. This crushing victory was the worst defeat the Mongols had experienced up to that time, and it was Ain Jalut which saved not only southern Syria and Egypt, but probably Africa and Greece from Mongol invasion.

The Mongols did not withdraw from Syria after their defeat in 1260. They continued to hold the north, and attempted to extend their lands at the expense of both Latins and Mameluks. But a second defeat at Homs in 1281 put an end to their attempt to conquer Egypt, and they settled themselves in Persia, where the Il-Khanate continued under the descendants of Hulagu until 1349.

These Il-Khans are the ones with whom the Latins sought alliance against the Mameluks. Hulagu, though himself a Moslem, had among his wives a Nestorian Christian, and his son Abaga (1265–81) was a Christian. The presence of these Christian khans in Persia gave the Latins the idea of an alliance to crush the Mameluks, but while there was much negotiation the one joint expedition which was undertaken failed, and the whole matter ended when Ahmed Khan (1281–84) turned Moslem. Under Ghazan Khan (1295–1304) the Il-Khans threw off their allegiance to the great khan and set themselves up as a wholly independent dynasty; but they did not long survive.

Meanwhile Kublai, another brother of Mangu who had been made governor of Honan, carried the war into south China in the years 1253 to 1257. He conquered Yunnan and Annam and, contrary to the practice of his house, spared the people of the lands conquered. In 1257, when Mangu died, Kublai refused to attend the kuraltai at Karakorum called by his brother Arikbuka, and instead held his own kuraltai in China, where he had himself proclaimed grand khan. Hulagu later accepted this kuraltai as legitimate, but Arikbuka and the descendants of Ogodai and Chagatai refused to concur in the election.

Kublai (1257–94) can be properly considered the last of the great khans of the Mongols as well as the first of the Yuan emperors of China. He conquered all of south China and Burma, ruling an empire that stretched from Korea and the Arctic waste on the north to the Malay archipelago on the south. He was successful in all his conquests by land, but never developed any sea power and was defeated in attempts to conquer Japan and Java. Kublai was far more the Chinese emperor than the Mongol khan; he was by religion a Buddhist, spoke Chinese, and built himself a new capital, the city of Kambalek or Peiping in China near the ancient capital of Yenking.

With Kublai the old Mongol empire disintegrated. The great khan ruled in China as a Chinese emperor, in Persia the Il-Khans became independent Moslem rulers; in the west, the Golden Horde ruled from Sarai over a Slav empire, and in the original home of the Mongols in the steppes the tribes began to disintegrate into the local divisions, which had characterized them before the unification by Chingiz. The khanate of Chagatai continued in name, but its rulers were relatively weak. The Mongols had met the nemesis of all barbarian nomads; as soon as they conquered the more civilized countries they took over some of the civilization of their subjects, lost their own primitive ferocity and vigor and were absorbed into the cultures of the various countries they had brought under their sway. In the case of the Mongols the change was rapid. Within a century from the time when they had come out of the steppes as unconquerable nomad warriors they had become settled Chinese or Persians. Where they still lived in the steppes they retained their primitive characteristics, but lost their cohesion and unity, and became the prey to civil war and feuds. They were to have a resurgence of their early splendor at the end of the fourteenth century, when under Timur, who came from the relatively barbarous Turkestan, they once again threatened the world, but Timur's empire, as we shall see, was but an ephemeral revival.

GOVERNMENT AND INSTITUTIONS OF THE MONGOLS

One of the most amazing aspects of the history of the Mongols was the efficient and enlightened government which they established for their empire. The khan was of course supreme lord, the chosen of heaven, and had apparently something of a sacerdotal character. But the fundamental laws of the empire were contained in the famous *Yassak,* or code given by Chingiz as the basic law for his people. This Yassak was at once administrative, civil, and criminal law, and was conspicuous for the severity of its criminal section, which imposed the death penalty for murder, major thefts, adultery, and other important offenses. In addition to the Yassak, the laws were developed from the writing down of the decisions given by the judges in cases brought before them.

The Mongols were quick to take over institutions of the people they had conquered if they seemed useful. Chingiz adopted the Uighur Turkish speech and written language, and modeled his chancery after that of the Uighurs. Later Mongol institutions were markedly influenced by those of China, where the nomads encountered the highest civilization of the East. In his work of establishing an organized state, Chingiz was ably assisted by Yelieu Chu'sai, a Chinese prince whom he captured in his conquest of north China. Yelieu became his chief advisor, chancellor, and intimate, continuing to influence the monarchs after the death of the old khan. He must be credited for much of the tempering of the natural savageness of the barbarians.

But in general it should be noted that the Mongols displayed towards their own subjects none of the ferocity they showed others. Their goal was the building of a great and prosperous state; if a captive was taken who could in any way benefit them, he was spared and put to work; if on the other hand he seemed to have no especial value he was promptly liquidated. The Mongols never kept quantities of captives, finding it simpler to kill them off.

Concerning the institutions of the empire under Chingiz himself, we have little information, but with the reign of Kuyuk, we begin to have the accounts of travelers from Europe. The accounts of John of Piano Carpini and William of Rubruck who visited the Mongol country in the years 1245 to 1255 give us valuable information concerning the customs of the Mongols in the days of Kuyuk and Mangu, while the famous Book of the Travels of Ser Marco Polo describes in detail, and with great accuracy, the high civilization of the court of Kublai.

The kuraltai was one of the most interesting of Mongol institutions. Piano Carpini was present at the kuraltai at which Kuyuk was elected in 1246 and has left an account of it. The princes of the house of Chingiz and the chief nobles came from all parts of the world to participate in the election of one of their number as the great khan. By the end of the century the family had grown so that the members of the immediate family made a very considerable assembly in themselves. These kuraltai, as we have seen, were always held back in the old homeland of Mongolia and it generally took months to collect all the participants.

The whole state was based on the army. The officers were known as the commanders of Tens, of Hundreds, of Thousands and of Ten Thousands, the latter being of course the highest ranking nobility. But in addition to these, there were the 10,000 members of the khan's bodyguard, who were privileged persons, a private in the guard ranking with an officer in the regular army. These men were bound to the khan by personal oaths not unlike the feudal obligations found in the West.

As early as the travels of Piano Carpini and Rubruck, the peace of the empire brought forth amazed comments on the part of foreigners. Crime was practically unknown, and a traveler or merchant could go from one end of the empire to the other in perfect safety. The disciplined obedience of the people to the law was a matter of amazement to European visitors, used to the practical anarchy of feudal Europe. The khan could demand anything of any of his people and they willingly gave it him. Piano

Carpini tells how the khan would collect maidens from all over the empire, and after selecting those he desired for himself, gave the others to his friends and retainers as marks of his favor.

Within the empire the khans kept up a system of roads, and a government post, which in the days of Kublai used 200,000 horses. If a man was in possession of a passport from the khan, horses and carts were supplied him for his journey and he was passed from post to post until he reached his destination. If he was not given the facilities of this post, travel was most difficult, as Friar John of Piano Carpini had occasion to know.

It is probably not safe to generalize on earlier Mongol institutions from the description given by Marco Polo of the government of Kublai, for by the end of the century they had changed materially, and Kublai was, as we have said, more a Chinese emperor than a Mongol khan. But whatever the conditions earlier, by the time Marco Polo saw them in China, the habits and institutions of the Mongols were certainly well advanced. Public hospitals were maintained by the state; food was distributed daily to the poor and needy, as many as 30,000 receiving the public dole every day; prices on all commodities were regulated by the government, and there was in use a paper currency which was valid throughout the empire. The use of this paper currency, stamped with the seal of the khan, and the habit of burning black stones (coal) are two of the things which most impressed Polo.

The city of Karakorum in the steppe not far from Lake Baikail, was a great city of tents. Essentially nomads, the Mongols had a capital which they could, and did, move around as the requirements for grazing demanded. But the tents were not the crude felt huts of the ordinary nomad, but magnificent chambers, with the walls lined with precious fabrics, and with luxurious appointments. Foreign craftsmen were to be found in Karakorum, William of Rubruck telling at length of William Buchier, the goldsmith of Paris, who had been captured in Hungary and who was working for the khan. He also met a woman from Metz, who was living in Karakorum with her Russian husband.

The thing which most appealed to Europeans, and which gave them a false idea of the Mongols, was the religious situation. The Mongols were originally shamanist, worshipping the great sky and other natural phenomena. But they were receptive to any and all religions, and when they conquered the Nestorian Christian Uighurs, they accepted Christianity along with their old beliefs. Complete religious tolerance was their policy, and pagans, Buddhists, Moslems, Jews, and Christians of all sects enjoyed equal freedom of religion under the khans. As we have seen, while Kublai became Buddhist, and Hulagu Moslem, the son of Hulagu was a Christian, as was the general Kitbuqa, and because Christians held high positions in the service of the khans, Western Europeans got the idea that the Mongols officially favored Christianity. This was fostered by the fact that in their conquest of Syria, Christians were given preferred positions over Moslems, but this was because they were at the time fighting Moslems, and trusted more those who were at odds religiously with their enemies. This utter indifference to religion was incomprehensible to Western minds, and by the latter part of the thirteenth century we find the rulers of Europe seeking the alliance of the Mongols against the Egyptians. As mentioned above, this fell through when the Il-Khans turned Moslem as did the khans of the Golden Horde, but for some years embassies were exchanged in a vain attempt to form an alliance with the Eastern Christian monarch, whom Western Europeans saw as the heir of the legendary Prester John.[2]

As we have mentioned, the Mongol dominion did not last long in most of the countries they conquered. Their dynasties in China and in Persia did not outlast the fourteenth century; that in Russia was a bit more permanent, and it is to Russia that we must now turn our attention.

RUSSIA TO THE RISE OF MOSCOW, 1113–1263

In the first period of Russian history, which we discussed in Chapter 8, we traced the rise of the principality of Kiev and its growth to a place of first importance as a commercial and cultural center. In the tenth and eleventh centuries, as we have seen, Kiev was one of the most advanced and prosperous of European cities, far ahead of the Western towns of the same period. In the twelfth and thirteenth centuries, however, when the West was coming into its own, Russia went into a period of decline. The supremacy of Kiev was ended with the closing of the trade routes by the barbaric Polovtsy, and, in place of the unified Kievan state, there developed three centers of Russian life in Suzdal, Galicia, and Novgorod. The Mongol conquest and the invasions by the Lithuanians, Germans, and Swedes, brought on a period of subjection to the East and hostility to the West which threw Russia back towards the East, and resulted in the eventual transfer of the seat of Russian culture and political life from the southwest to the northeast in the new state of Moscow.

The rota system of succession, established by Yaroslav the Wise produced, instead of the unity which its founder anticipated, continuous civil war between the various members of the ruling house. As we have seen, the

---

[2] Two monarchs have been credited with being Prester John: one is the Wang-khan of the Uighurs and the other is the Negus of Abyssinia. Both attributions have their ardent champions among modern scholars. It would seem that at first Prester John was found somewhere in Asia in the Turkish lands, but that later the legend was attributed to the Negus. Certainly it was Abyssinia that was considered the land of Prester John by the Portuguese in the fifteenth century, but there is reason to believe that earlier the Nestorian Turks were the subject of the legend. See below, p. 563.

proper line of succession was disregarded by the people of Kiev in 1113, when they called in as their Grand Prince, Vladimir Monomakh of Smolensk and Rostov. The reigns of Vladimir (1113–25) and his eldest son Mstislav (1125–32) mark the real end of the supremacy of Kiev. Both were able princes, who defended their territories against rival contenders and against the Polovtsy who were overrunning the plains of southern Russia. The death of Mstislav, however, inaugurated a period of civil war during which Kiev was repeatedly conquered and in which the center of power shifted from Kiev to Suzdal.

For over twenty-five years the throne of Kiev was disputed between the brothers and sons of Mstislav and the princes of the house of Cherni-gov. In 1159 it was finally conquered by Rostislav of Smolensk, who also ruled Novgorod, so that during his reign (1159–68) the whole of the old water route from the Baltic to the Black Sea was under the control of a single prince. But a new center had been developing meanwhile in the northeast, in Suzdal, where Yuri Dolgoruki, the youngest son of Vladimir, had been building up a strong state in the Rostov-Suzdal area, centering around a new city of Vladimir near the Volga. Colonists had been at-tracted to this new territory from the older parts of Russia, and the relative peace of Suzdal was most appealing after the continuous strife and har-rying of the Kievan region. Yuri had attempted to make himself lord of Kiev and had succeeded temporarily in 1154 to 1157, but it was in Suzdal that he built up his strength. The real founder of Suzdalian greatness was, however, Andrei Bogolubski, the son of Yuri, who built his princi-pality into a formidable military power and who attacked Kiev in 1168, sacking the city and destroying it. It is significant that Andrei, while assuming the title of Grand Prince of Kiev, did not personally remove to the old city, but ruled from his own town of Vladimir, relegating Kiev to the position of a provincial capital. This sack of Kiev in 1169 is generally considered as marking the end of the Kievan period of Russian history; a second sack by the Polovtsy in 1203 and the destruction by the Mongols in 1240 delivered the *coup de grace* to Kiev, which never thereafter re-covered her prosperity or importance, although it long remained a center of artistic and cultural life.

The removal of the capital to Vladimir by Andrei (1157–75) was sig-nificant in several ways. In the first place it shifted the center to the north and east where it was less subject to Western influences; secondly, Vladimir was a town built by the prince and lacking in any of the old traditions of municipal freedom which the older cities cherished. From the beginning of the Varangian rule the princes had had to compete with the local liberties of the towns, and the *vieche*, the popular assembly of the towns-men, had always played a considerable role in the government of the cities. It was the vieche of Kiev which installed Vladimir Monomakh in

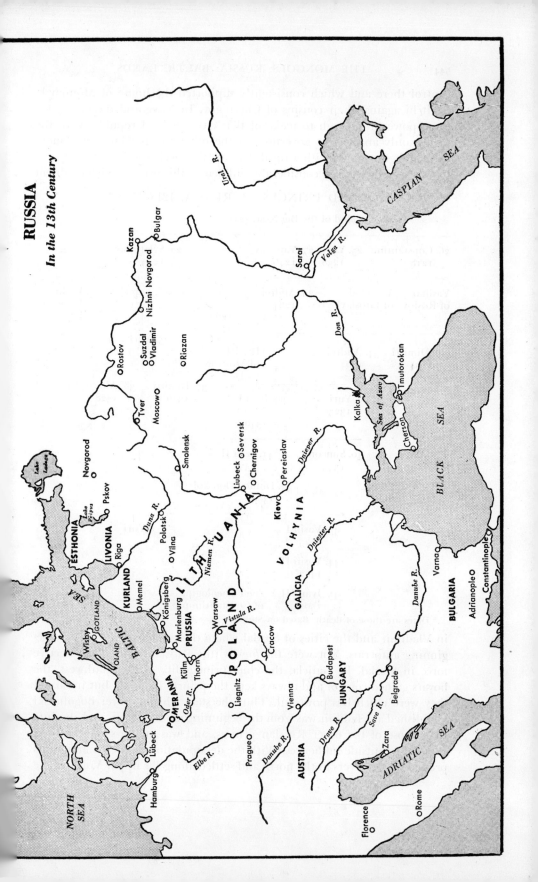

RUSSIA

In the 13th Century

NORTH SEA

BALTIC SEA

Hamburg
Lübeck
POMERANIA
Wisby
GOTLAND
OLAND
Elbe R.
Oder R.
Külm
Thorn
Marienburg
PRUSSIA
Königsberg
Memel
KURLAND
Riga
LIVONIA
ESTHONIA
Lake Peipus
Pskov
Novgorod
Lake Ladoga

Prague
AUSTRIA
Vienna
Danube R.
Liegnitz
Cracow
Warsaw
Vistula R.
POLAND
L I T H U A N I A
Polotsk
Vilna
Duna R.
Niemen R.
Smolensk
Tver
Moscow
Rostov
Suzdal
Vladimir
Riazan
Nizhni Novgorod
Kazan
Bulgar
Ural R.

Rome
Florence
ADRIATIC SEA
Zara
Save R.
Belgrade
Drave R.
HUNGARY
Budapest
Danube R.
GALICIA
VOLHYNIA
Dniester R.
Dnieper R.
Liubeck
Seversk
Chernigov
Kiev
Pereiaslav
Don R.
Sarai
Volga R.

BULGARIA
Adrianople
Constantinople
Varna
BLACK SEA
Cherson
Kalka
Sea of Azov
Tmutorokan
CASPIAN SEA

control there and which consistently supported the house of Monomak-havitchi against their cousins of Chernigov. In Novgorod the vieche be-came powerful enough to make of that city a virtual republic with the prince only an elective governor; in the other towns which were more intimately associated with a royal dynasty, the vieches were not so strong, but they still exercised considerable influence; this was completely absent

GRAND PRINCES OF RUSSIA, 1212–1505 *

24. Vsevelod of the Big Nest, 1212

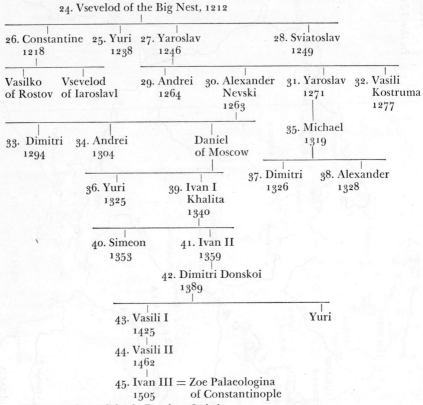

26. Constantine   25. Yuri   27. Yaroslav   28. Sviatoslav
    1218   1238   1246   1249

Vasilko   Vsevelod   29. Andrei   30. Alexander   31. Yaroslav   32. Vasili
of Rostov of Iaroslavl   1264   Nevski   1271   Kostruma
                                      1263   1277

                                                   35. Michael
                                                       1319

33. Dimitri   34. Andrei   Daniel
    1294   1304   of Moscow

                                                37. Dimitri   38. Alexander
                36. Yuri   39. Ivan I   1326   1328
                   1325   Khalita
                               1340

           40. Simeon   41. Ivan II
               1353   1359

                    42. Dimitri Donskoi
                         1389

           43. Vasili I   Yuri
               1425

           44. Vasili II
               1462

           45. Ivan III = Zoe Palaeologina
               1505   of Constantinople

* Dates are those of death. Based on Stokvis.

in Vladimir and the cities of Suzdal where the princes were from the be-ginning autocrats. Nor were the *boyars* (the Russian nobles) an effective force in Suzdal. In Galicia, the chief principality of the southwest, the boyars gained control and always kept the princes in check, but in Suzdal they were much less powerful. Thus the state which Andrei Bogolubski established at Vladimir was from the beginning more despotic and absolute than those of the other Russian princes, and was at the same time less exposed to outside influences. With the depopulation of Kiev, immigrants pressed up the rivers to the north and settled along the upper Volga where they established an essentially agricultural, as opposed to the earlier commercial, civilization.

In 1175 Andrei was murdered by a group of discontented boyars. In the civil war which followed the boyars were opposed by the people of Vladimir, who were ultimately successful in securing the throne for their candidate, Vsevelod III, "Big-Nest," a younger brother of Andrei, who ruled 1176 to 1212. Vsevelod continued the policies of Andrei in centralizing his authority; he conquered Riazan from Chernigov, defeated Novgorod and forced that proud city to accept a prince of his nomination and added greatly not only to the territories, but to the prestige of Vladimir. His reign is generally accepted as marking the zenith of the princes of Suzdal, for with his death the inevitable civil war broke out among his many sons. With the division of Suzdal among several petty dynasties the power of the grand princes again declined, and Vladimir, like Kiev before it, became the prize for which princes of various branches of the reigning house competed.

Meanwhile, a second principality of considerable importance had been developing in the southwest in the Volhynia-Galician area. At first separate states, Volhynia and Galicia were united by Roman Mstislavitch (1198–1205) who also ruled Kiev. Galicia was the most fertile and most populous part of all Russia, and was by far the wealthiest of the Russian states, but it lay on the western border where it was open to the attack of the Lithuanians, Poles, and Hungarians, and the princes of Galicia were never able to enforce their authority over the turbulent boyars who actually ruled the country. In spite of incessant civil wars and repeated invasions by Polovtsy and Lithuanians, Galicia developed a considerable prosperity, based on her rich agricultural land and on her good commercial position. In the thirteenth century there were over fifty towns in the country, and it was through Galicia that the main current of East-West traffic ran. It was overrun by the Mongols in 1240, but was never so completely subjected as were the northern and eastern principalities. Prince Daniel (1235–64) sought and received a royal crown from Pope Innocent IV, hoping thereby to interest the pope in his fate, but when he failed to get the expected aid from the West, he returned to the Orthodox fold, without however, relinquishing his title. Daniel paid tribute to the Mongols but ruled with relatively little interference from his overlords, and his reign was marked by successful wars against the Lithuanians, whom at one time he subjected to his rule. A second Mongol invasion in 1282, however, destroyed much of the prosperity of Galicia, which finally fell before the repeated attacks of her western neighbors, being incorporated into the kingdom of Poland in 1347.

In the twelfth century Smolensk, under the princes Mstislav the Brave and Mstislav the Daring, played an important role in Russian affairs. "The

two Mstislavs of Smolensk . . . dash around Kiev Russia as knight er-
rants, putting their heads into every wasps' nest"; [3] fighting in Kiev, Novgorod, Galicia, and leading the Russian princes in their first battle against
the Mongols at the Kalka in 1223.

The Mongol conquest changed the course of history in all of these
Russian principalities. In the years 1237 to 1240, as we have seen, the
Mongols overran and subjugated all of Russia except Novgorod, which
was far to the north and which was protected by marsh lands difficult
for the Mongol cavalry to cross. But in eastern and southern Russia the
"Tartar Yoke" was laid on the Russians until the end of the fifteenth century. In Galicia the rule was lighter than in the Suzdal area, and in both
the Mongols were content to allow the native princes to rule as long as they
remained subject and continued to pay tribute. Russian institutions continued to develop under the Mongol rule, and it was as the agents of the
khans that the princes of Moscow developed their power; but Russia had
been severely hurt by the ravages of the conquest and it took centuries to
regain the prosperity which she had enjoyed in the pre-Mongol days. While
Suzdal, Smolensk, Kiev, and Galicia were subject to the Mongols, the most
significant development in Russia took place in Novgorod.

"Lord Novgorod the Great," the wealthy city of the north which alone
escaped conquest by the Mongols, developed what was virtually a republican form of government. It will be recalled that under the rota
system Novgorod was allotted to the eldest son of the prince of Kiev, so
that the city never became the appanage of any dynasty as did Suzdal,
Galicia, Smolensk, and Chernigov. Most of the time Novgorod recognized
a vague suzerainty of the princes of Kiev or later of Vladimir, but she always had her own prince who was chosen by her own people. Unlike the
cities more closely controlled by princes, the vieche of Novgorod became
the real governing body of the city. Elective officials shared the power with
the prince and were not responsible to him; the prince was limited in his
powers much like the podestas of the Italian communes and it was the
corporate city itself which ruled in the north. The territories under the
control of Novgorod ran from the Urals, with their rich silver mines, into
the Finnish country of the north, with control of the eastern end of the
Baltic. Novgorod was the chief commercial city of Russia and through it
passed the trade between Siberia and eastern Russia and the Baltic. Furs
were the chief article of commerce, but there was also an extensive trade
in fish, whale oil, salt, amber, mica, and silver. While the merchants of
Novgorod carried on an active trade with the East, the trade with the
West was passive and merchants from Cologne, Lübeck, Bremen, and
Hamburg made regular journeys to the Eastern metropolis. In the fourteenth century, Novgorod was a member of the Baltic Hanse and partook
of the prosperity of that league.

[3] B. Pares, *History of Russia* (Knopf, 1926), p. 40.

Like Galicia, Novgorod was constantly threatened by her Western neighbors. The Swedes and Germans, as well as Poles and Lithuanians, attacked her domains, and the resistance which Novgorod presented to the Western attacks tended to throw her back towards the East and to prevent any Westernization. The greatest name in the history of northern Russia in the thirteenth century was Prince Alexander Nevski, who earned both his name and canonization, as the defender of the Orthodox church, by defeating the Swedes at the battle of the Neva in 1240, a victory which he followed up by crushing the Teutonic Knights at Lake Peipus in 1242, and the Lithuanians in 1245. He left Novgorod to become Grand Prince of Vladimir (1246–63) where he was the great patron of Orthodox monasticism and the defender of the Russians from the oppression of the Mongols. Alexander inaugurated the policy whereby the princes of Vladimir, and later those of Moscow, became the trusted servants of the khans, and in their capacity as the agents of the Mongols built up their own power until they could safely challenge that of their lords. It was Daniel, the youngest son of Alexander, who first established the principality of Moscow at the end of the thirteenth century.

THE BALTIC AND SCANDINAVIAN STATES

In their trade and in their attempts to control the eastern Baltic, the Russians came into conflict with a number of states which were growing up in the north. The closest neighbors to the Russians were the Lithuanians and Poles, but they also came into conflict with the Swedes and the Germans who were pushing eastward. While these states are of greater importance after 1300 than before, some mention of their early history must be included here.

The Lithuanians were one of the most backward of European nations. Pagan long after most of their neighbors had accepted Christianity, the Lithuanians lived in their swamps and marshes in a relatively barbaric state until the thirteenth century when they first achieved some degree of unity under Mindovg (ob. 1263). The prime cause of Lithuanian unification was common resistance to the Teutonic Knights who were advancing into Prussia and Livonia and threatening the Lithuanians. Mindovg built up a loose kingdom and received a crown from the pope when he accepted Christianity; but he soon relapsed into paganism as a result of his struggle with the Knights. During the height of his power Mindovg attacked Novgorod and was defeated by Alexander Nevski in 1245. After his death Lithuania relapsed into tribal anarchy for a while, and the real kingdom was established only by Gedymin in the fourteenth century.

The Teutonic Knights had meanwhile been establishing themselves in Prussia and along the Baltic coast. Founded after the Third Crusade as a military-religious order for Germans, the Knights had in 1229 transferred their activities to the conquest of pagan Prussia. The conquest of these lands had been begun earlier by an order known as the Knights of the Sword which had been founded in 1204 under the auspices of Innocent III to bring Christianity to the Livonians in co-operation with the new bishopric which had been founded at Riga. The Knights had begun the systematic reduction of the country, but in 1236 they were disastrously defeated by the natives. As a result they sought to strengthen themselves by allying to the more recently arrived Teutonic Knights. In 1237 the two orders were merged and the conquest begun again. Aided by the Poles and by the eastern German nobles, the Knights conquered Prussia, forcing conversion and subjection to their rule on the uncivilized inhabitants. They built new towns as they advanced, Thorn, Külm, Memel, Marien-burg, and Königsberg all being founded by the Knights during the course of their conquest. In 1240 the Knights attacked and captured the Russian city of Pskov, which was a dependency of Novgorod, but in the following year they and their Polish allies were defeated by the Mongols at Leignitz, and in 1242 they were driven out of Russia and their power seriously impaired by the disastrous defeat which they suffered at the hands of Alexander Nevski at Lake Peipus. This defeat encouraged the Prussians and Slavs to further resistance, and the order was only saved by a new crusade from Europe, led by Ottokar II of Bohemia in 1254. No sooner had the Knights recovered their position than they were again defeated in 1260, this time by Mindovg of Lithuania who overran Livonia. Again Prussia revolted. In putting down this revolt, which lasted thirteen years, the Knights practically exterminated the old Prussian population, filling the country with new colonists from Germany. In 1283 the conquest of Prussia was complete, and the country had become largely German in population. For the next century the Knights attempted to force their rule over Lithuania wthout success; however, in the middle of the fourteenth century the order ruled over Prussia, Esthonia, Livonia, Pomerania, and Kurland.

The greatest power in the Baltic was the kingdom of Denmark. The early history of the Scandinavian countries is shrouded in legend and obscurity: the tremendous expansion of the Scandinavians has already been discussed: their internal history is one of gradual development. The three kingdoms of Denmark, Norway, and Sweden developed at about the same time in the ninth and tenth centuries, when their monarchies emerged. This first period of their history—the Viking Age—was one in which they spread out to found colonies from Greenland to Novgorod. With the conversion of the Scandinavians to Christianity, churches were organized which generally supported the monarchies. Especially in Den-mark do we find a close alliance between church and king, the rulers of Denmark generally also supporting the clerical parties in their rival states.

By the end of the eleventh century definite kingdoms had been established in all three of the Scandinavian countries, but the kings of one not infrequently conquered the others so that the three crowns were united and separated in a most confusing manner. Canute, whom we have already seen as king of England, ruled Denmark and Norway as well, but at his death the three states separated. The first important king of Denmark after Canute was Waldemar the Great (1157–82) under whom the Danes expanded along the Baltic into the old Wendish country. His son Canute VI (1182–1202) and his grandson Waldmar II, the Conquerer (1202–41), pushed eastward along the south shore of the Baltic through Pomerania into Esthonia and Livonia, but their control over this area was but short-lived and the whole empire collapsed in a series of civil wars. Under Waldemar, the kingdom had been reorganized and a new semi-feudal nobility created, dependent on the monarchy. For a century (1157–1241) the Danish kings ruled with a loyal nobility, a friendly church and a prosperous commercial and peasant class. But civil war between the sons of Waldemar II, and a long struggle with the church, weakened the Danish monarchy, so that by 1282 the nobles and clergy forced Eric V Glipping to grant a charter of liberties which confirmed the privileges of the clergy and nobles and established the control of a parliament over the king.

In Sweden and in Norway the kings never achieved the power that those of Denmark did, the nobles always being stronger in relation to the crown. King Sverre of Norway (1184–1202) was perhaps the strongest ruler of that country, which he conquered and held against the opposition of the local clergy, the papacy and the nobles, resting his power on the solid support of the small free farmers and agricultural peasantry. The Norwegians attempted to expand at the expense of Iceland, Scotland, and the German towns along the Baltic, with singular lack of success in the latter instances. For a time under Eric, the Priest-hater (1280–99), Norway was forced to join the Baltic Hanse and to allow German merchants complete freedom of trade throughout the kingdom. In Sweden the outstanding figure of the period was Earl Birger Magnusson, who controlled the government (1248–66) and secured the election of his son as King Waldemar (1250–75). Birger suppressed the old nobles and established a new feudal nobility more dependent on the king, abolished serfdom, encouraged German colonists to establish themselves in Sweden, developed commerce with Germany, and in general tried to bring Sweden into line with Continental practices. He attempted expansion in the eastern Baltic, where Sweden already held Finland, but was defeated by Alexander Nevski at the Neva. In spite of a civil war between his sons, Sweden continued to prosper and develop commercially, considerable wealth being produced through mining.

Meanwhile there grew up along the Baltic coast that league of towns which under the name of the Baltic Hanse was to play so dominant a role in the history of the Baltic region and of European commerce in the thirteenth and fourteenth centuries. Since early times merchants from the German towns had banded together to secure privileges in distant countries and ports. By about 1000, German merchants are found in England and establishing a colony at Wisby on the island of Gotland. In 1157, merchants from Cologne and associated towns secured privileges from Henry II of England for trade in London, and towards the end of the century German merchants established a colony at Novgorod to attend to their business there. The greatest center of trade was, however, the Flemish town of Bruges, where the German merchants established a large colony or hanse. By the beginning of the thirteenth century, there were important commercial depots or hanses in Novgorod, London (the Steelyard), Bruges, Wisby, and other lesser ports. The mutual support of these oversea depots brought the German towns into close alliance for their mutual benefit and in the course of the century the organization of the Hanse, as an association of allied German cities, developed. Their aim was to secure for the members of the Hanse most favorable status in trading with other countries, and as far as possible secure monopolies of trade. Political alliances accompanied the commercial agreements, and the towns as a league were able to put effective pressure on a common enemy. In 1241 Lübeck and Hamburg allied; shortly thereafter Lübeck organized a league of Rostock, Wismar, Stralsund, and other towns in the old Wendish country. By the end of the thirteenth century, there were some nineteen members of the Hanse, and they had already had several occasions to show the value of their association. The associated towns fought and defeated Eric, the Priesthater, of Norway—forcing him to grant them most liberal privileges and adhere to the Hanse. Lübeck was from the first the leader in the Hanse and remained its dominant member. Some authorities will not admit the use of the term Hanse before the middle of the fourteenth century, when rival associations were reduced and the Hanse got a monopoly of trade, but this seems to be quibbling over terms, as the association had existed much earlier.[4]

Like the Scandinavian states, the Hanse was to become increasingly important in the fourteenth and fifteenth centuries; this later development will be noted in Chapter 39 below.

[4] J. W. Thompson (*The Middle Ages* [Knopf], II, 943). "When the absorption of these foreign hanses took place is uncertain, but when it did the Hanseatic League was founded. This formation occurred between 1350 and 1370 and it is therefore in this period that we are to look for the formation of the Hanseatic League." As Hanse means League, the term Hanseatic League is tautological: I prefer to speak of it as the Baltic Hanse.

✦✦✦

Book V

The Cultural Revival of the West

1100-1300

This section of the work discusses the cultural developments in the periods whose political events were described in the two preceding books. The age of the crusades and the great political popes was also the age of the Twelfth-Century Renaissance and scholasticism.

In the Twelfth-Century Renaissance, Western Europe acquired the cultural achievements of the Greeks and Arabs. While the East was stagnating intellectually in most things, the vigorous West appropriated the older learning and developed its own culture. Science, law, and classical literature were revived in the West and were studied in the cathedral schools and in the new, purely medieval, European institution, the university.

Vernacular literature also experienced a great development in French, German, English, Provençal, and Italian. While French literature was the most popular, and the chansons de geste of France spread their influence over all neighboring literatures, the supreme literary work of the Middle Ages was produced in Florence by Dante. In this period chivalry developed, and the daily life of the people improved immeasurably in material things. This age also produced the great churches of Europe, both Romanesque and Gothic—the finest ecclesiastical architecture the world has yet achieved, and the thirteenth century is often referred to as the Age of the Cathedrals.

St. Étienne, Caen
(*Romanesque*)

FRENCH CATHEDRALS

Amiens
(*Gothic*)

CHAPTER 32

THE TWELFTH-CENTURY
RENAISSANCE: UNIVERSITIES

❖

IN no field of activity is the ascendency of the West in the twelfth and
thirteenth centuries more pronounced than in that of cultural achievement. In our earlier chapter on intellectual developments we have noticed
that while the Byzantine and Moslem worlds maintained a high standard
of intellectual activity, the Latin West lagged far behind. But in the
twelfth and thirteenth centuries, in what we now term the Twelfth-Century
Renaissance, the West developed a vigorous intellectual life, absorbing
what was best of the Eastern cultures, and pushing forward to new accomplishments, eclipsing their Eastern neighbors. Thus this section will deal
essentially with the intellectual movements in Western Europe and but
scant attention will be paid to the Byzantines, whose chief importance in
this period lies primarily in the field of historical writing.

The Twelfth-Century Renaissance was one manifestation of that great
expenditure of Western energy which also produced the rise of the towns,
the revival of trade, the growth of national monarchies, and the crusades.
Its most tangible monuments are the great Gothic cathedrals of France,
Germany, and England, but it also gave rise to parliamentary institutions,
communal life, the universities, and a great literature both in Latin and
the vernacular. In the following chapters we shall endeavor to discuss,
however cursorily, the achievements of this age in education and philosophy, science, law, and historiography, and to describe the origins and
growth of the universities: thereafter we shall discuss the developments
in literature, and the artistic accomplishments of the whole medieval
period. With so much to cover we cannot hope to give the attention to
individual authors and scholars which we did in the earlier less productive
periods, and the discussion here must be recognized to be merely an introduction to the subject, which has been treated much more fully in
C. H. Haskins' *Renaissance of the Twelfth Century* and in other works
listed in our bibliography.

Fifty years ago it was common to think of the Middle Ages as a dark
unenlightened period when men thought only of salvation and the way to
accomplish it, when monastic ideals and virtues dominated a society
which was blissfully ignorant of the "spell of the classics" and interested
only in theological speculation. This old interpretation has now been

shown to be entirely fallacious: in fact the true Renaissance (if we admit such a term at all) occurred not in the fourteenth but in the twelfth century, and humanism was just as prevalent in twelfth-century Chartres as in fifteenth-century Florence. The Italian movement of the Quattrocento and the Cinquecento was merely a continuation of the intellectual revival which began in the twelfth century. In some things the Italians went beyond the accomplishments of their earlier predecessors, but in others, as in architecture, they fell behind. Further the Quattrocento movement was restricted largely to Italy, while the renaissance of the twelfth century included all the countries of western Europe: France, England, Spain, Italy, Germany, and the Low Countries. Its heart, however, was in France, where are found the finest cathedrals and where developed the great University of Paris, *"mater scientiorum."* Although many of the men who contributed most to this renaissance were not themselves French, their work centered in France and especially in Paris. "Germany has the empire, Italy the papacy, but France has the University of Paris."

Much of what the Twelfth-Century Renaissance accomplished can be seen by an examination of the *Speculum majus* of Vincent of Beauvais which was written about 1250. The work is divided into three parts: the *Speculum naturale, Speculum doctrinale* and *Speculum historiale.* There is absolutely nothing original about it and it is made up of quotations from other writers throughout, but it does reflect the increased knowledge of the age. About half of it deals with science, there being many quotations from the newly translated Arabic sources. The *Speculum naturale* consists of 32 books divided into 3718 chapters, the *Doctrinale* and *Historiale* being somewhat shorter, and the whole running to some 6000 folio pages. God and the heavens, man and the earth, the sciences, philosophy, theology, and universal history are all packed into this tremendous work. The organization is purely scholastic, with each topic broken down into subtopics and divisions. Although not in itself a great work, for it is remarkable only for the tremendous scope of the author's activities and interests, the *Speculum* does afford a good idea of the progress made during the intellectual revival of the twelfth and thirteenth centuries.

LANGUAGE AND GRAMMAR

There exists a popular fallacy that medieval Latin was necessarily bad Latin. This idea was promulgated by the humanists of the Italian Quattrocento, who insisted on returning to strictly classical forms and who cast aspersions on the Latin of the earlier period as barbarous and Gothic. There is no disputing the point that medieval Latin was not the same as classical; it did modify some of the more complex grammatical practices and it did include in its vocabularly many words which were wholly unknown to Cicero, but it was rather a new language than a badly corrupted one; it had expanded to include new words as every living language must expand. When the purists of the Renaissance purged it of all the medieval words and returned to strict classical usage, they killed the living Latin of the Middle Ages and produced the "dead language," which so bores the average modern student. The "romance" vernaculars developed from the complete breakdown of classical Latin: medieval Latin was still Latin but it had expanded to meet present needs.

If one is to understand what had been happening to Latin, he should try to say in words known to Shakespeare that "A dive-bomber dropped incendiary bombs on an ammunition dump, creating an explosion which destroyed all telephonic communications, railroad installations, and motor roads, wrecking a large number of tanks, refrigerator cars, and parked aircraft." Obviously the Bard would be hopelessly confused amidst such a vocabulary. It was equally impossible to say in Ciceronian phrase that "The penitent sinner confessed his heresy to the priest, and was given absolution, whereupon, proceeding to the high altar of the cathedral, he received the eucharist and was relieved of the excommunication which had been placed upon him by the bishop." Yet the Middle Ages needed these words as much as we need the technical vocabulary of our own time, and like ourselves, as new conditions arose, they adapted new words to express new ideas.

There was a further change from the classical in that words which had been in common use in Rome, but which were not accepted as good written Latin, received acceptance into polite vocabularies. It is hardly conceivable that Cicero himself used his magnificent vocabulary and phrases when ordering work done around his own kitchen. He very probably used the slang phrases which were the common speech of the Roman populace. And these words in the course of time slipped over from slang into good usage. The old literary words were forgotten and the words of daily speech replaced them; the vulgar Latin (so called because it was used by the *vulgus,* or multitude, and bearing no connotation of obscenity) of the Roman Empire became the literary Latin of the Middle Ages. Examples of such words are the use of *caballus* instead of *equus* for horse, *battalia* instead of *pugna* for battle, *viaticum* instead of *iter* for journey, *catus* instead of *felis* for cat, *focus* instead of *ignis* for fire. Also many German words crept in, such as *hundredum* for *centum* meaning a hundred. An interesting example is the word *equitatus* which originally meant a "riding," then became in classical Latin the word for cavalry, and then in medieval Latin reverted to its original meaning and became a foray or expedition. One has only to glance through the ten volumes of the Favre edition of DuCange's *Glossarium mediae et infimae latinitatis* (1883–87 ed.) to see the tremendous changes which affected the Latin language in the

Middle Ages. It is doubtful if it was a greater change than one would find in comparing an English dictionary of 1600 with one which includes all the terms used in World War II.

For a time in the early Middle Ages, it must be admitted that the rules of grammar were sadly neglected. Writers such as Gregory of Tours used grammatical construction which would have shocked any classicist, and the rules for agreement, the subjunctive, et al. were neglected woefully. But during the Twelfth-Century Renaissance classical grammar was revived and applied conscientiously, and the documents of the papal chancery, for example, are written in grammatically correct Latin, although they employed words which Cicero would not have known. In general there tended to be a simplification of style, so that a thirteenth-century chronicler is generally much easier to read than an Ausonius or even a Pliny, but the grammatical rules were observed, and the style was simple but correct. The involved rhetoric of the Quattrocento seems in many ways a retrograde movement rather than the improvement which its exponents were sure they had made.

Latin grammar was then well studied in the twelfth and thirteenth centuries. There were many dictionaries and phrase books which enjoyed a wide popularity. Rhetoric, prized by the ancient Romans for orations, was diverted in the Middle Ages into the art of epistolography. Men were not so concerned with flowery speeches but they did develop the style of their letters, and the manuals of correct letter writing of Alberic of Monte Cassino (fl. 1070) and of Boncompagno of Bologna (fl. 1220) taught an epistolary style which postulated rhythmical prose and rather florid phrases. The letters of Piero della Vigna, the chancellor of Frederick II, were collected and studied as perfect examples of the elegant style of epistolography. With the Italian Renaissance scholars turned back to oratory again, and the orator replaced the letter writer as the mentor of style.

LATIN POETRY

Latin poetry changed greatly from the classical styles. Classical poetry was entirely a matter of metre; medieval poetry developed rhyme. The classical metres were of course continued, and we find poems from the twelfth century in hexameters and pentameters, but rhyming verse was becoming increasingly popular, both in the hymns of the church and in the pagan drinking songs of the Goliardi. These Goliardi were students, organized into a sort of international fraternity under the patronage of St. Golias (Goliath) and sworn to the vows of poverty for others, chastity for none, and obedience to no one. They were found at all the universities, and were generally peripatetic. Their drinking and love songs are the most refreshing Latin poetry of the Middle Ages. They were often sacrilegious and ribald and quite frequently were profane parodies of religious hymns, but they were full of a pagan joy of life, which in itself is enough to refute the old theory that the Middle Ages was a period of religious austerity when men sought only the salvation of the soul. Goliardic songs praise wine, women, sport, and the easy life of pleasure; they condemn priests and find the four Beasts of the Apocalypse to be the pope, bishop, archdeacon, and dean. Probably the best known of the Goliardic songs is the *Gaudeamus Igitur,* which is still occasionally sung by students, and undoubtedly the most characteristic of their sentiments is the famous passage from the *Confession of Golias,* which reads, in the translation of J. A. Symonds: [1]

> In a public house to die, Is my resolution
> Let wine to my lips be nigh, At Life's dissolution:
> That will make the angels cry, With glad elocution,
> "Grant this toper, God on high, Grace and absolution!"

The authors of these poems are generally unknown but some of them have been shown to be the work of two poets known as the Primate and the Archpoet. The Primate was one Hugh, a canon of Orleans about 1140, and the Archpoet is known to have been a cleric of Cologne about 1160. The poems were once attributed to Walter Map, who may have written some of them, but who was certainly not the author of the entire corpus of verse.

Rhyme was also employed in the great hymns of the Middle Ages. The *Dies Irae* of Thomas of Celano, the *Stabat Mater* of Jacapone di Todi, the *Jerusalem the Golden* of Bernard Morlais of Cluny, and the hymns of St. Bernard, Adam de St. Victor, and others still hold honored places in our hymnals and attest the tremendous spiritual emotion which inspired the hymnologists of the twelfth and thirteenth centuries.

The sequences of Adam de St. Victor are generally considered to be the finest expression of medieval hymnology; the foremost didactic poet was Alan de Lille, the "universal doctor," whose *Anticlaudianus* is a complicated allegory in which the virtues, vices, senses and seven arts mingle with the pagan gods and with God and theology to point the moral that everything begins and ends in God, but that the human virtues and qualities must not fail to take their part.[2]

Medieval Latin poetry ran the gamut of forms and subjects from Alan to the Archpoet; the Twelfth-Century Renaissance was one of the great

[1] J. A. Symonds, *Wine, Women, and Song* (Chatto and Windus, 1925). This is the standard translation and the one which is generally quoted. Helen Waddell has a new translation in her *Medieval Latin Lyrics.*

[2] H. O. Taylor has a good analysis of the *Anticlaudianus* in his *Medieval Mind,* II, chap. 30.

periods for poetical composition and the reader can only be referred to the works of Haskins, Waddell, Taylor, Walsh and others for a more adequate discussion of the subject.

HUMANISM AND THE CLASSICS

Another popular misconception concerning the Middle Ages which was foisted upon posterity by the scholars of the Quattrocento is the idea that classical authors were not known and studied between the fall of Rome and the "rebirth" which began with Petrarch. This point of view merely shows the ignorance of the Italian Renaissance scholars of the interests of their predecessors. Modern scholarship has amply demonstrated that at no time in the Middle Ages were the classical authors wholly neglected and that in the period of the Twelfth-Century Renaissance and after they were studied avidly throughout western Europe. Analysis of medieval library catalogues shows a very respectable proportion of classical authors mingled in with the works of the church Fathers and works of Christian theology and dogmatics.[3]

Virgil was the most popular of the poets, but his personality underwent a strange metamorphosis and he was considered to be a great magician. He was also hailed for the Messianic dialogue which was supposed to prophesy the birth of Christ and as the great poet of the empire. Next in popularity to Virgil was Ovid, whose works were read by good clerics in an allegorical sense, although we may presume that some of the readers enjoyed the literal meaning of the *Art of Love* without worrying too much about its spiritual significance. Horace, Lucan, Statius, Juvenal, Persius, Claudius and Terence all appear in considerable numbers in the catalogues and in quotations in medieval works. Of the prose writers Cicero was most popular, with Seneca, Pliny the Elder, and Suetonius all ranking high. Pliny's *Natural History* was, however, too long for popular use and was known chiefly through the abridgement by Solinus.

Medieval authors delighted to write glosses on the classics, as the lawyers did on the legal texts, and there was a plethora of glosses on Virgil, Ovid, and other classical authors. The greatest center of twelfth-century humanism was the school of Chartres where William of Conches and the brothers Bernard and Thierry taught the classics, and where medieval humanism reached its peak in the person of John of Salisbury. John's classical education and his familiarity with ancient authors went beyond the ability to quote them on appropriate occasions and amounted to a real understanding and appreciation of them for their own sake. No scholar of the Quat-

---

[3] See H. Buttenwieser, "Popular Authors of the Middle Ages," *Speculum*, XVII (1942), 50–55, and J. S. Beddie, "Ancient Classics in Mediaeval Libraries," *Speculum*, V (1930), 3–20.

trocento deserves the name "humanist" more than John of Salisbury, who ended his life as the bishop of Chartres, where he had studied so long and so pleasantly. Humanism also flourished at the cathedral school of Orleans, and the familiarity with the classics was far more extensive than was generally conceded half a century ago.

Translators from the Arabic and Greek

While the Latin classics were never lost or forgotten in Western Europe, the Greek language and Greek works became generally unknown. There was a period when Greek scholarship flourished in the Irish monasteries, and there were always a few who had some knowledge of the language, but they were few, and it is generally correct to admit that the early Middle Ages in the West was a time when Greek was not known. Meanwhile the Greek classics, especially the scientific works, were translated into Arabic and studied by the Arabs, and it was from the Arabic that they passed into Western Europe. Very little direct translation from the Greek was done in the medieval period: that was the great contribution of the Italian Renaissance, but the knowledge of the Greeks was introduced into the West through the Arabic in the twelfth century.

While some translation was done in North Africa and in Syria, the two great centers for the work were Spain and Sicily, where under the patronage of enlightened monarchs like Roger II, Frederick II, and Alfonso the Wise, or prelates like Archbishop Raymond of Toledo and Bishop Michael of Tarazona, veritable schools of translators were established. We have already observed the intellectual activities of the Sicilian court; even more important was the great Toledo School, which developed in the early twelfth century. At first translation was done all over northern Spain, but it came to be centered in Toledo and it was there that the most work was done. In the second quarter of the twelfth century, we find a cosmopolitan group working in Spain: Plato of Tivoli, Adelard of Bath, Robert of Chester, Herman of Carinthia, John of Seville, and others. The greatest figure of the Toledo school was, however, Gerard of Cremona who flourished in the third quarter of the twelfth century, dying in 1187, and who translated some seventy-one known works in the fields of medicine, astronomy, astrology, alchemy, and mathematics. It is largely through the translations of Gerard that the works of Galen, Hippocrates, and Avicenna were known to the Latin world. Younger contemporaries of Gerard's were the Englishmen Daniel of Morley, Alfred of Sarechal, and Roger of Hereford; while in the thirteenth century, Michael Scot, Philip of Tripoli and Herman the German carried on the work of translation in Toledo. Much of the translation done by these men was faulty in the extreme, as they seldom knew both Arabic and Latin. A Jew would be employed to translate the work from Arabic into Spanish or Hebrew and the translator would then put it into Latin. All these changes did not tend towards accuracy and a work which had passed from Greek to Arabic to Spanish to Latin often bore but slight resemblance to the original. However, it was in this way that most of the great Greek scientific works were made available to Latin scholars. The works that came in through the Arabic were essentially scientific. Other Greek works were translated directly from the Greek, especially after the Fourth Crusade. Western scholars who visited Constantinople often brought back Greek works, which were then translated.

The importance of these translators can perhaps best be illustrated by examining the introduction of Aristotle into medieval Europe. The Old Logic, which had been translated by Boethius, had never been forgotten, but this was all the Aristotle which Abelard knew in 1120. By 1159 John of Salisbury knew the New Logic as well as the Old, part of it having been translated from the Greek and part from the Arabic. Then in the course of the latter twelfth century the scientific works were translated from the Arabic, Gerard of Cremona alone translating the *Physics, Caelo et Mundi, Meteorologica, Generatione et Corruptione* and others. The *Metaphysics* came in from both Greek and Arabic translations, and was banned at Paris because of the Arabic commentaries, which were translated along with the text. In the thirteenth century the *Politics, Ethics, Poetics,* and *Rhetoric* were all translated directly from the Greek by William of Moerbeke, the Latin bishop of Corinth (fl. 1260). At the same time many of the lesser scientific works were translated both from Arabic and Greek. We shall note below the great impact which the new Aristotle had on the thought of Western Europe, and how the synthesis of Aristotle with the Bible was the great work of the scholastics.

SCIENTIFIC LEARNING

One of the most important aspects of the Twelfth-Century Renaissance was the revival of science. With the introduction of Greek and Arabic science, the study of medicine, astronomy, mathematics, and the pseudo sciences of alchemy and astrology entered into a new vogue. Not only were the old scientific works studied, but a new spirit of scientific investigation developed, men making their own experiments to determine the truth of things. We have already noted the scientific interests of Frederick II; Adelard of Bath, Michael Scot, Albertus Magnus, Robert Grosseteste and Roger Bacon are merely the most illustrious among the many scientists who sought to fathom the knowledge of natural things by study and experiment.

In mathematics the old manuals of Bede, Boethius, and Isidore of Seville were now supplemented and supplanted by the works of Euclid,

Archimedes, Apollonius, and Ptolemy; and the algebra and trigonometry of Al Khwarizmi and other Arabic scholars were added. Hindu-Arabic numerals replaced the old cumbersome Roman numerals; the zero was first introduced in the twelfth century, and the new learning in mathematics was embodied in the works of Leonard of Pisa (fl. 1200–30) the greatest mathematician of the thirteenth century. "Mathematics" says Haskins, "had reached a point from which it was not to make notable advances until the time of Descartes. The decisive importance of the twelfth century is nowhere more evident." [4]

In the field of astronomy and astrology, the reception of Ptolemy's *Almagest* and the works of Al Khwarizmi, Al Fargani and others, and the use of new instruments (astrolobe, quadrant, etc.) greatly advanced the knowledge of the heavens. More immediately important, however, was the application of the celestial knowledge to man's own destiny. Astrology gained a popularity and credence which made the court astrologer the familiar consultant of every monarch. Ptolemy's *Quadropartitum* and the works of Albumasar, Al Kindi, and other Arab astrologers were translated and studied. The popularity of astrology was not impaired until Copernicus and Galileo ruined the whole science by demonstrating that the heavens did not revolve around the earth.

Alchemy was relatively unimportant in the twelfth century although there were translations of several Arabic alchemical works. The great days of the alchemists did not occur until early modern times.

Medicine was greatly improved by the introduction of Arabic anatomical and pharmaceutical works. Hippocrates and Galen were revived and the great *Canon* of Avicenna was translated. Constantine the African (fl. 1076) is credited with introducing the Arabic knowledge into southern Italy and founding the medical school at Salerno, and though we know that Salerno was active before this time, there can be little doubt that Constantine did influence the development of medicine there. In no field of learning was the East more advanced over the West, and even after the introduction of Arabic medicine, oriental doctors were preferred by many European rulers. Unfortunately, practical anatomy was little studied; some progress was made however, especially in the fields of curative and preventive medicine and pharmacology. The isolation of individuals suffering from contagious diseases was practiced in the thirteenth century—one of the greatest steps in medical history. Although physicians as a professional class were recognized by 1215, barber-surgeons and leeches were the ordinary practitioners when professional assistance was invoked at all, and most of the sick of medieval Europe were treated by the application of poultices made of herbs (which were occasionally effective) and by the exorcizing of demons and the saying of prayers and incantations. How very recent the

[4] C. H. Haskins, *Renaissance of the Twelfth Century*, p. 312.

science of medicine really is can best be realized when we recall the remedies applied by our ancestors in Colonial America only two centuries ago.

GEOGRAPHICAL KNOWLEDGE

In one field of science tremendous practical advances were made in the age of the crusades. While there was but little progress in theoretical geography and cosmography, in the practical knowledge of the earth tremendous strides were made. We have seen above that the ancient knowledge of geography was largely lost in the West, although carried on and increased by the Arabs, and that the horizon of the average medical man was limited to his own immediate district.

The crusades did much to change this. Pilgrims returning from Palestine wrote accounts of their travels; handbooks for travelers were prepared telling them all the sights to see in the Holy Land. With the tremendous increase of travel to the East resultant from the crusades, Palestine became almost as well known to the western European as was the land in the next county. The information was largely empirical and practical; men knew distances to foreign places and something of the nature of those places; they learned moreover the customs of foreign peoples and the commodities which could be secured from or sold to them.

Palestine was not the only country opened up to Western Europeans. The voyages of the Norsemen had brought them information concerning the Baltic lands and the islands of the Atlantic. Men began to travel more and to take a greater interest in their own countries as well as foreign parts. Illustrative of this tendency were the *Itinerary through Wales,* the *Description of Wales* and the *Topography of Ireland* written by Giraldus Cambrensis, a Welshman of the court of Henry II. Adam of Bremen described the Baltic regions and even Iceland and Greenland with considerable accuracy, but when he got to Prussia he filled the country with blue men with red faces and long hair, and with Amazons—beautiful women whose men were green and had the heads of dogs.

For the old legends persisted. The strange creatures, men and animals which had populated the world in the descriptions of Solinus and Isidore of Seville were still found just beyond the limits of the known lands on the medieval maps. The famous Hereford Map, drawn as late as 1314, still shows all the traditional creatures: giants, Amazons, cynocephali, antipodes, and strange men with only one foot consort on the outer portions of the map with centaurs, dragons, sphinxes, mandrakes, griffons and all the beasts of classical mythology as well as with elephants and crocodiles. The Garden of Eden is located in the Far East at the top of the map, and the circuit of the earth is surrounded by the waters of oceans into which flow the rivers of paradise.

Cosmography was still geocentric; the world was generally conceded to be a flat disc with Jerusalem as its hub. Near Jerusalem, at Mount Moriah, heaven and earth came nearest together, for it was there that Jacob saw the angels descend from paradise on a ladder. The location of hell was not definitely known, though many thought it to lie just beyond the hot sands of the Sahara, but Dante found the entrance not far from Florence.

One of the most popular legends of the twelfth century was that of Prester John, the fabulous Christian emperor who ruled the lands beyond Scythia and was the most powerful and wealthy of all the rulers of the earth. In his land flowed the traditional milk and honey; gold, silver and precious gems abounded everywhere, but the land was entirely free of serpents, scorpions, or any kind of poisonous reptile. When Europe first learned of the Mongols, and heard that they were Christians, they immediately accepted them as the subjects of Prester John until closer acquaintance disillusioned them.

The discovery of the East in the thirteenth century was fully as important as the discovery of the West in the fifteenth. The travels of John of Piano Carpini and William of Rubruk to the court of the Great Khan gave the West its first idea of the Mongol Empire, but the real splendors of Cathay were only revealed in the book of Marco Polo at the end of the thirteenth century. The descriptions of the magnificence of Cathay earned the adventurous Venetian the nick-name of *"Il Millione"* among his fellow-townsmen, but modern exploration and research have proven that on the whole Marco was a careful and conscientious observer, and that his wild tales were in fact the veriest truths. The sceptical reception of his account of burning stones (coal) and of paper money are merely indicative of the way in which his accurate statements were found incredible by his contemporaries.

But from such travelers' books as Marco Polo's the men of Western Europe heard of the East, and their horizon receded from their immediate neighborhoods to include far and fabled lands. When the land route to Cathay was closed, they sought to find the way thither by sea, and the discoveries of the Portuguese in the fifteenth century were largely inspired by the quest for Cathay and its incomparable riches.

SCHOLASTIC PHILOSOPHY

But the subject in which medieval scholars delighted more than any other was philosophy. With the revival of Aristotelianism as a result of the new translations from the Arabic and Greek, the Aristotelian concepts of philosophy became most popular and disturbed men greatly by their apparent contradictions of Holy Writ. The reconciliation of Aristotle and the Bible was the aim of the scholastic philosophers, and finally was resolved by St. Thomas Aquinas in his *Summa Theologicae,* the greatest monument of medieval philosophic and theological thought.

The problem which first interested the philsophers was the question of Universals. Was there a universal prototype of which apprehensible objects were replicas, or was the universal but a name applied to a generalization? Two schools of thought early developed: the Realists, of whom St. Anselm (1033–1109) and William de Champeaux were leaders, maintained that the universal was real, that there existed in the mind of God a real universal on which all earthly examples were patterned (*Universalia ante rem*). The Nominalists, on the other hand, led by Roscellinus (ob. 1121), insisted that only the apprehensible was real and that the universal was but a name (*Universalia post rem*). It would have been perfectly safe to argue *ad nauseam* about the universal dog, horse or man, but the philosophers almost at once got onto the dangerous ground of discussing such matters as the church, angels, the Holy Ghost, and other theological subjects. Catholic dogma had of necessity to accept the Realist point of view, for the very idea of the church as a divine institution postulated a recognition of the universal; Nominalism would have reduced the church to a number of congregations. Also to try to define the Trinity or the Holy Ghost from the Nominalist side produced indescribable difficulties. It was well enough to say that the universal man was merely a generalized name for a concept gained through observation of individual men, but how account for the Holy Ghost?

One of the most daring philosophers to attack this question was Peter Abelard (1079–1142), a Breton who became the most famous teacher at Paris in the early twelfth century. Abelard is best known for his unhappy love affair with Heloise, which he described in such detail in his *Historia Calamitatum*, and many who are familiar with the story of the great lovers fail to connect Abelard with the philosopher and teacher, who more than any other single man built the greatness of the schools of Paris. Abelard was the author of several theological works, commentaries on the Scriptures, and of some love songs which enjoyed a great vogue at the time, but his greatest work was the *Sic et Non* (*Yes and No*). In this impudent book, Abelard proposed a series of questions and then showed the answers given to them by the various church Fathers. The total lack of agreement among the Fathers was emphasized by this method of presentation, and Abelard did nothing to reconcile their differences. The book created a scandal and was subsequently burned along with other of his works, after he was condemned by the council of Sens (1141); but it became the model after which Peter Lombard organized his *Sentences*. Lombard, however, went on to reconcile the divergent opinions of the Fathers, so that his book became the standard textbook for theology, while Abelard's was cast into outer darkness.

Abelard was the completely questioning mind for whom reason was superior to faith. He naturally aroused the antagonism of such men as St. Bernard, who hounded him for years until he forced him out of the schools.

He had also provoked the enmity of William de Champeaux and Anselm of Laon, under both of whom he had studied, and both of whom he had bested in debate. But Abelard's fame as a teacher was great and his students many, even when he retreated to the Mount of St. Geneviève outside Paris and lectured in the open fields. Among the most famous of his students were Peter Lombard, John of Salisbury, Otto of Freising, Peter the Venerable, Arnold of Brescia, and Guibert de la Poirée (the latter two both charged with heresy later on).

In the matter of Universals, Abelard tried to compromise between the two extremes of Nominalism and Realism. He founded the school known as Conceptualism, which maintained that what was real was neither the universal in the mind of God, nor the individual, but the concept in the mind of man of the universal as comprehended by observation of the individuals. (*Universalia in re.*) This Conceptualism, under the name of modified realism, became an accepted belief of many theologians and philosophers later and was accepted generally by the church, but its author was too far ahead of his time and suffered because of it at the hands of the obscurantists. While it is to the eternal discredit of St. Bernard that he led the persecution of Abelard, it is to the eternal glory of Peter the Venerable of Cluny that he sheltered the ailing philosopher in his last years and gave him refuge behind the walls of a Cluniac house.

Abelard was directly responsible for the development of the schools at Paris. His quarrel with Champeaux caused the latter to withdraw from the cathedral school to St. Victor monastery; Abelard himself was refused permission to teach at Paris and so lectured at St. Geneviève nearby. It was from the fusion of the three schools—the cathedral, St. Geneviève, and St. Victor—that the University of Paris sprang.

Paris became early a center for the new Aristotelianism. Aristotle's *Physics* and *Metaphysics,* translated from the Arabic, became the subject of much philosophical study and speculation. The study of the *Metaphysics* was complicated by the fact that in translating it from the Arabic the commentary by the Moorish scholar, Averroes, had been translated along with the original text. Because of the doctrines of Averroes concerning the eternity of matter, his denial of individual salvation, and his pantheism, the books were banned at Paris until a papal commission could purge Aristotle of his Arabic accretions. Nevertheless a school of Averroists, under the leadership of Siger of Brabant, developed in the thirteenth century, to the great despair of the church.

But though Siger and his followers pursued Aristotle and Averroes into heresy, other scholars studied the Stygarite more orthodoxly. At Paris in the thirteenth century developed the great group of scholastic philosophers who were to accomplish the reconciliation of human knowledge with divine revelation. Albertus Magnus (1193–1280) a Dominican, who taught mostly at Cologne, was for a time a teacher at Paris. He was a thorough master of philosophy and theology, but his chief interest was in science on which he wrote prolifically. So familiar was he with all of the Aristotelian science that he was sometimes derisively called "Aristotle's ape" (a dig at both his enthusiasm for Aristotle and his own short stature). He was not only the first scientific mind of his age, but the teacher of St. Thomas Aquinas.

St. Thomas Aquinas (1225–74), the "Angelic doctor," came from a noble Italian family from the kingdom of Naples, one of his cousins, also named Thomas Aquinas, being count of Acerra and one of the trusted agents of Frederick II. He studied at Monte Cassino, Naples, Cologne, and Paris, remaining at Paris to teach. Later he left Paris to teach in Bologna, Rome, and other Italian cities. He died at the age of forty-eight on his way to the Council of Lyons in 1274.

Thomas is the greatest light of the Dominican order, and the greatest theologian of medieval Latin Christianity. His works fill more than sixty volumes and include treatises on philosophy, biblical exegesis, and commentaries, and above all the *Summa Theologica*. In the *Summa* St. Thomas gave Catholic doctrine its definitive form for centuries to come. He accomplished the thorny problem of reconciling the Bible and Aristotle by the single formula that faith supercedes reason. According to Thomas man can apprehend God's will in two ways—by direct revelation or by using his reasoning faculties, which God gave him that he might better comprehend His Will. Aristotle is the supreme perfection of the human mind and his reasoning is as correct as human reason can be; but there is always the possibility of error in any human reasoning, and therefore if there is found to be conflict between Aristotle and the Bible, the infallible revealed truths of the Holy Writ must be preferred to the excellent, but fallible, deductions of Aristotle's human mind.

A contemporary of St. Thomas was the Franciscan St. Bonaventura (1221–74), general of the order, official biographer of St. Francis, and the most eminent Franciscan theologian. His commentaries on Peter Lombard and his *Breviloquium* are masterpieces of theological exposition. He was more of a mystic than St. Thomas and differed from him on some points of theology, but his work is hardly less significant than that of the great Dominican.

Albertus, Thomas, and Bonaventura represent the climax of scholastic philosophy. With Duns Scotus (c. 1274–1308) another Franciscan, scholasticism began to become the sterile thing which made it the subject of such bitter denunciation by the later humanists. Men became enamored of the syllogism, and logic was employed to prove all sorts of ridiculous and trivial things. Duns Scotus carried this to such an extreme that he has given his name to the Dunce—the wise fool. With Scotus, and after him William of

Ockham (c. 1280–1349), faith was made so pre-eminent over reason that there was no purpose in applying reason to matters of theology, and logic became merely an intellectual exercise without much serious purpose.

Meanwhile at Oxford, Robert Grosseteste (1175–1253) and Roger Bacon (c. 1214–94) were asserting the superiority of the inductive method of scientific study. Bacon's reputation far exceeds his true importance, but he was a great teacher who popularized his theories and acquired a great celebrity. His imprisonment by his order (the Franciscan) for some of his radical ideas furthered the growth of his legend, until he came to be called the most original thinker of the Middle Ages, a designation which he does not deserve although he does rank high among scientists and philosophers.

The schools in which these philosophers did their work were the new universities, and we must now turn to the rise of this new institution.

RISE OF THE UNIVERSITIES

A distinctive development of the Twelfth-Century Renaissance was the rise of the universities; no modern institution is more purely medieval in its origin. In the seventh to tenth centuries, as we have seen, the monasteries were the chief centers of education in the West; then with the Carolingian Renaissance began the development of the cathedral schools, which grew into first importance as a result of the teaching of Gerbert and the dissemination of knowledge by his pupils. Chartres, Laon, Paris, Rheims, Orleans and other cathedral centers developed the schools in which the new studies of the Twelfth-Century Renaissance were pursued. Laon was pre-eminent in mathematics and logic, Paris in logic, Chartres was the great center of humanism. These cathedral schools flourished through the twelfth century, but as the century progressed their importance declined before the rise of the new universities. As the new sciences and subjects were introduced with the reception of the Arabic science and the Roman law, the new subjects crept into the curricula of the cathedral schools, and from some of them developed the universities.

The first school which is generally termed a university was the medical school at Salerno in southern Italy. As early as the middle of the eleventh century, Salerno had acquired a reputation as a center of medical studies, but as it never developed in any other line to any marked degree, it cannot be accepted as the founder of the university system. That distinction must go to the University of Bologna, which was established in the first part of the twelfth century as a center of legal studies, the greatness of the school being chiefly due to the fame of its celebrated teacher, Irnerius. At Bologna first developed those institutions which we consider characteristic of a university.

Paris developed its university from the fusion of three schools—the cathedral school of Notre Dame, the school at the abbey of St. Geneviève and the abbey school of St. Victor. It was a center of intellectual life under Peter Abelard in the first part of the twelfth century and thereafter continuously progressed. Oxford originated through a secession of masters and scholars from Paris during the struggle between Henry II and Thomas Becket. Montpellier, the last of the twelfth-century foundations, developed as a medical and legal center.

In the thirteenth century, many universities were founded, including Padua, Naples (the first state university), Orleans, Cambridge, Toulouse, and Salamanca. The fourteenth century saw the great development of the German universities with the foundation of Prague, Vienna, Heidelberg, Cologne, and the spread of the system to such outlying places as Buda, Cracow, and Lisbon.

Although the medieval universities were not as large as the modern, it must not be thought that they were by any means insignificant. It has been claimed that there were more students in the universities in the thirteenth century in proportion to the entire population than there are in the twentieth. Paris in her best days had, according to the very conservative estimates of Rashdall, the leading modern authority on the medieval universities, some six to seven thousand students, and Bologna had about the same number. Oxford varied from 1500 to 3000; Prague had about 1500, Toulouse around 2000, Heidelberg between 200 to 300. The 20,000 students of Paris and Bologna mentioned by some authorities are a decided exaggeration, but there is reason to believe that Oxford and Cambridge had within the vicinity of 10,000 students at a time when the entire population of England only totaled some three-and-a-half millions.

What was a university? The term *universitas* was not originally confined to the academic world. It meant merely "all of you"—a society. In fact the *universitas* and the *collegium* were not distinguishable, nor could either be differentiated from the *societas*. The university was originally the *universitas societas magistrorum disciplorumque*—a corporation, a gild of masters and students. Like the commercial and industrial gilds of the Middle Ages, the university was a gild of masters (masters of the science of the arts, or of theology, or law or medicine) with whom were associated students who were apprentices in the art or craft. The Italian craft gilds were termed *Arte*. In the trade gild there were masters, journeymen, and apprentices; in the chivalric there were knights, squires, and pages; in the academic there were masters, bachelors, and students. The Trinity was omnipresent.

The student entered under the tutelage of the masters and worked until he could pass certain examinations and be qualified to give his own lectures. Then he became a bachelor—the equivalent of the journeyman. As a bachelor he gave lectures on certain chapters of the standard text, until he had studied enough to qualify for his licentiate. It was when he passed his examination for the licentiate that the student was given a *license to teach*. He was not yet however a member of the gild of masters and only became a master upon his formal inception into the gild. Only after an elaborate and expensive ceremony of inception, which included gifts to all the masters and a huge banquet to which the masters and fellow students were alike invited (in some of the Spanish universities the licentiate had to supply a bull fight for the amusement of his guests), the licentiate was declared a full member of the masters' gild and was accorded the title of master of arts. Some schools at first used the titles "master" and "doctor" interchangeably, the difference being in which of the various faculties the student had qualified, i.e. master of arts, doctor of law or theology. The continental doctor of philosophy was of later origin, but in England today the masters is the ultimate degree for students in arts.

The university degree was then a license to teach, and the attainment of it gave the candidate the right to teach anywhere within the jurisdiction of the authority conferring the degree. As the universities developed on the whole from pre-existent cathedral schools, the license was usually conferred by the bishop of the diocese, or by one of his officials (the chancellor in Paris, the archdeacon in Bologna), and gave the new master the right to teach anywhere within the diocese. As there were seldom many institutions of learning within a single diocese the permission to teach was practically limited to permission to teach in the school from which the student was graduated. Schools in the Middle Ages were just as loath to accept work done in other institutions as they are today, and a master from one school had normally to stand re-examination before he could teach in another school than the one from which he had come. But some of the schools acquired at an early date extraordinary prestige and influence, and students from many countries attended them. These schools had to have a wider competence and so special privileges were granted them in bulls issued by either the pope or the emperor (the two powers which could claim to exercise universal dominion) which elevated them above the rank of the ordinary schools and gave their graduates the right to teach anywhere in Christendom. As all instruction was given in Latin this was possible as it would not be today with our multiplicity of tongues. Such a school with an oecumenical license was termed a *studium generale,* while the school whose graduates could only teach within the diocese was termed a *studium particularis.* To the *studium generale* students came from all parts of Europe and its members were rightly termed *universitas vestras.* And as time went on the term university became confined exclusively to these *studia generalia,* while the *studium particularis* remained merely a school. An exception to this is found in the schools which were declared to be *studium generale respectu regni* by kings, especially in Spain. These schools conferred a license valid anywhere within the kingdom, but they normally certified their position by securing a bull from the pope confirming their pretentions, and erecting them into regular *studia generalia*. There were further those great universities which could not show a papal or imperial bull, but were considered to be *studia generalia ex consuetudine*—traditionally and by common consent, universal schools. Oxford and Padua are the greatest examples of this class.

The university was, then, a corporation of scholars with a charter giving their graduates permission to teach anywhere in Christendom. The corporation consisted of the members of the various schools or faculties—arts, medicine, theology, civil and canon law. Except for arts, the faculties were headed by their deans, but in the organization of the arts faculty there were two great types—the Bologna type where the gild was composed of students, and the Paris type where it was made up of masters. All the other later universities corresponded generally to one or the other of these types. In both types the general group was divided into *nations,* each of which was a corporation in itself. At Bologna the two nations—the *Cismontane* and the *Transmontane*—were so distinct that to be entirely correct one should speak of the universities of Bologna. At Paris the four nations collectively formed the arts faculty. These nations were, as the name indicates, groups of students from a common homeland. In Bologna, the division was made between the Italian (*Cismontane*) and the non-Italian students; at Paris the four nations were the French, the English (or German), the Normans, and the Picards (which latter included the Flemish and Dutch scholars from the Low Countries). Of these the French, which included Italian and Spanish as well, by far outnumbered the others, sometimes equalling all three of them. Each nation had its own elected proctor and the proctors of the nations elected the rector, who was the administrative head of the entire university. The student pledged his loyalty to his nation and to its officers and the nation became the center of his academic life. From evidences found in the sermons and the court records, the nations were often on bad terms with each other and conflicts which often ended in free-for-all fights were not unknown among them.

The purpose of the nations, as indeed of the corporation of the university itself, was for protection and the maintenance of the rights of the scholars against the civil authorities and the townsmen. Town and gown were traditionally at odds, and the university jealously defended its privileges and its members against any exercise of arbitrary authority or any discrimination on the part of the townsfolk. The University of Paris, indeed, owed its original charter from the pope to an appeal made after a town and gown fight in which several students and citizens had been killed in a barroom brawl. Possessed of its own court with jurisdiction over its members and able to engage successfully in collective bargaining, the university was able to control prices and rents and to assure favorable treatment of its members. The independence of the university was materially increased by the fact that, having no buildings or "plant," the entire university could migrate at will, leaving a town which did not meet its demands and move to a more conciliatory community. For two years (1229–31) the University of Paris was "dispersed," the masters and scholars settling mostly at Angers, which thereupon came into prominence as a university. Many universities were founded as the results of migrations from older schools, Oxford from Paris, Cambridge from Oxford, Mantua from Bologna, Leipzig from Prague.

The organization of nations was, at Paris, characteristic of only the arts faculty. The other faculties, theology, canon law (civil law was prohibited at Paris by papal decree) and medicine, had their own organization under their deans. The dean had been the senior member and presiding officer of a chapter of cathedral canons and the title easily passed over to the president of a group of masters in a given faculty. In matters of ceremonial the rector of the university, representative of the arts faculty, took precedence over the deans of the higher faculties, and he was the spokesman for the corporation in dealings with outside authorities.

A feature of the organization of many of the medieval universities—especially those of the north which followed the Paris type—was the development of the *colleges*. What we call a college today was then termed a *faculty*, and they referred to the faculty of arts or of law. The medieval college was more like our fraternity or dormitory. It was a house in which a group of students lived as a community, and the college became the essential unit for many students. Their collegiate organization passed from Paris to Oxford and Cambridge and still remains the chief feature of the English system. The earliest college was that of the *Dixhuit* founded in Paris in 1180; it consisted of eighteen beds in the hospital which were given to needy students. Shortly thereafter the students secured a house of their own which became then the college property. The example was followed by others and the foundation of a college became a popular form of philanthropy. The most famous of the Parisian colleges was that founded in 1258 by Robert de Sorbonne, the confessor of King Louis IX. Founded for sixteen students in theology, four from each nation, it increased until it had a large membership and eventually gave its name to the arts department of the University of Paris which is now commonly referred to as the Sorbonne.

It was in these colleges that the libraries first developed, the graduates of each college leaving their books to the college. The university library developed later. It was also in the colleges that paid teachers first appeared in the north. The college would employ a tutor to direct the studies of the men belonging to the college. Gradually the tutors extended the sphere of their activities to students other than those in their own college. A tutorship with an assured income was preferable to the uncertain collection of fees from each student, which was the only means of livelihood for the regular university lecturers. In the south, Bologna first developed paid lectureships when they offered regular salaries to professors to lecture there, and thus guaranteed that they would not leave the city and go to another town.

In its physical appearance the medieval university differed considerably from the university of today. Except for the college buildings, which were private, it had no campus and no buildings, no registrar and no system of grades, no laboratories and no athletic field. The lectures were given by professors in their own houses or in buildings rented by them for that purpose. Irnerius, the great founder of the school of Bologna, is said to have lectured in the public square as there was no building large enough to accommodate his classes, but the average teacher held his classes in a room equipped with a lectern, from which he read, and with reeds on the floor on which the students sat. The students paid for each lecture or subscribed for the course, and if the professor missed a lecture he was obliged to refund to the students, who had subscribed, the proportionate amount of their fee. The method of study was the familiar lecture and discussion type, lectures by the professor being interspersed by discussions in which the students would debate problems with the teacher. Lectures were of two types—ordinary and extraordinary or cursory. The ordinary lectures were those given in the preferred hours by the masters and covered the more important books studied. The extraordinary lectures were given by either the master or by a bachelor assistant and came at less popular hours or on holidays. The three periods for the ordinary lectures were approximately from 6 to 9, from 2 to 4 and from 4:30 to 6 in the afternoon, thus giving one three-hour, one two-hour and one hour-and-a-half lecture each day. Extraordinary lectures could be given in the period 9 to 2 and were also given on saints days and holidays when the ordinary lectures were prohibited. This was because the attendance at the ordinary lectures was compulsory while that at the extraordinary was optional. As the rooms were unlighted and as the schools ran on the ecclesiastical schedule (matins, tierce, vespers) the hours above given are only approximate and varied from winter to summer. Teachers were expressly forbidden to lecture in the dark so that the students could not take down what they were saying. The courses of study in the medieval school were based essentially on certain books. In the arts course the *Grammar* of Priscan, the logical works of Aristotle, the *Isagogus* of Porphory and the *Topics* and *Divisions* of Boethius were among the required books studied for the bachelor's degree. For the licentiate the physical and scientific works of Aristotle were added. In theology the Bible and the *Sentences* of Peter Lombard were used, while Gratian and his successors contributed the texts of canon law. Medicine was based on Galen, Hippocrates, and Avicenna and the civil law was an intensive study of the Justinian *Digest*. The lecturer would dictate a passage from the text and then comment upon it, special questions arising from the lecture would become the subject of extra lectures, and discussions based upon the text or its interpretation took the place of our modern quiz. Statutes provided that the lectures be impromptu and not dictated from notes. The length of time required to complete the course varied with the institution and with the student. At Paris the arts course required a minimum of six years; theology required ten years, but the time was shortened if the student were already a bachelor of arts. As the students often entered the university at an early age—fourteen or fifteen— regulations carefully limited the minimum age of receiving the degree, and a Paris graduate could not begin to lecture in arts before the age of twenty-one or in theology before thirty-five.

A student himself declared his readiness to come up for his examination for his degree, and the university did not concern itself with him until he declared himself prepared. The examination was however a very serious matter, for it examined the student on all the work done at the university and lasted for hours or even days. When the examination had been successfully passed the student gave his inaugural dissertation—a lecture and defense of given theses—in which he debated against all comers on certain chosen subjects. From our present standards the medieval examination seems impossible, as the candidate has to know the texts by heart and be able to expound them for hours. However there seems to have been much leniency in the administration of the examination, and in some of the universities the sons of the higher nobility were excused without any examination. A sermon of Robert de Sorbonne, given as a baccalaureate sermon at Paris, reveals some interesting points about the examination. Robert was comparing the examinations which the students had just passed to the examination of the soul on the day of judgment—designed to show the rigors of God's judgment as compared with the laxity of the university. The students, we learn from this, could know on what texts they were to be examined and could "bone up" on them, they could pass with a grade of seventy-five per cent, the examination was conducted in private and few knew if the candidate failed; if he failed once he could try again a year later; and, sad to relate, gifts and the intercession of influential friends could often cause a favorable verdict or even the changing of the grade from failure to pass. Needless to say none of these ameliorations would be operative at the Day of Judgment.

The course of study was difficult and the examinations long. But there was a lighter side to university life. Not all the students' time was spent in onerous toil. Much of it seems to have been occupied with the tavern and its pleasures. Much of our information as to medieval student life comes from the contemporary records of the police courts where the extra-curricular activities of the students seem often to have led them. Statutes for the regulation of the students' lives also afford much light and we learn from them that students were not permitted to dance, wrestle, shoot bows and arrows, or throw stones in chapel.

A perusal of the statutes leaves one with the feeling that perhaps Robert de Sorbonne was right when he said of the students of Paris in the thir-teenth century that "Some of them are better acquainted with the rules of dice than with those of logic." Student letter-books reveal the student broke and in need of money, writing home, reporting his success at school and asking for funds to purchase ink, quills, and necessary supplies, while the songs of the Goliardi, the wandering students, reveal a tavern-haunting, wenching, quarrelsome crew. Clerics they may have been, but they were nonetheless youth.

CHAPTER 33

LAW, POLITICAL THEORY, AND HISTORIOGRAPHY

❖

REVIVAL OF ROMAN LAW

THE revival of interest in the Roman law and the growth of the great law school at Bologna was one of the most important aspects of the Twelfth-Century Renaissance. While the Justinian *Corpus* had been published in the West as well as in the East, it had never gotten a very secure hold in the Western provinces. The Germans, in their absorption of Roman laws and customs, had derived them rather from the older Theodosian code than from that of Justinian. As a result, the West lacked almost entirely the science of jurisprudence, which was based primarily on the *Digest*. The texts were extant but there was no one to study them until, in the twelfth century, Irnerius, a teacher at Bologna, began to lecture on the principles of the Roman law as found in the *Digest*.

The law of feudal Europe was, as we have seen, based on usage and custom and was essentially practical with very little theory. The revival of the Roman law resulted not only in the introduction of many principles of the laws themselves, but in the growth of a science of law. The application of the new science to both secular and ecclesiastical law stimulated the writing of many glosses and commentaries on the Roman law itself and also gave Gratian the necessary background and training for the codification of the *Corpus Juris Canonici* (ecclesiastical law) in his *Decretum*.

The work of Irnerius at Bologna was continued after his death (c. 1125) by his four great students: Jacobus, Bulgarus, Hugo, and Martinus. They followed the example of their teacher in writing glosses on articles of the *Code* and phrases of the *Digest*. The greatest of the glossators was Accursius, whose *Glossa Ordinaria* appeared about 1250, but he was only the last of a long line of teachers and writers which included such great figures as Azzo, Hugolinus, and Odofredus. After the glossators had written glosses on all the important parts of the Roman law, the commentators began their work, preparing lengthy commentaries which applied the rules of the law to the conditions of the times. The greatest of the postglossators or commentators was Bartolus of Sassaferrato (1314–57). The commentators were influenced by the passion for dialectic which dominated the schools, and went beyond the explanation of the texts which had been the chief work of the glossators. Their work was more scholastic, but they applied the law to the problems of their own society and made it a more virile element in the culture of the time.

These lawyers were not only teachers and writers, they were practitioners of the law; the four Bolognese doctors were found among the advisors of Frederick Barbarossa at the famous diet of Roncaglia where he laid down the platform for his rule in Italy. The new monarchs generally approved the revived Roman law, which tended to support the absolutism to which they aspired. Such phrases as "What the prince desires has the force of law," "The king is above law," and other principles of royal sovereignty which were found in the *Digest* were extremely useful to rulers like the two Fredericks, who aimed at replacing feudal monarchy with imperial absolutism.

The principles of the Roman law had always prevailed in the lands of southern Europe where the Gallo-Roman population had retained them as their custom law. France was divided into two great spheres, the lands of the written and of the custom law; but in the twelfth century, and increasingly in the thirteenth, Roman law principles found their way into the law books of the custom-law lands. The great books of feudal law in France, which date mostly from the thirteenth century: Beaumanoir, Pierre de Fontaines, *Les Establissements de St. Louis,* and *Le Livre de Jostice et de Plet,* which give the laws of Beauvais, Vermandois, Anjou, and Orleans, are all filled with quotations from the Roman law and with principles derived from it. Both the *Fuero Real* and the *Siete Partidas* of Castile show a strong Roman law influence. While the German *Sachsenspiegel* (early thirteenth century) is comparatively free of Roman influences and represents the old German law, the later *Schwabenspiegel* (c. 1275) and the glosses of the Sachsenspiegel are strongly colored by Roman. The reception of Roman law into Germany was at first theoretical and the full influence of the new law was not completely felt until the fifteenth century.

England alone of the great states of the West remained relatively immune to the Roman law. Master Vicarius taught Roman law in England in the days of Stephen, but Henry II forbade the teaching of the new law and opposed any attempt to introduce it in any large degree into his kingdom. He was intent on creating his own common law in which the Roman principles had no part. In Glanville's *De Legibus Angliae,* which reflects the law of the reign of Henry II, there is almost no influence of the Roman law; however, by the end of the reign of Henry III many Roman law principles had crept into the English law and are found perpetuated in Bracton's *De Legibus et Consuetudinibus Angliae.* But though Bracton shows traces of the Roman influence his work is essentially

English, and England never became a country of the Roman law, although Scotland, under French influence, did.

We have already noted the development of canon law. Gratian's *Decretum,* codifying the canons of the church, greatly facilitated the spread of the law which penetrated all Europe where the Roman church held sway. The conflict of jurisdictions in almost every country between the secular and the ecclesiastical courts, each practicing its own law, caused indescribable confusion and difficulty, although the legal as opposed to the jurisdictional problem was ameliorated somewhat when many of the principles of the canon law were assimilated into the civil codes.

POLITICAL THEORY

The spread of Roman and canon law, supporting as they did the claims of the empire and the papacy, had an important effect on the development of political theory. Much of the political thought of the twelfth and thirteenth centuries was expended on the question of imperial or papal supremacy, and the most significant political theories of the period are the authors of treatises to support the claims of either the popes or the emperors. The introduction of Aristotelian ideas, with the translation of his *Politics* into Latin, also strongly affected the political thought of the time. Among the most distinguished writers in this field was John of Salisbury (ob. 1180) who supported Becket against Henry II and who wrote the *Policraticus* or *Statesman's Book* in which he advanced the theory that a tyrant could be properly slain by his subjects. John distinguished scrupulously between the good king and the tyrant and was careful to point out that even the tyrant could not be slain for a private cause but only in the public good. He was an ardent defender of the papal supremacy and the doctrine of the "two swords" both belonging to the church, but he was a severe critic of ecclesiastical laxity and corruption.

In the writing of Gerhoh of Reichersberg (1094–1169) there is to be found a very reasonable position in which the author supports the superiority of the church in general, and approves the disciplining of errant princes, but in which the extreme pretentions of the church are denied. Thomas Aquinas (1225–74) in his *De Regimine Principum* likewise accepted the theory of papal superiority, but recognized the Aristotelian concept of natural rights of the secular state. He felt that lay states should be small.and suggested that the ruler could be deposed by his subjects if he ruled unjustly. But the conflict became much more bitter in the course of the thirteenth century and by the time of Boniface VIII and John XXII in the fourteenth we find papalists expressing the most extreme claims to world dominion.

In the *De potestate papae* of Augustinus Triumphus (ca. 1320) it was stated that the pope was the only power on earth and that all secular rulers held their authority from him and at his pleasure. This point of view was shared by Egidius Romanus and Alvarus Pelagius, who went even further than the pope in declaring the superiority of the ecclesiastical temporal power.

The greatest imperialist writer was Dante, who, in all his works but particularly in his *De Monarchia,* defended the supreme authority of the emperor. Dante systematically refuted all the papal arguments and then asserted the imperial ones. The *Donation of Constantine* he dismissed as invalid, since Constantine could not alienate the power he was empowered to defend, and his grant automatically invalidated itself by destroying his own position. Dante envisaged a world at peace under the benign rule of a universal emperor, under whom the church was a respected ministry. Dante combined scholastic logic, historical precedent, and plain common sense in his treatise, which may well be considered the swan song of the medieval empire. The secular position was asserted even more vigorously by supporters of Philip the Fair of France: Pierre Dubois, John of Paris, and de Nogaret.

An even more forcible attack on the papacy came from the pen of Marsiglio of Padua, whose *Defensor Pacis* (1324) set forth the principle that the church was not a monarchy at all, but was composed of the *"pars valentior"* as found in Aristotle. He was a supporter of Louis of Bavaria against John XXII and attacked the idea of any papal superiority. Not the pope but the greater part of the faithful governed the church, and the whole argument was a continuation of the conciliar theory advanced by Philip IV and his legist advisors. The maintenance of peace and orthodoxy were alike the duties of the state, and the church throughout was reduced to an inferior position of dependency. Though he spoke of the empire, Marsiglio obviously realized and approved the existence of several sovereign states, and his political theory is far closer to the modern than to the medieval.

HISTORICAL WRITING

In the field of historical literature the twelfth and thirteenth centuries witnessed a tremendous outpouring of works. In addition to the old world chronicles or the local annals, which were so characteristic of the earlier eras, there developed a great quantity of royal histories centering around the various monarchs and their courts. There was also a great increase in the histories of special events, wars or campaigns, such as the crusades. Most of this writing was done in Latin, but during the period under consideration the first great histories in the vernacular (excepting the *Anglo-*

Saxon Chronicle) were written and several of the most outstanding works were written in Old French. As there is such a quantity of historical material from these two centuries, we must of necessity be much more eclectic than in the earlier periods, and it will be impossible here to more than mention the outstanding historians of any country. On the other hand, as the material for them is so scattered, and they are neglected so uniformly in most texts, the historians will be treated in greater detail than the philosophers, poets, and scientists, about whom so much has been written elsewhere.

Byzantine

Among the Byzantines the old form of the world chronicle had become firmly entrenched and was not readily abandoned. Four universal chronicles which began with the Creation were written in the twelfth century by John Zonaras (to 1118); Constantine Manasses (to 1081 in verse); Michael Glykas (to 1118); and George Cedrenos (to 1057). All of these were compilations of earlier histories and are without great value as original works, though they sometimes include materials from older writers otherwise lost. Much more important were the history of John Cinnamus (1118–76), and those of Nicetas Choniates (1180–1206) and George Acropolitas (1203–61). Of these Cinnamus and Nicetas are most valuable for their accounts of the reigns of the later Comneni emperors, both for the internal history of the empire and for their relations with the Slavs, crusaders, and Western nations, while Nicetas is the best single Greek source for the Latin conquest of Constantinople in 1204. Acropolitas is the great historian of the Empire of Nicaea and incidentally of the Latin Empire of Constantinople, and the other Balkan states in the first half of the thirteenth century. He was continued by George Pachymeres (1261–1308) and later by Nicephorus Gregoras, who abridged Acropolitas and Pachymeres from 1204 to 1308 and continued them as an original work to 1359.

Histories of single reigns or events are found in the *Alexiade* of the Princess Anna Comnena, who wrote an epic poem eulogizing the deeds of her father Alexius I, probably the most remarkable piece of Byzantine historical writing in the entire period. Her account gives a valuable picture of the Byzantine reaction to the First Crusade, as well as a vivid story of Alexius' struggles with the Petchenegs and Cumans. Nicephorus Bryennius, Anna's husband, also wrote a history, much simpler than his learned wife's masterpiece, in which he traced the rise of the house of Comneni in the years 1070–79; his work is valuable for the detail on the period of anarchy before the accession of Alexius and for the Saljuq conquests in Asia Minor. While both of these works are profoundly prejudiced in favor of Alexius and the Comneni dynasty, they are of first importance for the study of this important period, Anna's characterizations of people she met at her father's court being especially valuable. Towards the end of the twelfth century Eustathius, bishop of Salonica, who is also noted for his commentaries on Homer, Pindar, and other classical poets and for his letters, wrote a history of the Norman conquest of Salonica in 1185, an important historical document which is only recently beginning to receive the attention it deserves.

It is worthy of note that only in the field of history did the Byzantines contribute much in this period. Michael Choniates, bishop of Athens, the brother of Nicetas, wrote a number of letters, sermons, and orations; Prodromos wrote essays, verse, satires, and philosophical tracts; and Nicephorus Blemmydes, the chief literary figure of the court of Nicaea, wrote copiously in the fields of philosophy, science, political philosophy, hagiography, and dogmatics, as well as leaving an autobiography which has considerable historical value. But apart from these the intellectual activity of the Byzantines was slight; they had obviously passed their meridian and had little to offer in competition with the great intellectual revival of Western Europe.

German

In Germany the monastic annals which were so important in the eleventh century were continued into the twelfth, and the chronicles of cities and bishoprics began to assume greater importance. The *Annals of Cologne,* which were a mere compilation of older works from the Creation to 1144, became for the period 1144 to 1238 a source of the first importance. World histories were also kept up, and Ekkehard of Aura, continuing an older universal history by Herman the Lame of Reichenau, wrote what in the opinion of J. W. Thompson, was "by all odds the best world chronicle of the Middle Ages." [1] Ekkehard covered the years 1099 to 1125, and included not only events in Germany and Italy, but also in France, England, Spain, and the crusades, giving one of the best accounts extant of the unfortunate crusade of 1101, in which he was a participant. Ekkehard's chronicle was continued (1126–1225) by Burchard of Ursburg.

"In Otto of Freising the German historiography of the Middle Ages reaches its highest point," said C. H. Haskins; [2] J. W. Thompson goes even farther in stating: "No other country in medieval Europe could boast so profound, so erudite, so philosophical an interpretation of history." [3] The *Chronicle of the Two Cities* was inspired by Augustine's *City of God* and attempts to tell the story of mankind from the Creation to 1146 with speculations as to the end of the world. In six books Otto got to the death

[1] J. W. Thompson, *History of Historical Writing* (Macmillan), I, 191.

[2] C. H. Haskins, *Renaissance of the Twelfth Century* (Harvard), p. 238.

[3] J. W. Thompson, *History of Historical Writing,* I, 195. Thompson's analysis of the *Chronicle* is inaccurate and must be read with caution.

of Gregory VII in 1085, the seventh book narrated the history of his own times to 1146 and is one of the most important of all medieval chronicles; the eighth book is devoted to considerations on the Day of Judgment and the future life. Throughout Otto's history runs a strong stream of theological thought, and Otto is never far from his preceptor St. Augustine. But he did develop a distinct philosophy of history and his work is far more than an ordinary chronicle of events. Certainly Otto shows the optimum absorption of the classics and the Church Fathers in the quotations which are sprinkled freely through his work. No mere annalist, Otto endeavored to explain the mysteries of human behavior in the pattern set by God. As a reflection of the theological, philosophical, historical, and classical training obtainable in the twelfth century, Otto's *Chronicle* occupies an almost unique position. But this was not Otto's only historical work. He also started a life of his nephew Frederick I but was able to carry it only to the year 1156. Although incomplete, the *Gesta Friderici* is of the utmost historical value, for Otto was in a position to know intimately the policies of his imperial nephew and the men who surrounded him. His history of the early years of Barbarossa is one of the most complete coverages of any reign in medieval history.[4]

A group of German historians of great importance were those who narrated the history of the eastward expansion of the Germans along the Baltic. Adam of Bremen's history of the bishops of Hamburg and Bremen, Helmhold's *Chronicle of the Slavs,* and Arnold of Lübeck's continuation of Helmhold tell the story of the eastward expansion of the Germans from the Carolingian times to the thirteenth century including much of the history of the Baltic kingdoms. The story of the final conquest of Prussia by the Teutonic Knights was told by a priest of the order, Peter of Duisberg, in the fourteenth century. Another work of first importance for the Slavic peoples of the East was Cosmos of Prague's *Chronicle of the Bohemians,* written in the early twelfth century and continued through to 1198.

Italian

The most important development in Italian historical writing was the growth of the city annals which, although some of them had been begun in the earlier period, reached their peak of importance in the twelfth and thirteenth centuries. As the Italian towns struggled for independence and grew with the newly developed commerce and industry, they began to chronicle the events in their local history. Several of these chronicles begin

---

[4] The work was continued (1156–60) by Rahewin, canon of Freising, but it does not live up to the standard of the first books written by Otto. The *Chronicle* was also continued to 1209 by Otto of St. Blaise and is one of the major sources for the period covered.

with the crusades, as it was that movement which so greatly stimulated the growth of the towns. The *Annals of Genoa,* begun by Cafaro in 1099 and continued through the thirteenth century, are a good example of a city chronicle beginning with the crusade. Local histories of varying importance were prepared in Cremona, Milan, Florence, Piacenza, Pisa, Ferrara, Bergamo, Brescia, Asti, and other Italian cities. Only a few like Pavia, Lucca, Parma, Perugia, and Bologna lack local annals or chronicles. One of the most interesting is the Venetian chronicle of Martino di Canale, which told the story of Venice from her foundation to 1275, and which is of first importance for the period 1250 to 1275 when Canale was recording events within his own memory. Interestingly, this chronicle was written in French, which Canale thought to be the most pleasant and expressive language of the time.

As could be expected, the city chronicles were most important in the north where urban life had developed farthest. Rome had no urban chronicle; the *Liber pontificalis* continued through the twelfth century, and lives of individual popes followed it in the thirteenth. Likewise in the south the town annals, though they existed, were of less importance than in the north.

The Norman conquest of southern Italy gave rise to a large number of historical works, several of which were hardly more than panegyrics on Robert Guiscard. William of Apulia's epic poem, the *Gesta Roberti,* Aimé of Monte Cassino's *History of the Normans,* and Geoffrey Malaterra's *History of Sicily* are all eulogies of Robert and his brother Roger. The later history of the Norman kingdom was told by Alexander of Telese, Romauld of Salerno, Fulco of Benevento, and Hugo Falcandus of Palermo; while most of these are partial to the Normans, Fulco is rabidly antagonistic to them.

For the period of Frederick II we have two biographies of the emperor, one by Nicholas of Jamsilla, favorable, and one by Saba Malaspina, hostile. The best history of Frederick is, however, the chronicle of Richard of San Germano, an imperial notary closely associated with the court. The chronicle of Rolandin of Padua is the best source for the life of Frederick's lieutenant Ezzelino da Romano.

A unique position among the Italian historians of the thirteenth century is held by Salimbene of Parma, a Franciscan friar, who wrote an autobiography which is one of the gems of medieval historical writing. Written in a chatty intimate style, Salimbene's book gives an unusually vivid picture of conditions in Italy: Frederick II, Innocent IV, St. Louis, Charles of Anjou, Joachim of Flora, John of Piano Carpini, and many other figures of the time appear in his story with pungent character analyses and comments. His work is a mine of information on the monastic conditions of the time, on the anarchy of Italian politics, and on the intellectual interests of the period.[5]

French

Probably the most important developments in French historical writing are the growth of the royal or ducal chronicles and the appearance of a number of important historical works in the French vernacular in the thirteenth century.

The old universal histories of the earlier era continued to be written, but they became on the whole more critical and better organized, with their sources more clearly indicated. The best examples of this kind of work were the chronicles of Robert of Auxerre (ob. 1214), Helinand (ob. c. 1215), Auberi de Trois Fontaines (ob. p. 1251), the *Rhyming Chronicle of the Kings of France* (to 1241) by Philippe Mouskes, and the *Speculum Historiale* of Vincent of Beauvais (1190–1264). All of these works have considerable historical value, especially for the periods contemporary with the lives of their authors, and all but Vincent demonstrate real critical historical craftsmanship. The *Speculum Historiale* is a part of the great encyclopedia written by Vincent discussed above, and is an amazing compilation of historical information from the Creation to 1250. In many ways the most interesting of all the universal chroniclers was Bernard Gui, the Dominican bishop and inquisitor (ob. 1331), who wrote a *Flores Chronicorum* from the birth of Christ to his own time, of which he prepared eight revisions in the years 1301 to 1331. This compilation was tremendously popular and was soon translated into French. In addition Gui wrote a *Chronicle of the Kings of France,* a collection of saints' lives, a history of the Dominican Order, a number of minor works on theology, doctrine and local history of the Toulouse region, and the famous *Practice of the Office of the Inquisition.* This last work is one of our best sources for the history of the Inquisition, especially in southern France, and it is for his writings on the Inquisition that Gui is best known today.

A work which enjoyed great popularity at the time was the *Grandes Chroniques de France,* a general compilation of materials on the kings of France prepared and kept up by the monks of the royal abbey of St. Denis. The work was originally begun at the instigation of Abbot Suger and was continued by later and less skillful hands until the end of the fifteenth century. While this work is not without some value, it is extremely unequal in its various parts and is on the whole a work of only secondary importance; but it had a tremendous vogue and was reproduced in many

---

[5] C. G. Coulton has translated much of Salimbene in his *From St. Francis to Dante* (1906) and H. O. Taylor has used him as the basis of his chapter "The World of Salimbene," a description of ecclesiastical life in *The Medieval Mind.*

manuscripts. Suger's reputation as a historian rests, however, not on his connection with the *Grandes Chroniques,* but on his excellent lives of Louis VI and Louis VII and on his account of his own work at St. Denis. These are all works of prime importance, written by the man who was the chief minister of the kings whose biographies he wrote. The *Life of Louis VII* is incomplete, as Suger died long before the king, but the *Life of Louis VI* is a masterpiece of medieval biography. Philip Augustus was not so fortunate in his biographers, the best account of his reign being that by Rigord and William the Breton. For many of the events of his reign we are better served by English than by French historians. With Joinville's *Life of St. Louis,* however, we come to what is considered by many to be the finest biography written in the Middle Ages, as well as one of the great monuments of Old French prose. The *Life* was written by Joinville (1225–1317), when he was in his eighties, at the request of Queen Joan of Navarre, to preserve the memory of the noble deeds and character of the king he loved so deeply. While the narrative deals chiefly with St. Louis' crusade, at the beginning and the end of the book are chapters dealing with the character and sayings of the king. The personality of no monarch of the medieval period stands out so clearly as does that of St. Louis in this intimate and inimitable biography. Other lives of St. Louis, but far inferior to Joinville's, were written by his confessor Geoffroi de Beaulieu, his chaplain William of Chartres, and the confessor of Queen Marguerite, William de Saint-Pathus. Geoffroi's work was the basis for the official biography of St. Louis written by the court historian of Philip III, William de Nangis. William wrote also a *Gesta Philippi III* for his patron and a *Chronicon* to 1303, which, although without great value, was very popular and often copied by later writers. In addition to these Latin works, William wrote a *Chronicle of the Kings of France* which was continued from 1303 to 1381. Written first in Latin, this was rewritten by William in French, which shows the increasing use of the vernacular at this time. Other historians who wrote in the vernacular, Villehardouin, and Robert de Clari, will be discussed under the head of crusader historiography.

Local histories were of course written as in the earlier period, and some of the most important French historians of the twelfth century were the chroniclers of special districts. Lambert of Ardres wrote a *Chronicle of Guines and Ardres* to 1203, while Gislebert of Mons' *History of Hainault* told the local history of that region from 1150 to 1195. One of the best of the historians of the Low Countries was Galbert of Bruges who wrote a history of Flanders for the years 1127 to 1128, with a detailed account of the murder of Count Charles the Good.

The history of Normandy was intimately connected with that of England, and the British historians naturally have much to say about it, but there existed a definite school of Norman historians of whom the greatest was Ordericus Vitalis (1075–1143). The *Ecclesiastical History of Normandy* written by this English-born monk of St. Evroul, includes in its nine books the history of Normandy, France, England, the abbey of St. Evroul, and the Norman expansion in Italy and on the First Crusade. A. Molinier terms Ordericus "the best French historian of the twelfth century." [6] Some of his material he gained at first hand from participants in the events recorded; much he derived from earlier sources which he used critically and discriminately. The style is easy and clear, and Ordericus brings out well the dramatic aspects of his narrative. Other Norman historians, less important that Ordericus but still of considerable value, are William of Poitiers, who wrote a biography of William the Conqueror, and William of Jumieges who did a history of Normandy which was continued to 1137 by Robert of Torigny, later abbot of Mont St. Michel. Robert was also the author of a continuation of a universal history by Sigebert of Gembloux from 1150 to 1186. Benoit de St. More also wrote a history of the Norman dukes to 1135 in verse, which is without originality. More important is the *Roman de Rou* of Wace, a verse history of the dukes of Normandy from Rollo to 1106. Written in Old French verse, the *Roman* has some of the qualities of an epic. English readers are more familiar with his *Roman de Brut,* the story of the British from Brutus on, which was translated into Anglo-Saxon by Layoman.

Before leaving France to discuss the English historians across the Channel, mention must be made of one of the most erudite and critical of the French writers, Guibert de Nogent (1053–1124), who wrote a history of the First Crusade, which he entitled the *Gesta Dei per Francos,* an autobiography, and a work on relics. Guibert was well versed in both Patristic and classical literature and his *Gesta Dei* was admittedly merely putting into better Latin the crude prose of the Anonymous *Gesta Francorum.* But he is better known for his critical and sceptical attitude towards relics, and for the denunciation of the communes, which is found in his *Autobiography.* He represented the clerical opposition to the emancipation of the communes, and nowhere can we get a clearer picture of the struggle of the towns for self-government than in his pages.

Special notice should also be given the historians of the crusade against the Albigensians: Pierre de Vaux-Cernay, William de Puylaurens, and the *Chanson de la Croisade des Albigois,* an epic poem begun by William de Tudele and completed by another hand. While Pierre was a devout partisan of de Montfort, both William de Puylaurens and William de Tudele were Catholics in the service of the counts of Toulouse and so more unbiased in their judgments. All three are valuable documents for the history of the vicious religious war.

[6] A. Molinier, *Les Sources de l'Histoire de France* (Picard, 1902), II, 220.

English

In no aspect of the Twelfth-Century Renaissance did England play a more brilliant role than in the writing of history. The twelfth and thirteenth were stirring centuries in England, and they called forth historians capable of properly commemorating their accomplishments. In England, as in France, there grew up a school of historians connected with the court, who based their works on official documents, but the greatest historical works were produced not at the court, but in the monasteries, such as Peterboro and St. Albans.

Of the court histories the most interesting is the anonymous *Gesta Henrici Secundi,* which was long erroneously attributed to Benedict of Peterboro. It is an official court chronicle full of chancery documents and the best single source for the reign of Henry II. It was copied almost verbatim, with additions, by Roger of Hoveden. Another official history, containing valuable documents, is the *Imagines historiarum* of Ralph of Diceto, dean of St. Pauls, which is important for the years 1183 to 1202. Closely related to historical writing were the works in law and government which were produced at the court of Henry II: the *Dialogus de Scaccario* (*Dialogue on the Exchequer*) by Richard Fitz-Neal (whom Bishop Stubbs thinks may have been the author of the *Gesta Henrici*), and the *De Legibus Angliae* of Ranulph Glanville, a royal justiciar. The former is a detailed description of the procedure in the exchequer, while Glanville's book is a treatise on law as practiced in the courts of Henry II.

Among the great monastic schools of historians the oldest was that of Northumbria, which traced its foundation back to Bede. In the early twelfth century Simeon of Durham wrote a universal history, based primarily on earlier materials but an original source for the period 1121 to 1129. This was continued by Richard and John of Hexham to 1154. The reigns of Stephen and Henry II were described in the history of William of Newburgh, who has been termed the "Father of historical criticism" by E. A. Freeman, and who is described by G. B. Adams as "the most modern of the twelfth century historians." Another important writer of this school was Roger of Hoveden, who wrote a history of England from 449 to 1201. The whole reign of Henry II was taken bodily from the *Gesta Henrici,* but Roger is original for the period 1193 to 1201. He includes the texts of many documents and covers much more than the history of England, being quite full on the Third Crusade and on affairs on the Continent. His work was continued by Walter of Coventry for the period 1202 to 1216, and is one of the most valuable sources for the reign of John.

Even more illustrious than the Northumbrian school was the group of historians who were connected with the monastery of St. Albans just outside of London. About 1180 the abbot of St. Albans established an official historian for the monastery, and Abbot John de Cella wrote a history covering the years 1195 to 1214. This was copied and continued in the *Flowers of History*, by Roger of Wendover, who added excellent original materials for the period 1216 to 1235. The school reached its height, however, in the continuator of Roger, Mathew Paris, whose *Chronicles* (Major and Minor) cover the years 1235 to 1259. Mathew Paris has often been acclaimed the greatest historian of the Middle Ages, a title which seems well merited by the vividness of his style and the wide scope of his information. In addition to events in England and France, Mathew has long sections on the happenings in Syria and the East, Italy, eastern Europe, and the best account of the Mongol invasions to be found in any Western chronicler. For the history of thirteenth century Europe in general there is no one to compare with Mathew, and he may justly be termed not only the greatest medieval but the greatest English historian. Mathew was continued by several hands but the work only became important again with Rishanger under the first two Edwards. Thereafter the St. Albans' school faded into insignificance.

Next to Mathew Paris in medieval English historiography must be rated William of Malmesbury, who is conceded the best English historian between Bede and Mathew. His *Gesta Regum* covers the years 449 to 1128, and his *Historia Novella* the period 1128 to 1142. He had a truly modern conception of historical writing, and the vividness of his descriptions and the ease of his style lift him far above the general level of his contemporaries.

Other English historians of lesser importance include Florence of Worcester, valuable for the period 1082 to 1117, and his continuator John of Worcester who carried his narrative down to 1141. The work was continued further by the monks of St. Edmundsbury, but declined in value and importance after 1141. Eadmer, a monk of Canterbury, wrote a history which is valuable for the accounts of Lanfranc and Anselm (1066–1121); Gervase of Canterbury supplies important information for the period 1188 to 1199, and Ralph of Coggeshall, a Cistercian abbot, whose chronicle covers the years 1066 to 1223, is valuable for the period after 1187. He gives much information on the crusade of Richard and is extremely useful for the reign of John. Richard's crusade was also treated by Richard of Devizes and by Ambroise (who will be discussed below). Of little value for political history, but full of information on twelfth-century social and economic conditions is the monastic chronicle of Joscelin of Brakelond. The history of Henry of Huntington, which was once rated very highly is now known to be inaccurate and rhetorical and without great significance.

The Crusades

The crusades as a movement produced in Western Europe not only a great physical and spiritual response but also a historiographical reaction. Never before had men attempted so much, never had their deeds been more worthy of recording, and the crusades developed a literature which must be considered separately from the histories of the various nations participating.

The First Crusade was the most productive of eye-witness accounts. The most valuable single narrative is the anonymous *Gesta Francorum,* written during the course of the crusade by a follower of Bohemond. The work is written in the simplest Latin of the time, and gives a straight-forward account of the events of the expedition as viewed by a man in the ranks of the army. This narrative was brought back to Europe (perhaps by Bohemond himself to serve as propaganda for his second expedition) and was immediately made the basis for a number of contemporary histories, the most important of which was the *Gesta Dei per Francos* of Guibert de Nogent. Scarcely less important than the *Gesta* is the *Historia Hierosolymitana* of Fulcher of Chartres, the chaplain of Baldwin I, whose chronicle covers not only the events of the crusade itself but the history of the Latin kingdom to 1127. Fulcher accompanied Baldwin to Edessa and so missed the siege of Antioch, but apart from that his account has the value of an eyewitness for the whole movement. The chronicler of the Provençals, and the third most important source for the First Crusade, was Raymond of Agiles, the chaplain of Raymond de St. Gilles, who participated in the entire crusade and has left a circumstantial account of it. Raymond is an ardent champion of the Holy Lance and his history gives the most detailed story of its discovery. Hardly inferior to the eyewitness accounts was the *Gesta Tancredi* of Raoul de Caen, the secretary of Tancred who wrote the biography of his hero from notes dictated by Tancred himself. Albert of Aix also, although he did not personally participate in the crusade, secured the materials for his history from returned crusaders, and is now accepted as a prime source for the crusade and the history of the kingdom to 1120. Closely akin to the work of Albert is the Old French poem, *Le Chanson d'Antioche,* which was apparently written by a trouvère eyewitness, but there has been much scholarly debate as to the relation of Albert and the *Chanson,* and the question whether they drew from each other is still unsolved.

In addition to these accounts, all of which can claim the authority of first-hand sources, are a number of contemporary histories, all based on the *Gesta Francorum* or Fulcher with little original material added. These works were formerly accepted as independent sources but are now recognized as secondary, if contemporary, accounts; they are Robert the Monk,

Tudebode, Baldric de Bourgueil, Guibert de Nogent, Lisard of Tours, and Fulco and Gilo.

The crusade of 1101 was chronicled by Cafaro, the author of the *Annales Ianuensis,* and by Ekkchard of Aura, both of whom took part in the disastrous expedition.

For the periods between the crusades from the West, the history of the Latin states becomes extremely scanty. Walter the Chancellor described the events in Antioch under Roger in the years 1115 to 1119, but the only work of first importance on the kingdom of Jerusalem in the twelfth century is the *History of the Deeds Done Across the Sea* by William, archbishop of Tyre (c. 1130–1185). Although no longer considered of especial value for the events of the First Crusade, William is the one great chronicler of the kingdom from 1127 to 1184. Archbishop of Tyre and chancellor of the kingdom, learned in Arabic as well as Latin, William was in a position to write authoritatively concerning the developments in Syria. If his chronology is sometimes slightly faulty, his genealogical and geographical information is excellent, and his intimate acquaintance with many of the principals of his history make his work lively and dramatic. William gives us by far the best account of the Second Crusade after it reached Syria.[7] The expedition of Louis VII from France to the East is elsewhere told by Odo de Deuil who accompanied the king, while that of Conrad III is given by Otto of Freising. An interesting episode in this crusade, the capture of Lisbon by the Anglo-German fleet, is the subject of a special narrative: *The Conquest of Lisbon.*

The Third Crusade produced almost as many historians as did the First. The Syrian story is best told in the *Histoire d'Eracles,* the Old French continuation of William of Tyre which runs in various recensions to 1228, 1231, 1261, and 1275. The first continuation was written by one Ernoul, a knight of Jerusalem, and gives the history of the crusade from the point of view of the Syrian nobility. Saladin's conquest of the kingdom was also recorded in the anonymous *Libellus de expugnatione terrae sanctae* and in an anonymous Latin continuation of William of Tyre. For the military expeditions from Europe we have the accounts of Tageno of Passau and Ansbert on Frederick Barbarossa, and Ambroise on Richard. Ambroise's *Estoire de la guerre sainte* is a long poem in Old French couplets, which gives a detailed account of Richard's crusade from his first departure from Europe to the treaty with Saladin. Strongly biased in favor of Richard and Guy de Lusignan, Ambroise is most hostile to Philip Augustus and to the local baronial party. Closely parallel to Ambroise is the *Itinerarium Regis Ricardi,* a Latin work written in England, which is so close as to seem a translation from Ambroise. The exact relationship

---

[7] On William see the excellent study of A. C. Krey, "William of Tyre," *Speculum,* XVI (1941), 149–66 and Krey's introduction to his translation of the *History.*

has not been definitely established, but the most recent theory is that both the French poem and the Latin prose work were derived from a French original prose text, now lost. Ambroise is probably the best single text for the history of Richard's crusade, but valuable supplementary materials are to be found in Roger of Hoveden, Richard of Devizes, and in a verse work by Haymarus, patriarch of Jerusalem (1194–1202).

The Fourth Crusade inspired one of the finest bits of medieval French prose in the *Conquest of Constantinople* by Geoffrey de Villehardouin. Villehardouin was one of the leaders of the crusade and prominent in the councils which guided its direction; his narrative is detailed and clear, explaining the diversion simply as a matter of circumstances. The work was attacked as an apology for the crusader chiefs, but more recently has been vindicated, and is now accepted as the correct interpretation of the crusade. A shorter account of the expedition was written, also in French, by Robert de Clari, a Picard knight, who gives the story as known to the men in the ranks and offers a good check on Villehardouin.

With the exception of Joinville's *Life of St. Louis* the later crusades did not give rise to literary work of the quality of the earlier. The best account of the Fifth Crusade is the *Conquest of Damietta* by Oliver of Paderborn, a German cleric who later became a cardinal. His history gives a detailed description of the siege and capture of Damietta and the expedition down the Nile, as well as considerable information about the Near Eastern lands at the time. His work was used by Jacques de Vitry in his history, which covers the events in the kingdom of Jerusalem in the late twelfth and early thirteenth centuries. Jacques was bishop of Acre and one of the most important preachers of the crusades; he is noted for his graphic and somewhat vitriolic style, his opinion of his parishioners being rather low.

Philip de Novare, a Cypriot jurist, wrote a history of the struggle of the Syrio-Cypriot barons against Frederick II and his baillies in the years 1229 to 1243, which was continued as *The Deeds of the Cypriots* (*Gestes des Chiprois*) through the early years of the fourteenth century. This was later translated into Italian and continued by Amadi and Florio Bustrone, but the only really great historian of Lusignan Cyprus was the Greek Leontios Makhairos, who wrote in the fifteenth century.

The crusades were described not only by the Latin but also by the Eastern Christian historians. A number of Armenian and Syriac chroniclers are valuable for various aspects of the movement. Mathew of Edessa, Michael the Syrian, Hayton of Armenia, and Gregory abul-Faradj (called Bar Hebraeus), all narrate the history of the crusade period from the point of view of the local Eastern Christian population.

The crusades also produced a considerable historical literature in Arabic. While many of these works are great chronicles covering long periods, there are also many local histories and a very considerable biographical literature. The only good Moslem account of the First Crusade is the *Damascus Chronicle* of Ibn al Qalanisi which gives the history of Damascus year by year from 1056 to 1160, with especial emphasis on the struggles with the Christians. Incidents of the early warfare between Frank and Moslem are recounted in the delightful *Memoirs* of Usamah ibn-Muniqdh (1095–1188), whose intimate gossipy souvenirs of his career as soldier and hunter give a fine insight into the manners and customs of the Arabic nobility of the twelfth century.

The rise of the Zanghids and Ayyubids brought on a group of historians who celebrated the deeds of Zanghi, Nureddin, and Saladin. Ibn al-Athir of Mosul (1160–1233) wrote not only a *History of the Atabegs of Mosul,* but a general chronicle of the years 1098 to 1230 in which he recounted the greatness of the Zanghids. Kemal ed-din (1192–1262) compiled a great history of Aleppo; Abu Chamah (1202–67) wrote a history of the reigns of Nureddin and Saladin, and Beha ed-din (1145–1234) wrote the best single biography of Saladin. The historical works of these men are the more important in that all of them were government officials, with access to official documents and often themselves privy to the inner councils of the rulers. Kemel ed-din was a vizier; Beha ed-din was an intimate of Saladin's and his biography is full of many personal touches. Biographies of the sultans as well as of most of the important men of the time were given in the great *Biographical Dictionary* of Ibn Kallikan (1211–82), a veritable mine of information about the ministers, scholars, and emirs of the Zanghid and Ayyubid periods. The *Annals* of Abu'l-Feda (1273–1331), although written later, have special value as their author was an Ayyubid prince of Hamah and well acquainted with the history of his house and area. The history of the later crusades is to be found primarily in the works of the Mameluk historians who wrote in the fourteenth and fifteenth centuries, but whose chronicles are of primary importance owing to their scrupulous citation of sources and historical accuracy. Among these should be noted Makrisi (1365–1442) who wrote a history of the crusade of St. Louis, as well as several other works on Egyptian history and archaeology, Badr ed-din al-Aini and Ibn Taghri Birdi, both fifteenth-century historians of the Mameluk sultans. Ibn Taghri Birdi is especially important for his references to social conditions and for his observations on economic data. While these writers were not at all contemporary with the crusades, they wrote of the relations with the Franks and are important sources for the history of the later crusade attempts. The greatest of all Moslem historians came, however, not from the East but from North Africa. Ibn Khaldun (1322–1406) was the foremost of all Moslem historians and the greatest historical philosopher of the Middle Ages; he is generally recognized to be the first great socio-economic historian, the first critical exponent of cultural history. With him Moslem historiography reached its zenith, and he is not only the greatest, but the last great Arabic historian.

CHAPTER 34

VERNACULAR LITERATURE AND CHIVALRY: THE CATHEDRALS

✢

GROWTH OF VERNACULAR LITERATURE

THE universities and the studies pursued there were essentially matters for the clergy. But intellectual life was by no means confined to the clerical profession, although it did enjoy almost a monopoly of the learned professions through the thirteenth century. The laity of the Middle Ages was far more literate than was formerly admitted, and the idea that no layman in medieval times could read or write must be discarded along with the Legend of the Year 1000.

It was among the laity and for its pleasure that the vernacular literatures developed. In Germany, Spain, Italy, England and above all in France both poems and prose were written in the vernacular throughout the twelfth and thirteenth centuries, Old French becoming the courtly language throughout western Europe. As we have seen, Canale in Venice and Philip de Novare in Cyprus both wrote their histories in French, and French was the language of literature in England, where Wace, Marie de France, King Richard, and others employed either French or Provençal for their literary works. Modern college courses in English literature too frequently devote themselves too exclusively to literature written in English, thus neglecting the great amount of work produced in both Latin and French.

We have already had occasion to note the use of the vernacular in historical writing. Villehardouin, de Clari, Joinville, the *Grandes Chroniques de France,* the *Eracles, Gestes des Chiprois, Guillaume le Marechal,* Ambroise, Hayton of Armenia, the *Chanson d'Antioche* and the *Chanson de la Croisade des Albigois* were all written in French, as were many others. Some of these were in prose, others in verse, but all employed the more familiar French language in preference to the more formal Latin.

Historical writing is seldom however the best literature. That Villehardouin and Joinville rise above the general level to become literary masterpieces is the exception, and on the whole it is in the field of more imaginative literature that the greatest literary monuments are found. In France, Germany, and Spain it was in the field of the epic *chansons de geste* or *romans d'aventure;* in Provence in the lyrics of the troubadours, that the best literary achievements were made. Italian vernacular literature is unimportant before Dante and can be omitted from our discussion until we consider the *Divine Comedy.*

THE OLD FRENCH EPIC CYCLES

Among the most interesting of the Old French poems are a number of epic cycles, each composed of a group of individual poems. The most important cycles are the Carolingian or national cycle; the Arthurian or Breton cycle; the cycle of the crusade; and the antique cycle about Troy and Alexander. The Carolingian cycle represents the *chansons de geste* at their best; the Arthurian is the supreme example of the *romans d'aventure.*

Between the Carolingian and Arthurian cycles great differences exist. According to J. Bédier, whose word is law in the matter of epic cycles, the *chansons de geste* were developed on the pilgrim roads, being narrated by unknown poets who sang them to the pilgrims journeying to a well-known shrine. The most famous example is the *Chanson de Roland,* which is the song of the pilgrim road through the Pyrenees to Santiago di Compestella. Others are associated with the pilgrimage to Rome, and A. Hatem has shown that part of the cycle of the crusade probably developed in connection with the pilgrim road at St. George of Lydda in Palestine. A later era was to give Geoffrey Chaucer the setting for his *Canterbury Tales* in the pilgrimage to the shrine of St. Thomas.

The *romans d'aventure,* on the other hand, were written, largely by known poets, for the amusement of the nobles in their castles. They were sung by minstrels as the nobles sat around the table in the great hall after dinner and provided amusement for the gentlefolk, much as the troubadour lyrics did in the courts of love in the Midi.

The chansons would naturally be hardier than the romans, and this is one of the main differences between them. Although both cycles were written at about the same time (i.e. eleventh through thirteenth centuries) they are utterly different in spirit and in the place accorded women in their stories. The pilgrim songs were designed for an essentially masculine audience, men who were facing hardship in fulfillment of a vow. The romans were for the pleasure of the ladies as they sat in their halls, and the feminine influence is strong on them. Henry Adams in his delightful *Mont Saint Michel and Chartres* compared the *Chanson de Roland* to the twelfth century romanesque architecture of the abbey of St. Michael and the romans to the thirteenth century Gothic of Chartres Cathedral, finding the former wholly masculine and militant and the latter devoted to the worship of the Virgin and women in general. But it was a difference of spirit, not of time, for some of the Arthurian stories are as old as the early Carolingian, and both continue through the thirteenth century.

On the whole the chansons are strictly feudal. Although the later stories are somewhat less brutal than the earlier ones, in all of them military prowess, hard blows given and received, vows kept or broken, enemies slaughtered in the name of God or the king are the predominating themes. Women play but minor roles, and when they do appear are either noble and competent wives and mothers or amorous wenches, in either case subordinate to the male. The deeds are the deeds of doughty men, and though exaggerated, have a basis in reality. There is also usually some vague historical incident which forms the basis of many of the stories of the chansons.

The Carolingian cycle includes between seventy and a hundred separate poems, all loosely connected by the fact that they center around the court of Charlemagne. The emperor is, however, but a minor figure in most of the tales; the heroes are his paladins, those brave knights whose accomplishments gave such lustre to his court. The greatest and probably the oldest of all the poems in the Carolingian cycle is the *Chanson de Roland,* which tells of the emperor's expedition into Spain to fight the Moors, of the black treason of Ganelon, and the heroic deeds and death of Roland at Roncevalles. It is a magnificent story of war, feudal loyalty and crusader zeal; love and the ladies play no part in it. Another poem which dates also from the eleventh century is the quite different *Pèlerinage de Charlemagne,* which recounts the deeds of the paladins on a pilgrimage which they are supposed to have made to Jerusalem. This poem is filled with a lusty humor and might be termed a good collection of tall tales in the section in which each hero seeks to outdo his comrades. The only possible relation to the *Roland* is in the names of the heroes participating.

On to Charlemagne were grafted a number of purely local legends and stories. Bédier finds these developing as the epics of local shrines and has identified most of them as to locale. The greatest of these local stories is the twenty-four-poem cycle of *Garin de Monglane* or of *Guillaume d'Orange,* an epic cycle in itself which is loosely grafted onto the Carolingian cycle by making the heroes vassals of the emperor. *Guillaume d'Orange, Girard de Vienne, Aymeri de Narbonne* show by their names the localization of the stories. In this cycle there is war against the Saracen, but also rebellion against the emperor, and feudal war among the barons themselves. Other local poems which were attached to the Charlemagne cycle include *Ogier le Danois, Girard de Rousillon, Les Quatre fils d'Aymon, Huon de Bordeaux* and others.

It should be noted that one tendency which runs through all the chansons is the family saga; in fact, Funck-Brentano has gone so far as to claim that all the chansons de geste were family poems extolling the virtues of a noble house.[1]

While this extreme statement of Funck-Brentano's cannot be accepted, there is no doubt as to the local and family interest in such poems as *Garin de Loherain, Raoul de Cambrai, Aymeri de Narbonne,* and *Guillaume d'Orange.* One aspect of this family interest was the building up of a hero's background with stories about his ancestors, and carrying the story down through generations of his descendants. Thus we find an *Enfances de Charlemagne* and a *Berthe aux grands pieds* developing purely fictitious parents for the emperor.

In the romans the poets allowed their imaginations to run unchecked; magic—both black and white, faery creatures, miraculous swords, love potions, enchanted princesses and all the impossibilities of faery legend abound in them. Perhaps this is due to their Celtic origin: Merlin and Morgan le Fay seem much more suited to Ireland or Cornwall than to France or Normandy, and Tristan is pure Celt, even when dressed up in the German of Gottfried von Strasbourg. In the Breton cycle the knights are forever rescuing damsels who have gotten themselves involved in the most dangerous and embarrassing situations, prowess in the boudoir is fully as important as valor in battle, men defend their honor and ladies lose theirs regularly through the poems. It would be grossly unfair to attribute this to the presence of a feminine audience. As Sidney Painter has so pungently remarked: "The composer of the songs dealt with what the knights of the day were interested in—war, feudal intrigue and light women. A high-born virgin burning with desire to climb into his bed has probably always been a favorite subject for man's daydreams." [2]

The Arthurian cycle deals with the adventures of King Arthur and the knights of his Round Table. The poems have no historical basis save in the fact that there may have been a British Arthur who fought the Saxons, but the Arthur of the poems is a feudal monarch of a faery country. Merlin the magician is one of the important characters in the cycle, and magic occurs throughout. Arthur secures his throne through a magic sword, at his death he is carried off to the magic land of Avalon by his faery cousin Morgan le Fay. Women may be said to dominate the Arthurian stories. While some heroes, like Gawain, roam fancy free through the stories, the grand passions of Lancelot for Guenivere and of Tristan for Yseult are the main themes of considerable parts of the cycle.

[1] F. Funck-Brentano, *The Middle Ages,* chapter 3. "The chanson de geste is the song of the family, composed to glorify the ancestors . . . 'Geste' means 'family' and especially so in the expression 'chanson de geste' by which epics are described." (pp. 50–52).

[2] S. Painter, *French Chivalry,* p. 104. Reprinted by permission of the publishers, the Johns Hopkins Univ. Press. This essay is by far the best treatment of chivalry in English and is indispensible for any study of the subject.

The Arthurian legends probably originated in Wales, Cornwall or Ireland and are found in good part in the Welsh *Mabinogian*. Written down in Latin in the pseudo-history of Geoffrey of Monmouth (c. 1100–1154) they were employed by Wace in his *Brut,* and carried across the Channel to France where they were written in French by Chrétien de Troyes (ca. 1160–80) at the court of Champagne. How far Chrétien was original and how far he derived his plots from older legends is a matter which is still disputed by Arthurian experts, but there can be little doubt but that he brought the stories together and fixed them in a form which they were to maintain for many years. Chrétien had little to say about Arthur personally; he dealt with Erec, Yvain, Lancelot, and Perceval, attaching to the Arthur stories the legend of the Holy Grail. From France the stories passed on to Germany where Wolfram von Eschenbach rewrote *Parzival*. Meanwhile *Tristan* had been brought over from Ireland to become a French romance by Berol and a German story by Gottfried von Strasbourg. Middle English versions of these stories also appeared and in the thirteenth century English prose romances further developed the legends. The *Grail, Merlin,* and *Lancelot* all appeared in English and in the following century Gawain reached his height in the story of *Gawain and the Grene Knight*. The literature on the Arthurian cycle makes an impressive bibliography and the student is referred to the studies of Ker, Weston, W. L. Jones, and Gollancz for further discussion of this cycle, which is still popular in the standard form given it by Sir Thomas Malory in the fifteenth century, the highly moralized transmogrification of Alfred Lord Tennyson in the Victorian era, or the cynical satires of our contemporary, Mr. John Erskine.

Classical antiquity also contributed the matter for epic poems in the twelfth century. The *Roman d'Alixandre,* the *Troie, Aeneas,* and *Thebes* dressed classical stories up in medieval costumes, and made the ancient heroes into feudal knights. The *Troie,* which was written by Benoit de St. More and dedicated to Queen Eleanor of Aquitaine, is considered the earliest of the romans which set the style for the courtly literature of the time.

An interesting cycle, and one which well illustrates the manner in which the epic cycles developed, is the cycle of the crusade. As we have seen, the story of the First Crusade was told in Old French verse by a contemporary poet in the *Chanson d'Antioche*. This is quite good history and is usable as an historical source of first importance for the movement. Then sometime after the crusade the *Conquête de Jerusalem* was written around the pilgrim shrine of St. George in Palestine. This is less historically accurate than the *Antioche,* but is not entirely without historical value and shows an intimate knowledge of the local geography. With these two historical poems as a starter, the growth of the cycle advanced rapidly. In *Les*

Chetifs, the adventures of a group of crusaders who wandered off from the First Crusade at Antioch is the subject of a romance full of heroic fights, alluring Moslem princesses, hairbreadth escapes and the other paraphernalia of romantic legend. The story is wholly fictitious save for the fact that the names of the heroes are derived from knights who took part in the crusade of 1101.

The next stage in the growth of the cycle was the creation of an appropriate ancestry for Godfrey de Bouillon, the hero of the *Chanson d'Antioche.* In *Les Enfances de Godefroi,* the youth of Godfrey is narrated and he is given as a childhood companion Kerbuqa, who came from Asia to learn chivalry in the West. The two boys go through numerous adventures, finally parting with the promise to meet in battle under the walls of Antioch. This, however, was not enough. The *Chevalier du Cygne,* the old story of the knight of the swan, was tacked on the front of the cycle to provide a fitting grandfather for the hero. The last two sections of the cycle are late in composition and show the degeneracy of the epic literary form. In the *Baudoin de Sebourc* and *Li Bastars de Bouillon* a wild conglomeration of adventures, enchantments, and heroic deeds are grafted on to the story, and the scene of the poem shifts all over Europe from Scotland and France to Sicily, Egypt, and Palestine. It is pure imaginative fiction, colored by a marked Flemish anticlericalism which makes the clergy the butt of jokes and derogatory remarks. The story ends in the usual manner with a number of marriages between the Christian heroes and Moslem princesses and between Moslem princes and the sisters of the Christian knights.

It should be observed that in these stories the Moslems are always converted.

The Moslem princesses invariably removed the handsome Christian captives from their fathers' dungeons and entertained them luxuriously and lasciviously in their own apartments. From the point of view of the composers of the *chansons* the great advantage of using Moslem ladies lay in the fact that eventually they could be converted. The baptism of a fair Saracen gave scope to their best lyrical efforts. The lady could be undressed and her charms and their effect on the knightly onlookers described in great detail all with the pious and worthy object of recounting a solemn religious ceremony.[3]

In addition to the cycles, there were, of course, many independent poems. The *Melusiné* told of the serpent woman who married the knight to become the ancestress of the house of Lusignan; *Aucassin and Nicolette* was a delightful story, part in verse and part prose, of the conventional boy-meets-girl variety, in which Aucassin, the son of a noble, loves the poor and humble Nicolette, but is prevented from marrying her by his father.

[3] S. Painter, *French Chivalry,* p. 103. Reprinted by permission of the publishers, Johns Hopkins Univ. Press.

How he was imprisoned for her sake, how she fled and he pursued her into the forest, how the lovely Saracen was converted and the obvious happy ending when the lovers are reunited is a familiar theme in the romances—and the general plot of most modern musical comedies. There are many other narrative poems but we cannot go into them here.

One of the most popular poetical works of the Middle Ages was the famous allegorical *Roman de la Rose*. Begun by William de Lorris about 1230 and completed by Jean de Meun about 1265, this poem of 12,780 lines starts as an allegory of the courts of love and rambles on to express the author's opinions on men, women, love, society, the church, secular institutions and anything else that came to his mind. William's idyllic and rather idiotic allegory was turned by Jean into a satire which had little to do with the original theme. The poem is very erudite and made a great impression on its contemporaries, but from our modern standards it is very dull stuff indeed.

Before leaving the subject of the epics, mention must be made of the cycle of *Renard the Fox,* the strictly bourgeois satire which poked fun at the chivalric poems. This animal epic deals with the varied adventures of Renard, the fox, the symbol of bourgeois cleverness, in his relations with the bear, lion, and wolf, who represent the powerful but stupid nobles. *Renard* went through many versions and was translated into German and English, passing into our children's literature as fables.

French and Provençal Lyrics

While the greatest individual works of Old French poetry were the epics, lyric poetry also developed, especially in the Midi. The form of the Provençal lyric seems to have been strongly influenced by the poetry of the Moors of Spain, and from Provence it spread into France and Italy. The center of Provençal literature was at first the court of Aquitaine, where William IX contributed many lyrics himself, and Eleanor was the patron of many troubadours. Provençal poetry always flourished in Aquitaine, Gascony, and Toulouse more than in Provence itself; after the destruction of the culture of the Midi by the Albigensian crusade, the troubadours fled to Italy where at the court of Frederick II they found a ready patron, and where developed a veritable school of Provençal literateurs.

The subject of the Provençal poets was primarily love. Bertrand de Born, it is true, expressed his joy in battles and carnage, but most of the poets dedicated themselves to more conventional love poems. The most common verse form was the *salut d'amour,* a letter in verse extolling the charms of the beloved and describing the tender passions aroused in the lover. Very popular also was the *tençon* in which poets debated a question of courtly love or behavior for the edification of the noble ladies in their audience. These tençons were often composed spontaneously by contestants in the courts of love, each author extemporizing verses to meet the points of his opponent. Proficiency in this art of extemporaneous poetry was admired among the southern French as among the Arabs.

The Provençal forms were also copied in northern France. Thibaut IV of Champagne, king of Navarre, wrote love songs to Blanche of Castile which have immortalized his lasting and correctly futile passion. Conon de Bethune, one of the leaders of the Third and Fourth crusades, wrote songs lamenting the necessity which took him to the East away from his lady-love. One of the most celebrated poems of the crusade was written by a lady who pointed out the great harm and evil which Jerusalem had done her in taking away her beloved.

Another popular verse form, both in Provençal and in northern French, was the *aube,* the song to the dawn which parted the lovers. *Rondeaux* were songs for dancing; the *sirviente* was often satirical and was not a love song. Over four hundred known troubadours are recorded as having written Provençal lyrics in a multitude of verse forms, but although there were many forms to choose from, the form, once chosen, was rigid and often quite complicated. The troubadour seldom sang his own compositions; he composed them and had them sung by minstrels who were professional entertainers. However, in the south it was considered correct for a troubadour occasionally to sing his own work, especially in contests of tençons, although in the north the trouvère never himself sang his verses. The sentiments expressed in the lyrics were usually as conventional as the forms of the verse; ideally the lady should be married, the lover has glimpsed her but once or twice, but so smitten with her charms has he become that he can think of nothing else. The verses should be sung under a balcony, and any fulfillment of his amorous desires was not mentioned as possible. Coarse physical love was on the whole frowned on by the courts of love, which set themselves on a high spiritual and emotional plane, but we need not infer from this that the men or women of the Midi were less amorously inclined than their northern contemporaries. Physical consummation had no part of courtly love; it was ideally unrealizable; if consummation happened to be achieved it was rather an accident than part of the game.

Although most of the troubadours are scarcely known by name, a number of them have left enough poems that they are well known. Raimbaut de Vaquiras, Peire Cardenal, Peire Vidal, Bernard de Ventadour, Jaufré Rudel, Bertrand de Born, and King Richard of England have all left lyrics which attest the high degree of technical perfection attained by these poets.

POETRY OUTSIDE OF FRANCE: DANTE

Much of the poetry of Germany, England, and Italy was the adaptation of stories or themes taken from the French, but in addition to this foreign literature, there developed in Germany and Spain what may be termed national epics. That of Spain was the story of the famous *Cid*, that adventurous knight who served Christian and Moslem alike in the border wars of the eleventh century and made himself independent lord of Valencia. In the epic, the Cid becomes the perfect Christian knight always eager to destroy the enemies of God and the king, but for an epic the poem has considerable historical basis in fact.

The German epic is the *Nibelungenlied,* the story of Siegfried, Brunhilde, Dietrich of Bern, and their fellows which is best known today as the vehicle for the tremendous music of Richard Wagner. This epic, written in the twelfth century and revised through the fourteenth, is full of spells and incantations, bloody fights and passionate love. It is characteristic of the German epic that while the action takes place generally in the court of tribal Burgundy, there is no central figure about whom the legends focus as in the case of Arthur or Charlemagne.

Lyric poetry also found expression in German in the songs of Walther von der Vogelweide, the great *minnesinger* (love poet) who sang of courtly love in the most approved fashion of the troubadours. Like the French and Provençal poets, Walther used his verse as a vehicle to express not only his conventional love sentiments, but his disapproval of the church and clergy. His criticism of the pope, Innocent III, for fomenting the Guelph-Ghibelline struggle in Germany has earned him a respected place among the patriotic writers of the German people.

The best English poetry was either of a religious nature or a fragment of the Arthurian story. Layamon's *Brut,* one of the most famous Old English poems, is little more than a translation of the *Brut* of Wace. Its chief importance is in connection with the transmission in English of the Arthurian materials and the other legends (Lear, etc.) which it derives from Wace.

The greatest poet of the Middle Ages, and the greatest Italian poet of any time, comes just at the end of our period in the person of Dante Aligheri. We have already noted the importance of this work in familiarizing us with the history of the period. Its literary effect was even greater, for it made the Tuscan dialect the language of literature in Italy, eclipsing the Neapolitan, Roman, Lombard, Venetian, and other rivals. No attempt will be made here to analyze this magnificent poem. Suffice it to note that it records the progress of the poet through Hell, Purgatory, and Paradise. Through the first two he is led by Virgil, through Paradise by Beatrice, his unattained beloved. The theology of the *Paradiso* is Thomistic, but the sins for which the sinners are suffering in the *Inferno* are rather those of Aristotle than those of the Church Fathers. In the lowest depth of Hell are the traitors: Brutus, Cassius, and Judas, those who betrayed God and the empire. Sexual sinners are found in the second circle, less severely punished than the gluttons, prodigals, or flatterers. Heretics occupy the sixth circle, much better off than those who have done violence to nature or art, magicians, hypocrites, thieves or fraudulent counsellors. In the crown of Heaven sits the emperor Henry VII, who tried to assert the imperial rule over Italy, while Hell awaits the coming of Boniface VIII, whose presence there was expected. But no description can in any way give even the most remote idea of the *Comedy,* and the student is again urged to read it for himself—preferably the story of Paolo and Francesca in canto V or that of Count Ugolino in canto XXXIII of the *Inferno.*

THE CATHEDRALS

To many people today the one contribution which made the medieval period at all significant was its architecture. The great cathedrals of Europe, dating from medieval times, are familiar to people who have otherwise no concept of the Middle Ages. Certainly these visible monuments of medieval culture afford impressive evidence of the artistic accomplishments of their builders. And to many there is no architectural form before or since which is as beautiful and inspiring as the graceful lines of Gothic architecture.

It has been said that it is impossible to genuinely admire both classical and medieval architecture. This is true to the extent that the vertical lines of Gothic and the horizontal lines of the classical do not generally appeal equally to a person. The beauty of each can be admired, but the one will produce an inner response which the other cannot induce. The great vistas of a Gothic church inspire an emotional reaction which is lacking in the colder perfection of Attic.

This chapter will not attempt a technical analysis of medieval architecture; that can best be had in technical works on art; we shall endeavor here to give some slight idea of the various styles (Byzantine, Romanesque, Gothic), and to show the place played by the cathedral in the life of the medieval community.

For the finest appreciation of medieval architecture, the student is referred to Henry Adams' brilliant *Mont Saint Michel and Chartres,* which is fundamentally an emotional and spiritual appreciation of Gothic art and the society which produced it. In my opinion no one has ever succeeded in capturing the spirit of Gothic as well as Adams, and reading his book for the first time is an experience which will never be forgotten. But Chartres is not the only great Gothic cathedral, and Bourges, Amiens, Rheims, the

Sainte Chapelle and others could as well have been taken as the point of departure.

Gothic is, moreover, only one (if the finest) of medieval architectural forms. There are beauties in the Byzantine and Romanesque which are as fine as those of Gothic; if Byzantine churches lack the graceful lines and magnificent vistas of the Gothic, they are resplendent in their mosaics and their use of colored marbles. Monreale, just outside Palermo, which combines Byzantine decoration with Romanesque design is, in the author's personal opinion, in many ways the most impressive building in Europe.

Basilica and Byzantine Styles

The earliest Christian churches were constructed on the model of Roman public buildings in what is known as the basilica form. They were rectangular buildings, with rows of columns marking out aisles and supporting a flat wooden roof. The main portion of the church, known as the nave, was flanked by the aisles; across the end of the nave and aisles ran a cross aisle, called the transept. On the other side of the transept, opposite the nave, was an extension, usually semi-circular in shape, called the apse. This gave the basilica roughly the shape of a cross, with the apse as the head. The walls of the center aisle of the nave were built up higher than the side aisles, so that above the lower side walls was raised a clerestory, in which were put windows to let in more light.

The interiors of many of the basilica were decorated with mosaics and colored stone, so that with the light streaming in through the clerestory, they presented a very colorful picture. The churches of San Apollinare in Ravenna and the late basilica of St. Pauls-outside-the-Walls in Rome are fine examples of basilican architecture.

While the basilica was the standard form of church construction, vaulted and domed churches soon began to be built. The dome probably came from Syria or Asia Minor and was used effectively on smaller churches which were often round or octagonal in shape. The use of the dome on a basilica presented great difficulties, however, for the space to be covered by the dome was the square area where the nave crossed the transept, and to put a round dome over a square area was obviously difficult. It was the ingenious architects of Justinian's great cathedral of Hagia Sophia in Constantinople who solved this problem. They did it by resting the dome on *pendentives:*—building up triangular concave walls at the four angles of the square and resting the dome on the circle they formed. Hagia Sophia is the greatest of all Byzantine churches and the model upon which countless others were based throughout the East and in parts of southern Europe. Outside of Constantinople, fine examples of Byzantine architecture are found in St. Marks at Venice, St. Front at Perigeux, San Vitale at Ravenna, and in many cities of south Russia, Sicily, and the Balkans. Moreover, Byzantine decoration was copied in many places where the architectural plan was not followed, so that the full extent of Byzantine influence in art is difficult to assess. In Germany and Italy under the Ottos, Byzantine influence was especially strong in the matters of carved ivories, manuscript illumination, and enamels. The strength of the Byzantine influence is well demonstrated by the group of domed churches in southern France, best respresented by St. Front at Perigeux, which were built in the Byzantine style in the great age of French cathedral building.

Until the recent uncovering of the mosaics at Hagia Sophia, the finest Byzantine mosaics in the West were thought to be in Ravenna and at Cefalu in Sicily. At Ravenna in the church of San Vitale are the famous mosaic portraits of Justinian and Theodora with their courts, at Sant Apollinare Nuovo is a fine frieze of saints clear around the nave just below the clerestory. At Cefalu the mosaics are badly damaged, but enough remains to judge of their brilliance and exquisite workmanship. But even these Western mosaics are surpassed by the work at Hagia Sophia which has been uncovered by the efforts of Mr. Thomas Whittemore and the Byzantine Institute with the co-operation of the Turkish Republic. The posthumous portrait of Justinian there is said to be even finer than that at Ravenna.

Although they are not as well done as some of the others, the mosaics at Monreale are among the most impressive in the world. For Monreale has what no other church possesses, the long vista of the columnar nave with its clerestory walls covered with mosaics leading to the apse with its single gigantic figure of Christ in benediction dominating the entire church.

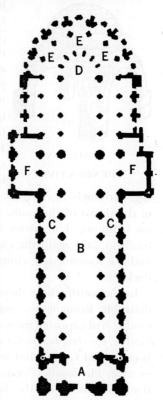

GROUND PLAN: RO-
MANESQUE CHURCH
St. Étienne, Caen

A. *Narthex*
B. *Nave*
C. *Side Aisles*
D. *Apse*
E. *Ambulatory*
F. *Transepts*

ROMANESQUE ARCHITECTURE

While the East was developing its domed churches, the West adhered to the simple wooden roofed basilica. Modifications were made in the Carolingian period but it was not until the eleventh century that Romanesque can be said to have been fully developed. The basic feature of Romanesque was a vaulted ceiling, at first a simple barrel vault extending the entire

length of the church, then a groined vault. This vaulting was necessary, as stone roofs had replaced the too inflammable wooden ones. The roof was still supported by heavy piers, the vault at first spanning the aisle from the wall supported by the piers. Then the vaulting was run not only between the piers across the aisles but between piers on the side walls. In this way the height of the vault was elevated somewhat. From the piers of the center aisle additional

DOME ON
PENDENTIVES

vaults ran over to those of the side walls. But to support the tremendous weight of stone vaulting, extremely heavy piers were needed. The side walls, which took some of the thrust of the vault, had to be heavy, and there was little space left for windows. The center aisle was higher than the side aisles, as in the basilicas, and again the clerestory afforded light, but this was not much, and the Romanesque churches in northern Europe were generally rather dark.

In the south where there was more sun, and where a cool building was desirable, Romanesque continued to hold sway long after the much lighter Gothic had captured most of the north. While the Italians speak of Italian Gothic, the style was never really understood there and their churches never became real Gothic, but were always essentially basilican or Romanesque in style. The façades (western front) of many Romanesque churches closely resembled those of the basilicas, with a high center aisle and lower side aisles, reflected by different heights of the façade. The façade of the cathedral of Pisa is one of the finest in the whole of eleventh century Italian Romanesque, with the baptistery and the campanile being separate buildings, not attached to the church. In France fine examples of Romanesque are to be found at Vezelay, Arles, Toulouse, Angoulême, Limoges, Poitiers, Le Puy, Clermont, and the cloister of the abbey of Moissac in the south,

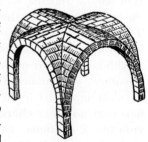

GROIN VAULT

and in the Norman churches at Bayeux, Rouen, and Mont St. Michel. Under the name of Norman architecture, Romanesque was popular in England, and was employed for at least parts of the churches at Durham, Norwich, Gloucester, Hereford, Winchester, Peterboro, and Exeter. In Italy, Romanesque was the prevalent form, notable examples being found in Palermo, Bari, Verona, Pavia, Piacenza, Lucca,

Milan (San Ambrogio) and San Miniato just outside Florence. The best German Romanesque is at Worms, Treves, Spires, Aix-la-Chapelle, and the Church of the Apostles at Cologne. It spread to the north where the cathedral of Lund in Sweden is a fine Romanesque building, and was carried to the East, as in the churches at Beirut and Tortosa.

THE DEVELOPMENT OF GOTHIC

While Romanesque was satisfactory for the south, it was too dark for the north, and architects sought some means whereby the churches could be better lighted. The solution to this problem was worked out by the builders of France, and consisted in substituting flying buttresses for the heavy masonry walls, and in breaking or pointing the arch. The flying buttresses —a heavy pier outside the building with a half-arch to the wall supporting the thrust of an arch inside—enabled the builders to lighten the walls and open more windows. The pointed arch enabled them to achieve height impossible in the Romanesque churches. Instead of the arch running from one pier to another, the arches were made higher, and pointed so that they met higher up, and the thrust of this pointed arch on the buttress was greatly reduced in comparison with a semicircular one at the same height and span. The whole thing was a matter of thrust and counter-thrust, resulting in the carrying of extremely heavy loads on relatively light walls and arches. The main piers, from which arches sprang in all directions, were massive, but the side piers could be much lighter and still bear the weight.

With the development of Gothic it became possible to have a much higher clerestory, pierced throughout with wider windows. As the side walls were also pierced, this enabled the churches to be quite light—an important consideration in the regions where days were short and the light less brilliant.

As the Gothic styles developed during the great age of cathedral building in the twelfth and thirteenth centuries, many churches were begun in Romanesque and finished in Gothic. Typical of these transition churches is Notre Dame at Paris, which is, however, chiefly Gothic. The greatest Gothic cathedrals are all found in northern France, at Amiens, Beauvais, Rheims, Bourges, Chartres, La Mans, Coutances, Rouen, and Strasbourg, but there are fine examples of Gothic at Albi in the south, at Antwerp, Brussels and Liége in the Low Countries, and at Cologne, Ulm, Ratisbon, Marburg, and Vienna in Germany. The only truly Gothic cathedral in Italy is Milan which was not built until the fifteenth century, although Florence, Siena, Orvieto, Assisi, Palermo, and others are termed Italian Gothic. In England, Canterbury, Litchfield, Lincoln, Salisbury, Wells and York are primarily in the early English style of Gothic though they frequently have later or Perpendicular additions. Westminster Abbey is a combination of all styles,

having been rebuilt in almost every period from the Saxon through the
Tudor, but much of it is Gothic from the reign of Henry III. Gothic architecture was also carried to the East by the crusaders, the cathedrals of
Nicosia, and Famagusta, and the Abbey of Lapais in Cyprus being splendid
examples of the style.

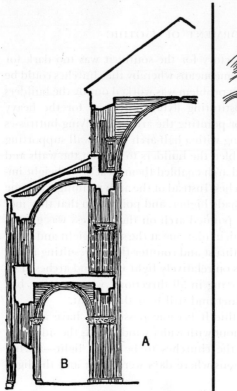

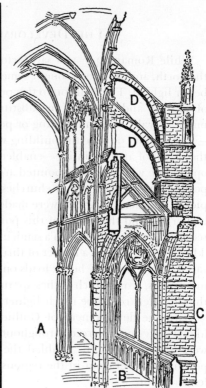

ROMANESQUE CHURCH   GOTHIC CATHEDRAL
St. Étienne, Caen   *Amiens*

CROSS SECTIONS
A. *Nave*
B. *Side Aisles*
C. *Buttress*
D. *Flying Buttresses*

The essential characteristics of both Romanesque and Gothic churches
are the long vaulted naves, the apses surrounded by chapels, the wide transepts, and the towers on the west front and over the crossing of the nave and
transept. The churches were almost invariably cruciform, with the apse
(containing the altar) at the east and the façade at the west. The façade con-

tained as many doors as there were aisles, usually three, but sometimes, as at Bourges, five. Above the doors on the façade was the rose window, and similar doors and roses were placed in each transept. In French Gothic the towers on the façade were the heaviest, in English the tower over the crossing of the nave and transept was usually the highest. There was the utmost variety in the matter of towers; Paris, Coutances, Chartres, Rheims, Amiens had heavy towers on the west with lighter and thinner towers over the crossing; the English went in for larger towers over the crossing; Wells, Ripon, Durham, York, Canterbury, Litchfield and Lincoln had towers on the west but a larger one at the crossing; Salisbury, Worcester, Norwich, Chichester, Gloucester, Hereford, and Chester had a tremendous tower over the crossing but none on the west front; Exeter had towers on the transepts only, Ely had one huge tower on the west and a smaller one on the crossing. The towers were often uneven in height or different in size and shape. The towers at Chartres were built at various times and are quite different; Strasbourg completed but one tower, the other not having been raised above the level of the roof. Beauvais has no façade or nave at all. There was a great rivalry among the various towns in the building of their cathedrals and each tried to outdo its neighbors; the people of Amiens built their cathedral to the extreme interior height of 141 feet; the men of Beauvais determined to build theirs even higher. They put up their church and reached the height of 154 feet, but unfortunately they had secured height without sufficient support and the whole roof fell in (1284). The apse was rebuilt, and later transepts were constructed, but the nave was never rebuilt and the church stands today without a nave or any façade. Inside, the builders were forced to insert extra piers between the original piers to support the weight and to tie them in with iron rods. The cathedral thus presents a rather confused picture and lacks the beauty of Amiens, Bourges, and others, but the good people of Beauvais have the distinction of having the highest vault in Europe (Bourges and Rheims are 125 ft.; Chartres 106).

One of the most interesting churches in France is the cathedral of Albi, which looks much more like a fortress than a church from outside. As Albi was the heart of the Catharist heresy, the Catholic bishop had to build a church which could be defended from attack. The result is a heavy building with one large tower on the west front, straight sides and a curved apse, surmounted by guard towers. It is built on a hill and a drawbridge leads to the entrance, but the interior is beautifully vaulted (the 59 ft. span of the vault being the widest in France).

SCULPTURE AND DECORATION

One of the characteristics of medieval architecture is the lavish employment of sculpture to ornament the building. And the sculpture is invariably organic; unlike the churches of Renaissance Italy where pictures were painted and hung in the churches, the decoration of Romanesque and Gothic churches was an integral part of the structure. The statues are parts of the piers, doorways, arches, and capitals. This is one reason why Gothic statuary has always that lean and emaciated look; the statue is one with the pier and partakes of its height and slenderness.

The chief places for sculptural decoration were the portals. On the west front was the three- or five-door portal, on the transepts were additional doors. These were regularly recessed back between heavy masonry piers, around which ran groups of statues. These statues represented saints, kings, the apostles, Christ, the Virgin, the virtues, vices, the arts. Various portals were devoted to special stories or episodes; the Last Judgment, the Last Supper, the Creation, flood, scenes from Old and New Testaments were depicted in the reliefs which surrounded the doors.

The best way to describe the sculptural decoration of a cathedral will be to examine one church in detail. Henry Adams has analyzed Chartres; let us look at Amiens. The cathedral of Notre Dame of Amiens was begun by Bishop Evrard de Fouilloy, who laid the first stone of his church in 1220. An earlier Romanesque church had been destroyed by fire in 1218, and the bishop had an opportunity to build the vast edifice of his dreams. The cost of construction was born chiefly by the local clergy and townspeople, but many outsiders, among them King Philip, contributed generously to the work. The nave was completed by 1236, the choir was finished in 1269, but the chapels are of later construction. The towers were not finished until much later, that on the north being completed only in 1366 and the south in 1402. The church consists of a three-aisle nave of six bays, flanked by chapels, a transept with three bays on each side, and an apse, which includes the choir, ambulatory and seven chapels. There are three doors on the façade, and one in each transept, with rose windows over the central western portal and over each of the transept doors. The façade mounts up five tiers: the portal, a gallery at the height of the triforium inside, a second gallery, the rose window, and the towers. The towers are uneven, the northern being higher than the southern. The great central portal was built between 1225 and 1236 and is in some ways the finest in France. The central door is dedicated to Christ, the two smaller ones to the Virgin and to St. Firmin, the first bishop of Amiens. In the central pier or trumeau of the main doorway is a great statue of Christ in benediction, resting his feet on the lion and the dragon. In the recesses of the main door are a series of the twelve apostles and four prophets. Each apostle and prophet is recognizable because of the standardized iconographical emblems. St. Peter carries the keys, St. Andrew bears a cross, St. Jacques has his shell, St. John a chalice, St. Paul a book and sword, St. Philip a stone. Figures of the lesser prophets adorn the outer face of the portal. In the tympanum, above the figure of Christ, is portrayed the Last Judgment. The tympanum is in four registers or friezes, the first showing the resurrection of the dead from their graves as angels blow trumpets. St. Michael sits in the middle weighing souls in a balance. In the frieze above, the souls are divided and sent to heaven or hell. Above this scene sits Christ in Judgment. He is surrounded by the Virgin, St. John the Evangelist and the symbols of the Passion. In the uppermost tier is again a head of Christ from whose mouth come two swords, while angels hold the sun and the moon. In the six ranges of carved figures which surround the tympanum are depicted: Abraham receiving the souls of the saved into his bosom, devils tormenting the damned in hell, the beasts of the Apocalypse, angels, martyrs, confessors, the Jewish patriarchs, and the wise and foolish virgins. In the spaces below the feet of the apostles are shown in bas-relief the virtues and vices, and below each of the prophets are scenes from his life.

In the southern portal of the west front, the place of honor in the center pier is held by the Virgin holding the Child in her arms. Under her feet is a serpent, and in the space below the statue are scenes from the story of Adam and Eve. The great statues on the right of the central statue show scenes in the life of Mary: the Annunciation, Visitation, Presentation at the Temple; on the left are the three wisemen offering gifts, Herod, Solomon, and the Queen of Sheba. The tympanum contains a lower frieze of Old Testament figures, above which are shown the death and assumption of the Virgin, and above that her coronation.

The door of St. Firmin has the saint in the central position, flanked on either side by other saints. The tympanum is devoted to scenes from the life of St. Firmin and the translation of his relics to Amiens. In the medallions below the feet of the saints are shown the signs of the zodiac and the months of the year with their various occupations.

Above the portals is a gallery of graceful columns; above this and directly below the rose is the gallery of the kings. Here are depicted the kings of France; similar galleries are found at Paris, Chartres, and Rheims.

The portal of the south transept is that of the Golden Virgin, so-called because the statue of the Virgin there was once covered with gold leaf. The trumeau figure is the Virgin holding the Child, immediately above her in the tympanum are eight figures: two angels and six saints, and also scenes from the lives of the various saints. The north transept, on the other hand, is only slightly ornamented. There is a statue of a bishop from the thirteenth century, a few bas-reliefs, and figures of animals and plants in the vaults. There are lovely rose windows in both transepts.

As will be observed from the above meagre description, the ornamentation of the Gothic church served a double purpose. It was organic in that it was part of the piers, walls or other integral parts of the building; it was never just tacked on unnecessarily. It was also functional in that it taught the parishoner the stories of the Bible, of the saints, and reminded him of moral precepts. The medieval cathedral has often been called "the Bible of the unlettered" or "Bible in stone" and such it truly was, for by looking at the sculptures around the doors the visitor was told the stories of the Testaments and reminded of the truths of religion. It must be remembered that medieval symbolism was rigid; each saint had his own attributes, each virtue and vice its own symbol. The most illiterate could recognize at once the familiar figures of apostles, saints, and the patriarchs.

One important feature of the medieval cathedral is almost entirely lacking at Amiens. It has no good glass outside of the rose windows, and the storied windows which are the glory of Chartres and Bourges are not to be found at Amiens. The windows also told stories of the Bible, the lives of the saints and other edifying subjects. Occasionally there was a window devoted to a secular theme, as in the Roland window at Chartres, which tells in glass medallions the story of the *Chanson de Roland*. But these are rare, and mostly the windows depicted the patron saint of the gild which paid for the glass. On the lower level are found the story windows; above, in the clerestory, where it is too high to distinguish small figures, the window is usually filled with a single huge figure of the saint. These windows give the churches they ornament a peculiar majesty. In the twelfth century, blue was the favorite color of the glass workers, in the thirteenth red, but the windows contain all shades of color. The very imperfections of the glass and the results of the weathering for centuries have given these windows shades and beauty which modern glass cannot entirely match.

Inside the church, the windows afford the chief decoration, but there is still much sculpture. The capitals of the columns are ornamented with figures, each one telling its story by allusion. There were often elaborately carved choir-screens, elaborate grills, and even sculptured seats in the choir. The screen at Amiens, which is one of the special treasures of the cathedral, is late, dating from the sixteenth century, but the symbolism is that of the thirteenth. For a comprehensive study of the iconography of the sculptures and decorations of medieval churches the reader is referred to Émile Male's *Religious Art in France in the Thirteenth Century*.

THE CATHEDRAL AND THE COMMUNITY

The cathedral was the heart and center of the medieval town. Its beauty was the crowning glory of municipal achievement, and there was an intense rivalry between towns as to which could have the finest church. We have already noticed how Beauvais' jealousy of Amiens brought it to grief. In the construction of the church all the people of the town took a personal part; they not only contributed money but they worked personally at the construction. It has been remarked that medieval men worked on their cathedrals in much the same manner that modern men rush home after work to tend their gardens. Working on the church afforded not only a relaxation and an interest but also definite spiritual benefits, and while the work was mainly done by professionals, there was always a certain amount of volunteer labor employed in the construction of the cathedral.

In the *parvis* (the square in front of the church) were held municipal meetings and ceremonies. The market often was set up near the church and fairs were frequently held there. In front of the church were performed the mystery and miracle plays, the earliest form of drama known to modern Europe. Nor was the commercial and social activity confined to the square in front of the church, but trafficking went on within the building itself, and the ambulatories served as promenades until well into modern times. Recently there has been a revival of the use of the parvis for entertainment. During the Paris World's Fair in 1937 a mystery play was performed in front of Notre Dame, using the façade of the cathedral as a back-drop. At the end the angels came out on the towers, and a powerful searchlight was turned on behind the rose, giving an effect incomparable in its beauty.

The construction of the medieval church often took many generations. Yet the idea that they all took centuries to build is quite false. Many of them were built with amazing rapidity, considering the conditions of labor at the time. Others took much longer, and of course there has never been an end to rebuilding and remodelling them. But even under modern conditions, the construction of St. John's the Divine has taken the better part of half a century, and we should marvel, not at the time it took to build such churches as Paris, Amiens, and Chartres, but at the speed with which the work was accomplished.

THE LESSER ARTS

We have already noticed sculpture in connection with architecture, and apart from its use in architectural embellishment, there was little sculpture in the Middle Ages. The statue *per se,* alone and isolated, was revived as a major sculptural type with the Italian renaissance. Painting likewise in the generally accepted sense had very little development before the fourteenth century. The statues of the medieval churches were always painted, and color was combined with sculpture. Incidentally, it should be remarked that the colors were also symbolical, and that each saint or prophet was usually associated with a single color. The Virgin, for example, was traditionally clad in blue. In the art of manuscript illumination and the painting of miniatures there was great work done, but the first great painter whose name is known in France was Jean Fouquet who flourished in the first half of the fifteenth century. Giotto and Cimabue in Italy were painting frescoes on the walls of buildings in the thirteenth century, but painting as an important art had to await the Quattrocento revival of art.

In the fields of embroidery, tapestries, and ivory carving, fine work was done throughout the Middle Ages, tapestries being made especially in the Byzantine Empire, but important works (such as the Bayeux embroidery) being produced in the West as well.

++

Book VI

The Decline of the Medieval World

1300-1500

This period is an age of transition from the medieval to the modern world; while it is often considered, under the name Renaissance, as the period of the birth of modern culture, it must also be recognized to be the decline of the medieval. In this period the Byzantine Empire dragged out its last years in obscurity until it was finally destroyed altogether by the Ottoman Turks in 1453. At the same time the church was undergoing schism and disruption, with the power of the popes declining through the Conciliar period. France and England were involved in the long struggle of the Hundred Year's War, and in both strong monarchs came to the fore at the end of the period to establish absolutisms. In Germany the old imperial idea gave way before the particularism of the great princes, the political weakness of the empire producing years of civil war, during which the great princes established their virtual independence of the emperor. In the East Moscow asserted herself against the Mongols to establish a new empire. The Baltic states became increasingly important, the cities of the Hanse dominating the commerce of northern Europe. Likewise in Italy, the cities grew, and this period witnessed the development of the many despotisms which characterize the Renaissance. The whole period is one in which decentralization and breakdown seem to be the chief characteristics.

Culturally there was a further advance in humanism, painting, science, and literature, and the intellectual movement of the Twelfth-Century Renaissance reached completion in the Italian Renaissance of the Quattrocento.

City Wall, York, England

MEDIEVAL TOWNS

Towers, San Gimignano, Italy

CHAPTER 35

THE FALL OF BYZANTIUM: TURKS AND MUSCOVITES

❖

IN the first chapter of this book we stated that medieval history was that period of history when the Byzantine Empire existed and continued to carry on the tradition of the old Roman Empire. We have seen the Eastern Empire assuming the ascendency in the period of the third to the seventh centuries, dominating the Western world in the seventh to twelfth centuries, and being eclipsed by the West in the twelfth and thirteenth. Now we must follow its declining fortunes through the fourteenth and into the fifteenth centuries, until it came to an ignominious end at the hands of the Ottoman Turks in 1453. While the empire was dragging out its lingering death, losing province after province until nothing was left, new powers arose and fell in the Balkans: Serbia reached her zenith and quickly declined; Tamerlane swept across nearer Asia like a tornado, leaving destruction in his wake; and the Mameluks in Egypt developed a far-flung empire, rich in the trade of the Indies; but by the end of the period both western Asia and southeastern Europe had fallen to the new and rising power of the Ottomans, who were almost unheard of when the era began. This chapter will endeavor to trace briefly the main course of these movements.

THE PALAEOLOGI, 1261–1453

When Michael VIII Palaeologus (1259–82) recaptured Constantinople from the Latins in 1261 there was every reason to believe that a revived Greek empire had arisen which would continue to dominate the East as the old empire had done for so many centuries. Michael held Nicaea and northern Anatolia, Constantinople and Thrace, Salonica and parts of Morea, and was recognized as suzerain by the despot of Epirus. It was a small empire as compared to the former state of the Macedonians or even of the Comneni:—Trebizond remained autonomous; Frankish states still maintained their independence in Greece; Venice and Genoa ruled the seas; Serbs and Bulgars controlled the Balkans—but Michael had shown himself the strongest of the various competing powers, and his astute diplomacy recaptured for Byzantium much of her former importance. Against Charles of Anjou, who most seriously threatened the empire from the west, Manuel built up an alliance with Aragon and Genoa, and helped to foment the rebellion in Sicily which broke Charles' power at the Sicilian Vespers. With his Eastern neighbors, he played a game of tortuous intrigue, allying at various times with Hulagu, the Mameluks, and the Mongols of the Golden Horde to preserve a balance of power. But Michael was "the first and also the last powerful emperor of restored Byzantium," [1] and with his son Andronicus II (1282–1328) began the civil war which was to destroy the empire internally, and so weaken it that it could offer little resistance to outside pressure.

It was Andronicus who invited to the East the Catalan Grand Company, which he employed against the Turks of Asia Minor. We have already seen how the Catalans got out of hand, established themselves at Gallipoli and eventually conquered the Latin duchy of Athens. Hardly had the empire recovered from the ravages of the Catalans, than civil war broke out between Andronicus II and his grandson. Andronicus II, to ensure the succession, crowned his son Michael IX co-emperor in 1295; but Michael died before his father in 1320, leaving a son Andronicus whose dissipations and license estranged his grandfather. Falling under the influence of an ambitious general, John Cantacuzenos, young Andronicus revolted against his grandfather and forced him to abdicate (1328). When Andronicus III (1328–41) was proclaimed emperor, the real power was in the hands of Cantacuzenos, who ruled the empire while the young emperor amused himself. When in 1341 Andronicus III died, leaving a minor heir John V only eleven years old, Cantacuzenos struck for personal empire. He had himself proclaimed Emperor John VI and assumed the crown at Adrianople shortly after John V had been crowned at the capital. The regents for John V were forced to recognize the usurpation, and the two Johns jointly ruled the empire, with Cantacuzenos actually controlling policy. He married one of his daughters to John V and another to the Turkish sultan, Orkhan. From 1347 to 1354 Cantacuzenos was supreme, but in 1354 John V asserted himself and, with the help of the Genoese, defeated his colleague, forcing him to abdicate and retire to a monastery.

This civil war offered an excellent opportunity to the neighbors of the empire to profit from its distress. The Ottoman Turks had taken Brusa and Nicomedia in the reign of Andronicus III and were established on the south shore of the Straits. In 1354 Cantacuzenos invited them into Europe as his allies, and they settled in Gallipoli whence it was found impossible to dislodge them. Meanwhile Stephen Dushan of Serbia (1331–55) had overthrown the Bulgarians in 1330 and had pushed south into Thessaly and Greece and east into Thrace. Allying first with John V and then with Cantacuzenos, Dushan pushed his conquests forward into the very heart of the empire. In 1346 he had himself crowned "Tsar of the Serbs and Romans" and there is no doubt that he envisaged himself as ruling over

---

[1] T. Florinsky, quoted in Vasiliev, *History of the Byzantine Empire*, II, 265.

a new empire to be formed by an amalgamation of the Serbo-Bulgarian and Byzantine states. During the civil war between John V and Cantacuzenos, Dushan ostensibly allied with John, and it was against this advance of the Serbs that Cantacuzenos called in the Turks. With the overthrow of Cantacuzenos in 1354, Dushan moved in on Adrianople, but death brought an end to all his schemes the following year, and the empire which he had created in the western Balkans fell apart after his death. Constantinople was saved from the Serbs, however, only to be more closely pressed by the Turks who occupied Adrianople in 1365.

The empire meanwhile continued to be torn by civil war. In 1376 John V was overthrown by his son Andronicus IV (1376–79). For three years Andronicus ruled with the support of the Genoese, but John V escaped from his prison, and, aided by the Turks, regained his throne. At the death of Andronicus in 1385, John V had his younger son Manuel crowned as co-emperor. This cut off the expectations of John, the son of Andronicus, who was stirred up by the Turks to revolt in 1390. He seized Constantinople and ruled for a few months in 1390 as John VII, but was soon driven out by Manuel, who peacefully succeeded to the throne at the death of John V in 1391.

Manuel II Palaeologus (1391–1425) was one of the ablest members of his house and in better times might well have given the empire a most successful reign. As it was, he labored hard to hold together what little remained to him of his empire, making repeated trips to Western Europe in vain attempts to secure substantial assistance against the Turks, who now surrounded him on all sides. In 1396 Western Europe answered the Turkish challenge by sending a considerable army of crusaders to the assistance of King Sigismund of Hungary, but the crusade was destroyed at Nicopolis, and its failure discredited further attempts for the time being. Manuel was able to secure some aid from France, under Marshal Boucicaut, who brought some Western knights to help defend Constantinople, which the Turks had besieged in 1397. But Boucicaut's forces were few, and it was only the invasion of Anatolia by Timur and the destruction of the Turkish forces at Angora in 1402 which saved Byzantium from falling to Sultan Bayazid at this time.

Manuel abdicated in 1425, turning the government over to his son John VIII (1425–48), who tried to bolster up his state by a series of marriage alliances. In 1439, John went to Italy to attend the church council of Ferrara-Florence, where he solemnly accepted the supremacy of the pope and sealed the union of the two churches in the hope that this would bring new crusades to rescue his city. But the desired help from the West was not forthcoming, and the Greeks repudiated the church union. A crusade was organized by Ladislas of Poland but it was defeated at Varna in 1444, and the Turks swept on into Europe. On the death of John VIII in 1448, the throne passed to his brother Constantine XI (1448–53) who had been despot of Morea.

During the years that Byzantium had been wasting away, a new center of Greek life and culture had developed in the peninsula of Morea, where the Greeks, operating out from their base at Mistra, had reconquered most of the peninsula and established a new intensely national state. The old Frankish states were uniformly reduced, only the Venetian possessions remaining in Latin hands; in 1446 Constantine had attempted to cross over to Attica and Boeotia but had been defeated by the Turks, who had taken Salonica in 1430 and had pushed south from there. But though the Turks checked its northern expansion, and even took the city of Corinth, the Greek state in Morea showed considerable signs of real vitality. It was from Morea, which he left to his brother Thomas, that Constantine came to be emperor of Constantinople in 1448. Although his succession to the throne was approved by the sultan, Constantine's reign was destined to be short, for in 1451 Muhammad II came to the Turkish throne determined to round out his possessions by the capture of Constantinople.

Muhammad began his attack on Constantinople by building the castle of Rumeli-Hisar on the European shore of the Bosphorus, directly across from the castle of Anatolici-Hisar which Bayazid had built. In these two castles were placed cannon which could throw stone balls of great weight, thus effectively cutting off the approach to the city by sea. A naval expedition against Morea created a diversion there which prevented any aid being sent the capital, and Muhammad sat down to besiege the coveted city.

Constantine's appeals for help brought some, but too little, aid. The Pope sent a cardinal, but no troops. Genoa sent seven hundred soldiers under the command of Giovanni Giustiniani, and some help was forthcoming from Venice, but the total garrison of the city amounted to only a few thousand men, while the Turks greatly outnumbered them, and their heavy artillery gave them an easy superiority. The siege began in earnest in early April 1453, and lasted until May 29th. The Turkish cannon pounded the city with tremendous stones which made breaches in the walls. When the Turkish ships were hauled overland across the point behind Galata and launched in the Golden Horn, in the rear of the defending Christian fleet, the fate of the city was sealed, but its citizens continued to put up a heroic defense. Finally on May 28, after the city had been weakened by weeks of artillery fire, starvation, and constant fighting, the Turks ordered a general assault. Constantine XI died on the walls, fighting as an ordinary soldier. The Turks breached the walls and entered the city which they put to sack. All who could escaped, but many were butchered by·the victorious Turks before they ended their orgy of loot. At last Hagia Sophia was solemnly "purified" and converted into a mosque, while Muhammad, forever after to be known as "the Conqueror," occupied the ancient palace of the Caesars.

The rest of the empire did not long survive. Morea was overrun in 1460, and Trebizond the year following. What Constantinople had meant as a Christian bulwark against the Turks was made manifest to Europe in the following generations when the Turks overran Hungary and reached Vienna in 1529. The fall of Constantinople caused a shudder of fear to run throughout Europe, but attempts to do anything about it were futile and ill-supported.

With the fall of Byzantium an era of world history ended. Nothing was more distinctly medieval than the Byzantine Empire, and the Middle Ages did not outlast its fall. The year 1453 is one of the few dates in history that do have a tremendous significance, and although we have carried our discussion on to somewhat later dates in some of the Western countries in order to complete movements already begun, it is with 1453 that the Middle Ages, and this book, rightly end. The city of the Caesars which so long had been the chief cultural, economic, and political city of Christendom, had fallen, and one can only agree with Wordsworth's lines on the fall of Venice that we

> . . . must grieve when even the shade
> of that which once was great, has passed away.

The Rise of the Ottoman Turks, 1240–1481

The Ottoman Turks, who effected the destruction of the Byzantine Empire in 1453, were relatively unknown when Manuel VIII triumphantly entered Constantinople in 1261. They first came into Anatolia as one of the tribes who had been displaced by the Mongol advance under Chingiz, and are first encountered as serving in the army of Jalal al-Din of Khwarizm against the Mongols. Driven westward, they entered Asia Minor where they became the mercenaries of the Saljuq sultans of Rum, who granted their leader, Urtoghrul, a fief on the frontier of the Byzantine Empire near Dorylaeum about 1240.

There they remained while the power of the sultans of Rum waned, becoming one of the twenty-six independent emirates which developed out of the old Saljuq state in the opening years of the fourteenth century. There is some question as to the composition of these Turks, and the most recent theory is that they were not a single tribe at all, but a military brotherhood, known as *Akhi*, much like the Christian Templars, who were recruited for war against the infidel. At any rate they established themselves firmly in northwestern Anatolia, where they expanded largely at the expense of the Greeks. They were checked temporarily by a severe defeat administered them by the Catalan Grand Company in 1304, but with the withdrawal of the Catalans they began their expansion again and captured Brusa in 1326. From the name of their leader Osman (1290–1326) whom they considered the real founder of their power, they took the name of Ottoman Turks or Osmanli.

Under Orkhan (1326–59), the son of Osman, the Turks continued their conquests in northeastern Asia Minor, taking Nicaea in 1329 and Nicomedia in 1337. Orkhan allied with John VI Cantacuzenos, whose daughter Theodora he married, and in 1354 first entered Europe with 6000 men at the invitation of Cantacuzenos. As we have seen, the Turks settled in Gallipoli and refused to depart. Instead they took advantage of the Greek civil war and the threat of Serbian invasion, to capture Adrianople in 1357. The Byzantines purchased the return of Adrianople temporarily, but Murad I (1359–89), Orkhan's son and successor, recaptured the city in 1365 and made it his capital the following year.

It is under Orkhan that the organization of the Turkish army is supposed to have been perfected by the sultan's brother, Ala-ad-Din. The army was composed of the familiar feudal cavalry (*Timariots*), a special paid non-feudal cavalry (*Spahis*), the regular infantry (*Akinji*), irregular shock troops (*Bashi-bazouks*), and the famous corps of the *Janissaries*. This famous corps was always a relatively small select body, and was recruited entirely from boys taken as blood tribute from the Christian peoples conquered by the Turks. The boys were taken from their homes and brought up in Turkish military barracks, where they were converted to Islam and taught the profession of arms. They became the most formidable infantry corps in Europe, and were fanatical in their service to the sultan, their master. Given special privileges, they became a Turkish Praetorian Guard, and eventually (in the seventeenth century) took over the characteristics of the Praetorians in the matter of deposing and installing sultans. They were generally held in reserve and thrown into battle when the enemies' forces had been weakened by the attack of the Bashi-bazouks and Spahis, with the result that they gained a reputation for invincibility which made them the terror of eastern Europe.

After moving his capital to Adrianople, Murad pushed inland in the Balkans. In 1366 he defeated the Bulgarians and reduced them to vassalage; southern Serbia and western Bulgaria were conquered at the battle of the Maritza in 1371 and Sofia was captured. The kings of Serbia and Bulgaria both accepted Turkish suzerainty in that year and the emperor John V became the vassal of the Turk two years later. Incursions were made into Morea where some of the Venetian holdings were taken, and in 1386 to 1387, Nish, Monastir, and Salonica were captured. A grand alliance was made between Lazar of Serbia, Sisman of Bulgaria and the Magyars, Albanians and Wallachians, all of whom combined to throw off

the Turkish lordship, but Murad crushed the coalition at the battle of
Kossovo in 1389. Murad was himself murdered in his tent on the battlefield of Kossovo by a Serb, but his son Bayazid I (1389–1402), called Ilderim,
or the Thunderbolt, succeeded immediately.

Under Murad I the conquest of Anatolia had also been pushed forward.
It is worthy of note that the Ottomans were a strong European power
before they began to expand extensively in Asia Minor, and that their
progress in Asia was slow as compared with their rapid conquest of the
Balkans. In Anatolia, the emir of Karamania, on the southern coast of the
peninsula, had made himself the most important of the Turkish rulers after
the break up of the Saljuq sultanate at Rum, and Karamania gave the
Ottomans the most serious opposition of any power they attacked.

Bayazid immediately followed the victory of Kossovo by further sub-
jugating Serbia and Bulgaria. Tirnovo was captured in 1393, which ended
the last remnants of the Bulgarian state, and Stephen Lazarovitch of Serbia
was forced to cede a large portion of his kingdom outright to the sultan,
becoming his vassal for a much reduced principality. With the Balkans
under control, Bayazid turned to Morea and Asia; several of the Aegean
islands were captured and Piraeus was attacked; the Greeks of Mistra were
defeated and Argos was added to the Turkish possessions. In Asia, Phrygia
and Bithynia were overrun by Turkish armies and Trebizond reduced to
vassalage.

The rapid advance of the Turks into Europe had alarmed all the West.
Manuel Palaeologus kept appealing for help; Pope Boniface IX preached
a crusade, and Sigismund of Hungary attacked the Turks, defeating them
in 1393. In 1396 a great crusade from the West, under the leadership of
John, count of Nevers, Enguerrand de Coucy, Boucicaut, the Count Palatine Ruprecht, the earl of Huntingdon and others, joined the forces of
the Hungarian monarch in a supreme effort to stop the Turk. The armies
met at Nicopolis, where, owing largely to the discipline of the Turkish
soldiers and the rash and undisciplined impetuosity of the Western knights,
the Christian army was annihilated. Only a few of the more important.
leaders escaped or were able to ransom themselves from captivity; thousands were massacred or carried into slavery, where many of them, like
Johann Schildtberger, who left a first-hand account of the expedition,
served in the army of the sultan.

The following year (1397) Bayazid began the siege of Constantinople.
We have seen how help was brought by Boucicaut from France, and aid
was also given by the Knights Hospitaller, who created a diversion by attacking Asia Minor from their stronghold at Rhodes. Bayazid was prevented from carrying through the siege to its final conclusion by the invasion of Anatolia by Timur, the Mongol khan from Samarkand.

Timur, called from his lameness Timur the Lame, or Tamerlane, was

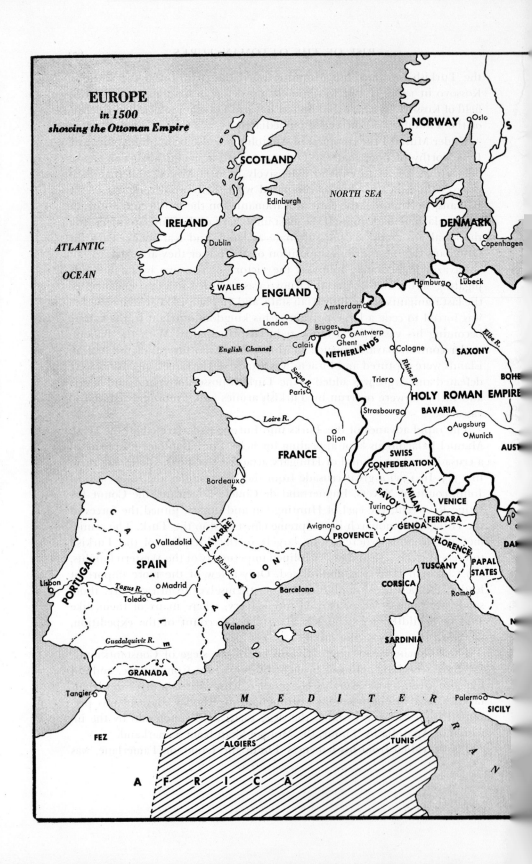

EUROPE
in 1500
showing the Ottoman Empire

NORWAY
Oslo

SCOTLAND
Edinburgh

NORTH SEA

IRELAND
Dublin

DENMARK
Copenhagen

ATLANTIC

OCEAN

Hamburg
Lübeck

WALES
ENGLAND

Amsterdam
London
Bruges
Antwerp
Ghent
Calais
NETHERLANDS
Cologne
Elbe R.
SAXONY

English Channel

Trier
Rhine R.
BOHE

Seine R.
Paris

HOLY ROMAN EMPIRE

Loire R.
Strasbourg
BAVARIA

Augsburg
Munich
AUST

Dijon

FRANCE

SWISS
CONFEDERATION

Bordeaux

SAVOY
MILAN
Turin
VENICE

Avignon
PROVENCE
FERRARA
GENOA

Valladolid
NAVARRE

Ebro R.

FLORENCE
TUSCANY
PAPAL
STATES

SPAIN
Madrid
Toledo
Tagus R.

CORSICA

Barcelona

Rome

Lisbon
PORTUGAL

CASTILE
ARAGON

Valencia

Guadalquivir R.

SARDINIA

GRANADA

Tangier

M E D I T E R
Palermo
SICILY

FEZ
ALGIERS
TUNIS

A F R I C A

born in Transoxiana about 1335 in territory subject to the Khans of Chagatai. In the confused politics of the crumbling Khanate, Timur won his way to control over Transoxiana in 1369. Then he turned south, and in 1380 to 1381 overran Khurasan, Kurdistan, and parts of Afghanistan and Persia. The spoils of his conquests were brought back to Samarkand, which became one of the wealthiest and most beautiful cities of the world, its buildings with their golden roofs reflecting the barbaric splendor of the khan. In 1391 and again in 1395, Tamerlane came into conflict with Tuktamish, khan of the Golden Horde, whom he defeated. It was in the course of his campaign against the Horde that he invaded Anatolia and took Siwas from the Ottomans in 1395. But he did not tarry in the West, turning instead to India where he conquered Kashmir, Delhi, and the northwestern provinces (1398). His empire by this time ran from the Sea of Aral to the Persian Gulf, from Delhi to Iraq; Transoxiana, Persia, Afghanistan, and Khurasan being ruled directly by the khan, with vassals ruling the peripheral districts. Then in 1401 he turned again to the west and overran Syria and Anatolia. Baghdad was captured and destroyed in 1401, after which Timur turned north into Asia Minor. There on a plain near Angora, the Mongol army of some 200,000 men met the Ottoman force of about 120,000 in the greatest battle of centuries on July 28, 1402. Bayazid was outgeneraled and outmaneuvered; the fine Turkish troops, who had brought such terror to Europe, were crushingly defeated by the warriors from farther Asia, and Bayazid was himself taken prisoner. Having thus destroyed the power of his most formidable adversary, Timur turned back to Syria where he took Aleppo and Damascus, with horrible slaughter, and defeated the forces sent against him by the Mameluks of Egypt. The great conqueror was then ready for his most cherished dream, the conquest of China, but he died while on the way there in 1405.

Tamerlane's empire fell apart immediately after his death. It had never had any real organization and had been always the creation of one man. Civil wars among his descendants, and local rebellions, caused the complete breakup of the empire which relapsed into a number of small contentious states. In the sixteenth century one of his descendants, Babar, established the line of the Great Moguls (Mongols) at Delhi which ruled India until the death of Aurangzeb in 1707. Meanwhile the Timurids were for the most part driven out of their many possessions, their home provinces of Transoxiana and Persia being lost about 1500.

The defeat of Angora threw the Ottoman empire into total confusion. Four sons of Bayazid struggled for the throne, Sulayman seizing Europe while his three brothers were fighting in Asia. In this civil war, Manuel Palaeologus succeeded for a time in regaining possession of Salonica and parts of his lost empire, but at the conclusion of the war in 1413, with the final victory of Muhammad I (1413–21) they were soon lost again. Muhammad, having defeated his brothers and secured the throne, continued aggressive wars, fighting the Venetians and invading Bosnia. He was succeeded at his death by his son, Murad II (1421–51), one of the greatest warriors in this house of conquerors.

Murad opened his reign with a siege of Constantinople in 1422, which however, he shortly abandoned to settle troubles which had arisen in Asia. He continued the war with Venice, taking Modon in Morea, and Salonica, which had been taken by the Venetians from the Greeks and was now surrendered to the Turks by its own inhabitants. In 1428 he defeated a coalition of Hungarian and Polish troops on the Danube but found himself unable to make any great headway against a revolt in Albania which was led by George Castriotes, famous under the name of Scanderbeg (1443–67). The increasing seriousness of their own positions caused the formation of a great alliance between Ladislas of Hungary and Poland, John Hunyadi of Transylvania and George Brancovic of Serbia. The allies won an initial victory at Sofia in 1443, but were severely defeated at Varna in the following year. In the campaign of Varna, the Christians had been aided by a number of crusaders from Western Europe, and the Crusade of Varna is generally considered as the last serious attempt to revive Western enthusiasm for a crusade against the Moslems. The remaining years of Murad's reign were marked by a second victory over Hunyadi at Kossovo (1448) and by the conquest of Greece as far as the Gulf of Corinth. While the Turkish arms were everywhere else successful, they were wholly unable to make any headway in Albania where Scanderbeg continued to hold out against them.

In 1451 Murad died and was succeeded by his son Muhammad II, the Conqueror (1451–81). Muhammad began his reign with an attack on Karamania which had withheld the usual homage, but his greatest achievement was the capture of Constantinople in 1453, as noted above. Although the conquest of Constantinople earned Muhammad his title of Conqueror and added the brightest jewel to his turban, it by no means ended his conquests. Muhammad was fortunate in that his two most formidable antagonists, John Hunyadi and Scanderbeg, died in 1456 and 1467 respectively, and he was able to overrun Serbia, Bosnia, and Albania. At the same time he conquered Morea, Trebizond, several of the Venetian islands, and forced the voivode of Wallachia, Vlad the Impaler, to accept his suzerainty and pay tribute (1462). In the next decade he turned to Asia where he defeated the sultan of Karamania and subjugated that country, thus eliminating the last remaining Turkish rival. A war with Persia brought Muhammad conquests in Armenia, while Azov and the Crimea were taken from the Mongols in 1475.

Only twice in his long career of conquest was Muhammad definitely defeated. He was unable to take Belgrade in 1456, and he was defeated in an attempt to take Rhodes from the Knights Hospitaller in 1480 to 1481. Both of these defeats were to be avenged by his great-grandson Sulayman the Magnificent in the following century. Thus at the death of Muhammad the Conqueror, in 1481, the Turkish Empire included all the Balkans as far as Belgrade, all of Anatolia, most of the northern and southern shores of the Black Sea, Greece and most of the Aegean islands and parts of Armenia. Western Europe seemed paralyzed; Pope Pius II tried in vain to launch a new crusade, but got almost no support for his plan. Only Venice actively opposed the Turks, and it was forced to pay tribute to save its Eastern possessions. At this time the Ottoman Empire was still essentially a European state, its Christian subjects far outnumbering its Moslem. The conquest of Syria and Egypt by Selim I (1512–20), the grandson of Muhammad, made the Turkish state for the first time since the reign of Murad I a predominantly Moslem power.

THE MAMELUKS AND THE KINGDOM OF CYPRUS, 1291–1517

While the Ottoman Turks were making themselves masters of Anatolia and the Balkans, the Mameluks of Egypt continued to dominate the Levant. We have seen above how they conquered the last of the crusader states of Syria at the end of the thirteenth century and extended their sway to include Egypt, Syria, and Arabia. The successors of Qalawun continued to rule until overthrown by their own Mameluk guard in 1390, and were succeeded by the new dynasty of the Burji Mameluks which lasted until 1517. The first line of Mameluks, the Bahri, had been mostly Turks or Mongols, and were generally Moslem-born. The twenty-three Burji sultans were nearly all Circassians, born Christian and converted to Islam after being sold into slavery, and they were even more oppressive to their subjects than the twenty-four Bahri sultans had been. The succession was always from Mameluk leader to Mameluk leader and there was never any passing of the throne from one member of a family to his descendants.[2] Foreign rulers in a conquered country, the Burji were unrestrained tyrants whose despotism was only checked by the assassination which was the lot of so many of them. Only a few deserve any remembrance and the whole period is one of decline. Syria was lost for a time to Timur, although it was subsequently regained; but the only real gain made in the entire period was the conquest of Cyprus in 1424 to 1426 by Sultan Barsbay, which temporarily reduced that kingdom to vassalage.

The prosperity of Mameluk Egypt lay in control of the trade routes between the Mediterranean and the Indian Ocean. Through its ports passed the jewels and spices of the East, and its merchants grew prosperous on the very active trade of which Egypt was the center. With tariffs of from

---

[2] For List of Sultans, see Appendix p. 765.

500 to 1000 per cent, the Mameluks made an extremely high profit on all trade passing through their country and were able to maintain in Egypt a high degree of luxury. However, these very tariffs which brought them such wealth caused their downfall, for the traders of the West sought for new routes to circumvent these tolls. The opening of the sea route to India by the Portuguese in the fifteenth century dealt a staggering blow to Mameluk prosperity. When Albuquerque with a Portuguese fleet closed the Red Sea, captured Sococtra and the mouth of the Persian Gulf, trade was deflected away from the Mameluk lands. By 1500 the economic ruin of the country was evident. It was a weakened and drained country that Selim I conquered from Qansuh al Ghouri and Tuman Bey, the last Mameluk sultans, in 1517.

In the period of their greatest strength, the Mameluks had faced the persistent enmity of two Christian powers in the eastern Mediterranean—the kingdom of Cyprus and the Knights Hospitaller of Rhodes. The Knights had fled to Cyprus after the fall of Acre in 1291, but had not long remained there as they conquered for themselves the island of Rhodes in 1308 to 1310. There they built a strong fortress, and a powerful navy which played an important role in patrolling the Mediterranean and securing the sea lanes for Christian commerce. The Knights were always ready to fight any Moslem and kept up a guerrilla war with both Mameluks and Turks. In 1344 they were the chief participants in the crusade against Smyrna, which took the city from the Turks, and the Knights garrisoned it for fifty years while it was in Christian hands. As we have already noted, they made a diversion into Asia to draw the Turks off from Constantinople in 1397, and they successfully resisted the attack of Muhammad the Conqueror in 1480 to 1481. They held their position at Rhodes until 1522 when Sulayman the Magnificent finally drove them out. They were then granted the island of Malta by the emperor Charles V, and removed there in 1530, to remain until the end of the eighteenth century. During the time that they were at Rhodes, the Knights could always be counted on for armed support of any venture against the Moslems, and they did much to keep the Turks from getting the control of the sea sooner than they did.

More interesting than the history of the Knights at Rhodes is that of the kingdom of Cyprus. It will be recalled that the kings of Cyprus had inherited the throne of Jerusalem in 1268 and ruled both kingdoms simultaneously. In 1291 when Acre and the other mainland cities fell, the refugees fled chiefly to Cyprus where they made the city of Famagusta the chief Christian trading center in the eastern Mediterranean. With their colonies on the mainland lost, the Italian cities established trading factories in Famagusta, Limassol, Larnaca, and the other Cypriot ports, and Cyprus became the chief emporium for the exchange of wares between the Christian and Moslem countries. The wealth of Famagusta became proverbial, and the many beautiful churches and palaces reflected the great prosperity of the city and island. Close relations were maintained with the Christian cities of Cilician Armenia—Sis, Adana, Adalia (Satalie), and the Cypriots interfered consistently in the political anarchy of the Armenian states.

In the reign of Peter I de Lusignan (1359–69) Cyprus took the lead in an attempt to revive the crusades. Voyaging to Europe, Peter visited the courts of the West in an attempt to recruit support for a crusade, and managed to raise a few vessels and some hundreds of men. He had already captured the cities of Gorighos and Adalia in Armenia from the Saljuqs; now in 1365 he turned against Egypt and led a crusade against Alexandria which succeeded in capturing the city, which was given over to plunder. The crusaders were obviously unable to retain possession of their prize, but they carried off the goods they found there and had considerable profit from the venture as well as great glory. However, the expedition was on the whole unfortunate, for the Egyptians were insulted thereby and took full revenge later.

With the murder of Peter I by a group of disaffected barons, and the accession of his minor son Peter II, civil war broke out in Cyprus, which was complicated by a war which developed between the Venetian and Genoese colonists in Famagusta. The net result was the capture of Famagusta by a Genoese fleet (1373) and the occupation of the city by the Genoese until the middle of the following century. In 1424 to 1426 the Egyptians repaid the insult of the capture of Alexandria by attacking Cyprus, defeating and capturing King Janus at the battle of Cheirokitia, and forcing him to accept the suzerainty of the sultan for his kingdom.

With Famagusta in the possession of the Genoese, and the suzerainty of the Mameluks recognized by the kings of Cyprus, the independence of the island seemed practically at an end, but the sultans were willing to accept tribute and verbal vassalage and interfered not at all in the internal affairs of the kingdom. At the death of King John II in 1458, the throne passed to his daughter Charlotte and her husband, Louis of Savoy, but James, a bastard of John II, attempted to seize the power and received the support of a large part of the nobility as well as the investiture by the sultan. Charlotte and Louis were driven out of the capital and besieged in Kyrenia, and finally, giving up all attempt to control the kingdom, fled to Italy. James was crowned and at once proceeded to drive the Genoese out of Famagusta. In his campaign against Genoa, James was aided by the Venetians resident in the island. To cement his alliance with Venice, he married Catherine Cornaro, the niece of one of the prominent Venetian merchants, and to give her a position worthy of a queen, she was officially adopted as the daughter of the Most Serene Republic. As a result, when

James died, the kingdom was left in the hands of the Venetian queen as regent for her infant son. Intense rivalry developed between two factions, one leaning on Venice and the other turning towards Aragon, but with the premature death of the infant king, the Venetian party gained complete control. In 1489 Catherine made over the kingdom to her adoptive parent, retired to Venice, and Cyprus became a Venetian colony. It was the last annexation made by Venice in the East and was the only gain in a period when it was steadily losing ground to the Turks. The Venetian control of Cyprus lasted until 1572, when it was taken from them by the Turks.

In all the years of the Lusignan and Venetian domination Cyprus was a commercial outpost of prime importance and great wealth. It was also a center of Christian opposition to the Moslem advance, and regularly allied with the Knights of Rhodes to check the Turkish domination of the eastern Mediterranean. With the loss of Cyprus in 1572, the last Christian bulwark disappeared in the East.

THE RISE OF MUSCOVITE RUSSIA, 1263–1505

While the Byzantine Empire was dying and the Ottoman Turks were building an empire in southeastern Europe, two powerful states were emerging in the northeast to carry on the traditions of Byzantium. At the time of the fall of Constantinople it would have been hard to tell whether Muscovy or Lithuania would become the chief power of eastern Europe, but both were clearly in the ascendent. "Two Romes have fallen and a third stands, a fourth is not to be" wrote a monk of Pskov in reference to Moscow,[3] which had become the seat of Orthodoxy after the fall of Constantinople. But at the time the Polish-Lithuanian kingdom seemed as powerful as Russia, and only the future was to prove that it was really Moscow and not Vilna or Warsaw which was to become the supreme power in the East.

At the beginning of the fourteenth century Moscow was only a small Russian principality under the rule of the Mongols of the Golden Horde. As we have already seen, Alexander Nevski (ob. 1263) had secured from the khan the position of deputy in Russia, an office which his successors exploited to the full to advance their authority over rival Russian princes. This office was not fixed in any one house, the khans appointing as Grand Prince whichever of the Russian princes they chose. For some years after the death of Alexander the title passed around among the princes of Vladimir and Tver, finally coming to rest in 1328 on Ivan I Khalita (Money-bags), the prince of Moscow.

While his brothers and cousins had struggled for the title of Grand Prince, the prince of Moscow, Daniel, the father of Ivan, had devoted

[3] Quoted in Platonov, *History of Russia* (Macmillan), p. 116.

himself to the building up of his own appanage. Moscow was geographically well situated to become the center of Russia as it lay in the very
heart of Great Russia and commanded the river traffic of that region.
Daniel, and after him Ivan, brought in colonists to settle the country, and
a prosperous if small state was erected around Moscow.

Ivan I (1328-41) secured not only the appointment from the khan as
Grand Prince, he obtained also the right to collect all the tribute from
Russia which was owed to the Mongols. To this power his sons, Simeon
(1341-53) and Ivan II (1353-59), added the right of adjudication over the
other princes, which gave them an evident superiority; as a chronicler
phrased it, the khan "put all the other princes under his hand." While
they were extremely subservient towards the khan, these princes ruled
despotically over their subjects, and laid the foundations for the autocracy
of the Tsars.

Equally important for the rise of Moscow was, moreover, the trans-
ference to that city of the seat of the Russian metropolitan. In 1299 the
metropolitan had fled Kiev, which was sinking to the position of a provincial town, and removed to Vladimir. In the struggle for supremacy
the metropolitan favored the princes of Moscow, and the ecclesiastical
seat was transferred there in the reign of Ivan I.

A more vigorous policy, and a leadership in the attempt to throw off the
"Tartar yoke," was begun by Dimitri Donskoi (1359-89) the son of Ivan
II. Dimitri came to the throne as a minor and had to win his way against
the opposition of the prince of Smolensk, but he had the support of the
metropolitan and the boyars, and was able to secure his appointment as
Grand Prince from the khan. He proved a strong and effective ruler, forcing
the other princes to respect his authority, and permanently reducing the
princes of Tver to a subordinate position. Dimitri's greatness comes, however, from his victory over the Mongols in 1380. For some time past the
Mongol power had been gradually weakening, due largely to civil wars
among the leaders of the Horde; in 1365 the Russians had driven off a
raiding expedition in Riazan, and in 1378 Dimitri had won a slight victory
over a Mongol force which had just burned Nizhni-Novgorod. At the same
time the Russians reduced the amount of their tribute. In 1380, Mamai,
who had become sole ruler of the Horde, determined to reassert the Mongol authority over the Russians and collected a large army, allying simultaneously with the Lithuanians. Oleg of Riazan immediately made his
peace with the khan, several of the other princes remained inactive, but
Dimitri of Moscow raised an army to oppose the invasion. The forces met
at Kulikovo on the Don on September 8, 1380, and the victory won by
Dimitri gave him his sobriquet of "Donskoi." Although the immediate
results of the battle were slight, and the Mongols returned two years later
to ravage Moscow and reimpose the tribute, the battle of Kulikovo had

tremendous psychological effects. It proved to the Russians that they could successfully oppose the dreaded Mongols, and it pointed the fact that leadership in any national effort must come from the princes of Moscow.

Dimitri died in 1389, in his thirty-ninth year, and the throne passed to his son Vasili I (1389–1425), whose reign was marked by further wars with the Mongols. But the day of the Golden Horde was past; in 1395 Tuktamish, the khan, was defeated by Timur, who subjugated the Russian Mongols to his widespread empire. Two new hordes established themselves in Kazan and in the Crimea, and the Mongols were too busy fighting amongst themselves to trouble much over the Russians.

This was most fortunate for Moscow, for at the death of Vasili, a civil war broke out between his son Vasili II (1425–62) and Yuri, the younger son of Dimitri. Yuri was defeated but his sons took up the challenge in turn and Vasili II was compelled to defend himself for several years against his cousins. Wars with the Mongols were still chronic, during one of which Vasili was captured by the Kazan Mongols, only being released on payment of a large ransom. In spite of all this Vasili was able to extend his territories considerably at the expense of his immediate neighbors and to leave to his son a state greatly enlarged and strengthened. It was during his reign that the metropolitan of Moscow declared the independence of the Russian Church from Constantinople, when the patriarch of Constantinople deserted the true faith and accepted the headship of Rome and the *Filioque* in the Creed at the Council of Florence (1439). A rival metropolitan, subject to Constantinople, was established at Kiev, but this only strengthened the position of Moscow as the one true center of Orthodoxy.

Meanwhile the western provinces of old Russia, including the old capital at Kiev, had passed under the rule of Lithuania. The first union of the Lithuanians under Mindvog (ob. 1263) has been noted above, but it was with the reign of Gedymin (1316–41) that Lithuania became an important state. Gedymin established a new capital at Vilna, and expanded thence to conquer Polotsk, Minsk, Kiev, and most of the Dnieper basin. His son Olgerd (1341–77) continued this expansion into Russia, capturing the Ukraine and reaching the shores of the Black Sea. Two thirds of the Lithuanian kingdom was inhabited by Russians, and the Russian element soon became dominant over the pagan Lithuanians. Including, as it did, the ancient capital, Lithuania promised to become the true successor of Kievan Russia, but this prospect of a strong Russian state in the west was destroyed by the marriage of Jagiello (1377–1434) the son of Olgerd, to Jadwiga, queen of Poland, and the conversion of the Lithuanians to Catholic Christianity. The union of Poland and Lithuania, whereby Jagiello became king of Poland under the name of Ladislas V, ended the struggle between Poland and Lithuania in the west, but resulted in internal difficulties between the adherents of the two churches. Many of the Lithuanian boyars fled to Moscow, others, who lived on the frontier, transferred themselves and their lands to the rule of the Muscovite prince, while still others sought autonomy for Lithuania under their own ruler. This was granted when Jagiello enfeoffed his cousin Vitovt with the Grand Duchy of Lithuania as a vassal state. The combined Polish-Lithuanian kingdom (when it was held together) was considerably the largest state in Europe at the time. Jagiello conquered Moldavia, Wallachia, and Bessarabia, making them vassals and extending his boundaries from the Baltic to the Danube and the Black Sea, while Vitovt pushed eastward annexing Smolensk. The virtual separation of Poland and Lithuania was continued after the death of Vitovt and Jagiello, when the lands were divided between the sons of Jagiello, Ladislas VI and Casimir. In 1447, however, Casimir inherited the Polish throne so that the two states were again reunited. At his death in 1492 the kingdom was again divided between his sons John Albert and Alexander, only to be reunited in 1501 when Alexander succeeded his brother on the throne of Poland. This union was destined to be permanent and there was no more question of a separate Lithuania.

Throughout this period, and for several generations to come, war with Moscow was endemic. Vitovt had at various times fought against, and allied with, the princes of Moscow, acting for a time as regent for the minor Vasili II. Thereafter there was warfare at intervals, Casimir supporting the revolt of the cousins of Vasili, and Moscow encouraging the disaffected Orthodox Lithuanian boyars. The whole social organization of Lithuania, which had been modeled after that of Kiev, was subjected to change, the more feudal Polish system being instituted. As Catholicism and acceptance of Polish customs were the roads to preferment in both Poland and Lithuania, many boyars accepted the change, but those who did not were extremely bitter. This internal disaffection, plus the newly awakened ambition of the princes of Moscow to rule all of old Russia, led to inevitable conflict, which lasted well into the reign of Ivan IV in the sixteenth century.

The reign of Ivan III, "the Great," of Moscow (1462–1505), the son of Vasili II, was one of the greatest importance in respect to the relations with Lithuania as well as in the general expansion of Moscow. Ivan can properly be considered the last of the princes of Moscow and the first tsar of Russia. When Ivan ascended the throne, Moscow, although it already possessed extensive territories, was closely hemmed in by rival states, the boundary of Tver being only fifty miles from the city of Moscow, and those of Lithuania and the Mongols less than seventy,[4] while the whole state was still, at least technically, under the suzerainty of the Mongols. Ivan began by attacking Novgorod, which had allied with Lithuania. In

[4] B. Pares. *History of Russia*, p. 84.

1471, he defeated an army sent out by Novgorod and forced on the city a treaty which recognized his overlordship while guaranteeing the freedom of the citizens; but the anti-Muscovite party in the city revolted and in 1478 after several expeditions against the city, Ivan canceled all the liberties of the former republic and reduced it to complete subjection. This was followed in 1494 by the expulsion of the German merchants of the Hanse, a move which destroyed the immense economic prosperity of "Lord Novgorod the Great." The annexation of Novgorod more than trebled the Muscovite territory, extending it to the Arctic and beyond the Urals. This tremendous expansion was augmented by the annexation of the other Russian principalities of Rostov, Riazan, and Tver (1463–85) and by the conquest from Lithuania of much of the land on the east of the Dnieper. Smolensk, Chernigov, and other territories were overrun by Ivan and brought under Muscovite dominion, although they were only formally annexed in the following reign. At first Ivan and Alexander of Lithuania had allied, Alexander marrying Ivan's daughter Helen, but Helen felt that she was badly treated and, as Ivan continued to accept the transfer to himself of lands belonging to Orthodox Lithuanian boyars, war broke out in 1500 in which Ivan conquered the considerable territory mentioned above. Ivan also made his power felt in the west in a war with Sweden although this led to nothing. It was Ivan III who ended the subjection of Russia to the Mongols. In 1480 he threw off all allegiance to the khan, allying with the khan of Crimea and reducing that of Kazan to vassalage. Ahmed, khan of the Golden Horde, invaded Russia, but withdrew without a pitched battle. Later Ivan assisted his ally, the khan of Crimea, in a campaign which broke up the Golden Horde entirely, while the khan assisted Ivan in his wars with Lithuania.

An event of first importance was the marriage of Ivan in 1472 to Zoe Palaeologina, the daughter of Thomas Palaeologus, despot of Morea. By this marriage Ivan became the heir of the Palaeologi, adopting their coat-of-arms of the double-headed eagle and assuming the Russian equivalent of the Greek title "autocrator." In his correspondence with foreign powers Ivan began to style himself "Tsar of all the Russians," and he had his eldest son crowned tsar. Ivan died without completing his work, but his son Vasili III (1505–33) filled in the gaps by annexing Pskov and Smolensk, and unifying the Russian state from the Arctic and the White Sea to Chernigov in the Ukraine, and from the Dnieper to beyond the Urals.

Not in ancient Kiev but in Moscow, had risen the new Christian state, which assuming the mantle of the Byzantine Empire, was to challenge and ultimately defeat the Ottoman Turks, and which has been for centuries consumed by the desire to gain possession of Tsargrad, the ancient city of the Caesars.

CHAPTER 36

THE DECLINE OF THE UNIVERSAL PAPACY

✢

THE AVIGNON PAPACY, 1305–78

THE fourteenth and fifteenth centuries dealt severely with many of the older medieval institutions. The Byzantine Empire, which dominated the early Middle Ages, weakened and passed away: the papacy, which in turn dominated the High Middle Ages, while not passing away, lost its oecumenical character and seriously declined in the same period. The church after winning its fight against the empire of the Hohenstaufens passed under the influence of France, and in the fourteenth century was less universally respected, as it seemed to become less spiritual and more worldly during its sojourn at Avignon and throughout the Schism. The Conciliar Movement attempted honest reform, but the movement failed, and as the prospects of reform from within diminished, open opposition and revolt increased until the Protestant Revolt shattered the unity of the church in the sixteenth century.

The seven Avignon popes who ruled from 1305 to 1378 were not bad men, or even bad popes, they were simply not the spiritual leaders which Western Christendon needed at the time. All were Frenchmen and often allowed their national feelings to color their policies, so that both Germany and England felt that the papacy was virtually a foreign and hostile power. Further, men felt with considerable justice that the papacy was too little interested in the business of saving souls and too much concerned with that of extracting money from its constituents. If there was but little development of doctrine, there was an amazing development in the financial bureaus and in new methods of papal taxation.

The period of the Avignon papacy is commonly referred to by the term "Babylonian Captivity of the Papacy," a phrase invented by Petrarch. In fact, while there was a certain amount of Babylonishness about the era, there was no captivity, for the popes preferred residence in Avignon to return to Rome. Not until after 1360 when the "free companies" were devastating southern France did Avignon lose its evident superiority as a place of residence. It is interesting to note how, as their real control over the peoples of Europe declined, the Avignon popes compensated to themselves by urging more and more extreme claims to oecumenical dominion.

The claims advanced by John XXII (1316–34) in his struggle with Louis of Bavaria were more extreme than even those propounded by Boniface VIII in the height of his arrogance. The struggle of empire and papacy in the fourteenth century was largely a paper war, but it produced the most vigorous statements on both sides, and if it lacked political significance, it was most important in the field of political theory.

Most of the Avignon popes were sincere and well-intentioned men; several of them labored diligently to revive the crusades in the East, and at least one of them (Urban V, 1362–70) was a learned and saintly character. But as a group they have gone down in history as luxurious, bureaucratic, rapacious politicians and businessmen. Clement V (1305–14) was a weak man completely dominated by Philip IV of France; John XXII (1316–34) aimed at the creation of a strong papal monarchy and is famous for his financial ingenuity; Benedict XII (1334–42) would like to have been a reformer but lacked the political acumen to secure his aims; Clement VI (1342–52) was devoted to the cause of the crusades, but was luxury-loving and morally lax; Innocent VI (1352–62) was well-meaning but weak; Urban V (1362–70), in character the best of them all, attempted to return to Rome and a more austere existence; Gregory XI (1370–78) was a great persecutor of heretics and zealous for the maintenance of the true faith. Individually they were no better and no worse than many of their predecessors or followers, but collectively they left a bad name, and were considered by many contemporaries as wolves rather than as shepherds of the flock. During the period of their pontificates, western Europe developed an extreme anticlericalism which we find reflected not only in the popular literature of the time, but in the great antipapal statutes like the English *Provisors* and *Praemunire,* and in the growth and spread of mysticism and heresy.

The financial exactions of the papacy developed along several lines; in general they were not so much innovations as extensions of rights previously held but relatively unexploited. The right of the pope to grant provisions (the appointment to benefices when they should become vacant) had long been recognized in certain instances, such as vacancies owing to the death of the holder while at Rome, but under John XXII this right was pushed to extremes, the pope granting provisions to practically all benefices, and often promising the same benefice to several persons. All episcopal sees were claimed by the popes as within their authority to provide, a claim which was bitterly resented not only by secular lords but by the local clergy. The spoils (personal property) of all deceased bishops were claimed for the papal treasury; special taxes were imposed on all visitors to Rome; bishops were charged what amounted to a heavy relief when they succeeded to their bishoprics; a tithe of all ecclesiastical incomes was rigorously collected, and special gifts were exacted in addition. True, this taxation was directed mainly against the clergy, but it came ultimately out of the pockets of the faithful, and clergy and laity alike resented the numerous vexatious exactions.

Papal jurisdiction was also extended beyond all reason. The pope could reverse any decision made in an inferior ecclesiastical court, and as the papal curia was also a court of first instance, it became customary to by-pass the lower courts and take the matter directly to Avignon. This not only cut down the income of the local clergy and increased that of the popes, but, due to the innumerable delays and the necessity of securing representatives at the court to champion the cases, tremendously increased the length and the expense of the proceedings.

Further there was considerable justified criticism of the way in which the monies thus exacted were spent. While no one could object to the endowment of schools or hiring troops for crusades against the Turks, men freely criticized the use of papal revenues to fight "crusades" against their political enemies in Italy (Venice, Milan, Verona et al.), which was a far greater source of outlay, as well as the lavish extravagance and luxury of the papal court. The English grew excessively bitter when the popes loaned money to France to hire troops for use in the Hundred Years' War, while the Germans came to feel that the papacy deliberately provoked civil war and confusion in their internal politics.

The papacy, however, hardly did more than reflect the general de-moralization of the whole church in this era. The bishops and even the parish clergy were generally more interested in their incomes than in their parishioners' souls, and absenteeism, pluralities, and concubinage were practically the rule among the local clergy. The curé would receive the revenues from several parishes, hiring vicars at miserable salaries to perform the duties of his offices, and thus filling the parish churches with ill-paid, uneducated, and incompetent chaplains. The decline of the secu lar cleary was paralleled by that of the monastic; rules were relaxed in most of the religious houses; vagrant monks were to be found everywhere outside their cloisters; the friars frankly abandoned their property, those who adhered to it (the Spirituals) being persecuted by John XXII to force them to conform.

Inevitably under such conditions heresy developed and attracted many followers. The Spiritual Franciscans were only one of a number of heretic groups which were dealt with by the Inquisition at this time. The Spirituals had long been under the influence of Joachim of Flora and the *Everlasting Gospel,* which predicted the advent of a third dispensation when monas-ticism and absolute poverty would prevail throughout the world. Under the name of Fratricelli they lapsed into definite heresy, denying the author-ity of the pope or their superiors. Some of the most able and ardent supporters of Louis of Bavaria, such as William of Ockham and Michael of Cesena, were drawn from the ranks of the Spiritual Franciscans who were condemned by John XXII.

While many pious souls lapsed into heresy through their denial of the authority of a corrupt clergy, others sought spiritual satisfaction in a devout mysticism. The fourteenth century was the great age of the German mystics, Master Eckehardt and Johann Tauler, as well as of the Flemish Ruysbroeck and Gerard Groote. The transcendental mysticism of the "New Devotion" which Groote taught, reached its finest expression in the following century in the *Imitation of Christ* by Thomas à Kempis still a widely read classic of devotional literature. Gerson, Nicholas of Cusa, and many of the men who were influential in the Conciliar Movement were strongly influenced by mysticism, and while some of the mystics were later declared heretics, many of them helped save the spirituality of the Catholic church during a period of general worldliness.

The residence of the popes at Avignon had been due primarily to the disturbed conditions of Rome and the Romagna at the opening of the fourteenth century, and one of the consistent goals of papal policy was the reduction of the Papal States to submission. In all the cities of the Romagna, local despots were establishing themselves regardless of the rights of the papacy, while in Rome itself the constant feuds of the Orsini, Colonna, and Gaetani kept the city in a state of anarchy. In 1347 a Roman demagogue, who had risen from the ranks of the common people, Cola di Rienzi, led a revolution which aimed at nothing less than the restoration of the ancient republic of Rome. Assuming the title of Tribune, Rienzi set up in Rome a well-ordered government, which forced the unruly nobles into temporary submission. At first the pope supported Rienzi in his struggle with the nobles, but when his true ideals became apparent Clement withdrew his support. After a brief period of success and power, Rienzi was driven from Rome by the nobles and forced to flee to Germany. Sent by the emperor to Avignon for trial as a heretic, Rienzi seemed to the pope to be a potentially useful tool, and was returned to Rome where in 1354 he was again made ruler of the city, with the backing of Cardinal Gil Albornoz, the commander of the papal army in Italy. This time, however, Rienzi had lost his former charm and popular appeal. He attempted to be a dictator and was soon overthrown and killed in a popular uprising.

Albornoz however continued his campaigns in the Romagna, and succeeded in reducing the petty despots, re-establishing the papal control over the ancient Patrimony of St. Peter. While trouble broke out again at the death of Albornoz, the authority of the papacy was strong enough that Urban V felt able to return to Rome. However he found conditions still too unsettled and went back to Avignon in the last year of his life. His successor Gregory XI was forced by public opinion and the persuasion of St. Catherine of Siena to remove from Avignon to Rome, and although he might have desired to return to France, death prevented this and he died in Rome in 1378.

THE GREAT SCHISM, 1378–1409

The cardinals who met at Rome to elect a new pope in April 1378 were mainly Frenchmen and would probably in the normal course of events have chosen another French pope. But the Roman populace threatened them with violence unless they elected a Roman or at least an Italian, and after a short and stormy conclave, the cardinals announced the election of Bartholemeo Prigano, archbishop of Bari, an Italian from the kingdom of Naples, whom they thought they could easily dominate. But Urban VI, as Prigano called himself, proved a quite different character than the cardinals had anticipated. Not only did he refuse to return to Avignon, as most of them wished, but he began to reduce the revenues of the cardinals, neglected to consult them, and in every way showed a determination to rule absolutely. In despair the cardinals went to Anagni, where in September they declared the election invalid as having been made under duress, and proceeded to elect Cardinal Robert of Geneva, who took the name of Clement VII and promptly returned to Avignon.

With two popes occupying the Fisherman's Seat, each excommunicating the other and claiming to be the only true pope, the nations of Europe were forced to decide for themselves where their allegiance should lie. The action taken by the various states was prompted more by political than by relgous or legal considerations. Clement was supported by France, Scotland, Navarre, Castile and Aragon. England, Gascony, and Flanders, who were hostile to France, accordingly became strong champions of Urban. Portugal, Bohemia, Hungary, and most of Germany also declared for Urban, while Italy was hopelessly divided on the question, local politics entering into this as into every other consideration in Italy. In Naples, where there was a disputed succession to the throne, Urban was favored by one faction and Clement by the other.

The Great Schism naturally caused much controversy between the supporters of the rival popes. It also tended to reduce the general control of the church over the laity, as such things as excommunication lost their strength and value when tossed about recklessly by rival popes. To be cut off from the communion of the church was a dreadful matter ordinarily, but no one was certain which pope really represented the true church so that no one could be sure whether he was excommunicated or not.

From the very beginning of the Schism the suggestion was made that a general council be summoned to solve the matter, and this was urged especially by the doctors of the University of Paris, led by Pierre d'Ailly.

But the French government supported Clement and the suggestion was suppressed for the time being. Clement sought to strengthen his position by sending French armies to conquer Italy, while Urban defended himself, the issue being fought out in Naples where Clement supported Louis of Anjou and Urban, Charles of Durazzo. But the whole thing became hopelessly confused when Urban broke with Charles and tried to take over the control of Naples personally. Six cardinals, who plotted to curb Urban by subjecting him to the College, were arrested by the pope, imprisoned, and finally executed. Finally Urban died in 1389, but his cardinals, rather than recognize Clement, elected another Neapolitan, Boniface IX (1389–1404). Boniface quickly mended his political fences in Naples, where he gave strong support to Charles' son, Ladislas, and showed himself in every way more conciliatory than Urban.

Jean Gerson and Pierre d'Ailly at the University of Paris again began their agitation for a general council, but this presented many difficulties, such as who had the authority to call a council, and people still hoped that the schism might be healed by the resignation of one or the other pope. This hope was increased when Clement died in 1394 and his successor at Avignon, Benedict XIII (1394–1424) agreed to abdicate if by so doing the schism could be healed. However, it soon became apparent that Benedict had no intention of fulfilling this promise, and repeated attempts to make him resign met with refusal. Each pope declared his willingness to abdicate, but each demanded that the other resign first, which naturally produced a total deadlock. An embassy from the English, French, and Castilian monarchs called upon both popes to resign and allow a new election, but both remained adamant. In 1398, the French clergy held a council in which they voted to renounce their allegiance to Benedict; Marshal Boucicaut marched on Avignon and for two months besieged the pope in his strong castle there, but the king of Aragon interceded in favor of the pope and the expedition was recalled. Local politics in France entered the picture, Orleans supporting Benedict and Burgundy opposing. By 1403 the pro-Benedict faction had gained so much strength that France again placed herself under his obedience, an action engineered by Orleans with the approval of the mad king, Charles VI. Things seemed to be very much where they had been a decade earlier.

The death of Boniface IX in 1404 hardly changed matters at all, as the Roman cardinals proceeded to elect a new pope Innocent VII (1404–6) who spent his brief pontificate in putting down a republican movement in Rome itself. He was succeeded by Gregory XII (1406–15), a Venetian, who agreed to resign if Benedict would do the same, and who meanwhile tried to arrange both a meeting of the two colleges of cardinals to plan a joint election if the way could be cleared, and a conference of the two popes themselves. The popularity of Gregory's proposals, and the threat of the withdrawal of French support if he refused, made Benedict more conciliatory, and arrangements were finally completed for a conference between the two popes at Savona, near Genoa. But Gregory developed misgivings at attending a conference to be held in territory obedient to his rival, and presented obstacles. Benedict went to Savona, thus gaining credit for willingness to co-operate, while Gregory hesitated at Siena. When the proposed negotiations broke down completely owing to Gregory's obstinacy, some of his cardinals revolted and met with some of Benedict's to arrange for mutual action.

THE COUNCIL OF PISA, 1409

Eight Roman and six Avignon cardinals met and agreed to summon a general council. France meanwhile, under the influence of the University of Paris, and no longer restrained by the duke of Orleans, who had been murdered, again threw off her allegiance to Benedict, refusing to recognize either pope. Both Benedict, who had fled to Aragon, and Gregory anticipated the action of the cardinals by summoning general councils, but by now no one trusted the sincerity of either pope. The fourteen cardinals renounced their obedience to either pope and summoned the council to meet at Pisa to heal the schism once and for all. England, France, Wenceslas of Germany and the states of northern Italy supported the rebel cardinals; Spain and Scotland remained loyal to Benedict, while Naples, Hungary, Venice, and a few other Italian states adhered to Gregory.

The Council of Pisa began its session in March 1409, and by June over five hundred clergy and laity had assembled. The rulers of France, England, Poland, Portugal, Burgundy, Savoy, and some of the German duchies and counties were represented, as well as delegates from thirteen universities, foremost among whom were representatives of Paris and Bologna. Commissions were at once appointed to prepare charges against both popes; as only heresy was adequate cause for the deposition of a pope, the commissioners had to dig out facts which indicated that the popes had had friendly dealings with heretics or had themselves engaged in sorcery. Witnesses were produced to attest these crimes, and formal charges were prepared against both Gregory and Benedict. In June the Council formally deposed both popes as heretics and schismatics. Then the twenty-four cardinals at Pisa formed themselves into a conclave to elect a new pope; each swore, if elected, to continue the work of the Council in the matter of church reform. The man elected was Alexander V (1409–10) who had been one of the most active cardinals in arranging for the Council. After providing for the summoning of local provincial councils immediately and a new general council in 1412 to carry out a program of reform, the Council of Pisa dissolved in August 1409.

The results of the Council of Pisa were not what its advocates had hoped. The supporters of Benedict and Gregory remained loyal to their previous allegiances and instead of there being two rival popes, there were now three. When Alexander died in 1410, the cardinals at once elected the Neapolitan Baldassare Cossa, not without considerable suspicion of bribery and intimidation, as Pope John XXIII (1410–15). The qualifications of the new pope were, to say the least, unusual. He had gained wealth and notoriety as a pirate in his youth, before he found in the church an easier road to power. He had studied law at Bologna, entered the church and been made cardinal by Boniface IX, who employed him as an administrator. He had a peculiar genius for the tortuous paths of Italian political intrigue, and had been a leader in the calling of the Council of Pisa. Under Alexander he had captured Rome for the Conciliar pope, though Alexander had never reached the Holy City and it was John who made a triumphal entry there in 1411. One of John's close allies and friends was the Florentine banker and politician Cosimo di Medici, and the tomb of Pope John in the Baptistery of Florence still attests the close relations between these two Italian political opportunists. It is hardly to be expected that such a man would be vigorous in the matter of church reform; he conquered Avignon by arms, secured the recognition of Sigismund of Luxemburg, king of Hungary and emperor-elect of Germany, and for a time won over Ladislas of Naples. But he soon broke with Ladislas, and opposition began to develop rapidly among those who were sincerely anxious for church reform and a true end to the Schism. Once again the cry for the general council was raised, and Sigismund was approached with the proposition that he, as emperor, should convene it.

To anticipate the demand for the council, John held a council at Rome in 1412, but it was a small affair and accomplished nothing, being adjourned for lack of attendance. Hardly was the council ended than Ladislas attacked Rome and drove out the pope. The expulsion of Pope John from Rome threw him into the hands of Sigismund who was in Italy at the time. John needed the imperial support, and to get it had to agree to the summoning of a general council at Constance in 1414. Although personally reluctant, John issued the bulls summoning the council (to which Sigismund had already invited the secular princes) and the Council of Constance began its session on November 5, 1414.

THE COUNCIL OF CONSTANCE, 1414–18

The Council of Constance, which was said to have been attended by as many as 40,000 people, ecclesiastical and lay (though that figure is undoubtedly exaggerated), was one of the most important gatherings in

European history. Its agenda included three major items: the healing of the Schism, reform of the church, and the suppression of heresy. Of the three the healing of the Schism was by far the most important in the minds of the participants.

As the delegates were slow in assembling, little was accomplished in the first weeks of the Council, the most important action being the beginning of the trial of the Bohemian heresiarch, John Huss, whose trial began in December 1414 and dragged on until his final condemnation and execution in July 1415. The doctrines of Huss will be discussed below in the section on heresy and can be passed over here, except to note that in the matter of heresy the Council was in agreement and able to act with urgency.

One of the first problems confronting the Council was the question of organization. Pope John was strongly supported by the Italian clergy, who made up the largest single unit at the meeting. To secure the predominance of the Italians, it was proposed that formal voting be done by head, each bishop and abbot being given one vote. This suggestion was vigorously opposed by the English, German, and French representatives, who urged that every cleric who held a degree in theology or law be given a vote, but that formal voting be done by nations, as in the organization of the universities. This latter view prevailed and four nations were organized—the German, English, French, and Italian. When the Spanish representatives later came to the Council, a fifth Spanish nation was added.

The Council then demanded the resignation of all three popes. Gregory agreed to abdicate at once; John said that he would resign if both the other popes would do the same, but Benedict absolutely refused to recognize the authority of the Council in any way, only consenting to an interview with Sigismund at Nice where proposals for union might be discussed. As Benedict's refusal was anticipated, John's promise of abdication was, of course, meaningless.

John was still officially pope and felt himself indispensable to the Council. Hoping to bring them to complete recognition of his position by a drastic act, the pope fled the Council in March 1415 and took refuge in Germany. But the result of John's flight was the opposite from what he had anticipated. Instead of approving him as the true pope, the Council asserted its own supremacy. In decrees passed in the fifth general session, the Council stated that the authority of the Council was superior to that of any pope, that it held its power directly from God, was supreme in matters of faith and doctrine, and that it had the right to depose any pope who obstructed it in the exercise of its authority. John was ordered to return at once or to stand charges of heresy and schism.

A long list of charges were prepared against John, including the familiar ones of heresy, sorcery, simony, and immorality. To these were added the accusations of murdering Alexander V, of selling a head of John the

Baptist for 50,000 ducats, and of promoting schism by his flight from Constance. Witnesses were heard and the pope was convicted on fifty-four counts. John was declared deposed, and was arrested and imprisoned in Germany. The abdication of Gregory was received a short while thereafter, and all that remained was to secure the resignation of Benedict. But Benedict proved extremely difficult. Sigismund went to Perpignan to confer with him, but could arrive at no conclusion. After several months of negotiation, the emperor gave up and withdrew to Narbonne where he was joined by envoys from the Spanish kingdoms who signed an agreement repudiating Benedict, but stipulating that no new pope be elected until they should have sent representatives to the Council. As the last of the Spanish delegates did not reach Constance until March 1417, this seriously delayed any action towards healing the schism. Then in July, Benedict was formerly deposed and Odo Colonna was elected Pope Martin V by a special electoral college which consisted not only of the cardinals, but of representatives of the five nations (November 1417).

Meanwhile serious dissensions had split the Council, which had been working on the matter of church reform. The outbreak of war between England and France in 1415 had produced strained relations between their respective delegates and what one nation favored was sure to be opposed by the other. There was disagreement as to whether a new pope should be elected before the reform program had been drawn up; the extent of the papal power and its limitations offered occasion for heated argument; the whole question of the relations of pope and Council was reopened. In general English and Germans stood together against the Italians and French but these party lines broke down on individual issues. The Council did manage to pass the decree *Frequens* which ordered that a general council should be held five years after the end of the Council of Constance, another seven years after that, and that councils should be held regularly at stated intervals thereafter. It was also provided that in case of another schism, a council should be convened automatically. When Pope Martin was elected he was presented with eighteen specific points demanding reform and a committee was appointed to confer with him concerning them.

But the election of the new pope had accomplished the work that was paramount in the eyes of the members of the Council and the zeal for reform waned. Martin issued a few decrees touching on reform, declared the matter closed, and dissolved the Council in April 1418, ordering a new council to assemble at Pavia five years hence. Meanwhile the pope had arranged concordats with England, Germany, and France regulating such matters as the papal provisions, ecclesiastical taxation, etc. As none of these really went to the heart of things, they were uniformly acceptable to all parties. After three and a half years the Council of Constance was over, and the delegates could go home feeling that they had solved the chief problem of the Schism, and had disposed of a pernicious heretic, even though they had not done all they set out to do in the general matter of reform. In healing the Schism the Council of Constance had ended the *raison d'être* of the councils, and the papacy was strong enough to neglect reform and to ignore the decree stating the superiority of the councils.

The Councils of Basel and Ferrara-Florence, 1431–49

It soon became evident that Martin V had no intention of seriously pursuing any drastic policy of church reform. Although elected by a council, Martin was a firm believer in the supremacy of the papal monarchy and was opposed to any diminution of its power. He could not avoid the summoning of the council ordered for Pavia in 1423, but he immediately transferred it to Siena and after a year of petty discussion, in which the only practical accomplishment was the renewal of decrees against heretics, the pope dissolved the council for lack of attendance.

Meanwhile the successes of the Hussites in Bohemia made the convocation of a real council a matter of urgency to the secular powers. The pope was forced by pressure from the emperor and other princes to convene the next council as required by the decree *Frequens,* and it was called for Basel in 1431. Cardinal Julian Caesarini was appointed by the pope to preside over the Council, but before the prelates could hold their opening session, Martin V died. The cardinals at once elected as his successor a Venetian who took the papal name of Eugenius IV (1431–47). When the Council of Basel began its sessions, it was so badly attended that its dissolution seemed imminent, but further Hussite victories caused an increase in attendance as men were convinced that the only way to deal with the Hussites was through the Council. The Council at once sent an invitation to the Hussite leaders to confer with them with the hope of effecting an understanding. Unfortunately, before he had heard of the great increase in attendance at the Council, Eugenius had issued bulls dissolving the Council and summoning a new one to meet at Bologna for 1433. The Council, sure that the pope misunderstood the situation, refused to accept the dissolution and passed a decree that no one could dissolve or move a council without its own consent. For the next two years the Council struggled with the pope, who at first refused to recognize its existence and then attempted to limit its jurisdiction. Finally in 1433 Eugenius was constrained to accept the Council and grant approval of all its acts. Meanwhile Hussite delegates had appeared at Basel and begun discussions which resulted in the split in the Hussite party into an extreme and a moderate wing, the latter being reconciled with the church.

Their success in the Hussite negotiations and in forcing the hand of the pope emboldened the prelates at Basel to attack the matter of reform with extreme measures. In 1435, they issued decrees which abolished all annates and all payments for any ecclesiastical appointments. Further measures limited appeals to Rome, ordered regular diocesan synods, limited the power of the general interdict, and generally reduced the papal power and revenues. Eugenius at first delayed any reply, but finally in 1436, after the Council had passed a decree demanding an oath from the pope to accept the decree of Constance concerning the supremacy of the councils, he flatly accused the Council of meddling in matters which were none of its business. The pope recalled his legates and threatened to dissolve the Council. The Council retaliated by bringing charges against the pope and convicting him of fomenting a schism (1437). Eugenius ordered the Council to cease its criticism and to remove itself to Ferrara where he had convened another council.

One of the chief subjects on the agenda of the Council had been the question of a projected union with the Greek Church. As we have seen, the Byzantines, in desperation at the continued threat of the Turks, had appealed to the West and offered union as the price of military help. Both pope and Council had tried to persuade the Greeks that they were the power with which to deal, but the Council had refused to meet a Greek demand that the council be held at a port. In discussing this matter the Council had split badly between those who favored adjourning to some town acceptable to the Greeks and those who insisted that it meet at either Basel or Avignon. The pope meanwhile convened the council for Ferrara, and papal ships sent to Constantinople brought the Greeks to that city.

The council was not destined to remain long at Ferrara, for an outbreak of the plague caused it to move within a few months to Florence, where the Greeks were lavishly entertained by the Medici. The clergy at Basel refused to participate in the Ferrara-Florence Council, though Caesarini and the cardinals abandoned them to go to the new council. While the pope and the theologians at Florence were arguing over the question of the procession of the Holy Spirit and the matter of papal supremacy over the Eastern patriarch, the Council of Basel went ahead with the deposition of Eugenius and the election of their own pope—Amadeus, duke of Savoy, who took the name Felix V (1439-49).

The union which was reached at Florence was ephemeral and was not accepted in Constantinople, where popular sentiment ran so high that the emperor was afraid even to officially publish the decree. The metropolitan of Kiev did, and received a Roman cardinal's hat as a reward, but, apart from Isidore of Kiev and Bessarion, few Greek clergy were really convinced, and the union remained a dead letter.

Meanwhile the Council of Basel had been steadily losing support outside. The control of the Council fell into the hands of the extremists; the more conservative members left; and several states including France officially withdrew their support. Charles VII of France forbade his clergy to attend either the Basel or Ferrara councils, holding instead his own national council at Bourges, which promulgated a number of the Basel reforms, wherein the papal control was reduced and the royal increased, in the Pragmatic Sanction of Bourges (1438). A German council at Mainz ratified most of the acts of Basel but deplored the attitude of the Council in regard to the pope.

Strengthened by the success with the Greeks and by the decline in prestige of the Council of Basel, Eugenius at his Council of Florence issued new decrees denying the supremacy of councils over popes, and declaring the right of the pope to adjourn, transfer or dissolve any council (1439). This Council continued to meet in Florence until 1443 when it was transferred to Rome where it continued for a while under the papal eye, until it gradually broke up.

The remnants of the Council of Basel still continued to sit although they were by now practically devoid of any support. When Germany was officially reconciled with the papacy in 1448 the Conciliar party lost its last vestige of strength; the emperor Frederick III ordered the city of Basel to expel the Council, which sadly removed itself to Lausanne in 1448. The death of Eugenius brought to the papal throne Nicholas V (1447–55) who was more tolerant of the Basel group than Eugenius had been, and negotiations were begun for healing the breach between pope and Council. In 1449 Felix, the Conciliar antipope, abdicated in favor of Nicholas, and the Council voted its own dissolution in April 1449. The history of the papacy in the later fifteenth century will be discussed below under Italian politics where it more properly belongs.

The Conciliar Movement had solved the problem which originally brought it into being: the Schism was healed and the papacy restored to its former position of power. And in so doing it had destroyed itself, for the revived and strengthened papacy would not tolerate the existence of the councils as rivals to its authority. For a few years, during the Council of Constance, the Council had ruled the church in the absence of any pope, a precedent which Basel would like to have followed. No pope could encourage such a tendency. The Council of Constance had decreed the superiority of the Council, which that of Florence had denied. The other great problems which confronted the councils were not solved. Church reform could not be accomplished by a council without the consistent support of the popes, and it was not until the Council of Trent (1545–64) that the reform demanded in the fourteenth century was really accomplished. Nor was the problem of heresy successfully met, for earnest reformers despaired of reform from within and broke into open revolt in the following century. It is not going too far to say that the failure of the Conciliar Movement precipitated the Protestant Revolt.

THE SPREAD OF HERESY: JOHN WYCLIFFE, 1374–1414

As noted above the narrow nationalism and rapaciousness of the Avignon popes and the divided allegiances during the Schism caused the papacy to lose much of its oecumenical position and to decline sharply in prestige. Soon pious souls sought spiritual consolation in an exalted mysticism, many became open critics of the papal system, a few went further and became definite heretics, questioning the authority of the church and the truth of some of its doctrines.

Had the political and economic condition been propitious, either John Wycliffe, the Englishman, or John Huss, the Bohemian, might have been the founder of the Protestant Revolt instead of Martin Luther, but the time was not yet ripe, and both of these reformers went too far in their departures from orthodoxy. Luther's more conservative revolt found a ready acceptance in the sixteenth century in a world disgusted with the worldliness of a corrupt church, which the more radical teachings of Wycliffe and Huss could not inspire in the fourteenth century while men still hoped that reform could be accomplished within the church through the agency of the councils. But both of these early reformers influenced those who came later, and the Protestant Revolt grew in ground prepared by the earlier teachings of the two great fourteenth-century heresiarchs.

John Wycliffe (c. 1324–84) was a teacher at Oxford and one of the greatest theologians in England, with a great reputation as both scholar and preacher, before he became the great heresiarch. It is possible to trace the development of his theological radicalism through several distinct stages and to note how he burgeoned forth under persecution. Until 1374 Wycliffe was a perfectly orthodox professor of theology at Oxford and it was a political issue which first brought him into the field of active opposition to the papacy. As we have seen, the English strongly resented the partiality which the Avignon popes showed towards their enemy France. The Statutes of *Provisors* and *Praemunire,* depriving the pope of the right to appoint to English vacancies and forbidding any appeals to Rome, had been passed in 1351 and 1353, and since the beginning of the Hundred Years' War England had refused to pay the seven hundred marks a year tribute owed the papacy since the surrender of John to Innocent III.

In 1374 Wycliffe was selected as one of the English ambassadors to attend a meeting at Bruges to negotiate for a truce with French and papal representatives. It was during this mission that Wycliffe first came into contact with John of Gaunt, duke of Lancaster, who was to be his patron and friend for the rest of his life. On his return from this mission Wycliffe published the first of the works which made him a heretic in the eyes of the church. In the *Determinatio de Domino,* Wycliffe pointed out that the English throne was based on the right of conquest and not on any papal grant; that the pope through failure to defend his vassal had broken the feudal tie and that he had even acted against his vassal in giving comfort to his enemies; that the pope was rather the vassal of the king for the lands held by the church in England; that when Innocent III received England from John he was guilty of simony and the act therefore illegal, and that in any case John had not had the power to make such a surrender; and finally that England could not be said to pay a tribute of seven hundred marks a year as that sum was utterly inadequate for tribute from such a great country and could only be considered as a gift granted the pope by the English sovereign. These arguments strongly appealed to Englishmen already stirred to patriotic sentiments by the French war, and Wycliffe became a champion of the national cause, commanding large audiences wherever he preached. During the course of the next few years, he went beyond this position to declare that the pope had no more control of the Keys than did any parish priest, and that the church would be better off if her lands were to be seized by the temporal lords and she were forced to return to Apostolic poverty and live off her tithes.

This was clearly heresy; Bishop William Courtenay of London summoned Wycliffe to answer to charges at St. Pauls in February 1377. Wycliffe went, but was attended by John of Gaunt, and when John felt that his protégé was not being given courteous treatment, he ordered his men to clear the hall. A riot ensued between the followers of the duke and those of the bishop, during which Wycliffe and Duke John departed. Courtenay appealed to the pope who issued a bull condemning nineteen of Wycliffe's statements as erroneous and dangerous, and ordered the archbishop of Canterbury to imprison Wycliffe until his case could be heard before the papal court. Once again Wycliffe was cited to appear for trial, and again he was rescued by court influence and the mob. The faculty of theology at Oxford examined Wycliffe's writings and found the ideas true and sound, though unfortunately phrased. These attacks on Wycliffe seem to have driven him into a more extreme position and his views became rapidly more violent and heretical. He attacked the papacy, demanding a complete surrender of all temporal possessions, demanded that monks and friars be put to work, as they were inspired by the devil and not by God, declared that most of the popes were themselves damned by the sinfulness of their own lives, and proposed the erection of a national English church independent of Rome. In line with the accepted Conciliar theories, he claimed that the church was the body of the faithful and not merely the clergy, but he went much further when he stated that neither pope nor priest had the power to excommunicate, as that power lay only with God. Likewise he maintained that absolution was wholly in the power of God, as no cleric on earth can presume to forgive sin. He denied the validity of auricular confession, and anticipated Luther in claiming that true contrition and repentance felt in the heart of the sinner were sufficient and did not need confession to be effective. Scripture was, he maintained, the only source of faith and law, and should be interpreted literally, not allegorically; any contradiction of the Scripture was heresy but the denial of other teachings of the church was not.

But his two chief heresies were his denial of transubstantiation in the eucharist and his theory that the sacraments could not be administered by a priest who was himself in mortal sin, which denied the doctrine of the indelibility of the priesthood as acquired through ordination. A priest himself guilty of sin, said Wycliffe, was a corrupt vessel and incapable of transmitting God's grace to others; any sacraments administered by sinful priests were invalid. As for transubstantiation, he asserted that Christ existed only spiritually in the bread and wine, and that it was sacrilege to presume any physical change in the purely symbolic ceremony. As the substance cannot be separated from the accident, and there is no change in the accident, there can be no change in the substance, and transubstantiation does not take place.

These sentiments, many of which are commonplaces in Protestant doctrines today, were most radical heresies in the fourteenth century. But they found popular acceptance with many, and a group of Wycliffe's disciples, organized as the Poor Priests (more commonly called Lollards), went all over England preaching his doctrines. One of them, John Ball, who pushed to extremes the doctrine of the sinful priest, went so far as to maintain that a sinful ruler need not be obeyed, thus anticipating Luther's doctrine of the Godly Prince, and preached an equality of man which mounted to pure democracy and social equality. Ball was one of the men most influential in stirring up the great Peasant Revolt in 1381.

The Peasant Revolt, which was blamed by many on Wycliffe's teachings, lost Wycliffe much of his standing at court. His doctrines had been condemned, without mentioning him by name, at Oxford earlier in that same year, and John of Gaunt had already ordered him to stop all preaching. Wycliffe did not personally sympathize with the revolting peasants, but there can be little doubt that his teachings did have an effect in precipitating the movement and he was somewhat discredited by it. In 1382 he was again tried for heresy by Courtenay, now archbishop of Canterbury, who declared ten articles heretical and an additional fourteen erroneous. Wycliffe was forbidden ever to preach or to lecture again; an appeal to the royal council and to Parliament did him no good, as he was suspect in connection with the recent rebellion, and he was forced to retire to Lutterworth, where he spent the remaining years of his life writing tracts and preparing his English translation of the Bible. He was finally summoned to appear for trial at Rome, and expressed his perfect willingness to go, but as he was paralytic he was not able to travel. He died in December 1384.

The investigation of his works continued after his death. In 1413 his books were ordered burned, and in 1417 the Council of Constance ordered that his body be removed from consecrated ground and his bones thrown in the river. Meanwhile his doctrines spread throughout England. By 1401 the heresy had become so widespread that Parliament passed the statute *De Heretico Comburendo* (For the Burning of Heretics) but it was not until the accession of Henry V in 1413 that this punishment was enforced at all strenuously. In 1414, led by Sir John Oldcastle, some 20,000 Lollards revolted, but the movement was suppressed and Oldcastle burned as a heretic three years later. Thereafter persecution was the rule until the outbreak of the civil War of the Roses when it died down to be resumed again under Henry VII. In its later years Lollardry became almost exclusively a peasant movement and deteriorated badly owing to the fact that none of the books of Wycliffe could be had and the Lollards were forced to fall back on oral tradition which often became corrupted. By the end of the fifteenth century, Lollardry was practically stamped out in England, but a few Lollards remained in the southwestern counties to join the Lutheran movement when it was introduced into England in the sixteenth century.

John Huss, 1410–71

But if Wycliffism was suppressed in England, it was transported to Bohemia where it became the basis of the teachings of John Huss. Bohemia in the latter part of the fourteenth century was undergoing a nationalist Czech reaction against the incursions of German clergy, merchants, miners, and politicians who came in with the house of Luxemburg. Huss' teachings became inextricably involved with this Czech nationalism and thereby gained great support. That an English heresy should appear in Bohemia when it was not prevalent in France or Germany might at first seem difficult to explain, but the reason is a simple one. Anne of Bohemia married Richard II of England and took with her to England a number of Bohemian priests. After her death these clergy returned to Bohemia and brought back with them the books and ideas of the English preacher and heretic. The new teachings were studied avidly by the teachers at Prague, among whom was John Huss, a professor of philsophy and a popular Czech preacher. Huss was deeply impressed by Wycliffe's writings and translated many of his works into Czech. He had already gained a great reputation as the leader of the Czech faction in a university quarrel which resulted in the withdrawal of all the German students from Prague, whence they seceded to found the University of Leipzig. In 1410 Pope Alexander ordered that the Wycliffian writings be seized and burned; Huss objected and was excom-

municated. In defiance of the papal bull Huss continued preaching, attempts of the archbishop to suppress him being nullified by the support he
received from Wenceslas, king of Bohemia. Pope John XXIII ordered him
to come to Rome but he refused. Then, in 1412, John XXIII issued indulgences to raise money for his war with Naples. Both Huss and Jerome of
Prague, a fellow-Wycliffian, denounced indulgences issued for such a purpose. In this Huss did not deny at all the theory of the indulgence, but did
oppose their use for political purposes. A student riot burned the papal
bulls announcing the indulgences, and when the leaders were arrested and
executed Huss denounced their executioners as murderers and said the special Mass for martyrs over them. By this time Huss had become too radical
for most of his colleagues on the faculty who joined with the archbishop of
Prague in condemning him. Prague was placed under an interdict as long
as Huss preached there, but he had a tremendous popular following and
was still supported by the king. Although Wenceslas did persuade him to
leave Prague, Huss continued his preaching in the country, the interdict
following him around wherever he went. It was at this time that he wrote
his greatest book, the *De ecclesia,* in which he set forth most of his doctrines.

Huss followed Wycliffe in general in his teachings concerning the inva-
lidity of sacraments administered by sinful priests and in his reliance on
Scripture as the only source of faith. He went on to point out that bulls
issued by sinful popes were without validity and that popes were often far
from infallible. The pope should have no temporal power and should not
engage in war, indulgences issued for that purpose being invalid. He did
not follow Wycliffe in his denial of transubstantiation, but admitted the
Real Presence in the eucharist; but he developed a new line of heresy in his
teaching that the church was not the visible body of the clergy but all the
elect of God—those predestined to salvation—living or dead. The introduction of predestination into his concept of the church raised a doctrine
which had been declared heretical when advocated by Gottschalk in the
ninth century, and which was to be reaffirmed by John Calvin.

In 1413 the pope in the Council of Rome officially pronounced Wycliffism to be heresy; Wenceslas appointed a commission to investigate the
question in Bohemia, but when he found the orthodox clergy unwilling to
compromise at all, threw in his lot with the Hussites and deprived the orthodox of their posts, appointing Hussite sympathizers. Meanwhile Huss
sent a copy of his *De ecclesia* to Gerson in Paris, who found in it some
twenty errors, especially objecting to the doctrine of the sinful priest.

But although Wenceslas was willing to support the heretics in Bohemia,
his brother and heir Sigismund of Hungary, the emperor-elect, was, as we
have seen, most anxious for the healing of the Schism and the restoration of
orthodoxy. Having persuaded John XXIII to convene the Council of Constance, Sigismund demanded that Huss appear before the Council, offering

him a safe-conduct to attend. Huss accepted and went to Constance, where he was at once arrested and imprisoned.

The only explanation of Huss' willingness to appear at Constance lies in his supreme confidence in the righteousness of his beliefs and in his ability to convince others of his orthodoxy. Throughout his trial he stoutly maintained that he was a true Catholic and that it was his opponents who were in error. The lead in the examination of Huss was taken by Gerson and Pierre d'Ailly, and from their point of view Huss was given every opportunity to defend himself and to recant his errors. The Council had found 260 errors in Wycliffe, many of which Huss was charged with accepting; in his own works some thirty-nine errors and heresies were discovered. Since his departure from Bohemia, some of his followers had begun to advocate the use of double communion (the giving of both the bread and the wine to the laity) and Huss had approved of this in a letter, which was now brought up against him. As a suspected heretic, he was given no chance to argue his case, but was compelled to answer "Yes" or "No" to specific questions. Both Sigismund and d'Ailly urged him to recant his heresies but he steadfastly refused, insisting that only his own conscience was right and that he could not accept the decisions of the Council when they ran counter to his own beliefs. Recognizing in Huss a heretic of the worst stamp, Sigismund abandoned him, canceling the safe-conduct (which of course was invalid when issued to a proven heretic) and turned him over to the mercy of the Council. The Council ordered all his works to be burned, and after repeated attempts to force him to recant had failed, condemned him as an obstinate heretic and turned him over to the Count Palatine, the secular lord of Constance, for execution (July 1415). His colleague Jerome of Prague was likewise burned a year later; he had recanted his errors but had later denied his recantation.

The news of Huss' execution—martyrdom to his followers—raised a storm of protest in Bohemia which quickly broke out into open revolt. Wenceslas was indifferent; his queen Sophia and the Czech nobles were actively Hussite. Bohemia became almost completely Hussite, but as early as 1417 when they drew up their first Articles of Faith, the conservative and radical elements among the Hussites began to differ on matters of doctrine, anticipating the rift which was to result in the formation of two distinct parties, the Calixtines and Taborites. The Calixtines were very nearly orthodox except that they adhered to the doctrine of the sinful priest and the practice of double communion; the Taborites on the other hand went farther in their heresies, denying purgatory, prayers for the dead, and the use of images or incense in churches.

The pope and Sigismund both brought pressure to bear on Wenceslas to suppress the spread of heresy in Bohemia, but as Queen Sophia still favored the Hussites the indolent king would do little. The pope accordingly

preached crusades against the Hussites, five crusades being launched between 1420 and 1431. Against all of these the Hussites, led by the Taborites
John Ziska and Procop, were victorious, and Bohemia might well have remained Hussite had not civil war broken out between the Calixtines and
Taborites.

When the Council of Basel met, they invited the Hussites to confer with
them in the matter of settling their differences. To win over the Calixtines,
the Council agreed to allow double communion and to give the church in
Bohemia a privileged position. This compromise successfully won over the
Calixtines but drove the Taborites to renewed opposition. However, in
1434 an army of Calixtines defeated Procop and the Taborites at Lipany
and destroyed their power. Much of the strength of the Hussites had lain in
the fact that when Wenceslas died in 1419, the throne passed to his brother
Sigismund, already king of Hungary and emperor of Germany. As Sigismund was known to favor the Germans, the Czech nobles and people
united in keeping him out of the country, and Hussitism was the national
religion of the Czechs in opposition to the orthodox Germans. The defeat
of the Taborites enabled Sigismund to occupy Bohemia in 1436 and to restore the kingship which had been suspended since 1419. The Hussite movement was, however, far from dead and continued to trouble Bohemia for
the rest of the century, the control of the country remaining in the hands of
the moderate Calixtines. In 1458 they secured the election of one of their
number, George Podiebrad, as king. When King George rejected an attempt of Pope Pius II to revoke the compact of Basel and withdraw double
communion, the pope deposed him and gave the crown to Corvinus of Hungary, but George defeated Corvinus and held the throne until his death
in 1471. A mission of John of Capistrano to convert the Hussites proved
equally fruitless, and Hussitism continued in Bohemia through the Lutheran Revolt when many of them accepted Lutheranism. In 1618, at the
opening of the Thirty Years' War, Bohemia was predominately Protestant,
but by 1648 Protestantism had been virtually stamped out, although the
Bohemian Brethren still continue as the Moravian Church.

Thus we find that by the end of the fifteenth century the church had lost
much of her position of supremacy and the predecessors of Protestantism
had already begun to make themselves felt in Europe. The popes after 1447
hardly aspired to oecumenical position; they were Italian humanists, scholars, and politicians, who were concerned with the new learning or with
founding states for their relatives. It was to require the tremendous impact
of the Protestant Revolt and the Catholic Reformation of the sixteenth
century to restore the papacy to a position of spiritual leadership, and when
that happened a large part of Europe had been lost completely to the
Roman Church.

CHAPTER 37

FRANCE AND ENGLAND:
THE FOURTEENTH CENTURY

✤

FRANCE UNDER THE SONS OF PHILIP IV, 1314–28

THE sons of Philip IV who ruled France in succession to each other from 1314 to 1328 merely continued the work of their father. The chief interest of the period is in the dynastic succession, when fortuitously and through expediency the so-called Salic Law was established in France, but of far greater importance was the gradual evolution of administration which continued along the lines begun under Philip IV.

Louis X (1314–16) was confronted at his accession with one of those baronial revolts which always followed an especially strong rule in France. The old ministers of Philip IV were overthrown, de Marigny being hanged at his own gallows at Montfauçon, and the nobles forced the king to grant charters giving greater powers to the provincial estates and reducing those of the central government. Nevertheless in his reign the organization of the *Chambre des Comtes* was perfected and the *Grand Conseil* became an independent body. Philip IV had consulted with a number of ministers and nobles; under his son the body took definite form and became a regular council of twenty-four princes and important lords with considerable power in its own hands, acting in matters which the king could not attend to personally. The Parlement of Paris also tightened up its organization and increased its competence, establishing fixed sessions, departmental subdivisions, and extending its rights over appeals.

When Louis X died he left an infant daughter, and his wife pregnant. The child, when born a boy, was immediately proclaimed King John I, but it died almost immediately and the throne passed to Louis' younger brother Philip V (1316–22), passing over the claims of the four-year-old daughter Jeanne. The whole matter was one of expediency; it seemed far better that Philip should be king than that he should continue as regent through a long minority, and the matter was handled with tact and ease. The development of administration continued through the reign of Philip V, who was a conscientious and hard-working ruler, but local opposition defeated some of the king's plans for increased centralization, and heavy taxation made the king unpopular with his subjects.

When Philip died in 1322, he too left only daughters, and the throne

KINGS OF FRANCE, 1270–1515

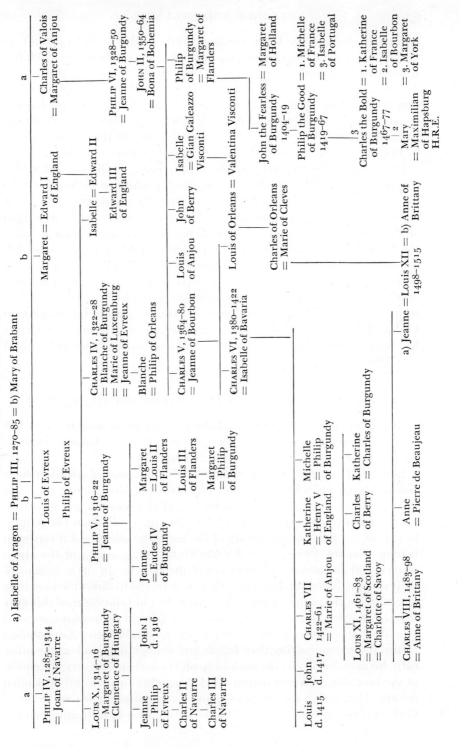

again was given to the king's younger brother, Charles IV (1322–28), to avoid the complications of a long regency. After the precedent set by Philip, it was easy for Charles to advance his own claims and secure the throne. The short reign of Charles IV is notable chiefly for the attempts of the king, supported by Pope John XXII, to secure his own election as Holy Roman emperor in opposition to Louis of Bavaria, schemes which came to nothing. At Charles' death in 1328, also without male heirs, the throne was claimed by Philip of Valois, a cousin, the son of Philip IV's younger brother.

It was at this time that the royal lawyers, to justify Philip's accession, discovered the Salic Law, which, it was claimed, prohibited succession to the throne of France through a female line. Actually the claim of Philip VI (1328–50) was based on expediency and the precedents of accession of 1316 and 1322, and the law was merely a legal fiction which justified the act after the event. Its importance lay in the fact that it excluded the claims of Edward III of England, who was the grandson of Philip IV through Isabelle. Ordinarly the son of a daughter would have better claims than the son of a brother, but the "discovery" of the Salic Law gave Philip of Valois the better claim, and Edward did not press his claims, performing homage to Philip after his coronation. A few years later, in 1337, when other factors had led him to war anyway, Edward renounced his allegiance and revived his claims to the French crown.

ENGLAND UNDER EDWARD II AND EDWARD III, 1307–37

In England the death of Edward I also produced a baronial reaction, but there the movement took a more constitutional form, the barons seeking to wrest control of the government from the king.

Edward II (1307–27) was a weak, selfish man, endowed with but little political sense and wholly dominated by favorites. Chief among these was one Pier Gaveston, whom Edward made earl of Cornwall, and who arrogantly domineered over the lords whose lineage made them the natural leaders of the English community of the realm. So offensive did Gaveston become that the barons in 1308 came armed to a meeting of the king's council and demanded the expulsion of the favorite. In the statement of their case the barons declared that they were bound to direct the king if he strayed from the path of virtue, and that it was in fulfillment of this duty that they sought the banishment of Gaveston. Edward reluctantly consented to exile Pier to Ireland, but within a year he recalled him. Gaveston returned more domineering than before and deliberately insulted the other earls, his enemies. Under the leadership of Thomas of Lancaster, the cousin of the king, the earls and barons banded together in 1310 and demanded reform. They forced the king to appoint a committee known as the Lords Ordainers to serve for a year as the royal executive in instituting reform.

The following year they presented their program, calling for annual parliaments, responsibility of all royal ministers to Parliament, parliamentary control over war and the coinage, and demanding the expulsion of Gaveston and other royal favorites.

Had the Ordainers been men of a more liberal stamp, and led by a statesman of ability instead of a reactionary, selfish baron like Lancaster, this program might have been a great step in English constitutional development, but it was in reality no more than a reaffirmation of the ideas of the Provisions of Oxford. The Parliament, as far as they were concerned, meant only the barons, and parliamentary limitation of the crown was actually merely a control exercised by the barons.

Edward was constrained to accept the Ordinance, but refused to abandon Gaveston whom he hid in a royal castle. The earls took up arms, captured Gaveston and beheaded him (1312); Edward armed to avenge his friend, but the lords made their submission and an armistice was arranged in 1313. The situation in Scotland, where Robert Bruce had united the country against the English, demanded all the king's attention, so that he was forced to accept the excuses of Lancaster and his partisans. In 1314, however, the Scots won their great victory at Bannockburn which ended all hope of successful English control in the northern kingdom. Discontent was rife throughout England, the political situation being aggravated by bad crops, famine, the plague, and rebellion in the Marches and in Wales. While popular resentment at the extravagance of the king ran high, and Lancaster had the Ordinance reissued in Parliament, Edward proceeded to develop new favorites in the de Spencers, father and son, and plotted to avenge himself on Lancaster at the first opportunity. In 1322 war broke out between the king and the Ordainers over a minor incident. At Boroughbridge the royal forces won a decisive victory over the barons, and Edward had his revenge when Lancaster and three other earls were beheaded as traitors. In the Statute of York, issued in the same year, Edward restored the old order before the Ordinance, and returned to a royal despotism dominated by favorites.[1]

For the next four years, Edward and the de Spencers tryrannized over England, taxing heavily and ruling badly. English arms continued to meet

[1] It was long maintained that the Statute of York granted Commons the right to participate in all matters of legislation. This view still has its defenders, but has been attacked with great cogency in a number of recent studies wherein the "community of the realm" has been reduced to the barons, the consent has been limited to taxation alone, and the whole thing has been discounted as merely a convenient phrase. Such eminent authorities as C. H. McIlwain, Gaines Post, G. T. Lapsley, W. A. Morris, G. L. Haskins, M. V. Clarke, H. G. Richardson, G. Sayles and others have discussed the problem at great length in books and articles. Probably the best summaries of the question with divergent points of view are to be found in Strayer, "Statute of York and the Community of the Realm" in the *Amer. His. Rev.* XLVII (1941); W. A. Morris "Magnates and the Community of the Realm in Parliament" in *Medievalia et Humanistica* I (1943); and G. L. Haskins' several studies.

defeat in Scotland; there was trouble with France over the Gascon frontier; the barons smouldered in their resentment, and the clergy were stirred up against the king by Adam Orton, bishop of Hereford. In 1325 Queen Isabelle was sent to France to arrange a treaty with her brother, and there met Roger Mortimer, a Marcher lord who had fled to France after the fall of the Ordainers. The Queen and the Marcher lord soon became intimate, and conspired to rid themselves and England of the incompetent king. In September 1326 they landed in England with an armed force and declared open war on Edward. London and most of the country rose in support of the injured queen; Edward fled to Wales, only to be captured and brought back to prison, while both the de Spencers were executed. In a parliament of January 1327, Orton demanded that young Edward III replace his father on the throne, and when this was seen to have popular approval, articles were drawn up against Edward II.

The king was given the opportunity to abdicate rather than face deposition, and agreed to do so on receiving promises of personal safety and honorable treatment. But these promises were broken and the miserable king was murdered in his prison before the year was out. Meanwhile Edward III, then aged fourteen, was proclaimed king and received the homages of the realms. Isabelle and Mortimer were recognized as regents during the minority.

The bad rule of Edward II was followed by a worse rule by Isabelle and Mortimer, the latter taking the title of Earl of March. The scandal of their irregular union was aggravated by the rapaciousness of their financial exactions and the ineptitude of their foreign policy, which was one of general appeasement. Bruce was recognized as king of Scotland; an indemnity was paid and land was ceded to France to settle the Gascon border trouble, while homage was performed to both Charles IV and later to Philip VI for the English possessions in France. The barons became restive, Henry of Lancaster taking his father's place as leader of the opposition; but Mortimer frustrated their plans and maneuvered Edmund of Kent, the younger brother of Edward II, into open treason for which he was executed. The execution of his uncle, added to the suggestions offered by Lancaster, decided young Edward III to assert himself and overthrow the regent. Mortimer was arrested by partisans of the king, charged with treason, tried in Parliament and executed (1330); Isabelle was allowed to retire to honorable seclusion. In 1358, after taking the veil of the sisters of Santa Clara, she died.

Edward III (1327–77) was not a great king, but he was an honest one. His talents were entirely in the military line where his personal bravery made him conspicuous. He was a chivalrous knight, with the best virtues of that class, his courage being far more conspicuous than his intellect. Under him England experienced a considerable constitutional development chiefly because the king and Parliament were able to work together and the king, who was more interested in his wars than in internal politics, proved willing to accept parliamentary limitations of his prerogative in return for a steady flow of supply.

The whole reign was colored by the war which broke out with France in 1337 but, largely owing to the king's preoccupation with the war, Parliament gained significant powers. In the matter of personnel the clergy withdrew into Convocation and the Parliament divided into the two distinct houses of Lords and Commons, while the Council became clearly differentiated from Parliament. In the sphere of competence, Parliament gained complete control of the voting of supply and for a time regulated expenditures; ministerial responsibility to Parliament was established in 1341 and in 1376 impeachment of royal officials was begun. Within Parliament the Commons took the lead and Commons' petitions came to be the accepted means of initiating legislation. While most of the judicial work was done by Council, the court of Parliament also developed the right to try all peers and to hear appeals on error.

It was under Edward III that the English Parliament passed the great antipapal statutes of Provisors (1351) and Praemunire (1353), the first of which invalidated all papal provisions in England and required that English sees be filled by English men, while the second declared that appeals to Rome from any English court were treason. Economic matters also occupied much of the attention of Edward's Parliaments, the agricultural situation undergoing great changes through development of the system of enclosures and the substitution of free for servile labor. As it had long been more profitable to raise sheep for wool than to engage in produce or grain farming, large areas were enclosed for pasture with a consequent loss of arable land. The lords also discovered that they could operate more cheaply with hired labor than they could with the old servile tenantry, who received compensation for their boon work which often amounted to more than the work was worth. The lord found that he could make much more out of the land if he freed the serfs, took the land into his own possession and either had it farmed by hired labor or turned it into sheep pastures. This had been going on steadily throughout the fourteenth century when the ravages of the Black Death in 1348–50 suddenly changed the whole picture by reducing the number of laborers and forcing up the price of hired hands. To meet this emergency, Parliament passed the famous Statute of Laborers of 1351 which decreed that no laborer could receive more than the wage paid him in 1346 before the Black Death. But the law of supply and demand was stronger than any Parliamentary statute and both employers and workers joined in violating the Statute. In 1361 an act was passed which punished with branding any laborer who left his job for one bringing higher pay, but even this proved ineffective. The situation continued to get worse throughout the reign and finally resulted in the great Peasant Revolt of 1381 under Richard II.

In foreign commerce the government also took a hand. To mitigate against smuggling, and to guarantee the use of English ships in the carrying trade, a Staple was established at Calais (after that city was captured) through which all goods going from or coming to England must pass. This was augmented in the reign of Richard II in 1381 by the first of the Navigation Acts, which were to become standard British policy through the eighteenth century. It was economics as much as politics that led England into the Hundred Years' War with France, and to that conflict we must now turn our attention.

THE FIRST PHASE OF THE HUNDRED YEARS' WAR, 1337–60

The ostensible excuse for the English attack on France which began in 1337 was Edward's claim to the French throne, which he advanced as the son of Isabelle, the daughter of Philip IV. However, this excuse was thought up only after the war had practically begun and the true causes must be sought in Flanders, Gascony, and Scotland.

In Scotland, the French had consistently supported the house of Bruce against the English and had helped restore David Bruce to his throne in 1341 against the opposition of Edward III. The Gascon trouble was a continuation of the old border dispute and conflict of jurisdictions which had troubled Anglo-French relations under Edward I and Philip IV, and which had gotten worse rather than better as time passed. The occasional conflicts of French and English ships in the Channel also continued with considerable damage to shipping on both sides. But the worst cause of trouble was Flanders where England supported the towns against their count, who had the backing of France.

A popular rising of the townsmen had driven Count Louis de Nevers of Flanders from possession of much of his lands. Louis appealed for help to his suzerain Philip VI, who brought a French army into Flanders, which routed the forces of the townsmen at Cassel (August 1328). The merchants turned to England with which they were closely connected owing to the cross-Channel trade in wool. In 1336, Count Louis arrested all English merchants in Flanders, confiscating their goods; Edward retaliated by seizing all Flemish merchants and by prohibiting the export of all wool to Flanders, which shut down the weaving industry there for lack of raw materials. The Flemish burghers rose under Jacques van Artevelde of Ghent in 1337, got control of most of the county and brought about the removal of the English embargo. Meanwhile Philip had declared Gascony confiscated to the French crown, so that Edward owed no allegiance to the French monarchy. Largely to assuage the consciences of the Flemings, Edward assumed the title of King of France and sent a formal defiance to Philip (November 1337).

Several theories have been advanced as to the true aims of Edward in declaring war on France. One interpretation is that he hoped to gain the complete independence of Guyenne from French suzerainty and expected by claiming the whole of France to force a cession of his full control over the southern provinces. Another is that his real goal was Scotland, and he wished to engage France so that she could offer no assistance to the Scots in their resistance. There is little reason to believe that Edward himself ever took seriously his claim to the French crown, but it gave him a strong weapon with which to demand concessions that he did want.

In 1337, France was by far the greater country of the two, with a larger army and greater resources. But the French army was the old feudal array, with the heavily-armed knights forming its most effective arm, and infantry playing a relatively minor role. The English on the other hand relied mainly on the archers, who wielded the long bows with deadly effect. Instead of knights serving for stipulated periods, the English forces were mercenaries paid by the king and ready to serve indefinitely; they were either professional "companies," recruited by a leader and hired by the king, or the yeoman militia who made up the bulk of the archers. Further, Edward was in a much better financial position than Philip. The war was popular in England and Parliament voted supplies willingly, so that the English forces were better equipped and supplied than were the rather badly equipped and wholly disorganized French. England also had allies: Edward had built up a grand coalition which included the Flemish towns, the emperor Louis of Bavaria, the lords of Brabant, Hainault, Juliers, and others. Philip was supported by Pope Clement VI, who excommunicated all the enemies of the king of France: but as the English clergy stood solidly behind their king this did not trouble Edward at all.

The military operations of the war were slow in getting under way. In 1339 Edward led an expedition to Picardy but accomplished nothing and withdrew. The first important battle of the war occurred on June 24, 1340 at Sluys off the coast of Flanders, when the French navy attacked the English ships which were bringing troops to the Continent. The English won a signal victory, which gave them complete control of the Channel, but Edward was unable to win any marked victories on land and consented to a truce.

The failure of the English to win anything on land was due to the fact that at this time the art of defense was much more highly developed than that of offense. Edward could win any pitched battle in which he could engage the French, but he could not successfully storm a town or castle. His whole tactic in these campaigns was to ravage the country and try to make the French attack him on the open field; as long as they refused an open battle and stayed behind the walls of their castles and towns, no decisive engagement could take place. Not until the use of cannon and gunpowder was well developed did offensive warfare catch up with the defensive perfection which had been achieved in the stone castles of the thirteenth and fourteenth centuries.

The Hundred Years' War was a succession of isolated campaigns broken by numerous truces. Actually it lasted from 1337 to 1453—well over the hundred years, but the years in which fighting was officially going on were much fewer. The war is generally divided into five main periods: 1. 1337–64 when the English were victorious; 2. 1364–80 when the French recouped their losses piece by piece in the reign of Charles V; 3. 1380–1415 when the war lagged and both countries engaged in civil conflict; 4. 1415–29 when the English swept everything before them; and 5. 1429–53 when the French again slowly recaptured all they had lost and finally expelled the English from all of France except Calais. For only relatively short periods during this time was there actual official war between the two countries, but at almost no time was there peace in France.

When a truce was signed between Edward and Philip in 1340 the fighting was merely transferred to a different theatre. Count John III of Brittany died in 1341 and his succession was disputed between his younger brother, John de Montfort, and Charles of Blois, the husband of his niece. Completely reversing their previous positions in the matter of female inheritance, Philip supported Charles who claimed through the female line, Edward assisting John who stood on the Salic Law. While the English occupied lower Brittany, French forces helped Charles seize most of the county. At the same time Edward lost the support of Louis of Germany, and a Flemish uprising overthrew and killed Van Artevelde (1345). In 1346 Edward reopened hostilities on a major scale by invading Normandy, where he captured Caen and struck north towards Flanders. Philip determined to cut him off and destroy him, and at Crécy the English were caught between the sea and the French army, and forced to stand on August 25, 1346. The French cavalry charged valiantly against the English long bowmen and pikemen and lost their lives in a magnificent gesture. The English victory was crushing, the French suffered tremendous losses and were utterly routed. The road to the north lay open before Edward who proceeded to the siege of Calais.

But if the English could win in the open field they still had great difficulty in siege operations, and it was not until after six months that Calais was starved into surrender. Calais was made an English town, settlers were brought over from England and the city served as a continental base for Britain until its final loss in 1558. Meanwhile John de Montfort was successful in Brittany and Queen Philippa of England, who had been left in control during her husband's absence overseas, defeated a Scottish invasion of northern England at Neville's Cross (October 1346). England was everywhere victorious and France sued for peace. The truce, which was signed at Calais on September 28, 1347, lasted until after the death of Philip VI (1350).

Both sides were exhausted. The Black Death ravaged both countries with its terrible toll of lives; the costs of the war had drained the resources of both kingdoms. We have already noted how the English Parliament took advantage of Edward's financial necessities to establish its own control over finance; the French Estates General failed to accomplish the same end. Many new taxes were raised in France:—the *gabelle,* the tax on salt, which as Edward III said made Philip truly a Salic king, being the most famous—and special levies were made on clergy and nobles, while the Estates were called upon to vote extra supplies. Loans were also floated with the papacy which at this time was wholly French in its sympathies. The financial demands of the crown were not without their effect in increasing the importance of the French Estates General, but it was the provincial Estates rather than the national body which really profited. Meanwhile France received two important cessions of territory when she acquired Montpellier from the king of Majorca, and Dauphiné from Humbert II. By the terms of the sale of Dauphiné to France, the district was to become the property of the eldest son of the king and was to retain its own local individuality; but by this acquisition France first reached her natural eastern border in the Alps.

John the Good (1350–64) who succeeded to the throne of France on the death of his father Philip VI in 1350, was a model of chivalry and knightly virtue, but an ineffectual king. Fortunately he relied somewhat on the advice of his son, the future Charles V, who was shrewd and diplomatic, later showing himself to be possessed of all the qualifications for a king which his father lacked. From the beginning of the reign there was border fighting around Guyenne, but the war on any large scale only began again in 1355 when Edward, the Black Prince, issued out from his headquarters at Bordeaux to harry the French lands south of the Loire. This method of warfare became characteristic of the conflict; bypassing strong castles, the armies would make long plundering raids into the enemy's country, burning villages and carrying off animals and crops. Neither side gained much from these raids, but the country was ruinously devastated. In 1355 Prince Edward overran Languedoc in a campaign in which he ravaged the country and brought back much booty to Bordeaux.

Meanwhile a new leader had risen to prominence in the person of Charles the Bad, king of Navarre, the son of Jeanne, the daughter of King Louis X. If the Salic Law were to be denied and succession through the female line recognized, it was Charles, as heir of the eldest line, who had the best claims to the throne. As it was, he held Navarre, Evreux, and other fiefs in Normandy where he had a very considerable following. At first Charles was friendly to King John, whose daughter he married, but in 1354 he broke with the king when he murdered one of John's favorites, Charles de la Cerda of Spain, constable of France. Having broken with the king, Charles turned to Edward to whom he proposed a partition of France. To prevent this, King John offered Charles complete forgiveness and had him invited to a banquet at Rouen. When Charles came, he was arrested by the king's men and thrown into prison; his followers at once appealed to Edward to avenge him.

Edward accepted the overtures of the Navarrese party; all lower Normandy revolted and declared for England while the Black Prince started north from Bordeaux to join the Norman insurgents. The French gathered at Chartres to prevent the Black Prince from crossing the Loire and forced him back into Poitou. There at Maupertuis, near Poitiers, on September 19, 1356 Prince Edward defeated the French, commanded by King John, in a victory which was at least the equal of Crécy. King John and his son, Philip of Burgundy, were captured along with many other knights, and the French army was again routed. Poitiers confirmed the decision of Crécy that the mounted knights were no match for the longbow, but the French were not yet able to learn the lesson thus taught. It took Nicopolis and Agincourt before they finally realized the change that had come over military tactics in the previous century.

The capture of King John and his subsequent imprisonment in England left France without a recognized head. Charles of Normandy, the dauphin, was declared regent at once but found his control challenged by the Estates General, which had already begun to assert itself under the leadership of Etienne Marcel, the provost of the merchants of Paris.

In December 1355, the Estates had granted supply only at the expense of reorganizing the administration. It was stipulated that the money voted was to be used for the enlistment of troops to be recruited by the officers of the Estates, and the king was forced to agree to consult the Estates before demanding any new tax of any kind. When, after Poitiers, the regent needed more money—to provide for the ransom of the king and to raise new levies—the Estates demanded the election of a Council of State to advise the crown in all matters of internal government and the prosecution of the war. In 1357 was issued the *Grande Ordonnance* wherein the Estates promised a heavy tax, but demanded extensive reforms in administration and the responsibility of all royal officers to the Estates. They were to have representatives on the king's council, to have control over the coinage and the collection of taxes, and to be allowed to meet on their own initiative. They also demanded the punishment of the king's evil councillors and the release from prison of Charles of Navarre. Meanwhile Navarre escaped from his prison and came to Paris where he made common cause with Marcel. Then, as Charles had not dismissed some of his councillors whom the Estates opposed, two of his most trusted lieutenants were murdered by the orders of Marcel (1358).

The dauphin fled Paris and summoned the Estates to meet at Compiègne. Marcel and Navarre fortified Paris and prepared to resist, while the dauphin collected an army and laid siege to the city. Meanwhile bands of mercenary troops, the infamous "free companies," were ravaging northern France, Normandy and Picardy, and were approaching Paris itself. These companies of mercenaries, organized under their own captains, had been employed by both sides during the war, and failed to disband when truces were signed, continuing to harry the country at will. The only difference was that during the truce they pillaged the lands of both the French and the English instead of devoting their attacks to the territories held by the enemy.

In the midst of this confusion broke out the *Jacquerie,* a revolt of the peasants of the Île de France, Beauvaisis, Picardy, and Champagne. The destruction caused by the free companies was one of the principle causes for this peasant insurrection, but they blamed the government for its inability to keep peace, and wreaked their vengeance and hate on their lords, burning chateaux and expelling the nobles. Marcel, without entirely approving the peasant movement, attempted to use it for his own ends. But Charles of Navarre could not favor the peasantry against his own class, and descended on the hapless peasants with great vigor. Thus the dauphin and Navarre found themselves fighting a common war against the rebellious peasants and Marcel, while they were fighting against each other for the control of Paris. In the suppression of the Jacquerie, over 20,000 peasants are said to have been killed, and the country was further devastated. With the revolt settled, Navarre and the dauphin resumed their struggle for Paris. Navarre invited in the English who occupied the city, but the Parisians were so bitterly anti-English that Marcel was forced to dismiss the English garrison. Shortly thereafter, Marcel was himself murdered and the dauphin entered Paris in triumph, which enabled him to force the surrender of Charles of Navarre.

King John in London was meanwhile negotiating a treaty with England. The Treaty of London made over to England all the old Plantagenet possessions in France from Normandy through Gascony, fifteen provinces in all, and agreed to pay a ransom of four million crowns. When this treaty was sent to France, both the dauphin and the Estates refused to ratify it, and war began again. Edward III led an army in a raid across France, reaching Rheims but capturing no important cities. He besieged Paris but was unable to capture it, and allowed the papal legate to begin negotiations for a peace.

The treaty was negotiated at Bretigny in May 1360 and was solemnly ratified at Calais in October. By its terms Edward renounced all claims to the throne of France and was given full and free ownership of eleven counties, including all the old Plantagenet lands south of the Loire (Poitou, Limousin, Perigord, Guyenne et al.) and the districts of Pontheiu, Guines, and Montreuil, including the city of Calais in the north. The ransom for King John was set at three million crowns of which 600,000 were to be paid before the release of the king. However Edward was willing to mitigate this to a degree, and liberated John when only 400,000 crowns had been paid over, taking hostages, among whom was John's son, Louis duke of Anjou, for the balance of the ransom. Edward's renunciation

FRANCE AT THE
TREATY OF BRETIGNY
*showing conquests
made by the
English, 1337–69*

of his claims and John's surrender of the suzerainty of Guyenne were not to be effective until the other terms of the treaty had been fulfilled. By 1363 the transfer of most of the land to England had been effected, but although John exhausted every resource in his attempt to raise money, he was still several million crowns short. While John was still trying to find money, his son, Louis of Anjou, broke his parole and escaped to France. John, ever the chivalrous and impractical knight, at once insisted on returning to captivity in England until the entire ransom should be paid. He was honorably received in England, but died after a few months, in April 1364, probably the most constructive thing he ever did for his country.

THE WAR UNDER CHARLES V, 1364–80

Charles V, the Wise (1364–80), lacked entirely his father's military prowess but possessed instead a native shrewdness, a fine touch in diplomacy, and a tendency to despotism. Moreover he was a good judge of character and picked able ministers and officers whom he bound to himself

and who served him loyally. There was no need for the king to be a military
hero when he could enlist the services of a Bertrand du Guesclin, and the
great constable won back for his king almost all the lands which had
been lost in the previous reigns. In contrast to the first period of the war
there were no great battles, no overwhelming victories; instead there was a
slow, steady pushing forward of the French control until almost nothing
was left to the English.

The reign opened favorably with the defeat of Charles of Navarre and
the winning over of John de Montfort of Brittany. In the Breton war which
had been going along throughout this entire period, John, assisted by the
English under Sir John Chandos, had finally defeated his rival and made
himself unchallenged count of Brittany. But in 1365 French diplomacy
succeeded in winning him over and he became the vassal of King Charles,
throwing his support to France.

With the cessation of the English, Navarrese, and Breton wars the
problem of the free companies became even more acute. These organized
brigands roved all over France leaving only destruction in their wake;
getting rid of these dangerous and unruly bands became one of the chief
problems of both the French and English governments in France. We
have already seen how one of these companies, the Navarrese Company,
was sent to Greece where they overran Thebes and Morea. The great bulk
of the "free companies" were diverted by Charles V in 1365 into Castile,
where Pedro the Cruel and his half-brother, Henry of Trastamara, were
fighting for the crown. King Charles declared himself in favor of Henry
and sent du Guesclin to Spain at the head of a large army of the freebooters; Edward, the Black Prince, at once took the other side and led
a force of the mercenaries to the support of Pedro. A great battle was
fought at Navarette (Nájera) in April 1367 which secured the throne for
Pedro and successfully killed off many of the mercenaries on both sides—
the essential cause for the campaign. The Black Prince went back to
Bordeaux and du Guesclin finally overthrew Pedro, installing Henry as
king of Castile.

In France meanwhile, King Charles set about organizing a new army
recruited, like the English, in part from "free companies" and in part
from native peasantry trained as archers (though they still clung to the
cross bow). He also developed some artillery which was just coming into
use, and began the building of a royal navy based on Rouen, with which
he was able to wrest control of the seas from the English in 1372. To
finance this Charles resorted to heavy indirect taxation—sales taxes etc.—
and levied a hearth tax, the *fouage,* which quickly became the most hated
form of taxation. After the experience of his regency, Charles consulted
the Estates but sparingly, relying rather on a group of intimate councillors.

Charles won a diplomatic victory of no mean importance when he secured the hand of Margaret, heiress of Louis, count of Flanders, for his brother Philip of Burgundy. She had previously been bethrothed to Edmund of Cambridge, which would have tied Flanders closely to England, but Charles persuaded the pope to revoke the dispensation issued for this marriage, and bribed Count Louis to give his daughter to Philip. This was the foundation of the fortunes of the house of Valois-Burgundy with its great wealth in the Low Countries.

The war with England broke out again in 1369. Charles claimed suzerainty over Gascony and was supported by a revolt of the Gascon nobles who resented the strong rule of the Black Prince. In a campaign of skirmishes and small gains du Guesclin slowly occupied most of the English south, being careful not to engage in any large pitched battles but to confine the fighting to sieges and minor engagements. Then in 1376 the Black Prince died, to be followed the next year by Edward III. England now suffered from a minority while the king's uncles disputed the control, and the French were able to make conspicuous gains. In 1378 John of Brittany returned to the English alliance only to be declared forfeit and have his county taken away from him by du Guesclin. Charles of Navarre was found guilty of treason and his lands occupied by the constable. At the death of King Charles in 1380, France had regained all her territory except Calais, Cherbourg, Brest, Bordeaux, and Bayonne, and the war became a very desultory affair on both sides until a truce was arranged in 1396.

CHAPTER 38

FRANCE AND ENGLAND:
THE FIFTEENTH CENTURY

❖

CIVIL WAR IN FRANCE AND IN ENGLAND, 1380–1415

FOR thirty years both France and England lost interest in the war while they engaged in dynastic struggles at home. The death of Charles V left the throne to his twelve-year-old son Charles VI (1380–1422), under the regency of his uncles, Louis of Anjou, Philip of Burgundy, John of Berry, and Louis of Bourbon. Anjou was appointed regent, but the custody of the young king's person was entrusted to Burgundy and his maternal uncle of Bourbon, who could have no interest in the succession. On his deathbed Charles V had ordered that the *fouage* and other unpopular taxes should be cancelled, with the result that when the new government attempted to collect them there was a general uprising. The government maintained that Charles had meant only to forgive all arrears in the taxes due at his death, but the people insisted that the king had ordered that the taxes should not be collected in the future. A Paris mob, known as the *maillotins* from mallets they carried, attacked the government buildings, burning the archives, murdering some of the tax collectors and opening the jails. Similar risings took place in Rouen and other cities of the kingdom. In 1382 the Flemings again revolted, electing as their leader Philip van Artevelde, the son of Jacques their former champion. Philip of Burgundy acted with firmness; raising a considerable army he defeated the Flemings at Roosebeke (November 1382), where van Artevelde was killed, and put down the rising with great cruelty. Then he turned on Paris, and, in 1383, Burgundy and Berry suppressed the revolts throughout France, executing the rebels wholesale. Anjou had meanwhile gone to Italy where he was endeavoring to assert claims to the crown of Naples, thus leaving France to the mercies of his brothers. From 1383 to 1388, Burgundy dominated the government of France, arranging a marriage alliance between Charles and Isabelle of Bavaria. He planned a great expedition against England, but it came to nothing owing to the opposition of Berry, who feared his brother's pre-eminence. Finally in 1388 King Charles threw off the tutelage of his uncles and declared himself ready to rule personally.

Charles turned at first to the former ministers of his father, called derisively the *marmousets* by the dukes, but the dominating figure soon became the younger brother of the king, Louis duke of Orleans, a charming, extravagant, selfish, ambitious man who completely controlled his weak-willed brother. It was Orleans who was the strong influence in securing the support of France for the Avignon popes during the Schism. From the very beginning there was hostility between Orleans and his uncle of Burgundy, each of whom sought to dominate the crown. Charles VI probably sincerely wished to reform the administration and the shattered finances of his country, but he was fundamentally weak, and while the state was very nearly bankrupt and the expenses of the war were more than the kingdom could stand, Charles and Louis of Orleans spent great sums in useless entertainments, balls, banquets, and festivities at court.

Then in August 1392 King Charles was seized with a fit of insanity. At first the attacks were not of long duration and were spaced at rather long intervals, but they became increasingly worse until the king was a hopeless madman with but few lucid intervals. Louis of Orleans and Philip of Burgundy both stepped into the breach to govern the realm for the mad king. All of the marmousets were driven from office and any attempt at reform was dropped. In 1396 a truce was arranged with England, ending the war which was so distasteful to both parties by now; England kept Calais and parts of Gascony and the friendship of the two nations was guaranteed by the marriage of Richard II to Isabelle, the infant daughter of King Charles.

The struggle between Orleans and Burgundy was intensified when Philip of Burgundy died in 1404 and was succeeded by his son John the Fearless (1404–19). Inheriting Burgundy, Flanders, Artois, Champagne and several minor counties, John gained by marriage Hainault, Holland, Brabant, and Limburg, thus setting Burgundy well on the way to the establishment of the "Middle Kingdom" which was to be the goal of his grandson Charles. John was rash and intemperate, and, feeling himself the first lord of the realm, resented the predominance of Orleans. The two princes differed on every conceivable issue, supporting rival popes, rival emperors, and different foreign policies. Louis had the support of the queen, Isabelle of Bavaria, whose lover he was purported to be, and through her the control over the king. In November 1407 John of Burgundy thought to settle the matter by having Orleans murdered in a Paris street.

Although supported by the city of Paris, where he caused John Petit to defend the murder by invoking the theory of tyrannicide, John of Burgundy had stirred up a hornets' nest against himself. Valentine Visconti the widow of the murdered duke, Charles of Orleans his son, Bernard of Armagnac, the father of Charles' wife, and Queen Isabelle, were the nucleus of a party which included the dukes of Berry, Bourbon, and Brittany. Burgundy turned to England offering alliance, but the *Armagnacs* (as the Orleanist party was thereafter to be known) outbid him and signed an alliance with Henry IV whereby the English monarch was to receive all of Aquitaine in return for help against Burgundy. John of Burgundy at Paris declared himself the protector of the French people and attacked the Armagnacs at Bourges. But an ephemeral truce was effected at Auxerre in 1412 while the English ravaged Normandy on their own.

In 1413, probably at the instigation of the duke of Burgundy, the Estates General of the north were summoned to meet at Paris. At once they began to draw up plans for reform, supported by Burgundy. While the Estates were working on their program, the Paris mob, led by one Simon Caboche, took matters into their own hands. Claiming that the reforms were not being sincerely undertaken, and that there were traitors in the council of the king, the Cabochiens stormed the Bastile and invaded the royal palace. King Charles was at the moment in one of his saner periods. He joined the mob and promised to enforce their demands. An *Ordonnace cabochienne* of 258 articles was prepared which demanded that all officials be elected rather than appointed, set up new advisory councils, reduced the number of royal officials, and gave strict control of taxation and expenditure to the elected assemblies. This ordinance was promulgated in May 1413, but was never put into effect. It was the work of the University members of the Estates and not at all what the mob wanted, and they expressed their displeasure by rioting. There was a short reign of terror in which the mob killed several of the ministers and forced Burgundy to flee. Then the dauphin Louis, who had gone over to the Armagnacs, with the support of the upper bourgeoisie got control of the city and inaugurated a "white terror." Burgundy retreated to Flanders where he collected an army and returned as far as St. Denis, but he was unable to take Paris, and the Armagnac rule was strong enough that the Parisians, who were generally Burgundian, could not rise in his favor. Duke John was declared outlawed; a royal army sacked Soissons but was defeated at Arras, and a truce was made which left the Armagnacs in Paris and in control of all the governmental posts. This was the situation in France when Henry V renewed the English claims to France and began the war anew.

Meanwhile England had also been suffering from civil disturbances, though the results were not as disastrous as in France. On the death of Edward III in 1377 the throne passed to his grandson Richard II (1377–99), the son of the Black Prince. As in the case of Charles VI of France, the regency was taken over by the uncles of the youthful king, John of Gaunt, duke of Lancaster, playing the leading role. In England too, Parliament had become more demanding towards the end of the reign of the old king, the famous "Good Parliament" of 1376 having refused grant of supply until grievances were redressed, and having impeached the lord chamberlain for peculation. This was the first use of impeachment to control a minister of the crown; it was also the first appearance of the speaker of the Commons as an important leader of Parliament. This effrontery of the Parliament was punished by John of Gaunt who imprisoned the speaker, but a precedent had been set which was never to be lost.

England also suffered from a peasant uprising. The Great Revolt of 1381 was touched off by the imposition of a poll tax, but its underlying causes were the resentment of the peasants at the attempts to restore villeinage, and that of the artisans at the incursions of foreign competition, while all of the laboring classes resented the restrictive legislation which had been passed since the Black Death. As we have seen above, the egalitarian preaching of John Ball may also have had some part in stirring up the revolutionary movement.

The revolt began in Essex and Kent but rapidly spread to other parts of the country. Under Wat Tyler, the rebels marched on London where King Richard met them and promised to redress their grievances, granting an immediate abolition of all serfdom and banalities. So far the movement had not been especially violent, but the rebels got into London where they began to pillage and riot, murdering the archbishop of Canterbury, the lord treasurer, and several royal officials. While the king continued to offer concessions, the burgesses of London rose against the rebels, killing Tyler and a number of his followers. The death of Wat Tyler ended the most serious part of the revolt, and the local insurrections in Cambridge, Norwich, and York were quickly suppressed. The net result of the whole affair was that all the royal concessions were revoked and the peasants were, if anything, worse off than before.

Meanwhile King Richard was building up a court party around Michael de la Pole, earl of Suffolk, and Robert de Vere, earl of Oxford, to offset the predominance of his uncle of Lancaster. At the same time a third, baronial, party was forming around Thomas of Woodstock, earl of Gloucester, another uncle of the king. While Lancaster took control of the foreign war, and led a "crusade" into Spain to secure that country to the obedience of Pope Urban and to his own possession, Gloucester allied with Parliament to oppose the royal party. The earl of Suffolk was impeached and imprisoned but was promptly released by the king. Gloucester, Warwick, Arundel, and some of the other earls took up arms, and calling themselves the "Lords Appellant" marched on London where they seized control of the government. Under their guidance the "Merciless Parliament" of 1388 impeached and executed two of the king's ministers, issuing a general proscription of the royalists. For more than a year the Lords Appellant ruled, before the king felt able to strike back. Then in 1389 Richard declared himself able to govern alone, demanded the resignation of several ministers appointed by the Lords and took over the government into his own hands. Against the opposition of Gloucester and his colleagues, King Richard and Lancaster had made common cause, and for several years Duke John played a leading role in the councils of the king. For eight years (1389–97) there was a close co-operation between king and Parliament, ministerial responsibility to Parliament being recognized at least in theory.

The death of Anne of Bohemia, Richard's wife, in 1395, removed a restraining influence, which had contributed much to these years of good rule. Anne was able to sway her husband and during her lifetime he often followed her advice with good results. Her death, which threw him back on himself, caused him to develop more despotic tendencies and to deteriorate rapidly into a selfish despot. His second wife, Isabelle of France, whom he married in 1396, was only six years old and obviously played no significant part in national affairs.

In the last two years of his reign, from 1397 to 1399, Richard was an almost unbridled tyrant. Haxey, who ventured to criticize royal expenditure in Parliament, was arrested and condemned to death, only the intercession of some powerful bishops saving his life—a case which was to become famous in the history of parliamentary privilege. But the real goal of the king was revenge on the Lords Appellant who had so humiliated him a decade before. Determined to suppress them, Richard charged them all with treason in 1397 to 1398 and secured sentences against them; Gloucester was murdered, Arundel executed, Warwick imprisoned and Derby banished.

It was while Henry of Derby was in exile that his father John of Lancaster died and he inherited the duchy. When the king confiscated all the lands of the duchy to the royal fisc, Henry broke into open revolt and landed in Yorkshire where he was joined by the Percies of Northumberland, the earl of Westmorland, et al. Richard meanwhile had gone to Ireland to put down rebellion there. Hearing of the revolt of the barons, he returned to Britain but found the country already lost to him. He retreated to Wales but was pursued and captured. There in prison he abdicated the throne, but this was not enough, and Parliament solemnly heard charges against him and formally declared his deposition. Then after investigating the claims advanced by Derby, Parliament proclaimed that Henry of Derby was by grace of God and act of Parliament declared king of England.

The throne which Henry IV (1399–1413) ascended was none too secure, as his hereditary claims were distinctly inferior to those of several of his cousins. He had always to respect the prerogatives of Parliament which had in large measure given him the throne, and he was confronted with the problem of adequately rewarding the barons who had assisted him in his rebellion. Further, his title was by no means universally recognized and the whole reign is marked by a series of revolts. War with Scotland broke out almost immediately; Henry invaded the northern kingdom only to be stopped at Edinburgh (1400), but a Scottish invasion of England was defeated by the Percies at Homildon Hill (1402), which ended any serious threat from the Scots. More serious was the rebellion of Owen Glendower of Wales, who proclaimed Welsh independence and allied with France. Aided by a French fleet, Glendower managed to hold out for several years and it was not until 1409 that Prince Henry, the king's eldest son, brought the revolt to an end. While the Welsh war was just getting under way, Henry was faced with a great rebellion of the Percies who felt that they had not received their due. Northumberland, his son Harry Hotspur, Worcester, Edmund Mortimer earl of March, and others allied with Glendower and met the royal forces at Shrewsbury in July 1403. The king was victorious; Hotspur was killed, Worcester executed, and the others dispersed. But two years later there was an attempt to put Mortimer (who was descended from Lionel of Clarence) on the throne, in which the duke of York was implicated. A second rebellion that same year (1405) involved Mortimer, Northumberland, Glendower, and Archbishop Richard Scrope of York. The capture and execution of Archbishop Scrope caused Henry to lose much support, as the clerical position of the popular archbishop made him, in the eyes of many, immune from such drastic punishment.

Scrope's rebellion was the last important revolt to disturb the reign of Henry IV, and the last eight years of Henry's life were marked chiefly by the rise of the Beauforts, and the struggle between Prince Henry and Archbishop Thomas Arundel of Canterbury. Matters had come to an open breach between King Henry and his son when the old king died in March 1413, and Henry V (1413–22) came to the throne.

Internal affairs play but a minor role in the reign of Henry V, the entire interest of the reign centering in the renewal of the Hundred Years' War. The most significant internal events were the Lollard revolt led by Sir John Oldcastle, which occurred in the years 1413 to 1417, and the conspiracy of Richard of Cambridge in 1415. We should also point out that in the reigns of Henry IV and Henry V great gains were made by Parliament, which began to secure control of the initiative in legislation. In 1407 Parliament had demanded the right to initiate all money bills, and in 1414 claimed that no law was valid to which Parliament had not given its assent. It is in this period that Parliament secured the right to prepare bills and have them accepted as presented, which made these bills become the chief source of statutes. At the same time that Parliament was thus increasing her powers, the Council became a permanent body instead of one which met only on occasion when called. It is not true, as was once taught, that Parliament developed in the Lancastrian period while Council rose in the Yorkist. Both bodies prospered in the Lancastrian era and both were rather neglected under the more despotic and irresponsible Yorkists.

THE ENGLISH CONQUEST, 1415–29

In 1415, having secured the neutrality of Burgundy by treaty, Henry V again advanced his claims to the French throne and invaded Normandy. His motives were undoubtedly mixed; he hoped to turn men's minds from internal dissatisfaction by waging a successful foreign war, and he wished to recapture as much as he could of the old Plantagenet inheritance. Claiming the crown gave him the same lever that Edward III had possessed in his negotiations with France.

The war began with the siege and capture of Harfleur on the coast of Normandy near the mouth of the Seine. Then, following the same general tactic as that employed by Edward III in 1346, Henry turned north towards Calais. The battle which took place at Agincourt, on St. Crispin's day, October 25, 1415 was almost a repetition of Crécy; the French cavalry charged the English pike and long bowmen, their horses were killed and their lines thrown into confusion. Once again a small, lightly-armed English infantry force (13,000 men) had defeated a larger, heavier French cavalry (50,000 men), and the victory won by the "happy few" at Agincourt was decisive for the entire campaign. Henry pushed on to Calais whence he returned to England in victory. The French retreated in despair to Paris, while both Burgundian and Armagnac troops ravaged the country round about the capital. Henry tightened his entente with Burgundy, formed an alliance with Sigismund of Germany, and then in 1417 renewed his invasion of Normandy. Systematically the English proceeded to reduce the Norman duchy; Caen was besieged and taken, the smaller towns fell quickly, and it was not until Rouen was reached in July 1418 that the steady march was halted. The siege of Rouen lasted six months, the city only surrendering after starvation had reduced it to its last extremities. Only Chateau Gaillard and Mont St. Michel remained unconquered, and Chateau Gaillard fell towards the end of 1419.

Meanwhile John of Burgundy had captured Paris in May 1418, where he removed Queen Isabelle, with whom he had recently formed an alliance. The Armagnacs retreated south of the Loire, where they proclaimed the dauphin Charles regent at Bourges. Frantic negotiations ensued between the three governments; Burgundy proclaimed himself the defender of France against the English and treated with the dauphin, then negotiated with Henry for a partition of the kingdom; the dauphin treated with both Burgundy and England. During the course of these tortuous negotiations Duke John had a conference with the dauphin on a bridge at Montereau on September 10, 1419. Hardly had the conference begun than the dauphin's men fell on the duke and his companions and murdered them.

The murder of John of Burgundy resolved the diplomatic tangle for there could no longer be any question of rapprochement between Burgundy and the Armagnacs. John's son, Philip the Good (1419–67) at once entered into a close treaty of alliance with Henry and negotiated the Treaty of Troyes between Henry and the mad King Charles (May 21, 1420). By this treaty Henry was to marry Charles' daughter Katherine, and to inherit the throne of France on the death of the king; in the meantime Henry should act as regent for his father-in-law. The marriage took place in June and Henry was officially recognized as regent and heir apparent. The rest of the year was spent in cleaning out the Armagnac garrisons in northern

FRANCE IN 1429
*showing conquests
made in the campaigns,
1415–29, and the
positions of the two
monarchies at the advent
of Jeanne d'Arc.*

France. The dauphin Charles was cited to appear for trial before the Council and Parlement, and declared forfeit when he did not appear. After reorganizing the administration of Normandy, Henry returned to England to secure the English ratification of the treaty. While he was gone rebellion broke out in Normandy, and the English were badly defeated in a battle at Baugé in Anjou. Henry returned to France and was engaged in putting down the last Armagnac strongholds around Meaux and Compiègne when he died on August 31, 1422. Within two months Charles VI followed him to the grave on October 21, 1422.

The deaths of Henry V and Charles VI left the throne of France, under the terms of the Treaty of Troyes, to Henry VI, an infant nine months old. A double regency was arranged for the two uncles of the little king, John of Bedford becoming regent for France, and Humphrey of Gloucester governing England. The rule of Bedford was in general quite successful; he won several engagements and pushed the English conquests south to the Loire where in October 1428 the earl of Salisbury began the siege of Orleans. The dauphin at Bourges became so discouraged that he seriously contemplated flight to Scotland or surrendering his kingdom and retiring to Dauphiné. It was at this crucial moment that Jeanne d'Arc arrived to change the whole fortune of war and bring victory to the shattered French nation.

JEANNE D'ARC AND THE LAST YEARS OF THE WAR, 1429–53

Jeanne d'Arc (she is officially St. Jeanne d'Arc in the Catholic Church) accomplished a major miracle. She was not a great general, not a great soldier, but she infused into the Armagnac soldiers a confidence in their final victory and a certainty that God was on their side that enabled the good generals in their forces to lead them to astounding victories. Dunois, Richemont, La Trémoille, Gilles de Rais, were all able captains, but they led dispirited troops who had no confidence in themselves or their leaders. Jeanne gave them not only confidence but assurance of celestial aid and direction. She provides probably the greatest example of the importance of morale in the history of warfare.

Her effect on the English and Burgundians was hardly less than on the Armagnacs; whether she came from God or from the Devil, men doubted not that she had some supernatural power and naturally hesitated to pit themselves against her. The English feared the witch as much as the French trusted in the saint. The conclusion was foregone.

The actual generalship of Jeanne's campaigns must be credited to Dunois, the famous Bastard of Orleans, who was in some ways the best commander in the Armagnac forces. He saw the advantage that Jeanne could bring to his men and exploited her to the full. Between them they raised the siege of Orleans between April 29 and May 6, 1429, and gave the Armagnacs their first taste of real victory.

The dash to Rheims to secure the crown for Charles was strategically mad but had a tremendous moral significance. No self-respecting general would have left his base of supplies so far to the rear and gone cutting across enemy country in a mad drive to secure an empty crown. But Jeanne did, and the dauphin, now crowned King of France in the cathedral of Rheims, where the kings were wont to receive their consecration, had a much greater prestige than the "king of Bourges." It was a magnificent, mad gamble—and it worked.

With the king crowned, Jeanne's mission was ended, and after that glorious foray she met with little success. Her attack on Paris failed, and Jeanne was herself wounded at St. Denis. Shortly thereafter she was captured by the Burgundians in a skirmish at Compiègne. The story of her sale to the English, of her trial and execution at Rouen, are too familiar to require discussion here. Pierre Cauchon acted correctly according to his lights in destroying the witch who was convicted by the regular procedure of the Inquisition. The English were following an accepted practice when they burned the relapsed heretic and witch. The most astounding thing in the whole trial is the way in which Charles VII allowed her to be sacrificed. For that, Charles will always bear a brand of infamy, which his feeble motions to clear her reputation in 1450 did nothing to remove. "Charles the Well Served" has gone down in history as "Charles the Ungrateful" and obloquy will always be his meed. Whether he could have secured her release is beside the point: he never moved a finger to attempt it, though she had given him a throne.

After the meteoric career of Jeanne, the Armagnac victories continued. Dunois and Richemont advanced on Chartres and St. Denis. Bedford died, and Burgundy finally agreed to accept the alliance of the king. By the Treaty of Arras (1435) Burgundy gave his support to Charles, receiving Macon, Auxerre, and the Somme towns from St. Quentin to St. Valery, and a guarantee of independence. With Burgundy on the royal side and Bedford dead, the English had no chance. Richemont took Paris in April 1436 and the king entered the capital the following November. There was a general popular movement against the English throughout France. When a truce was made in 1444, France had reconquered everything save Normandy and Guyenne, and these last provinces were reconquered in 1449 to 1453. Rouen opened her gates to the French, forcing Talbot to surrender; Bordeaux held out to the last but was forced to capitulate by Dunois. No treaty ended the Hundred Years' War; in 1453 both sides were exhausted and stopped fighting. Only Calais remained to England of all that she had so proudly conquered less than half a century earlier.

Jeanne embodied something which was beginning to affect Frenchmen in the fifteenth century—a spirit of nationalism. If they did not feel themselves French, at least they did feel themselves different from the English—they called them *"les Goddams"* and commented on their uncouth preference for beer over wine. To say that it was French nationalism is probably going too far, for they could as well have developed a sense of Burgundian nationalism as French, but they did develop a feeling of solidarity against a foreigner, which is the beginning of nationalism, and the victories of the French king, which were rendered possible by the uplift in morale produced by Jeanne d'Arc made the French king the center of this new feeling of unity. The same tendency was at work in England; it is not pure coincidence that Henry IV was the first English king to speak English naturally rather than French, or that it was in the same generation that Geoffrey Chaucer wrote his *Canterbury Tales* in the English tongue. The old feudal world was passing and a new world of national states was emerging. In England, in France, in Hussite Bohemia, men felt themselves united as members of a common nation, as heirs of a common heritage. The old localism was dying, giving way to the far more dangerous and demanding cult of nationalism.

FRANCE AND BURGUNDY TO THE END OF THE CENTURY

The French monarchy which emerged from the Hundred Years' War was in many ways stronger than it had been at the beginning of the struggle. During the war the Estates General had for a time threatened to take over the control of the government, but they had failed to accomplish this, and the monarchy came out the stronger. The French kingdom, unlike the English, was too large for a single representative assembly to govern it well. The expenses of the delegates to the meetings of the Estates General were high and the constituencies were glad when they could avoid sending them. Provincial estates did all the work that was necessary and the national body never really found its essential place. The king soon learned how to do without it, and as the people never learned how to use it to their own advantage, the institution died out naturally. Meanwhile the Estates had for so long meekly voted the king extraordinary supplies and grants that these became taken for granted, the crown continuing to collect them without any special authorization. The local assemblies remained to conduct local business; in them the local usages were codified into laws, the *coutumiers*.

Further the crown had been strengthened by the development of the army which took place in the latter years of the war. The army remained in the royal service after the enemy against whom it had been organized was gone. It was a professional army of trained soldiers, equipped with the new artillery, owing its loyalty to its paymaster. It became one of the most important agents in establishing the French royal absolutism.

The greatest threat to the French crown lay in the existence of the great appanage dukedoms which had been created for the younger sons of the kings. These appanage nobility combined great territorial holdings with potential claims to the crown itself; what a menace their conflicting rivalries could be had been demonstrated in the reign of the mad Charles VI when Burgundy and Orleans brought the country into civil war. The growth of the Burgundian state was one of the most important developments of the fifteenth century, and the destruction of the appanages was the great work of Louis XI.

We have already seen the early rise of the dukes of Burgundy. The appanage had been created by King John for his younger son Philip the Bold (1363–1404), who was given the duchy and county of Burgundy. To this Philip added Flanders, Rethel, Nevers, and part of Artois by his marriage to Margaret of Flanders. Further territories in the Low Countries were added when a double marriage was arranged with the count of Holland,

Zeeland, Hainault, Brabant and Limburg, whereby the count married the daughter of Duke Philip while his sister married John the Fearless (1404–19). These lands were annexed to the Burgundian possessions by Duke Philip the Good (1419–67) at the death of the count, and the territories were further rounded out by the purchase of Namur and Luxemburg, and by the acquisition of the rest of Artois and the Somme towns by the Treaty of Arras (1435).

Philip the Good aspired to unite his lands in the Low Countries with those in Burgundy by securing Alsace and Lorraine but was unable to effect this acquisition. Philip also negotiated with the emperor Frederick III for a royal title, but satisfactory terms could never be reached, and the dream of the recreation of the Middle Kingdom was passed on to his son Charles the Bold (1467–77).

FRANCE AND BURGUNDY
*showing the lands
held by Charles
the Bold.*

Under Philip the Good, the Burgundian state became one of the leading powers of Europe. Rich with the wealth of the industrially developed Low Countries, occupying an area of the highest strategic importance, and with an army that was second to none in personnel and equipment, Duke Philip was able to play an important role in the politics of both France and Germany. The court of Burgundy became also a great artistic center, the dukes patronizing such artists as Claus Sluter of Dijon, and the Flemings, Jan van Eyck and Rogier van der Weyden. The weaving of tapestries and the painting of miniatures reached a high point of perfection in the Burgundian lands, while the library, which was begun under Philip the Bold, was soon the best in northern Europe. The Burgundian court became also a great center of courtly chivalry, with elaborate pageants, splendid tournaments, and a degree of luxury in living which was impossible to the poorer monarchs of France. In 1430 Philip the Good founded the knightly

Order of the Golden Fleece, the most magnificent of the chivalrous military orders.

While Duke Philip was building up Burgundy, Charles VII was trying to hold France together against numerous baronial revolts and civil disturbances. The mendacity and miserliness of Charles VII deserved less loyalty than he received from his subjects, and he was truly Charles, *"le bien servi."* He chose his chief ministers from the bourgeois class, which he favored over the nobility, allowing them to feather their own nests well so long as they served him faithfully. But he would not support them if their activities provoked too much criticism, and he permitted the ruin of his friend and financier, Jacques Coeur, with the same cold callousness that he had shown in the trial of Jeanne d'Arc.

Such a monarch was bound to inspire baronial rebellions, and the nobles found a leader in the person of the dauphin, Louis, who cordially hated his father. In 1440 a major revolt known as the *Praguerie* broke out, led by the dukes of Bourbon, Brittany, and Alençon, with the aim of forcing the abdication of the king and the setting up of a regency under the dauphin. But Richemont managed to put down the rebellion and the dauphin was banished to his own estates in Dauphiné, where he continued to intrigue against his father, allying closely with Philip of Burgundy. Consequently, when Charles died in 1461, Louis XI (1461–83) came to the throne with the blessings of Duke Philip. Louis was one of the ablest, if one of the most unappealing, of the kings of France. Sly, crafty, treacherous, always scheming involved plots, always ready to use and cast aside any minister or ally, miserly, addicted to low company, shabby in his personal appearance, superstitious and personally rather timid, Louis XI deserves the soubriquet, "King Spider," by which he is commonly known. Yet this unpleasant individual succeeded in destroying the great appanages and in uniting France under the king into a strong national monarchy.

The reign opened with a revolt of the nobles led by Charles, count of Charolais, the son of Philip of Burgundy, in 1464. Organizing what they termed "The League of the Public Welfare," Charolais, Brittany, Bourbon, Dunois, Armagnac, Berry, Albret, Lorraine and others took the field against the king and even brought their forces up to besiege Paris. But Louis defeated them in detail and made separate truces with them individually, destroying their unity and buying them off with individual concessions. Meanwhile royal agents stirred up rebellion in the lands of the princes. Typical of Louis diplomacy was his treatment of his brother, Charles of Berry: to win him over the king granted him Normandy in 1465; then in 1468 the king assembled the Estates at Tours and put through a declaration that Normandy was an inalienable part of the domain and could not be granted away. He thereupon invaded and occupied the duchy, forcing Berry to accept a cash pension in lieu of his appanage. Brittany and Bourbon were likewise bought off with cash and pensions until they could be defeated by arms.

With Charles the Bold of Charolais, who succeeded to the duchy of Burgundy in 1467, Louis was less fortunate. He arranged an interview at Peronne and was negotiating with Charles when word was received that Liége had revolted under the inspiration of royal agents. Charles was furious and imprisoned the king, who only gained his liberty by personally assisting the duke to put down the Liége rebellion and making great concessions to Burgundy and the other nobles. To fortify himself against France, the duke of Burgundy forced Louis to grant Champagne to Charles of Berry, but after this concession had been made and Louis was free, he persuaded Berry to exchange Champagne for Guyenne, thus isolating the allies (1469).

The struggle between Louis XI and Charles the Bold was one of great dramatic interest. The two men were such opposites; Charles was rash, brave, lavish, chivalrous, a dreamer of great dreams and a poor diplomat, while Louis was niggardly, cautious, and careful of every detail. Charles placed his trust in battles—Louis in court litigation and diplomatic intrigue. Louis assembled the Estates and secured the repudiation of the Treaty of Peronne and the condemnation of Charles. Charles organized a new league against the king. While Charles invaded northern France, Louis conquered Guyenne and Brittany and subsidized rebellion in the Burgundian lands. Both sides intrigued with England, Louis supporting the Lancastrians while Charles allied with York, marrying Margaret, the sister of Edward IV. But Louis was willing to pay out money when needed, and when Edward IV invaded France in 1475, he bought him off by paying a heavy indemnity and an annual subsidy.

Charles then became involved in imperial politics and turned his attention to the east and to the creation of his Middle Kingdom. He attacked Lorraine and the Swiss (who received aid from France) while he negotiated with the emperor for a royal title. But he was badly defeated by the Swiss and killed in a battle at Nancy in January 1477, and all his plans died with him, as he left as his heir only a daughter Mary. Louis at once seized ducal Burgundy and the Somme area. An attempt to seize the county of Burgundy was frustrated by the resolute resistance of the inhabitants, and the king was also baulked in his attempt to get control of Mary whom he wished to marry to his son Charles. Instead of Charles, Mary married Maximilian of Hapsburg, duke of Austria, the son of Emperor Frederick III, thus interposing a strong force against the schemes of Louis. For five years there was a state of semi-hostility between Louis and Maximilian, until, after Mary's death, Maximilian agreed to a treaty whereby his daughter Margaret was betrothed to Charles and was assigned Artois and comital Burgundy as her dot (1482).

Louis was more successful in gaining control of the other appanages and fiefs. Alençon, Armagnac, and St. Pol were all declared forfeit to the crown owing to the treason and rebellion of their lords: Guyenne was reunited at the death of Duke Charles; Bourbon and Orleans were tied to the crown by marriage alliances to Louis' own daughters. One of the most important acquisitions was the Angevin inheritance, which included Anjou, Provence, Maine, Bar, and claims to the throne of Naples, which passed into the royal domain when the line of René of Anjou died out. Rousillon and Cerdagne were also acquired by a treaty with Aragon, and when Louis XI died in 1483, only Brittany remained unabsorbed into the domain of the kings of France.

The acquisition of Brittany was accomplished by Charles VIII (1483–98). Duke Francis died leaving the duchy to his daughter Anne who became the object of the solicitude of Austria, England, and Spain, who were anxious to prevent Brittany being absorbed by France. The little duchess was quickly married by proxy to Maximilian, but French armies invaded the duchy and, as Maximilian got no help to his supporters, the duchess was persuaded to reconsider the matter. The marriage was declared invalid; Charles' engagement to Maximilian's daughter was broken, and Charles and Anne were married. Thus Brittany was incorporated into the French kingdom, while Artois and the county of Burgundy reverted to Maximilian. Concessions were made to Spain by ceding her Roussillon, and England was bought off with cash. France was at last united; her diplomatic position was good, and Charles was able to prepare for the invasion of Italy to enforce his claims to Naples.

The Italian expedition of Charles VIII (1495–96) marks the beginning of a new era in the history both of France and of Italy. The old problems of the French monarchy were solved: the king was absolute in a unified country, the institutions of her absolutism had been established on a firm basis, her economic prosperity had increased tremendously during the last half century, and France was ready to take the initiative in foreign expansion and to assert herself as the leading power in western Europe.

England at the End of the Century

While France was ending a period of civil war and developing a strong centralized monarchy, England became involved in a civil war which is very reminiscent of the French struggle in the first part of the century. A mad king, rival dukes, regencies, war and intrigue marked the Wars of the Roses as they had the Burgundian-Armagnac struggle in France.

And at their end there came the strong despotism of the Tudors. In both countries the monarchy emerged from a period of civil war stronger and more absolute, while the old noble houses were in both countries largely eliminated. The reign of Henry VI (1422–61) has much in common with that of his grandfather Charles VI of France. The insanity which first showed itself in Charles, reappeared in his English grandson, and the royal cousins and uncles struggled for power in England much as they had in France.

During the minority of Henry VI (1422–37) the regency was held by the king's uncles, John of Bedford in France and Humphrey of Gloucester in England. But the Beaufort family, descended from the second wife of John of Gaunt, contested the rule of Gloucester and built up a strong party which, allying with the Council, strictly limited the power of Duke Humphrey. When Henry declared himself of age in 1437, the Beauforts and William de la Pole of Suffolk took over the administration of the kingdom, while Gloucester went into opposition. It was Suffolk who arranged the treaty with France whereby Henry married Margaret of Anjou, and his influence over the king was sufficient that he secured in 1447 the impeachment of his rival Gloucester. The death of Gloucester during the trial raised more than a suspicion of foul play, but Suffolk carried on with the royal support, and managed to have the duke of York, who became the leader of the opposition, sent as governor to Ireland, a thankless post which effectively removed him from English politics.

The failure of the war in France, however, reacted against Suffolk, who was impeached in 1450 and murdered shortly thereafter. Meanwhile a peasant rebellion, led by one Jack Cade, had captured London, demanding the dismissal of the royal ministers and the repeal of the Statute of Laborers. Although the army sent against the rebels mutinied and joined the revolt, the bishops were finally able to make peace so that the rebels were pardoned and sent home, but Cade was himself executed for violence committed after the peace had been negotiated.

In 1450 Richard of York returned from Ireland, and in the following year his partisans demanded that he be recognized as heir presumptive. Parliament however supported Edmund Beaufort, duke of Somerset, and demanded that York be declared forfeit as a traitor. At this critical moment Henry VI went insane (1453). The Council, which was friendly to York, summoned him to take over as regent for the insane king, arresting Somerset and imprisoning him in the Tower. In 1454 York was officially named protector for the young Edward, the infant child of Henry VI and Margaret of Anjou, but when Henry regained his sanity the following year, York was summarily dismissed and Somerset returned to favor.

Resolved not to be done out of the power which he considered to be rightly his, York armed, supported by the powerful Richard Neville, earl

KINGS OF ENGLAND, 1307–1509

EDWARD II, 1307–27 = Isabelle, daughter of Philip IV of France

Children of Edward II and Isabelle:

- EDWARD III, 1327–77 = Philippa of Hainault
- John of Cornwall
- Jeanne = David of Scotland

Children of Edward III:

- Edward the Black Prince = Joan of Kent
  - RICHARD II, 1377–99 = Anne of Bohemia = Isabelle of France
- Lionel of Clarence
  - Philippa = Roger Mortimer
    - Roger Mortimer
      - Edmund
        - Anne = Richard of York
- John of Gaunt = Blanche of Lancaster a = Catherine Swynford b
  - (a) HENRY IV, 1399–1413 = Mary Bohun
    - HENRY V, 1413–22 = Katherine of France
      - HENRY VI, 1422–61 = Margaret of Anjou
        - Edward
    - John of Bedford
    - Humphrey of Gloucester
  - (b) John Beaufort of Somerset
    - John Beaufort of Somerset
      - Margaret Beaufort = Edmund Tudor of Richmond (son of Owen Tudor and Katherine of France)
        - HENRY VII, 1485–1509 = Elizabeth of York
  - (b) Henry Cardinal Beaufort
  - Joan = James I of Scotland
- Thomas of Gloucester
- Edmund of York
  - Richard of Cambridge
    - Richard of York
      - EDWARD IV, 1461–83 = Elizabeth Woodville
        - EDWARD V, 1483
        - Richard of York
        - Elizabeth = Henry VII
      - George of Clarence d. 1478
      - RICHARD III, 1483–85 = Anne Neville of Warwick
      - Margaret = Charles of Burgundy
      - Elizabeth = John of Suffolk

of Warwick. The rebels marched on London, encountered a royal army under Somerset at St. Albans (May 22, 1455) and won a decisive victory in which Somerset was killed. When Henry relapsed into insanity later that year, York was again proclaimed regent, only to again be dismissed when the king recovered his reason. War broke out anew and in 1459 York was defeated at Ludlow and forced to flee to Ireland while Warwick sought refuge at Calais. A hand-picked Parliament convicted York and Warwick of treason, but the rebel leaders returned, defeated the royal forces at Northampton (July 1460) and secured the possession of the person of the mad king. York then claimed the throne as the proper heir of Edward III, but Parliament refused this claim, granting only that he should succeed to Henry VI, to the prejudice of the latter's son Edward.

Queen Margaret, meanwhile, had placed herself at the head of the Lancastrian party and recruited an army. In December 1460 she met York at the battle of Wakefield in which the duke was killed, and followed up this victory by a second battle of St. Albans in which Warwick was routed. These gains were offset by the victory won by Edward of York, the son of Richard, who defeated a royalist army at Mortimer's Cross and entered London. On February 26, 1461 Edward IV was proclaimed king in London, but before he could be crowned he had to defeat a new army raised by Margaret at Towton (March 1461). While Queen Margaret and Prince Edward fled, Edward IV returned to be solemnly crowned at Westminster.

The Yorkist dynasty rested its claims on their hereditary right through Philippa of Clarence, an elder line of descent from Edward III than that of the Lancastrians, but their real strength lay in the support given them by Warwick and the great nobles. For three years Edward and Warwick continued to work in harmony, several Lancastrian movements being suppressed at their inceptions, but in 1464 a rift was created between the king and the great earl when Edward married Elizabeth Woodville and began to shower favors on her relatives. Disagreement over foreign policy also entered into the matter, as Edward allied with Burgundy, while Warwick favored Louis XI of France. From 1464 to 1469 relations between the king and Warwick became increasingly strained; then Warwick broke with Edward and placed himself behind George of Clarence, Edward's younger brother, whom he proposed as king. The king met the rebels at the battle of Edgecote, only to be captured by Warwick, but the rule of the earl was unpopular and a rebellion in Lincolnshire caused his overthrow. After being defeated in Stanford, Warwick and Clarence fled to France (1470). There Warwick and Queen Margaret were brought together by the astute diplomacy of Louis XI, who saw a chance to strike at Charles of Burgundy through his allies. A treaty was arranged whereby Warwick's daughter was to marry Prince Edward and the powerful earl threw his support to the Lancastrian side.

In 1470 Warwick, Margaret, and their partisans landed in England. The strong rule of Edward IV had raised many enemies and the country responded readily to Warwick's appeal. Edward fled without fighting and took refuge in the Burgundian Low Countries; Henry VI was rescued from his imprisonment in the Tower and put back on the throne, and a proscription of Yorkists began.

But mad Henry, and vindicative Margaret and Warwick, proved no more able to hold popular support than had Edward IV. In 1471 Edward returned, was welcomed by the nobles, and won a crushing victory at Barnet. Warwick was killed and Edward entered London to resume the throne.

Queen Margaret fled to the western counties where she proceeded to raise another army. On May 4, 1471, the Lancastrian forces, led by Somerset and Devon, were again defeated by Edward at Tewkesbury, where Prince Edward was killed and Queen Margaret captured. With this defeat the Lancastrian opposition collapsed, and when Henry VI died shortly thereafter, Edward IV seemed secure on his throne.

From 1471 to 1483 Edward IV ruled as an absolute monarch. He was successful in a short campaign which he made in France as the ally of Charles of Burgundy, filling his coffers with the indemnity which Louis XI payed him to withdraw. But even confiscations of Lancastrian estates and French subsidies were insufficient for the expenses of his government, and Edward became increasingly unpopular for the heavy exactions which he levied on his people. His rule was largely personal; while Council was larger than previously the king consulted it less than had his predecessors, and if Edward summoned frequent Parliaments he dictated to them, destroying the initiative which they had gained under the first Lancastrians. The ordinary method of inaugurating legislation in the Lancastrian period had been by the Commons' petitions or bills; under Edward the official bills, drawn up by the crown, became the only common form of statute. Bills of attainder, whereby an enemy of the king was declared to have been guilty of treason by parliamentary enactment, were also commonly employed. This innovation was a powerful weapon to an autocrat who could control his Parliament. If the king wished to do away with a man, and could find no legal grounds for convicting him, he would simply introduce a bill of attainder which declared that the person had been guilty of treason, and could thus legislate a conviction, which could not have been obtained by the ordinary legal procedure. One of the most famous bills of attainder passed under Edward IV was against his brother George of Clarence who had broken with the king and was accused of treason. A bill of attainder was passed upon Clarence, but he was opportunely drowned (possibly by his other brother Richard of Gloucester) in a butt of Malmsey wine before sentence could be carried out.

When Edward IV died in 1483, the throne passed to his twelve-year-old son, Edward V, under the regency of Richard of Gloucester. At once there developed a struggle between the regent and the young king's maternal relatives, the Woodvilles, which resulted in the overthrow and execution of the chief members of that family. Then in 1483 Richard usurped the throne, had Edward IV's marriage to Elizabeth Woodville declared illegal and his children illegitimate, and himself crowned. To assure himself that there would be no further trouble from Edward V or his brother the infant duke of York, the two princes were murdered in the Tower.

But more than the murder of two small princes was needed to keep the crown on the head of Richard III, Buckingham, who had been his chief supporter in his stroke for the throne, rebelled and had to be put down; and hardly had Buckingham been defeated and executed than a new rebellion was begun by Henry Tudor, earl of Richmond, a Lancastrian of the Beaufort line. On August 22, 1485 Henry defeated Richard at the battle of Bosworth Field; the hunchbacked king was killed (for lack of a horse according to Shakespeare) and Henry Tudor assumed the crown by right of conquest and with the approval of Parliament.

The character of Richard III has long been blackened as that of a villainous murderer, but it must be remembered that his fame has been preserved to us largely through the accounts written by partisans of the Tudor dynasty. More sober analysis seems to indicate that Richard III was a conscientious, hard-working king, who favored the commercial middle class, pursued an intelligent economic policy, and embodied in himself many of the best features of the Renaissance despots, who were making such a success of the business of politics in Italy. In fact Richard was an "Italian despot" on an English throne, and therein probably lies the story of his failure.

With the advent of the Tudor dynasty, England left the Middle Ages to enter into modern times. As in France the old feudal nobility was largely gone; the Wars of Lancaster and York had been costly in the lives of the nobles, though they had not been especially destructive to the prosperity of the middle or lower classes. But few ancient families survived the battle of Bosworth Field and the nobility of the Tudors was mostly a new nobility which arose in the service of the dynasty.

The period was one in which constitutional development was set back. After two centuries of warfare men were happy to settle down to peace even if it was peace secured by a despotism. The gains made by Parliament in the last Plantagenet and early Lancastrian reigns were lost under the Yorkists; Parliament continued to function but with its initiative gone and its powers sadly restricted. It became merely an agency for the expression of the royal will. But England had what France lacked—a tradition of parliamentary importance which gave the Parliaments of the seventeenth century precedents to which to turn. The sixteenth century was an age of despotic governments everywhere, and both France and England followed the fashion. But England went back to her parliamentarianism in the seventeenth century, whereas France remained absolute until the end of the eighteenth. That this was true was in large part a result of the events and conditions of the fourteenth and fifteenth centuries.

CHAPTER 39

GERMANY AND CENTRAL EUROPE

✠

T HE history of Germany and central Europe in the fourteenth and fifteenth centuries is a confused and complex story which can only be
treated here in its broadest outlines. In general the period is characterized
in Germany by the transfer of power from the emperor to the great territorial princes, and by creation of strong princely domains in the hands
of the Hapsburg, Luxemburg, Wittelsbach, and Hohenzollern families.
At the same time the cities and the knights become more independent, and
Germany tended to break down into that mass of semi-sovereign units
which characterized it in the early modern period. While some of the
emperors still continued to demonstrate an interest in Italy, on the whole
Italian affairs play a minor part in German politics, and the Hohenstaufen dream of the German-Italian Empire faded before the more
practical policy of developing strong family principalities within Germany. The political center of Germany, which had lain in the north in
the period of the Saxon emperors, had shifted to the southwest with the
Salians and Hohenstaufens; now it shifted again to the southeast and
centered in Hapsburg Austria, Wittelsbach Bavaria, and the Luxemburg
domains in Bohemia.

HAPSBURG VS LUXEMBURG, 1273–1347

When Rudolph of Hapsburg was elected king in 1273, his chief quali-
fication for the throne was his relative insignificance. The great princes
were anxious to have as emperor a man whom they felt would be incapable
of dominating the scene, and Rudolph was elected largely as a means of
frustrating the ambitions of Ottokar of Bohemia. This policy of electing
a weak candidate was to be followed through several elections until the
princes discovered that each emperor used his imperial position to build
up the possessions of his own house and raised up a new powerful dynasty.
In 1274 the Imperial Diet at Nuremburg authorized Rudolph to recover for the empire all lands alienated since the deposition of Frederick
II, an act aimed at Ottokar of Bohemia, who had taken Austria, Styria,
Carinthia, and Carniola in 1246. Ottokar was summoned to the Diet, and
when he refused, his lands were declared forfeit. War ensued in which
Rudolph was victorious at the battle of the Marchfeld (August 1278), and
Ottokar was forced to surrender all his lands to the emperor, receiving

back only Bohemia as a fief. In 1278 Ottokar broke the peace and invaded Austria, only to be killed. Rudolph then invested his own sons with the Austrian lands (1282), having gained the consent of the princes to the grant. Thus the petty dynast from Swabia secured for his family rich territories in the east and made his house one of the strongest families in Germany.

In fact the Hapsburgs became so strong that when Rudolph died in 1291 the princes passed over his son Albert of Austria and chose instead the insignificant Adolph of Nassau (1291–98). Albert was not the man to stand by while another got the throne, and at once broke out in revolt. For seven years Adolph endeavored to defend his position, but in 1298 the princes deposed him and elected Albert (1298–1308). Adolph was killed in the fighting soon thereafter and Albert became king.

Albert of Austria is known primarily for his alliance with Philip IV against Boniface VIII and for the outbreak of Swiss rebellion which began in his reign. He attempted to follow his father's example of adding territory to the family holdings, and was able to get his son Rudolph elected king of Bohemia, but Rudolph died and the whole scheme fell through. His policy of extending his family possessions in the south had precipitated the revolt of the Forest Cantons and the union of Schwyz, Uri, and Unterwalden into a federal alliance (1291), which received the support of Adolph of Nassau. Albert put down the rebellion and held the Swiss in check, but the revolt blazed out afresh after his murder in 1298, the Swiss consistently supporting the enemies of the Hapsburgs.

On the death of Albert, the princes once again repudiated the Hapsburg candidate and chose a relatively unimportant noble, Henry count of Luxemburg, who ascended the throne as Henry VII (1308–13). In this election, Philip IV of France had tried to secure the throne for his brother, Charles of Valois, and it was to avoid either the French or the Hapsburg princes that the German electors selected Henry, the brother of the archbishop of Treves, who was half French and utterly unimportant. Henry VII combined both the old and the new policies of empire. At home he strengthened the possessions of his own house by securing the throne of Bohemia for his son John when the Czech nobles deposed their king, Henry of Carinthia (1310); but he was also anxious to secure the imperial crown at Rome, and engaged in an expensive and futile Italian expedition (1310–13). He received the Lombard crown at Pavia, established imperial vicars in Lombardy, allied with the Visconti of Milan, fought his way into Rome, and was crowned in St. Peters, June 29, 1312. He was, however, unable to hold the city and withdrew to the north where he besieged Florence without success. The imperial expedition raised the hopes of the Ghibellines throughout Italy, and Dante accorded Henry a distinguished place in Paradise for his attempt to "liberate" Florence, but the expedition was, on the whole,

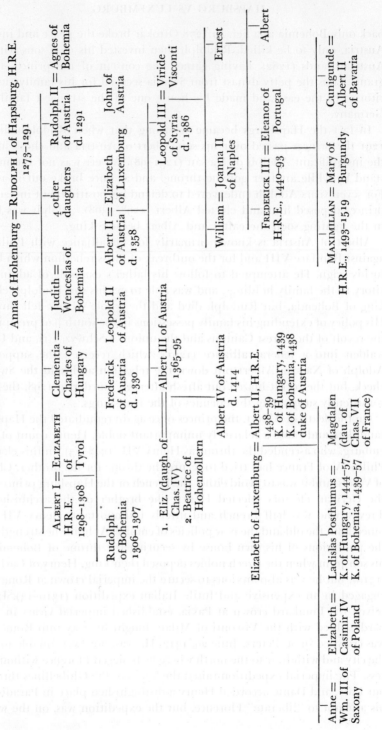

THE HOUSE OF HAPSBURG

unsuccessful, and Henry died while preparing to carry the war against Robert of Naples.

When the German princes met to elect a successor to Henry, there were two major candidates; John of Bohemia, the minor son of the deceased emperor, and Frederick of Austria. In November 1313, however, Frederick was defeated in battle by Louis, duke of Bavaria, and the Luxemburg supporters transferred their votes to Louis as a strong anti-Hapsburg candidate. Five electors voted for Louis while four cast their ballots for Frederick. War

THE HOUSE OF LUXEMBURG

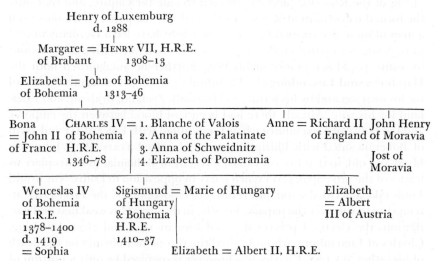

```
                    Henry of Luxemburg
                          d. 1288
                            |
            Margaret = HENRY VII, H.R.E.
            of Brabant        1308-13
                      |
        Elizabeth = John of Bohemia
        of Bohemia      1313-46
                |
    ┌──────────┬───────────────────────────────────┬──────────────────┬──────────────┐
   Bona      CHARLES IV = 1. Blanche of Valois    Anne = Richard II   John Henry
   = John II of Bohemia |  2. Anna of the Palatinate    of England    of Moravia
   of France  H.R.E.    |  3. Anna of Schweidnitz                         |
              1346-78   |  4. Elizabeth of Pomerania                   Jost of
                                                                       Moravia

    ┌──────────────┬───────────────────────────────────┬──────────────┐
   Wenceslas IV   Sigismund = Marie of Hungary        Elizabeth
   of Bohemia     of Hungary|                          = Albert
   H.R.E.         & Bohemia |                          III of Austria
   1378-1400      H.R.E.    |
   d. 1419        1410-37   |
   = Sophia                 Elizabeth = Albert II, H.R.E.
```

broke out between the two camps and Louis won the day and the empire at the battle of Mühldorf (September 28, 1322). He at once used his position to put his son Louis in possession of the vacant margravate of Brandenburg.

But Louis was not yet secure on his throne, for he had neglected to obtain the approval of the pope. John XXII, who was most jealous of papal prerogatives, ordered him to give up the government, which he had usurped and which he was exercising without proper authority. Louis replied by a decree in which he stated that election was all that was required to qualify an emperor, and that papal approval was unnecessary. John excommunicated Louis, who promptly championed the cause of the Spiritual Franciscans and declared the pope a heretic. It was in the course of the pamphlet-war which developed out of this controversy that Marsiglio of Padua wrote his famous *Defensor pacis,* in which he maintained the supremacy of the state over the church, and Augustinus Triumphus presented his extreme statement of papal claims.

In 1325, Louis IV put an end to the opposition of the Hapsburgs by granting Duke Frederick a condominium, whereby Frederick was to be joint ruler of Germany with the king, and Louis was free to turn his attention to his struggle with the pope. In 1327 to 1330 he made an expedition to Italy, where he was crowned at Rome by four lay delegates of the city and an anti-pope was set up, Marsiglio of Padua being appointed imperial vicar in Rome. But when the emperor withdrew from Italy his appointees were overthrown and the papal authority was re-established.

But the struggle with the papacy had united the German princes behind Louis. In 1338 an Imperial Diet passed the law *Licet juris,* which declared as part of the fundamental law that the man elected by the electors was "King of the Romans," and empowered to rule the empire, and that only the formal coronation at Rome was the right of the pope. Had Louis been a man of more determined character, he might have led a Germany united in opposition to papal claims, but he was himself vacillating and anxious to secure papal acceptance of his title. Further he antagonized both the Hapsburgs and Luxemburgs by his fumbling attempts to secure the Tyrol for his own son and by his seizure of Hainault, Zeeland, Brabant, and Friesland for his wife. Already there had been bad blood between the emperor and the house of Luxemburg when Louis allied with Edward III and John of Bohemia sided with Philip VI in the Hundred Years' War. John was blind and old, so that his son Charles, regent of Bohemia, took his place as leader of the pro-papal, pro-French party in opposition to Louis. Nor would Louis take a decided stand, but refused to enforce firmly the *Licet juris,* attempting to win over the papacy. Finally, in disgust at his weakness and vacillation, the electoral princes deposed him in 1346 and elected as king, Charles of Luxemburg, who inherited the throne of Bohemia on the death of his father at Crécy. Charles was however recognized by only a portion of the princes, while most of the towns supported Louis. There was desultory war between them until Louis died while hunting in October 1347, leaving the throne free for his rival.

THE LUXEMBURG EMPERORS, 1347–1437

Charles IV (1347–78) was one of the greatest kings of Bohemia which he favored above all other parts of the empire, but as a German emperor he rather neglected his obligations. Maximilian later termed him "The father of Bohemia and the step-father of the empire," [1] an apt phrase, for his interests were mainly devoted to building up his eastern kingdom. But his very preoccupation with Bohemia led to his promulgation in Germany of the famous Golden Bull of 1356, whereby he established the Seven Electors, and granted to the electoral princes regalian rights which made them vir-

[1] Quoted in Privité-Orton, *History of Europe, 1198–1378,* p. 307 (Putnam's & Methuen).

tually independent. As Bryce phrased it: "he legalized anarchy and called it a constitution." [2]

The Golden Bull regularized a procedure which had been current in the empire for some time. Always ideally elective, the empire had become in practice hereditary under the Salian and Hohenstaufen, but the princes had always theoretically preserved their right to elect the monarch. Certain princes early developed as the important figures in any election but there was considerable dispute as to just who the electors were. The archbishops of Cologne, Treves, and Mainz were accepted without question, but there were several contestants for the lay electorships. By the Golden Bull, the claims of Bavaria to electoral status were ignored, as Charles was the avowed enemy of the Wittelsbachs and would not permit two electorships in the same family, and the electorates were conferred upon the princes of Saxony, Brandenburg, the Palatinate, and the king of Bohemia.[3]

Charles followed the usual procedure of building up his own family possessions. To his inherited kingdom of Bohemia (with Moravia and Silesia) he added Brandenburg, Lower Lusatia, and the Upper Palatinate. Further, in 1364 he signed a treaty with the Hapsburgs which provided that if either house became extinct their possessions should revert to the other, a document from which the Hapsburgs, not the Luxemburgs, were eventually to profit.

Twice Charles journeyed into Italy: in 1354 to 1355 he went to Rome for his coronation, and in 1368 to 1369 he escorted Pope Urban V back to the Holy City. Neither expedition was of any significance, except that Charles sold imperial titles throughout Italy and thereby benefited his treasury. Meanwhile in Germany he encouraged the local peace associations, the *Landfrieden,* which became one of the most powerful organizations in the empire and did much to diminish the anarchy which was developing in the disorganized condition of the country. On the other hand, he fought actively against the free imperial towns, supporting the princes against the city leagues. But his defeat by the Swabian League forced him to grant concessions which ultimately facilitated the growth of urban liberties. His chief work was however the building up the Bohemian state, a task to which he devoted his best energies. Under Charles, Prague became an important intellectual and economic center; the university was founded, and Czech literature was patronized. Although most of the clergy and many of the officials were Germans, Charles favored the Czechs, giving them the best posts, and employing Czechs in imperial offices whenever possible.

[2] James Bryce, *The Holy Roman Empire,* p. 233 (Macmillan, 1886 ed.).

[3] This was later changed in 1623 when the electorship of the Palatinate was transferred to Bavaria. Then in 1648 both Bavaria and the Palatinate were recognized as electors, making eight electors until 1692 when Hanover was created as a ninth. But Bavaria died out in 1777.

Charles set the crown on his work when he secured the election of his son Wenceslas, who was his heir in Bohemia, as King of the Romans in 1376. Thus when he died in 1378 the succession was assured.

It was during the reign of Charles IV that the final steps were taken in the winning of Swiss independence. Kept down by Albert of Austria, the Swiss received imperial support from Louis the Bavarian in their struggle to free themselves from Duke Leopold who had inherited that part of the Hapsburg lands. In 1315 the army of the Swiss confederation defeated Leopold at Morgarten, another battle in which infantry demonstrated their superiority over mailed knights. The victory of Morgarten brought new members to the confederation, when the towns of Zurich, Berne and Lucerne joined the league, and the confederated cantons were strong enough to seize control of Glarus and Zug. Although Charles IV assisted the Hapsburgs against the Swiss, they continued to grow in strength, and in 1386 defeated and killed Duke Leopold III at the crushing victory of Sempach. This was followed by defeating Duke Albert III of Austria at Nafels in 1388, after which a treaty was concluded (1394) recognizing the autonomy of the eight cantons. In these wars the Swiss pikemen acquired a great reputation as soldiers, which they increased when they defeated Charles the Bold of Burgundy in the latter part of the fifteenth century. In the sixteenth century the Swiss infantry were the most prized mercenaries in the armies of the various European monarchs, and Switzerland paid much of her expenses from the money earned by hiring out her sons as soldiers. The Swiss Guards of the Vatican today are a relic of the time when the Swiss held the first rank for military prowess.

Wenceslas (1378–1400), who succeeded his father on the thrones of Bohemia and Germany, was even more devoted to Bohemia and the aggrandizement of his family than Charles had been. Well educated and handsome, he was at the same time lethargic and vacillating, and as he grew older he spent more and more of his time in an alcholic daze, avoiding through intoxication the issues which he did not wish to face.

In the struggle between the towns and the knights, Wenceslas was indifferent until forced to take sides, when he supported the knights and princes; but in the main he stayed in Bohemia, completely ignoring Germany, and exerting himself only to support the pretentions of his brother, Sigismund of Brandenburg, for the throne of Hungary. In the all-important matter of the papal schism, Wenceslas seemed content to do nothing and when he finally exerted himself to attend a conference with Charles VI of France at Rheims to discuss the matter, the emperor was drunk through most of the proceedings. Annoyed beyond endurance at his lethargy, the electors finally decided on his deposition. Wenceslas was summoned to appear at a Diet in June 1400, but refused to leave Bohemia, whereupon the princes proceeded with the election of a new emperor, Rupert of Wittelsbach, the elector of the Palatinate. Wenceslas refused to recognize Rupert, but made no especial attempt to retain his title, remaining in Bohemia, where, as we have seen, he allowed the Hussite movement to develop.

Rupert of the Palatinate (1400-10) was well intentioned, but weak and not overly intelligent. He planned a great expedition to Italy to get back control over Milan, which had been given to its duke by Wenceslas, but received little support and got no further than Venice when he was forced to return home for lack of funds. He quarreled with the powerful archbishop of Mainz, broke with many of his supporters over the question of the Council of Pisa, and was threatened with a general revolt when he died in 1410.

The election of 1410 was a disputed one, both candidates being members of the house of Luxemburg. While one party among the electors favored Sigismund, a minority elected Jost of Moravia, his cousin. Wenceslas, who still claimed the title for himself, cast his vote for Jost. However Jost died opportunely and the influence of Frederick of Hohenzollern, burgrave of Nuremburg, was sufficient to secure the re-election of Sigismund, Wenceslas giving a grudging approval.

Sigismund (1410-37) was a gallant, handsome, well-educated, eloquent and urbane man of most pleasing qualities. His most conspicuous vice was his extreme lustfulness, but as a ruler his worst liability was a tendency to rush into matters with great enthusiasm and then to drop them altogether; he always had several schemes afoot at the same time and seldom carried them to completion. He was moreover profligate in the extreme and was always out of funds, resorting to all sorts of expedients to raise the money for his ordinary household expenses. His interests were divided between war with the Turks over his kingdom of Hungary, healing the schism of the church, increasing his possessions and power in Germany, and reasserting imperial prestige in Italy. In all of them he made some progress, but in none of them was he entirely successful.

We have already encountered Sigismund as fighting the Turks at Nicopolis (1396) and as convoking the Council of Constance (1414). In 1412 to 1414 he campaigned in Italy where he attempted to force Venice to surrender lands on the Dalmatian coast, which they had taken from Hungary. But he found that he could not afford the time or money which the campaign would cost, and so abandoned it, making peace with the republic, and returning to Germany to be crowned king at Aix-la-Chapelle (1414). For the next year he was busy at Constance, but in 1416 he went to England where he allied with Henry V against France.

In 1415 Sigismund rewarded the services of his friend Frederick of Hohenzollern by granting him the electorate of Brandenburg, which was to remain the possession of his family until the twentieth century, and which was to become the ruling state in all Germany. About the same time he established the house of Wettin in Saxony, another dynasty that was to last to the present century. A close alliance was made with the Hapsburgs when Sigismund married his daughter Elizabeth to Albert V of Austria and recognized the Austrian duke as his heir apparent and protégé for the imperial succession. In 1419, at the death of Wenceslas, Sigismund inherited the kingdom of Bohemia, but was unable to enforce his rule there until 1436, owing to the opposition of the Hussite nobles. Against these Hussites Sigismund launched many expeditions, but was for years unsuccessful, until their unity was broken by internal disputes. In 1433 Sigismund fulfilled one of his cherished desires when he went to Italy and received the imperial crown in St. Peter's from Pope Eugenius, whom he agreed to support against the Council of Basel. He died in December 1437, just short of seventy, after a life of almost continuous activity. With him the male line of the house of Luxemburg ended, its titles and lands passing through his daughter to her husband, Albert of Austria.

Sigismund was not a great king, but he was certainly one of the best in the Germany of the later Middle Ages, and around his name many legends accumulated. He was a colorful personality with an unbounded ambition and tireless energy. The story told on him when opening the Council of Constance, that when someone ventured to criticize his Latin, he replied *"Imperator sum, et super grammaticam"* is undoubtedly apocryphal, but characterizes rather well the confident, arrogant emperor.

THE HAPSBURG EMPERORS, 1437–93

Albert of Austria was elected King of the Romans in accordance with the wishes of Sigismund against the rival candidacy of Frederick of Hohenzollern; the imperial title never passed out of the possession of his house until the extermination of the Austrian Empire in 1918, though Hohenzollerns were later to prevail over the Hapsburgs.

His reign, however, lasted but a few months, as he died in Hungary while fighting the Turks in 1439, before he had had an opportunity to do much of anything. At the time of his death his wife was pregnant, and the child born after its father's death turned out to be a son, Ladislas Posthumus, who was recognized as duke of Austria and king of Bohemia and Hungary. Meanwhile the electors met and chose the head of the cadet line of the Hapsburgs, Frederick of Styria as emperor.

Frederick III (1440–93) was without doubt the most ineffective monarch ever to rule Germany. His lassitude even outdid that of Wenceslas and he did not have the redeeming vices of the Luxemburger. He spent his life in the study of astrology and in devising acrostics with the letters AEIOU which he formed into the mottoes *"Austria est imperare orbi universa"* and

"Alles Erdreich ist Osterreich unterthan." His one interest was in the aggrandisement of his family, of which he rested assured since the stars predicted a glorious future for his house. This left Frederick nothing to do about it—which is exactly what he did.

For some years Frederick sat on the fence in the struggle between the pope and Council of Basel, but eventually, in 1477, a concordat was arranged whereby he decided in favor of the pope in return for the promise of the imperial crown and a cash subsidy. In 1452 he went to Rome where he was solemnly crowned—the last Holy Roman emperor to receive the imperial crown at Rome. In 1457 when Ladislas Posthumus died, both the Bohemian and Hungarian magnates refused to elect Frederick as their king, Bohemia going to George Podiebrad (1458-71), while the Hungarians elected Matthias Corvinus (1458-90). Nor was Frederick popular in Austria; there after the death of his brother Albert, with whom he had jointly held the old Hapsburg lands, Frederick faced opposition on the part of his nobles as well as intermittent attacks by the Turks. Finally in 1485 Matthias Corvinus of Hungary captured Vienna, forcing Frederick to flee to western Germany. The emperor was able to regain his capital only at the cost of surrendering eastern Austria to the Hungarian king. Meanwhile the dukes of Burgundy were forcing him to cede them imperial territories in the west, although Frederick was able to stall off the granting of the royal title which Charles the Bold desired (1473). Frederick's one positive act was the securing of the hand of Mary of Burgundy, the heiress of Charles the Bold, for his son Maximilian, who was elected King of the Romans during his father's lifetime in 1486. In fact Maximilian, who possessed the energy and ambition which his father so grossly lacked, at once took charge, and Frederick died in innocuous obscurity in 1493. He was the last of the medieval emperors—the last to be crowned in Rome, and the last in point of policy, for with Maximilian the Hapsburg empire of modern times began.

And the Germany he ruled had changed also. The old feudal ties remained only in theory and the new Germany was a country of strong, virtually independent princes, prosperous, politically-conscious towns, and imperial knights, each of whom lorded it without restraint in his own small domain. Never strongly unified, Germany had by 1500 broken down into a myriad local units with very little cohesion. The Holy Roman Empire was dying, and the Germany of the Lutheran Godly Prince and the *"Cuius regio"* was just ahead.

BOHEMIA

As the history of Bohemia, Hungary and Poland was so closely bound up with that of Germany in the fourteenth and fifteenth centuries little need be said here about any of them, but it may be well to pick up some loose threads.

Bohemia, as we have seen, passed on the death of the last Premyslid, Wenceslas III, to John of Luxemburg, the son of Henry VII. John was a romantic and chivalrous knight-errant, who wandered over Europe, becoming ruler of Lombardy for a time in 1331 to 1333, and dying in the French lines at Crécy. Although he generally neglected Bohemia, it was under his rule that Silesia and Upper Lusatia were added to the Czech kingdom, and that the great influx of Germans took place in Bohemia. His son Charles (1347–78) raised Bohemia to a position of pre-eminence in Germany, making Prague the cultural capital of the empire, but with Wenceslas (1378–1419) a decline set in and Bohemia was torn by the Hussite wars. During the years 1420 to 1433 the real leaders in Bohemia were John Ziska and Procop the Great who led the Hussites to victory against the repeated crusades, which were sent against them by Sigismund and the papacy. After the defeat of the Taborites and the short rule of Sigismund, Bohemia passed to Albert of Austria. Civil war broke out when a number of the nobles called in Ladislas of Poland, but Ladislas was defeated and Ladislas Posthumus inherited his father's throne (1439–57). The Hussites, who recognized that their surrender to the papacy had been bought with false promises, asserted themselves and established a regency for the young king under George Podiebrad, a prominent Calixtine Hussite noble. Podiebrad ruled as regent until 1453, giving Bohemia the ablest rule it had enjoyed in many years, and when Ladislas died in 1457, the former regent was unanimously elected king.

George Podiebrad (1458–71) began his own rule by interfering in Germany, where for a time he dreamed of replacing Frederick III as emperor, but he was soon involved in a struggle with the popes which brought him back to Bohemia to defend the liberties of the Calixtine church there. The papacy was determined to force the Bohemians back into complete orthodoxy and denounced the concessions made at Basel. King George defied the papal excommunication and defended his country against Catholic rebellion within and invasion by Matthias Corvinus of Hungary. However the Catholic party elected Matthias king, and he was contesting the throne when Podiebrad died. To prevent the absorption of Bohemia into Hungary, King George had designated as his successor Ladislas, the son of Casimir IV of Poland, who was accordingly recognized as king by the majority of the Czech nobles, although the Hungarian party still held out until the death of Corvinus, when Ladislas was also elected king of Hungary.

HUNGARY

Hungary likewise had undergone several changes of dynasty in the period since the extermination of the old Arpad house in 1301. After a short period of civil war, the throne went to Charles Robert (Carobert) of Anjou, the grandson of Charles II of Anjou and Marie of Hungary. Charles I (1308–42) spent most of his reign putting down the local dynasties of Hungary and establishing instead a new feudal nobility dependent on the crown. He encouraged immigration and built up towns by encouraging commerce and industry in an attempt to make Hungary a Western nation. His son, Louis I the Great (1342–82), continued his father's policy of Westernization, building Gothic churches in the French style, encouraging the arts and letters, and founding the University of Pécs. His court at Buda became one of the leading cultural centers of Europe, reflecting the Franco-Italian taste of the king. He spent some years in a fruitless war in Naples where he attempted to avenge the murder of his brother Andrew, the husband of Joanna I, but although he conquered Naples and enforced his rule there for a time (1347–50), he finally abandoned the idea and turned to more pressing problems nearer home. One of these was the conquest from Venice of Zara and parts of the Dalmatian coast, which he accomplished in 1356 to 1358. Louis allied with Genoa in the war of Chioggia, and although Venice defeated Genoa, the peace negotiated in 1381 recognized the Hungarian possession of the disputed Dalmatian territories. To the southeast, Louis fought Stephen Dushan of Serbia without any success, but at the death of the great tsar in 1355 he was able to establish his suzerainty over parts of northern Serbia and Croatia. He also forced his overlordship on the voivode of Wallachia, but his control was never very effective in any of these regions. This interference in the Balkans of course brought him into conflict with the Turks, over whom he won a victory in 1366 at Vidin in Bulgaria. In 1370 on the death of his uncle, Casimir III of Poland, Louis inherited the claims of his mother Elizabeth, and was elected king by the Polish nobles, but he never paid much attention to this kingdom, governing it through regents.

At the death of Louis, his two kingdoms were divided between his daughters, Marie inheriting Hungary and Jadwiga, Poland. Marie was married to Sigismund of Luxemburg who claimed his wife's inheritance, but was opposed by Charles of Durazzo-Naples. Charles had strong support in Croatia and southern Hungary and managed to seize the throne for a year (1385–86) but was murdered, Sigismund becoming king of Hungary in 1387. It was as Hungarian king that Sigismund took part in the disastrous crusade of Nicopolis, and throughout his reign the Turks threatened his eastern frontiers. His attempts to claim the Bohemian throne also involved Hungary in war with the Hussites, and Venice took the op-

portunity to recapture Dalmatia. During this time first came into prominence John Hunyadi, voivode of Transylvania, the Hungarian champion
against the Turks.

At the death of Sigismund, the throne of Hungary passed, along with all
his other titles, to Albert of Austria, but at Albert's death the Hungarian
nobles refused to accept Ladislas Posthumus and chose instead Ladislas
of Poland who ruled Hungary (1440–44) until his death in the crusade
of Varna. At the death of Ladislas of Poland, Ladislas Posthumus was
recognized as king with Hunyadi as regent, but Hunyadi was killed in
driving the Turks back from Belgrade in 1456 and King Ladislas died the
year following. Passing over the claims of Frederick III, the Hungarian
nobles elected as their king Matthias Corvinus, the son of John Hunyadi.

Matthias Corvinus (1458–90) just missed being one of the greatest
rulers of Europe. He brought Hungary to a new peak of prestige and
prosperity, subdued the nobles, reorganized the administration and the
courts, increased taxes and the ability of the country to pay them, and
developed a first-rate standing army. He was a great patron of writers and
artists and developed a great library at Buda; in fact he was in every
way a model despot of the Italian Renaissance type. In his wars with the
Turks he was successful, achieving a deserved reputation as a brave and
able warrior. But he wasted the substance of his country in the pursuit of
a false dream of imperial conquest. Instead of concentrating his energies
on the war with the Turks, he attempted to conquer both Bohemia and Austria and dreamed of replacing Frederick III on the imperial throne. In his
Bohemian and Austrian wars he was moderately successful; though he
never could dispossess George Podiebrad in Bohemia, he had strong support there and retained some supporters in Bohemia until the time of his
death. In Austria, as we have seen, he captured Vienna and forced Frederick to cede him all of the eastern part of the duchy. Certainly he made
Hungary the leading power of central Europe, but though he made himself feared in Germany, Bohemia, and Poland, he failed to stop the power
which was soon thereafter to overrun and subjugate his kingdom.

At the death of Corvinus without heirs, the throne of Hungary passed
to Ladislas Jagiellian who had already acquired Bohemia in 1471 and
who united the two eastern monarchies until his death in 1516. Ladislas
was a weak sovereign, who lost most of the gains made by Corvinus and
Podiebrad, and who devoted much of his attention to securing favorable
relations with the Hapsburgs. A double marriage alliance joined the
two houses, and in 1491 Ladislas signed the Treaty of Pressburg with
Maximilian whereby he agreed that should his own line fail of male heirs
his inheritance should pass to the Hapsburgs. This treaty went into effect
in the early seventeenth century and resulted in the establishment of the

Hapsburg empire in both Bohemia and Hungary. Meanwhile, however, most of Hungary had fallen to the Turks (1526).

POLAND

Poland has always suffered from the fact that her frontiers were never obviously fixed on any natural boundaries and from the individualism and separatist tendencies of her people. The Piast dynasty, which had been founded in the tenth century, had, as we have seen, organized the Polish state and brought it to a high degree of power in the eleventh century. Under Boleslav III (1102–38) the country had been divided into five great principalities: Great Poland, Silesia, Masovia, Cracow, and Sandomir, each of which was an appanage with its own Piast dynasty. The lord of Cracow was Grand Prince, and to him the others were theoretically subject. But this arrangement in no wise relieved Poland of the usual dynastic struggles, and the only result was to enable the nobles to get an unusual amount of control over their princes. The advent of the Teutonic Knights in the early thirteenth century (1228) and the Mongol invasions of a few years later completed the disruption of Poland which fell into truly sorry days by the end of the century. At the very beginning of the fourteenth century Poland was subject for a time to Bohemia, but her independence was asserted by Ladislas (Vladislav) IV (1305–33) who made himself Grand Prince and made considerable headway in uniting the various provinces and enforcing his rule over the nobles. But he was opposed by the Piast dynasties of Silesia and Mazovia, the Bohemians and the Teutonic Knights, and his reign was a series of wars against his enemies on all fronts. To gain allies Ladislas married his daughter to Charles I of Hungary (thus establishing the relationship with the Hungarian Angevins), while his son Casimir married the daughter of Gedymin of Lithuania.

Casimir III (1333–70) abandoned his father's attempts to control the north and west and concentrated on the southeast, where after a long war with Lithuania, he secured the possession of Galicia. He secured the alliance of Hungary by recognizing his sister's son Louis of Hungary as his heir, stipulating that the Polish kingdom should retain its own institutions and officials. Casimir issued the first code of Polish laws and founded the University of Cracow (1364), but he made great concessions to the nobles, which established them as a distinct and privileged class. Under Casimir, Poland developed a new prosperity, the condition of the peasantry being greatly improved with the abolition of serfdom, and new towns being formed largely from Jewish and German colonists. A broader toleration of Jews than was common at the time attracted multitudes of Jews to Poland, which from then on became the great center of Jewish life in eastern Europe.

Louis of Anjou-Hungary (1370–82) had relatively little interest in his Polish kingdom and was mainly anxious to secure its possession for one of his daughters. He granted the Polish nobles the Charter of Koszyce in

KINGS OF POLAND AND GRAND DUKES OF LITHUANIA

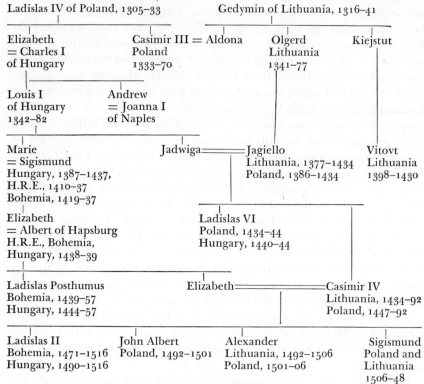

Ladislas IV of Poland, 1305–33   Gedymin of Lithuania, 1316–41

Elizabeth
= Charles I
of Hungary

Casimir III = Aldona
Poland
1333–70

Olgerd
Lithuania
1341–77

Kiejstut

Louis I
of Hungary
1342–82

Andrew
= Joanna I
of Naples

Marie
= Sigismund
Hungary, 1387–1437,
H.R.E., 1410–37
Bohemia, 1419–37

Jadwiga=====Jagiello
Lithuania, 1377–1434
Poland, 1386–1434

Vitovt
Lithuania
1398–1430

Elizabeth
= Albert of Hapsburg
H.R.E., Bohemia,
Hungary, 1438–39

Ladislas VI
Poland, 1434–44
Hungary, 1440–44

Ladislas Posthumus
Bohemia, 1439–57
Hungary, 1444–57

Elizabeth==============Casimir IV
Lithuania, 1434–92
Poland, 1447–92

Ladislas II
Bohemia, 1471–1516
Hungary, 1490–1516

John Albert
Poland, 1492–1501

Alexander
Lithuania, 1492–1506
Poland, 1501–06

Sigismund
Poland and
Lithuania
1506–48

1374 which further greatly increased their privileges, exempting them from all taxation and reducing the powers of the crown to the benefit of the noble class. At his death in 1382, the Polish nobles refused to accept his daughter Marie and her husband Sigismund as their rulers, but in 1384 consented to the election of the younger daughter, Jadwiga (1384–99), whom they married off to Jagiello of Lithuania (1386). Jagiello was forced to grant even further concessions to the Polish nobles (Charter of Cracow, 1433) while Lithuania, as we have seen, became virtually independent under Vitovt. Jagiello won a crushing victory over the Teutonic Knights in 1410 at Tannenberg, but left them in control of the coast by the Treaty of Thorn the year following.

Jagiello (called Ladislas V of Poland) was succeeded by his son, Ladislas

VI (1434–44), who was elected king of Hungary in 1440. Far more interested in Hungary than in Poland, Ladislas concerned himself almost exclusively with the affairs of his southern kingdom, especially in the wars against the Turks. It was in the ill-fated campaign at Varna that he lost his life in 1444. After a three-year interregnum during which the nobles enjoyed a pleasant anarchy, the throne of Poland passed by election to Casimir IV (1447–92) the younger brother of Ladislas, who had been ruling Lithuania which was now reunited with Poland.

Casimir IV was always more interested in Lithuania than in Poland, much of his energies being spent in keeping the Lithuanians satisfied so that they would not turn to Moscow. He antagonized the Polish nobles, but was able to benefit from a division in their ranks and secured the support of the lesser nobles against the greater princes. In the Statute of Nieszawa he recognized the rights of the lesser nobles to be consulted in all matters of war and peace or in legislation. This alliance of the crown with the lesser nobles strengthened the monarchy against the greater nobles, but made the king dependent on the approval of the several provincial diets. The fame of Casimir, however, rests on his great victory over the Teutonic Knights and his annexation of West Prussia. The Prussian people had become restive under the stern rule of the Knights and had organized themselves into protective leagues. One of these leagues assisted the Poles at Tannenburg in 1410, and the Prussians had forced the Grand Master to allow the formation of a Landtag. But the Landtag was ignored and the Prussians reduced to their former unhappy condition. In 1440 the townsmen and nobles organized a great Prussian League and placed themselves under the protection of the king of Poland. In March 1454 Casimir officially proclaimed the annexation of Prussia to Poland, and Polish troops moved into the disputed territory. The Knights defended themselves valiantly, and for several years the war went badly for Casimir, but with the aid of the Prussians and Czech mercenaries, he finally defeated the Knights in 1462, forcing on them the second Treaty of Thorn (1466), whereby the order surrendered West Prussia, with Kulm, Marienburg, and Danzig, to the Poles. Danzig was permitted to be self-governing under the Polish crown, but the rest of West Prussia was incorporated into Poland. This gave Poland her long-desired outlet to the sea, and effectively cut East Prussia off from Germany. The immediate cause of World War II may be said to have traced back to this treaty of 1466, as this was the first appearance of the Polish Corridor in history.

While Casimir wisely refused to accept the crown of Bohemia when it was offered to him by the pope and kept on good terms with George Podiebrad, he did allow his son to accept it in 1471, a move which brought him into difficulties with Matthias Corvinus of Hungary. However, as we have seen, Ladislas eventually acquired both the Bohemian and Hungarian thrones, while his younger brothers John Albert (1492–1501) and Alexander succeeded their father on the thrones of Poland and Lithuania. John Albert is best known for the Statute of Piotrkow in 1496 which gave the nobles further privileges at the expense of the burghers and peasants and virtually re-established serfdom in Poland. At his death in 1501 Poland and Lithuania were permanently united when Alexander of Lithuania was elected king of Poland (1501–06).

The Scandinavian Kingdoms and the Hanse, 1286–1501

The history of the Scandinavian countries in the fourteenth and fifteenth centuries is a story of the gradual development of monarchical institutions, a feudal nobility and national churches, while throughout the whole runs the conflict between the Scandinavian monarchs and the German Hanse towns.

King Eric VI Menved (1286–1320) of Denmark spent his life attempting to strengthen the royal power against the great nobles and the church, but met with little success, being forced to recognize extensive immunities and privileges of the church. The fortunes of the monarchy dropped even further in the reign of his brother Christopher II (1320–32) who was driven from his throne by rebellious nobles and who lost nearly all of the royal domain. For eight years after the death of Christopher there was complete anarchy, ended by the accession of Waldemar IV (1340–75) the son of Christopher, who spent his long reign in regaining the lands and powers his father had lost. Waldemar tried to break the control of the Hanse towns over the commerce of Denmark, and engaged in two wars with them, during the course of which the Hanse sacked Copenhagen. Although successful in the first war (1361–63), Waldemar was defeated by a coalition of the Hanse, Sweden, and Mecklenburg in the second (1368–70) and was forced to sign the humiliating Treaty of Stralsund (1370) whereby the Hanse recovered all their commercial privileges, received cities and revenues in Scania and throughout Denmark, and were given the right to be consulted in the election of any Danish monarch. This treaty assured the complete dominance of the Hanse in the Baltic and marked the zenith of its power.

The Scandinavian monarchies were strengthened by the Union of Kalmar in 1397, whereby the three crowns were all united in a single person. Margaret, the daughter of Waldemar IV of Denmark, married Haakon VI of Norway and became regent of both kingdoms for her minor son Olaf. She was then chosen as regent of Sweden, so that in 1387 she ruled over all three countries. In 1397 she proclaimed the Union of Kalmar, whereby the three crowns were united but each kingdom retained its own institutions and officers. The Union was never ratified by the assemblies of the various states concerned, but became nonetheless effective throughout the lives of Margaret and her immediate successors. It was broken in 1448 when Sweden separated itself to elect its own king, but the union of Denmark and Norway was made permanent and lasted in fact until 1814. Under the Union, the leading role was played by Denmark, and the rivalries of the nobles kept the union from ever being too complete, but it did represent a step towards unification and greater royal power than had been known for some time.

With the death of Margaret in 1412, the control passed to her grand-nephew Eric (1412–39) who carried on a prolonged war with the Hanse and with Holstein, finally annexing the disputed territory of Schleswig. However, revolt broke out in Sweden which spread to the other kingdoms and resulted in the deposition of Eric, and the election of Christopher of Wittelsbach, his cousin. Christopher proved quite incompetent, relying for support mainly on the alliance of the Hanse towns, which regained all their old privileges. When Christopher died in 1448, Denmark elected Christian of Oldenburg, who was also proclaimed in Norway in 1450, but Sweden went her own way, electing as king Knut Knutsson, a leader of their own nobility. In 1457 the Swedes tired of Knut and drove him out, calling in Christian, but the real power lay in the hands of the great baron, Sten Sture, and after 1501 the power of the Danish king was no longer recognized in Sweden.

With all commerce in the hands of the German Hanse merchants, and with the great nobles ruling their lands practically unchecked, it is small wonder that the Scandinavian countries did not develop greatly in this period. Scandinavian towns, such as Bergen, did, indeed, grow into great prominence, but it was only as they were depots of the Hanse, and the prosperity accrued to the Germans rather than to the native population. In Sweden, where the German influence was less pronounced, there was some commercial and industrial development, and a strong national spirit came into being, which was fostered by the foundation of the University of Upsala in 1477. It was not however until the rise of the house of Vasa in the sixteenth century that Sweden emerged as an important power, and the dynastic wars between the three countries long kept any of them from enjoying a peaceful prosperity.

Meanwhile the mighty Hanse began to lose its monopoly of trade in the north. The league was split by internal squabbles, the more democratic towns quarreling with the old oligarchies. Although the Hanse continued to be powerful throughout the fifteenth century it was slowly losing ground, and many of the towns passed under the control of territorial princes who restricted the liberties of the merchants. As the national princes developed, they resented the German trade monopoly; Edward IV expelled the Hanse merchants from London and closed the Steelyard in 1468; Ivan III destroyed their factory at Novgorod in 1494; the dukes of Burgundy fostered the growth of Flemish and Dutch towns which were not members of the Hanse; and the electors of Brandenburg placed restrictions on the Hanse in their territories. In the chronic wars between the Hanse and Denmark, the Danish monarchs sheltered pirates who preyed on the Hanse commerce greatly disrupting trade. There were even civil wars between members of the Hanse, Cologne defying the authority of the league and siding with England when Edward fought it. The unity of the Hanse broke down, and minor leagues were formed within its membership which resented the domination of Lübeck. But the Hanse continued as long as the Baltic remained the one great center of north European trade; it was the development of the Atlantic carrying trade that really put an end to the prosperity and domination of the Hanse in the sixteenth century.

CHAPTER 40

ITALY AND THE IBERIAN STATES

❖

ITALY

If the history of England and France, of Germany and the East, shows on the whole a decline in the fourteenth and fifteenth centuries, the same cannot be said for Italy, where the fifteenth century was, in many ways, the highest point ever reached since classical antiquity. At no time since the days of ancient Rome has Italian culture so blossomed forth, and at no time has Italian influence been so great as in the Quattrocento. Yet while we can speak of Italian culture and the Italian Renaissance, it must be remembered that there was never an Italy. Political disorganization, too, reached its peak in this century of extremes; and the very individualism of the petty states is generally conceded to have had some considerable influence on the growth of personal individualism within them. The intellectual accomplishments of the Italians will be discussed in the following chapter; here we must endeavor to trace a path through the intricate maze of politics which marked the development of the despotisms and republics of the Trecento and Quattrocento.

We have already seen how Italy, torn by Guelph and Ghibelline struggles in practically every town, began to develop despotisms in the late thirteenth century, and have noted how such men as Ezzelino da Romano and Uberto Pallavicini were the precursors of the despots of the following age. The same general characteristics which marked the Italian towns in the late thirteenth century continued to distinguish them through the Quattrocento: Venice and Florence remained republics, though the republican institutions of Florence were adapted to the rule of political bosses who actually controlled the city: Milan, Verona, Padua, Ferrara, Mantua, Bologna, Rimini continued to be ruled by despots with varying degrees of legitimacy; while Naples was always a kingdom under a relatively absolute monarch from the days of the Normans to the liberation by Garibaldi. The leading states in this period, as in the preceding, were: Milan, Venice, Florence, Rome and Naples, and, in the struggle for supremacy in the peninsula, these states developed a technique of diplomacy and a concept of the balance of power, which were to be followed by the greater states of Europe in the succeeding centuries.

The incipient nationalism, which we have seen taking root in England, France, and Bohemia, had no part in the Italian scheme. There intense local patriotism animated men's minds, and if there were those who dreamed of a united Italy, it was always an Italy united in subjection to their own particular city or dynasty. It was an age of unscrupulous *real-politik,* which fittingly gave birth to that master of subterfuge, mendacity and political immorality, Niccolo Machiavelli.

The general political trend was towards the growth of personal absolutism, whether cloaked in legitimate titles or exercised through demagogery. The despots acquired their titles in various ways: some were families who received title as imperial vicars, such as the Visconti of Milan, or the Scaligeri of Verona; others were *condottieri* (captains of companies of mercenary troops) such as Francesco Sforza; some, like the Estensi of Ferrara, the Malatesta in Rimini, and the Montefeltri in Urbino were old feudal dynasties; while in some towns the elected captains of the popolo or podestas made their control hereditary, as in the cases of the Carrara in Padua, Gonzaga in Mantua and Scotti in Piacenza. In Florence, the Medici, in Bologna, the Bentivogli and in Perugia, the Baglioni, were all wealthy burgesses who bribed their way into power through exercise of their great wealth; while at the end of the period we find a new type of despot in the houses of the Farnese in Parma, Riario in Forli, Della Rovere in Urbino, and Borgia in the Romagna, all of whom owed their elevation to papal nepotism. But whatever their origin, the characteristics of these despots were much the same. They were brutal, unscrupulous, ambitious men, who were at the same time patrons of the arts and letters; men who murdered an enemy, applauded a poet or orator, or seduced a pretty woman with equal ease and pleasure. They hung pictures on their walls and enemies on their gibbets; wrote poetry and plotted treason; built churches and burned villages; excelled in courtly etiquette and inhuman tortures; lived lustily and died violently. When the poet Aretino wished to blackmail men such as these, he did not seek to expose dark crimes, unnatural vices, strange lusts or brutal murders—of these they were not ashamed; he mulcted good cash out of them by insinuating that they wrote bad verses, painted poorly, or were deficient in polite and courteous speech or manners. It was an age of extremes: violence and urbanity, cruelty and artistry, superstition and cold intellectuality. Only religion failed to burgeon in the intense, extravagant life of Renaissance Italy.

The political history of Renaissance Italy runs from the Italian expedition of the emperor Henry VII in 1310 to 1313 to that of King Charles VIII of France in 1494 to 1495. During that period the Big Five (Milan, Florence, Venice, Rome and Naples) secured their predominance over all lesser rivals and managed to preserve a precarious and ever-shifting balance of power between themselves. But if we devote our attention to the history of these five, it must not be forgotten that other cities, such as

Verona, Ferrara, Urbino, Bologna, Rimini, Padua et al. were enjoying an active political life of their own, duplicating in miniature the characteristics of the larger states.

VENICE

At the opening of the fourteenth century Venice was still almost exclusively a maritime commercial city. Its whole interest lay in trade and in the colonial empire which it had built up in the Adriatic, Aegean, and eastern Mediterranean. Resolutely turning its back to the Continent, Venice faced the sea, and only necessity caused it to alter its policy and seek inland expansion on the Italian mainland. Throughout the fourteenth century until final victory was won, the chief concern of Venice was the struggle with Genoa for the domination of the eastern waters; in the fifteenth it continued fighting to maintain itself in the East, but fought a losing battle against the Turks, who ultimately destroyed its Levantine empire.

Venetian tradition tells the incident that the Doge Tomasso Mocenigo on his deathbed in 1423 warned the Venetians against the election of Francesco Foscari as he would divert Venice from its true interests on the sea into a disastrous policy of expansion by land, which would impoverish and destroy the state. The Venetians however elected Foscari and with him deliberately chose the policy of intervention in Italian affairs. This story does in part indicate the general shift of Venetian policy at this time, but Venice had already cast envious eyes landward before 1423, and retained an interest in the sea long after that date.

The maintenance of the navy and maritime supremacy entailed, however, the control of some hinterland territories whence Venice could derive the timber and other materials needed for ship-building, and it was this that first turned Venice's attention to expansion on the mainland.

Venice's first attempt to acquire territory in Italy failed in 1308 to 1310, when it sought the annexation of Ferrara, but was defeated by papal forces. Thereafter Venice turned back to the sea, allowing eastern Lombardy to fall into the hands of the Scaliger lords of Verona. Under Can Grande della Scala, Verona expanded over its neighbors, absorbing Padua and ultimately controlling a congeries of states which extended from Lucca on the west to Treviso on the east. This expansion of Verona resulted in the formation of a league of Venice, Florence, Milan, and several minor Lombard towns, which in 1336 to 1338 defeated Verona and reduced the Scaligeri to their original lordship. Padua was restored to the house of Carrara, but under Venetian control, and Treviso was defintely annexed to Venice, giving the republic its first territorial acquisition on the Italian mainland.

Further inland expansion was halted by the war with Genoa which broke out soon thereafter and which occupied all Venice's attention for half a century. The fighting began in the Black Sea colonies, and soon spread throughout the Mediterranean. At first Venice, aided by Aragon, was successful in defeating a Genoese fleet off Sicily, but Genoa retaliated by allying with Milan and destroying the Venetian fleet at Sapienza off the coast of Greece (1354). A peace was arranged the following year, but the conflicting colonial and commercial rivalries of the two republics soon brought them into conflict again, trouble breaking out in the Aegean and in Cyprus. Genoa allied with Hungary and the Carrara of Padua to attack Venice in the War of Chioggia (1378–80), in which the allied forces besieged Venice in its own lagoons, occupying the village of Chiogga just outside Venice. The opportune arrival of the Venetian Eastern fleet enabled them to cut off the Genoese and administer on them a crushing defeat, from which the Ligurian republic never recovered.

But if the ancient feud with Genoa was finally successfully ended, expansion had brought Venice other enemies: Hungary and Austria resented the expansion along the Adriatic and in the region of Treviso; the Turks were already threatening the Eastern colonies, and Milan was jealous of the gains of Venice in northeastern Italy. In 1388 Milan occupied Padua and threatened Venice on its own borders, but Venice managed to regain control of Padua, and at the death of Gian Galeazzo Visconti in 1402 took the offensive, overthrowing the Carraras and annexing Padua, Verona, Vicenza, and other neighboring lands (1405).

Throughout the fifteenth century, Venice was engaged in almost perpetual wars with Milan in Italy and the Turks in the East. In 1416, Pietro Loredano won a great victory over the Turks at Gallipoli, which was followed by the occupation of Salonica a few years later. But the Turks soon captured Salonica and in the next decades Venice lost also possessions in Euboea and other Aegean islands. By 1479, when peace was made with the sultan, Venice had been stripped of most of her Eastern empire and was forced to pay tribute for what remained. The only advance in this area was the acquisition of Cyprus in 1489, but Venice retained sufficient strength to consistently oppose the Turkish advance for another century.

Meanwhile the republic had expanded westward into Lombardy in a war with Milan (1425–32) acquiring as a result Brescia, Bergamo, and other Lombard towns, which welcomed the moderately lenient rule of the republic in preference to that of Milan. The war with Milan was endemic throughout the rest of the century; Venice interfered in Milanese affairs at the death of Filippo Maria Visconti in 1447, and supported first the republic of San Ambrogio and then Francesco Sforza. But Sforza proved too dangerous a neighbor and Venice allied with Naples against him. But no alliance was permanent in fifteenth-century Italy, and we find Venice and the papacy allying to take the offensive against Milan, Florence, and Naples in a series of wars in the years 1466 to 1470 and 1480 to 1484. As a result of the War of Ferrara of 1482 to 1484, Venice reached the limits of its permanent territorial expansion in Italy.

In all this period the Venetian constitution remained practically unchanged. In 1310, as we have seen above, the conspiracy of Bajamonte Tiepolo caused the creation of the Council of Ten, that super-legal tribunal, whose secret sessions determined the policy of the state and the lives of its citizens. Resenting the virtual impotence of the dogeship under this system, Doge Marino Falerio in 1354 plotted to overthrow the constitution and massacre many of the leading members of the nobility. But his conspiracy was discovered and the doge was himself tried by the Ten and beheaded. It was the second and last attempt to overthrow the oligarchical constitution under which the city of the lagoons had risen to a place of world power. The rule of Venice over dependencies was liberal though stern; they were allowed considerable local freedom as long as they remained completely loyal to Venice and contributed to its wealth and greatness. There is probably no country in the world which so completely absorbed the interests of its sons as did Venice; into the construction of churches, palaces, and public buildings went the best efforts and the treasure of the citizens. Perhaps the obvious and lavish display of wealth in Venice was not always in the best taste, but it proved the pride of Venetians in their lovely city on whose beautification and ornamentation they squandered the fruits of their wide-flung commercial enterprise.

MILAN

Although in some ways Venice was the strongest state of Italy, Milan was the most typical of the Renaissance city-states, and it was its policies that most directly influenced those of its neighbors. Throughout the thirteenth century, as we have seen, Milan led the Italian towns in their opposition to imperial domination, while, within, the control of the city was contested between the Guelph Della Torre and the Ghibelline Visconti families. In 1287 Matteo Visconti was chosen capitano del populo, securing the title of imperial vicar seven years later. His position was secured completely by the Italian journey of the emperor Henry VII in 1311, after which the Della Torre ceased to figure as rivals, and in 1317, when John XXII excommunicated all imperial vicars, Matteo quietly assumed the title of General Lord of Milan in his own right. Under Matteo, Milan ruled over Pavia, Piacenza, Tortona, Bergamo and Alessandria, but Matteo was unsuccessful in an attempt to enforce his control over Genoa.

After the death of Matteo in 1322, the Visconti fortunes declined for a time as those of the Scaligeri of Verona went up, but with Archbishop Giovanni Visconti, the third son of Matteo, who succeeded to the temporal as well as spiritual headship of the city in 1349, a second period of Milanese expansion began. Giovanni established the rule of Milan over all west and central Lombardy, secured the submission of Genoa (1353), and even pushed his control into the Romagna to include Bologna. At his death in 1354 the seigneury was divided into three parts which were given to his three nephews, a violent crew who proceeded to fight each

THE VISCONTI AND SFORZA OF MILAN

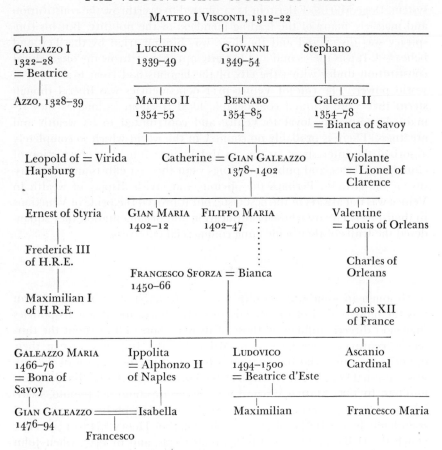

MATTEO I VISCONTI, 1312–22

GALEAZZO I 1322–28 = Beatrice   LUCCHINO 1339–49   GIOVANNI 1349–54   Stephano

Azzo, 1328–39   MATTEO II 1354–55   BERNABO 1354–85   Galeazzo II 1354–78 = Bianca of Savoy

Leopold of = Virida Hapsburg   Catherine = GIAN GALEAZZO 1378–1402   Violante = Lionel of Clarence

Ernest of Styria   GIAN MARIA 1402–12   FILIPPO MARIA 1402–47   Valentine = Louis of Orleans

Frederick III of H.R.E.   FRANCESCO SFORZA = Bianca 1450–66   Charles of Orleans

Maximilian I of H.R.E.   Louis XII of France

GALEAZZO MARIA 1466–76 = Bona of Savoy   Ippolita = Alphonzo II of Naples   LUDOVICO 1494–1500 = Beatrice d'Este   Ascanio Cardinal

GIAN GALEAZZO 1476–94 ====Isabella   Maximilian   Francesco Maria
       Francesco

other, while a coalition led by Venice forced them to abandon Bologna. Finally the state was reunited by Gian Galeazzo (1378–1402) who inherited Pavia in 1378, and succeeded to Milan by murdering his uncle, Bernabo, in 1385.

Gian Galeazzo Visconti, "the Viper of Milan," was the greatest of the Visconti and was the dominant figure in Italian politics of his day. He consolidated his rule over all Lombardy, captured Padua, invaded Tuscany and captured Pisa, even forcing his suzerainty over Siena, Lucca, Assisi, and Perugia. He recaptured Bologna, and was contemplating the conquest of Florence when he died in 1402.

To secure a title worthy of his state, Gian Galeazzo purchased from the emperor Wenceslas the title of Duke of Milan, and when, after the deposition of Wenceslas, Rupert attempted to deprive him of it, he defeated the imperial forces and proudly retained his title and position.

Gian Galeazzo was the perfect Italian Renaissance despot. Cruel and treacherous, he was at the same time a benevolent despot, giving Milan an excellent rule. He abolished privileges, equalized and reduced taxation, introduced measures to insure the public health, established governmental medical inspection and quarantine of contagious diseases, insisted on an honest and efficient administration, and made of Milan the best governed autocracy in Europe. He was also a great builder, beginning the erection of the cathedral of Milan and the beautiful Certosa of Pavia. To encourage trade he built a canal from Milan to Pavia, and so built up the prosperity of his state that it was able to float government bonds at the relatively low rate of ten per cent.

In international affairs Gian Galeazzo brought Milan to a new height: his own wife was the daughter of King John of France; his daughter, Valentine, married Louis of Orleans, and his sister, Violante, Lionel of Clarence. For a time it seemed that the union of all northern Italy was to be accomplished by Milan, but Florence and Venice kept up a dogged resistance, which had its reward after the death of the duke in 1402.

If Gian Galeazzo represents the best in Renaissance despotism, his sons who succeeded him represent the very worst. Gian Maria (1402–12), the elder, is infamous for his habit of hunting human beings, turning his fierce boar hounds on the track of a helpless fugitive and hunting him down as one would a wild beast. His career of lust and violence was ended by the daggers of assassins in 1412, and his brother Filippo Maria succeeded. Filippo Maria (1402–47), an ugly misshapen creature, spent his life in constant fear of assassination, surrounding himself with guards, living in the fortress and seldom venturing into the city. He developed an elaborate system of spies whom he employed to watch his generals and ministers as well as his enemies.

Under the sons of Gian Galeazzo, Milan lost much of the territory conquered by the great duke. There was almost continuous war with Venice, Florence, and the papacy in which the smaller Lombard towns changed hands back and forth with the varying fortunes of war. This was the age of great condottieri—Carmagnola, Ficino Cane, Piccinini, and Francesco Sforza—all of whom served whatever master paid them best, on occasion capturing a town for one master and then either selling it out to the enemy or keeping it for themselves. Ficino Cane made himself lord of Tortona, Novara, Vercelli, and Alessandria, these towns being secured by Milan through the marriage of Filippo Maria to the widow of the condottiere. Venice showed an unusual independence when she executed Carmagnola for treason. Much more common was the bribing of the generals by marriage alliances, such as that contracted by Francesco Sforza and the daughter of Filippo Maria.

The career of Francesco Sforza is so characteristic of Renaissance Italy that it deserves some detailed consideration. Sforza had been employed by the Milanese to command against the Venetian army led by Carmagnola. Winning certain territories for his employer, the condottiere seized them for himself, forcing Filippo Maria to recognize him as lord of Cremona and Pontremoli and to give him the hand of his illegitimate daughter, Bianca. This humiliated the Visconti who began to plot the overthrow of his unwelcome son-in-law. Sforza retaliated by going over to the enemy and accepting the command of a Venetian-Florentine army against Milan. Then in 1447 Filippo Maria died leaving no legitimate heir. The Milanese proclaimed the republic of San Ambrogio, against which Venice promptly declared war. Sforza then reversed himself and became the general of the Milanese troops against Venice. Accepted as the defender of Milan, Sforza found it an easy matter to suppress the republic and proclaim himself duke (1450). As duke he cemented an alliance with Florence and made peace with Venice, which was willing to accept a truce as she was troubled by the Turkish war. To secure himself the more firmly Sforza then negotiated a double marriage alliance with Naples, and made an alliance with Louis XI of France, whereby in return for assistance against the League of the Public Welfare, he received the city of Genoa, which had previously been annexed by France.

Like Gian Galeazzo, Francesco Sforza was a conscientious ruler and labored to develop the economic prosperity of his duchy. He built the great Martesana Canal (the first to use large locks) as well as several smaller canals, which facilitated the shipment of goods throughout Lombardy. He completed the building of the cathedral of Milan, and the Certosa of Pavia, begun by Gian Galeazzo, and began the construction of the famous Sforza palace in Milan. He was also a great patron of scholars and humanists, the greatest light of his court being Francesco Filelfo.

The son of Francesco Sforza and Bianca Visconti, Galeazzo Sforza (1466–76) had more in common with his maternal grandfather than with his father. He was cruel and capricious, extravagant and tyrannical; the ten years of his misrule ended with his assassination by a group of young men inspired by the example of Brutus and Cassius who had rid Rome of a tyrant. But the hereditary succession was well enough established that the throne could pass to his minor son, Gian Galeazzo, under the regency of his mother, Bona of Savoy.

One of the first acts of the regent was the exile of the brothers of her late husband, Ascanio and Ludovico "Il Moro," but internal dissention and pressure from Naples secured the return of the duke's uncles and the overthrow of the regent in 1479. Thereafter Ludovico ruled as regent for young Gian Galeazzo whom he married to Isabella, the daughter of his friend Ferrante of Naples. The triple alliance of Milan, Naples, and Florence was renewed and strengthened for a time, but Ludovico refused to allow the young duke any share in the government, and his wife Beatrice d'Este slighted the duchess Isabella, who appealed to her father. Ferrante interferred in Milan to secure the rights of his son-in-law against the regent, who, finding himself isolated, appealed to France against Naples. In 1492 Ludovico purchased for himself the title of duke from the emperor Maximilian, to whom he gave his niece Bianca in marriage, but he kept this investiture secret until the death of Gian Galeazzo two years later, a demise possibly caused by poison administered over a period of time by Ludovico. With the throne vacant, Ludovico allowed himself to be elected duke, producing thereafter the imperial investiture previously secured.

The significance of Ludovico's appeal to Charles VIII of France against Naples will be discussed below, but the invitation opened Italy to a new era of invasion from the north, which led to the long struggle between France and Spain for the control of the peninsula and to the capture of Milan itself by the French in the Italian wars of the sixteenth century.

Ludovico, like his father Francesco, was a great patron of scholars and artists, the court of Milan being rendered illustrious through the residence there of Leonardo da Vinci who worked under the patronage of the duke, assisting him in several engineering projects, and designing numerous canals and buildings. Bramante also added to the glory of Milan at his time with buildings which commanded the great admiration of his contemporaries.

FLORENCE

While Venice and Milan were securing the control of northern Italy, Florence was rising to a position of dominance in Tuscany. Throughout the fourteenth century Florence continued under the republican constitution of the Ordinances of Justice without being able to end the incessant civil strife which marked its political life. Florence withstood the attack of the emperor Henry VII and preserved itself from imperial domination, only to be defeated by Lucca which was rising to power under Castruccio Castracani (1325). To secure aid against Lucca, which was allied with Milan, Florence placed itself under the protection of Duke Charles of Calabria, the son of Robert of Naples, but that busy prince, who had his finger in several political pies at the same moment, could only send forces under his cousin Walter de Brienne, duke of Athens, which scarcely held their own against Castracani. The death of Castracani and Duke Charles ended the threat of the moment and Florence returned to democracy and civil feuds. After a number of years of fruitless experimentation, the Florentines offered the seigneury of their city to Walter de Brienne, who was appointed capitano del populo but who conducted himself as despot of Florence. After a year of Walter's tyranny (1342–43) he was violently driven out by the Florentines, who were determined never again to risk the development of a despotism by entrusting too much power to any individual.

But if Florence was saved from becoming a despotism, it could not evolve a satisfactory democratic government, the wealthier merchants and bankers and the proletariat drifting farther and farther apart in their desires and aspirations. The great Guelph oligarchic families, the *populo grasso,* gained increasing power, at the expense of the *populo minuto,* and by 1345 social revolt began to be felt in Florence.

The great rebellion of the lower classes did not occur, however, until 1378, when, supported by Salvestro di Medici and some of the newer nobles, the *Ciompi,* a group of the lower proletarians, revolted in a bloody uprising. But the revolt was premature; the concessions gained were soon after revoked. Di Medici was exiled and the oligarchs returned to power. For the next few decades Florence was engaged in rather continuous war against Milan and its ally Pisa. The threat of a Milanese conquest of Tuscany was ended with the death of Gian Galeazzo in 1402, as we have seen, and Florence followed up the advantage by capturing Pisa and reducing it to total subjection in 1406. The conquest of Pisa made Florence the dominant power in Tuscany, the other cities offering submission with but little opposition. This expansion brought Florence into further conflict with Milan against whom Florence allied with Venice.

In the long struggle with Milan the leadership of Florence had been held by the family of Albizzi, who stood for the old oligarchy and the greater gilds, but towards the end of the war, in 1427, a new popular leader arose in the person of Giovanni di Medici, who managed to secure a revision of the taxes to the benefit of the lower classes.

The leadership of the popular party was carried on by Cosimo di Medici, the son of Giovanni. Failure in a campaign against Lucca caused his banishment in 1433, but in the following year he returned as the popular hero, was given the title of *"Pater Patriae,"* and secured the exile of the Albizzi and the oligarchic leaders. From 1434 dates the beginning of the Medici "boss rule" over Florence.

Under Cosimo and his successors Florence was practically a despotism, but the republican forms were carefully preserved and the Medici themselves seldom held any office in the state. Cosimo somewhat resembled the

Roman Augustus, who established the principate while retaining all the old republican offices. The Medici control was based on the great wealth of the family banking house and a cleverly manipulated political machine; while the officers of state were still selected by lot from panels of the citizens, none but Medici partisans were listed on the panels. The old constitution was retained, the priors still governed the city, there were still the multiplicity of special commissions to handle domestic and foreign affairs— but all of them were drawn from Medici party men, and behind them all was the Medici "boss," who maintained a consistent policy throughout the rapidly shifting series of public officials. While embassies from foreign states were officially accredited to the Signoria, they actually conferred with Cosimo, and it was he who dictated the policy of Florence both in internal and foreign affairs.

Under the Medici, Florence reached the height of its glory as the greatest center of Renaissance culture and art. It also took on a new importance in political matters, holding the balance of power between the rival states of Italy. Cosimo recognized that Florence's natural allies were Milan and Naples, as opposed to the papacy and Venice, and the triple alliance was largely his creation. He was the ally of Francesco Sforza, whom he helped to seize the throne of Milan; he blocked papal advance into Tuscany, establishing instead a Florentine hegemony over parts of the Romagna and Umbria, but he was the lavish host to the Council of Florence in 1439, entertaining the pope and the Byzantine emperor with a magnificent display of luxury and elegance.

Cosimo could easily have made himself despot of Florence, but he preferred to remain behind the scenes pulling the strings. While there was inevitably some opposition to the Medici control, it was on the whole extremely popular, the Florentines basking in the relative peace and security which the Medici absolutism afforded them. When Cosimo died in 1464, after thirty years of rule, his place was taken by his son Pietro (1464–69) who continued his father's policies, and passed the family position on to his sons Lorenzo "the Magnificent" (1469–92) and Guiliano. Under Lorenzo and Guiliano the opposition made a bold stroke to rid Florence of the Medici in the famous Pazzi Conspiracy in 1478 in which a group of disaffected nobles, backed by the pope, attempted the assassination of the brothers. Guiliano was killed, but Lorenzo escaped, and the general uprising which the conspirators expected turned instead into a great demonstration of popular support for the Medici. The conspirators were tortured and killed, and the net result of the affair was to establish Lorenzo even more firmly in control of the city. It was shortly after this that Lorenzo gained his greatest diplomatic triumph. The pope, Sixtus IV, was the confirmed enemy of the Medici and had intrigued against them with Naples, so that Ferrante of Naples aided in the attack on Lorenzo.

Florence countered with an alliance with Milan and Venice and began negotiations with France. Then Lorenzo went himself to Naples where he persuaded Ferrante to abandon the pope and join the alliance against him. This diplomatic stroke isolated the pope and made Florence the central power in Italian politics. Lorenzo's popularity at home was unbounded, and he took the occasion to reorganize the constitution, creating a new Council of Seventy as the chief governmental body, and assuring that its members should of course be good Mediceans.

Lorenzo died in 1492, when the expedition of Charles VIII was already being planned. Fra Girolamo Savonarola, the Dominican prophet, who denounced the worldliness of the Medicean court, was already prophesying the scourge of God which was to descend on Florence as the punishment for its sins. The history of Florence in the decades immediately following the death of Lorenzo justified the gloomy prophecies of the gaunt Dominican, but the Age of Lorenzo the Magnificent still remains the high point of Florentine civilization. The literary and artistic accomplishments which were the glory of Medicean Florence will be discussed in the next chapter.

ROME AND THE PAPAL STATES

The history of the Papal States while the papacy was at Avignon is a story of factional strife in Rome itself and the rise of petty despotisms in the various towns of the Romagna. We have already noted how Rome became a republic temporarily under Cola da Rienzi (1347) and how the great military cardinal, Gil Albornoz, finally brought Rome and the Papal States back into subjection to the church. Petty dynasts had established themselves throughout the cities of the Romagna; the Manfredi of Faenza, the Malatesta of Rimini, the Ordelaffi of Forli and Cesena, and the Montefeltri of Urbino being but the chief of the many lesser despotisms established. Albornoz brought these tyrants to terms, re-establishing the rule of the church over the entire territory, and establishing the *Constitutiones aegidianae* (1357), a code of laws which were to remain in force until the opening of the nineteenth century. His general policy was to make war on the despots until he had reduced them to submission and then allow them to continue ruling their cities as papal vicars.

With the re-establishment of a strong papacy after the Schism and Conciliar Movement, the popes became more than ever Italian princes, interested primarily in Italian affairs. Nicholas V (1447–55), the last pope of the Concilar period, was also the first of the Renaissance popes who were scholars and men of letters rather than churchmen. Before his elevation to the papacy, Tomasso Parentucelli had been the librarian of Cosimo de Medici in Florence and had laid the foundations for the great Medicean library there. As pope he continued his interest in books and libraries, founding the Vatican Library and employing many humanists and scholars as papal secretaries. Under his patronage, Poggio, Alberti, and Lorenzo Valla all held papal offices and began to make Rome a center of the new learning.

Nicholas was succeeded by Calixtus III (1455–68), an Aragonese cardinal of the Borgia family, who had no interest in scholarship or in religion and who is chiefly noted for his generous treatment of his relatives. He did make some gestures towards organizing a crusade against the Turks, but his prime interest was in founding the fortunes of his family, especially his nephew, Roderigo, whom he created a cardinal. He was succeeded by another humanist, Aeneas Silvius Piccolomini of Siena, who had won a great reputation as a scholar, historian, and diplomat. He had played an important part in the confused diplomacy during the struggle between the pope and the Council of Basel, switching from Council to pope and being chiefly instrumental in securing the imperial adherence to the papal side. He had also been a poet, and was the author of some scandalous verses which he spent great effort, after his election to the papacy, in endeavoring to suppress. As Pius II (1458–64), while he was favorable to the humanists, he was more concerned with the crusade against the Turks, and died while vainly endeavoring to organize an expedition against Constantinople.

One characteristic marked all the popes of this period—that was an eager nepotism and a tendency to bestow on their relatives offices in the church and church lands. None of the popes of the later fifteenth century were free of this, and several of them allowed it to become the dominating interest of their pontificates. Nicholas V and Pius II were the best of the lot, for they were themselves scholars and contributed to the intellectual movements of the time; further, both took their papal duties seriously; but even Pius founded the fortunes of the Piccolomini family while occupying the See of Peter.

Paul II (1464–71) was a member of the Venetian house of Barbo, and his policy was essentially Venetian, his chief concern being a crusade against the Turks to recapture Venetian colonies in the East. However, the crusade was badly defeated off Euboea (Negroponte) in 1470, and Paul resigned himself to building up a great collection of jewels and to encouraging horse racing. Paul was the enemy of the humanists whom he expelled from Rome. His closing of the Roman Academy and persecution of the scholars has left him a bad reputation. His successor Sixtus IV (1471–84) of the Genoese family of Della Rovere, was primarily interested in founding principalities for his nephews the Riarios. He engaged in the Pazzi conspiracy in an attempt to secure Florence for one of them, and for years kept Italy embroiled as a result of his ambitious political ventures. He was, however, a great patron of artists, and was responsible for the building of the famous Sistine Chapel with its decoration by Pinturicchio, Perugino, Ghirlandaio, et al. Sixtus ranks with Julius II (his nephew, 1503–13) as the great builder and patron of artists.

Innocent VIII (Giovanni Cibo, a Genoese), who ruled from 1484 to 1492, is best known as the first pope to openly recognize his children and as the pope who opened a public bank in Rome to sell pardons and indulgences. Apart from meddling in Neapolitan politics, where he stirred up a revolt against King Ferrante and supported the Angevin claims, his pontificate is without interest. The dominant person in the curia was Cardinal Guliano della Rovere (later Pope Julius II) who directed papal policy throughout the pontificate of the indolent and luxury-loving Innocent. On the death of the pope, Della Rovere failed of election to the papacy, however, and the throne passed to Cardinal Roderigo Borgia (the nephew of Calixtus III), who as Pope Alexander VI (1492–1503) brought the papacy to a new low of degradation. Alexander's chief ambition was the creation of principalities for his children, especially the infamous Caesar Borgia, who conquered most of the Romagna and was well on his way to establish a Borgian duchy in central Italy when his father's death put an abrupt end to his schemes. Alexander's daughter Lucrezia, the wife of Alfonso d'Este of Ferrara, does not deserve the reputation as a *femme fatale* which is usually accorded her. Her famous poisons are largely legendary, and after she got away from the influence of her father, she proved herself a reasonably respectable Renaissance lady. It was Alexander who was the expert at poisoning, and Caesar who excelled in murder and torture; Lucrezia herself was an innocent tool in the hands of her thoroughly degenerate family.

It is small wonder that the stench of Rome reached even as far as Germany where it so offended the nostrils of Martin Luther that he deliberately broke with the papacy. Even Lorenzo di Medici, who was certainly no puritan, warned his son that Rome was a "sink of iniquity." Thus the Middle Ages ended with its most ennobling institution, the church, sunk into a slough of degeneracy and corruption. It took the Protestant movement to produce the Counter-Reformation of the church in the sixteenth century.

NAPLES AND SICILY

Except for its geographical location, Naples had not too much in common with the rest of Italy in the fourteenth century, although in the fifteenth it began to participate in the movement of the Renaissance. While the other Italian states were republics or despotisms, Naples remained a monarchy of the old feudal type. The two states of Naples and Sicily went their own ways under different dynasties, Naples under the descendants of Charles of Anjou, and Sicily under the Aragonese kings, and not until they were united in 1435 by Alfonso the Magnanimous did the two states again have a common history. The story of Sicily is bound up with that of Aragon, that of Naples is closely tied to Hungary and to the politics of the Italian communes.

Robert the Good (1309–43) who succeeded his father Charles II on the throne of Naples, was a dominant figure in Italian politics for many years, as he was the leader of the Guelph factions throughout the country. To him turned the Guelphs whenever they were threatened by Ghibelline forces, and he gained great influence as the leader of the opposition when Henry VII and Louis of Bavaria made their expeditions into Italy. Robert's son, Charles of Calabria, died before his father, leaving only daughters, and in an attempt to secure the succession, Robert arranged the marriage of his granddaughter Joanna to her cousin Andrew, the son of King Charles Robert of Hungary.

Joanna I (1343–82) had but little affection for her husband who attempted to rule for himself, giving the best posts in the kingdom to his Hungarian friends. In 1345 Andreas was brutally murdered by a party of Neapolitan barons, and although she later procured a papal brief exonerating her from any complicity in the murder, Joanna may well have been privy to the crime. Louis of Hungary, Andreas' brother, invaded Naples to avenge his brother's murder, occupying the kingdom and executing the nobles who had been involved in the plot (1347–50). But the Hungarian rule was violently opposed by most of the Neapolitans, so that when Joanna married Louis of Tarento, the barons rallied to their side and expelled the foreigners. Throughout her reign Joanna had to contend with baronial rebellions, in which the barons generally invoked Hungarian aid. Finally, after the death of her fourth husband, Joanna adopted as her heir Louis of Anjou, the brother of King Charles V of France. Against the succession of Louis, Charles of Durazzo, a great-grandson of Charles II, set up his own claims as head of the Hungarian party. Joanna was captured by Charles, whose mercenaries strangled the unhappy queen, and Charles of Durazzo was proclaimed Charles III of Naples. But Charles soon became involved in Hungarian affairs, where he secured the crown for a year, only to lose his life in 1386. The throne of Naples then passed to his minor son, Ladislas (1386–1414), the succession being challenged by the Angevin party. This struggle between Angevin and Hungarian dominated the history of Naples for several decades, each party supporting rival popes during the Schism, until Ladislas finally overcame his enemies and established himself firmly on the throne. Louis II of Anjou twice invaded Naples, supported by the popes of the Council of Pisa, but Ladislas defended his kingdom and even carried the war into the Papal States which he occupied for a time. It was Ladislas' attack on

Rome in 1414 which prompted John XXIII to agree to the summoning of the Council of Constance. In the same year Ladislas died, leaving the throne to his sister Joanna II. A series of lovers swayed the weak will of the voluptuous queen, whose husband, Jacques de Bourbon, was imprisoned for three years, after which he fled to France. The government deteriorated into practical anarchy, the queen's current lovers holding the high posts of government irrespective of their obvious incapacities. The Angevin claims were revived and Louis III of Anjou invaded the kingdom. To offset this danger, Joanna adopted as her heir Alfonso of Aragon and Sicily, but when Alfonso landed in southern Italy, he proved so successful that Joanna feared him worse than Louis and reversed her decision, denouncing Alfonso and adopting Louis as her heir. Louis died and Joanna recognized his brother, René of Provence, as her heir, but the Aragonese party continued to gain strength, and after Joanna died in 1435, René was driven from the country and Alfonso proclaimed king.

Alfonso the Magnanimous (1435-58) brought peace and a considerable measure of prosperity to his new kingdom. In fact he preferred Naples to any of his other domains, and subordinated the interests of both Aragon and Sicily to those of his latest acquisition. Under him the Neapolitan Renaissance reached its height, as he was the patron of artists and scholars, but Naples never rivaled Florence or Milan as a center of intellectual or artistic achievement.

Alfonso rather consistently allied with Milan, supporting at first the Visconti and later the Sforza. Although his accession to the throne was opposed by Pope Eugenius IV, he won over the pope and maintained an alliance with Rome. His chief desire was to insure the succession of Naples to his illegitimate son Ferrante (Ferdinand) whom he had legitimated and recognized as his heir in Naples. Aragon and Sicily were bequeathed to his brother so that the union of Naples and Sicily was broken again.

Ferrante (1458-94) was one of the worst of the Renaissance rulers, his reign being a long series of baronial revolts and wars with the papacy and with the Angevins. In general he supported the alliance with Milan and Medicean Florence, and in internal affairs he attempted to carry on his father's constructive work. We have already seen how he broke with Florence to support Rome in the Pazzi conspiracy only to be won back by Lorenzo and how he interferred in Milan in favor of Gian Galeazzo against Ludovico "Il Moro." The breach with Il Moro was fatal, for the wily duke of Milan turned to France, where King Charles VIII had inherited the old Angevin claims to Naples on the extinction of the house of Anjou. It was to press these claims that Charles VIII invaded Italy in 1494. Ferrante abdicated and his son Alfonso II came to the throne, but the hatred of the father carried over to the son, and the Neapolitans welcomed the French monarch who would rid them of the house of Aragon. In 1495, after a successful progress down the length of Italy, Charles VIII came to Naples where he had himself crowned king.

The Italian expedition of Charles VIII inaugurated a new period in Italian history. After several centuries of relatively undisturbed local development, Italy once again became the battleground for the greater powers of Europe: France, Spain, and the empire struggling for control throughout the first part of the sixteenth century. When the Italian wars were over, Italy was prostrate; the Renaissance passed across the Alps, and Italy relapsed into centuries of political and intellectual stagnation under the domination of foreign powers and the Inquisition.

SPAIN AND PORTUGAL

CASTILE AND ARAGON, 1312–1492

The history of the kingdoms of Castile and Aragon in the fourteenth and fifteenth centuries is largely a story of civil war and anarchy in both states, but both monarchs made significant gains, and the period ends with the union of the two thrones in the absolute monarchy of Ferdinand and Isabella.

In Castile the reign of Alfonso XI (1312–50) was marked by the great battle of the Rio Saludo (1340) in which the war against the Moslems was brought to an end by a crushing victory over the Moors of Africa. This was the last great battle of the Reconquista, and thereafter there was generally peace between the Christian and Moslem powers until the final capture of Granada in 1492. The existence of Granada was an important factor in the life of Spain, for the Christian monarchs were constrained to follow a policy of religious toleration as long as there was an independent Moslem state on their frontier. Only after Granada became impotent were the Catholic Kings able to introduce that policy of utter intolerance which is associated with the terrifying name of the Spanish Inquisition.

At the death of Alfonso in 1350, civil war broke out between his son Pedro IV, "the Cruel" (1350–69), and his illegitimate half-brother, Henry of Trastamara. In this war the house of Trastamara was supported by the French, with whom Castile had allied at the beginning of the Hundred Years' War, while the English led by the Black Prince aided Pedro. At first Pedro and the English were successful, winning the battle of Navarette (Nájera) in 1367; but Pedro's penchant for murder and his inhuman brutalities disgusted the Black Prince, who withdrew, so that Henry of Trastamara and du Guesclin were able to overthrow Pedro at Monteil in 1369.

As we have seen, this campaign materially relieved France by liquidating many of the bands of free companies which were terrorizing the country in the truce between the French and English crowns.

Henry II of Trastamara (1369–79) repaid the help given him by France when he defeated an English fleet off La Rochelle (1372), enabling the French to get control of the Atlantic and the Channel and weakening the English position in Guyenne. In 1375 Henry arranged a marriage alliance with Aragon whereby his son John married Eleanor the daughter of Pedro IV of Aragon; as a result of this alliance Ferdinand, the younger son of John of Castile, later ascended the throne of Aragon.

The reigns of John I (1379–90), Henry III (1390–1406), and John II (1406–54) were relatively unimportant. John I attempted to conquer Portugal but was defeated, and all three monarchs were strictly limited by the powers of the nobles and the towns. One of the most important groups in Castile at this time was the *Mesta,* a great association of sheep growers, who combined to regulate the wool trade. Wool was one of the prime industries of medieval Spain, Spanish wool vying with English in the markets of Flanders and Italy. The Mesta included the sheep raisers both great and small, whose migrant herds wandered across Castile searching out the best pasture lands. This seasonal migration of the sheep was an important factor in the economic life of medieval Castile.

Under John II the real power in Castile was wielded by Alvaro de Luna, the Grand Master of the Order of Santiago, who strengthened the power of the crown but stirred up a tremendous antagonism in the process. His presumption at last reached such a degree that the queen and even the king resented the dominance of the favorite, and Alvaro was summarily executed. King John was twice married, to Marie of Aragon and to Isabella of Portugal. By his first wife he had one son, Henry, who succeeded as Henry IV (1454–74), while by Isabelle he had a son, Alfonso, and a daughter, Isabella. Henry IV proved an even worse king than his father, and the favorite who assumed control, Beltran de la Cueva, had all the arrogance without the statesmanship of Alvaro. So intimate did Beltran become with both Henry and his queen Joanna of Portugal, that the child which Joanna bore in 1462, although admitted as his own by Henry, was commonly called Joanna La Beltraneja. When Henry had the Cortes recognize little Joanna as his heir, a party of the nobles supported by the king of Aragon, used the presumed illegitimacy of the child as an excuse for revolt. In 1464 the nobles deposed King Henry and embarked in civil war. They were defeated in battle but were able to coerce Henry into accepting his brother Alfonso as his heir. Alfonso, however, gave every appearance of being a strong man unwilling to accept dictation from the nobles, and it was most convenient for them that he died of the plague. In fact his death was announced three days before it actually occurred, a

KINGS OF CASTILE AND ARAGON, 1312–1516

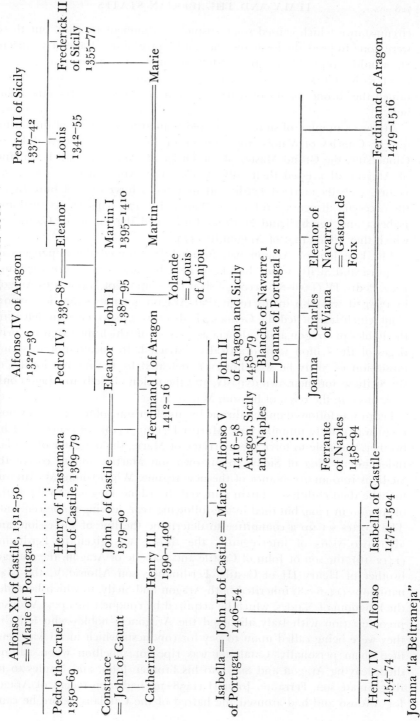

circumstance which caused some suspicious comment to arise, but there were none to press the issue and the nobles proclaimed Isabella as queen. She would accept only the title of heir-apparent and insisted on an agreement with Henry (Treaty of Toros de Guisando) whereby the king retained the throne for his own lifetime, but acknowledged Isabella as his heir.

At once a number of suitors appeared requesting the hand of the future queen: Charles of Valois, the brother of Louis XI; Richard duke of Gloucester; the Grand Master of the Order of Alcantara; and Ferdinand of Aragon all pressed their suit. Against the expressed desires of King Henry, Isabella married Ferdinand in 1469, a forged papal bull giving the necessary dispensation for the alliance. In 1474, King Henry died and Isabella and her husband Ferdinand ascended the throne of Castile, to which they added that of Aragon in 1479.

The kingdom of Aragon had meanwhile reunited the appanages of Majorca and Sicily, which had been held by cadet lines since 1276 and 1302. Pedro IV (1336–87) accomplished the reunion of Majorca to Aragon in 1349; it was also in his reign that Aragon got possession of Sardinia from which it expelled the Genoese. Pedro further succeeded in defeating the nobles of Aragon and Valencia as a result of which the extensive privileges of the Union were drastically restricted. In an attempt to secure possession of Sicily he was, however, defeated by the intense loyalty of the Sicilians for their own dynasty, and the union of Sicily to Aragon only took place in the reign of his son, Martin I.

Pedro was followed on the throne by his elder son John (1387–95) whose reign was utterly unimportant. Martin I (1395–1410) who succeeded his brother, was able to force the marriage of Marie, the daughter of the last independent king of Sicily, to his own son Martin, and to coerce the Sicilians into an acceptance of the new regime. When young Martin and his wife died childless, Martin annexed the island kingdom to the realm of Aragon in 1409, but died in the following year, leaving no descendants. The Cortes set up a committee to determine the line of succession, and after two years of interregnum, the throne was given to Ferdinand (1412–16), the son of John of Castile and Isabelle of Aragon, the younger brother of Henry III of Castile. Ferdinand's son Alfonso V, the Magnanimous (1416–58) inherited both Aragon and Sicily, to which he added the kingdom of Naples, which he acquired by conquest in 1435. Alfonso's preoccupation with Italy alienated the Aragonese nobles who felt that they were being called upon to pay for conquests which in no way benefited them personally. Catalonia was ripe for rebellion when Alfonso died, leaving Aragon and Sicily to his brother John, and Naples to his illegitimate son, Ferrante. John II (1458–79) had been regent of Aragon for Alfonso and had aroused the hatred of the Catalans before he came to the throne. His struggles with his son Charles of Viana, from whom he seized the kingdom of Navarre which Charles had acquired by marriage, caused an open revolt of the Catalans who championed the cause of the younger man. John turned for help to France, and in return for the cession of Rousillon and Cerdagne, purchased assistance from Louis XI which enabled him to put down the rebellion. The timely death of Charles (probably by poison as the Catalans insisted) left the field open for negotiation, and a settlement was reached whereby Navarre went to John's daughter, Eleanor, and her husband Gaston de Foix, while his younger son, Ferdinand, inherited Aragon and Sicily. The Catalans still resisted, and went so far as to offer the crown of Catalonia in succession to Henry IV of Castile, a Portuguese prince, and King René of Provence. None of these claimants were able to effect any great victory, however, and King John finally captured Barcelona in 1472, putting an end to the revolt. Meanwhile he had won a great diplomatic victory when he secured the hand of Isabella of Castile for his son Ferdinand in 1469.

The marriage of Ferdinand and Isabella was unacceptable to many parties. The Castilian nobles resented it; Louis XI of France protested; and Alfonso, "the African," of Portugal, who was betrothed to La Beltraneja, claimed the throne for his fiancée.

The ensuing conflict was more critical for Spain, and indeed for Europe, than any of the combatants suspected. Victory for Alfonso would have united Castile with Portugal; the two realms would have shared the results of the great discoveries and conquests that were occurring and about to occur in Africa, Asia, and America, and Castile would probably have avoided entanglement in the feuds of Italy.[1]

In 1479, however, Alfonso was defeated and forced to recognize the accession of Isabella to the Castilian throne. La Beltraneja became a nun; John II of Aragon died, and Ferdinand and Isabella succeeded to the combined thrones of Castile and Aragon. They had already in 1478 established the Office of the Inquisition which was to become the chief agent in establishing not only religious orthodoxy but political absolutism.

Ferdinand and Isabella were able to introduce the Inquisition because already they had determined to break with Granada. In 1476 the king of Granada had taken advantage of the Castilian civil war to stop the payment of tribute and in 1481 he attacked a Castilian border fortress. The following year the Castilians began the systematic invasion of Granada; Malaga fell in 1487, Granada itself was besieged and after eighteen months resistance was forced to surrender in January 1492. The last Moorish state in the peninsula was thus conquered and the united kingdom of Spain

---

[1] W. T. Waugh, *History of Europe 1378-1494*, pp. 394-95. Reprinted by permission of the publishers, G. P. Putnam's Sons, New York and Methuen & Co., London.

established. While the union of Castile and Aragon was merely a personal one, the monarchs built an absolutism which made them supreme in both states and ensured the permanent and more complete fusion at a later date. At the same time overseas expansion was begun, the Canary Islands being captured, and the expedition of Christopher Columbus being sent out to seek a new route to Cathay through the uncharted expanses of the Western ocean.

THE EXPANSION OF PORTUGAL, 1279–1498

While Castile and Aragon were achieving their unification, Portugal was beginning to lay the foundations for the colonial empire that was to raise her to the rank of a first-rate power in the sixteenth century.

King Diniz (1279–1325) was the real founder of Portuguese prosperity; he was devoted to the economic and cultural improvement of his kingdom, not only encouraging agriculture and commerce, but founding the University of Coimbra. In 1294 he began what was to become one of the most lasting features of Portuguese policy when he signed a commercial treaty with England and began the close relations of the two countries which were to continue for centuries, and which resulted in the English preference for Port wine. His son Alfonso IV (1325–57) is best known for his participation in the battle of the Rio Saludo against the Moors, and for the civil war which broke out between the king and his heir Pedro over the murder of Pedro's mistress by his father's orders. However, he continued Diniz' intelligent economic policy, as did Pedro I (1357–67), who is remembered for codifying the laws and enforcing strict justice. Pedro also ended the ancient struggle with the church to the advantage of the monarchy, greatly restricting ecclesiastical jurisdiction and establishing a more uniform legal system. Pedro's son Ferdinand I (1367–83) involved Portugal in war with Castile, in which the Portuguese relied on help from England which did not amount to much. The Castilian navy defeated the English, besieged Lisbon and forced Ferdinand to make a peace whereby his only daughter married John of Castile.

However, Castilian hopes for the annexation of Portugal were dashed by the revolt of John of Avis, Ferdinand's illegitimate half-brother who seized control from the regent after the death of Ferdinand and was proclaimed king by the Cortes. The Castilians invaded, only to be severely defeated at Aljubarotta (1385), a victory which assured the throne to John and guaranteed Portuguese independence of Castile. King John I (1385–1433) the founder of the house of Avis, was an extremely able ruler, who held firm to the English alliance and devoted himself to developing the internal resources of his country. In 1386 he signed a permanent alliance with England, marrying the daughter of John of Gaunt and closely allying Portugal and England. It was in his reign that the first Portuguese expansion overseas began with the conquest of Ceuta in northern Morocco in 1415. Ceuta had long been a stronghold of pirates, so that its conquest had an important effect in facilitating trade in the western Mediterranean and through the Straits of Gibraltar. The capture of Ceuta also directed the attention of the Portuguese towards Africa and anticipated the con-

KINGS OF PORTUGAL, 1279–1521

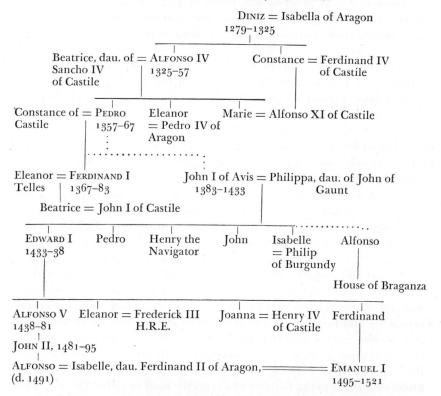

quests of the succeeding generations. It was John's third son, Prince Henry the Navigator, however, who did most towards directing Portugal towards a career of overseas expansion. He built an observatory and founded a school of navigation at Sagres, whence he sent out ships to explore the coasts of Africa and the isles of the Atlantic. Prince Henry was the Grand Master of the military-religious Order of Christ and was motivated in his explorations as much by crusading and missionary zeal as he was by a desire for geographical knowledge, but the results of his work were greater in the more mundane sphere than in the religious. The Madeira Islands were discovered in 1418 to 1419, the Azores in 1427, while in 1434 Portuguese ships sent out by Prince Henry rounded Cape Bojador and two

years later explored the Guinea Coast of Africa. The economic value of
these explorations was immediately realized; from the Madeiras was
brought the fine wine which under the name of Malmsey became so great
a staple of Portuguese trade, and even more important, in 1441 black slaves
were first brought back to the markets of Lisbon.

The opening up of the slave trade did more to encourage the exploration
of Africa than had the pious desires of Prince Henry for missionary fields
to conquer. Rapid progress was made in pushing down the west coast
of Africa where Portuguese colonies were soon established with a regular
government, their control of the area being sanctioned by a papal bull in
1454.

Meanwhile Henry's brother, Edward I (1433–38), had attempted to
expand into Tangier, but had been driven back with grievous losses in
1437. Under Edward's son, Alfonso V, "the African" (1438–81), the
Portuguese sent three expeditions against Morocco, finally succeeding in
capturing Casablanca and Tangier (1471). As we have seen, Alfonso was
defeated in an attempt to make himself king of Castile in 1476 and the
reign was otherwise marked by civil disturbances; but it was under Alfonso that the *Ordenacoes Affonsinas,* the great code of Portuguese law,
was issued (1446). Alfonso was succeeded by his son John II (1481–95) who
established a royal absolutism, breaking the power of the nobles and erecting a despotism of the approved fifteenth-century type. In the opening
years of his reign he was faced with a baronial rebellion, led by Ferdinand
of Braganza, an illegitimate descendant of John I, who was supported by
Ferdinand and Isabella. In his suppression of this revolt, John executed
great numbers of the nobles, but he retained a considerable popularity
with the middle classes and his reign was on the whole one of increased
prosperity and intellectual accomplishment. Meanwhile the flow of slaves
and African gold was enriching the Portuguese, and they were pressing
ever southward in their exploration. In 1486, Bartholomew Diaz rounded
the Cape of Good Hope at the southern point of Africa and sailed five
hundred miles into the Eastern waters on the road to India. In 1497, Vasco
da Gama finally reached India, proving the possibility of reaching the
east by sailing south. Within the next two decades Almeida, Albuquerque,
and Suarez were to build a Portuguese empire in the East and get a
monopoly of the Indian trade. Meanwhile Spain had begun to expand
to the West; the sea road to Cathay had been discovered and a new world
had been revealed to Europe. The Modern Age had begun.

CHAPTER 41

CULTURAL DEVELOPMENTS: FOURTEENTH AND FIFTEENTH CENTURIES

❖

ACCORDING to an idea once popular but now generally repudiated the Italian Renaissance was a wonderful rebirth of intellectual and artistic life, when men cast off the shackles of medieval obscurantism and burgeoned forth into the new light of modern knowledge. This is no longer thought to be true by any reputable historians, it being now recognized that the Middle Ages were not all dark and that the Italian developments were but a carrying on of intellectual movements found in France and other countries in the twelfth century. No longer can we accept those treatments which discuss the period under such headings as: the Revival of the Individual, the Revival of Literature, the Revival of Art, Science, etc. For these "revivals" did not take place. Men studied the classics for themselves in the twelfth century as avidly as they did in the fifteenth; John of Salisbury, or even Lupus de Ferriéres, were as good humanists as Petrarch or Poggio, only they were less ostentatious about it. It has often been maintained that the Italian Renaissance produced a great turn to vernacular literature as a new form of expression. More vernacular writing was done it is true, but it must be remembered that this was largely so because the attempts of the humanists to "purify Latin" rendered Latin no longer capable of expressing men's thoughts and forced them to the vernacular. Latin was killed; the living language of the thirteenth century was murdered and embalmed by the humanists who refused to employ any word not known to Cicero and thus effectively destroyed it as a means of expression. We have already pointed out the difficulty of expressing any current ideas in an idiom of a past age. When the humanists turned the clock back, they cut out all the words which had been introduced into the language to express new ideas and institutions. To carry out the analogy of the earlier chapter, they forced men to talk about atom bombs in the words of Shakespeare. And men, finding that the language could no longer adequately express their ideas, turned to the newer vernacular tongues which were able to do so. Then, having turned to them, they developed the theory of the superiority of the vernacular and wrote books to show why the vernaculars were the better forms of literary expression. The first of these works was Dante's *De Vulgaro Eloquentia,* a Latin work asserting the superiority of the Italian language. A parallel work was later written by Du Bellay in his *Defense and Illustration of the French Language* (1549), which was, with greater consistency, written in French.

It cannot be denied that there was in the period of the Renaissance a development of individualism. There were more great artists in the Renaissance, though there was no more great art than in the earlier period. The difference is that we know the names of the painters, sculptors, and architects of the fourteenth and fifteenth centuries while those of the twelfth and thirteenth are largely anonymous. The cathedrals were built not by any man but by a gild; they were co-operative objects and we do not know to any large extent the names of the men who contributed to their building. In the fourteenth century, we begin to know the identities of the artists as individuals and we can speak of the work of Massaccio, Ghirlandaio, Botticelli, and others, but it is doubtful that any work of art produced in the Renaissance was superior to some of the medieval sculptures, such as the Virgin of Amiens, or to the glass windows of Chartres.

Although there was a great development of science in the period of the late Renaissance, the scientific work was done mainly after the turn of the sixteenth century and so does not fall within the limits of this book. The fourteenth and fifteenth centuries did not maintain the level of scientific work done in the period of the Twelfth-Century Renaissance, and contributed nothing worth discussing here. Likewise in the field of philosophy these centuries produced generally stagnant and uninspiring works. Scholasticism had become stultified and barren; the best minds of the age deliberately turned away from philosophy to study the new humanities.

To sum up broadly the accomplishments of the last two centuries of the medieval world, we may say that there was a marked increase in vernacular literature, a general decline in historical writing, a tremendous advance in painting, a decline in architecture, and a quantitative increase in humanism. New times brought in new tastes; men found their pleasure in different forms of learning and artistic expression, and in some of these great strides were made. But the whole development was essentially an extension of the general intellectual and artistic movements which had been engendered in the Middle Ages.

HUMANISM AND THE "SPELL OF THE CLASSICS"

Traditionally, one of the greatest accomplishments of the Italian Renaissance was the great revival of classical study, the discovery of ancient manuscripts long neglected, and the development of the humanist attitude of love of classical authors for their own sakes. That this attitude was current in the Middle Ages we have already shown, and that many authors were "discovered" in the Renaissance is becoming increasingly questionable as our studies into medieval humanism are continued. But we cannot deny that in fourteenth-century Italy there arose a generation of men who sincerely loved the ancient authors and who brought them into a general popularity which they had not previously enjoyed. Education, and with it the study of the classics, was put on a much broader basis. Instead of being the delight of the few, classical studies became the passion of many, and intellectualism became socially correct. This is reflected in the despots, who, if they could not themselves be scholars, at least felt it necessary to have around their courts a coterie of humanists and litterateurs, under whose patronage the letters and arts of the period flourished.

The first great name in Renaissance humanism is of course Francesco Petrarca (1304–74) the great champion and popularizer of the "new learning." Born in Arezzo, of Florentine parentage, Petrarch spent his life in Avignon and in various parts of Italy, receiving a poet's crown in Rome in 1341 and enjoying at other times the hospitality of Milan, Parma, and other cities. He even visited Prague where he was honored by Charles IV. Petrarch's great contribution to humanism lay not so much in his own writings as in his work in popularizing the classics. He made people "classic conscious" and set the vogue firmly on the courts of Italy. He never knew Greek, but his oft-expressed regrets at this deficiency did much to establish the knowledge of Greek as a very real desideratum for scholars. His *Familiar Letters,* Latin letters addressed to Homer, Cicero, Virgil, Ovid, Seneca, and other illustrious ancient authors, enjoyed a tremendous vogue and helped popularize the works of the authors concerned. His greatest work was a long and tedious Latin epic, the *Africa,* which he wrote in Virgilian hexameters and which no one reads today. It was long, labored, erudite, and tedious. He is much better known for his *Sonnets to Laura,* written in Italian, and, in the best tradition of the troubadours, addressed to a lady whom he had scarcely met. These poems set the form of the fourteen-line Italian or Petrarchian sonnet which became the most popular verse form in the centuries following its invention and which is still today a standard form for sonnets. It is ironical that both Petrarch and his follower, Giovanni Boccaccio (1313–75), are better known today for their vernacular than for their Latin works. Boccaccio studied some Greek and was as ardent a Latin humanist as Petrarch, but no one now reads his *Genealogy of the Gods,* a tremendous collection of classical mythological lore, while his collection of Italian tales, the *Decameron,* is still popularly read everywhere, especially among high-school students who have heard of it as a lusty and ribald book. The *Decameron* was the first of a long series of works which strung together short stories on a slender framework of continuity, and established the form of the modern short novel more than any other single work. It was not, however, original, having been anticipated by the *Gesta Romanorum,* and having derived much both in form and content from the *Arabian Nights.*

Petrarch and Boccaccio are unquestionably the greatest names in the early Italian Renaissance. Some scholars include Dante as a Renaissance author, but he was so typically medieval in all his ideas that he belongs rather at the end of the Middle Ages than in the Renaissance and has so been considered in this volume. The work of Petrarch in popularizing the classics was carried on in Florence by Coluccio Salutati (1331–1406), the secretary of the republic, an ardent devotee of Cicero, who collected about himself a group of eager students and first made Florence the center of humanist activities. It was due to the great interest in the classics at Florence at this time that Manuel Chrysoloras came from Constantinople to Italy to begin the teaching of Greek there. From Chrysoloras and his pupils sprang the intense study of Greek throughout fifteenth-century Italy.

Among the younger men of the circle of Salutati and Chrysoloras were Leonardo Bruni (1370–1444) who translated much of Plato and Aristotle and who wrote a History of Florence; Carlo Marsuppini (1399–1453), who became so involved with classical culture that he renounced Christianity and became a pagan; Niccolo Niccoli (1363–1437), the bibliophile and collector of manuscripts; and Poggio Bracciolini (1380–1459), who achieved fame as a collector and discoverer of manuscripts, as an historian of Florence, and as the author of a series of scurrilous and scandalous essays, the *Facetiae,* which enjoyed an immense popularity. Poggio was himself puritanical and ascetic, although in his writing he descended to the worst obscenities, and he denounced the corruption of the clergy and the world in scathing satires written in the most elegant Latin. The chief objects of his hatred were the rival humanists, Francesco Filelfo (1398–1481), who enlivened the Visconti court at Milan, and Lorenzo Valla (1407–57), who enjoyed the patronage of Alfonso of Naples and of Pope Nicholas V.

Poggio represents two of the most significant facets of Renaissance humanism: the collection of manuscripts and the study of Greek. A great impetus to the latter was afforded by the Council of Ferrara-Florence, which brought many Greek ecclesiastics to Italy. While most of them returned to the East after the Council, some stayed on to acquire great reputations as teachers. Among these was George Gemisthos Plethon (1355–1450) from Mistra in Morea, a devout Neo-Platonist who brought to Florence that cult of Plato which became almost a religion among its devotees. So popular was Gemisthos, that, although he returned to Greece, his body was brought back to Italy for burial by Pandolfo Malatesta, despot of Rimini, who accorded him the veneration properly due a saint. Another eminent Greek who came to the Council of Florence and stayed was Bessarion, a Greek archbishop who was sincerely converted to the Roman creed, and received a cardinal's hat as his reward. He was a great collector of manuscripts, his collection of over six hundred, which he gave to the Library of San Marco at Venice, forming the basis for the classical collection there. Another Greek scholar who developed a great reputation in Italy was John Argyropulous, who came to Italy in 1441 and lectured on Plato in Florence from 1456 to 1471. After the fall of Constantinople there was a great deluge of Greeks into Italy, so that no individual teacher stands out as did these earlier ones.

While men were learning Greek and perfecting their classical Latin, they also collected libraries of manuscripts. Poggio became famous for his many trips to monasteries all over Europe in search of ancient codices, but he was only one of many such collectors. Filelfo, his great rival, visited Constantinople whence he brought back manuscripts of the Attic poets and philosophers; Guarino da Verona (1370–1460) one of the greatest teachers of the time, also went to Constantinople where he gathered manuscripts as well as pursuing his study of Greek. But the greatest of the manuscript collectors was Giovanni Aurispa (1374–1450), who brought back from Byzantium no less than 238 volumes of Greek writings, including works of Euripides, Sophocles, and other dramatists and the historian Thucydides.

The collection of manuscripts produced a group of professional dealers who would search around, find a new manuscript, employ scribes to make several copies of the work, and sell them to the wealthy collectors. Of these the most famous was Vespasiano di Bisticci (1421–98), who not only supplied codices to the great and wealthy but wrote the *Lives of the Illustrious Men of the Fifteenth Century*, a collection of short biographies which give us intimate pictures of many of the leading figures of the time, such as Alfonso of Naples, Federigo of Urbino, Cosimo di Medici, and various popes and cardinals who were patrons of the author. Among the great collectors of libraries were Duke Federigo of Urbino who collected more than seven hundred manuscripts and who disdained the new art of printing, refusing to have a printed book in his collection; Pope Nicholas V, who as Tomasso Parentucelli had been the librarian of Cosimo di Medici, and who collected not only the large library for his patron in Florence but later as pope laid the foundations for the great Vatican Library. The Vatican collection soon outstripped all the others, having a total of 3600 volumes by the end of the century, while the Medicean Library in Florence, even after it had been increased by Lorenzo, boasted only about 1050.

With the development of printing, of course, libraries became much larger. The first printing press to use movable type was set up in Mainz by Johann Gutenberg ca. 1450 and the famous so-called "Gutenberg Bible" was published in 1454. Printing soon crossed the Alps into the friendly Italian atmosphere, the first Italian presses being established in Rome and Venice by German printers in the 1460's. The greatest of all Renaissance presses was that of Aldo Manuzio of Venice (1450–1515), who used Petrarch's handwriting as the model for his type, ever since known as Italic. Aldo was himself a humanist and employed humanists to edit the books he published. Using a small format, he printed books in quantities so that he was able to sell them at reduced prices, thus tremendously popularizing the owning of books. Aldo published classical works both in Latin and Greek, but he also printed books in the vernacular, bringing out the works of many contemporary writers. The great Dutch humanist, Erasmus, worked for a time for the Aldine press, several of his own works being first published by it.

Meanwhile scholarship and humanistic studies flourished throughout Italy. In evaluating the work of the humanists two distinct periods must be observed: in the first men collected manuscripts, perfected their Latin style and endeavored to absorb classical style and thought. In the younger generation they went beyond this to produce original work of their own, modeled after the classic, but revealing great originality. If Marsilio Ficino (1433–99) the Platonist, a protégé of Cosimo de Medici's, worshipped Plato blindly and uncritically, Pico della Mirandola (1463–94) was himself a real philosopher, defending Platonic philosophy as superior to Christianity after an intensive study of both Plato and Christian theology. In the circle of the Medici were found several of those *uomini universali* who were so admired in the Renaissance, men whose infinite versatility made them proficient in everything to which they turned their hands. Such a man was Leon Batista Alberti (1404–72) a practicing architect, who also composed music, wrote treatises on education, painting and architecture, wrote a comedy which he passed off as a classical work, did research in optics, and enjoyed a great reputation as an athlete, excelling especially in the broad jump. Lorenzo di Medici was himself a versatile dillettante who wrote poetry of a very superior sort. Of Lorenzo, J. A. Symonds has written:—

Lorenzo was a man of marvelous variety and range of mental power. . . . While he never for one moment relaxed his grasp of politics, among philosophers he passed for a sage, among men of letters for an original and graceful poet, among scholars for a Grecian sensitive to every nicety of Attic idiom, among artists for an amateur gifted with refined discernment and consummate taste. Pleasure-seekers knew in him the libertine . . . The pious extolled him as an author of devotional lauds and mystery plays, a profound theologian, a critic of sermons. He was no less famous for his jokes and repartees than for his pithy apothegms and maxims, as good a judge of cattle as of statues, as much at home in the bosom of his family as in the riot of an orgy, as ready to discourse on Plato as to plan a campaign or to plot the death of a dangerous citizen.[1]

[1] J. A. Symonds, *The Revival of Learning*, pp. 320–21. Reprinted by permission of the publishers, Henry Holt & Co.

Even more brilliant and versatile than Lorenzo was his intimate friend Angelo Poliziano (1454–94) probably the greatest universal scholar and poet of the Italian Renaissance. Brought up in Florence as a ward of the Medici, Poliziano was writing Latin epigrams at the age of thirteen. Above all the other humanists he showed a complete absorption of the spirit of the classical authors, his works including not only translations from the Greek poets, but many original Italian poems of great merit. In addition to numerous love songs, he composed two major works, the *Orfeo* (written at seventeen) an epic about Orpheus, and the *Giostra,* which told the romance of Guiliano di Medici and his love, Simonetta. He was in addition a celebrated teacher, being the tutor to Lorenzo's own children as well as lecturing publicly in Florence. He had a great influence in the extension of the Renaissance across the Alps as, together with Pico, he was the inspiration of the Englishmen, Grocyn and Linacre, and the German, Johann Reuchlin.

Although Florence was the greatest center of humanism, not all the great humanists were Florentines. Filelfo, as we have seen, spent his best years in Milan, though he also worked in Rome and Naples for shorter periods. The Renaissance at Rome centered around two great humanist popes, Nicholas V and Pius II, both of whom had made considerable names for themselves as scholars before their election to the papacy. Nicholas (Tomasso Parentucelli) had, as we have seen, assisted in the building of the library of Cosimo di Medici in Florence, and when he went to the papacy, he determined to make Rome the equal of Florence as a center of humanism. In addition to founding the Vatican Library, he was also the patron of scholars, bringing such men as Poggio, Guarino da Verona, and Lorenzo Valla to Rome where he made them papal secretaries. Pius II (Aeneas Sylvius Piccolomini) had been a most worldly humanist before his election to the papacy, and had acquired an enviable reputation as a scholar, historian, and man of letters. As pope, however, he proved a disappointment to his former colleagues, for he devoted himself almost exclusively to the cause of a crusade against the Turks and did little to encourage scholarship at Rome. The Roman Renaissance in letters had to wait until the beginning of the sixteenth century when Giovanni di Medici, the son of Lorenzo, ascended the papal throne as Leo X (1513–21) and transferred from Florence to Rome the patronage of the Medici house. The Roman Academy, founded in 1460, was essentially antiquarian and archaeological in its interests rather than literary.

In Naples, humanism was patronized by Alfonso the Magnanimous and Ferrante, but it produced no one of the calibre of the Florentine group. Antonio Beccadelli (1394–1471) a Sicilian, had the distinction of writing a work which was so indecent as to provoke the indignation of Poggio, but which had a great popular vogue for a time. He was also the author of a life of Alfonso, but beyond a certain degree of scholarship and a fine style, his works were lacking in any originality. The head of the Neapolitan Academy, which was essentially literary, was Jovianus Pontanus (1426–1503), a notable orator and accomplished stylist, but without further distinction. The one man of original genius associated with Naples was Lorenzo Valla (1407–57) a Roman, who came to the court of Alfonso after teaching in Pavia, Milan, Genoa, Ferrara, and Mantua. He was interested in grammar and philology and developed historical and literary criticism to a high degree. He has been termed the father of modern historical criticism for his famous attack on the Donation of Constantine, which he proved from internal evidence to be a forgery. He also extended his critical approach to the histories of Livy and Eusebius, the latinity of the Vulgate, the Apostles' Creed, the writings of St. Augustine, and the Fathers. Epicurean and anti-clerical, he denounced the clergy, especially the monks, and became a distinct thorn in the flesh of the church. Pope Nicholas V, not wishing to let so dangerous a man remain at liberty, brought him to Rome where he made him a papal secretary and set him to work translating and editing Thucydides and other Greek historians, a harmless occupation which kept him out of mischief.

There remain to be noted two remarkable teachers, Guarino da Verona (1374–1460), who taught at Ferrara at the court of the Estensi, and Vittorino da Feltre (1378–1446), who established at Mantua, under the patronage of Gianfrancesco Gonzaga, a new type of school which emphasized the humanities, history, and physical training instead of the older seven arts. Vittorino is one of the great names in the history of education, and among his pupils were some of the leading patrons of learning, such as Federigo di Montefeltro of Urbino, Ippolito Sforza, and the Gonzagas. The school was unusual in its emphasis on physical education and also in that it was coeducational, the girls studying along with the boys.

HISTORIOGRAPHY

The writing of history did not enjoy as prominent a place in the literature of the fourteenth and fifteenth centuries as it had in the two centuries preceding. In general there was a marked decline; there are few really important German historians and England produced nothing to compare with the earlier epoch. Only in France and in Italy was there truly significant historical authorship, and even the great figures of the Burgundian school were narrators of chivalrous deeds rather than analytical historians. Probably the greatest single contribution to history was Lorenzo Valla's application of scholarly criticism to historical materials noted above.

England, which had produced so many great historians during the Middle Ages, declined most conspicuously. There were a few chronicles, such as those of Rishanger, Nicholas Trevet, and Peter Langtoft who described the reign of Edward I, and the St. Albans school expired with considerable distinction in the writings of Thomas Walsingham, who covered the years 1272 to 1422. But on the whole the historians were decidedly second or third-rate, works like the *Flores Historiarum* (1259–1326) or Ralph of Higden's *Polychronicon,* a popular universal history, replacing the excellent histories of the earlier centuries. English history for this period must be derived from the official documents, which fortunately become very numerous and complete in this era.

Spain produced two important writers: Ramon Muntaner's history of the Catalan Grand Company and Lopez de Ayala's chronicle of Spain, written in the early years of the fifteenth century, both being excellent narratives of adventure and prowess. In Germany there is nothing of importance beyond some of the town chronicles.

The greatest historians outside of Italy were the Franco-Burgundian group who chronicled the events of the Hundred Years' War and the reigns of Louis XI and Charles VIII. In general these historians were narrators of military campaigns, essentially interested in the great deeds of individual heroes, and while their books are still good reading, presenting vivid accounts of stirring deeds, they lack any deep insight into historical values. The first of this group was Jehan le Bel who chronicled the years 1326 to 1361 and whose work afforded much of the material for the later chronicles of Jean Froissart. Froissart is *par excellence* the chronicler of chivalry; his spirited accounts of the battles and skirmishes of the Hundred Years' War have made the events of that period familiar to every generation of schoolboys and have immortalized the names of Sir John Chandos and other heroes of the wars. But Froissart's chronicle of the years 1326 to 1399 is little more than a collection of stories of individual heroism, of battles won and noble deeds done, and the historical significance of the events in no wise seemed to concern the chronicler. Froissart was continued for the years 1400 to 1444 by Enguerrand de Monstrelet, whose chronicle follows the pattern of the earlier work, sharing its qualities and defects. Georges Chastellain also wrote a narrative of the years 1418 to 1474, of which only parts have been preserved, that is vivid in its description of men and events. All of these writers covered a wide field describing the wars in Cyprus and the East as well as those in France, England, Spain, and Western Europe. The greatest of them all was Philippe de Commines, a trusted servant of Charles the Bold, Louis XI, and Charles VIII, who wrote memoirs of the years 1464 to 1498, through the Italian expedition of King Charles. Commines is much more a historian than his predecessors, evaluating men and institutions, and producing a work which was unquestionably the greatest achievement of French historiography since Joinville. Froissart and Commines present an interesting contrast: the ideals of chivalry which were Froissart's chief concern interested Commines not at all; Commines was cynical and materialistic in contrast to Froissart's idealism; Froissart wrote with a far more graphic pen than did Commines, but Commines showed a true insight into history, which the romantic chronicler lacked altogether.

Apart from these great figures, the most important French historical writing was done in biography. Christine de Pisan wrote a life of Charles V; Cuvelier composed a verse biography of du Guesclin; and Louis II of Bourbon and Marshal Boucicaut were the subjects of extensive biographies. Among the best of the lives were those of Charles VII and Louis XI by Thomas Basin whose vivid descriptions of the sufferings of France as a result of the war stand out in marked contrast to Froissart's. Froissart dealt only with the nobles, ignoring completely the peasantry and lesser folk; Basin wrote movingly of the misery of the little people caught in the grip of the war, giving the seamy side of Froissart's splendid tapestry. His writings are somewhat reduced in value by his total lack of objectivity. He had suffered greatly personally at the hands of Louis XI and had been given refuge in Burgundy, events which colored his history, making Louis thoroughly dastardly and Charles of Burgundy more heroic. Basin is also to be remembered for his defense of Jeanne d'Arc, whom he felt to be divinely inspired.

Two journals of the period, that of Nicholas Baye (1400–17) and the anonymous *Journal d'un bourgeois de Paris* (1405–49) afford intimate pictures of life in Paris in the fifteenth century. Baye, an official of the Paris Parlement, especially commented on the actions taken by the Parlement, often making caustic comments on the men involved. The *Bourgeois* was much less well informed on matters of state, but is no less valuable for his pictures of daily life in Paris under the French, English, and Burgundians. In his intimate journal we can see as nowhere else the irritation of the bourgeois at the various governments which ruled the city, his annoyance at the scarcity of goods and the high prices asked, and his keen interest in the events, great and trivial, which transpired in and about the city.

It is interesting to note that all these historians wrote in the French language and that Latin, as a means of historical exposition, was almost entirely obsolete by this time. The same is true of the Italian historians, most of whom wrote in the vernacular, although some of the humanists preferred to write in Latin.

As might be expected, Florence was a center of historical writing as of everything else at this time. Most of the Italian historians devoted themselves to narrating the history of their own city or the lives of illustrious men. We have already noticed that Leonardo Bruni and Poggio wrote histories of Florence; but these erudite works of the humanists rank, as histories, far below the history of Florence of the Villanis. This history, begun by Giovanni Villani, was continued by his brother, Matteo, and completed by his nephew, Filippo. All told it covered the history of Florence from the founding of the city to the year 1365. Giovanni's part which comes to 1346 is the best, while that of Filippo covering the years 1362 to 1365 is far inferior, being too rhetorical, but the whole work is unsurpassed as the history of a city, including not only its politics but shrewd observations as to economic conditions. Indeed the Villani's seem to have been enamored of statistics, and they supply figures as to national income, public expenditures, costs of campaigns and public buildings, and the banking operations of the leading Florentine houses. The work is a mine for students of social and economic history and enables us to be more familiar with the economy of fourteenth-century Florence than with al- most any other medieval city. Matteo's description of the effects of the plague of 1348 in Florence is almost unique, not only for his figures on the casualties, but for his observations on the effects on public morality.

The Villani chronicle was continued by Gino Capponi from 1379 to 1419. Capponi was at one time gonfaloniere and Florentine governor of Pisa, so that he was intimately acquainted with the inside story of the events he chronicled. He is the last of the medieval chroniclers, as op- posed to the new humanist historians who patterned their work on Livy. This new type of history is found in the Latin histories of Bruni (to 1415) and Poggio (to 1455), and reaches its high point in the *Historia Fiorentina* of Niccolo Machiavelli (1469–1527) which tells the story of Florence from the foundation of the city to the death of Lorenzo in 1492. Although best known for his *Prince*, Machiavelli's *Historia* is probably the greatest single historical work written by an Italian and was the first product of that great group of Florentine historians which included Francesco Guicciardini (1482–1540), the author of a monumental history of Italy from 1494 to 1534. Machiavelli was entirely modern and had nothing of the medieval in his make-up, so that he properly falls both in time and in spirit into the sixteenth century. He does, however, mark the end of an epoch; when such a man could win universal acclaim, the Middle Ages were gone, and modern times had come.

If Florence produced the outstanding historians, Milan and Venice were not far behind. The history of Milan was chronicled by Piero De- cembrio, Giovanni Simonetta, and Bernardino Corio, of whom Corio was by far the most outstanding. His History of Milan from about 1250 to 1499 covered all the great period of the Visconti and the Sforza when Milan was at her height. The annals of Venice were written by Bernardo Giustiniani and Domenico Malipiero to the year 1500. The greatest Ve- netian historical work, however, covers the early sixteenth century—the fifty-nine volumes of the *Diary* of Marino Sanudo the Younger (1466–

1535). Another valuable diary of this time was that of Johann Burckhard, the papal secretary whose journal affords a detailed description of Rome and the papacy from Innocent VIII through Julius II.

As could be expected in an age when individualism ran rampant, biography was a popular form of historical composition. Sycophant scholars wrote lives of many of their patrons, many of them mediocre but some of them good. Lives of statesmen, artists, scholars, poets, and prelates were all composed for the glory of the subjects and the profit of the authors. Among the best biographies of the period are Boccaccio's *Life of Dante*, and Decembrio's *Life of Filippo Maria Visconti*. Collective lives of great men were popuplar, the outstanding being Vespasiano's *Lives of Illustrious Men* cited above, Platina's *Lives of the Popes* and Vasari's famous *Lives of the Painters*. The single work of greatest importance, however, was neither chronicle or biography but Lorenzo Valla's work on the Donation of Constantine, which laid the foundations for modern historical criticism by carefully examining the document to determine its authenticity.

In the field of political thought, the fourteenth century is marked by the struggle between John XXII and Louis of Bavaria which produced the writings of Marsiglio of Padua and Egidius Romanus noted above. In the following period the Conciliar doctrines assumed first place, especially the works of Jean Gerson and Nicholas of Cusa which defended the position of the Councils as opposed to the papal monarchy. The old medieval ideas and controversies were passing, and a new science of statecraft was being empirically developed in Italy, which was to have its first philosophical protagonist in Machiavelli. Meanwhile in England, Sir John Fortescue was writing his praise of the laws of England and Wycliffe was developing his theory of dominium, both concepts that were to have great influence in the succeeding eras.

LITERATURE

In the centuries under consideration in this chapter vernacular literature developed to such an extent in all the countries of Europe that we can only attempt here to indicate the most outstanding authors and works. In France, England, Spain, Italy, and Germany there was a great production of works in the vernacular, some of which are of prime importance as literary compositions, while most of them have value in showing the development of the languages. We have already noted that the vernacular came to be used almost exclusively for historical writing; it also became the accepted vehicle for poetry and even for some didactic works.

In France the greatest names of the fourteenth century are the poets Guillaume de Machaut (ob. 1377) and Eustache Deschamps (ob. 1410), both of them prolific writers who employed numerous verse forms. The ballad and rondeaux were the most popular types of lyric, but Machaut indulged also in epic composition, his *Prise d'Alexandrie* commemorating the conquest of Alexandria by Peter de Lusignan. The works of both these poets are in general artificial and somewhat pedantic and, though they are the best the century produced, cannot be rated as great works of literature. The fifteenth century produced better writers. Charles d'Orleans (ob. 1465), the son of Louis, duke of Orleans, not only wrote charming lyrics himself, but collected a large library and was the patron of poets. Christine de Pisan (ob. 1431), a Venetian woman domiciled in France, wrote some of the best lyrics of the time, combining considerable learning with a personal emotion. Important in popularizing classical themes as the subjects of French lyric poetry was Alain Chartier (ob. 1440) who enjoyed a great renown in his own day, but by far the greatest poet of France in this whole period was the vagabond scholar, thief and ne'er-do-well, François Montcorbier, who took the name of his adopted father and is known as François Villon (1431–80). Villon's poems are incorported in two works, the *Grand* and *Petit Testaments,* in which he facetiously bequeaths to friends and enemies the good and bad things of life. Interspersed through the *Testaments* are the immortal ballads which give Villon a recognized position as the greatest poet of medieval France. His work shows occasionally the influence of Deschamps, Chartier, and perhaps even Machaut, but he brought to his poems a vitality lacking in the more polished and artificial work of his predecessors. Villon is the great poet of Paris—of the Parisian underworld, the world of thieves, prostitutes, and drunkards. He is cynical, morbid, sarcastic—and passionately French. The fear of death, presumably on the gibbet, lay always on him, and there is in his writing much of the macabre character which expressed itself in the contemporary pictures of the Dance of Death. In his most famous ballad he queries "Where are the snows of yesteryear?" as he recalls the great and noble ladies who have passed beyond; another ballad reminds men of the great lords who are dead, ending always with the refrain "But where is the mighty Charlemagne?" The *Regrets de la belle heaulmiere* is one of the most bitter and poignant laments for lost love and beauty in any language; the *Ballad of Those about to be Hanged* ("The rather pray, God grant us of his grace"), the *Ballad of Villon in Prison* ("Will you all leave poor Villon here to rot?") and others reveal the disillusioned libertine fearing death, but in one of his best ballads, the *Ballad of the Women of Paris,* Villon reveals the true Parisian, who prefers in all the world the city whose women speak the best—

Prince, aux dames Parisiennes	Prince, to the women of Paris
De bien parler donnes le prix	Give the prize for beautiful speech
Quoy qu'on die d'Italiennes	Whatever one says of Italians
Il n'est bon bec que de Paris.	There's no tongue like that of Paris.

In England and Italy, where vernacular literature had not developed in the earlier period as it had in France, the last centuries of the Middle Ages were of the greatest importance, as it was in this time that the languages took definite form. In both countries the vernacular emerged as the accepted literary language, and in both the genius of one man fixed a particular dialect as the accepted form of the national speech. In Italy this was accomplished, as we have seen, by Dante who made the Tuscan dialect the Italian language. In England the poems of Geoffrey Chaucer (1340–1400) and the translation of the Bible by John Wycliffe established the Midlands dialect as the English tongue. English also replaced the Norman-French as the language of the courts and of noble society, although the historians and scholars still clung to Latin.

Geoffrey Chaucer's *Canterbury Tales* occupies in English literature a position comparable to Dante's *Divine Comedy* in Italian. The various pilgrims who assembled for the journey to the shrine of St. Thomas at Canterbury are vividly depicted in sometimes gentle and often bitter phrases. The knight, parson, monk, prioress, pardoner, the wife of Bath— all are familiar to us as our own neighbors through the graphic verse of Chaucer; and if he treated the gentry kindly, he excoriated the clergy for their laxity and rapaciousness. The *Prologue* which introduces the characters is generally more interesting than the individual tales, which are frequently familiar themes. The form of the work resembles Boccaccio's *Decameron* in that it is a series of stories told by a number of individuals, who have been brought together and who tell the tales to pass the time of their enforced companionship. Chaucer's genius lay in his selection of characters and in his depiction of them, as well as in his mastery of language, rather than in any freshness of his plot.

Before Chaucer, Langland (or someone else if the work was not really by Langland) had also drawn some very realistic characters in the *Vision of Piers the Plowman* (ca. 1370) an allegory in which the simple plowman leads assorted characters in their search for St. Truth. Conscience, False, Glutton, the Seven Sins, and the other familiar allegorical figures appear in the story, whose plot and general style is reminiscent of the *Roman de la Rose,* but there are some extremely vivid descriptions of the peasants and burgesses which make the work an historical as well as a literary document of considerable importance. It is one of the earliest works to concern itself primarily with the common man rather than the nobles, and reflects the changing social conditions of the era in which it was written.

John Gower (ca. 1325–1408) is especially interesting as showing the transition from Latin and French to English. His earlier poems were in Latin or French, but later on he wrote his *Confessio Amantis* in English. This is a collection of stories, largely derived from Ovid, into which the author worked much scholarly erudition and comment. The era is also notable for a large number of English poems based on the French chansons and romances, which were done over into English. There were also notable original English works such as the *Pearl, Gawain and the Grene Knight,* and *Hereward.*

In Italy, a tremendous stimulus was given to vernacular writing by the work of Petrarch and Boccaccio, both of whom composed their best known works in the vernacular. The use of Italian as a literary language had been fixed by Dante, but Petrarch added the sonnet form and further popularized the new idiom. As we have seen, the composition of Italian lyrics was considered an essential attribute of the *uomo universale* and was indulged in by many humanists. We have noted the poems of Lorenzo di Medici and Poliziano, who are only two, if among the best, of the Italian lyricists.

Important work was also done in the field of the epic. Luigi Pulci (1432–90), a poet (not a humanist) of the Medici circle, wrote, about 1483, an epic poem, the *Morgante Maggiore,* which narrated a number of amusing and absurd adventures of Roland and his knights. The poem takes its name from the giant Morgante who becomes one of Roland's companions. The story of Ganelon and Roland and the death of Roland are retold, on occasion the poetry reaching epic quality, but in general Pulci burlesqued the chivalrous stories in a gentle parody. It is burlesque rather than satire, for Pulci's purpose was obviously to amuse and there is no serious purpose underlying his work. He laughed at the chansons and their heroics, and parodied them unmercifully in the earlier part of his work, ending however with a stirring retelling of the story of Roncevalles.

The Roland story received further treatment at the hands of Matteo Maria Boiardo (1434–94) who was one of the leading figures of the Estensi court at Ferrara. Boiardo had received a humanistic education and was proficient in Greek and Latin, but he was fascinated with the old epic legends. In his *Orlando Innamorato* he wove together characters from the Roland cycle, the Arthurian legends and Eastern fable into an amazing patchwork story of the infatuation of Orlando (Roland) for the fair Saracen princess, Angelica. Unfortunately Angelica loves not Orlando but his closest friend Rinaldo (Oliver) and much of the story is the contest of the two heroes for the maiden's affections—a competition which does not affect their mutual affection and loyalty for each other. Merlin, Morgan le Fay, Charlemagne, the Queen of the Amazons, and a myriad scattered characters are introduced; the action jumps from France and Italy to Tartary and back with no noticeable lapses of time. Love philtres, lethal draughts, magic fountains and all the familiar magical paraphernalia are present, one of the best episodes of the story being Orlando's theft of the magic armor of Hector. Boiardo wrote seriously, and did not poke gentle fun at his characters as did Pulci. His poem shows the complete corruption and utter transmogrification of the old epics in Italian hands. Boiardo never completed his poem and the story was continued in the *Orlando Furioso* of Ludovico Ariosto (1474–1535), the poem which ranks next to the *Divine Comedy* among the masterpieces of Italian verse.

Ariosto, who wrote at Ferrara in the early sixteenth century, is generally considered to be the finest poetical craftsman of the Italian Renaissance. His work has been compared to a tapestry in which each scene is complete and perfect, but in which there is little continuity. The poem lacks the freshness of Boiardo's and is more cynical and sophisticated. Orlando loses his wits and goes through the poem a madman. Mythological characters abound and the magic is even more omnipresent than in Boiardo, but it is not taken seriously. One of the gems of the poem is the scene in which Astolfo, searching for Orlando's lost wits, secures the golden chariot of St. John the Evangelist to make a trip to the moon. The moon is full of the things which have been lost or discarded on earth; there he finds Orlando's lost wits in a bottle, but in the search he turns up such items as women's virtue and other qualities which are no longer cherished on earth. Although Ariosto wrote in the sixteenth century and properly falls outside the limits of this book, he was the last great exponent of the epic tradition, however altered it may have become by his time, and his subject matter may be considered medieval, though his treatment and literary style are distinctly modern.

ARCHITECTURE, SCULPTURE, AND PAINTING

The fourteenth and fifteenth centuries are one of the greatest periods in the history of the arts and are best left to art historians.[2] However some slight mention must be made of them here, as they were so important an aspect of the life of the period. In discussing the art of this era we must distinguish between the later Gothic art which continued until the sixteenth century, and the new Renaissance art which developed in Italy in the fifteenth. Renaissance art reached its height in Italy only in the sixteenth century and belongs properly to modern rather than medieval history, so that it will be touched upon but lightly in this volume. The Gothic art of northern Europe, which was more characteristically medieval, declined after 1500 to be replaced by the new forms engendered in Italy and falls more fittingly into our discussion of the decline of the medieval world. Even in this northern art, however, there was a tendency towards greater naturalism and a departure from the formalism of the medieval styles.

[2] The student is especially referred to the excellent manual by D. M. Robb and J. J. Garrison, *Art in the Western World* (2nd ed. 1942, Harpers). Some of the illustrations in this book are due to the courtesy of Dr. Robb.

In architecture the period is marked by the development of Flamboyant Gothic in both ecclesiastical and secular building. Instead of the simple graceful lines of early Gothic, there was a multiplicity of vaulting and an tremendous increase in decoration, The ceilings of Flamboyant churches are a mass of cross vaultings, with arches bisecting each other at all possible angles. Tracery became more complex and involved. Arches within arches appear in both vaults and windows, and all the simple grace of the earlier Gothic is lost. The cathedrals of Milan and Exeter, the façade of Rouen and the cloisters at Gloucester are good examples of this style. More interesting are the secular buildings, the town halls and gild houses, such as the Doges' palace in Venice, the Palais de Justice in Rouen, the town halls in Bruges, Brussels, and Antwerp, the house of Jacques Coeur at Bourges, and the gild halls in many Flemish towns. In all of these there is the almost lace-like tracery and elaboration of ornament characteristic of the fourteenth century.

In sculpture, the late Gothic was characterized by an attempt at naturalism. In both sculpture and painting the Low Countries produced the finest examples of this style under the patronage of the Valois dukes of Burgundy. Claus Sluter (ob. 1405), a Fleming who worked at Dijon, produced in his *Well of Moses* a group of figures carved with deep emotion and great naturalism. The same may be said for the Flemish painters Jan van Eyck (ob. 1440), Rogier van der Weyden (ob. 1464), Hugo van der Goes (ob. 1482) and Hans Memling (ob. 1494). The great *Adoration of the Lamb*, painted by van Eyck as the altarpiece for the church of St. Bavon in Ghent, shows the continued influence of the miniature painters of an earlier age, but the figures are more naturalistic. This work is hardly a single piece, but rather a series of disconnected scenes, like a tapestry, but each scene is done to perfection. Jan Van Eyck also demonstrated a fidelity to life in his portraits, that of the burgher Arnolfini and his wife being especially notable. Van der Weyden and Van der Goes likewise instilled a new human equality into their figures, Van der Goes' Virgin being a human woman rather than the ethereal figure of earlier painters. The greatest figure in this school of Flemish painters was Hans Memling who excelled in portraiture, his faces revealing a fine sensitivity and his pictures generally exhibiting a close attention to detail. The passion for earthiness, as opposed to the ethereal, reached its height in the work of Jerome Bosch (ob. 1516) whose figures are bitter caricatures displaying a vivid if morbid imagination and a keen sense of the grotesque and macabre. Bosch has been justly compared with some of the surrealists of the most modern era.

Preoccupation with death and damnation was one of the characteristics of the fourteenth and fifteenth centuries. "Dances of Death"—pictorial representations of Death carrying off people of all classes—were popular everywhere. We have noted François Villon's preoccupation with death, and the same motif appears in the popular mystery plays of the period. The fifteenth century seems to have been assailed with a mass psychosis, which demonstrated itself in such societies as the Flagellants, and which was undoubtedly produced in part by the repeated epidemics of the plague which so afflicted Europe.

In France, the greatest of the late medieval painters was Jean Fouquet (ca. 1415–82) whose portraits reveal a keen portrayal of character, his *Virgin and Child* combining a placidity of mein with a natural grace and beauty which is utterly charming.

Gothic art enjoyed a particular impetus in Italy in the work of Niccolo Pisano (ob. 1280) who was, however, strongly influenced by classical figures which he had studied on funerary monuments in the Campo Santo of Pisa. Niccolo was however alone in his classical tendency, and his successors were more completely Gothic in their inspiration. His son, Giovanni Pisano, and his pupil, Arnolfo of Florence, produced pulpits and bas-reliefs which continued the influence of the master, but Florentine Gothic art reached its perfection in the reliefs on the campanile by Giotto (1266–1336) and the tabernacle for the church of Or San Michele by Andrea Orcagna (ob. 1368). Giotto is equally famous as a painter; his frescoes departed radically from the Byzantine style of his master Cimabue, and reveal a sense of humanity and a seeking after naturalness unprecedented in Italian painting, which has given him an honored place as the first great Renaissance painter. Later artists of the school of Giotto, who combined human expression with something of the old Byzantine formalism, were Fra Angelico (1387–1455) and Benozzo Gozzoli (1420–97), both of whom excelled in colorful pageantry.

If the Flemings and the other artists of the Gothic type show the last expression of the medieval spirit, the new humanism was revealing itself in Italy in the work of a group of sculptors and painters, who owed much to the study of antiquity, but more to the study of nature. That they cannot be called simply copyists of the classical is proven by the vitality and emotion portrayed in their works. Classical sculpture sought ever repose and placidity, the temperate calm and moderation which was the ancient ideal. The Renaissance artists lacked this altogether and strove instead to portray strong emotions. They studied the ancients for the beauty of their lines and techniques, but they followed the medieval artists in their attempts to show passion, action, and emotion. The work of this group began in the fifteenth century but reached its zenith only in the sixteenth, so that the artists we shall discuss were in many cases only the precursors of greater figures of a later generation. The greatest age came just at the turn of the sixteenth century with such figures as Leonardo da Vinci (1452–1519), Michaelangelo (1475–1564), and Raphael (1483–1520).

The classical influence made itself felt in all forms of art. In architecture it inspired Brunelleschi (1377–1446) who superimposed a great dome on the Gothic cathedral which Arnolfo di Cambio had begun in Florence. Brunelleschi also designed the Pitti Palace which is almost wholly classical in style. Other architects who copied more or less the classical forms were Leon Batista Alberti (already encountered as a humanist) who did the Rucellai Palace in Florence and remodeled older churches in Ravenna and Mantua, and Michellozzo (1396–1472), the favorite architect of Cosimo di Medici, who built the Riccardi Palace, the residence of the Medicis in the fifteenth century.

Sculpture, which throughout the Middle Ages had been ancillary to architecture, came into its own as a separate art, the discovery of the great sculptures of antiquity giving a tremendous impetus to the production of individual isolated statues. But naturalism, even more than classicism, inspired the sculptors of the fifteenth century. It was with reason that of all the classic figures discovered the most popular should be the *Laöcoon,* one of the few ancient statues to portray vivid emotion. The first great sculptor of the Renaissance was Ghiberti (1378–1455) who spent from 1401 to 1447 making the bronze doors of the Baptistery at Florence. They are bas-reliefs depicting scenes from the Bible and are similar to those found on the Gothic churches except that the figures are so much more fluid and animated and that Ghiberti achieved a sense of perspective hitherto unknown. The superb quality of the craftsmanship and the genius of design have caused these doors to be termed "The Gates of Paradise." A sculptor who infused a new life into his figures, and who produced works of an amazing variety, was Donatello (1386–1466). Donatello was the first modern artist to produce a rounded nude (*David*) or an equestrian statue (*Gattamelata*). The equestrian statue of Gattamalata is strongly influenced by classical examples, the condottieri being depicted in ancient armor, but the work portrays a character of expression which is quite foreign to the placid calm of the Roman figures. Donatello also did statues of *John the Baptist, Judith, St. George,* and a number of bas-reliefs (*The Singing Gallery*). His statue of Poggio Bracciolini on the Duomo is almost grotesque in its realism, and is familiarly known as *Lo Zuccone* (The Pumpkinhead). Tremendous action and muscular tension is seen in the *Hercules and Antaeus* of Antonio Pollaiulo (1432–98) one of the statues which ornament the Loggia dei Lanzi in Florence.

Andrea Verrochio (1435–88), a pupil of Donatello's, continued the style of his master, exceeding anything he had done in his famous statue of *Bartolomeo Colleoni,* which stands outside the church of Sts. Giovanni and Paolo in Venice. The haughty and contemptuous sneer on the face of the condottieri dramatically displays the pride. and cruelty of the man, and the tremendous force and vigor of the whole statue, man and beast, make it one of the outstanding statues of all time. Lucca della Robbia (1400–82) is sometimes rated among the great sculptors of the fifteenth century, chiefly because of his use of terra cotta as a medium for sculpture. He modeled many Madonnas but specialized in children, his most celebrated work being the *Bambini* which decorate the façade of the orphanage in Florence and which have been reproduced *ad nauseam* on Christmas seals, calendars, and talcum-powder cans. Jacopo della Quercia, a Sienese, although a notable sculptor in his own right, is best known as the teacher of the mighty Michaelangelo, some of whose earliest pieces fall within our period.

Painting developed even more spectacularly than did sculpture in the early years of the Italian Renaissance. We have already seen that Giotto, Fra Angelico, and Gozzoli transformed the Byzantino-Gothic style with a new naturalness and life. The great exponent of realism in painting was, however, Masaccio (1401–28) whose frescoes in the Church of the Carmine in Florence were to start a new school of realistic painting. His paintings are remarkable for their action and dramatic movement. At first neglected, Masaccio later came to have a dominant influence over Florentine painters, the chief among his disciples being Fra Filippo Lippi (1406–69). Lippi painted Madonnas, who were obviously Florentine women of his own day, and his children are far from aesthetic. While he painted ecclesiastical subjects, the approach of the good friar was distinctly earthly. "In Piero della Francesca (ca. 1416–92) is found the painter with a more natural gift for an art than any man in the century. . . . In all of Italian painting there is no master whose work is so restrained, so deliberate and discriminating." [3] Piero was not a Florentine, but an Umbrian, and his chief works are to be found in Arezzo and Borgo San Sepolcro. He was a master of perspective, on which he wrote a learned treatise.

Domenico Ghirlandaio (1449–97) also reproduced precisely what he saw. His religious pictures are all realistic, the Virgin and Mary Magdalene being two Florentine women conversing in Florence with the Arno in the background. Ghirlandaio is not rated the equal of many of his contemporaries, although his lavish colors and precision of detail make him extremely interesting to the layman: one of his chief bids for fame was that he was the teacher of Michaelangelo. Another realist, one who specialized in the human body and painted mostly nudes, was Luca Signorelli (1441–1523) who anticipated Michaelangelo in his study of anatomy. His greatest work is a fresco in the church at Orvieto, depicting the torments of the damned in Hell, a scene which he fills with naked spirits writhing in all possible positions to reveal the play of muscles. Signorelli's Hell is a far more vivid place than the Hells of the medieval artists, and anticipated the modern illustrations of Dante by Gustave Doré.

There was a marked return to the conventional in the work of Sandra Botticelli (1444–1510) whose allegorical and mythological pictures are done

[3] Robb and Garrison, *Art in the Western World*, pp. 645–46.

in a semi-stylized manner which emphasized spirituality and symbolism at the expense of naturalism. Perugino (1446–1524) and his pupil Pinturicchio (1454–1513) of the Umbrian school, also returned somewhat to the spiritual, rejecting the complete realism of men like Lippi. Perugino was a master of landscape backgrounds, though his central figures are stiff. Pinturicchio is best known for his scenes from the life of Pius II in the cathedral of Siena and for his pictures in the Sistine Chapel at Rome. It was from him that Raphael, a student of Perugino's, derived the inspiration for the lovely Madonnas for which he is so famous.

The work of most of the leading artists of the late fifteenth century can be studied in the Sistine Chapel. In its decoration Pope Sixtus employed the best artists of the time, and its walls include paintings by Perugino, Pinturicchio, Botticelli, Ghirlandaio, Signorelli, and others. Later, Julius II hired Michaelangelo to complete the room with his *Last Judgment* on the end wall and his pictures on the ceiling.

Meanwhile in Venice a separate school was developing which was to become the most notable of all for its use of color. The real founders of this group were the Bellinis, Jacopo (1395–1470), and his sons, Giovanni (1430–1516) and Gentile (1429–1507). Closely connected with them was Mantegna of Padua (1431–1506), who married Jacopo's daughter. Mantegna, who is best known for his murals in Padua and Mantua, developed a fine eye for detail, each flower in his backgrounds or each piece of armor on his figures being painted with the utmost exactitude. Gentile Bellini was especially skillful in perspective and the painting of architectural detail; his brother Giovanni was one of the greatest portraitists of all time; strongly influenced by Mantegna in his passion for detail, Giovanni added a feeling for expression which is shown equally in the stern features of his portrait of Doge Loredano and in the serene and beautiful faces of his Madonnas. Of Giovanni, Reinach remarks: "Giovanni Bellini, who lived eighty-six years, passed through such a variety of stages that he was a school of painting in himself, rather than a single painter . . . In his laborious life this great artist traversed all the road that led from Mantegna to Titian." [4]

Other great figures of the Venetian school are Carpaccio (1460–1522) and Giorgione (1478–1510). Carpaccio united the Bellini's use of color with an ability to narrate a story in his paintings; his scenes from the life of St. Ursula are packed with action and at the same time show every attention to the details of the rich backgrounds. Giorgione, the master of Titian, was the supreme Venetian artist in the painting of the human body as demonstrated by his *Venus,* now in the Dresden gallery. Only a few of Giorgione's pictures have been preserved, but his influence is clear in the works of Titian and Tintoretto in the next generation.

[4] S. Reinach, *Apollo* (rev. ed. 1924, Scribners), pp. 172–74.

In Venice, better than in the other centers of art, one may observe a characteristic, carried over from the medieval, which is one of the charming features of Renaissance art. Whatever the subject matter, whether it be Biblical scenes or classical subjects, the figures and the settings are always local and contemporary. The *Last Supper* is held in an Italian dining hall, the *Marriage at Cana* takes place in a Venetian palace; apostles, saints, and Roman warriors wear the costumes of the fifteenth century. We can get a good idea of contemporary Venice from the background scenes in the pictures of the artists of this school.

There remains for discussion the most universal genius of the Italian Renaissance, Leonardo da Vinci (1452–1519), the pupil of Verrocchio, who served as architect and engineer for Ludovico Il Moro, who called himself a sculptor, who experimented with a flying machine, and who is universally recognized as one of the greatest masters of painting the world has ever produced.

Leonardo's works are relatively few. His colossal statue of Francesco Sforza was destroyed and we have no example of his sculpture. We do possess, however, his sketchbooks with the cartoons of works projected which give some idea of his capacity in this line. His painting speaks for itself, in the magnificent, if badly damaged, *Last Supper* in the church of San Ambrogio in Milan, and the *Mona Lisa Giaconda,* the *Virgin with St. Anne,* and the *Virgin of the Rocks,* all of which are in the Louvre. There exist in addition a number of unfinished pictures and cartoons, as well as several doubtful paintings attributed to Leonardo, but the four known works are sufficient to establish his greatness, in color, character, action and a combination of humanity with high spirituality.

The remaining great artists of the Renaissance fall outside of our period, but with Leonardo, art reached a perfection which has never been surpassed (if equalled) and the fifteenth century can well be said to have gone out amidst a blaze of unprecedented glory in the artistic field.

REFLECTIONS BY WAY OF EPILOGUE

✛

"**B**UT where are the snows of yesteryear?" cried François Villon, and well might a man have questioned thus in the closing years of the fifteenth century. Gradually and imperceptibly the medieval world had passed away making way for the modern, and if some looked to the future there were always those who mourned the past. Of the institutions, movements, and beliefs that characterized the medieval world most had vanished. The stable unities—the unity of the church and the unity of the state—had both perished. The Byzantine Empire had fallen before the Turk; the Holy Roman Empire was but a shadowy mantel on the shoulders of the Hapsburg monarchs; the oecumenical papacy had been rent with schism and was about to be overthrown by the Protestant Revolt of which the foundations had already been laid. Chivalry was gone; feudalism and the feudal society had perforce yielded to the pressure of the rising middle class; feudal monarchs had become absolute sovereigns, and the political theory of a John of Salisbury had been cast aside for the practical precepts of a Marsiglio and Machiavelli. The narrow horizon of the medieval man had been pushed back to include unknown lands to the east, south, and west. The world was in a state of change.

Much of the medieval world had ended of course by 1300. The great days of both empires, East and West, had been past by then; the papacy had fallen in the humiliation of Anagni before the new strength of national monarchies; the crusades were ended. But for two centuries the old institutions hung on, and it was not until the end of the fifteenth century that it was wholly apparent how complete the change had become. As Roman civilization survived the end of the empire in the West from the fourth to the seventh century, so did medieval civilization continue from the end of the thirteenth to that of the fifteenth century.

But if the old order was dead, there was yet much of it which carried over into the new. Many of our modern institutions come to us directly from the Middle Ages:—our parliamentary system, our universities, our system of banking and credit, our municipal institutions, our religious organization and much of the dogma of many of our creeds, our very languages and the literatures which have developed in them, all these and more we owe to the medieval period of our history. Of tangible remains we can point to our great churches and the contents of our museums:— to tapestries, statues, carved ivories, to poems, histories, philosophical and scientific works. However much the machine age has removed us from our medieval ancestors in many of the incidents of our daily lives, yet most of us come daily into contact with something which we owe to the Middle Ages, and those of us who enjoy the academic or ecclesiastical professions are constantly surrounded by medieval souvenirs.

It would be pleasant to think that we might be able to gain from the history of the Middle Ages some principles which might be of benefit to us in molding our own society. But Clio is rather exploited as an attorney than revered as a teacher. Historical precedents and historical bases are sought for the most preposterous claims today, and it is rather too much to hope that we can really learn much from the past. But the study of past civilizations cannot but disturb, however mildly, our complacence concerning the permanence of our own peculiar culture. We have seen in this volume how the center of civilization moved from Rome to Constantinople only to return to the West after a few hundred years. The Moslem states rose, reached almost unparalleled heights of material splendor, and fell with amazing rapidity. Our Western nations came to the fore in the twelfth century; since then they have continuously developed and expanded until at the beginning of the twentieth the whole world was patterned on our mode of life. But in eastern Europe a new power has rejected those institutions and beliefs which we hold most dear, and it may well be that once again the world will be divided between two separate and distinct culture centers in the East and West. It is even not impossible that there might again develop the three centers—the Latin, the Byzantino-Russian, and the Moslem which divided the world for several centuries. Clio is no fortune-teller; she only claims to be able to advise, by pointing out past experiences, those things which might be done under similar circumstances in the present or future. But one fact she can assert:—no civilization falls from outside pressure alone; it is invariably due to internal decay and corruption, to the loss of its own ideals and integrity, that any nation or civilization has succumbed. Not Rome, nor Byzantium, Baghdad nor Cairo, fell for any reason other than their own internal demoralization. Professor Arnold Toynbee feels the need for a spiritual regeneration if Western society is to be saved. This may perhaps be true, but it is evident that if we are *not* saved, the fault will lie "not in our stars, but in ourselves."

APPENDICES

✤

LIST OF POPES

Sylvester I, 314–335 [*Roman*]
Mark, 336 [*Roman*]
Julius I, 337–352 [*Italian*]
Liberius, 352–355/365–366 [*Roman*]
[Felix II, antipope, 355–365]
Damasus I, 366–384 [*Roman*]
[Ursinus, 366–367, antipope]
Siricius, 384–399 [*Roman*]
Anastius I, 399–401 [*Italian*]
Innocent I, 401–417 [*Roman*]
Zosimus, 417–418 [*Greek*]
[Eulalius, 418–419, antipope]
Boniface I, 418–422 [*Roman*]
Celestine I, 422–432 [*Roman*]
Sixtus III, 432–440 [*Roman*]
Leo I, 440–461 [*Roman*]
Hilary, 461–468 [*Sardinian*]
Simplicius, 468–483 [*Roman*]
Felix III, 483–492 [*Italian*]
Gelasius I, 492–496 [*Roman*]
Anastasius II, 496–498 [*Roman*]
Symmachus, 498–514 [*Sardinian*]
[Lawrence, 498–505, antipope]
Hormisdas, 514–523 [*Roman*]
John I, 523–526 [*Tuscan*]
Felix IV, 526–530 [*Italian*]
[Dioscorus, 530, antipope]
Boniface II, 530–532 [*Roman*]
John II, 533–535 [*Roman*]
Agapetus, 535–536 [*Roman*]
Sylverius, 536–537 [*Italian*]
Vigilius, 537–555 [*Roman*]
Pelagius I, 556–561 [*Roman*]
John III, 561–574 [*Roman*]
Benedict I, 575–579 [*Roman*]
Pelagius II, 579–590 [*Roman*]
Gregory I, 590–604 [*Roman*]
Sabinianus, 604–606 [*Tuscan*]

Boniface III, 607 [*Greek*]
Boniface IV, 608–615 [*Italian*]
Deusdedit, 615–618 [*Roman*]
Boniface V, 619–625 [*Neapolitan*]
Honorius I, 625–638 [*Italian*]
Severinus, 640 [*Roman*]
John IV, 640–642 [*Dalmatian*]
Theodore I, 642–649 [*Greek*]
Martin I, 649–653 [*Tuscan*]
Eugenius I, 654–657 [*Italian*]
Vitalian, 657–672 [*Italian*]
Adeodatus, 672–676 [*Roman*]
Donus, 676–678 [*Italian*]
Agatho, 678–681 [*Sicilian*]
Leo II, 682–683 [*Sicilian*]
Benedict II, 684–685 [*Roman*]
John V, 685–686 [*Syrian*]
Conon, 686–687 [*Greek*]
[Theodore II, 687, antipope]
[Pascal I, 687–692, antipope]
Sergius I, 687–701 [*Syrian*]
John VI, 701–705 [*Greek*]
John VII, 705–707 [*Greek*]
Sisinnius, 708 [*Syrian*]
Constantine, 708–715 [*Syrian*]
Gregory II, 715–731 [*Roman*]
Gregory III, 731–741 [*Syrian*]
Zacharias, 741–752 [*Greek*]
Stephen, 752 [*Roman*]
Stephen II, 752–757 [*Roman*]
Paul I, 757–767 [*Roman*]
[Constantine and Philip, 767–768, antipopes]
Stephen III, 768–772 [*Sicilian*]
Adrian I (Colonna), 772–795 [*Roman*]
Leo III, 795–816 [*Italian*]
Stephen IV, 816–817 [*Roman*]
Pascal I, 817–824 [*Roman*]

Eugenius II, 824–827 [Roman]
Valentine, 827 [Italian]
Gregory IV, 827–844 [Roman]
[John VIII, 844, antipope]
Sergius II, 844–847 [Roman]
Leo IV, 847–855 [Roman]
Benedict III, 855–858 [Roman]
[Anastasius III, 855, antipope]
[John IX, 855–857, antipope]
Nicholas I, 858–867 [Roman]
Adrian II, 867–872 [Roman]
John VIII, 872–882 [Roman]
Martin II, 882–884 [Tuscan]
Adrian III, 884–885 [Roman]
Stephen V, 885–891 [Roman]
Formosas, 891–896 [Italian]
Boniface VI, 896 [Roman]
Stephen VI, 896–897 [Roman]
Romanus, 897 [Roman]
Theodore II, 897 [Roman]
John IX, 898–900 [Italian]
Benedict IV, 900–903 [Roman]
Leo V, 903 [Italian]
Christopher, 903–904 [Roman]
Sergius III, 904–911 [Roman]

Anastasius III, 911–913 [Roman]
Lando, 913–914 [Roman]
John X, 914–928 [Italian]
Leo VI, 928 [Italian]
Stephen VII, 929–931 [Italian]
John XI (son of Marozia), 931–936 [Roman]
Leo VII, 936–939 [Italian]
Stephen VIII, 939–942 [Roman]
Martin III, 942–946 [Roman]
Agapetus II, 946–955 [Roman]
John XII (son of Alberic), 955–963 [Roman]
Leo VIII, 963–964 (Roman?)
Benedict V, 964 [Roman]
John XIII, 965–972 [Roman]
Benedict VI, 973–974 [Italian]
[Boniface VII, 974, antipope]
Benedict VII, 974–983 [Roman]
John XIV, 983–984 [Lombard]
Boniface VII, 984–985 [Roman]
John XV, 985–996 [Roman]
Gregory V (Bruno), 996–999 [German]
[John XVI, 997–998, antipope]

Sylvester II (Gerbert of Aurillac), 999–1003 [French]
John XVII, 1003 [Italian]
John XVIII (Phasian), 1003–9 [Roman]
Sergius IV (Peter Bocca), 1009–12 [Roman]
Benedict VIII (John of Tusculum), 1012–24 [Roman]
[Gregory VI, 1012, antipope]
John XIX (Romanus, Duke of Rome, bro. of Benedict VIII), 1024–32
Benedict IX (Theophilactus of Tusculum, nephew of John XIX), 1032–45
[Sylvester III, 1045, antipope]
Gregory VI (John Gratian), 1045–46 [Roman]
Clement II (Suidger), 1046–47 [German]
Damasus II (Pappo), 1048 [German]
Leo IX (Bruno, b. of Toul), 1049–54 [German]
Victor II (Geberhard, b. of Eichstadt), 1055–57 [German]
Stephen IX (Frederick of Lorraine, abbot of Monte Cassino), 1057–58 [German]
Benedict X (John, b. of Velletri), 1058–59 [Italian]
Nicholas II (Gerard, b. of Florence), 1058–61 [Burgundian]
Alexander II (Anselm, b. of Lucca), 1061–73 [Milanese]
[Honorius II (Cadulous, b. of Parma), 1061–72, antipope]
Gregory VII (Hildebrand), 1073–85 [Tuscan]
[Clement III (Guibert, arb. of Ravenna), 1084–1100, antipope]

Victor III (Desiderius, ab. of Monte Cassino), 1087 [*Italian*]

Urban II (Eudes de Lagery, b. of Ostia), 1088–99 [*French*]

Paschal II (Ranier, ab. of San Lorenzo), 1099–1118 [*Italian*]

[Theoderich, 1100, antipope]

[Albert, 1102, antipope]

[Sylvester IV, 1105–11, antipope]

Gelasius II (John of Gaeta), 1118–19 [*Italian*]

[Gregory VIII, 1118–21, antipope]

Calixtus II (Guy of Burgundy, arb. Vienne), 1119–24 [*Burgundian*]

Honorius II (Lambert, b. of Ostia), 1124–30 [*Italian*]

[Celestine II, 1124, antipope]

Innocent II (Gregory Papi), 1130–43 [*Italian*]

[Anacletus II (Pierleoni), 1130–38, antipope]

[Victor IV, 1138, antipope]

Celestine II (Guy), 1143–44 [*Tuscan*]

Lucius II (Gerard of Bologna), 1144–45 [*Italian*]

Eugenius III (Bernard of Pisa), 1145–53 [*Italian*]

Anastasius IV (Conrad), 1153–54 [*Roman*]

Adrian IV (Nicholas Breakspear), 1154–59 [*English*]

Alexander III (Roland Bandinelli), 1159–81 [*Tuscan*]

[Victor IV (Octavian), 1159–64, antipope]

[Pascal III (Guy of Crema), 1164–68, antipope]

[Calixtus III (John, b. of Jerusalem), 1168–79, antipope]

[Innocent III (Lando), 1179–80, antipope]

Lucius III (Ubaldo, b. of Ostia), 1181–85 [*Tuscan*]

Urban III (Huberto Crivelli, arb. of Milan), 1185–87 [*Lombard*]

Gregory VIII (Albert de Morra), 1187 [*Italian*]

Clement III (Paul Scolaro), 1187–91 [*Roman*]

Celestine III (Hyacinth Bobocard), 1191–98 [*Roman*]

Innocent III (Lothaire de Segni), 1198–1216 [*Roman*]

Honorius III (Cencio Savelli), 1216–27 [*Roman*]

Gregory IX (Ugolino de Segni, b. of Ostia), 1227–41 [*Roman*]

Celestine IV (Geoffrey de Castiglione), 1241 [*Lombard*]

Innocent IV (Sinibaldo Fieschi), 1243–54 [*Genoese*]

Alexander IV (Reinald de Segni, b. of Ostia, nephew of Greg. IX), 1254–61 [*Roman*]

Urban IV (Jacques Pantaleon), 1261–64 [*French*]

Clement IV (Guy Foulquois), 1265–68 [*French*]

Gregory X (Thealdo Visconti), 1271–76 [*Lombard*]

Innocent V (Pierre de Tarantaise), 1276 [*French*]

Adrian V (Ottoboni Fieschi, nephew of Inno. IV), 1276 [*Genoese*]

John XXI (Peter, arb. of Braga), 1276–77 [*Portuguese*]

Nicholas III (John Gaetani Orsini), 1277–80 [*Roman*]

Martin IV (Simon de Brion), 1281–85 [*French*]

Honorius IV (James Savelli), 1285–87 [*Roman*]

Nicholas IV (Jerome of Ascali), 1288–92 [*Italian*]

Celestine V (Peter Morrone), 1294 [*Italian*]

Boniface VIII (Benedetto Gaetani), 1294–1303 [*Roman*]
Benedict XI (Nicholas Boccasino), 1303–4 [*Italian*]
Clement V (Bertrand de Got), 1305–14 [*French*]
John XXII (Jacques d'Euse), 1316–34 [*French*]
[Nicholas V (Pierre de Corbiere), 1328–30, antipope]
Benedict XII (Jacques Fournier), 1334–42 [*Gascon*]
Clement VI (Pierre Rogier), 1342–52 [*French*]
Innocent VI (Etienne d'Albert), 1352–62 [*French*]
Urban V (Guillaume de Grimoard), 1362–70 [*French*]
Gregory XI (Pierre Rogier, nephew of Clement VI), 1370–78 [*French*]

* * * * * * *

Roman Line

Urban VI (Bartholomeo Prigano), 1378–89 [*Neapolitan*]
Boniface IX (Pietro Tomacelli), 1389–1404 [*Neapolitan*]
Innocent VII (Cosmato de Meliorati), 1404–6 [*Neapolitan*]
Gregory XII (Angelo Cornaro), 1406–15 [*Venetian*]

Avignon Line: Antipopes

Clement VII (Robert de Geneva), 1378–94 [*French*]
Benedict XIII (Pedro de Luna), 1394–1424 [*Aragonese*]

Conciliar Line: Antipopes

Alexander V (Piero Philargo, arb. of Milan), 1409–10 [*Cretan*]
John XXIII (Baldassare Cossa), 1410–15 [*Neapolitan*]

* * * * * * * * * *

Martin V (Odo Colonna), 1417–31 [*Roman*]
[Clement VIII, 1424–29, antipope]
[Benedict XIV, 1424, antipope]
Eugenius IV (Gabriel Condolmaro), 1431–47 [*Venetian*]
[Felix V (Amadeo, D. of Savoy), 1439–49, antipope]
Nicholas V (Tomasso Parentucelli), 1447–55 [*Tuscan*]
Calixtus III (Alfonso Borgia), 1455–58 [*Aragonese*]
Pius II (Aeneas Silvius Piccolomini), 1458–64 [*Tuscan*]
Paul II (Pietro Barbo), 1464–71 [*Venetian*]
Sixtus IV (Francesco della Rovere), 1471–84 [*Genoese*]
Innocent VIII (Giovanni Baptisto Cibo), 1484–92 [*Genoese*]
Alexander VI (Roderigo Borgia, nephew of Calixtus III), 1492–1503 [*Spanish*]

EMPERORS OF THE EASTERN ROMAN EMPIRE, 306–1453

Constantine I, 306–337

Constantius, 337–361 [*son of Constantine I*], Constantine II, 337–340 and Constans, 337–50, his brothers, coemperors

Julian, 361–363 [*nephew of Constantine I*]

Jovian, 363–364

Valens, 364–378 [*his brother Valentinian I, 364–375 in West*]

Theodosius I, 379–395 [*Gratian, 375–383 and Valentinian II, 375–392, the sons of Valentinian and brothers-in-law of Theodosius, in West*]

Arcadius, 395–408 [*son of Theodosius*] [*His brother Honorius, 395–423 in West*]

Theodosius II, 408–450 [*son of Arcadius*] [*Valentinian III, nephew of Honorius in West*]

Marcian, 450–457 [*brother-in-law of Theodosius II: husband of Pulcheria*]

Leo I, 457–474

Leo II, 474 [*grandson of Leo I*]

Zeno, 474–491 [*husband of Verina the daughter of Leo I and mother of Leo II*]

Anastasius, 491–518 [*husband of Verina*]

Justin I, 518–527

Justinian I, 527–565 [*nephew of Justin I*]

Justin II, 565–578 [*nephew of Justinian I*]

Tiberius II, 578–582 [*son-in-law of Justin II*]

Maurice, 582–602 [*son-in-law of Tiberius II*]

Phocas, 602–610

Heraclius, 610–641

Constantine III and Heracleonas 641 [*sons of Heraclius*]

Constans II, 641–668 [*son of Constantine III*]

Constantine IV, 668–685 [*son of Constans II*]

Justinian II, 685–695 [*son of Constantine IV*]

Leontius, 695–698

Tiberius III, 698–705

Justinian II, restored, 705–711

Philip, 711–713

Anastasius, 713–715

Theodosius III, 715–717

Leo III the Isaurian, 717–741

Constantine V, 741–775 [*son of Leo III*]

Leo IV, 775–780 [*son of Constantine V*]

Constantine VI, 780–797 [*son of Leo IV*]

Irene, 797–802 [*widow of Leo IV, mother of Constantine VI*]

Nicephorus I, 802–811

Stauracius, 811 [*son of Nicephorus*]

Michael I, 811–813 [*son-in-law of Nicephorus*]

Leo V the Armenian, 813–820

Michael II the Amorian, 820–829

Theophilus, 829–842 [*son of Michael II*]

Michael III, 842–867 [*son of Theophilius; regency of his mother Theodora and her brother, Caesar Bardas 842–866*]

Basil I the Macedonian, 867–886

Leo VI, 886–912 and Alexander, 886–913 [*sons of Basil I*]

Constantine VII Porphyrogenitos, 913–959 [*son of Leo VI*]

Romanus I Lecapenus, 919–944, coemperor [*father-in-law of Constantine VII*]

Constantine, 944–945, coemperor [*brother-in-law of Constantine VII*]

Romanus II, 959–963 [*son of Constantine VII*]

Basil II Bulgaroctenos, 963–1025 and Constantine VIII, 963–1028 [*sons of Romanus*]

Nicephorus II Phocas 963–969, coemperor [*husband of Theophano, the mother of Basil II*]

John Tzimisces, 969–976, coemperor [*husband of Theodora, the sister of Romanus II*]

Zoe, 1028–50 and Theodora, 1028–56 [*daughters of Constantine VIII*]

Romanus III Argyrus, 1028–34 [*husband of Zoe*]

Michael IV, 1034–41 [*husband of Zoe*]

Michael V, 1041–42 [*nephew of Michael IV, adopted by Zoe*]

Constantine IX, 1042–54 [*husband of Zoe*]

Michael VI, 1056–57 [*adopted by Theodora*]

Isaac I Comnenus, 1057–59

Constantine X Ducas, 1059–67

Romanus IV Diogenes, 1067–71 [*husband of Eudocia, the widow of Constantine X*]

Michael VII, 1071–78 [*son of Constantine X and Eudocia*]

Nicephorus III Botoniates, 1078–81 [*husband of Marie the widow of Michael VII*]

Alexius I Comnenus, 1081–1118 [*nephew of Isaac Comnenus*]

John II Comnenus, 1118–43 [*son of Alexius*]

Manuel I, 1143–80 [*son of John*]

Alexius II, 1180–83 [*son of Manuel*]

Andronicus I, 1183–85 [*cousin of Manuel*]

Isaac II Angelus, 1185–95

Alexius III Angelus, 1195–1203 [*brother of Isaac II*]

Isaac II restored, 1203–04 and Alexius IV [*his son*]

Alexius V Ducas Murtzuphles, 1204 [*son-in-law of Alexius III*]

Theodore I Lascaris, 1204–22 [*son-in-law of Alexius III; at Nicaea*]

John III Vatatses, 1222–54 [*son-in-law of Theodore I*]

Theodore II, 1254–58 [*son of John III*]

John IV, 1258–61 [*son of Theodore II*]

Michael VIII Palaeologus, 1259–82 [*restored empire to Constantinople*]

Andronicus II, 1283–1328 [*son of Michael VIII*]

Michael IX, 1295–1320 coemperor [*son of Andronicus II*]

Andronicus III, 1328–41 [*son of Michael IX*]

John V, 1341–76 [*son of Andronicus III*]

John VI Cantacuzenos, 1347–54 coemperor [*father-in-law of John V*]

Andronicus IV, 1376–79 [*son of John V*]

John V, restored, 1379–91

John VII, 1390 [*son of Andronicus IV, grandson of John V*]

Manuel II, 1391–1425 [*younger son of John V, uncle of John VII*]

John VIII, 1425–48 [*son of Manuel II*]

Constantine XI, 1448–53 [*younger brother of John VIII*]

THE UMAYYAD CALIPHS OF DAMASCUS AND CORDOVA

Caliphs of Damascus

1. Mu'awiyah, 661–680 (son of Abu-Sufyan; great-grandson of Umayyah)
2. Yazid I, 680–683 (son of Mu'awiyah 1)
3. Mu'awiyah II, 683 (son of Yazid 2)
4. Marwan I, 683–685 (great-grandson of Umayyah, through Hakam)
5. Abd al Malik, 685–705 (son of Marwan 4)
6. Walid I, 705–715 (eldest son of Abd al Malik 5)
7. Sulayman, 715–717 (second son of Abd al Malik 5)
8. Umar II, 717–720 (son of Abd al Aziz, the son of Marwan 4)
9. Yazid II, 720–724 (third son of Abd al Malik 5)
10. Hisham, 724–743 (fourth son of Abd al Malik 5)
11. Walid II, 743–744 (son of Yazid 9)
12. Yazid III, 744 (son of Walid 6)
13. Ibrahim, 744 (younger son of Walid 6)
14. Marwan II, 744–750 (son of Muhammad the son of Marwan 4)

Emirs and Caliphs of Cordova

1. Abd ar Rahman I, 756–788 (son of Mu'awiyah, son of Hisham 10)
2. Hisham I, 788–796 (son of Abd ar Rahman 1)
3. Hakam I, 796–822 (son of Hisham 2)
4. Abd ar Rahman II, 822–52 (son of Hakam 3)
5. Muhammad I, 852–886 (son of Abd ar Rahman 4)
6. Al Mundhir, 886–888 (elder son of Muhammad 5)
7. Abdullah, 888–912 (younger son of Muhammad 5)
8. Abd ar Rahman III, 912–961 (grandson of Abdullah 7) [First Caliph 929]
9. Hakam II, 961–976 (eldest son of Abd ar Rahman 8)
10. Hisham II, 976–1009 (son of Hakam 9)
11. Muhammad II, 1009 (great-grandson of Abd ar Rahman 8)
12. Sulayman, 1009–10 (great-grandson of Abd ar Rahman 8)
11a. Muhammad, restored, 1010
10a. Hisham II, restored, 1010–13
12a. Sulayman, restored, 1013–16
[Reign of Ali Nasir ben Hammud of Malaga, 1016–18]
13. Abd ar Rahman IV, 1018 (great-grandson of Abd ar Rahman 8)
[Reigns of Kasim ben Hammud and Yahya of Malaga, 1018–22]
14. Abd ar Rahman V, 1023 (brother of Muhammad 11)
15. Muhammad III, 1023–24 (great-grandson of Abd or Rahman 8)
[Reign of Yahya again, 1024–25]
16. Hisham III, 1027–31 (brother of Abd ar Rahman 13)

THE ABBASID CALIPHS

1. Abu al Abbas al Saffah, 750–754
2. Al Mansur, 754–775 (brother of Al Saffah 1)
3. Al Mahdi, 775–785 (son of Al Mansur 2)
4. Al Hadi, 785–786 (son of Al Mahdi 3)
5. Harun al Rashid, 786–809 (son of Al Mahdi 3)
6. Al Amin, 809–813 (son of Al Rashid 5)
7. Al Mamun, 813–833 (son of Al Rashid 5)

8. Al Mu'tasim, 833–842 *(son of Al Rashid 5)* [*Removal to Samarra*]
9. Al Wathiq, 842–847 *(son of Al Mu'tasim 8)*
10. Al Mutawakkil, 847–861 *(son of Al Mu'tasim 8)* [*Murdered by guards*]
11. Al Muntasir, 861–862 *(son of Al Mutawakkil 10)*
12. Al Mustain, 862–866 *(son of Muhammad, the eldest son of Al Mu'tasim 8)*
13. Al Mu'tazz, 866–869 *(son of Al Mutawakkil 10)*
14. Al Muhtadi, 869–870 *(son of Al Wathiq 9)*
15. Al Mu'tamid, 870–892 *(son of Al Mutawakkil 10)*
16. Al Mu'tadid, 892–902 *(son of Al Muwaffak, younger son of Al Mutawakkil 10)*
    [*Return from Samarra*]
17. Al Muktafi, 902–908 *(son of Al Mu'tadid 16)*
18. Al Muqtadir, 908–932 *(son of Al Mu'tadid 16)*
19. Al Qahir, 932–934 *(son of Al Mu'tadid 16)*
20. Al Radi, 934–940 *(son of Al Muqtadir 18)*
21. Al Muttaqi, 940–944 *(son of Al Muqtadir 18)*
22. Al Mustakfi, 944–946 *(son of Al Muktafi 17)* [*Buwayhids gain control*]
23. Al Muti, 946–974 *(son of Al Muqtadir 18)*
24. Al Ta'i, 974–991 *(son of Al Muti 23)*
25. Al Qadir, 991–1031 *(son of Al Muttaqi 21)*
26. Al Qaim, 1031–75 *(son of Al Qadir 25)* [*Buwayhids overthrown by Saljuqs*]
27. Al Muqtadi, 1075–94 *(grandson of Al Qaim 26)*
28. Al Mustazhir, 1094–1118 *(son of Al Muqtadi 27)*
29. Al Mustarshid, 1118–35 *(son of Al Mustazhir 28)*
30. Al Rashid, 1135–36 *(son of Al Mustarshid 29)*
31. Al Muqtafi, 1136–60 *(son of Al Mustazhir 28)*
32. Al Mustanjid, 1160–70 *(son of Al Muqtafi 31)*
33. Al Mustadi, 1170–80 *(son of Al Mustanjid 32)*
34. Al Nasir, 1180–1225 *(son of Al Mustadi 33)* [*End of Saljuq control.*]
35. Al Zahir, 1225–26 *(son of Al Nasir 34)*
36. Al Mustansir, 1226–42 *(son of Al Zahir 35)*
37. Al Mustasim, 1242–58 *(son of Al Mustansir 36)* [*Mongol Conquest*]

THE FATIMID CALIPHS OF EGYPT

1. Al Mahdi, 909–934
2. Al Qaim, 934–946 *(son of Al Madhi 1)*
3. Al Mansur, 946–952 *(son of Al Qaim 2)*
4. Al Mu'izz, 952–975 *(son of Al Mansur 3)*
5. Al Aziz, 975–996 *(son of Al Mu'izz 4)*
6. Al Hakim, 996–1021 *(son of Al Aziz 5)*
7. Al Zahir, 1021–35 *(son of Al Hakim 6)*
8. Al Mustansir, 1035–94 *(son of Al Zahir 7)*
9. Al Mustali, 1094–1101 *(son of Al Mustansir 8)*
10. Al Amir, 1101–30 *(son of Al Mustali 9)*
11. Al Hafiz, 1130–49 *(grandson of Al Mustansir 8, son of Muhammad, a younger son)*
12. Al Zafir, 1149–54 *(younger son of Al Hafiz 11)*
13. Al Fa'iz, 1154–60 *(son of Al Zafir 12)*
14. Al Adid, 1160–71 *(grandson of Al Hafiz 11, son of Yusuf an elder son)*

THE MAMELUK SULTANS OF EGYPT

Bahri Dynasty

1. Aibek, 1250–57 (*slave of Al Salih Ayyub, and husband of Shajar al Durr*)
2. Nureddin Ali, 1257–59 (*son of Aibek 1*)
3. Qutuz, 1259–60 (*slave of Al Salih*)
4. Baybars, 1260–77 (*slave of Al Salih*)
5. Barakah, 1277–79 (*son of Baybars 4*)
6. Salamish, 1279 (*son of Baybars 4*)
7. Qalawun, 1279–90 (*slave of Al Salih*)
8. Khalil, 1290–93 (*son of Qalawun 7*)
9. Al Nasir, 1293–94 (*son of Qalawun 7*)
10. Ketbogha, 1294–96 (*slave of Qalawun 7*)
11. Lajin, 1296–98 (*slave of Qalawun 7*)
9a. Al Nasir, restored, 1298–1308
12. Baybars II, 1308–9 (*slave of Qalawun 7*)
9b. Al Nasir, restored, 1309–40
13. Abu Bakr, 1340–41 (*son of Nasir 9*)
14. Kujuk, 1341–42 (*son of Nasir 9*)
15. Ahmas, 1342 (*son of Nasir 9*)
16. Ismail, 1342–45 (*son of Nasir 9*)
17. Kamil Shaban, 1345–46 (*son of Nasir 9*)
18. Muzzaffer, 1346–47 (*son of Nasir 9*)
19. Hasan, 1347–51, 1354–61 (*son of Nasir 9*)
20. Salih, 1351–54 (*son of Nasir 9*)
21. Muhammad, 1361–63 (*son of Muzzaffer 18*)
22. Aschraf Shaban, 1363–76 (*son of Husayn son of Nasir 9*)
23. Aladin Ali, 1376–81 (*son of Aschraf Shaban 22*)
24. Salih Hajii, 1381–82, 1389–90 (*son of Aschraf Shaban 22*)

Burji Dynasty

1. Barkuk, 1382–89, 1391–98
2. Faraj, 1398–1405, 1406–12
3. Abd al Aziz, 1405–6
   [Caliph al Mustasin, 1412]
4. Al Muayyad, 1412–21
5. Muzaffar Ahmed, 1421
6. Zahir Tatar, 1421
7. Salih Muhammad, 1421
8. Barsabey, 1422–38
9. Al Aziz Yusuf, 1438
10. Jakmak, 1438–53
11. Uthman, 1453

12. Aschraf Inal, 1453–60
13. Nasir Ahmed, 1460–61
14. Kushkadam, 1461–67
15. Yalbey, 1467
16. Timurbugha, 1467–68
17. Kaitbey, 1468–95
18. Nasir Muhammad, 1495
19. Qansuh, 1498–99
20. Janbalat, 1499–1500
21. Qansuh al Ghouri, 1500–16
22. Tuman Bey, 1516–17

BIBLIOGRAPHY

✜

The list of books which follow are only meant to supplement the bibliographies given in L. J. Paetow's *Guide to the Study of Medieval History* (Appleton-Century-Crofts, rev. ed., 1931). Many books have appeared since the publication of the last edition of Paetow, and until the appearance of the new edition, which is now being prepared by Professor Gray C. Boyce of Northwestern University, a useful purpose can be served by giving some indication of the more important works which have come out since 1930. A few of the most significant earlier works are included in these lists, where they seem of such especial importance as to deserve particular notice, but in the main this bibliography comprises those works which are not to be found in Paetow. A useful supplement for what it covers is the list of works appearing in Europe during the war-years 1940–46, published in the *Progress of Medieval and Renaissance Studies in the United States and Canada*, XIX (1947), but this list limits itself to Continental publications and omits all British or American works. Unfortunately Paetow does not include works on English history; the list in that field is therefore somewhat more comprehensive than in others, although the reader is referred to the bibliography in W. E. Lunt, *History of England* (Harpers, rev. ed., 1938) for more complete coverage of works on England.

Hardly less important than Paetow is C. P. Farrar and E. P. Evans, *Bibliography of English Translations from Medieval Sources* (Columbia University, "Records of Civilization," 1946), which meets a long-felt demand for a comprehensive listing of English translations and obviates the necessity of citing here editions of sources. The names of the authors are found in this text; the translations can be found in Farrar and Evans, and there is little use in repeating the information here.

For lists of works in English only, J. W. Thompson, *Reference Studies in Medieval History* (3 vols. Chicago, 1923) has value as it includes many periodical articles not included in Paetow, but the listing is uncritical and sometimes faulty.

GENERAL HISTORIES OF THE MIDDLE AGES

The most important single work in English is the *Cambridge Medieval History* (8 vols. Cambridge Univ. Press and Macmillan, 1911–36), which has chapters on almost every aspect of medieval history, with excellent bibliographies for each volume and chapter. Within the last twenty years has been started the publication of several new series of which some are already nearing completion. The "Methuen's Medieval and Modern History" (G. P. Putnams Sons) has already published Z. N. Brooke, *History of Europe, 911–1198* (1938); C. W. Privité-Orton, *Europe, 1198–1378* (1937); and W. T. Waugh, *Europe, 1378–1494* (1932); while

J. H. Baxter, *Europe 476–911* is announced as in preparation. In France, the "Peuples et Civilisations" series (F. Alcan), edited by L. Halphen and P. Sagnac includes L. Halphen, *Les Barbares* (2nd ed. 1930), L. Halphen, *L'Essor de l'Europe* (1932; rev. ed., 1941) and Pirenne, Renaudet, Perroy, and Handelsman, *La Fin du moyen âge* (2 vols. 1931). In G. Glotz, "Histoire générale" series (Les Presses Universitaires) the section on "Histoire du Moyen Age" has: Lot, Pfister, et Ganshof, *Les Destinées de l'empire en occident, 395–888* (1928); A. Fliche, *L'Europe occidentale 888–1125* (1930); Diehl et Marcais, *Le Monde oriental, 395–1081* (1936); E. Jordan, *L'Allemagne et l'Italie aux XII et XIII siècles* (1939); C. Petit-Dutaillis et P. Guinard, *L'Essor des états d'occident* (1937); R. Fawtier, *L'Europe occidentale, 1270–1380* (1940); J. Calmette et E. Deprez. *L'Europe occidentale de la fin du XIV siècle aux guerres d'Italie* (2 vols. 1937–39); Pirenne, Cohen, et Focillon, *La Civilization occidentale au moyen âge* (1933); and Diehl, Guilland, Grousset, et Economos, *Le Monde oriental, 1081–1453* (1945). Several volumes have also appeared in the "Evolution de l'Humanité" series, (Renaissance du Livre) many of which have been translated into English in the "History of Civilization" series (London, Trubner and N.Y. Knopf) and are listed separately. Like the "Evolution," the Cavaignac "Histoire du Monde" series (Boccard) does not attempt a continuous history, but deals with individual periods in separate volumes which are cited below by title.

A brilliant synthetic treatment of the whole Middle Ages is given in N. Iorga *Essai de synthèse de l'histoire de l'humanité,* II (Paris, Gamber, 1927) and in H. Pirenne *History of Europe to the XVI Century* (Norton, 1939). The most recent general treatment in English above the textbook level is that of J. W. Thompson, *The Middle Ages* (2 vols. Knopf, 1931). Older general works will be found listed in Paetow.

General Works on Special Periods

A brilliant presentation of early medieval history (and the one followed in viewpoint in this text) is found in H. Pirenne *Mohammed and Charlemagne* (Norton, 1939). H. S. L. B. Moss, *The Birth of the Middle Ages* (Oxford, 1935) is a delightfully written essay on the period 395–814. F. Lot, *End of the Ancient World and the Beginning of the Middle Ages* (Knopf, 1931, "His. Civil.") affords a comprehensive overall treatment of the decline of the empire and the barbarian states with emphasis on the development in the West.

For the High Middle Ages a very informative volume is J. Calmette *Le Monde féodale* ("Coll. Clio," rev. ed., Presses Universitaires, 1942). E. P. Cheyney, *The Dawn of a New Era* (Harpers, 1936), and the first chapters of E. S. Lucas *Renaissance and Reformation* (Harpers, 1934) are recent interpretations of the fourteenth and fifteenth centuries. W. K. Ferguson, *The Renaissance* (Holt, 1939) is a useful volume in the "Berkshire Series."

Reference Books and Atlases

W. E. Langer, *Encyclopedia of World History* (Houghton Mifflin, 1940) provides a fund of chronological data, with genealogies, lists of rulers, etc. This most useful date book is a thorough revision of the old Ploetz *Epitome of Universal History* and is the accepted work for reference as to dates, spellings of names, etc. Unfortunately it is not infallible and there are several errors, especially in the sections dealing with Byzantium.

W. R. Shepherd's *Historical Atlas* (Holt) went into its seventh edition in 1929 and is still the most useful general historical atlas. For further reference works see Paetow pp. 1–46.

COLLECTIONS OF ESSAYS

Several *festschrift* volumes have appeared since the publication of Paetow. Among the American volumes are: *Persecution and Liberty: Essays in Honor of George Lincoln Burr* (Century, 1931); *Essays in History and Political Theory in Honor of Charles H. McIlwain* (Harvard, 1936); and *Medieval and Historiographical Essays in Honor of James Westphall Thompson* (Chicago, 1938).

PERIODICALS

The past two decades have witnessed the birth of several new periodicals devoted to medieval studies. *The Progress of Medieval and Renaissance Studies in the United States and Canada* (Univ. Colorado) which began in 1923, has expanded under the editorship of Professor S. H. Thomson to include review articles and extensive bibliographies in special fields, as well as the annual publications of medievalists.

Thomson is also the editor and founder of *Medievalia et Humanistica* (Boulder, Colo.) which began publication in 1943 and has now issued five fasciculi. *Traditio* (N.Y. Cosmopolitan Science and Art Service Co.), devoted to ancient and medieval culture, first appeared in 1943. *Byzantina-Metabyzantina* (N.Y., Society for Promotion of Byzantine and Modern Greek Studies) an American journal of Byzantine studies, issued its first volume in 1946. *Medium Aevum* is the organ for the Society for the study of Medieval Languages and Literature, which publishes at Oxford both the journal and a series of monographs. The Pontifical Institute at Ottawa publishes *Medieval Studies,* which has been appearing regularly since 1939.

TEXTBOOKS

The last two decades have witnessed a goodly number of one-volume textbooks. To list only the American texts we find: G. C. Sellery and A. C. Krey, *Medieval Foundations of Western Civilization* (Harpers, 1929); E. M. Hulme, *The Middle Ages* (Holt, 1929; rev. ed., 1938); J. W. Thompson, *History of the Middle Ages* (Norton, 1931, a condensation of his two-volume work); W. O. Ault, *Europe in the Middle Ages* (Heath, 1932; rev. ed., 1937); S. M. Brown, *Medieval Europe* (Harcourt, 1932; rev. ed., 1935); C. Stephenson, *Medieval History* (Harpers, 1935; rev. ed., 1943; an abridgement of this work was issued as *A Brief Survey of Medieval Europe,* 1941); R. W. Collins, *A History of Medieval Civilization* (Ginn,

1936); J. W. Thompson and E. N. Johnson, *An Introduction to Medieval Europe* (Norton, 1937, a completely new work, and although based on Thompson's two-volume history, it contains much additional material); L. C. MacKinney, *The Medieval World* (Rinehart, 1938); J. R. Strayer and D. C. Munro, *The Middle Ages* (Appleton-Century-Crofts, 1942, a new book, based on the older Munro and Sontag volume [1928] but completely reorganized and rewritten); J. O'Sullivan and J. F. Burns, *Medieval Europe* (Appleton-Century-Crofts, 1943).

SOURCEBOOKS

While the great vogue for sourcebooks has abated since the early decades of the century, in addition to the volumes listed in Paetow, there now are: J. F. Scott, A. Hyma and A. H. Noyes, *Readings in Medieval History* (Appleton-Century-Crofts, 1933: includes both source readings and selections from modern writers, a very useful volume for collateral readings); G. C. Coulton, *Life in the Middle Ages* (4 vols. Cambridge Univ. Press and Macmillan, 1928–30); R. C. Cave and H. H. Coulson, *Source Book for Medieval Economic History* (Bruce, 1936); C. Stephenson and F. C. Marcham, *Sources of English Constitutional History* (Harpers, 1937); R. McKeon, *Selections from Medieval Philosophers* (2 vols. Scribners, 1929–30); H. Bettenson, *Documents of the Christian Church* (Oxford, 1947). The University of Pennsylvania "Translation and Reprints from the Original Sources of European History" has also inaugurated a Third Series since 1941, the new volumes differing from the older series in that each volume is a single chronicle or collection of documents. The "Records of Civilization" edited by A. P. Evans (Columbia) has increased tremendously in the past two decades, with volumes in almost every important field of medieval history. These works are listed in Farrar and Evans *Bibliography* which itself forms part of the series.

The "Fathers of the Church," a new project for publishing patristic writings, undertaken by the Cima Press, New York, brought out its first two volumes in 1947.

THE ROMAN EMPIRE AND THE BARBARIAN INVASIONS

Two volumes by M. Rostovtzeff, *History of the Ancient World: Rome* (Oxford, 1931), and *Social and Economic History of the Roman Empire* (Oxford, 1926) have added much to our knowledge of the late Roman Empire. The most complete treatment is the *Cambridge Ancient History,* Vol. XII, 193–394 A.D. (Cambridge Univ. Press and Macmillan, 1939) with excellent bibliographies. The political history is also well treated in H. D. M. Parker *History of the Roman World 138–337* A.D. (Methuen, 1935). J. B. Bury, *The Invasions of Europe by the Barbarians* (Macmillan, 1928) is a useful supplement to his earlier studies on the *Later Roman Empire.* F. Lot, *The End of the Ancient World* (Knopf, 1931) is a translation of his earlier French work, and he has since covered the field again in *Les Invasions barbares et le peuplement de l'Europe* (2 vols. Paris, 1937).

One of the most significant works in this field is A. Dopsch *The Economic and Social Foundations of European Civilization* (Harcourt, 1937). A very useful short introduction, especially suitable for undergraduate reading, is that of R. F. Arragon, *The Transition from the Ancient to the Medieval World* (Holt, 1936, "Berkshire Studies"). Reference should also be made to the works of Pirenne, Lot, Moss, and Halphen mentioned above.

On the subject of the Church in the Roman Empire are: W. W. Hyde, *Paganism and Christianity in the Roman Empire* (Univ. Penna., 1946); E. R. Goodenough, *The Church in the Roman Empire* (Holt, 1931, "Berkshire Studies"); K. M. Setton, *Christian Attitude towards the Emperor in the Fourth Century* (Columbia, 1941).

Byzantine Empire

The best single history of the Byzantine Empire in English is A. A. Vasiliev, *History of the Byzantine Empire* (2 vols. Univ. Wisconsin, 1928–29; a new edition is now in preparation). There have appeared since the publication of Paetow: S. Runciman, *Byzantine Civilisation* (Longmans, 1933); B. Diener, *Imperial Byzantium* (Little Brown, 1938; not recommended); N. Iorga, *La Vie byzantine* (3 vols. Bucharest, 1934) and his *Byzance après Byzance* (Bucharest, 1935); C. Diehl, *Les grandes problèmes de l'histoire byzantine* (Paris, 1943); G. I. Bratianu, *Etudes byzantines* (Paris, 1938), and L. Bréhier, *Le Monde byzantine,* vol. I *Vie et mort de Byzance* (Paris, 1947, "Evol. Hum.").

Diehl's *History of the Byzantine Empire* (Princeton, 1925) is still the best brief treatment, and the volumes by J. B. Bury, *History of the Later Roman Empire* (2 vols., Macmillan, 1889; rev. ed. of first part, 2 vols. 1923) and *History of the Later Roman Empire 802–867,* (Macmillan, 1912) are unequaled for the period covered. The fourth volume of the *Cambridge Medieval History* (Cambridge Univ. Press and Macmillan, 1923) is devoted to the history of Byzantium, 717–1453, and is standard. Important recent works are those in the Glotz series cited above.

P. Lemerle, *Philippes et la Macédoine orientale à l'époque chretienne et byzantine* (2 vols., Paris, Boccard, 1945) is a most significant recent monograph in the field of Byzantine history. Lemerle has also written a *Histoire de Byzance* (1943) and *Le style byzantin* (1943).

Works on special subjects not included in Paetow include: S. Runciman, *The Emperor Romanus Lecapenus* (Cambridge, 1929); A. A. Vasiliev, *The Russian Attack on Constantinople in 860* (Med. Acad., 1946); P. Charanis, *Church and State in the Later Roman Empire* (Wisconsin, 1939); J. M. Hussey, *Church and Learning in the Byzantine Empire, 867–1185* (Oxford, 1937); S. der Nersessian, *Armenia and the Byzantine Empire* (Harvard, 1945); G. Buckler, *Anna Comnena* (H. Milford, 1929).

The biographies of the various emperors listed in Paetow still afford an excellent means of reading Byzantine history; especially noteworthy are the works of G. Schlumberger (*Nicéphore Phocas,* Paris, 1890, and *L'Epopée byzantine,* 3 vols., Paris, 1890–1905) and F. Chalandon *(Alexis Comnène,* Paris, 1900, and *Les Comnènes, Jean et Manuel,* Paris, 1910). Diehl's *Byzantine Portraits* (Knopf, 1927) is a delightful series of sketches which amply repay reading for their literary as well as their historical merit.

The standard handbook for Byzantine art is still Diehl's *Manuel de l'art byzantin* (2 vols. Paris, 1925–26). The recent work of the Byzantine Institute at Hagia Sophia is bringing to light new information on that church, which is being published by Dr. Whittemore seriatim. See also E. H. Swift, *Hagia Sophia* (Columbia, 1940). For literature and the historians the only thorough work is still K. Krumbacher, *Geschichte der Byzantinischen Litteratur* (Munich, 2nd ed., 1897).

G. Moravesik, *Byzantinoturcica* (2 vols., Budapest, 1942–43) has brought to date the Byzantine literature on the Huns, Turks, Bulgars, etc.

The Digenes Akrites epic has been made the subject of special study by Henri Grégoire in a number of articles and in a special volume (N.Y. 1941).

Much of the most significant work in the field of Byzantine studies has been published in the periodicals *Byzantion* (Brussels, 1924–) *Byzantinoslavica* (Prague), *Revue des étucles byzantines* (Paris, 1943–), and in the new American journal *Byzantina-Metabyzantina* cited above. The *Dumbarton Oaks Papers*, published by the Byzantine Institute of Harvard University at Dumbarton Oaks, Washington, D.C., of which the third volume appeared in 1946 presents articles on Byzantine culture, especially the fine arts.

THE MOSLEM WORLD

P. K. Hitti *History of the Arabs* (Macmillan, 3rd ed., 1946) has superseded all other works in English as a general history of the Arabs. An abridged form of this work, published under the title *The Arabs* (Princeton, 1943), is most useful for a rapid survey of Arab history and civilization. G. E. von Grunbaum, *Medieval Islam* (Chicago, 1946) is a study of the institutions and culture of the Moslems. Collections of articles on aspects of Moslem culture are found in *The Legacy of Islam* (Oxford, 1931), edited by T. Arnold and A. Guillaume, and in *The Arab Heritage* (Princeton, 1944) edited by N. A. Faris.

Several biographical studies of the period of Harun al Rashid—biographies of Harun by St. John Philby (London, 1933) and by G. Audisio (McBride, 1931), and *Two Queens of Baghdad* by N. Abbott (Chicago, 1946)—are popular and without great historical merit.

Recent works include Gaudefroy-Demombynes et Platonov, *Le Monde musulman et byzantin jusqu'aux croisades* (Paris, 1931; "Hist. Monde"), primarily on the Arabs and Russians with a very short section on Byzantium; B. Lewis, *The Origins of Isma'ilism* (Cambridge: Heffer, 1940). Attention should also be called to De Lacy O'Leary *History of the Fatimid Caliphate* (Routledge and Dutton, 1923; omitted by Paetow). There has also been a new translation of the Koran: M. Pickthall, *The Meaning of the Glorious Koran* (Knopf, 1930).

On the Mongols there have appeared recently three volumes by René Grousset: *L'Empire Mongol* (Paris, 1940, "Hist. Monde"), *Conquerant du monde* [Chinghiz] (Paris, 1944) and *L'Empire des steppes* (Paris, 1939); L. Bouvat, *L'Empire mongol: Timur* (Paris, 1927, "Hist. Monde"); M. Prawden, *The Mongols* (Macmillan, 1940) and the popular *March of the Barbarians* by Harold Lamb (Doubleday Doran, 1940) whose biographies of *Genghis Khan* and *Tamerlane* (McBride, 1927–28) have gone into many editions.

A recent work on Persia is A. Christenson, *L'Iran sous les Sassanides* (Copenhagen, 2nd. ed., 1944). The standard history of Persia is P. Sykes, *History of Persia* (2 vols., 2nd. ed., Macmillan, 1921). On the Ottoman Turks, in addition to H. A. Gibbons, *Foundation of the Ottoman Empire* (Century, 1916), should be noted the very important work of Paul Wittek *The Rise of the Ottoman Empire* (London, Royal Asiatic Soc., 1938) and the excellent article by R. Blake and W. Langer "The Rise of the Ottoman Turks," *American Historical Review*, XXXVII (1932).

The Church and the Papacy

A. Fliche, *La Chrétienté mediévale* (Paris, 1929, "Hist. Monde") and G. Schnürer *L'Eglise et la civilisation au moyen âge* (2 vols., Paris, 1933–35) are excellent recent works. Among standard books in English are J. A. Foakes-Jackson, *Introduction to the History of Christianity* (Macmillan, 1921), D. S. Schaff, *History of the Christian Church* Vol. V; *The Middle Ages,* (Scribners, 1907), and the works of H. C. Lea especially his *History of the Inquisition* (3 vols. Macmillan, 1888). A recent history of the Inquisition is that of J. Guiraud, *Histoire de l'Inquisition au moyen âge,* (2 vols. Paris, 1935–38).

Several significant biographies have appeared recently: T. S. R. Boase, *Boniface VIII* (Constable, 1933); L. E. Binns, *Innocent III* (Methuen, 1931), A. J. Mac-Donald, *Hildebrand, a Life of Gregory VII* (Methuen, 1932); H. X. Arquillière, *Saint Grégoire VII* (Paris, 1934); T. Jalland, *Life and Times of St. Leo the Great* (Macmillan, 1941); J. McCann, *St. Benedict* (Methuen, 1937); W. Williams, *St. Bernard of Clairvaux* (Manchester, 1935); H. Bett, *Nicholas of Cusa* (Methuen, 1932); M. Spinka, *John Hus and the Czech Reform* (Chicago, 1941). Helen Waddell discussed the early ascetics in *The Desert Fathers* (Holt, 1936). Monasticism has been studied in: D. Knowles, *The English Monastic Order* (Cambridge, 1939); R. F. Bennett, *The Early Dominicans* (Cambridge, 1937), J. B. Mahn, *L'Ordre Cistercien* (Paris, 1945); J. F. O'Sullivan, *The Cistercian Settlements in Wales and Monmouthshire* (Fordham, 1948); and R. M. Huber, *Documented History of the Franciscan Order, 1182–1517* (Milwaukee, 1945). Two volumes have been added to G. C. Coulton's *Five Centuries of Religion,* as has a third volume of A. Fliche, *La Réforme grégorienne* (3 vols. Louvain, 1924–37). The fourteenth and fifteenth centuries have been studied recently in: L. E. Binns, *Decline and Fall of the Medieval Papacy* (Methuen, 1934); A. Flick, *The Decline of the Medieval Church* (2 vols. Knopf, 1930), and E. F. Jacob, *Essays on the Conciliar Epoch* (Manchester, 1943). W. E. Lunt has published two significant works: *Financial Relations of the Papacy with England to 1327* (Med. Acad., 1939) and *Papal Revenues in the Middle Ages* (2 vols. Columbia, 1934, "Records"). In the "Records" also appeared a selection of *The Correspondence of Gregory VII,* translated by E. Emerton (1932).

A very useful volume which compresses a great deal into a little space is S. Packard *Europe and the Church under Innocent III* (Holt, 1927, "Berkshire Studies"). In the "Berkshire Studies" also appear S. Baldwin, *Organization of Medieval Christianity* and E. R. Goodenough, *The Church in the Roman Empire.*

On special aspects of Church history should be noted: R. W. Emery, *Heresy and the Inquisition in Narbonne* (Columbia, 1941); A. C. Howland, ed., *The*

Minor Historical Writings of Henry Charles Lea (Pennsylvania, 1942) and *Materials Towards a Study of the History of Witchcraft by H. C. Lea* (3 vols. Penna.; 1939).

CAROLINGIAN EMPIRE

A. Kleinclaus, *Charlemagne* (Paris, 1934) is a definitive biography. L. Halphen, *Charlemagne et l'empire carolingien* (Paris, 1947) and Halphen's edition of Einhard's *Vie de Charlemagne* (Paris, 1938); J. W. Thompson, *The Dissolution of the Carolingian Fisc* (California, 1935); L. Auzias, *L'Aquitaine carolingienne 778–987* (Toulouse, 1937) are recent works on the Carolingians.

THE NORSE INVASIONS

T. D. Kendrick, *History of the Vikings* (Scribners, 1930); A. Olrik, *Viking Civilization* (Norton, 1930); S. A. Anderson, *Viking Enterprise* (Columbia, 1936) have appeared since the last edition of Paetow.

THE GERMAN EMPIRE

The publication of G. Barraclough's *Medieval Germany* (2 vols., Blackwell, 1938) has forced a reinterpretation of the old ideas concerning Saxon and Hohenstaufen Germany. Barraclough's conclusions, which are given in the first volume, have been worked over in more popular form in his *Origins of Modern Germany* (Blackwell, 1946) and should be read by any serious student of the subject. A. Fliche, *La querelle des investitures* (Paris, 1946) is the most recent work on this problem. E. N. Johnson, *Secular Activities of the German Episcopate* (Nebraska, 1932) is a detailed study of the role of the clergy in German government and politics.

Three biographies of Frederick II have appeared in English recently: E. Kantorowicz, *Frederick II* (R. Smith, 1931); P. Wiegler, *The Infidel Emperor and His Struggle Against the Pope* (Routledge, 1930); and G. Slaughter, *The Amazing Frederic* (Macmillan, 1947). B. Jarrett has a biography of *The Emperor Charles IV* (Sheed & Ward, 1935). There are some very good chapters on Germany in the *Cambridge Medieval History* and in the volumes by Brooke, Privité-Orton, and Waugh in the Methuen series. James Bryce, *Holy Roman Empire* (London, 1873, and repeated editions since) still remains a classic interpretation of the empire. ·The *Chronicle of the Two Cities of Otto of Freising*, which was translated by C. C. Mierow in the "Records of Civilization" in 1928 is to be followed soon by the translation of his *Gesta Frederici* in the same series.

RUSSIA AND THE SLAVIC STATES

G. Vernadsky, *Ancient Russia* and *Kievan Russia* (Yale, 1944, 1948) are the most recent authoritative studies of medieval Russia. A. Eck, *Le Moyen Age russe* (Paris, 1933) is another valuable recent work. Kluchevsky, *History of Russia* (Vols. I and II, Dutton, 1911–12) are still of prime importance. F. Nowak, *Medieval Slavdom and the Rise of Russia* (Holt, 1930, "Berkshire Studies") is a convenient short account. G. Vernadsky has translated *Medieval Russian Laws* (Columbia, 1948, "Records").

S. Runciman, *History of the First Bulgarian Empire* (Bell, 1930) and C. A. Macartney, *The Magyars in the Ninth Century* (Cambridge, 1930) are important studies in the early history of those peoples.

ITALY

Of first importance is F. Schevill, *History of Florence* (Harcourt, 1936). The older works are listed in Paetow and reliance must still be placed on them generally, particularly the works of Symonds, Villari, Browning, et al., H. Kretschmayr, *Geschichte von Venedig* (2 vols. to 1516, Gotha, 1905–20) is still the best critical history of Venice. W. F. Butler, *The Lombard Communes* (Unwin, 1906) has not been surpassed in that field. A. C. Krey, *Florence, a City that Art Built* (Minnesota, 1936); R. Lopez, *Genova marinara nel ducento* (Milan, 1933); and D. M. B. de Mesquita, *Giangaleazzo Visconti* (Cambridge, 1941) are recent studies.

NORMAN SICILY

The most significant single work in this field to appear since 1930 is C. Cahen, *Le Regime féodale de l'Italie normande* (Paris, 1940). Lynn White, *Latin Monasticism in Norman Sicily* (Med. Acad., 1938) presents an authoritative study of this special subject. T. C. Van Cleve, *Markward of Anweiler* (Princeton, 1937) is a biography of the regent for Frederick II, which gives considerable detail on this troubled period. *The Greatest Norman Conquest* by J. W. Osborne (Dutton, 1937) is a popular history of the conquest to 1101.

The best brief accounts in English are still to be found in C. H. Haskins *The Normans in European History* (Houghton Mifflin, 1915) and in the chapter by F. Chalandon in *The Cambridge Medieval History* (Vol. V, 1926). There are good chapters on Sicily, Naples, and Spain in J. Longnon, *Les Français d'Outremer* (Paris, 1929).

SPAIN

The standard work in English is still R. Merriman, *Rise of the Spanish Empire* (Vol. I, Macmillan, 1918). There are good chapters by R. Altemira in the *Cambridge Medieval History*, Vols. VI, VII and VIII; Vol. VIII also contains a chapter on Portugal by E. Prestage. Among recent works should be noted: R. M. Pidal *The Cid and his Spain* (Murray, 1934); H. J. Chaytor, *History of Aragon and Catalonia* (Methuen, 1933); and a translation of R. Altemira *History of Spanish Civilization* (London, 1930). M. E. Madden, *Political Theory and Law in Medieval Spain* (Fordham, 1930) is a study of constitutional development as well as law and theory.

FRANCE

The great work for the history of France is E. Lavisse *Histoire de France* (18 vols. Paris, 1900–11) of which eight volumes deal with the medieval period. Also important for the study of medieval France are A. Luchaire, *Histoire des institutions monarchiques de la France, 987–1180* (2 vols. Paris, 1891) and his *Social France in the Time of Philip Augustus* (Holt, 1912). An interesting volume is F. Funck-Brentano, *The Middle Ages* (Putnams, 1923). Among significant recent books on medieval France are C. Petit-Dutaillis, *Feudal Monarchy in France and England* (Knopf, 1936); J. Strayer, *Administration of Normandy under St. Louis* (Med. Acad., 1932); C. H. Taylor and J. R. Strayer, *Studies in Early French Taxation* (Harvard, 1939); E. Perroy, *La Guerre de cent ans* (Paris, 1945); W. H. Newman, *Le Domain royal sous les premiers Capétiens* (Paris, 1937). G. Digard, *Philippe le Bel et le Sainte Siège* (2 vols. Paris, 1936) gives an exhaustive treatment of Philip's struggle with Boniface VIII. S. Painter, *The Scourge of God, Peter of Dreux* (Hopkins, 1937) and M. V. Rosenberg, *Eleanor of Aquitaine* (Houghton Mifflin, 1937) are well written biographies. A Cartellieri, *The Court of Burgundy* has been translated into English (Knopf, 1929). C. H. Haskins *Normans in European History* (Houghton Mifflin, 1915) and J. Longnon *Les Français d'Outremer au moyen âge* (Paris, 1929) are both excellent studies of French expansion.

ENGLAND

As there is no coverage of medieval England in Paetow this list will be more complete than most. The student is, however, referred to the bibliographies in W. E. Lunt, *History of England* (Harpers, rev. ed., 1938) for more complete bibliographies.

For the general narrative history of England there are two important sets of works. The Oman series published by Methuen and Putnams and the Hunt-Poole *Political History of England* by Longmans. The new *Oxford History of England* has as yet no volumes on medieval history except Stenton, *Anglo-Saxon England* (1943). In the Oman series are: C. Oman, *England Before the Norman Conquest* (3rd. ed., 1919), H. W. C. Davis, *England under the Normans and Angevins* (6th ed., 1919), K. H. Vickers, *England in the Later Middle Ages* (2nd. ed., 1919). In the Hunt-Poole series are: T. Hodgkin, *England to 1066;* G. B. Adams, *England, 1066–1216;* T. F. Tout; *England, 1216–1377;* and C. Oman, *England, 1377–1485* (various editions).

The most recent histories of Anglo-Saxon England are those of Stenton (Oxford, 1943) and R. H. Hodgkin (2 vols. Oxford, 1935). For the Norman-Plantagenet epoch are the series of biographies by Kate Norgate: *England under the Angevin Kings* (2 vols. Macmillan, 1887), *Richard Lion Heart* (1924), *John Lackland* (1902), *The Minority of Henry III* (1912); F. M. Powicke, *Loss of Normandy, 1189–1204* (Manchester, 1913), *Stephen Langton* (Oxford, 1928) and *King Henry III and the Lord Edward* (2 vols. Oxford, 1947). S. Painter, *William Marshal* (Hopkins, 1933) is a delightfully written biography of the great regent. C. Bemont, *Simon de Montfort* came out in a new edition in 1930 (Oxford); N. Denholm-Young, has a biography of *Richard of Cornwall* (Blackwell, 1947). The story of the Barons'

War has been told recently in an excellent volume by R. F. Treharne, *The Baronial Plan of Reform* (Manchester, 1932). H. Johnstone, *Edward of Carnarvon, 1284–1307* (Manchester, 1946) actually covers more than her title indicates; T. F. Tout, *The Place of Edward II in English History* had a revised edition in 1936 (Manchester); and *Richard II* was the subject of a biography by A. Steel (Cambridge, 1941). Older biographies of especial merit are S. Armitage-Smith, *John of Gaunt* (Constable, 1904); K. H. Vickers, *Humphrey Duke of Gloucester* (Constable, 1907) and G. M. Trevelyan, *England in the Age of Wycliffe* (Longmans, 1909).

In the field of Constitutional History there have been several recent works: J. E. A. Jolliffe, *Constitutional History of Medieval England* (Van Nostrand, 1937) is full, but confusing and should not be attempted by the beginner, although it should be stimulating to advanced students. W. A. Morris, *Constitutional History of England to 1216* (Macmillan, 1930), G. B. Adams, *Constitutional History of England* (Holt, rev. ed., 1934) and A. B. White, *Making of the English Constitution* (Putnams, 1925) are good brief accounts. The great classic is still Stubbs, *Constitutional History of England* (3 vols. Oxford, various editions since 1874) with which should be read C. Petit-Dutaillis, *Studies Supplementary to Stubbs* (4 vols. Manchester, 1908–30). G. B. Adams: *The Origin of the English Constitution* and his *Councils and Courts in Anglo-Norman England* (Yale, 1912, 1926); F. M. Stenton, *First Two Centuries of English Feudalism* (Oxford, 1932); J. F. Baldwin, *The Kings' Council in England during the Middle Ages* (Oxford, 1913); J. H. Round, *Feudal England* (Sonnenschein, 1895), *Geoffrey de Mandeville* (Longmans, 1892), *Kings' Serjeants* (Nisbet, 1911) all deal with constitutional problems. Some recent studies in constitutional history are G. L. Haskins, *Statute of York* (Harvard, 1935); B. Wilkinson, *Studies in Constitutional History of the XIII and XIV Centuries* (Manchester, 1937) and S. B. Chrimes, *English Constitutional Ideas of the Fifteenth Century* (Cambridge, 1936).

On Magna Carta see W. S. McKechnie, *Magna Carta* (Maclehose, Glasgow, rev. ed., 1914); F. Thompson, *The First Century of Magna Carta* (Minnesota, 1925); and the *Magna Carta Commemoration Essays* (London, Royal Hist. Soc. 1917).

For the history of Parliament the most recent study is G. L. Haskins, *The Growth of English Representative Government* (Pennsylvania, 1948). Other important works on this subject are: C. H. McIlwain, *The High Court of Parliament* (Yale, 1910); A. F. Pollard, *The Evolution of Parliament* (Longmans, 1920); H. L. Gray, *The Influence of the Commons on Early Legislation* (Harvard, 1932); D. Pasquet, *Origins of the House of Commons* (Cambridge, 1925); W. V. Clarke, *Medieval Representation and Consent* (Longmans, 1936); D. B. Weske, *Convocation of the Clergy* (S.P.C.K., 1937).

A great impetus to the study of administrative history was given by the publication of T. F. Tout, *Chapters in the Administrative History of Medieval England* (4 vols. Manchester, 1920–28). Since then have appeared G. P. Cuttino, *English Diplomatic Administrations, 1259–1339* (Oxford, 1940); and two volumes of *The English Government at Work, 1327–1336*, Vol. I. *Central and Prerogative Administration* by J. F. Willard and W. A. Morris; Vol. II. *Fiscal Administration* by W. A: Morris and J. R. Strayer (Med. Acad., 1940–47). Finance was also discussed in J. R. Ramsey, *The Revenues of the Kings of England* (2 vols. Oxford, 1925). The great classic for the history of law is still unquestionably F. Pollock and F. W. Maitland, *History of English Law to the Death of Edward I* (2 vols. Cambridge, 2 ed., 1899), invaluable for the study of English feudalism.

Feudalism (including Manorialism)

Carl Stephenson, *Mediaeval Feudalism* (Cornell, 1942) is an extremely useful brief outline of the whole subject, admirably adapted to class use, largely supplanting the older *Feudal Regime* of Seignobos. F. L. Ganshof, *Qu'est-ce que la féodalité?* (Brussels, 1944) is another short treatment which analyses feudal institutions. There has also been a fourth edition of J. Calmette's very valuable *La société féodale* (Paris, 1938) which is still probably the best treatment in a short compass. Among longer works on the subject have appeared two very important studies: M. Bloc, *La société féodale* (2 vols., Paris, 1939-40) and H. Mitteis, *Lehnrecht and Staatsgewalt* (Weimar, 1933).

C. E. Odegaard, *Vassi and Fideles in the Carolingian Empire* (Harvard, 1945), A. Dopsch, *Beneficialwesen und Feudalität* (Vienna, 1932), and H. Krawinkel, *Untersuchen zum frankischen Benefizialrecht* (Weimar, 1936) are recent studies in the Frankish origins of feudalism. The classic work on feudal origins is still, however, P. Guilhiermoz, *Essai sur les origines de la noblesse en France au moyen âge* (Paris, 1902).

M. Sczaniecki, *Essai sur les fief-rentes* (Paris, 1946) studies the subject of money fiefs, while English serjeanty tenure has been investigated by E. G. Kimball in *Serjeanty Tenure in Medieval England* (Yale, 1936). There have been a number of valuable studies of feudalism in various countries: S. Painter, *Studies in the History of the English Barony* (Johns Hopkins, 1943); N. Denholm-Young, *Seignorial Administration in England* (Oxford, 1937); S. E. Gleason, *An Ecclesiastical Barony of the Middle Ages: the Bishopric of Bayeux* (Harvard, 1936); C. Cahen, *Le régime féodale de l'Italie normande* (Paris, 1940); Olivier-Martin, *Histoire de la coutume de la prévoté et vicomté de Paris* (2 vols. Paris, 1922-30); F. M. Stenton, *The First Two Centuries of English Feudalism* (Oxford, 1932); C. Petit-Dutaillis, *Feudal Monarchy in France and England* (Knopf, 1936); J. L. LaMonte, *Feudal Monarchy in the Latin Kingdom of Jerusalem* (Med. Acad., 1932); G. Barraclough, *Medieval Germany* (Oxford, 1938).

Indispensable still are F. Pollock and F. W. Maitland, *History of English Law* (Cambridge, 2nd. ed., 1898) and A. Luchaire, *Manuel des institutions françaises* (Paris, 1892).

For Manorialism the first volume of the *Cambridge Economic History* edited by J. H. Clapham and E. Power (Cambridge, 1941) is now the most complete study of medieval agrarian institutions. A useful short survey is N. Neilson, *Medieval Agrarian Economy* (Holt, 1936, "Berkshire Studies"). A. Déléage, *La Vie rurale en Bourgogne jusqu'au debut du onzième siècle* (3 vols. Paris, 1941) is an intensive and scholarly study of the manorial conditions in Burgundy. M. Bloch, *Les caractères originaux de l'histoire rurale française* (Oslo, 1931); K. W. D. Fedden, *Manor Life in Old France* (Columbia, 1933); C. H. Bell, *Peasant Life in Old German Epics* (Columbia, 1931, "Records"); G. C. Homans, *English Villagers of the*

Thirteenth Century (Harvard, 1940): A. E. Levett *Studies in Manorial History* (Oxford, 1938): H. S. Bennett, *Life on the English Manor* (Cambridge, 1937) all deal with manorial and peasant conditions.

COMMERCE AND THE TOWNS

Of first importance is H. Pirenne, *Economic and Social History of Medieval Europe* (Harcourt, 1936) which briefly and brilliantly summarizes the opinions of the great authority in this field. J. W. Thompson followed his *Economic and Social History of the Middle Ages* (Century, 1928) with an *Economic and Social History of Europe in the Later Middle Ages, 1300–1530* (Century, 1931). H. Laurent, *Un grand commerce d'exportation au moyen âge* (Paris, 1935) is a study of the Flemish wool trade; E. H. Byrne, *Genoese Shipping in the XII–XIII Centuries* (Med. Acad., 1930), R. Lopez, *Studi sull'economia Genovese nel medio evo* (Turin, 1936) and F. C. Lane, *Venetian Ships and Shipbuilders* (Hopkins, 1934) deal with aspects of Italian commerce and industry. E. Lipson *Economic History of England*, Vol. I (Black, 1929) covers trade and industry as well as agriculture.

The early chapters of H. Heaton, *Economic History of Europe* (Harpers, 1936) are excellent for the Middle Ages. P. Boissonade, *Life and Work in Medieval Europe* (trans. E. Power, Knopf, 1927) is the best general treatment of both Byzantine and Western industry and commerce. An important work in the field of commercial history was the publication of Pegalotti *Practica della mercatura* by Allan Evans (Med. Acad. 1936).

H. Pirenne, *Les Villes et les institutions urbaines* (2 vols. Paris, 1939), C. Petit-Dutaillis, *Les communes françaises* ("Evol. Human.," 1947), and C. Stephenson, *Borough and Town* (Med. Acad., 1933) present the currently accepted theory as to the origin and character of the medieval town. Their conclusions are challenged to a certain degree by J. Tait, *The Medieval English Borough* (Manchester, 1936).

THE CRUSADES

The decades since 1930 have been especially productive of good books in the history of the Crusades. D. C. Munro, *The Kingdom of the Crusaders* (Appleton-Century-Crofts, 1935) is a delightful account of the crusades and the kingdom of Jerusalem through the twelfth century. René Grousset, *Histoire des croisades* (3 vols. Paris, 1934–36) and his *L'Empire du levant* (Paris, 1946) are eminently readable histories of considerable scholarly merit. Two monumental works in the field are Claude Cahen, *La Syrie du Nord à l'époque du croisades* (Paris, 1940) a splendid study of Antioch and northern Syria, and Sir George Hill's definitive *History of Cyprus* (3 vols. Cambridge, 1940–48) of which Vols. II and III deal with the Frankish period. Both of these magnificent works rank with R. Röhricht's *Geschichte des Königreichs Jerusalem* (Innsbruck, 1898), as the great definitive histories of the subjects covered. At the other end of the scholarly scale Harold Lamb's two volumes, *Iron Men and Saints,* and *The Flame of Islam* (Doubleday Doran, 1930–31) are interesting popular accounts.

On the subject of propaganda and theory of the Crusades are M. Villey, *Les Croisades* (Paris, 1942); C. Erdmann, *Die Entstehung des Kreuzzugsgedankens*

(Stuttgart, 1935); P. Rousset, *Les Origins et les caractères de la première croisade* (Neuchatel, 1945); and P. Throop, *Criticism of the Crusade* (Amsterdam, 1940). Biographies include: R. Nicholson, *Tancred* (Chicago, 1940), J. C. Andressohn, *Ancestry and Life of Godfrey of Bouillon* (Indiana, 1947), M. Baldwin, *Raymond III of Tripolis* (Princeton, 1936), J. Longnon, *Geoffroy de Villehardouin* (Paris, 1939). R. B. Yewdale, *Bohemond I of Antioch* (Princeton, 1924).

On the institutions of the Latin kingdom are: J. L. LaMonte, *Feudal Monarchy in the Latin Kingdom of Jerusalem* (Med. Acad., 1932); D. Hayek, *Le Droit franc en Syrie* (Paris, 1925); M. Grandclaude's indispensable *Etude critique sur les livres des Assises de Jérusalem* (Paris, 1923), and J. Richard, *Le Comté de Tripoli 1102–87* (Paris, 1945). The period of the later crusades has come in for special notice in the works of A. S. Atiya, *The Crusade in the Later Middle Ages* (Methuen, 1938) and *The Crusade of Nicopolis* (Methuen, 1934) which open up a whole new field of investigation and reveal the importance of the attempts to revive the crusades after the fall of Acre. O. Halecki has discussed, in a special monograph, *The Crusade of Varna* (New York Polish Institute, 1943). R. Grousset has recently published a *Histoire de l'Armenie* (1947) and a popular *L'Épopée des croisades* (1939). K. M. Setton, *Catalan Domination of Athens, 1311–1388* (Med. Acad., 1948) is a recent and authoritative treatment of that difficult period.

Two important new texts are G. Recoura, *Les Assises de Romanie* (Paris, 1930) and E. Faral's edition of Villehardouin (2 vols. Paris, 1938–39).

Many original sources have been translated recently: *William of Tyre* by E. Babcock and A. C. Krey (2 vols. 1943). The *Conquest of Lisbon* by C. W. David (1936), *Robert de Clari* by E. H. McNeal (1936), *Ambroise* and *Philip de Novare* by J. L. LaMonte and M. J. Hubert (1941, 1936)—(all in the "Records of Civilization"); *The Damascus Chronicle* by H. A. R. Gibb (Luzac, 1931); *Anna Comnena* by A. S. Dawes (Trubner, 1928); *Fulcher of Chartres,* Book I, by E. M. McGinty and *Oliver of Paderborn* by J. J. Gavigan are in the "Translations and Reprints, Third Series." *Odo de Deuil* by V. G. Berry appeared in 1948 in the "Records."

The military architecture of the crusaders is the subject of two handsome volumes by P. Deschamps *Les Chateaux de croisés en terre sainte* (Paris, 1934–39) of which the first volume deals exclusively with Crac-des-Chevaliers. T. E. Lawrence, *Crusaders' Castles* (2 vols. Oxford, Blackwell, 1936) presents a new interpretation concerning the influence of Eastern and Western building which runs counter to all accepted theories on the subject. The literary cycle of the crusades is studied by A. Hatem, *Les poèmes épiques des croisades* (Paris, 1932).

The University of Pennsylvania Press announces the future publication (about 1952–53) of an international co-operative *History of the Crusades* in five volumes, which should be the definitive work on all aspects of the crusades when it appears, and the "Records" has in prospect an anthology of the historians of the crusades.

Intellectual Developments

While many new books have appeared in this field since 1928 several of the items listed in Paetow are still the indispensable works on the subject. E. K. Rand, *The Founders of the Middle Ages* (Harvard, 1928) is a delightful series of essays by a man who was himself a great classicist and humanist. P. de Labriolle, *History and Literature of Latin Christianity* (Knopf, 1925) is a most useful guide to the early writers. More recent works on the early period include: E. S. Duckett *Latin Writers of the Fifth Century* (Holt, 1930) and *Gateway to the Middle Ages* (Macmillan, 1938); F. P. Cassidy, *Molders of the Medieval Mind* (Herder, 1944); M. Laistner, *Thought and Letters in Western Europe, 500–900* (Dial, 1931), especially fine on the Carolingian Renaissance; and the recent study in cultural relationships by W. Levison, *England and the Continent in the Eighth Century* (Oxford, 1946). Individual authors have been discussed in H. M. Barrett, *Boethius* (Macmillan, 1940); H. R. Patch, *The Tradition of Boethius* (Oxford, 1935); H. Dudden, *Life and Times of St. Ambrose* (2 vols. Oxford, 1935); A. H. Thompson, *Bede, his Life, Times and Writings* (Oxford, 1935) and C. H. Beeson, *Lupus of Ferrières* (Med. Acad., 1930).

H. O. Taylor, *Classical Heritage of the Middle Ages* (Macmillan, rev. ed., 1911) and *The Medieval Mind* (2 vols. Macmillan, 4 ed., 1927) are good general surveys of the whole subject. For the Twelfth-Century Renaissance the great works are those of C. H. Haskins: *The Renaissance of the Twelfth Century* (Harvard, 1927), *The Rise of Universities* (Holt, 1923); *Studies in Medieval Science* (Harvard, 1924) and *Studies in Medieval Culture* (Oxford, 1929); the last two are collections of essays. A revised edition of H. Rashdall, *The Universities of Europe in the Middle Ages* was issued under the editorship of F. M. Powicke and A. B. Emden (3 vols. Oxford, 1936). Another important study of universities is S. d'Irsay, *Histoire des universités* (2 vols. Paris, 1933). L. Thorndike has brought together a collection of translated sources for medieval universities in his *University Records and Life* (Columbia, 1944, "Records"). *The Medieval Library* is the subject of a series of articles edited by J. W. Thompson (Chicago, 1939). J. W. Thompson *The Literacy of the Laity in the Middle Ages* (California, 1939) does much to remedy the old idea that learning was confined to the clergy.

PHILOSOPHY

M. de Wulf, *Histoire de la philosophie médiévale* (of which an English translation was published by Longmans in 1925–26) appeared in a sixth edition (Louvain, 1934). E. Gilson, *The Spirit of Medieval Philosophy* and *Reason and Revelation in the Middle Ages* appeared in English translations in 1936 and 1938. A. C. McGiffert, *History of Christian Thought* (2 vols. Scribner's, 1932) reviews the whole subject. S. Moncrieff, *Letters of Abelard and Heloise* (Knopf, 1929), is a good translation of the famous letters.

SCIENCE

Various aspects of medieval scientific development are treated in: L. C. Mac-Kinney, *Early Medieval Medicine* (Hopkins, 1937); D. Riesmann, *The Story of Medicine in the Middle Ages* (Hoeber, 1935); and L. Thorndike, *History of Magic and Experimental Science* (6 vols., Macmillan and Columbia, 1923–40).

POLITICAL THEORY

The most important book in this subject to appear in the last twenty years is C. H. McIlwain, *Growth of Political Thought in the West* (Macmillan, 1932) which is especially fine on the medieval period. A. J. Carlyle, *History of Medieval Political Theory in the West* (8 vols. Edinburgh, Blackwood, 1903–36) has been completed in eight volumes; this work is by far the most complete study of the subject in any language. Recent studies include: F. Kern, *Kingship and Law in the Middle Ages* (Blackwell, 1939); N. Iung, *Alvaro Pelayo* (Paris, 1931), G. Lagarde, *Marsile de Padove* (Paris, 1934).

HISTORIOGRAPHY

The best general work on medieval historiography is J. W. Thompson, *History of Historical Writing* (2 vols. Macmillan, 1942). Useful older works are the "Early Chroniclers of Europe" (S.P.C.K.) series (U. Balzani, *Italy;* G. Masson, *France;* J. Gairdner, *England*). The best source for editions and texts is A. Molinier, *Les Sources de l'histoire de France* (6 vols. Paris, 1901–6). A. Potthast, *Bibliotheca historica medii aevi* (2 vols. Berlin, 2 ed., 1896) also analyses sources. For the Byzantine historians see K. Krumbacher, *Geschichte der Byzantinischen Litteratur* (Munich, 2 ed., 1897). Most of the important chroniclers have been translated either into English or French; for English translations see Farrar and Evans *Bibliography*. The introductions to texts or translations usually discuss the work of the author and provide useful information; see especially the works translated in the "Records of Civilization" series.

GEOGRAPHY

G. H. T. Kimble, *Geography in the Middle Ages* (Methuen, 1938) gives an excellent general study of the subject. A. P. Newton, *The Great Age of Discovery* (Univ. London, 1932) and J. E. Gillespie, *A History of Geographical Discovery, 1400–1800* (Holt, 1933, "Berkshire Studies") are useful volumes. Percy Sykes, *The Quest for Cathay* (Black, 1936) studies the travelers to China. H. C. Adams, *Travellers' Tales* (Boni, 1927) takes up various legends and beliefs concerning geography in the Middle Ages in a popular style. R. Beazley, *The Dawn of Modern Geography* (3 vols. J. Murray, 1897–1906) is still the most exhaustive treatment of the matter, and attention should also be given to A. P. Newton, *Travel and Travellers of the Middle Ages* (Knopf, 1926) and J. K. Wright, *Geographical Lore of the Time of the Crusaders* (Amer. Geog. Soc., 1925). A recent study of Marco Polo is H. H. Hunt, *Venetian Adventurer* (Stanford, 1942).

LITERATURE AND CHIVALRY

The whole subject of chivalry has received a scintillating and brilliant treatment in Sidney Painter, *French Chivalry* (Hopkins, 1940). R. L. Kilgour, *Decline of Chivalry as shown in the French Literature of the Late Middle Ages* (Harvard,

1937), C. B. West, *Courtoisie in Anglo-Norman Literature* (Oxford, 1938), M. A. Gist, *Love and War in the Middle English Romances* (Pennsylvania, 1947), all deal with special periods or aspects of the subject. Andreas Capellanus, *Art of Courtly Love* has been translated by J. J. Parry (Columbia, 1941, "Records").

H. Waddell, *Medieval Latin Lyrics* (Constable, 1929) is a translation of Latin poetry which in large part superseded J. A. Symonds' *Wine, Women and Song*. Her *Wandering Scholars* (Houghton Mifflin, 1927) is a delightful picture of medieval student life.

C. C. Abbott, *Early Medieval French Lyrics* (London, 1932), U. T. Holmes, Jr., *A History of Old French Literature, from the Origins to 1300* (Appleton-Century-Crofts, 1948), C. S. Lewis, *The Allegory of Love* (Oxford, 1936), R. S. Loomis and R. Willard, *Medieval English Verse and Prose, in Modernized Versions* (Appleton-Century-Crofts, 1948) are recent works. The *Cambridge History of English Literature*, Vol. I (Putnam's, 1907) and G. Paris, *Medieval French Literature* (Dent, 1903) are standard. C. V. Langlois, *La Vie en France au moyen âge* (4 vols. Paris, 1924–28) and J. Bédier, *Les Légendes épiques; recherches sur la formation des chansons de geste* (4 vols. Paris, 3rd ed., 1930) are works of fundamental importance.

ARCHITECTURE AND ART

For an interpretation of medieval art and its place in the medieval world, Henry Adams, *Mont Saint Michel and Chartres* (Houghton Mifflin, 1913) is unequaled. D. M. Robb and J. J. Garrison, *Art in the Western World* (Harpers, 1935) is a very useful manual. There have been several important works on various aspects of medieval art: C. R. Morey, *Christian Art* (Longmans, 1935), *Early Christian Art* (Princeton, 1942) and *Medieval Art* (Norton, 1942); A. Gardner, *Medieval Sculpture in France* (Cambridge, 1931); H. Gardner, *Art through the Ages* (Harcourt, 1936); B. Berenson, *Italian Painting of the Renaissance* (Oxford, 1930). Two handsomely illustrated volumes are: L. Deshairs et P. Léon, *L'Art des origines à nos jours* (2 vols., Larousse, 1932–33) and L. van Puyvelde, *Les Primitifs Flamands* (Brussels, 1947). For Italian art *The Wonders of Italy* (Florence, 7th ed., 1937) is most useful.

Our description of Amiens is taken largely from A. Boinet, *La Cathédrale d'Amiens* (Paris, 1926) in M. Aubert's convenient series *Petits Monographies des grands edifices de la France* (Laurens). For the iconography of medieval art the classic work is Emile Male, *Religious Art in France in the XIII Century* (Dutton, 1913). Banister Fletcher, *History of Architecture* (Scribner's, 6th ed., 1921) is a mine of information on comparative architecture.

INDEX

✜

SINCE NO accepted standard for medieval nomenclature has ever been developed any index of medieval materials is of necessity both hard to prepare and difficult to use. The present index is no exception, but I hope it is a usable one. To simplify matters as much as possible I have set up a few general rules, from which I have deviated only when the individual circumstance seems to demand it.

All emperors, kings, queens, sultans, and other reigning princes have been indexed under their first names, and have been listed under their highest titles. Thus Charles of Anjou, king of Naples, will be found under Charles of Naples, not Anjou. In the case of queens, however, as their origin was generally more important than their final title, the listing has been based on their provenance; thus Eleanor of Aquitaine, queen of France and England, is found under Eleanor of Aquitaine, and comes before Eleanor of Aragon, queen of Castile. In general, first names have been used, unless the persons are best known by their family names. Peter Abelard, Geoffrey Chaucer, and Giovanni Boccaccio are obviously found under their last names, and so are the Byzantines, who early developed patronymics and are usually spoken of by their last names. This has also been done in the cases of the great Italian families (Este, Sforza, Visconti, Medici) and in some other instances (Bigods, Montforts, et al). In some instances (John of Gaunt, John de Brienne, Robert Guiscard, et al), a man is so well known by one form of his name that it would be disconcerting to find him listed under his title.

Square brackets have been used throughout the index to indicate the page on which a person is found on a genealogical table. Names on the tables not mentioned in the text have not been indexed. Brackets also indicate variant names under which an individual was known; parentheses are used for family names or lesser titles of persons indexed under their highest title. Explanatory characterizations of places and things are also in parentheses.

Several terms have been used rather freely in identifying entries in this index: "Byzantine" is used for rulers in the East after Theodosius I; "city" includes all urban communities irrespective of their size or ecclesiastical status; "historian" and "artist" describe wide varieties of accomplishments in these general fields; *cited* as used for modern authors includes both quotations from and references to the subject.

Many things have been most deliberately omitted from the index. Churches (especially when used as illustrations of styles of architecture), titles of books or works of art, individuals when used comparatively, characters in literature, and place names where the reference is merely incidental: all have been left out. However, it is hoped that the index will be found a satisfactory guide to the important subjects considered in the book.